Contents

ON THE ROAD

CHRIS HILL/GETTY IMAGES ©

Western Europe

Ireland
p381

Britain
p109

The Netherlands
p499

Germany
p257

Belgium &
Luxembourg
p73

France
p181

Switzerland
p639

Austria
p39

Portugal
p525

Spain
p561

Italy
p417

Greece
p333

THIS EDITION WRITTEN AND RESEARCHED BY

Alexis Averbuck, Kerry Christiani, Emilie Filou, Duncan Garwood,
Anthony Ham, Catherine Le Nevez, Sally O'Brien,
Andrea Schulte-Peevers, Helena Smith, Neil Wilson

PLAN YOUR TRIP

CHÂTEAU VERSAILLES, FRANCE P202

BRUGES, BELGIUM P93

ON THE ROAD

PETE SEAWARD/LONELY PLANET ©

JOSEIGNACIOSOTO/GETTY IMAGES ©

Contents

GIANT'S CAUSEWAY P410, NORTHERN IRELAND

Welcome to Western Europe

Western Europe's intricate tapestry of countries and cultures is woven together by rich history; artistic, architectural and culinary treasures; enduring traditions and cutting-edge trends.

Living History

In Western Europe, history is all around you: in prehistoric Cro-Magnon caves, in otherworldly tombs and stone circles, in the tumbledown remains of Greek temples and Roman bathhouses, in ostentatious castles and palaces where power was wielded and geopolitical boundaries were shaped and reshaped, in the winding streets and broad boulevards of its stately cities, and at poignant sites including the D-Day beaches and the remnants of the Berlin Wall. Understanding Europe's long and often troubled history is a vital part of figuring out what makes this pastiche of countries what they are today.

Extraordinary Art & Architecture

Western Europe's architectural heritage has given rise to iconic, instantly recognisable landmarks such as Rome's gladiatorial Colosseum, Cologne's cathedral, London's Big Ben and Paris' art nouveau Eiffel Tower, along with contemporary additions. This environment is inextricably tied to the artistic legacy of Western Europe: the home of virtuosos from Michelangelo to Monet, Da Vinci to Dalí, Botticelli to Banksy, it continues to inspire boundary-pushing artists while monumental and intimate museums, galleries and public spaces showcase their exceptional works.

Thriving Culture

Distinct cultures, defined by their language, customs, specialities, idiosyncrasies, style and way of life, make Western Europe a fascinating place to travel. Especially along country borders, you can see where cultures intertwine and overlap. You'll also see subtle cultural shifts between each country's regions, and the influence of trade and immigration over the centuries, creating cultural melting pots. Wherever you travel, allow time to soak up the vibe in parks and gardens, at time-honoured and innovative new festivals, and in neighbourhood pubs and cafes where you can watch the world go by.

Celebrated Food & Drink

Western Europe is united by its passion for eating and drinking with gusto. Every country has its own unique flavours, incorporating olive oils and sun-ripened vegetables in the hot south, rich cream and butter in cooler areas, fresh-off-the-boat seafood along the coast, delicate river and lake fish, and meat from fertile mountains and pastures. Each country has its own tipples, too, spanning renowned wines, beers, stouts and ciders, and feistier firewater including premeal *apéritifs* and postmeal *digestifs*.

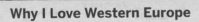

Why I Love Western Europe

By Catherine Le Nevez, Writer

What I love most about Western Europe is that its diversity is so accessible. Its grand old-world cities, contemporary metropolises, vibrant towns and exquisite cobbled villages are just hours apart, along with surf beaches, sun-baked islands, vineyards, lavender and tulip fields, dark forests and snowy peaks. The fantastic transport network here makes it easy to zip back and forth between countries to check out old haunts and new openings and catch exhibitions, concerts and festivals. It's the perfect place for spontaneous discoveries, which, to me, are the highlights of travelling.

For more about our writers, see page 704.

Above: Monte de Santa Luzia (p555), Viana do Castelo, Portugal

Western Europe

Causeway Coast
Hike the Giant's Causeway (p410)

Amsterdam
Cruise the Golden Age canals (p501)

London
Catch fabulous theatre and concerts (p112)

Paris
Scale the iconic Eiffel Tower (p184)

Granada
Admire the Alhambra palace complex (p624)

Champagne
Sip the legend at its source (p210)

The Matterhorn
Marvel at Switzerland's mightiest mountain (p647)

Barcelona
Gaudí's La Sagrada Família astounds (p584)

Shetland Islands

Orkney Islands

Outer Hebrides

SCOTLAND

Aberdeen

NORTHERN IRELAND

Edinburgh

Newcastle-upon-Tyne

North Sea

Belfast

Isle of Man

ENGLAND

Frisian Islands

Galway

Dublin

Irish Sea

York

IRELAND

BRITAIN

Cork

St George's Channel

WALES

Cambridge

NETHERLANDS

Oxford

Cardiff

London

Amsterdam

Bruges

Düsseldorf

Plymouth

Brighton

Brussels

BELGIUM

ATLANTIC OCEAN

English Channel

Channel Islands

Caen

LUXEMBOURG

Luxembourg City

St-Malo

CHAMPAGNE

Rennes

Paris

Strasbourg

Loire

Orleans

Basel

Nantes

Dijon

Bern

FRANCE

Geneva

Limoges

Lyon

VALAIS

Santiago de Compostela

Gijón

Bay of Biscay

Bordeaux

Santander

Toulouse

Monaco

San Sebastián

PYRENEES

Marseille

Nice

MONACO

Porto

Douro

Andorra La Valla

ANDORRA

Golfe du Lion

Zaragoza

Barcelona

Madrid

PORTUGAL

Tagus

SPAIN

Mediterranean Sea

Lisbon

Évora

Guadiana

Valencia

Mallorca

Menorca

Palma De Mallorca

Ibiza

Balearic Islands

Faro

Seville

Murcia

Granada

Strait of Gibraltar

Constantine

MOROCCO

ALGERIA

NORWAY
Oslo ✪

SWEDEN
Stockholm ✪

kagerrak

DENMARK
Copenhagen ✪
Zealand
Bornholm

Stralsund
Hamburg
Schwerin
Bremen
Elbe
Berlin ✪

GERMANY

Erfurt
Frankfurt-
am-Main

Dresden

Stuttgart
Munich
Zurich
LIECHTENSTEIN
Vaduz
SWITZERLAND
ALPS
Milan
ITALY
Genoa
Pisa
Bologna
TUSCANY
Perugia
Ligurian Sea
Corsica
(Fr)
Ajaccio
Elba
Rome ✪

FINLAND
Helsinki ✪
Åland
✪ Tallinn
ESTONIA
Saaremaa

St Petersburg

Moscow ✪

RUSSIA

Gotland
Baltic Sea
Öland

Rīga ✪
LATVIA

LITHUANIA
Vilnius ✪
RUSSIA
✪ Kaliningrad

BELARUS
Minsk ✪

POLAND

Warsaw ✪

UKRAINE
✪ Kiev
Dnieper

Prague ✪ **CZECH REPUBLIC**

SLOVAKIA
CARPATHIAN MOUNTAINS

MOLDOVA
Chişinău ✪

Bratislava ✪
Vienna ✪
Salzburg
AUSTRIA
SLOVENIA
Ljubljana ✪
CROATIA
Zagreb ✪
Budapest ✪
HUNGARY

ROMANIA
Bucharest ✪

San Marino
SAN MARINO
BOSNIA & HERZEGOVINA
Sarajevo ✪
SERBIA
MONTENEGRO
Podgorica ✪
KOSOVO
Priština ✪
Skopje ✪
MACEDONIA
Tirana ✪
ALBANIA
Bari

Black Sea

BULGARIA
Sofiya ✪

İstanbul

Sea of Marmara

Naples
Salerno
APPENINES
Adriatic Sea
Sassari
Sardinia
(It)
Cagliari
Tyrrhenian Sea

Thessaloniki

TURKEY

Corfu
Ioannina
Aegean Sea
Lesvos
Evia
Athens ✪

Aeolian Islands
Palermo
Sicily
Syracuse
Pantelleria
Tunis ✪
TUNISIA
MALTA
Valletta ✪

Tripoli

Ionian Sea
Ionian Islands

Cyclades Islands
GREECE

Dodecanese Islands
Crete

Berlin
Learn about the infamous Wall (p260)

Munich
Beer halls and beer gardens (p283)

Vienna
Imperial Vienna's architectural legacy dazzles (p42)

Venice
Romantic waterways and exceptional art (p450)

Rome
Survey the Palatino's evocative ruins (p419)

Tuscany
Vineyards bathed in golden light (p462)

Santorini
Whitewashed island with spectacular sunsets (p356)

Western Europe's
Top 26

1

Eiffel Tower, Paris

1 Initially designed as a temporary exhibit for the 1889 Exposition Universelle (World Fair), the elegant, webbed-metal art nouveau design of Paris' Eiffel Tower (p184) has become the defining fixture of the French capital's skyline. Its recent 1st-floor refit incorporates two glitzy new glass pavilions housing interactive history exhibits; outside them, peer d-o-w-n through glass flooring to the ground below. Visit at dusk for the best day and night views of the glittering City of Light, and toast making it to the top at the sparkling champagne bar.

Live Music, London

2 Music lovers will hear London calling – from the theatres, concert halls, nightclubs, pubs and even tube stations, where on any given night countless performers take to the stage. Find your own iconic London experience, whether it's the Proms at the Royal Albert Hall (p136), an East End singalong around a pub piano, a classic musical in the West End, a superstar DJ set at Fabric (p133), the city's top-rated club, or a floppy-fringed guitar band at a local boozer. Royal Albert Hall

2

Ancient Rome

3 Rome's famous seven hills (there are actually nine) offer superb vantage points. The Palatino is a gorgeous green expanse of ruins, towering pines and unforgettable views over the Colosseum and the Roman Forum (p419), containing the remains of temples, basilicas and public spaces. This was the social, political and commercial hub of the Roman Empire, where Romulus supposedly founded the city and where ancient Roman emperors lived. As you walk the cobbled paths you can almost sense the ghosts in the air.

Colosseum

Venice

4 There's something especially atmospheric about Venice (p450) on a sunny winter's day. With fewer tourists around and the light sharp and clear, it's the perfect time to lap up the magic of the romantic waterways. Ditch your map and wander Dorsoduro's shadowy back lanes while imagining secret assignations and whispered conspiracies at every turn. Then linger in two of Venice's top galleries, the Galleria dell'Accademia (p451) and the Peggy Guggenheim Collection (p452); the latter houses works by many of the giants of 20th-century art.

Imperial Vienna

5 Imagine what you could do with unlimited riches and Austria's top architects at your disposal and you have Vienna of the Habsburgs. The graceful Hofburg (p42) whisks you back to the age of empires as you marvel at the treasury's imperial crowns, the equine ballet of the Spanish Riding School and the chandelier-lit apartments fit for an empress. The palace is rivalled in grandeur only by the 1441-room Schloss Schönbrunn and the baroque Schloss Belvedere, both set in exquisite landscaped gardens. Hofburg

Remembering the Wall, Berlin

6 Even after more than a quarter of a century, it's hard to comprehend how the Berlin Wall separated the city. The best way to examine its ramifications is to make your way – on foot or by bike – along the Berlin Wall Trail. Passing the Brandenburger Tor (Brandenburg Gate; p261) and analysing graffiti at the East Side Gallery (p265), the path brings it into context. It's heartbreaking and hopeful and sombre, but integral to understanding Germany's capital today. Detail of a mural by César Olhagaray, East Side Gallery

Tuscany

7 Battalions of books, postcards and TV shows try to capture the essence of the enchanting Italian region of Tuscany (p462), but nothing can match experiencing it for yourself. Monumental art cities and picture-perfect towns, including its magnificent capital Florence, as well as tower-famed Pisa and medieval Siena, are filled with Renaissance treasures, vying for visitors' attention with medieval monasteries and rolling hills ribboned by ancient vineyards bathed in golden light. Also seeking attention is some of Italy's finest food and wine.

The Matterhorn

8 It graces Toblerone packages and evokes stereotypical 'Heidi' scenes, but nothing prepares you for the allure of the Matterhorn (p647). When you arrive at the timber-chalet-filled village of Zermatt, Switzerland's mightiest mountain soars above you, mesmerising you with its chiselled, majestic peak. Gaze at it from a tranquil cafe terrace, hike in its shadow along the tangle of alpine paths above town with cowbells clinking in the distance or pause on a ski slope to contemplate its sheer size.

GEHRING/GETTY IMAGES ©

SVETOSLAVA SLAVOVA/GETTY IMAGES ©

Barcelona's La Sagrada Família

9 The Modernista brainchild of Antoni Gaudí remains a work in progress close to a century after the architect's death. Fanciful and profound, inspired by nature and barely restrained by a Gothic style, Barcelona's La Sagrada Família (p588) climbs skyward; when completed, the highest tower will be more than half as high again as today's. The improbable angles and departures from architectural convention confound but the decorative detail of the passion and nativity facades are worth studying for hours.

Beer-Drinking in Munich

10 The southern German state of Bavaria is synonymous with brewing, and Munich (the country's third-largest city), has an astounding variety of places to drink. There's the rollicking Oktoberfest festival of course, and then there are the famous beer halls, from the huge, such as Hofbräuhaus (p288) complete with oompah bands, to the traditional and wonderful, such as Augustiner Bräustuben (p288), inside the Augustiner brewery. There are also sprawling, high-spirited beer gardens like Chinesischer Turm, where you can enjoy a frothy, refreshing stein. Oktoberfest beer hall

Alhambra, Granada

11 In Spain's sultry southern Andalucía region in the city of Granada is the Alhambra (p624). The world's most refined example of Islamic art, it's the enduring symbol of 800 years of the Moorish rule of Al-Andalus. The Alhambra's red fortress towers dominate the Granada skyline against the Sierra Nevada's snowcapped peaks, while its geometric Generalife gardens complement the exquisite detail of the Palacios Nazaríes, where Arabic inscriptions proliferate in the stuccowork. Put simply, this is Spain's most beautiful monument. Wall detail, Palacios Nazaríes, Alhambra

HANS-PETER MERTEN/GETTY IMAGES ©

ECLYPSE78/SHUTTERSTOCK ©

Castles, Luxembourg

12 Beyond the gleaming banks and financial centres that help make Luxembourg Europe's wealthiest country, the grand duchy is a picturesque patchwork of undulating fields, wooded hills and deep-cut river valleys. Take in Luxembourg City's extraordinary fortifications along 'Europe's most beautiful balcony', the pedestrian promenade Chemin de la Corniche (p100), which winds along the 17th-century city ramparts. Further afield, Luxembourg's bucolic countryside retains impressive castle ruins. Château de Bourscheid (p104)

Champagne

13 Name-brand Champagne houses such as Mumm, Mercier and Moët & Chandon, in the main towns of Reims (p210) and Épernay (p211), are known the world over. But what's less well known is that much of Champagne's best liquid gold is made by thousands of small-scale *vignerons* (winemakers) in hundreds of villages. Dozens welcome visitors for a taste and the chance to shop at producers' prices, making the region's scenic driving routes the best way to sample fine bubbly amid rolling vineyards and gorgeous villages. Champagne house, Épernay

Navigating Amsterdam's Canals

14 The Dutch capital is a watery wonderland. Amsterdam made its fortune in maritime trade, and its Canal Ring (p501) was constructed during the city's Golden Age. Stroll along the canals and check out its narrow, gabled houses and thousands of houseboats, or relax on a cafe terrace. Better still, go for a ride. Cruises and boat rentals abound. From boat level you'll see a whole new set of architectural details, such as the ornamentation bedecking the bridges and, come nightfall, glowing lights reflecting in the ripples.

Santorini

15 On first view, startling Santorini (Thira; p356) grabs your attention and doesn't let go. The submerged caldera, surrounded by lava-layered cliffs topped by villages that look like a sprinkling of icing sugar, is one of nature's great wonders, best experienced by a walk along the clifftops from the main town of Fira to the northern village of Oia (p356). The precariousness and impermanence of the place is breathtaking. Recover from your effort with Santorini's ice-cold Yellow Donkey beer as you wait for its famed picture-perfect sunset. *Oia*

Causeway Coast, Northern Ireland

16 Hiking the Causeway Coast (p409) takes you through some of Northern Ireland's most inspiring coastal scenery. Its grand geological centrepiece is the Giant's Causeway, a World Heritage–listed natural wonder incorporating 40,000 hexagonal basalt columns, formed by cooling lava 60 million years ago. Another highlight of this other-worldly hiking route is the nerve-testing challenge of the Carrick-a-Rede Rope Bridge (p410) swaying above the rock-strewn water. *Carrick-a-Rede Rope Bridge*

15

16

Alfama, Lisbon

17 With its labyrinthine alleyways, hidden courtyards and curving, shadow-filled lanes, the Alfama (p527) is a magical place to lose all direction and delve into the soul of the Portuguese capital. On the journey, you'll pass breadbox-sized grocers, brilliantly tiled buildings and cosy taverns filled with easygoing chatter, with the aroma of chargrilled sardines and the mournful rhythms of fado (traditional Portuguese melancholic song) drifting in the breeze. Then you round a bend and catch sight of steeply pitched rooftops leading down to the glittering river, the Tejo.

Slow-Boating on the Rhine

18 A boat ride through the romantic Rhine Valley (p308) between Koblenz and Mainz is one of Germany's most memorable experiences. As you sit back on deck, glorious scenery drifts slowly past like a slide show: vineyard-clad hills, idyllic riverside towns and, every now and then, a mighty medieval castle. Stop off for a hearty meal, sample a few of the local wines and spend an hour or two wandering around a half-timbered village – the Rhine is a guaranteed highlight of any Western Europe trip.

KAVALENKAU/SHUTTERSTOCK ©

TONY SOUTER/GETTY IMAGES ©

Bath

19 Britain has many beautiful cities, but Bath (p144) is the belle of the ball. The Romans built a health resort to take advantage of the steaming-hot water bubbling to the surface here; the springs were rediscovered in the 18th century and Bath became the place to see and be seen in British high society. Today, Bath's Georgian architecture of sweeping crescents, grand townhouses, and Palladian mansions (not to mention Roman remains, a beautiful abbey and a 21st-century spa) make the former home town and inspiration of novelist Jane Austen a must. Roman Baths (p144)

The Netherlands by Bike

20 The nation where everyone rides bikes (p513) to commute, to shop, to socialise or just for the sheer enjoyment is perfectly designed for cyclists. Much of the landscape is famously below sea level and pancake-flat; you can glide alongside canals, tulip fields and windmills; there are more than 32,000km of dedicated bike paths; rental outlets are everywhere; and except for motorways there's virtually nowhere bicycles can't go. Even if you just take the occasional spin, it'll be a highlight of your travels. Family cycling, Amsterdam

Beer & Chocolate, Belgium

21 Belgium (p73) has a brew for all seasons, and then some. The range of Belgian beer is exceptional, and each variety is served in its own special glass. You can sip a selection in timeless cafes, hidden in the cores of Belgium's great art cities – Ghent, Bruges, Antwerp and Brussels – with their unique blends of medieval and art nouveau architecture; try Au Bon Vieux Temps (p82). Belgium also has an unparalleled range of chocolate shops selling melt-in-the-mouth pralines incorporating classic and intriguing new flavour combinations.

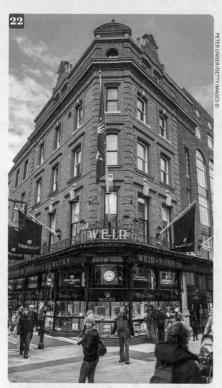

PETER UNGER/GETTY IMAGES ©

KRAINOC KALLSTROM/SHUTTERSTOCK ©

Dublin

22 Ireland's capital city (p383) contains all the attractions and distractions of an international metropolis, but manages to retain the intimacy and atmosphere of a small town. Whether you're strolling stately St Stephen's Green, viewing prehistoric treasures and Celtic art at the superb National Museum of Ireland – Archaeology, or learning about Ireland's hard-fought path to independence at Kilmainham Gaol, you're never far from a friendly pub where the craic is flowing. And, of course, you can sink a pint of the black stuff at the original Guinness brewery.

Edinburgh

23 Edinburgh (p162) is a city of many moods, famous for its exuberant festivals and especially lively in the summer. The Scottish capital is also well worth visiting out of season, to see Edinburgh Castle (p162) silhouetted against the blue spring sky with yellow daffodils gracing the slopes below; to see its gardens strewn with autumnal leaves; or witness fog cloaking the spires of the Old Town, with rain on the cobblestones and a warm glow beckoning from the window of a pub on a chilly winter's day. Edinburgh Castle

Skiing in Chamonix

24 Skiing, mountaineering, trekking, canyoning, rafting, you name it, French mountaineering mecca Chamonix (p225), in the glaciated Mont Blanc massif, has it all and more. Afterwards, toast your triumphs at Chamonix' chic après-ski bars before getting up the next day to tackle the area's outdoor challenges all over again. And even if you're not an adrenaline junkie, year-round you can take the vertiginous Téléphérique de l'Aiguille du Midi cable car from Chamonix to the top of Aiguille du Midi and marvel at the Alpine scenery unfolding.

Salzburg

25 If Salzburg (p57) didn't exist, someone would have to invent it to keep all the acolytes who visit each year happy. A Unesco World Heritage Site with 17th-century cobbled streets, Salzburg's baroque old town looks much as it did when Mozart lived here, both from ground level and from the Festung Hohensalzburg (p59) fortress high above. For many, this is first and foremost *The Sound of Music* country, where you can be whisked into the gorgeous steep hills that are alive with tour groups year-round.

Ancient Greece

26 Follow the path of history over Greece's landscape. From Athens' renowned Acropolis (p335) to the monastery-crowned rock spires of Meteora (p346), Greece offers some of Europe's most impressive historical sights, including the Temple of Delphi (p346) perched above the Gulf of Corinth; Olympia (p345), home to the first Olympic Games; Epidavros' acoustically perfect theatre (p345) and its mystical Sanctuary of Asclepius, an ancient healing centre. Parthenon, Acropolis, Athens

Need to Know

For more information, see Survival Guide (p667)

Currency

Euro (€) Austria, Belgium, France, Germany, Greece, Ireland, Italy, Luxembourg, Netherlands, Portugal, Spain
Pound (£) UK
Swiss franc (Sfr) Switzerland

Money

ATMs are widespread. Credit card usage varies by country; Visa and MasterCard are the most widely accepted.

Visas

Generally not required for stays of up to 90 days for citizens of most Western countries (Australia, USA etc). The Schengen Agreement (no passport controls at borders between member countries) applies to most areas; the UK and Ireland are exceptions. Nationals of other countries (eg China and India) will need a Schengen visa, which is good for a maximum stay of 90 days in a six-month period.

When to Go

Dry climate
Warm summer, mild winter
Mild year-round
Mild summer, very cold winter
Cold climate

Ireland
GO Jun–Aug

Britain
GO Apr–Sep

Germany
GO Jul–Aug & Dec

France
GO Apr–Oct

Spain
GO Sep–Nov & Mar–May

Italy
GO Mar–Jun & Sep–Nov

Greece
GO Apr–May & Sep–Oct

High Season
(Jun–Aug)

➡ Visitors arrive and Europeans hit the road; prices peak.

➡ Beautiful weather means that everybody is outside at cafes.

➡ Businesses in major cities often have seasonal closures around August.

Shoulder
(Apr & May, Sep & Oct)

➡ Moderate weather with frequent bright, clear days.

➡ Almost everything is open.

➡ Considered high season in some places such as Italy's big art cites (Rome, Florence, Venice).

Low Season
(Nov–Mar)

➡ Outside of ski resorts and Christmas markets, much is closed in regional areas.

➡ Perfect for enjoying major cities where indoor attractions and venues stay open.

➡ Prices often plummet.

Useful Websites

Lonely Planet (www.lonely planet.com/europe) Destination info, hotel bookings, traveller forums and more.

The Man in Seat 61 (www.seat61.com) Comprehensive information about travelling Europe by train.

Ferrylines (www.ferrylines.com) Excellent portal for researching ferry routes and operators throughout Europe.

Michelin (www.viamichelin.com) Calculates the best driving routes and estimates toll and fuel costs.

BBC News (www.bbc.co.uk/news) Find out what's happening before you arrive.

Europa (http:europa.eu) Official website of the European Union.

Important Numbers

EU-wide general emergency	112
UK general emergency	999

Tipping

Adding another 5% to 10% to a bill at a restaurant or cafe for good service is common across Western Europe, although tipping is never expected.

Daily Costs

Budget: Less than €100

➡ Dorm bed: €20–€50

➡ Double room in budget property per person: €60–€100

➡ Excellent markets; restaurant main: under €12

➡ Local bus/train tickets: €5–€10

Midrange: €100–€250

➡ Double room in midrange hotel per person: €80–€160

➡ Restaurant main: €12–€25

➡ Museum admission: free–€15

➡ Short taxi trip: €10–€20

Top End: More than €250

➡ Iconic hotels

➡ Destination restaurants

➡ Duty-free refunds from stylish shopping

What to Take

Sandals or thongs (flip-flops) For rocky Mediterranean beaches.

Raincoat, waterproof jacket or umbrella For the weather that keeps Europe green.

Phrasebook For rewarding experiences interacting with locals.

Earplugs To sleep peacefully in the heart of boisterous culture.

Travel plug (adaptor)

Pocket knife with corkscrew Corked wine bottles are the norm; screw caps are rare (just remember to pack it in your checked-in luggage).

Smart clothes For chic venues.

Comfortable shoes For all that walking you'll be doing – many cities and towns are best explored on foot.

Arriving in Western Europe

Major gateway airports in Western Europe include the following:

Schiphol Airport, Amsterdam (p523; www.schiphol.nl) Trains (20 minutes) to the centre.

Heathrow Airport, London (p177; www.heathrowairport.com) Trains (15 minutes) and tube (one hour) to the centre.

Aéroport de Charles de Gaulle, Paris (p200; www.aeroports deparis.fr) Many buses (one hour) and trains (30 minutes) to the centre.

Frankfurt Airport, Frankfurt (p308; http://www.frankfurt-airport.com) Trains (15 minutes) to the centre.

Leonardo da Vinci Airport–Fiumicino, Rome (p437; www.adr.it) Buses (one hour) and trains (30 minutes) to the centre.

Getting Around

Air Cheap airfares make it easy to fly from one end of the continent to the other.

Bicycle From coasting along the flat Netherlands landscape alongside canals to tackling mountainous trails in Italy, Western Europe is ideal for cycling. Bike-rental outlets abound.

Boat Relax at sea on board ferries between Ireland and Britain, Britain and the continent, Spain and Italy, Italy and Greece.

Car In Britain and Ireland, drive on the left; in continental Europe, drive on the right. Car hire is readily available throughout Western Europe. Non-EU citizens might consider leasing a vehicle, which can work out cheaper.

Train Trains go almost everywhere; they're often fast and usually frequent.

For much more on **getting around**, see p678.

If You Like...

Castles & Palaces

Strategically designed castles and vast royal palaces surrounded by extravagant grounds continue to astound visitors.

Versailles Opulence abounds in the palace's shimmering Hall of Mirrors and sumptuous fountained gardens. (p202)

Neuschwanstein In the heart of the Bavarian Alps, this is everyone's (including Disney's) castle fantasy. (p292)

Conwy Castle With eight defensive towers, this Welsh fortress is what a serious castle should look like. (p161)

Hofburg An imperial spectacle, Vienna's Hofburg exemplifies royal excess. (p42)

Alhambra Spain's exquisite Islamic palace complex in Granada is a World Heritage–listed marvel. (p624)

Gravensteen The counts of Flanders' turreted stone castle looms over the beautiful Belgian city of Ghent. (p91)

Kilkenny Castle Majestic riverside castle in the delightful Irish town of Kilkenny. (p393)

Château de Bourscheid Luxembourg's most evocative medieval ruined castle. (p104)

Historic Sites

Western Europe is layered in millennia upon millennia of history that you can explore today.

Stonehenge Britain's most iconic – and mysterious – archaeological site, dating back some 5000 years. (p143)

Pompeii Wander the streets and alleys of this great ancient city, buried by a volcanic eruption. (p480)

Athens Ancient Greek wonders include the Acropolis, Ancient Agora, Temple of Olympian Zeus and more. (p334)

Amsterdam's Canal Ring Stroll the Dutch capital's Golden Age canals lined with gabled buildings. (p501)

Bruges Beautiful Renaissance town in Belgium with gables, canals, bell towers and a beguiling overall harmony. (p93)

Dachau Germany's first Nazi concentration camp is a harrowing introduction to WWII's horrors. (p290)

West Belfast Falls and Shankill Rds are emblazoned with murals expressing local political and religious passions. (p405)

Cultural Cuisine

Every country in Western Europe has its own delicious delicacies; the following are just a taster.

Spanish tapas Small dishes of every description; cured Iberian ham or a perfect stuffed olive...

Greek mezedhes Shortened to *meze*, these tasting dishes include *dolmadhes* (stuffed vine leaves) and *oktapodi* (octopus).

British fish and chips Cod expertly battered, fried and served with chips and quality vinegar is sublime.

German Wurst Germany has hundreds of varieties of sausage – often the source of great local pride.

Austrian Wiener schnitzel Made with veal, this tender, breadcrumbed delicacy is the real deal.

French bread *Boulangeries* (bakeries) in France turn out still-warm, crusty baguettes and richer treats like buttery croissants.

Dutch cheese The tastiest hard, rich *oud* (old) Gouda varieties have strong, complex flavours.

Belgian chocolate Buy a box of velvety, extravagant confections.

Italian pizza The best are wood-fired, whether Roman (thin crispy base) or Neapolitan (higher, doughier base).

Portuguese custard tarts Portugal's *pastéis de nata* is a must-try.

Swiss fondue Dip bread into a bubbling pot of melted emmental and Gruyère cheese and white wine.

Local Tipples

Europe packs a large variety of beer and wine into a small space: virtually every region has at least one renowned liquid creation.

Belgian beer Belgium is famed for its lagers, white beers, abbey beers and monastery-brewed 'Trappist beers'.

Bordeaux and Burgundy wines Tour the vineyards where France's finest reds are produced. (p229)

Champagne Visit century-old cellars to sip France's feted bubbles. (p210)

Portuguese port Enjoy port-wine tastings across the Rio Douro from Porto at Vila Nova da Gaia. (p555)

English ales Served at room temperature, so the flavours – from fruity to bitter – come through.

Tuscan Chianti The warm burnt-umber colours of the iconic Italian region are palpable in every glass.

German riesling This classic white wine is renowned for its quality.

Scotch whisky Have a dram of Scotland's signature distilled spirit aged in oak barrels for three-plus years.

MATT MUNRO/GETTY IMAGES ©

Top: Neuschwanstein Castle (p292), Bavaria, Germany
Bottom: *Pastéis de nata* (custard tarts) from Portugal (p525)

Cafes & Bars

Whether it's a coffee savoured for an hour or a pint with a roomful of new friends, you'll find plenty of places to imbibe like a local.

Vienna's coffee houses Unchanged in decades and redolent with an air of refinement. (p50)

Irish pubs Guinness' iconic stout tastes best on home turf, expertly hand-pulled in a traditional pub.

Parisian cafes Opening onto wicker-chair-strewn terraces, Paris' cafes are the city's communal lounge rooms. (p197)

Dutch brown cafes Cosy, candlelit havens named for the old tobacco stains on the walls. (p507)

Brussels' bars Historic treasures hidden in alleys around the Bourse serve Belgian beer, including spontaneously fermented lambic. (p82)

Greek tavernas Sip anise-flavoured ouzo in Greece's rustic tavernas.

Outdoor Fun

Don't just stare at the beautiful scenery, dive right into it, no matter the season.

Strolling the English countryside England's entire countryside seems tailor-made for beautiful, memorable walking.

Cycling the Netherlands Pedal past the creaking windmills and shimmering canals of the gloriously flat, tulip-filled Dutch countryside. (p513)

Skiing year-round Head to the glaciers near Austria's alpine city Innsbruck for downhill action. (p64)

Windsurfing the Mediterranean The wind is always howling in Tarifa, Spain, the windsurfing capital of Europe.

Hillwalking in Ireland The starkly beautiful Connemara region is prime hillwalking country with wild, remote terrain. (p404)

Hiking the Alps Hundreds of kilometres of trails web Switzerland's Jungfrau region, with jaw-dropping views. (p653)

Beaches

From blindingly white Mediterranean sand lapped by cobalt blue waters to pounding Atlantic surf, beaches abound in Western Europe.

St-Tropez Plage de Pampelonne is studded with the French Riviera's most glamorous drinking and dining haunts. (p245)

Lefkada Cliffs drop to broad swaths of white sand and turquoise waters on this untrammelled Greek island. (p374)

Menorca Beaches are tucked away in little coves like pearls in oysters on this Spanish Balearic island. (p612)

Baleal Pumpin' Portuguese surf beach. (p544)

Nightlife

Throbbing nightclubs, historic theatres and intimate venues are all part of the scene after dark.

Berlin Countless cutting-edge clubs, where DJs experiment with the sounds of tomorrow. (p273)

London Dozens of theatre productions, from crowd-pleasing musicals to serious drama, take to London's stages nightly. (p134)

Ibiza Mythical European clubbing scene with a near-perfect mix of decadent beach bars and all-night clubs. (p614)

Paris Romantic strolls amid the lit-up splendour can end in jazz clubs, cafes, cabarets and more. (p198)

Madrid Night-time energy never abates in a city where life is lived on the streets 24/7. (p574)

Art

From ancient artefacts to creations that defy comprehension, Europe's art is ever-evolving.

Louvre Paris' pièce de résistance is one of the world's largest and most diverse museums. (p189)

Tate Modern London's modern-art museum fills a huge old power station on the banks of the Thames. (p117)

Galleria degli Uffizi Florence's crowning glory contains the world's greatest collection of Italian Renaissance art. (p463)

Rijksmuseum The Netherlands' premier art trove is packed with old masters. (p503)

Madrid The golden mile's Prado, Reina Sofía and Thyssen represent one of Europe's richest art concentrations. (p564)

Vatican Museums Crane your neck to see Michelangelo's Sistine Chapel ceiling frescoes. (p423)

Centre Belge de la Bande Dessinée Brussels' comic museum occupies an art nouveau building. (p81)

Architecture

The architecture in Western Europe spans the centuries and is as diverse as the continent itself.

Beach, Lefkada (p374), Greece

Notre Dame Paris' gargoyled cathedral is a Gothic wonder. (p188)

Meteora Late-14th-century monasteries perch dramatically atop enormous rocky pinnacles in Meteora, Greece. (p346)

La Sagrada Família Gaudí's singular work in progress, Barcelona's cathedral boggles the mind. (p588)

Pantheon Commissioned during Augustus' reign, the portico of Rome's Pantheon is graced by Corinthian columns. (p424)

Grand Place Brussels' showpiece central square is ringed by gilded guild houses. (p76)

Overblaak Development This late-20th-century Rotterdam complex incorporates a 'forest' of 45-degree-tilted cube-shaped apartments. (p516)

Shard London's dramatic splinterlike building is a contemporary icon. (p121)

Music

Classical music of royalty, soulful songs of the masses, pop culture that changed the world and much, much more.

Staatsoper Vienna's state opera is the premier venue in a city synonymous with classical music. (p51)

Teatro alla Scala Italian opera is soul-stirring in the crimson-and-gilt splendour of Milan's opera house. (p445)

Irish music The Emerald Isle hums with music pubs; Galway (p401) on the west coast has a cornucopia.

Fado Portuguese love the melancholy, nostalgic songs of fado. Hear it in Lisbon's atmospheric Alfama district (p527)

Andalucia The heartland of passionate flamenco, Spain's best-loved musical tradition, capturing the spirit of the nation. (p616)

Scenic Journeys

There are beautiful journeys aplenty in Europe, from the Highlands of Scotland to the soaring, snow-covered peaks of the Swiss Alps.

Scottish Highlands The Inverness–Kyle of Lochalsh route is one of Britain's great scenic train journeys. (p171)

Cinque Terre Five picture-perfect Italian villages linked by a trail along beaches, vineyards and olive groves. (p440)

Romantic Rhine Valley Storybook German river cruise past forested hillsides, craggy cliffs, terraced vineyards and idyllic half-timbered villages. (p308)

Bernina Express The Unesco-recognised train route between Tirano and St Moritz is one of Switzerland's most spectacular. (p661)

Month by Month

is the lavish Opernball (Opera Ball; p47).

January

The frosty first month of the year isn't Western Europe's most festive. But museum queues are nonexistent, cosy cafes have crackling fireplaces and it's a great time to ski.

✨ Hogmanay

An enormous, raucous Edinburgh street party, Hogmanay sees in the New Year in Scotland. It's replicated Europe-wide as main squares resonate with champagne corks and fireworks.

☆ Vienna Ball Season

If you've dreamed of waltzing at Vienna's grand balls, you won't want to miss the Austrian capital's ball season, when 300 or so balls are held in January and February. The most famous

February

Carnival in all its manic glory sweeps through Catholic regions of continental Europe – cold temperatures are forgotten amid masquerades, street festivals and general bacchanalia. Couples descend on romantic destinations like Paris for Valentine's Day.

✨ Carnevale

In the pre-Lent period before Ash Wednesday (10 February 2016; 1 March 2017), Venice goes mad for masks. Costume balls, many with traditions centuries old, enliven the social calendar in this storied old city like no other event. Even those without a coveted invite are swept up in the pageantry. (p455)

✨ Carnaval

Pre-Lent is celebrated with greater vigour in Maastricht than anywhere else in Northern Europe. While the rest of the Netherlands hopes the canals will freeze for ice skating, this Dutch corner cuts loose with a celebration that would have

done its former Roman residents proud.

✨ Karneval

Germany doesn't leave the pre-Lent season solely to its neighbours. Karneval (Fasching) is celebrated with abandon in the traditional Catholic regions of the country, including Cologne (p313), much of Bavaria, along the Rhine and deep in the Black Forest.

March

Blooms appear in parks and gardens, leaves start greening city avenues and festivities begin to flourish. And days get longer – the last Sunday morning of the month ushers in daylight saving time.

✨ St Patrick's Day

Parades and celebrations are held on 17 March in Irish towns big and small to honour St Patrick. While elsewhere the day is a commercialised romp of green beer, in his home country it's a time to celebrate with friends and family.

April

Spring arrives with a burst of colour, from

the glorious bulb fields of the Netherlands to the blossoming orchards of Spain. On the southernmost beaches it's time to shake the sand out of the umbrellas.

✵ Semana Santa

Procession of penitents and holy icons in Spain, notably in Seville, during Easter week (from 20 March 2016; 9 April 2017). Throughout the week thousands of members of religious brotherhoods parade in traditional garb. (p618)

✵ Settimana Santa

Italy celebrates Holy Week with processions and passion plays. By Holy Thursday (24 March 2016; 13 April 2017), Rome is thronged with the faithful and even nonbelievers are swept up in the emotion and piety of hundreds of thousands of faithful flocking to the Vatican and St Peter's Basilica.

✵ Greek Easter

The most important festival in the Greek Orthodox calendar. The emphasis is on the Resurrection so it's a celebratory event – the most significant part is midnight on Easter Saturday (30 April 2016; 15 April 2017) when fireworks explode. The night before, candlelit processions hit the streets.

✵ Feria de Abril

A week-long party held in the southern Spanish city of Seville in late April to counterbalance the religious peak of Easter. The many beautiful old squares of this gorgeous city come alive during the long, warm

nights the nation is known for. (p618)

✵ Koningsdag

On 27 April (26 April if the 27th is a Sunday) the Netherlands celebrates Koningsdag (King's Day), the birthday of King Willem-Alexander. There are events nationwide but especially in Amsterdam, where – uproarious partying, music and outrageous orange get-ups aside – there's a giant flea market.

May

Outdoor activities and cafe terraces come into their own. Expect nice weather anywhere but especially in the south throughout the Mediterranean regions. Yachts ply the harbours while beautiful people take to the sun lounges.

☆ Cannes Film Festival

Celebrities, would-be celebrities and plenty of starstruck spectators hit the French Riviera's glitziest seafront, La Croisette, during Cannes' famous film festival (www.festival-cannes.com), held over two weeks in May.

☆ Brussels Jazz Marathon

Brussels swings to around-the-clock jazz performances (www.brusselsjazzmarathon.be) for three days over the second-last weekend in May. Free performances are everywhere from open stages in city squares to tight-packed cafes and pubs, and encompass everything from zydeco to boogie-blues.

✵ Queima das Fitas

Fado (traditional melancholic song) fills the air in the Portuguese town of Coimbra, whose annual highlight is this boozy festival of traditional music and revelry during the first week in May, when students celebrate the end of the academic year. (p547)

✵ Karneval der Kulturen

This joyous street carnival (www.karneval-berlin.de) celebrates Berlin's multicultural tapestry with parties, global nosh and a fun parade of flamboyantly costumed dancers, DJs, artists and musicians.

June

The huge summer travel season hasn't started yet but the sun has burst through the clouds, the weather is gorgeous and long daylight hours peak during the summer solstice (between 20 and 22 June).

✵ Festa de Santo António

In Portugal's capital, the Festa de Santo António (Festival of Saint Anthony), from 12 June to 13 June, wraps up the three-week Festas de Lisboa (www.festasdelisboa.com), with processions and dozens of street parties; it's liveliest in the Alfama.

✵ Festa de São João

Elaborate processions, live music on Porto's plazas and merrymaking take place in Portugal's second city. Squeaky plastic hammers (available for sale everywhere) come out for the unusual custom of whacking one another. Everyone is fair game – don't expect mercy. (p552)

🎊 Lëtzebuerger Nationalfeierdag

Held on 23 June, Luxembourg National Day is the grand duchy's biggest event – a celebration of the birth of the grand duke (though it has never actually fallen on a grand ducal birthday).

☆ Glastonbury Festival of Contemporary Performing Arts

One of England's favourite outdoor events is Glastonbury's long weekend of music, theatre and New Age shenanigans. More than 100,000 turn up to writhe in Pilton Farm's grassy fields (or deep mud). (p149)

🎊 Gay Pride

European Gay Pride celebrations take place on a summer weekend usually in late June but at times as late as August. Amsterdam (www.amsterdamgaypride. org) hosts the world's only waterborne pride parade.

July

Visitors have arrived from around the world and outdoor cafes, beer gardens and beach clubs are hopping. Expect beautiful weather anywhere you go.

🎊 Il Palio

Siena's great annual event is the Palio (2 July and 16 August), a pageant culminating in a bareback horse race round Il Campo. The city is divided into 17 *contrade* (districts), of which 10 compete for the *palio* (silk banner).

☆ Montreux Jazz Festival

It's not just jazz: big-name rock acts also hit the shores of Lake Geneva during the first two weeks of July (www.montreuxjazz.com). The cheaper music festival Paleo (www.paleo.ch) takes place in Nyon, between Geneva and Lausanne, in the second half of July.

🎊 Running of the Bulls

From 6 to 14 July, Pamplona, Spain, hosts the famous Sanfermines festival (aka Encierro or 'Running of the Bulls'; p605), when the city is overrun with thrill-seekers, curious onlookers and, yes, bulls.

🎊 Bastille Day

Fireworks and military processions mark France's national day, 14 July. It's celebrated in every French town and city, with the biggest festivities in Paris, where the storming of the Bastille prison kick-started the French Revolution.

☆ De Gentse Feesten

The charming Belgian city of Ghent is transformed into a 10-day party of music and theatre; a highlight is a vast techno celebration called 10 Days Off (www. gentsefeesten.be).

☆ Festival d'Avignon

In France's lavender-scented Provence region, hundreds of artists take to the stage and streets of Avignon during July's world-famous Festival d'Avignon (www.festival-avignon. com). The fringe Festival Off (www.avignonleoff. com) runs from early July to early August.

August

Everybody's on the move as major European city businesses shut down and residents head off to enjoy the traditional month of holiday. If it's near the beach, from Germany's Baltic to Spain's Balearic, it's mobbed.

☆ Salzburg Festival

Austria's most renowned classical music festival, the Salzburger Festspiele attracts international stars from late July to the end of August. That urbane person who looks like a famous cellist sitting by you having a glass of wine probably is. (p60)

🎊 Street Parade

In Switzerland, it's Zürich's turn to let its hair down with an enormous techno parade (www.streetparade. com). All thoughts of numbered accounts are forgotten as bankers and everybody else parties to deep-base thump, thump, thump.

🎊 Notting Hill Carnival

For three days during the last weekend of August, London's Notting Hill echoes to the beats of calypso, ska, reggae and soca at London's most vibrant outdoor carnival, where the local Caribbean community shows the city how to party. (p125)

☆ Edinburgh International Festival

Three weeks of innovative drama, comedy, dance, music and more, held in Edinburgh. Two weeks overlap with the celebrated 3½-week Fringe Festival (www.edfringe.com), which draws innovative acts from around the globe. Catch cutting-edge comedy, drama and productions that defy description. (p163)

September

It's cooling off in every sense, from the northern countries to the romance started on an Ibiza dance floor. But it's often the best time to visit, with pleasant weather and thinner crowds.

☆ Venice International Film Festival

The Mostra del Cinema di Venezia is Italy's top film festival and one of the world's top indie film fests. Judging is seen as an indication of what to look for at the next year's Oscars. (p455)

✕ Galway Oyster Festival

National and World Oyster Opening Championships are just the start of this spirited seafood festival in Ireland's colourful west-coast city of Galway, with tastings, talks, cooking demonstrations and plenty of live music and merry-making. (p401)

⚝ Festes de la Mercè

Barcelona knows how to party until dawn and it outdoes itself around 24 September for the Festes de la Mercè: four days of concerts, dancing, *castellers* (human-castle builders), fireworks and *correfocs* (a parade of firework-spitting dragons and devils). (p590)

October

October heralds an autumnal kaleidoscope, along with bright, crisp days, cool, clear nights and excellent cultural offerings, with prices and visitor numbers way down. Daylight saving ends on the last Sunday morning of the month.

🍷 Oktoberfest

Germany's legendary beer-swilling party originates from the marriage celebrations of Crown Prince Ludwig in 1810. Munich's Oktoberfest (www.oktoberfest.de; p283) runs for the 15 days before the first Sunday in October. Millions descend for whopping 1L steins of beer and carousing that has no equal.

☆ Festival at Queen's

Belfast hosts the UK's second-biggest arts festival (www.belfastfestival.com) for three weeks in late October/early November in and around Queen's University, celebrating the intellectual and the creative.

November

Leaves have fallen and snow is about to in much of Europe. Even in the temperate zones around the Mediterranean it can get chilly, rainy and blustery. Most seasonal attractions have closed for the year.

⚝ Guy Fawkes Night

Bonfires and fireworks flare up across Britain on 5 November recalling the failed antigovernment 'gunpowder plot' from 1605 to blow up the parliament (Fawkes was in charge of the explosives). Go to high ground in London to see glowing explosions erupt everywhere.

December

Twinkling fairy lights, brightly decorated Christmas trees and shop windows, and outdoor ice-skating rinks make December a magical month to be in Western Europe, where every region has its own traditions.

🔒 Christmas Markets

Christmas markets are held across many European counties, particularly Germany (p296) and Austria, whose most famous are Nuremberg's Christkindlmarkt and Vienna's Weihnachtsmarkt. Warm your hands through your mittens holding a hot mug of mulled wine and find that special present.

👁 Natale

Italian churches set up an intricate crib or *presepe* (nativity scene) in the lead-up to celebrating Christmas. Some are quite famous, most are works of art and many date back hundreds of years and are venerated for their spiritual ties.

Itineraries

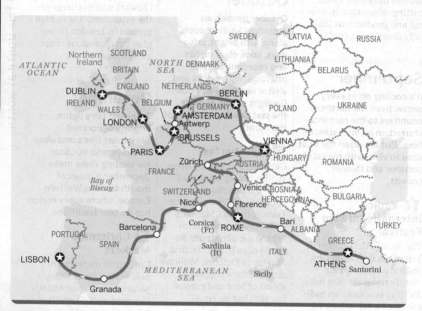

6 WEEKS Ultimate Europe

Have limited time but want to see a bit of everything? Hit the highlights on this trip. Start in **Dublin**, sampling its vibrant pubs and traditional Irish craic. From Ireland, fly to **London** for great theatre. Then catch the Eurostar train through the English Channel tunnel to unmissable **Paris**.

Travel north to **Brussels** for amazing beer and chocolate, then further north to free-spirited **Amsterdam**, making time to cruise its canals. Go east, stopping for a cruise on the Rhine, and spend a few days exploring (and surviving) the legendary nightlife in **Berlin**. Next, visit **Vienna** for architectural and classical-music riches. Zigzag west to **Zürich** and the Swiss Alps for awe-inspiring ski slopes and vistas.

Head to canal-laced **Venice**, art-filled **Florence** and historic **Rome**. Train it to **Bari** and take a ferry to **Athens**, then explore island beaches, starting with the stunning **Santorini**. Connect by air or go by ferry and train to the French Riviera (aka the Côte d'Azur) to check out quintessential Mediterranean destinations such as **Nice**. Continue to **Barcelona**, then the Moorish towns of southern Spain like **Granada**. End your trip in the hilly quarters of **Lisbon**, toasting your grand journey with Portugal's port wine.

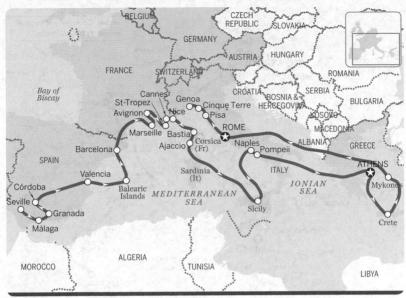

 Mediterranean Europe

Beautiful weather and breathtaking scenery are the draws of this comprehensive tour that takes in famous towns and cities from antiquity to the present. Start in southern Spain in orange-blossom-filled **Seville** and soak up the architecture, sunshine and party atmosphere. Make your way up the eastern coast past the Moorish town of **Málaga** and on to **Granada** and **Córdoba**. Then it's back to the coast at **Valencia**, home of Spain's famous rice dish paella, for a ferry hop to the parties and beaches of the **Balearic Islands**.

Back on the mainland, **Barcelona** brims with the architecture of Gaudí. From here, head into France's fabled Provence region, where in **Marseille** you can see the fortress that was inspiration for the novel *The Count of Monte Cristo*. Then leave the sea for Provence's lush hills and lavender-scented towns around the rampart-hooped city of **Avignon**. On to the French Riviera and its playground for the rich and famous, **St-Tropez**. The charming seaside city **Nice** is a perfect jumping-off point for other nearby coastal hot spots such as **Cannes**.

Cruise by ferry to Corsica and experience the traditional lifestyle of quiet fishing villages. Hit the bustling old port of **Bastia**, Napoléon Bonaparte's home town **Ajaccio**, then the glittering harbour of Bonifacio to hop on a ferry south to Sardinia and on to **Sicily** to visit colossal temples and its famous volcano, Mt Etna.

Catch a ferry to **Naples**, on the Italian mainland, and take a trip to **Pompeii**. Move east to Brindisi for a ferry to Greece that passes rocky coasts seen by mariners for millenniums, landing in Patra. Head to **Athens** to wonder at the Greek capital's ancient treasures before boarding a plane or ferry to magical islands such as **Crete** and **Mykonos**. Return to Italy, taking time to wander amid the ruins and piazzas of **Rome**. Continue north through Tuscany, stopping at **Pisa** to see its famous 'leaning tower'. Finish up along the Ligurian coast, travelling via the coastal villages making up the **Cinque Terre**, strung between plunging cliffs and vine-covered hills, to the port city of **Genoa**.

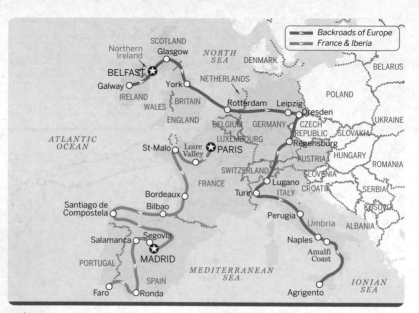

Backroads of Europe

4 WEEKS

You've done the major capitals, now see the rest of Europe. The far west of Ireland is rugged and uncrowded; start in bohemian **Galway**, departure point for the wild Connemara region and windswept Aran Islands, then travel to Northern Ireland – **Belfast** in particular. Head across to the dynamic Scottish city of **Glasgow**. Swing south to the walled English city of **York**. Hop across to the Netherlands, where buzzing **Rotterdam** is a veritable gallery of modern and cutting-edge architecture.

Travel to the dynamic eastern German cities of **Leipzig** and **Dresden**. Turn south via the stunning Bavarian student hub of **Regensburg** to the temperate Swiss town of **Lugano**, on the shores of its sparkling namesake lake. Cross into Italy and stop at the cultured city of **Turin**, with its regal *palazzi* (mansions) and baroque piazzas, followed by beautiful Umbria spots such as **Perugia**. In Italy's south, explore frenetic **Naples** and the winding **Amalfi Coast**, with villages perched above the glittering sea. Scoot over to Sicily to experience its ancient and colourful culture. Marvel at the Grecian Valley of Temples in **Agrigento**, which rival anything in Greece itself.

France & Iberia

2 WEEKS

Get a feel for three of Europe's most distinct countries on this relatively compact jaunt. Start in **Paris**, of course. Visit the châteaux of the **Loire Valley**, then take the fast TGV train to Brittany. Walk the 17th-century ramparts encircling **St-Malo** and sample authentic Breton cider. Track south along the Atlantic coast, where red wine reaches its pinnacle around **Bordeaux**. Cross the border to the Basque city of **Bilbao**, best known for the magnificent Guggenheim Museum, before continuing to the pilgrimage shrine of **Santiago de Compostela**.

Spain's art-filled capital, **Madrid**, is prime for night owls: an evening of tapas and drinks in tiny bars can postpone dinner until midnight. Spend a day exploring the Roman aqueduct and storybook castle in beautiful **Segovia**. Don't skip the sandstone splendour of lively **Salamanca**. Use a car to explore the many hill towns of Andalucía. Narrow, winding roads traverse sunburnt landscapes and olive orchards before reaching the whitewashed buildings of **Ronda**, whose 1785-built Plaza de Toros is considered the national home of bullfighting. Finally, go west via Seville to Portugal's pretty Algarve region, finishing in **Faro**.

Top: Erasmusbrug (Erasmus Bridge), Rotterdam (p515), Netherlands

Bottom: Positano (p485), Amalfi Coast, Italy

TARATATA/GETTY IMAGES ©

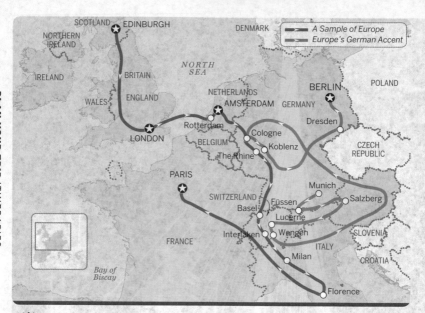

2 WEEKS A Sample of Europe

Watching Europe from the window of a train or gazing at the sea rolling past the handrail of a ferry – that's the way generations of travellers have explored the continent, and it's still as idyllic today.

Start in the engaging Scottish capital **Edinburgh**, then take the train to pulsating **London** and on to Harwich for a ferry crossing to Hoek van Holland. From here, trains connect to the dynamic, contemporary Dutch city of **Rotterdam** and the fabled, gabled canalscapes of **Amsterdam**.

Take a fast train to **Cologne** and then relax on a river cruise down the alluring **Rhine**. Alight at Mainz and connect by train through **Basel** to **Interlaken** for the slow-moving trains and trams that wend through the majestic Alps. Next take a train past rugged scenery to stylish **Milan**. From here, fast trains zip to Tuscany's capital, **Florence**, a veritable Renaissance time capsule, then snuggle up on a night train to **Paris**, feeling the romance in the rhythm of the rails.

2 WEEKS Europe's German Accent

Brush up on your Deutsch on this central European jaunt. Fly into **Munich**, home to famous beer halls and beer gardens. Head into the Alps and behold the most enchanting castle on a hilltop you'll ever see: the real-life model for Disney's Sleeping Beauty's castle, Neuschwanstein, in tiny **Füssen**. A short jaunt east brings you to Austria's harmonious combination of hills and music: **Salzburg**. Travel west to Switzerland's lakeside city of **Lucerne**, where iconic half-timbered bridges cross glacier-cold waters. Ascend to one of the cosy chalets of **Wengen**, where an imposing wall of glacier-capped alpine peaks looms before you.

Head north into Germany and catch a high-speed train to **Cologne** to see its stunning cathedral and explore its lively Altstadt (old town). Set aside a day for a river cruise up the Rhine from **Koblenz**, gliding past steep hillsides covered in vineyards and crowned by castles. Take another high-speed train east to irrepressible **Dresden** and delve into its vibrant cultural scene. Finish in **Berlin**, revelling in its heady history, galleries, hip neighbourhoods and unrivalled nightlife.

On the Road

Austria

Best Places to Eat

➜ Mini (p49)

➜ Tian (p49)

➜ Der Steirer (p56)

➜ Esszimmer (p61)

➜ Chez Nico (p65)

Best Places to Stay

➜ Pension Sacher (p48)

➜ Schlossberg Hotel (p55)

➜ Haus Ballwein (p60)

➜ Hotel Weisses Kreuz (p65)

➜ Hotel Edelweiss (p67)

Why Go?

For such a small country, Austria has made it big. This is, after all, the land where Mozart was born, Strauss taught the world to waltz and Julie Andrews grabbed the spotlight with her twirling entrance in *The Sound of Music*. This is where the Habsburgs built their 600-year empire, and where past glories still shine in the resplendent baroque palaces and chandelier-lit coffee houses of Vienna, Innsbruck and Salzburg. This is a perfectionist of a country and whatever it does – mountains, classical music, new media, castles, cake, you name it – it does exceedingly well.

Beyond its grandiose cities, Austria's allure lies outdoors. And whether you're schussing down the legendary slopes of Kitzbühel, climbing high in the Alps of Tyrol or pedalling along the banks of the sprightly Danube, you'll find the kind of inspiring landscapes that no well-orchestrated symphony, camera lens or singing nun could ever quite do justice to.

When to Go
Vienna

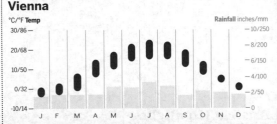

Jul & Aug Alpine hiking in Tyrol, lake swimming in Salzkammergut and lots of summer festivals.

Sep & Oct New wine in vineyards near Vienna, golden forest strolls and few crowds.

Dec & Jan Christmas markets, skiing in the Alps and Vienna waltzing into the New Year.

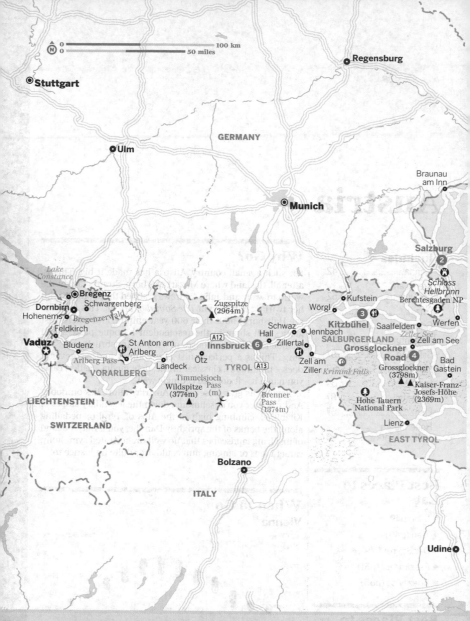

Austria Highlights

1 Discover the opulent Habsburg palaces, coffee houses and cutting-edge galleries of **Vienna** (p42).

2 Survey the baroque cityscape of **Salzburg** (p57) from the giddy height of 900-year-old Festung Hohensalzburg.

3 Send your spirits soaring from peak to peak hiking and skiing in **Kitzbühel** (p67).

4 Buckle up for a roller-coaster ride of Alps and glaciers on the **Grossglockner Road** (p68), one of Austria's greatest drives.

Brno

CZECH REPUBLIC

Drosendorf

Retz

Horn

Hollabrunn

Passau

UPPER AUSTRIA

Freistadt

Krems an
der Donau

Dürnstein

Stockerau

SLOVAKIA

Linz

7 Danube Valley

The
Wachau

Tulln

1 Vienna

Schwechat

Bratislava

Traun

Danube (Donau)

A1

Melk

St Pölten

Ansfelden

Mödling

A4

Wels

Amstetten

Baden bei Wien

Neusiedl
am See

5 Salzkammergut

Steyr

A2

Neusiedler
See

Gmunden

Waidhofen an
der Ybbs

Wiener
Neustadt

Eisenstadt

Mondsee

Traunkirchen

Hoher Nock
(1963m)

Ebensee

St
Gilgen

Wolfgangsee

Bad Ischl

Mariazell

Mürzzuschlag

Gloggnitz

Nationalpark
Kalkalpen

Bad Aussee

Oberpullendorf

Hallstatt

Obertraun

Eisenerz

BURGENLAND

A10

Schladming

A9

Admont

Kapfenberg

STYRIA

Radstadt

Leoben

Bruck
an der Mur

Oberwart

Unzmarkt-
Frauenburg

Hundertwasser
Spa

Tamsweg

Judenburg

Köflach

Graz

Bad
Blumau

Murau

Voitsberg

HUNGARY

Rennweg

CARINTHIA

Wolfsberg

Spittal an
der Drau

A2

Bad
Radkersberg

Feldkirchen

Klagenfurt

Villach

Wörthersee

Völkermarkt

Drava

SLOVENIA

CROATIA

Ljubljana

Zagreb

5 Dive into the crystal-clear
lakes of **Salzkammergut**
(p62), Austria's summer
playground.

6 Whiz up to the Tyrolean
Alps in Zaha Hadid's space-age

funicular from picture-perfect
Innsbruck (p64).

7 Explore the romantic
Wachau and technology
trailblazer Linz in the **Danube
Valley** (p52).

ITINERARIES

Two Days

Spend this entire time in **Vienna**, making sure to visit the Habsburg palaces and Stephansdom before cosying up in a *Kaffeehaus* (coffee house). At night, check out the pumping bar scene.

One Week

Spend two days in Vienna, plus another day exploring the **Wachau** (Danube Valley) **wine region**, a day each in **Salzburg** and **Innsbruck**, one day exploring the **Salzkammergut lakes**, and finally one day in St Anton am Arlberg or Kitzbühel hiking or skiing (depending on the season).

VIENNA

📄 01 / POP 1.79 MILLION

Few cities in the world waltz so effortlessly between the present and the past like Vienna. Its splendid historical face is easily recognised: grand imperial palaces and bombastic baroque interiors, revered opera houses and magnificent squares.

But Vienna is also one of Europe's most dynamic urban spaces. A stone's throw from Hofburg (the Imperial Palace), the MuseumsQuartier houses some of the world's most provocative contemporary art behind a striking basalt facade. In the Innere Stadt (Inner City), up-to-the-minute design stores sidle up to old-world confectioners, and Austro-Asian fusion restaurants stand alongside traditional *Beisl* (small taverns). In this Vienna, it's OK to mention poetry slam and Stephansdom in one breath.

Throw in the mass of green space within the confines of the city limits and the 'blue' Danube (Donau) cutting a path east of the historical centre, and this is a capital that is distinctly Austrian.

⊙ Sights

Heading into the Innere Stadt will take you to a different age. Designated a Unesco World Heritage Site, the heart of the city is blessed with a plethora of architectural wonders that hint at Vienna's long and colourful history.

★ Hofburg
PALACE

(Imperial Palace; www.hofburg-wien.at; 01, Michaelerkuppel; 🚊 1A, 2A Michaelerplatz, Ⓜ Herrengasse, 🚋 D, 1, 2, 71, 46, 49 Burgring) FREE Nothing symbolises the culture and heritage of Austria more than its Hofburg, home base of the Habsburgs from 1273 to 1918. The oldest section is the 13th-century **Schweizerhof** (Swiss Courtyard), named after the Swiss

guards who used to protect its precincts. The Renaissance **Swiss gate** dates from 1553. The courtyard adjoins a larger courtyard, **In der Burg**, with a monument to Emperor Franz II adorning its centre. The palace now houses the Austrian president's offices and a raft of museums.

★ Kaiserappartements
PALACE

(Imperial Apartments; www.hofburg-wien.at; 01, Michaelerplatz; adult/child €11.50/7, with guided tour €13.50/8; ⊙ 9am-5.30pm; Ⓜ Herrengasse) The Kaiserappartements (Imperial Apartments), once the official living quarters of Franz Josef I and Empress Elisabeth, are dazzling in their chandelier-lit opulence. One section, known as the **Sisi Museum**, is devoted to Austria's most beloved empress. It has a strong focus on the clothing and jewellery of Austria's monarch. Audioguides – available in 11 languages – are also included in the admission price. Admission on guided tours includes the Kaiserappartements plus the Sisi Museum.

★ Kaiserliche Schatzkammer
MUSEUM

(Imperial Treasury; www.kaiserliche-schatzkammer.at; 01, Schweizerhof; adult/under 19yr €12/free; ⊙ 9am-5.30pm Wed-Mon; Ⓜ Herrengasse) The Schatzkammer (Imperial Treasury) contains secular and ecclesiastical treasures of priceless value and splendour – the sheer wealth of this collection of crown jewels is staggering. As you walk through the rooms you see magnificent treasures such as a golden rose, diamond-studded Turkish sabres, a 2680-carat Colombian emerald and, the highlight of the treasury, the imperial crown.

Albertina
GALLERY

(www.albertina.at; 01, Albertinaplatz 3; adult/child €11.90/free; ⊙ 10am-6pm Thu-Tue, to 9pm Wed; 🖽; Ⓜ Karlsplatz, Stephansplatz, 🚋 D, 1, 2, 71 Kärntner Ring/Oper) Once used as the Habsburg's imperial apartments for guests, the Albertina is now a repository for the greatest collection of graphic art in the world. The permanent Batliner Collection – with paintings covering the period from Monet to Picasso – and the high quality of changing exhibitions are what really make the Albertina so worthwhile visiting.

Haus der Musik   MUSEUM
(www.hdm.at; 01, Seilerstätte 30; adult/child €12/5.50, with Mozarthaus Vienna €17/7; ☺10am-10pm; ♿; Ⓜ Karlsplatz, ⓐD, 1, 2 Kärntner Ring/Oper) The Haus der Musik is an interesting and unusual museum as it manages to explain the world of sound in an amusing and highly interactive way (in English and German) for both children and adults. Exhibits are spread over four floors and cover everything from how sound is created, through to Vienna's Philharmonic Orchestra and street noises.

Kaisergruft   CHURCH
(Imperial Burial Vault; www.kaisergruft.at; 01, Neuer Markt; adult/child €5/2.50; ☺10am-6pm; Ⓜ Stephansplatz, Karlsplatz, ⓐD, 1, 2, 71 Kärntner Ring/Oper) The Kaisergruft beneath the **Kapuzinerkirche** (Church of the Capuchin Friars) is the final resting place of most of the Habsburg royal family, including Empress Elisabeth.

★**Stephansdom**   CHURCH
(St Stephan's Cathedral; www.stephanskirche.at; 01, Stephansplatz; ☺6am-10pm Mon-Sat, from 7am Sun, main nave & Domschatz audio tours 9-11.30am & 1-5.30pm Mon-Sat, 1-5.30pm Sun; Ⓜ Stephansplatz) Vienna's Gothic masterpiece Stephansdom, or Steffl (Little Stephan) as it's nicknamed, is Vienna's pride and joy. A church has stood here since the 12th century, and reminders of this are the Romanesque **Riesentor** (Giant Gate) and **Heidentürme**. From the exterior, the first

IMPERIAL ENTERTAINMENT

The world-famous **Vienna Boys' Choir** (Wiener Sängerknaben; www.wienersaenger knaben.at) performs on Sunday at 9.15am (late September to June) in the Burgkapelle (Royal Chapel) in the Hofburg. **Tickets** (☑533 99 27; www.hofburg kapelle.at; 01, Schweizerhof; Sun Burgkapelle performance €9-35; Ⓜ Herrengasse) should be booked around six weeks in advance. The group also performs regularly in the Musikverein.

Another throwback to the Habsburg glory days is the **Spanish Riding School** (Spanische Hofreitschule; ☑533 90 31; www.srs.at; 01, Michaelerplatz; performances €31-190; ⓐ1A, 2A Michaelerplatz, Ⓜ Herrengasse), where Lipizzaner stallions gracefully perform equine ballet to classical music. For **morning training** (adult/child/family €14/7/28; ☺10am-noon Tue-Fri Feb-Jun & mid-Aug-Dec) sessions, same-day tickets are available at the nearby **visitor centre** (Michaelerplatz 1; ☺9am-4pm; Ⓜ Herrengasse).

thing that will strike you is the glorious tiled **roof**, with its dazzling row of chevrons and Austrian eagle. Inside, the magnificent Gothic stone **pulpit** presides over the main nave, fashioned in 1515 by an unknown artisan.

Pestsäule   MEMORIAL
(Plague Column; 01, Graben; Ⓜ Stephansplatz) Graben is dominated by the knobbly outline of this memorial, designed by Fischer von Erlach in 1693 to commemorate the 75,000 victims of the Black Death.

★**Kunsthistorisches Museum**   MUSEUM
(Museum of Art History, KHM; www.khm.at; 01, Maria-Theresien-Platz; adult/under 19yr incl Neue Burg museums €14/free; ☺10am-6pm Tue-Sun, to 9pm Thu; ♿; Ⓜ Museumsquartier, Volkstheater) One of the unforgettable experiences of being in Vienna will be a visit to the Kunsthistorisches Museum, brimming with works by Europe's finest painters, sculptors and artisans. Occupying a neoclassical building as sumptuous as the art it contains, the museum takes you on a time-travel treasure hunt from Classical Rome to Egypt and the Renaissance. If time is an issue, skip straight to the **Picture Gallery**, where you'll want to dedicate at least an hour or two to Old Masters.

Central Vienna

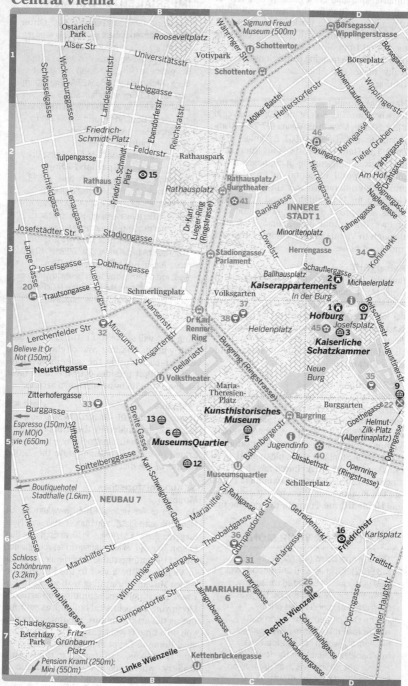

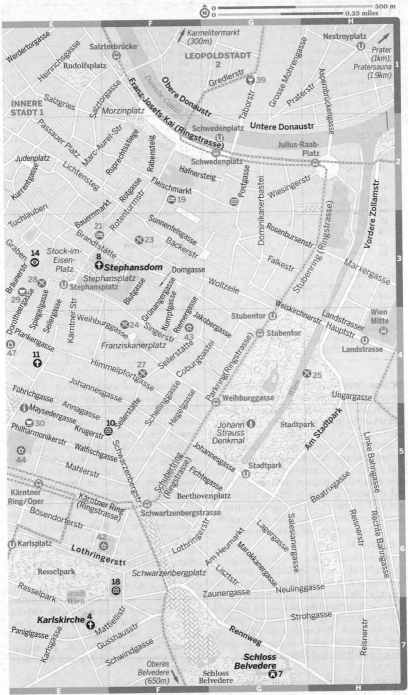

500 m
0.25 miles

E F G H

Werdertorgasse
Heinrichsgasse
Rudolfsplatz
Salztorbrücke
Karmelitermarkt
(300m)
LEOPOLDSTADT
2
Nestroyplatz
Prater
(1km);
Pratersauna
(1.9km)
1

Salzgries
Salztorgasse
Franz-Josefs-Kai (Ringstrasse)
Donaukanal
Obere Donaustr
Gredlerstr
39
Grosse Mohrengasse
Aspernbrückengasse
Taborstr

INNERE
STADT 1
Passauer Platz
Marc-Aurel-Str
Morzinplatz
Untere Donaustr
Schwedenplatz
Julius-Raab-
Platz
Praterstr

Judenplatz
Lichtensteg
Ruprechtsstiege
Rabensteig
Hafnersteig
Schwedenplatz
Postgasse
Wiesingerstr
Dominikanerbastei
Vordere Zollamtstr
2

Kurrentgasse
Rotgasse
Fleischmarkt
19
Rotenturmstr
Sonnenfelsgasse
Rosenbursenstr
Stubenring (Ringstrasse)
Marxergasse

Tuchlauben
Bauernmarkt
Brandstätte
21
23
Bäckerstr
Falkestr
Wien
Mitte

Graben
14
Stock-im-
Eisen-
Platz
8 Stephansdom
Domgasse
Wollzeile
Weiskirchnerstr
Landstrasser
Hauptstr
Landstrasse
3

Braünerstr
28
29
Stephansplatz
Stephansplatz
Blutgasse
Grünangergasse
Kumpfgasse
Riemergasse
Jakobergasse
Stubentor
Stubentor
Coburgbastei

Dorotheergasse
Spiegelgasse
Seilergasse
Kärntner Str
Weihburggasse
24
Singerstr
Seilerstätte
43
25
Ungargasse
4

47
11
Himmelpfortgasse
27
Hegelgasse
Parking (Ringstrasse)
Weihburggasse

Führichgasse
Maysedergasse
Annagasse
Johannesgasse
Schellinggasse
Johann
Strauss
Denkmal
Stadtpark
Am Stadtpark

Philharmonikerstr
30
Krugerstr
10
Walfischgasse
Schwarzenbergstr
Johannesgasse
Fichtegasse
Stadtpark
5

44
Mahlerstr
Schubertring (Ringstrasse)
Beethovenplatz
Beatrixgasse
Linke Bahngasse
Rechte Bahngasse

Kärntner
Ring/Oper
Bösendorferstr
Kärntner Ring
(Ringstrasse)
42
Schwartzenbergstrasse
Schwarzenbergstr
Lothringerstr
Reisnerstr

Karlsplatz
Lothringerstr
Resselpark
Stadt
Wien
18
Schwarzenbergplatz
Am Heumarkt
Lisztstr
Marokkanergasse
Lagergasse
Salesianergasse
Neulinggasse
Zaunergasse
6

Resselpark
Karlskirche
4
Mattiellistr
Gusshausstr
Schwindgasse
Paniglgasse
Karlsgasse
Rennweg
Strohgasse
Reisnerstr
7

Oberes
Belvedere
(650m)
Schloss
Belvedere
Schloss
Belvedere
7

E F G H

Central Vienna

⭐ **MuseumsQuartier** MUSEUM
(Museum Quarter; www.mqw.at; 07, Museumsplatz; ⊙information & ticket centre 10am-7pm; ⓂMuseumsquartier, Volkstheater) The Museums-Quartier is a remarkable ensemble of museums, cafes, restaurants and bars inside former imperial stables designed by Fischer von Erlach. This breeding ground of Viennese cultural life is the perfect place to hang out and watch or meet people on warm evenings. With more than 60,000 sq metres of exhibition space, the complex is one of the world's most ambitious cultural spaces.

➡ **Leopold Museum**
(www.leopoldmuseum.org; 07, Museumsplatz 1; adult/child €12/7, audioguide €3.50; ⊙10am-6pm Wed-Mon, to 9pm Thu; ⓂMuseumsquartier, Volkstheater) The undoubted highlight of a visit to the MuseumsQuartier is the Leopold Museum, a striking white limestone gallery that showcases the world's largest collection of Egon Schiele paintings, alongside some fine Klimts and Kokoschkas.

➡ **MUMOK**
(Museum Moderner Kunst, Museum of Modern Art; www.mumok.at; 07, Museumsplatz 1; adult/child €10/free; ⊙2-7pm Mon, 10am-7pm Tue-Sun, to 9pm Thu; ⓂMuseumsquartier, Volkstheater, 🚋49 Volkstheater) The dark basalt edifice and sharp corners of the Museum Moderner Kunst are a complete contrast to the MuseumsQuartier's historical sleeve. Inside, MUMOK is crawling with Vienna's finest collection of 20th-century art, centred on fluxus, nouveau realism, pop art and photo-realism.

Secession LANDMARK, GALLERY
(www.secession.at; 01, Friedrichstrasse 12; adult/child €9/5.50, audioguide €3; ⊙10am-6pm Tue-Sun; ⓂKarlsplatz) In 1897, 19 progressive artists swam away from the mainstream Künstlerhaus artistic establishment to form the Vienna Secession (*Sezession*). Among their number were Klimt, Josef Hoffman, Kolo Moser and Joseph M Olbrich. Olbrich designed the new exhibition centre of the Secessionists, which combined sparse functionality with stylistic motifs. Its biggest draw is Klimt's exquisitely gilded *Beethoven Frieze*.

Wien Museum
MUSEUM

(www.wienmuseum.at; 04, Karlsplatz 8; adult/under 19yr €8/free, 1st Sun of month free; ☺10am-6pm Tue-Sun; Ⓜ Karlsplatz) The Wien Museum presents a fascinating romp through Vienna's history, from Neolithic times to the mid-20th century, putting the city and its personalities in a meaningful context. Exhibits are spread over three floors, including spaces for two temporary exhibitions.

★ Schloss Belvedere
PALACE, GALLERY

(www.belvedere.at; Oberes Belvedere adult/child €12.50/free, Unteres Belvedere €11/free, combined ticket €19/free; ☺10am-6pm; Ⓜ Taubstummengasse, Südtiroler Platz, Ⓖ D, 71 Schwarzenbergplatz) Belvedere is a masterpiece of total art and one of the world's finest baroque palaces, designed by Johann Lukas von Hildebrandt (1668–1745) for Prince Eugene of Savoy. The first of the palace's two buildings is the **Oberes Belvedere** (Upper Belvedere), showcasing Gustav Klimt's *The Kiss* (1908), the perfect embodiment of Viennese art nouveau, alongside other late-19th- to early-20th-century Austrian works. The lavish **Unteres Belvedere** (Lower Belvedere), with its richly frescoed **Marmorsaal** (Marble Hall), sits at the end of sculpture-dotted gardens.

Prater
PARK

(www.wiener-prater.at; Ⓜ Praterstern) This large park encompasses meadows, woodlands, an amusement park (the **Würstelprater**) and one of the city's most visible icons, the **Riesenrad**. Built in 1897, this 65m-high Ferris wheel of *The Third Man* fame affords far-reaching views of Vienna.

Sigmund Freud Museum
HOUSE, MUSEUM

(www.freud-museum.at; 09, Berggasse 19; adult/child €9/4; ☺10am-6pm; Ⓜ Schottentor, Schottenring, Ⓖ D Schlickgasse) Sigmund Freud is a bit like the telephone – once he happened, there was no going back. This is where Freud spent his most prolific years and developed his groundbreaking theories; he moved here with his family in 1891 and stayed until he was forced into exile by the Nazis in 1938.

Schloss Schönbrunn
PALACE

(www.schoenbrunn.at; 13, Schönbrunne Schlossstrasse 47; Imperial Tour with audioguide adult/child €11.50/8.50, Grand Tour €14.50/9.50; ☺8.30am-5.30pm; Ⓜ Hietzing) The Habsburgs' overwhelmingly opulent summer palace is now a Unesco World Heritage Site. Of the palace's 1441 rooms, 40 are open to the public; the Imperial Tour takes you into 26 of these.

Fountains dance in the French-style formal gardens. The gardens harbour the world's oldest zoo, the **Tiergarten**, founded in 1752; a 630m-long hedge maze; and the **Gloriette**, whose roof offers a wonderful view over the palace grounds and beyond.

Because of the popularity of the palace, tickets are stamped with a departure time and there may be a time lag, so buy your ticket straight away and then explore the gardens.

🏃 Activities

The **Donauinsel** (Danube Island) features swimming areas and paths for walking and cycling. The **Alte Donau** (Old Danube) is a landlocked arm of the Danube, a favourite of sailing and boating enthusiasts, swimmers, walkers, fisherfolk and, in winter (when it's cold enough), ice skaters.

🎊 Festivals & Events

Pick up a copy of the monthly booklet of events from the tourist office.

Opernball
CULTURAL

(www.wiener-staatsoper.at; ☺Jan/Feb) Of the 300 or so balls held in January and February, the Opernball (Opera Ball) is number one. Held in the Staatsoper, it's a supremely

---

SPIN OF THE RING

One of the best deals in Vienna is a self-guided tour on tram 1 or 2 of the monumental **Ringstrasse** boulevard encircling much of the Innere Stadt, which turned 150 in 2015. For the price of a single ticket you'll take in the neo-Gothic **Rathaus** (City Hall; www.wien.gv.at; 01, Rathausplatz 1; ☺ guided tours 1pm Mon, Wed & Fri; Ⓜ Rathaus, Ⓖ D, 1, 2 Rathaus) **FREE**, the Greek Revival–style parliament, the 19th-century **Burgtheater** (National Theatre; ✆514 44 4440; www.burgtheater.at; 01, Universitätsring 2; seats €5-51, standing room €2.50, students €8; ☺ box office 9am-5pm Mon-Fri; Ⓜ Rathaus, Ⓖ D, 1, 2 Rathaus) and the baroque **Karlskirche** (St Charles Church; www.karlskirche.at; Karlsplatz; adult/child €8/4; ☺9am-5.30pm Mon-Sat, 11.30am-5.30pm Sun; Ⓜ Karlsplatz), among other sights.

lavish affair, with the men in tails and women in shining white gowns.

Wiener Festwochen
ART
(www.festwochen.at; ⊘mid-May–late June) Wide-ranging program of arts from around the world.

Donauinselfest
MUSIC
(https://donauinselfest.at; ⊘late Jun) FREE Held over three days on a weekend in late June, the Donauinselfest features a feast of rock, pop, folk and country performers, and attracts almost three million onlookers. Best of all, it's free!

Musikfilm Festival
FILM
(http://filmfestival-rathausplatz.at; 01, Rathausplatz; ⊘Jul & Aug) Once the sun sets in July and August, the Rathausplatz is home to free screenings of operas, operettas and concerts.

Viennale Film Festival
FILM
(✆526 59 47; www.viennale.at; ⊘late Oct–early Nov) The country's best film festival features fringe and independent films from around the world. It is held every year, with screenings at numerous locations around the city.

Christkindlmärkte
CHRISTMAS MARKET
(www.christkindlmarkt.at; ⊘mid-Nov–25 Dec) Vienna's much-loved Christmas market.

🛌 Sleeping

my MOjO vie
HOSTEL €
(✆0676-551 11 55; http://mymojovie.at; 07, Kaiserstrasse 77; dm/d/tr/q €26/56/81/104; @🛜; Ⓜ Burggasse Stadthalle) An old-fashioned cage lift rattles up to these incredible backpacker digs. Everything you could wish for is here – design-focused dorms, a kitchen with free supplies, netbooks for surfing, guidebooks for browsing and even musical instruments for your own jam session.

Believe It Or Not
HOSTEL €
(✆0676-550 00 55; www.believe-it-or-not-vienna.at; 07, Myrthengasse 10; dm €26-30; @🛜; Ⓜ Volkstheater) It may seem nondescript on the face of things, but you really won't believe what a cosy, homely hostel this is. We love the dorms with mezzanine-style beds, the laid-back lounge, kitchen with free basics and laptops for guest use.

Pension Kraml
PENSION €
(✆587 85 88; www.pensionkraml.at; 06, Brauergasse 5; s €35, d €48-78, tr €69-87, q €110-120; @🛜; Ⓜ Zieglergasse) Tucked peacefully down a backstreet five minutes' walk south of Mari-

ahilfer Strasse, this family-run pension looks back on 150 years of history and prides itself on old-school hospitality and comfort.

★ Pension Sacher
PENSION €€
(✆533 32 38; www.pension-sacher.at; 01, Rothenturmstrasse 1; apt €100-152; ❄🛜; Ⓜ Stephansplatz) Filled with chintzy knick-knacks, florals and solid wood furnishings, these super-central, spacious apartments are lovingly kept by the Sacher family of chocolate-cake fame. There's everything you need to feel right at home and the views of Stephansdom are phenomenal.

Hotel Rathaus Wein & Design
BOUTIQUE HOTEL €€
(✆400 11 22; www.hotel-rathaus-wien.at; 08, Lange Gasse 1; s/d/tr €150/210/240; ❄@🛜; Ⓜ Rathaus, Volkstheater) Each of the open-plan, minimalist-chic rooms at this boutique hotel is dedicated to an Austrian winemaker and the minibar is stocked with premium wines from the growers themselves.

Boutiquehotel Stadthalle
HOTEL €€
(✆982 42 72; www.hotelstadthalle.at; 15, Hackengasse 20; s €80-120, d €118-188; 🛜; Ⓜ Schweglerstrasse) 🍃 Welcome to Vienna's most eco-aware hotel, which has a roof fragrantly planted with lavender. Bursts of purple, pink and peach enliven rooms that blend modern with polished antiques. An organic breakfast is served in the ivy-draped courtyard garden.

Hollmann Beletage
PENSION €€
(✆961 19 60; www.hollmann-beletage.at; 01, Köllnerhofgasse 6; d €159-229, tr €179-259, q €199-300, ste from €390; @🛜; Ⓜ Schwedenplatz, 🚋1, 2 Schwedenplatz) This minimalist establishment offers style and clean lines throughout. A terrace and lounge where you can enjoy free snacks at 2pm are bonuses, as is the small hotel cinema and the free use of an iPad.

🍴 Eating

Self-caterers can stock up at central Hofer, Billa and Spar supermarkets. Some have delis that make sandwiches to order. *Würstel Stand* (sausage stands) are great for a cheap bite on the run.

Trzesniewski
SANDWICHES €
(www.trzesniewski.at; 01, Dorotheergasse 1; bread & spread €1.20; ⊘8am-7pm Mon-Fri, 9am-5pm Sat; Ⓜ Stephansplatz) Possibly the finest sandwich shop in Austria, Trzesniewski has been serving spreads and breads to the entire spectrum of munchers for over 100 years.

DON'T MISS

FOOD MARKET FINDS

The sprawling **Naschmarkt** (06, Linke & Rechte Wienzeile; ⊙ 6am-7.30pm Mon-Fri, to 6pm Sat; Ⓜ Karlsplatz, Kettenbrückengasse) is the place to *nasch* (snack) in Vienna. Stalls are piled high with meats, fruits, vegetables, cheeses, olives, spices and wine. There are also plenty of cafes dishing up good-value lunches, along with delis and takeaway stands.

Bio-Markt Freyung (01, Freyungasse; ⊙ 9am-6pm Fri & Sat; Ⓜ Herrengasse, Schottentor) sells farm-fresh produce, as does the bustling **Karmelitermarkt** (02, Karmelitermarkt; ⊙ 6am-7.30pm Mon-Fri, to 5pm Sat; Ⓜ Taborstrasse, 🚊 2 Karmeliterplatz). Head to the Saturday farmers market at the latter for brunch at one of the excellent deli-cafes.

Bitzinger Würstelstand am Albertinaplatz SAUSAGE STAND €
(01, Albertinaplatz; sausages €1.70-4.30; ⊙ 8am-4am; Ⓜ Karlsplatz, Stephansplatz, 🚊 Kärntner Ring/Oper) Vienna has many sausage stands but this one located behind the Staatsoper is hands down one of the best.

★**Mini** FUSION €€
(📞 0595-44 83; www.minirestaurant.at; 06, Marchettigasse 11; mains €16-24; ⊙ 11.30am-midnight; Ⓜ Pilgramgasse) A slick, vaulted interior provides the backdrop for Hungarian cuisine with a pinch of global personality at Mini. Starters like wild-boar soup warm you up nicely for bright, flavour-packed mains like swordfish in white-wine mushroom sauce. The two-course lunch is a snip at €7.90.

Meierei im Stadtpark AUSTRIAN €€
(📞 713 31 68; http://steirereck.at; 03, Am Heumarkt 2a; set breakfasts €20-24, mains €11-20, 6-cheese selection €11; ⊙ 8am-11pm Mon-Fri, 9am-7pm Sat & Sun; 📶; Ⓜ Stadtpark) Embedded in the greenery of the Stadtpark, the Meierei serves a bountiful breakfast until noon. It's most famous, though, for its goulash served with leek roulade (€18), and its selection of 120 types of cheese.

Gasthaus Pöschl AUSTRIAN €€
(📞 513 52 88; 01, Weihburggasse 17; mains €9-18; ⊙ noon-midnight; Ⓜ Stubentor) Close to pretty Franziskanerplatz, this small, wood-panelled *Beisl* brims with Viennese warmth and

bonhomie. Austrian classics like *Tafelspitz* (boiled beef) and schnitzel are cooked to a T.

Figlmüller BISTRO €€
(📞 512 61 77; www.figlmueller.at; 01, Wollzeile 5; mains €13-23; ⊙ 11am-10.30pm; 📶; Ⓜ Stephansplatz) The Viennese would simply be at a loss without Figlmüller. This famous *Beisl* has some of the biggest and best schnitzels in the business.

★**Tian** VEGETARIAN €€€
(📞 890 46 65; www.tian-vienna.com; 01, Himmelpfortgasse 23; 2-/3-course lunch €26/32, 4-/8-course evening menu €81-120; ⊙ noon-midnight Mon-Sat; 📶; Ⓜ Stephansplatz, 🚊 2 Weihburggasse) Stealthy charm meets urban attitude at this lounge-style, Michelin-starred restaurant that takes vegetarian cuisine to delicious heights. Lunch menus offer the best value; you can also enjoy a drink in the delightful wine bar.

🍷 **Drinking & Nightlife**

Pulsating bars cluster north and south of the Naschmarkt, around Spittelberg and along the Gürtel (mainly around the U6 stops of Josefstädter Strasse and Nussdorfer Strasse).

Vienna's *Heurigen*, or wine taverns, cluster in the wine-growing suburbs to the north, southwest, west and northwest of the city. Opening times are approximately from 4pm to 11pm, and wine costs around €3 per *Viertel* (250mL).

★**Dachboden** BAR
(http://25hours-hotels.com; 07, Lerchenfelder Strasse 1-3; ⊙ 2pm-1am Tue-Fri, noon-1am Sat, noon-10pm Sun; 📶; Ⓜ Volkstheater) Housed in the circus-themed 25hours Hotel, Dachboden has big-top views of Vienna's skyline from its decked terrace. DJs spin jazz, soul and funk on Wednesday and Friday nights.

Weinfach Vinothek & Bar WINE BAR
(www.weinfach.at; 02, Taborstrasse 11a; ⊙ 5-10pm Tue-Sat; 🚊 2 Gredlerstrasse) This bright, modern wine store and bar extends the warmest of welcomes. The well-edited, 90-variety wine list traverses the entire Austrian spectrum and the sharing plates of local cheese and Carinthian salami are perfect for grazing. The clued-up staff arrange regular tastings and events.

Palmenhaus BAR
(www.palmenhaus.at; 01, Burggarten; ⊙ 11.30am-midnight Mon-Thu, 10am-1am Fri & Sat, 10am-11pm Sun; Ⓜ Karlsplatz, Museumsquartier, 🚊 D, 1, 2, 71

DON'T MISS

COFFEE HOUSE CULTURE

Vienna's legendary *Kaffeehauser* (coffee houses) are wonderful places for people-watching, daydreaming, chatting and browsing the news. Most serve light meals alongside mouth-watering cakes and tortes. Expect to pay around €8 for a coffee with a slice of cake. Here are five favourites:

Café Sperl (www.cafesperl.at; 06, Gumpendorfer Strasse 11; ⊙7am-11pm Mon-Sat, 11am-8pm Sun; 🗑; Ⓜ Museumsquartier, Kettenbrückengasse) With its gorgeous *Jugendstil* (art nouveau) fittings, grand dimensions, cosy booths and unhurried air, Sperl is one of the finest coffee houses in Vienna. The must-try is Sperl Torte, an almond-and-chocolate-cream dream.

Café Leopold Hawelka (www.hawelka.at; 01, Dorotheergasse 6; ⊙8am-1am Mon-Sat, 10am-1am Sun; Ⓜ Stephansplatz) Dark, moody and picture-plastered, this late-1930s coffee house was once the hang-out of artists and writers – Friedensreich Hundertwasser, Elias Canetti, Arthur Miller and Andy Warhol included.

Demel (www.demel.at; 01, Kohlmarkt 14; ⊙9am-7pm; 🚍1A, 2A Michaelerplatz, Ⓜ Herrengasse, Stephansplatz) An elegant and regal cafe within sight of the Hofburg, Demel's speciality is the Ana Demel Torte, a calorie-bomb of chocolate and nougat.

Café Sacher (www.sacher.com; 01, Philharmonikerstrasse 4; ⊙8am-midnight; Ⓜ Karlsplatz, 🚍D, 1, 2, 71 Kärntner Ring/Oper) Fancy, chandelier-lit Sacher is celebrated for its Sacher Torte, a rich chocolate cake with apricot jam once favoured by Emperor Franz Josef.

Espresso (http://espresso-wien.at; 07, Burggasse 57; ⊙7.30am-1am Mon-Fri, 10am-1am Sat & Sun; Ⓜ Volkstheater, 🚍49 Siebensterngasse/Kirchengasse) For a fresh take on the coffee-house scene, stop by this retro-cool blast from the 1950s, where hipsters linger over espressos with a kick and brunch.

Burgring) Housed in a beautifully restored *Jungendstil* (art nouveau) palm house, the Palmenhaus opens onto a terrific garden terrace in summer.

Phil　BAR
(www.phil.info; 06, Gumpendorfer Strasse 10-12; ⊙5pm-1am Mon, 9am-1am Tue-Sun; Ⓜ Museumsquartier, Kettenbrückengasse) A retro bar, book and record store, Phil attracts a bohemian crowd happy to squat on kitsch furniture your grandma used to own. The vibe is as relaxed as can be.

Volksgarten Pavillon　BAR
(www.volksgarten-pavillon.at; 01, Burgring 1; ⊙11am-2am Apr–mid-Sep; 🗑; Ⓜ Volkstheater, 🚍D, 1, 2, 71 Dr-Karl-Renner-Ring) Volksgarten Pavillon is a lovely 1950s-style pavilion with views of Heldenplatz.

Das Möbel　BAR
(http://dasmoebel.at; 07, Burggasse 10; ⊙2pm-midnight Mon-Fri, from 10am Sat & Sun; 🗑; Ⓜ Volkstheater) Das Möbel wins points for its furniture, consisting entirely of one-off pieces produced by local designers – and everything is for sale.

Pratersauna　CLUB
(www.pratersauna.tv; 02, Waldsteingartenstrasse 135; ⊙club 9pm-6am Wed-Sun, pool 1-9pm Fri & Sat Jun-Sep; Ⓜ Messe-Prater) Pool, cafe, bistro and club converge in a former sauna – these days, you'll sweat it up on the dance floor any given night.

Volksgarten ClubDiskothek　CLUB
(www.volksgarten.at; 01, Burgring 1; cover from €6; ⊙10pm-4am or later Tue & Thu-Sat; Ⓜ Museumsquartier, Volkstheater, 🚍D, 1, 2, 71 Dr-Karl-Renner-Ring) A hugely popular club, superbly located near the Hofburg, Volksgarten serves a clientele eager to see and be seen.

☆ Entertainment

Vienna is, and probably will be till the end of time, the European capital of opera and classical music. The line-up of music events is never-ending and even the city's buskers are often classically trained musicians.

Box offices generally open from Monday to Saturday and sell cheap (€3 to €6) standing-room tickets around an hour before performances.

For up-to-date listings, visit www.falter.at (in German).

Staatsoper
OPERA

(✆514 44 7880; www.wiener-staatsoper.at; 01, Opernring 2; Ⓜ Karlsplatz, ⓓD 1, 2 Kärntner Ring/Oper) The Staatsoper is *the* premiere opera and classical music venue in Vienna. Productions are lavish, formal affairs, where people dress up accordingly.

Musikverein
CONCERT VENUE

(✆505 81 90; www.musikverein.at; 01, Bösendorferstrasse 12; seats €25-89, standing room €4-6; ⊙ box office 9am-8pm Mon-Fri, to 1pm Sat; Ⓜ Karlsplatz) The opulent Musikverein holds the proud title of the best acoustics of any concert hall in Austria, which the Vienna Philharmonic Orchestra makes excellent use of.

Porgy & Bess
JAZZ

(✆512 88 11; www.porgy.at; 01, Riemergasse 11; tickets around €18; ⊙ concerts 7pm or 8.30pm; Ⓜ Stubentor, ⓓ2 Stubentor) Quality is the cornerstone of Porgy & Bess' continuing popularity. Its program is loaded with modern jazz acts from around the globe.

Burg Kino
CINEMA

(✆587 84 06; www.burgkino.at; 01, Opernring 19; Ⓜ Museumsquartier, ⓓD, 1, 2 Burgring) The Burg Kino shows only English-language films. It has regular screenings of *The Third Man*, Orson Welles' timeless classic set in post-WWII Vienna.

🔒 Shopping

In the alley-woven Innere Stadt, go to Kohlmarkt for designer chic, Herrengasse for antiques and Kärntnerstrasse for high-street brands. Tune into Vienna's creative pulse in the idiosyncratic boutiques and concept stores in Neubau, especially along Kirchengasse and Lindengasse.

Dorotheum
ANTIQUES

(www.dorotheum.com; 01, Dorotheergasse 17; ⊙10am-6pm Mon-Fri, 9am-5pm Sat; Ⓜ Stephansplatz) The Dorotheum is among the largest auction houses in Europe. For the casual visitor it's more like a museum than an auction space, housing everything from antique toys and tableware to autographs, antique guns and, above all, lots of quality paintings.

ℹ Information

Many cafes and bars offer free wi-fi for their customers. Free public hot-spots include Rathausplatz, Naschmarkt and Prater. See www.lonelyplanet.com.au/austria/vienna for more information.

Airport Information Office (⊙7am-10pm) Full services, with maps, Vienna Card and walk-in hotel booking. Located in the Vienna International Airport arrival hall.

Allgemeines Krankenhaus (✆404 000; www.akhwien.at; 09, Währinger Gürtel 18-20) Emergency rooms available at this hospital.

Jugendinfo (Vienna Youth Information; ✆4000 84 100; www.jugendinfowien.at; 01, Babenbergerstrasse 1; ⊙2-7pm Mon-Wed, 1-6pm Thu-Sat; Ⓜ Museumsquartier, ⓓ Burgring) Jugendinfo offers various reduced-priced event tickets for 14 to 26 year olds.

Main Post Office (01, Fleischmarkt 19; ⊙7am-10pm Mon-Fri, 9am-10pm Sat & Sun; Ⓜ Schwedenplatz, ⓓ1, 2 Schwedenplatz)

Police Station (✆31 310; 01, Schottenring 7-9; Ⓜ Schottentor)

Tourist Info Wien (✆245 55; www.wien.info; 01, Albertinaplatz; ⊙9am-7pm; ☎; Ⓜ Stephansplatz, ⓓD, 1, 2, 71 Kärntner Ring/Oper) Vienna's main tourist office, with a ticket agency, hotel booking service, free maps and every brochure under the sun.

ℹ Getting There & Away

AIR

For details on flying to Vienna, see the Getting There & Away section, p70.

BOAT

Fast hydrofoils travel eastwards to Bratislava (one way €20 to €35, 1¼ hours) daily from April to October. From May to September, they also travel twice weekly to Budapest (one way/return €109/125, 5½ hours). Bookings can be made through **DDSG Blue Danube** (✆01-58 880; www.ddsg-blue-danube.at; Handelskai 265, Vienna; Ⓜ Vorgartenstrasse).

BUS

Vienna currently has no central bus station. National Bundesbuses arrive and depart from several different locations, depending on the destination. Bus lines serving Vienna include **Eurolines** (✆0900 128 712; www.eurolines.

ℹ GETTING INTO TOWN

The fastest transport into the centre is **City Airport Train** (CAT; www.cityairporttrain.com; return adult/child €19/free; ⊙ departs airport 6.06am-11.36pm, departs city 5.36am-11.06pm), which runs every 30 minutes and takes 16 minutes between the airport and Wien Mitte; book online for a €2 discount. The S-Bahn (S7) does the same journey (single €4.40) but in 25 minutes.

com; Erdbergstrasse 200; ⊘ 6.30am-9pm Mon-Fri; Ⓜ Erdberg).

CAR & MOTORCYCLE

The Gürtel is an outer ring road that joins up with the A22 on the north bank of the Danube and the A23 southeast of town. All the main road routes intersect with this system, including the A1 from Linz and Salzburg, and the A2 from Graz.

TRAIN

Vienna is one of central Europe's main rail hubs. **Österreichische Bundesbahn** (ÖBB; Austrian Federal Railway; www.oebb.at) is the main operator. There are direct services and connections to many European cities. Sample destinations include Budapest (€29 to €37, 2½ to 3¼ hours), Munich (€93, 4½ to five hours), Paris (€51 to €142, 11½ to 13 hours), Prague (€49, 4¼ hours) and Venice (€49 to €108, seven to 11 hours).

Vienna's main station is the Hauptbahnhof, formerly the Südbahnhof. Following a massive construction project, it became partially operational in December 2012 and is set for completion in 2015. In the meantime, some long-distance trains are being rerouted among the rest of Vienna's train stations, including the Westbahnhof and Wien Meidling. Further train stations include Franz-Josefs-Bahnhof (which handles trains to/from the Danube Valley), Wien Mitte and Wien Nord.

ⓘ Getting Around

BICYCLE

Vienna's city bike scheme is called **Citybike Wien** (Vienna City Bike; www.citybikewien.at; 1st hr free, 2nd/3rd hr €1/2, per hr thereafter €4), with more than 120 bicycle stands across the city. A credit card is required to rent bikes – just swipe your card in the machine and follow the instructions (in a number of languages).

PUBLIC TRANSPORT

Vienna's unified public transport network encompasses trains, trams, buses, and underground (U-Bahn) and suburban (S-Bahn) trains. Free maps and information pamphlets are available from **Wiener Linien** (🖉 7909-100; www.wienerlinien.at).

All tickets must be validated at the entrance to U-Bahn stations and on buses and trams (except for weekly and monthly tickets).

Singles cost €2.20. A 24-hour ticket costs €7.60, a 48-hour ticket €13.30 and a 72-hour ticket €16.50. Weekly tickets (valid Monday to Sunday) cost €16.20.

THE DANUBE VALLEY

The stretch of Danube between Krems and Melk, known locally as the Wachau, is arguably the loveliest along the entire length of the mighty river. Both banks are dotted with ruined castles and medieval towns, and lined with terraced vineyards. Further upstream is the industrial city of Linz, Austria's avant-garde art and new technology trailblazer.

Krems an der Donau

🖉 02732 / POP 24,085

Sitting on the northern bank of the Danube against a backdrop of terraced vineyards, Krems marks the beginning of the Wachau. It has an attractive cobbled centre, some good restaurants and the gallery-dotted **Kunstmeile** (Art Mile; www.kunstmeile-krems.at).

⊙ Sights & Activities

Kunsthalle GALLERY
(www.kunsthalle.at; Franz-Zeller-Platz 3; admission €10; ⊘ 10am-5pm Tue-Sun) The flagship of Krems' Kunstmeile, an eclectic collection of galleries and museums, the Kunsthalle has a program of small but excellent changing exhibitions.

🛏 Sleeping

Arte Hotel Krems HOTEL €€
(🖉 71123; www.arte-hotel.at; Dr-Karl-Dorrek-Strasse 23; s/d €109/159; 🅿 🛜) This cutting-edge art hotel has 91 large, well-designed rooms with big retro prints and patterns complementing the funky '60s-style furniture.

Hotel Unter den Linden HOTEL €€
(🖉 82 115; www.udl.at; Schillerstrasse 5; s €67-87, d €90-118; 🛜) This big, family-run hotel has knowledgeable and helpful owners, 39 bright, welcoming rooms and a convenient location in Krems itself.

ⓘ ON YOUR BIKE

Many towns in the Danube Valley are part of a bike-hire network called **Nextbike** (🖉 02742-229 901; www.nextbike.at; per hr €1, 24hr €8). After registering using a credit card (either by calling the hotline or on the website), €1 is deducted and you can begin renting bicycles.

ℹ Information

Krems Tourismus (☑ 82 676; www.krems.info; Utzstrasse 1; ⊙ 9am-6pm Mon-Fri, 11am-6pm Sat, 11am-4pm Sun, shorter hours in winter) Helpful office well stocked with info and maps.

ℹ Getting There & Away

Frequent daily trains connect Krems with Vienna's Franz-Josefs-Bahnhof (€15.90, one hour) and Melk (€12.70, 1½ hours).

Melk

☑ 02752 / POP 5187

With its sparkling and majestic abbey-fortress, Melk is a highlight of any visit to the Danube Valley. Many visitors cycle here for the day – wearily pushing their bikes through the cobblestone streets.

◉ Sights

Stift Melk   MONASTERY
(Benedictine Abbey of Melk; www.stiftmelk.at; Abt Berthold Dietmayr Strasse 1; adult/child €10/5.50, with guided tour €12/7.50; ⊙ 9am-5.30pm May-Sep, tours 11am & 2pm Oct-Apr) Of the many abbeys in Austria, this one is the most famous. Possibly Lower Austria's finest, the monastery church dominates the complex with its twin spires and high octagonal dome. The interior is baroque gone barmy, with regiments of smirking cherubs, gilt twirls and polished faux marble. The theatrical high-altar scene, depicting St Peter and St Paul (the church's two patron saints), is by Peter Widerin. Johann Michael Rottmayr created most of the ceiling paintings, including those in the dome.

🛏 Sleeping & Eating

Restaurants and cafes with alfresco seating line the Rathausplatz.

Hotel Restaurant zur Post   HOTEL €€
(☑ 523 45; www.post-melk.at; Linzer Strasse 1; s €65-85, d €108-125; [P][@][🛜]) A bright and pleasant hotel in the heart of town offering 25 large, comfortable rooms in plush colours with additional touches such as brass bed lamps.

ℹ Information

The centrally located **tourist office** (☑ 511 60; www.stadt-melk.at; Kremser Strasse 5; ⊙ 9.30am-6pm Mon-Sat, to 4pm Sun Apr-Oct, 9am-5pm Mon-Thu, to 2.30pm Fri Nov-Mar) has maps and plenty of useful information.

ℹ Getting There & Away

Boats leave from the canal by Pionierstrasse, 400m north of the abbey. There are hourly trains to Vienna (€16.30, 1¼ hours).

Linz

☑ 0732 / POP 193,814

In Linz beginnt's (It begins in Linz) goes the Austrian saying, and it's spot on. The technology trailblazer and European Capital of Culture 2009 is blessed with a leading-edge cyber centre and world-class contemporary-art gallery.

◉ Sights & Activities

★ **Ars Electronica Center**   MUSEUM
(www.aec.at; Ars Electronica Strasse 1; adult/child €8/6; ⊙ 9am-5pm Tue-Fri, to 9pm Thu, 10am-6pm Sat & Sun) The technology, science and digital media of the future are in the spotlight at Linz' biggest crowd-puller, the Ars Electronica Center. In the labs you can interact with robots, animate digital objects, convert your name to DNA and (virtually) travel to outer space.

Lentos   GALLERY
(www.lentos.at; Ernst-Koref-Promenade 1; adult/child €8/4.50, guided tours €3; ⊙ 10am-6pm Tue-Sun, to 9pm Thu) Overlooking the Danube, the rectangular glass-and-steel Lentos is strikingly illuminated by night. The gallery guards one of Austria's finest modern-art collections, including works by Warhol, Schiele, Klimt, Kokoschka and Lovis Corinth, which sometimes feature in the large-scale exhibitions.

Mariendom   CATHEDRAL
(Herrenstrasse 26; ⊙ 7.30am-7pm Mon-Sat, 8am-7.15pm Sun) Also known as the Neuer Dom, this neo-Gothic giant of a cathedral lifts your gaze to its riot of pinnacles, flying buttresses and filigree traceried windows.

Pöstlingberg   VIEWPOINT
Linz spreads out beneath you atop Pöstlingberg (537m). It's a precipitous 30-minute ride aboard the narrow-gauge **Pöstlingbergbahn** (Hauptplatz; adult/child return €5.80/3; ⊙ 6am-10.30pm Mon-Sat, 7.30am-10.30pm Sun)

ℹ LINZ CARD

The Linz Card, giving entry to major sights and unlimited use of public transport, costs €15/25 for one/three days.

from the Hauptplatz. This gondola features in the *Guinness Book of World Records* as the world's steepest mountain railway – quite some feat for such a low-lying city!

🛏 Sleeping & Eating

Hotel am Domplatz
DESIGN HOTEL €€

(✐77 30 00; www.hotelamdomplatz.at; Stifterstrasse 4; d €125-145, ste €300; ❋ @ ⊜) Sidling up to the neo-Gothic Neuer Dom, this glass-and-concrete cube reveals streamlined interiors in pristine whites and blonde wood that reveal a Nordic-style aesthetic. Wind down with a view at the rooftop spa.

k.u.k. Hofbäckerei
CAFE €

(Pfarrgasse 17; coffee & cake €3-6; ⊙6.30am-6.30pm Mon-Fri, 7am-12.30pm Sat) The Empire lives on at this gloriously stuck-in-time cafe. Here Fritz Rath bakes the best Linzer Torte in town – rich, spicy and with lattice pastry that crumbles just so.

Cook
INTERNATIONAL €€

(✐78 13 05; www.cook.co.at; Klammstrasse 1; mains €9.50-16; ⊙11.30am-2.30pm Mon, 11.30am-2.30pm & 6-10pm Tue-Fri) Tossing Scandinavian and Asian flavours into the same pan may seem like folly, but Cook somehow manages to pull it off. A clean-lined, crisp interior forms the backdrop for dishes such as fish soup with a generous pinch of chilli.

ℹ Information

Hotspot Linz (www.hotspotlinz.at) Free wi-fi at 120 hot spots in the city, including Ars Electronica Center and Lentos.

Tourist Information Linz (✐7070 2009; www.linz.at; Hauptplatz 1; ⊙9am-7pm Mon-Sat, 10am-7pm Sun) Brochures, accommodation listings, a free room-reservation service and a separate Upper Austria information desk can be found here. It's open shorter hours in winter.

ℹ Getting There & Around

AIR

Ryanair flies to the Blue Danube Airport (p71), 13km southwest of Linz. An hourly shuttle bus (€2.90, 20 minutes) links the airport to the main train station.

PUBLIC TRANSPORT

Single bus and tram tickets cost €2, and day passes €4.

TRAIN

Linz is halfway between Salzburg and Vienna on the main road and rail routes. Trains to Salzburg (€25.30, 1¼ hours) and Vienna (€33.60, 1½ hours) leave at least twice hourly.

THE SOUTH

Austria's two main southern states, Styria (Steiermark) and Carinthia (Kärnten), often feel worlds apart from the rest of the country, both in climate and attitude. Styria is a blissful amalgamation of genteel architecture, rolling green hills, vine-covered slopes and soaring mountains. Its capital, Graz, is one of Austria's most attractive cities. A fashion-conscious crowd heads to sun-drenched Carinthia in summer. Sidling up to Italy, the region exudes an atmosphere that's as close to Mediterranean as this staunch country gets.

Graz

✐0316 / POP 269,997

Austria's second-largest city is probably its most relaxed and, after Vienna, its liveliest for after-hours pursuits. It's an attractive place with bristling green parkland, red rooftops and a small, fast-flowing river gushing through its centre. Architecturally, it has Renaissance courtyards and provincial baroque palaces complemented by innovative modern designs. The surrounding countryside, a mixture of vineyards, mountains, forested hills and thermal springs, is within easy striking distance.

⊙ Sights

Graz is a city easily enjoyed by simply wandering aimlessly. Admission to all of the Joanneum museums with a 24-hour ticket costs €11/4 for adults/children.

★ Neue Galerie Graz
GALLERY

(www.museum-joanneum.at; Joanneumsviertel; adult/child €8/3; ⊙10am-5pm Tue-Sun; ⊜; ⊟1, 3, 4, 5, 6, 7 Hauptplatz) The Neue Galerie is the crowning glory of the three museums inside the Joanneumsviertel museum complex. The stunning collection on level 0 is the highlight. Though not enormous, it showcases richly textured and colourful works by painters such as Ernst Christian Moser, Ferdinand Georg Waldmüller and Johann Nepomuk Passini. Egon Schiele is also represented here.

Kunsthaus Graz
GALLERY

(www.kunsthausgraz.at; Lendkai 1; adult/child €8/3; ⊙10am-5pm Tue-Sun; ⊟1, 3, 6, 7 Südtiroler

Platz) Designed by British architects Peter Cook and Colin Fournier, this world-class contemporary-art space is a bold creation that looks something like a space-age sea slug. Exhibitions change every three to four months.

Schloss Eggenberg PALACE
(Eggenberger Allee 90; adult/child €11.50/5.50; ⊙ tours 10am-4pm Tue-Sun Palm Sun-Oct; 🚃 1 Schloss Eggenberg) Graz' elegant palace was created for the Eggenberg dynasty in 1625 by Giovanni Pietro de Pomis (1565–1633) at the request of Johann Ulrich (1568–1634). Admission is on a highly worthwhile guided tour during which you learn about the idiosyncrasies of each room, the stories told by the frescoes and about the Eggenberg family itself.

Murinsel BRIDGE
(🚃 4, 5 Schlossplatz/Murinsel, 🚃 1, 3, 6, 7 Südtiroler Platz) Murinsel is a constructed island-cum-bridge of metal and plastic in the middle of the Mur. This modern floating landmark contains a cafe, a kids' playground and a small stage.

Schlossberg VIEWPOINT
(1hr ticket for lift or funicular €2.10; 🚃 4, 5 Schlossbergplatz) **FREE** Rising to 473m, Schlossberg is the site of the original fortress where Graz was founded and is topped by the city's most visible icon – the **Uhrenturm**. Its wooded slopes can be reached by a number of bucolic and strenuous paths, but also by lift or Schlossbergbahn funicular. Take tram 4 or 5 to Schlossplatz/Murinsel for the lift.

Landeszeughaus MUSEUM
(Styrian Armoury; www.museum-joanneum.at; Herrengasse 16; adult/child €8/3; ⊙ 10am-5pm Mon & Wed-Sun; 🚃 1, 3, 4, 5, 6, 7 Hauptplatz) You won't need to have a passion for armour and weapons to enjoy what's on show at the Landeszeughaus. More than 30,000 pieces of glistening weaponry are housed here.

Burg CASTLE, PARK
(Hofgasse; 🚃 30 Schauspielhaus, 🚃 1, 3, 4, 5, 6, 7 Hauptplatz) **FREE** Graz' 15th-century Burg today houses government offices. At the far end of the courtyard, on the left under the arch, is an ingenious **double staircase** (1499) – the steps diverge and converge as they spiral. Adjoining it is the **Stadtpark**, the city's largest green space.

🛏 Sleeping

Hotel Daniel HOTEL €
(🕿 711 080; www.hoteldaniel.com; Europaplatz 1; r €64-81, breakfast €11; 🅿 ❄ @ 🤶; 🚃 1, 3, 6, 7 Hauptbahnhof) The Daniel is a design hotel with slick, minimalist-style rooms. You can rent a Vespa or e-bike for €15 per day, or a Piaggio APE for €9 per hour.

★ Schlossberg Hotel HOTEL €€
(🕿 80 70-0; www.schlossberg-hotel.at; Kaiser-Franz-Josef-Kai 30; s €115-135, d €150-185, ste €210-250; 🅿 @ 🤶 ❄; 🚃 4, 5 Schlossbergbahn) Central but secluded, four-star Schlossberg is blessed with a prime location at the foot of its namesake. Rooms are well sized and decorated in the style of a country inn. The rooftop terrace with views is perfect for an evening glass of wine.

Hotel zum Dom HOTEL €€
(🕿 82 48 00; www.domhotel.co.at; Bürgergasse 14; s €74, d €89-169, ste €189-294; 🅿 ❄ 🤶; 🚃 30 Palais Trauttmansdorff/Urania, 🚃 1, 3, 4, 5, 6, 7 Hauptplatz) Ceramic art crafted by a local artist lends character to graceful Hotel zum Dom, whose individually furnished rooms come either with steam/power showers or whirlpools. One suite even has a terrace whirlpool.

🍴 Eating

Aside from the following listings, there are plenty of cheap eats near Universität Graz, particularly on Halbärthgasse, Zinzendorfgasse and Harrachgasse.

Stock up for a picnic at the **farmers markets** (⊙ 6am-1pm Mon-Sat) on Kaiser-Josef-Platz

---

HUNDERTWASSER SPA

East Styria is famed for its thermal springs. Fans of Friedensreich Hundertwasser's playful architectural style won't want to miss the surreal **Rogner-Bad Blumau** (🕿 03383-51 00; www.blumau.com; adult/child Mon-Fri €42/23, Sat & Sun €51/28; ⊙ 9am-11pm), 50km east of Graz. The spa has all the characteristics of his art, including uneven floors, grass on the roof, colourful ceramics and golden spires. Overnight accommodation includes entry to the spa. Call ahead to book treatments from sound meditation to invigorating Styrian elderberry wraps.

and Lendplatz. For **fast-food stands**, head for Hauptplatz and Jakominiplatz.

★ Der Steirer
AUSTRIAN, TAPAS €€

(☑703 654; www.dersteirer.at; Belgiergasse 1; tapas €2, lunch menu €7.90, mains €10-22.50; ☺11am-midnight; ☑; ☐1, 3, 6, 7 Südtiroler Platz) This Styrian neo-*Beisl* (bistro pub) and wine bar has a small but fantastic selection of local dishes, including a great goulash, and Austro-tapas if you just feel like nibbling.

Landhauskeller
AUSTRIAN €€

(☑83 02 76; Schmiedgasse 9; mains €11.50-28.50; ☺11.30am-midnight Mon-Sat; ☐1, 3 ,4, 5, 6, 7 Hauptplatz) What started as a spit-and-sawdust pub in the 16th century has evolved into an atmospheric, medieval-style restaurant serving specialities such as its four different sorts of *Tafelspitz* (prime broiled beef).

🍷 Drinking & Nightlife

The bar scene in Graz is split between three main areas: around the university; adjacent to the Kunsthaus; and on Mehlplatz and Prokopigasse (dubbed the 'Bermuda Triangle').

La Enoteca
WINE BAR

(www.laenoteca.at; Sackstrasse 14; ☺5-11pm Mon, 11.30am-11pm Tue-Fri, 10am-11pm Sat; ☐1, 3, 4, 5, 6, 7 Hauptplatz) This small wine bar has an informal, relaxed atmosphere and courtyard seating, making it an ideal place to enjoy a Schilcher Sekt (sparkling rosé) with mixed antipasti.

Kulturhauskeller
BAR, CLUB

(Elisabethstrasse 30; ☺9pm-5am Tue-Sat; ☐7 Lichtenfelsgasse) The raunchy Kulturhauskeller is a popular student hang-out with a great cellar-pub feel and a Wednesday karaoke night.

ℹ️ Information

Graz Tourismus (☑80 75; www.graztourismus.at; Herrengasse 16; ☺10am-6pm; ☎; ☐1, 3, 4, 5, 6, 7 Hauptplatz) Graz' main tourist office, with loads of free information on the city, and helpful and knowledgeable staff.

ℹ️ Getting There & Away

AIR

Graz airport (p71) is located 10km south of the centre and is served by carriers including **Air Berlin** (www.airberlin.com), which connects the city with Berlin.

BICYCLE

Bicycle rental is available from **Bicycle** (☑82 13 57; www.bicycle.at; Körösistrasse 5; per 24hr €10, Fri-Mon €16; ☺7am-1pm & 2-6pm Mon-Fri).

PUBLIC TRANSPORT

Single tickets (€2.10) for buses, trams and the Schlossbergbahn are valid for one hour, but you're usually better off buying a 24-hour pass (€4.80).

TRAIN

Trains to Vienna depart hourly (€37, 2½ hours), and six daily go to Salzburg (€48.20, four hours). International train connections from Graz include Ljubljana (€30 to €40, 3½ hours) and Budapest (€51 to €73, 5½ hours).

Klagenfurt

☑0463 / POP 96,640

With its captivating location on Wörthersee and more Renaissance than baroque beauty, Klagenfurt has a distinct Mediterranean feel. Carinthia's capital makes a handy base for exploring Wörthersee's lakeside villages and elegant medieval towns to the north.

⊙ Sights & Activities

Boating and swimming are usually possible from May to September.

★ Wörthersee
LAKE

Owing to its thermal springs, the Wörthersee is one of the region's warmer lakes (an average 21°C in summer) and is great for swimming, lakeshore frolicking and water sports. The 50km **cycle path** around the lake is one of the 'Top 10' in Austria. In summer the tourist office cooperates with a hire company for bicycles (per day/week €11/45), which can be picked up and dropped off at points around the lake.

Europapark
PARK

The green expanse and its *Strandbad* (beach) on the shores of the Wörthersee are centres for splashy fun, and especially good for kids. The park's biggest draw is **Minimundus** (www.minimundus.at; Villacher Strasse 241; adult/child €13/8; ☺9am-7pm Mar-Sep; ☑), a 'miniature world' with 140 replicas of the

---

ℹ️ FREE TOURS

Free guided tours depart from Klagenfurt's tourist office at 10am every Friday and Saturday.

world's architectural icons, downsized to a scale of 1:25. To get here, take bus 10, 11, 12 or 22 from Heiligengeistplatz.

🛏 Sleeping & Eating

When you check into accommodation in Klagenfurt, ask for a *Gästekarte* (guest card), entitling you to discounts.

Hotel Geyer   HOTEL €€
(☑ 578 86; www.hotelgeyer.com; Priesterhausgasse 5; s €70-88, d €102-135, q €155-170; P 🛜) Expect modern and comfortable rooms in this three-star hotel. Bonuses are the sauna and steam bath, and free use of the fitness centre around the corner.

Restaurant Maria Loretto   AUSTRIAN €€
(☑ 24 465; Lorettoweg 54; mains €16-26; ☺ 10am-midnight Wed-Mon) Situated on a headland above Wörthersee, this characterful restaurant is easily reached by foot from the *Strandbad*. It does a very good trout and some flavoursome meat dishes. Reserve for an outside table.

ℹ Information

Tourist Office (☑ 53 722 23; www.klagenfurt-tourismus.at; Neuer Platz 1, Rathaus; ☺ 8am-6pm Mon-Fri, 10am-5pm Sat, 10am-3pm Sun) Sells Kärnten Cards and books accommodation.

ℹ Getting There & Around

AIR
Klagenfurt's airport (p71) is 3km north of town. The low-cost airline **Germanwings** (www.germanwings.com) flies to Vienna, and Berlin, Hamburg and Cologne in Germany.

BUS
Bus drivers sell single tickets (€2.10) and 24-hour passes (€4.70). Bus 40/42 shuttles between the Hauptbahnhof and the airport.

TRAIN
Two hourly direct trains run from Klagenfurt to Vienna (€52, four hours) and Salzburg (€39, 3¼ hours). Trains to Graz depart every two to three hours (€40, three hours). Trains to western Austria, Italy, Slovenia and Germany go via Villach (€6.70, 24 to 37 minutes, two to four per hour).

SALZBURG

☑ 0662 / POP 147,825
The joke 'If it's baroque, don't fix it' is a perfect maxim for Salzburg; the tranquil Old Town

burrowed below steep hills looks much as it did when Mozart lived here 250 years ago.

A Unesco World Heritage Site, Salzburg's overwhelmingly baroque old town is entrancing both at ground level and from Hohensalzburg fortress high above. Across the fast-flowing Salzach River rests Schloss Mirabell, surrounded by gorgeous manicured gardens.

If this doesn't whet your appetite, then bypass the grandeur and head straight for kitsch-country by joining a tour of *The Sound of Music* film locations.

⦿ Sights

★ Dom   CATHEDRAL
(Cathedral; Domplatz; donations accepted; ☺ 8am-7pm Mon-Sat, 1-7pm Sun) Gracefully crowned by a bulbous copper dome and twin spires, the Dom stands out as a masterpiece of baroque art. Bronze portals symbolising faith, hope and charity lead into the cathedral. In the nave, intricate stucco and Arsenio Mascagni's ceiling frescoes recounting the Passion of Christ guide the eye to the polychrome dome.

Dommuseum   MUSEUM
(www.domquartier.at; Kapitelplatz 6; DomQuartier ticket adult/child €12/4; ☺ 10am-5pm Wed-Mon) The Dommuseum is a treasure trove of sacred art. A visit whisks you past a cabinet of Renaissance curiosities crammed with crystals, coral and oddities such as armadillos and pufferfish, through rooms showcasing gem-encrusted monstrances, stained glass and altarpieces, and into the Long Gallery, which is graced with 17th- and 18th-century paintings, including Paul Troger's chiaroscuro *Christ and Nicodemus* (1739).

★ Residenz   PALACE
(www.domquartier.at; Residenzplatz 1; DomQuartier ticket adult/child €12/4; ☺ 10am-5pm Wed-Mon) The crowning glory of Salzburg's new DomQuartier, the Residenz is where the prince-archbishops held court until Salzburg became part of the Habsburg Empire in the 19th century. An audio-guide tour takes in the exuberant state rooms, lavishly adorned with tapestries, stucco and frescoes by Johann Michael Rottmayr.

The 3rd floor is given over to the Residenzgalerie, where the focus is on Flemish and Dutch masters. Must-sees include Rubens' *Allegory on Emperor Charles V* and Rembrandt's chiaroscuro *Old Woman Praying*.

Salzburg

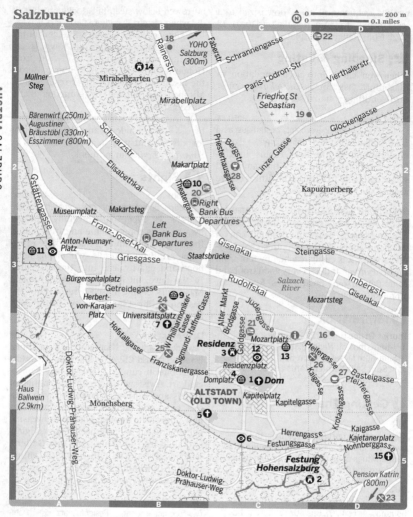

Residenzplatz
SQUARE

With its horse-drawn carriages, palace and street entertainers, this stately baroque square is the Salzburg of a thousand postcards. Its centrepiece is the **Residenzbrunnen**, an enormous marble fountain ringed by four water-spouting horses and topped by a conch-shell-bearing Triton.

Salzburg Museum
MUSEUM

(www.salzburgmuseum.at; Mozartplatz 1; adult/child €7/3; ⊙9am-5pm Tue-Sun, to 8pm Thu) Housed in the baroque Neue Residenz palace, this flagship museum takes you on a fascinating romp through Salzburg past and present. Ornate rooms showcase everything from Roman excavations to prince-archbishop portraits. There are free guided tours at 6pm every Thursday.

Erzabtei St Peter
CHURCH

(St Peter's Abbey; St Peter Bezirk 1-2; catacombs adult/child €2/1.50; ⊙ church 8am-noon & 2.30-6.30pm, cemetery 6.30am-7pm, catacombs 10am-6pm) A Frankish missionary named Rupert founded this abbey church and monastery in around 700, making it the oldest in the German-speaking world. The cemetery is

Salzburg

home to the **catacombs**, cave-like chapels and crypts hewn out of the Mönchsberg cliff face.

★Festung Hohensalzburg
FORT

(www.salzburg-burgen.at; Mönchsberg 34; adult/child/family €8/4.50/18.20, incl Festungsbahn funicular €11.30/6.50/26.20; ⊙9am-7pm) Salzburg's most visible icon is this mighty 900-year-old cliff-top fortress, one of the biggest and best preserved in Europe. It's easy to spend half a day up here, roaming the ramparts for far-reaching views over the city's spires, the Salzach River and the mountains. The fortress is a steep 15-minute jaunt from the centre or a speedy ride in the glass **Festungsbahn funicular** (Festungsgasse 4).

Stift Nonnberg
CHURCH

(Nonnberg Convent; Nonnberggasse 2; ⊙7am-dusk) A short climb up the Nonnbergstiege staircase from Kaigasse or along Festungsgasse brings you to this Benedictine convent, founded 1300 years ago and made famous as *the* nunnery in *The Sound of Music*. You can visit the beautiful rib-vaulted church, but the rest of the convent is off-limits.

Kollegienkirche
CHURCH

(Universitätsplatz; ⊙8am-6pm) Johann Bernhard Fischer von Erlach's grandest baroque design is this late-17th-century university church, with a striking bowed facade. The high altar's columns symbolise the Seven Pillars of Wisdom.

Mozarts Geburtshaus
MUSEUM

(Mozart's Birthplace; www.mozarteum.at; Getreidegasse 9; adult/child €10/3.50, incl Mozart-Wohnhaus €17/5; ⊙9am-5.30pm) Wolfgang Amadeus Mozart, Salzburg's most famous son, was born in this bright-yellow townhouse in 1756 and spent the first 17 years of his life here.

Mozart-Wohnhaus
MUSEUM

(Mozart's Residence; www.mozarteum.at; Makartplatz 8; adult/child €10/3.50, incl Mozarts Geburtshaus €17/5; ⊙9am-5.30pm) Mozart's one-time residence showcases family portraits, documents and instruments. An audioguide accompanies your visit, serenading you with opera excerpts. Alongside family portraits and documents, you'll find Mozart's original fortepiano.

Museum der Moderne
GALLERY

(www.museumdermoderne.at; Mönchsberg 32; adult/child €8/6; ⊙10am-6pm Tue-Sun, to 8pm Wed) Straddling Mönchsberg's cliffs, this contemporary glass-and-marble oblong of

 SALZBURG CARD

The money-saving **Salzburg Card** (1-/2-/3-day card €27/36/42) gets you entry to all of the major sights, a free river cruise, unlimited use of public transport (including cable cars) plus numerous discounts on tours and events. The card is €3 cheaper in the low season and half price for children aged 15 and under.

a gallery stands in stark contrast to the fortress. The gallery shows first-rate temporary exhibitions of 20th- and 21st-century art. There's a free guided tour of the gallery at 6.30pm every Wednesday. The **Mönchsberg Lift** (Gstättengasse 13; one way/return €2.10/3.40, incl gallery €9.70/6.80; ◷8am-7pm Thu-Tue, to 9pm Wed) whizzes up to the gallery year-round.

Schloss Mirabell — PALACE
(Mirabellplatz 4; ◷ Marble Hall 8am-4pm Mon, Wed & Thu, 1-4pm Tue & Fri, gardens dawn-dusk) `FREE` Prince-Archbishop Wolf Dietrich had this splendid palace built for his mistress Salome Alt in 1606. Johann Lukas von Hildebrandt, of Schloss Belvedere fame, gave it a baroque makeover in 1721. The lavish **Marmorsaal** (Marble Hall), replete with stucco, marble and frescoes, is free to visit and provides a sublime backdrop for evening chamber concerts. For stellar fortress views, stroll the fountain-dotted gardens. *The Sound of Music* fans will naturally recognise the Pegasus statue and the steps where the von Trapps practised 'Do-Re-Mi'.

☞ Tours

If you would rather go it alone, the tourist office has four-hour iTour audioguides (€9), which take in big-hitters such as the Residenz, Mirabellgarten and Mozartplatz.

Fräulein Maria's Bicycle Tours — BICYCLE TOUR
(www.mariasbicycletours.com; Mirabellplatz 4; adult/child €30/18; ◷9.30am May-Sep, plus 4.30pm Jun-Aug) Belt out *The Sound of Music* faves as you pedal on one of these jolly 3½-hour bike tours, taking in film locations including the Mirabellgarten, Stift Nonnberg, Schloss Leopoldskron and Hellbrunn. No advance booking is necessary; just turn up at the meeting point on Mirabellplatz.

Salzburg Panorama Tours — BUS TOUR
(☎87 40 29; www.panoramatours.com; Mirabellplatz; ◷office 8am-6pm) Boasts the 'original *Sound of Music* Tour' (€40) as well as a huge range of others, including Altstadt walking tours (€15), Mozart tours (€25) and Bavarian Alps and Salzkammergut excursions (€40).

Segway Tours — TOUR
(www.segway-salzburg.at; Wolf-Dietrich-Strasse 3; City/Sound of Music tour €33/60; ◷ tours 10.30am, 1pm & 3pm Apr-Oct) These guided Segway tours take in the big sights by zippy battery-powered scooter. Trundle through the city on a one-hour ride or tick off *The Sound of Music* locations on a two-hour tour.

Bob's Special Tours — BUS TOUR
(☎84 95 11; www.bobstours.com; Rudolfskai 38; ◷office 8.30am-5pm Mon-Fri, 1-2pm Sat & Sun) Minibus tours to *The Sound of Music* locations (€45), the Bavarian Alps (€45) and Grossglockner (€90). Prices include a free hotel pick-up for morning tours starting at 9am. Reservations essential.

✮✮ Festivals & Events

Mozartwoche — MUSIC
(Mozart Week; www.mozarteum.at; ◷late Jan) World-renowned orchestras, conductors and soloists celebrate Mozart's birthday with a feast of his music.

Salzburg Festival — ART
(Salzburger Festspiele; www.salzburgerfestspiele. at; ◷late Jul-Aug) You'll need to book tickets months ahead for this venerable summer festival, running since 1920.

🛏 Sleeping

★Haus Ballwein — GUESTHOUSE €
(☎82 40 29; www.haus-ballwein.at; Moosstrasse 69a; s €42-49, d €63-69, apt €98-120; P🐾) With its bright, pine-filled rooms, mountain views, free bike hire and garden, this place is big on charm. The largest, quietest rooms face the back and have balconies and kitchenettes. It's a 10-minute trundle from the Altstadt; take bus 21 to Gsengerweg.

YOHO Salzburg — HOSTEL €
(☎87 96 49; www.yoho.at; Paracelsusstrasse 9; dm €20-24, s €41, d €67-77; @🐾) Free wi-fi, secure lockers, comfy bunks, plenty of cheap beer and good-value schnitzels – what more could a backpacker ask for? Except, perhaps, a merry sing along with *The Sound of Music* screened daily (yes, *every* day). The friendly crew can arrange tours, adventure sports such as rafting and canyoning, and bike hire.

Pension Katrin — PENSION €€
(☎83 08 60; www.pensionkatrin.at; Nonntaler Hauptstrasse 49b; s €64-70, d €112-122, tr €153-168, q €172-188; P🐾) With its flowery garden, bright and cheerful rooms and homemade goodies at breakfast, this pension is one of the homiest in Salzburg. The affable Terler family keeps everything spick and span. Take bus 5 from the Hauptbahnhof to Wäschergasse.

Hotel Am Dom — BOUTIQUE HOTEL €€
(☎84 27 65; www.hotelamdom.at; Goldgasse 17; s €90-160, d €130-280; ✳🐾) Antique meets

boutique at this Altstadt hotel, where the original vaults and beams of the 800-year-old building contrast with razor-sharp design features.

Arte Vida
GUESTHOUSE €€

(⌨87 31 85; www.artevida.at; Dreifaltigkeitsgasse 9; s €59-129, d €86-140, apt €150-214; ⓢ) Arte Vida has the boho-chic feel of a Marrakesh riad, with its lantern-lit salon, communal kitchen and serene garden. Asia and Africa have provided the inspiration for the rich colours and fabrics that dress the individually designed rooms, all with DVD players and iPod docks.

Hotel Mozart
HISTORIC HOTEL €€

(⌨87 22 74; www.hotel-mozart.at; Franz-Josef-Strasse 27; s €95-105, d €140-155, tr €160-175; P ⓢ) An antique-filled lobby gives way to spotless rooms with comfy beds and sizeable bathrooms at the Mozart.

✕ Eating

Self-caterers can find picnic fixings at the **Grünmarkt** (Green Market; Universitätsplatz; ⊘7am-7pm Mon-Fri, 6am-3pm Sat).

Bärenwirt
AUSTRIAN €€

(⌨42 24 04; www.baerenwirt-salzburg.at; Müllner Hauptstrasse 8; mains €9.50-20; ⊘11am-11pm) Sizzling and stirring since 1663, Bärenwirt combines a woody, hunting-lodge-style interior with a river-facing terrace. Go for hearty *Bierbraten* (beer roast) with dumplings, locally caught trout or organic wild-boar bratwurst. The restaurant is 500m north of Museumplatz.

Triangel
AUSTRIAN €€

(⌨84 22 29; Wiener-Philharmoniker-Gasse 7; mains €10-19; ⊘noon-midnight Tue-Sat) The menu is market-fresh at this arty bistro, where the picture-clad walls pay tribute to Salzburg Festival luminaries. It does gourmet salads, a mean Hungarian goulash with organic beef, and delicious homemade ice cream.

Green Garden
VEGETARIAN €€

(⌨0662-841201; Nonntaler Hauptstrasse 16; mains €9.50-14.50; ⊘noon-3pm & 5.30-10pm Tue-Sat; ⓓ) 𝒞 The Green Garden is a breath of fresh air for vegetarians and vegans. Locavore is the word at this bright, modern cottage-style restaurant, pairing dishes like wild herb salad, saffron risotto with braised fennel and vegan fondue with organic wines in a totally relaxed setting.

Zwettler's
AUSTRIAN €€

(⌨84 41 99; www.zwettlers.com; Kaigasse 3; mains €9-18; ⊘4pm-2am Mon, 11.30am-2am Tue-Sat, 11.30am-midnight Sun) This gastro-pub has a lively buzz on its pavement terrace. Local grub such as schnitzel with parsley potatoes and goulash goes well with a cold, foamy Kaiser Karl wheat beer.

★ Esszimmer
FRENCH €€€

(⌨87 08 99; www.esszimmer.com; Müllner Hauptstrasse 33; 3-course lunch €38, tasting menus €75-118; ⊘noon-2pm & 6.30-9.30pm Tue-Sat) Andreas Kaiblinger puts an innovative spin on market-driven French cuisine at Michelin-starred Esszimmer. Eye-catching art, playful backlighting and a glass floor revealing the Almkanal stream keep diners captivated, as do gastro showstoppers inspired by the seasons. Buses 7, 21 and 28 to Landeskrankenhaus stop close by.

🍷 Drinking & Nightlife

You'll find the biggest concentration of bars along both banks of the Salzach; the hippest are around Gstättengasse and Anton-Neumayr-Platz.

★ Augustiner Bräustübl
BREWERY

(www.augustinerbier.at; Augustinergasse 4-6; ⊘3-11pm Mon-Fri, from 2.30pm Sat & Sun) Who says monks can't enjoy themselves? Since 1621, this cheery monastery-run brewery has been serving potent homebrews in Stein tankards in the vaulted hall and beneath the chestnut trees in the 1000-seat beer garden.

Enoteca Settemila
WINE BAR

(Bergstrasse 9; ⊘5-11pm Tue-Thu, from 3pm Fri & Sat) This bijou wine shop and bar brims with the enthusiasm and passion of Rafael Peil and Nina Corti. Go to sample their well-edited selection of wines, including Austrian, organic and biodynamic ones, with *taglieri* – sharing plates of cheese and *salumi* (cold cuts) from small Italian producers.

220 Grad
CAFE

(Chiemseegasse 5; ⊘9am-7pm Tue-Fri, to 6pm Sat) Famous for freshly roasted coffee, this retro-chic cafe serves probably the best espresso in town and whips up superb breakfasts.

ℹ Information

Many hotels and bars offer free wi-fi, and there are several cheap internet cafes near the train station. *Bankomaten* (ATMs) are all over the place.

> ### ⓘ DOMQUARTIER
>
> Salzburg's historic centre shines more brightly than ever since the opening of the DomQuartier in May 2014. A single ticket (adult/child €12/4) gives you access to all five sights in the complex, including the Residenz, Dommuseum and Erzabtei St Peter. For more details, visit www.domquartier.at.

Tourist Office (889 87 330; www.salzburg. info; Mozartplatz 5; ⊘9am-7pm) Helpful tourist office with a ticket-booking service.

ⓘ Getting There & Away

AIR

Low-cost airlines including **Ryanair** (www.ryanair. com) and **easyJet** (www.easyjet.com) serve Salzburg airport (p71), 5.5km west of the city centre.

BUS

Buses depart from just outside the Hauptbahnhof on Südtiroler Platz. For bus timetables and fares, see www.svv-info.at and www.postbus.at.

TRAIN

Fast trains leave frequently for Vienna (€51, 2½ hours) via Linz (€25, 1¼ hours). There is a two-hourly express service to Klagenfurt (€39, three hours). There are hourly trains to Innsbruck (€45, two hours).

ⓘ Getting Around

TO/FROM THE AIRPORT

Bus 2 runs from the Hauptbahnhof (€2.50, 19 minutes) to the airport.

BICYCLE

Top Bike (www.topbike.at; Staatsbrücke; per day €15; ⊘10am-5pm) Bicycle rental joint with half-price rental for kids. The Salzburg Card yields a 20% discount.

BUS

Bus drivers sell single (€2.50) and 24-hour (€5.50) tickets; these are cheaper when purchased in advance from machines (€1.70 and €3.40 respectively).

AROUND SALZBURG

Schloss Hellbrunn PALACE

(www.hellbrunn.at; Fürstenweg 37; adult/child/family €10.50/5/25; ⊘9am-5.30pm, to 9pm Jul & Aug; 🅿) A prince-archbishop with a wicked sense of humour, Markus Sittikus built Italianate Schloss Hellbrunn as a 17th-century summer palace and an escape from his Residenz functions. The ingenious trick fountains and water-powered figures are the big draw. When the tour guides set them off, expect to get wet! Admission includes entry to the baroque palace. The rest of the sculpture-dotted gardens are free to visit. Look out for *The Sound of Music* pavilion of 'Sixteen Going on Seventeen' fame.

Bus 25 runs to Hellbrunn, 4.5km south of Salzburg, every 20 minutes from Rudolfskai in the Altstadt.

Werfen

📵 06468 / POP 2963

More than 1000m above Werfen in the Tennengebirge mountains is **Eisriesenwelt** (www.eisriesenwelt.at; adult/child €11/6, incl cable car €22/12; ⊘9am-3.45pm May-Oct, to 4.45pm Jul & Aug). Billed as the world's largest accessible ice caves, this glittering ice empire is a once-seen-never-forgotten experience. Wrap up warm for subzero temperatures. Well below the caves is **Burg Hohenwerfen** (adult/child/family €11/6/26.50, incl lift €14.50/8/34.50; ⊘9am-5pm Apr-Oct; 🅿), a formidable cliff-top fortress dating from 1077.

Both the ice caves and fortress can be visited as a day trip from Salzburg if you start early (tour the caves first and be at the castle by 3.15pm for the falconry show); otherwise consult the **tourist office** (📵53 88; www. werfen.at; Markt 24; ⊘9am-5pm Mon-Fri) for accommodation options.

Werfen is 45km south of Salzburg on the A10/E55 motorway. Trains run frequently to Salzburg (€8.60, 40 minutes). In summer, minibuses (return adult/child €6.50/4.90) run every 25 minutes between Eisriesenstrasse in Werfen and the car park, a 20-minute walk from the cable car to Eisriesenwelt.

SALZKAMMERGUT

A wonderland of glassy blue lakes and tall craggy peaks, Austria's Lake District is a long-time favourite holiday destination. The peaceful lakes attract visitors in droves, who come to boat, fish, swim or just laze on the shore.

Bad Ischl is the region's transport hub, but Hallstatt is its true jewel. For info visit **Salzkammergut Touristik** (📵0613-224 000; www.salzkammergut.co.at; Götzstrasse 12; ⊘9am-

7pm). The Salzkammergut Card (€4.90, available May to October) provides up to 30% discounts on sights, ferries, cable cars and some buses.

Hallstatt

📞 06134 / POP 788

With pastel-hued homes, swans and towering mountains on either side of a glassy green lake, Hallstatt looks like some kind of greeting card for tranquillity. Now a Unesco World Heritage Site, Hallstatt was settled 4500 years ago and over 2000 graves have been discovered in the area, most of them dating from 1000 to 500 BC.

⊙ Sights & Activities

Salzwelten MINE
(www.salzwelten.at; funicular return plus tour adult/child/family €26/13/54, tour only €19/9.50/40; ⊙9.30am-4.30pm late Apr–late Oct) The fascinating Salzwelten is situated high above Hallstatt on Salzberg (Salt Mountain) and is the lake's major cultural attraction. The German–English tour details how salt is formed and the history of mining, and takes visitors down into the depths on miners' slides – the largest is 60m, during which you have your photo taken.

Beinhaus CHURCH
(Bone House; Kirchenweg 40; admission €1.50; ⊙10am-6pm May-Oct) This small charnel house contains rows of neatly stacked skulls, painted with decorative designs and the names of their former owners. Bones have been exhumed from the overcrowded graveyard since 1600, and the last skull in the collection was added in 1995.

Hallstätter See LAKE
(boat hire per hr from €11) You can hire boats and kayaks to get out on the lake, or scuba dive with the **Tauchclub Dachstein** (📞0664-88 600 481; www.dive-adventures.at; intro course from €35).

🛏 Sleeping & Eating

⭐**Pension Sarstein** GUESTHOUSE €
(📞82 17; Gosaumühlstrasse 83 ; d €64-80, apt €70-120; 🅿) The affable Fischer family takes pride in its little guesthouse a few minutes' walk along the lake from central Hallstatt. The old-fashioned rooms are nothing flash, but they are neat, cosy and have balconies with dreamy lake and mountain views. Family-sized apartments come with kitchenettes.

WORTH A TRIP

OBERTRAUN

Near Hallstatt, Obertraun has the intriguing **Dachstein Rieseneishöhle** (www.dachstein-salzkammergut.com; tour adult/child €14.30/8.30; ⊙core tour 9.20am-4pm May-late Oct). These caves are millions of years old and extend into the mountain for almost 80km in places.

From Obertraun it's also possible to catch a cable car to **Krippenstein** (return adult/child €28/15.50; ⊙May-Oct), where you'll find the freaky **5 Fingers viewing platform**, which protrudes over a sheer cliff face – not for sufferers of vertigo.

Restaurant zum Salzbaron EUROPEAN €€
(📞82 63; Marktplatz 104; mains €16-23; ⊙11.30am-10pm; 🌐🅿) One of the best gourmet acts in town, the Salzbaron is perched alongside the lake inside the Seehotel Grüner Baum and serves a seasonal pan-European menu; local trout features strongly in summer.

ℹ Information

Tourist Office (📞82 08; www.dachstein-salzkammergut.at; Seestrasse 99; ⊙9am-5pm Mon-Fri, to 1pm Sat) Turn left from the ferry to reach this office. It stocks a free leisure map of lakeside towns, and hiking and cycling trails.

ℹ Getting There & Away

BOAT
The last ferry connection leaves Hallstatt train station at 6.50pm (€2.50, 10 minutes). Ferry excursions do the circuit of Hallstatt Lahn via Hallstatt Markt, Obersee, Untersee and Steeg return (€12, 90 minutes) three times daily from July to early September.

TRAIN
Hallstatt train station is across the lake. The boat service from there to the village coincides with train arrivals. About a dozen trains daily connect Hallstatt and Bad Ischl (€4.30, 27 minutes).

TYROL

With converging mountain ranges behind lofty pastures and tranquil meadows, Tyrol (also Tirol) captures a quintessential Alpine panoramic view. Occupying a central position is Innsbruck, the region's jewel, while in

WORTH A TRIP

BREGENZERWALD

Only a few kilometres southeast of Bregenz, the forest-cloaked slopes, velvet-green pastures and limestone peaks of the Bregenzerwald unfold. In summer it's a glorious place to spend a few days hiking the hills and filling up on homemade cheeses in alpine dairies. Winter brings plenty of snow, and the area is noted for its downhill and cross-country skiing. The **Bregenzerwald tourist office** (📞05512-23 65; www.bregenzerwald.at; Impulszentrum 1135, Egg; ⊙9am-5pm Mon-Fri, 8am-1pm Sat) has information on the region.

the northeast and southwest are superb ski resorts. In the southeast, separated somewhat from the main state since part of South Tyrol was ceded to Italy at the end of WWI, lies the protected natural landscape of the Hohe Tauern National Park, an alpine wonderland of 3000m peaks, including the country's highest, the Grossglockner (3798m).

Innsbruck

📞 0512 / POP 124,579

Tyrol's capital is a sight to behold. The mountains are so close that within 25 minutes it's possible to travel from the heart of the city to over 2000m above sea level. Summer and winter outdoor activities abound, and it's understandable why some visitors only take a peek at Innsbruck proper before heading for the hills. But to do so is a shame, for Innsbruck has its own share of gems, including an authentic medieval Altstadt (Old Town), inventive architecture and vibrant student-driven nightlife.

◎ Sights

Hofkirche   CHURCH
(www.tiroler-landesmuseum.at; Universitätstrasse 2; adult/child €5/free; ⊙9am-5pm Mon-Sat, 12.30-5pm Sun) Innsbruck's pride and joy is the Gothic Hofkirche, one of Europe's finest royal court churches. It was commissioned in 1553 by Ferdinand I, who enlisted top artists of the age such as Albrecht Dürer, Alexander Colin and Peter Vischer the Elder. Top billing goes to the empty **sarcophagus of Emperor Maximilian I** (1459–1519), a masterpiece of German Renaissance sculpture, elaborately carved from black marble.

Goldenes Dachl & Museum   MUSEUM
(Golden Roof; Herzog-Friedrich-Strasse 15; adult/child €4/2; ⊙10am-5pm, closed Mon Oct-Apr) Innsbruck's golden wonder is this Gothic oriel, built for Emperor Maximilian I and glittering with 2657 fire-gilt copper tiles. An audioguide whizzes you through the history in the museum; look for the grotesque tournament helmets designed to resemble the Turks of the rival Ottoman Empire.

Hofburg   PALACE
(Imperial Palace; www.hofburg-innsbruck.at; Rennweg 1; adult/child €8/free; ⊙9am-5pm) Demanding attention with its imposing facade and cupolas, the Hofburg was built as a castle for Archduke Sigmund the Rich in the 15th century, expanded by Emperor Maximilian I in the 16th century and given a baroque makeover by Empress Maria Theresia in the 18th century. The centrepiece of the lavish rococo state apartments is the 31m-long **Riesensaal** (Giant's Hall).

Bergisel   VIEWPOINT
(www.bergisel.info; adult/child €9.50/4.50; ⊙9am-6pm) Rising above Innsbruck like a celestial staircase, this glass-and-steel ski jump was designed by much-lauded Iraqi architect Zaha Hadid. It's 455 steps or a two-minute funicular ride to the 50m-high **viewing platform**, with a breathtaking panorama of the Nordkette range, Inntal and Innsbruck. Tram 1 trundles here from central Innsbruck.

Schloss Ambras   CASTLE
(www.schlossambras-innsbruck.at; Schlosstrasse 20; adult/child/family €10/free/18; ⊙10am-5pm; ♿) Picturesquely perched on a hill and set among beautiful gardens, this Renaissance pile was acquired in 1564 by Archduke Ferdinand II, then ruler of Tyrol, who transformed it from a fortress into a palace. Don't miss the centrepiece **Spanische Saal** (Spanish Hall), the dazzling **armour collection** and the gallery's Velázquez and van Dyck originals.

ℹ CITY SAVERS

The **Innsbruck Card** allows one visit to Innsbruck's main sights/attractions, a return journey on lifts and cable cars, unlimited use of public transport including the Sightseer bus, and three-hour bike rental. It's available at the tourist office and costs €33/41/47 for 24/48/72 hours.

Stadtturm TOWER
(Herzog-Friedrich-Strasse 21; adult/child €3/1.50; ☺10am-8pm) Climb this tower's 148 steps for 360-degree views of the city's rooftops, spires and surrounding mountains.

🏃 Activities

Anyone who loves playing in the great outdoors will be itching to head up into the Alps in Innsbruck.

Nordkettenbahnen FUNICULAR
(www.nordkette.com; one way/return to Hungerburg €4.60/7.60, Seegrube €16.50/27.50, Hafelekar €18.30/30.50; ☺Hungerburg 7am-7.15pm Mon-Fri, 8am-7.15pm Sat & Sun, Seegrube 8.30am-5.30pm daily, Hafelekar 9am-5pm daily) Zaha Hadid's space-age funicular runs every 15 minutes, whizzing you from the Congress Centre to the slopes in no time. Walking trails head off in all directions from **Hungerburg** and **Seegrube**. For more of a challenge, there is a downhill track for mountain bikers and two fixed-rope routes *(Klettersteige)* for climbers.

Patrolled by inquisitive alpine sheep, the 2334m summit of **Hafelekar** affords tremendous views over Innsbruck to the snowcapped giants of the Austrian Alps, including 3798m Grossglockner.

Inntour ADVENTURE SPORTS
(www.inntour.com; Leopoldstrasse 4; ☺9am-6.30pm Mon-Fri, to 5pm Sat & Sun) Based at Die Börse, Inntour arranges all manner of thrillseeking pursuits, including canyoning (€80), tandem paragliding (€105), whitewater rafting (€45) and bungee jumping from the 192m Europabrücke (€140).

🛏 Sleeping

The tourist office has lists of private rooms costing between €20 and €40 per person.

Nepomuk's HOSTEL €
(☎584 118; www.nepomuks.at; Kiebachgasse 16; dm €24, d €58; 🖧) Could this be backpacker heaven? Nepomuk's sure comes close, with its Altstadt location, well-stocked kitchen and high-ceilinged dorms with homely touches like CD players. The delicious breakfast in attached Cafe Munding, with homemade pastries, jam and fresh-roasted coffee, gets your day off to a grand start.

Pension Paula GUESTHOUSE €
(☎292 262; www.pensionpaula.at; Weiherburggasse 15; s €35-46, d €60-70, tr €92, q €104; 🅿) This pension occupies an alpine chalet and has super-clean, homely rooms (most with

FREE GUIDED HIKES

From late May to October, Innsbruck Information (p66) arranges daily guided hikes, from sunrise walks to half-day mountain jaunts. The hikes are free with a Club Innsbruck Card, which you receive automatically when you stay overnight in Innsbruck. Pop into the tourist office to register and browse the program.

balconies). It's up the hill towards the zoo and has great vistas across the city.

★Hotel Weisses Kreuz HISTORIC HOTEL €€
(☎594 79; www.weisseskreuz.at; Herzog-Friedrich-Strasse 31; s €39-80, d €73-149; 🅿@🖧) Beneath the arcades, this atmospheric Altstadt hotel has played host to guests for 500 years, including a 13-year-old Mozart. With its wood-panelled parlours, antiques and twisting staircase, the hotel oozes history with every creaking beam. Rooms are supremely comfortable, the staff are charming and breakfast is a lavish spread.

Weisses Rössl GUESTHOUSE €€
(☎583 057; www.roessl.at; Kiebachgasse 8; s €70-110, d €100-160; @🖧) An antique rocking horse greets you at this 16th-century guesthouse. The vaulted entrance leads up to spacious rooms recently revamped with blonde wood, fresh hues and crisp white linen. The owner is a keen hunter and the restaurant (mains €10 to €18) has a meaty menu.

🍴 Eating

Markthalle MARKET €
(www.markthalle-innsbruck.at; Innrain; ☺7am-6.30pm Mon-Fri, to 1pm Sat) Fresh-baked bread, Tyrolean cheese, organic fruit, smoked ham and salami – it's all under one roof at this riverside covered market.

Cafe Munding CAFE €
(www.munding.at; Kiebachgasse 16; cake €2-4; ☺8am-8pm) Stop by this 200-year-old cafe for delicious cakes – try the moist chocolate raspberry Haustorte or the chocolate-marzipan Mozarttorte – and freshly roasted coffee.

★Chez Nico VEGETARIAN €€
(☎0650-451 06 24; www.chez-nico.at; Maria-Theresien-Strasse 49; 2-course lunch €14.50, 7-course menu €60; ☺6.30-10pm Mon & Sat,

noon-2pm & 6.30-10pm Tue-Fri; 🖉) Take a petite bistro and a Parisian chef with a passion for herbs, *et voilà*, you get Chez Nico. Nicolas Curtil (Nico) cooks seasonal, all-vegetarian delights along the lines of smoked aubergine wonton and chanterelle-apricot goulash. You won't miss the meat, we swear.

Die Wilderin AUSTRIAN €€
(📋562 728; www.diewilderin.at; Seilergasse 5; mains €11-18; ⏱5pm-2am Tue-Sat, 4pm-midnight Sun) 🍴 Take a gastronomic walk on the wild side at this modern-day hunter-gatherer of a restaurant, where chefs take pride in local sourcing and using top-notch farm-fresh and foraged ingredients. The menu sings of the seasons, be it asparagus, game, strawberries or winter veg. The vibe is urbane and relaxed.

Himal ASIAN €€
(📋588 588; Universitätsstrasse 13; mains €9.50-14.50; ⏱11.30am-2.30pm & 6-10.30pm Mon-Sat, 6-10pm Sun; 🖉) Friendly and intimate, Himal delivers vibrant, robust Nepalese flavours. Spot-on curries (some vegetarian) are mopped up with naan and washed down with mango lassis. The two-course €8.10 lunch is cracking value.

🍷 Drinking & Nightlife

Moustache BAR
(www.cafe-moustache.at; Herzog-Otto-Strasse 8; ⏱11am-2am Tue-Sun; 🕾) Playing Spot-the-Moustache (Einstein, Charlie Chaplin and co) is the preferred pastime at this retro bolthole, with a terrace overlooking pretty Domplatz and Club Aftershave in the basement.

Hofgarten Café BAR
(www.tagnacht.at; Rennweg 6a; ⏱7pm-4am Tue & Fri-Sat) DJ sessions and a tree-shaded beer garden are crowd-pullers at this trendy cafe-cum-bar set in the greenery of Hofgarten.

360° BAR
(Rathaus Galerien; ⏱10am-1am Mon-Sat) Grab a cushion and drink in 360-degree views of the city and Alps from the balcony that skirts this spherical, glass-walled bar. It's a nicely chilled spot for a coffee or sundowner.

ℹ Information

Innsbruck Information (📋598 50; www. innsbruck.info; Burggraben 3; ⏱9am-6pm) Main tourist office with truckloads of info on the city and surrounds, including skiing and walking.

ℹ Getting There & Away

AIR
EasyJet flies to Innsbruck Airport (p71), 4km west of the city centre.

CAR & MOTORCYCLE
Heading south by car through the Brenner Pass to Italy, you'll hit the A13 toll road (€8). Toll-free Hwy 182 follows the same route, although it is less scenic.

TRAIN
Fast trains depart at least every two hours for Bregenz (€37, 2½ hours), Salzburg (€45, two hours), Kitzbühel (€20.40, 1½ hours) and Munich (€41, 1¾ hours). There are several daily services to Lienz (€15.40, 3¾ hours).

ℹ Getting Around

Single tickets on buses and trams cost €1.80 from machines or €2 from the driver. A 24-hour ticket is €4.50. Bus F runs between the airport and Maria-Theresien-Strasse.

OTHER TOWNS WORTH A VISIT

Fancy exploring further? Here are some towns, resorts and valleys in Austria that you may want to consider for day trips or longer visits.

Zillertal Storybook Tyrol, with a steam train, snow-capped Alps and outdoor activities aplenty.

Bad Ischl Handsome spa town and a fine base for visiting the region's five lakes.

Zell am See An alpine beauty on the shores of its namesake lake. Gateway to the epic Grossglockner Road.

Eisenstadt The petite capital of Burgenland is known for its wonderful palace and famous former resident, composer Haydn.

Schladming Styrian gem in the glacial Dachstein mountains. Great for skiing, hiking, biking and white-water rafting on the Enns River.

Kitzbühel

☑ 05356 / POP 8211

Kitzbühel began life in the 16th century as a silver- and copper-mining town, and today preserves a charming medieval centre despite its other persona – as a fashionable and prosperous winter resort. It's renowned for the white-knuckled Hahnenkamm downhill ski race in January and the excellence of its slopes.

🏃 Activities

In winter there's first-rate intermediate skiing and freeriding on **Kitzbüheler Horn** to the north and **Hahnenkamm** to the south of town. A one-day ski pass in the peak season costs €49.

Dozens of summer **hiking trails** thread through the Kitzbühel Alps; the tourist office gives walking maps and runs free guided hikes for guests staying in town. The Flex-Ticket covering all cable cars costs €46 for three out of seven days.

🛏 Sleeping & Eating

Rates leap by up to 50% in the winter season.

Snowbunny's Hostel   HOSTEL €
(☑ 067-6794 0233; www.snowbunnys.co.uk; Bichlstrasse 30; dm €25-45, d €80-120; @ 🖥) This friendly, laid-back hostel is a bunny-hop from the slopes. Dorms are fine, if a tad dark; breakfast is DIY-style in the kitchen. There's a TV lounge, ski storage room and cats to stroke.

★ Hotel Edelweiss   HOTEL €€
(☑ 752 52; www.edelweiss-kitzbuehel.at; Marchfeldgasse 2; d incl half board €210-230; P 🖥) Near the Hahnenkammbahn, Edelweiss oozes Tyrolean charm with its green surrounds, alpine views, sauna and cosy interiors. Your kindly hosts Klaus and Veronika let you pack up a lunch from the breakfast buffet and serve delicious five-course dinners.

Huberbräu Stüberl   AUSTRIAN €€
(☑ 656 77; Vorderstadt 18; mains €8.50-18; ⊙8am-midnight Mon-Sat, from 9am Sun) An old-world Tyrolean haunt with vaults and pine benches, this tavern favours substantial portions of Austrian classics, such as schnitzel, goulash and dumplings, cooked to perfection.

ℹ Information

Tourist Office (☑ 666 60; www.kitzbuehel.com; Hinterstadt 18; ⊙8.30am-6pm Mon-Fri,

---

WORTH A TRIP

KRIMML FALLS

The thunderous, three-tier **Krimmler Wasserfälle** (Krimml Falls; www.wasserfaelle-krimml.at; adult/child €3/1; ⊙ticket office 8am-6pm mid-Apr–Oct) is Europe's highest waterfall at 380m, and one of Austria's most unforgettable sights. The **Wasserfallweg** (Waterfall Trail), which starts at the ticket office and weaves gently uphill through mixed forest, has numerous viewpoints with photogenic close-ups of the falls. It's about a two-hour round-trip walk.

The pretty alpine village of Krimml has a handful of places to sleep and eat – contact the **tourist office** (☑ 72 39; www.krimml.at; Oberkrimml 37; ⊙8am-noon & 2-6pm Mon-Fri, 8.30-10.30am & 4.30-6.30pm Sat) for more information.

Buses run year-round from Krimml to Zell am See (€10.20, 1¼ hours, every two hours), with frequent onward train connections to Salzburg (€19.60, 1½ hours). The village is about 500m north of the waterfall, on a side turning from the B165. There are parking spaces near the falls.

9am-6pm Sat, 10am-noon & 4-6pm Sun) The central tourist office has loads of info in English and a 24-hour accommodation board.

ℹ Getting There & Away

Trains run frequently from Kitzbühel to Innsbruck (€20.40, 1¾ hours) and Salzburg (€29.80, 2½ hours). For Kufstein (€11, one hour), change at Wörgl.

It's quicker and cheaper to reach Lienz by bus (€15.30, two hours, every two hours) than train.

Lienz

☑ 04852 / POP 11,903

With the jagged Dolomites crowding its southern skyline, the capital of East Tyrol is a scenic staging point for travels through the Hohe Tauern National Park.

◉ Sights & Activities

A €36 day pass covers skiing on the nearby **Zettersfeld** and **Hochstein** peaks. However, the area is more renowned for its 100km of cross-country trails; the town fills up for the annual Dolomitenlauf cross-country skiing race in mid-January.

Schloss Bruck
CASTLE

(www.museum-schlossbruck.at; Schlossberg 1; adult/child €7.50/2.50, combined admission with Aguntum €10.50/8.50; ⊙10am-6pm, closed Mon Sep-May) Lienz' famous medieval fortress has a museum chronicling the region's history, as well as Roman artefacts, Gothic winged altars and local costumes. The castle tower is used for changing exhibitions; a highlight for art enthusiasts is the **Egger-Lienz-Galerie** devoted to the emotive works of Albin Egger-Lienz.

Aguntum
MUSEUM, RUINS

(www.aguntum.info; Stribach 97; adult/child €7/4, combined admission with Schloss Bruck €10.50/8.50; ⊙9.30am-4pm May-Oct) Excavations are still under way at the Aguntum archaeological site in nearby Dölsach to piece together the jigsaw puzzle of this 2000-year-old *municipium*, which flourished as a centre of trade and commerce under Emperor Claudius. Take a stroll around the excavations, then visit the glass-walled museum to explore Lienz' Roman roots.

🛏 Sleeping & Eating

The tourist office can point you in the direction of good-value guesthouses and camping grounds.

Goldener Fisch
HOTEL €€

(☑621 32; www.goldener-fisch.at; Kärntnerstrasse 9; s/d €65/110; 🅿🛜) The chestnut-tree-shaded beer garden is a big draw at this family friendly hotel. The rooms are light and modern – if not fancy – and you can wind down in the sauna and herbal steam baths.

Kirchenwirt
AUSTRIAN €€

(☑625 00; www.kirchenwirt-lienz.at; Pfarrgasse 7; mains €9.50-29; ⊙9am-11.30pm Sun-Thu, to 1.30am Fri & Sat) Up on a hill opposite Stadtpfarrkirche St Andrä, this is Lienz' most atmospheric restaurant. Dine on a selection of local dishes under the vaults or on the streamside terrace. The lunch special costs under €10.

ⓘ Information

Tourist Office (☑050 212 400; www.lienzer dolomiten.net; Europaplatz 1; ⊙8.30am-6pm Mon-Fri, 9am-noon & 2-5pm Sat, 8.30-11am Sun) Staff will help you find accommodation (even private rooms) free of charge.

ⓘ Getting There & Away

There are several daily services to Innsbruck (€15.40 to €20.40, 3¼ to 4½ hours). Trains run every two hours to Salzburg (€38.90, 3½ hours). To head south by car, you must first divert west or east along Hwy 100.

Hohe Tauern National Park

Straddling Tyrol, Salzburg and Carinthia, this national park is the largest in the Alps; a 1786-sq-km wilderness of 3000m peaks, alpine meadows and waterfalls. At its heart lies **Grossglockner** (3798m), Austria's highest mountain, which towers over the 8km-long Pasterze Glacier, best seen from the outlook at **Kaiser-Franz-Josefs-Höhe** (2369m).

The 48km **Grossglockner Road** (www. grossglockner.at; Hwy 107; car/motorcycle €34.50/24.50; ⊙May-early Nov) from Bruck in Salzburgerland to Heiligenblut in Carinthia is one of Europe's greatest alpine drives. A feat of 1930s engineering, the road swings giddily around 36 switchbacks, passing jewel-coloured lakes, forested slopes and wondrous glaciers.

The major village on the Grossglockner Road is **Heiligenblut**, famous for its 15th-century pilgrimage church. Here the **tourist office** (☑27 00; www.heiligenblut.at; Hof 4; ⊙9am-noon & 2-6pm Mon-Fri, 3-6pm Sat & Sun) can advise on guided ranger hikes, mountain hiking and skiing. The village also has a spick-and-span **Jugendherberge** (☑22 59; www.oejhv.or.at; Hof 36; dm/s/d €22/30/52; 🅿🖥).

Bus 5002 runs frequently between Lienz and Heiligenblut on weekdays (€16.40, one hour), less frequently at weekends.

VORARLBERG

Vorarlberg has always been a little different. Cut off from the rest of Austria by the snow-capped Arlberg massif, this westerly region has often associated itself more with nearby Switzerland than distant Vienna, and also provides a convenient gateway to Germany and Liechtenstein.

The capital, **Bregenz**, sits prettily on the shores of Lake Constance and holds the **Bregenzer Festspiele** (Bregenz Festival; ☑05574-4076; www.bregenzerfestspiele.com; ⊙late Jul-late

Aug) in July/August, when opera is performed on a floating stage on the lake.

The real action here, though, is in the Arlberg region, shared by Vorarlberg and neighbouring Tyrol. Some of the country's best downhill and off-piste skiing – not to mention après-ski partying – is in **St Anton am Arlberg**, where the first ski club in the Alps was founded in 1901. The centrally located **tourist office** (☑05446-226 90; www.stantonamarlberg.com; Dorfstrasse 8; ☺8am-6pm Mon-Fri, 9am-6pm Sat, 9am-noon & 2-5pm Sun) has maps, and information on accommodation and activities.

A ski pass covering the whole Arlberg region and valid for all 85 ski lifts costs €49.50/276 for one/seven days in the high season.

Accommodation is mainly in small B&Bs. Many budget places (rates from €30 per person) are booked months in advance.

St Anton is on the main railway route between Bregenz (€20.40, 1½ hours) and Innsbruck (€21.20, 1¼ hours). It's close to the eastern entrance of the Arlberg Tunnel, the toll road connecting Vorarlberg and Tyrol (€8.50).

SURVIVAL GUIDE

❶ Directory A–Z

ACCOMMODATION

From simple mountain huts to five-star hotels fit for kings – you'll find the lot in Austria. Tourist offices invariably keep lists and details, and some arrange bookings for free or for a nominal fee. Some useful points:

➡ Book ahead for the high seasons: July and August and December to April (in ski resorts).

➡ Some hostels and some rock-bottom digs have an *Etagendusche* (communal shower).

➡ In mountain resorts, high-season prices can be up to double the prices charged in the low season (May to June and October to November).

SLEEPING PRICE RANGES

Prices include a private bathroom and breakfast unless otherwise stated.

€ less than €80

€€ €80 to €200

€€€ more than €200

COUNTRY FACTS

Area 83,871 sq km

Capital Vienna

Country Code ☑43

Currency Euro (€)

Emergency ☑112

Language German

Money ATMs widely available; banks open Monday to Friday

Visas Schengen rules apply

➡ Some resorts issue a *Gästekarte* (guest card) when you stay overnight, offering discounts on things such as cable cars and admission.

Some useful websites include the following:
Austrian Hotelreservation (www.austrian-hotelreservation.at)
Austrian National Tourist Office (www.austria.info)
Bergfex (www.bergfex.com)
Camping in Österreich (www.campsite.at)

Accommodation Types

Alpine huts There are 236 huts in the Austrian Alps maintained by the **Österreichischer Alpenverein** (ÖAV, Austrian Alpine Club; www.alpenverein.at). Bed prices for nonmembers are from €20 in a dorm; ÖAV members pay half-price. Meals or cooking facilities are often available.

Camping Austria has some 500 camping grounds, many well equipped and scenically located. Prices can be as low as €5 per person or small tent and as high as €12. Many close in winter, so phone ahead to check. Search by region at www.camping-club.at (in German).

Hostels In Austria around 100 hostels (*Jugendherberge*) are affiliated with Hostelling International (HI). Facilities are often excellent. Four- to six-bed dorms with shower/toilet are the norm, though some places also have doubles and family rooms. See www.oejhv.or.at or www.oejhw.at for details.

Private rooms *Privatzimmer* (private rooms) are cheap (often about €50 per double). On top of this, you will find *Bauernhof* (farmhouses) in rural areas, and some *Öko-Bauernhöfe* (organic farms).

Rental accommodation *Ferienwohnungen* (self-catering apartments) are ubiquitous in Austrian mountain resorts. Contact a local tourist office for lists and prices.

ACTIVITIES

Austria is a wonderland for outdoorsy types, with much of the west given over to towering alpine peaks. Opportunities for hiking and mountaineering are boundless in Tyrol, Salzburgerland and the Hohe Tauern National Park, all of which have extensive alpine hut networks (see www.alpenverein.at). Names like St Anton, Kitzbühel and Mayrhofen fire the imagination of serious skiers, but you may find cheaper accommodation and lift passes in little-known resorts; visit www.austria.info for the lowdown.

BUSINESS HOURS

Banks 8am to 3pm Monday to Friday, to 5.30pm Thursday

Cafes 7.30am to 8pm; hours vary widely

Clubs 10pm to late

Post offices 8am to noon and 2pm to 6pm Monday to Friday, 8am to noon Saturday

Pubs 6pm to 1am

Restaurants noon to 3pm and 7pm to 11pm

Shops 9am to 6.30pm Monday to Friday, 9am to 5pm Saturday

Supermarkets 9am to 8pm Monday to Saturday

DISCOUNT CARDS

Discount Rail Cards See p72 for more information.

Student & Youth Cards International Student Identity Cards (ISIC) and European Youth Card (Euro<26; check www.euro26.org for discounts) will get you discounts at most museums, galleries and theatres. Admission is generally a little higher than the price for children.

INTERNET RESOURCES

ÖAV (www.alpenverein.at) Austrian Alpine Club

ÖBB (www.oebb.at) Austrian Federal Railways

Österreich Werbung (www.austria.info) National tourism authority

MONEY

Austria's currency is the euro. An approximate 10% tip is expected in restaurants. Pay it directly to the server; don't leave it on the table.

PUBLIC HOLIDAYS

New Year's Day (Neujahr) 1 January

Epiphany (Heilige Drei Könige) 6 January

Easter Monday (Ostermontag) March/April

Labour Day (Tag der Arbeit) 1 May

Whit Monday (Pfingstmontag) Sixth Monday after Easter

Ascension Day (Christi Himmelfahrt) Sixth Thursday after Easter

Corpus Christi (Fronleichnam) Second Thursday after Whitsunday

Assumption (Maria Himmelfahrt) 15 August

National Day (Nationalfeiertag) 26 October

All Saints' Day (Allerheiligen) 1 November

Immaculate Conception (Mariä Empfängnis) 8 December

Christmas Day (Christfest) 25 December

St Stephen's Day (Stephanitag) 26 December

TELEPHONE

➜ Austrian telephone numbers consist of an area code followed by the local number.

➜ The country code is 🖉43 and the international access code is 🖉00.

➜ The mobile network works on GSM 1800 and is compatible with GSM 900 phones. Phone shops sell prepaid SIM cards for about €10.

➜ Phonecards in different denominations are sold at post offices and *Tabak* (tobacconist) shops. Call centres are widespread in cities, and many internet cafes are geared for Skype calls.

TOURIST INFORMATION

Tourist offices, which are dispersed far and wide in Austria, tend to adjust their hours from one year to the next, so business hours may have changed slightly by the time you arrive.

Austrian National Tourist Office (ANTO; www.austria.info) The Austrian National Tourist Office has a number of overseas offices. There is a comprehensive listing on the ANTO website.

VISAS

Schengen visa rules apply. The Austrian Foreign Ministry website www.bmeia.gv.at lists embassies.

🛈 Getting There & Away

AIR

Among the low-cost airlines, Air Berlin flys to Graz, Innsbruck, Linz, Salzburg and Vienna, easyJet to Innsbruck, Salzburg and Vienna, and Ryanair to Linz, Salzburg and Bratislava (for Vienna).

EATING PRICE RANGES

Price ranges in this chapter are for a two-course meal excluding drinks.

€ less than €15

€€ €15 to €30

€€€ more than €30

Following are the key international airports in Austria (and neighbouring Slovakia):

Airport Bratislava (Letisko; +421 2 3303 3353; www.bts.aero) Airport Letisko Bratislava is connected to Vienna International Airport and Vienna Erdberg (U3) by almost hourly buses (one way/return €7.70/14.40, 1¾ hours). Book online at www.slovaklines.sk.

Blue Danube Airport Linz (🖉7221 6000; www.linz-airport.at; Flughafenstrasse 1, Hörsching) Austrian Airlines, Lufthansa, Ryanair and Air Berlin are the main airlines servicing the Blue Danube Airport, 13km southwest of the centre.

Graz Airport (🖉0316-29 020; www.flughafen-graz.at) Graz airport is located 10km south of the centre and is served by carriers including Air Berlin, which connects the city with Berlin.

Innsbruck Airport (🖉0512-22 525; www.innsbruck-airport.com; Fürstenweg 180) EasyJet flies to Innsbruck Airport, 4km west of the city centre.

Kärnten Airport (🖉41 500; www.klagenfurt-airport.com; Flughafenstrasse 60-66) Klagenfurt's airport is 3km north of town and served by the low-cost airline germanwings.

Salzburg Airport (🖉858 00; www.salzburg-airport.com; Innsbrucker Bundesstrasse 95) Salzburg airport, a 20-minute bus ride from the city centre, has regular scheduled flights to destinations all over Austria and Europe.

Vienna International Airport (🖉01-7007 22 233; www.viennaairport.com) Vienna International Airport has good connections worldwide. The airport is in Schwechat, 18km southeast of Vienna.

LAND

Bus

Buses depart from Austria for as far afield as England, the Baltic countries, the Netherlands, Germany and Switzerland. But most significantly, they provide access to Eastern European cities small and large – from the likes of Sofia and Warsaw, to Banja Luka, Mostar and Sarajevo.

Services operated by **Eurolines** (www.eurolines.at) leave from Vienna and from several regional cities.

Car & Motorcycle

There are numerous entry points into Austria by road from Germany, the Czech Republic, Slovakia, Hungary, Slovenia, Italy and Switzerland. All border-crossing points are open 24 hours.

Standard European insurance and paperwork rules apply.

Train

Austria has excellent rail connections. The main services in and out of the country from the west normally pass through Bregenz, Innsbruck or Salzburg en route to Vienna. Express services to Italy go via Innsbruck or Villach; trains to Slovenia are routed through Graz.

Trains from Vienna run to many Eastern European destinations, including Bratislava, Budapest, Prague and Warsaw; there are also connections south to Italy via Klagenfurt and north to Berlin. Salzburg is within sight of the Bavarian border, and there are many trains Munich-bound and beyond from the baroque city. Innsbruck is on the main rail line from Vienna to Switzerland, and two routes also lead to Munich. Look out for the fast, comfortable RailJet services to Germany and Switzerland.

For online timetables and tickets, visit the **ÖBB** (Österreichische Bundesbahnen; Austrian Federal Railways; 🖉24hr hotline 05 1717; www.oebb.at) website. SparSchiene (discounted tickets) are often available when you book online in advance and can cost as little as a third of the standard train fare.

RIVER & LAKE

Hydrofoils run to Bratislava and Budapest from Vienna; slower boats cruise the Danube between the capital and Passau. The **Danube Tourist Commission** (www.danube-river.org) has a country-by-country list of operators and agents who can book tours.

ℹ Getting Around

AIR

Austrian Airlines (www.austrian.com) The national carrier offers several flights daily between Vienna and Graz, Innsbruck, Klagenfurt, Linz and Salzburg.

BICYCLE

➡ All cities have at least one bike shop that doubles as a rental centre; expect to pay around €10 to €15 per day.

➡ Most tourist boards have brochures on cycling facilities and plenty of designated cycling routes within their region.

➡ You can take bicycles on any train with a bicycle symbol at the top of its timetable. For regional and long-distance trains, you'll pay an extra 10% on your ticket price. It costs €12 to take your bike on international trains.

BOAT

Services along the Danube are generally slow, scenic excursions rather than functional means of transport.

BUS

Postbus (🖉24hr 05 17 17; www.postbus.at) Postbus services usually depart from outside train stations. In remote regions, there are fewer services on Saturday and often none on Sunday.

ESSENTIAL FOOD & DRINK

➡ **Make it meaty** Go for a classic Wiener schnitzel, *Tafelspitz* (boiled beef with horseradish sauce) or *Schweinebraten* (pork roast). The humble *Wurst* (sausage) comes in various guises.

➡ **On the side** Lashings of potatoes, either fried *(Pommes)*, roasted *(Bratkartoffeln)*, in a salad *(Erdapfelsalat)* or boiled in their skins *(Quellmänner)*; or try *Knödel* (dumplings) and *Nudeln* (flat egg noodles).

➡ **Kaffee und Kuchen** Coffee and cake is Austria's sweetest tradition. Must-tries: flaky apple strudel, rich, chocolatey Sacher Torte and *Kaiserschmarrn* (sweet pancakes with raisins).

➡ **Wine at the source** Jovial locals gather in rustic *Heurigen* (wine taverns) in the wine-producing east, identified by an evergreen branch above the door. Sip crisp Grüner Veltliner whites and spicy Blaufränkisch wines.

➡ **Cheese fest** Dig into gooey *Käsnudeln* (cheese noodles) in Carinthia, *Kaspressknodel* (fried cheese dumplings) in Tyrol and *Käsekrainer* (cheesy sausages) in Vienna. The hilly Bregenzerwald is studded with dairies.

CAR & MOTORCYCLE

A *Vignette* (toll sticker) is imposed on all motorways; charges for cars/motorbikes are €8.70/5 for 10 days and €25.30/12.70 for two months. *Vignette* can be purchased at border crossings, petrol stations and *Tabak* shops. There are additional tolls (usually €2.50 to €10) for some mountain tunnels.

Speed limits are 50km/h in built-up areas, 130km/h on motorways and 100km/h on other roads.

Multinational car-hire firms Avis, Budget, Europcar and Hertz all have offices in major cities. The minimum age for hiring small cars is 19 years, or 25 years for larger, 'prestige' cars. Customers must have held a driving licence for at least a year. Many contracts forbid customers to take cars outside Austria, particularly into Eastern Europe. Crash helmets are compulsory for motorcyclists.

TRAIN

Austria has a clean, efficient rail system, and if you use a discount card it's very inexpensive.
➡ Disabled passengers can use the 24-hour
☑ 05 17 17 customer number for special travel assistance; do this at least 24 hours ahead of travel (48 hours ahead for international services). Staff at stations will help with boarding and alighting.

➡ Fares quoted are for 2nd-class tickets.
➡ ÖBB (p71) is the main operator, supplemented with a handful of private lines. Tickets and timetables are available online.
➡ It's worth seeking out RailJet train services connecting Vienna, Graz, Villach, Salzburg, Innsbruck, Linz and Klagenfurt, as they travel up to 200km/h.
➡ Reservations in 2nd class within Austria cost €3.50 for most express services; recommended for travel on weekends.

Rail Passes

Depending on the amount of travelling you intend to do in Austria, rail passes can be a good deal.

Eurail Austria Pass This handy pass is available to non-EU residents; prices start at €129 for three days' unlimited 2nd-class travel within one month. See the website at www.eurail.com for all options.

Interrail Passes are for European residents and include One Country Pass Austria (three/four/six/eight days €131/154/187/219). Youths under 26 receive substantial discounts. See www.interrail.eu for all options.

Vorteilscard Reduces fares by at least 45% and is valid for a year, but not on buses. Bring a photo and your passport or ID. It costs adult/under 26 years/senior €99/19/29.

Belgium & Luxembourg

Best Places to Eat

➡ De Stove (p96)

➡ De Ruyffelaer (p98)

➡ L'Ogenblik (p82)

➡ In 't Nieuwe Museum (p96)

Best Places to Stay

➡ Hôtel Le Dixseptième (p80)

➡ Hôtel Simoncini (p101)

➡ Auberge Aal Veinen (p104)

➡ B&B Dieltiens (p96)

Why Go?

Stereotypes of comic books, chips and sublime chocolates are just the start in eccentric little Belgium; its self-deprecating people have quietly spent centuries producing some of Europe's finest art and architecture. Bilingual Brussels is the dynamic yet personable EU capital, but also sports what's arguably the world's most beautiful city square. Flat, Flemish Flanders has many other alluring medieval cities, all easily linked by regular train hops. In hilly, French-speaking Wallonia, the attractions are contrastingly rural – castle villages, outdoor activities and extensive cave systems.

Independent Luxembourg, the EU's richest country, is compact and hilly with its own wealth of castle villages. The grand duchy's capital city is famed for banking but also sports a fairytale Unesco-listed historic old town. And from the brilliant beers of Belgium to the sparkling wines of Luxembourg's Moselle Valley, there's plenty to lubricate some of Europe's best dining. Welcome to the good life.

When to Go
Brussels

Pre-Easter weekends Belgium hosts many of Europe's weirdest carnivals, not just at Mardi Gras.

Feb & Mar Both countries symbolically burn the spirit of winter on the first weekend after Carnival.

Jul & Aug Countless festivals, hotels packed at the coast but cheaper in Brussels and Luxembourg City.

Belgium & Luxembourg Highlights

❶ Come on weekdays off-season to appreciate the picture-perfect canal scenes of medieval **Bruges** (p93), without the tourist overload.

❷ Be wooed by underappreciated **Ghent** (p89), one of Europe's greatest all-round discoveries.

❸ Savour the 'world's most beautiful square', then seek out the remarkable cafes, chocolate shops and art nouveau survivors in **Brussels** (p76).

❹ Follow fashion to hip yet historic **Antwerp** (p85).

❺ Spend the weekend in Unesco-listed **Luxembourg City** (p100) then head out to the grand duchy's evocative castle villages.

❻ Ponder the heartbreaking futility of WWI in Flanders' fields around meticulously rebuilt **Ypres** (p97).

❼ Explore the caves and castles of rural **Wallonia** (p99).

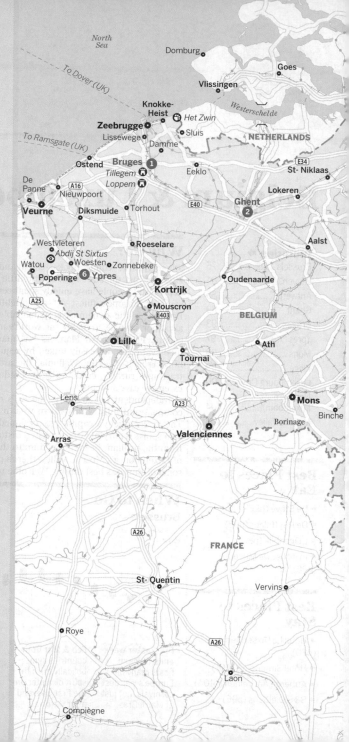

ITINERARIES

Four Days

Just long enough to get a first taste of Belgium's four finest 'art cities': Bruges, Ghent, Brussels and Antwerp, all easy jump-offs or short excursions while you're train-hopping between Paris and Amsterdam. **Bruges** is the fairy-tale 'Venice of the north', **Ghent** has similar canalside charms without the tourist hordes, and **Brussels**' incomparable Grand Place is worth jumping off any train for, even if you have only a few hours to spare. Cosmopolitan **Antwerp** goes one step further, adding in fashion and diamonds. If you're overnighting make sure to hit Brussels on a weekend and Bruges on a weekday to get the best deals on accommodation.

Ten Days

Add an extra night in each of the above and consider stops in **Mechelen** and **Lier**, practising your French in **Mons** and **Tournai** on the 'back route' to France or in **Luxembourg** en route to Koblenz, Germany.

BRUSSELS

POP 1.14 MILLION

Like the country it represents, Brussels (Bruxelles, Brussel) is a surreal, multilayered place pulling several disparate identities into one enigmatic core. It subtly seduces with great art, tempting chocolate shops and classic cafes. Meanwhile a confusing architectural smorgasbord pits awesome art nouveau and 17th-century masterpieces against shabby suburbanism and the glass-faced anonymity of the EU area. Note that Brussels is officially bilingual, so all names – from streets to train stations – have both Dutch and French versions, but for simplicity we use only the French versions in this chapter.

◉ Sights

◉ Central Brussels

★ Grand Place   SQUARE

(Ⓜ Gare Centrale) Brussels' incomparable central square tops any itinerary. Its splendidly spired Gothic **Hôtel de Ville** (City Hall; Pl Guillaume II) was the only building to escape bombardment by the French in 1695, quite ironic considering that it was their main target. Today the pedestrianised square's splendour is due largely to its intact **guildhalls**, rebuilt by merchant guilds after 1695 and fancifully adorned with gilded statues.

Manneken Pis   MONUMENT

(cnr Rue de l'Étuve & Rue du Chêne; Ⓜ Gare Centrale) From Rue Charles Buls, Brussels' most unashamedly touristy shopping street, chocolate and trinket shops lead the camera-toting hoards three blocks to the Manneken Pis. This fountain-statue of a little boy taking a leak is comically tiny and a perversely perfect national symbol for surreal Belgium. Most of the time the tiny statue's nakedness is largely hidden beneath a costume relevant to an anniversary, national day or local event: his ever-growing wardrobe is partly displayed at the **Maison du Roi** (Musée de la Ville de Bruxelles; Grand Pl; Ⓜ Gare Centrale).

★ Musées Royaux des Beaux-Arts   GALLERY

(Royal Museums of Fine Arts; ☑ 02-508 32 11; www.fine-arts-museum.be; Rue de la Régence 3; adult/BrusselsCard/6-25yr €8/free/2, with Magritte Museum €13; ☉ 10am-5pm Tue-Sun; Ⓜ Gare Centrale, Parc) This prestigious museum incorporates the **Musée d'Art Ancien** (ancient art); the **Musée d'Art Moderne** (modern art), with works by surrealist Paul Delvaux and fauvist Rik Wouters; and the purpose-built **Musée Magritte**. The 15th-century Flemish Primitives are wonderfully represented in the Musée d'Art Ancien: there's Rogier Van der Weyden's *Pietà* with its hallucinatory dawn sky, Hans Memling's refined portraits, and the richly textured *Madonna with Saints* by the Master of the Legend of St Lucy.

★ MIM   MUSEUM

(Musée des Instruments de Musique; ☑ 02-545 01 30; www.mim.be; Rue Montagne de la Cour 2; adult/concession €12/8; ☉ 9.30am-5pm Tue-Fri, 10am-5pm Sat & Sun; Ⓜ Gare Centrale, Parc) Strap on a pair of headphones then step on the automated floor panels in front of the precious instruments (including world instruments and Adolphe Sax's inventions) to hear them being played. As much of a highlight as the Musical Instrument Museum itself, is its premises – the art nouveau Old England building. This former department store was built in 1899 by Paul Saintenoy and has a panoramic rooftop *café* (pub/bar) and outdoor terrace.

Palais de Justice   HISTORIC BUILDING
(Place Poelaert; Ⓜ Louise, 🚌 92, 94) When constructed in 1883, this gigantic domed law court was Europe's biggest building. From outside, rooftop panoramas look towards the distant Atomium and Koekelberg Basilica. A glass elevator leads down into the quirky, downmarket but gentrifying Marolles quarter.

◉ Beyond the Centre

★**Musée Horta**   MUSEUM
(📞 02-543 04 90; www.hortamuseum.be; Rue Américaine 25; adult/child €8/4; ⊙ 2-5.30pm Tue-Sun; Ⓜ Horta, 🚌 91, 92) The typically austere exterior doesn't give much away, but Victor Horta's former home (designed and built 1898–1901) is an art nouveau jewel. The stairwell is the structural triumph of the house – follow the playful knots and curlicues of the banister, which become more exuberant as you ascend, ending at a tangle of swirls and glass lamps at the skylight, glazed with citrus-coloured and plain glass.

Cantillon Brewery   BREWERY
(Musée Bruxellois de la Gueuze; 📞 02-521 49 28; www.cantillon.be; Rue Gheude 56; admission €7; ⊙ 9am-5pm Mon-Fri, 10am-5pm Sat; Ⓜ Clemenceau) Beer lovers shouldn't miss this unique living brewery-museum. Atmospheric and family run, it's Brussels' last operating lambic brewery and still uses much of the original 19th-century equipment. After a brief explanation, visitors take a self-guided tour, including the barrel rooms where the beers mature for up to three years in chestnut wine-casks. The entry fee includes two taster-glasses of Cantillon's startlingly acidic brews.

★**Musée du Cinquantenaire**   MUSEUM
(📞 02-741 72 11; www.kmkg-mrah.be; Parc du Cinquantenaire 10; adult/child/BrusselsCard €5/free/free; ⊙ 9.30am-5pm Tue-Fri, from 10am Sat & Sun; Ⓜ Mérode) This astonishingly rich, global collection ranges from Ancient Egyptian sarcophagi to Meso-American masks, to icons to wooden bicycles. Decide what you want to see before coming or the sheer scope can prove overwhelming. Visually attractive spaces include the medieval stone carvings set around a neogothic cloister and the soaring Corinthian columns (convincing fibreglass props) that bring atmosphere to an original AD 420 mosaic from Roman Syria. Labelling is in French and Dutch so the English-language audioguide (€3) is worth considering.

Atomium   MONUMENT, MUSEUM
(www.atomium.be; Sq de l'Atomium; adult/student/BrusselsCard €11/6/9; ⊙ 10am-6pm; Ⓜ Heysel, 🚌 51) The space-age Atomium looms 102m over north Brussels' suburbia resembling a steel alien from a '60s Hollywood movie. It consists of nine house-sized metallic balls linked by steel tube-columns containing escalators and lifts. The balls are arranged like a school chemistry set to represent iron atoms in their crystal lattice...except these are 165 billion times bigger. It was built as a symbol of postwar progress for the 1958 World's Fair and became an architectural icon, receiving a makeover in 2006.

Waterloo Battlefield   HISTORIC SITE
(www.waterloo1815.be) A day trip from Brussels, Waterloo Battlefield (20km south) is where the course of European history changed in June 1815 with the final defeat of Napoleon. Today the rolling fields are marked by the striking cone of a grassy hill topped with a great bronze lion. You can climb it (adult/child €6/4) from the **visitor centre**, which offers a range of battle-related activities. TEC bus W from Bruxelles-Midi gets you within 800m. Don't use Waterloo train station, which is 5km away.

☞ Tours

Brussels Bike Tours   CYCLING
(📞 0484 89 89 36; www.brusselsbiketours.com; tour incl bicycle rental adult/student €25/22; ⊙ 10am Feb-Nov, 10am & 3pm Apr-Sep) Tours start from the Grand Place, taking 3½ hours including stops for beer and *frites*.

> ## ❶ BRUSSELSCARD
>
> The **BrusselsCard** (www.brusselscard.be; 24/48/72hr €24/36/43) allows free visits to more than 30 Brussels-area museums and free transport but you'll need to be a hyperactive museum fan to save much money. On the first Wednesday afternoon of each month many museums are free.

Central Brussels

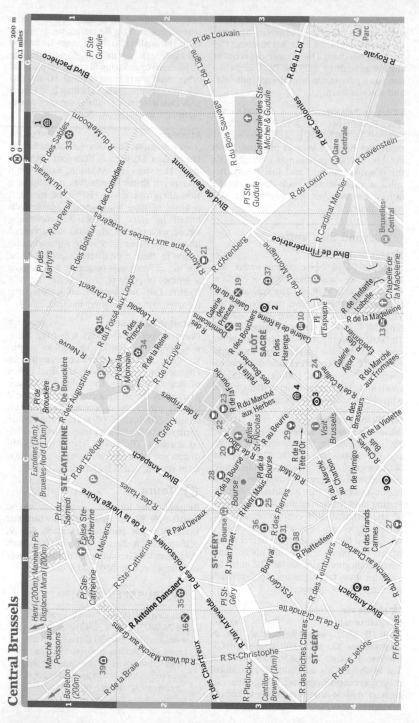

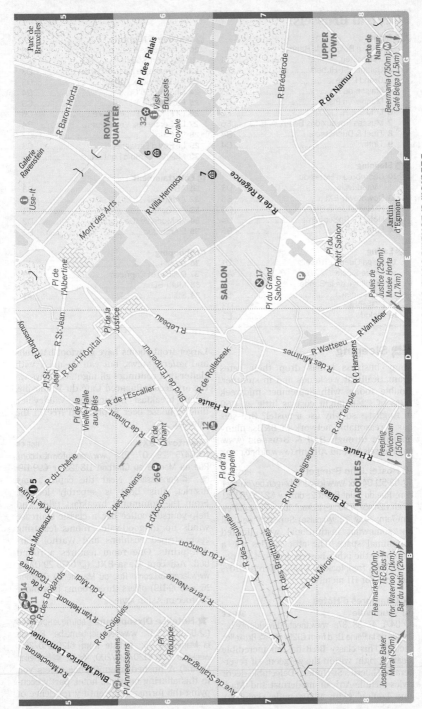

Parc de Bruxelles

UPPER TOWN

Pl des Palais

R Bréderode

Porte de Namur

Beermania (750m); Café Belga (1.5km)

R de Namur

R Baron Horta

ROYAL QUARTER

32 Visit Brussels

Pl Royale

6

Galerie Ravenstein

Use-It

7

R de la Régence

Jardin d'Egmont

Mont des Arts

R Villa Hermosa

SABLON

Pl du Petit Sablon

Palais de Justice (250m); Musée Horta (1.7km)

Pl de l'Albertine

17 Pl du Grand Sablon

R Van Moer

R St-Jean

Pl de la Justice

R Lebeau

R Watteeu

R des Minimes

R C Hanssens

R de l'Hôpital

R Duquesnoy

Pl St-Jean

R de Rollebeek

R de l'Escalier

Bld de l'Empereur

R Haute

R du Temple

Peeping Policeman (150m)

Pl de la Vieille Halle aux Blés

R de Dinant

Pl de Dinant

12

R Haute

R du Chêne

Pl de la Chapelle

R Notre Seigneur

MAROLLES

5

R de l'Étuve

R des Alexiens

26

R d'Accolay

R Blaes

R des Moineaux

R des Ursulines

R des Brigittines

R du Miroir

Flea market (200m); TEC Bus W (for Waterloo) (1km); Bar du Matin (2km)

14

R de l'Goutière

30 11

R des Bogards

R Van Helmont

R du Midi

R Terre-Neuve

R du Poinçon

Blvd Maurice Lemonnier

R des Soignies

Pl Rouppe

R d Moucherons

Anneessens

Pl Anneessens

Ave de Stalingrad

Josephine Baker Mural (50m)

Central Brussels

🛏 Sleeping

Many business hotels drop their rates dramatically at weekends and in summer. Double rooms with September midweek rates of €240 might cost as little as €69 in August – so why use a hostel? Brussels has a reasonable network of B&Bs, many bookable through **Bed & Brussels** (www.bnb-brussels.be) and **Airbnb** (www.airbnb.com).

HI Hostel John Bruegel   HOSTEL €
(☏ 02-511 04 36; www.jeugdherbergen.be/brussel.htm; Rue du Saint Esprit 2; dm/tw €27.20/63.30, youth €24.45/57.90; ⊙ lockout 10am-2pm, curfew 1am-7am; ⊛ @ ☎; Ⓜ Louise) Superbly central but somewhat institutional with limited communal space. The attic singles are a cut above the other hostels. Internet €2 per hour, wi-fi free, lockers €1.50. There's a 10% discount for HI members.

★ Chambres d'Hôtes du Vaudeville   B&B €€
(☏ 0471 47 38 37; www.theatreduvaudeville.be; Galerie de la Reine 11; d from €120; ☎; ⓠ Bruxelles Central) This classy B&B has an incredible location right within the gorgeous (if reverberant) Galeries St-Hubert. Delectable decor styles include African, modernist and 'Madame Loulou' (with 1920s nude sketches).

Larger front rooms have clawfoot bathtubs and *galerie* views, but can be noisy with clatter that continues all night. Get keys via the art-deco-influenced Café du Vaudeville, where breakfast is included. Vaudeville's unique house beer is provided free in the minibar.

Downtown-BXL   B&B €€
(☏ 0475 29 07 21; www.downtownbxl.com; Rue du Marché au Charbon 118-120; r €99-119; ☎; ⓠ Anneessens) Near the capital's gay district, this B&B is superbly located. From the communal breakfast table and help-yourself coffee bar, a classic staircase winds up to good-value rooms featuring zebra-striped cushions and Warhol Marilyn prints. One room features a round bed. Adjacent **Casa-BXL** (☏ 0475 29 07 21; www.lacasabxl.com; Rue du Marché au Charbon 16; r €109-119) offers three rooms in a more Moroccan-Asian style.

★ Hôtel Le Dixseptième   BOUTIQUE HOTEL €€€
(☏ 02-517 17 17; www.ledixseptieme.be; Rue de la Madeleine 25; s/d/ste from €120/140/250, weekend from €120/120/200; ⊛ ☎; ⓠ Bruxelles Central) A hushed magnificence greets you in this alluring boutique hotel, partly occupying the former 17th-century residence of

the Spanish ambassador. The coffee-cream breakfast room retains original cherub reliefs. Spacious executive suites come with four-poster beds. Across a tiny enclosed courtyard-garden in the cheaper rear section, the Creuz Suite has its bathroom tucked curiously into a 14th-century vaulted basement. Lifts stop between floors so you'll need to deal with some stairs.

✗ Eating

Fin de Siècle   BELGIAN €
(Rue des Chartreux 9; mains €11.25-20; ☺bar 4.30pm-1am, kitchen 6pm-12.30am; ☐Bourse) From *carbonade* (beer-based hotpot) and *kriek* (cherry beer) chicken to mezzes and tandoori chicken, the food is as eclectic as the decor in this low-lit cult place. Tables are rough, music constant and ceilings purple. To quote the barman, 'there's no phone, no bookings, no sign on the door...we do everything to put people off, but they still keep coming'.

Mokafé   SWEETS €
(☏02-511 78 70; Galerie du Roi; waffles from €3; ☺7.30am-11.30pm; ⓂDe Brouckère) Locals get their waffles in this old-fashioned cafe under the glass arch of the Galeries-St Hubert. It's a little timeworn and dowdy inside, but wicker chairs in the beautiful arcade provide you with a view of passing shoppers.

★ Henri   FUSION €€
(☏02-218 00 08; www.restohenri.be; Rue de Flandre 113; mains €15-20; ☺noon-2pm Tue-Fri & 6-10pm Tue-Sat; ⓂSte-Catherine) In an airy white space on this street to watch, Henri concocts tangy fusion dishes like tuna with ginger, soy and lime, artichokes with scampi, lime and olive tapenade, or Argentinean fillet steak in parsley. There's an astute wine list, and staff who know their stuff.

Le Cercle des Voyageurs   BRASSERIE €€
(☏02-514 39 49; www.lecercledesvoyageurs.com; Rue des Grands Carmes 18; mains €15-21; ☺11am-midnight; ☎; ⓂAnnessens, ☐Bourse) Invite Phileas Fogg for coffee to this delightful bistro featuring globes, an antique-map ceiling and a travel library. If he's late, flick through an old *National Geographic* in your colonial leather chair. The global brasserie food is pretty good, and the free live music fantastic: piano jazz on Tuesdays and experimental on Thursdays. Other gigs in the cave have a small entrance fee.

Belga Queen Brussels   BELGIAN €€
(☏02-217 21 87; www.belgaqueen.be; Rue du Fossé aux Loups 32; mains €16-25, weekday lunch €16; ☺noon-2.30pm & 7pm-midnight; ⓂDe Brouckère) Belgian cuisine is given a chic, modern twist within a magnificent, if reverberant, 19th-century bank building. Classical stained-glass ceilings and marble columns are hidden behind an indecently hip oyster

COMIC-STRIP CULTURE

In Belgium, comic strips *(bande dessinée)* are revered as the 'ninth art'. Serious comic fans might enjoy Brussels' comprehensive **Centre Belge de la Bande Dessinée** (Belgian Comic Strip Centre; ☏02-219 19 80; www.comicscenter.net; Rue des Sables 20; adult/concession €8/6; ☺10am-6pm Tue-Sun; ⓂRogier) in a distinctive Horta-designed art-nouveau building.

Comic shops include **Brüsel** (www.brusel.com; Blvd Anspach 100; ☺10.30am-6.30pm Mon-Sat, from noon Sun; ☐Bourse) and **Multi-BD** (www.multibd.com; Blvd Anspach 122-124; ☺10.30am-7pm Mon-Sat, 12.30-6.30pm Sun; ☐Bourse). There's even a cartoon-based cafe-restaurant, **Le Village de la Bande Dessinée** (☏02-523 13 23; www.comicscafe.be; Place du Grand Sablon 8; snacks from €6; ☺11am-11pm Tue-Sun; ☐Louise), complete with Tintin statue and original Hergé sketches.

More than 40 cartoon murals enliven Brussels buildings; our favourites include the following:

Tibet & Duchâteau (Rue du Bon Secours 9; ☐Bourse)

Josephine Baker Mural (Rue des Capucins 9; ⓂPorte de Hal)

Tintin (Rue de l'Étuve; ☐Bourse)

Peeping Policeman (Rue Haute; ⓂLouise)

Mannekin Pis Displaced Mural (Rue de Flandre; ⓂSte-Catherine)

BOURSE CAFES

Many of Brussels' most iconic cafes are within stumbling distance of the Bourse. Don't miss century-old **Falstaff** (www.lefalstaff.be; Rue Henri Maus 17; ☉10am-1am; ⓖBourse) with its festival of stained-glass ceilings, or **Le Cirio** (Rue de la Bourse 18; ☉10am-midnight; ⓖBourse), a sumptuous yet affordable 1866 marvel full of polished brasswork serving great-value pub meals. Three more classics are hidden up shoulder-wide alleys: the medieval yet unpretentious **A l'Image de Nostre-Dame** (off Rue du Marché aux Herbes 5; ☉noon-midnight Mon-Fri, 3pm-1am Sat, 4-10.30pm Sun; ⓖBourse); the 1695 Rubenseque **Au Bon Vieux Temps** (Impasse Saint Michel; ☉11am-midnight; ⓖBourse), which sometimes stocks ultra-rare Westvleteren beers (€10!); and lambic specialist **À la Bécasse** (www.alabecasse.com; Rue de Tabora 11; ☉11am-midnight, to 1am Fri & Sat; ⓜGare Centrale), with its vaguely Puritanical rows of wooden tables.

counter and wide-ranging beer and cocktail bar (open noon till late). In the former bank vaults beneath, there's a cigar lounge that morphs into a nightclub after 10pm Wednesday to Saturday.

★ **L'Ogenblik**　　　　　　FRENCH €€€
(☏02-511 61 51; www.ogenblik.be; Galerie des Princes 1; mains €23-29, lunch €12; ☉noon-2.30pm & 7pm-midnight; ⓖBourse) It may be only a stone's throw from Rue des Bouchers, but this timeless bistro with its lace curtains, resident cat, marble-topped tables and magnificent wrought-iron lamp feels a world away. They've been producing French classics here for more than 30 years, and the expertise shows. Worth the price for a special meal in the heart of town.

🍷 Drinking & Nightlife

Cafe culture is one of Brussels' greatest attractions. On the Grand Place itself, 300-year-old gems, like Le Roy d'Espagne and Chaloupe d'Or are magnificent but predictably pricey. Go out of the centre a little to explore the city's new brand of laid-back hipster bars, most decorated in minimal upcycled style, and hosting DJ nights and live music events: try Café Belga, BarBeton or Bar du Matin.

★ **La Fleur en Papier Doré**　　　PUB
(www.goudblommekeinpapier.be; Rue des Alexiens 53; ☉11am-midnight Tue-Sat, to 7pm Sun; ⓖBruxelles Central) The nicotine-stained walls of this tiny *café*, adored by artists and locals, are covered with writings, art and scribbles by Magritte and his surrealist pals, some of which were reputedly traded for free drinks. *Ceci n'est pas un musée*, quips a sign on the door, reminding visitors to buy a drink and not just look around.

Moeder Lambic Fontainas　　BEER HALL
(www.moederlambic.com; Place Fontainas 8; ☉11am-1am Sun-Thu, to 2am Fri & Sat; ⓖAnnessens, Bourse) At the last count they were serving 46 artisinal beers here, in a contemporary rather than old-world setting: walls are bare brick and hung with photos and the booths are backed with concrete. They dish up great quiches and cheese and meat platters. The mood is upbeat and the music loud.

À la Mort Subite　　　　　　CAFE
(☏02-513 13 18; www.alamortsubite.com; Rue Montagne aux Herbes Potagères 7; ☉11am-1am Mon-Sat, noon-midnight Sun; ⓜGare Centrale) An absolute classic unchanged since 1928, with lined-up wooden tables, arched mirror panels and entertainingly brusque service.

☆ Entertainment

★ **L'Archiduc**　　　　　　　JAZZ
(☏02-512 06 52; www.archiduc.net; Rue Antoine Dansaert 6; beer/wine/cocktails €2.50/3.60/8.50; ☉4pm-5am; ⓖBourse) This intimate, split-level, art-deco bar has been playing jazz since 1937. It's an unusual two-tiered circular space that can get incredibly packed but remains convivial. You might need to ring the doorbell. Saturday concerts are free (5pm), Sundays bring in international talent and admission charges vary.

La Monnaie/De Munt　　OPERA, THEATRE
(www.lamonnaie.be; Place de la Monnaie; ⓜDe Brouckère) Grand and glittering theatre, opera and dance venue.

Art Base
LIVE MUSIC

(☑ 02-217 29 20; www.art-base.be; Rue des Sables 29; ☺ Fri & Sat; M Rogier) One of the best little venues in town for music fans with eclectic tastes. Located opposite the Comic Museum, it resembles someone's living room. But the programming is first rate, and it's worth taking a punt on Greek *rebetiko*, Indian classical music, Argentinian guitar or whatever else is playing.

AB
LIVE MUSIC

(Ancienne Belgique; ☑ 02-548 24 00; www.ab concerts.be; Blvd Anspach 110; ⛴ Bourse) The AB's two auditoriums are favourite venues for mid-level international rock bands and acts such as Jools Holland and Madeleine Peyroux, plus plenty of home-grown talent. The ticket office is located on Rue des Pierres. There's a good on-site bar-restaurant that opens at 6pm (bookings essential).

🛍 Shopping

Tourist-oriented shops selling chocolate, beer, lace and Atomium baubles stretch between the Grand Place and Manneken Pis. For better chocolate shops in calmer, grander settings, peruse the resplendent **Galeries St-Hubert** (www.galeries-saint-hubert.com; off Rue du Marché aux Herbes; M Gare Centrale) or the upmarket Sablon area, or visit the daily **flea market** (Place du Jeu-de-Balle; ☺ 6am-2pm). Antwerp more than Brussels is Belgium's fashion capital, but Rue Antoine Dansaert has several cutting-edge boutiques including **Stijl** (www.stijl.be; Rue Antoine Dansaert 74; M Ste-Catherine).

Supermarkets sell a range of Belgian beers relatively cheaply but for wider selections and the relevant glasses, try **Beermania** (www.beermania.be; Chaussée de Wavre 174; ☺ 11am-9pm Mon-Sat; M Porte de Namur) or the very personal little **Délices et Caprices** (www.the-belgian-beer-tasting-shop.be; Rue des Bouchers 68; ☺ 2-8pm Thu-Mon; M Gare Centrale).

ℹ Information

ATMs are widespread. Exchange agency rates are usually best around the Bourse. As well as the following there are info counters at Brussels Airport and Bruxelles-Midi station. For planning advice, author recommendations, traveller reviews and insider tips see www.lonelyplanet.com/belgium/brussels.

Use-It (☑ 02-218 39 06; www.use-it.travel/cities/detail/brussels; Galerie Ravenstein 17; ☺ 10am-6.30pm Mon-Sat; ☎; M Ste-Catherine) Meeting place for young travellers, with free coffee and tea and a list of live-music events written up by the door. They do a free alternative city tour at 2pm on Monday, with the emphasis on social history and nightlife. The printed material is first rate, with a quirky city map, a guide for wheelchair users and a beer pamphlet.

Visit Brussels (☑ 02-513 89 40; www.visit brussels.be; Hôtel de Ville; ☺ 9am-6pm; ⛴ Bourse) Visit Brussels has stacks of city-specific information as well as handy fold-out guides (independently researched) to the best shops, restaurants and pubs in town. The Rue Royale (Rue Royale 2; ☺ 9am-6pm Mon-Fri, 10am-6pm Sat-Sun; M Parc) office is much less crowded than the Grand Place one. Here you'll also find the Arsène50 (☑ 02-512 57 45; www.arsene50.be; ☺ 12.30-5.30pm Tue-Sat) desk, which provides great discounts for cultural events.

ℹ Getting There & Away

BUS

Eurolines (☑ 02-274 13 50; www.eurolines.be; Rue du Progrès 80; ☺ 5.45am-8.45pm; ⛴ Gare du Nord) International bus service Eurolines has buses departing from Bruxelles-Nord train station.

TRAIN

Brussels has two major stations. All main domestic trains from Brussels stop at both stations as do some Amsterdam services. Eurostar, TGV and Thalys high-speed trains stop only at Bruxelles-Midi (Brussel-Zuid). That's not in the best part of town so, on arrival, jump straight onto any local service for the four-minute hop to more conveniently central Bruxelles-Central.

Consult www.belgianrail.be for timetable information.

ℹ Getting Around

TO/FROM BRUSSELS AIRPORT
Taxi
Fares start around €40. Very bad idea in rush-hour traffic.

Train
Four per hour (5.30am to 11.50pm) costing €8.50. It takes 20 minutes to reach Bruxelles-Central, 24 minutes to Bruxelles-Midi.

TO/FROM CHARLEROI AIRPORT
Charleroi Airport is also known as Brussels-South.

Bus
L'Elan (www.voyages-lelan.be) Direct services operated by L'Elan run half-hourly to Bruxelles-Midi station (single/return

WORTH A TRIP

BRUSSELS TO ANTWERP

Direct Brussels–Antwerp trains take just over half an hour. But if you're not in a hurry consider stopping en route at a couple of other historic cities, not more than a minor diversion by train: Leuven (30 minutes) then Mechelen (22 minutes). In both towns the station is around 15 minutes' walk from the centre. And both have imaginative accommodation, including hostels, if you're too charmed to move on.

€14/23); last services to/from the airport are 8.30pm/9.25pm. It should take one hour, but allow far more time at rush hour.

Train

TEC bus A (€5, 18 minutes) links at least hourly from Charleroi Airport to Charleroi-Sud station, a 50-minute train ride from Brussels.

BICYCLE

FietsPunt/PointVelo (www.recyclo.org; Carrefour de l'Europe 2; per 1/3 days €7.50/15; ⊙7am-7pm Mon-Fri; ⊠ Bruxelles-Central) Rents long term; it's on the left as you leave Bruxelles-Central station by the Madeleine exit.

Villo! (☑078-05 11 10; www.en.villo.be; subscription day/week €1.60/7.65) Has 180 automated pick-up/drop-off short-term rental stands. Credit card required; read the online instructions carefully.

PUBLIC TRANSPORT

STIB/MIVB (www.stib.be) tickets are sold at metro stations, newsagents and on buses and trams. Single-/five-/10-journey tickets valid for one hour from validation cost €2.10/8/12.50 including transfers. Unlimited one/two/three-day passes cost €7/13/17. Airport buses are excluded.

FLANDERS

Leuven

POP 97,600

Lively, self-confident Leuven (Louvain in French; www.leuven.be) is Flanders' oldest university town and home to the vast **Stella Artois brewery** (www.breweryvisits.com; Vuurkruisenlaan; admission €8.50; ⊙9am-7.30pm Tue-Sat). Its greatest attraction is a flamboyant 15th-century **Stadhuis** (Grote Markt 9;

tour €4; ⊙tour 3pm) lavished with exterior statuary. Other architectural attractions are patchy due to heavy damage sustained in 20th-century wars, but the iconic **university library** has been rebuilt. Twice. **Muntstraat** is a loveable medieval alley full of restaurants and **Oude Markt** is a very lively square of wall-to-wall bars that hum till the wee hours.

The most interesting option for accommodation is the grand mansion housing **Oude Brouwerei Keyser Carel** (☑016 22 14 81; www.keysercarel.be; Lei 15; s/d €105/120), while homely **Leuven City Hostel** (☑016 84 30 33; www.leuvencityhostel.com; Ravenstraat 37; dm/d €23/54; ⊙reception 4-8pm; @♠) and stylish B&B **Casa Bollicine** (☑0497 83 97 17; www.casabollicine.be; Parijsstraat 7; s/d €120/150; ♠) are good, relatively central accommodation choices. Directly behind the station, around 1km east, the HI Hostel **Jeugdherberg De Blauwput** (☑016 63 90 62; www.leuven-hostel.com; Martelarenlaan 11a; dm/d €24.60/58, youth dm/d €22.30/54.20; ⊙@♠) makes a good choice for those wanting to sleep near Brussels Airport, a mere 16 minutes away by train.

Mechelen

POP 82,300

Belgium's religious capital, Mechelen (Malines in French) has the **St-Romboutskathedraal** (http://sintromboutstoren.mechelen.be; Grote Markt; ⊙8.30am-6pm) **FREE**, a cathedral featuring a 97m, 15th-century tower that soars above a particularly memorable central market square. There are other splendid churches on Keizerstraat where the courthouse and theatre were both once royal palaces in the days when the Low Countries were effectively run from Mechelen. Other top sights include the brilliant **Speelgoedmuseum** (☑015 55 70 75; www.speelgoedmuseum.be; Nekkerstraat 21; adult/child €8/5.50; ⊙10am-5pm Tue-Sun), a toy museum, and the **Schepenhuis gallery tower** on IJzerenleen, a street of fine baroque facades leading towards the main station passing close to **Vismarkt**, the compact bar-cafe zone. There's a modern HI Hostel, the **Hostel De Zandpoort** (☑015 27 85 39; www.mechelen-hostel.com; Zandpoortvest 70; dm/tw €24.60/58, youth dm/tw €22.30/54.10; ⊙check-in 5-10pm; P♠), or try stylish **Martins Patershof** (☑015 46 46 46; www.martinshotels.com;

Karmelietenstraat 4; from €149; ▣ 🛜), set in a 1867 Franciscan monastery.

Antwerp

POP 511,700

Cosmopolitan, confident and full of contrasts, Antwerp (Antwerpen in Dutch, Anvers in French) was one of northern Europe's foremost cities in the 17th century when it was also home to Pieter Paul Rubens, diplomat, philosopher and northern Europe's greatest baroque artist. Today it's once again in the ascendant, attracting art lovers and fashion moguls, clubbers and diamond dealers.

◎ Sights

◎ City Centre

Brabo Fountain   STATUE
(Grote Markt) As with every great Flemish city, Antwerp's medieval heart is a classic Grote Markt (marketplace). Here the triangular, pedestrianised space features the voluptuous, baroque Brabo Fountain depicting Antwerp's hand-throwing legend. Flanked on two sides by very photogenic guildhalls, the square is dominated by an impressive Italo-Flemish Renaissance-style stadhuis (town hall), completed in 1565.

Het Steen   CASTLE
(Steenplein) On a riverside knoll, Het Steen is a dinky but photogenic castle from AD 1200 occupying the site of Antwerp's original Gallo-Roman settlement. Outside is a humorous **statue of Lange Wapper**, a tall folkloric 'peeping Tom' figure showing off his codpiece to two diminutive onlookers. Directly north, the misnamed **Maritime Park** is a long, open-sided wrought-iron shed displaying a historic **barge collection**. There is nothing to see inside.

Onze-Lieve-Vrouwekathedraal   CATHEDRAL
(www.dekathedraal.be; Handschoenmarkt; adult/concession €6/4; ⊙10am-5pm Mon-Fri, to 3pm Sat, to 4pm Sun) Belgium's finest Gothic cathedral was 169 years in the making (1352–1521). Wherever you wander in Antwerp, its gracious, 123m-high spire has a habit of popping unexpectedly into view and rarely fails to jolt a gasp of awe. The sight is

particularly well framed when looking up Pelgrimstraat in afternoon light.

★**Museum Plantin-Moretus**   HISTORIC BUILDING
(www.museumplantinmoretus.be; Vrijdag Markt 22; adult/child €8/1; ⊙10am-5pm Tue-Sun) The idea of giving a museum Unesco World Heritage status might seem odd, until you've seen this fabulous place. Once home to the world's first industrial printing works, it has been a museum since 1876. The medieval building and 1622 **courtyard garden** alone are worth the visit. Highlights include the 1640 **library**, the historic **bookshop** (room 4), and rooms 11 and 21 for their gilt leather 'wallpaper'. Then there's a priceless collection of manuscripts, tapestries and the world's oldest printing press.

Fashion District   AREA
In the space of just a few streets, you'll find dozens of designer boutiques, both Belgian and international, along with a variety of streetwear, end-of-line discounters, secondhand shops and more mainstream chains. Simply stroll Nationalestraat, Lombardenvest, Huidevettersstraat and Schuttershofstraat, not missing Kammenstraat for retro labels and urban scrawl.

Rubenshuis   MUSEUM
(www.rubenshuis.be; Wapper 9-11; adult/child €8/1, audio guide €2; ⊙10am-5pm Tue-Sun) Restored along original lines, the 1611 building was built as home and studio by celebrated painter Pieter Paul Rubens. Rescued from ruins in 1937, the building is architecturally indulgent with baroque portico, rear facade and formal garden. The furniture dates from Rubens' era but was not part of the original decor. Ten Rubens canvases are displayed, including one where Eve appears to glance lustfully at Adam's fig leaf.

★**Antwerpen-Centraal**   LANDMARK
With its neo-Gothic facade, vast main hall and splendidly proportioned dome, the 1905 Antwerpen-Centraal train station is one of

---

🛈 ANTWERP CARD

An **Antwerp Card** (www.visitantwerpen.be; 24/48/72hr €25/32/37) will usually save you money if you visit at least four of the city's splendid museums.

Antwerp

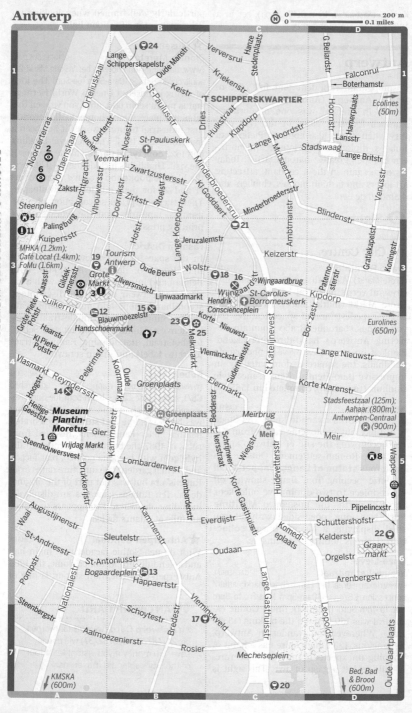

N

0   200 m
0   0.1 miles

'T SCHIPPERSKWARTIER

Ecolines
(50m)

Eurolines
(650m)

Stadsfeestzaal (125m);
Aahaar (800m);
Antwerpen-Centraal
(900m)

**Museum
Plantin-
Moretus**

KMSKA
(600m)

Bed, Bad
& Brood
(600m)

Antwerp

the city's premier landmarks. It was rated by *Newsweek* as one of the world's five most beautiful stations. It's also very practical, the multilevel platforms having had a full 21st-century makeover.

⊙ Meir

If walking from the main train station to Groenplaats, revel in the grand, statue-draped architecture of pedestrianised Meir and Leystraat. The gilt-overloaded **Stadsfeestzaal** (www.stadsfeestzaal.com; Meir 76; ⊙9.30am-7pm Mon-Sat) is one of the world's most indulgently decorated shopping malls. Watch top-quality chocolates being made behind **Chocolate Line** (www.thechocolate line.be; ⊙10.30am-6.30pm), a shop that fills a mural-lined room of the 1745 **Paleis op de**

Meir (www.paleisopdemeir.be; Meir 50; tour €8; ⊙tour 2pm Tue-Sat).

⊙ 't Zuid

Around 1km south of the Fashion District, 't Zuid is a conspicuously prosperous area dotted with century-old architecture, hip bars, fine restaurants and museums. The classic centrepiece art gallery, **KMSKA** (www.kmska.be; Leopold De Waelplaats), is closed for renovation until 2017, but there's still **MHKA** (☑03-238 59 60; www.muhka.be; Leuvenstraat 32; adult/child €8/1; ⊙11am-6pm Tue-Sun, to 9pm Thu) for contemporary conceptual art, and outstanding **FoMu** (Foto-Museum; ☑03-242 93 00; www.fotomuseum.be; Waalsekaai 47; adult/child €8/3; ⊙10am-5pm Tue-Sun) for photography.

🛏 Sleeping

Over 40 B&Bs can be sorted by price or map location on www.bedandbreakfast-antwerp. com, but relatively few are central.

★**Pulcinella** HOSTEL €
(☑03-234 03 14; www.jeugdherbergen.be; Bo-gaardeplein 1; dm/tw €26.80/32.40; @🛜) This giant, tailor-made HI Hostel is hard to beat for its Fashion District location and cool modernist decor. HI members save €3.

ABhostel HOSTEL €
(☑0473 57 01 66; www.abhostel.com; Kattenberg 110; mixed dm/tw €19/50; ⊙reception noon-3pm & 6-8pm; 🛜) This adorable family-run hostel has lots of little added extras to make it comfy. Its inner-suburban setting is 20-minutes' walk east of Antwerpen-Centraal station, past inexpensive shops, ethnic restaurants and African wig shops. Across the street is the brilliantly unpretentious local pub **Plaza Real** (⊙from 8pm Wed-Sun), owned by a band member of dEUS.

★**Bed, Bad & Brood** B&B €€
(☑03-248 15 39; www.bbantwerp.com; Justitie-straat 43; s/d/q €75/85/135; ☒@) In a 1910, belle-epoque-style townhouse near the vast Gerechtshof (former courthouse), BB&B has squeaky wooden floors, high ceilings, some old-fashioned furniture and a remarkable spaciousness for a B&B in this price range. Owners are assiduously keen to help. Get off trams 12 or 24 at the Gerechtshof with its verdigris statues of justice. Two-night minimum stay often applies.

Hotel O
HOTEL €€

(☑03-500 89 50; www.hotelokathedral.com; Handschoenmarkt 3; r €89-129) The immediate selling point here is an unbeatable location, staring across a square at the cathedral frontage. Behind an intriguing little foyer of 1950s radios, the all-black decor is relieved by mid-sized rooms with giant Rubens prints spilling over onto the ceilings. Note that there's a second Hotel O above Nero Brasserie in Het Zuid.

✗ Eating

For cheap, central snacks, stroll Hoogstraat, near the cathedral. For cosy if pricier options look in parallel Pelgrimstraat (with its 'secret' medieval alley, Vlaaikeusgang) or the picturesque lanes leading to Rubens' wonderful St-Carolus-Borromeuskerk. There are many more excellent options in 't Zuid, north and west of KMSKA.

't Brantyser
EUROPEAN €

(☑03-233 18 33; www.brantyser.be; Hendrik Conscienceplein 7; snacks €6-12.50, mains €17-26; ⊙11.15am-10pm) The cosy, double-level Brantyser gets the antique clutter effect just right while its enviable terrace surveys one of Antwerp's most appealing pedestrian squares. Other restaurants nearby might be more refined, but the food here is tasty and portions generous. Try the *visschotel*, a delicious melange of seafoods and fish pieces in a creamy herb sauce.

Aahaar
INDIAN, VEGAN €

(www.aahaar.com; Lange Herentalsestraat 23; buffet €10; ⊙noon-3pm & 5.30-9.30pm Mon-Fri, 1-9.30pm Sat & Sun; ☑) Unpretentious and popular little place for vegan/vegetarian Jain-Indian food including an eat-all-you-like buffet with five mains, two sweets and rice.

★ De Groote Witte Arend
BELGIAN €€

(☑03-233 50 33; www.degrootewittearend.be; Reyndersstraat 18; mains €13-24; ⊙10.30am-midnight, kitchen 11.30am-3pm & 5-10pm; ☎) Retaining the Tuscan stone arcade of a 15th- and 17th-century convent building, this relaxed central gem combines the joys of a good beer bar with the satisfaction of well-cooked, sensibly priced Flemish home cuisine, notably *stoemp, stoofvlees/carbonnades* and huge portions of rabbit in rich Westmalle sauce.

Kathedraalcafe
BELGIAN €€

(Torfbrug 10; mains €14-24.50, sandwiches €8.50; ⊙noon-11pm) This ivy-clad medieval masterpiece has an astounding interior decked with angels, saints, pulpits and several deliciously sacrilegious visual jokes. Good, if pricey, sandwiches supplement the mussels, vol-au-vents and other typical local favourites. Outside dining hours, or after 11pm, come for a beer: they have St Bernardus Tripel on draught.

♟ Drinking & Nightlife

To sound like a local, stride into a pub and ask for a *bolleke*. Don't worry, that means a 'little bowl' (ie glass) of De Koninck, the city's favourite ale. Cheap places to try it include classic *cafés* **Oud Arsenaal** (Pijpelincxstraat 4; ⊙10am-10pm Wed-Fri, 7.30am-7.30pm Sat & Sun), **De Kat** (Wolstraat 22) and the livelier **Pelikaan** (www.facebook.com/cafepelikaan; Melkmarkt 14; ⊙8.30am-3am). Mechelseplein bars including **Korsåkov** (Mechelseplein 21; snacks €3.50-5.50, Primus/Chouffe €2/2.50; ⊙10am-4am) open till very late, as do countless other great options around KMSKA in the 't Zuid area.

Den Bengel
PUB

(www.cafedenengel.be; Grote Markt 5; ⊙9am-2am) Sixteenth-century guildhall pub with fabulous cathedral views from the terrace.

Bierhuis Kulminator
PUB

(Vleminckveld 32; ⊙4pm-midnight Tue-Sat, from 8pm Mon) Classic beer pub boasting 700 mostly Belgian brews, including notably rare 'vintage' bottles laid down to mature for several years like fine wine.

Normo
CAFE

(www.normocoffee.com; Minderbroedersrui 30; coffees €2-3.50, muffins €2; ⊙10am-7pm Mon-Fri, to 6pm Sat) Coffee is an art at Normo, from the science-project dripping station to the exposed brick walls, attractively battered tiles and bearded baristas.

Red & Blue
CLUB

(www.redandblue.be; Lange Schipperskapelstraat 11; ⊙11pm-7am Thu-Sat; ☑7) Great dance venue with decent-sized yet still intimate dance floor. It's most famous for its Saturday gay night. There's also a Thursday student night, TGIT (www.thankgoditsthursday.be), Fridays see a mixed crowd groove to house music, and some Sundays there are classic 1970s-style discos.

Café Local
CLUB

(www.cafelocal.be; Waalsekaai 25; cover €7-15; ☉10pm-late Wed-Sun; ⬚4) Popular, friendly 't Zuid nightclub with a Mexican trading post-themed bar-island. Wednesdays are formal (collared shirts required), Thursday student nights are free (18 to 25 year olds), Fridays are for over 40s, and Paradise Saturdays see deckchairs and palm fronds appear. On the first Sunday of each month the music takes a salsa-merengue turn.

☆ Entertainment

For listings consult www.weekup.be/antwerpen/week; www.zva.be in summer; and www.gratisinantwerpen.be for free events.

deSingel
PERFORMING ARTS

(☑03-248 28 28; www.desingel.be; Desguinlei 25) Two concert halls offering a highly innovative program of classical music, international theatre and modern dance.

De Muze
JAZZ

(☑03-226 01 26; http://jazzmuze.be; Melkmarkt 15; ☉noon-4am) Very appealing triple-level gabled *café* with an Escher-like interior hosting great live jazz from 10pm Monday to Saturday (but not Wednesday or Thursday in summer).

❶ Information

Tourism Antwerp (☑03-232 01 03; www.visitantwerpen.be; Grote Markt 13; ☉9am-5.45pm Mon-Sat, to 4.45pm Sun & holidays) Tourism Antwerp is a central tourist office with a branch on level zero of Antwerpen-Centraal train station.

❶ Getting There & Away

BUS

Many regional buses (eg to Lier) leave from near Ecolines.

Ecolines (www.ecolines.net; Paardenmarkt 65) Ecolines services for Eastern Europe depart from near Antwerpen-Berchem train station, 2km southeast of Antwerpen-Centraal. The ticket agent is Euro-Maror.

Eurolines (☑03-233 86 62; www.eurolines.com; Van Stralenstraat 8; ☉9am-5.45pm Mon-Fri, to 3.15pm Sat) International Eurolines buses depart from points near Franklin Rooseveltplaats.

TRAIN

Regular services to Bruges (€14.80, 75 minutes), Brussels (€7.30, 35-49 minutes) and Ghent (€9.40, 46 minutes). High-speed service to Amsterdam.

❶ Getting Around

Franklin Rooseveltplaats and Koningin Astridplein are hubs for the integrated network of **De Lijn** (www.delijn.be) buses and trams (some running underground metro-style).

Ghent

POP 251,100

Known as Gent in Dutch and Gand in French, Ghent is like a grittier Bruges without the crush of tourists. Nonetheless it sports photogenic canals, medieval towers, great cafes and some of Belgium's most inspired museums. Always a lively student city, Ghent goes crazy in mid-July during the 10-day **Gentse Feesten** (www.gentsefeesten.be; ☉Jul), featuring street theatre, jazz and techno music.

◉ Sights

Most major sights are strolling distance from Korenmarkt, the westernmost of three interlinked squares that form the heart of Ghent's historic core.

---

❶ SEE MORE OF GHENT

The good-value **CityCard Gent** (www.visitgent.be; 2-/3-day ticket €30/35) provides three days' free city transport and entrance to all the sights reviewed (except boat tours) plus much more including the dynamic industrial museum, **MIAT** (Museum voor Industriële Archeologie en Textiel; www.miat.gent.be; Minnemeers 9; adult/youth €6/2; ☉10am-6pm Tue-Sun), the eclectic **Design Museum** (www.designmuseumgent.be; J Breydelstraat 5; adult/concession €8/6; ☉10am-6pm Tue-Sun) and the interactive city museum **STAM** (www.stamgent.be; Bijloke Complex; adult/concession €8/6; ☉10am-6pm Tue-Sun; ⬚4). In Citadelpark near Gent-St-Pieters station, fine-art gallery **MSK** (Museum voor Schone Kunsten; ☑09-240 07 00; www.mskgent.be; Citadelpark; adult/youth €8/2; ☉10am-6pm Tue-Sun) and the cutting-edge **SMAK** (Museum of Contemporary Art; www.smak.be; Citadelpark; adult/youth €12/2, 10am-1pm Sun free; ☉10am-6pm Tue-Sun; ⬚5) exhibition space are also included.

Ghent Centre

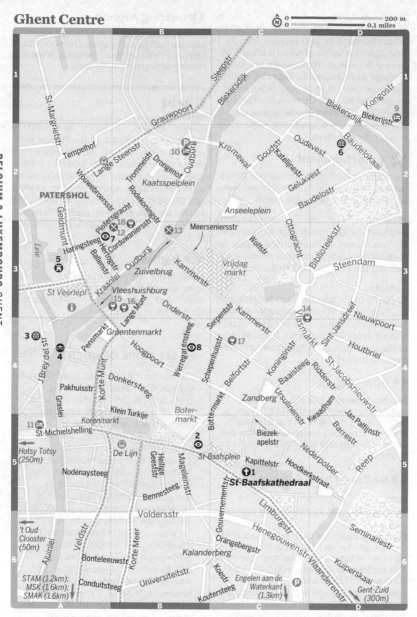

★**St-Baafskathedraal**   CHURCH
(www.sintbaafskathedraal.be;   St-Baafsplein;
☺8.30am-6pm Apr-Oct, to 5pm Nov-Mar) St-Baafs
cathedral's towering interior has some fine
stained glass and an unusual combination
of brick vaulting with stone tracery. A €0.20
leaflet guides you round the cathedral's numerous art treasures, including a big original
Rubens opposite the stairway that leads down
into the partly muralled crypts. However,
most visitors come to see just one magnificent
work – the Van Eycks' 1432 'Flemish Primitive'

Ghent Centre

masterpiece, *The Adoration of the Mystic Lamb* (adult/child/audio guide €4/1.50/1).

Belfort BELFRY
(Botermarkt; adult/concession €6/2; ⊙10am-5.30pm) Ghent's soaring, Unesco-listed, 14th-century belfry is topped by a large dragon, and it's become something of a city mascot. You'll meet two previous dragon incarnations on the climb to the top (mostly by lift) but other than some bell-making exhibits the real attraction is the view. Enter through the **Lakenhalle**, Ghent's cloth hall that was left half-built in 1445 and only completed in 1903.

Werregarensteeg STREET
(www.ghentizm.be) Graffiti is positively encouraged as an art form in this tiny central alley.

Grasbrug VIEWPOINT
To admire Ghent's towers and gables at their most photogenic, stand just west of the Grasbrug bridge at dusk. It's a truly gorgeous scene, though the appealing waterfront facades of Graslei aren't as old as they look – these 'medieval' warehouses and townhouses were largely rebuilt to make Ghent look good for the 1913 World's Fair.

Canal trips depart from either end of the Grasbrug and nearby Vleeshuisbrug bridges.

Gravensteen CASTLE
(www.gravensteengent.be; St-Veerleplein; adult/child €10/6; ⊙10am-6pm Apr-Oct, 9am-5pm Nov-Mar) Flanders' quintessential 12th-century stone castle comes complete with moat, turrets and arrow slits. It's all the more remarkable considering that during the 19th century the site was converted into a cotton mill. Meticulously restored since, the interior sports the odd suit of armour, a guillotine and torture devices. The relative lack of furnishings is compensated for by a hand-held 45-minute movie guide, which sets a tongue-in-cheek historical costumed drama in the rooms, prison pit and battlements.

Patershol NEIGHBOURHOOD
(www.patershol.be) Dotted with half-hidden restaurants, enchanting Patershol is a web of twisting cobbled lanes whose old-world houses were once home to leather tradesmen and to the Carmelite Fathers (Paters), hence the name. An aimless wander here is one of the city's great pleasures.

⛱ Sleeping

Ghent offers innovative accommodation in all budget ranges. Websites www.gent-accommodations.be and www.bedandbreakfast-gent.be help you gauge availability in the city's numerous appealing B&Bs.

★**Engelen aan
de Waterkant** B&B €€
(☑09-223 08 83; www.engelenaandewaterkant.be; Ter Platen 30; s/d €120/140) Two 'angel' rooms are an opportunity for the interior-designer owner to experiment and for guests to soak up the special atmosphere in a 1900 townhouse overlooking the tree-lined canal.

Simon Says GUESTHOUSE €€
(☑09-233 03 43; www.simon-says.be; Sluizeken 8; d €110; ⊛) Two fashionably styled guest rooms above an excellent coffee shop in a brightly coloured corner house with art nouveau facade.

Uppelink HOSTEL €€
(☑09-279 44 77; www.hosteluppelink.com; Sint-Michielsplein 21; dm €27.50-37.50, s €52, tw €62) Within a classic step-gabled canalside house, the show-stopping attraction at this super-central new hostel is the unbeatable view of Ghent's main towers as seen from the breakfast room and from the biggest,

cheapest dorms. Smaller rooms have little view, if any.

Hostel 47
HOSTEL €€

(☑0478 71 28 27; www.hostel47.com; Blekerijstraat 47-51; dm €26.50-29.50, d €66, tr €90; 🕑) Unusually calm yet pretty central, this inviting hostel has revamped a high-ceilinged historic house with virginal white walls, spacious bunk rooms and designer fittings. Free lockers and cursory breakfast with Nespresso coffee; no bar.

✗ Eating

Enchanting Patershol (p91) is a web of twisting cobbled lanes with old-world houses that are now interspersed with small restaurants. Others jostle for summer terrace space on Graslei's gorgeous canalside terrace. There's fast food around Korenmarkt and great-value Turkish options along Sleepstraat. Numerous vegetarian and organic choices feature on the tourist office's free Veggieplan Gent guide map. Thursday is Veggieday.

't Oud Clooster
TAVERNA €

(☑09-233 78 02; www.toudclooster.be; Zwartezusterstraat 5; mains €9-18; ⊙noon-2.30pm & 6-10.30pm Mon-Fri, noon-2.30pm & 5-10.30pm Sat, 5-10.30pm Sun) Mostly candlelit at night, this atmospheric double-level 'pratcafe' is built into sections of what was long ago a nunnery, hence the sprinkling of religious statues and cherub lamp-holders. Well-priced cafe food is presented with unexpected style. Try the original curry-cream *Spaghetti Oud Clooster*.

Soup Lounge
SOUP €

(www.souplounge.be; Zuivelbrug 4; small/large soup €4/5, sandwiches €2.80; ⊙10am-6pm) At this bright, central '70s-retro soup kitchen, each bowlful comes with add-your-own cheese and croutons, two rolls and a piece of fruit. Canal views are free.

Amadeus
RIBS €

(☑09-225 13 85; www.amadeusspareribrestaurant. be; Plotersgracht 8/10; mains €13.75-18.75; ⊙6.30-11pm) All-you-can-eat spare ribs at four Ghent addresses, all within ancient buildings that are full of atmosphere, bustle and cheerful conversation.

♟ Drinking & Entertainment

Try the snug Hot Club de Gand (www.hot clubdegand.be; Schuddevisstraatje-Groentenmarkt

15b; ⊙11.30am-late) for live jazz, gyspy or blues music, Hotsy Totsy (www.hotsytotsy.be; Hoogstraat 1; ⊙6pm-1am Mon-Fri, 8pm-2am Sat & Sun) for free Thursday jazz, and beautifully panelled Rococo (Corduwaniersstraat 5; ⊙from 10pm) for candlelit conversation. Het Waterhuis aan de Bierkant (www.waterhuisaandebierkant.be; Groentenmarkt 12; ⊙11am-1am) has the best beer choice including its own brews, Pink Flamingo's (www.pinkflamingos.be; Onderstraat 55; ⊙noon-midnight Mon-Wed, noon-3am Thu-Sat, 2pm-midnight Sun) is a retro-kitsch bar, and Charlatan (www.charlatan.be; Vlasmarkt 9; ⊙7pm-late Tue-Sun during term) is the place for raucous partying and eclectic live music.

ⓘ Information

Ghent Tourist Office (☑09-266 56 60; www. visitgent.be; Oude Vismijn, St-Veerleplein 5; ⊙9.30am-6.30pm mid-Mar–mid-Oct, to 4.30pm mid-Oct–mid-Mar) Very helpful for free maps and accommodation bookings.

ⓘ Getting There & Away

BUS

Some longer distance buses depart from **Gent-Zuid bus station** (Woodrow Wilsonplein), others from various points around Gent-St-Pieters train station.

TRAIN

Gent-Dampoort One kilometre west of the old city, this is the handiest station but only some trains stop here, including three hourly runs to Antwerp (€9.40, fast/slow 42/64 minutes) and an hourly Bruges service (€6.50, 36 minutes).

Gent-St-Pieters Located 2.5km south of the city centre, this is the main station for Brussels (€8.90, 35 minutes, twice hourly). From here there are five hourly hops to Bruges (fast/slow 24/42 minutes).

ⓘ Getting Around

BICYCLE

Max Mobiel (www.max-mobiel.be; Vokselslaan 27; per day/week/month €9/25/30) Two minutes' walk south of Gent-St-Pieters station. Branch kiosk at Gent-Dampoort station.

BUS & TRAM

One-hour/all-day tickets cost €1.30/5 if purchased ahead of time from ticket machines or De Lijn offices beside **Gent-St-Pieters** (⊙7am-1.30pm & 2-7pm Mon-Fri) or in the **centre** (www. delijn.be; Cataloniestraat 4; ⊙10.15am-5pm Mon-Sat). Handy tram 1 runs from Gent-St-Pieters through the centre passing within walking distance of most major sites.

Bruges

POP 117,400

Cobblestone lanes, dreamy canals, soaring spires and whitewashed almshouses combine to make central Bruges (Brugge in Dutch) one of Europe's most picture-perfect historic cities. The only problem is that everyone knows of these charms, and the place gets mobbed.

◉ Sights

The real joy of Bruges is simply wandering alongside the canals, soaking up the atmosphere. To avoid the worst crowds, explore east of pretty Jan van Eyckplein.

Markt SQUARE

The heart of ancient Bruges, the old market square is lined with pavement cafes beneath step-gabled facades. The buildings aren't always quite as medieval as they look, but together they create a fabulous scene and even the neo-Gothic post office is architecturally magnificent. The scene is dominated by the Belfort, Belgium's most famous belfry whose iconic octagonal tower is arguably better appreciated from afar than by climbing 366 claustrophobic steps to the top.

Historium MUSEUM

(www.historium.be; Markt 1; adult/child €11/5.50; ◷10am-6pm) An 'immersive' one-hour audio and video tour, the lavish Historium aims to take you back to medieval Bruges: you can survey the old port or watch Van Eyck paint. It's a little light on facts so for many it will be a diversion from the real sights of the city, perhaps best for entertaining kids on a rainy day.

Burg SQUARE

Bruges' 1420 Stadhuis (City Hall; Burg 12) is smothered in statuettes and contains a breathtaking Gotische Zaal (Gothic Hall; Burg; adult/concession €4/3; ◷9.30am-5pm), featuring dazzling polychromatic ceilings, hanging vaults and historicist murals. Tickets include entry to part of the early baroque Brugse Vrije (Burg 11a; ◷9.30am-noon & 1.30-4.30pm) next door. With its gilt highlights and golden statuettes, this palace was once the administrative centre for a large autonomous territory ruled from Bruges between 1121 and 1794.

★ Groeningemuseum GALLERY

(www.brugge.be; Dijver 12; adult/concession €8/6; ◷9.30am-5pm Tue-Sun) Bruges' most celebrated art gallery, an astonishingly rich collection whose strengths are in superb Flemish Primitive and Renaissance works, depicting the conspicuous wealth of the city with glitteringly realistic artistry. In room 2 are meditative works including Jan Van Eyck's 1436 radiant masterpiece *Madonna with Canon George Van der Paele* (1436) and the *Madonna* by the Master of the Embroidered Foliage, where the rich fabric of the Madonna's robe meets the 'real' foliage at her feet with exquisite detail.

★ Museum St-Janshospitaal MUSEUM

(Memlingmuseum; Mariastraat 38; adult/child €8/free; ◷9.30am-5pm Tue-Sun) In the restored chapel of a 12th-century hospital building with superb timber beamwork, this museum shows various torturous-looking medical implements, hospital sedan chairs and a gruesome 1679 painting of an anatomy class. But it is much better known for six masterpieces by 15th-century artist Hans Memling, including the enchanting reliquary of St Ursula. This gilded oak reliquary looks like a mini Gothic cathedral, painted with scenes from the life of St Ursula, including highly realistic Cologne cityscapes.

Brouwerij De Halve Maan BREWERY

(☏050 33 26 97; www.halvemaan.be; Walplein 26; ◷10.30am-6pm, closed mid-Jan) Founded in 1856, this is the last family *brouwerij* (brewhouse) in central Bruges. Multilingual guided visits (tours €7.50; ◷11am-4pm, to 5pm Sat), lasting 45 minutes, depart on each hour. They include a tasting but can sometimes be rather crowded. Alternatively, you can simply sip one of the excellent *Brugse Zot* (Bruges Fool, 7%) or *Straffe Hendrik* (Strong Henry, 9%) beers in the appealing brewery *café*.

Begijnhof BEGIJNHOF

(Wijngaardstraat; ◷6.30am-6.30pm) FREE Bruges' delightful *begijnhof* originally dates from the 13th century. Although the last *begijn*

ℹ BRUGES CITY CARD

A Bruges City Card (www.bruggecitycard.be; 48/72hr €46/49) gets you into numerous museums and scores you a free canal boat tour (adult/child €7.60/3.40; ◷10am-6pm Mar–mid-Nov) and discounts on bicycle rental.

Bruges

N
0   200 m
0   0.1 miles

Sledestr
Raamstr
Ezelstr
Poitevinstr
Pottenmakersstr
Rozendal
Zakske
Oude Zak
13
Grauwwerkersstr
Vlamingstr
Kortewinkel
Kipstr
Spanjaardstr
Genthof
Woensdag-markt
18 Strostr
St-Annarei
Verversdijk
Spiegelrei
Spinolarei
Koningstr
Hoornstr
Boomgaardstr
Academiestr
Kraanrei
Jan Van
Eyckplein
St-Jansstr
St-Walburgastr
Naaldenstr
Kuipersstr
St-Jakobsstr
Willaertstr
A
St-Jansplein
Leeuwstr
Geerwijnstr
St-Jakobs-plein
Muntplein
Moerstr
Geldmuntstr
Biekorf
Bus Stop
Eiermarkt
Philipstockstr
Twijnstr
21
Hoogstr
Peerdenstr
In 't Nieuwe
Museum
(400m);
Bauhaus
(800m)
Groenerei
Burgstr
7
8
Ontvangersstr
Helmstr
Haanstr
Kopstr
St-Amandsstr
15
6 9 5
Gare
Steenhouwersdijk
Meestr
Predikherenstr
Wulfhagestr
Giststr
Zilverstr
Steenstr
St-Niklaasstr
17
Canal Cruises
16
Fish
Market
J.Suvestr
Waalsestr
10
Cactus
Muziekcentrum
(850m)
Noordzandstr
Dweersstr
Simon
Stevinplein
19
Loppemstr
Oude Burg
Wollestr
Canal
Cruises
't Pandreitje
Eekhoutstr
Park
Koningin
Astridpark
't
Zand
Zuidzandstr
Korte Vulderstr
Mariastr
Heilige
Geeststr
Guido
Gezelle-plein
Nieuwstr
Canal
Cruises
Dijver
Canal
Cruises
1
Groeningemuseum
Eekhoutpoortstr
Garenmarkt
Stallizerstr
Godshuis
St-Trudo
In &
Uit Brugge
Goezeputstr
St Salvatorskerkhof
St-Bonifaciusbrug
Hof
Arents
Groeninge
20
St-Jan-in-de-Meers
11
Museum St-
Janshospitaal
2
Mariastr
Nieuwe Gentweg
Koning Albertlaan
Westmeers
Oostmeers
Zonnekemeers
Canal
Cruises
Stoofstr
Walstr
Walplein
4
Oude Gentweg
Wijngaardstr
3
Wijngaardplein
Noordstr
Katelijnestr
Sulferbergstr
Gentpoortvest
Eiland
14
12
(250m)
Minnewater
Minnewater
Park

has long since passed away, today residents of the pretty, whitewashed garden complex include a convent of Benedictine nuns. Despite the hoards of summer tourists, the *begijnhof* remains a remarkably tranquil haven. In spring a carpet of daffodils adds to the quaintness of the scene. Outside the 1776 gateway bridge lies a tempting, if predictably tourist-priced, array of terraced restaurants, lace shops and waffle peddlers.

Bruges

⊙ **Top Sights**
1 Groeningemuseum.............................C4
2 Museum St-Janshospitaal.................B4

⊙ **Sights**
3 Begijnhof...B6
4 Brouwerij De Halve Maan..................C5
5 Brugse Vrije.....................................C3
6 Burg..C3
Gotische Zaal.............................. (see 9)
7 Historium..C2
8 Markt..C2
9 Stadhuis..C3

⊜ **Sleeping**
10 B&B Dieltiens...................................D3
11 Baert B&B.......................................A5
12 't Keizershof....................................A6

⊗ **Eating**
13 De Bottelier.....................................A1
14 De Stoepa..A6
15 De Stove..B3
16 Est Wijnbar......................................C3

⊙ **Drinking & Nightlife**
17 De Garre..C3
18 Herberg Vlissinghe...........................D1
19 't Brugs Beertje................................B3

⊗ **Entertainment**
20 Concertgebouw................................A5
21 Retsin's Lucifernum.........................D2

⟲ Tours

Quasimodo BUS
(☑ 050 37 04 70; www.quasimodo.be) Quasimo-do has minibus Triple Treat tours (under/over 26 €45/55) at 9am on Monday, Wednesday and Friday from February to mid-December which visit a selection of castles plus the fascinating WWII coastal defences near Ostend. Its Flanders Fields tours (under/over 26 €45/55) at 9am Tuesday to Sunday, April to October, visits Ypres Salient.

Quasimundo BICYCLE
(☑ 050 33 07 75; www.quasimundo.eu; adult/student €28/26; ☉ Mar-Oct) Guided bicycle tours around Bruges (2½ hours, morning) or via Damme to the Dutch border (four hours, afternoon). Bike rental included. Book ahead.

🛏 Sleeping

Although there are well over 250 hotels and B&Bs, accommodation can still prove oppressively overbooked from Easter to September,

over Christmas and especially at weekends, when two-night minimum stays are commonly required. In the lowest seasons (early November, late January), midrange options sometimes give big last-minute discounts. An all-night touch-screen computer outside the main tourist office displays hotel availability and contact information. The website www.brugge.be has a booking engine.

't Keizershof HOTEL €
(☑ 050 33 87 28; www.hotelkeizershof.be; Oostermeers 126; s €35-47, d €47; P 🛜) Remarkably tasteful and well kept for this price, the seven simple rooms with shared bathrooms are above a former brasserie-*café* decorated with old radios (now used as the breakfast room). Free parking.

Bauhaus HOSTEL €
(☑ 050 34 10 93; www.bauhaus.be; Langestraat 145; hostel dm/tw €16/50, hotel s/d €16/50, 2-4 person apt per weekend from €240; @ 🛜) One of Belgium's most popular hang-outs for young travellers, this virtual backpacker 'village' incorporates a bustling hostel, apartments, a nightclub, internet cafe and a little chill-out room that's well hidden behind the reception and laundrette section at Langestraat 145. Simple and slightly cramped dorms are operated with key cards; hotel-section double rooms have private shower cubicles. Bike hire is also available. Take bus 6 or 16 from the train station.

★ Baert B&B B&B €€
(☑ 050 33 05 30; www.bedandbreakfastbrugge.be; Westmeers 28; s/d €80/90) In a 1613 former stable this is one of very few places in Bruges where you'll get a private canalside terrace

---

WHAT'S A BEGIJNHOF?

Usually enclosed around a central garden, a *begijnhof* (*béguinage* in French) is a pretty cluster of historic houses originally built to house lay sisters. The idea originated in the 12th century when many such women were left widowed by their crusader-knight husbands. Today 14 of Flanders' historic *begijnhoven* have been declared Unesco World Heritage sites with great examples at Diest, Lier, Turnhout, Kortrijk and Bruges, which also has dozens of smaller *godshuizen* (almshouses).

(flower-decked, though not on the loveliest canal section). Floral rooms have bathrooms across the landing; bathrobes are provided. A big breakfast spread is served in a glass verandah, and extras include a welcome drink and a pack of chocolates.

★ **B&B Dieltiens** B&B €€

(☑ 050 33 42 94; www.bedandbreakfastbruges.be; Waalsestraat 40; s €60-80, d €70-90, tr €90-100) Old and new art fills this lovingly restored classical mansion, which remains an appealingly real home run by charming musician hosts. Superbly central yet quiet. They also operate a holiday flat nearby in a 17th-century house.

✖ Eating

Est Wijnbar TAPAS €

(☑ 050 33 38 39; www.wijnbarest.be; Braambergstraat 7; mains €9.50-12.50, tapas €3.50-9.50; ⊘ 4pm-midnight Wed-Sun; ☑) This attractive little wine bar – the building dates back to 1637 – is an especially lively spot on Sunday nights, when you can catch live jazz, blues and occasionally other musical styles from 8.30pm. It's also a pleasantly informal supper spot, with *raclette,* pasta, snacks and salads on the menu, and tasty desserts.

★ **De Stove** BISTRO €€

(☑ 050 33 78 35; www.restaurantdestove.be; Kleine St-Amandsstraat 4; mains €19-33, menu without/with wine €48/65; ⊘ noon-1.30pm Sat & Sun, 7-9pm Fri-Tue) Just 20 seats keep this gem intimate. Fish caught daily is the house speciality, but the monthly changing menu also includes the likes of wild boar fillet on oyster mushrooms. Everything, from the bread to the ice cream, is homemade. Despite perennially rave reviews, this calm, one-room, family restaurant remains friendly, reliable and inventive, without a hint of tourist tweeness.

★ **In 't Nieuwe Museum** PUB €€

(☑ 050 33 12 22; www.nieuw-museum.com; Hooistraat 42; mains €16-22; ⊘ noon-2pm & 6-10pm Thu-Tue, closed lunch Sat) So called because of the museumlike collection of brewery plaques, money boxes and other mementoes of cafe life adorning the walls, this family-owned local favourite serves five kinds of *dagschotel* (dish of the day) for lunch (€7 to €12.50), and succulent meat cooked on a 17th-century open fire in the evenings.

De Bottelier MEDITERRANEAN €€

(☑ 050 33 18 60; www.debottelier.com; St-Jakobsstraat 63; mains from €16; ⊘ lunch & dinner Tue-Fri, dinner Sat) Decorated with hats and old clocks, this adorable little restaurant sits above a wine shop overlooking a delightful handkerchief of canalside garden. Pasta/veg dishes cost from €9/13.50. Diners are predominantly local. Reservations are wise.

De Stoepa BISTRO €€

(☑ 050 33 04 54; www.stoepa.be; Oostmeers 124; ⊘ noon-2pm & 6pm-midnight Tue-Sat, noon-3pm & 6-11pm Sun) A gem of a place in a peaceful residential setting with a slightly hippie/ Buddhist feel. Oriental statues, terracotta-coloured walls, a metal stove and wooden floors and furniture give a homey but stylish feel. Best of all though is the leafy terrace garden. Tuck into its upmarket bistro-style food.

☕ Drinking & Nightlife

Beer-specialist cafes include **'t Brugs Beertje** (www.brugsbeertje.be; Kemelstraat 5; ⊘ 4pm-midnight Mon, Thu & Sun, to 1am Fri & Sat) and alley-hidden **De Garre** (☑ 050 34 10 29; www.degarre.be; Garre 1; ⊘ noon-midnight Mon-Thu, to 1am Fri & Sat) serving its own fabulous 11% Garre house brew. Old-world classic **Herberg Vlissinghe** (☑ 050 34 37 37; www. cafevlissinghe.be; Blekerstraat 2; ⊘ 11am-10pm Wed & Thu, to midnight Fri & Sat, to 7pm Sun) dates from 1515. Eiermarkt, just north of Markt, has many plain but lively bars, with DJs and seemingly endless happy hours. If you're feeling brave, have a drink with a self-proclaimed vampire at the wildly eccentric **Retsin's Lucifernum** (☑ 0476 35 06 51; www. lucifernum.be; Twijnstraat 6-8; admission incl drink €6; ⊘ 8-11pm Sun).

☆ Entertainment

Concertgebouw CONCERT VENUE

(☑ 050 47 69 99; www.concertgebouw.be; 't Zand 34; tickets from €10) Bruges' stunning 21st-century concert hall is the work of architects Paul Robbrecht and Hilde Daem and takes its design cues from the city's three famous towers and red bricks. Theatre, classical music and dance are regularly staged. The tourist office is situated at street level.

Cactus Muziekcentrum LIVE MUSIC

(☑ 050 33 20 14; www.cactusmusic.be; Magdalenastraat 27) Though small, this is the city's top venue for contemporary and world music, both live bands and international DJs. It also organises festivals including July's **Cactus Music Festival** (www.cactusfestival.be; ⊙ Jul), held in the Minnewater park at the southern edge of the old city.

ℹ️ Information

Bruggecentraal (www.bruggecentraal.be) has events listings.

In & Uit Brugge (☑ 050 44 46 46; www.brugge.be; 't Zand 34; ⊙10am-6pm Mon-Sun) The tourist office is situated at street level of the big, red Concertgebouw concert hall with a branch at the train station. Standard city maps cost €0.50, comprehensive guide pamphlets €2. Excellent **Use-It guide-maps** (www.use-it.be) are free if you ask for one.

ℹ️ Getting There & Away

Bruges' train station is about 1.5km south of the Markt, a lovely walk via the Begijnhof.

Antwerp (€14.80, 75 minutes) Twice hourly.

Brussels (€14.10, one hour) Twice hourly.

Ghent (€6.50, fast/slow 24/42 minutes) Five hourly; two continue to more central Gent-Dampoort.

Ypres (Ieper in Dutch) Take a train to Roeselare (€5, fast/slow 22/33 minutes), then bus 94 or 95: both buses pass key WWI sites en route.

ℹ️ Getting Around

BICYCLE

B-Bike (☑ 0499 70 50 99; Zand Parking 26; per hr/day €4/12; ⊙10am-7pm Apr-Oct)

Rijwielhandel Erik Popelier (☑ 050 34 32 62; www.fietsenpopelier.be; Mariastraat 26; per hr/half/full day €4/8/12, tandem €10/17/25; ⊙10am-6pm) Good bicycles for adults and kids; helmets for hire, free map, no deposit.

BUS

To get from the train station to Markt, take any bus marked 'Centrum'. For the way back, buses stop at Biekorf, just northwest of Markt on Kuiperstraat.

Ypres

POP 34,900

During WWI (1914–18), historic Ypres (pronounced 'eepr'; Ieper in Dutch) was bombarded into oblivion while futile battles raged between trench networks in the surrounding poppy fields. Today, many medieval buildings have been meticulously rebuilt and the battlefields in Ypres' rolling agricultural hinterland (called the Ypres Salient) are a moving reminder of the horrors of war, with their seemingly endless graveyards and memorials.

⊙ Sights

⊙ Central Ypres

Grote Markt   SQUARE
The brilliantly rebuilt **Lakenhallen**, a vast Gothic edifice originally serving as the 13th-century cloth market, dominates this very photogenic central square. It sports a 70m-high belfry, reminiscent of London's Big Ben, and hosts the gripping museum **In Flanders Fields** (www.inflandersfields.be; Lakenhallen, Grote Markt 34; adult/youth €9/4-5; ⊙10am-6pm Apr–mid-Nov, to 5pm Tue-Sun mid-Nov–Mar), a multimedia WWI experience honouring ordinary people's experiences of wartime horrors. It's very highly recommended. The ticket allows free entry to three other minor city museums.

Menin Gate   MEMORIAL
(Menenpoort) A block east of Grote Markt, the famous Menin Gate is a huge stone gateway straddling the main road at the city moat. It's inscribed with the names of 54,896 'lost' British and Commonwealth WWI troops whose bodies were never found.

⊙ Ypres Salient

Many WWI sites are in rural locations that are awkward to reach without a car or tour bus. But the following are all within 600m of Ypres–Roeselare bus routes 94 and 95 (once or twice hourly weekdays, five daily weekends), so could be visited en route between Ypres and Bruges.

LAST POST
....
At 8pm daily, traffic through the Menin Gate is halted while buglers sound the **Last Post** (www.lastpost.be; ⊙8pm) in remembrance of the WWI dead, a moving tradition started in 1928. Every evening the scene is different, possibly accompanied by pipers, troops of cadets or maybe a military band.

BELGIUM & LUXEMBOURG YPRES

Memorial Museum
Passchendaele 1917   MUSEUM
(www.passchendaele.be; Ieperstraat 5; admission
€7.50; ⊙10am-6pm Feb-Nov; 🚌94) In central
Zonnebeke village, **Kasteel Zonnebeke**
(www.zonnebeke.be) is a lake-fronted Normandy chalet-style mansion built in 1922
to replace a castle bombarded into rubble
during WWI. It now hosts a tourist office,
cafe and a particularly polished WWI museum charting local battle progressions with
plenty of multilingual commentaries. The
big attraction here is descending into its
multiroom 'trench experience' with low-lit,
wooden-clad subterranean bunk rooms and
a soundtrack to add wartime atmosphere.
Entirely indoors, explanations are much
more helpful here than in 'real' trenches
elsewhere.

Tyne Cot   CEMETERY
(⊙24hr, visitor centre 9am-6pm Feb-Nov; 🚌94)
FREE Probably the most visited Salient site,
this is the world's biggest British Commonwealth war cemetery, with 11,956 graves. A
huge semicircular wall commemorates another 34,857 lost-in-action soldiers whose
names wouldn't fit on Ypres' Menin Gate.
The name Tyne Cot was coined by Northumberland fusiliers who fancied that German
bunkers on the hillside here looked like Ty-
neside cottages. Two such dumpy concrete
bunkers sit amid the graves, with a third
partly visible through the metal wreath beneath the central white Cross of Sacrifice.

Deutscher Soldatenfriedhof   CEMETERY
FREE The area's main German WWI cemetery is smaller than Tyne Cot but arguably more memorable, amid oak trees and
trios of squat, mossy crosses. Some 44,000
corpses were grouped together here, up to
10 per granite grave slab, and four eerie
silhouette statues survey the site. Entering
takes you through a black concrete 'tunnel'
that clanks and hisses with distant war
sounds, while four short video montages
commemorate the tragedy of war. It's beyond the northern edge of Langemark on
bus route 95.

🖙 Tours

Over the Top   BUS
(📞0472 34 87 47; www.overthetoptours.be;
Meensestraat 41; tours €40; ⊙9am-12.30pm,
1.30-5.30pm & 7.30-8.30pm) A WWI specialist
bookshop towards the Menin Gate, offering

twice-daily, half-day guided minibus tours of
the Ypres Salient.

British Grenadier   BUS
(📞057 21 46 57; www.salienttours.be; Meensestraat 5; short/long tour €30/38; ⊙9.30am-1pm,
2-6pm & 7.30-8.30pm) Two Ypres tours – the
2½-hour option takes in Hill 60, the Cater-
pillar Crater and the German Bayernwald
trench complex, while the standard four-
hour tour covers every site on the Salient.

🛏 Sleeping & Eating

Ariane Hotel   HOTEL €€
(📞057 21 82 18; www.ariane.be; Slachthuisstraat
58; s/d from €89/109; 🅿🛜) This peaceful,
professionally managed, large hotel has a
designer feel to the rooms and popular restaurant while wartime memorabilia dots the
spacious common areas.

B&B Ter Thuyne   B&B €€
(📞057 36 00 42; www.terthuyne.be; Gustave de
Stuersstraat 19; d €95; @) Three comfortable rooms that are luminously bright and
scrupulously clean, but not overly fashion-
conscious.

★ Main Street Hotel   GUESTHOUSE €€€
(📞057469633; www.mainstreet-hotel.be; Rijselse-
straat 136; d €180-260; 🛜) Jumbling funky
eccentricity with historical twists and luxurious comfort, this is a one-off that simply
oozes character. The smallest room is designed like a mad professor's experiment,
the breakfast room has a Tiffany glass ceiling...and so it goes on!

★ De Ruyffelaer   FLEMISH €€
(📞057 36 60 06; www.deruyffelaer.be; Gustave
de Stuersstraat 9; mains €15-21, menus €24-33;
⊙11.30am-3.30pm Sun, 5.30-9.30pm Thu-Sun)
Traditional local dishes served in an adorable,
wood-panelled interior with chequerboard
floors and a brocante decor, including dried
flowers, old radios and antique biscuit tins.

ℹ Information

Toerisme Ieper (📞057 23 92 20; www.ieper.be;
Grote Markt 34; ⊙9am-6pm) The well-equipped
tourist office is within the Lakenhallen.

ℹ Getting There & Around

BICYCLE
Hotel Ambrosia (📞057 36 63 66; www.
ambrosiahotel.be; D'Hondtstraat 54; standard/
electric bike per day €12/30; ⊙7.30am-7pm)
Bicycle rentals.

BUS

Services pick up passengers in Grote Markt's northeast corner (check the direction carefully!). For Bruges take Roeselare-bound routes 94 or 95 then change to train.

TRAIN

Services run hourly to Ghent (€11.50, one hour) and Brussels (€17.50, 1¾ hours) via Kortrijk (€5.30, 30 minutes), where you could change for Bruges or Antwerp.

WALLONIA

Parlez-vous français? You'll need to in hilly Wallonia, Belgium's French-speaking southern half. Wallonia's cities do have their charms, though none quite manage to outshine the many Flemish 'art cities'. Wallonia's foremost attractions are mostly rural – outdoor activities, fabulous caves and ancient rural castles. This is where you'll really appreciate having your own wheels for easier access.

Mons

POP 93,100

It's fair to say that historic Mons (Bergen in Dutch) was a little slow off the starting blocks in embracing its role as European City of Culture in 2015, with many projects well behind schedule: Santiago Calatrava's train station won't open till 2018. The cube-like modern **BAM gallery** (Musée des Beaux-Arts; ☑065 40 53 24; www.bam.mons.be; Rue Neuve 8; adult/concession €8/5; ⊙hours vary) is worth a visit though, and other attractions include the 80m baroque **Beffroi** (belfry), the oversized 15th-century church of **Ste-Waudru** (www.waudru.be; Place du Chapitre; ⊙9am-6pm) and the attractive **Grand Place**. This great square comes to life on Trinity Sunday when the festivities of the **Ducasse** (www.ducasse demons) reach a raucous culmination with a George versus the dragon battle.

Dream Hotel (☑065 32 97 20; www.dream-mons.be; Rue de la Grand Triperie 17; s/d €75/90; P@) offers accommodation in a quirkily decorated 19th-century chapel. For eating, tavern-style local favourite **Henri** (☑065 35 23 06; Rue d'Havré 41; ⊙noon-2.30pm & 6.30-9pm Tue-Sat, noon-2.30pm Sun & Mon) has been serving Mons dishes since 1956, while for an unforgettable dinner in 17th-century style don't miss the **Salon des Lumières** (☑0474 29 25 84; www.salondeslumieres.com;

Rue du Mirroir 23; mains €16.50-20; ⊙7-10pm Wed-Sun, from 6pm winter).

Liège

POP 196,200

Beneath its brutally disfigured, post-industrial surface, sprawling Liège (Luik in Dutch) is a living architectural onion concealing layer upon layer of history. Fine churches abound, as befits a city that spent 800 years as the capital of an independent principality run by bishops. Proudly free-spirited citizens are disarmingly friendly and no Belgian city bubbles with more joie de vivre.

The somewhat grimy historic zone has several excellent museums. The **Grand Curtius** (www.grandcurtiusliege.be; Féronstrée 136; adult/child €9/free; ⊙10am-6pm Wed-Mon) presents a millennium's development of decorative arts, and art gallery **Musée des Beaux-Arts** (www.beauxartsliege.be; Féronstrée 86; adult/youth €5/3; ⊙10am-6pm Tue-Sun) is richly endowed, if a bit brutal architecturally.

Love it or loathe it, Liège is quirky and oddly compulsive, especially during its chaotic 15 August **festival**, held just across the river in the self-declared 'republic' of Outremeuse where there's a handy **Auberge de**

Jeunesse (☑04-344 56 89; www.lesauberges dejeunesse.be; Rue Georges Simenon 2; dm/s/d €23/36.50/54.75; @). The most appealing central accommodation options are the cosy little **Hôtel Hors Château** (☑04-250 60 68; www.hors-chateau.be; Rue Hors Château 62; s/d/ste €78/95/125; ☎) and the dramatic **Crowne Plaza** (☑04-222 94 94; www.crowne plazaliege.be; Mont St-Martin 9; r €109-690). For real Liègois food dine at **Le Bistrot d'en Face** (☑04-223 15 84; www.lebistrotdenface.be; Rue de la Goffe 10; mains €15-18; ⊙noon-2.30pm & 7-10.30pm Wed-Sun, closed lunch Sat) or **Amon Nanesse** (www.maisondupeket.be; Rue de l'Epée 4; meals €10.50-19.50; ⊙10am-2am, kitchen noon-2.30pm & 6-10.30pm).

Liège's great archtectural masterpiece is its 21st-century **Guillermins train station**, shaped vaguely like a giant concrete manta-ray. That's on the Brussels–Frankfurt mainline, though Liège-Palais station is far more central.

LUXEMBOURG

Ruled by its own monarchy, the Grand Duchy of Luxembourg is famed for its banks but visually it's mostly an undulating series of pretty wooded hills dotted with castle villages. These are made accessible from the attractive capital city by excellent roads and a very well organised single-price public transport system. Luxembourg has its own language, Lëtzeburgesch, in which *moien* is the standard greeting. But most Luxem-bourgers also speak French and German.

Luxembourg City

POP 100,000

World Heritage–listed Luxembourg City sits high on a promontory overlooking the deep-cut valleys of the Pétrusse and Alzette

---

ℹ **LUXEMBOURG CARD**

The brilliant value **Luxembourg Card** (www.ont.lu/en/luxembourg-card; 1-/2-/3-day adult €11/19/27, family €28/48/68), marked LC in reviews, allows free admission to most of the grand duchy's main attractions and unlimited use of public transport nationwide. You can buy it from tourist offices, museums or certain hotels.

Rivers. These gorges were the key to the city's defence from AD 963 when Count Sigefroi (or Siegfried) of Ardennes built a castle here. Luxembourg eventually grew to become one of Europe's strongest for-tresses, earning the nickname 'Gibraltar of the North'. In 1867 the majority of the for-tifications were removed as part of a treaty to reduce tensions between France and Ger-many, though a remarkable mass of bastion remnants and tunnels survives, providing visitors with spectacular viewpoints over-looking the old quarters of Clausen, Pfaffen-thal and the Grund.

⊙ Sights

⊙ Old Town

Within the compact, mostly pedestrianised Old Town all sights are walking distance from each other. Access to the fairy-tale Grund area is easiest using a public elevator on Plateau du St-Esprit.

★**Chemin de la Corniche**   PROMENADE
This pedestrian promenade has been hailed as 'Europe's most beautiful balcony'. It winds along the course of the 17th-century city ramparts with views across the river canyon towards the hefty fortifications of the Wenzelsmauer (Wenceslas Wall). Across Rue Sigefroi, the rampart-top walk contin-ues along Blvd Victor Thorn to the Dräi Tier (Triple Gate) tower.

★**Musée d'Histoire de la
Ville de Luxembourg**   MUSEUM
(Luxembourg City History Museum; www.mhvl.lu; 14 Rue du St-Esprit; adult/LC €5/free; ⊙10am-6pm Tue-Sun, to 8pm Thu) This remarkably engrossing and interactive museum hides within a series of 17th-century houses, including a former 'holiday home' of the Bishop of Orval. A lovely garden and open terrace offer great views.

Royal Palace   PALACE
(17 Rue du Marché-aux-Herbes; tours €7; ⊙guided tours 4pm Mon-Sat mid-Jul & Aug) Photogenically a-twitter with little pointy turrets, this 1573 palace has been much extended over the years. It now houses the Grand Duke's office with parliament using its 1859 annexe. For a brief period in summer the palace opens for gently humorous 45-minute **guided tours**, which deal mostly with the Duke's family history. From the medieval-gothic dining

room, the palace's interior style morphs into sumptuous gilded romanticism upstairs.

MNHA
MUSEUM

(Musée National d'Histoire et d'Art; www.mnha.lu; Marché-aux-Poissons; adult/LC €7/free; ☉10am-6pm Tue-Sun, to 8pm Thu) Startlingly modern for its Old Town setting, this unusual museum offers a fascinating if uneven coverage of art and history. It starts deep in an excavated rocky basement with exhibits of Neolithic flints then sweeps you somewhat unevenly through Gallic tomb chambers, Roman mosaics and Napoleonic medals to an excellent if relatively small art gallery. Cezanne and Picasso get a look-in while Luxembourg's Expressionist artist Joseph Kutter (1894–1941) gets a whole floor.

Cathédrale Notre Dame
CHURCH

(Blvd Roosevelt; ☉10am-noon & 2-5.30pm) Most memorable for its distinctively elongated black spires, the 17th-century cathedral contains a tiny but highly revered Madonna-and-child idol (above the altar) and the graves of the royal family (in the crypt).

Spuerkeess
MUSEUM, ARCHITECTURE

(Banque et Caisse d'Épargne de l'État; www.bcee.lu; 1 Place de Metz) **FREE** In a dramatic, century-old, castle-style building, Spuerkeess is the state savings bank, and hosts an intriguing **Bank Museum** (☉9am-5.30pm Mon-Fri) tracing 150 years of tradition and innovation in banking, from piggy banks to ATMs and bank robbers.

◉ Kirchberg

Luxembourg's shiny-glass business district and Eurocrat 'ghetto' is across the Pont Grande-Duchesse Charlotte, the city's giant, iconic red bridge.

★Mudam
GALLERY

(www.mudam.lu; 3 Parc Dräi Eechelen; adult/LC €7/free; ☉11am-8pm Wed-Fri, to 6pm Sat-Mon) Ground-breaking exhibitions of modern, installation and experiential art are hosted in this airy architectural icon designed by IM Pei. The museum's collection includes everything from photography to fashion, design and multimedia. The glass-roofed cafe makes a decent lunch/snack spot.

To find Mudam, take bus 1, 13 or 16 to 'Philharmonie', walk around the striking Philharmonie and descend past Hotel Melia. One Friday a month it's open to 10pm.

🛏 Sleeping

Luxembourg City's accommodation scene is heavy with business options but online rates are slashed at weekends and in summer.

Auberge de Jeunesse
HOSTEL €

(☎22 68 89; luxembourg@youthhostels.lu; 2 Rue du Fort Olizy; dm/s/d €20.90/34.90/57.80, HI members €23.90/37.90/59; P❄✳@☎; ♿9) This state-of-the-art hostel has very comfortable, sex-segregated dorms with magnetic-key entry systems. There are good-sized lockers (bring padlock), laundry facilities and masses of relaxing space including a great terrace from which to admire views to the old city. It's a short but steep walking descent from the Casemates area using a stepped path from near the 'Clausen Plateau Altmunster' bus stop.

★Hôtel Simoncini
HOTEL €€

(☎22 28 44; www.hotelsimoncini.lu; 6 Rue Notre Dame; s/d Mon-Thu from €155/175, Fri-Sun €125/145; @☎) A delightful contemporary option in the city centre, the Simoncini's foyer is a modern-art gallery and the smart, bright rooms have slight touches of retro-cool. There's free wi-fi in the lobby, and plug-in internet in rooms.

★Hôtel Parc Beaux-Arts
BOUTIQUE HOTEL €€€

(☎26 86 76 1; www.parcbeauxarts.lu; 1 Rue Sigefroi; ste Mon-Thu advance/rack rates €190/400, Fri-Sun from €135; @☎) Exuding understated luxury, this charming little hotel comprises a trio of 18th-century houses containing 10 gorgeous suites. Each features original artworks by contemporary artists, oak floors, Murano crystal lamps and a fresh rose daily. Seek out the 'secret' lounge hidden away in the original timber eaves.

🍴 Eating

Tree-shaded Place d'Armes overflows with terrace seating in summer and covers all bases from fast food to ritzy resto. Cheaper terraced places can be found on or near relatively unexotic Place de Paris, while for intimate and more original dining options, hunt out the tiny alleys and passages collectively nicknamed Ilôt Gourmand, directly behind the palace.

Anabanana
VEGAN €

(www.anabanana.lu; 117 Rue de la Tour Jacob; sandwich/lunch/dinner €5/12/19; ☉noon-2pm Tue-Fri, 7-10pm Tue-Sat; ✏) Quaint, colourful little

Luxembourg City

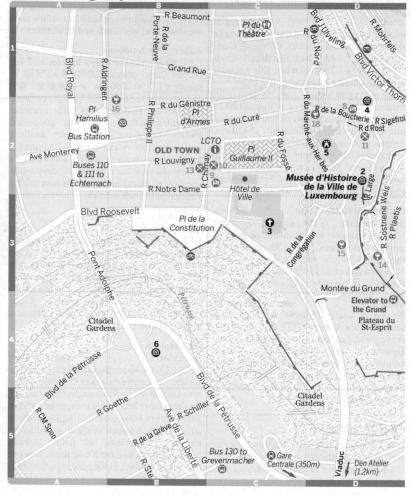

vegan-fusion restaurant with a fixed dinner choice that changes daily. Juice €4.50, no alcohol.

Bosso
FRENCH, GERMAN €

(www.bosso.lu; 7 Bisserwée; mains €8.50-16; ⏰5pm-midnight Mon-Thu, from 11am Fri-Sun) In summer, the biggest attraction of this good-value Grund restaurant is the hidden courtyard garden where seating is attractively tree-shaded. Try the *flammeküeche*, wafer-thin Alsatian 'pizzas' made with sour cream instead of tomato sauce, various takes on potato rösti or just linger over a drink.

Cathy Goedert
CAFE, BAKERY €

(www.cathygoedert.lu; 8 Rue Chimay; ⏰8am-6pm Tue-Sat, 9am-6pm Sun) This gleaming patisserie/boulangerie/cafe is a good option on Sunday when Luxembourg generally shuts up shop. Sumptuous cakes and pastries, plus a good variety of teas and coffees.

Á la Soupe
SOUP €

(www.alasoupe.net; 9 Rue Chimay; breakfast €3.50-7, soup €4.90-7.30; ⏰9am-7.30pm Mon-Sat) Central and minimally stylish soup station serving Moroccan and detox soups, as well as classic chicken.

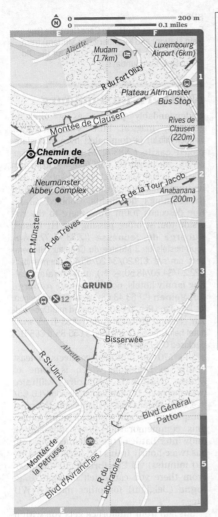

Luxembourg City

◎ Top Sights
1 Chemin de la Corniche E2
2 Musée d'Histoire de la Ville
   de Luxembourg D2

◎ Sights
Bank Museum .... (see 6)
3 Cathédrale Notre Dame C3
4 MNHA D2
5 Royal Palace D2
6 Spuerkeess B4

⊜ Sleeping
7 Auberge de Jeunesse F1
8 Hôtel Parc Beaux-Arts D2
9 Hôtel Simoncini C2

⊗ Eating
10 Á la Soupe C2
11 Am Tiirmschen D2
12 Bosso E3
13 Cathy Goedert B2

◉ Drinking & Nightlife
14 Café des Artistes D3
15 De Gudde Wëllen D3
16 L'Interview B2
17 Liquid Café E3
18 Urban Bar D2

declausen.com) form the city's liveliest youth scene. For more atmosphere, try a couple of places in Grund: either boho **Café des Artistes** (22 Montée du Grund; ⊙ Tue-Sun) or tucked-away **Liquid Café** (www.liquid.lu; 17 Rue Münster; ⊙ 5pm-1am Mon-Fri, from 8pm Sat & Sun). Fun central cafe-bars include **Urban Bar** (www.urban.lu/urbancity.html; 2 Rue de la Boucherie; ⊙ noon-late, kitchen 1-6pm), **L'Interview** (Rue Aldringen; ⊙ 7.30am-1am) and **De Gudde Wëllen** (www.deguddewellen.lu; 17 Rue du St-Esprit; ⊙ 5pm-1am Tue-Thu, 6pm-3am Fri & Sat), which has live-music nights featuring everything from drum and bass to Balkan folk. Some 700m west of Gare Centrale, factory-like **Den Atelier** (☑ 49 54 66; www.atelier.lu; 54 Rue de Hollerich) hosts a fine range of alternative music gigs.

❶ Information

Bibliothèque Municipale (Municipal Library; 3 Rue Génistre; ⊙ 10am-7pm Tue-Fri, to 6pm Sat) Sign up (with ID) for one hour's free internet. No printing.

LCTO (Luxembourg City Tourist Office; ☑ 22 28 09; www.lcto.lu; Place Guillaume II; ⊙ 9am-6pm Mon-Sat, from 10am Sun) Free city maps, walking-tour pamphlets and event guides.

Am Tiirmschen   LUXEMBOURG €€
(☑ 26 27 07 33; www.amtiirmschen.lu; 32 Rue de l'Eau, Ilôt Gourmand; mains €13-26; ⊙ noon-2pm Tue-Fri, 7-10.30pm Mon-Sat) This is a great place to sample typical Luxembourg dishes, but it also serves good fish and French options in case your companions don't fancy *kniddelen* (dumplings) or smoked pork. It has a semi-successful mix of old and pseudo-old decor with heavy, bowed beams.

▼ Drinking & Entertainment

Nearly a dozen themed bar-restaurant clubs in the **Rives de Clausen** (www.rives

ℹ Getting There & Away

BUS

Useful international connections from beside the train station include Bitburg (bus 401, 1¼ hours) and Trier (bus 118, one hour).

TRAIN

Gare Centrale is 1km south of the old city. There are **left-luggage lockers** (Gare Centrale; per day €3; ☉ 6am-9.30pm) at the far north end of platform 3; these are inaccessible at night.

There are trains to the following destinations:

Brussels (€39, two hours)

Diekirch (€2, 30 minutes) Hourly via Ettelbrück.

Liège (from €36.20, 2½ hours) Every two hours via Clervaux (one hour) and Coo (1¾ hours).

Paris (from €56, 145 minutes) By TGV.

Trier (€9-20, 50 minutes) Hourly, several continuing to Koblenz (€46.20, 130 minutes).

ℹ Getting Around

TO/FROM LUXEMBOURG AIRPORT

Luxembourg Airport (www.lux-airport.lu) is 6km east of Place d'Armes, 20 minutes by bus 16.

BICYCLE

Vélo en Ville (☑ 47 96 23 83; 8 Bisserwée; per half day/full day/weekend/week €12.50/20/37.50/100; ☉10am-noon & 1-8pm Apr-Sep, 7am-3pm Mar & Oct) Mountain bikes and free cycle-routes pamphlet available; tandems cost double. Renters under 26 get 20% discounts.

Velóh (☑ 800 611 00; www.en.veloh.lu; subscription per week/year €1/15; ☉24hr) Luxembourg City's short-hop bicycle-rental scheme works in a similar way to Brussels' Villo! (p84). As long as you return the bicycle within 30 minutes to any of 72 stations, each ride is free. The initial subscription is payable by bank card at one of 25 special stands.

ℹ LUXEMBOURG'S SIMPLIFIED TRANSPORT SYSTEM

Using bus, train or any combination, travel between any two points in the entire country (except border stations) costs €2/4 for two hours/one day. Buy tickets aboard buses, at train stations or in post offices.

See www.autobus.lu and www.cfl.lu for timetables.

BUS

Frequent buses shuttle to Gare Centrale (the train station) and Kirchberg (for Mudam) from Place Hamilius, the main bus stand for the Old Town. Fewer on Sundays.

Northern Luxembourg

Understandably popular as a weekend get-away, magical little **Vianden** (www.vianden-info.lu) is dominated by a vast slate-roofed **castle** (☑ 83 41 08 1; www.castle-vianden.lu; adult/child/LC €6/2/free; ☉10am-4pm Nov-Feb, to 5pm Mar & Oct, to 6pm Apr-Sep) and its impregnable stone walls glow golden in the evening's floodlights. Cobbled Grand Rue descends 700m from there to the riverside tourist office passing the HI Hostel, **Auberge de Jeunesse** (☑83 41 77; www.youthhostels.lu; 3 Montée du Château; HI members dm/s/d €19.20/34.20/55.40, nonmembers €22.20/34.20/48.50; ☻🛜), and several appealling family hotels, notably unique **Auberge Aal Veinen** (☑83 43 68; www.hotel-aal-veinen.lu; 114 Grand Rue; d €80; ☉closed mid-Dec–mid-Jan; 🛜) and **Hôtel Heintz** (☑83 41 55; www.hotel-heintz.lu; 55 Grand Rue; s €55-85, d €65-110; ☉closed Oct-Easter; 🛜).

Bus 570 (18 minutes) connects at least hourly to **Diekirch**, which is home to **Musée National d'Histoire Militaire** (www.mnhm.lu; 110 Rue Bamertal; adult/LC €5/free, WWII veterans free; ☉10am-6pm), the most comprehensive and visual of many museums commemorating 1944's devastating midwinter Battle of the Ardennes. Diekirch has twice-hourly trains to Luxembourg City (40 minutes) via **Ettelbrück** (10 minutes). From there you can catch buses to **Bastogne** (Belgium) for other major WWII sites.

Bus 545 from Ettelbrück gets you within 2km of isolated **Château de Bourscheid** (www.bourscheid.lu; adult/senior/LC €5/4/free; ☉9.30am-6pm Apr–mid-Oct, 11am-4pm mid-Oct–Mar), Luxembourg's most evocative medieval ruined castle, and trains run north towards Liège via pretty **Clervaux**, home to a convincingly rebuilt castle that hosts the world-famous **Family of Man photography exhibition** (www.steichencollections.lu; adult/senior €6/4, under 21 free; ☉noon-6pm Wed-Sun Mar-Jan), established in 1955 and intended as a manifesto for peace. Bus 663 (32 minutes) departs for Vianden at 8.30am, 10am, 2pm and 5pm.

Echternach

POP 5600

Echternach is home to sparse Roman excavations and Luxembourg's most important religious building, a sombre neo-Romanesque basilica rebuilt after merciless WWII bombing.

The town makes a useful base for hiking the well-signposted **Müllerthal Trails** (www.mullerthal-trail.lu) through shoulder-wide microgorges. Trail E1 (11.7km) starts from Echternach bus station, reached via pedestrianised, cafe-lined Rue de la Gare from the attractive main square. Mountain bikes (half/full day €8/15) can be rented from Echternach's modern **HI hostel** (Auberge de Jeunesse; ☑72 01 58; www.youthhostels.lu; HI members dm/s/d €21.20/36.20/53.40, non-members €24.20/39.20/60; ☺reception 8-10am & 5-10pm; 🅿😊🛜), set in a lakeside country park 2km south of town. To get there head 800m southwest to the fire station (bus stop Centre de Secours on route 110 Luxembourg City–Echternach), then walk 1.2km southeast in the direction of Rodenhof (Roudenhaff). Bus 111 (55 minutes, hourly) takes an alternative route to Luxembourg City via Berdorf.

Moselle Valley

Smothering the Moselle River's steeply rising banks are the neatly clipped vineyards that produce Luxembourg's balanced rieslings, fruity rivaners and excellent *crémants* (sparkling *méthode traditionelle* wines). Taste a selection at the grand **Caves Bernard-Massard** (☑75 05 45 1; www.bernard-massard.lu; 8 Rue du Pont; tour adult/child/LC from €7/4/free; ☺9.30am-6pm Apr-Oct) in central **Grevenmacher**, where frequent 20-minute winery tours are multilingual and spiced with humour. The Enner der Bréck bus stop outside is on bus routes 130 from Rue Heine in Luxembourg City (55 minutes, once or twice hourly).

Rentabike Miselerland (www.entente-moselle.lu/rentabike-miselerland; per day €10, LC free) bicycles can be rented from Grevenmacher's Butterfly Garden, allowing you to cycle along the riverside route via several other wineries. Return the bicycle at Remich bus station where bus 175 returns to Luxembourg City.

SURVIVAL GUIDE

ℹ️ Directory A–Z

ACCOMMODATION

Tourist offices often provide free accommodation-booking assistance.

B&Bs Rooms rented in local homes *(gastenkamers/chambres d'hôtes)* can be cheap and cheerful but some offer standards equivalent to a boutique hotel (up to €160 for a double). Discounts of around €10 per room are common if you stay at least a second night.

Camping Opportunities are plentiful, especially in the Ardennes. For extensive listings see www.campingbelgique.be (Wallonia), www.camping.be (Flanders) and www.camping.lu (Luxembourg).

Holiday houses *Gîtes* are easily rented in **Wallonia** (www.gitesdewallonie.be) and **Luxembourg** (www.gites.lu), but minimum stays apply and there's a hefty 'cleaning fee' on top of quoted rates.

Hostels Typically charge around €20 to €26 for dormitory beds, somewhat less in Bruges. HI hostels (*jeugdherbergen* in Dutch, *auberges de jeunesse* in French) affiliated with **Hostelling International** (www.youthhostels.be) charge €3 less for members, and some take off €2 for under-26-year-olds. Prices usually include sheets and a basic breakfast. Always read the conditions.

Short-term apartments Bookable through sites including www.airbnb.com and www.wimdu.com.

ACTIVITIES

In mostly flat **Flanders** (www.fietsroute.org), bicycles are a popular means of everyday travel

---

SLEEPING PRICE RANGES

Prices include a double room with a private bathroom, except in hostels or where otherwise specified. Rates quoted are for high season, which is May to September in Bruges, Ypres and the Ardennes, but September to June in business cities. Top-end business establishments in Brussels and Luxembourg City often cut prices radically at weekends and in summer.

€ less than €60

€€ €60 to €140

€€€ more than €140

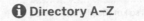

COUNTRY FACTS

Area 30,278 sq km (Belgium), 2586 sq km (Luxembourg)

Capitals Brussels (Belgium), Luxembourg City (Luxembourg)

Country Codes 32 (Belgium), 352 (Luxembourg)

Currency Euro (€)

Emergency 112

Languages Dutch, French, German, Lëtzeburgesch

Money ATMs are widely available; banks open Monday to Friday

Visas Schengen rules apply

and many roads have dedicated cycle lanes. In **Wallonia** (www.wallonie.be), the hilly terrain favours mountain bikes (VTT).

Canoeing and kayaking are best in the Ardennes, but don't expect rapids of any magnitude.

Local tourist offices have copious information about bicycle paths and sell regional hiking maps.

BUSINESS HOURS

Opening hours given in the text are for high season. Many tourism-based businesses reduce their hours off season.

Banks 9am to 3.30pm Monday to Friday, Saturday mornings too in Luxembourg

Brasseries 11am to midnight

Clubs 11pm to 6am Friday to Sunday

Pubs and cafes 1am or later

Restaurants 11.30am to 2.30pm and 6.30 to 10.30pm

Shops 10am to 6pm Monday to Saturday, some close for lunch; limited opening on Sunday in Belgium

Supermarkets 9am to 8pm Monday to Saturday, some open Sundays

INTERNET RESOURCES

Belgium (www.belgiumtheplaceto.be)
Flanders (www.visitflanders.com)
Luxembourg (www.ont.lu)
Wallonia (www.wallonia.be)

MONEY

➡ Banks usually offer better exchange rates than exchange bureaus (*wisselkantoren* in Dutch, *bureaux de change* in French), though often only for their banking clients, especially in Luxembourg.

➡ ATMs are widespread, but often hidden within bank buildings.

➡ Tipping is not expected in restaurants or cabs: service and VAT are always included.

PUBLIC HOLIDAYS

School holidays are July and August (slightly later in Luxembourg); one week in early November; two weeks at Christmas; one week around Carnival (February/March); two weeks at Easter; and one week in May (Ascension).

Public holidays are as follows:

New Year's Day 1 January
Easter Monday March/April
Labour Day 1 May
Ascension Day Fortieth day after Easter
Whit Monday Seventh Monday after Easter
National Day (Luxembourg) 23 June
Flemish Community Festival 11 July (Flanders only)
National Day (Belgium) 21 July
Assumption 15 August
Francophone Community Festival 27 September (Wallonia only)
All Saints' Day 1 November
Armistice Day 11 November (Belgium only)
German-Speaking Community Festival 15 November (eastern cantons only)
Christmas Day 25 December

TELEPHONE

➡ Dial full numbers: there's no optional area code.

➡ The international telephone code is 1234 for Belgium and 12410 for Luxembourg.

TOURIST INFORMATION

Excellent free info-maps of each major city are given away by youth hostels or available to download from www.use-it.travel.

VISAS

Schengen visa rules apply. Embassies are listed at www.diplomatie.belgium.be/en and www.mae.lu.

❶ Getting There & Away

AIR

Brussels Airport (BRU; www.brusselsairport. be) is Belgium's main long-haul gateway. Budget airlines **Ryanair** (www.ryanair.com) and **WizzAir** (www.wizzair.com) use the misleadingly named Brussels–South Charleroi Airport, which is actually 55km south of Brussels, 6km north of the ragged, post-industrial city of Charleroi (an hour south of Brussels). These budget airlines offer cheap deals to numerous European destinations.

Luxembourg Airport (www.lux-airport.lu) has various European connections including **EasyJet** (www.easyjet.com) budget flights to London Gatwick.

LAND
Bus

Ecolines (p89) operates from Brussels and Antwerp to various destinations in Eastern Europe.

Eurolines (www.eurolines.eu) is a Europe-wide network. Pre-bookings are compulsory but, although nine Belgian cities are served, only Brussels, Antwerp, Ghent and Liège have ticket offices.

Useful local cross-border buses include De Panne–Dunkerque and Luxembourg City–Trier.

Car & Motorcycle
➡ Border crossings are not usually controlled.
➡ Diesel is cheaper than unleaded. Both are cheaper in Luxembourg than almost anywhere else in Western Europe.
➡ As in France, give way to the right.
➡ Motorways are toll-free, with a speed limit of 120km/h in Belgium and 130km/h in Luxembourg.

EuroStop (www.eurostop.be; per 100km €4) EuroStop matches paying hitchhikers with drivers for long-distance international rides.

Train
There are excellent train links with neighbouring countries.
➡ Amsterdam, Paris, Cologne and London are all under 2½ hours from Brussels by high-speed train. Liège, Luxembourg City and Antwerp are also on high-speed international routes. Go via Tournai to reach France by train if you want to avoid such lines and their compulsory reservations.
➡ For comprehensive timetables and international bookings, see www.belgianrail.be or www.cfl.lu.
➡ Railcards are valid on standard services but there are surcharges for high-speed lines including **Eurostar** (www.eurostar.com) to London and Lille, **Thalys** (www.thalys.com) to Amsterdam and Paris and **Fyra** (www.b-europe.com) to Amsterdam.
➡ **ICE** (www.db.de) runs high-speed trains that cover the route Brussels–Liège–Aachen–Cologne–Frankfurt (3¼ hours), while **TGV**

ESSENTIAL FOOD & DRINK

Belgium's famous lagers (eg Stella Artois) and white beers (Hoegaarden) are now global brands. But what has connoisseurs really drooling are the robust, rich 'abbey' beers (originally brewed in monasteries), and the 'Trappist beers' (that still are). Chimay, Rochefort, Westmalle and Orval are the best known. But for beer maniacs the one that really counts is ultra-rare Westvleteren XII.

Dining is a treat in Belgium and Luxembourg, where meals are often described as being French in quality, German in quantity. Classic, home-style dishes include the following:

➡ **Chicons au gratin** Endive rolled in ham and cooked in cheese/béchamel sauce.
➡ **Filet Américain** A blob of raw minced beef, typically topped with equally raw egg yolk.
➡ **Judd mat gaardebounen** Luxembourg's national dish: smoked pork-neck in a cream-based sauce with chunks of potato and broad beans.
➡ **Kniddelen** Dumplings.
➡ **Mosselen/moules** Steaming cauldrons of in-the-shell mussels, typically cooked in white wine and served with a mountain of *frites* (chips).
➡ **Paling in 't groen** Eel in a sorrel or spinach sauce.
➡ **Stoemp** Mashed veg-and-potato dish.
➡ **Vlaamse stoverij/carbonade flamande** Semi-sweet beer-based meat casserole.
➡ **Waterzooi** A cream-based chicken or fish stew.

EUROLINES BUSES FROM BELGIUM

LINE	STANDARD PRICE (€)	SUPER-PROMO PRICE (€)	DURATION (HR)	FREQUENCY
Brussels–Amsterdam	20	9	3½-4½	up to 9 daily
Brussels–Frankfurt	46	24	6	2 daily
Brussels– London	51	9	6 (day), 8½ (night)	2 daily
Bruges–London	48	9	4¼	4 weekly, daily in holidays
Brussels–Paris	34	19	4	10 daily

(www.sncf.com) links to numerous French destinations, albeit bypassing central Paris.

➡ To avoid high-speed surcharges, useful 'ordinary' cross-border services include Liège–Aachen, Tournai–Lille, Antwerp–Rosendaal (for Amsterdam) and Luxembourg–Trier.

SEA

P&O (www.poferries.com) operates a Zeebrugge–Hull route. Pedestrians cost from UK£120 one way. Fourteen hours overnight.

ⓘ Getting Around

BICYCLE

Cycling is a great way to get around in flat Flanders, less so in chaotic Brussels or undulating Wallonia. The Belgian countryside is riddled with cycling routes and most tourist offices sell helpful regional cycling maps.

➡ Bike hire is available in or near most major train stations. Short-hop hire schemes are available in Brussels, Antwerp, Namur and Luxembourg City.

➡ Bikes on the train are free in Luxembourg. In Belgium it costs €5 one way (or €8 all day) on top of the rail fare. A few busy city-centre train stations don't allow bicycle transport.

BUS & TRAM

Regional buses are well coordinated with Belgium's rail network, but in rural regions you can still find that relatively short distances can involve long waits. In Brussels and Antwerp, trams that run underground are called *premetro*.

CAR & MOTORCYCLE

➡ Motorways are toll free.

➡ Speed limits are 50km/h in most towns (30km/h near schools), 70km/h to 90km/h on inter-town roads, and 120km/h on motorways in Belgium (130km/h in Luxembourg).

➡ The maximum legal blood alcohol limit is 0.05%.

➡ Car hire is available at airports and major train stations, but is usually cheaper from city-centre offices.

TAXI

Taxis must usually be pre-booked but there are ranks near main stations. Tips and taxes are always included in metered fares.

TRAIN

NMBS/SNCB (Belgian Railways; ☎ 02 528 28 28; www.b-rail.be) NMBS/SNCB trains are non-smoking. B-Excursions are good-value, one-day excursion fares including return rail ticket plus selected entry fees. Weekend Return Tickets valid from 7pm Friday to Sunday night cost just 20% more than a single but on weekdays a return costs twice the single price.

Britain

Best Traditional British Pubs

➡ Star Inn (p146)

➡ Bear Inn (p149)

➡ Old Thatch Tavern (p151)

➡ Blue Bell (p156)

➡ Café Royal Circle Bar (p166)

Best Museums

➡ Victoria & Albert Museum (p121)

➡ Ashmolean Museum (p147)

➡ National Railway Museum (p154)

➡ Kelvingrove Art Gallery & Museum (p167)

➡ Science Museum (p121)

Why Go?

Few places cram so much history, heritage and scenery into such a compact space as Britain. Twelve hours is all you'll need to travel from one end to the other, but you could spend a lifetime exploring – from the ancient relics of Stonehenge and Avebury, to the great medieval cathedrals of Westminster and Canterbury, and the magnificent country houses of Blenheim Palace and Castle Howard.

In fact, Britain isn't really one country at all, but three. While they haven't always been easy bedfellows, the contrasts between England, Wales and Scotland make this a rewarding place to visit. With a wealth of rolling countryside, stately cities, world-class museums and national parks to explore, Britain really is one of Europe's most unmissable destinations. And despite what you may have heard, it doesn't rain *all* the time – but even so, an umbrella and a raincoat will certainly come in handy.

When to Go
London

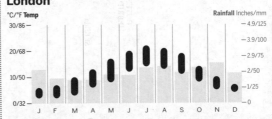

Easter–May Fewer crowds, especially in popular spots like Bath, York and Edinburgh.

Jun–Aug The weather is at its best but the coast and national parks are busy.

Mid-Sep–Oct Prices drop and the weather is often surprisingly good.

Britain Highlights

1 Explore the streets of one of the world's greatest capital cities, **London** (p112).

2 Visit Roman baths and admire grand Georgian architecture in **Bath** (p144).

3 Enjoy a Shakespeare play in the town of his birth, **Stratford-upon-Avon** (p150).

4 Marvel at the mountainous landscape of Wales' **Snowdonia National Park** (p161).

5 Delve into the history – Roman, Viking and medieval – of **York** (p154).

6 Get lost among the dreaming spires of **Oxford** (p147).

7 Step back in time wandering around the great trilithons

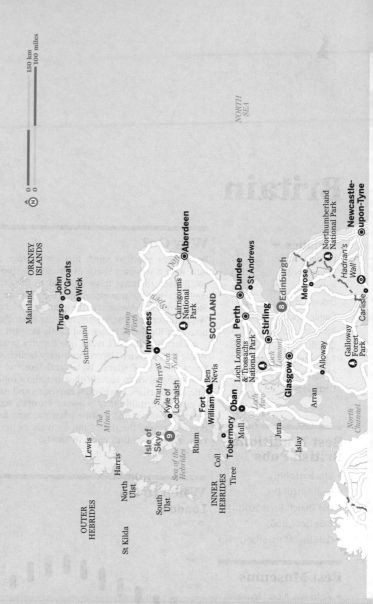

SHETLAND ISLANDS
Mainland

ORKNEY ISLANDS
Mainland

ATLANTIC OCEAN

Thurso
O'Groats
Wick

Sutherland

OUTER HEBRIDES

Lewis

Harris

St Kilda

North Uist

South Uist

The Minch

Strathfarrar
Loch Ness
Inverness
Moray Firth
Dee
Don
Aberdeen
Cairngorms National Park
SCOTLAND

Isle of Skye
Kyle of Lochalsh

Sea of the Hebrides

Rhum

Ben Nevis
Fort William

Tobermory
Oban
Mull
Coll
Tiree
INNER HEBRIDES

Loch Linnhe
Loch Awe

Jura
Islay
Arran

North Channel

Loch Lomond & Trossachs National Park
Loch Lomond

Dundee
St Andrews
Perth
Stirling
Glasgow
Edinburgh **8**
Alloway

Galloway Forest Park **4**

Melrose

Carlisle
Hadrian's Wall
Northumberland National Park **4**
Newcastle-upon-Tyne

NORTH SEA

150 km
100 miles
N

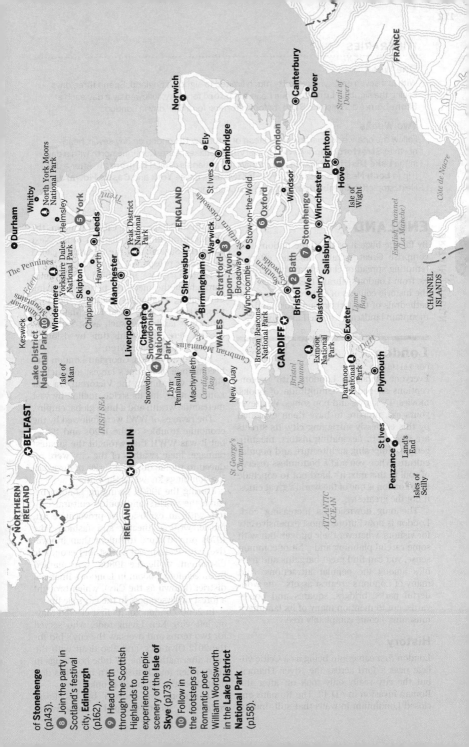

Durham

Whitby

North York Moors National Park

Helmsley

York 5

Leeds

Skipton •

Yorkshire Dales National Park

Haworth •

Manchester

Chipping •

Peak District National Park

Liverpool •

Chester

Snowdonia National Park

Snowdon •

Llyn Peninsula

Machynlleth •

Cardigan Bay

New Quay •

Cambrian Mountains

WALES

Brecon Beacons National Park

Wynchcombe •

CARDIFF ✪

Shrewsbury

Birmingham

Warwick •

Stratford-upon-Avon 3

Broadway •

Stow-on-the-Wold

Northern Cotswolds

Southern Cotswolds

Bristol 2 **Bath**

Wells •

Glastonbury •

Exmoor National Park 4

Exeter •

Dartmoor National Park 4

Plymouth •

Lyme Bay

St Ives •

Penzance •

Land's End

Isles of Scilly

Norwich

Ely •

Cambridge

St Ives •

ENGLAND

Oxford 6

London 1

Windsor •

Stonehenge 7

Winchester ✪

Salisbury •

Canterbury •

Dover •

Strait of Dover

Brighton • **Hove**

Isle of Wight

English Channel (La Manche)

FRANCE

Côte de Nacre

CHANNEL ISLANDS

The Pennines

Eden

Cumbrian Mountains

Keswick •

Isle of Man

Windermere 10

Lake District National Park

BELFAST ✪

NORTHERN IRELAND

IRELAND

DUBLIN ✪

IRISH SEA

St George's Channel

ATLANTIC OCEAN

Trent

Severn

Dart

Bristol Channel

Wye

ENGLAND

ITINERARIES

One Week

With just seven days, you're pretty much limited to sights in England. Spend three days seeing the sights in **London**, then head to **Oxford** for a day, followed by a day each at **Stonehenge** and historic **Bath**, before returning for a final day in London.

Two Weeks

Follow the one-week itinerary, but instead of returning to London on day seven, head north to **Stratford-upon-Avon** for everything Shakespeare. Continue north with a day in the **Lake District**, followed by two days in Scotland's capital **Edinburgh**. After a day trip to **Loch Ness**, recross the border for two days to see **York** and **Castle Howard**. Next, stop off in **Cambridge** on the way back to London.

ENGLAND

By far the biggest of the three nations that comprise Great Britain, England offers a tempting spread of classic travel experiences, from London's vibrant theatre scene and the historic colleges of Oxford, to the grand cathedrals of Canterbury and York and the mountain landscapes of the Lake District.

London

POP 7.51 MILLION

Everyone comes to London with preconceptions shaped by a multitude of books, movies, TV shows and pop songs. Whatever yours are, prepare to have them exploded by this endlessly intriguing city. Its streets are steeped in fascinating history, magnificent art, imposing architecture and popular culture. When you add a bottomless reserve of cool to this mix, it's hard not to conclude that London is one of the world's great cities, if not the greatest.

The only downside is increasing cost: London is now Europe's most expensive city for visitors, whatever their budget. But with some careful planning and a bit of common sense, you can find great bargains and freebies among the popular attractions. And many of London's greatest assets – its wonderful parks, bridges, squares and boulevards, not to mention many of its landmark museums – come completely free.

History

London first came into being as a Celtic village near a ford across the River Thames, but the city really only took off after the Roman invasion in AD 43. The Romans enclosed Londinium in walls that still find an echo in the shape of the City of London (the city's central financial district) today. Next came the Saxons, and the town they called Lundenwic prospered.

London grew in global importance throughout the medieval period, surviving devastating challenges such as the 1665 plague and the 1666 Great Fire. Many of its important landmarks such as St Paul's Cathedral were built at this time by visionary architect Christopher Wren.

By the early 1700s, Georgian London had become one of Europe's largest and richest cities. It was during the Victorian era that London really hit its stride, fuelled by vast mercantile wealth and a huge global empire.

The ravages of WWI were followed by the economic troubles of the 1920s and 1930s, but it was WWII that wrought the greatest damage: huge swathes of the city were reduced to rubble during a series of devastating bombings known as the Blitz.

During the 1960s, Swinging London became the world's undisputed cultural capital, with an explosion of provocative art, music, writing, theatre and fashion. The 1970s proved more turbulent than innovative, with widespread unrest and economic discontent, while the 1980s were marked by an economic boom in London's financial district (known as the City), which brought a forest of skyscrapers to the city's skyline.

In 2000 London got its first elected Mayor, left-wing Ken Livingstone, who served for two terms and oversaw the city's bid for the 2012 Olympics, and also dealt with the grim aftermath of the 7/7 tube bombings in 2005, when four British-born terrorists detonated bombs, killing 52 people.

Livingstone was ousted by his Eton-educated, blonde-mopped Conservative

London

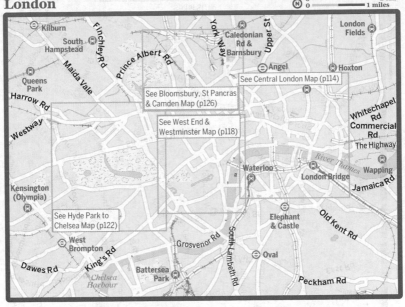

rival, Boris Johnson, in 2008. Johnson was re-elected in 2012 and oversaw the Queen's Golden Jubilee celebrations, followed by the city's hugely successful stint as Olympics host.

⊙ Sights

⊙ Westminster & St James's

★ Westminster Abbey   CHURCH
(Map p118; ☑020-7222 5152; www.westminster-abbey.org; 20 Dean's Yard, SW1; adult/child £20/9, verger tours £5; ⊙9.30am-4.30pm Mon, Tue, Thu & Fri, to 7pm Wed, to 2.30pm Sat; ⊖Westminster) Westminster Abbey is a mixture of architectural styles, but considered the finest example of Early English Gothic (1190–1300). It's not merely a beautiful place of worship, though. The Abbey serves up the country's history cold on slabs of stone. For centuries the country's greatest have been interred here, including 17 monarchs, from Henry III (died 1272) to George II (1760).

Houses of Parliament   HISTORIC BUILDING
(Map p118; www.parliament.uk; Parliament Sq, SW1; ⊖Westminster) FREE Officially called the Palace of Westminster, the Houses of Parliament's oldest part is 11th-century Westminster Hall, which is one of only a few sections that survived a catastrophic fire in 1834. Its roof, added between 1394 and 1401, is the earliest known example of a hammerbeam roof. Most of the rest of the building is a neo-Gothic confection built by Charles Barry (1795–1860) and Augustus Pugin (1812–1852).

Buckingham Palace   PALACE
(Map p118; ☑020-7766 7300; www.royalcollection.org.uk; Buckingham Palace Rd, SW1; adult/child £20.50/11.80; ⊙9.30am-7.30pm late Jul-Aug, to 6.30pm Sep; ⊖St James's Park, Victoria, Green Park) Built in 1703 for the Duke of Buckingham, Buckingham Palace replaced St James's Palace as the monarch's official London residence in 1837. When she's not giving her famous wave to far-flung parts of the Commonwealth, Queen Elizabeth II divides her time between here, Windsor and, in summer, Balmoral. To know if she's at home, check whether the yellow, red and blue standard is flying.

★ Tate Britain   GALLERY
(www.tate.org.uk; Millbank, SW1; ⊙10am-6pm, to 10pm 1st Fri of month; ⊖Pimlico) FREE You'd think that Tate Britain might have suffered since its sexy sibling, Tate Modern, took half its collection and all of the limelight across the river. On the contrary, the venerable Tate Britain, built in 1897 by Henry Tate,

Central London

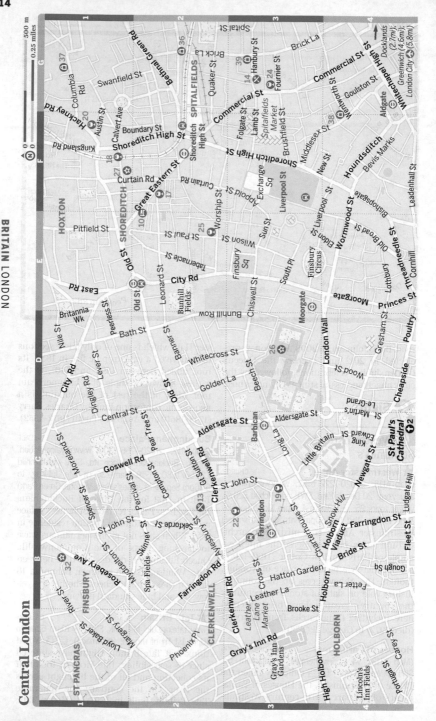

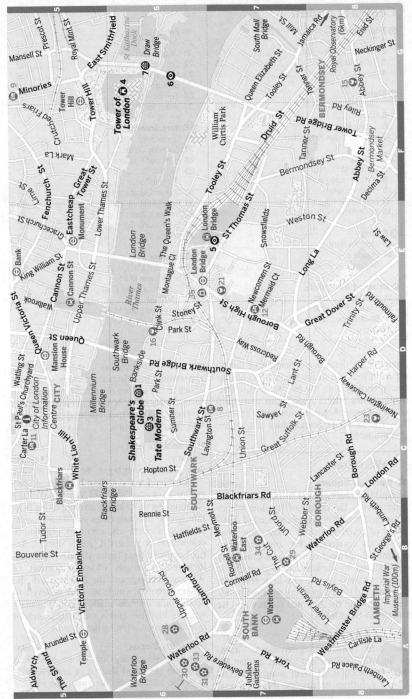

BRITAIN LONDON

stretched its definitive collection of British art from the 16th to the late 20th centuries out splendidly. Join the free 45-minute **thematic tours** (11am, noon, 2pm and 3pm) and 15-minute **Art in Focus talks** (1.15pm Tue, Thu and Sat). Audioguides (£3.50) are also available.

◉ West End

★ Trafalgar Square   SQUARE
(Map p118; ⊖ Charing Cross) In many ways Trafalgar Sq is the centre of London, where rallies and marches take place, tens of thousands of revellers usher in the New Year and locals congregate for anything from communal open-air cinema and Christmas celebrations to various political protests. It is dominated by the 52m-high **Nelson's Column** and ringed by many splendid buildings, including the National Gallery and **St Martin-in-the-Fields**.

★ National Gallery   GALLERY
(Map p118; www.nationalgallery.org.uk; Trafalgar Sq, WC2; ⏱ 10am-6pm Sat-Thu, to 9pm Fri; ⊖ Charing Cross) FREE With some 2300 European paintings on display, this is one of the richest art galleries in the world. There are seminal paintings from every important epoch in the history of art from the mid-13th to the early 20th century, including works by Leonardo da Vinci, Michelangelo, Titian, Van Gogh and Renoir.

National Portrait Gallery   GALLERY
(Map p118; www.npg.org.uk; St Martin's Pl, WC2; ⏱ 10am-6pm Sat-Wed, to 9pm Thu & Fri; ⊖ Charing Cross, Leicester Sq) FREE What makes the National Portrait Gallery so compelling is its familiarity; in many cases you'll have heard of the subject (royals, scientists, politicians, celebrities) or the artist (Andy Warhol, Annie Leibovitz, Sam Taylor-Wood). Highlights include the famous 'Chandos portrait' of William Shakespeare, the first artwork the gallery acquired (in 1856) and believed to be the only likeness made during the playwright's lifetime, and a touching sketch of novelist Jane Austen by her sister.

Piccadilly Circus   SQUARE
(Map p118; ⊖ Piccadilly Circus) John Nash had originally designed Regent St and Piccadilly in the 1820s to be the two most elegant

streets in town but, curbed by city planners, couldn't realise his dream to the full. He would certainly be disappointed with what Piccadilly Circus has become: swamped with visitors, flanked by flashing advertisement panels and surrounded by shops flogging tourist tat.

Madame Tussauds MUSEUM
(Map p122; ☑ 0870 400 3000; www.madame-tussauds.com/london; Marylebone Rd, NW1; adult/child £30/26; ⊙ 9.30am-5.30pm; ● Baker St) Madame Tussauds offers photo ops for days with your dream celebrity at the A-List Party (Daniel Craig, Lady Gaga, George Clooney, David and Victoria Beckham), the Bollywood gathering (Hrithik Roshan, Salman Khan) and the Royal Appointment (the Queen, Harry, William and Kate). If you're into politics, get up close and personal with Barack Obama or even London Mayor Boris Johnson.

👁 The City

⭐ St Paul's Cathedral CHURCH
(Map p114; www.stpauls.co.uk; St Paul's Churchyard, EC4; adult/child £16.50/7.50; ⊙ 8.30am-4.30pm Mon-Sat; ● St Paul's) Dominating the City of London with the world's second-largest church domes (and weighing in at around 65,000 tonnes), St Paul's Cathedral was designed by Christopher Wren after the Great Fire and built between 1675 and 1710. The site is ancient hallowed ground with four other cathedrals preceding Wren's English Baroque masterpiece here, the first dating from 604.

⭐ Tower of London CASTLE
(Map p114; ☑ 0844 482 7777; www.hrp.org.uk/toweroflondon; Tower Hill, EC3; adult/child £22/11, audioguide £4/3; ⊙ 9am-5.30pm Tue-Sat, 10am-5.30pm Sun & Mon, to 4.30pm Nov-Feb; ● Tower Hill) The unmissable Tower of London (actually a castle of 20-odd towers) offers a window on to a gruesome and quite compelling history. This was where two kings and three queens met their death and countless others were imprisoned. Come here to see the colourful Yeoman Warders (or Beefeaters), the spectacular **Crown Jewels**, the soothsaying ravens and armour fit for a king.

Tower Bridge BRIDGE
(Map p114; ● Tower Hill) London was a thriving port in 1894 when elegant Tower Bridge was built. Designed to be raised to allow ships

DON'T MISS

BRITISH MUSEUM

The vast **British Museum** (Map p118; ☑ 020-7323 8000; www.britishmuseum.org; Great Russell St, WC1; ⊙ 10am-5.30pm Sat-Thu, to 8.30pm Fri; ● Russell Sq, Tottenham Court Rd) FREE isn't just the nation's largest museum, it's one of the oldest and finest anywhere in the world. Among the must-see antiquities are the **Rosetta Stone**, the key to deciphering Egyptian hieroglyphics, discovered in 1799; the controversial **Parthenon Sculptures**, stripped from the walls of the Parthenon in Athens by Lord Elgin (the British ambassador to the Ottoman Empire); and the Anglo-Saxon **Sutton Hoo relics**. The **Great Court** was restored and augmented by Norman Foster in 2000 and now has a spectacular glass-and-steel roof.

You'll need multiple visits to savour even the highlights here; take advantage of the 15 free half-hour **Eye Opener** tours between 11am and 3.45pm daily, focusing on different parts of the collection. Various multimedia iPad tours are also available (adult/child £5/3.50).

to pass, electricity has now taken over from the original steam and hydraulic engines. A lift leads up from the northern tower to the **Tower Bridge Exhibition** (Map p114; www.towerbridge.org.uk; adult/child £8/3.40; ⊙ 10am-6pm Apr-Sep, 9.30am-5.30pm Oct-Mar; ● Tower Hill), where the story of its building is recounted within the upper walkway.

👁 South Bank

⭐ Tate Modern MUSEUM
(Map p114; www.tate.org.uk; Queen's Walk, SE1; ⊙ 10am-6pm Sun-Thu, to 10pm Fri & Sat; 🔊 ♿; ● Blackfriars, Southwark or London Bridge) FREE One of London's most popular attractions, this outstanding modern and contemporary art gallery is housed in the creatively revamped **Bankside Power Station** south of the **Millennium Bridge**. A spellbinding synthesis of funky modern art and capacious industrial brick design, Tate Modern has been extraordinarily successful in bringing challenging work to the masses. A stunning extension is aiming for a 2016 completion

West End & Westminster

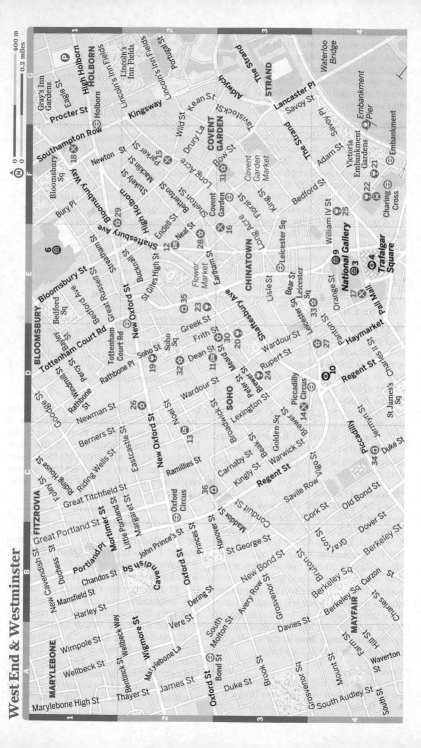

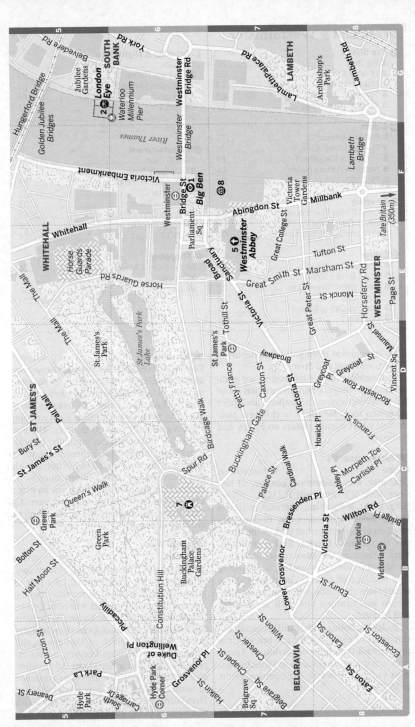

BRITAIN LONDON

West End & Westminster

date. Free guided highlights tours depart at 11am, noon, 2pm and 3pm daily.

Audioguides (in five languages) are available for £4 – they contain information about 50 artworks across the gallery and offer suggested tours for adults or children. Note the late-night opening hours on Friday and Saturday.

★ Shakespeare's Globe
HISTORIC BUILDING

(Map p114; www.shakespearesglobe.com; 21 New Globe Walk, SE1; adult/child £13.50/8; ⊙9am-5.30pm; 🚻; ⊖Blackfriars, Southwark or London Bridge) Today's Londoners may flock to Amsterdam to misbehave, but back in the bard's day they'd cross London Bridge to Southwark. Free from the city's constraints, they could settle down to whoring, bear-baiting and heckling of actors. The most famous theatre was the Globe, where a genius playwright was penning hits such as *Macbeth* and *Hamlet*.

Today's Globe, a faithful reconstruction of oak beams, handmade bricks, lime plaster and thatch, is the vision of American actor and director Sam Wanamaker, who sadly died before the opening night in 1997.

★ London Eye
VIEWPOINT

(Map p118; ☑ 0871 781 3000; www.londoneye.com; adult/child £21/15; ⊙10am-8pm; ⊖Waterloo) Standing 135m high in a fairly flat city, the London Eye affords views 25 miles in every direction, weather permitting. Each rotation takes a gracefully slow 30 minutes. The Eye draws 3.5 million visitors annually; at peak times (July, August and school holidays) it may seem like they are all in the queue with you. Save money and shorten queues by buying tickets online, or cough up an extra £10 to showcase your fast-track swagger. Alternatively, visit before 11am or after 3pm to avoid peak density.

Imperial War Museum
MUSEUM

(www.iwm.org.uk; Lambeth Rd, SE1; ⊙10am-6pm; ⊖Lambeth North) FREE Fronted by a pair of intimidating 15in naval guns, this riveting museum is housed in what was once Bethlehem Royal Hospital, also known as Bedlam. Although the museum's focus is on military action involving British or Commonwealth troops during the 20th century, it also explores war in the wider sense. After extensive refurbishment, the museum reopened in summer 2014, with new state-of-the-art First World War Galleries to mark the 100th anniversary of the start of WWI.

Shard
NOTABLE BUILDING

(Map p114; www.the-shard.com; 32 London Bridge St, SE1; adult/child £29.95/23.95; ⊙10am-10pm; ⊜London Bridge) Puncturing the skies above London, the dramatic splinter-like form of the Shard has rapidly become an icon of the town. The **viewing platforms** on floors 68, 69 and 72 are open to the public and the views are, as you'd expect from a 244m vantage point, sweeping, but they come at a hefty price – book online to save £5.

As well as the viewing platform, the Shard will be home to flats, hotels and restaurants; the first three opened over the summer in 2013.

⊙ Kensington & Hyde Park

This area is called the Royal Borough of Kensington and Chelsea, and residents are certainly paid royally, earning the highest incomes in the UK (shops and restaurants will presume you do, too).

★ Victoria & Albert Museum
MUSEUM

(V&A; Map p122; www.vam.ac.uk; Cromwell Rd, SW7; ⊙10am-5.45pm Sat-Thu, to 10pm Fri; ⊜South Kensington) FREE The Museum of Manufactures, as the V&A was known when it opened in 1852, was part of Prince Albert's legacy to the nation in the aftermath of the successful Great Exhibition of 1851, and its original aims – which still hold today – were the 'improvement of public taste in design' and 'applications of fine art to objects of utility'. It's done a fine job so far.

★ Natural History Museum
MUSEUM

(Map p122; www.nhm.ac.uk; Cromwell Rd, SW7; ⊙10am-5.50pm; ⊜South Kensington) FREE This colossal building is infused with the irrepressible Victorian spirit of collecting, cataloguing and interpreting the natural world. The main museum building is as much a reason to visit as the world-famous collection within.

★ Science Museum
MUSEUM

(Map p122; www.sciencemuseum.org.uk; Exhibition Rd, SW7; ⊙10am-6pm; ⊜South Kensington) FREE With seven floors of interactive and educational exhibits, this scientifically spellbinding museum will mesmerise adults and children alike, covering everything from early technology to space travel.

Hyde Park
PARK

(Map p122; ⊙5.30am-midnight; ⊜Marble Arch, Hyde Park Corner, Queensway) At 145 hectares, Hyde Park is central London's largest open space. Henry VIII expropriated it from the Church in 1536, when it became a hunting ground and later a venue for duels, executions and horse racing. The 1851 Great Exhibition was held here, and during WWII the park became an enormous potato field. These days, it's an occasional concert venue (Bruce Springsteen, the Rolling Stones, Madonna) and a full-time green space for fun and frolics, including boating on the **Serpentine**.

⊙ Hampstead & North London

With one of London's best high streets and plenty of green space, increasingly hip Marylebone is a great area to wander.

★ ZSL London Zoo
ZOO

(www.londonzoo.co.uk; Outer Circle, Regent's Park, NW1; adult/child £26/18.50; ⊙10am-5.30pm Mar-Oct, to 4pm Nov-Feb; ⊜Camden Town) These famous zoological gardens have come a long way since being established in 1828, with massive investment making conservation, education and breeding the name of the game. Highlights include **Penguin Beach, Gorilla Kingdom, Animal Adventure** (the new childrens' zoo) and **Butterfly Paradise**. Feeding sessions or talks take place during the day. Arachnophobes can ask about the zoo's Friendly Spider Programme, designed to cure fears of all things eight-legged and hairy.

Regent's Park
PARK

(www.royalparks.org.uk; ⊙5am-dusk; ⊜Regent's Park, Baker St) The most elaborate and ordered of London's many parks, this one was created around 1820 by John Nash, who planned to use it as an estate to build palaces for the aristocracy. Although the plan never quite came off, you can get some idea of what Nash might have achieved from the buildings along the Outer Circle.

⊙ Greenwich

An extraordinary cluster of buildings has earned 'Maritime Greenwich' its place on Unesco's World Heritage list. It's also famous for straddling the hemispheres; this is the degree zero of longitude, home of the Greenwich Meridian and Greenwich Mean Time.

BRITAIN LONDON

Hyde Park to Chelsea

0 500 m
0 0.25 miles

WESTBOURNE GROVE

Harrow Rd
Sutherland Ave
Shirland Rd
Bourne Tce
Senior St
Maida Ave
Blomfield Rd
Grand Union Canal
Warwick Avenue
Warwick Ave
Howley Pl
St Mary's Tce
Little Venice
Royal Oak
Westway
Harrow Rd
Westway
Westbourne Park Villas
Ranelagh Bridge
Porchester Rd
Bishop's Bridge Rd
Harrow Rd
Church St
Hall Pl
Edgware Rd
Penfold St
Penfold St
Broadway
Lisson Gve
Marylebone St
Melcombe Pl
Bell St
Marylebone Rd
Gloucester Pl Rd
York Tce
Allsop Pl
Baker St
Marylebone High St
Wimpole St
Aybrook St
Manchester St
Paddington St
Baker St
Gloucester Pl
Dorset St
Blandford St
Montagu Sq
Bryanston Sq
York St
Crawford St
Seymour Pl
Brown St
George St
Upper Berkeley St
Edgware Rd
Connaught St
Thayer St
Wigmore St
James St
Oxford St
Bond St
Duke St
Orchard St
Portman Sq
Portman St
Seymour St
North Row
Park St
Grosvenor Sq
South Audley St
Culross St
Park St
South St
Park La

MAYFAIR

Marble Arch
Cumberland Gate

MARYLEBONE

Marylebone Rd
Old Marylebone Rd
Edgware Rd
Westway
Harrow Rd
North Wharf Rd
South Wharf Rd
Sale Pl
Star St
Praed St
Sussex Gdns
Norfolk Cres
Norfolk Sq
Albion St
Hyde Park St
Bayswater Rd
Gloucester Sq
Hyde Park Gdns
The Ring
North Ride
The Ring
Cumberland Gate

Hyde Park

Buck Hill Walk

The Long Water

PADDINGTON
Paddington
Paddington Basin
Eastbourne Tce
Cleveland Tce
Westbourne Tce
Spring St
Westbourne Tce
Gloucester Tce
Devonshire Tce
Craven Tce
Lancaster Gate
Lancaster Tce
Lancaster Gate

Kensington Gardens
Budge's Walk

WESTBOURNE GROVE
Harrow Rd
Westway
Rough Trade West (500m)
Talbot Rd
Hereford Rd
Westbourne Park Villas
Orsett Tce
Westbourne Tce
Newtown Rd
Chepstow Rd
Chepstow Pl
Dawson Pl
Pembridge Villas
Kensington Gardens Sq
Leinster Sq
Ossington St
Moscow Rd
Bayswater
Queensway
Inverness Tce
Queensborough Tce
Porchester Tce
Leinster Tce
Craven Tce
Queen's Gdns
Cleveland Tce

BAYSWATER
Bayswater Rd
Bayswater Rd

Notting Hill Gate
Notting Hill Gate
Portobello Road Market (600m)
Chepstow Rd

Queensway

5
19
22
10
4
12

Greenwich is easily reached on the DLR train (to Cutty Sark station), or by boat – Thames River Services depart from Westminster Pier (one hour, every 40 minutes) and Thames Clippers depart from the London Eye (35 minutes, every 20 minutes).

★ Royal
Observatory   HISTORIC BUILDING
(www.rmg.co.uk; Greenwich Park; adult/child £7.70/3.60; ☉10am-5pm; 🚊DLR Cutty Sark, 🚊DLR Greenwich, 🚊Greenwich) Rising south of Queen's House, idyllic **Greenwich Park** climbs up the hill, affording stunning views of London from the Royal Observatory, which Charles II had built in 1675 to help solve the riddle of longitude.

Success was confirmed in 1884 when Greenwich was designated as the prime meridian of the world, and Greenwich Mean Time (GMT) became the universal measurement of standard time.

In the north of the observatory is lovely **Flamsteed House** and the **Meridian Courtyard** (where you can stand with your feet straddling the western and eastern hemispheres); admission is by ticket. The southern half contains the highly informative and free **Astronomy Centre** and the **Peter Harrison Planetarium** (adult/child £6.50/4.50).

**Old Royal Naval
College**   HISTORIC BUILDING
(www.oldroyalnavalcollege.org; 2 Cutty Sark Gardens, SE10; ☉10am-5pm, grounds 8am-6pm; 🚊DLR Cutty Sark) FREE Designed by Wren, the Old Royal Naval College is a magnificent example of monumental classical architecture. Parts are now used by the University of Greenwich and Trinity College of Music, but you can visit the **chapel** and the extraordinary **Painted Hall**, which took artist Sir James Thornhill 19 years to complete. Yeomen-led tours of the complex leave at noon daily, taking in areas not otherwise open to the public (£6, 60 minutes).

**National Maritime
Museum**   MUSEUM
(www.rmg.co.uk/national-maritime-museum; Romney Rd, SE10; ☉10am-5pm, Sammy Ofer Wing & ground fl galleries to 8pm Thu; 🚊DLR Cutty Sark) FREE Narrating the long and eventful history of seafaring Britain, this museum is a top Greenwich attraction. Exhibits are arranged thematically, with highlights including **Miss Britain III** (the first boat to top 100mph on open water) from 1933, the 19m-long **golden state barge** built in 1732 for Frederick, Prince of Wales, and the huge **ship's propeller** installed on level one. Families will love these, as well as the **ship simulator** and the 2nd floor **children's gallery**, where kids can let rip.

Cutty Sark   LANDMARK
(www.rmg.co.uk/cuttysark; King William Walk, SE10; adult/child £13.50/7; ☉10am-5pm; 🚊DLR Cutty Sark) This Greenwich landmark, the last of the great clipper ships to sail between China and England in the 19th century, reopened in spring 2012 after serious fire damage. Luckily half of the ship's furnishings and equipment, including the mast, had been removed for conservation at the time of the conflagration.

◉ **Outside Central London**

Kew Gardens   GARDENS
(www.kew.org; Kew Rd; adult/child £15/3.50; ☉10am-6.30pm Apr-Aug, earlier closing Sep-Mar;

Kew Pier, Kew Bridge, Kew Gardens) In 1759 botanists began rummaging around the world for specimens to plant in the 3-hectare Royal Botanic Gardens at Kew. They never stopped collecting, and the gardens, which have bloomed to 120 hectares, provide the most comprehensive botanical collection on earth (including the world's largest collection of orchids). Recognised as a Unesco World Heritage Site, the gardens can easily swallow a day's exploration; for those pressed for time, the Kew Explorer (adult/child £4/1) hop-on/hop-off road train takes in the main sights.

Hampton Court Palace — PALACE

(www.hrp.org.uk/HamptonCourtPalace; adult/child/family £17.50/8.75/43.80; ☉ 10am-6pm Apr-Oct, to 4.30pm Nov-Mar; Hampton Court Palace, Hampton Court) Built by Cardinal Thomas Wolsey in 1514 but coaxed from him by Henry VIII just before Wolsey (as chancellor) fell from favour, Hampton Court Palace is England's largest and grandest Tudor structure. It was already one of the most sophisticated palaces in Europe when, in the 17th century, Christopher Wren designed an extension. The result is a beautiful blend of Tudor and 'restrained baroque' architecture. You could easily spend a day exploring the palace and its 24 hectares of riverside gardens.

Tours

One of the best ways to orientate yourself when you first arrive in London is with a 24-hour hop-on/hop-off pass for the double-decker bus tours. The buses loop around interconnecting routes throughout the day, providing a commentary as they go. The price includes a river cruise and three walking tours. You'll save a couple of pounds by booking online.

Original Tour — BUS

(www.theoriginaltour.com; adult/child/family £29/14/86; ☉ every 20min 8.30am-5.30pm) A hop-on hop-off option with a river cruise thrown in as well as three themed walks: Changing of the Guard, Rock 'n' Roll and Jack the Ripper.

Big Bus Tours — BUS

(www.bigbustours.com; adult/child/family £32/12/76; ☉ every 20min 8.30am-6pm Apr-Sep, to 5pm Oct & Mar, to 4.30pm Nov-Feb) Informative commentaries in eight languages. The ticket includes a free river cruise with City Cruises and three thematic walking tours (Royal London, Harry Potter film locations

> ### BIG BEN
>
> The Houses of Parliament's most famous feature is the clock tower known as **Big Ben** (Map p118). Strictly speaking, however, Big Ben is the tower's 13-tonne bell, named after Benjamin Hall, commissioner of works when the tower was completed in 1858.

and Ghosts by Gaslight). Online booking discounts available.

Festivals & Events

University Boat Race — SPORTS

(www.theboatrace.org) A posh-boy grudge match held annually since 1829 between the rowing crews of Oxford and Cambridge Universities (late March).

Virgin Money London Marathon — SPORTS

(www.virginmoneylondonmarathon.com) Up to half a million spectators watch the whippet-thin champions and bizarrely clad amateurs take to the streets in late April.

Trooping the Colour — PARADE

Celebrating the Queen's official birthday (in June), this ceremonial procession of troops, marching along the Mall for their monarch's inspection, is a pageantry overload.

Meltdown Festival — MUSIC

(www.southbankcentre.co.uk) The Southbank Centre hands over the curatorial reigns to a legend of contemporary music (such as David Bowie, Morrissey or Patti Smith) to pull together a full program of concerts, talks and films in late June.

Wimbledon Lawn Tennis Championships — SPORTS

(www.wimbledon.com) The world's most splendid tennis event takes place in late June.

Pride — GAY & LESBIAN

(www.prideinlondon.org) The big event on the gay and lesbian calendar; a Technicolor street parade heads through the West End in late June or early July, culminating in a concert in Trafalgar Sq.

Notting Hill Carnival — CARNIVAL

(www.thenottinghillcarnival.com) Every year, for three days during the last weekend of August, Notting Hill echoes to the calypso, ska, reggae and soca sounds of the Notting

Bloomsbury, St Pancras & Camden

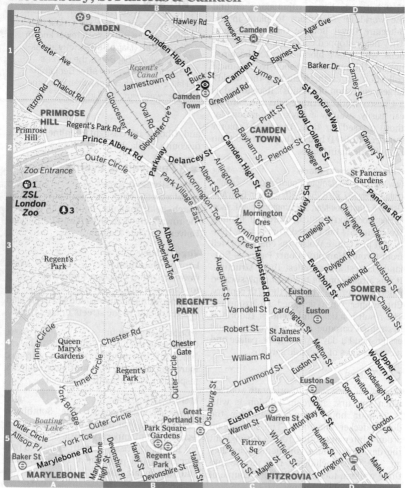

Hill Carnival. Launched in 1964 by the local Afro-Caribbean community, keen to celebrate its culture and traditions, it has grown to become Europe's largest street festival (up to one million people) and a highlight of London's annual calendar. A further undisputed attraction is the food.

🛏 Sleeping

When it comes to accommodation, London is one of the most expensive places in the world. Budget is pretty much anything below £100 per night for a double; double rooms ranging between £100 and £200 per night are considered midrange; more expensive options fall into the top-end category. Public transport is good, so you don't need to sleep at Buckingham Palace to be at the heart of things.

🛏 West End

YHA London Oxford Street   HOSTEL **£**
(Map p118; ☎ 020-7734 1618; www.yha.org.uk; 14 Noel St, W1; dm/tw from £18/46; @🗢; ⊖Oxford Circus) The most central of London's eight

worked as a scribe and members of the Clash made an appearance in 1978. Rooms feature pod beds (including storage space) in four- to 16-bed dormitories (there is a female aisle). There's a top kitchen with a huge dining area and a busy bar in the basement.

London St Pancras YHA HOSTEL £
(☎ 020-7388 9998; www.yha.org.uk; 79 Euston Rd, NW1; dm/r from £20/61; @ 🛜; ⊖ King's Cross St Pancras) This 185-bed hostel has modern, clean dorms sleeping four to six (nearly all with private facilities) and some private rooms. There's a good bar and cafe, although there are no self-catering facilities.

Seven Dials Hotel HOTEL ££
(Map p118; ☎ 020-7240 0823; www.sevendials hotellondon.com; 7 Monmouth St, WC2; s/d/tr/q £95/105/130/150; 🛜; ⊖ Covent Garden, Tottenham Court Rd) The Seven Dials is a clean and comfortable almost-budget option in a very central location. Half of the 18 rooms face onto charming Monmouth St; the ones at the back don't get much of a view but are quieter.

Arosfa Hotel B&B ££
(☎ 020-7636 2115; www.arosfalondon.com; 83 Gower St, WC1; s/tw/d/tr/f incl breakfast £83/128/135-155/155/185; 🛜; ⊖ Goodge St) The old Arosfa has come a long way, with Philippe Starck furniture in the lounge and a new modern look. The 17 rooms are less lavish, with cabin-like bathrooms in many of them. About half have been refurbished; they are small but remain good value. There are a

YHA hostels is also one of the most intimate, with just 104 beds and excellent shared facilities: we love the fuchsia kitchen and the bright, funky lounge. Dormitories have three and four beds and there are doubles and twins. Internet costs £1 per 20 minutes on their computers; wi-fi is £5/9 per day/week.

Clink78 HOSTEL £
(☎ 020-7183 9400; www.clinkhostels.com; 78 King's Cross Rd, WC1; dm/r from £10/25; @ 🛜; ⊖ King's Cross St Pancras) This fantastic 500-bed hostel is housed in a 19th-century magistrates courthouse where Dickens once

couple of family rooms; room 4 looks onto a small garden.

Dean Street Townhouse
BOUTIQUE HOTEL **£££**

(Map p118; ☑ 020-7434 1775; www.deanstreet townhouse.com; 69-71 Dean St, W1; r £260-450; ❀ ⓢ; ⊖ Tottenham Court Rd) This 39-room gem in the heart of Soho has a wonderful boudoir atmosphere with its Georgian furniture, retro black-and-white tiled bathroom floors, beautiful lighting and girly touches (Cowshed bathroom products, hairdryer *and* straighteners in every room!). 'Medium' and 'bigger' rooms have four-poster beds and antique-style bathtubs right in the room.

The City

London St Paul's YHA
HOSTEL **£**

(Map p114; ☑ 020-7236 4965; www.yha.org.uk; 36 Carter Lane, EC4; dm £17-25, d £40-50; @ ⓢ; ⊖ St Paul's) This 213-bed hostel, housed in a heritage-listed building, stands in the very shadow of St Paul's. Dorms have between three and 11 beds, and twins and doubles are available. There's a licensed cafeteria (breakfast £5, dinner from £6 to £8) but no kitchen, plus a lot of stairs and no lift. There's a seven-night maximum stay.

Hotel Indigo Tower Hill
BOUTIQUE HOTEL **££**

(Map p114; ☑ 0843 208 7007; www.hotelindigo. com/lontowerhill; 142 Minories, EC3; r weekend/ weekday from £100/200; ❀ ⓢ; ⊖ Aldgate) A welcome addition to the City's accommodation scene is this new branch of the US InterContinental group's boutique-hotel chain. The 46 differently styled rooms all feature four-poster beds, iPod docking stations and a 'unique scent' system that allows you to choose your own fragrance. Larger-than-life drawings and photos of the neighbourhood won't let you forget where you are.

South Bank

Immediately south of the river is good if you want to immerse yourself in workaday London and still be central.

St Christopher's Village
HOSTEL **£**

(Map p114; ☑ 020-7939 9710; www.st-christophers.co.uk; 163 Borough High St, SE1; dm/r from £15.90/50; @ ⓢ; ⊖ London Bridge) This 185-bed place is the flagship of a hostel chain

with basic but cheap and clean accommodation (the bathrooms are looking a little tired however). There's a roof garden with bar, barbecue and excellent views of the Shard skyscraper, as well as a cinema and Belushi's bar below for serious partying. Dorms have four to 14 beds.

★ Citizen M
BOUTIQUE HOTEL **££**

(Map p114; ☑ 020-3519 1680; www.citizenm.com/ london-bankside; 20 Lavington St, SE1; r £109-199; ❀ @ ⓢ; ⊖ Southwark) If Citizen M had a motto, it would be 'less fuss, more comfort'. The hotel has done away with things it considers superfluous (room service, reception, bags of space) and instead gone all out on mattresses and bedding (heavenly super king-size beds), state-of-the-art technology (everything in the room from mood-lighting to TV is controlled through a tablet computer) and superb decor.

Kensington & Hyde Park

This classy area offers easy access to the museums and big-name fashion stores, but at a price that reflects the upmarket surroundings.

Number Sixteen
HOTEL **£££**

(Map p122; ☑ 020-7589 5232; www.firmdalehotels. com/hotels/london/number-sixteen; 16 Sumner Pl, SW7; s from £174, d £228-360; ❀ @ ⓢ; ⊖ South Kensington) With uplifting splashes of colour, choice art and a sophisticated-but-fun design ethos, ravishing Number Sixteen is four properties in one and a lovely (and rather labyrinthine) place to stay. There are 41 individually designed rooms, a cosy drawing room and a fully stocked library. And wait till you see the idyllic, long back garden set around a fish pond, or have breakfast in the light-filled conservatory.

Ampersand Hotel
BOUTIQUE HOTEL **£££**

(Map p122; ☑ 020-7589 5895; www.ampersand hotel.com; 10 Harrington Rd; s & d £372; ❀ @ ⓢ; ⊖ South Kensington) Housed in the old Norfolk Hotel building, a light, fresh and bubbly feel fills the new Ampersand, its (narrow) corridors and (stylish but smallish) rooms decorated with wallpaper designs celebrating the nearby arts and sciences of South Kensington's museums, a short stroll away. The wrapping recently off, there's a spring in its step, zest in the service and an eagerness to please.

Clerkenwell, Shoreditch & Spitalfields

★ Hoxton Hotel
HOTEL £

(Map p114; ☑ 020-7550 1000; www.hoxtonhotels. com; 81 Great Eastern St, EC2; r from £59; ❋ @ ⟨; ⊜ Old St) This is hands down the best hotel deal in London. In the heart of Shoreditch, this sleek 208-room hotel aims to make its money by being full each night. You get an hour of free phone calls, free computer terminal access in the lobby, free printing and breakfast from Prêt à Manger. Rooms are small but stylish.

Notting Hill & West London

West London's Earl's Court district is lively, cosmopolitan and so popular with travelling antipodeans that it's been nicknamed Kangaroo Valley.

Tune Hotel
HOTEL £

(Map p122; ☑ 020-7258 3140; www.tunehotels.com; 41 Praed St, W2; r £35-80; ❋ @ ⟨; ⊜ Paddington) This new 137-room Malaysian-owned budget hotel offers super-duper rates for early birds who book a long way in advance. The ethos is you get the bare bones – a twin or double room, the cheapest without window – and pay for add-ons (towel, wi-fi, TV) as you see fit, giving you the chance to just put a roof over your head, if that's all you need.

Barclay House
B&B ££

(☑ 020-7384 3390; www.barclayhouselondon.com; 21 Barclay Rd, SW6; r £110-125; @ ⟨; ⊜ Fulham Broadway) The two dapper, thoroughly modern and comfy bedrooms in this charmingly ship-shape Victorian house are a dream, from the Philippe Starck shower rooms, walnut furniture, new double-glazed sash windows and underfloor heating to the small, thoughtful details (fumble-free coat hangers, drawers packed with sewing kits and maps). The cordial, music-loving owners – bursting with tips and handy London knowledge – concoct an inclusive, homely atmosphere. Usually there is a four-night minimum stay.

Rockwell
BOUTIQUE HOTEL ££

(Map p122; ☑ 020-7244 2000; www.therockwell.com; 181-183 Cromwell Rd, SW5; s/ste from £90/160, d £100-150; ❋ @ ⟨; ⊜ Earl's Court) With an understated-cool design ethos, things are muted, dapper and more than a tad minimalist at 'budget boutique' 40-room Rockwell. Spruce and stylish, all rooms have shower, the mezzanine suite is an absolute peach and the three rooms (LG1, 2 and 3) giving on to the garden are particularly fine.

La Suite West
BOUTIQUE HOTEL £££

(Map p122; ☑ 020-7313 8484; www.lasuitewest.com; 41-51 Inverness Tce, W2; r £179-489; ❋ @ ⟨; ⊜ Bayswater) The black-and-white foyer of the Anouska Hempel–designed La Suite West – bare walls, a minimalist slit of a fireplace, an iPad for guests' use on an otherwise void white marble reception desk – presages the OCD neatness of rooms hidden away down dark corridors. The straight lines, spotless surfaces and sharp angles are accentuated by impeccable bathrooms and softened by comfortable beds and warm service.

✕ Eating

Dining out in London has become so fashionable that you can hardly open a menu without banging into a celebrity chef. The range and quality of eating options has increased enormously over the last few decades.

✕ West End

★ Koya
NOODLES £

(Map p118; www.koya.co.uk; 49 Frith St, W1; mains £7-15; ⊙ noon-3pm & 5.30-10.30pm; ⊜ Tottenham Court Rd, Leicester Sq) Arrive early or late if you don't want to queue at this excellent Japanese eatery. Londoners come for their fill of authentic udon noodles (served hot or cold, in soup or with a cold sauce), the efficient service and very reasonable prices.

Orchard
VEGETARIAN £

(Map p118; www.orchard-kitchen.co.uk; 11 Sicilian Ave, WC1; mains £6.50-7; ⊙ 8am-4pm Mon-Fri; ☑; ⊜ Holborn) A boon for vegetarians in central London is this delightful retro-style cafe on a quiet pedestrian street. Mains include specialities like broccoli and Yorkshire blue cheese pie, and a sarnie (that's a sandwich to Londoners) and mug of soup is just £4.95. Desserts are unusual – try the toasted oat and currant cake with Horlicks icing.

★ Brasserie Zédel
FRENCH ££

(Map p118; ☑ 020-7734 4888; www.brasseriezedel.com; 20 Sherwood St, W1; mains £8.75-30; ⊙ 11.30am-midnight Mon-Sat, to 11pm Sun; ⟨; ⊜ Piccadilly Circus) This brasserie in the renovated art deco ballroom of a former Piccadilly hotel is the French-est eatery west of Calais. Choose from among the usual favourites, including *choucroute alsacienne* (sauerkraut with sausages and charcuterie) and duck leg confit with Puy lentils. The set menus (£8.25/11.75 for two/three courses) and *plats du jour* (£12.95) offer excellent value.

North Sea Fish Restaurant
FISH & CHIPS ££

(www.northseafishrestaurant.co.uk; 7-8 Leigh St, WC1; mains £10-20; ⊙noon-2.30pm & 5.30-10.30pm Mon-Sat, 1-6pm Sun; ⊖Russell Sq) The North Sea sets out to cook fresh fish and potatoes – a simple ambition in which it succeeds admirably. Look forward to jumbo-sized plaice or halibut fillets, deep-fried or grilled, and a huge serving of chips. There's takeaway next door if you can't face the rather austere dining room.

Great Queen Street
BRITISH ££

(Map p118; ✉020-7242 0622; 32 Great Queen St, WC2; mains £14-20; ⊙noon-2.30pm & 6-10.30pm Mon-Sat, 1-4pm Sun; ⊖Holborn) The menu at what is one of Covent Garden's best places to eat is seasonal (and changes daily), with an emphasis on quality, hearty dishes and good ingredients – there are always delicious stews, roasts and simple fish dishes. The atmosphere is lively, with a small bar downstairs. The staff are knowledgeable about the food and wine they serve and booking is essential.

National Dining Rooms
BRITISH ££

(Map p118; ✉020-7747 2525; www.peytonand byrne.co.uk; 1st fl, Sainsbury Wing, National Gallery, Trafalgar Sq, WC2; mains £12.50-17.50; ⊙10am-5.30pm Sat-Thu, to 8.30pm Fri; ⊖Charing Cross) Chef Oliver Peyton's restaurant at the National Gallery styles itself as 'proudly and resolutely British', and what a great idea. The menu features an extensive and wonderful selection of British cheeses for a light lunch. For something more filling, go for the county menu, a monthly changing menu honouring regional specialities from across the British Isles.

Hawksmoor Seven Dials
STEAKHOUSE £££

(Map p118; ✉020-7420 9390; www.thehawksmoor. com; 11 Langley St, WC2; steak £18-34, 2-/3-course express menu £24/27; ⊙noon-3pm & 5-10.30pm Mon-Sat, noon-9.30pm Sun; ☎; ⊖Covent Garden) Legendary among London carnivores for its mouth-watering and flavour-rich steaks from British cattle breeds, Hawksmoor's

sumptuous Sunday roasts, burgers and well-executed cocktails are other show-stoppers. Book ahead.

✖ South Bank

For a feed with a local feel, head to Borough Market or Bermondsey St.

M Manze
BRITISH £

(www.manze.co.uk; 87 Tower Bridge Rd, SE1; mains £2.40-6.25; ⊙11am-2pm Mon-Thu, 10am-2.30pm Fri & Sat; ⊖Borough) Dating to 1902, M Manze (Italian roots) started off as an ice-cream seller before moving on to selling its legendary staples: pies. It's a classic operation, from the lovely tile work to the traditional working-man's menu: pie and mash, pie and liquor and you can take your eels jellied or stewed.

★Skylon
MODERN EUROPEAN ££

(Map p114; ✉020-7654 7800; www.skylon-restaurant.co.uk; 3rd fl, Royal Festival Hall, South-bank Centre, Belvedere Rd, SE1; grill mains £12.50-30, restaurant 2-/3-course meal £42/48; ⊙grill noon-11pm Mon-Sat, noon-10.30pm Sun, restaurant noon-2.30pm & 5.30-10.30pm Mon-Sat, noon-4pm Sun; ☎; ⊖Waterloo) Named after the defunct 1950s tower, this excellent restaurant on top of the refurbished Royal Festival Hall is divided into grill and fine-dining sections by a large bar (⊙noon-1am Mon-Sat, to 10.30pm Sun; ⊖Waterloo). The decor is cutting-edge 1950s: muted colours and period chairs (trendy then, trendier now), while floor-to-ceiling windows bathe you in magnificent views of the Thames and the City.

✖ Kensington & Hyde Park

★Pimlico Fresh
CAFE £

(86 Wilton Rd, SW1; mains from £4.50; ⊙7.30am-7.30pm Mon-Fri, 9am-6pm Sat & Sun; ⊖Victoria) A wholesome choice for a healthy breakfast or lunch, this friendly two-room cafe cooks up fine homemade dishes from pies, soups, baked beans on toast and lasagne to warming bowls of porridge laced with honey, maple syrup, banana, yoghurt or sultanas, while making regular forays into creative cuisine. There's an invigorating choice of fresh fruit juices, and steaming glasses of spicy apple winter warmer fend off the cold in chillier months.

Wasabi JAPANESE £
(Map p122; www.wasabi.uk.com; Kensington Arcade, Kensington High St, W8; mains £5-8; ⊙10am-10pm Mon-Sat, 11am-9pm Sun; ⊖High St Kensington) Large, bright sit-down and take-out branch of this superb Japanese sushi and bento chain, with fantastic rice sets, noodles, rolls and salads, all good value and perfect for a fast lunch. Branches all over central London.

Tom's Kitchen MODERN EUROPEAN ££
(Map p122; ☑020-7349 0202; www.tomskitchen. co.uk; 27 Cale St, SW3; breakfast £2.50-15, mains £12.75-27; ⊙8-11.30am, noon-2.30pm & 6-10.30pm Mon-Fri, 10am-3.30pm & 6-10.30pm Sat & Sun; ⊖South Kensington) Celebrity chef Tom Aikens' restaurant serves excellent food, including award-winning breakfasts and pancakes.

★**Dinner by Heston Blumenthal** MODERN BRITISH £££
(Map p122; ☑020-7201 3833; www.dinnerbyheston. com; Mandarin Oriental Hyde Park, 66 Knightsbridge, SW1; 3-course set lunch £38, mains £28-42; ⊙noon-2.30pm & 6.30-10.30pm; ☎; ⊖Knightsbridge) Sumptuously presented Dinner is a gastronomic tour de force, taking diners on a journey through British culinary history (with inventive modern inflections). Dishes carry historical dates to convey context, while the restaurant interior is a design triumph, from the glass-walled kitchen and its overhead clock mechanism to the large windows onto the park.

✗ Clerkenwell, Shoreditch & Spitalfields

From the hit-and-miss Bangladeshi restaurants of Brick Lane to the Vietnamese strip on Kingsland Rd, the East End's cuisine is as multicultural as its residents. Clerkenwell's hidden gems are well worth digging for; Exmouth Market is a good place to start.

Poppies FISH & CHIPS ££
(Map p114; www.poppiesfishandchips.co.uk; 6-8 Hanbury St, E1; mains £7-16; ⊙11am-11pm Mon-Thu, to 11.30pm Fri & Sat, to 10.30pm Sun; ☎; ⊖Shoreditch High St, Liverpool St) Glorious re-creation of a 1950s East End chippy, complete with waitstaff in pinnies and hairnets, and retro memorabilia. As well as the usual fishy suspects, it does jellied eels, homemade tartare sauce and mushy peas, and you can wash it all down with a glass of wine or beer. Also does a roaring takeaway trade.

WANT MORE?
For in-depth information, reviews and recommendations at your fingertips, head to the Apple App Store to purchase Lonely Planet's *London City Guide* iPhone app.
Alternatively, head to **Lonely Planet** (lonelyplanet.com/england/london) for planning advice, author recommendations, traveller reviews and insider tips.

Modern Pantry FUSION £££
(Map p114; ☑020-7553 9210; www.themodern pantry.co.uk; 47-48 St John's Sq, EC1; mains £14-21.50; ⊙noon-3pm Tue-Fri, 11am-4pm Sat & Sun, 6-10.30pm Tue-Sat; ☎; ⊖Farringdon) This three-floor Georgian town house in the heart of Clerkenwell has a cracking all-day menu, which gives almost as much pleasure to read as to eat from. Ingredients are combined sublimely into unusual dishes such as tamarind miso marinated onglet steak or panko and parmesan crusted veal escalope. The breakfasts are great, too, though sadly portions can be on the small side. Reservations recommended for the evenings.

✗ Notting Hill & West London

Taquería MEXICAN £
(Map p122; www.taqueria.co.uk; 139-143 Westbourne Grove; tacos £5-7.50; ⊙noon-11pm Mon-Fri, 10am-11.30pm Sat, noon-10.30pm Sun; ☎; ⊖Notting Hill Gate) ✔ You won't find fresher, limper (they're not supposed to be crispy!) tacos anywhere in London because these ones are made on the premises. It's a small casual place with a great vibe. Taquería is also a committed environmental establishment: the eggs, chicken and pork are free-range, the meat British, the fish MSC-certified and the milk and cream organic.

Ledbury FRENCH £££
(☑020-7792 9090; www.theledbury.com; 127 Ledbury Rd, W11; 4-course set lunch £50, 4-course dinner £95; ⊙noon-2pm Wed-Sun & 6.30-9.45pm daily; ☎; ⊖Westbourne Park, Notting Hill Gate) Two Michelin stars and swooningly elegant, Brett Graham's artful French restaurant attracts well-heeled diners in jeans with designer jackets. Dishes – such as roast sea bass with broccoli stem, crab and black quinoa, or saddle of roe deer with beetroot, pinot lees and

BRITAIN LONDON

bone crisp potato – are triumphant. London gastronomes have the Ledbury on speed-dial, so reservations are crucial.

Drinking & Nightlife

As long as there's been a city, Londoners have loved to drink – and, as history shows, often immoderately. Clubland is no longer confined to the West End, with megaclubs scattered throughout the city wherever there's a venue big enough, cheap enough or quirky enough to hold them. The big nights are Friday and Saturday. Admission prices vary widely; it's often cheaper to arrive early or prebook tickets.

West End

Gordon's Wine Bar
BAR

(Map p118; www.gordonswinebar.com; 47 Villiers St, WC2; ⊙11am-11pm Mon-Sat, noon-10pm Sun; ⊜Embankment) Gordon's is a victim of its own success; it is relentlessly busy and unless you arrive before the office crowd does (generally around 6pm), you can forget about getting a table. It's cavernous and dark, and the French and New World wines are heady and reasonably priced. You can nibble on bread, cheese and olives. Outside garden seating in summer.

French House
BAR

(Map p118; www.frenchhousesoho.com; 49 Dean St, W1; ⊙noon-11pm Mon-Sat, noon-10.30pm Sun; ⊜Leicester Sq) French House is Soho's legendary boho boozer with a history to match: this was the meeting place of the Free French Forces during WWII, and De Gaulle is said to have drunk here often, while Dylan Thomas, Peter O'Toole and Francis Bacon all ended up on the wooden floor at least once.

Spuntino
BAR

(Map p118; www.spuntino.co.uk; 61 Rupert St, W1; mains £6-10; ⊙noon-midnight Mon-Wed, to 1am Thu-Sat, to 11pm Sun; ⊜Piccadilly Circus) Speakeasy decor meets creative fusion American-Italian food at Rupert St cool customer Spuntino. Grab a seat at the bar or one of the counters at the back, but put aside time to queue (no reservations and no phone).

Terroirs
WINE BAR

(Map p118; www.terroirswinebar.com; 5 William St, WC2; ⊙noon-11pm Mon-Sat; ⊜Charing Cross Rd) Fab two-floor spot for a pre-theatre glass or some expertly created charcuterie, with

informative staff, affordable £10 lunch specials, a lively, convivial atmosphere and a breathtaking list of organic wines.

LAB
COCKTAIL BAR

(Map p118; ☑020-7437 7820; www.labbaruk.com; 12 Old Compton St, W1; ⊙4pm-midnight Mon-Sat, to 10.30pm Sun; ⊜Leicester Sq, Tottenham Court Rd) A long-standing Soho favourite for almost two decades, the London Academy of Bartenders (to give it its full name) has some of the best cocktails in town. The list is the size of a small book but, fear not, if you can't make your way through it, just tell the bartenders what you feel like and they'll concoct something divine.

South Bank

★40 Maltby Street
WINE BAR

(Map p114; www.40maltbystreet.com; 40 Maltby St, SE1; ⊙5.30-10pm Wed & Thu, 12.30-2pm & 5.30-10pm Fri, 11am-5pm Sat) This tunnel-like wine-bar-cum-kitchen sits under the railway arches taking trains in and out of London Bridge. It is first and foremost a wine importer focusing on organic vintages but its hospitality venture has become incredibly popular. The wine recommendations are obviously top-notch (most of them by the glass) and the food – simple, gourmet bistro fare – is spot on.

George Inn
PUB

(Map p114; ☑020-7407 2056; www.national trust.org.uk/george-inn; 77 Borough High St, SE1; ⊙11am-11pm; ⊜London Bridge) This magnificent old boozer is London's last surviving galleried coaching inn, dating from 1676 and mentioned in Dickens' *Little Dorrit*. It is on the site of the Tabard Inn, where the pilgrims in Chaucer's *Canterbury Tales* gathered before setting out (well lubricated, we suspect) on the road to Canterbury, Kent.

Anchor Bankside
PUB

(Map p114; 34 Park St, SE1; ⊙11am-11pm Sun-Wed, to midnight Thu-Sat; ⊜London Bridge) Firmly anchored in many guidebooks (including this one) – but with good reason – this riverside boozer dates to the early 17th century (subsequently rebuilt after the Great Fire and again in the 19th century). Trips to the terrace are rewarded with superb views across the Thames but brace for a constant deluge of drinkers.

🍷 Clerkenwell, Shoreditch & Spitalfields

Jerusalem Tavern PUB

(Map p114; www.stpetersbrewery.co.uk; 55 Britton St, EC1; ☉11am-11pm Mon-Fri; 🛜; ⊖Farringdon) Starting life as one of the first London coffee houses (founded in 1703), with the 18th-century decor of occasional tile mosaics still visible, the JT is an absolute stunner, though sadly it's both massively popular and tiny, so come early to get a seat.

Book Club BAR

(Map p114; 🖉 020-7684 8618; www.wearetbc.com; 100 Leonard St, EC2A; ☉8am-midnight Mon-Wed, to 2am Thu & Fri, 10am-2am Sat & Sun; 🛜; ⊖Old St) This former Victorian warehouse has been transformed into an innovative temple to good times. Spacious and whitewashed with large windows upstairs and a basement bar below, it hosts a real variety of offbeat events, such as spoken word, dance lessons and life drawing, as well as a varied program of DJ nights.

Fabric CLUB

(Map p114; www.fabriclondon.com; 77a Charterhouse St, EC1; admission £8-18; ☉10pm-6am Fri, 11pm-8am Sat, 11pm-6am Sun; ⊖Farringdon) This most impressive of superclubs is still the first stop on the London scene for many international clubbers. The crowd is hip and well dressed without overkill, and the music – electro, techno, house, drum and bass and dubstep – is as superb as you'd expect from London's top-rated club.

Ten Bells PUB

(Map p114; cnr Commercial & Fournier Sts, E1; ☉11am-11pm Mon-Sat, noon-10.30pm Sun; ⊖Liverpool St) This landmark Victorian pub, with its large windows and beautiful tiles, is perfect for a pint after a wander round Spitalfields Market. It's famous for being one of Jack the Ripper's pick-up joints, although

---

GAY & LESBIAN LONDON

Generally, London's a safe place for lesbians and gays. It's rare to encounter any problem with sharing rooms or holding hands in the inner city, although it would pay to keep your wits about you at night and be conscious of your surroundings.

The West End, particularly Soho, is the visible centre of gay and lesbian London, with numerous venues clustered around Old Compton St – but many other areas have their own mini scenes.

The easiest way to find out what's going on is to pick up the free press from a venue (*Boyz*, *QX*); the gay section of *Time Out* (www.timeout.com/london/lgbt) is also useful. Some venues to get you started:

George & Dragon (Map p114; 2 Hackney Rd, E2; ☉6-11pm; ⊖Old St) Once a scuzzy local pub, the George was taken over and decorated with the owner's grandma's antiques (antlers, racoon tails, old clocks), cardboard cut-outs of Cher and fairy lights, turning this one-room pub into what has remained the epicentre of the Hoxton scene for more than a decade.

Edge (Map p118; www.edgesoho.co.uk; 11 Soho Sq, W1; ☉4pm-1am Mon-Thu, noon-to 3am Fri & Sat, 4-11.30pm Sun; 🛜; ⊖Tottenham Court Rd) Overlooking Soho Sq in all its four-storey glory, the Edge is London's largest gay bar and heaves every night of the week. There are dancers, waiters in skimpy outfits, good music and a generally super-friendly vibe. There's also a straight presence, as it's so close to Oxford St. So much the better.

Heaven (Map p118; www.heavennightclub-london.com; Villiers St, WC2; ☉11pm-5am Mon, Thu & Fri, 10pm-5am Sat; ⊖Embankment, Charing Cross) This long-standing, perennially popular gay club under the arches beneath Charing Cross station has always been host to good club nights. Monday's Popcorn (mixed dance party, all-welcome door policy) has to be one of the best weeknight's clubbing in the capital. The celebrated G-A-Y takes place here on Thursday (G-A-Y Porn Idol), Friday (G-A-Y Camp Attack) and Saturday (plain ol' G-A-Y).

Popstarz (Map p118; www.popstarz.org; The Den, 18 West Central St, WC1; ☉10pm-4am Fri; ⊖Tottenham Court Rd) This grand dame of gay indie has been revitalised by a recent transfer to the heart of the West End. It's popular with a studenty, friendly, mixed crowd. There are three rooms of great indie pop.

these days it attracts a rather more salubrious and trendy clientele.

Worship St

Whistling Shop
COCKTAIL BAR

(Map p114; ☑020-7247 0015; www.whistlingshop. com; 63 Worship St, EC2; ⊗5pm-midnight Tue, to 1am Wed & Thu, to 2am Fri & Sat; ⊜Old St) A 'Victorian' drinking den that takes cocktails to a molecular level, the Whistling Shop (as Victorians called a place selling illicit booze) serves expertly crafted and highly unusual concoctions using potions conjured up in its on-site lab. Try a Panacea, Black Cat Martini or the Bosom Caresser (made with formula milk). There's an incredible array of interesting spirits, as well as a Dram Shop for a private party, and an Experience Room for the really adventurous.

Cargo
CLUB

(Map p114; www.cargo-london.com; 83 Rivington St, EC2; admission free-£16; ⊗noon-1am Mon-Thu, to 3am Fri & Sat, to midnight Sun; ⊜Old St) Cargo is one of London's most eclectic clubs. Under its brick railway arches you'll find a dance-floor room, bar and outside terrace. The music policy is innovative and varied, with plenty of up-and-coming bands also on the menu. Food is available throughout the day.

🍸 Notting Hill, Bayswater & Paddington

Churchill Arms
PUB

(Map p122; www.churchillarmskensington.co.uk; 119 Kensington Church St, W8; ⊗11am-11pm Mon-Wed, to midnight Thu-Sat, noon-10.30pm Sun; 🐸; ⊜Notting Hill Gate) With its cascade of geraniums and Union Jack flags swaying in the breeze, the Churchill Arms is quite a sight on Kensington Church St. Renowned for its Winston memorabilia and dozens of knick-knacks on the walls, the pub is a favourite of both locals and tourists. The attached conservatory has been serving excellent Thai food for two decades (mains £6 to £10).

Windsor Castle
PUB

(Map p122; www.thewindsorcastlekensington.co.uk; 114 Campden Hill Rd, W11; ⊗noon-11pm Mon-Sat, noon-10.30pm Sun; 🐸; ⊜Notting Hill Gate) A classic tavern on the brow of Campden Hill Rd, this place has history, nooks and charm on tap. It's worth the search for its historic compartmentalised interior, roaring fire (in winter), delightful beer garden (in summer) and affable regulars (most always). Legend

attests the bones of Thomas Paine (author of *Rights of Man*) are in the cellar.

Earl of Lonsdale
PUB

(277-281 Portobello Rd, W11; ⊗noon-11pm Mon-Fri, 10am-11pm Sat, noon-10.30pm Sun; ⊜Notting Hill Gate, Ladbroke Grove) Named after the *bon vivant* founder of the AA (Automobile Association, *not* Alcoholics Anonymous), the Earl is peaceful during the day, with a mixture of old biddies and young hipsters inhabiting the reintroduced snugs. There are Samuel Smith's ales, a fantastic backroom with sofas, banquettes, open fires and a magnificent beer garden.

🍷 Greenwich & South London

Trafalgar Tavern
PUB

(☑020-8858 2909; www.trafalgartavern.co.uk; 6 Park Row, SE10; ⊗noon-11pm Mon-Thu, to midnight Fri & Sat, to 10.30pm Sun; 🚊DLR Cutty Sark) Lapped by the brown waters of the Thames, this elegant tavern with big windows looking onto the river is steeped in history. Dickens apparently knocked back a few here – and used it as the setting for the wedding breakfast scene in *Our Mutual Friend* – and prime ministers Gladstone and Disraeli used to dine on the pub's celebrated whitebait.

Ministry of Sound
CLUB

(Map p114; www.ministryofsound.com; 103 Gaunt St, SE1; admission £16-25; ⊗11pm-6.30am Fri & Sat; ⊜Elephant & Castle) This legendary club-cum-enormous-global-brand (four bars, four dance floors) lost some 'edge' in the early noughties but, after pumping in top DJs, the Ministry has firmly rejoined the top club ranks. Fridays is the Gallery trance night, while Saturday sessions offer the *crème de la crème* of house, electro and techno DJs.

☆ Entertainment

Theatre

London is a world capital for theatre and there's a lot more than mammoth musicals to tempt you into the West End. On performance days, you can buy half-price tickets for West End productions (cash only) from the official agency TKTS (Map p118; www. tkts.co.uk; Leicester Sq, WC2; ⊗10am-7pm Mon-Sat, noon-4pm Sun; ⊜Leicester Sq). The booth is the one with the clock tower; beware of touts selling dodgy tickets. For more, see www.officiallondontheatre.co.uk or www. theatremonkey.com.

National Theatre THEATRE
(Map p114; ☑020-7452 3000; www.nationaltheatre.org.uk; South Bank, SE1; ⊖Waterloo) England's flagship theatre showcases a mix of classic and contemporary plays performed by excellent casts in three theatres (Olivier, Lyttelton and Dorfman). Outstanding artistic director Nicholas Hytner (who stepped down in March 2015) oversaw a golden decade at the theatre, with landmark productions such as *War Horse*. There are also constant surprises in the program.

Royal Court Theatre THEATRE
(Map p122; ☑020-7565 5000; www.royalcourttheatre.com; Sloane Sq, SW1; ⊖Sloane Sq) Equally renowned for staging innovative new plays and old classics, the Royal Court is among London's most progressive theatres and has continued to foster major writing talent across the UK.

Tickets for concessions are £6 to £10, and £10 for everyone on Monday (four 10p standing tickets sold at the Jerwood Theatre Downstairs); tickets for under 26s are £8. Check the theatre's Facebook page for the lastest on cheap tickets.

Old Vic THEATRE
(Map p114; ☑0844 871 7628; www.oldvictheatre.com; The Cut, SE1; ⊖Waterloo) Never has there been a London theatre with a more famous artistic director. American actor Kevin Spacey took the theatrical helm in 2003, looking after this glorious theatre's program. The theatre does both new and classic plays, and its cast and directors are consistently high-profile.

Young Vic THEATRE
(Map p114; ☑020-7922 2922; www.youngvic.org; 66 The Cut, SE1; ⊖Waterloo, ⊖Southwark) This ground-breaking theatre is as much about showcasing and discovering new talent as it is about people discovering theatre. The Young Vic showcases actors, directors and plays from across the world, many of which tackle contemporary political or cultural issues such as the death penalty, racism or corruption, often blending dance and music with acting.

Donmar Warehouse THEATRE
(Map p118; ☑0844 871 7624; www.donmarwarehouse.com; 41 Earlham St, WC2; ⊖Covent Garden) The cosy Donmar Warehouse is London's 'thinking person's theatre'. The new artistic director, Josie Rourke, has staged some interesting and unusual productions such as the Restoration comedy *The Recruiting Officer*, by George Farquhar, and a restaging of Conor McPherson's *The Weir*.

Live Music
KOKO LIVE MUSIC
(www.koko.uk.com; 1a Camden High St, NW1; ⊙7-11pm Sun-Thu, to 4am Fri & Sat; ⊖Mornington Cres) Once the legendary Camden Palace, where Charlie Chaplin, the Goons and the Sex Pistols have all performed, KOKO is keeping its reputation as one of London's better gig venues. The theatre has a dance floor and decadent balconies, and attracts an indie crowd with Club NME on Friday. There are live bands almost every night of the week.

100 Club LIVE MUSIC
(Map p118; ☑020-7636 0933; www.the100club.co.uk; 100 Oxford St, W1; admission £8-20; ⊙check website for gig times; ⊖Oxford Circus, Tottenham Court Rd) This legendary London venue has always concentrated on jazz, but it's also spreading its wings to swing and rock. It once showcased Chris Barber, BB King and the Stones, and was at the centre of the punk revolution and the '90s indie scene. It hosts dancing swing gigs and local jazz musicians, as well as the occasional big name.

Roundhouse LIVE MUSIC
(www.roundhouse.org.uk; Chalk Farm Rd, NW1; ⊖Chalk Farm) The Roundhouse was once home to 1960s avant-garde theatre, then was a rock venue, then it fell into oblivion for a while before reopening a few years back. It holds great gigs and brilliant performances, from circus to stand-up comedy, poetry slam and improvisation sessions. The round shape of the building is unique and generally well used in the staging.

Ronnie Scott's JAZZ
(Map p118; ☑020-7439 0747; www.ronniescotts.co.uk; 47 Frith St, W1; ⊙7pm-3am Mon-Sat, to midnight Sun; ⊖Leicester Sq, Tottenham Court Rd) Ronnie Scott originally opened his jazz club on Gerrard St in 1959 under a Chinese gambling den. The club moved to its current location six years later and became widely known as Britain's best jazz club. Gigs are at 8.30pm (8pm Sunday) with a second one at 11.15pm Friday and Saturday, and are followed by a late show until 2am. Expect to pay between £20 and £50.

Comedy

Comedy Store
COMEDY

(Map p118; ☑0844 871 7699; www.thecomedy store.co.uk; 1a Oxendon St, SW1; admission £8-23.50; ⊖Piccadilly Circus) This was one of the first (and is still one of the best) comedy clubs in London. Wednesday and Sunday night's Comedy Store Players is the most famous improvisation outfit in town, with the wonderful Josie Lawrence; on Thursdays, Fridays and Saturdays Best in Stand Up features the best on London's comedy circuit.

Comedy Cafe
COMEDY

(Map p114; ☑020-7739 5706; www.comedycafe. co.uk; 68 Rivington St, EC2; admission free-£12; ⊙Wed-Sat; ⊖Old St) A major venue, the Comedy Cafe is purpose built for, well, comedy, hosting some good comedians. It can be a little too try-hard and wacky, but it's worth seeing the Wednesday night try-out spots for some wincing entertainment.

Soho Theatre
COMEDY

(Map p118; ☑020-7478 0100; www.sohotheatre. com; 21 Dean St, W1; admission £10-25; ⊖Tottenham Court Rd) The Soho Theatre has developed a superb reputation for showcasing new comedy-writing talent and comedians. It's also hosted some top-notch stand-up or sketch-based comedians including Alexei Sayle and Doctor Brown. Tickets cost between £10 and £20.

Classical Music, Opera & Dance

Royal Albert Hall
CONCERT VENUE

(Map p122; ☑020-7589 8212, 0845 401 5045; www.royalalberthall.com; Kensington Gore, SW7; ⊖South Kensington) This Victorian concert hall hosts classical-music, rock and other performances, but is most famously the venue for the BBC-sponsored Proms. Booking is possible, but from mid-July to mid-September Proms punters also queue for £5 standing (or 'promenading') tickets that go on sale one hour before curtain-up. Otherwise, the box office and prepaid tick-

---

ROLL OUT THE BARROW

London has more than 350 markets selling everything from antiques and curios to flowers and fish. Some, such as Camden and Portobello Road, are full of tourists, while others exist just for the locals.

Columbia Road Flower Market (Map p114; Columbia Rd, E2; ⊙8am-3pm Sun; ⊖Old St) A real explosion of colour and life, this weekly market sells a beautiful array of flowers, pot plants, bulbs, seeds and everything you might need for the garden. A lot of fun, even if you don't buy anything, the market gets really packed so go as early as you can, or later on, when the vendors sell off the cut flowers cheaply. It stretches from Gossett St to the Royal Oak pub.

Borough Market (Map p114; www.boroughmarket.org.uk; 8 Southwark St, SE1; ⊙11am-5pm Thu, noon-6pm Fri, 8am-5pm Sat; ⊖London Bridge) Located here in some form or another since the 13th century, 'London's Larder' has enjoyed an astonishing renaissance in the past decade. Always overflowing with food lovers, inveterate gastronomes, wide-eyed newcomers, guidebook-toting visitors and all types in between, this fantastic market has become firmly established as a sight in its own right.

Along with a section devoted to quality fresh fruit, exotic vegetables and organic meat, there's a fine-foods retail market, with the likes of home-grown honey and homemade bread plus loads of free samples. Throughout, takeaway stalls supply sizzling gourmet sausages, chorizo sandwiches and quality burgers in spades, filling the air with meaty aromas. Shoppers get queuing for cheeses at Neal's Yard Dairy, wait in line at the Monmouth Coffee Company and the Spanish deli Brindisa (www.brindisa.com), line up for takeaways at Roast, shop at butcher Ginger Pig and down pints of ale at Rake. The market simply heaves on Saturdays (get here early for the best pickings).

Camden Market (Camden High St, NW1; ⊙10am-6pm; ⊖Camden Town, Chalk Farm) Although, or perhaps because, it stopped being cutting-edge several thousand cheap leather jackets ago, Camden Market gets a whopping 10 million visitors each year and is one of London's most popular attractions. What started out as a collection of attractive craft stalls by Camden Lock on the Regent's Canal now extends most of the way from Camden Town tube station to Chalk Farm tube station.

et collection counter are both through door 12 (south side of the hall).

Barbican
PERFORMING ARTS
(Map p114; ☎020-7638 8891, 0845 121 6823; www.barbican.org.uk; Silk St, EC2; ⊜Barbican) Home to the wonderful London Symphony Orchestra and its associate orchestra, the lesser-known BBC Symphony Orchestra, the arts centre hosts scores of other leading musicians each year as well, focusing in particular on jazz, folk, world and soul artists. Dance is another strong point here.

Southbank Centre
CONCERT VENUE
(Map p114; ☎020-7960 4200; www.southbank centre.co.uk; Belvedere Rd, SE1; ⊜Waterloo) The Southbank Centre's overhauled **Royal Festival Hall** (Map p114; ☎020-7960 4242; www.southbankcentre.co.uk; admission £6-60; ⊜Waterloo) seats 3000 in a now-acoustic amphitheatre and is one of the best places for catching world and classical music artists. The sound is fantastic, the programming impeccable and there are frequent free gigs in the wonderfully expansive foyer. There are more eclectic gigs at the smaller **Queen Elizabeth Hall** (QEH; Map p114; ☎020-7960 4200; www.southbankcentre.co.uk; ⊕5-11.30pm daily; ⊜Waterloo) and **Purcell Room** (Map p114), including talks and debates, dance performances, poetry readings and so forth.

Royal Opera House
OPERA
(Map p118; ☎020-7304 4000; www.roh.org.uk; Bow St, WC2; tickets £7-250; ⊜Covent Garden) The £210 million redevelopment for the millennium gave classic opera a fantastic setting in London, and coming here for a night is a sumptuous – if pricey – affair. Although the program has been fluffed up by modern influences, the main attractions are still the opera and classical ballet – all are wonderful productions and feature world-class performers.

Sadler's Wells
DANCE
(Map p114; ☎0844 412 4300; www.sadlerswells.com; Rosebery Ave, EC1; tickets £10-49; ⊜Angel)

Portobello Road Market (www.portobellomarket.org; Portobello Rd, W10; ⊕8am-6.30pm Mon-Wed, Fri & Sat, to 1pm Thu; ⊜Notting Hill Gate, Ladbroke Grove) Portobello Road Market is an iconic London attraction with an eclectic mix of street food, fruit and veg, antiques, curios, collectibles, vibrant fashion and trinkets. Although the shops along Portobello Rd open daily and the fruit and veg stalls (from Elgin Cres to Talbot Rd) only close on Sunday, the busiest day by far is Saturday, when antique dealers set up shop (from Chepstow Villas to Elgin Cres).

Broadway Market (www.broadwaymarket.co.uk; London Fields, E8; ⊕9am-5pm Sat; ⊜Bethnal Green) There's been a market down this pretty street since the late 19th century, the focus of which has these days become artisan food, arty knick-knacks, books, records and vintage clothing. A great place on a Saturday, followed by a picnic at **London Fields** (www.hackney.gov.uk; ⊛; ⊠55, 277, ⊠London Fields) park.

Brixton Market (www.brixtonmarket.net; Electric Ave & Granville Arcade; ⊕8am-6pm Mon, Tue & Thu-Sat, 8am-3pm Wed; ⊜Brixton) A heady, cosmopolitan blend of silks, wigs, knock-off fashion, Halal butchers and the occasional Christian preacher on Electric Ave. Tilapia fish, pig's trotters, yams, mangoes, okra, plantains and Jamaican *bullah* cakes (gingerbread) are just some of the exotic products on sale.

Sunday UpMarket (Map p114; www.sundayupmarket.co.uk; Old Truman Brewery, Brick Lane, E1; ⊕10am-5pm Sun; ⊜Liverpool St) Market where young designers sell wonderful clothes, music and crafts, and the excellent food hall has worldwide grub, from Ethiopian vegie dishes to Japanese delicacies. If you've got the stamina, top it all off with a browse round Spitalfields.

Brick Lane Market (Map p114; www.visitbricklane.org; Brick Lane, E1; ⊕8am-2pm Sun; ⊜Liverpool St) Takes over a vast area with household goods, bric-a-brac, secondhand clothes and cheap fashion. You can even stop off and play carrom (similar to billiards).

Petticoat Lane Market (Map p114; Wentworth St & Middlesex St, E1; ⊕9am-2pm Sun-Fri; ⊜Aldgate) The famous lane itself has been renamed Middlesex St. The market, however, soldiers on, selling cheap consumer items and clothes.

The theatre site dates from 1683 but was completely rebuilt in 1998; today it is the most eclectic and modern dance venue in town, with experimental dance shows of all genres and from all corners of the globe. The Lilian Baylis Studio stages smaller productions.

Shopping

Department Stores

London's famous department stores are an attraction in themselves, even if you're not interested in buying.

Selfridges
DEPARTMENT STORE

(Map p122; www.selfridges.com; 400 Oxford St, W1; ⊙9.30am-9pm Mon-Sat, 11.30am-6.15pm Sun; ⊜Bond St) Selfridges loves innovation – it's famed for its inventive window displays by international artists, gala shows and, above all, its amazing range of products. It's the trendiest of London's one-stop shops, with labels such as Boudicca, Luella Bartley, Emma Cook, Chloé and Missoni; an unparalleled food hall; and Europe's largest cosmetics department.

Fortnum & Mason
DEPARTMENT STORE

(Map p118; www.fortnumandmason.com; 181 Piccadilly, W1; ⊙10am-9pm Mon-Sat, noon-6pm Sun; ⊜Piccadilly Circus) London's oldest grocery store, now into its fourth century, refuses to yield to modern times. Its staff are still dressed in old-fashioned tailcoats and it keeps its glamorous food hall supplied with hampers, cut marmalade, speciality teas and so on. Downstairs is an elegant wine bar as well as elegant kitchenware, luxury gifts and perfumes.

Liberty
DEPARTMENT STORE

(Map p118; www.liberty.co.uk; Great Marlborough St, W1; ⊙10am-8pm Mon-Sat, noon-6pm Sun; ⊜Oxford Circus) An irresistible blend of contemporary styles in an old-fashioned mock-Tudor atmosphere, Liberty has a huge cosmetics department and an accessories floor, along with a breathtaking lingerie section, all at very inflated prices. A classic London souvenir is a Liberty fabric print especially in the form of a scarf.

Harrods
DEPARTMENT STORE

(Map p122; www.harrods.com; 87 Brompton Rd, SW1; ⊙10am-8pm Mon-Sat, 11.30am-6pm Sun; ⊜Knightsbridge) Both garish and stylish at the same time, perennially crowded Harrods is an obligatory stop for London's tourists, from the cash strapped to the big, big spenders.

The stock is astonishing and you'll swoon over the spectacular food hall.

Harvey Nichols
DEPARTMENT STORE

(Map p122; www.harveynichols.com; 109-125 Knightsbridge, SW1; ⊙10am-8pm Mon-Sat, 11.30am-6pm Sun; ⊜Knightsbridge) At London's temple of high fashion, you'll find Chloé and Balenciaga bags, the city's best denim range, a massive make-up hall with exclusive lines, great jewellery and the fantastic restaurant, Fifth Floor.

Music

As befitting a global music capital, London has a wide range of music stores.

Ray's Jazz
MUSIC

(Map p118; www.foyles.co.uk; 2nd fl, 107 Charing Cross Rd, WC2; ⊙9.30am-9pm Mon-Sat, 11.30am-6pm Sun; ⊜Tottenham Court Rd) Quiet and serene with friendly and helpful staff, this shop on the 2nd floor of Foyles bookshop has one of the best jazz selections in London.

Rough Trade West
MUSIC

(☑020-7229 8541; www.roughtrade.com; 130 Talbot Rd, W11; ⊙10am-6.30pm Mon-Sat, 11am-5pm Sun; ⊜Ladbroke Grove) With its underground, alternative and vintage rarities, this home of the eponymous punk-music label remains a haven for vinyl junkies.

Bookshops

Foyles
BOOKS

(Map p118; www.foyles.co.uk; 107 Charing Cross Rd, WC2; ⊙9.30am-9pm Mon-Sat, 11.30am-6pm Sun; ⊜Tottenham Court Rd) This is London's most legendary bookshop, where you can bet on finding even the most obscure of titles. The lovely **cafe** is on the 1st floor where you'll also find **Grant & Cutler**, the UK's largest foreign-language bookseller. Ray's Jazz is up on the 2nd floor.

Daunt Books
BOOKS

(Map p122; www.dauntbooks.co.uk; 83 Marylebone High St, W1; ⊙9am-7.30pm Mon-Sat, 11am-6pm Sun; ⊜Baker St) An original Edwardian bookshop, with oak panels and gorgeous skylights, Daunt is one of London's loveliest travel bookshops. It has two floors and stocks general fiction and nonfiction titles as well.

ⓘ Information

City of London Information Centre (Map p114; www.visitthecity.co.uk; St Paul's Churchyard, EC4; ⊙9.30am-5.30pm Mon-Sat, 10am-4pm Sun; ⊜St Paul's) Tourist information, fast-track tickets to City attractions and guided walks (adult/child £6/4).

ⓘ Getting There & Away

BUS & COACH
The London terminus for long-distance buses (called 'coaches' in Britain) is **Victoria Coach Station** (164 Buckingham Palace Rd, SW1; ⓔVictoria).

TRAIN
Most of London's main-line rail terminals are linked by the Circle line on the tube.

Charing Cross Canterbury

Euston Manchester, Liverpool, Carlisle, Glasgow

King's Cross Cambridge, Hull, York, Newcastle, Edinburgh, Aberdeen

Liverpool Street Stansted airport (Express), Cambridge

London Bridge Gatwick airport, Brighton

Marylebone Birmingham

Paddington Heathrow airport (Express), Oxford, Bath, Bristol, Exeter, Plymouth, Cardiff

St Pancras Gatwick and Luton airports, Brighton, Nottingham, Sheffield, Leicester, Leeds, Paris Eurostar

Victoria Gatwick airport (Express), Brighton, Canterbury

Waterloo Windsor, Winchester, Exeter, Plymouth

ⓘ Getting Around

TO/FROM THE AIRPORTS
Gatwick
Main-line trains run every 15 minutes between Gatwick's South Terminal and Victoria (from £15, 37 minutes), hourly at night, or to/from St Pancras (from £10, 56 minutes) via London Bridge, City Thameslink, Blackfriars and Farringdon.

Gatwick Express (www.gatwickexpress.com; one way/return £19.90/34.90) trains run to/from Victoria every 15 minutes from 5am to 11.45pm (first/last train 3.30am/12.32am).

The **EasyBus** (www.easybus.co.uk; one way £10, return from £12) minibus service between Gatwick and Earl's Court (from 4.25am to 1am, about 1¼ hours, every 30 minutes) can cost as little as £2, depending on when you book. You're charged extra if you have more than one carry-on and one check-in bag.

Heathrow
The cheapest option from Heathrow is the Underground (tube). The Piccadilly line is accessible from every terminal (£5.70, one hour to central London, departing from Heathrow every five minutes from around 5am to 11.30pm).

Faster, and much more expensive, is the **Heathrow Express** (www.heathrowexpress.com; one way/return £21/34) train to Paddington station (15 minutes, every 15 minutes, 5.12am to 11.48pm). You can purchase tickets on board (£5 extra), from self-service machines (cash and credit cards accepted) at both stations, or online.

London City
The Docklands Light Railway (DLR) connects London City Airport to the tube network, taking 22 minutes to reach Bank station (£4.70). A black taxi costs around £30 to/from central London.

Luton
There are regular National Rail services from St Pancras (£13.90, 29 to 39 minutes) to Luton Airport Parkway station, where a shuttle bus (£1.60) will get you to the airport within 10 minutes. EasyBus minibuses head from Victoria, Earl's Court and Baker St to Luton (from £2 if booked in advance); allow 1½ hours, every 30 minutes. A taxi costs around £100 to £110.

Stansted
The **Stansted Express** (☏ 0845 850 0150; www.stanstedexpress.com) connects with Liverpool Street station (one way/return

ⓘ OYSTER CARD

The Oyster card is a smart card on which you can store credit towards 'prepay' fares, as well as Travelcards valid for periods from a day to a year. Oyster cards are valid across the entire public transport network in London. When entering a station, simply touch your card on a reader (they have a yellow circle with the image of an Oyster card on them) and then touch again on your way out. The system will deduct the appropriate amount of credit from your card. For bus journeys, you only need to touch once upon boarding.

The benefit is that fares for Oyster card users are lower than standard ones. If you make many journeys during the day, you will never pay more than the appropriate Travelcard (peak or off peak) once the daily 'price cap' has been reached.

Oyster cards can be bought (£5 refundable deposit required) and topped up at any Underground station, travel information centre or shop displaying the Oyster logo.

To get your deposit back along with any remaining credit, simply return your Oyster card at a ticket booth.

£23.40/33.20, 46 minutes, every 15 minutes, 6am to 12.30am).

EasyBus (p139) has services between Stansted and Baker St (1¼ hours, every 20 minutes). The Airbus A6 links with Victoria Coach Station (£11, allow 1¾ hours, at least every 30 minutes).

National Express (www.nationalexpress.com) runs buses to Stansted from Liverpool St station (£9 one way, 80 minutes, every 30 minutes).

BICYCLE

Central London is mostly flat, relatively compact and the traffic moves slowly – all of which makes it surprisingly good for cyclists. It can get terribly congested though, so you'll need to keep your wits about you – and lock your bike (including both wheels) securely.

Bikes can be hired from numerous self-service docking stations through **Barclays Cycle Hire Scheme** (☑ 0845 026 3630; www.tfl.gov.uk). The hire access fee is £2 for 24 hours or £10 per week. On top of that are the ride fees: the first 30 minutes is free (making the bikes perfect for short hops), or £1/4/6/15 for one hour/90 minutes/two hours/three hours.

CAR

Don't. London was recently rated Western Europe's second-most congested city (congratulations Brussels). In addition, you'll pay £10 per day congestion charge (7am to 6pm weekdays) simply to drive into central London. If you're hiring a car to continue your trip around Britain, take the tube or train to a major airport and pick it up from there.

PUBLIC TRANSPORT

London's public transport is excellent, with tubes, trains, buses and boats getting you wherever you need to go. **TFL** (www.tfl.gov.uk), the city's public transport provider, is the glue that binds the network together. Its website has a handy journey planner and information on all services, including taxis.

Boat

Thames Clippers (www.thamesclippers.com) runs regular commuter services between Embankment, Waterloo, Blackfriars, Bankside, London Bridge, Tower, Canary Wharf, Greenwich, North Greenwich and Woolwich piers (adult/child £6/3) from 7am to midnight (from 9.30am weekends).

Bus

Buses run regularly during the day, while less frequent night buses (prefixed with the letter 'N') wheel into action when the tube stops. Single-journey bus tickets (valid for two hours) cost £2.40 (£1.40 on Oyster, capped at £4.40 per day); a weekly pass is £20.20. Buses stop on request, so clearly signal the driver with an outstretched arm.

Underground & Docklands Light Railway

The tube extends its subterranean tentacles throughout London and into the surrounding counties, with services running every few minutes from roughly 5.30am to 12.30am (7am to 11.30pm Sunday). The Docklands Light Railway (DLR) links the City to Docklands, Greenwich and London City Airport.

Lines are colour-coded (red for the Central Line, yellow for the Circle Line, black for the Northern Line and so on). It helps to know the direction you're travelling in (ie northbound or southbound, eastbound or westbound) as well as the terminus of the line you're travelling on. If you get confused, don't worry, as copies of the tube's famous map are posted everywhere, showing how the 14 different routes intersect. Be warned, however – the distances between stations on the tube map aren't remotely to scale.

Single fares cost from £2.30/4.80 with/without an Oyster card.

TAXI

London's famous black cabs are available for hire when the yellow light above the windscreen is lit. Fares are metered, with flag fall of £2.40 and the additional rate dependent on time of day, distance travelled and taxi speed. A 1-mile trip will cost between £5.60 and £8.80.

Minicabs are a cheaper alternative to black cabs and will quote trip fares in advance. Only use drivers from proper agencies; licensed minicabs aren't allowed to tout for business or pick you up off the street without a booking.

 MAPS

There was a time when no Londoner would be without a pocket-sized *London A–Z* map-book. It's a great resource if you don't have a smartphone. You can buy them at newsstands and shops everywhere. For getting around the London Underground system (the tube), maps are free at underground stations.

Around London

'When you're tired of London, you're tired of life' said 18th-century Londoner Samuel Johnson. But he wasn't living in an age when too many days on the tube can leave you exhausted and grouchy. Luckily, the capital is surprisingly close to some excellent day trips; Windsor and Eton are two gems that are an easy train ride from the capital.

Windsor & Eton

POP 31,000

Dominated by the massive bulk and heavy influence of Windsor Castle, these twin towns have a rather surreal atmosphere, with the morning pomp and ceremony of the changing of the guards in Windsor and the sight of school boys dressed in formal tailcoats wandering the streets of Eton.

◉ Sights

★**Windsor Castle**   CASTLE, PALACE
(www.royalcollection.org.uk; Castle Hill; adult/child £19/11; ☉9.45am-5.15pm) The largest and oldest occupied fortress in the world, Windsor Castle is a majestic vision of battlements and towers. It's used for state occasions and is one of the Queen's principal residences; if she's at home, you'll see the Royal Standard flying from the Round Tower. Join a free guided tour (every half-hour) or take a multilingual audio tour of the lavish state rooms and beautiful chapels. Note, some sections may be off-limits on any given day if they're in use.

Eton College   NOTABLE BUILDING
(www.etoncollege.com) Eton is the largest and most famous public (meaning very private) school in England, and arguably the most enduring and illustrious symbol of England's class system. At the time of writing, it wasn't possible to visit the school due to building work, but check the visitors tab on its website to see whether tours have resumed.

❶ Information

Royal Windsor Information Centre (www.windsor.gov.uk; Old Booking Hall, Windsor Royal Shopping Arcade; ☉9.30am-5pm) Pick up a heritage walk brochure (50p).

❶ Getting There & Away

Trains from Windsor Central station on Thames St go to London Paddington (£9.80, 27 to 43 minutes), and from Windsor Riverside station to London Waterloo (£9.80, 56 minutes). Services run half-hourly from both stations.

Canterbury

POP 43,432

Canterbury tops the charts for English cathedral cities. Many consider the World Heritage-listed cathedral that dominates its centre

THE MAKING OF HARRY POTTER

Whether you're a fairweather fan or a full-on Pothead, this studio **tour** (☏0845 084 0900; www.wbstudiotour.co.uk; Studio Tour Dr, Leavesden; adult/child £31/24; ☉9am-9.30pm) is well worth the admittedly hefty admission price. You'll need to prebook your visit for an allocated timeslot and then allow two to three hours to do the complex justice. It starts with a short film before you're ushered through giant doors into the actual set of Hogwarts' Great Hall – the first of many 'wow' moments. You'll find the studio near Watford, northwest of London – shuttle buses run from Watford Junction station.

BRITAIN CANTERBURY

to be one of Europe's finest, and the town's narrow medieval alleyways, riverside gardens and ancient city walls are a joy to explore.

◉ Sights

★**Canterbury Cathedral**   CATHEDRAL
(www.canterbury-cathedral.org; adult/concession £10.50/9.50, tour adult/concession £5/4, audio tour adult/concession £4/3; ☉9am-5pm Mon-Sat, 12.30-2.30pm Sun) A rich repository of more than 1400 years of Christian history, the Church of England's mother ship is a truly extraordinary place with an absorbing history. This Gothic cathedral, the highlight of the city's World Heritage Sites, is southeast England's top tourist attraction as well as a place of worship. It's also the site of English history's most famous murder: Archbishop Thomas Beckett was done in here in 1170. Allow at least two hours to do the cathedral justice.

⌂ Sleeping

Arthouse B&B   B&B ££
(☏07976 725457; www.arthousebandb.com; 24 London Rd; r £75; ℗☎) A night at Canterbury's most laid-back digs, housed in a 19th-century fire station, is a bit like sleeping over at a really cool art student's pad. The theme is funky and eclectic, with furniture by local designers and artwork by the instantly likeable artist owners, who have a house-studio out back.

Kipp's Independent Hostel
HOSTEL £

(☑ 01227-786121; www.kipps-hostel.com; 40 Nunnery Fields; dm/s/d £19.50/28.50/57; @ 🛜) Occupying a red-brick town house in a quietish residential area less than a mile from the city centre, these superb backpacker digs enjoy a homely atmosphere, clean (though cramped) dorms and rave reviews.

✗ Eating & Drinking

Tiny Tim's Tearoom
CAFE £

(34 St Margaret's St; mains £7-9; ☺ 9.30am-5pm Tue-Sat, 10.30am-4pm Sun) Swish 1930s English tearoom offering hungry shoppers big breakfasts bursting with Kentish ingredients, and tiers of cakes, crumpets, cucumber sandwiches and scones plastered in clotted cream.

Goods Shed
MARKET, RESTAURANT ££

(www.thegoodsshed.co.uk; Station Rd West; mains £12-20; ☺ market 9am-7pm Tue-Sat, 10am-4pm Sun, restaurant 8am-9.30pm Tue-Sat, 9am-3pm Sun) Farmers market, food hall and fabulous restaurant rolled into one, this converted warehouse by the Canterbury West train station is a hit with everyone from self-caterers to sit-down gourmets.

The chunky wooden tables sit slightly above the market hubbub but in full view of its appetite-whetting stalls, and daily specials exploit the freshest farm goodies England has to offer.

ℹ Information

Tourist Office (☑ 01227-378100; www.canterbury.co.uk; 18 High St; ☺ 9am-5pm Mon-Wed, Fri & Sat, to 7pm Thu, 10am-5pm Sun) Located in the Beaney House of Art & Knowledge. Staff can help book accommodation, excursions and theatre tickets.

ℹ Getting There & Away

There are two train stations: Canterbury East for London Victoria and Dover; and Canterbury West for London's Charing Cross and St Pancras stations. Connections include Dover Priory (£8, 25 minutes, every 30 minutes), London St Pancras (£34, one hour, hourly) and London Victoria/Charing Cross (£28.40, 1¾ hours, two to three hourly).

Salisbury

POP 43,335

Centred on a majestic cathedral topped by the tallest spire in England, the gracious city

AVEBURY

While the tour buses usually head straight to Stonehenge, prehistoric purists make for **Avebury Stone Circle**. Though it lacks the dramatic trilithons ('gateways') of its sister site across the plain, Avebury is the largest stone circle in the world and a more rewarding place to visit simply because you can get closer to the giant boulders.

A large section of Avebury village is actually inside the circle, meaning you can sleep, or at least have lunch and a pint, inside the mystic ring.

To get here, buses 5, 6 and 96 run from Salisbury (1¾ hours, hourly Monday to Saturday, five on Sunday).

of Salisbury has been an important provincial city for more than 1000 years.

◉ Sights

★ Salisbury Cathedral
CATHEDRAL

(☑ 01722-555120; www.salisburycathedral.org.uk; Cathedral Close; requested donation adult/child £6.50/3; ☺ 9am-5pm Mon-Sat, noon-4pm Sun) England is endowed with countless stunning churches, but few can hold a candle to the grandeur and sheer spectacle of 13th-century Salisbury Cathedral. This early English Gothic–style structure has an elaborate exterior decorated with pointed arches and flying buttresses, and a sombre, austere interior designed to keep its congregation suitably pious. Its statuary and tombs are outstanding. Don't miss the daily tower tours and the cathedral's original, 13th-century copy of the Magna Carta. It's best experienced on a **Tower Tour** (adult/child £10/8; ☺ 1-5pm daily).

★ Salisbury Museum
MUSEUM

(☑ 01722-332151; www.salisburymuseum.org.uk; 65 Cathedral Close; adult/child £5/2; ☺ 10am-5pm Mon-Sat, plus noon-5pm Sun Jun-Sep) The hugely important archaeological finds here include the Stonehenge Archer: the bones of a man found in the ditch surrounding the stone circle – one of the arrows found alongside probably killed him. With gold coins dating from 100 BC and a Bronze Age gold necklace, it's a powerful introduction to Wiltshire's prehistory.

🛏 Sleeping & Eating

Salisbury YHA HOSTEL £
(☑ 0845 371 9537; www.yha.org.uk; Milford Hill; dm/d £18/28; P @ 🛜) A real gem: neat rooms in a rambling Victorian house, with a cafe-bar, laundry and dappled gardens, too.

★ St Ann's House BOUTIQUE B&B ££
(☑ 01722-335657; www.stannshouse.co.uk; 32 St Ann St; s £59-64, d £89-110; 🛜) The aromas wafting from breakfast may well spur you from your room: great coffee; baked peaches with raspberry, honey and almonds; poached eggs and Parma ham. Utter elegance reigns upstairs, where well-chosen antiques, warm colours and Turkish linen ensure a supremely comfortable stay.

Cloisters PUB ££
(www.cloisterspubsalisbury.co.uk; 83 Catherine St; mains £9-13; ⊘ 11am-3pm & 6-9pm Mon-Fri, 11am-9pm Sat & Sun) The building dates from 1350, it's been a pub since the 1600s and today improbably warped beams reinforce an age-old vibe. It's a convivial spot for tasty beef-and-ale pie, sausage and mash or fancier foods such as an impressive lamb shank slow-braised in red wine.

ℹ Information

Tourist Office (☑ 01722-342860; www.visit wiltshire.co.uk; Fish Row; ⊘ 9am-5pm Mon-Fri, 10am-4pm Sat, 10am-2pm Sun)

ℹ Getting There & Away

BUS
National Express services include Bath (£11, 1¼ hours, one daily), Bristol (£11, 2¼ hours, one daily) and London (£17, three hours, three daily) via Heathrow. Tour buses leave Salisbury for Stonehenge regularly.

TRAIN
Trains run half-hourly from London Waterloo (£38, 1¾ hours). Hourly connections include Bath (£10, one hour), Bristol (£11, 1¼ hours) and Exeter (£25, two hours).

Stonehenge

This compelling ring of monolithic stones has been attracting a steady stream of pilgrims, poets and philosophers for the last 5000 years and is easily Britain's most iconic archaeological site.

ℹ STONE CIRCLE ACCESS VISITS

Visitors to Stonehenge normally have to stay outside the stone circle. But on **Stone Circle Access Visits** (☑ 0870 333 0605; www.english-heritage.org.uk; adult/child £21/12.60) you get to wander round the core of the site, getting up-close views of the bluestones and trilithons. The walks take place in the evening or early morning, so the quieter atmosphere and the slanting sunlight add to the effect. Each visit only takes 26 people; to secure a place book at least two months in advance.

The landscape around **Stonehenge** (☑ 0870 333 1181; www.english-heritage.org.uk; adult/child incl visitor centre £14/8.30; ⊘ 9am-8pm Jun-Aug, 9.30am-7pm Apr, May & Sep, 9.30am-5pm Oct-Mar) is undergoing a long-overdue revamp, which should dramatically improve the experience of those visiting when it's completed. But even before the changes, and despite the huge numbers of tourists who traipse around the perimeter, Stonehenge still manages to be a mystical, ethereal place – a haunting echo from Britain's forgotten past, and a reminder of the people who once walked the many ceremonial avenues across Salisbury Plain.

Even more intriguingly, it's still one of Britain's great archaeological mysteries: despite countless theories about what the site was used for, ranging from a sacrificial centre to a celestial timepiece, no one knows for sure what drove prehistoric Britons to expend so much time and effort on its construction.

Stonehenge now operates by timed tickets, meaning if you want guaranteed entry you have to book in advance. If you're planning a high-season visit, it's best to secure your ticket well in advance.

ℹ Getting There & Around

BUS
There is no public transport to the site. The **Stonehenge Tour** (☑ 0845 072 7093; www. thestonehengetour.info; adult/child £26/16) leaves Salisbury's railway and bus stations half-hourly from June to August, and hourly from September to May.

TAXI
Taxis charge £40 to go to Stonehenge from Salisbury, wait for an hour and come back.

Bath

POP 90,144

Britain is littered with beautiful cities, but precious few can hold a candle to Bath, founded on top of a network of natural hot springs. Bath's heyday was during the 18th century, when local entrepreneur Ralph Allen and the father-and-son architects John Wood the Elder and Younger, turned this sleepy backwater into the toast of Georgian society, and constructed fabulous landmarks such as the Circus and Royal Crescent.

⊙ Sights

★Roman Baths   MUSEUM

(☎01225-477785; www.romanbaths.co.uk; Abbey Churchyard; adult/child/family £13.50/8.80/38; ⊗9am-6pm, to 9pm Jul & Aug) In typically ostentatious style, the Romans constructed a complex of bathhouses above Bath's three natural hot springs, which emerge at a steady 46°C (115°F). Situated alongside a temple dedicated to the healing goddess Sulis Minerva, the baths now form one of the best-preserved ancient Roman spas in the world, encircled by 18th- and 19th-century

Bath

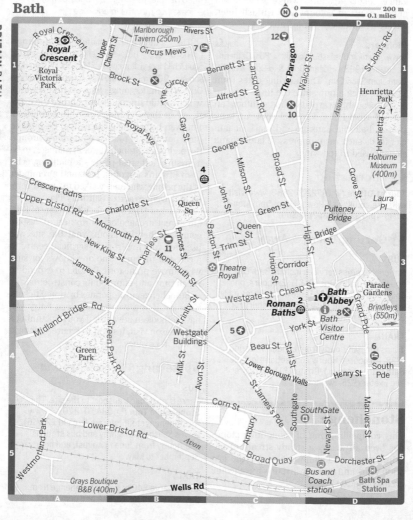

buildings. As Bath's premier attraction, the Roman Baths can get very, very busy. Avoid the worst crowds by buying tickets online, visiting early on a midweek morning, and avoiding July and August.

★ **Royal Crescent**   HISTORIC SITE
Bath is justifiably celebrated for its glorious Georgian architecture, and it doesn't get any grander than on Royal Crescent, a semicircular terrace of majestic town houses overlooking the green sweep of Royal Victoria Park. Designed by John Wood the Younger (1728–82) and built between 1767 and 1775, the houses appear perfectly symmetrical from the outside, but the owners were allowed to tweak the interiors to their own specifications; consequently no two houses on the Crescent are quite the same.

★ **Bath Abbey**   CHURCH
(☑ 01225-422462; www.bathabbey.org; requested donation £2.50; ☉ 9am-6pm Mon-Sat, 1-2.30pm & 4.30-5.30pm Sun) Looming above the city centre, Bath's huge abbey church was built between 1499 and 1616, making it the last great medieval church raised in England. Its most striking feature is the west facade, where angels climb up and down stone ladders, commemorating a dream of the founder, Bishop Oliver King. **Tower tours** (towertours@bathabbey.org; adult/child £6/3; ☉ 10am-5pm Apr-Aug, to 4pm Sep-Oct, 11am-4pm

Jan-Mar, to 3pm Nov & Dec) leave on the hour from Monday to Friday, or every half-hour on Saturdays, but don't run on Sundays.

Holburne Museum   GALLERY
(☑ 01225-388569; www.holburne.org; Great Pulteney St; ☉ 10am-5pm) FREE Sir William Holburne, the 18th-century aristocrat and art fanatic, amassed a huge collection that now forms the core of the Holburne Museum, in a lavish mansion at the end of Great Pulteney St. Fresh from a three-year refit, the museum houses a roll-call of works by artists including Turner, Stubbs, William Hoare and Thomas Gainsborough, as well as 18th-century majolica and porcelain. Temporary exhibitions incur a fee.

Jane Austen Centre   MUSEUM
(☑ 01225-443000; www.janeausten.co.uk; 40 Gay St; adult/child £8/4.50; ☉ 9.45am-5.30pm) Bath is known to many as a location in Jane Austen's novels, including *Persuasion* and *Northanger Abbey*. Though Austen only lived in Bath for five years from 1801 to 1806, she remained a regular visitor, and a keen student of the city's social scene. This museum houses memorabilia relating to the writer's life in Bath, and there's a Regency tearoom that serves crumpets and cream teas in suitably frilly surroundings.

⊨ Sleeping

Bath YHA   HOSTEL £
(☑ 0845 371 9303; www.yha.org.uk; Bathwick Hill; dm £13-20, d from £29; ☉ reception 7am-11pm; ℗ @ 🛜) Split across an Italianate mansion and a modern annexe, this impressive hostel is a steep climb (or a short hop on bus 18) from the city centre. The listed building means the rooms are huge, and some have period features such as cornicing and bay windows.

★ **Halcyon**   HOTEL £££
(☑ 01225-444100; www.thehalcyon.com; 2/3 South Pde; d £125-145; 🛜) Just what Bath needed: a smart city-centre hotel that doesn't break the bank. Situated on a terrace of townhouses off Manvers St, the Halcyon offers style on a budget: uncluttered rooms, contemporary bed linen and Philippe Starck bath fittings.

Rooms vary in size and are spread out over three floors – inconvenient as there's no lift. Self-catering apartments (£150 to £300 per night) are also available in a separate building at 15a George St.

THE THERMAE BATH SPA

Taking a dip in the Roman Baths might be off-limits, but you can still sample the city's curative waters at this fantastic modern **spa complex** (📞0844-888 0844; www.thermaebathspa.com; Bath St; ⏰9am-10pm, last entry 7.30pm), housed in a shell of local stone and plate glass. Tickets includes steam rooms, waterfall showers and a choice of two swimming pools. The showpiece attraction is the open-air rooftop pool, where you can bathe with a backdrop of Bath's cityscape – a don't-miss experience, best appreciated at dusk.

Grays Boutique B&B
B&B £££

(📞01225-403020; www.graysbath.co.uk; Upper Oldfield Park; d £120-195; 🛜) An elegant B&B straight out of an interiors magazine. All the rooms are individual: some with feminine flowers or polka-dot prints, others maritime stripes, but all simple and stylish (we particularly liked room 2, with its French bed and bay window). Breakfast is served in the conservatory, with eggs, milk and bacon from local farms.

The owners run a smaller but equally smart B&B on the east side of town, **Brindleys** (📞01225-310444; www.brindleysbath.co.uk; 14 Pulteney Gardens; d £110-185).

★Queensberry Hotel
HOTEL £££

(📞01225-447928; www.thequeensberry.co.uk; 4 Russell St; d £115-225; 🅿🛜) The quirky Queensberry is Bath's best boutique spoil. Four Georgian town houses have been combined into one seamlessly stylish whole. Some rooms are cosy in gingham checks and country creams, others feature bright upholstery, original fireplaces and free-standing tubs. The Olive Tree Restaurant is excellent, too. Rates exclude breakfast.

✖ Eating & Drinking

Sam's Kitchen Deli
CAFE £

(📞01225-481159; www.samskitchendeli.co.uk; 61 Walcot St; lunch £8-10; ⏰8am-5pm Mon-Sat, to 10pm every 2nd Fri) Situated on Bath's hippest street, Sam's is a perfect lunch spot, with set dishes (including a daily roast) served from pans on the counter. With its

dilapidated piano and reclaimed furniture, it's the epitome of a shabby-chic cafe, and very popular. There are live gigs every other Friday.

Café Retro
CAFE £

(📞01225-339347; 18 York St; mains £5-11; ⏰9am-5pm Mon-Sat, 10am-5pm Sun) A poke in the eye for the corporate coffee chains. The paint job's scruffy, the crockery's ancient and none of the furniture matches, but that's all part of the charm: this is a cafe from the old school, and there's nowhere better for burgers, butties (sandwiches) or cake. Takeaways (in biodegradable containers) are available from Retro-to-Go next door.

★Circus
MODERN BRITISH ££

(📞01225-466020; www.thecircuscafeandrestaurant.co.uk; 34 Brock St; mains lunch £8.30-13.50, dinner £16.50-18.50; ⏰10am-10pm Mon-Sat) Chef Ali Golden has turned this bistro into one of Bath's destination addresses. Her taste is for British dishes with a continental twist, à la Elizabeth David: rabbit, guinea-fowl, roast chicken, spring lamb, infused with herby flavours and rich sauces. It occupies the ground floor and basement of a town house near the Circus. Reservations recommended.

Marlborough Tavern
GASTROPUB ££

(📞01225-423731; www.marlborough-tavern.com; 35 Marlborough Bldgs; lunch £9-13, dinner mains £13.50-21.50; ⏰noon-11pm) The queen of Bath's gastropubs, with food that's closer to a fine-dining restaurant – think duo of venison and pork tenderloin rather than bog-standard meat-and-two-veg. Chunky wooden tables and racks of wine behind the bar give it an exclusive, classy feel.

★Colonna & Smalls
CAFE

(www.colonnaandsmalls.co.uk; 6 Chapel Row; ⏰8am-5.30pm Mon-Sat, 10am-4pm Sun) A connoisseur's coffeehouse. The espressos and cappuccinos are, quite simply, second to none – so if you care about your caffeine, you won't want to miss it. Proper coffee nuts can even take a barista training course.

★Star Inn
PUB

(www.star-inn-bath.co.uk; 23 The Vineyards, off The Paragon; ⏰noon-11pm) Not many pubs are registered relics, but the Star is – it still has many of its 19th-century bar fittings. It's the brewery tap for Bath-based Abbey Ales;

some ales are served in traditional jugs, and you can even ask for a pinch of snuff in the 'smaller bar'.

ℹ Information

Bath Visitor Centre (✆ 0906 711 2000, accommodation bookings 0844 847 5256; www.visit bath.co.uk; Abbey Churchyard; ⊙ 9.30am-5pm Mon-Sat, 10am-4pm Sun) Sells the **Bath Visitor Card** (http://visitbath.co.uk/special-offers/ bath-visitor-card; £3). The general enquiries line is charged at the premium rate of 50p per minute.

ℹ Getting There & Away

BUS

Bath's **bus and coach station** (Dorchester St; ⊙ 9am-5pm Mon-Sat) is near the train station. National Express coaches run directly to London (£17, 3½ hours, eight to 10 daily) via Heathrow.

TRAIN

Bath Spa station is at the end of Manvers St. Many services connect through Bristol (£7.10, 15 minutes, two or three per hour), especially to the north of England. Direct services include London Paddington/London Waterloo (£42, 1½ hours, half-hourly) and Salisbury (£16.90, one hour, hourly).

Oxford

POP 134,300

Oxford is a privileged place, one of the world's most famous university towns. The city is a wonderful place to ramble: the oldest of its 39 separate colleges dates back almost 750 years, and little has changed inside the hallowed walls since then (with the notable exception of female admissions, which only began in 1878).

◉ Sights

Not all Oxford's colleges are open to the public. Check www.ox.ac.uk/colleges for full details.

★ Ashmolean Museum

MUSEUM

(www.ashmolean.org; Beaumont St; ⊙ 10am-5pm Tue-Sun; 🅿) **FREE** Britain's oldest public museum, second in repute only to London's British Museum, was established in 1683 when Elias Ashmole presented the university with the collection of curiosities amassed by the well-travelled John Tradescant, gardener to Charles I. A 2009 makeover has left the museum with new interactive features, a giant atrium, glass walls revealing galleries on different levels and a beautiful rooftop restaurant.

★ Christ Church

COLLEGE

(www.chch.ox.ac.uk; St Aldate's; adult/child £8/6.50; ⊙ 10am-4.30pm Mon-Sat, 2-4.30pm Sun) The largest of all of Oxford's colleges and the one with the grandest quad, Christ Church is also its most popular. Its magnificent buildings, illustrious history and latter-day fame as a location for the Harry Potter films have tourists coming in droves. The college was founded in 1524 by Cardinal Thomas Wolsey, who suppressed the monastery existing on the site to acquire the funds for his lavish building project.

Magdalen College

COLLEGE

(www.magd.ox.ac.uk; High St; adult/child £5/4; ⊙ 1-6pm) Set amid 40 hectares of lawns, woodlands, river walks and deer park, Magdalen (*mawd*-lin), founded in 1458, is one of the wealthiest and most beautiful of Oxford's colleges. It has a reputation as an artistic college, and some of its famous

BRITAIN OXFORD

THE COTSWOLDS

Gorgeous villages built of honey-coloured stone, thatched cottages and atmospheric churches draw crowds of visitors to the Cotswolds. If you've ever coveted exposed beams or lusted after a cream tea in the afternoon, there's no finer place to fulfil your fantasies. This is prime tourist territory, however, and the most popular villages can be besieged by traffic in summer.

Travel by public transport requires careful planning and patience; for the most flexibility and the option of getting off the beaten track, your own car is unbeatable. Alternatively, the **Cotswolds Discoverer card** (1-/3-day bus pass £10/25, train pass £8.30/20) gives you unlimited travel on participating bus or train routes.

students have included writers Julian Barnes, Alan Hollinghurst, CS Lewis, John Betjeman, Seamus Heaney and Oscar Wilde, not to mention Edward VIII, TE Lawrence 'of Arabia' and Dudley Moore.

Merton College
COLLEGE

(www.merton.ox.ac.uk; Merton St; admission £3; ⊙ 2-5pm Mon-Fri, 10am-5pm Sat & Sun) Founded in 1264, Merton is the oldest of the three original colleges and the first to adopt collegiate planning, bringing scholars and tutors together into a formal community and providing a planned residence for them. Its distinguishing architectural features include large gargoyles whose expressions suggest that they're about to throw up, and the charming 14th-century **Mob Quad** – the first of the college quads.

Bodleian Library
LIBRARY

(✆ 01865-287400; www.bodley.ox.ac.uk; Catte St; tours £5-13; ⊙ 9am-5pm Mon-Sat, 11am-5pm Sun) Oxford's Bodleian Library is one of the oldest public libraries in the world and quite possibly the most impressive one you'll ever see. Casual visitors are welcome to wander around the central quad and visit the exhibition space in the foyer. For £1 you can also access the Divinity School, but the rest of the complex can only be visited on guided tours (check online or at the information desk for times; it pays to book ahead).

MESSING ABOUT ON THE RIVER
....

An unmissable Oxford experience, **punting** is all about sitting back and quaffing Pimms (the quintessential English summer drink) as you watch the city's glorious architecture float by. Which, of course, requires someone else to do the hard work – punting is far more difficult than it appears. If you decide to go it alone, a deposit is usually charged. Most punts hold five people including the punter. Hire them from **Magdalen Bridge Boathouse** (✆ 01865-202643; www.oxfordpunting. co.uk; High St; chauffered per 30min £25, self-punt per hour £20; ⊙ 9.30am-dusk Feb-Nov) or **Cherwell Boat House** (✆ 01865-515978; www.cherwellboathouse. co.uk; 50 Bardwell Rd; per hour £15-18; ⊙ 10am-dusk mid-Mar–mid-Oct).

Radcliffe Camera
LIBRARY

(Radcliffe Sq) The Radcliffe Camera is the quintessential Oxford landmark and one of the city's most photographed buildings. The spectacular circular library/reading room, filled with natural light, was built between 1737 and 1749 in grand Palladian style, and has Britain's third-largest dome. The only way to see the interior is to join one of the extended tours (£13, 90 minutes) of the Bodleian Library.

🛏 Sleeping

Central Backpackers
HOSTEL £

(✆ 01865-242288; www.centralbackpackers.co.uk; 13 Park End St; dm £22-28; @ 🛜) A friendly budget option located above a bar and right in the centre of town, this small hostel has basic, bright and simple rooms that sleep four to 12 people, a rooftop terrace and a small lounge with satellite TV.

★ Oxford Coach & Horses
B&B ££

(✆ 01865-200017; www.oxfordcoachandhorses. co.uk; 62 St Clements St; s/d from £115/130; 🅿 🛜) Once a coaching inn, this 18th-century building has been painted powder blue and given a fresh, modern makeover. Rooms are spacious and light-filled, and the ground floor has been converted into a large, attractive breakfast room.

Burlington House
B&B ££

(✆ 01865-513513; www.burlington-house.co.uk; 374 Banbury Rd, Summertown; s/d from £70/97; 🅿 🛜) Twelve big, bright and elegant rooms with patterned wallpaper and splashes of colour are available at this Victorian merchant's house. The fittings are luxurious and the bathrooms immaculate; the service is attentive; and breakfast comes complete with organic eggs and granola. It has good public transport links to town.

Remont Guesthouse
B&B ££

(✆ 01865-311020; www.remont-oxford.co.uk; 367 Banbury Rd, Summertown; r £112-142; 🅿 @ 🛜) All modern style, subtle lighting and plush furnishings, this 25-room guesthouse has rooms decked out in cool neutrals with silky bedspreads, abstract art and huge plasma-screen TVs. There's also a sunny garden.

🍴 Eating

★ Edamame
JAPANESE £

(www.edamame.co.uk; 15 Holywell St; mains £6-8; ⊙ 11.30am-2.30pm Wed-Sun, 5-8.30pm Thu-Sat) The queue out the door speaks volumes

GLASTONBURY

To many people, Glastonbury is synonymous with the **Glastonbury Festival of Contemporary Performing Arts** (www.glastonburyfestivals.co.uk), a majestic (and frequently mud-soaked) extravaganza of music, theatre, dance, cabaret, carnival, spirituality and general all-round weirdness that's been held on and off farmland in Pilton, just outside Glastonbury, for the last 40-something years (bar the occasional off-year to let the farm recover).

The town owes much of its spiritual fame to nearby **Glastonbury Tor** (NT; www.nationaltrust.org.uk/glastonbury-tor), a grassy hump about a mile from town, topped by the ruins of St Michael's Church. According to local legend, the tor is said to be the mythical Isle of Avalon, King Arthur's last resting place. It's also allegedly one of the world's great spiritual nodes, marking the meeting point of many mystical lines of power known as ley lines.

There is no train station in Glastonbury, but bus 376/377 runs to Wells (17 minutes, every 15 minutes) and Bristol (1½ hours, every half hour).

about the quality of food here. This tiny joint, all light wood and friendly bustle, is the best place in town for authentic Japanese cuisine. Arrive early and be prepared to wait.

★ **Rickety Press**   MODERN BRITISH ££
(☑ 01865-424581; www.thericketypress.com; 67 Cranham St; mains £13-17; ⊘ noon-2.30pm & 6-9.30pm) Hidden in the backstreets of Jericho, this old corner pub serves up beautifully presented, tasty food in casual surrounds. Call in for lunch or before 7pm for a great-value express menu (two/three courses £13/15).

Door 74   MODERN BRITISH ££
(☑ 01865-203374; www.door74.co.uk; 74 Cowley Rd; mains £10-14; ⊘ noon-3pm & 5-11pm Tue-Fri, 10am-11pm Sat, 11am-4pm Sun) This cosy little place woos its fans with a rich mix of British and Mediterranean flavours and friendly service. The menu is limited and the tables tightly packed, but the food is consistently good and weekend brunches (full English breakfast, pancakes etc) supremely filling. Book ahead.

Café Coco   MEDITERRANEAN ££
(☑ 01865-200232; www.cafecoco.co.uk; 23 Cowley Rd; breakfast £4-10, lunch £7-12; ⊘ 10am-midnight Thu-Sat, 10am-5pm Sun) This Cowley Rd institution is a popular brunching destination for the hip and hungry, and is decorated with classic posters on the walls and a bald plaster-cast clown in an ice bath. The menu ranges from cooked breakfasts and waffles to pizza, salads, Mediterranean mains and pecan pie.

 Drinking & Nightlife

★ **Bear Inn**   PUB
(www.bearoxford.co.uk; 6 Alfred St; ⊘ 11am-11pm; 🛜) Arguably Oxford's oldest pub (there's been a pub on this site since 1242), this atmospheric creaky place requires all but the most vertically challenged to duck their heads when passing through doorways. There's a curious tie collection on the walls and ceiling (though you can no longer exchange yours for a pint), and there are usually a couple of worthy guest ales.

Eagle & Child   PUB
(www.nicholsonspubs.co.uk/theeagleandchild oxford; 49 St Giles; ⊘ 11am-11pm; 🛜) Affectionately known as the 'Bird & Baby', this atmospheric place, dating from 1650, was once the favourite haunt of authors JRR Tolkien and CS Lewis. Its wood-panelled rooms and selection of real ales still attract a mellow crowd.

Turf Tavern   PUB
(www.theturftavern.co.uk; 4 Bath Pl; ⊘ 11am-11pm) Hidden down a narrow alleyway, this tiny medieval pub (dating from at least 1381) is one of the town's best loved; it's where US president Bill Clinton famously 'did not inhale'. Home to 11 real ales, it's always packed with a mix of students, professionals and lucky tourists who manage to find it. Plenty of outdoor seating.

 Information

Tourist Office (☑ 01865-252200; www.visitoxfordandoxfordshire.com; 15-16 Broad St; ⊘ 9.30am-5pm Mon-Sat, 10am-3.30pm Sun)

BLENHEIM PALACE

One of the country's greatest stately homes, **Blenheim Palace** (www.blenheimpalace. com; adult/child £22/12, park & gardens only £13/6.50; ⊙10.30am-5.30pm daily, closed Mon & Tue Nov–mid-Feb) is a monumental baroque fantasy designed by Sir John Vanbrugh and Nicholas Hawksmoor between 1705 and 1722. Now a Unesco World Heritage Site, it's home to the 11th Duke of Marlborough. Highlights include the **Great Hall**, a vast space topped by 20m-high ceilings adorned with images of the first duke in battle; the most important public room, the opulent **Saloon**; the three **state rooms** with their plush decor and priceless china cabinets; and the magnificent 55m **Long Library**. You can also visit the **Churchill Exhibition**, dedicated to the life, work and writings of Sir Winston, who was born at Blenheim in 1874.

Blenheim Palace is near the town of Woodstock, a few miles northwest of Oxford. To get there, Stagecoach bus S3 (£3.50, 35 minutes, every half hour, hourly on Sunday) runs from George St in Oxford.

ⓘ Getting There & Away

BUS

Oxford's main bus/coach station is at Gloucester Green, with frequent services to London (£14, 1¾ hours, every 15 minutes). There are also regular buses to/from Heathrow and Gatwick airports.

TRAIN

Oxford's train station has half-hourly services to London Paddington (£25, 1¼ hours) and roughly hourly trains to Birmingham (£27, 1¼ hours). Hourly services also run to Bath (£18, 1½ hours) and Bristol (£28, one to two hours), but require a change at Didcot Parkway.

Stratford-upon-Avon

POP 22,187

William Shakespeare was born in Stratford in 1564 and died here in 1616. The various buildings linked to his life form the centrepiece of a tourist attraction that verges on a cult of personality. Experiences range from the tacky (Bard-themed tearooms) to the humbling (Shakespeare's modest grave in Holy Trinity Church) and the sublime (a play by the world-famous Royal Shakespeare Company).

◉ Sights & Activities

★ Shakespeare's
Birthplace   HISTORIC BUILDING

(⌨ 01789-204016; www.shakespeare.org.uk; Henley St; incl Nash's House & New Place & Halls Croft £15.90/9.50; ⊙9am-5.30pm Jul-Sep, to 5pm Oct-Jun) Start your Shakespeare quest at the house where the world's most popular playwright supposedly spent his childhood days. In fact, the jury is still out on whether this really was Shakespeare's birthplace, but devotees of the Bard have been dropping in since at least the 19th century, leaving their signatures scratched onto the windows. Set behind a modern facade, the house has restored Tudor rooms, live presentations from famous Shakespearean characters, and an engaging exhibition on Stratford's favourite son.

Anne Hathaway's
Cottage   HISTORIC BUILDING

(⌨ 01789-204016; www.shakespeare.org.uk; Cottage Lane, Shottery; adult/child £9.50/5.50; ⊙9am-5pm mid-Mar–Oct) Before tying the knot with Shakespeare, Anne Hathaway lived in Shottery, a mile west of the centre of Stratford, in this delightful thatched farmhouse. As well as period furniture, it has gorgeous gardens and an orchard and arboretum, with examples of all the trees mentioned in Shakespeare's plays. A footpath (no bikes allowed) leads to Shottery from Evesham Pl.

Holy Trinity Church   CHURCH

(⌨ 01789-266316; www.stratford-upon-avon.org; Old Town; Shakespeare's grave adult/child £2/1; ⊙8.30am-6pm Mon-Sat, 12.30-5pm Sun Apr-Sep, reduced hours Oct-Mar) The final resting place of the Bard is said to be the most visited parish church in all of England. Inside are handsome 16th- and 17th-century tombs (particularly in the Clopton Chapel), some fabulous carvings on the choir stalls and, of course, the grave of William Shakespeare, with its ominous epitaph: 'cvrst be he yt moves my bones'.

🛏 Sleeping

Stratford-upon-Avon YHA
HOSTEL £

(☑ 0845 371 9661; www.yha.org.uk; Hemmingford House, Alveston; dm/d from £19/40; P @ 🛜) Set in a large 200-year-old mansion, 1.5 miles east of the town centre along Tiddington Rd, this superior hostel attracts travellers of all ages. Of its 32 rooms and dorms, 16 are en suite. There's a canteen, bar and kitchen. Buses 18 and 18A run here from Bridge St. Wi-fi is available in common areas.

Legacy Falcon
HOTEL ££

(☑ 0844 411 9005; www.legacy-hotels.co.uk; Chapel St; d/f from £83/113; P 🛜) Definitely request a room in the original 15th-century building, not the soulless modern annexe or dingy 17th-century garden house of this epicentral hotel. This way you'll get the full Tudor experience – creaky floorboards, wonky timbered walls and all. Open fires blaze in the wi-fi'd public areas; rooms have wired broadband but the best asset is the unheard-of-for-Stratford free car park.

White Sails
GUESTHOUSE ££

(☑ 01789-550469; www.white-sails.co.uk; 85 Evesham Rd; d from £100; ❄) Plush fabrics, framed prints, brass bedsteads and shabby-chic tables and lamps set the scene at this gorgeous and intimate guesthouse on the edge of the countryside. The four individually furnished rooms come with flatscreen TVs, climate control and glamorous bathrooms.

🍴 Eating & Drinking

Sheep St is clustered with eating options, mostly aimed at theatregoers (look out for good-value pretheatre menus).

Fourteas
TEAROOM £

(☑ 01789-293908; www.thefourteas.co.uk; 24 Sheep St; dishes £3-7, afternoon tea with/without Prosecco £17/12.50; ⊙ 9.30am-5pm Mon-Fri, 9am-5.30pm Sat, 11am-4pm Sun) Breaking with Stratford's Shakespearian theme, this tearoom takes the 1940s as its inspiration with beautiful old teapots, framed posters and staff in period costume. As well as premium loose-leaf teas and homemade cakes, there are hearty breakfasts, delicious sandwiches (fresh poached salmon, brie and grape), a hot dish of the day and indulgent afternoon teas.

Edward Moon's
MODERN BRITISH ££

(☑ 01789-267069; www.edwardmoon.com; 9 Chapel St; mains £10-18; ⊙ 12.30-3pm & 5-10pm Mon-Fri, noon-10pm Sat & Sun) Named after a famous travelling chef who cooked up the flavours of home for the British colonial service, this snug eatery serves delicious, hearty English dishes, many livened up with herbs and spices from the East.

★ Old Thatch Tavern
PUB

(http://oldthatchtavernstratford.co.uk; Greenhill St; ⊙ 11.30am-11pm Mon-Sat, noon-6pm Sun; 🛜) To truly appreciate Stratford's olde-worlde atmosphere, join the locals for a pint at the town's oldest pub. Built in 1470, this thatched-roofed, low-ceilinged treasure has great real ales and a gorgeous summertime courtyard.

Dirty Duck
PUB

(Black Swan; Waterside; ⊙ 11am-11pm Mon-Sat, to 10.30pm Sun) Also called the 'Black Swan', this enchanting riverside alehouse is the only pub in England to be licensed under two names. It's a favourite thespian watering hole, with a roll-call of former regulars (Olivier, Attenborough et al) that reads like a who's who of actors.

☆ Entertainment

★ Royal Shakespeare Company
THEATRE

(RSC; ☑ 0844 800 1110; www.rsc.org.uk; Waterside; tickets £10-62.50) Coming to Stratford without seeing a Shakespeare production would be like visiting Beijing and bypassing the Great Wall. The three theatre spaces run by the world-renowned Royal Shakespeare Company have witnessed performances by such legends as Lawrence Olivier, Richard Burton, Judi Dench, Helen Mirren, Ian McKellan and Patrick Stewart.

> ### ⓘ SHAKESPEARE HISTORIC HOMES
>
> Five of the most important buildings associated with Shakespeare contain museums that form the core of the visitor experience at Stratford. All are run by the Shakespeare Birthplace Trust (www.shakespeare.org.uk).
>
> Tickets for the three houses in town: **Shakespeare's Birthplace**, **Nash's House & New Place** and **Halls Croft** cost adult/child £15.90/9.50. If you also visit **Anne Hathaway's Cottage** and **Mary Arden's Farm**, buy a combination ticket covering all five properties (adult/child £23.90/14).

WORTH A TRIP

WARWICK

Regularly namechecked by Shakespeare, the town of Warwick is a treasure-house of medieval architecture. It is dominated by the soaring turrets of **Warwick Castle** (☑ 0871 265 2000; www.warwick-castle.com; castle adult/child £22.80/16.80, castle & dungeon £28.80/24, Kingdom Ticket incl castle, dungeon & exhibition £30.60/27; ☉ 10am-6pm Apr-Sep, to 5pm Oct-Mar; Ⓟ), founded in 1068 by William the Conqueror, and later the ancestral home of the Earls of Warwick. It's now been transformed into a major tourist attraction by the owners of Madame Tussauds, with kid-centred activities and waxworks populating the private apartments.

Stagecoach buses 16 and X18 go to Stratford-upon-Avon (£5.40, 40 minutes, half-hourly). Trains run to Birmingham (£7.50, 40 minutes, half-hourly), Stratford-upon-Avon (£5.40, 30 minutes, hourly) and London (£28.80, 1½ hours, every 20 minutes).

Stratford has two grand stages – **the Royal Shakespeare Theatre** and the **Swan Theatre** on Waterside – as well as the smaller **Courtyard Theatre** (☑ 0844 800 1110; www.rsc.org.uk; Southern Lane). Contact the RSC for the latest news on performance times. There are often special deals for under 25-year-olds, students and seniors, and a few tickets are held back for sale on the day of the performance, but get snapped up fast. Book well ahead.

ⓘ Information

Tourist Office (☑ 01789-264293; www.shakespeare-country.co.uk; Bridge Foot; ☉ 9am-5.30pm Mon-Sat, 10am-4pm Sun) Just west of Clopton Bridge on the corner with Bridgeway.

ⓘ Getting There & Away

BUS

National Express coaches and other bus companies run from Stratford's Riverside bus station (behind the Stratford Leisure Centre on Bridgeway). Destinations include Birmingham (£8.40, one hour, twice daily), London Victoria (£17, three hours, three daily) and Oxford (£10.70, one hour, twice daily). Bus 16 runs to Warwick (£5.40, 40 minutes, half-hourly).

TRAIN

From Stratford train station, trains run to Birmingham (£7.30, 50 minutes, half-hourly) and London Marylebone (£9, two hours, up to two per hour).

Cambridge

POP 123,900

Abounding with exquisite architecture, oozing history and tradition, and renowned for its quirky rituals, Cambridge is a university town extraordinaire. The tightly packed core of ancient colleges, the picturesque 'Backs' (college gardens) leading on to the river and the leafy green meadows that surround the city give it a far more tranquil appeal than its historic rival Oxford.

◉ Sights

Cambridge University comprises 31 colleges, though not all are open to the public. Opening hours are only a rough guide, so contact the colleges or the tourist office for more information.

★**King's College Chapel**   CHAPEL

(☑ 01223-331212; www.kings.cam.ac.uk/chapel; King's Pde; adult/child £7.50/free; ☉ non-term 9.45am-4.30pm, term 9.45am-3.15pm Mon-Sat, 1.15-2.30pm Sun) In a city crammed with show-stopping buildings, this is the scene-stealer. Grandiose, 16th-century King's College Chapel is one of England's most extraordinary examples of Gothic architecture. Its inspirational, intricate 80m-long, fan-vaulted ceiling is the world's largest and soars upwards before exploding into a series of stone fireworks. This hugely atmospheric space is a fitting stage for the chapel's world-famous choir; hear it in full voice during the magnificent, free, evensong (in term time only – 5.30pm Monday to Saturday, 10.30am and 3.30pm Sunday).

★**Trinity College**   COLLEGE

(www.trin.cam.ac.uk; Trinity St; adult/child £2/1; ☉ 10am-4.30pm, closed early Apr–mid-Jun) The largest of Cambridge's colleges, Trinity offers an extraordinary Tudor gateway, an air of supreme elegance and a sweeping Great Court – the largest of its kind in the world. It also boasts the renowned and suitably musty **Wren Library** (☉ noon-2pm Mon-Fri), containing 55,000 books dated before 1820 and more than 2500 manuscripts. Works include those by Shakespeare, St Jerome,

Newton and Swift – and AA Milne's original *Winnie the Pooh;* both Milne and his son, Christopher Robin, were graduates.

The Backs   PARK
Behind the Cambridge colleges' grandiose facades and stately courts, a series of gardens and parks line up beside the river. Collectively known as the Backs, the tranquil green spaces and shimmering waters offer unparalleled views of the colleges and are often the most enduring image of Cambridge for visitors. The picture-postcard snapshots of college life and graceful bridges can be seen from the riverside pathways and pedestrian bridges – or the comfort of a chauffeur-driven punt.

Fitzwilliam Museum   MUSEUM
(www.fitzmuseum.cam.ac.uk; Trumpington St; donation requested; ⊙10am-5pm Tue-Sat, noon-5pm Sun) [FREE] Fondly dubbed 'the Fitz' by locals, this colossal neoclassical pile was one of the first public art museums in Britain, built to house the fabulous treasures that the seventh Viscount Fitzwilliam bequeathed to his old university. Expect Roman and Egyptian grave goods, artworks by many of the great masters and some more quirky collections: banknotes, literary autographs, watches and armour.

🛏 Sleeping

Cambridge YHA   HOSTEL £
(☑0845 371 9728; www.yha.org.uk; 97 Tenison Rd; dm/d £21/30; @⊙) Busy, recently renovated, popular hostel with compact dorms and good facilities near the railway station.

Cambridge Rooms   B&B ££
(www.universityrooms.com/en/city/cambridge/home; s/d from £45/75) For an authentic taste of university life check into a student room in one of a range of colleges. Accommodation varies from functional singles (with shared bathroom) overlooking college courts to more modern, en suite rooms in nearby annexes. Breakfast is often in the hall (the students' dining room).

Worth House   B&B ££
(☑01223-316074; www.worth-house.co.uk; 152 Chesterton Rd; s £65-75, d £65-100; P⊙) The welcome is wonderfully warm, the great-value rooms utterly delightful. Soft grey and cream meets candy-stripe reds, fancy bathrooms boast claw-footed baths and tea trays are full of treats. There's also a three-person,

self-catering apartment (per week £550) two doors down.

✕ Eating & Drinking

Fitzbillies   BAKERY, CAFE £
(www.fitzbillies.com; 52 Trumpington St; cafe mains £6-16; ⊙8am-5pm Mon-Wed, 9am-9.30pm Thu-Sat, 10am-5pm Sun) Cambridge's oldest bakery has a soft, doughy place in the hearts of generations of students, thanks to its ultrasticky Chelsea buns and other sweet treats. Pick up a bag-full to take away or munch in comfort in the quaint cafe next door.

Oak   BISTRO ££
(☑01223-323361; www.theoakbistro.co.uk; 6 Lensfield Rd; mains £12-20; set lunch 2/3 courses £13/16; ⊙noon-2.30pm & 6-9.30pm Mon-Sat) Truffles (white and black), olive pesto and rosemary jus are the kind of flavour intensifiers you'll find at this friendly but classy neighbourhood eatery where locally sourced duck, fish and beef come cooked just so. The set lunch is a bargain.

Chop House   BRITISH ££
(www.cambscuisine.com/cambridge-chop-house; 1 Kings Pde; mains £14-20; ⊙noon-10.30pm Mon-Sat, to 9.30pm Sun) The window seats here deliver some of the best views in town – onto King's College's hallowed walls. The food is pure English establishment too: hearty steaks and chops and chips, plus a scattering of fish dishes and suet puds. Sister restaurant **St John's Chop House** (21-24 Northampton St) sits near the rear entrance to St John's College.

Newton and Swift – and AA Milne's original *Winnie the Pooh;* both Milne and his son, Christopher Robin, were graduates.

Newton and Swift – and AA Milne's original *Winnie the Pooh;* both Milne and his son, Christopher Robin, were graduates.

The Backs   PARK
Behind the Cambridge colleges' grandiose facades and stately courts, a series of gardens and parks line up beside the river. Collectively known as the Backs, the tranquil green spaces and shimmering waters offer unparalleled views of the colleges and are often the most enduring image of Cambridge for visitors. The picture-postcard snapshots of college life and graceful bridges can be seen from the riverside pathways and pedestrian bridges – or the comfort of a chauffeur-driven punt.

Fitzwilliam Museum   MUSEUM
(www.fitzmuseum.cam.ac.uk; Trumpington St; donation requested; ⊙10am-5pm Tue-Sat, noon-5pm Sun) [FREE] Fondly dubbed 'the Fitz' by locals, this colossal neoclassical pile was one of the first public art museums in Britain, built to house the fabulous treasures that the seventh Viscount Fitzwilliam bequeathed to his old university. Expect Roman and Egyptian grave goods, artworks by many of the great masters and some more quirky collections: banknotes, literary autographs, watches and armour.

🛏 Sleeping

Cambridge YHA   HOSTEL £
(☑0845 371 9728; www.yha.org.uk; 97 Tenison Rd; dm/d £21/30; @⊙) Busy, recently renovated, popular hostel with compact dorms and good facilities near the railway station.

Cambridge Rooms   B&B ££
(www.universityrooms.com/en/city/cambridge/home; s/d from £45/75) For an authentic taste of university life check into a student room in one of a range of colleges. Accommodation varies from functional singles (with shared bathroom) overlooking college courts to more modern, en suite rooms in nearby annexes. Breakfast is often in the hall (the students' dining room).

Worth House   B&B ££
(☑01223-316074; www.worth-house.co.uk; 152 Chesterton Rd; s £65-75, d £65-100; P⊙) The welcome is wonderfully warm, the great-value rooms utterly delightful. Soft grey and cream meets candy-stripe reds, fancy bathrooms boast claw-footed baths and tea trays are full of treats. There's also a three-person,

self-catering apartment (per week £550) two doors down.

✕ Eating & Drinking

Fitzbillies   BAKERY, CAFE £
(www.fitzbillies.com; 52 Trumpington St; cafe mains £6-16; ⊙8am-5pm Mon-Wed, 9am-9.30pm Thu-Sat, 10am-5pm Sun) Cambridge's oldest bakery has a soft, doughy place in the hearts of generations of students, thanks to its ultrasticky Chelsea buns and other sweet treats. Pick up a bag-full to take away or munch in comfort in the quaint cafe next door.

Oak   BISTRO ££
(☑01223-323361; www.theoakbistro.co.uk; 6 Lensfield Rd; mains £12-20; set lunch 2/3 courses £13/16; ⊙noon-2.30pm & 6-9.30pm Mon-Sat) Truffles (white and black), olive pesto and rosemary jus are the kind of flavour intensifiers you'll find at this friendly but classy neighbourhood eatery where locally sourced duck, fish and beef come cooked just so. The set lunch is a bargain.

Chop House   BRITISH ££
(www.cambscuisine.com/cambridge-chop-house; 1 Kings Pde; mains £14-20; ⊙noon-10.30pm Mon-Sat, to 9.30pm Sun) The window seats here deliver some of the best views in town – onto King's College's hallowed walls. The food is pure English establishment too: hearty steaks and chops and chips, plus a scattering of fish dishes and suet puds. Sister restaurant **St John's Chop House** (21-24 Northampton St) sits near the rear entrance to St John's College.

★**Midsummer House**   MODERN BRITISH £££
(☑ 01223-369299; www.midsummerhouse.co.uk;
Midsummer Common; 5/7/10 courses £45/75/95;
⊘ noon-1.30pm Wed-Sat, 7-9pm Tue-Sat) At the
region's top tables chef Daniel Clifford's
double Michelin-starred creations are
distinguished by depth of flavour and immense technical skill. Sample braised oxtail,
coal-baked celeriac and scallops with truffle before dollops of dark chocolate, blood
orange and marmalade ice cream. Wine
flights start at £55.

Eagle   PUB
(www.gkpubs.co.uk; Benet St; ⊘ 9am-11pm Mon-
Sat, to 10.30pm Sun) Cambridge's most famous
pub has loosened the tongues and pickled
the grey cells of many an illustrious academic – among them Nobel Prize–winning
scientists Crick and Watson, who discussed
their research into DNA here (note the
blue plaque by the door). Fifteenth-century,
wood-panelled and rambling, its cosy rooms
include one with WWII airmens' signatures
on the ceiling. The food, served all day, is
good, too.

ℹ Information

Tourist Office (☑ 0871 226 8006; www.
visitcambridge.org; Peas Hill; ⊘ 10am-5pm
Mon-Sat, plus 11am-3pm Sun Apr-Oct)

ℹ Getting There & Away

BUS
From Parkside there are regular **National
Express** (www.nationalexpress.com) buses to
London Gatwick airport (£20, 4½ hours, hourly),
Heathrow airport (£17, four hours, hourly) and
Oxford (£15, 3½ hours, every 30 minutes).

TRAIN
The train station is off Station Rd, which is off
Hills Rd. Destinations include London Kings
Cross (£18, one hour, two to four per hour) and
Stansted airport (£15, 30 minutes to 1¼ hours,
two per hour).

York

POP 181,100

Nowhere in northern England says 'medieval' quite like York, a city of extraordinary
historical wealth that has lost little of its pre-
industrial lustre. Its spider's web of narrow
streets is enclosed by a magnificent circuit of
13th-century walls and the city's rich heritage
is woven into virtually every brick and beam.

◉ Sights

★**York Minster**   CHURCH
(www.yorkminster.org; Deangate; adult/child £10/
free, combined ticket incl tower £15/5; ⊘ 9am-
5.30pm Mon-Sat, 12.45-5.30pm Sun, last admission
5pm) The remarkable York Minster is the
largest medieval cathedral in all of Northern
Europe, and one of the world's most beautiful Gothic buildings. Seat of the archbishop
of York, primate of England, it is second in
importance only to Canterbury, seat of the
primate of *all* England – the separate titles
were created to settle a debate over the true
centre of the English church. If this is the
only cathedral you visit in England, you'll
still walk away satisfied.

★**Jorvik Viking Centre**   MUSEUM
(www.jorvik-viking-centre.co.uk;   Coppergate;
adult/child £9.95/6.95; ⊘ 10am-5pm Apr-Oct, to
4pm Nov-Mar) Interactive multimedia exhibits aimed at bringing history to life often
achieve exactly the opposite, but the much-
hyped Jorvik manages to pull it off with
aplomb. It's a smells-and-all reconstruction of the Viking settlement unearthed
here during excavations in the late 1970s,
brought to you courtesy of a 'time-car'
monorail that transports you through 9th-
century Jorvik. You can reduce time waiting
in the queue by booking your tickets online
and choosing the time you want to visit (£1
extra).

★**City Walls**   ARCHAEOLOGICAL SITE
(⊘ 8am-dusk) **FREE** If the weather's good,
don't miss the chance to walk the City Walls,
which follow the line of the original Roman
walls and give a whole new perspective on
the city. Allow 1½ to two hours for the full
circuit of 4.5 miles or, if you're pushed for
time, the short stretch from **Bootham Bar**
to **Monk Bar** is worth doing for the views
of the minster.

★**National Railway
Museum**   MUSEUM
(www.nrm.org.uk;   Leeman Rd; ⊘ 10am-6pm;
P ♿) **FREE** While many railway museums
are the sole preserve of lone men in anoraks
comparing dog-eared notebooks and getting high on the smell of machine oil, coal
smoke and nostalgia, this place is different.
York's National Railway Museum – the biggest in the world, with more than 100 locomotives – is so well presented and crammed
with fascinating stuff that it's interesting
even to folk whose eyes don't mist over at

the thought of a 4-6-2 A1 Pacific class thundering into a tunnel.

Yorkshire Museum
MUSEUM

(www.yorkshiremuseum.org.uk; Museum St; adult/child £7.50/free; ⊙10am-5pm) Most of York's Roman archaeology is hidden beneath the medieval city, so the recently revamped displays in the Yorkshire Museum are invaluable if you want to get an idea of what Eboracum was like. There are maps and models of Roman York, funerary monuments, mosaic floors and wall paintings, and a 4th-century bust of Emperor Constantine.

Shambles
STREET

The Shambles takes its name from the Saxon word *shamel,* meaning 'slaughterhouse' – in 1862 there were 26 butcher shops on this street. Today the butchers are long gone, but this narrow cobbled lane, lined with 15th-century Tudor buildings that overhang so much they seem to meet above your head, is the most picturesque in Britain, and one of the most visited in Europe, often crammed with visitors intent on buying a tacky souvenir before rushing back to the tour bus.

☞ Tours

Ghost Hunt of York
WALKING

(www.ghosthunt.co.uk; adult/child £5/3; ⊙tours 7.30pm) The kids will just love this award-winning and highly entertaining 75-minute tour laced with authentic ghost stories. It begins at the Shambles, whatever the weather (it's never cancelled) and there's no need to book: just turn up and wait till you hear the handbell ringing...

Yorkwalk
WALKING

(www.yorkwalk.co.uk; adult/child £6/5; ⊙tours 10.30am & 2.15pm Feb-Nov) Offers a series of two-hour walks on a range of themes, from the classics – Roman York, the snickelways (narrow alleys) and City Walls – to walks focused on chocolates and sweets, women in York, and the inevitable graveyard, coffin and plague tour. Walks depart from Museum Gardens Gate on Museum St; there's no need to book.

🛏 Sleeping

Despite the inflated prices of the high season, it is still tough to find a bed during midsummer.

★ Fort
HOSTEL £

(☎01904-620222; www.thefortyork.co.uk; 1 Little Stonegate; dm from £22, d from £68; 🛜) This new boutique hostel showcases the work of young British designers, creating affordable accommodation with a dash of character and flair. There are six- and eight-bed dorms, along with half a dozen doubles, but don't expect a peaceful retreat – the central location is in the middle of York's nightlife, and there's a lively club downstairs (earplugs are provided!).

York YHA
HOSTEL £

(☎0845 371 9051; www.yha.org.uk; 42 Water End, Clifton; dm/q from £21/99; P@🛜) Originally the Rowntree (Quaker confectioners) mansion, this handsome Victorian house makes a spacious and child-friendly youth hostel, with most of its rooms four-bed dorms. Often busy, so book early. It's about a mile northwest of the city centre; there's a riverside footpath from Lendal Bridge (poorly lit, so avoid after dark). Alternatively, take bus 2 from the train station or Museum St.

Abbeyfields
B&B ££

(☎01904-636471; www.abbeyfields.co.uk; 19 Bootham Tce; s/d from £55/84; 🛜) 🍳 Expect a warm welcome and thoughtfully arranged bedrooms here, with chairs and bedside lamps for comfortable reading. Breakfasts are among the best in town, with sausage and bacon from the local butcher, freshly laid eggs from a nearby farm and the aroma of newly baked bread.

Elliotts B&B
B&B ££

(☎01904-623333; www.elliottshotel.co.uk; 2 Sycamore Pl; s/d from £55/75; P@🛜) A beautifully converted 'gentleman's residence', Elliotts leans towards the boutique end of the guesthouse market, with stylish and elegant rooms and some designer touches such as contemporary art and colourful textiles. An excellent location, both quiet and central.

ℹ YORK PASS

If you plan on visiting a lot of sights, you can save yourself some money by using a **York Pass** (www.yorkpass.com; 1/2/3 days adult £36/48/58, child £20/24/28). It grants you free access to more than 70 pay-to-visit sights in Yorkshire, including all the major attractions in York. Available at York Tourist Office, or you can buy online.

★**Middlethorpe Hall**   HOTEL **£££**
(☑ 01904-641241; www.middlethorpe.com; Bishopthorpe Rd; s/d from £139/199; P ⑤) This breathtaking 17th-century country house is set in eight hectares of parkland, once the home of diarist Lady Mary Wortley Montagu. The rooms are divided between the main house, restored courtyard buildings and three cottage suites. All the rooms are beautifully decorated with original antiques and oil paintings that have been carefully selected to reflect the period.

✕ Eating & Drinking

★**Mannion's**   CAFE, BISTRO **£**
(☑ 01904-631030; www.mannionandco.co.uk; 1 Blake St; mains £5-9; ⊙ 9am-5.30pm Mon-Sat, 10am-5pm Sun) Expect to queue for a table at this busy bistro (no reservations), with its maze of cosy, wood-panelled rooms and selection of daily specials. Regulars on the menu include eggs Benedict for breakfast, a chunky Yorkshire rarebit made with home-baked bread, and lunch platters of cheese and charcuterie from the attached deli. Oh, and pavlova for dessert.

Cafe No 8   CAFE, BISTRO **££**
(☑ 01904-653074; www.cafeno8.co.uk; 8 Gillygate; 2-/3-course meal £18/22, Fri & Sat £22/27; ⊙ 10am-10pm; ⑤ ⊞) 🍴 A cool little place with modern artwork mimicking the Edwardian stained glass at the front, No 8 offers a day-long menu of classic bistro dishes using fresh local produce, including duck breast with blood orange and juniper, and Yorkshire pork belly with star anise, fennel and garlic. It also does breakfast daily (mains £5) and Sunday lunch (three courses £25). Booking recommended.

**Parlour at
Grays Court**   CAFE **££**
(www.grayscourtyork.com; Chapter House St; mains £8-14; ⊙ 10am-5pm; ⑤) An unexpected find in the heart of York, this 16th-century house (now a hotel) has more of a country atmosphere. Enjoy gourmet coffee and cake in the sunny garden, or indulge in a light lunch in the historic setting of the oak-panelled Jacobean gallery. The menu runs from Yorkshire rarebit to confit duck, and includes traditional afternoon tea (£18.50).

Bettys   TEAROOM **££**
(www.bettys.co.uk; St Helen's Sq; mains £6-14, afternoon tea £18.50; ⊙ 9am-9pm; ⊞) Old-school afternoon tea, with white-aproned waiters, linen tablecloths and a teapot collection arranged along the walls. The house speciality is the Yorkshire Fat Rascal, a huge fruit scone smothered in melted butter, but the smoked haddock with poached egg and hollandaise sauce (seasonal) is our favourite lunch dish. No bookings – queue for a table at busy times.

★**Blue Bell**   PUB
(53 Fossgate; ⊙ 11am-11pm Mon-Sat, noon-10.30pm Sun) This is what a real English pub looks like – a tiny, 200-year-old wood-panelled room with a smouldering fireplace, decor untouched since 1903, a pile of ancient board games in the corner, friendly and efficient bar staff, and Timothy Taylor and Black Sheep ales on tap. Bliss, with froth on top – if you can get in (it's often full).

ℹ Information

York Tourist Office (☑ 01904-550099; www.visityork.org; 1 Museum St; ⊙ 9am-6pm Mon-Sat, 10am-5pm Sun Apr-Sep, shorter hours Oct-Mar) Visitor and transport info for all of Yorkshire, plus accommodation bookings, ticket sales and internet access.

ℹ Getting There & Away

BUS

For timetable information call **Traveline Yorkshire** (☑ 0871 200 2233; www.yorkshiretravel.net). All local and regional buses stop on Rougier St, about 200m northeast of the train station.

There are **National Express** (☑ 0871 781 8181; www.nationalexpress.com) coaches to London (£31, 5½ hours, three daily), Birmingham (£29, 3½ hours, one daily) and Newcastle (£15.20, 2¾ hours, two daily).

TRAIN

York is a major railway hub with frequent direct services to Birmingham (£45, 2¼ hours), Newcastle (£16, one hour), Leeds (£13.50, 25 minutes), London's King's Cross (£80, two hours), Manchester (£17, 1½ hours) and Scarborough (£8, 50 minutes). There are also trains to Cambridge (£65, three hours), changing at Peterborough.

Castle Howard

Stately homes may be two a penny in England, but you'll have to try hard to find one as breathtakingly stately as **Castle Howard** (www.castlehoward.co.uk; adult/child house & grounds £14/7.50, grounds only £9.50/6; ⊙ house 11am-4.30pm Apr-Oct, grounds 10am-5pm Mar-Oct

& Dec, to 4pm Nov, Jan & Feb; $\boxed{P}$), a work of theatrical grandeur and audacity, and one of the world's most beautiful buildings. It's instantly recognisable from its starring role in the 1980s TV series *Brideshead Revisited* and in the 2008 film of the same name.

It's 15 miles northeast of York; **Stephenson's of Easingwold** (www.stephensonsof easingwold.co.uk) operates a bus service (£7.50 return, 40 minutes, three times daily Monday to Saturday) from York.

Chester

Marvellous Chester is one of English history's greatest legacies. Its red-sandstone wall, which today gift-wraps a tidy collection of Tudor and Victorian buildings, was built during Roman times. The town was then called Castra Devana, and was the largest Roman fortress in Britain.

◉ Sights

★ City Walls
LANDMARK

A good way to get a sense of Chester's unique character is to walk the 2-mile circuit along the walls that surround the historic centre. Originally built by the Romans around AD 70, the walls were altered substantially over the following centuries but have retained their current position since around 1200. The tourist office's *Walk Around Chester Walls* leaflet is an excellent guide.

★ Rows
ARCHITECTURE

Besides the City Walls, Chester's other great draw is the Rows, a series of two-level galleried arcades along the four streets that fan out in each direction from the **Central Cross**. The architecture is a handsome mix of Victorian and Tudor (original and mock) buildings that house a fantastic collection of individually owned shops.

Chester Cathedral
CATHEDRAL

($\boxed{\mathcal{J}}$ 01244-324756; www.chestercathedral.com; 12 Abbey Sq; admission £3; ⊙9am-5pm Mon-Sat, 1-4pm Sun) Originally a Benedictine abbey built on the remains of an earlier Saxon church dedicated to St Werburgh (the city's patron saint), Chester Cathedral was shut down in 1540 as part of Henry VIII's dissolution frenzy, but reconsecrated as a cathedral the following year. Although the cathedral itself was given a substantial Victorian facelift, the 12th-century cloister and its surrounding buildings are essentially unaltered and

retain much of the structure from the early monastic years.

🛏 Sleeping

Chester Backpackers
HOSTEL £

($\boxed{\mathcal{J}}$ 01244-400185; www.chesterbackpackers.co.uk; 67 Boughton; dm/s/d from £16/22/34; ⓢ) Comfortable dorm rooms with nice pine beds in a typically Tudor white-and-black building. It's just a short walk from the city walls and there's also a pleasant garden.

★ Stone Villa
B&B ££

($\boxed{\mathcal{J}}$ 01244-345014; www.stonevillachester.co.uk; 3 Stone Pl, Hoole Rd; s/d from £45/75; $\boxed{P}$ ⓢ; ▣9) Twice winner of Chester's B&B of the Year in the last 10 years, this beautiful villa has everything you need for a memorable stay. Elegant bedrooms, a fabulous breakfast and welcoming, friendly owners all add up to one of the best lodgings in town. The property is about a mile from the city centre.

✕ Eating

Joseph Benjamin
MODERN BRITISH ££

($\boxed{\mathcal{J}}$ 01244-344295; www.josephbenjamin.co.uk; 134-140 Northgate St; mains £13-17; ⊙9am-5pm Tue & Wed, 9am-midnight Thu-Sat, 10am-5pm Sun) A bright star in Chester's culinary firmament is this combo restaurant, bar and deli that delivers carefully prepared local produce to take out or eat in. Excellent sandwiches and gorgeous salads are the mainstay of the takeout menu, while the more formal dinner menu features fine examples of modern British cuisine.

Bar Lounge
MODERN BRITISH ££

(www.barlounge.co.uk; 75 Watergate St; mains £11-18) One of the most popular spots in town is this bistro-style bar that serves up good burgers, pies and a particularly tasty beer-battered haddock and chips. There's a heated outdoor terrace for alfresco drinks.

ℹ Getting There & Away

BUS

National Express ($\boxed{\mathcal{J}}$ 08717 81 81 81; www. nationalexpress.com) coaches stop on Vicar's Lane, just opposite the tourist office. Destinations include Liverpool (£8.20, one hour, four daily), London (£23, 5½ hours, three daily) and Manchester (£7.70, 1¼ hours, three daily).

TRAIN

The train station is about a mile from the city centre. City Rail Link buses are free for people with rail tickets. Destinations include Liverpool

(£6.65, 45 minutes, hourly), London Euston (£65, 2½ hours, hourly) and Manchester (£12.60, one hour, hourly).

Lake District National Park

A dramatic landscape of ridges, lakes and peaks, including England's highest mountain, Scafell Pike (978m), the Lake District is one of Britain's most scenic corners. The awe-inspiring geography here shaped the literary personae of some of Britain's best-known poets, including William Wordsworth.

Often called simply the Lakes, the national park and surrounding area attract around 15 million visitors annually. But if you avoid summer weekends it's easy enough to miss the crush, especially if you do a bit of hiking.

There's a host of B&Bs and country-house hotels in the Lakes, plus more than 20 YHA hostels, many of which can be linked by foot if you wish to hike.

ⓘ Information

Brockhole National Park Visitor Centre
(✆015394-46601; www.lake-district.gov.uk; ⊘10am-5pm Easter-Oct, to 4pm Nov-Easter) In a 19th-century mansion 3 miles north of Windermere on the A591, this is the Lake District's flagship tourist office, and also has a teashop, an adventure playground and gardens.

ⓘ Getting There & Around

BUS

There's one daily National Express coach from London Victoria (£37, eight hours) via Lancaster and Kendal.

The main local bus operator is **Stagecoach** (www.stagecoachbus.com); you can download timetables from the website.

Bus 555 Lancaster to Keswick; stops at all the main towns including Windermere and Ambleside.

Bus 505 (Coniston Rambler) Kendal, Windermere, Ambleside and Coniston.

TRAIN

To get to the Lake District by train, you need to change at Oxenholme (on the London Euston to Glasgow line) for Kendal and Windermere, which has connections from London Euston (£99, 3½ hours), Manchester Piccadilly (£23, 1½ hours) and Glasgow (£52, 2¾ hours).

Windermere

POP 8432

Windermere – the lake and the town of the same name – has been a centre for Lakeland tourism since the first steam trains arrived in 1847. The station is still there, making this an excellent gateway.

Windermere Lake Cruises (✆015395-31188; www.windermere-lakecruises.co.uk; tickets from £2.70) offers scheduled boat trips across the lake from the lakeside settlement of Bowness-on-Windermere.

🛏 Sleeping

Archway   B&B £
(✆015394-45613; www.the-archway.com; 13 College Rd, Windermere Town; d £50-86) Value is the name of the game here: this place is a no-nonsense, old-fashioned, home-away-from-home. Some of the rooms have fell views, and the breakfast is enormous, but there's no parking.

**Lake District
Backpackers Lodge**   HOSTEL £
(✆015394-46374; www.lakedistrictbackpackers. co.uk; High St, Windermere Town; dm/r £16/36; @) Not the fanciest hostel in the Lake District, but these Windermere digs are about the only option in town for backpackers. There are two small four-bed dorms, plus two private rooms with a double bed and a single bed above.

Boundary   B&B ££
(✆015394-48978; www.theboundaryonline.co.uk; Lake Rd, Windermere Town; d £100-191; P ☎) Not the cheapest sleep in Windermere, but definitely one of the swishest. Owners Steve and Helen have given this Victorian house a sleek, boutique makeover: chic decor, monochrome colours, retro furniture and all. Steve's a cricket obsessive, so all the rooms are named after famous batsmen.

Grasmere

Grasmere is a gorgeous little Lakeland village, all the more famous because of its links with Britain's leading Romantic poet, William Wordsworth.

Literary pilgrims come to **Dove Cottage** (✆015394-35544; www.wordsworth.org.uk; adult/child £7.50/4.50; ⊘9.30am-5.30pm), his former home, where highlights include some fine portraits of the man himself, a cabinet containing his spectacles, and a set of scales used by his pal de Quincey to weigh out opium. At **St Oswald's Church** (Church Stile) you'll see a memorial to the poet, and in the churchyard you'll find his grave.

To cure any sombre thoughts, head for **Sarah Nelson's Gingerbread Shop** (www.grasmeregingerbread.co.uk; Church Cottage; ⊙9.15am-5.30pm Mon-Sat, 12.30-5pm Sun) and stock up on Grasmere's famous confectionery.

Keswick

POP 5257

The main town of the north Lakes, Keswick sits beside lovely Derwent Water, a silvery curve studded by wooded islands and crisscrossed by puttering cruise boats, operated by the **Keswick Launch** (☑017687-72263; www.keswick-launch.co.uk; round-the-lake adult/child £9.25/4.50).

🛏 Sleeping

Keswick YHA   HOSTEL £
(☑0845 371 9746; keswick@yha.org.uk; Station Rd; dm £13-21; @) Keswick's YHA is a beauty, lodged inside a converted woollen mill by the clattering River Rothay, and renovated thanks to the benevolence of a generous doctor. Dorms are cosy, there's an excellent cafe, and some rooms even have balconies over Fitz Park.

★Howe Keld   B&B ££
(☑017687-72417; www.howekeld.co.uk; 5-7 The Heads; s £58, d £110-130; P🛜) This gold-standard B&B pulls out all the stops: goose-down duvets, slate-floored bathrooms, chic colours and locally made furniture. The best rooms have views across Crow Park and the golf course, and the breakfast is a pick-and-mix delight. Free parking is available on the Heads if there's space.

Linnett Hill   B&B ££
(☑017687-44518; www.linnetthillkeswick.co.uk; 4 Penrith Rd; s/d £45/80; 🛜) Much recommended by travellers, this lovingly run B&B has lots going for it: crisp white rooms, a great location near Fitz Park and keen prices that stay the same year-round. Breakfast is good too: there's a blackboard of specials to choose from, and the dining room has gingham-check tablecloths and a crackling woodburner.

HILL TOP

The cute-as-a-button farmhouse of **Hill Top** (NT; ☑015394-36269; www.national trust.org.uk/hill-top; adult/child £9/4.50; ⊙10.30am-4.30pm Sat-Thu mid-Feb–Oct, longer hours Jul & Aug) is a must for Beatrix Potter fans: it was her first house in the Lake District, and is also where she wrote and illustrated several of her famous tales.

The cottage is in Near Sawrey, 2 miles from Hawkshead and Ferry House. The **Cross Lakes Experience** (www.lakedistrict.gov.uk/visiting/planyourvisit/travelandtransport/crosslakes; ⊙Apr-Nov) stops en route from Ferry House to Hawkshead.

WALES

Lying to the west of England, Wales is a nation with Celtic roots, its own language and a rich historic legacy. While some areas in the south are undeniably scarred by coal mining and heavy industry, Wales boasts a landscape of wild mountains, rolling hills, rich farmland and the bustling capital city of Cardiff.

Cardiff

POP 324,800

The capital of Wales since only 1955, Cardiff has embraced its new role with vigour, emerging as one of Britain's leading urban centres in the 21st century.

🎯 Sights

⊙ Central Cardiff

★Cardiff Castle   CASTLE
(www.cardiffcastle.com; Castle St; adult/child £12/9, incl guided tour £15/11; ⊙9am-5pm) Cardiff Castle is, quite rightly, the city's leading attraction. There's a medieval keep at its heart, but it's the later additions that capture the imagination of many visitors: during the Victorian era extravagant mock-Gothic features were grafted onto this relic, including a clock tower and a lavish banqueting hall.

OTHER BRITISH PLACES WORTH A VISIT

Some places in Britain we recommend for day trips or longer visits:

Cornwall The southwestern tip of Britain is ringed with rugged granite seacliffs, sparkling bays, picturesque fishing villages and white sandy beaches.

Liverpool The city's waterfront is a World Heritage Site crammed with top museums including the International Slavery Museum and the Beatles Story.

Hadrian's Wall One of the country's most dramatic Roman ruins, a 2000-year-old procession of abandoned forts and towers marching across the lonely landscape of northern England.

Glen Coe Scotland's most famous glen combines those two essential qualities of Highlands landscape: dramatic scenery and deep history.

Pembrokeshire Wales' western extremity is famous for its beaches and coastal walks, as well as being home to one of Britain's finest Norman castles.

★**Wales Millennium Centre** ARTS CENTRE

(☑029-2063 6464; www.wmc.org.uk; Bute Pl; tours £6; ☉tours 11am & 2.30pm) FREE The centrepiece and symbol of Cardiff Bay's regeneration is the superb Wales Millennium Centre, an architectural masterpiece of stacked Welsh slate in shades of purple, green and grey topped with an overarching bronzed steel shell. Designed by Welsh architect Jonathan Adams, it opened in 2004 as Wales' premier arts complex, housing major cultural organisations such as the Welsh National Opera, National Dance Company, National Orchestra, Literature Wales, HiJinx Theatre and Ty Cerdd (Music Centre of Wales).

Doctor Who Experience EXHIBITION

(☑0844 801 2279; www.doctorwhoexperience. com; Porth Teigr; adult/child £15/11; ☉10am-5pm Wed-Mon, daily school holidays, last admission 3.30pm) The huge success of the reinvented classic TV series *Doctor Who*, produced by BBC Wales, has brought Cardiff to the attention of sci-fi fans worldwide. City locations have featured in many episodes, and the first two series of the spin-off *Torchwood* were also set in Cardiff Bay. Capitalising on Timelord tourism, this interactive exhibition is located right next to the BBC studios where the series is filmed – look out for the Tardis hovering outside.

🛏 Sleeping

★**River House Backpackers** HOSTEL £

(☑029-2039 9810; www.riverhousebackpackers. com; 59 Fitzhamon Embankment; dm/r incl breakfast from £18/42; @ 🛜) Professionally run by a young brother-and-sister team and a pair of fluffy cats, the River House has a well-equipped kitchen, small garden and cosy TV lounge. The private rooms are basically small dorm rooms and share the same bathrooms. A free breakfast of cereal and toast is provided.

St David's Hotel & Spa HOTEL ££

(☑029-2045 4045; www.thestdavidshotel.com; Havannah St; r from £119; @ 🛜 ≋) A glittering, glassy tower topped with a sail-like flourish, St David's epitomises Cardiff Bay's transformation from wasteland to desirable address. Almost every room has a small private balcony with a bay view. The exterior is already showing signs of wear and tear, but the rooms have been recently renovated.

Park Plaza HOTEL ££

(☑029-2011 1111; www.parkplazacardiff.com; Greyfriars Rd; r from £86; 🛜 ≋) Luxurious without being remotely stuffy, the Plaza has all the five-star facilities you'd expect from an upmarket business-orientated hotel. The snug reception sets the scene, with a gas fire blazing along one wall and comfy wingback chairs. The rear rooms have leafy views over the Civic Centre.

🍴 Eating

★**Coffee Barker** CAFE £

(Castle Arcade; mains £4-7; ☉8.30am-5.30pm Mon-Sat, 10.30am-4.30pm Sun; 🛜 👶) Slink into an armchair, sip on a silky coffee and snack on salmon scrambled eggs or a sandwich in what is Cardiff's coolest cafe. There are plenty of magazines and toys to keep everyone amused.

Goat Major PUB £
(www.sabrain.com/goatmajor; 33 High St; pies £7.50; ⊙ kitchen noon-6pm Mon-Sat, to 4pm Sun; 🛜) A solidly traditional wood-lined pub with armchairs, a fireplace and Brains Dark real ale on tap, the Goat Major's gastronomic contribution comes in the form of its selection of homemade savoury pot pies served with chips. Try the Wye Valley pie, a mixture of buttered chicken, leek, asparagus and Tintern Abbey cheese.

Conway GASTROPUB ££
(📞 029-2022 4373; www.knifeandforkfood.co.uk; 58 Conway Rd; mains £10-15; ⊙ noon-11pm; 🍴) With a sun-trap front terrace and a pleasantly laid-back vibe, this wonderful corner pub chalks up its delicious 'seasonal, fresh and local' offerings daily. Kids get their own menu, while the grownups can ponder the large selection of wines served by the glass.

ⓘ Information

Cardiff Tourist Office (📞 029-2087 3573; www.visitcardiff.com; Old Library, The Hayes; ⊙ 9.30am-5.30pm Mon-Sat, 10am-4pm Sun) Cardiff's main tourist office stocks Ordnance Survey maps and Welsh books, and offers an accommodation booking service and internet access.

ⓘ Getting There & Away

BUS

National Express travels to London (£19, 3½ hours), Birmingham (£27, 2¾ hours) and Bristol (£6, 1¼ hours).

TRAIN

Arriva Trains Wales (www.arrivatrainswales. co.uk) operates all train services in Wales. Direct services from Cardiff include London

---

WORTH A TRIP

CONWY CASTLE
....
On the north coast of Wales, the historic town of Conwy is utterly dominated by the Unesco-designated cultural treasure of **Conwy Castle** (Cadw; 📞 01492-592358; www.cadw.wales.gov.uk; Castle Sq; adult/child £5.75/4.35; ⊙ 9.30am-5pm; 🅿), the most stunning of all Edward I's Welsh fortresses. Built between 1277 and 1307 on a rocky outcrop, it has commanding views across the estuary and Snowdonia National Park.

Paddington (£39, 2¼ hours) and Bristol (£13, 35 minutes).

Snowdonia National Park

Snowdonia National Park (Parc Cenedlaethol Eryri; www.eryri-npa.gov.uk) was founded in 1951 (making it Wales' first national park). Around 350,000 people travel to the national park to climb, walk or take the train to the summit of Mt Snowdon, Wales' highest mountain.

Snowdon

No Snowdonia experience is complete without coming face-to-face with Snowdon (1085m). On a clear day the views stretch to Ireland and the Isle of Man. Even on a gloomy day you could find yourself above the clouds. At the top is the striking **Hafod Eryri** (⊙ 10am to 20min before last train departure; 🛜) visitor centre, opened in 2009 by Prince Charles.

Six paths of varying length and difficulty lead to the summit, all taking around six hours return, or you can cheat and catch the **Snowdon Mountain Railway** (📞 0844 493 8120; www.snowdonrailway.co.uk; return diesel adult/child £27/18, steam £35/25; ⊙ 9am-5pm mid-Mar–Oct), opened in 1896 and still the UK's only public rack-and-pinion railway.

However you get to the summit, take warm, waterproof clothing, wear sturdy footwear and check the weather forecast before setting out.

🛌 Sleeping & Eating

Snowdon Ranger YHA HOSTEL £
(📞 0800 019 1700; www.yha.org.uk; dm/tr/q £19/57/73; 🅿 @) On the A4085, 5 miles north of Beddgelert at the trailhead for the Snowdon Ranger Path, this former inn has its own adjoining lakeside beach. Accommodation is basic.

Bryn Gwynant YHA HOSTEL £
(📞 0800 019 5465; www.yha.org.uk; Nantgwynant; dm/tw/f £19/50/73; ⊙ Mar-Oct; 🅿) Of all of the park's youth hostels, Bryn Gwynant has the most impressive building and the most idyllic setting, occupying a grand Victorian mansion looking over a lake to Snowdon – although it's certainly not flash inside. It's located 4 miles east of Beddgelert, near the start of the Watkin Path.

ⓘ Getting There & Away

The **Welsh Highland Railway** (☑ 01766-516000; www.festrail.co.uk; adult/child return £35/31.50) and **Snowdon Sherpa** (☑ 0870 608 2608) buses link various places in Snowdonia with the town of Bangor, which can be reached by train from London Euston (£86, 3¼ hours, hourly).

SCOTLAND

Despite its small size, Scotland has many treasures crammed into its compact territory – big skies, lonely landscapes, spectacular wildlife, superb seafood and hospitable, down-to-earth people. From the cultural attractions of Edinburgh to the heather-clad hills of the Highlands, there's something for everyone.

Edinburgh

POP 440,000

Edinburgh is a city that just begs to be explored. From the imposing castle to the Palace of Holyroodhouse to the Royal Yacht Britannia, every corner turned reveals sudden views and unexpected vistas – green sunlit hills, a glimpse of rust-red crags, a blue flash of distant sea. But there's more to Edinburgh than sightseeing – there are top shops, world-class restaurants and bacchanalian bars to enjoy.

◉ Sights

★Edinburgh Castle   CASTLE
(www.edinburghcastle.gov.uk; adult/child incl audioguide £16/9.60; ⊙9.30am-6pm Apr-Sep, to 5pm Oct-Mar, last admission 45min before closing; 🚌23, 27, 41, 42) Edinburgh Castle has played a pivotal role in Scottish history, both as a royal residence – King Malcolm Canmore (r 1058–93) and Queen Margaret first made their home here in the 11th century – and as a military stronghold. The castle last saw military action in 1745; from then until the 1920s it served as the British army's main base in Scotland. Today it is one of Scotland's most atmospheric and most popular tourist attractions.

★Real Mary
King's Close   HISTORIC BUILDING
(☑0845 070 6244; www.realmarykingsclose.com; 2 Warriston's Close, High St; adult/child

£12.95/7.45; ⊙10am-9pm daily Apr-Oct, to 11pm Aug, 10am-5pm Sun-Thu, 10am-9pm Fri & Sat Nov-Mar; 🚌23, 27, 41, 42) Edinburgh's 18th-century City Chambers were built over the sealed-off remains of Mary King's Close, and the lower levels of this medieval Old Town alley have survived almost unchanged amid the foundations for 250 years. Now open to the public, this spooky, subterranean labyrinth gives a fascinating insight into the everyday life of 17th-century Edinburgh. Costumed characters lead tours through a 16th-century town house and the plague-stricken home of a 17th-century gravedigger. Advance booking recommended.

★National Museum
of Scotland   MUSEUM
(www.nms.ac.uk; Chambers St; fee for special exhibitions; ⊙10am-5pm; 🚌2, 23, 27, 35, 41, 42, 45) FREE Broad, elegant Chambers St is dominated by the long facade of the National Museum of Scotland. Its extensive collections are spread between two buildings, one modern, one Victorian – the golden stone and striking modern architecture of the new building, opened in 1998, is one of the city's most distinctive landmarks. The five floors of the museum trace the history of Scotland from geological beginnings to the 1990s, with many imaginative and stimulating exhibits – audioguides are available in several languages.

★Royal Yacht
Britannia   SHIP
(www.royalyachtbritannia.co.uk; Ocean Terminal; adult/child £12.75/7.75; ⊙9.30am-6pm Jul-Sep, to 5.30pm Apr-Jun & Oct, 10am-5pm Nov-Mar, last admission 90min before closing; 🚕; 🚌11, 22, 34, 35, 36) Built on Clydeside, the former Royal Yacht Britannia was the British royal family's floating holiday home during their foreign travels from the time of her launch in 1953 until her decommissioning in 1997, and is now moored permanently in front of Ocean Terminal. The tour, which you take at your own pace with an audioguide (included in admission fee and available in 20 languages), lifts the curtain on the everyday lives of the royals, and gives an intriguing insight into the Queen's private tastes.

Scottish Parliament
Building   NOTABLE BUILDING
(☑0131-348 5200; www.scottish.parliament.uk; Horse Wynd; ⊙9am-6.30pm Tue-Thu, 10am-5.30pm

Mon, Fri & Sat in session, 10am-6pm Mon-Sat in recess; 🕾; 🖵 35, 36) **FREE** The Scottish parliament building, built on the site of a former brewery, was officially opened by HM the Queen in October 2005. Designed by Catalan architect Enric Miralles (1955–2000), the ground plan of the parliament complex represents a 'flower of democracy rooted in Scottish soil' (best seen looking down from Salisbury Crags). Free, one-hour guided tours (advance booking recommended) include a visit to the Debating Chamber, a committee room, the Garden Lobby and an MSP's (Member of the Scottish Parliament) office.

Palace of Holyroodhouse
PALACE

(www.royalcollection.org.uk; Horse Wynd; adult/child £11.30/6.80; ◷ 9.30am-6pm Apr-Oct, to 4.30pm Nov-Mar; 🕾; 🖵 35, 36) This palace is the royal family's official residence in Scotland, but is more famous as the 16th-century home of the ill-fated Mary, Queen of Scots. The highlight of the tour is **Mary's Bed Chamber**, home to the unfortunate queen from 1561 to 1567. It was here that her jealous first husband, Lord Darnley, restrained the pregnant queen while his henchmen murdered her secretary – and favourite – Rizzio. A plaque in the neighbouring room marks the spot where he bled to death.

🛏 Sleeping

★ Malone's Old Town Hostel
HOSTEL £

(☑ 0131-226 7648; www.maloneshostel.com; 14 Forrest Rd; dm £16-25; @ 🕾) No fancy decor or style credentials here, but it has got the basics right: it's clean, comfortable and friendly, and set upstairs from an Irish pub where guests get discounts on food and drink. The cherry on the cake is its superbly central location, an easy walk from the Royal Mile, the castle, the Grassmarket and Princes St.

Smart City Hostel
HOSTEL £

(☑ 0131-524 1989; www.smartcityhostels.com; 50 Blackfriars St; dm £24-28, tr £99; @ 🕾) A big, modern hostel, with a convivial cafe where you can buy breakfast, and mod cons such as keycard access and charging stations for mobile phones, MP3 players and laptops. Lockers in every room, a huge bar and a central location just off the Royal Mile make

this a favourite among the young, party-mad crowd – don't expect a quiet night!

★ Southside Guest House
B&B ££

(☑ 0131-668 4422; www.southsideguesthouse. co.uk; 8 Newington Rd; s/d £75/95; 🕾) Though set in a typical Victorian terrace, the Southside transcends the traditional guesthouse category and feels more like a modern boutique hotel. Its eight stylish rooms ooze interior design, standing out from other Newington B&Bs through the clever use of bold colours and modern furniture. Breakfast is an event, with Bucks fizz (champagne mixed with orange juice) on offer to smooth the rough edges off your hangover!

B+B Edinburgh
HOTEL ££

(☑ 0131-225 5084; www.bb-edinburgh.com; 3 Rothesay Tce; d/ste from £110/170; 🕾) Built in 1883 as a grand home for the proprietor of the *Scotsman* newspaper, this Victorian extravaganza of carved oak, parquet floors, stained glass and elaborate fireplaces was given a designer makeover in 2011 to create a striking contemporary hotel. Rooms on the 2nd floor are the most spacious, but the smaller top-floor rooms enjoy the finest views.

No 45
B&B ££

(☑ 0131-667 3536; www.edinburghbedbreakfast. com; 45 Gilmour Rd; s/d £70/140; 🕾) A peaceful setting, large garden and friendly owners contribute to the appeal of this Victorian terraced house, which overlooks the local bowling green. The decor is a blend of 19th and 20th century, with bold Victorian reds, pine floors and period fireplace in the lounge, a rocking horse and art nouveau lamp in the hallway, and a 1930s vibe in the three spacious bedrooms.

FESTIVAL CITY

Edinburgh boasts a frenzy of festivals throughout the year, including the world-famous **Edinburgh Festival Fringe** (☑ 0131-226 0026; www.edfringe. com), held over 3½ weeks in August. The last two weeks overlap with the first two weeks of the **Edinburgh International Festival** (☑ 0131-473 2099; www. eif.co.uk). See www.edinburghfestivals. co.uk for more.

Central Edinburgh

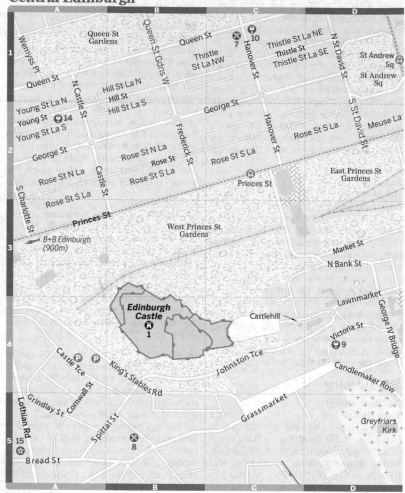

✗ Eating

★ Mums

CAFE **£**

(www.monstermashcafe.co.uk; 4a Forrest Rd; mains £6-9; ⊙9am-10pm Mon-Sat, 10am-10pm Sun; 🚌23, 27, 41, 42) ✐ This nostalgia-fuelled cafe serves up classic British comfort food that wouldn't look out of place on a 1950s menu – bacon and eggs, bangers and mash, shepherd's pie, fish and chips. But there's a twist – the food is all top-quality nosh freshly prepared from local produce, including Crombie's gourmet sausages. There's even a wine list, though we prefer the real ales and Scottish-brewed cider.

David Bann

VEGETARIAN **£**

(☎0131-556 5888; www.davidbann.com; 56-58 St Mary's St; mains £9-13; ⊙noon-10pm Mon-Fri, 11am-10pm Sat & Sun; 🖋; 🚌35) ✐ If you want to convince a carnivorous friend that cuisine à la veg can be as tasty and inventive as a meat-muncher's menu, take them to David Bann's stylish restaurant – dishes such as parsnip and blue cheese pudding, and

BRITAIN EDINBURGH

scallop with apple, jerusalem artichoke and sorrel; and juniper-smoked pigeon with wild garlic flowers and beetroot.

Dogs BRITISH ££
(☑0131-220 1208; www.thedogsonline.co.uk; 110 Hanover St; mains £10-15; ⊙noon-4pm & 5-10pm; ▣23, 27) ⊘ One of the coolest tables in town, this bistro-style place uses cheaper cuts of meat and less-well-known, more-sustainable species of fish to create hearty, no-nonsense dishes such as lamb sweetbreads on toast, baked coley with *skirlie* (fried oatmeal and onion), and devilled liver with bacon and onions.

★Kitchin SCOTTISH £££
(☑0131-555 1755; www.thekitchin.com; 78 Commercial Quay; mains £33-38, 3-course lunch £28.50; ⊙12.15-2.30pm & 6.30-10pm Tue-Thu, to 10.30pm Fri & Sat; ⏻; ▣16, 22, 35, 36) Fresh, seasonal, locally sourced Scottish produce is the philosophy that has won a Michelin star for this elegant but unpretentious restaurant. The menu moves with the seasons, of course, so expect fresh salads in summer and game in winter, and shellfish dishes such as seared scallops with endive *tarte tatin* when there's an 'r' in the month.

spiced aduki bean and cashew pie, are guaranteed to win converts.

★Timberyard SCOTTISH ££
(☑0131-221 1222; www.timberyard.co; 10 Lady Lawson St; mains £16-21; ⊙noon-9.30pm Tue-Sat; ⏻; ▣2, 35) ⊘ Ancient worn floorboards, cast-iron pillars, exposed joists and tables made from slabs of old mahogany create a rustic, retro atmosphere in this slow-food restaurant where the accent is on locally sourced produce from artisan growers and foragers. Typical dishes include seared

🍷 Drinking & Nightlife

Bow Bar
PUB

(80 West Bow; 🚌23, 27, 41, 42) One of the city's best traditional-style pubs (it's not as old as it looks), serving a range of excellent real ales and a vast selection of malt whiskies, the Bow Bar often has standing-room only on Friday and Saturday evenings.

★Café Royal
Circle Bar
PUB

(www.caferoyaledinburgh.co.uk; 17 West Register St; 🚌all Princes St buses) Perhaps *the* classic Edinburgh pub, the Cafe Royal's main claims to fame are its magnificent oval bar and its Doulton tile portraits of famous Victorian inventors. Sit at the bar or claim one of the cosy leather booths beneath the stained-glass windows, and choose from the seven real ales on tap.

BrewDog
BAR

(www.brewdog.com; 143 Cowgate; 📶; 🚌36) The Edinburgh outpost of Scotland's self-styled 'punk brewery', BrewDog stands out among the grimy, sticky-floored dives that line the Cowgate, with its cool, industrial-chic designer look. As well as its own highly rated beers, there's a choice of four guest real ales.

Oxford Bar
PUB

(www.oxfordbar.co.uk; 8 Young St; 🚌19, 36, 37, 41, 47) The Oxford is that rarest of things: a real pub for real people, with no 'theme', no music, no frills and no pretensions. 'The Ox' has been immortalised by Ian Rankin, author of the Inspector Rebus novels, whose fictional detective is a regular here.

Bramble
COCKTAIL BAR

(www.bramblebar.co.uk; 16a Queen St; 🚌23, 27) One of those places that easily earns the title 'best-kept secret', Bramble is an unmarked cellar bar where a maze of stone and brick hideaways conceals what is arguably the city's best cocktail venue. No beer taps, no fuss, just expertly mixed drinks.

Cabaret Voltaire
CLUB

(www.thecabaretvoltaire.com; 36-38 Blair St; 🚌all South Bridge buses) An atmospheric warren of stone-lined vaults houses this self-consciously 'alternative' club, which eschews huge dance floors and egotistical DJ worship in favour of a 'creative crucible' hosting an eclectic mix of DJs, live acts, comedy, theatre, visual arts and the spoken word. Well worth a look.

☆ Entertainment

The comprehensive source for what's on is *The List* (www.list.co.uk).

★Sandy Bell's
LIVE MUSIC

(www.sandybellsedinburgh.co.uk; 25 Forrest Rd) This unassuming pub is a stalwart of the traditional music scene (the founder's wife sang with The Corries). There's folk music almost every evening at 9pm, and from 3pm Saturday and Sunday, plus lots of impromptu sessions.

Henry's Cellar Bar
LIVE MUSIC

(www.henryscellarbar.com; 16 Morrison St; admission free–£5) One of Edinburgh's most eclectic live-music venues, Henry's has something going on most nights of the week, from rock and indie to 'Balkan-inspired folk', funk to hip-hop to hardcore, staging both local bands and acts from around the world. Open till 3am at weekends.

ℹ Information

Edinburgh Information Centre (☑0131-473 3868; www.edinburgh.org; Princes Mall, 3 Princes St; ⊙9am-9pm Mon-Sat, 10am-8pm Sun Jul & Aug, 9am-7pm Mon-Sat, 10am-7pm Sun May, Jun & Sep, 9am-5pm Mon-Wed, to 6pm Thu-Sun Oct-Apr) Includes an accommodation booking service, currency exchange, gift and bookshop, internet access and counters selling tickets for Edinburgh city tours and Scottish Citylink bus services.

ℹ Getting There & Away

AIR
Edinburgh Airport (p177), 8 miles west of the city, has numerous flights to other parts of Scotland and the UK, Ireland and mainland Europe.

BUS
Scottish Citylink (☑0871 266 3333; www.citylink.co.uk) buses connect Edinburgh with all of Scotland's cities and major towns, including Glasgow (£7.30, 1¼ hours, every 15 minutes), Stirling (£8, one hour, hourly) and Inverness (£30, 3½ to 4½ hours, hourly). National Express operates a direct coach service from London (£26, 10 hours, one daily).

It's also worth checking with **Megabus** (☑0900 160 0900; www.megabus.com) for cheap intercity bus fares from Edinburgh to London, Glasgow and Inverness.

TRAIN
The main terminus in Edinburgh is Waverley train station, in the heart of the city. Trains arriving from, and departing for, the west also stop at

Haymarket station, which is more convenient for the West End.

First ScotRail (📞 0845 755 0033; www. scotrail.co.uk) operates a regular shuttle service between Edinburgh and Glasgow (£13.20, 50 minutes, every 15 minutes), and frequent daily services to all Scottish cities, including Stirling (£8.30, one hour, twice hourly Monday to Saturday, hourly Sunday) and Inverness (£72, 3½ hours). There are also regular trains to London Kings Cross (£85, 4½ hours, hourly) via York.

Glasgow

POP 634,680

With a population around 1½ times that of Edinburgh, and a radically different history rooted in industry and trade rather than politics and law, Glasgow stands in complete contrast to the capital. The city offers a unique blend of friendliness, energy, dry humour and urban chaos, and also boasts excellent art galleries and museums – including the famous Burrell Collection – as well as numerous good-value restaurants, countless pubs, bars and clubs, and a lively performing-arts scene.

Just 50 miles to the west of Edinburgh, Glasgow makes an easy day trip by train or bus.

◉ Sights

Glasgow's main square in the city centre is grand **George Square**, built in the Victorian era to show off the city's wealth, and dignified by statues of notable Scots, including Robert Burns, James Watt, John Moore and Sir Walter Scott.

★**Kelvingrove Art Gallery & Museum**   GALLERY, MUSEUM
(www.glasgowmuseums.com; Argyle St; ⊙10am-5pm Mon-Thu & Sat, 11am-5pm Fri & Sun; 🖭) FREE A magnificent stone building, this grand Victorian cathedral of culture is a fascinating and unusual museum, with a bewildering variety of exhibits. You'll find fine art alongside stuffed animals, and Micronesian shark-tooth swords alongside a Spitfire plane, but it's not mix 'n' match: rooms are carefully and thoughtfully themed, and the collection is a manageable size. There's an excellent room of Scottish art, a room of fine French Impressionist works, and quality Renaissance paintings from Italy and Flanders.

★**Burrell Collection**   GALLERY
(www.glasgowmuseums.com; Pollok Country Park; ⊙10am-5pm Mon-Thu & Sat, 11am-5pm Fri & Sun) FREE One of Glasgow's top attractions was amassed by wealthy industrialist Sir William Burrell then donated to the city and is housed in an outstanding museum, in a park 3 miles south of the city centre. Burrell collected all manner of art from his teens to his death at 97, and this idiosyncratic collection of treasure includes everything from Chinese porcelain and medieval furniture to paintings by Degas and Cézanne. It's not so big as to be overwhelming, and the stamp of the collector lends an intriguing coherence.

★**Riverside Museum**   MUSEUM
(www.glasgowmuseums.com; 100 Pointhouse Pl; ⊙10am-5pm Mon-Thu & Sat, 11am-5pm Fri & Sun;

THE GENIUS OF CHARLES RENNIE MACKINTOSH

Charles Rennie Mackintosh (1868–1928) is to Glasgow what Gaudí is to Barcelona. A designer, architect and master of the art-nouveau style, his quirky, linear and geometric designs are seen all over Glasgow. Many of his buildings are open to the public, though his masterpiece, the **Glasgow School of Art**, was closed after being badly damaged by fire in 2014. If you're a fan, the **Mackintosh Trail ticket** (£10), available at the tourist office or any Mackintosh building, gives you a day's free admission to all his creations, plus unlimited bus and subway travel. Highlights include the following:

Willow Tearooms (www.willowtearooms.co.uk; 217 Sauchiehall St; ⊙9am-5pm Mon-Sat, 11am-5pm Sun; 🖭) FREE

Mackintosh House (www.hunterian.gla.ac.uk; 82 Hillhead St; ⊙10am-5pm Tue-Sat, 11am-4pm Sun) FREE

House for an Art Lover (📞 0141-353 4770; www.houseforanartlover.co.uk; Bellahouston Park, Dumbreck Rd; adult/child £4.50/3; ⊙10am-4pm Mon-Wed, to 12.30pm Thu-Sun)

Glasgow

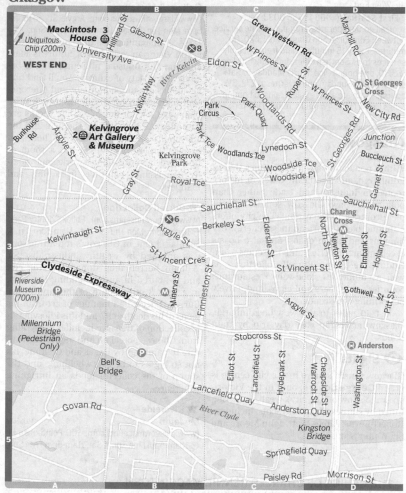

📶 ♿) **FREE** This visually impressive modern museum at Glasgow Harbour (west of the centre – get bus 100 from the north side of George Sq, or the Clyde Cruises boat service) owes its striking curved forms to British-Iraqi architect Zaha Hadid. A transport museum forms the main part of the collection, featuring a fascinating series of cars made in Scotland, plus assorted railway locos, trams, bikes (including the world's first pedal-powered bicycle from 1847) and model Clyde-built ships.

Glasgow Cathedral   CHURCH

(HS; www.historic-scotland.gov.uk; Cathedral Sq; ⏰ 9.30am-5.30pm Mon-Sat, 1-5pm Sun Apr-Sep, closes 4.30pm Oct-Mar) **FREE** Glasgow Cathedral has a rare timelessness. The dark, imposing interior conjures up medieval might and can send a shiver down the spine. It's a shining example of Gothic architecture, and, unlike nearly all Scotland's cathedrals, survived the turmoil of the Reformation mobs almost intact. Most of the current building dates from the 15th century.

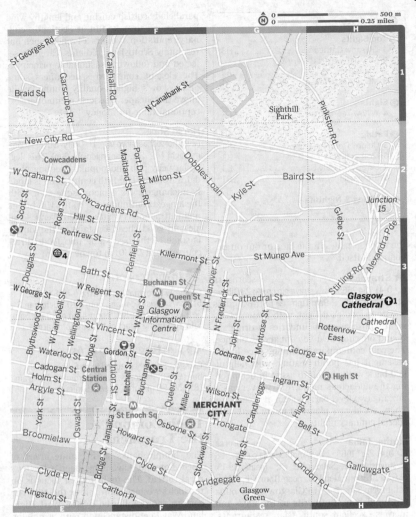

✖ Eating & Drinking

★ Saramago
Café Bar   CAFE £

(www.facebook.com/saramagocafebar; 350 Sauchiehall St; light meals £3-9; ☺ food 10am-10pm Mon-
Wed, 10am-11.30pm Thu-Sat, noon-11.30pm Sun;
🛜🖭) In the airy atmosphere of the Centre
for Contemporary Arts, this place does a
great line in eclectic vegan fusion food, with
a range of top flavour combinations from
around the globe. The upstairs bar has a
great deck on steep Scott St and packs out
inside with a friendly hipstery crowd enjoying the eclectic DJ sets and quality tap beers.

Chippy Doon
the Lane   FISH & CHIPS £

(www.thechippyglasgow.com; McCormick Lane, 84
Buchanan St; meals £6-10; ☺noon-9.30pm; 🛜)
🖋 Don't be put off by its location in a down-
at-heel alleyway off the shopping precinct:
this is a cut above your average chip shop.
Sustainable seafood is served in a chic space,
all old-time brick, metal archways and jazz.
Otherwise, chow down on your takeaway at

Glasgow

◉ Top Sights
1 Glasgow Cathedral H3
2 Kelvingrove Art Gallery &
   Museum A2
3 Mackintosh House A1

◉ Sights
4 Willow Tearooms E3

✖ Eating
5 Chippy Doon the Lane F4
6 Mother India B3
7 Saramago Café Bar E3
8 Stravaigin B1

◉ Drinking & Nightlife
9 Horse Shoe F4

the wooden tables in the lane or out on Buchanan St itself.

★ Stravaigin   SCOTTISH ££
(☏ 0141-334 2665; www.stravaigin.co.uk; 28 Gibson St; mains £10-18; ☺ 9am-11pm; ☏) Stravaigin is a serious foodie's delight, with a menu constantly pushing the boundaries of originality and offering creative culinary excellence. The cool contemporary dining space in the basement has booth seating, and helpful, laid-back waiting-staff to assist in deciphering the audacious menu. Entry-level has a buzzing two-level bar; you can also eat here. There are always plenty of menu deals and special culinary nights.

Mother India   INDIAN ££
(☏ 0141-221 1663; www.motherindia.co.uk; 28 Westminster Tce, Sauchiehall St; mains £9-15; ☺ 5.30-10.30pm Mon-Thu, noon-11pm Fri, 1-11pm Sat, 1-10pm Sun; ☏✎♿) Glasgow curry buffs forever debate the merits of the city's numerous excellent south Asian restaurants, and Mother India features in every discussion. It may lack the trendiness of some of the up-and-comers but it's been a stalwart for years, and the quality and innovation on show is superb. The three separate dining areas are all attractive and they make an effort for kids, with a separate menu.

★ Ubiquitous Chip   SCOTTISH £££
(☏ 0141-334 5007; www.ubiquitouschip.co.uk; 12 Ashton Lane; 2-/3-course lunch £16/20, mains £23-27, brasserie mains £9-14; ☺ noon-2.30pm & 5-11pm; ☏) ✐ The original champion of Scottish produce, this is legendary for its un-

paralleled Scottish cuisine and lengthy wine list. Named to poke fun at Scotland's culinary reputation, it offers a French touch but resolutely Scottish ingredients, carefully selected and following sustainable principles. The elegant courtyard space offers some of Glasgow's highest-quality dining, while above the cheaper brasserie menu offers exceptional value for money.

Horse Shoe   PUB
(www.horseshoebar.co.uk; 17 Drury St; ☺ 10am-midnight Mon-Sat, 11am-midnight Sun) This legendary city pub and popular meeting place dates from the late 19th century and is largely unchanged. It's a picturesque spot, with the longest continuous bar in the UK, but its main attraction is what's served over it – real ale and good cheer. Upstairs in the lounge is some of the best value pub food (three-course lunch £4.50) in town.

ⓘ Information

Glasgow Information Centre (☏ 0845 225 5121; www.visitscotland.com; 170 Buchanan St; ☺ 9am-6pm Mon-Sat, noon-4pm or 10am-5pm Sun; ☏) In the heart of the shopping area.

ⓘ Getting There & Away

Glasgow is easily reached from Edinburgh by bus (£7.30, 1¼ hours, every 15 minutes) or train (£12.50, 50 minutes, every 15 minutes).

Loch Lomond & the Trossachs

The 'bonnie banks' and 'bonnie braes' of Loch Lomond have long been Glasgow's rural retreat. The main tourist focus is on the loch's western shore, along the A82. The eastern shore, followed by the West Highland Way long-distance footpath, is quieter. The region's importance was recognised when it became the heart of **Loch Lomond & the Trossachs National Park** (www.lochlomond-trossachs.org) – Scotland's first national park, created in 2002.

The nearby Trossachs is a region famous for its thickly forested hills and scenic lochs. It first gained popularity in the early 19th century when curious visitors came from across Britain, drawn by the romantic language of Walter Scott's poem *Lady of the Lake,* inspired by Loch Katrine, and his novel *Rob Roy,* about the derring-do of the region's most famous son.

The main centre for Loch Lomond boat trips is Balloch, where **Sweeney's Cruises** (☏01389-752376; www.sweeneyscruises.com; Balloch Rd, Balloch) offers a range of outings, including a one-hour cruise to Inchmurrin and back (adult/child £8.50/5, departs hourly).

Loch Katrine Cruises (☏01877-376315; www.lochkatrine.com; Trossachs Pier; 1hr cruise adult/child £13/8; ⊙Easter-Oct) runs boat trips from Trossachs Pier at the eastern tip of Loch Katrine. At 10.30am there's a departure to Stronachlachar at the other end of the loch before returning. One of these is the fabulous centenarian steamship *Sir Walter Scott*.

🛏 Sleeping & Eating

Oak Tree Inn   INN **££**
(☏01360-870357; www.oak-tree-inn.co.uk; Balmaha; dm/s/d £30/50/85; 🅿🛜) An attractive traditional inn built in slate and timber, this offers bright modern guest bedrooms for pampered hikers, super-spacious superior chambers, self-catering cottages and two four-bed bunkrooms for hardier souls. The rustic restaurant brings locals, tourists and walkers together and dishes up hearty meals that cover lots of bases (mains £9 to £12, food noon to 9pm). There's lots of outdoor seating and it brews its own beers.

★Roman Camp Hotel   HOTEL **£££**
(☏01877-330003; www.romancamphotel.co.uk; Main St; s/d/superior £110/160/210; 🅿🛜) Callander's best hotel is centrally located but feels rural, set by the river in beautiful grounds. Endearing features include a lounge with blazing fire and a library with a tiny secret chapel. It's an old-fashioned warren of a place with four grades of room; standards are certainly luxurious, but superiors are even more appealing, with period furniture, excellent bathrooms, armchairs and fireplace.

The upmarket restaurant is open to the public. Reassuringly, the name refers not to toga parties but to a ruin in the adjacent fields.

★Drover's Inn   PUB FOOD **££**
(☏01301-704234; www.thedroversinn.co.uk; Ardlui; bar meals £8-12; ⊙11.30am-10pm Mon-Sat, 11.30am-9.30pm Sun; 🛜) This is one howff (drinking den) you shouldn't miss – a low-ceilinged place just north of Ardlui with smoke-blackened stone, barmen in kilts, and walls festooned with moth-eaten stags'

heads and stuffed birds. The bar, where Rob Roy allegedly dropped by for pints, serves hearty hill-walking fuel and hosts live folk at weekends. We recommend this more as an atmospheric place to eat and drink than somewhere to stay.

★Callander Meadows   SCOTTISH **££**
(☏01877-330181; www.callandermeadows.co.uk; 24 Main St; lunch £10, mains £12-16; ⊙9am-9pm Thu-Sun; 🛜) Informal but smart, this well-loved restaurant in the centre of Callander occupies the two front rooms of a house on the main street. There's a contemporary flair for presentation and unusual flavour combinations, but a solidly British base underpins the cuisine. There's a great beer/coffee garden out the back, where you can also eat. Opens daily from June to September.

ℹ Getting There & Away

Balloch, at the southern end of Loch Lomond, can be easily reached from Glasgow by bus (£4.50, 1½ hours, at least two per hour) or train (£5.10, 45 minutes, every 30 minutes).

For exploring the Trossachs, your own transport is recommended.

Inverness

Inverness, the primary city and shopping centre of the Highlands, has a great location astride the River Ness at the northern end of the Great Glen. It's a jumping-off point for exploring northern Scotland, with the railway line from Edinburgh branching east to Elgin and Aberdeen, north to Thurso and Wick, and west to Kyle of Lochalsh (the nearest train station to the Isle of Skye). The latter route is one of Britain's great scenic rail journeys.

🛏 Sleeping

Bazpackers Backpackers Hotel   HOSTEL **£**
(☏01463-717663; www.bazpackershostel.co.uk; 4 Culduthel Rd; dm/tw £17/44; @🛜) This may be Inverness' smallest hostel (34 beds), but it's hugely popular. It's a friendly, quiet place – the main building has a convivial lounge centred on a wood-burning stove, and a small garden and great views (some rooms are in a separate building with no garden). The dorms and kitchen can be a bit cramped, but the showers are great.

DON'T MISS

STIRLING CASTLE

Hold Stirling and you control Scotland. This maxim has ensured that a fortress of some kind has existed here since prehistoric times. You cannot help drawing parallels with Edinburgh Castle, but many find **Stirling Castle** (HS; www.stirlingcastle.gov.uk; adult/child £14/7.50; ⊙9.30am-6pm Apr-Sep, to 5pm Oct-Mar) more atmospheric – the location, architecture, historical significance and commanding views combine to make it a grand and memorable sight.

The current castle dates from the late 14th to the 16th century, when it was a residence of the Stuart monarchs. The undisputed highlight of a visit is the fabulous, recently restored **Royal Palace**. The idea was that it should look brand new, just as when it was constructed by French masons under the orders of James V in the mid-16th century with the aim of impressing his new (also French) bride and other crowned heads of Europe. The suite of six rooms – three for the king, three for the queen – is a sumptuous riot of colour. Particularly notable are the fine fireplaces, the **Stirling Heads** – modern reproductions of painted oak discs in the ceiling of the king's audience chamber – and the fabulous series of tapestries that have been painstakingly woven over many years.

Stirling is 35 miles northwest of Edinburgh, and easily reached by train (£8.30, one hour, twice hourly Monday to Saturday, hourly Sunday).

★**Trafford Bank** B&B ££
(☑01463-241414; www.traffordbankguesthouse. co.uk; 96 Fairfield Rd; d £120-132; P🖥) Lots of word-of-mouth rave reviews for this elegant Victorian villa, which was once home to a bishop, just a mitre-toss from the Caledonian Canal and 10 minutes' walk west from the city centre. The luxurious rooms include fresh flowers and fruit, bathrobes and fluffy towels – ask for the Tartan Room, which has a wrought-iron king-size bed and Victorian roll-top bath.

Ardconnel House B&B ££
(☑01463-240455; www.ardconnel-inverness.co.uk; 21 Ardconnel St; r per person £35-40; 🖥) The six-room Ardconnel is one of our favourites – a terraced Victorian house with comfortable en suite rooms, a dining room with crisp white table linen, and a breakfast menu that includes Vegemite for homesick antipodeans. Kids under 10 not allowed.

✕ Eating

★**Café 1** BISTRO ££
(☑01463-226200; www.cafe1.net; 75 Castle St; mains £10-24; ⊙noon-2.30pm & 5-9.30pm Mon-Fri, noon-2.30pm & 6-9.30pm Sat) Café 1 is a friendly and appealing bistro with candlelit tables amid elegant blonde-wood and wrought-iron decor. There is an international menu based on quality Scottish produce, from Aberdeen Angus steaks to crisp pan-fried sea bass and meltingly tender pork belly. The set lunch

menu (two courses for £8) is served noon to 2.30pm Monday to Saturday.

Contrast Brasserie BRASSERIE ££
(☑01463-223777; www.glenmoristontownhouse. com; 20 Ness Bank; 2-course lunch £10.95, 2-course early bird £12.95, à la carte £4.95-25) Book early for what we think is one of the best-value restaurants in Inverness – a dining room that drips designer style, with smiling professional staff and truly delicious food prepared using fresh Scottish produce. The two-course lunch menu and three-course early bird menu (£16, 5pm to 6.30pm) are bargains.

ℹ Information

Inverness Tourist Office (☑01463-252401; www.visithighlands.com; Castle Wynd; internet access per 20min £1; ⊙9am-6pm Mon-Sat, 9.30am-5pm Sun Jul & Aug, 9am-5pm Mon-Sat, 10am-4pm Sun Jun, Sep & Oct, 9am-5pm Mon-Sat Apr & May) Bureau de change and accommodation booking service; also sells tickets for tours and cruises. Opening hours limited November to March.

ℹ Getting There & Away

BUS

Buses depart from **Inverness bus station** (Margaret St). Coaches from London (£45, 13 hours, one daily direct) are operated by **National Express** (☑08717 81 81 78; www.gobycoach. com); more frequent services require a change at Glasgow. Other routes include Edinburgh (£30, 3½ to 4½ hours, hourly) and Portree on the Isle of Skye (£25, 3¼ hours, three daily).

TRAIN

Trains depart from Inverness for Kyle of Lochalsh (£22, 2½ hours, four daily Monday to Saturday, two Sunday); this is one of Britain's most scenic railway lines.

There's one direct train from London each day (£100, eight to nine hours); others require a change at Edinburgh.

Loch Ness

Deep, dark and narrow, Loch Ness stretches for 23 miles between Inverness and Fort Augustus. Its bitterly cold waters have been extensively explored in search of the elusive Loch Ness monster, but most visitors see her only in cardboard cut-out form at the monster exhibitions. The village of **Drumnadrochit** is a hotbed of beastie fever, with two monster exhibitions battling it out for the tourist dollar.

Sights & Activities

Loch Ness Centre & Exhibition   INTERPRETATION CENTRE
(☑ 01456-450573; www.lochness.com; adult/child £7.45/4.95; ☺ 9.30am-6pm Jul & Aug, to 5pm Easter-Jun, Sep & Oct, 10am-3.30pm Nov-Easter; ℗) This Nessie-themed attraction adopts a scientific approach that allows you to weigh the evidence for yourself. Exhibits include the original equipment – sonar survey vessels, miniature submarines, cameras and sediment coring tools – used in various monster hunts, as well as original photographs and film footage of sightings. You'll find out about hoaxes and optical illusions, as well as learning a lot about the ecology of Loch Ness – is there enough food in the loch to support even one 'monster', let alone a breeding population?

Urquhart Castle   CASTLE
(HS; ☑ 01456-450551; adult/child £7.90/4.80; ☺ 9.30am-6pm Apr-Sep, to 5pm Oct, to 4.30pm Nov-Mar; ℗) Commanding a brilliant location 1.5 miles east of Drumnadrochit, with outstanding views (on a clear day), Urquhart Castle is a popular Nessie-watching hotspot. A huge visitor centre (most of which is beneath ground level) includes a video theatre (with a dramatic 'unveiling' of the castle at the end of the film)

and displays of medieval items discovered in the castle.

Nessie Hunter   BOAT TOUR
(☑ 01456-450395; www.lochness-cruises.com; adult/child £15/10; ☺ Easter-Oct) One-hour monster-hunting cruises, complete with sonar and underwater cameras. Cruises depart from Drumnadrochit hourly (except 1pm) from 9am to 6pm daily.

ℹ Getting There & Away

Scottish Citylink (☑ 0871 266 3333; www.citylink.co.uk) and **Stagecoach** (www.stagecoachbus.com) buses from Inverness to Fort William run along the shores of Loch Ness (six to eight daily, five on Sunday); those headed for Skye turn off at Invermoriston. There are bus stops at Drumnadrochit (£3.20, 30 minutes) and Urquhart Castle car park (£3.50, 35 minutes).

Isle of Skye

POP 9900

The Isle of Skye is the biggest of Scotland's islands (now linked to the mainland by a bridge at Kyle of Lochalsh), a 50-mile-long smorgasbord of velvet moors, jagged mountains, sparkling lochs and towering sea cliffs. It takes its name from the old Norse *sky-a*, meaning 'cloud island', a Viking reference to the often mist-enshrouded **Cuillin Hills**, Britain's most spectacular mountain range. The stunning scenery is the main attraction, including the cliffs and pinnacles of the **Old Man of Storr**, **Kilt Rock** and the **Quiraing**, but there are plenty of cosy pubs to retire to when the rain clouds close in.

Portree is the main town, with Broadford a close second; both have banks, ATMs, supermarkets and petrol stations.

Sights & Activities

Dunvegan Castle   CASTLE
(☑ 01470-521206; www.dunvegancastle.com; adult/child £10/7; ☺ 10am-5.30pm Apr–mid-Oct; ℗) Skye's most famous historic building, and one of its most popular tourist attractions, Dunvegan Castle is the seat of the chief of Clan MacLeod. It has played host to Samuel Johnson, Sir Walter Scott and, most famously, Flora MacDonald. The oldest parts are the 14th-century keep and dungeon but most of it dates from the 17th to 19th centuries.

Skye Tours

BUS TOUR

(☑ 01471-822716; www.skye-tours.co.uk; adult/child £35/30; ☺ Mon-Sat) Five-hour sightseeing tours of Skye in a minibus, departing from the tourist office car park in Kyle of Lochalsh (close to Kyle of Lochalsh train station).

🛏 Sleeping

Portree, the island's capital, has the largest selection of accommodation, eating places and other services.

Bayfield Backpackers

HOSTEL £

(☑ 01478-612231; www.skyehostel.co.uk; Bayfield; dm £18; P @ 🛜) Clean, central and modern, this hostel provides the best backpacker accommodation in town. The owner really makes you feel welcome, and is a fount of advice on what to do and where to go in Skye.

Ben Tianavaig B&B

B&B ££

(☑ 01478-612152; www.ben-tianavaig.co.uk; 5 Bosville Tce; r £75-88; P 🛜) 🍴 A warm welcome awaits from the Irish-Welsh couple that runs this appealing B&B bang in the centre of town. All four bedrooms have a view across the harbour to the hill that gives the house its name and breakfasts include free-range eggs and vegetables grown in the garden. Two-night minimum stay April to October; no credit cards.

★ Tigh an Dochais

B&B ££

(☑ 01471-820022; www.skyebedbreakfast.co.uk; 13 Harrapool; d £90; P) A cleverly designed modern building, Tigh an Dochais is one of Skye's best B&Bs – a little footbridge leads to the front door, which is on the 1st floor. Here you'll find the dining room (gorgeous breakfasts) and lounge offering a stunning view of sea and hills; the bedrooms (downstairs) open onto an outdoor deck with that same wonderful view.

Peinmore House

B&B £££

(☑ 01478-612574; www.peinmorehouse.co.uk; r £135-145; P 🛜) Signposted off the main road about 2 miles south of Portree, this former manse has been cleverly converted into a guesthouse that is more stylish and luxurious than most hotels. The bedrooms and bathrooms are huge (one bathroom has an armchair in it!), as is the choice of breakfast (kippers and smoked haddock on the menu), and there are panoramic views to the Old Man of Storr.

Eating

Café Arriba

CAFE £

(☑ 01478-611830; www.cafearriba.co.uk; Quay Brae; mains £5-10; ☺ 7am-6pm daily May-Sep, 8am-5pm Thu-Sat Oct-Apr; 🍴) Arriba is a funky little cafe, brightly decked out in primary colours and offering delicious flatbread melts (bacon, leek and cheese is our favourite) as well as the best choice of vegetarian grub on the island, ranging from a vegie breakfast fry-up to falafel wraps with hummus and chilli sauce. Also serves excellent coffee.

★ Harbour View Seafood Restaurant

SEAFOOD ££

(☑ 01478-612069; www.harbourviewskye.co.uk; 7 Bosville Tce; mains £14-19; ☺ noon-3pm & 5.30-11pm Tue-Sun) The Harbour View is Portree's most congenial place to eat. It has a homely dining room with a log fire in winter, books on the mantelpiece and bric-a-brac on the shelves. And on the table, superb Scottish seafood such as fresh Skye oysters, seafood chowder, king scallops, langoustines and lobster.

❶ Getting There & Away

BOAT

Despite the bridge, there are still a couple of ferry links between Skye and the mainland. Ferries also operate from Uig on Skye to the Outer Hebrides.

Mallaig to Armadale (www.calmac.co.uk; per person/car £4.65/23.90) The Mallaig to Armadale ferry (30 minutes, eight daily Monday to Saturday, five to seven on Sunday) is very popular on weekends and in July and August, so book ahead if you're travelling by car.

Glenelg to Kylerhea (www.skyeferry.co.uk; car with up to four passengers £15; ☺ Easter-mid Oct) Runs a tiny vessel (six cars only) on the short Kylerhea to Glenelg crossing (five minutes, every 20 minutes). The ferry operates from 10am to 6pm daily (till 7pm June to August).

BUS

There are buses to Portree from Kyle of Lochalsh (£6.50, one hour, six daily) and Inverness (£24, 3¼ hours, three daily).

SURVIVAL GUIDE

❶ Directory A–Z

ACCOMMODATION

Accommodation can be difficult to find during holidays (especially around Easter and New

SLEEPING PRICE RANGES

Our reviews refer to double rooms with a private bathroom, except in hostels or where otherwise specified. Quoted rates are for a double room in high season.

£ less than £60 (£100 in London)

££ £60 to £130 (£100 to £200 in London)

£££ more than £130 (£200 in London)

Year) and major events (such as the Edinburgh Festival). In summer, popular spots (York, Canterbury, Bath etc) get very crowded, so booking ahead is essential. Local tourist offices often provide an accommodation booking service for a small fee.

Hostels There are two types of hostels in Britain: those run by the **Youth Hostels Association** (www.yha.org.uk) and **Scottish Youth Hostels Association** (www.syha.org.uk), and independent hostels, most of which are listed in the **Independent Hostels Guide** (www.independenthostelguide.co.uk). The simplest hostels cost around £15 per person per night. Larger hostels with more facilities are £18 to £25. London's YHA hostels cost from £30.

B&Bs The B&B (bed and breakfast) is a great British institution. At smaller places it's pretty much a room in somebody's house; larger places may be called a 'guesthouse' (halfway between a B&B and a full hotel). Prices start from around £25 per person for a simple bedroom and shared bathroom; for around £30 to £35 per person you get a private bathroom – either down the hall or an en suite.

Hotels There's a massive choice of hotels in Britain, from small town houses to grand country mansions, from no-frills locations to boutique hideaways. At the bargain end, single/double rooms cost from £40/50. Move up the scale and you'll pay £100/150 or beyond.

Camping Campsites range from farmers' fields with a tap and basic toilet, costing from £3 per person per night, to smarter affairs with hot showers and many other facilities, charging up to £13. You usually need all your own equipment.

ACTIVITIES

Britain is a great destination for outdoor enthusiasts. Walking and cycling are the most popular activities – you can do them on a whim, and they're the perfect way to open up some beautiful corners of the country.

Cycling

Compact Britain is an excellent destination to explore by bike. Popular regions to tour include southwest England, the Yorkshire Dales, Derbyshire's Peak District, Mid-Wales and the Scottish Borders. Bike-hire outlets are widespread; rates range from £10 per day to £60 per week.

The 10,000-mile **National Cycle Network** (www.nationalcyclenetwork.org.uk) is a web of quiet roads and traffic-free tracks that pass through busy cities and remote rural areas.

Sustrans (www.sustrans.org.uk) is another useful organisation, and publishes a wide range of maps, guides and planning tools.

Walking & Hiking

Hiking is a hugely popular pastime in Britain, especially in scenic areas such as Snowdonia, the Lake District, the Yorkshire Dales and the Scottish Highlands. Various long-distance routes cross the countryside, including the **Coast to Coast** (www.thecoasttocoastwalk.info), the **Cotswold Way** (www.nationaltrail.co.uk/cotswold), the **West Highland Way** (☑ 01389-722600; www.west-highland-way.co.uk) and the **South West Coast Path** (www.southwestcoastpath.com).

The **Ramblers Association** (www.ramblers.org.uk) is the country's leading walkers' organisation.

BUSINESS HOURS

Standard opening hours:

Banks 9.30am to 4pm or 5pm Monday to Friday; main branches 9.30am to 1pm Saturday

Post Offices 9am to 5pm (5.30pm or 6pm in cities) Monday to Friday, 9am to 12.30pm Saturday (main branches to 5pm)

Pubs 11am to 11pm Sunday to Thursday, 11am to midnight or 1am Friday and Saturday

Restaurants lunch noon to 3pm, dinner 6pm to 10pm; hours vary widely

COUNTRY FACTS

Area 88,500 sq miles

Capitals London (England and the United Kingdom), Cardiff (Wales), Edinburgh (Scotland)

Country Code ☑ 44

Currency Pound sterling (£)

Emergency ☑ 999 or ☑ 112

Languages English, Welsh, Scottish Gaelic

Money ATMs are widespread; credit cards widely accepted

Population 61.4 million

Visas Schengen rules do not apply

Shops 9am to 5pm Monday to Saturday, 10am to 4pm Sunday

GAY & LESBIAN TRAVELLERS

Britain is generally a tolerant place for gays and lesbians. London, Manchester and Brighton have flourishing gay scenes, and in other size-able cities (even some small towns) you'll find communities not entirely in the closet. That said, you'll still find pockets of homophobic hostility in some areas. Resources include the following:

Diva (www.divamag.co.uk)

Gay Times (www.gaytimes.co.uk)

London Lesbian & Gay Switchboard (www.llgs.org.uk)

INTERNET RESOURCES

Traveline (www.traveline.org.uk) Timetables and travel advice for public transport across Britain.

Visit Britain (www.visitbritain.com) Comprehensive national tourism website.

MONEY

➡ The currency of Britain is the pound sterling (£). Paper money (notes) comes in £5, £10, £20 and £50 denominations, although some shops don't accept £50 notes.

➡ ATMs, often called cash machines, are easy to find in towns and cities.

➡ Most banks and some post offices offer currency exchange.

➡ Visa and MasterCard credit and debit cards are widely accepted in Britain. Nearly every-where uses a 'Chip and PIN' system (instead of signing).

➡ Smaller businesses may charge a fee for credit card use, and some take cash or cheque only.

➡ Tipping is not obligatory. A 10% to 15% tip is fine for restaurants, cafes, taxi drivers and pub meals; if you order drinks and food at the bar, there's no need to tip.

➡ Travellers cheques are rarely used.

PUBLIC HOLIDAYS

In many areas of Britain, bank holidays are just for the banks – many businesses and visitor attractions stay open.

 SCOTTISH POUNDS

Scottish banks issue their own sterling banknotes. They are interchangeable with Bank of England notes, but you'll sometimes run into problems outside Scotland – shops in the south of Eng-land may refuse to accept them. They are also harder to exchange once you get outside the UK, though British banks will always exchange them.

SCHOOL HOLIDAYS

Roads get busy and hotel prices go up during school holidays.

Easter Holiday Week before and week after Easter.

Summer Holiday Third week of July to first week of September.

Christmas Holiday Mid-December to first week of January.

There are also three week-long 'half-term' school holidays – usually late February (or early March), late May and late October. These vary between Scot-land, England and Wales.

New Year's Day 1 January

Easter March/April (Good Friday to Easter Monday inclusive)

May Day First Monday in May

Spring Bank Holiday Last Monday in May

Summer Bank Holiday Last Monday in August

Christmas Day 25 December

Boxing Day 26 December

SAFE TRAVEL

Britain is a remarkably safe country, but crime is not unknown in London and other cities.

➡ Watch out for pickpockets and hustlers in crowded areas popular with tourists, such as around Westminster Bridge in London.

➡ When travelling by tube, tram or urban train services at night, choose a carriage containing other people.

➡ Many town centres can be rowdy on Friday and Saturday nights when the pubs and clubs are emptying.

➡ Unlicensed minicabs – a bloke with a car earning money on the side – operate in large cities, and are worth avoiding unless you know what you're doing.

TELEPHONE

The UK uses the GSM 900/1800 network, which covers the rest of Europe, Australia and New Zealand, but isn't compatible with the North American GSM 1900. Most modern mobiles can function on both networks – but check before you leave home just in case.

Area codes in the UK do not have a standard format or length (eg Edinburgh ☑ 0131, London ☑ 020, Ambleside ☑ 015394). In our reviews, area codes and phone numbers have been listed together, separated by a hyphen.

Other codes include ☑ 0500 or ☑ 0800 for free calls, ☑ 0845 for local rates, ☑ 087 for

ℹ PRACTICALITIES

DVD PAL format (incompatible with NTSC and Secam).

Newspapers Tabloids include the *Sun* and *Mirror,* and *Daily Record* (in Scotland); quality 'broadsheets' include (from right to left, politically) the *Telegraph, Times, Independent* and *Guardian.*

Radio Main BBC stations and wavelengths are Radio 1 (98–99.6MHz FM), Radio 2 (88–92MHz FM), Radio 3 (90–92.2MHz FM), Radio 4 (92–94.4MHz FM) and Radio 5 Live (909 or 693AM). National commercial stations include Virgin Radio (1215Hz MW) and nonhighbrow classical specialist, Classic FM (100–102MHz FM). All are available on digital.

TV All TV in the UK is digital. Leading broadcasters include BBC, ITV and Channel 4. Satellite and cable TV providers include Sky and Virgin Media.

Weights & Measures Britain uses a mix of metric and imperial measures (eg petrol is sold by the litre but beer by the pint; mountain heights are in metres but road distances are in miles).

national rates and ☑ 089 or ☑ 09 for premium rates. Mobile phones start with ☑ 07 and calling them is more expensive than calling a landline. Dial ☑ 100 for an operator and ☑ 155 for an international operator as well as reverse-charge (collect) calls.

➡ To call outside the UK, dial ☑ 00, then the country code (☑ 1 for USA, ☑ 61 for Australia etc), the area code (you usually drop the initial zero) and the number.

➡ For directory enquiries, a host of agencies compete for your business and charge from 10p to 40p; numbers include ☑ 118 192, ☑ 118 118, ☑ 118 500 and ☑ 118 811.

TIME

Britain is on GMT/UTC. The clocks go forward for 'summer time' one hour at the end of March and go back at the end of October. The 24-hour clock is used for transport timetables.

VISAS

European Economic Area (EEA) nationals don't need a visa to visit (or work in) Britain. Citizens of Australia, Canada, New Zealand, South Africa and the USA can visit for up to six months (three months for some nationalities), but are prohibited from working. For more info see www.ukvisas.gov.uk.

ℹ Getting There & Away

AIR
London Airports

London is served by five airports; Heathrow and Gatwick are the busiest.

Gatwick (LGW; www.gatwickairport.com) Britain's number-two airport, mainly for international flights, 30 miles south of central London.

London City (LCY; www.londoncityairport.com)
London Heathrow Airport (www.heathrow airport.com) The UK's major hub welcoming flights from all over the world.

Luton (LTN; www.london-luton.co.uk) Some 35 miles north of central London, well known as a holiday-flight airport.

Stansted (STN; www.stanstedairport.com) About 35 miles northeast of central London, mainly handling charter and budget European flights.

Regional Airports

Bristol Airport (www.bristolairport.co.uk) Flights from all over Europe as well as some popular holidays destinations in North Africa and North America.

Cardiff Airport (☑ 01446-711111; www.cardiff-airport.com)

Edinburgh Airport (☑ 0844 448 8833; www.edinburghairport.com) Edinburgh Airport, 8 miles west of the city, has numerous flights to other parts of Scotland and the UK, Ireland and mainland Europe. **FlyBe/Loganair** (☑ 0871 700 2000; www.loganair.co.uk) operates daily flights to Inverness, Wick, Orkney, Shetland and Stornoway.

Glasgow International Airport (GLA; ☑ 0844 481 5555; www.glasgowairport.com) Ten miles west of the city, Glasgow International Airport handles domestic traffic and international flights.

Liverpool John Lennon Airport (☑ 0870 750 8484; www.liverpoolairport.com; Speke Hall Ave)

Manchester Airport (☑ 0161-489 3000; www.manchesterairport.co.uk) Manchester Airport, south of the city, is the largest airport outside London and is served by 13 locations throughout Britain as well as more than 50 international destinations.

ESSENTIAL FOOD & DRINK

Britain once had a reputation for bad food, but the nation has enjoyed something of a culinary revolution in the last decade or so, and you can often find fine dining based on fresh local produce.

➡ **Fish & chips** Long-standing favourite, best sampled in coastal towns.

➡ **Haggis** Scottish icon, mainly offal and oatmeal, traditionally served with 'tatties and neeps' (potatoes and turnips).

➡ **Sandwich** Global snack today, but an English invention from the 18th century.

➡ **Laverbread** Laver is a type of seaweed, mixed with oatmeal and fried to create this traditional Welsh speciality.

➡ **Ploughman's lunch** Bread and cheese – pub menu regular, perfect with a pint.

➡ **Roast beef & Yorkshire pudding** Traditional lunch on Sunday for the English.

➡ **Cornish pasty** Savoury pastry, southwest speciality, now available country-wide.

➡ **Real ale** Traditionally brewed beer, flavoured with malt and hops and served at room temperature.

➡ **Scotch whisky** Spirit distilled from malted and fermented barley, then aged in oak barrels for at least three years.

Newcastle International Airport (☑ 0871 882 1121; www.newcastleairport.com) Seven miles north of the city off the A696, the airport has direct services to many UK and European cities as well as long-haul flights to Dubai. Tour operators fly charters to the USA, Middle East and Africa.

LAND
Bus & Coach

The international network **Eurolines** (www.eurolines.com) connects a huge number of European destinations via the Channel Tunnel or ferry crossings.

Services to and from Britain are operated by **National Express** (www.nationalexpress.com).

Train

The quickest way to Europe from Britain is via the Channel Tunnel. High-speed **Eurostar** (www.eurostar.com) passenger services shuttle at least 10 times daily between London and Paris

EATING PRICE RANGES

The prices we quote are for a main course at dinner unless otherwise indicated. The symbols used in each review indicate the following price ranges:

£ less than £9

££ £9 to £18

£££ more than £18

(2½ hours) or Brussels (two hours) via the Channel Tunnel. The normal one-way fare between London and Paris/Brussels costs £140 to £180; cheaper fares as low as £39 one way are possible via advance booking and by travelling off-peak.

Vehicles use the **Eurotunnel** (www.eurotunnel.com) at Folkestone in England or Calais in France. The trains run four times an hour from 6am to 10pm, then hourly. The journey takes 35 minutes. The one-way cost for a car and passengers is between £75 and £165 depending on time of day; promotional fares often bring it down to £55.

Travelling between Ireland and Britain, the main train–ferry–train route is Dublin to London, via Dun Laoghaire and Holyhead. Ferries also run between Rosslare and Fishguard or Pembroke (Wales), with train connections on either side.

SEA

Ferries sail from southern England to French ports in a couple of hours; other routes connect eastern England to the Netherlands, Germany and northern Spain, and Ireland from southwest Scotland and Wales.

The main ferry routes between Britain and mainland Europe include Dover to Calais or Boulogne (France), Harwich to Hook of Holland (Netherlands), Hull to Zeebrugge (Belgium) or Rotterdam (Netherlands), and Portsmouth to Santander or Bilbao (Spain). Routes to and from Ireland include Holyhead to Dun Laoghaire.

Competition from the Eurotunnel and budget airlines means ferry operators discount heavily at certain times of year. The short cross-channel routes such as Dover to Calais or Boulogne can be as low as £20 for a car plus up to five passengers, although around £50 is more likely. If you're a foot passenger, or cycling, crossings can start from as little as £10 each way.

Broker sites covering all routes and options include www.ferrybooker.com and www.direct ferries.co.uk.

Brittany Ferries (www.brittany-ferries.com)

DFDS Seaways (www.dfds.co.uk)

Irish Ferries (www.irishferries.com)

P&O Ferries (www.poferries.com)

Stena Line (www.stenaline.com)

ⓘ Getting Around

For getting around Britain, your first choice is car or public transport. Having your own car makes the best use of time and helps reach remote places, but rental, fuel costs and parking can be expensive – so public transport is often the better way to go.

Cheapest but slowest are long-distance buses (called coaches in Britain). Trains are faster but much more expensive.

AIR

Britain's domestic air companies include **British Airways** (BA; www.britishairways.com), **Flybe/ Loganair** (☑ 0871 700 2000; www.loganair. co.uk), **EasyJet** (EZY; www.easyjet.com) and **Ryanair** (FR; www.ryanair.com). On most shorter routes (eg London to Newcastle, or Manchester to Bristol), it's often faster to take the train once airport downtime is factored in.

BUS

Long-distance buses (coaches) nearly always offer the cheapest way to get around. Many towns have separate stations for local buses and intercity coaches; make sure you're in the right one.

National Express (www.nationalexpress. com) is England's main coach operator. North of the border, **Scottish Citylink** (www.citylink. co.uk) is the leading coach company. Tickets are cheaper if you book in advance and travel at quieter times. As a rough guide, a 200-mile trip (eg London to York) will cost around £15 to £30 if booked a few days in advance.

Also offering cheap fares (if you're lucky, from £1) is **Megabus** (www.megabus.com), which serves about 30 destinations around Britain.

Bus Passes

National Express offers discount passes to full-time students and under-26s, called Young Persons Coachcards. They cost £10 and give 30% off standard adult fares. Also available are coachcards for people over 60, families and travellers with a disability.

For touring the country, National Express offers Brit Xplorer passes, allowing unlimited travel for seven days (£79), 14 days (£139) and 28 days (£219).

CAR & MOTORCYCLE

Most overseas driving licences are valid in Britain for up to 12 months from the date of entry.

Rental

Car rental is expensive in Britain; you'll pay from around £120 per week for the smallest model, or £250 per week for a medium-sized car (including insurance and unlimited mileage). All the major players including Avis, Hertz and Budget operate here.

Using a rental-broker site such as **UK Car Hire** (www.ukcarhire.net) or **Kayak** (www.kayak.com) can help find bargains.

It's illegal to drive a car or motorbike in Britain without (at least) third-party insurance. This is included with all rental cars.

Road Rules

The *Highway Code,* available in bookshops (or at www.gov.uk/highway-code), contains everything you need to know about Britain's road rules. The main ones to remember:

➡ Always drive on the left.

➡ Give way to your right at junctions and roundabouts.

➡ Always use the left-hand lane on motorways and dual carriageways, unless overtaking (passing).

➡ Wear seatbelts in cars and crash helmets on motorcycles.

➡ Don't use a mobile phone while driving.

➡ Don't drink and drive; the maximum blood-alcohol level allowed is 80mg/100mL (0.08%) in England and Wales, 50mg/100mL (0.05%) in Scotland.

➡ Yellow lines (single or double) along the edge of the road indicate parking restrictions; red lines mean no stopping whatsoever.

➡ Speed limits are 30mph in built-up areas, 60mph on main roads, and 70mph on motorways and dual carriageways.

ⓘ TRAVELINE

Traveline (☑ 0871 200 2233; www. traveline.info) is a very useful information service covering bus, coach, taxi and train services nationwide.

TRAIN

About 20 different companies operate train services in Britain, while Network Rail operates tracks and stations. For some passengers this system can be confusing at first, but information and ticket-buying services are mostly centralised. If you have to change trains, or use two or more train operators, you still buy one ticket – valid for the whole journey. The main railcards and passes are also accepted by all train operators.

National Rail Enquiries (☑ 08457 48 49 50; www.nationalrail.co.uk) provides booking and timetable information for Britain's entire rail network.

Classes

Rail travel has two classes: 1st and standard. Travelling 1st class costs around 50% more than standard. At weekends some train operators offer 'upgrades' to first class for an extra £5 to £25 on top of your standard class fare, payable on the spot.

Costs & Reservations

The earlier you book, the cheaper it gets. You can also save if you travel 'off-peak' (ie the days and times that aren't busy). If you buy online, you can have the ticket posted (UK addresses only), or collect it from station machines on the day of travel.

There are three main fare types:

Anytime Buy anytime, travel anytime – usually the most expensive option.

Off-peak Buy anytime, travel off-peak (what is off-peak depends on the journey).

Advance Buy in advance, travel only on specific trains (usually the cheapest option).

Train Passes

If you're staying in Britain for a while, passes known as railcards (www.railcard.co.uk) are available:

16–25 Railcard For those aged 16 to 25, or a full-time UK student.

Senior Railcard For anyone over 60.

Family & Friends Railcard Covers up to four adults and four children travelling together.

Railcards cost £30 (valid for one year, available from major stations or online) and get 33% discount on most train fares, except those already heavily discounted. With the Family card, adults get 33% and children get 60% discounts, so the fee is easily repaid in a couple of journeys.

Regional Passes

Various local train passes are available covering specific areas and lines – ask at a local train station to get an idea of what's available.

National Passes

For country-wide travel, **BritRail** (www.britrail.net) passes are available for visitors from overseas. They must be bought in your country of origin (not in Britain) from a specialist travel agency. Available in seven different versions (eg England only; Scotland only; all Britain; UK and Ireland) for periods from four to 30 days.

France

Why Go?

France has so much to entice travellers – renowned gastronomy, iconic sights, splendid art heritage, a fabulous outdoors. You could sample it all in a week, but you'll invariably feel as though you've only scratched the surface of this big country.

Visiting France is certainly about seeing the big sights, but it's just as much about savouring life's little pleasures: a stroll through an elegant city square, a coffee on a sunny pavement terrace, a meal that lasts well into the afternoon or night, a scenic drive punctuated with photo stops and impromptu farm or vineyard visits. The French are big on their *art de vivre* (art of living) and you should embrace it, too.

Best Places to Eat

➡ Le Musée (p223)
➡ Café Saint Régis (p196)
➡ Restaurant Le Pim'pi (p231)
➡ Le Genty-Magre (p233)
➡ Le Café des Épices (p237)

Best Places for History

➡ Grotte de Lascaux (p227)
➡ D-Day beaches (p207)
➡ The Somme (p204)
➡ Pont du Gard (p235)
➡ Musée Carnavalet (p192)

When to Go
Paris

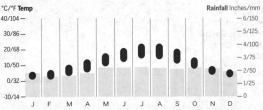

Dec–Mar Christmas markets in Alsace, snow action in the Alps and truffles in the south.

Apr–Jun France is at its springtime best, with good weather and no crowds.

Sep Cooling temperatures, abundant local produce and the *vendange* (grape harvest).

France Highlights

1 Gorge on the iconic sights and sophistication of Europe's most hopelessly romantic city, **Paris** (p184).

2 Relive the French Renaissance with extraordinary châteaux built by kings and queens in the **Loire Valley** (p215).

3 Do a Bond and swoosh down slopes in the shadow of Mont Blanc in **Chamonix** (p225).

4 Dodge tides, stroll moonlit sand and immerse yourself in legend at island abbey **Mont St-Michel** (p207).

5 Savour ancient ruins, modern art, markets, lavender and hilltop villages in slow-paced **Provence** (p235).

6 Taste bubbly in ancient *caves* (cellars) in **Épernay** (p211), the heart of Champagne.

7 Tuck into France's halest piggy-driven cuisine in a traditional *bouchon* in **Lyon** (p220).

8 Hit the big time at Monaco's sumptuous **Casino de Monte Carlo** (p247).

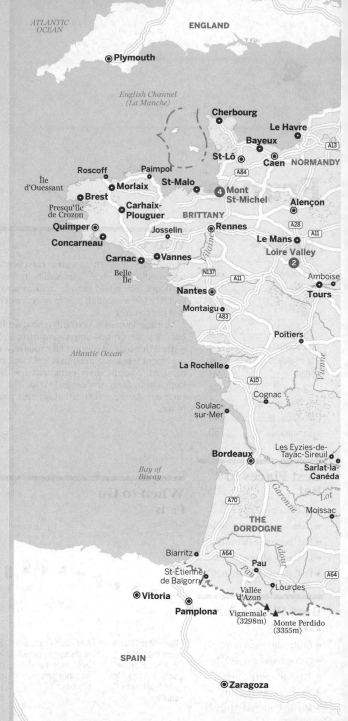

ITINERARIES

One Week

Start with a couple of days exploring **Paris**, taking in the Louvre, the Eiffel Tower, Notre Dame, Montmartre and a boat trip along the Seine. Day trip to magnificent **Versailles** and then spend the rest of the week in **Normandy** to visit WWII's D-Day beaches and glorious Mont St-Michel. Or head east to **Champagne** to sample the famous bubbly and visit Reims' magnificent cathedral.

Two Weeks

With Paris and surrounds having taken up much of the first week, hop on a high-speed TGV down to **Avignon** or **Marseille** and take in the delights of Provence's Roman heritage, its beautiful hilltop villages and its famous artistic legacy. Finish your stay with a few days in **Nice**, enjoying its glittering Mediterranean landscapes and sunny cuisine. Alternatively, head southwest to elegant **Bordeaux** and its world-famous vineyards before pushing inland to the **Dordogne** with its hearty gastronomy and unique prehistoric-art heritage.

PARIS

POP 2.2 MILLION

What can be said about the sexy, sophisticated City of Lights that hasn't already been said myriad times before? Quite simply, this is one of the world's great metropolises – a trendsetter, market leader and cultural capital for over a thousand years and still going strong.

As you might expect, Paris is strewn with historic architecture, glorious galleries and cultural treasures galore. But the modern-day city is much more than just a museum piece: it's a heady hotchpotch of cultures and ideas – a place to stroll the boulevards, shop till you drop, flop riverside or simply do as the Parisians do and watch the world buzz by from a streetside cafe. Savour every moment.

◉ Sights

◉ Left Bank

★ Eiffel Tower   LANDMARK

(Map p186; ☎ 08 92 70 12 39; www.tour-eiffel.fr; Champ de Mars, 5 av Anatole France, 7e; lift to top adult/child €15/10.50, lift to 2nd fl €9/4.50, stairs to 2nd fl €5/3, lift 2nd fl to top €6; ⊙ lifts & stairs 9am-midnight mid-Jun–Aug, lifts 9.30am-11pm, stairs 9.30am-6.30pm Sep–mid-Jun; Ⓜ Bir Hakeim or RER Champ de Mars-Tour Eiffel) No one could imagine Paris today without it. But Gustave Eiffel only constructed this elegant, 320m-tall signature spire as a temporary exhibit for the 1889 World Fair. Luckily, the art nouveau tower's popularity assured its survival. Prebook tickets online to avoid long ticket queues.

Lifts ascend to the tower's three levels; change lifts on the 2nd level for the final ascent to the top. Energetic visitors can walk as far as the 2nd level using the south pillar's 704-step stairs.

★ Musée d'Orsay   MUSEUM

(Map p186; www.musee-orsay.fr; 62 rue de Lille, 7e; adult/child €11/free; ⊙ 9.30am-6pm Tue, Wed & Fri-Sun, to 9.45pm Thu; Ⓜ Assemblée Nationale or RER Musée d'Orsay) Recently renovated to incorporate richly coloured walls and increased exhibition space, the home of France's national collection from the impressionist, postimpressionist and art nouveau movements spanning the 1840s and 1914 is the glorious former Gare d'Orsay railway station – itself an art nouveau showpiece – where a roll-call of masters and their world-famous works are on display.

Top of every visitor's must-see list is the museum's painting collections, centred on the world's largest collection of impressionist and post-impressionist art.

Musée du Quai Branly   MUSEUM

(Map p186; www.quaibranly.fr; 37 quai Branly, 7e; adult/child €8.50/free; ⊙ 11am-7pm Tue, Wed & Sun, 11am-9pm Thu-Sat; Ⓜ Alma Marceau or RER Pont de l'Alma) No other museum in Paris so inspires travellers, armchair anthropologists and those who simply appreciate the beauty of traditional craftsmanship. A tribute to the diversity of human culture, Musée du Quai Branly presents an overview of indigenous and folk art. Its four main sections focus on Oceania, Asia, Africa and the Americas.

An impressive array of masks, carvings, weapons, jewellery and more make up the body of the rich collection, displayed in a refreshingly unique interior without rooms or high walls.

Musée Rodin   GARDENS, MUSEUM
(Map p186; www.musee-rodin.fr; 79 rue de Varenne, 7e; adult/child museum incl garden €6/free, garden only €2/free; ⊙10am-5.45pm Tue & Thu-Sun, to 8.45pm Wed; ⓂVarenne) Sculptor, painter, sketcher, engraver and collector Auguste Rodin donated his entire collection to the French state in 1908 on the proviso that it dedicated his former workshop and showroom, the beautiful 1730 Hôtel Biron, to displaying his works. They're now installed not only in the mansion itself, but in its rose-clambered garden – one of the most peaceful places in central Paris and a wonderful spot to contemplate his famous work *The Thinker*.

Purchase tickets online to avoid queuing.

Les Catacombes   CEMETERY
(Map p186; www.catacombes.paris.fr; 1 av Colonel Henri Roi-Tanguy, 14e; adult/child €8/free; ⊙10am-8pm Tue-Sun, last admission 7pm; ⓂDenfert Rochereau) Paris' most macabre sight is its underground tunnels lined with skulls and bones. In 1785 it was decided to rectify the hygiene problems of Paris' overflowing cemeteries by exhuming the bones and storing them in disused quarry tunnels and the Catacombes were created in 1810.

After descending 20m (via 130 narrow, dizzying spiral steps) below street level, you follow the dark, subterranean passages to reach the ossuary itself (2km in all). Exit back up 83 steps onto rue Remy Dumoncel, 14e.

Panthéon   HISTORIC BUILDING
(Map p190; www.monum.fr; place du Panthéon, 5e; adult/child €7.50/free; ⊙10am-6.30pm Apr-Sep, to 6pm Oct-Mar; ⓂMaubert-Mutualité, Cardinal Lemoine or RER Luxembourg) Overlooking the city from its Left Bank perch, the Panthéon's stately neoclassical dome stands out as one of the most recognisable icons in the Parisian skyline. Originally a church and now a mausoleum, it has served since 1791 as the resting place of some of France's greatest thinkers, including Voltaire, Rousseau, Braille and Hugo. An architectural masterpiece, the interior is impressively vast (if slightly soulless) and certainly worth a wander. The dome is closed for renovations through 2015 (other structural work will continue through 2022).

Jardin du Luxembourg   PARK
(Map p190; numerous entrances; ⊙hours vary; ⓂSt-Sulpice, Rennes or Notre Dame des Champs, or RER Luxembourg) This inner-city oasis of formal terraces, chestnut groves and lush lawns has a special place in Parisians' hearts. Napoléon dedicated the 23 gracefully laid-out hectares of the Luxembourg Gardens to the children of Paris, and many residents spent their childhood prodding 1920s wooden **sailboats** (per 30min €3; ⊙Apr-Oct) with long sticks on the octagonal **Grand Bassin** pond, watching puppets perform Punch & Judy–type shows at the **Théâtre du Luxembourg** (Map p190; www.marionnettesduluxembourg.fr; tickets €4.80; ⊙usually 3.30pm Wed, 11am & 3.30pm Sat & Sun, daily during school holidays; ⓂNotre Dame des Champs), and riding the *carrousel* (merry-go-round) or **ponies** (Map p190).

Église St-Sulpice   CHURCH
(Map p190; http://pss75.fr/saint-sulpice-paris; place St-Sulpice, 6e; ⊙7.30am-7.30pm; ⓂSt-Sulpice) In 1646 work started on the twin-towered Church of St Sulpicius, lined inside with 21

ⓘ **MUSEUM DISCOUNTS & FREEBIES**

If you plan on visiting a lot of museums, pick up a **Paris Museum Pass** (http://en.parismuseumpass.com; 2/4/6 days €42/56/69) or a **Paris City Passport** (www.parisinfo.com; 2/3/5 days €71/103/130), which also includes public transport and various extras. The passes get you into 60-odd venues in and around Paris, bypassing (or reducing) long ticket queues. Both passes are available from the Paris Convention & Visitors Bureau (p200).

Permanent collections at most city-run museums are free, but temporary exhibitions usually command a fee. Admission to national museums is reduced for those aged over 60 and reduced or free for those under 26, so don't buy a Paris Museum Pass or Paris City Passport if you qualify.

National museums are also free for everyone on the first Sunday of each month, except the Arc de Triomphe, Conciergerie, Musée du Louvre, Panthéon and Tours de Notre Dame, which are only free on the first Sunday of the month November to March.

Greater Paris

Seine

Île de la Grande Jatte

Porte de St-Ouen

Bd Bessières

Porte de Clichy

Av Bineau

Péreire Lavallois

R de Rome

La Fourche

Av Charles de Gaulle

Av Niel

Av de Wagram

Bd Malesherbes

Place de Clichy

Av des Ternes

Bd de Courcelles

Jardin d'Acclimatation

Mare St-James

Lac Pour le Patinage

Neuilly Porte Maillot Palais des Congrès

Av Mac Mahon

Av Hoche

Bd Haussmann

St-Augustin

Gare St-Lazare

Pl du Maillot de Lattre de Tassigny

4

Charles de Gaulle Étoile

24

28

Auber

Allée de Longchamp

Avenue Foch

Av Foch

25

16

Av des Champs-Élysées

Bois de Boulogne

Lac Inférieur

Av Kléber

10

Cours la Reine

Jardin des Tuileries

Avenue Henri Martin

Trocadéro

Jardins du Trocadéro

Q d'Orsay

Q Anatole France

Eiffel Tower

Q Branly

7

Av Bosquet

19

Esplanade des Invalides

6

Musée d'Orsay

3

Musée d'Orsay

2

Boulain-Villiers

Lac Supérieur

11

Champ de Mars-Tour Eiffel

Av de Suffren

Av de la Motte-Picquet

École Militaire

8

Bd des Invalides

20

Av Mozart

Avenue du Président Kennedy

Bir Hakeim

17

Av de Saxe

Bd Raspail

R de Rennes

Porte d'Auteuil

13

Javel

Av Émile Zola

R de Sèvres

Ste-Périne

Seine

R de la Convention

14

26

Av Maine

9

Boulevard Victor

R Lecourbe

R de Vaugirard

Gare Montparnasse

Bd Raspail

R de la Croix Nivert

Bd Victor

R de Vouillé

Issy–Val de Seine

Bd Lefebvre

Porte de Vanves

Av du Maine

R d'Alésia

Île St-Germain

Jacques Henri Lartigue

Bd Périphérique

Issy Ville

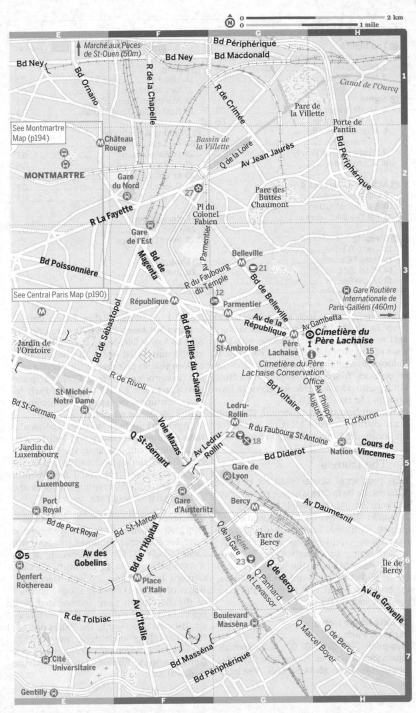

Greater Paris

side chapels, and it took six architects 150 years to finish. What draws most visitors isn't its striking Italianate facade with two rows of superimposed columns, its Counter Reformation–influenced neoclassical decor or even its frescoes by Eugène Delacroix but its setting for a murderous scene in Dan Brown's *The Da Vinci Code*.

You can hear the monumental, 1781-built organ during 10.30am Mass on Sunday or the occasional Sunday-afternoon concert.

◉ The Islands

Paris' twin set of islands could not be more different. Île de la Cité is bigger, full of sights and very touristy (few people live here).

Smaller Île St-Louis is residential and quieter, with just enough boutiques and restaurants – and legendary ice-cream maker Berthillon – to attract visitors. The area around Pont St-Louis, the bridge across to the Île de la Cité, and Pont Louis-Philippe, the bridge to the Marais, is one of the most romantic spots in Paris.

★ Cathédrale Notre
Dame de Paris　　　　　　CATHEDRAL
(Map p190; ☑ 01 53 10 07 00; www.cathedrale deparis.com; 6 place du Parvis Notre Dame, 4e; cathedral free, towers adult/child €8.50/free, treas-

ury €2/1; ⊙cathedral 7.45am-6.45pm Mon-Sat, to 7.15pm Sun, towers 10am-6.30pm, to 11pm Fri & Sat Jul & Aug; Ⓜ Cité) Notre Dame, Paris' most visited unticketed site with upwards of 14 million visitors crossing its threshold a year, is a masterpiece of French Gothic architecture. It was the focus of Catholic Paris for seven centuries, its vast interior accommodating 6000-plus worshippers.

Highlights include its three spectacular **rose windows**, **treasury** and bell **towers**, which can be climbed. From the North Tower, 400-odd steps spiral to the top of the western facade, where you'll find yourself face-to-face with frightening gargoyles and a spectacular view of Paris.

Conciergerie　　　　　　MONUMENT
(Map p190; www.monuments-nationaux.fr; 2 bd du Palais, 1er; adult/child €8.50/free, joint ticket with Sainte-Chapelle €12.50; ⊙9.30am-6pm; Ⓜ Cité) A royal palace in the 14th century, the Conciergerie later became a prison. During the Reign of Terror (1793–94) alleged enemies of the Revolution were incarcerated here before being brought before the Revolutionary Tribunal next door in the Palais de Justice. Top-billing exhibitions take place in the beautiful, Rayonnant Gothic Salle des Gens d'Armes, Europe's largest surviving medieval hall.

◉ Right Bank

★ **Musée du Louvre**   MUSEUM
(Map p190; ☑ 01 40 20 53 17; www.louvre.fr; rue
de Rivoli & quai des Tuileries, 1er; adult/child €12/
free; ⏰ 9am-6pm Mon, Thu, Sat & Sun, to 9.45pm
Wed & Fri; Ⓜ Palais Royal–Musée du Louvre) Few
art galleries are as prized or daunting as the
Musée du Louvre, Paris' pièce de résistance
no first-time visitor to the city can resist.
This is, after all, one of the world's largest
and most diverse museums. Showcase to
35,000 works of art – from Mesopotamian,
Egyptian and Greek antiquities to masterpieces by artists such as da Vinci, Michelangelo and Rembrandt – it would take nine
months to glance at every piece, rendering
advance planning essential.

★ **Cimetière du Père Lachaise**   CEMETERY
(Map p186; ☑ 01 43 70 70 33; www.pere-lachaise.
com; 16 rue du Repos & bd de Ménilmontant, 20e;
⏰ 8am-6pm Mon-Fri, 8.30am-6pm Sat, 9am-
6pm Sun; Ⓜ Père Lachaise or Gambetta) FREE
The world's most visited cemetery, Père
Lachaise, opened in 1804. Its 70,000 ornate,
even ostentatious, tombs of the rich and/or
famous form a verdant, 44-hectare sculpture
garden. The most visited are those of 1960s
rock star Jim Morrison (division 6) and Oscar Wilde (division 89). Pick up cemetery
maps at the **conservation office** (Map p186;
16 rue du Repos, 20e; ⏰ 8.30am-12.30pm & 2-5pm
Mon-Fri; Ⓜ Père Lachaise), near the main bd de
Ménilmontant entrance.

Arc de Triomphe   LANDMARK
(Map p186; www.monuments-nationaux.fr; place
Charles de Gaulle, 8e; adult/child €9.50/free;
⏰ 10am-11pm Apr-Sep, to 10.30pm Oct-Mar;
Ⓜ Charles de Gaulle–Étoile) If anything rivals
the Eiffel Tower as the symbol of Paris, it's
this magnificent 1836 monument to Napoléon's 1805 victory at Austerlitz, which
he commissioned the following year. The
intricately sculpted triumphal arch stands
sentinel in the centre of the Étoile ('star')
roundabout. From the viewing platform on
top of the arch (50m up via 284 steps and
well worth the climb) you can see the dozen
avenues.

Centre Pompidou   MUSEUM
(Map p190; ☑ 01 44 78 12 33; www.centre
pompidou.fr; place Georges Pompidou, 4e; museum,
exhibitions & panorama adult/child €13/free;
⏰ 11am-9pm Wed-Mon; 🕾; Ⓜ Rambuteau) The
Pompidou Centre has amazed and delighted
visitors ever since it opened in 1977, not just
for its outstanding collection of modern art –
the largest in Europe – but also for its radical architectural statement. The dynamic
and vibrant arts centre delights with its irresistible cocktail of galleries and cutting-edge
exhibitions, hands-on workshops, dance
performances, cinemas and other entertainment venues. The exterior, with its street
performers and fanciful fountains (place
Igor Stravinsky), is a fun place to linger.

Basilique du Sacré-Cœur   BASILICA
(Map p194; www.sacre-coeur-montmartre.com;
place du Parvis du Sacré-Cœur; dome adult/child
€6/4, cash only; ⏰ 6am-10.30pm, dome 9am-7pm
Apr-Sep, to 5.30pm Oct-Mar; Ⓜ Anvers) Although
some may poke fun at Sacré-Cœur's unsubtle
design, the view from its parvis is one of
those perfect Paris postcards. More than just
a basilica, Sacré-Cœur is a veritable experience, from the musicians performing on the
steps to the groups of friends picnicking on
the hillside park. Touristy, yes. But beneath it
all, Sacré-Cœur's heart still shines gold.

Musée Picasso   ART MUSEUM
(Map p190; ☑ 01 42 71 25 21; www.museepicasso
paris.fr; 5 rue de Thorigny, 3e; admission €11;
⏰ 11.30am-6pm Tue-Fri, 9.30am-6pm Sat & Sun;

ⓘ THE LOUVRE: TICKETS & TOURS

To best navigate the collection, opt for a
self-guided **thematic trail** (1½ to three
hours; download trail brochures in advance from the website) or a self-paced
multimedia guide (€5). More formal,
English-language **guided tours** depart
from the Hall Napoléon, which also has
free English-language maps.

The main entrance and ticket windows are covered by the 21m-high
Grande Pyramide, a glass pyramid
designed by the Chinese-born American
architect IM Pei. If you don't have the
Museum Pass (which gives you priority), you can avoid the longest queues
(for security) outside the pyramid by
entering the Louvre complex via the underground shopping centre **Carrousel
du Louvre** (Map p190; www.carrouseldu-
louvre.com; 99 rue de Rivoli; ⏰ 8am-11pm,
shops 10am-8pm; 🕾; Ⓜ Palais Royal–
Musée du Louvre). You'll need to queue up
again to buy your ticket once inside.

Central Paris

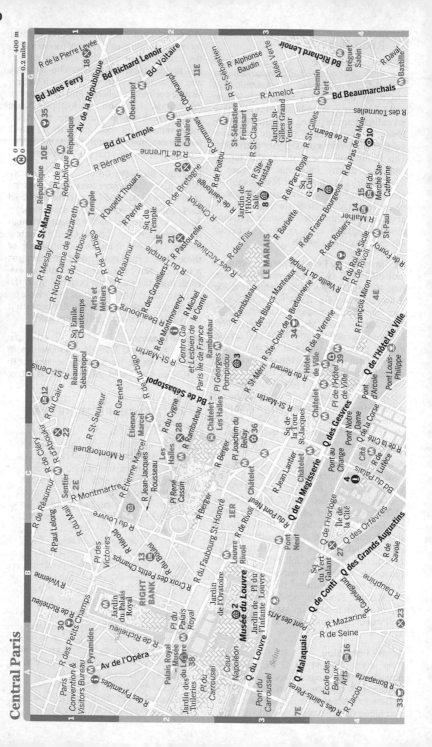

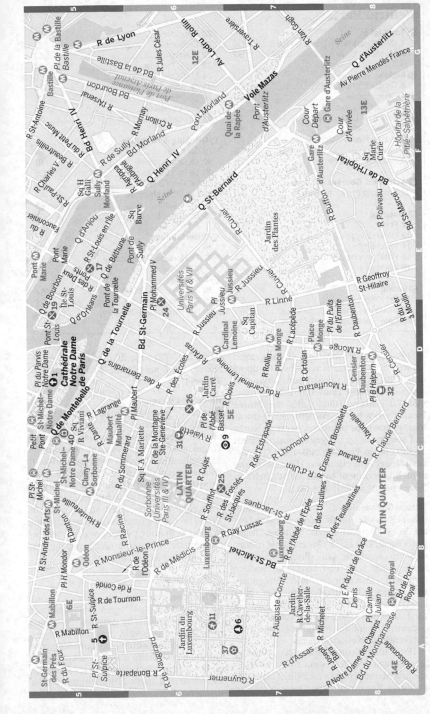

Central Paris

Ⓜ St-Paul or Chemin Vert) One of Paris' most beloved art collections reopened its doors in late 2014 after a massive renovation and much controversy. Housed in the stunning, mid-17th-century Hôtel Salé, the Musée Picasso woos art lovers with 5000 drawings, engravings, paintings, ceramic works and sculptures by the *grand maître* (great master) Pablo Picasso (1881–1973). The extraordinary collection was donated to the French government by the artist's heirs in lieu of paying inheritance tax.

Musée Carnavalet   MUSEUM
(Map p190; www.carnavalet.paris.fr; 23 rue de Sévigné, 3e; ⊙10am-6pm Tue-Sun; Ⓜ St-Paul, Chemin Vert or Rambuteau) FREE This engaging history museum, spanning Gallo-Roman times to modern day, is in two *hôtels particuliers* (private mansions): mid-16th-century Renaissance-style Hôtel Carnavalet and late-17th-century Hôtel Le Peletier de St-Fargeau. Some of the nation's most important documents, paintings and other objects from the French Revolution are here.

Don't miss Georges Fouquet's stunning art nouveau jewellery shop from rue Royale, and Marcel Proust's cork-lined bedroom in his bd Haussmann apartment where he wrote his 7350-page literary cycle *À la Recherche du Temps Perdu* (Remembrance of Things Past).

Place des Vosges   SQUARE
(Map p190; place des Vosges, 4e; Ⓜ St-Paul or Bastille) Inaugurated in 1612 as place Royale and thus Paris' oldest square, place des Vosges is a strikingly elegant ensemble of 36 symmetrical houses with ground-floor arcades, steep slate roofs and large dormer windows arranged around a leafy square with four symmetrical fountains and an 1829 copy of a mounted statue of Louis XIII. The square received its present name in 1800 to honour the Vosges *département* (administrative division) for being the first in France to pay its taxes.

⌕ Tours

★ **Parisien d'un jour –
Paris Greeters**   WALKING TOUR
(www.parisgreeters.fr; by donation) See Paris through local eyes with these two- to three-hour city tours. Volunteers – knowledgeable Parisians passionate about their city in the main – lead groups (maximum six people) to their favourite spots. Minimum two weeks' notice needed.

Fat Tire Bike Tours CYCLING
(Map p186; ☑ 01 56 58 10 54; www.fattirebiketours.
com) Day and night bike tours of the city,
both in central Paris and further afield to
Versailles and Monet's garden in Giverny.

Bateaux-Mouches BOAT TOUR
(Map p186; ☑ 01 42 25 96 10; www.bateaux
mouches.com; Port de la Conférence, 8e; adult/
child €13.50/5.50; ☺ Apr-Dec; Ⓜ Alma Marceau)
The largest river cruise company in Paris
and a favourite with tour groups. Cruises
(70 minutes) run regularly from 10.15am to
11pm April to September and 13 times a day
between 11am and 9pm the rest of the year.
Commentary is in French and English. It's
located on the Right Bank, just east of the
Pont de l'Alma.

Paris Walks WALKING TOUR
(☑ 01 48 09 21 40; www.paris-walks.com; adult/
child €12/8) Long established and highly
rated by our readers, Paris Walks offers two-
hour thematic walking tours (art, fashion,
chocolate, the French Revolution etc).

🛌 Sleeping

The Paris Convention & Visitors Bureau
(p200) can find you a place to stay (no booking fee, but you need a credit card), though
queues can be long in high season. To rent
an apartment, try **Paris Attitude** (www.paris
attitude.com).

🛏 Left Bank

Hôtel Vic Eiffel BOUTIQUE HOTEL €
(Map p186; www.hotelviceiffel.com; 92 bd Garibaldi, 15e; s/d from €99/109; 🛜; Ⓜ Sèvres-Lecourbe)
Outstanding value for money, this pristine
hotel with chic orange and oyster-grey
rooms (two are wheelchair accessible) is a
short walk from the Eiffel Tower, with the
metro on the doorstep. Budget-priced Classic rooms are small but perfectly functional;
midrange Superior and Privilege rooms offer increased space. Friendly staff go out of
their way to help.

⭐**Hôtel Félicien** BOUTIQUE HOTEL €€
(Map p186; ☑ 01 83 76 02 45; www.hotelfelicien-
paris.com; 21 rue Félicien David, 16e; d €120-280;
❄ @ 🛜 🗫; Ⓜ Mirabeau) The price–quality
ratio at this chic boutique hotel, squirrelled
away in a 1930s building, is outstanding. Exquisitely designed rooms feel more five-star
than four, with 'White' and 'Silver' suites on
the hotel's top 'Sky floor' more than satisfy-

ing their promise of indulgent cocooning.
Romantics, eat your heart out.

Sublim Eiffel DESIGN HOTEL €€
(Map p186; ☑ 01 40 65 95 95; www.sublimeiffel.
com; 94 bd Garibaldi, 15e; d from €140; ❄ 🛜;
Ⓜ Sèvres-Lecourbe) There's no forgetting
what city you're in with the Eiffel Tower
motifs in reception and rooms (along with
Parisian street-map carpets and metro-
tunnel-shaped bedheads) plus glittering
tower views from upper-floor windows.
Edgy design elements also include cobblestone staircase carpeting (there's also a lift/
elevator) and, fittingly in *la ville lumière*,
technicoloured in-room fibre-optic lighting. The small wellness centre/hamam
offers massages.

L'Hôtel BOUTIQUE HOTEL €€€
(Map p190; ☑ 01 44 41 99 00; www.l-hotel.com; 13
rue des Beaux Arts, 6e; d €275-495; ❄ @ 🛜 🗫;
Ⓜ St-Germain des Prés) In a quiet quayside
street, this award-winning hostelry is the
stuff of romance, Parisian myths and urban
legends. Rock- and film-star patrons fight to
sleep in room 16, where Oscar Wilde died
in 1900 and which is now decorated with a
peacock motif, or in the art deco room 36
(which entertainer Mistinguett once stayed
in), with its huge mirrored bed.

🛏 Right Bank

⭐**Mama Shelter** DESIGN HOTEL €
(Map p186; ☑ 01 43 48 48 48; www.mamashelter.
com; 109 rue de Bagnolet, 20e; s/d from €79/89;
❄ @ 🛜; ☒ 76, Ⓜ Alexandre Dumas or Gambetta) Coaxed into its zany new incarnation
by uberdesigner Philippe Starck, this former car park offers what is surely the best
value accommodation in the city. Its 170
supercomfortable rooms feature iMacs,
trademark Starck details such as a
chocolate-and-fuchsia colour scheme,
concrete walls and even microwave ovens,
while a rooftop terrace and cool pizzeria
add to the hotel's street cred.

Cosmos Hôtel HOTEL €
(Map p186; ☑ 01 43 57 25 88; www.cosmos-
hotel-paris.com; 35 rue Jean-Pierre Timbaud, 11e; s
€62-75, d €68-75, tr/q €85/94; 🛜; Ⓜ République)
Cheap, brilliant value and just footsteps
from the nightlife of rue JPT, Cosmos is a
shiny star with retro style on the budget-
hotel scene. It has been around for 30-odd
years but, unlike most other hotels in the
same price bracket, Cosmos has been treated

Montmartre

Montmartre

to a thoroughly modern makeover this century. Breakfast is €8.

★ Loft
APARTMENT €€

(Map p194; ☑ 06 14 48 47 48; www.loft-paris.fr; 7 cité Véron, 18e; apt €100-270; ☎; Ⓜ Blanche) Book months in advance to secure one of the stylish apartments in this gem, which offers an intimacy that simply cannot be replicated in a hotel. Just around the corner from the Moulin Rouge, this apartment block offers choices ranging from a two-person studio to a loft that can fit a large family or group. The owner, a culture journalist, is a great resource.

Hôtel Jeanne d'Arc
HOTEL €€

(Map p190; ☑ 01 48 87 62 11; www.hoteljeanne darc.com; 3 rue de Jarente, 4e; s €72, d €98-120, q €250; ☎; Ⓜ St-Paul) About the only thing wrong with this gorgeous address is everyone knows about it; book well in advance. Games to play, a painted rocking chair for tots in the bijou lounge, knick-knacks everywhere and the most extraordinary mirror in the breakfast room create a real 'family home' air in this 35-room house.

Hôtel Emile
DESIGN HOTEL €€

(Map p190; ☑ 01 42 72 76 17; www.hotelemile.com; 2 rue Malher, 4e; s €170, d €180-230, ste €350; ✻☎; Ⓜ St-Paul) Prepare to be dazzled – literally. Retro B&W, geometrically patterned carpets, curtains, wallpapers and drapes dress this chic hotel, wedged between boutiques and restaurants in the Marais. Pricier 'top floor' doubles are just that, complete with breathtaking outlook over Parisian roofs and chimney pots.

Breakfast, included in the price, is on bar stools in the lobby; open the cupboard to find the 'kitchen'.

Edgar
BOUTIQUE HOTEL €€

(Map p190; ☑ 01 40 41 05 19; www.edgarparis. com; 31 rue d'Alexandrie, 2e; d €235-295; ✻☎; Ⓜ Strasbourg St-Denis) Twelve playful rooms, each decorated by a different team of artists or designers, await the lucky few who secure a reservation at this former convent/ seamstress workshop. Milagros conjures up all the magic of the Far West, while Dream echoes the rich imagination of childhood with surrealist installations.

Breakfast is served in the popular downstairs restaurant, and the hidden tree-shaded square is a fabulous location.

★ Hôtel Molitor
BOUTIQUE HOTEL €€€

(☑ 01 56 07 08 50; www.mltr.fr; 2 av de la porte Molitor, 16e; d from €270; ✻@☎✉; Ⓜ Michel Ange Molitor) Famed as Paris' swishest swimming pool in the 1930s (where the bikini made its first appearance, no less) and hot spot for graffiti art in the 1990s, the Molitor is one seriously mythical address. The art deco complex, built in 1929 and abandoned from 1989, has been restored to stunning effect.

Hôtel Crayon
BOUTIQUE HOTEL €€€

(Map p190; ☑ 01 42 36 54 19; www.hotelcrayon.com; 25 rue du Bouloi, 1er; s/d €311/347; ✻☎; Ⓜ Les Halles or Sentier) Line drawings by French artist Julie Gauthron bedeck walls and doors at this creative boutique hotel. The pencil *(le crayon)* is the theme, with 26 rooms sporting a different shade of each floor's chosen colour – we love the coloured-glass shower doors and the books on the bedside table that guests can swap and take home. Online deals often slash rates by more than 50%.

Eating

✕ Left Bank

★ JSFP Traiteur
DELICATESSEN €

(Map p190; http://jsfp-traiteur.com; 8 rue de Buci, 6e; dishes €3.40-5.70; ☉ 9.30am-8.30pm; ☑; Ⓜ Mabillon) Brimming with big bowls of salad, terrines, pâté and other prepared delicacies, this deli is a brilliant bet for quality Parisian 'fast food' such as quiches in a variety of flavour combinations (courgette and chive, mozzarella and basil, salmon and spinach...) to take to a nearby park, square or stretch of riverfront.

Le Comptoir du Panthéon
CAFE, BRASSERIE €

(Map p190; ☑ 01 43 54 75 56; 5 rue Soufflot, 5e; salads €11-13, mains €12.40-15.40; ☉ 7am-1.45am; ☎; Ⓜ Cardinal Lemoine or RER Luxembourg) Enormous, creative meal-size salads are the reason to pick this as a dining spot. Magnificently placed across from the domed Panthéon on the shady side of the street, its pavement terrace is big, busy and oh so Parisian – turn your head away from Voltaire's burial place and the Eiffel Tower pops into view.

Le Casse Noix
MODERN FRENCH €€

(Map p186; ☑ 01 45 66 09 01; www.le-cassenoix.fr; 56 rue de la Fédération, 15e; 2-/3-course lunch menus €21/26, 3-course dinner menu €33; ☉ noon-2.30pm & 7-10.30pm Mon-Fri; Ⓜ Bir Hakeim) Proving that

DON'T MISS

TOP THREE FOR SWEET TREATS

The French have something of a sweet tooth – from breakfast *viennoiseries* (sweet baked goods) to fabulous desserts, crêpes and ice creams, sweets are part and parcel of the gastronomy. Here are our top Parisian picks for a treat:

Ladurée (Map p186; www.laduree.com; 75 av des Champs-Élysées, 8e; pastries from €1.50; ☺7.30am-11.30pm Mon-Fri, 8.30am-12.30am Sat, 8.30am-11.30pm Sun; Ⓜ George V) Its macarons are so famous they seldom need introducing.

Berthillon (Map p190; 31 rue St-Louis en l'Île, 4e; 2-/3-/4-ball cone or tub €2.50/5.50/7; ☺10am-8pm Wed-Sun; Ⓜ Pont Marie) Berthillon is to ice cream what Château Lafite Rothschild is to wine: the Holy Grail. There are 70-odd flavours to choose from, including seasonal ones.

Dessance (Map p190; ☎01 42 77 23 62; www.dessance.fr; 74 rue des Archives, 3e; desserts à la carte €19, 4-course dessert menu €36-44; ☺3-11pm Wed-Fri, noon-midnight Sat & Sun; ☝; Ⓜ Arts et Métiers) Incredible as it sounds, this restaurant only serves desserts – although some of the 'dishes' may surprise you.

a location footsteps from the Eiffel Tower doesn't mean compromising on quality, quantity or authenticity, 'the nutcracker' is a neighbourhood gem with a cosy retro interior, affordable prices and exceptional cuisine that changes by season and by the inspiration of owner/chef Pierre Olivier Lenormand, who has honed his skills in some of Paris' most fêted kitchens. Book ahead.

Les Pipos   WINE BAR €€
(Map p190; ☎01 43 54 11 40; www.les-pipos.com; 2 rue de l'École Polytechnique, 5e; mains €13.90-26.90; ☺8am-2am Mon-Sat; Ⓜ Maubert-Mutualité) A feast for the eyes and the senses, this *bar à vins* is above all worth a visit for its food. The bistro standards (boeuf bourguignon) and *charcuteries de terroir* (regional cold meats and sausages) are mouth-watering, as is the cheese board, which includes all the gourmet names (bleu d'Auvergne, St-Félicien, St-Marcellin). No credit cards.

L'AOC   TRADITIONAL FRENCH €€
(Map p190; ☎01 43 54 22 52; www.restoaoc.com; 14 rue des Fossés St-Bernard, 5e; 2-/3-course lunch menus €21/29, mains €19-36; ☺noon-2.30pm & 7.30-10.30pm Tue-Sat; Ⓜ Cardinal Lemoine) *'Bistrot carnivore'* is the strapline of this ingenious restaurant concocted around France's most respected culinary products. The concept is Appellation d'Origine Contrôlée (AOC), meaning everything has been reared or produced according to strict guidelines. The result? Only the best! Choose between meaty favourites (steak tartare) or the rotisserie menu, ranging from roast chicken to suckling pig.

★**Restaurant David Toutain**   GASTRONOMIC €€€
(Map p186; ☎01 45 51 11 10; http://davidtoutain.com; 29 rue Surcouf, 7e; lunch menus €42, lunch & dinner menus €68-98; ☺noon-2.30pm & 8-10pm Mon-Fri; Ⓜ Invalides) Prepare to be wowed: David Toutain pushes the envelope at his eponymous new restaurant with some of the most creative high-end cooking in Paris today. Mystery degustation courses include unlikely combinations such as smoked eel in green-apple and black-sesame mousse, or candied celery and truffled rice pudding with artichoke praline (stunning wine pairings available).

⊁ The Islands

★**Café Saint Régis**   CAFE €
(Map p190; http://cafesaintregisparis.com; 6 rue Jean du Bellay, 4e; salads & mains €14.50-28; ☺7am-2am; ☎; Ⓜ Pont Marie) Hip and historical with an effortless dose of retro vintage thrown in, Le Saint Régis – as those in the know call it – is a deliciously Parisian hangout any time of day. From pastries for breakfast to a mid-morning pancake, brasserie lunch or early evening oyster platter, Café St-Regis gets it just right. Come midnight it morphs into a late-night hot spot.

Les Voyelles   MODERN FRENCH €€
(Map p190; ☎01 46 33 69 75; www.les-voyelles.com; 74 quai des Orfèvres, 4e; plat du jour €12, 2-/3-course menus €17/22.50; ☺8am-midnight Tue-Sat; Ⓜ Pont Neuf) This new kid on the block is worth the short walk from Notre Dame. The Vowels – spot the letters casually scattered between books and beautiful objects on the shelves lining the intimate 'library' dining room – is thoroughly contemporary, with a menu ranging from finger

food to full-blown dinner to match. Its pavement terrace is Paris gold.

Right Bank

Candelaria
MEXICAN €

(Map p190; www.candelariaparis.com; 52 rue Saintonge; tacos €3.20-3.75, quesadillas & tostadas €3.50, lunch menu €11.50; ⊙ noon-midnight Thu-Sat, to 11pm Sun-Wed; M Filles du Calvaire) You need to know about this terribly cool taqueria to find it. Made of pure, unadulterated hipness in that brazenly nonchalant manner Paris does so well, clandestine Candelaria serves delicious homemade tacos, quesadillas and tostadas in a laid-back setting – squat at the bar in the front or lounge out back around a shared table with bar stools or at low coffee tables.

Le Miroir
BISTRO €€

(Map p194; ☑ 01 46 06 50 73; http://restaurant miroir.com; 94 rue des Martyrs, 18e; lunch menu €19.50, dinner menus €27-34; ⊙ noon-2.30pm & 7.30-11pm Tue-Sat; M Abbesses) This unassuming modern bistro is smack in the middle of the Montmartre tourist trail, yet it remains a local favourite. There are lots of delightful pâtés and rillettes to start off with – guinea hen with dates, duck with mushrooms, haddock and lemon – followed by well-prepared standards like stuffed veal shoulder.

Pirouette
NEOBISTRO €€

(Map p190; ☑ 01 40 26 47 81; 5 rue Mondétour, 1er; lunch menu €18, 3-/6-course dinner menu €40/60; ⊙ noon-2.30pm & 7.30-10.30pm Mon-Sat; M Les Halles) In one of the best restaurants in the vicinity of the old 'belly of Paris', chef Tomy Gousset's crew is working wonders at this cool loft-like space, serving up tantalising creations ranging from seared duck, asparagus and Buddha's hand fruit to rum baba with chantilly and lime. Some unique ingredients and a new spin for French cuisine.

Blue Valentine
MODERN FRENCH €€

(Map p190; ☑ 01 43 38 34 72; http://blue valentine-restaurant.com; 13 rue de la Pierre Levée, 11e; 2-/3-course menu €29/36, 8-course tasting menu €54; ⊙ noon-2.30pm & 7.30-11pm Wed-Mon, bar 7pm-2am; M République) This thoroughly modern bistro with retro decor in the increasingly gourmet 11e was a hit the moment it opened in late 2013. A hip crowd flocks here for well-crafted cocktails and Japanese chef Saito Terumitsu's exquisite dishes flavoured with edible flowers and a profusion of herbs. The menu is small – just three dishes to choose from per course – but memorable.

★ Frenchie
BISTRO €€€

(Map p190; ☑ 01 40 39 96 19; www.frenchie-restaurant.com; 5-6 rue du Nil, 2e; prix fixe menu €48; ⊙ 7-11pm Mon-Fri; M Sentier) Tucked down an alley you wouldn't venture down otherwise, this bijou bistro with wooden tables and old stone walls is iconic. Frenchie is always packed and for good reason: excellent-value dishes are modern, market-driven (the menu changes daily with a choice of two dishes) and prepared with just the right dose of unpretentious creative flair by French chef Gregory Marchand.

🍷 Drinking & Nightlife

The line between bars, cafes and bistros is blurred at best. It costs more to sit at a table than to stand at the counter, more on a fancy square than a backstreet, more in the 8e than in the 18e. After 10pm many cafes charge a pricier *tarif de nuit* (night rate).

Left Bank

★ Au Sauvignon
WINE BAR

(Map p186; 80 rue des St-Pères, 7e; ⊙ 8.30am-10pm Mon-Sat, to 9pm Sun; M Sèvres-Babylone) Grab a table in the evening sun at this wonderfully authentic *bar à vin* or head to the quintessential bistro interior, with an original zinc bar, tightly packed tables and hand-painted ceiling celebrating French viticultural tradition. A plate of *casse-croûtes au pain Poilâne* – toast with ham, pâté, terrine, smoked salmon, foie gras etc – is the perfect accompaniment.

★ Le Batofar
CLUB

(Map p186; www.batofar.org; opp 11 quai François Mauriac, 13e; ⊙ bar 12.30pm-midnight Tue, to 6am Wed-Fri, 6pm-6am Sat; M Quai de la Gare or Bibliothèque) This much-loved, red-metal tugboat has a rooftop bar that's terrific in summer, and a respected restaurant, while the club underneath provides memorable underwater acoustics between its metal walls and portholes. Le Batofar is known for its edgy, experimental music policy and live performances, mostly electro-oriented but also incorporating hip-hop, new wave, rock, punk or jazz.

Le Verre à Pied
CAFE

(Map p190; http://leverreapied.fr; 118bis rue Mouffetard, 5e; ⊙ 9am-9pm Tue-Sat, 9.30am-4pm

BAR-HOPPING STREETS

Prime Parisian streets for a soirée:

Rue Vieille du Temple, 4e Marais cocktail of gay bars and chic cafes.

Rue Oberkampf, 11e Edgy urban hang outs.

Rue de Lappe, 11e Boisterous Bastille bars and clubs.

Rue de la Butte aux Cailles, 13e Village atmosphere and fun local haunts.

Rue Princesse, 6e Student and sports bars.

Sun; M Censier Daubenton) This *café-tabac* is a pearl of a place where little has changed since 1870. Its nicotine-hued mirrored wall, moulded cornices and original bar make it part of a dying breed, but the place oozes the charm, glamour and romance of an old Paris everyone loves, including stall holders from the rue Mouffetard market who yo-yo in and out.

Les Deux Magots   CAFE
(Map p190; www.lesdeuxmagots.fr; 170 bd St-Germain, 6e; ⊙7.30am-1am; M St-Germain des Prés) If ever a cafe summed up St-Germain des Prés' early-20th-century literary scene, it's this former hang-out of anyone who was anyone. You will spend *beaucoup* to sip a coffee in a wicker chair on the terrace shaded by dark-green awnings and geraniums spilling from window boxes, but it's an undeniable piece of Parisian history.

Le Pub St-Hilaire   PUB
(Map p190; 2 rue Valette, 5e; ⊙3pm-2am Mon-Thu, 3pm-4am Fri, 4pm-4am Sat, 4pm-midnight Sun; M Maubert-Mutualité) 'Buzzing' fails to do justice to the pulsating vibe inside this student loved pub. Generous happy hours last several hours and the place is kept packed with a trio of pool tables, board games, music on two floors, hearty bar food and various gimmicks to rev up the party crowd (a metre of cocktails, 'be your own barman' etc).

🍷 Right Bank

★**St James Paris**   BAR
(Map p186; ☑01 44 05 81 81; www.saint-james-paris.com; 43 rue Bugeaud, 16e; drinks €15-25, Sun brunch €65; ⊙7-11pm; 🛜; M Porte Dauphine) It might be a hotel bar, but a drink at St James might well be one of your most memorable in Paris. Tucked behind a stone wall, this historic mansion opens its bar each evening to nonguests – and the setting redefines extraordinary. Winter drinks are in the library, in summer they're in the impossibly romantic garden.

★**Le Barbouquin**   CAFE
(Map p186; www.lebarbouquin.fr; 3 rue Ramponeau, 20e; ⊙10.30am-6pm Tue-Sat; M Belleville) There is no lovelier spot to relax in a vintage armchair over a cup of organic tea or freshly juiced carrot-and-apple cocktail after a hectic morning at Belleville market. Secondhand books – to be borrowed, exchanged or bought – line one wall and the twinset of pavement-terrace tables outside sit on magnificently graffitied rue Dénoyez. Breakfast and weekend brunch.

Le Baron Rouge   WINE BAR
(Map p186; 1 rue Théophile Roussel, 12e; ⊙10am-2pm & 5-10pm Tue-Fri, 10am-10pm Sat, 10am-4pm Sun; M Ledru-Rollin) Just about the ultimate Parisian wine-bar experience, this place has barrels stacked against the bottle-lined walls. As unpretentious as you'll find, it's a local meeting place where everyone is welcome and it's especially busy on Sunday after the **Marché d'Aligre** (Map p186; http://marchedaligre.free.fr; rue d'Aligre, 12e; ⊙8am-1pm & 4-7.30pm Tue-Sat, 8am-1.30pm Sun; M Ledru-Rollin) wraps up. All the usual suspects – cheese, charcuterie and oysters – will keep your belly full.

La Fourmi   BAR
(Map p194; 74 rue des Martyrs, 18e; ⊙8am-1am Mon-Thu, to 3am Fri & Sat, 10am-1am Sun; M Pigalle) A Pigalle institution, La Fourmi hits the mark with its high ceilings, long zinc bar and unpretentious vibe. Get up to speed on live music and club nights or sit down for a reasonably priced meal and drinks.

Le Rex Club   CLUB
(Map p194; www.rexclub.com; 5 bd Poissonnière, 2e; ⊙midnight-7am Thu-Sat; M Bonne Nouvelle) Attached to the art deco Grand Rex cinema, this is Paris' premier house and techno venue where some of the world's hottest DJs strut their stuff on a 70-speaker, multidiffusion sound system.

☆ Entertainment

To find out what's on, buy *Pariscope* (€0.50) or *L'Officiel des Spectacles* (€0.50; www.offi.

fr) at Parisian news kiosks. Both are published on Wednesday. The most convenient place to buy concert, performance or event tickets is megastore **Fnac** (Map p186; ☑08 92 68 36 22; www.fnactickets.com), which has numerous branches in town. If you go on the day of a performance, you can snag a half-price ticket (plus €3 commission) for ballet, theatre, opera and other performances at the discount-ticket outlet **Kiosque Théâtre Madeleine** (Map p194; opp 15 place de la Madeleine, 8e; ⊙12.30-8pm Tue-Sat, to 4pm Sun; Ⓜ Madeleine).

Moulin Rouge CABARET
(Map p194; ☑01 53 09 82 82; www.moulinrouge.fr; 82 bd de Clichy, 18e; Ⓜ Blanche) Immortalised in the posters of Toulouse-Lautrec and later on screen by Baz Luhrmann, the Moulin Rouge twinkles beneath a 1925 replica of its original red windmill. Yes, it's rife with bus-tour crowds. But from the opening bars of music to the last high kick it's a whirl of fantastical costumes, sets, choreography and sparkling wine. Booking advised.

Au Limonaire LIVE MUSIC
(Map p194; ☑01 45 23 33 33; http://limonaire.free.fr; 18 cité Bergère, 9e; ⊙6pm-2am Tue-Sat, from 7pm Sun & Mon; Ⓜ Grands Boulevards) This perfect little wine bar is one of the best places to listen to traditional French *chansons* (songs) and local singer-songwriters. Performances begin at 10pm Tuesday to Saturday and 7pm on Sunday. Entry is free; reservations are recommended if you plan on dining.

Palais Garnier OPERA
(Map p194; ☑08 92 89 90 90; www.operadeparis.fr; place de l'Opéra, 9e; Ⓜ Opéra) The city's original opera house is smaller than its Bastille counterpart, but has perfect acoustics. Due to its odd shape, some seats have limited or no visibility – book carefully. Ticket prices and conditions (including last-minute discounts) are available from the **box office** (Map p194; cnr rues Scribe & Auber; ⊙11am-6.30pm Mon-Sat).

Point Éphémère LIVE MUSIC
(Map p186; www.pointephemere.org; 200 quai de Valmy, 10e; ⊙12.30pm-2am Mon-Sat, 12.30-11pm Sun; 🔊; Ⓜ Louis Blanc) This arts and music venue by the Canal St-Martin attracts an underground crowd from noon till past midnight, for drinks, meals, concerts, dance nights and even art exhibitions. At the time of writing there were three different food trucks setting up shop here three days a week after 7pm.

Le Baiser Salé LIVE MUSIC
(Map p190; www.lebaisersale.com; 58 rue des Lombards, 1er; ⊙daily; Ⓜ Châtelet) Known for its Afro and Latin jazz, and jazz fusion concerts, the Salty Kiss combines big names and unknown artists. The place has a relaxed vibe, with sets usually starting at 7.30pm or 9.30pm.

FRANCE PARIS

GAY & LESBIAN PARIS

The Marais (4e), especially the areas around the intersection of rue Ste-Croix de la Bretonnerie and rue des Archives, and eastwards to rue Vieille du Temple, has been Paris' main centre of gay nightlife for some three decades.

The single best source of info on gay and lesbian Paris is the **Centre Gai et Lesbien de Paris** (CGL; Map p190; ☑01 43 57 21 47; www.centrelgbtparis.org; 63 rue Beaubourg, 3e; ⊙centre & bar 3.30-8pm Mon-Fri, 1-7pm Sat, library 6-8pm Mon-Wed, 3.30-6pm Fri, 5-7pm Sat; Ⓜ Rambuteau or Arts et Métiers), with a large library and happening bar.

The following aare some top choices:

Open Café (Map p190; www.opencafe.fr; 17 rue des Archives, 4e; ⊙11am-2am; Ⓜ Hôtel de Ville) The wide terrace is prime for people-watching.

Scream Club (Map p190; www.scream-paris.com; 18 rue du Faubourg du Temple, 11e; admission €15; ⊙midnight-7am Sat; Ⓜ Belleville or Goncourt) Saturday's the night at 'Paris' biggest gay party'.

3w Kafé (Map p190; 8 rue des Écouffes, 4e; ⊙8pm-3am Wed & Thu, to 5.30am Fri & Sat; Ⓜ St-Paul) The name of this sleek spot stands for 'women with women'.

Queen (Map p186; ☑01 53 89 08 90; www.queen.fr; 102 av des Champs-Élysées, 8e; ⊙11.30pm-6.30am; Ⓜ George V) Don't miss disco night.

La Champmeslé (Map p190; www.lachampmesle.com; 4 rue Chabanais, 2e; ⊙4pm-dawn Mon-Sat; Ⓜ Pyramides) Cabaret nights, fortune telling and art exhibitions attract an older lesbian crowd.

🛍 Shopping

Guerlain
PERFUME

(Map p186; ☑ spa 01 45 62 11 21; www.guerlain. com; 68 av des Champs-Élysées, 8e; ☺ 10.30am-8pm Mon-Sat, noon-7pm Sun; ⓜ Franklin D Roosevelt) Guerlain is Paris' most famous parfumerie, and its shop (dating from 1912) is one of the most beautiful in the city. With its shimmering mirror and marble art deco interior, it's a reminder of the former glory of the Champs-Élysées. For total indulgence, make an appointment at its decadent spa.

Paris Rendez-Vous
CONCEPT STORE

(Map p190; 29 rue de Rivoli, 4e; ☺ 10am-7pm Mon-Sat; ⓜ Hôtel de Ville) Only the city of Paris could be so chic as to have its own designer line of souvenirs, sold in its own ubercool concept store inside the Hôtel de Ville. Shop here for everything from clothing and homewares to Paris-themed books, toy sailing boats and signature Jardin du Luxembourg's Fermob chairs. *Quel style!*

Marché aux Puces de St-Ouen
MARKET

(www.marcheauxpuces-saintouen.com; rue des Rosiers, av Michelet, rue Voltaire, rue Paul Bert & rue Jean-Henri Fabre; ☺ 9am-6pm Sat, 10am-6pm Sun, 11am-5pm Mon; ⓜ Porte de Clignancourt) This vast flea market, founded in the late 19th century and said to be Europe's largest, has more than 2500 stalls grouped into a dozen *marchés* (market areas), each with its own speciality (eg Paul Bert for 17th-century furniture, Malik for clothing, Biron for Asian art). There are miles upon miles of 'freelance' stalls; come prepared to spend some time.

Shakespeare & Company
BOOKS

(Map p190; www.shakespeareandcompany.com; 37 rue de la Bûcherie, 5e; ☺ 10am-11pm Mon-Fri, from 11am Sat & Sun; ⓜ St-Michel) This bookshop is the stuff of legends. A kind of spell descends as you enter, weaving between nooks and crannies overflowing with new and secondhand English-language books. The original shop (12 rue l'Odéon, 6e; closed by the Nazis in 1941) was run by Sylvia Beach and became the meeting point for Hemingway's 'Lost Generation'. Readings by emerging and illustrious authors take place at 7pm most Mondays; it also hosts workshops and festivals.

Galeries Lafayette
DEPARTMENT STORE

(Map p194; http://haussmann.galerieslafayette.com; 40 bd Haussmann, 9e; ☺ 9.30am-8pm Mon-Sat, to 9pm Thu; ⓜ Auber or Chaussée d'Antin) *Grande dame* department store Galeries Lafayette is spread across the main store (whose magnificent stained-glass dome is over a century old), **men's store** and **homewares** store, and includes a gourmet emporium.

Catch modern art in the **gallery** (www. galeriedesgaleries.com; 1st fl; ☺ 11am-7pm Tue-Sat) 🆓; a **fashion show** (☑ bookings 01 42 82 30 25; ☺ 3pm Fri Mar-Jul & Sep-Dec by reservation); a free, windswept rooftop panorama; or take a break at one of its 19 restaurants and cafes.

ℹ Information

DANGERS & ANNOYANCES

Metro stations best avoided late at night include: Châtelet–Les Halles and its corridors; Château Rouge in Montmartre; Gare du Nord; Strasbourg St-Denis; Réaumur Sébastopol; and Montparnasse Bienvenüe.

Pickpocketing and thefts from handbags and packs is a problem wherever there are crowds (especially of tourists).

MEDICAL SERVICES

American Hospital of Paris (☑ 01 46 41 25 25; www.american-hospital.org; 63 bd Victor Hugo, Neuilly-sur-Seine; ⓜ Pont de Levallois) Private hospital; emergency 24-hour medical and dental care.

Hôpital Hôtel Dieu (☑ 01 42 34 82 34; www. aphp.fr; 1 place du Parvis Notre Dame, 4e; ⓜ Cité) One of the city's main government-run public hospitals; after 8pm use the emergency entrance on rue de la Cité.

Pharmacie Les Champs (☑ 01 45 62 02 41; Galerie des Champs-Élysées, 84 av des Champs-Élysées, 8e; ☺ 24hr; ⓜ George V)

TOURIST INFORMATION

Paris Convention & Visitors Bureau (Office du Tourisme et des Congrès de Paris; Map p190; www.parisinfo.com; 27 rue des Pyramides, 1er; ☺ 9am-7pm May-Oct, 10am-7pm Nov-Apr; ⓜ Pyramides) Main branch of the Paris Convention & Visitors Bureau, about 500m northwest of the Louvre.

ℹ Getting There & Away

AIR

There are three main airports in Paris:

Aéroport de Charles de Gaulle (p254) Most international airlines fly to CDG, 28km northeast of the centre of Paris. In French, the airport is commonly called 'Roissy'.

Aéroport d'Orly (ORY; ☑ 01 70 36 39 50; www. aeroportsdeparis.fr) Located 19km south of Paris but not as frequently used by international airlines.

Aéroport de Beauvais (BVA; ☑ 08 92 68 20 66; www.aeroportbeauvais.com) Not really in Paris at all (it's 75km north of Paris) but used by some low-cost carriers.

BUS

Gare Routière Internationale de Paris-Galliéni (☑ 08 92 89 90 91; 28 av du Général de Gaulle; Ⓜ Galliéni) The city's international bus terminal is in the eastern suburb of Bagnolet; it's about a 15 minute metro ride to the more central République station.

TRAIN

Paris has six major train stations serving both national and international destinations:

Gare du Nord (rue de Dunkerque, 10e; Ⓜ Gare du Nord) Trains to/from the UK, Belgium, Germany and northern France.

Gare de l'Est (bd de Strasbourg, 10e; Ⓜ Gare de l'Est) Trains to/from Germany, Switzerland and eastern areas of France.

Gare de Lyon (bd Diderot, 12e; Ⓜ Gare de Lyon) Trains to/from Provence, the Riviera, the Alps and Italy. Also serves Geneva.

Gare d'Austerlitz (bd de l'Hôpital, 13e; Ⓜ Gare d'Austerlitz) Trains to/from Spain and Portugal, and non-TGV trains to southwestern France.

Gare Montparnasse (av du Maine & bd de Vaugirard, 15e; Ⓜ Montparnasse Bienvenüe) Trains to/from western France (Brittany, Atlantic coast) and southwestern France.

Gare St-Lazare (rue St-Lazare & rue d'Amsterdam, 8e; Ⓜ St-Lazare) Trains to Normandy.

For mainline train information, check **SNCF** (www.sncf-voyages.com).

❶ Getting Around

TO/FROM THE AIRPORTS

Getting into town is straightforward and inexpensive thanks to a fleet of public-transport options. Bus drivers sell tickets. Children aged four to 11 years pay half-price on most services.

Aéroport de Charles de Gaulle

RER B line (€9.50, approximately 50 minutes, every 10 to 15 minutes) Stops at Gare du Nord, Châtelet–Les Halles and St-Michel–Notre Dame stations in the city centre. Trains run from 5am to 11pm; there are fewer trains on weekends.

RATP bus 351 (€5.70, 60 minutes, every 30 minutes, 5.30am to 11pm) Links the airport with Place de la Nation.

Roissybus (€10.50, 45 to 60 minutes, every 15 minutes, 5.30am to 11pm) Links the airport with Opéra.

Taxi Costs €50, more at nights and weekends. Allow 40 minutes to the centre, more at rush hour.

Aéroport d'Orly

RER B and Orlyval (€10.90, 35 minutes, every four to 12 minutes, 6am to 11pm) The nearest RER station to the airport is Antony, where you connect on the dedicated Orlyval.

Air France bus 1 (€12.50, one hour, every 20 minutes, 5am to 11pm) Links the airport with Gare Montparnasse, Invalides and Arc de Triomphe.

Taxi Costs around €40, more at nights and weekends. Allow 30 minutes to the centre, more at rush hour.

Aéroport de Beauvais

The **Beauvais shuttle** (€17, 1¼ hours) links the airport with metro station Porte Maillot.

BICYCLE

The **Vélib'** (http://en.velib.paris.fr; day/week subscription €1.70/8, bike hire up to 30min/60min/90min/2hr free/€1/2/4) bike-share scheme puts 20,000-odd bikes at the disposal of Parisians and visitors to get around the city. There are around 1800 docking stations; bikes are available around the clock.

BOAT

Batobus (www.batobus.com; Port de Solférino, 7e; 1-/2-day pass €16/18; ⊙ 10am-9.30pm Apr-Aug, to 7pm rest of year) Batobus runs glassed-in trimarans that dock every 20 to 25 minutes at eight small piers along the Seine: Eiffel Tower, Musée d'Orsay, St-Germain des Prés, Notre Dame, Jardin des Plantes, Hôtel de Ville, Musée du Louvre and Champs-Élysées. Buy tickets online, at ferry stops or at tourist offices. You can also buy a 2-/3-day ticket covering L'Open Tour buses too for €45/49.

PUBLIC TRANSPORT

Paris' public transit system is operated by the **RATP** (www.ratp.fr).

➡ The same RATP tickets are valid on the metro, RER, buses, trams and Montmartre funicular. A single ticket/carnet of 10 costs €1.70/13.70.

➡ One ticket covers travel between any two metro stations (no return journeys) for 1½ hours; you can transfer between buses and between buses and trams, but not from metro to bus or vice versa.

➡ Keep your ticket until you exit the station or risk a fine.

Bus

➡ Buses run from 5.30am to 8.30pm Monday to Saturday, with certain evening lines continuing until midnight or 12.30am, when the hourly **Noctilien** (www.noctilien.fr) night buses kick in.

➡ Short bus rides (ie rides in one or two bus zones) cost one ticket; longer rides require two.

→ Remember to punch single-journey tickets in the *composteur* (ticket machine) next to the driver.

Metro & RER

Paris' underground network consists of 14 numbered metro lines and the five suburban RER lines (designated by the letters A to E).

Trains usually start around 5.30am and finish sometime between 12.35am and 1.15am (2.15am Friday and Saturday).

Tourist Passes

The **Mobilis Card** allows unlimited travel for one day in two to five zones (€6.80 to €16.10) on the metro, the RER, buses, trams and suburban trains; while the **Paris Visite** 'Paris+ Suburbs+Airports' pass allows unlimited travel (including to/from airports), plus discounted entry to museums and activities, and costs €22.85/34.70/59.50 for one/two/five days.

Passes are sold at larger metro and RER stations, SNCF stations and the airports.

Travel Passes

If you're staying in Paris more than three or four days, the cheapest and easiest way to use public transport is to get a rechargeable **Navigo** (www. navigo.fr) pass.

Weekly/monthly passes beginning on a Monday/first day of the month cost €20.40/67.10. You'll also need to pay €5 for the Navigo card and provide a passport photo.

TAXI

→ The flag fall is €2.50, plus €1 per kilometre within the city limits from 10am to 5pm Monday to Saturday (Tarif A; white light on meter).

→ It's €1.24 per kilometre from 5pm to 10am, all day Sunday, and on public holidays (Tarif B; orange light on meter).

→ The first piece of luggage is free; additional bags cost €1.

→ Taxis will often refuse to take more than three passengers.

→ You can flag taxis on the street, wait at official stands or phone/book online with **Taxis G7** (✆ 36 07; www.taxisg7.fr) or **Taxis Bleus** (✆ 01 49 36 10 10; www.taxis-bleus.com).

AROUND PARIS

Versailles

POP 88,470

Louis XIV – the Roi Soleil (Sun King) – transformed his father's hunting lodge into the monumental Château de Versailles in the mid-17th century, and it remains France's most famous, grandest palace. Situated in the prosperous, leafy and bourgeois suburb of Versailles, 28km southwest of Paris, the baroque château was the kingdom's political capital and the seat of the royal court from 1682 up until the fateful events of 1789, when revolutionaries massacred the palace guard and dragged Louis XVI and Marie Antoinette back to Paris, where they were ingloriously guillotined.

⊙ Sights

Château Versailles   PALACE
(✆ 01 30 83 78 00; www.chateauversailles.fr; passport ticket incl estate-wide access adult/child €18/ free, with musical events €25/free, palace €15/ free; ⊙ 9am-6.30pm Tue-Sat, to 6pm Sun Apr-Oct, to 5.30pm Tue-Sun Nov-Mar; M RER Versailles-Château–Rive Gauche) Works on the Château began in 1661 under the guidance of architect Louis Le Vau (Jules Hardouin-Mansart took over from Le Vau in the mid-1670s); painter and interior designer Charles Le Brun; and landscape artist André Le Nôtre, whose workers flattened hills, drained marshes and relocated forests to create the magnificent geometric **gardens** (except during musical events admission free; ⊙ gardens 9am-8.30pm Apr-Oct, 8am-6pm Nov-Mar, park 7am-8.30pm Apr-Oct, 8am-6pm Nov-Mar).

Le Brun and his hundreds of artisans decorated every moulding, cornice, ceiling and door of the interior with the most luxurious and ostentatious of appointments: frescoes, marble, gilt and woodcarvings, many with themes and symbols drawn from Greek and Roman mythology. The opulence reaches its peak in the **Galerie des Glaces** (Hall of Mirrors), a 75m-long ballroom with 17 huge mirrors on one side and, on the other, an equal number of windows looking out over the gardens and the setting sun.

The château has undergone relatively few alterations since its construction, though almost all the interior furnishings disappeared during the Revolution and many of the rooms were rebuilt by Louis-Philippe (r 1830–48).

⊙ Getting There & Away

The easiest way to get to/from Versailles is aboard RER line C5 (€3.25, 45 minutes, every 15 minutes) from Paris' Left Bank RER stations to Versailles-Château–Rive Gauche, 700m southeast of the chateau.

Chartres

POP 40,675

The magnificent 13th-century **Cathédrale Notre Dame** (www.cathedrale-chartres.org; place de la Cathédrale; ⊙ 8.30am-7.30pm daily year-round, to 10pm Tue, Fri & Sun Jun-Aug) of Chartres, crowned by two very different spires – one Gothic, the other Romanesque – rises from rich farmland 88km southwest of Paris and dominates the medieval town.

The cathedral's west, north and south entrances have superbly ornamented triple portals and its 105m-high **Clocher Vieux** (Old Bell Tower), also called the Tour Sud (South Tower), is the tallest Romanesque steeple still standing. Superb views of three-tiered flying buttresses and the 19th-century copper roof, turned green by verdigris, reward the 350-step hike up the 112m-high **Clocher Neuf** (New Bell Tower, also known as North Tower).

Inside, 172 extraordinary stained-glass windows, mainly from the 13th century, form one of the most important ensembles of medieval stained glass in the world. The three most exquisite – renowned for the depth and intensity of their tones, famously known as 'Chartres blue' – are above the west entrance and below the rose window.

ⓘ Getting There & Away

Frequent SNCF trains link Paris' Gare Montparnasse (€15.60, 55 to 70 minutes) with Chartres.

Giverny

The tiny village of Giverny (pop 516), 74km northwest of Paris, was the **home of impressionist Claude Monet** (⊘ 02 32 51 28 21; www.fondation-monet.com; 84 rue Claude Monet;

adult/child €9.50/5, incl Musée des Impressionnismes Giverny €16.50/8; ⊙ 9.30am-6pm Apr-Oct) for the last 43 years of his life. You can visit the artist's pastel-pink house and famous gardens with lily pond, Japanese bridge draped in purple wisteria, and so on. Early to late spring, daffodils, tulips, rhododendrons, wisteria and irises bloom in the flowery gardens, followed by poppies and lilies. By June, nasturtiums, roses and sweet peas are in flower, while September is the month to see dahlias, sunflowers and hollyhocks.

The nearest train station is **Vernon**, 7km west of Giverny, from where shuttle buses (€8 return, three to six daily April to October) shunt passengers to Giverny. There are around 15 trains a day from Paris Gare St-Lazare (€14.30, 50 minutes).

LILLE & THE SOMME

When it comes to culture, cuisine, beer, shopping and dramatic views of land and sea, the friendly Ch'tis (residents of France's northern tip) and their region compete with the best France has to offer. Highlights include Flemish-style Lille, the cross-Channel shopping centre of Calais, and the moving battlefields and cemeteries of WWI.

Lille

POP 232,210

Lille may be the country's most underrated major city. In recent decades, this once-grimy industrial metropolis has transformed itself – with generous government help – into a glittering and self-confident cultural and commercial hub. Highlights of the city include an attractive Old Town with a strong Flemish accent, renowned art museums, stylish shopping and a cutting-edge, student-driven nightlife.

◉ Sights

Palais des Beaux Arts   ART MUSEUM
(Fine Arts Museum; ☏ 03 20 06 78 00; www.pba-lille.fr; place de la République; adult/child €6.50/free; ⊙ 2-5.30pm Mon, 10am-5.30pm Wed-Sun; Ⓜ République Beaux Arts) Lille's world-renowned Fine Arts Museum displays a truly first-rate collection of 15th- to 20th-century paintings, including works by Rubens, Van Dyck and Manet. Exquisite porcelain and faience (pottery), much of it of local provenance, is on the ground floor, while in the basement

you'll find classical archaeology, medieval statuary and 18th-century scale models of the fortified cities of northern France and Belgium. Information sheets in French, English and Dutch are available in each hall.

Musée d'Art Moderne, d'Art Contemporain et d'Art Brut – LaM
ART MUSEUM

(☑ 03 20 19 68 68; www.musee-lam.fr; 1 allée du Musée, Villeneuve-d'Ascq; adult/child €7/free; ☉ 10am-6pm Tue-Sun) Colourful, playful and just plain weird works of modern and contemporary art by masters such as Braque, Calder, Léger, Miró, Modigliani and Picasso are the big draw at this renowned museum and sculpture park in the Lille suburb of Villeneuve-d'Ascq, 9km east of Gare Lille-Europe. Take metro line 1 to Pont de Bois, then bus line 4 (10 minutes) to Villeneuve-d'Ascq-LaM.

★☆ Festivals & Events

★ Braderie de Lille
FLEA MARKET

On the first weekend in September Lille's entire city centre – 200km of footpaths – is transformed into the Braderie de Lille, billed as the world's largest flea market. It runs nonstop – yes, all night long – from 2pm on Saturday to 11pm on Sunday, when street sweepers emerge to tackle the mounds of mussel shells and old *frites* (French fries) left behind by the merrymakers.

The extravaganza – with stands selling antiques, local delicacies, handicrafts and more – dates from the Middle Ages, when Lillois servants were permitted to hawk their employers' old garments for some extra cash. Lille's tourist office can supply you with a free map of the festivities.

🛏 Sleeping & Eating

Auberge de Jeunesse
HOSTEL €

(☑ 03 20 57 08 94; www.hifrance.org; 12 rue Malpart; dm incl breakfast €23; P @ 🛜; M Mairie de Lille, République Beaux-Arts) This central former maternity hospital has 163 beds in rooms for two to eight, kitchen facilities and free parking. A few doubles have en-suite showers. Lockout is from 11am to 3pm (to 4pm Friday to Sunday).

Hotel Kanaï
HOTEL €€

(☑ 03 20 57 14 78; www.hotelkanai.com; 10 rue de Bethune; d €75-140; ❄ @ 🛜; M Rihour) In the heart of Lille's pedestrian zone, this enticing hotel offers reasonably priced rooms with a clean modern design; pick of the bunch are rooms 102 and 302, with large picture windows and plenty of natural light. All come with coffee makers, attractive tiled bathrooms, crisp linen and excellent bedding. One complaint: there's no lift.

★ Meert
PATISSERIE €

(☑ 03 20 57 07 44; www.meert.fr; 27 rue Esquermoise; waffles from €3; ☉ 9.30am-9.30pm Tue-Sat, 9am-6pm Sun; M Rihour) A delightful spot for morning coffee or mid-afternoon tea, this elegant tearoom dating to 1761 is beloved for its retro decor and its *gaufres* (waffles) filled with Madagascar vanilla paste. The tearoom's 1830s-vintage chocolate shop next door has a similarly old-fashioned atmosphere.

Le Bistrot Lillois
FLEMISH €

(☑ 03 20 14 04 15; 40 rue de Gand; mains €10-15; ☉ noon-2pm & 7.30-10pm Tue-Sat) This place owes its reputation to a menu based solidly on expertly prepared regional specialities. The highlight of the menu is *os à moëlle* (marrow bone), but other dishes worth trying include *carbonade flamande* (braised beef stewed with Flemish beer, spice bread and brown sugar) and *potjevleesch* (jellied chicken, pork, veal and rabbit).

ℹ Information

The **tourist office** (☑ 03 59 57 94 00; www.lilletourism.com; place Rihour; ☉ 9am-6pm Mon-Sat, 10am-noon & 2-5pm Sun & holidays; M Rihour) has walking itineraries of the city (€3).

ℹ Getting There & Away

AIR

Aéroport de Lille (www.lille.aeroport.fr) is connected to all major French cities and a number of European destinations too.

TRAIN

Lille has two train stations: Gare Lille-Flandres for regional services and Paris' Gare du Nord (€35 to €61, one hour, 14 to 24 daily), and ultramodern Gare Lille-Europe for all other trains, including Eurostars to London and TGVs/Eurostars to Brussels-Nord (€19 to €30, 35 minutes, 12 daily).

The Somme

The First Battle of the Somme, a WWI Allied offensive waged in the villages and woodlands northeast of Amiens, was designed to relieve pressure on the beleaguered French troops at Verdun. On 1 July 1916, British, Commonwealth and French troops 'went over the top' in a massive assault along a 34km front. But German positions proved virtually unbreachable, and on the first day of the battle an astounding 21,392 British troops were killed and another 35,492 were wounded. Most casualties were infantrymen mown down by German machine guns. By the time the offensive was called off in mid-November, a total of 1.2 million lives had been lost on both sides. The British had advanced 12km, the French 8km.

Between 2014 and 2018, a number of events will commemorate the Centenary of WWI throughout the region – it's well worth timing your trip around them.

◎ Sights & Activities

The battlefields and memorials are numerous and relatively scattered – joining a tour can therefore be a good option, especially if you don't have your own transport. Respected operators include **Battlefields Experience** (☑ 03 22 76 29 60; www.the battleofthesomme.co.uk) and **Western Front Tours** (www.westernfronttours.com.au; ⊙ mid-Mar–mid-Nov).

Historial de la Grande Guerre   WAR MUSEUM
(Museum of the Great War; ☑ 03 22 83 14 18; www.historial.org; Château de Péronne, Péronne; adult/child incl audioguide €7.50/4; ⊙ 10am-6pm, closed mid-Dec–mid-Feb) The best place to begin a visit to the Somme battlefields – especially if you're interested in WWI's historical and cultural context – is the outstanding Historial de la Grande Guerre in the town of Péronne, about 60km east of Amiens. Tucked inside Péronne's massively fortified château, this award-winning museum tells the story of the war chronologically, with equal space given to the German, French and British perspectives on what happened, how and why.

Beaumont-Hamel Newfoundland Memorial   WAR MEMORIAL
(☑ 03 22 76 70 86; www.veterans.gc.ca; Beaumont-Hamel) This evocative memorial preserves part of the Western Front in the state it was in at fighting's end. The zigzag trench system, which still fills with mud in winter, is clearly visible, as are countless shell craters and the remains of barbed-wire barriers. A path leads to an orientation table at the top of the 'Caribou mound', where a bronze caribou statue is surrounded by plants native to Newfoundland. Beaumont-Hamel is 9km

WORTH A TRIP

LOUVRE-LENS

Opened with fanfare in 2012 in Lens, 35km southwest of Lille, the innovative **Louvre-Lens** (☑ 03 21 18 62 62; www.louvrelens.fr; 99 rue Paul Bert, Lens; ⊙ 10am-6pm Wed-Mon) showcases hundreds of treasures from Paris' venerable Musée du Louvre in a purpose-built, state-of-the-art exhibition space.

Unlike its Parisian cousin, there's no permanent collection here. Instead, the museum's centrepiece, a 120m-long exhibition space called the **Galerie du Temps**, displays a limited but significant, ever-rotating collection of 200-plus pieces from the original Louvre, spanning that museum's full breadth and diversity of cultures and historical periods.

A second building, the glass-walled **Pavillon de Verre**, displays temporary themed exhibits. Rounding out the museum are educational facilities, an auditorium, a restaurant and a park.

Lens is accessible by regular TGV trains from Paris' Gare du Nord (€28.50 to €51, 65 to 70 minutes), as well as regional trains from Lille (from €6.80, 40 minutes).

north of Albert; follow the signs for 'Memorial Terreneuvien'.

🛏 Sleeping & Eating

★ **Au Vintage**   B&B €
(☑ 06 83 03 45 26, 03 22 75 63 28; www.chambresdhotes-albert.com; 19 rue de Corbie, Albert; d incl breakfast €65-85; P 🜹) This B&B is an absolute spoil from start to finish. It occupies an elegant brick mansion with two rooms and a family suite that are furnished with taste and flair.

Our fave is Rubis, with its super-size bathroom. Evelyne and Jacky are delightful, cultured hosts who enjoy sharing their knowledge about the battlefields with their guests – in good English.

Butterworth Farm   B&B €
(☑ 06 22 30 28 02, 03 22 74 04 47; www.butterworth-cottage.com; route de Bazentin, Pozières; d incl breakfast €65; P 🜹) Beloved by Australians and Brits, this well-run venture is an excellent base. Well-tended, fresh guest

rooms are in a converted barn, the facade of which is covered with wood panels.

There's a garden, filled with flowers and herbs, for lounging in, and breakfasts are copious.

Le Tommy BRASSERIE €
(☑ 03 22 74 82 84; 91 route d'Albert, Pozières; mains €8-12; ☉ 11am-3pm) This no-frills, slightly eccentric eatery on the main road in Pozières is ideal for a light lunch comprising a main course and dessert, or a sandwich. It also houses a small museum with WWI memorabilia and artifacts.

ℹ Information

The tourist offices in **Péronne** (☑ 03 22 84 42 38; www.hautesomme-tourisme.com; 16 place André Audinot, Péronne; ☉ 10am-noon & 2-6pm Mon-Sat) and **Albert** (☑ 03 22 75 16 42; www. tourisme-paysducoquelicot.com; 6 rue Émile Zola, Albert; ☉ 9am-12.30pm & 1.30-6.30pm Mon-Sat, 9am-1pm Sun) both have plenty of information in English and can help with booking tours and accommodation.

ℹ Getting There & Away

You will need your own transport to visit WWI sights. Alternatively, join a tour.

NORMANDY

Famous for cows, cider and Camembert, this largely rural region (www.normandie-tourisme.fr) is one of France's most traditional, and most visited, thanks to world-renowned sights such as the Bayeux Tapestry, the historic D-Day beaches and spectacular Mont St-Michel.

Bayeux

POP 13,350

Bayeux has become famous throughout the English-speaking world thanks to a 68m-long piece of painstakingly embroidered cloth: the 11th-century Bayeux Tapestry, whose 58 scenes vividly tell the story of the Norman invasion of England in 1066.

The town is also one of the few in Normandy to have survived WWII practically unscathed, with a centre crammed with 13th- to 18th-century buildings, wooden-framed Norman-style houses, and a spectac-

ular Norman Gothic cathedral. It makes a great base for exploring D-Day beaches.

⊙ Sights

★ **Bayeux Tapestry** TAPESTRY
(☑ 02 31 51 25 50; www.tapestry-bayeux.com; rue de Nesmond; adult/child incl audioguide €9/4; ☉ 9am-6.30pm mid-Mar–mid-Nov, to 7pm May-Aug, 9.30am-12.30pm & 2-6pm mid-Nov–mid-Mar) The world's most celebrated embroidery depicts the conquest of England by William the Conqueror in 1066 from an unashamedly Norman perspective. Commissioned by Bishop Odo of Bayeux, William's half-brother, for the opening of Bayeux' cathedral in 1077, the 68.3m-long cartoon strip tells the dramatic, bloody tale with verve and vividness.

Musée d'Art et d'Histoire Baron Gérard MUSEUM
(MAHB; ☑ 02 31 92 14 21; www.bayeuxmuseum. com; 37 rue du Bienvenu; adult/child €7/4; ☉ 9.30am-6.30pm May-Sep, 10am-12.30pm & 2-6pm Oct-Apr) Opened in 2013, this is one of France's most gorgeously presented provincial museums. The exquisite exhibits cover everything from Gallo-Roman archaeology to medieval art to paintings from the Renaissance to the 20th century, including a fine work by Gustave Caillebotte. Other highlights include impossibly delicate local lace and Bayeux-made porcelain. Housed in the former bishop's palace.

🛏 Sleeping & Eating

Les Logis du Rempart B&B €
(☑ 02 31 92 50 40; www.lecornu.fr; 4 rue Bourbesneur; d €60-100, tr €110-130; 🛜) The three rooms of this delightful *maison de famille* ooze old-fashioned cosiness. Our favourite, the Bajocasse, has parquet floor and Toile de Jouy wallpaper. The shop downstairs is the perfect place to stock up on top-quality, homemade cider and *calvados* (apple brandy).

Hôtel d'Argouges HOTEL €€
(☑ 02 31 92 88 86; www.hotel-dargouges.com; 21 rue St-Patrice; d/tr/f €140/193/245; ☉ closed Dec & Jan; 🅿 🛜) Occupying a stately 18th-century residence with a lush little garden, this graceful hotel has 28 comfortable rooms with exposed beams, thick walls and Louis XVI–style furniture. The breakfast room,

hardly changed since 1734, still has its original wood panels and parquet floors.

★**La Reine Mathilde** PATISSERIE €
(47 rue St-Martin; cakes from €2.20; ⊙9am-7.30pm Tue-Sun) This sumptuously decorated patisserie and *salon de thé* (tearoom), ideal for a sweet breakfast or a relaxing cup of afternoon tea, hasn't changed much since it was built in 1898.

Le Pommier NORMAN €€
(✆02 31 21 52 10; www.restaurantlepommier.com; 38-40 rue des Cuisiniers; lunch menus €15-18, other menus €21-39.50; ⊙noon-2pm & 7-9pm, closed Sun Nov-Feb; ✐) At this romantic restaurant, delicious Norman classics include steamed pollock and Caen-style tripe. A vegetarian menu – a rarity in Normandy – is also available, with offerings such as soybean steak in Norman cream.

❶ Information

The **tourist office** (✆02 31 51 28 28; www. bayeux-bessin-tourisme.com; pont St-Jean; ⊙9.30am-12.30pm & 2-6pm Mon-Sat) covers both Bayeux and the surrounding region, including D-Day beaches.

❶ Getting There & Away

Trains link Bayeux with Caen (€6.60, 20 minutes, hourly), from where there are connections to Paris' Gare St-Lazare and Rouen.

D-Day Beaches

Early on 6 June 1944, Allied troops stormed 80km of beaches north of Bayeux, codenamed (from west to east) Utah, Omaha, Gold, Juno and Sword. The landings on D-Day – called *Jour J* in French – ultimately led to the liberation of Europe from Nazi occupation. For context, see www.normandiememoire.com and www.6juin1944.com.

The most brutal fighting on D-Day took place 15km northwest of Bayeux along the stretch of coastline now known as **Omaha Beach**, today a glorious stretch of fine golden sand partly lined with sand dunes and summer homes. **Circuit de la Plage d'Omaha**, a trail marked with a yellow stripe, is a self-guided tour along the beach, surveyed from a bluff above by the huge **Normandy American Cemetery & Memorial** (www.abmc.gov; Colleville-sur-Mer; ⊙9am-6pm mid-Apr–mid-Sep, to 5pm rest of year). Featured in the opening scenes of Steven Spielberg's *Saving Private Ryan,* this is the largest American cemetery in Europe.

Caen's high-tech, hugely impressive **Mémorial – Un Musée pour la Paix** (Memorial – A Museum for Peace; ✆02 31 06 06 44; www.memorial-caen.fr; esplanade Général Eisenhower; adult/child €19/11.50; ⊙9am-7pm daily mid-Feb–mid-Nov, 9.30am-6.30pm Tue-Sun mid-Nov–mid-Feb, closed 3 weeks in Jan) uses sound, lighting, film, animation and lots of exhibits to graphically explore and evoke the events of WWII, the D-Day landings and the ensuing Cold War.

☞ Tours

Normandy Tours GUIDED TOUR
(✆02 31 92 10 70; www.normandy-landing-tours. com; 26 place de la Gare, Bayeux; adult/student €62/55) Offers well-regarded four- to five-hour tours of the main sites starting at 8.15am and 1.15pm on most days, as well as personally tailored trips. Based at Bayeux' Hôtel de la Gare, facing the train station.

Tours by Mémorial – Un Musée pour la Paix MINIBUS TOUR
(✆02 31 06 06 45; www.memorial-caen.fr; adult/child morning €64/64, afternoon €81/64; ⊙9am & 2pm Apr-Sep, 1pm Oct-Mar, closed 3 weeks in Jan) Excellent year-round minibus tours (four to five hours), with cheaper tours in full-size buses (€39) from June to August. Rates include entry to Mémorial – Un Musée pour la Paix. Book online.

Mont St-Michel

On a rocky island opposite the coastal town of Pontorson, connected to the mainland by a narrow causeway, the sky-scraping turrets of the abbey of **Mont St-Michel** (✆02 33 89 80 00; www.monuments-nationaux.fr; adult/child incl guided tour €9/free; ⊙9am-7pm, last entry 1hr before closing) provide one of France's iconic sights. The surrounding bay is notorious for its fast-rising tides: at low tide, the Mont is surrounded by bare sand for miles around; at high tide, just six hours later, the bay is submerged.

From the **tourist office** (✆02 33 60 14 30; www.ot-montsaintmichel.com; ⊙9am-12.30pm & 2-6pm Sep-Jun, 9am-7pm Jul & Aug), at the base of Mont St-Michel, a cobbled street winds up to the **Église Abbatiale** (Abbey Church), incorporating elements of both Norman and Gothic architecture. Other notable sights include the arched **cloître** (cloister), the barrel-roofed **réfectoire** (dining hall), and the Gothic **Salle des Hôtes** (Guest Hall), dating from 1213. A one-hour tour is included with admission; English tours run hourly in summer, twice daily (11am and 3pm) in winter. In July and August, Monday to Saturday, there are illuminated *nocturnes* (night-time visits) with music from 7pm to midnight.

If you'd like to stay in the Mont itself, **Hôtel Du Guesclin** (☑ 02 33 60 14 10; www. hotelduguesclin.com; Grande Rue, Mont St-Michel; d €80-95; ⊗ closed Wed night & Thu Apr-Jun & Oct–mid-Nov, hotel closed mid-Nov–Mar) is your best bet, with five of the 10 rooms offering stupendous views of the bay. Much better value and with magical views of the Mont is Vent des Grèves, a lovely B&B 1km east of La Caserne.

ⓘ Getting There & Away

Transdev bus 1 links the Mont St-Michel La Caserne parking lot (2.5km from the Mont itself, which you access by free shuttle) with Pontorson (€3, 18 minutes), the nearest train station. From Pontorson, there are two to three daily trains to/from Bayeux (€23.90, 1¾ hours) and Caen (€26.10, 1¾ hours).

BRITTANY

Brittany is for explorers. Its wild, dramatic coastline, medieval towns, thick forests and the eeriest stone circles this side of Stonehenge make a trip here well worth the detour from the beaten track. This is a land of prehistoric mysticism, proud tradition and culinary wealth, where locals remain fiercely independent, where Breton culture (and cider) is celebrated and where Paris feels a very long way away indeed.

Quimper

POP 66,911

Small enough to feel like a village – with its slanted half-timbered houses and narrow cobbled streets – and large enough to buzz as the troubadour of Breton culture, Quimper (pronounced *kam-pair*) is the thriving capital of Finistère (meaning 'land's end').

⊙ Sights

Cathédrale St-Corentin   CHURCH
(place St-Corentin; ⊗ 8.30am–noon & 1.30-6.30pm Mon-Sat, 8.30am–noon & 2-6.30pm

Sun) At the centre of the city is Quimper's cathedral with its distinctive kink, said to symbolise Christ's inclined head as he was dying on the cross. Construction began in 1239 but the cathedral's dramatic twin spires weren't added until the 19th century. High on the west facade, look out for an equestrian statue of King Gradlon, the city's mythical 5th-century founder.

Musée
Départemental Breton   MUSEUM
(☑ 02 98 95 21 60; www.museedepartemental breton.fr; 1 rue du Roi Gradlon; adult/child €5/3; ⊗ 9am-12.30pm & 1-5pm Tue-Sat, 2-5pm Sun) Beside the Cathédrale St-Corentin, recessed behind a magnificent stone courtyard, this superb museum showcases Breton history, furniture, costumes, crafts and archaeology, in a former bishop's palace.

🛏 Sleeping & Eating

Hôtel Manoir des Indes   HOTEL €€
(☑ 02 98 55 48 40; www.manoir-hoteldesindes. com; 1 allée de Prad ar C'hras; s €99-125, d €158-189; P 🛇 🅿 ▨) This stunning hotel conversion, located in an old manor house just a short drive from the centre of Quimper, has been restored with the globe-trotting original owner in mind. Decor is minimalist and modern, with Asian objets d'art and lots of exposed wood. It's located a five-minute drive west of Quimper, a little way north of the D100.

Crêperie du Quartier   CRÊPERIE €
(☑ 02 98 64 29 30; 16 rue du Sallé; mains €5-9; ⊗ noon-2pm Mon-Sat, 7-10pm Mon, Wed, Fri & Sat) In a town where the humble crêpe is king, this cosy stone-lined place is one of the best. Its wide-ranging menu includes a *galette* of the week and, to follow up, you can go for a crêpe stuffed with apple, caramel, ice cream, almonds and chantilly.

ⓘ Information

The **tourist office** (☑ 02 98 53 04 05; www. quimper-tourisme.com; place de la Résistance; ⊗ 9am-7pm Mon-Sat, 10am-12.45pm & 3-5.45pm Sun Jul & Aug, 9.30am-12.30pm & 1.30-6.30pm Mon-Sat, 10am-12.45pm Sun Jun & Sep) has information about the wider area.

ⓘ Getting There & Away

Frequent trains serve Paris' Gare Montparnasse (€55 to €65, 4¾ hours).

THE MORBIHAN MEGALITHS

Pre-dating Stonehenge by about a hundred years, **Carnac** is home to the world's greatest concentration of megalithic sites. There are more than 3000 of these upright stones scattered across the countryside between **Carnac-Ville** and **Locmariaquer** village, most of which were erected between 5000 BC and 3500 BC. No one's quite sure what purpose these sites served, or how the original builders hacked and hauled these vast granite blocks.

Because of severe erosion, the sites are usually fenced off to allow vegetation to regrow. **Guided tours** run in French year-round and in English early July to late August. Sign up at the **Maison des Mégalithes** (☑ 02 97 52 29 81; www.carnac.monuments-nationaux.fr; rte des Alignements; tour adult/child €6/free; ☺ 9.30am-7.30pm Jul & Aug, to 5pm Sep-Apr, to 6pm May & Jun). Opposite, the largest menhir field – with no fewer than 1099 stones – is the **Alignements du Ménec**, 1km north of Carnac-Ville. From here, the D196 heads northeast for about 1.5km to the **Alignements de Kermario**. Climb the stone observation tower midway along the site to see the alignment from above. Another 500m further on are the **Alignements de Kerlescan**, while the **Tumulus St-Michel**, 400m northeast of the Carnac-Ville tourist office, dates back to at least 5000 BC.

For background, Carnac's **Musée de Préhistoire** (☑ 02 97 52 22 04; www.museede carnac.fr; 10 place de la Chapelle, Carnac-Ville; adult/child €6/2.50; ☺ 10am-6pm) chronicles life in and around Carnac from the Palaeolithic and Neolithic eras to the Middle Ages.

St-Malo

POP 48,800

The mast-filled port of fortified St-Malo is inextricably tied up with the deep briny blue: the town became a key harbour during the 17th and 18th centuries, functioning as a base for merchant ships and government-sanctioned privateers, and these days it's a busy cross-Channel ferry port and summertime getaway.

☉ Sights

Walking on top of the sturdy 17th-century ramparts (1.8km) affords fine views of the old walled city known as **Intra-Muros** (Within the Walls), or Ville Close; access the ramparts from any of the city gates.

Cathédrale St-Vincent   CATHEDRAL
(place Jean de Châtillon; ☺ 9.30am-6pm) The city's centrepiece was constructed between the 12th and 18th centuries. During the ferocious fighting of August 1944 the cathedral was badly hit; much of its original structure (including its spire) was reduced to rubble. The cathedral was subsequently rebuilt and reconsecrated in 1971. A mosaic plaque on the floor of the nave marks the spot where Jacques Cartier received the blessing of the bishop of St-Malo before his 'voyage of discovery' to Canada in 1535.

Musée d'Histoire de St-Malo   MUSEUM
(☑ 02 99 40 71 57; www.ville-saint-malo.fr/culture/les-musees; Château; adult/child €6/3; ☺ 10am-12.30pm & 2-6pm Apr-Sep, Tue-Sun Oct-Mar) Within **Château de St-Malo**, built by the dukes of Brittany in the 15th and 16th centuries, this museum looks at the life and history of the city through nautical exhibits, model boats and marine artefacts, as well as an exhibition covering the city's cod-fishing heritage. There's also background info on the city's sons, including Cartier, Surcouf, Duguay-Trouin and the writer Chateaubriand.

⊨ Sleeping & Eating

Hôtel San Pedro   HOTEL €
(☑ 02 99 40 88 57; www.sanpedro-hotel.com; 1 rue Ste-Anne; s €65-69, d €75-83; ☑ ☜) Tucked at the back of the old city, the San Pedro has a cool, crisp, neutral-toned decor with subtle splashes of yellow paint, friendly service, great breakfast, private parking (€10) and a few bikes available for free. It features 12 rooms on four floors served by a miniature lift (forget those big suitcases!); two rooms come with sea views.

★ **L'Absinthe**   MODERN FRENCH €€
(☑ 02 99 40 26 15; www.restaurant-absinthe-cafe. fr; 1 rue de l'Orme; mains €18-24, menus €28-45; ☺ noon-2pm & 7-10pm) Hidden away in a quiet street near the covered market, this fab (and

WORTH A TRIP

CULINARY CANCALE

No day trip from St-Malo is tastier than one to **Cancale**, an idyllic Breton fishing port 14km east, famed for its offshore *parcs à huîtres* (oyster beds).

Learn all about oyster farming at the **Ferme Marine** (☑ 02 99 89 69 99; www.ferme-marine.com; corniche de l'Aurore; adult/child €7/3.70; ⊙ guided tours in French 11am, 3pm & 5pm Jul–mid-Sep, in English 2pm), and afterwards lunch on oysters fresh from their beds at the **Marché aux Huîtres** (Pointe des Crolles; 12 oysters from €4; ⊙ 9am-6pm), the local oyster market atmospherically clustered around the Pointe des Crolles lighthouse.

Buses stop behind the church on place Lucidas and at Port de la Houle, next to the fish market. **Keolis St-Malo** (www.ksma.fr) has year-round services to and from St-Malo (€1.25, 30 minutes).

very French) eatery is housed in an imposing 17th-century building. Ingredients fresh from the nearby market are whipped into shape by the talented chef, Stéphane Brebel, and served in cosy surrounds. The wine list is another hit, with an all-French cast from white to red and rosé.

ⓘ Information

Tourist Office (☑ 08 25 13 52 00; www.saint-malo-tourisme.com; esplanade St-Vincent; ⊙ 9am-7.30pm Mon-Sat, 10am-6pm Sun) Just outside the walls.

ⓘ Getting There & Away

Brittany Ferries (www.brittany-ferries.com) sails between St-Malo and Portsmouth; **Condor Ferries** (www.condorferries.co.uk) runs to/from Poole via Jersey or Guernsey.

TGV train services go to Paris' Gare Montparnasse (€52 to €64, three hours, up to 10 daily).

CHAMPAGNE

Known in Roman times as Campania, meaning 'plain', the agricultural region of Champagne is synonymous these days with its world-famous bubbly. This multi-million-dollar industry is strictly protected under French law, ensuring that only grapes grown in designated Champagne vineyards can truly lay claim to the hallowed title. The town of Épernay, 30km south of the regional capital of Reims, is the best place to head for *dégustation* (tasting); a self-drive **Champagne Routes** (www.tourisme-en-champagne.com) wends its way through the region's most celebrated vineyards.

Reims

POP 184,652

Over the course of a millennium (from 816 to 1825), some 34 sovereigns – among them two dozen kings – began their reigns in Reims' famed cathedral. Meticulously reconstructed after WWI and again following WWII, the city – whose name is pronounced something like 'rance' and is often anglicised as Rheims – is endowed with handsome pedestrian zones, well-tended parks, lively nightlife and a state-of-the-art tramway.

◉ Sights & Activities

The bottle-filled cellars (10°C to 12°C – bring a sweater!) of 10 Reims-area Champagne houses can be visited by a guided tour that ends, *naturellement*, with a tasting session.

★ Cathédrale Notre Dame   CATHEDRAL

(www.cathedrale-reims.culture.fr; place du Cardinal Luçon; tower adult/child €7.50/free, incl Palais du Tau €11/free; ⊙ 7.30am-7.30pm, tower tours hourly 11am-4pm Tue-Sun May-Sep) Imagine the egos and extravagance of a French royal coronation. The focal point of such bejewelled pomposity was Reims' resplendent Gothic cathedral, begun in 1211 on a site occupied by churches since the 5th century. The interior is a rainbow of stained-glass windows; the finest are the western facade's 12-petalled **great rose window**, the north transept's **rose window** and the vivid **Chagall** creations (1974) in the central axial chapel. The tourist office rents audioguides (€6) for self-paced cathedral tours.

Basilique St-Rémi   BASILICA

(place du Chanoine Ladame; ⊙ 8am-7pm) **FREE** This 121m-long former Benedictine abbey church, a Unesco World Heritage Site, mixes Romanesque elements from the mid-11th century (the worn but stunning nave and transept) with early Gothic features from the latter half of the 12th century (the choir, with a large triforium gallery and, way up top, tiny clerestory windows). Next door, **Musée St-Rémi** (53 rue Simon; adult/child €4/free; ⊙ 2-6.30pm Mon-Fri, to 7pm Sat & Sun), in a 17th- and 18th-century abbey, features local Gallo-Roman archaeology, tapestries and 16th- to 19th-century military history.

Palais du Tau   MUSEUM
(http://palais-tau.monuments-nationaux.fr; 2 place du Cardinal Luçon; adult/child €7.50/free, incl cathedral tower €11/free; ⊙ 9.30am-12.30pm & 2-5.30pm Tue-Sun) A Unesco World Heritage Site, this former archbishop's residence, constructed in 1690, was where French princes stayed before their coronations – and where they hosted sumptuous banquets afterwards. Now a museum, it displays truly exceptional statuary, liturgical objects and tapestries from the cathedral, some in the impressive, Gothic-style Salle de Tau (Great Hall).

Mumm   CHAMPAGNE HOUSE
(☎ 03 26 49 59 70; www.mumm.com; 34 rue du Champ de Mars; 1hr tours incl tasting €14-25; ⊙ tours 9am-5pm daily, shorter hours & closed Sun winter) Mumm (pronounced 'moom'), the only *maison* in central Reims, was founded in 1827 and is now the world's third-largest producer (almost eight million bottles a year). Engaging and edifying one-hour tours take you through cellars filled with 25 million bottles of fine bubbly. Wheelchair accessible. Phone ahead if possible.

Taittinger   CHAMPAGNE HOUSE
(☎ 03 26 85 45 35; www.taittinger.com; 9 place St-Niçaise; tours €16.50-45; ⊙ 9.30am-5.30pm, shorter hours & closed Sun winter) The headquarters of Taittinger are an excellent place to come for a clear, straightforward presentation on how Champagne is actually made – there's no claptrap about 'the Champagne mystique' here. Parts of the cellars occupy 4th-century Roman stone quarries; other bits were excavated by 13th-century Benedictine monks. No need to reserve. Situated 1.5km southeast of Reims centre; take the Citadine 1 or 2 bus to the St-Niçaise or Salines stops.

🛏 Sleeping & Eating

Les Telliers   B&B €€
(☎ 09 53 79 80 74; http://telliers.fr; 18 rue des Telliers; s €67-83, d €79-114, tr €115-134, q €131-155; P 🐾) Enticingly positioned down a quiet alley near the cathedral, this bijou B&B extends one of Reims' warmest *bienvenues*. The high-ceilinged rooms are big on art-

deco character, handsomely decorated with ornamental fireplaces, polished oak floors and the odd antique. Breakfast costs an extra €9 and is a generous spread of pastries, fruit, fresh-pressed juice and coffee.

L'Éveil des Sens   BISTRO €€
(☎ 03 26 35 16 95; www.eveildessens-reims.com; 8 rue Colbert; menus €30-38; ⊙ 12.15-2pm & 7.15-10pm, closed Sun & Wed) The 'awakening of the senses' is a fitting name for this terrific bistro. Monochrome hues and white linen create a chic yet understated setting for market-fresh cuisine delivered with finesse. Nicolas Lefèvre's specialities appear deceptively simple on paper, but the flavours are profound – be it scallops with tangy Granny Smith apple or braised beef ravioli on white bean velouté.

ℹ Information

Tourist Office (☎ 03 26 77 45 00; www.reims-tourisme.com; 2 rue Guillaume de Machault; ⊙ 9am-7pm Mon-Sat, 10am-6pm Sun)

ℹ Getting There & Away

From Reims' train station, 1km northwest of the cathedral, there are services to Paris' Gare de l'Est (€36 to €44, one hour, 12 to 17 daily) and Épernay (€6.80, 30 minutes, 19 daily).

Épernay
POP 24,600
Prosperous Épernay, 25km south of Reims, is the self-proclaimed *capitale du champagne* and home to many of the world's most celebrated Champagne houses. Beneath the town's streets, some 200 million bottles of Champagne are slowly being aged, just waiting to be popped open for some fizz-fuelled celebration.

◉ Sights & Activities

★ **Avenue de Champagne**   STREET
Épernay's handsome avenue de Champagne fizzes with *maisons de champagne*

(Champagne houses). The boulevard is lined with mansions and neoclassical villas, rebuilt after WWI. Peek through wrought-iron gates at Moët's private **Hôtel Chandon**, an early 19th-century pavilion-style residence set in landscaped gardens, which counts Wagner among its famous past guests. The haunted-looking **Château Perrier**, a red-brick mansion built in 1854 in neo-Louis XIII style, is aptly placed at number 13! The roundabout presents photo ops with its giant cork and bottle-top.

Moët & Chandon CHAMPAGNE HOUSE
(✆03 26 51 20 20; www.moet.com; 20 av de Champagne; adult incl 1/2 glasses €21/28, 10-18yr €10; ☻tours 9.30-11.30am & 2-4.30pm, closed Sat & Sun late Jan–mid-Mar) Flying the Moët, French, European and Russian flags, this prestigious *maison* offers frequent one-hour tours that are among the region's most impressive, offering a peek at part of its 28km labyrinth of *caves* (cellars). At the shop you can pick up a 15L bottle of Brut Impérial for just €1500; a standard bottle will set you back €31.

Champagne Domi Moreau VINEYARD TOUR
(✆06 30 35 51 07, after 7pm 03 26 59 45 85; www.champagne-domimoreau.com; tours €25-30; ☻tours 9.30am & 2.30pm except Wed & 2nd half of Aug) This company runs scenic and insightful three-hour minibus tours, in French and English, of nearby vineyards. Pick-up is across the street from the tourist office. It also organises two-hour vineyard tours by bicycle (€25). Call ahead for reservations.

🛏 Sleeping

Parva Domus B&B €€
(✆06 73 25 66 60; www.parvadomusrimaire.com; 27 av de Champagne; d €100, ste €110; ☎) Brilliantly situated on the avenue de Champagne, this vine-swathed B&B is kept spick and span by the amiable Rimaire family. Rooms have a countrified feel, with wood floors, floral fabrics and pastel colours. Sip a glass of house Champagne on the terrace or in the elegant living room.

★**La Villa Eugène** BOUTIQUE HOTEL €€€
(✆03 26 32 44 76; www.villa-eugene.com; 84 av de Champagne; d €154-333, ste €375-390; P✳☎☎) Sitting handsomely astride the avenue de Champagne in its own grounds with an outdoor pool, La Villa Eugène is a class act. It's lodged in a beautiful 19th-century town mansion that once belonged to the Mercier family. The roomy doubles exude understated elegance, with soft, muted hues and the odd antique. Splash out more for a private terrace or four-poster.

🍴 Eating & Drinking

La Grillade Gourmande REGIONAL CUISINE €€
(✆03 26 55 44 22; www.lagrilladegourmande.com; 16 rue de Reims; menus €19-57; ☻noon-2pm & 7.30-10pm Tue-Sat) This chic, red-walled bistro is an inviting spot to try chargrilled meats and dishes rich in texture and flavour, such as crayfish pan-fried in Champagne and lamb cooked until meltingly tender in rosemary and honey. Diners spill out onto the covered terrace in the warm months.

★**C Comme** CHAMPAGNE BAR
(www.c-comme.fr; 8 rue Gambetta; light meals €7.50-14.50, 6-glass Champagne tasting €33-39; ☻10am-8.30pm Sun-Wed, 10am-11pm Thu, 10am-midnight Fri & Sat) The downstairs cellar has a stash of 300 different varieties of Champagne; sample them (from €5.50 a glass) in the softly lit bar-bistro upstairs. Accompany with a tasting plate of regional cheese, charcuterie and rillettes. We love the funky bottle-top tables and relaxed ambience.

ℹ Information

The **tourist office** (✆03 26 53 33 00; www.ot-epernay.fr; 7 av de Champagne; ☻9.30am-12.30pm & 1.30-7pm Mon-Sat, 10.30am-1pm & 2-4.30pm Sun; ☎) has English brochures and maps.

ℹ Getting There & Away

The **train station** (place Mendès-France) has direct services to Reims (€6.80, 30 minutes, 19 daily) and Paris' Gare de l'Est (€23.60, 1¼ hours to 2¾ hours, 16 daily).

ALSACE & LORRAINE

Teetering on the tempestuous frontier between France and Germany, the neighbouring regions of Alsace and Lorraine are where the worlds of Gallic and Germanic culture collide. Half-timbered houses, lush vineyards and forest-clad mountains hint at Alsace's Teutonic leanings, while Lorraine is indisputably Francophile.

Strasbourg

POP 271,708

Strasbourg is the perfect overture to all that is idiosyncratic about Alsace – walking a fine tightrope between France and Germany and between a medieval past and a progressive future, it pulls off its act in inimitable Alsatian style. Roam the old town's twisting alleys lined with crooked half-timbered houses à la Grimm, feast in cosy *winstubs* (Alsatian taverns), and marvel at how a city that does Christmas markets and gingerbread so well can also be home to the glittering EU Quarter and France's second-largest student population.

◉ Sights

★ Cathédrale
Notre-Dame

CATHEDRAL

(place de la Cathédrale; astronomical clock adult/child €2/1.50, platform adult/child €5/2.50; ⊙ 7am-7pm, astronomical clock tickets sold 9.30-11am, platform 9am-7.15pm; ⓖ Grand'Rue) Nothing prepares you for your first glimpse of Strasbourg's Cathédrale Notre-Dame, completed in all its Gothic grandeur in 1439. The lace-fine facade lifts the gaze little by little to flying buttresses, leering gargoyles and a 142m spire. The interior is exquisitely lit by 12th- to 14th-century **stained-glass windows**, including the western portal's jewel-like rose window. The Gothic-meets-Renaissance **astronomical clock** strikes solar noon at 12.30pm with a parade of figures portraying the different stages of life and Jesus with his apostles.

Grande Île

HISTORIC QUARTER

(ⓖ Grand'Rue) History seeps through the twisting lanes and cafe-rimmed plazas of Grande Île, Strasbourg's Unesco World Heritage–listed island bordered by the River Ill. These streets – with their photogenic line-up of wonky, timber-framed houses in sherbet colours – are made for aimless ambling. They cower beneath the soaring magnificence of the cathedral and its sidekick, the gingerbready 15th-century **Maison Kammerzell** (rue des Hallebardes), with its ornate carvings and leaded windows. The alleys are at their most atmospheric when lantern-lit at night.

Petite France

HISTORIC QUARTER

(ⓖ Grand'Rue) Criss-crossed by narrow lanes, canals and locks, Petite France is where artisans plied their trades in the Middle Ages. The half-timbered houses, sprouting veritable thickets of scarlet geraniums in summer, and the riverside parks attract the masses, but the area still manages to retain its Alsatian charm, especially in the early morning and late evening. Drink in views of the River Ill and the **Barrage Vauban** from the much-photographed **Ponts Couverts** (Covered Bridges) and their trio of 13th-century towers.

🛏 Sleeping & Eating

Villa Novarina

DESIGN HOTEL €€

(🖉 03 90 41 18 28; www.villanovarina.com; 11 rue Westercamp; s €87-157, d €117-257, ste €237-537; 🅿✳🛜🖥; ⓖ Droits de l'Homme) New-wave design is pitched just right at this light-flooded 1950s villa near Parc de l'Orangerie. Slick without being soulless, rooms and suites are liberally sprinkled with art and overlook gardens. Breakfast places the accent on organic, regional produce. There's a heated pool, whirlpool and spa for quiet moments. It's a 10-minute walk south of Droits de l'Homme tram stop.

★ Cour du Corbeau

BOUTIQUE HOTEL €€€

(🖉 03 90 00 26 26; www.cour-corbeau.com; 6-8 rue des Couples; r €140-175, ste €220-260; ✳🛜; ⓖ Porte de l'Hôpital) A 16th-century inn lovingly converted into a boutique hotel, Cour du Corbeau wins you over with its half-timbered charm and location, just steps from the river. Gathered around a courtyard, rooms blend original touches like oak parquet and Louis XV furnishings with mod cons such as flat-screen TVs.

Bistrot et Chocolat

CAFE €

(www.bistrotetchocolat.net; 8 rue de la Râpe; snacks €7.50-11, brunch €12.50-26.50; ⊙ 11am-7pm Mon-Thu, 10am-9pm Fri-Sun; 🖉🚻; ⓖ Grand'Rue) Chilled bistro hailed for its solid and liquid organic chocolate (ginger is superb), day specials and weekend brunches.

★ La Cuiller à Pot

ALSATIAN €€

(🖉 03 88 35 56 30; www.lacuillerapot.com; 18b rue Finkwiller; mains €17.50-26.50; ⊙ noon-2.30pm & 7-10.30pm Tue-Fri, 7-10.30pm Sat; ⓖ Musée d'Art Moderne) Run by a talented husband-wife team, this little Alsatian dream of a restaurant rustles up fresh regional cuisine. Its well-edited menu goes with the seasons, but might include such dishes as fillet of beef with wild mushrooms, and homemade gnocchi and escargots in parsley jus. Quality is second to none.

❶ Information

The **tourist office** (☑ 03 88 52 28 28; www.otstrasbourg.fr; 17 place de la Cathédrale; ⊙9am-7pm daily; ⓖ Grand'Rue) has maps in English (€1).

❶ Getting There & Away

AIR

Strasbourg's international **airport** (☑ 03 88 64 67 67; www.strasbourg.aeroport.fr) is 17km southwest of the city centre (towards Molsheim).

TRAIN

Direct services go to both European and French cities. Destinations include:

Brussels-Nord €80 to €185, 5¼ hours, three daily

Lille €96 to €140, four hours, 17 daily

Lyon €75 to €145, 4½ hours, 14 daily

Metz €26 to €42, two hours, 20 daily

Paris €75 to €134, 2¼ hours, 19 daily

Metz

POP 122,149

Straddling the confluence of the Moselle and Seille Rivers, Metz is Lorraine's graceful capital. Its Gothic marvel of a cathedral, Michelin star–studded dining scene, beautiful yellow-stone **Old Town** and regal **Quartier Impérial** (up for Unesco World Heritage status) are a joy to discover.

◉ Sights

★**Cathédrale St-Étienne**   CATHEDRAL

(place St-Étienne; audioguide €7, combined ticket treasury & crypt adult/child €4/2; ⊙8am-6pm, treasury & crypt 9.30am-12.30pm & 1.30-5.30pm Mon-Sat, 2-6pm Sun) The lacy golden spires of this Gothic cathedral crown Metz' skyline. Exquisitely lit by kaleidoscopic curtains of 13th- to 20th-century stained glass, the cathedral is nicknamed 'God's lantern' and its sense of height is spiritually uplifting. Notice the flamboyant **Chagall windows** in startling jewel-coloured shades of ruby, gold, sapphire, topaz and amethyst in the ambulatory, which also harbours the **treasury**. The sculpture of the **Graoully** ('grau-lee'), a dragon said to have terrified pre-Christian Metz, lurks in the 15th-century **crypt**.

Centre Pompidou-Metz   GALLERY

(www.centrepompidou-metz.fr; 1 parvis des Droits de l'Homme; adult/child €7/free; ⊙11am-6pm Mon & Wed-Fri, 10am-8pm Sat, 10am-6pm Sun) Designed by Japanese architect Shigeru Ban, with a curved roof resembling a space-age Chinese hat, the architecturally innovative Centre Pompidou-Metz is the star of the city's art scene. The satellite branch of Paris' Centre Pompidou draws on Europe's largest collection of modern art to stage ambitious temporary exhibitions, such as the avant-garde works of German artist Hans Richter and the bold graphic works of American conceptual artist Sol LeWitt. The dynamic space also hosts cultural events, talks and youth projects.

🛏 Sleeping & Eating

Hôtel de la Cathédrale   HISTORIC HOTEL €€

(☑ 03 87 75 00 02; www.hotelcathedrale-metz.fr; 25 place de Chambre; d €75-120; ❧) You can expect a friendly welcome at this classy little hotel, occupying a 17th-century town house in a prime spot right opposite the cathedral. Climb the wrought-iron staircase to your classically elegant room, with high ceilings, hardwood floors and antique trappings. Book well ahead for a cathedral view.

La Table de Pol   MODERN FRENCH €€

(☑ 03 87 62 13 72; www.latabledepol.fr; 1/3 rue du Grand Wad; menus €17-46; ⊙noon-2pm & 7-9pm

Tue-Sat) Intimate lighting and cheek-by-jowl tables keep the mood mellow in this friendly bistro, which serves winningly fresh dishes prepared with market produce, along the lines of lamb filet mignon in a herb crust and cod filet with asparagus – all cooked to a T.

ⓘ Information

The **tourist office** (☑ 03 87 55 53 76; http://tourisme.mairie-metz.fr; 2 place d'Armes; ⊙ 9am-7pm Mon-Sat, 10am-5pm Sun) has free walking-tour maps.

ⓘ Getting There & Away

Metz' ornate early-20th-century **train station** (place du Général de Gaulle) has a supersleek TGV linking Paris with Luxembourg. Direct trains:

Luxembourg €16.20, 45 minutes, 40 daily
Paris €60 to €75, 1½ hours, 15 daily
Strasbourg €26.40, 1½ hours, 16 daily

THE LOIRE VALLEY

One step removed from the French capital, the Loire was historically the place where princes, dukes and notable nobles established their country getaways, and the countryside is littered with some of the most extravagant architecture outside Versailles.

Blois

POP 48,393

Blois' historic château was the feudal seat of the powerful counts of Blois, and its grand halls, spiral staircases and sweeping courtyards provide a whistlestop tour through the key periods of French architecture.

◉ Sights

★ **Château Royal de Blois**　CHÂTEAU
(☑ 02 54 90 33 33; www.chateaudeblois.fr; place du Château; adult/child €9.80/5, audioguide €4, English tours Jul & Aug free; ⊙ 9am-6.30pm Apr-Sep, to 7pm Jul & Aug, shorter hours rest of year) Intended more as an architectural showpiece (look at that ornately carved facade!) than a military stronghold, Blois' château bears the creative mark of several successive French kings. It makes an excellent introduction to the châteaux of the Loire Valley, with elements of Gothic (13th century), Flamboyant Gothic (1498–1503), early Renaissance (1515–24) and classical (1630s) architecture in its four grand wings.

The most famous feature of the Renaissance wing, the royal apartments of François I and Queen Claude, is the **loggia staircase**, decorated with salamanders and curly Fs (heraldic symbols of François I).

Maison de la Magie　MUSEUM
(www.maisondelamagie.fr; 1 place du Château; adult/child €9/5; ⊙ 10am-12.30pm & 2-6.30pm Apr-Aug, 2-6.30pm Mon-Fri, 10am-12.30pm & 2-6.30pm Sat & Sun Sep) Opposite the château you can't miss the former home of watchmaker, inventor and conjurer Jean Eugène Robert-Houdin (1805–71), whose name was later adopted by American magician Harry Houdini. Dragons emerge roaring from the windows on the hour, while the museum inside hosts daily **magic shows**, exhibits on the history of magic, displays of optical trickery and a short historical film about Houdini.

🛏 Sleeping & Eating

Côté Loire　HOTEL €
(☑ 02 54 78 07 86; www.coteloire.com; 2 place de la Grève; r €59-95; 🖥) Spotless rooms come in cheery checks, bright pastels and the odd bit of exposed brick; some have Loire views. Breakfast (€10.50) is served on a quaint interior wooden deck, and the restaurant (*menus* €21 to €31) dishes up delicious local cuisine. Find it a block off the river, southwest of Pont Jaques Gabriel.

★ **La Maison de Thomas**　B&B €€
(☑ 02 54 46 12 10; www.lamaisondethomas.fr; 12 rue Beauvoir; r incl breakfast €90; 🖥) Four spacious rooms and a friendly welcome await travellers at this beautiful B&B on a pedestrianised street halfway between the château and the cathedral. There's bike storage in the interior courtyard and a wine cellar where you can sample local vintages.

Les Banquettes Rouges　FRENCH €€
(☑ 02 54 78 74 92; www.lesbanquettesrouges.com; 16 rue des Trois Marands; menus €17.50-32.50; ⊙ noon-2pm & 7-10pm Tue-Sat) Handwritten slate menus and wholesome food distinguish the Red Benches: pork with chorizo and rosemary, duck with lentils, and *fondant au chocolat* to top it off.

ℹ Information

Tourist Office (☏ 02 54 90 41 41; www.
bloischambord.com; 23 place du Château;
☉ 9am-7pm Apr-Sep, to 5pm Oct-Mar) Helpful,
and sells joint château tickets. Download the
Visit Blois smartphone app.

ℹ Getting There & Away

BUS

TLC (☏ 02 54 58 55 44; www.tlcinfo.net) operates buses from Blois' train station (€2) to
Chambord (line 3; 25 to 40 minutes, two Monday
to Saturday) and Cheverny (line 4; 45 minutes,
three Monday to Friday, one Saturday).

TRAIN

The **Blois-Chambord train station** (av Jean
Laigret) is 600m uphill from Blois' château.

Amboise €7, 20 minutes, 13 daily

Paris From €28.60, 1½ to two hours, 26 daily

Tours €10.90, 40 minutes, 13 daily

Around Blois

Château de Chambord

For full-blown château splendour, you can't
top **Chambord** (☏ information 02 54 50 40
00, tour & spectacle reservations 02 54 50 50 40;
www.chambord.org; adult/child €11/9, parking €4;
☉ 9am-6pm Apr-Sep, 10am-5pm Oct-Mar), constructed from 1519 by François I as a lavish
base for hunting game in the Sologne forests
but eventually used for just 42 days during
the king's 32-year reign (1515–47).

The château's most famous feature is
its **double-helix staircase**, attributed by
some to Leonardo da Vinci, who lived in
Amboise (34km southwest) from 1516 until
his death three years later. The most interesting rooms are on the 1st floor, including
the **king's and queen's chambers** (complete with interconnecting passages to enable late-night hijinks) and a wing devoted
to the thwarted attempts of the Comte de
Chambord to be crowned Henri V after the
fall of the Second Empire.

Several times daily there are 1½-hour
guided tours (€4) in English.

Chambord is 16km east of Blois and accessible by bus.

Château de Cheverny

Thought by many to be the most perfectly proportioned château of all, **Cheverny**
(☏ 02 54 79 96 29; www.chateau-cheverny.fr; adult/
child €9.50/6.50; ☉ 9am-7pm Apr-Sep, 10am-5pm
Oct-Mar) has hardly been altered since its

CHÂTEAUX TOURS

Hard-core indie travellers might balk at the idea of a tour, but don't dismiss it out of
hand, especially if you don't have your own transport.

Minibus

Many private companies offer a choice of well-organised itineraries, taking in various
combinations of châteaux (plus wine-tasting tours). Half-day trips cost between €23 and
€36; full-day trips range from €50 to €54. Entry to the châteaux isn't included, although
you'll likely get a discount on tickets. Reserve via the Tours **tourist offices** (☏ 02 47 70 37
37; www.tours-tourisme.fr; 78-82 rue Bernard Palissy; ☉ 8.30am-7pm Mon-Sat, 10am-12.30pm &
2.30-5pm Sun Apr-Sep, shorter hours rest of year) or Amboise tourist office, from where most
tours depart.

Bicycle

The Loire Valley is mostly flat and thus excellent cycling country.

Loire à Vélo (www.loireavelo.fr) Maintains 800km of signposted routes. Pick up a guide
from tourist offices, or download route maps, audioguides and bike-hire details online.

Détours de Loire (☏ 02 47 61 22 23; www.locationdevelos.com) Has a bike-rental shop in
Blois and can deliver bikes; it also allows you to collect/return bikes along the route for a
small surcharge. Classic bikes cost €15/60 per day/week.

Les Châteaux à Vélo (☏ in Blois 02 54 78 62 52; www.chateauxavelo.com; per day €12-14)
Has 400km of marked trails around Blois, Chambord, Cheverny and Chaumont-sur-
Loire; shuttle minibus available, as well as free route maps and MP3 guides online.

construction between 1625 and 1634. Inside is a formal dining room, bridal chamber and children's playroom (complete with Napoléon III–era toys), as well as a guards' room full of pikestaffs, claymores and suits of armour.

Many priceless art works (including the *Mona Lisa*) were stashed in the château's 18th-century **Orangerie** during WWII. Near the château's gateway, the **kennels** house pedigreed French pointer/English foxhound hunting dogs still used by the owners of Cheverny; feeding time, the **Soupe des Chiens**, takes place daily at 5pm April to September.

Cheverny is 16km southeast of Blois and accessible by bus.

Amboise

POP 13,375

The childhood home of Charles VIII and the final resting place of Leonardo da Vinci, elegant Amboise, 23km northeast of Tours, is pleasantly perched along the southern bank of the Loire and overlooked by its fortified château.

◉ Sights

Château Royal d'Amboise   CHÂTEAU
(☑02 47 57 52 23; www.chateau-amboise.com; place Michel Debré; adult/child €10.70/7.20, with audioguide €14.70/10.20; ⊙9am-7pm Jul & Aug, to 6pm Apr-Oct, shorter hours Nov-Mar) Elegantly tiered on a rocky escarpment above town, this easily defendable castle presented a formidable prospect to would-be attackers – but saw little military action. It was more often a weekend getaway from the official royal seat at Blois. Charles VIII (r 1483–98), born and bred here, was responsible for the château's Italianate remodelling in 1492. Today just a few of the original 15th- and 16th-century structures survive, notably the Flamboyant Gothic wing and **Chapelle St-Hubert**, the final resting place of Leonardo da Vinci. They have thrilling views to the river, town and gardens.

Le Clos Lucé   HISTORIC BUILDING
(☑02 47 57 00 73; www.vinci-closluce.com; 2 rue du Clos Lucé; adult/child €14/9, joint family tickets reduced; ⊙9am-8pm Jul & Aug, 9am-7pm Feb-Jun, Sep & Oct, 9am-6pm Nov & Dec, 10am-6pm Jan; ⊕) Leonardo da Vinci took up residence at this grand manor house in 1516 on the invitation of François I. An admirer of the Italian Renaissance, François named da Vinci 'first painter, engineer and king's architect'. Already 64 by the time he arrived, da Vinci spent his time sketching, tinkering and dreaming up new contraptions, scale models of which are now displayed throughout the home and its expansive **gardens**. Visitors tour rooms where da Vinci worked and the bedroom where he drew his last breath on 2 May 1519.

🛏 Sleeping & Eating

Au Charme Rabelaisien   B&B €€
(☑02 47 57 53 84; www.au-charme-rabelaisien.com; 25 rue Rabelais; d incl breakfast €92-179; P❄🛜🏊) At this calm haven in the centre, Sylvie offers the perfect small B&B experience. Mixing modern fixtures with antique charm, three comfy rooms share a flower-filled garden, pool and free enclosed parking. The spacious Chambre Nature is delightfully secluded and only a few steps from the pool. Breakfasts are fab.

Chez Bruno   BISTRO €
(☑02 47 57 73 49; www.bistrotchezbruno.com; 38-40 place Michel Debré; mains €8-12; ⊙lunch & dinner Tue-Sat) Uncork a host of local vintages in a lively contemporary setting just beneath the towering château. Tables of chatting visitors and locals alike dig into delicious, inexpensive regional cooking. If you're after Loire Valley wine tips, this is the place to come.

ℹ Information

The **tourist office** (☑02 47 57 09 28; www.amboise-valdeloire.com; quai du Général de Gaulle; ⊙9.30am-6pm Mon-Sat, 10am-1pm & 2-5pm Sun, closed Sun Nov-Mar) offers walking tours.

ℹ Getting There & Around

From the **train station** (bd Gambetta, 1.5km north of the château), there are services to Blois (€7, 20 minutes, 13 daily) and Paris' Gare d'Austerlitz (€15, 1¾ hours, four daily).

Around Amboise

Château de Chenonceau

Spanning the languid Cher River via a series of supremely graceful arches, the castle of

Chenonceau ([🖰]02 47 23 90 07; www.chenon ceau.com; adult/child €12.50/9.50, with audio-guide €17/13.50; ⊙9am-7pm Apr-Sep, shorter hours rest of year; ⊛) is one of the most elegant and unusual in the Loire Valley. You can't help but be swept up in the magical architecture, the fascinating history of prominent female owners, the glorious setting and the landscaped parkland.

The château's interior is crammed with wonderful furniture and tapestries, stunning original tiled floors and a fabulous art collection including works by Tintoretto, Correggio, Rubens, Murillo, Van Dyck and Ribera. The pièce de résistance is the 60m-long window-lined **Grande Gallerie** spanning the Cher.

Make time to visit the **gardens**, too: it seems as if there's one of every kind imaginable (maze, English, vegetable, playground, flower...).

The château is located 10km southeast of Amboise. **Touraine Fil Vert** (www.touraine filvert.com; tickets €2.20) runs two daily buses from Amboise (15 minutes, Monday to Saturday).

Château d'Azay-le-Rideau

Romantic, moat-ringed **Azay-le-Rideau** ([🖰]0247454204; www.azay-le-rideau.monuments-nationaux.fr/en; adult/child €8.50/free; ⊙9.30am-6pm Apr-Sep, to 7pm Jul & Aug, 10am-5.15pm Oct-Mar) is wonderfully adorned with slender turrets, geometric windows and decorative stonework, wrapped up within a shady landscaped park. Built in the 1500s on a natural island in the middle of a river, the château is one of the Loire's loveliest: Honoré de Balzac called it a 'multifaceted diamond set in the River Indre'.

Its most famous feature is its open **loggia staircase**, in the Italian style, overlooking the central courtyard and decorated with the salamanders and ermines of François I and Queen Claude.

Azay-le-Rideau is 26km southwest of Tours. The château is 2.5km from the train station, where there are eight daily services to Tours (€5.80, 30 minutes).

BURGUNDY & THE RHÔNE VALLEY

If there's one place in France where you're really going to find out what makes the nation tick, it's Burgundy. Two of the country's

enduring passions – food and wine – come together in this gorgeously rural region. If you're a sucker for hearty food and the fruits of the vine, you'll be in seventh heaven.

Dijon
POP 155,900

Filled with elegant medieval and Renaissance buildings, dashing Dijon is Burgundy's capital, and the spiritual home of French mustard. Its lively Old Town is wonderful for strolling and shopping, interspersed with some snappy drinking and dining.

⊙ Sights

Palais des Ducs et des
États de Bourgogne PALACE
(Palace of the Dukes & States of Burgundy; place de la Libération) Once home to Burgundy's powerful dukes, this monumental palace with a neoclassical facade overlooks place de la Libération, Old Dijon's magnificent central square dating from 1686. The palace's eastern wing houses the outstanding Musée des Beaux-Arts, whose entrance is next to the **Tour de Bar**, a squat 14th-century tower that once served as a prison.

Musée des Beaux-Arts ART MUSEUM
([🖰]03 80 74 52 09; http://mba.dijon.fr; audioguide €4; ⊙9.30am-6pm Wed-Mon May-Oct, 10am-5pm Nov-Apr) **FREE** Housed in the monumental Palais des Ducs, these sprawling galleries (works of art in themselves) constitute one of France's most outstanding museums. The star attraction, reopened in September 2013 after extensive renovations, is the wood-panelled **Salle des Gardes**, which houses the ornate, carved late-medieval sepulchres of dukes John the Fearless and Philip the Bold. Other sections focus on Egyptian art, the Middle Ages in Burgundy and Europe, and six centuries of European painting, from the Renaissance to modern times.

🛏 Sleeping & Eating

Hôtel du Palais HOTEL €
([🖰]03 80 65 51 43; www.hoteldupalais-dijon. fr; 23 rue du Palais; s €59-79, d €65-89, q €119; ✳⊛) Newly remodelled and upgraded to three-star status, this inviting hotel in a 17th-century *hôtel particulier* (private mansion) offers excellent value. The 13 rooms range from cosy, inexpensive 3rd-floor doubles tucked under the eaves to spacious, high-ceilinged family suites with

MAD ABOUT MUSTARD

If there is one pilgrimage to be made in Dijon it is to **Moutarde Maille** (✐03 80 30 41 02; www.maille.com; 32 rue de la Liberté; ⊙10am-7pm Mon-Sat), the factory boutique of the company that makes Dijon's most famous mustard. The tangy odours of the sharp sauce assault your nostrils instantly upon entering and there are 36 kinds to buy, including cassis-, truffle- or celery-flavoured; sample three on tap.

Or head to **Moutarderie Fallot** (Mustard Mill; ✐03 80 22 10 10; www.fallot. com; 31 rue du Faubourg Bretonnière; adult/child €10/8; ⊙tasting room 9.30am-6pm Mon-Sat, tours 10am & 11.30am Mon-Sat mid-Mar–mid-Nov, plus 3.30pm & 5pm Jun-Sep, by arrangement rest of year) in neighbouring Beaune, where Burgundy's last family-run, stone-ground mustard company offers tours of its facilities and mustard museum. Reserve ahead at Beaune tourist office.

abundant natural light. The location is unbeatable, on a quiet side street five minutes' walk from supercentral place de la Libération.

Chez Léon REGIONAL CUISINE €€
(✐03 80 50 01 07; www.restochezleon.fr; 20 rue des Godrans; mains €17-23, lunch menus €15-19, dinner menus €25-29; ⊙noon-2pm & 7-10.30pm Tue-Sat) From bœuf bourguignon to *andouillettes* (chitterling sausages), this is the perfect primer course in hearty regional fare celebrated in a cosy and joyful atmosphere. The dining room is cluttered but there's outdoor seating in warmer months.

ⓘ Information

The **tourist office** (✐08 92 70 05 58; www.visit dijon.com; 11 rue des Forges; ⊙9.30am-6.30pm Mon-Sat, 10am-6pm Sun Apr-Sep, shorter hours rest of year) offers tours and maps.

ⓘ Getting There & Away

BUS

Transco (✐03 80 11 29 29; www.cotedor.fr/ cms/transco-horaires) buses stop in front of the train station; tickets (€1.50) are sold on board. Bus 44 goes to Nuits-St-Georges and Beaune.

TRAIN

Connections from Dijon's **train station** (rue du Dr Rémy) include the following:

Lyon-Part Dieu Regional train/TGV €31/36, two/1½ hours, 25 daily

Marseille TGV €89, 3½ hours, six direct daily

Paris Gare de Lyon Regional train/TGV €45/65, three/1½ hours, 25 daily

Beaune

POP 22,620

Beaune (pronounced 'bone'), 44km south of Dijon, is the unofficial capital of the Côte d'Or. This thriving town's *raison d'être* and the source of its *joie de vivre* is wine.

⊙ Sights & Activities

Beaune's amoeba-shaped old city is enclosed by **stone ramparts** sheltering wine cellars.

Hôtel-Dieu des Hospices de Beaune HISTORIC BUILDING
(www.hospices-de-beaune.com; rue de l'Hôtel-Dieu; adult/child €7/3; ⊙9am-6.30pm) Built in 1443, this magnificent Gothic hospital (until 1971) is famously topped by stunning turrets and pitched rooftops covered in multicoloured tiles. Interior highlights include the barrel-vaulted **Grande Salle** (look for the dragons and peasant heads up on the roof beams); the mural-covered **St-Hughes Room**; an 18th-century **pharmacy** lined with flasks once filled with elixirs and powders; and the multipanelled masterpiece **Polyptych of the Last Judgement** by 15th-century Flemish painter Rogier van der Weyden, depicting Judgment Day in glorious technicolour.

Marché aux Vins WINE TASTING
(www.marcheauxvins.com; 2 rue Nicolas Rolin; ⊙10am-7pm Apr-Oct, 10am-noon & 2-7pm Nov-Mar) Sample seven wines for €11, or 10 for €15, in the candle-lit former Église des Cordeliers and its cellars. Wandering among the vintages takes about an hour. The finest wines are at the end; look for the *premier crus* and the *grand cru* (wine of exceptional quality).

🛏 Sleeping & Eating

⭐**Les Jardins de Loïs** B&B €€
(✐03 80 22 41 97; www.jardinsdelois.com; 8 bd Bretonnière; incl breakfast r €149, ste €180-190, apt €280-350; ☞) An unexpected oasis in the middle of the city, this luxurious B&B

A TRIP BETWEEN VINES

Burgundy's most renowned vintages come from the **Côte d'Or** (Golden Hillside), a range of hills made of limestone, flint and clay that runs south from Dijon for about 60km. The northern section, the **Côte de Nuits**, stretches from Marsannay-la-Côte south to Corgoloin and produces reds known for their robust, full-bodied character. The southern section, the **Côte de Beaune**, lies between Ladoix-Serrigny and Santenay and produces great reds and whites.

Tourist offices provide brochures. The signposted **Route des Grands Crus** (www. road-of-the-fine-burgundy-wines.com) visits some of the most celebrated Côte de Nuits vineyards; mandatory tasting stops for oenophiles seeking nirvana include 16th-century **Château du Clos de Vougeot** (✆ 03 80 62 86 09; www.closdevougeot.fr; Vougeot; adult/child €5/2.50; ⊙ 9am-6.30pm Apr-Sep, 9-11.30am & 2-5.30pm Oct-Mar, closes 5pm Sat year-round, which has excellent guided tours, and **L'Imaginarium** (✆ 03 80 62 61 40; www. imaginarium-bourgogne.com; av du Jura, Nuits-St-Georges; adult incl basic/grand cru tasting €8/15, child €5; ⊙ 2-7pm Mon, 10am-7pm Tue-Sun, an entertaining wine museum in Nuits-St-Georges.

Wine & Voyages (✆ 03 80 61 15 15; www.wineandvoyages.com; tours from €53) and **Alter & Go** (✆ 06 23 37 92 04; www.alterandgo.fr; tours from €70), with an emphasis on history and winemaking methods, run minibus tours in English; reserve online or at the Dijon tourist office.

encompasses several ample rooms, including two suites and a 135-sq-metre top-floor apartment with drop-dead gorgeous views of Beaune's rooftops. The vast garden, complete with rose bushes and fruit trees, makes a dreamy place to sit and enjoy wine grown on the hotel's private *domaine*. Free parking.

Le Bacchus MODERN BURGUNDIAN €€
(✆ 03 80 24 07 78; 6 Faubourg Madeleine; lunch menus €14-16.50, dinner menus €26.50-33; ⊙ noon-1.30pm & 7-10pm) The welcome is warm and the food exceptional at this small restaurant just outside Beaune's centre. Multilingual co-owner Anna works the tables while her partner Olivier whips up market-fresh menus that blend classic flavours (steak with Fallot mustard) with tasty surprises (gazpacho with tomato-basil ice cream). Save room for splendid desserts such as Bourbon vanilla crème brûlée, flambéed at your table.

ⓘ Information

The **tourist office** (✆ 03 80 26 21 30; www. beaune-tourisme.fr; 6 bd Perpreuil; ⊙ 9am-6.30pm Mon-Sat, 9am-6pm Sun) has lots of info about nearby vineyards.

ⓘ Getting There & Away

BUS

Bus 44 links Beaune with Dijon (€1.50, 1½ hours, two to seven daily), stopping at Côte d'Or villages such as Nuits-St-Georges.

TRAIN

Trains run to the following destinations:
Dijon €7.80, 25 minutes, 40 daily
Paris Gare de Lyon €75, 2¼ hours, two daily
Lyon-Part Dieu €26.50, 1¾ hours, 16 daily

Lyon

POP 499,800

Gourmets, eat your heart out: Lyon is *the* gastronomic capital of France, with a lavish table of piggy-driven dishes and delicacies to savour. The city has been a commercial, industrial and banking powerhouse for the past 500 years, and is France's third-largest city, with outstanding art museums, a dynamic nightlife, green parks and a Unesco-listed Old Town.

◉ Sights

◎ Vieux Lyon

Old Lyon, with its cobblestone streets and medieval and Renaissance houses below

Fourvière hill, is divided into three quarters: St-Paul (north), St-Jean (middle) and St-Georges (south). Lovely old buildings languish on **rue du Bœuf, rue St-Jean** and **rue des Trois Maries**.

Listen out for the chime of the **astronomical clock** of the partly Romanesque **Cathédrale St-Jean** (place St-Jean, 5e; ☉8.15am-7.45pm Mon-Fri, to 7pm Sat & Sun; Ⓜ Vieux Lyon), striking the hour at noon, 2pm, 3pm and 4pm.

⊙ Fourvière

Over two millennia ago, the Romans built the city of Lugdunum on the slopes of Fourvière. Today, Lyon's 'hill of prayer' – topped by the **Basilique Notre Dame de Fourvière** (www.fourviere.org; place de Fourvière, 5e; rooftop tour adult/child €6/3; ☉8am-7pm; funicular Fourvière) and the **Tour Métallique**, an Eiffel Tower–like structure built in 1893 and used as a TV transmitter – affords spectacular views of the city. Footpaths wind uphill, but the **funicular** (place Édouard Commette, 5e; one way €1.70) is less taxing.

⊙ Presqu'île, Confluence & Croix-Rousse

Lyon's city centre lies on this 500m- to 800m-wide peninsula bounded by the rivers Rhône and Saône.

The centrepiece of main square **place des Terreaux** is a 19th-century fountain sculpted by Frédéric-Auguste Bartholdi, creator of the Statue of Liberty. The **Musée des Beaux-Arts** (www.mba-lyon.fr; 20 place des Terreaux, 1er; adult/child incl audioguide €7/free; ☉10am-6pm Wed, Thu & Sat-Mon, 10.30am-6pm Fri; Ⓜ Hôtel de Ville) showcases France's finest collection of sculptures and paintings outside of Paris.

Lyonnais silks are showcased at the **Musée des Tissus** (www.musee-des-tissus.com; 34 rue de la Charité, 2e; adult/child €10/7.50, after 4pm €8/5.50; ☉10am-5.30pm Tue-Sun; Ⓜ Ampère). Next door, the **Musée des Arts Décoratifs** (34 rue de la Charité, 2e; free with Musée des Tissus ticket; ☉10am-noon & 2-5.30pm Tue-Sun) displays 18th-century furniture, tapestries, wallpaper, ceramics and silver. Laid out in the 17th century, **place Bellecour** – one of Europe's largest public squares – is pierced by an equestrian **statue of Louis XIV**. South of here, past Gare

de Perrache, lies **Lyon Confluence** (www.lyon-confluence.fr), the city's newest neighbourhood, where the Rhône and Saône meet. Trendy restaurants line its quays, and the ambitious **Musée des Confluences** (www.museedesconfluences.fr; 28 bd des Belges, 6e), a science-and-humanities museum inside a futuristic steel-and-glass transparent crystal, is also located here.

North of place Bellecour, the charming hilltop quarter of **Croix Rousse** is famed for its lush outdoor food market and silk-weaving tradition, illustrated by the **Maison des Canuts** (www.maisondescanuts.com; 10-12 rue d'Ivry, 4e; adult/child €6.50/3.50; ☉10am-6.30pm Mon-Sat, guided tours 11am & 3.30pm Mon-Sat; Ⓜ Croix Rousse).

🛏 Sleeping

Auberge de Jeunesse du Vieux Lyon　　　　　HOSTEL €

(☏04 78 15 05 50; www.fuaj.org/lyon; 41-45 montée du Chemin Neuf, 5e; dm incl breakfast €19.50-24; ☉reception 7am-1pm, 2-8pm & 9pm-1am; @🐾; Ⓜ Vieux Lyon, funicular Minimes) Stunning city views unfold from the terrace of Lyon's HI-affiliated hostel, and from many of the (mostly six-bed) dorms. Bike parking, kitchen and laundry (wash-dry per load €4) facilities are available, and there's an on-site bar. To avoid the tiring 10-minute climb from Vieux Lyon metro station, take the funicular to Minimes station and walk downhill.

Mama Shelter　　　　　　　　　　HOTEL €€

(☏04 78 02 58 00; www.mamashelter.com/en/lyon; 13 rue Domer; r €89-149; P✳@🐾; Ⓜ Jean Macé) Lyon's branch of this trendy hotel chain has sleek decor, carpets splashed with calli-graffiti, firm beds, plush pillows, modernist lighting and big-screen Macs offering free in-room movies. A youthful crowd fills the long bar at the low-lit restaurant. The residential location 2km outside the centre may feel remote, but it's only three metro stops from Gare Part-Dieu and place Bellecour.

Lyon Renaissance　　　　　　APARTMENT €€

(☏04 27 89 30 58; www.lyon-renaissance.com; 3 rue des Tourelles, 5e; apt €95-115; 🐾; Ⓜ Vieux Lyon) Friendly owners Françoise and Patrick rent these two superbly situated Vieux Lyon apartments with beamed ceilings and kitchen facilities. The smaller 3rd-floor walk-up

Lyon

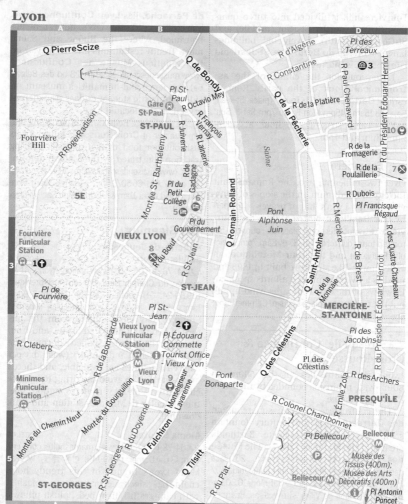

sleeps two, with windows overlooking a pretty tree-shaded square. A second unit, opposite Vieux Lyon's most famous medieval tower, has a spacious living room with ornamental fireplace and fold-out couch, plus a mezzanine with double bed.

★**Cour des Loges**　　　　　HOTEL €€€
(☎04 72 77 44 44; www.courdesloges.com; 2-8 rue du Bœuf, 5e; d €190-485, junior ste €340-655; ❀@☎☒; Ⓜ Vieux Lyon) Four 14th- to 17th-century houses wrapped around a *traboule* (secret passage) with preserved features such as Italianate loggias make this an exquisite place to stay. Individually decorated rooms woo with designer bathroom fittings and bountiful antiques, while decadent facilities include a spa, an elegant restaurant (menus €85 to €105), swish cafe (lunch menu €17.50, mains €22 to €30) and cross-vaulted bar.

Lyon

⊙ Sights
1 Basilique Notre Dame de
  Fourvière A3
2 Cathédrale St-Jean B4
3 Musée des Beaux-Arts......................D1

🛏 Sleeping
4 Auberge de Jeunesse du Vieux
  Lyon A4
5 Cour des Loges B2
6 Lyon Renaissance B2

⊗ Eating
7 Le Musée...D2
8 Les Adrets B3

● Drinking & Nightlife
9 (L'A)Kroche.....................................B4
10 Harmonie des Vins D2

market has nearly five dozen stalls selling countless gourmet delights. Pick up a round of runny St Marcellin from legendary cheesemonger Mère Richard, and a knobbly Jésus de Lyon from Charcuterie Sibilia. Or enjoy a sit-down lunch of local produce, especially enjoyable on Sundays when local families congregate for shellfish and white-wine brunches.

Les Adrets BOUCHON €€
(📋04 78 38 24 30; 30 rue du Bœuf, 5e; lunch menu €17.50, dinner menus €27-45; ⊗ noon-1.30pm & 7.45-9pm Mon-Fri; Ⓜ Vieux Lyon) This atmospheric spot serves an exceptionally good-value lunch *menu* (including wine and coffee). The mix is half classic *bouchon* fare, half alternative choices such as Parma ham and truffle risotto, or duck breast with roasted pears.

★ Le Musée BOUCHON €€
(📋04 78 37 71 54; 2 rue des Forces; lunch/dinner menus €23/28; ⊗ noon-2pm & 7.30-9.30pm Tue-Sat; Ⓜ Cordeliers) Housed in the stables of Lyon's former Hôtel de Ville, this delightful *bouchon* serves a splendid array of meat-heavy Lyonnais classics alongside veggie-centric treats such as roasted peppers with fresh goat cheese. The daily changing menu features 10 appetisers and 10 main dishes, plus five scrumptious desserts, all served on cute china plates at long family-style tables.

✗ Eating

Lyon's sparkling restaurant line-up embraces all genres: French, fusion, fast and international, as well as traditional Lyonnais *bouchons* (small, friendly bistros serving local city cuisine).

**★ Les Halles de
Lyon Paul Bocuse** MARKET €
(www.hallespaulbocuse.lyon.fr; 102 cours Lafayette, 3e; ⊗ 7am-10.30pm Tue-Sat, to 4.30pm Sun; Ⓜ Part-Dieu) Lyon's famed indoor food

ⓘ LYON CITY CARD

The excellent-value **Lyon City Card** (www.en.lyon-france.com/Lyon-City-Card; 1/2/3 days adult €22/32/42, child €13.50/18.50/23.50) offers free admission to every Lyon museum and a number of attractions. The card also includes unlimited city-wide transport on buses, trams, the funicular and the metro. Full-price cards are available at the tourist office, or save 10% by booking online.

L'Ourson qui Boit   FUSION €€

(☑ 04 78 27 23 37; 23 rue Royale, 1er; lunch/dinner menus €18/28; ⊘ noon-1.30pm & 7.30-9.30pm Mon, Tue & Thu-Sat; Ⓜ Croix Paquet) On the fringes of Croix Rousse, Japanese chef Akira Nishigaki puts his own splendid spin on French cuisine, with plenty of locally sourced fresh vegetables and light, clean flavours. The ever-changing menu of two daily entrées and two main dishes is complemented by good wines, attentive service and delicious desserts. Well worth reserving ahead.

🍷 Drinking & Entertainment

Cafe terraces on place des Terreaux buzz with all-hours drinkers, as do the British, Irish and other-styled pubs on nearby rue Ste-Catherine, 1er, and rue Lainerie and rue St-Jean, 5e, in Vieux Lyon.

Floating bars with DJs and live bands rock until around 3am aboard the string of *péniches* (river barges) moored along the Rhône's left bank. Scout out the section of quai Victor Augagneur between Pont Lafayette (metro Cordeliers or Guichard) and Pont de la Guillotière (metro Guillotière).

Harmonie des Vins   WINE BAR

(www.harmoniedesvins.fr; 9 rue Neuve, 1er; ⊘ 10am-2.30pm & 6.30pm-1am Tue-Sat; 🛜; Ⓜ Hôtel de Ville, Cordeliers) Find out all about French wine at this charm-laden wine bar replete with old stone walls, contemporary furnishings and tasty food.

(L'A)Kroche   BAR

(www.lakroche.fr; 8 rue Monseigneur Lavarenne, 5e; ⊘ 4pm-1am Tue-Sat, 4-9pm Sun & Mon; Ⓜ Vieux Lyon) Hip cafe-bar with six dozen flavours of rum, daily happy hours and frequent live music with no cover charge.

★ Le Sucre   LIVE MUSIC

(www.le-sucre.eu; 50 quai Rambaud, 2e; ⊘ 6pm-midnight Wed & Thu, 7pm-6am Fri & Sat) Down in the Confluence neighbourhood, Lyon's newest and most innovative club hosts DJs, live shows and eclectic arts events on its super-cool roof terrace atop a 1930s sugar factory, La Sucrière.

ⓘ Information

Tourist Office (☑ 04 72 77 69 69; www.lyon-france.com; place Bellecour, 2e; ⊘ 9am-6pm; Ⓜ Bellecour) In the centre of Presqu'île, Lyon's exceptionally helpful, multilingual and well-staffed main tourist office offers a variety of city walking tours and sells the Lyon City Card. There's a smaller branch (av du Doyenné, 5e; ⊘ 10am-5.30pm; Ⓜ Vieux Lyon) just outside the Vieux Lyon metro station.

ⓘ Getting There & Away

AIR

Lyon-St-Exupéry Airport (www.lyonaeroports.com), 25km east of the city, serves 120 direct destinations across Europe and beyond, including many budget carriers.

BUS

In the Perrache complex, **Eurolines** (☑ 08 92 89 90 91, 04 72 56 95 30; www.eurolines.fr; Gare de Perrache) and Spain-oriented **Linebús** (☑ 04 72 41 72 27; www.linebus.com; Gare de Perrache) have offices on the bus-station level of the Centre d'Échange (follow the 'Lignes Internationales' signs).

TRAIN

Lyon has two main-line train stations with direct TGV services: **Gare de la Part-Dieu** (Ⓜ Part-Dieu), 1.5km east of the Rhône, and **Gare de Perrache** (Ⓜ Perrache).

Frequent TGV services include the following:

Dijon €36, 1½ hours

Marseille €52, 1¾ hours

Paris Charles de Gaulle Airport €95, two hours

Paris Gare de Lyon €73, two hours

ⓘ Getting Around

Tramway **Rhônexpress** (www.rhonexpress.fr; adult/child/youth €15.70/free/13) links the airport with Part-Dieu train station in under 30 minutes.

Buses, trams, a four-line metro and two funiculars linking Vieux Lyon to Fourvière are run by **TCL** (www.tcl.fr). Public transport runs from around 5am to midnight. Tickets cost €1.70.

Time-stamp tickets on all forms of public transport or risk a fine.

Bikes are available from 200-odd bike stations thanks to **Vélo'v** (www.velov.grandlyon.com; first 30min free, next 30min €1, each subsequent 30min period €2).

THE FRENCH ALPS

Hiking, skiing, majestic panoramas – the French Alps have it all when it comes to the great outdoors. But you'll also find excellent gastronomy, good nightlife and plenty of history.

Chamonix

POP 9050 / ELEV 1037M

With the pearly white peaks of the Mont Blanc massif as a sensational backdrop, being an icon comes naturally to Chamonix. First 'discovered' by Brits William Windham and Richard Pococke in 1741, this is the mecca of mountaineering. Its knife-edge peaks, plunging slopes and massive glaciers have enthralled generations of adventurers and thrill-seekers ever since. Its après-ski scene is equally pumping.

Sights

Aiguille du Midi   VIEWPOINT

A jagged finger of rock soaring above glaciers, snowfields and rocky crags, 8km from the hump of Mont Blanc, the Aiguille du Midi (3842m) is one of Chamonix' most distinctive geographical features. If you can handle the altitude, the 360-degree views of the French, Swiss and Italian Alps from the summit are (quite literally) breathtaking. Year-round, you can float in a cable car from Chamonix to the Aiguille du Midi on the vertiginous **Téléphérique de l'Aiguille du Midi** (www.compagniedu montblanc.co.uk; place de l'Aiguille du Midi; adult/child return to Aiguille du Midi €55/47, to Plan de l'Aiguille summer €29.50/25, winter €16/14; ⊙1st ascent btwn 7.10am & 8.30am, last ascent btwn 3.30pm & 5pm).

Le Brévent   VIEWPOINT

The highest peak on the western side of the Chamonix Valley, Le Brévent (2525m) has tremendous views of the Mont Blanc massif, myriad hiking trails, ledges to paraglide from and the summit restaurant **Le Panoramic**. Reach it on the **Télécabine de Planpraz** (www.compagniedumontblanc.co.uk; adult/child one way €13.20/11.20, return €16/13.60), 400m west of the tourist office, and then the **Téléphérique du Brévent** (www.compagniedumontblanc.co.uk; 29 rte Henriette d'Angeville; adult/child one way €22/18.70, return €29.50/25; ⊙mid-Dec–mid-Apr & mid-Jun–mid-Sep). Plenty of family-friendly trails begin at **Planpraz** (2000m).

Mer de Glace   GLACIER

France's largest glacier, the glistening 200m-deep Mer de Glace (Sea of Ice) snakes 7km down on the northern side of Mont Blanc, moving up to 1cm an hour (about 90m a year). The **Train du Montenvers** (www.compagniedumontblanc.co.uk; adult/child one way €24/20.40, return €29.50/25; ⊙closed late Sep–mid-Oct), a picturesque, 5km-long cog railway opened in 1909, links Chamonix' Gare du Montenvers with Montenvers (1913m), from where a cable car takes you down to the glacier and the **Grotte de la Mer de Glace** (⊙closed last half of May & late Sep–mid-Oct), an ice cave whose frozen tunnels and ice sculptures change colour like mood rings.

Activities

The ski season runs from mid-December to mid-April. Summer activities – hiking, canyoning, mountaineering etc – generally start in June and end in September. The **Compagnie des Guides de Chamonix** (☑04 50 53 00 88; www.chamonix-guides.com; 190 place de l'Église, Maison de la Montagne; ⊙8.30am-noon & 2.30-7.30pm, closed Sun & Mon late Apr–mid-Jun & mid-Sep–mid-Dec) is the most famous of all the guide companies and has guides for virtually every activity, whatever the season.

Sleeping

Gîte Le Vagabond   HOSTEL €

(☑04 50 53 15 43; www.gitevagabond.com; 365 av Ravanel-le-Rouge; dm €21, sheets €5.50, d incl breakfast €101; ⊙reception 8-10am & 4.30-10.30pm; 🛜) In a 150-year-old stage-coach inn, Chamonix' hippest bunkhouse has rooms with four to six beds and a buzzing bar with a great log fire in winter. Situated 850m southwest of Chamonix' town centre.

★ **Hôtel Richemond** HOTEL €€
(☑ 04 50 53 08 85; www.richemond.fr; 228 rue du Docteur Paccard; s/d/tr €75/120/153; ☺ closed mid-Apr–mid-Jun & mid-Sep–mid-Dec; ☎) In a grand old building constructed in 1914 (and run by the same family ever since), this hotel – as friendly as it is central – has 52 spacious rooms with views of either Mont Blanc or Le Brévent; some are pleasantly old-fashioned, others recently renovated in white, black and beige, and three still have cast-iron bath-tubs. Outstanding value.

Auberge du Manoir HOTEL €€
(☑ 04 50 53 10 77; www.aubergedumanoir.com; 8 rte du Bouchet; s/d/tr €130/150/220; ☺ closed 2 weeks in late Apr & 2 weeks in autumn; ☎) This beautifully converted farmhouse, ablaze with geraniums in summer, offers 18 pine-panelled rooms that are quaint but never cloying, pristine mountain views, an outdoor hot tub, a sauna and a bar whose open fire keeps things cosy. Family owned.

✕ Eating

Papillon CAFE €
(416 rue Joseph Vallot; mains €5-8; ☺ 11am-8pm Mon-Sat, 4-8pm Sun mid-Dec–early May & mid-Jun–early Oct; ☑) A British-owned hole-in-the-wall take-out place that does great home-made curries, chilli con carne, Italian-style meatballs, noodle soup and deli-style sandwiches. Has plenty of vegie, vegan and gluten-free options.

★ **Le Cap Horn** FRENCH €€
(☑ 04 50 21 80 80; www.caphorn-chamonix.com; 78 rue des Moulins; lunch menu €20, other menus €29-39; ☺ noon-1.30pm or 2pm & 7-9pm or 10pm daily year-round) Housed in a gorgeous, two-storey chalet decorated with model sailboats – joint homage to the Alps and Cape Horn – this highly praised restaurant, opened in 2012, serves French and Asian-inflected dishes such as pan-seared duck breast with honey and soy sauce, fisherman's stew and, for dessert, *souffle au Grand Marnier*. Reserve for dinner Friday and Saturday in winter and summer.

Munchie FUSION €€
(☑ 04 50 53 45 41; www.munchie.eu; 87 rue des Moulins; mains €19-24; ☺ 7pm-2am daily, closed 2 weeks May & mid-Oct–Nov) Franco-Asian fusion has been the lip-smacking mainstay of this casual, Swedish-skippered restaurant since 1997. Specialities such as steak with spicy Béarnaise sauce are presented with

panache. Reservations recommended during the ski season.

🍷 Drinking & Nightlife

Nightlife rocks in Chamonix. In the centre, riverside rue des Moulins boasts a line-up of après-ski joints serving food as well as booze.

MBC MICROBREWERY
(Micro Brasserie de Chamonix; www.mbchx.com; 350 rte du Bouchet; ☺ 4pm-2am Mon-Thu, 10am-2am Fri-Sun) Run by four Canadians, this trendy microbrewery is fab. Be it with their phenomenal burgers (€10 to €15), cheesecake of the week, live music (Sunday from 9.30pm) or amazing beers, MBC delivers. Busiest from 5pm to 11pm.

Chambre Neuf BAR
(272 av Michel Croz; ☺ 7am-1am daily year-round; ☎) Chamonix' most spirited après-ski party (4pm to 8pm), fuelled by a Swedish band and dancing on the tables, spills out the front door of Chambre Neuf. Wildly popular with seasonal workers.

La Terrasse BAR
(43 place Balmat; ☺ 4pm-2am Mon-Fri, 1pm-2am Sat & Sun, closed May & Nov; ☎) Overlooking Chamonix' main square and the river, this British-style pub – take the spiral staircase for the best views – serves pub grub from 4.30pm to 10.30pm and then gives itself over to music (live or DJed) and dancing. Staff are British.

ⓘ Information

Tourist Office (☑ 04 50 53 00 24; www.chamonix.com; 85 place du Triangle de l'Amitié; ☺ 9am-12.30pm & 2-6pm, longer hours winter & summer) Information on accommodation, activities, the weather and cultural events.

ⓘ Getting There & Away

BUS

From **Chamonix bus station** (☑ 04 50 53 01 15; place de la Gare; ☺ 8-11.30am & 1.15-6.15pm winter, shorter hours rest of year), next to the train station, **SAT-Mont Blanc** (☑ 04 50 78 05 33; www.sat-montblanc.com) operates five daily buses to/from Geneva airport (one way/return €30/50, 1½ to two hours). Advance bookings only.

TRAIN

The Mont Blanc Express narrow-gauge train trundles from St-Gervais-Le Fayet station, 23km west of Chamonix, to Martigny in Switzerland, stopping in Chamonix en route. There are nine to 12 return trips daily between Chamonix and St-Gervais (€5.50, 45 minutes). From St-Gervais-Le Fayet, there are trains to major French cities.

THE DORDOGNE

Tucked in the country's southwestern corner, the Dordogne fuses history, culture and culinary sophistication in one unforgettably scenic package. The region is best known for its sturdy *bastides* (fortified towns), clifftop châteaux and spectacular prehistoric cave paintings.

Sarlat-la-Canéda

POP 10,105

A picturesque tangle of honey-coloured buildings and medieval architecture, Sarlat-la-Canéda is incredibly scenic and perennially popular with visitors.

⊙ Sights

Part of the fun of Sarlat is getting lost in its twisting alleyways and backstreets. **Rue Jean-Jacques Rousseau** and **rue Landry** are good starting points, but for the grandest buildings and *hôtels particuliers* explore **rue des Consuls**.

Sarlat Markets MARKET
(place de la Liberté & rue de la République; ⊙8.30am-1pm Wed, 8.30am-6pm Sat) For an introductory French market experience visit Sarlat's heavily touristed Saturday market, which takes over the streets around Cathédrale St-Sacerdos. Depending on the season, delicacies include local mushrooms and duck- and goose-based products such as foie gras. Get *truffe noir* (black truffle) at the winter **Marché aux Truffes** (⊙Sat morning Dec-Feb). An atmospheric, largely organic **night market** (⊙6-10pm) operates on Thursday. Seasoned market-goers may prefer others throughout the region.

DON'T MISS

PREHISTORIC PAINTINGS

Fantastic prehistoric caves with some of the world's finest **cave art** is what makes the Vézère Valley so very special. Most of the caves are closed in winter, and get very busy in summer. Visitor numbers are strictly limited, so you'll need to reserve well ahead.

Of the valley's 175 known sites, the most famous include **Grotte de Font de Gaume** (📞05 53 06 86 00; http://eyzies.monuments-nationaux.fr; adult/child €7.50/free; ⊙guided tours 9.30am-5.30pm Sun-Fri mid-May–mid-Sep, 9.30am-12.30pm & 2-5.30pm Sun-Fri mid-Sep–mid-May), 1km northeast of Les Eyzies. About 14,000 years ago, prehistoric artists created the gallery of over 230 figures, including bison, reindeer, horses, mammoths, bears and wolves, of which 25 are on permanent display.

About 7km east of Les Eyzies, **Abri du Cap Blanc** (📞05 53 06 86 00; adult/child €7.50/free; ⊙guided tours 9.30am-5.30pm Sun-Fri mid-May–mid-Sep, 9.30am-12.30pm & 2-5.30pm Sun-Fri mid-Sep–mid-May) showcases an unusual sculpture gallery of horses, bison and deer.

Then there is **Grotte de Rouffignac** (📞05 53 05 41 71; www.grottederouffignac.fr; Rouffignac-St-Cernin-de-Reilhac; adult/child €7/4.60; ⊙9-11.30am & 2-6pm Jul & Aug, 10-11.30am & 2-5pm mid-Apr–Jun, Sep & Oct, closed Nov–mid-Apr), sometimes known as the 'Cave of 100 Mammoths' because of its painted mammoths. Access to the caves, hidden in woodland 15km north of Les Eyzies, is aboard a trundling electric train.

Star of the show goes hands down to **Grotte de Lascaux** (📞05 53 51 95 03; www.semitour.com; Montignac; adult/child €9.90/6.40, joint ticket with Le Thot €13.50/9.40; ⊙guided tours 9am-7pm Jul & Aug, 9.30am-6pm Apr-Jun, 9.30am-noon & 2-6pm Sep & Oct, shorter hours rest of year, closed Jan), 2km southeast of Montignac, featuring an astonishing menagerie including oxen, deer, horses, reindeer and mammoths, as well as an amazing 5.5m bull, the largest cave drawing ever found. The original cave was closed to the public in 1963 to prevent damage to the paintings, but the most famous sections have been meticulously recreated in a second cave nearby – a massive undertaking that required some 20 artists and took 11 years.

Cathédrale St-Sacerdos CATHEDRAL

(place du Peyrou) Once part of Sarlat's Cluniac abbey, the original abbey church was built in the 1100s, redeveloped in the early 1500s and remodelled again in the 1700s, so it's a real mix of styles. The belfry and western facade are the oldest parts of the building, while the nave, organ and interior chapels are later additions.

🛏 Sleeping & Eating

Villa des Consuls B&B €€

(☑ 05 53 31 90 05; www.villaconsuls.fr; 3 rue Jean-Jacques Rousseau; d €95-110, apt €150-190; @ 🛜) Despite its Renaissance exterior, the enormous rooms at Villa des Consuls are modern through and through, with shiny wood floors and sleek furnishings. Several delightful self-contained apartments dot the town, all offering the same mix of period plushness – some also have terraces overlooking the town's rooftops.

★**Le Quatre Saisons** REGIONAL CUISINE €€

(☑ 05 53 29 48 59; www.4saisons-sarlat-perigord. com; 2 côte de Toulouse; menus from €19; ⊙ 12.30-2pm & 7.30-9.30pm Thu-Mon; 🖉🖭) A reliable local favourite, hidden in a beautiful stone house on a narrow alley leading uphill from rue de la République. The food is honest and unfussy, taking its cue from market ingredients and regional flavours. The most romantic tables have cross-town views.

ℹ Information

Tourist Office (☑ 05 53 31 45 45; www. sarlat-tourisme.com; 3 rue Tourny; ⊙ 9am-7pm Mon-Sat, 10am-1pm & 2-6pm Sun May-Aug, shorter hours Sep-Apr; 🛜) Sarlat's tourist office is packed with info, but often gets overwhelmed by visitors; the website has it all.

ℹ Getting There & Away

The **train station** (av de la Gare), 1.3km south of the old city, serves Périgueux (€15.90, 1¾ hours, four daily) and Les Eyzies (€9.80, 50 minutes to 2½ hours, four daily), both via Le Buisson.

THE ATLANTIC COAST

With quiet country roads winding through vine-striped hills and wild stretches of coastal sands interspersed with misty islands, the Atlantic coast is where France gets back to nature. If you're a surf nut or beach bum, the sandy bays around Biarritz will be right up your alley, while oenophiles can sample the fruits of the vine in the high temple of French winemaking, Bordeaux.

Bordeaux

POP 236,000

The new millennium was a turning point for the city long nicknamed La Belle au Bois Dormant (Sleeping Beauty), when the mayor, ex-prime minister Alain Juppé, roused Bordeaux, pedestrianising its boulevards, restoring its neoclassical architecture and implementing a high-tech public-transport system. Today the city is a Unesco World Heritage Site and, with its merry student population and 2.5 million-odd annual tourists, scarcely sleeps at all.

◎ Sights

The 4km-long riverfront esplanade incorporates playgrounds and bicycle paths.

Cathédrale St-André CATHEDRAL

(place Jean Moulin) Lording over the city, and a Unesco World Heritage Site prior to the city's classification, the cathedral's oldest section dates from 1096; most of what you see today was built in the 13th and 14th centuries. Exceptional masonry carvings can be seen in the north portal.

CAPC Musée d'Art Contemporain GALLERY

(rue Ferrère, Entrepôt 7; temporary exhibitions adult/child €5/2.50; ⊙ 11am-6pm Tue & Thu-Sun, to 8pm Wed) Built in 1824 as a warehouse for French colonial produce like coffee, cocoa, peanuts and vanilla, the cavernous Entrepôts Lainé creates a dramatic backdrop for cutting-edge modern art at the CAPC Musée d'Art Contemporain. Entry to the permanent collection is free but there is a cover charge for any temporary exhibitions.

Musée des Beaux-Arts GALLERY

(20 cours d'Albret; ⊙ 11am-6pm daily mid-Jul–mid-Aug, closed Tue rest of year) FREE The evolution of Occidental art from the Renaissance to the mid-20th century is on view at Bordeaux's Musée des Beaux-Arts, which occupies two wings of the 1770s-built Hôtel de Ville, either side of the Jardin de la Mairie (an elegant public park). The museum was established in 1801; highlights include 17th-century Flemish, Dutch and Italian paintings. Temporary exhibitions are regularly hosted at its nearby annexe, **Galerie des Beaux-Arts** (place du Colonel Raynal;

ON THE WINE TRAIL

Thirsty? The 1000-sq-km wine-growing area around the city of Bordeaux is, along with Burgundy, France's most important producer of top-quality wines. Whet your palate with Bordeaux tourist office's introductory wine-and-cheese courses (€25).

Serious students of the grape can enrol in a two-hour (€39) or two- to three-day (€390 to €690) course at the **École du Vin** (Wine School; ☑ 05 56 00 22 66; www. bordeaux.com) inside the **Maison du Vin de Bordeaux** (3 cours du 30 Juillet).

Bordeaux has more than 5000 estates where grapes are grown, picked and turned into wine. Smaller châteaux often accept walk-in visitors, but at many places, especially better-known ones, you have to reserve in advance. If you have your own wheels, one of the easiest to visit is **Château Lanessan** (☑ 05 56 58 94 80; www.lanessan.com; Cussac-Fort-Medoc; ⊙ 9am-noon & 2-6pm).

Favourite vine-framed villages brimming with charm and tasting/buying opportunities include medieval **St-Émilion** and port town **Pauillac**. In **Arsac-en-Médoc**, Philippe Raoux's vast glass-and-steel wine centre, **La Winery** (☑ 05 56 39 04 90; www.winery.fr; Rond-point des Vendangeurs, D1; ⊙ 10am-7pm), stuns with concerts and contemporary art exhibitions alongside tastings to determine your *signe œnologique* ('wine sign'; booking required).

Many châteaux close during October's *vendange* (grape harvest).

adult/child €5/2.50; ⊙ 11am-6pm daily mid-Jul–mid-Aug, closed Tue rest of year).

🛏 Sleeping

Hôtel Notre Dame
HOTEL €

(☑ 05 56 52 88 24; 36-38 rue Notre Dame; s €53-70, d €61-79; 🛜) Location is the key selling point of this good-value hotel. It's within an easy stroll of the town centre, just back from the river and in the middle of a lovely village-like neighbourhood of antique shops and relaxed cafes. It also has a wheelchair-accessible room.

Ecolodge des Chartrons
B&B €€

(☑ 05 56 81 49 13; www.ecolodgedeschartrons. com; 23 rue Raze; s €107-205, d €119-228; 🛜) Hidden away in a little side street off the quays in Bordeaux's Chartrons wine-merchant district. The owner-hosts of this *chambre d'hôte*, Veronique and Yann, have stripped back and limewashed the stone walls of an old house, scrubbed the wide floorboards and brought in recycled antique furniture to create a highly memorable place to stay.

★ L'Hôtel Particulier
BOUTIQUE HOTEL €€€

(☑ 05 57 88 28 80; www.lhotel-particulier.com; 44 rue Vital-Carles; apt from €89, d from €203; 🛜) When you step into this fabulous boutique hotel, with its secret courtyard garden, and find a thousand eyes staring at you from the reception walls and lampshades made only of feathers, you realise you've stumbled upon somewhere special. The rooms don't disappoint – they are highly extrav-agant affairs with huge fireplaces, carved ceilings, freestanding bath-tubs and quality furnishings.

There are also great value, fully equipped apartments ideal for a longer stay.

🍴 Eating

Place du Parlement, rue du Pas St-Georges, rue des Faussets and place de la Victoire are loaded with dining addresses, as is the old waterfront warehouse district around quai des Marques – great for a sunset meal or drink.

★ Le Cheverus Café
BISTRO €

(☑ 05 56 48 29 73; 81-83 rue du Loup; menus from €12.50; ⊙ noon-3pm & 7-9pm Mon-Sat) In a city full of neighbourhood bistros, this one, smack in the city centre, is one of the most impressive. It's friendly, cosy and chaotically busy (be prepared to wait for a table at lunchtime). The food tastes fresh and home-cooked and it dares to veer slightly away from the bistro standards of steak and chips.

Karl
INTERNATIONAL €€

(☑ 05 56 81 01 00; place du Parlement; breakfast from €5.50; ⊙ 8.30am-7.30pm) Simply *the* place in town for a morning-after-the-night-before brunch. These range from light continental-style affairs to the full works with salmon, cheeses, hams and eggs. It's just as good for a snack at any time of the day and is perpetually packed with a young crowd.

SATURDAY-MORNING OYSTERS

A classic Bordeaux experience is a Saturday morning spent slurping oysters and white wine from one of the seafood stands to be found at **Marché des Capucins** (six oysters & glass of wine €6; ⊙7am-noon Sat). Afterwards, you can peruse the stalls while shopping for the freshest ingredients for a picnic in one of the city's parks. To get there, head south down cours Pasteur and, once at place de la Victoire, turn left onto rue Élie Gintrec.

La Tupina REGIONAL CUISINE €€€
(⌨05 56 91 56 37; www.latupina.com; 6 rue Porte de la Monnaie; menus €18-74, mains €27-45) Filled with the aroma of soup simmering inside an old *tupina* ('kettle' in Basque) over an open fire, this white-tableclothed place is feted far and wide for its seasonal southwestern French specialities such as a mini casserole of foie gras and eggs, milk-fed lamb or goose wings with potatoes and parsley.

❶ Information

Main Tourist Office (⌨05 56 00 66 00; www.bordeaux-tourisme.com; 12 cours du 30 Juillet; ⊙9am-7pm Mon-Sat, 9.30am-6pm Sun) Runs an excellent range of city and regional tours. There's a small-but-helpful branch (⌨05 56 91 64 70; ⊙9am-noon & 1-6pm Mon-Sat, 10am-noon & 1-3pm Sun) at the train station.

❶ Getting There & Away

AIR
Bordeaux Airport (www.bordeaux.aeroport.fr) is in Mérignac, 10km west of the city centre, with domestic and international services.

TRAIN
From Gare St-Jean, 3km from the centre, at least 16 trains daily serve Paris' Gare Montparnasse (€73, three hours).

Biarritz

POP 26,067

Edge your way south along the coast towards Spain and you arrive in stylish Biarritz, just as ritzy as its name suggests. The resort took off in the mid-19th century (Napoléon III had a rather soft spot for the place) and it

still shimmers with architectural treasures from the belle époque and art deco eras. Big waves – some of Europe's best – and a beachy lifestyle are a magnet for Europe's hip surfing set.

◉ Sights & Activities

Biarritz' *raison d'être* is its fashionable beaches, particularly central **Grande Plage** and **Plage Miramar**, lined end to end with sunbathing bodies on hot summer days. North of Pointe St-Martin, the adrenaline-pumping surfing beaches of **Anglet** (the final 't' is pronounced) continue northwards for more than 4km. Take bus 10 or 13 from the bottom of av Verdun (just near av Édouard VII).

Musée de la Mer MUSEUM
(⌨05 59 22 75 40; www.museedelamer.com; esplanade du Rocher de la Vierge; adult/child €14/10; ⊙9.30am-midnight Jul & Aug, 9.30am-8pm Apr-Jun, Sep & Oct, shorter hours rest of year) Housed in a wonderful art deco building, Biarritz's Musée de la Mer is seething with underwater life from the Bay of Biscay and beyond, including huge aquariums of sharks and dainty tropical reef fish, as well as exhibits on fishing recalling Biarritz's whaling past. It's the seals, though, that steal the show (feeding time, always a favourite with children, is at 10.30am and 5pm). In high season it's possible to have the place almost to yourself by visiting late at night.

Cité de l'Océan MUSEUM
(⌨05 59 22 75 40; www.citedelocean.com; 1 av de la Plage; adult/child €11/7.30; ⊙10am-10pm Jul & Aug, 10am-7pm Easter, Apr-Jun, Sep & Oct, shorter hours rest of year) We don't really know whether it's fair to call the Cité de l'Océan a mere 'museum'. At heart it's simply a museum of the ocean but this is entertainment, cutting-edge technology, theme park and science museum all rolled into one. During a visit you will learn all you ever wanted to know about the ocean and (sort of) ride in a submarine to watch giant squid and sperm whales do battle.

⌂ Sleeping

Auberge de Jeunesse de Biarritz HOSTEL €
(⌨05 59 41 76 00; www.hihostels.com; 8 rue Chiquito de Cambo; dm incl sheets & breakfast €25.40; ⊙reception 9am-noon & 6-10pm, closed mid-Dec–early Jan; @🛜) This popular place offers

outdoor activities including surfing. From the train station, follow the railway line westwards for 800m.

Hôtel Mirano
BOUTIQUE HOTEL €€

(☏05 59 23 11 63; www.hotelmirano.fr; 11 av Pasteur; d €72-132; 🅿🛜) Squiggly purple, orange and black wallpaper and oversized orange perspex light fittings are some of the rad '70s touches at this boutique retro hotel. Oh, and there's a flirty Betty Boop in the bar. The staff go above and beyond the call of duty in order to please. All up, it's one of the best deals in town.

✖ Eating

See-and-be-seen cafes and restaurants line Biarritz' beachfront. Anglet's beaches are also becoming increasingly trendy, with cafes strung along the waterfront.

★ Restaurant le Pim'pi
FRENCH €€

(☏05 59 24 12 62; 14 av Verdun; menus €14-28, mains €17; ☺noon-2pm Tue, noon-2pm & 7-9.30pm Wed-Sat) This is a small and resolutely old-fashioned place unfazed by all the razzmatazz around it. The daily specials are chalked up on a blackboard – most are of the classic French bistro style but are produced with such unusual skill and passion that many consider this one of the town's better places to eat.

Bistrot des Halles
BASQUE €€

(☏05 59 24 21 22; 1 rue du Centre; mains €17-19; ☺noon-2pm & 7.30-10.30pm Tue-Sat) One of a cluster of restaurants along rue du Centre that get their produce directly from the nearby covered market, this bustling place stands out from the pack by serving excellent fish and other fresh modern French market fare from the blackboard menu, in an interior adorned with old metallic advertising posters. Open daily during Easter and the summer holidays.

Drinking & Nightlife

Great bars stud rue du Port Vieux, place Clemenceau and the central food-market area.

Miremont
CAFE

(☏05 59 24 01 38; www.miremont-biarritz.com; 1bis place Georges-Clemenceau; hot chocolate from €5; ☺9am-8pm) Operating since 1880, this grande dame harks back to the time when belle-époque Biarritz was the beach resort of choice for the rich and glamorous. Today it still attracts perfectly coiffed hairdos (and that's just on the poodles) but the less chic are also welcome to come and partake of a fine selection of tea and cakes.

Ventilo Caffé
BAR

(rue du Port Vieux; ☺closed Tue Oct-Easter) Dressed up like a boudoir, this funky place continues its domination of the Biarritz young and fun bar scene.

ℹ Information

Tourist office (☏05 59 22 37 10; www.biarritz.fr; square d'Ixelles; ☺9am-7pm Jul & Aug, shorter hours rest of year)

FRANCE BIARRITZ

WORTH A TRIP

DUNE DU PILAT

This colossal sand dune (sometimes referred to as the Dune de Pyla because of its location in the resort town of Pyla-sur-Mer), 65km west of Bordeaux, stretches from the mouth of the Bassin d'Arcachon southwards for almost 3km. Already the largest in Europe, it's spreading eastwards at 4.5m a year – it has swallowed trees, a road junction and even a hotel.

The view from the top – approximately 114m above sea level – is magnificent. To the west you can see the sandy shoals at the mouth of the Bassin d'Arcachon, including the **Banc d'Arguin bird reserve** and Cap Ferret. Dense dark-green pine forests stretch from the base of the dune eastwards almost as far as the eye can see.

Take care swimming in this area: powerful currents swirl out to sea from the deceptively tranquil *baïnes* (little bays).

Although an easy day trip from Bordeaux, the area around the dune is an enjoyable place to kick back for a while. Most people camp in one of the swag of seasonal campgrounds; see www.bassin-arcachon.com.

ℹ Getting There & Away

AIR

Biarritz-Anglet-Bayonne Airport (www.biarritz.aeroport.fr), 3km southeast of Biarritz, is served by several low-cost carriers.

BUS

ATCRB (www.transports-atcrb.com) runs services down the coast to the Spanish border.

TRAIN

Biarritz-La Négresse train station, 3km south of town, is linked to the centre by bus A1.

LANGUEDOC-ROUSSILLON

Languedoc-Roussillon comes in three distinct flavours: Bas-Languedoc (Lower Languedoc), land of bullfighting, rugby and robust red wines; Haut Languedoc (Upper Languedoc), a mountainous, sparsely populated terrain made for lovers of the great outdoors; and Roussillon, to the south, snug against the rugged Pyrenees and frontier to Spanish Catalonia.

Languedoc's traditional centre, Toulouse, was shaved off when regional boundaries were redrawn almost half a century ago, but we've chosen to include it in this section.

Toulouse

POP 446,200

Elegantly set at the confluence of the Canal du Midi and the River Garonne, this vibrant southern city – nicknamed *la ville rose* (the pink city) after the distinctive hot-pink stone used in many buildings – is one of France's liveliest metropolises. Busy, buzzy and bustling with students, this riverside dame has a history stretching back more than 2000 years and has been a hub for the aerospace industry since the 1930s. With a thriving cafe and cultural scene, a wealth of impressive *hôtels particuliers* and an enormously atmospheric old quarter, France's fourth-largest city is one place you'll love to linger.

◉ Sights & Activities

Place du Capitole   SQUARE

Toulouse's magnificent main square is the city's literal and metaphorical heart, where Toulousains turn out en masse on sunny evenings to sip a coffee or an early aperitif at a pavement cafe. On the eastern side is the 128m-long facade of the **Capitole** (rue Gambetta & rue Romiguières, place du Capitole; ◷10am-7pm), the city hall, built in the 1750s. Inside is the **Théâtre du Capitole**, one of France's most prestigious opera venues, and the over-the-top, late-19th-century **Salle des Illustres** (Hall of the Illustrious).

To the south of the square is the city's **Vieux Quartier** (Old Quarter), a tangle of lanes and leafy squares brimming with cafes, shops and eateries.

Cité de l'Espace   MUSEUM

(🖉08 20 37 72 33; www.cite-espace.com/en; av Jean Gonord; adult €20.50-24, child €15-17.50; ◷10am-7pm Jul & Aug, closes at 5pm or 6pm rest of year, closed Jan) This fantastic space museum on the city's eastern outskirts explores Toulouse's interstellar industry. The hands-on exhibits include a shuttle simulator, planetarium, 3D cinema and simulated observatory, plus full-scale replicas of iconic spacecraft including the Mir Space Station and a 53m-high Ariane 5 space rocket. Multilingual audioguides allow you to explore at your own pace. To get there, catch bus 15 from allée Jean Jaurès to the last stop, from where it's a 500m walk.

Basilique St-Sernin   CHURCH

(place St-Sernin; ◷8.30am-noon & 2-6pm Mon-Sat, 8.30am-12.30pm & 2-7.30pm Sun) With its soaring spire and unusual octagonal tower, this red-brick basilica is one of France's best-preserved Romanesque structures. Inside, the soaring nave and delicate pillars harbour the tomb of St Sernin, sheltered beneath a sumptuous canopy. The basilica was once an important stop on the Chemin de St-Jacques pilgrimage route.

Musée des Augustins   MUSEUM

(www.augustins.org; 21 rue de Metz; adult/child €4/free; ◷10am-6pm, to 9pm Wed) Like most big French cities, Toulouse has a fabulous fine arts museum. Located within a former Augustinian monastery, it spans the centuries from the Roman era through to the early 20th century. The highlights are the French rooms, with Delacroix, Ingres and Courbet representing the 18th and 19th centuries, and works by Toulouse-Lautrec and Monet among the standouts from the 20th-century collection. Don't miss the 14th-century cloister gardens. The entrance is on rue de Metz.

Airbus Factory Tours   TOUR
(☑05 34 39 42 00; www.manatour.fr/lva; tours adult/child €15.50/13) Hardcore plane-spotters can arrange a guided tour of Toulouse's massive JL Lagardère Airbus factory, 10km west of the city in Colomiers. The main factory tour includes a visit to the A380 production line; there's also a longer 'Panoramic Tour', which takes in other sections of the 700-hectare site via bus. All tours must be booked in advance online or by phone, and non-EU visitors have to book at least two days ahead. Remember to bring a passport or photo ID.

⌂ Sleeping

Hôtel La Chartreuse   HOTEL €
(☑05 61 62 93 39; www.chartreusehotel.com; 4bis bd de Bonrepos; s/d/f €52/59/73) The nicest of a cluster of basic hotels that line the riverbanks near the station. It's clean, friendly and quiet, with a back garden patio for breakfast. The rooms are spartan, but the rates are dirt cheap.

★Côté Carmes   B&B €€
(☑06 83 44 87 55; www.cote-carmes.com; 7 rue de la Dalbade; r €85-110) Elegant in the way only the French can manage, this charming B&B has three rooms straight out of an interiors catalogue. Louvre doors, parquet floors, exposed brick and upcycled furniture give it a slinky, designer feel; Chambre Paradoux is the roomiest, and has a private balcony. Breakfast is a spoil, too, with *viennoiseries*, smoothies and macaroons.

Hôtel St-Sernin   BOUTIQUE HOTEL €€€
(☑05 61 21 73 08; www.hotelstsernin.com; 2 rue St-Bernard; d from €135; ☎) Parisian expats have renovated this pied-à-terre near the Basilique St-Sernin, and it has a modern, metropolitan style, with small-but-sleek rooms, the best of which have floor-to-ceiling windows overlooking the basilica.

✕ Eating

Bd de Strasbourg, place St-Georges and place du Capitole are perfect spots for summer dining alfresco. Rue Pargaminières is the street for kebabs, burgers and other late-night student grub.

Faim des Haricots   VEGETARIAN €
(☑05 61 22 49 25; www.lafaimdesharicots.fr; 3 rue du Puits Vert; menus €11-15.50; noon-3pm & 6-10pm daily; ☑) A budget favourite, this 100% vegie restaurant serves everything *à volonté* (all you can eat). There are five courses, including a quiche, a buffet salad, a hot dish and a pudding; €15.50 buys you the lot including an aperitif and coffee.

Solilesse   BISTRO €€
(☑09 83 34 03 50; www.solilesse.com; 40 rue Peyrolières; 3-course menu lunch/dinner €17.50/28.50; noon-2.30pm Wed-Sat & 8-10pm Tue-Sat) Punky chef Yohann Travostino has turned his bistro into one of the city's hottest dining addresses. He previously worked in Mexico and California, so his food blends French style with zingy west coast flavours. The industrial decor (black tables, steel, brick) echoes the modern food.

★Le Genty-Magre   FRENCH €€€
(☑05 61 21 38 60; www.legentymagre.com; 3 rue Genty Magre; mains €16-28, menu €38; 12.30-2.30pm & 8-10pm Tue-Sat) Classic French cuisine is the order of the day here, but lauded chef Romain Brard has plenty of modern tricks up his sleeve too. The dining room feels inviting, with brick walls, burnished wood and down-lights. It's arguably the best place in the city to try traditional rich dishes such as *confit de canard* or cassoulet.

ⓘ Information

Tourist Office (☑05 61 11 02 22; www.toulouse-tourisme.com; square Charles de Gaulle; 9am-7pm daily) In a grand building on square Charles de Gaulle.

ⓘ Getting There & Away

AIR
Toulouse-Blagnac Airport (www.toulouse.aeroport.fr/en), 8km northwest of the centre, has frequent domestic and European flights. A **Navette Aéroport Flybus** (Airport Shuttle; ☑05 61 41 70 70; www.tisseo.fr) links it with town.

TRAIN
Gare Matabiau (bd Pierre Sémard), 1km northeast of the centre, is served by frequent TGVs to Bordeaux (€22 to €29, two hours) and east to Carcassonne (€14, 45 minutes to one hour).

Carcassonne
POP 49,100
Perched on a rocky hilltop and bristling with zigzag battlements, stout walls and spiky turrets, the fortified city of Carcassonne

looks like something out of a children's storybook from afar. It's most people's perfect idea of a medieval castle, and it's undoubtedly an impressive spectacle – not to mention one of the Languedoc's biggest tourist draws. The **tourist office** (☑ 04 68 10 24 30; www.tourisme-carcassonne.fr; 28 rue de Verdun; ☺ 9am-7pm daily Jul & Aug, shorter hours rest of year) can help with tours and bookings.

◉ Sights

★ La Cité
FORTRESS

(☺ Porte Narbonnaise 9am-7pm Jul & Aug, to 5pm Sep-Jun) Carcassonne's rampart-ringed fortress is one of the Languedoc's most recognisable landmarks. Built on a steep spur of rock, it's been used as a defensive stronghold for nigh on 2000 years. The fortified town is encircled by two sets of battlements and 52 stone towers, topped by distinctive 'witch's hat' roofs (added by the architect Viollet-le-Duc during 19th-century restorations). The main gateway of **Porte Narbonnaise** leads into the citadel's interior, a maze of cobbled lanes and courtyards, now mostly lined by shops and restaurants.

Château Comtal
CASTLE

(adult/child €8.50/free; ☺ 10am-6.30pm Apr-Sep) The entrance fee lets you look around the castle itself, enjoy an 11-minute film and join an optional 30- to 40-minute guided tour of the ramparts (tours in English, July and August). Descriptive panels around the castle, in both French and English, are explicit. For more detail, invest in an audioguide (1/2 people €4.50/6).

🛏 Sleeping & Eating

La Maison Vieille
B&B €€

(☑ 04 68 25 77 24; www.la-maison-vieille.com; 8 rue Trivalle; d €85-95; 🖥) As charming a B&B as you'll find in Carcassonne. In an old mansion, the rooms are supremely tasteful: Barbecane in blues, Cité with exposed brick, Prince Noir with an in-room bath, Dame Carcas with floaty fabrics and vintage luggage. There's a walled courtyard for breakfast, and the location is ideal for Villes Haute and Basse. Rue Trivalle lies just east of the Pont Vieux.

Bloc G
BISTRO €€

(☑ 04 68 47 58 20; www.bloc-g.com; 112 rue Barbacane; 3-course lunch €15, dinner mains €15-25; ☺ noon-2.30pm Tue-Sat, 7-10.30pm Wed-Sat) This modern diner offers far better food than most places in the citadel, for half the price.

Its modern style – white walls, white chairs, white tables – is matched with modern food: a short menu of salads and *tarte salées* for lunch, and creative versions of southwest classics for supper. Great local wines by the glass, too.

ⓘ Getting There & Away

There are frequent trains to Toulouse (€14, 45 minutes to one hour).

Nîmes

POP 146,500

This lively city boasts some of France's best-preserved classical buildings, including a famous Roman amphitheatre, although the city is most famous for its sartorial export, *serge de Nîmes* – better known to cowboys, clubbers and couturiers as denim.

◉ Sights

A **Pass Nîmes Romaine** (adult/child €11.50/9), valid for three days, covers all Roman sights; buy one at the first place you visit.

★ Les Arènes
ROMAN SITES

(www.arenes-nimes.com; place des Arènes; adult/child €9/7; ☺ 9am-8pm Jul & Aug, shorter hours rest of year) Nîmes' twin-tiered amphitheatre is the best-preserved in France. Built around 100 BC, the arena would have seated 24,000 spectators and staged gladiatorial contests and public executions, and it still provides an impressive venue for gigs, events and summer bullfights. An audioguide provides context as you explore the arena, seating areas, stairwells and corridors (rather marvellously known to Romans as *vomitories*), and afterwards you can view replicas of gladiatorial armour and original bullfighters' costumes in the museum.

Maison Carrée
ROMAN SITES

(place de la Maison Carrée; adult/child €5.50/4; ☺ 10am-8pm Jul & Aug, shorter hours rest of year) Constructed in gleaming limestone around AD 5, this temple was built to honour Emperor Augustus' two adopted sons. Despite the name, the Maison Carrée (Square House) is actually rectangular – to the Romans, 'square' simply meant a building with right angles. The building is beautifully preserved, complete with stately columns and triumphal steps; it's worth paying the admission to see the interior, but probably worth skipping the lame 3D film.

✺ Festivals & Events

Féria de Pentecôte & Féria des Vendanges   BULLFIGHTING

Nîmes becomes more Spanish than French during its two *férias* (bullfighting festivals): the five-day Féria de Pentecôte (Whitsuntide Festival) in June, and the three-day Féria des Vendanges on the third weekend in September. Each is marked by daily *corridas* (bullfights).

🛏 Sleeping & Eating

Auberge de Jeunesse   HOSTEL €

(✆04 66 68 03 20; www.hinimes.com; 257 chemin de l'Auberge de Jeunesse, La Cigale; dm/d €16.45/38; ☺reception 7.30am-1am) It's out in the sticks, 4km from the bus and train stations, but this hostel has lots in its favour: spacious dorms, family rooms, a garden with space for camping, and a choice of self-catering kitchen or cafe. Take bus I, direction Alès or Villeverte, and get off at the Stade stop.

Hôtel de l'Amphithéâtre   HOTEL €€

(✆04 66 67 28 51; www.hoteldelamphitheatre. com; 4 rue des Arènes; s/d/f €72/92/130) Down a narrow backstreet leading away from Les Arènes, this tall town house ticks all the boxes: smart rooms with shabby-chic furniture and balconies overlooking place du Marché; a sleek palette of greys, whites and taupes; and a great buffet breakfast. It's run by an expat Cornishman and his French wife.

★Le Cerf à Moustache   BISTRO €€

(✆09 81 83 44 33; 38 bd Victor Hugo; mains €14-35; ☺11.45am-2pm & 7-11pm Tue-Sat) Despite its weird name, the Deer with the Moustache has quickly established itself as one of Nîmes' top bistros, with quirky decor (including reclaimed furniture and a wall full of old-book doodles), matched by chef Julien Salem's creative take on the classics. Go basic with burgers and risotto, or upmarket with crusted lamb and chunky steaks.

❶ Information

Tourist Office (✆04 66 58 38 00; www. ot-nimes.fr; 6 rue Auguste; ☺8.30am-8pm Mon-Fri, 9am-7pm Sat, 10am-6pm Sun Jul & Aug, shorter hours rest of year) There's also a seasonal annexe (☺usually Jul & Aug) on esplanade Charles de Gaulle.

❶ Getting There & Away

AIR

Ryanair is the only airline to use Nîmes' **airport** (✆04 66 70 49 49; www.nimes-aeroport.fr), 10km southeast of the city on the A54.

BUS

Edgard (www.edgard-transport.fr) runs services to Pont du Gard (40 minutes, hourly Monday to Saturday) from the bus station (next to the train station).

TRAIN

From the **train station** (bd Talabot), there are more than 12 TGVs a day to/from Paris' Gare de Lyon (€62.50 to €111, three hours). Other destinations include Avignon (€8.50, 30 minutes).

Pont du Gard

Southern France has some fine Roman sites, but for audacious engineering, nothing can top Unesco World Heritage Site **Pont du Gard** (✆04 66 37 50 99; www.pontdugard.fr; car & up to 5 passengers €18, after 8pm €10; ☺visitor centre & museum 9am-8pm Jul & Aug, shorter hours rest of year), 21km northeast of Nîmes. This three-tiered aqueduct was once part of a 50km-long system of water channels, built around 19 BC to transport water from Uzès to Nîmes. The scale is huge: 48.8m high, 275m long and graced with 35 precision-built arches, the bridge was sturdy enough to carry up to 20,000 cubic metres of water per day. Each block was carved by hand and transported here from nearby quarries – no mean feat, considering the largest blocks weigh over 5 tonnes.

The **Musée de la Romanité** provides background on the bridge's construction, while kids can try out educational activities in the **Ludo** play area. Nearby, the 1.4km **Mémoires de Garrigue** walking trail winds upstream through typically Mediterranean scrubland, and offers some of the best bridge views.

There are large car parks on both banks of the river, about a 400m walk from the bridge.

PROVENCE

Provence conjures up images of rolling lavender fields, blue skies, gorgeous villages, wonderful food and superb wine. It certainly delivers on all those fronts, but it's not just worth visiting for its good looks – dig a little deeper and you'll also discover the multicultural metropolis of Marseille, the artistic haven of Aix-en-Provence and the old Roman city of Arles.

Marseille

POP 859,360

Marseille grows on you with its fusion of cultures, souk-like markets, millennia-old port and *corniches* (coastal roads) along rocky inlets and sun-baked beaches. Once the butt of French jokes, the *cité phocéenne* (in reference to Phocaea, the ancient Greek city located in modern-day Turkey, from where Marseille's settlers, the Massiliots, came) is looking fabulous after its facelift as the European Capital of Culture in 2013.

◎ Sights

★Vieux Port   HISTORIC QUARTER

(Ⓜ Vieux Port) Ships have docked for more than 26 centuries at the city's birthplace, the colourful Old Port. The main commercial docks were transferred to the Joliette area north of here in the 1840s, but the old port remains a thriving harbour for fishing boats, pleasure yachts and tourists. The free **Cross-Port Ferry** (◎ 10am-1.15pm & 2-7pm) in front of the town hall is a fun way to get out on the water, however briefly.

★Musée des Civilisations de l'Europe et de la Méditerranée   MUSEUM

(MuCEM; Museum of European & Mediterranean Civilisations; 🖉 04 84 35 13 13; www.mucem.org; 1 esplanade du J4; Fort St-Jean free, J4 adult/child €8/5; ◎ 9am-8pm Jul & Aug, 11am-7pm May, Jun, Sep & Oct, 11am-6pm Nov-Apr; 🚻; Ⓜ Vieux Port or Joliette) The icon of the 'new' Marseille, this stunning museum is split across two dramatically contrasting sites, linked by a vertigo-inducing foot bridge. On one side is lumbering **Fort St-Jean**, founded in the 13th century by the Knights Hospitaller of St John of Jerusalem and rebuilt by Louis XIV in the 17th century; and on the other, the contemporary **J4**, a shoebox with breath-

taking 'lace' skin designed by Algerian-born, Marseille-educated architect Rudi Ricciotti.

Le Panier   HISTORIC QUARTER

(Ⓜ Vieux Port) From the Vieux Port, hike north up to this fantastic history-woven quarter, dubbed Marseille's Montmartre as much for its sloping streets as its artsy ambience. In Greek Massilia it was the site of the *agora* (marketplace), hence its name, which means 'the basket'. During WWII the quarter was dynamited and afterwards rebuilt. Today it's a mishmash of lanes hiding artisan shops, *ateliers* (workshops) and terraced houses strung with drying washing.

Basilique Notre Dame de la Garde   CHURCH

(Montée de la Bonne Mère; ◎ 7am-8pm Apr-Sep, 7am-7pm Oct-Mar) This opulent 19th-century Romano-Byzantine basilica occupies Marseille's highest point, La Garde (162m). Built between 1853 and 1864, it is ornamented with coloured marble, murals depicting the safe passage of sailing vessels and superb mosaics. The hilltop gives 360-degree panoramas of the city. The church's bell tower is crowned by a 9.7m-tall gilded statue of the Virgin Mary on a 12m-high pedestal. It's a 1km walk from the Vieux Port, or take bus 60 or the tourist train.

Château d'If   ISLAND, CASTLE

(www.if.monuments-nationaux.fr; adult/child €5.50/free; ◎ 10am-6pm May-Sep, shorter hours rest year) Immortalised in Alexandre Dumas' classic 1844 novel *Le Comte de Monte Cristo* (The Count of Monte Cristo), the 16th-century fortress-turned-prison Château d'If sits on the tiny island Île d'If, 3.5km west of the Vieux Port. Political prisoners were incarcerated here, along with hundreds of Protestants, the Revolutionary hero Mirabeau, and the Communards of 1871.

Frioul If Express (www.frioul-if-express.com; 1 quai des Belges) boats leave for Château d'If (€10.10 return, 20 minutes, around 15 daily) from the Vieux Port.

🛏 Sleeping

Hôtel Hermès   DESIGN HOTEL €

(🖉 04 96 11 63 63; www.hotelmarseille.com; 2 rue Bonneterie; s €64, d €85-102; ✳ 🛜; Ⓜ Vieux Port) Nothing to do with the Paris design house, this excellent-value hotel has a rooftop terrace with panoramic Vieux Port views. Grab breakfast (€9) on a tray in the bright ground-floor breakfast room and ride the lift to the 5th floor for breakfast à la rooftop. Contemporary rooms have white walls and a splash of lime-green or red to complement their Scandinavian-like design.

★ **Hôtel Edmond Rostand**   DESIGN HOTEL €€
(☑ 04 91 37 74 95; www.hoteledmondrostand.com; 31 rue Dragon; d €90-115, tr €127-141; ✿ @ 🛜; Ⓜ Estrangin-Préfecture) Turn a blind eye to the grubby outside shutters of this excellent-value Logis de France hotel in the Quartier des Antiquaires. Inside, decor is a hip mix of contemporary design and vintage, with a great sofa area for lounging and 16 rooms dressed in crisp white and soothing natural hues. Some rooms overlook a tiny private garden, others the Basilique Notre Dame de la Garde.

★ **Au Vieux Panier**   B&B €€
(☑ 04 91 91 23 72; www.auvieuxpanier.com; 13 rue du Panier; d €100-140; Ⓜ Vieux Port) The height of Le Panier shabby chic, this super-stylish *maison d'hôte* woos art lovers with original works of art. Each year artists are invited to redecorate, meaning its six rooms change annually. Staircases and corridors are like an art gallery and a drop-dead gorgeous rooftop terrace peeks across terracotta tiles to the sea on the horizon.

✕ Eating

The Vieux Port overflows with restaurants, but choose carefully. Head to cours Julien and its surrounding streets for world cuisine.

★ **Café Populaire**   BISTRO €
(☑ 04 91 02 53 96; 110 rue Paradis; tapas €8-16, mains €19-23; ⊙ noon-2.30pm & 8-11pm Tue-Sat; Ⓜ Estrangin-Préfecture) Vintage furniture, old books on the shelves and a fine collection of glass soda bottles lend a retro air to this trendy, 1950s-styled *jazz comptoir* (counter) – a restaurant despite its name. The crowd is chic and smiling chefs in the open kitchen mesmerise with daily specials like king prawns *à la plancha* or beetroot and coriander salad.

★ **Le Café des Épices**   MODERN FRENCH €€
(☑ 04 91 91 22 69; www.cafedesepices.com; 4 rue du Lacydon; 2-/3-course lunch menu €25/28, dinner menu €45; ⊙ noon-3pm & 6-11pm Tue-Fri, noon-3pm Sat; 🍴; Ⓜ Vieux Port) One of Marseille's best chefs, Arnaud de Grammont, infuses his cooking with a panoply of flavours: squid-ink spaghetti with sesame and

---

WORTH A TRIP

LES CALANQUES

Marseille abuts the wild and spectacular **Parc National des Calanques** (www.calanques-parcnational.fr), a 20km stretch of high, rocky promontories, rising from brilliant-turquoise Mediterranean waters.

The sheer cliffs are occasionally interrupted by small idyllic beaches, some impossible to reach without a kayak. Amongst the most famous are the calanques of Sormiou, Port-Miou, Port-Pin and En-Vau.

October to June, the best way to see the Calanques is to hike and the best access is from the small town of Cassis. The **tourist office** (☑ 08 92 39 01 03; www.ot-cassis.com; quai des Moulins; ⊙ 9am-6.30pm Tue-Sat, 9.30am-12.30pm & 3-6pm Sun, shorter hours low season) has maps. In July and August, trails close because of fire danger: take a boat tour from Marseille or Cassis; sea kayak with **Raskas Kayak** (www.raskas-kayak.com); drive; or take a bus.

---

perfectly cooked scallops, or coriander- and citrus-spiced potatoes topped by the catch of the day. Presentation is impeccable, the decor playful, and the colourful outdoor terrace between giant potted olive trees nothing short of superb.

Le Rhul   SEAFOOD €€€
(☑ 04 91 52 01 77; www.lerhul.fr; 269 corniche Président John F Kennedy; bouillabaisse €53; ⊙ noon-2pm & 5-9pm; 🚌 83) This long-standing classic has atmosphere (however kitschy): a 1940s seaside hotel with Mediterranean views. This is one of the most reliably consistent spots for real bouillabaisse.

♥ Drinking & Entertainment

Options for a coffee or something stronger abound on both quays at the Vieux Port. Cafes crowd cours Honoré d'Estienne d'Orves, 1er, a large open square two blocks south of quai de Rive Neuve.

La Caravelle   BAR
(34 quai du Port; ⊙ 7am-2am; Ⓜ Vieux Port) Look up or miss this standout upstairs hideaway, styled with rich wood and leather, a zinc bar and yellowing murals. If it's sunny, snag a

coveted spot on the port-side terrace. On Fridays, there's live jazz from 9pm to midnight.

Espace Julien LIVE MUSIC
(☑04 91 24 34 10; www.espace-julien.com; 39 cours Julien; Ⓜ Notre Dame du Mont–Cours Julien) Rock, *opérock*, alternative theatre, reggae, hip hop, Afro groove and other cutting-edge entertainment all appear on the bill; the website lists gigs.

❶ Tourist Information

The **tourist office** (☑04 91 13 89 00; www.marseille-tourisme.com; 11 La Canebière; ☯9am-7pm Mon-Sat, 10am-5pm Sun; Ⓜ Vieux Port) has plenty of information about the city and the Calanques.

❶ Getting There & Away

AIR
Aéroport Marseille-Provence (p254), 25km northwest in Marignane, has numerous budget flights to various European destinations. Shuttle buses link it with the Marseille train station (€8.20, 25 minutes, every 20 minutes).

BOAT
The **passenger ferry terminal** (www.marseille-port.fr; Ⓜ Joliette) is 250m south of place de la Joliette, 1er. **SNCM** (☑08 91 70 18 01; www.sncm.fr; 61 bd des Dames; Ⓜ Joliette) boats sail to Corsica, Sardinia and North Africa.

TRAIN
From Marseille's Gare St-Charles, trains including TGVs go all over France and Europe. Services include:

Avignon €29.50, 35 minutes
Lyon €65, 1¾ hours
Nice €37, 2½ hours
Paris Gare de Lyon €113, three hours

❶ Getting Around

Marseille has two metro lines, two tram lines and an extensive bus network, all run by **RTM** (☑04 91 91 92 10; www.rtm.fr; 6 rue des Fabres; ☯8.30am-6pm Mon-Fri, 8.30am-noon & 1-4.30pm Sat; Ⓜ Vieux Port), where you can obtain information and transport tickets (€1.50).

Pick up a bike from 100-plus stations across the city with **Le Vélo** (www.levelo-mpm.fr).

Aix-en-Provence

POP 144,274
Aix-en-Provence is to Provence what the Left Bank is to Paris: a pocket of bohemian chic crawling with students. It's hard to believe that 'Aix' (pronounced ex) is just 25km from chaotic, exotic Marseille. The city has been a cultural centre since the Middle Ages (two of the town's most famous sons are painter Paul Cézanne and novelist Émile Zola), but for all its polish, it's still a laid-back Provençal town at heart.

◉ Sights

A stroller's paradise, Aix's highlight is the mostly pedestrian old city, **Vieil Aix**. South of cours Mirabeau, the **Quartier Mazarin** was laid out in the 17th century, and is home to some of Aix's finest buildings.

★**Atelier Cézanne** MUSEUM
(☑04 42 21 06 53; www.atelier-cezanne.com; 9 av Paul Cézanne; adult/child €5.50/free; ☯10am-noon & 2-5pm) Cézanne's last studio, 1.5km north of the tourist office on a hilltop, was painstakingly preserved (and recreated: not all the tools and still-life models strewn around the room were his) as it was at the time of his death. Though the studio is inspiring, none of his works hang there. Take bus 1 or 20 to the Atelier Cézanne stop or walk the 1.5km from town.

Cours Mirabeau HISTORIC QUARTER
No avenue better epitomises Provence's most graceful city than Cours Mirabeau, a fountain-studded street sprinkled with Renaissance *hôtels particuliers* and crowned with a summertime roof of leafy plane trees. Named after the revolutionary hero Comte de Mirabeau, it was laid out in the 1640s. Cézanne and Zola hung out at **Les Deux Garçons** (53 cours Mirabeau; ☯7am-2am), one of a clutch of busy pavement cafes.

Musée Granet MUSEUM
(www.museegranet-aixenprovence.fr; place St-Jean de Malte; adult/child €5/free; ☯11am-7pm Tue-Sun) Housed in a 17th-century priory of the Knights of Malta, this exceptional museum is named after the Provençal painter François Marius Granet (1775–1849), who donated a large number of works. Its collections include 16th- to 20th-century Italian, Flemish and French works. Modern art reads like a who's who: Picasso, Léger, Matisse, Monet, Klee, Van Gogh and Giacometti, among others. Nine works by Cézanne are the museum's pride and joy. Excellent temporary exhibitions.

VAN GOGH'S ARLES

If the winding streets and colourful houses of Arles seem familiar, it's hardly surprising – Vincent van Gogh lived here for much of his life in a yellow house on place Lamartine, and the town regularly featured in his canvases. His original house was destroyed during WWII, but you can still follow in Vincent's footsteps on the evocative **Van Gogh walking circuit** – the **tourist office** (☑04 90 18 41 20; www.arlestourisme.com; esplanade Charles de Gaulle, bd des Lices; ☉9am-6.45pm Apr-Sep, to 4.45pm Mon-Fri & 12.45pm Sun Oct-Mar; ☎) sells maps (€1). You won't see many of the artist's masterpieces in Arles, however, although the modern art gallery **Fondation Vincent Van Gogh** (☑04 90 49 94 04; www.fondation-vincentvangogh-arles.org; 33 ter rue du Docteur Fanton; adult/child €9/4; ☉11am-7pm Tue-Sun Apr–mid-Sep, to 6pm mid-Sep–Mar) always has one on show, as well as contemporary exhibitions inspired by the Impressionist.

Two millennia ago, Arles was a major Roman settlement. The town's 20,000-seat amphitheatre, known as the **Arènes** (Amphithéâtre; adult/child incl Théâtre Antique €5.50/free; ☉9am-8pm Jul & Aug, to 7pm May, Jun & Sep, shorter hours rest of year), is nowadays used for bullfights.

There are buses to/from Aix-en-Provence (€10.50, 1½ hours) and regular trains to/from Nîmes (€8.60, 30 minutes), Marseille (€15.30, 55 minutes) and Avignon (€7.50, 20 minutes).

🛏 Sleeping

Hôtel les Quatre Dauphins   BOUTIQUE HOTEL €
(☑04 42 38 16 39; www.lesquatredauphins.fr; 54 rue Roux Alphéran; s €62-72, d €72-87; ✳ ☎ ☎) This sweet 13-room hotel slumbers in a former private mansion in one of the loveliest parts of town. Rooms are fresh and clean, with excellent modern bathrooms. Those with sloping, beamed ceilings in the attic are quaint but not for those who cannot pack light – the terracotta-tiled staircase is not suitcase-friendly.

★ L'Épicerie   B&B €€
(☑06 08 85 38 68; www.unechambreenville.eu; 12 rue du Cancel; d €100-130; ☎) This intimate B&B is the fabulous creation of born-and-bred Aixois lad Luc. His breakfast room recreates a 1950s grocery store, and the flowery garden out back is perfect for excellent evening dining and weekend brunch (book ahead for both). Breakfast is a veritable feast. Two rooms accommodate families of four.

🍽 Eating

★ Jacquou Le Croquant   SOUTHWEST, PROVENÇAL €
(☑04 42 27 37 19; www.jacquoulecroquant.com; 2 rue de l'Aumône Vielle; plat du jour €10.90, menus from €14; ☉noon-3pm & 7-11pm) This veteran address, around since 1985, stands out on dozens of counts: buzzy jovial atmosphere, flowery patio garden, funky interior, early evening opening, family friendly, hearty homecooking, a menu covering all price ranges and so forth. Cuisine from southwestern France is its speciality, meaning lots of duck, but the vast menu covers all bases.

Le Petit Verdot   FRENCH €€
(☑04 42 27 30 12; www.lepetitverdot.fr; 7 rue d'Entrecasteaux; mains €15-25; ☉7pm-midnight Mon-Sat) Delicious menus are designed around what's in season, and paired with excellent wines. Meats are often braised all day and vegetables are tender, stewed in delicious broths. Save room for an incandescent dessert. Lively dining occurs around tabletops made of wine crates (expect to talk to your neighbour), and the gregarious owner speaks multiple languages.

ℹ Information

The **tourist office** (☑04 42 16 11 61; www.aixenprovencetourism.com; 300 av Giuseppe Verdi; ☉8.30am-7pm Mon-Sat, 10am-1pm & 2-6pm Sun, to 8pm Mon-Sat Jun-Sep; ☎) sells tickets for guided tours and events.

ℹ Getting There & Away

BUS

From Aix's **bus station** (☑08 91 02 40 25, 04 42 91 26 80; place Marius Bastard), a 10-minute walk southwest from La Rotonde, routes include Marseille (€5.70, 25 minutes) and Avignon (€17.40, 1¼ hours).

TRAIN

The only useful train from Aix's tiny **city centre train station** (av Victor Hugo) is to/from Marseille (€8.20, 45 minutes). Aix TGV station, 15km away and accessible by shuttle bus from the bus station (€3.70), serves most of France; Marseille (€6.20) is a mere 12 minutes away.

Avignon

POP 92,078

Hooped by 4.3km of superbly preserved stone ramparts, this graceful city is the belle of Provence's ball. Its turn as the papal seat of power has bestowed Avignon with a treasury of magnificent art and architecture, none grander than the massive medieval fortress and papal palace, the Palais des Papes. Famed for its annual performing arts festival, these days Avignon is a lively student city and an ideal spot from which to step out into the surrounding region.

⊙ Sights

Palais des Papes　　　　　　　PALACE
(Papal Palace; www.palais-des-papes.com; place du Palais; adult/child €11/9, with Pont Saint Bénezet €13.50/10.50; ⊙9am-8pm Jul, 9am-8.30pm Aug, shorter hours Sep-Jun) Palais des Papes, a Unesco World Heritage Site, is the world's largest Gothic palace. Built when Pope Clement V abandoned Rome in 1309, it was the papal seat for 70-odd years. The immense scale testifies to the papacy's wealth; the 3m-thick walls, portcullises and watchtowers show its insecurity.

It takes imagination to picture the former luxury of these bare, cavernous stone halls, but multimedia audioguides (€2) assist. Highlights include 14th-century chapel frescoes by Matteo Giovannetti, and the Chambre du Cerf with medieval hunting scenes.

Pont Saint Bénezet　　　　　　BRIDGE
(bd du Rhône; adult/child €5/4, with Palais des Papes €13.50/10.50; ⊙9am-8pm Jul, 9am-8.30pm Aug, shorter hours Sep-Jun) Legend says Pastor Bénezet had three saintly visions urging him to build a bridge across the Rhône. Completed in 1185, the 900m-long bridge with 20 arches linked Avignon with Villeneuve-lès-Avignon. It was rebuilt several times before all but four of its spans were washed away in the 1600s. Don't be surprised if you spot someone dancing; in France, the bridge is known as Pont d'Avignon after the nursery rhyme: 'Sur le pont d'Avignon/L'on y danse, l'on y danse...' (On Avignon Bridge, all are dancing...).

★☆ Festivals & Events

Hundreds of artists take to the stage and streets during the world-famous **Festival d'Avignon** (www.festival-avignon.com; ⊙Jul) and the fringe **Festival Off** (www.avignonleoff.com), held early July to early August.

⊨ Sleeping

Hôtel Mignon　　　　　　　HOTEL €
(☑04 90 82 17 30; www.hotel-mignon.com; 12 rue Joseph Vernet; s €40-60, d €65-77, tr €80-99, q €105; ❋@⊛) Bathrooms might be tiny and the stairs up, steep and narrow, but Hôtel Mignon (literally 'Cute Hotel') remains excellent value. Its 16 rooms are clean and comfortable, and the hotel sits on Avignon's smartest shopping street. Breakfast is €7.

Le Limas　　　　　　　　B&B €€
(☑04 90 14 67 19; www.le-limas-avignon.com; 51 rue du Limas; s/d/tr from €130/150/250; ❋@⊛) This chic B&B in an 18th-century town house, like something out of *Vogue Living*, is everything designers strive for when mixing old and new: state-of-the-art kitchen and minimalist white decor complementing antique fireplaces and 18th-century spiral stairs. Breakfast on the sun-drenched terrace is divine, darling.

✗ Eating

Place de l'Horloge's touristy cafes have so-so food.

Ginette et Marcel　　　　　　CAFE €
(☑04 90 85 58 70; 27 place des Corps Saints; tartines €4-7; ⊙11am-11pm Wed-Mon; ⊛) With tables and chairs on one of Avignon's most happening plane-tree-shaded squares, this vintage cafe styled like a 1950s grocery store is a charming spot to hang out and people-watch over a *tartine* (open-faced sandwich), tart, salad or other light dish – equally tasty for lunch or an early evening *apéro* (pre-dinner drink). Kids adore Ginette's cherry- and violet-flavoured cordials, and Marcel's glass jars of old-fashioned sweets.

★83.Vernet　　　　　MODERN FRENCH €€
(☑04 90 85 99 04; www.83vernet.com; 83 rue Joseph Vernet; lunch/dinner menu €19.50/€24-30; ⊙noon-3pm & 7pm-1am Mon-Sat) Forget flowery French descriptions. The menu is straightforward and to the point at this

strikingly contemporary address, magnificently at home in the 18th-century cloistered courtyard of a medieval college. Expect pan-seared scallops, squid à la plancha and beef steak in pepper sauce on the menu, and watch for weekend events that transform the lounge-style restaurant into the hippest dance floor in town.

ℹ Information

Tourist Office (☑ 04 32 74 32 74; www.avignon-tourisme.com; 41 cours Jean Jaurès; ⊘9am-6pm Mon-Fri, to 6pm Sat, 10am-noon Sun Apr-Oct, shorter hours rest of year) Organises guided walking tours of the city, and has plenty of information on other tours and activities, including boat trips and lunch cruises on the River Rhône, and wine-tasting trips to nearby Côtes du Rhône vineyards.

ℹ Getting There & Away

BUS
The bus station is down the ramp to the right as you exit the train station. Services include Marseille (€22, 35 minutes) and Nîmes (€1.50, 1¼ hours).

TRAIN
Avignon has two stations: Gare Avignon TGV, 4km southwest in Courtine, and Gare Avignon Centre, with services to/from Arles (€7.50, 20 minutes) and Nîmes (€9.70, 30 minutes).

Some TGVs to/from Paris (€123, 3½ hours) stop at Gare Avignon Centre, but TGVs to/from Marseille (€25, 30 minutes) and Nice (€60, 3¼ hours) only use Gare Avignon TGV.

In July and August, a direct Eurostar service operates on Saturday to/from London (from €140, six hours).

THE FRENCH RIVIERA & MONACO

With its glistening seas, idyllic beaches and fabulous weather, the French Riviera (Côte d'Azur in French) screams exclusivity, extravagance and excess. It has been a favourite getaway for the European jet set since Victorian times and there is nowhere more chichi or glam in France than St-Tropez, Cannes and super-rich, sovereign Monaco.

Nice
POP 348,195
Riviera queen Nice is what good living is all about – shimmering shores, the very best of Mediterranean food, a unique historical heritage, free museums, a charming Old Town, exceptional art and alpine wilderness within an hour's drive.

◉ Sights

★**Vieux Nice** HISTORIC QUARTER
(⊘food markets 6am-1.30pm Tue-Sun) Nice's old town, a mellow-hued rabbit warren, has scarcely changed since the 1700s. Retracing its history – and therefore that of the city – is a highlight, although you don't need to be a history buff to enjoy a stroll in this atmospheric quarter. Vieux Nice is as alive and prominent today as it ever was.

Promenade des Anglais ARCHITECTURE
Palm-lined promenade des Anglais, paid for by Nice's English colony in 1822, is a fine stage for a stroll. It's particularly atmospheric in the evening, with Niçois milling about

DON'T MISS

THE CORNICHES

Some of the Riviera's most spectacular scenery stretches east between Nice and Monaco. A trio of *corniches* (coastal roads) hugs the cliffs between the two seaside cities, each higher up the hill than the last. The middle *corniche* ends in Monaco; the upper and lower continue to Menton near the French–Italian border.

Corniche Inférieure (lower) Skimming the glittering, villa-studded shoreline, this road is all about belle époque glamour, the height of which can be seen at the extravagant **Villa Ephrussi de Rothschild** (www.villa-ephrussi.com; St-Jean-Cap Ferrat; adult/child €13/10; ⊘10am-6pm Mar-Oct, 2-6pm Nov-Feb) in St-Jean-Cap Ferrat.

Moyenne (middle) Corniche The jewel in the Riviera crown undoubtedly goes to Èze, a medieval village spectacularly located on a rocky outcrop with dazzling views of the Med.

Grande (upper) Corniche The epitomy of 'scenic drive', with sublime panoramas unfolding at every bend. Stop in La Turbie for dramatic views of Monaco.

and epic sunsets. Don't miss the magnificent facade of **Hôtel Negresco**, built in 1912, or art deco **Palais de la Méditerranée**, saved from demolition in the 1980s and now part of a 4-star palace. The promenade follows the whole Baie des Anges (4km) and has a cycle and skating lane.

Musée Matisse
ART MUSEUM
(www.musee-matisse-nice.org; 164 av des Arènes de Cimiez; ⊙ 10am-6pm Wed-Mon) FREE Located about 2km north of the centre in the leafy quarter of Cimiez, this museum houses a fascinating assortment of works by Matisse documenting the artist's stylistic evolution, including oil paintings, drawings, sculptures, tapestries and Matisse's signature famous paper cut-outs. The permanent collection is displayed in a red-ochre 17th-century Genoese villa overlooking an olive-tree-studded park. Temporary exhibitions are hosted in the futuristic basement building. Explanations in French only.

🛏 Sleeping

Hôtel Solara
HOTEL €
(☑ 04 93 88 09 96; www.hotelsolara.com; 7 rue de France; s/d/tr/q €65/85/120/150; ❄ ⚛ ☎) Were it not for its fantastic location on pedestrian rue de France and the sensational terraces that half the rooms boast, we'd say the Solara was an honest-to-goodness budget-friendly choice with impeccable rooms. But with those perks (and did we mention the small fridges in each room for that evening rosé?), it is a hidden gem.

★ Nice Pebbles
SELF-CONTAINED €€
(☑ 04 97 20 27 30; www.nicepebbles.com; 1-/3-bedroom apt from €107/220; ❄ ☎) Have you ever dreamt of feeling like a real Niçois? Coming back to your designer pad in Vieux Nice, opening a bottle of ice-cold rosé and feasting on market goodies? Nice Pebbles' concept is simple: offering the quality of a 4-star boutique hotel in holiday flats. The apartments (one to three bedrooms) are gorgeous and equipped to high standards.

Nice Garden Hôtel
BOUTIQUE HOTEL €€
(☑ 04 93 87 35 62; www.nicegardenhotel.com; 11 rue du Congrès; s/d €75/100; ❄ ☎) Behind heavy iron gates hides this little gem of a hotel: the nine beautifully appointed rooms, the work of the exquisite Marion, are a subtle blend of old and new and overlook a delightful garden with a glorious orange tree.

Amazingly, all this charm and peacefulness is just two blocks from the promenade.

Eating

Niçois nibbles include *socca* (a thin layer of chickpea flour and olive oil batter), *salade niçoise* and *farcis* (stuffed vegetables). Restaurants in Vieux Nice are a mixed bag, so choose carefully.

★ La Rossettisserie
FRENCH €
(☑ 04 93 76 18 80; www.larossettisserie.com; 8 rue Mascoïnat; mains €14.50; ⊙ noon-2pm & 7.30-10pm Mon-Sat) The Rossettisserie (a lovely play on the word rotisserie – roast house – and Rossetti, the name of the nearby square) only serves succulent, roast meat – beef, chicken, veal, lamb or pork. It is cooked to perfection and comes with a choice of heavenly homemade mash, ratatouille or sauté potatoes and a mixed salad. The vaulted dining room in the basement is stunning.

Chez Palmyre
FRENCH €
(☑ 04 93 85 72 32; 5 rue Droite; menu €17; ⊙ noon-1.30pm & 7-9.30pm Mon-Fri) A new chef has breathed new life into this fabulously atmospheric little restaurant, seemingly unchanged for its long life. The kitchen churns out Niçois standards with a light hand, service is sweet and the price fantastic; book ahead, even for lunch.

L'Escalinada
NIÇOIS €€
(☑ 04 93 62 11 71; www.escalinada.fr; 22 rue Pairolière; menu €26, mains €19-25; ⊙ noon-2.30pm & 7-11pm) This charming restaurant has been one of the best places in town for Niçois cuisine for the last half-century: try melt-in-your-mouth homemade gnocchi with tasty *daube* (Provençal beef stew), grilled prawns with garlic and herbs or Marsala veal stew. The staff are delightful and the welcome *kir* (white wine sweetened with blackcurrant syrup) is on the house. No credit cards.

🍷 Drinking & Entertainment

Vieux Nice's streets are stuffed with bars and cafes. There is a vibrant live-music scene.

Les Distilleries Idéales
CAFE
(www.lesdistilleriesideales.fr; 24 rue de la Préfecture; ⊙ 9am-12.30am) Whether you're after an espresso on your way to the cours Saleya market or an *apéritif* (complete with cheese and charcuterie platters, €5.60) before trying out one of Nice's fabulous restaurants,

Nice

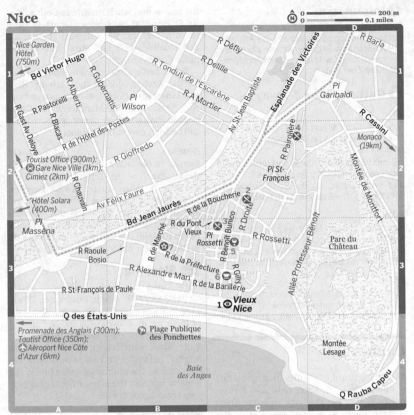

Nice

Les Distilleries is one of the most atmospheric bars in town. Tables on the small street terrace are ideal for watching the world go by. Happy hour is from 6pm to 8pm.

L'Abat-Jour   BAR
(25 rue Benoît Bunico; ◎6.30pm-2.30am) With its vintage furniture, rotating art exhibitions and alternative music, L'Abat-Jour is all the rage with Nice's young and trendy crowd. The basement has live music or DJ sessions as the night darkens.

Chez Wayne's   LIVE MUSIC
(www.waynes.fr; 15 rue de la Préfecture; ◎10am-2am) Raucous watering hole Chez Wayne's is a typical English pub that looks like it's been plucked out of London, Bristol or Leeds. It features excellent live bands every night and has the best atmosphere in town. The pub is also sports-mad and shows every rugby, football, Aussie Rules, tennis and cricket game worth watching.

ℹ Information

Tourist Office (☎ 08 92 70 74 07; www.
nicetourisme.com; 5 promenade des Anglais;
☻ 9am-6pm Mon-Sat) There's also a branch at
the train station (av Thiers; ☻ 8am-7pm Mon-
Sat, 10am-5pm Sun).

ℹ Getting There & Away

AIR

Nice Côte d'Azur airport (p254) is 6km west
of Nice, by the sea. A taxi to Nice centre costs
around €30.

Buses 98 and 99 link the airport terminal with
Nice's centre and Nice train station (€6, 35 minutes, every 20 minutes). Bus 110 (€20, hourly)
links the airport with Monaco (30 minutes).

BOAT

Nice is the main port for ferries to Corsica.
SNCM (www.sncm.fr; quai du Commerce) and
Corsica Ferries (www.corsicaferries.com; quai
du Commerce) are the two main companies.

TRAIN

From Nice's train station, 1.2km north of the
beach, there are frequent services to Cannes (€7,
40 minutes) and Monaco (€3.80, 25 minutes).

Cannes

POP 73,671

Most have heard of Cannes and its celebrity film festival. The latter only lasts for two
weeks in May, but the buzz and glitz linger
all year thanks to regular visits from celebrities who come here to indulge in designer
shopping, beaches and the palace hotels of
the Riviera's glammest seafront, bd de la
Croisette.

◉ Sights & Activities

La Croisette   ARCHITECTURE
The multi-starred hotels and couture shops
that line the famous bd de la Croisette (aka
La Croisette) may be the preserve of the rich
and famous, but anyone can enjoy the palm-
shaded promenade and take in the atmosphere. In fact, it's a favourite among Cannois
(natives of Cannes), particularly at night
when it is lit with bright colours.

Îles de Lérins   ISLAND
Although just 20 minutes away by boat,
these tranquil islands feel far from the madding crowd. **Île Ste-Marguerite**, where
the mysterious Man in the Iron Mask was
incarcerated during the late 17th century, is
known for its bone-white beaches, eucalyp-

tus groves and small marine museum. Tiny
Île St-Honorat has been a monastery since
the 5th century: you can visit the church
and small chapels and stroll through the
monks' vineyards.

Boats leave Cannes from quai des Îles
on the western side of the harbour. **Riviera Lines** (www.riviera-lines.com; quai Laubeuf)
runs ferries to Île Ste-Marguerite and **Compagnie Planaria** (www.cannes-ilesdelerins.com;
quai Laubeuf) covers Île St-Honorat.

Beaches   SWIMMING
Cannes is blessed with sandy beaches, although much of the stretch along bd de la
Croisette is taken up by private beaches.
This arrangement leaves only a small strip
of free sand near the Palais des Festivals
for the bathing hoi polloi; the much bigger
Plage du Midi (bd Jean Hibert) and **Plage de
la Bocca**, west of Vieux Port, are also free.

☐ Sleeping

Hôtel Alnéa   HOTEL €
(☎ 04 93 68 77 77; www.hotel-alnea.com; 20 rue
Jean de Riouffe; s/d €70/90; ❄ 🛜) A breath
of fresh air in a town of stars, Noémi and
Cédric have put their heart and soul into
their hotel, with bright, colourful rooms,
original paintings and numerous little details such as the afternoon coffee break, the
honesty bar and the bike or *boules* (to play
pétanque) loans. No lift.

Hôtel de Provence   HOTEL €€
(☎ 04 93 38 44 35; www.hotel-de-provence.com;
9 rue Molière; s/d from €108/118; ❄ 🛜) A tall
town house with pale yellow walls and
lavender blue shutters, the exterior of the
Hôtel de Provence is true to its name. Inside, however, the design is more minimalist chic than quaint Provençal, with plenty
of clean white lines. The hotel's strength is
its height, with almost every room sporting
a balcony or terrace.

✗ Eating

PhilCat   DELICATESSEN €
(La Pantiéro; sandwiches & salads €4.50-6;
☻ 8.30am-5pm; ✍) Don't be put off by Phil-
lipe and Catherine's unassuming prefab
cabin on La Pantiéro: this is Cannes' best
lunch house. Huge salads, made to order, are
piled high with delicious fresh ingredients.
Or if you're *really* hungry, try one of their
phenomenal *pan bagna* (a moist sandwich
bursting with Provençal flavours).

THE SCENT OF THE CÔTE D'AZUR

Mosey some 20km northwest of Cannes to inhale the sweet smell of lavender, jasmine, mimosa and orange-blossom fields. In **Grasse**, one of the world's leading perfume centres, dozens of perfumeries create essences to sell to factories (for aromatically enhanced foodstuffs and soaps) as well as to prestigious couture houses – the highly trained noses of local perfume-makers can identify 3000 scents in a single whiff.

Learn about three millennia of perfume-making at the **Musée International de la Parfumerie** (MIP; www.museesdegrasse.com; 2 bd du Jeu de Ballon; adult/child €4/free; 10.30am-5.30pm Wed-Mon;) and watch the process firsthand during a guided tour at **Fragonard perfumery** (www.fragonard.com; 20 bd Fragonard; tour free; 9am-6pm), the easiest to reach on foot. The **tourist office** (04 93 36 66 66; www.grasse.fr; place de la Buanderie; 9am-12.30pm & 2-6pm Mon-Sat;) has information on other perfumeries and field trips to local flower farms. Roses are picked mid-May to mid-June, jasmine July to late October.

Aux Bons Enfants FRENCH €€
(www.aux-bons-enfants.com; 80 rue Meynadier; menu €23, mains €16; noon-2pm & 7-10pm Tue-Sat) A people's-choice place since 1935, this informal restaurant cooks up wonderful regional dishes such as *aïoli garni* (garlic and saffron mayonnaise served with fish and vegetables), *daube* (a Provençal beef stew), and *rascasse meunière* (pan-fried rockfish), all in a convivial atmosphere. Make no plans for the afternoon after lunching here. No credit cards or reservations.

Mantel MODERN EUROPEAN €€
(04 93 39 13 10; www.restaurantmantel.com; 22 rue St-Antoine; menus €35-60; noon-2pm Fri-Mon, 7.30-10pm Thu-Tue) Discover why Noël Mantel is the hotshot of the Cannois gastronomic scene at his refined old-town restaurant. Service is stellar and the seasonal cuisine divine: try the wonderfully tender glazed veal shank in balsamic vinegar or the original poached octopus *bourride*-style. Best of all though, you get not one but two desserts from the mouthwatering dessert trolley.

ⓘ Information

Tourist Office (04 92 99 84 22; www.cannes-destination.fr; Palais des Festivals, bd de la Croisette; 9am-7pm) The place to book guided tours of the city and get information on what to do and see in Cannes.

ⓘ Getting There & Away

BUS
From the **bus station** (place Cornut-Gentille), buses serve Nice (€1.50, 1½ hours, every 15 minutes) and Nice airport (€20, 50 minutes, half-hourly).

TRAIN
From Cannes train station there are at least hourly services to/from Nice (€7, 40 minutes), Grasse (€4.30, 30 minutes), Monaco (€9.40, one hour) and Marseille (€32, two hours).

St-Tropez

POP 4571

In the soft autumn or winter light, it's hard to believe the pretty terracotta fishing village of St-Tropez is a stop on the Riviera celebrity circuit. It seems far removed from its glitzy siblings further up the coast, but come spring or summer, it's a different world: the population increases tenfold, prices triple and fun-seekers pile in to party till dawn, strut around the luxury-yacht-packed Vieux Port and enjoy the creature comforts of exclusive A-listers' beaches in the Baie de Pampelonne.

◉ Sights & Activities

About 4km southeast of town is the start of **Plage de Tahiti** and its continuation, the famous **Plage de Pampelonne**, studded with St-Tropez' most legendary drinking and dining haunts.

Place des Lices SQUARE
St-Tropez's legendary and very charming central square is studded with plane trees, cafes and *pétanque* players. Simply sitting on a cafe terrace watching the world go by or jostling with the crowds at its extravaganza of a twice-weekly **market** (place des Lices; 8am-1pm Tue & Sat), jam-packed with

FRANCE ST-TROPEZ

everything from fruit and veg to antique mirrors and flip-flops (thongs), is an integral part of the St-Tropez experience.

Musée de l'Annonciade ART MUSEUM
(place Grammont; adult/child €6/free; ☺10am-1pm & 2-6pm Wed-Mon) In a gracefully converted 16th-century chapel, this small but famous art museum showcases an impressive collection of modern art infused with that legendary Côte d'Azur light. Pointillist Paul Signac bought a house in St-Tropez in 1892 and introduced others to the area. The museum's collection includes his *St-Tropez, Le Quai* (1899) and *St-Tropez, Coucher de Soleil au Bois de Pins* (1896).

🛏 Sleeping & Eating

Multistar campgrounds abound on the road to Plage de Pampelonne. Quai Jean Jaurès at the Vieux Port is littered with restaurants and cafes.

Hôtel Lou Cagnard HOTEL €€
(☑04 94 97 04 24; www.hotel-lou-cagnard.com; 18 av Paul Roussel; d €81-171; ☺Mar-Oct; ✻🐾) Book well ahead for this great-value courtyard charmer, shaded by lemon and fig trees, and owned by schooled hoteliers. The pretty Provençal house with lavender shutters has its very own jasmine-scented garden, strung with fairy lights at night. Bright and beautifully clean rooms are decorated with painted Provençal furniture. Five have ground-floor garden terraces. The cheapest rooms have private washbasin and stand-up bath-tub but share a toilet; most rooms have air-con.

Hôtel Le Colombier HOTEL €€
(☑04 94 97 05 31; http://lecolombierhotel.free.fr; impasse des Conquettes; d/tr from €105/235; ☺mid-Apr–mid-Nov; ✻🐾) An immaculately clean converted house, five minutes' walk from place des Lices, the Colombier's fresh, summery decor is feminine and uncluttered,

> **ℹ ACCOMMODATION WARNING**
>
> Accommodation can be impossible to find, not to mention prohibitively expensive, during the Cannes Film Festival and the Monaco Grand Prix (both held in May). This applies to the coast between Menton and Cannes. July and August are busy everywhere, so book well in advance.

with bedrooms in shades of white and vintage furniture.

★**La Tarte Tropézienne** CAFE, BAKERY €
(www.latartetropezienne.fr; place des Lices; mains €13-15; ☺6.30am-7.30pm, lunch noon-3pm) This cafe-bakery is the original creator of the eponymous cake, and therefore the best place to buy St-Tropez's delicacy. But to start, choose from delicious daily specials, salads and sandwiches, which you can enjoy in the bistro inside or on the little terrace outside.

La Plage des Jumeaux SEAFOOD €€€
(☑04 94 58 21 80; www.plagedesjumeaux.com; rte de l'Épi, Pampelonne; mains €25-40; ☺noon-3pm; ✻⊞) The top pick of St-Tropez's beach restaurants, Les Jumeaux serves beautiful seafood (including fabulous whole fish, ideal to share) and sun-bursting salads on its dreamy white-and-turquoise striped beach. Families are well catered for, with playground equipment, beach toys and a kids' menu.

ℹ Information

Tourist Office (☑08 92 68 48 28; www.sainttropeztourisme.com; quai Jean Jaurès; ☺9.30am-1.30pm & 3-7.30pm Jul & Aug, 9.30am-12.30pm & 2-7pm Apr-Jun, Sep &Oct, to 6pm Mon-Sat Nov-Mar) Has a kiosk in Parking du Port in July and August.

ℹ Getting There & Away

From the **bus station** (☑04 94 56 25 74; av du Général de Gaulle), buses run by VarLib (☑04 94 24 60 00; www.varlib.fr; tickets €3) serve Ramatuelle (€3, 35 minutes) and St-Raphaël train station (€3, 1¼ hours). There are four daily buses to Toulon-Hyères airport (€3, 1½ hours).

Monaco

POP 32,020

Squeezed into just 200 hectares, this confetti principality may be the world's second-smallest country (the Vatican is smaller), but what it lacks in size it makes up for in attitude. Glitzy, glam and screaming hedonism, Monaco is truly beguiling.

It is a sovereign state but has no border control. It has its own flag (red and white) and national holiday (19 November), and it uses the euro even though it's not part of the EU.

You can easily visit Monaco as a day trip from Nice, a short train ride away.

◉ Sights

★ Musée Océanographique de Monaco
AQUARIUM

(www.oceano.mc; av St-Martin; adult/child €14/7; ⊘10am-6pm) Stuck dramatically to the edge of a cliff since 1910, the world-renowned Musée Océanographique de Monaco, founded by Prince Albert I (1848–1922), is a stunner. Its centrepiece is its aquarium, with a 6m-deep lagoon where sharks and marine predators are separated from colourful tropical fishes by a coral reef. Upstairs, two huge colonnaded rooms retrace the history of oceanography and marine biology (and Prince Albert's contribution to the field) through photographs, old equipment, numerous specimens and interactive displays.

Le Rocher
HISTORIC QUARTER

Monaco Ville, also called Le Rocher, thrusts skywards on a pistol-shaped rock. It's this strategic location overlooking the sea that became the stronghold of the Grimaldi dynasty. Built as a fortress in the 13th century, the **palace** is now the private residence of the Grimaldis. It is protected by the Carabiniers du Prince; **changing of the guard** takes place daily at 11.55am.

Jardin Exotique
GARDENS

(www.jardin-exotique.mc; 62 bd du Jardin Exotique; adult/child €7.20/3.80; ⊘9am-dusk) Home to the world's largest succulent and cactus collection, from small echinocereus to 10m-tall African candelabras, the gardens tumble down the slopes of Moneghetti through a maze of paths, stairs and bridges. Views of the principality are spectacular and the gardens are delightful. Your ticket also gets you a 35-minute **guided tour** round the **Grottes de l'Observatoire**.

⌊≜ Sleeping

Monaco is no budget destination when it comes to accommodation. Budget-conscious travellers should stay in nearby Nice and visit as a day trip.

Hôtel Miramar
HOTEL €€

(☑93 30 86 48; www.miramar.monaco-hotel.com; 1 av du Président JF Kennedy; s/d €160/185; ❋✿) This modern hotel with rooftop-terrace restaurant is a great option right by the port. Seven of the 11 rooms have fabulous balconies overlooking the yachts. The hotel was entirely refurbished in 2014, giving the 1950s building a proper 21st-century make-over.

✕ Eating

Supermarché Casino
BOULANGERIE €

(17 bd Albert, 1er; pizza slices & sandwiches from €3.20; ⊘8.30am-midnight Mon-Sat, to 9pm Sun; ☑) It's not so much the supermarket that's worth knowing about as its excellent streetside bakery and pizzeria, which churns out freshly prepared goodies. A saviour for those keen to watch the pennies.

La Montgolfière
FUSION €€

(☑97 98 61 59; www.lamontgolfiere.mc; 16 rue Basse; mains €14-27; ⊘noon-2pm & 7.30-9.30pm Mon, Tue & Thu-Sat) This tiny fusion wonder is an unlikely find amid the touristy jumble of Monaco's historic quarter. But what a great idea Henri and Fabienne Geraci had to breathe new life into the Rocher. The couple have spent a lot of time in Malaysia, and Henri's fusion cuisine is outstanding, as is Fabienne's welcome in their pocket-sized dining room.

Café Llorca
MODERN FRENCH €€

(☑99 99 29 29; www.cafellorca.mc; Grimaldi Forum, 10 av Princesse Grace; menu €22, mains €15-19; ⊘noon-3pm Mon-Fri) This is Michelin-starred chef Alain Llorca's gift to lunch-goers: fabulous modern French cuisine with a fusion twist at affordable prices. The two-course lunch menu including a glass of wine is a steal. In spring/summer, make a beeline (and book) for the tables on the terrace overlooking the sea.

♟ Drinking & Entertainment

Brasserie de Monaco
MICROBREWERY

(www.brasseriedemonaco.com; 36 rte de la Piscine; ⊘noon-2am) Tourists and locals rub shoulders at Monaco's only microbrewery, which crafts rich organic ales and lager, and serves tasty (if pricey) antipasti plates. The brasserie regularly hosts live music and shows major sports events. Happy hour runs from 6.30pm to 8.30pm.

★ Casino de Monte Carlo
CASINO

(www.montecarlocasinos.com; place du Casino; admission Salon Europe/Salons Privés €10/20; ⊘Salon Europe 2pm-late daily, Salons Privés from 4pm Thu-Sun) Gambling – or simply watching the poker-faced gamble – in Monte Carlo's grand marble-and-gold casino is part and parcel of the Monaco experience. The building and atmosphere are an attraction in its own right and you need not play huge sums. To enter the casino, you must be at least 18.

ℹ️ Information

TELEPHONE

Calls between Monaco and France are international calls. Dial 🗷 00 followed by Monaco's country code (🗷 377) when calling Monaco from France or elsewhere abroad. To phone France from Monaco, dial 🗷 00 and France's country code (🗷 33).

TOURIST INFORMATION

Tourist Office (www.visitmonaco.com; 2a bd des Moulins; ☉ 9am-7pm Mon-Sat, 11am-1pm Sun) Smartphone users should download the tourist office's excellent app called Monaco Travel Guide.

ℹ️ Getting There & Away

Monaco's **train station** (av Prince Pierre) has frequent trains to Nice (€3.80, 25 minutes), and east to Menton (€2.10, 15 minutes) and beyond into Italy. Bus 100 goes to Nice (€1.50, 45 minutes) along the Corniche Inférieure.

CORSICA

The rugged island of Corsica (Corse in French) is officially a part of France but remains fiercely proud of its own culture, history and language. It's one of the Mediterranean's most dramatic islands, with a bevy of beautiful beaches, glitzy ports and a mountainous, maquis-covered interior to explore, as well as a wild, independent spirit all of its own.

Ajaccio

POP 67,477

Ajaccio, Corsica's main metropolis, is all class and seduction. Looming over this elegant port city is the spectre of Corsica's great general: Napoléon Bonaparte was born here in 1769 and the city is dotted with statues and museums relating to him (starting with the main street in Ajaccio, cours Napoléon).

👁 Sights & Activities

Kiosks on the quayside opposite place du Maréchal Foch sell tickets for seasonal **boat trips** around the Golfe d'Ajaccio and **Îles Sanguinaires** (adult/child €25/15), and excursions to the **Réserve Naturelle de Scandola** (adult/child €55/35).

Palais Fesch – Musée des Beaux-Arts ART MUSEUM

(www.musee-fesch.com; 50-52 rue du Cardinal Fesch; adult/child €8/5; ☉ 10.30am-6pm Mon, Wed & Sat, noon-6pm Thu, Fri & Sun May-Sep, to 5pm Oct-Apr) One of the island's must-sees, this superb museum established by Napoléon's uncle has France's largest collection of Italian paintings outside the Louvre. Mostly the works of minor or anonymous 14th- to 19th-century artists, there are also canvases by Titian, Fra Bartolomeo, Veronese, Botticelli and Bellini. Look out for *La Vierge à l'Enfant Soutenu par un Ange* (Mother and Child Supported by an Angel), one of Botticelli's masterpieces. The museum also houses temporary exhibitions.

Maison Bonaparte HOUSE MUSEUM

(🗷 04 95 21 43 89; www.musees-nationaux-napoleoniens.org; rue St-Charles; adult/child €7/free; ☉ 10.30am-12.30pm & 1.15-6pm Tue-Sun Apr-Sep, to 4.30pm Oct-Mar) Napoléon spent his first nine years in this house. Ransacked by Corsican nationalists in 1793, requisitioned by English troops from 1794 to 1796, and eventually rebuilt by Napoléon's mother, the house became a place of pilgrimage for French revolutionaries. It hosts memorabilia of the emperor and his siblings, including a glass medallion containing a lock of his hair. A comprehensive audioguide (€2) is available in several languages.

🛏 Sleeping & Eating

Hôtel Marengo HOTEL €

(🗷 04 95 21 43 66; www.hotel-marengo.com; 2 rue Marengo; d/tr €90/110; ☉ Apr-Oct; ❄️🛜) For something near to the sand, try this charmingly eccentric small hotel. Rooms have a balcony, there's a quiet flower-filled courtyard and reception is an agreeable clutter of tasteful prints and personal objects. Find it down a cul-de-sac off bd Madame Mère.

⭐**Hôtel Demeure Les Mouettes** BOUTIQUE HOTEL €€€

(🗷 04 95 50 40 40; www.hotellesmouettes.fr; 9 cours Lucien Bonaparte; d €160-340; ☉ Apr-Oct; ❄️🏊🛜) This peach-coloured 19th-century colonnaded mansion right on the water's edge is a dream. Views of the bay of Ajaccio from the (heated) pool and terrace are exquisite: dolphins can often be spotted very early in the morning or in the evenings. Inside, the decor is one of understated elegance and service is 4 stars.

Don Quichotte   BRASSERIE €
(✏ 04 95 21 27 30; 7 rue des Halles; mains €10-18; ☺ noon-2pm & 7-11pm Mon-Sat) Tucked behind the fish market, this inconspicuous brasserie is something of a hidden gem: the cuisine is light, fresh and generous, and an absolute bargain. Don't miss the fabulous *moules à la Corse* (Corsican-style mussels: tomato, cream, pancetta, onion, chestnut) with homemade fries – simply divine.

A Nepita   BISTRO €€
(✏ 04 95 26 75 68; 4 rue San Lazaro; 2-/3-course menu €24/29; ☺ noon-2pm Mon-Fri, 8-10pm Thu-Sat) Ajaccio's rising culinary star is winning plaudits and loyal followers for its modern French cuisine and elegant setting. It's a nice change from hearty traditional Corsican fare, although the island isn't forgotten: the menu changes daily and uses only the freshest local products, including seasonal seafood and vegetables.

ℹ Information

Tourist Office (✏ 04 95 51 53 03; www.ajaccio-tourisme.com; 3 bd du Roi Jérôme; ☺ 8am-7pm Mon-Sat, 9am-1pm Sun; 🖥)

ℹ Getting There & Away

AIR
Bus 8 (€4.50, 20 minutes) links **Aéroport d'Ajaccio Napoléon Bonaparte** (www.2a.cci.fr/Aeroport-Napoleon-Bonaparte-Ajaccio.html), 8km east, with Ajaccio's train and bus stations.

BOAT
Boats to/from Toulon, Nice and Marseille depart from Ajaccio's **Terminal Maritime et Routier** (✏ 04 95 51 55 45; quai L'Herminier).

BUS
Local bus companies have ticket kiosks inside the ferry terminal building, the arrival/departure point for buses.

TRAIN
From the **train station** (place de la Gare), services include Bastia (€21.60, four hours, five daily).

Bastia

POP 43,539

The bustling old port of Bastia has an irresistible magnetism. Allow yourself at least a day to drink in the narrow old-town alleyways of Terra Vecchia, the seething Vieux Port, the dramatic 16th-century citadel perched up high, and the compelling history museum.

⊙ Sights & Activities

Terra Vecchia   HISTORIC QUARTER
A spiderweb of narrow lanes, Terra Vecchia is Bastia's heart and soul. Shady **place de l'Hôtel de Ville** hosts a lively morning market on Saturday and Sunday. One block west, baroque **Chapelle de l'Immaculée Conception** (rue des Terrasses), with its elaborately painted barrel-vaulted ceiling, briefly served as the seat of the short-lived Anglo-Corsican parliament in 1795. Further north is **Chapelle St-Roch** (rue Napoléon), with an 18th-century organ and trompe l'œil roof.

Vieux Port   PORT
Bastia's Vieux Port is ringed by pastel-coloured tenements and buzzy brasseries, as well as the twin-towered **Église St-Jean Baptiste** (4 rue du Cardinal Viale Préla). The best views of the harbour are from the hillside

FRANCE BASTIA

FRENCH TOWNS WORTH A VISIT

We couldn't possibly squeeze the whole of France into one chapter, so here are some more towns and regions worth considering for longer stays.

Alta Rocca Corsica may be an island, but its cultural heart is its mountainous hinterland.

Annecy A postcard-perfect medieval town with alpine landscapes in the background.

Arras Exceptional Flemish architecture and subterranean WWI sites.

Beaujolais An area known for its fruity red wines, and Beaujolais Nouveau (young wine drunk at just six weeks).

Cathar fortresses Travel back to the Middle Ages among Languedoc's crumbling fortresses.

Étretat Admire Mother Nature's work of art on Étretat's chalk-white cliffs.

Luberon Explore Provence's famed rolling hills and hilltop villages.

park of **Jardin Romieu**, reached via a gorgeous old stately staircase that twists uphill from the waterfront.

Terra Nova   HISTORIC QUARTER
Above Jardin Romieu looms Bastia's amber-hued citadel, built from the 15th to 17th centuries as a stronghold for the city's Genoese masters. Inside, the Palais des Gouverneurs houses the **Musée de Bastia** (☑ 04 95 31 09 12; www.musee-bastia.com; place du Donjon; adult/child €5/2.50; ⊙ 10am-6pm Tue-Sun Apr-Oct, shorter hours rest of year), which retraces the city's history. A few streets south, don't miss the majestic **Cathédrale Ste-Marie** (rue de l'Évêché) and nearby **Église Ste-Croix** (rue de l'Évêché), featuring gilded ceilings and a mysterious black-oak crucifix found in the sea in 1428.

🛏 Sleeping & Eating

Hôtel Central   HOTEL €€
(☑ 04 95 31 69 72; www.centralhotel.fr; 3 rue Miot; s/d/apt €80/90/150; 🌐 🛜) From the vintage, black-and-white tiled floor in the entrance to the sweeping staircase and eclectic jumble of plant pots in the minuscule interior courtyard, this family-run address oozes 1940s grace. The hotel's pedigree dates to 1941 and the vintage furnishings inside the 19th-century building don't disappoint. The three apartments, with fully equipped kitchen, are great for longer stays.

★ Raugi   ICE CREAM €
(www.raugi.com; 2 rue du Chanoine Colombani; ice cream from €2; ⊙ 9.30am-midnight Tue-Sat Oct-May, 9.30am-12.30pm & 2.30pm-1am Mon-Sat Jun-Sep) Going strong since 1937, Raugi is a Bastia institution. Flavours range from bog-standard raspberry, lemon and so on to Corsican chestnut, mandarin, fig, aromatic *senteur de maquis* (scent of Corsican herbal scrubland) and sweet *myrte* (myrtle). The *verrines glacées* (ice-cream desserts, €4.70) are out of this world.

Le Lavezzi   MODERN FRENCH €€
(☑ 04 95 31 05 73; 8 rue St-Jean; mains €21-35, lunch menus €22) A boutique address that design-loving gourmets will love: think turquoise polished concrete floor and brightly coloured Alexander McQueen–style chairs – fabulous and funky. The real heart stealer is the twinset of 1st-floor balconies above the water with prime old-port views. Modern cuisine injects a fusion zest into classic meat and fish dishes.

❶ Information

Tourist Office (☑ 04 95 54 20 40; www.bastia-tourisme.com; place St-Nicolas; ⊙ 8am-6pm Mon-Sat, to noon Sun; 🛜) Organises guided tours of the city and has plenty of information about Cap Corse.

❶ Getting There & Away

AIR
Aéroport Bastia-Poretta (www.bastia.aeroport.fr), 24km south, is linked by bus (€9, 35 minutes, 10 daily) with the Préfecture building in town.

BOAT
Ferry companies have information offices at **Bastia port** (www.bastia.port.fr); they are usually open for same-day ticket sales a couple of hours before sailings. Ferries sail to/from Marseille, Toulon and Nice (mainland France), and Livorno, Savona, Piombino and Genoa (Italy).

BUS & TRAIN
The **bus station** (1 rue du Nouveau Port) is north of place St-Nicolas. Additional bus stops are scattered around town. There are daily train services to Ajaccio (€21.60, four hours, five daily).

Bonifacio
POP 2994

With its glittering harbour, dramatic perch atop creamy white cliffs, and a stout citadel teetering above the cornflower-blue waters of the Bouches de Bonifacio, this dazzling port is an essential stop. Just a short hop from Sardinia, Bonifacio has a distinctly Italianate feel: sun-bleached town houses, dangling washing lines and murky chapels cram the web of alleyways of the old citadel, while, down below on the harbourside, brasseries and boat kiosks tout their wares to the droves of day trippers.

◉ Sights

★ Citadel   HISTORIC QUARTER
(Haute Ville) Much of Bonifacio's charm comes from strolling the citadel's shady streets, several spanned by arched aqueducts designed to collect rainwater to fill the communal cistern opposite **Église Ste-Marie Majeure**. From the marina, the paved steps of **montée du Rastello** and **montée St-Roch** bring you up to the citadel's old gateway, **Porte de Gênes**, complete with an original 16th-century drawbridge.

👉 Tours

SPMB   BOAT TOUR
(☎04 95 10 97 50; www.spmbonifacio.com; Port de Bonifacio) Don't leave Bonifacio without taking a boat trip around its extraordinary coastline, where you'll get the best perspective of the town's precarious position on top of the magnificent chalky cliffs. The one-hour itinerary (adult/child €17.50/12) includes several *calanques* (deep rocky inlets), views of the Escalier du Roi d'Aragon and the **Grotte du Sdragonato** (Little Dragon Cave), a vast watery cave with a natural rooftop skylight.

🛏 Sleeping & Eating

Hôtel Le Colomba   HOTEL €€
(☎04 95 73 73 44; www.hotel-bonifacio-corse.fr; rue Simon Varsi; d €112-147; ⊘Mar-Nov; ❃ 🛜) Occupying a tastefully renovated 14th-century building, this beautiful hotel is a delightful address in a picturesque (steep) street, bang in the heart of the old town. Rooms are simple and smallish, but fresh and pleasantly individual: wrought-iron bedsteads and country fabrics in some, carved bedheads and checkerboard tiles in others. Breakfast in a vaulted room is another highlight.

Kissing Pigs   CORSICAN €
(☎04 95 73 56 09; 15 quai Banda del Ferro; mains €11-20) Soothingly positioned by the harbour, this widely acclaimed restaurant and wine bar serves savoury fare in a seductively cosy interior, complete with wooden fixtures and swinging sausages. It's famed for its cheese and charcuterie platters; for the indecisive, the combination *moitié-moitié* (half-half) is perfect. The Corsican wine list is another hit.

ℹ Information

Tourist Office (☎04 95 73 11 88; www.bonifacio.fr; 2 rue Fred Scamaroni; ⊘9am-7pm mid-Apr–mid-Oct, 10am-5pm Mon-Fri mid-Oct–mid-Apr; 🛜)

ℹ Getting There & Away

AIR
A taxi into town from **Aéroport de Figari-Sud-Corse** (www.2a.cci.fr/Aeroport-Figari-Sud-Corse.html), 20km north, costs about €45.

BOAT
Sardinia's main ferry operators, **Moby** (www.moby.it) and **Saremar** (www.saremar.it), run seasonal boats between Bonifacio and Santa Teresa Gallura (Sardinia); sailing time is 50 minutes.

SURVIVAL GUIDE

ℹ Directory A–Z

ACCOMMODATION
Many tourist offices make room reservations, often for a fee of €5; many only do so if you stop by in person. In the French Alps, ski-resort tourist offices operate a central reservation service.

B&Bs
For charm, a heartfelt *bienvenue* (welcome) and home cooking, it's hard to beat a *chambre d'hôte* (B&B). Pick up lists at local tourist offices or online.

Fleurs de Soleil (www.fleursdesoleil.fr) Selective collection of 550 stylish *maisons d'hôte*, mainly in rural France.

Gîtes de France (www.gites-de-france.com) France's primary umbrella organisation for B&Bs and self-catering properties (*gîtes*). Search by region, theme (charm, with kids, by the sea, gourmet, great garden etc), activity (fishing, wine tasting etc) or facilities (pool, dishwasher, fireplace, baby equipment etc).

Samedi Midi Éditions (www.samedimidi.com) Country, mountain, seaside... Choose your *chambre d'hôte* by location or theme (romance, golf, design, cooking courses).

Camping
➜ Most campgrounds open March or April to October.

➜ Euro-economisers should look for good-value but no-frills *campings municipaux* (municipal camping grounds).

➜ Accessing campgrounds without your own transport can be difficult in many areas.

➜ Camping in nondesignated spots (*camping sauvage*) is illegal in France.

FRANCE DIRECTORY A–Z

COUNTRY FACTS

Area 551,000 sq km

Capital Paris

Country Code ☎33

Currency Euro (€)

Emergency ☎112

Language French

Money ATMs everywhere

Visas Schengen rules apply

SLEEPING PRICE RANGES

Our reviews refer to the cost of a double room with private bathroom, except in hostels or where otherwise specified. Quoted rates are for high season and exclude breakfast unless otherwise noted:

€ less than €90 (€130 in Paris)

€€ €90 to €190 (€130 to €200 in Paris)

€€€ more than €190 (€200 in Paris)

Websites with listings searchable by location and facilities include:

Camping en France (www.camping.fr)

Camping France (www.campingfrance.com)

HPA Guide (http://camping.hpaguide.com)

Hostels

Hostels range from funky to threadbare.

➡ A dorm bed in an *auberge de jeunesse* (youth hostel) costs €20 to €50 in Paris, and anything from €15 to €35 in the provinces; sheets are always included and often breakfast, too.

➡ To prevent outbreaks of bed bugs, sleeping bags are no longer permitted.

➡ All hostels are nonsmoking.

Hotels

➡ French hotels almost never include breakfast in their advertised nightly rates.

➡ Hotels in France are rated with one to five stars; ratings are based on objective criteria (eg size of entry hall), not service, decor or cleanliness.

➡ A double room has one double bed (or two singles pushed together); a room with twin beds is more expensive, as is a room with bathtub instead of shower.

ACTIVITIES

From glaciers, rivers and canyons in the Alps to porcelain-smooth cycling trails in the Dordogne and Loire Valley – not to mention 3200km of coastline stretching from Italy to Spain and from the Basque country to the Straits of Dover – France's landscapes are ripe for exhilarating outdoor escapes.

➡ The French countryside is criss-crossed by a staggering 120,000km of *sentiers balisés* (marked walking paths), which pass through every imaginable terrain in every region of the country. No permit is needed to hike.

➡ The best-known trails are the *sentiers de grande randonnée* (GR), long-distance paths marked by red-and-white-striped track indicators.

➡ For complete details on regional activities, courses, equipment rental, clubs, companies and organisations, contact local tourist offices.

BUSINESS HOURS

➡ French business hours are regulated by a maze of government regulations, including the 35-hour working week.

➡ The midday break is uncommon in Paris but, in general, gets longer the further south you go.

➡ French law requires most businesses to close Sunday; exceptions include grocery stores, *boulangeries,* florists and businesses catering to the tourist trade.

➡ In many places shops close on Monday.

➡ Many service stations open 24 hours a day and stock basic groceries.

➡ Restaurants generally close one or two days of the week.

➡ Museums tend to close on Monday or Tuesday.

➡ Standard hours are as follows:

Banks 9am to noon, 2 to 5pm Monday to Friday or Tuesday to Saturday

Bars 7pm to 1am Monday to Saturday

Cafes 7am or 8am to 10pm or 11pm Monday to Saturday

Club 10pm to 3am, 4am or 5am Thusday to Saturday

Post offices 8.30am or 9am to 5pm or 6pm Monday to Friday, 8am to noon Saturday

Restaurants noon to 2.30pm (or 3pm in Paris), 7pm to 11pm (or 10pm to midnight in Paris)

Shops 9am or 10am to 7pm Monday to Saturday (often closed noon to 1.30pm)

Supermarkets 8.30am to 7pm Monday to Saturday, to 12.30pm Sunday

GAY & LESBIAN TRAVELLERS

The rainbow flag flies high in France, one of Europe's most liberal countries when it comes to homosexuality.

➡ Paris has been a thriving gay and lesbian centre since the late 1970s.

➡ Bordeaux, Lille, Lyon, Toulouse and many other towns have active communities.

➡ Attitudes towards homosexuality tend to be more conservative in the countryside and villages.

➡ Same-sex marriage has been legal in France since May 2013.

➡ Gay Pride marches are held in major French cities from mid-May to early July.

Online, try the following websites:

France Queer Resources Directory (www.france.qrd.org) Gay and lesbian directory.

Gaipied (www.gayvox.com/guide3) Online travel guide to France, with listings by region, by Gayvox.

INTERNET RESOURCES

France 24 (www.france24.com/en/france) French news in English.

Paris by Mouth (http://parisbymouth.com) Capital dining and drinking.

Rendez-Vous en France (www.rendezvousenfrance.com) Official French government tourist office website.

Wine Travel Guides (www.winetravelguides.com) Practical guides to France's wine regions.

LANGUAGE COURSES

➨ All manner of French-language courses are available in Paris and provincial towns and cities; most also arrange accommodation.

➨ Prices and courses vary greatly; the content can often be tailored to your specific needs (for a fee).

➨ The website www.europa-pages.com/france lists language schools in France.

Alliance Française (Map p186; www.alliancefr.org; 101 bd Raspail, 6e, Paris; Ⓜ St-Placide) French courses (minimum one week) for all levels. *Intensif* courses meet for four hours a day five days a week; *extensif* courses involve nine hours' tuition a week.

Eurocentres (www.eurocentres.com) This affiliation of small, well-organised schools has three addresses in France: in Amboise in the charming Loire Valley, in La Rochelle and Paris.

LEGAL MATTERS

➨ French police have wide powers of stop-and-search and can demand proof of identity at any time.

➨ Foreigners must be able to prove their legal status in France (eg passport, visa, residency permit).

➨ French law doesn't distinguish between hard and soft drugs; penalties can be severe (including fines and jail sentences).

MONEY

Credit and debit cards are accepted almost everywhere in France.

➨ Some places (eg 24-hour petrol stations and some *autoroute* toll machines) only take credit cards with chips and PINs.

➨ In Paris and major cities, *bureaux de change* (exchange bureaus) are fast and easy, are open long hours and offer competitive exchange rates.

For lost cards, call your credit card company:

Amex (☑ 01 47 77 70 00)

MasterCard (☑ 08 00 90 13 87)

Visa (Carte Bleue; ☑ 08 00 90 11 79)

PUBLIC HOLIDAYS

The following *jours fériés* (public holidays) are observed in France:

New Year's Day (Jour de l'An) 1 January

Easter Sunday & Monday (Pâques & Lundi de Pâques) Late March/April

May Day (Fête du Travail) 1 May

Victoire 1945 8 May – WWII armistice

Ascension Thursday (Ascension) May – celebrated on the 40th day after Easter

Pentecost/Whit Sunday & Whit Monday (Pentecôte & Lundi de Pentecôte) Mid-May to mid-June – celebrated on the seventh Sunday after Easter

Bastille Day/National Day (Fête Nationale) 14 July – *the* national holiday

Assumption Day (Assomption) 15 August

All Saints' Day (Toussaint) 1 November

Remembrance Day (L'onze Novembre) 11 November – WWI armistice

Christmas (Noël) 25 December

TELEPHONE

Mobile Phones

➨ French mobile phone numbers begin with ☑ 06 or ☑ 07.

➨ France uses GSM 900/1800, which is compatible with the rest of Europe and Australia but not with the North American GSM 1900 or the totally different system in Japan (though some North Americans have tri-band phones that work here).

➨ It is usually cheaper to buy a local SIM card from a French provider such as Orange, SFR, Bouygues and Free Mobile than to use international roaming. To do this, ensure your phone is 'unlocked'.

➨ Recharge cards are sold at most *tabacs* (tobacconist-newsagents) and supermarkets.

Phone Codes & Useful Numbers

Calling France from abroad Dial your country's international access code, then ☑ 33 (France's country code), then the 10-digit local number *without* the initial zero.

Calling internationally from France Dial ☑ 00 (the international access code), the *indicatif* (country code), the area code (without the initial zero if there is one) and the local number.

Directory inquiries For national *service des renseignements* (directory inquiries) dial ☑ 11 87 12 or use the service for free online at www.118712.fr.

Emergency numbers Can be dialled from public phones without a phonecard.

VISAS

For up-to-date details on visa requirements, check the **Ministère des Affaires Étrangères** (Ministry of Foreign Affairs; Map p186; www.diplomatie.gouv.fr; 37 quai d'Orsay, 7e).

ESSENTIAL FOOD & DRINK

When you think of France it is pretty easy to start drooling over its world-renowned cuisine. Here are some taste sensations to get your mouth watering:

➡ **Fondue & raclette** Warming cheese dishes in the French Alps.

➡ **Oysters & white wine** Everywhere on the Atlantic coast, but especially in Cancale and Bordeaux.

➡ **Bouillabaisse** Marseille's signature hearty fish stew, eaten with croutons and *rouille* (garlic-and-chilli mayonnaise).

➡ **Foie gras & truffles** The Dordogne features goose and 'black diamonds' from December to March. Provence is also good for indulging in the aphrodisiacal fungi.

➡ **Piggy-part cuisine** Lyon is famous for its juicy *andouillette* (pig-intestine sausage), a perfect marriage with a local Côtes du Rhône red.

➡ **Champagne** Tasting in century-old cellars is an essential part of Champagne's bubbly experience.

➡ **Bordeaux & Burgundy wines** You'll find France's signature reds in every restaurant; now find out more by touring the vineyards.

Visa requirements:

➡ EU nationals and citizens of Iceland, Norway and Switzerland need only a passport or national identity card to enter France and stay in the country, even for stays of over 90 days. Citizens of new EU member states may be subject to various limitations on living and working in France.

➡ Citizens of Australia, the USA, Canada, Israel, Hong Kong, Japan, Malaysia, New Zealand, Singapore, South Korea and many Latin American countries do not need visas to visit France as tourists for up to 90 days. For longer stays of over 90 days, contact your nearest French embassy or consulate.

➡ Other people wishing to come to France as tourists have to apply for a Schengen Visa.

➡ Tourist visas cannot be changed into student visas after arrival. However, short-term visas are available for students sitting university-entrance exams in France.

➡ Citizens of Australia, Canada, Japan and New Zealand aged between 18 and 30 are eligible for a 12-month, multiple-entry **Working Holiday Visa** (Permis Vacances Travail).

EATING PRICE RANGES

Price ranges refer to a two-course meal.

€ less than €20

€€ €20 to €40

€€€ more than €40

Getting There & Away

AIR

International airports include the following; there are many smaller ones serving European destinations only.

Aéroport de Charles de Gaulle (CDG; www.aeroportsdeparis.fr)

Aéroport d'Orly (www.aeroportsdeparis.fr)

Aéroport Marseille-Provence (MRS; ☑ 04 42 14 14 14; www.marseille.aeroport.fr)

Aéroport Nice Côte d'Azur (http://societe.nice.aeroport.fr)

LAND

Bus

Eurolines (☑ 08 92 89 90 91; www.eurolines.eu), a grouping of 32 long-haul coach operators, links France with cities all across Europe and in Morocco and Russia. Discounts are available to people under 26 and over 60. Make advance reservations, especially in July and August.

Car & Motorcycle

A right-hand-drive vehicle brought to France from the UK or Ireland must have deflectors affixed to the headlights to avoid dazzling oncoming traffic.

Departing from the UK, **Eurotunnel Le Shuttle** (☑ in France 08 10 63 03 04, in UK 08443-35 35 35; www.eurotunnel.com) trains whisk bicycles, motorcycles, cars and coaches in 35 minutes from Folkestone through the Channel Tunnel to Coquelles, 5km southwest of Calais. Shuttles run 24 hours a day, with up to three departures an hour during peak periods. The earlier you book, the less you pay. Fares for a car, including up to nine passengers, start at €30.

Train

→ Rail services – including a dwindling number of overnight services to/from Spain, Italy and Germany, and Eurostar services to/from the UK – link France with virtually every country in Europe.

→ Book tickets and get train information from **Rail Europe** (www.raileurope.com). In France, ticketing is handled by **SNCF** (www.voyages-sncf.com); internet bookings are possible, but it won't post tickets outside France.

SEA

Regular ferries travel to France from the UK, Ireland and Italy.

Brittany Ferries (www.brittany-ferries.co.uk) Links between England/Ireland and Brittany and Normandy.

P&O Ferries (www.poferries.com) Ferries between England and northern France.

SNCM (www.sncm.fr) Ferries between France and Sardinia.

ⓘ Getting Around

AIR

Air France (www.airfrance.com) and its subsidiaries **Hop!** (www.hop.com) and **Transavia** (www.transavia.com) control the lion's share of France's domestic airline industry.

Budget carriers offering flights within France include **EasyJet** (www.easyjet.com), **Twin Jet** (www.twinjet.net) and **Air Corsica** (www.air corsica.com).

BUS

Buses are widely used for short-distance travel within *départements,* especially in rural areas with relatively few train lines (eg Brittany and Normandy). Unfortunately, services in some regions are infrequent and slow, in part because they were designed to get children to school rather than transport visitors around the countryside.

BICYCLE

France is a great place to cycle, and French train company SNCF does its best to make travelling with a bicycle easy; see www.velo.sncf.com for full details.

Most French cities and towns have at least one bike shop that rents out mountain bikes (VTT; around €15 a day), road bikes (VTCs) and cheaper city bikes. You have to leave ID and/or a deposit (often a credit-card slip) that you forfeit if the bike is damaged or stolen. A growing number of cities have automatic bike-rental systems.

CAR & MOTORCYCLE

A car gives you exceptional freedom and allows you to visit more remote parts of France. But it can be expensive and, in cities, parking and traffic are frequently a major headache. Motorcyclists will find France great for touring, with winding roads of good quality and lots of stunning scenery.

→ All drivers must carry a national ID card or passport; a valid driving licence (*permis de conduire;* most foreign licences can be used in France for up to a year); car-ownership papers, known as a *carte grise* (grey card); and proof of third-party (liability) insurance.

→ Many French motorways (*autoroutes*) are fitted with toll (*péage*) stations that charge a fee based on the distance you've travelled; factor in these costs when driving.

→ To hire a car you'll usually need to be over 21 and in possession of a valid driving licence and a credit card. Automatic transmissions are very rare in France; you'll need to order one well in advance.

TRAIN

France's superb rail network is operated by the state-owned **SNCF** (www.sncf.com); many rural towns not on the SNCF train network are served by SNCF buses.

→ The flagship trains on French railways are the superfast TGVs, which reach speeds in excess of 200mph and can whisk you from Paris to the Côte d'Azur in as little as three hours.

→ Before boarding any train, you must validate (*composter*) your ticket by time-stamping it in a

---

CONNECTIONS

→ High-speed trains link Paris' Gare du Nord with London's St Pancras (via the Channel Tunnel/Eurostar rail service) in just over two hours; Gare du Nord is also the point of departure for speedy trains to Brussels, Amsterdam and Cologne.

→ Many more trains make travelling between the French capital and pretty much any city in every neighbouring country a real pleasure.

→ Regular bus and rail links cross the French–Spanish border via the Pyrenees, and the French–Italian border via the Alps and the southern Mediterranean coast.

SNCF TRAIN FARES & DISCOUNTS

The Basics

➡ 1st-class travel, where available, costs 20% to 30% extra.

➡ Ticket prices for some trains, including most TGVs, are pricier during peak periods.

➡ The further in advance you reserve, the lower the fares.

➡ Children under four travel for free (€9 to any destination if they need a seat).

➡ Children aged four to 11 travel for half price.

Discount Tickets

Prem's The SNCF's most heavily discounted, use-or-lose tickets are sold online, by phone and at ticket windows/machines a maximum of 90 days and a minimum of 14 days before you travel.

Bons Plans A grab-bag of cheap options for different routes/dates, advertised online under the tab 'Dernière Minute' (Last Minute).

iDTGV Cheap tickets on advance-purchase TGV travel between about 30 cities; only sold at www.idtgv.com.

Discount Cards

Reductions of 25% to 60% are available with several discount cards (valid for one year):

Carte Jeune (€50) Available to travellers aged 12 to 27.

Carte Enfant+ (€75) For one to four adults travelling with a child aged four to 11.

Carte Sénior+ (€50) For travellers over 60.

composteur, one of those yellow posts located on the way to the platform.

Rail Passes

Residents of Europe (who do not live in France) can purchase an **InterRail One Country Pass** (www.interrailnet.com; 3/4/6/8 days €216/237/302/344, 12-25yr €147/157/199/222), which entitles its bearer to unlimited travel on SNCF trains for three to eight days over the course of a month.

For non-European residents, Rail Europe (p255) offers the **France Rail Pass** (www.francerailpass.com; 3/6/9 days over 1 month €211/301/388).

You need to really rack up the kilometres to make these passes worthwhile.

Germany

Best Castles & Palaces

➡ Schloss Neuschwanstein (p292)

➡ Burg Eltz (p311)

➡ Wartburg (p281)

➡ Schloss Sanssouci (p272)

Best Iconic Sights

➡ Brandenburger Tor (Gate) (p261)

➡ Holstentor (p325)

➡ Kölner Dom (p312)

➡ Frauenkirche (p275)

Why Go?

Prepare for a roller coaster of feasts, treats and temptations as you take in Germany's soul-stirring scenery, spirit-lifting culture, old and bold architecture, big-city beauties, romantic castles and towns with half-timbered buildings.

Few countries have had as much impact on the world as Germany, which has given us the printing press, the automobile, aspirin and MP3 technology. This is the birthplace of Martin Luther, Albert Einstein and Karl Marx, of Bach, Beethoven, the Brothers Grimm and other heavyweights who have left their mark on human history.

Germany's story-book landscapes will also likely leave an even bigger imprint on your memories. There's something undeniably artistic in the way the scenery unfolds from the windswept maritime north to the off-the-charts splendour of the Alps. As much fun as it may be to rev up the engines on the autobahn, do slow down to better appreciate this complex and fascinating country.

When to Go
Berlin

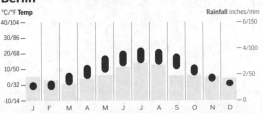

Jun–Aug Warm summers cause Germans to shed their clothes; night never seems to come.

Sep Radiant foliage and sunny skies invite outdoor pursuits, with festivals (Oktoberfest!) galore.

Dec It's icy, it's cold but lines are short and Alpine slopes and twinkly Christmas markets beckon.

Germany Highlights

1 Discover your inner party animal in **Berlin** (p260); save sleep for somewhere else as there's no time here with the clubs, museums, bars and ever-changing zeitgeist.

2 Time your journey for **Oktoberfest** (p283), Munich's bacchanal of suds, or just soak up the vibe in a beer garden.

3 Go slow in Germany's alluring small towns like **Bamberg** (p297), with winding lanes, smoked beer (!) and a lack of cliché.

4 Compare the soaring peaks of the Dom in **Cologne** (p312) with the slinky glasses of the city's famous beer.

5 Go cuckoo in the **Black Forest** (p299), discovering

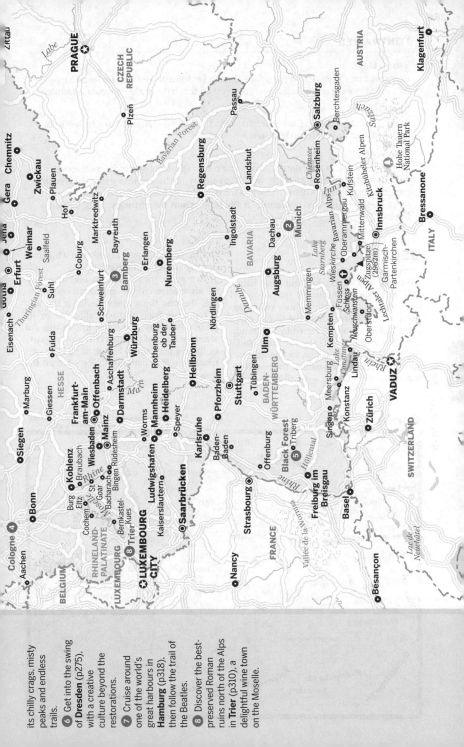

its chilly crags, misty peaks and endless trails.

6 Get into the swing of **Dresden** (p275), with a creative culture beyond the restorations.

7 Cruise around one of the world's great harbours in **Hamburg** (p318), then follow the trail of the Beatles.

8 Discover the best-preserved Roman ruins north of the Alps in **Trier** (p310), a delightful wine town on the Moselle.

ITINERARIES

Three Days

Come on, that's all you got? If the answer is really yes, drive the **Romantic Road**, stopping in Rothenburg ob der Tauber and Füssen, then spend the rest of your time in **Munich**.

Five Days

Spend a couple of days in **Berlin**, head down to **Dresden** and **Nuremberg** for half a day each and wrap up your trip in **Munich**.

One Week

This gives you a little bit of time to tailor a tour beyond the highlights mentioned above. Art fans might want to build **Cologne** or **Düsseldorf** into their itinerary; romantics could consider **Heidelberg**, a Rhine cruise or a trip down the **Romantic Road**; while nature types are likely to be lured by **Garmisch-Partenkirchen**, **Berchtesgaden** or the **Black Forest**.

BERLIN

☎ 030 / POP 3.5 MILLION

Bismarck and Marx, Einstein and Hitler, JFK and Bowie, they've all shaped – and been shaped by – Berlin, whose richly textured history stares you in the face at every turn. You might be distracted by the trendy, edgy, gentrified streets, by the bars bleeding a laid-back cool factor, by the galleries sprouting talent and pushing the envelope, but make no mistake – reminders of the German capital's past assault you while modernity sits around the corner.

Renowned for its diversity and tolerance, its alternative culture and night-owl stamina, the best thing about Berlin is the way it reinvents itself and isn't shackled by its unique past. And the world knows this – a steady stream of Germans from other parts of the country and a league of global expatriates are flocking here to see what all the fuss is about.

GERMANY BERLIN

Berlin

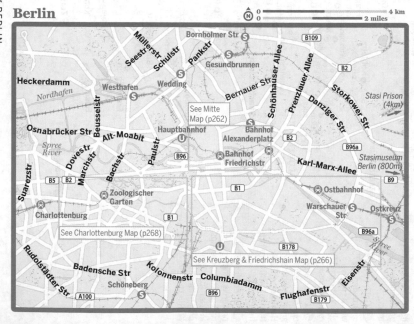

⊙ Sights

Key sights like the Reichstag, the Brandenburger Tor, Fernsehturm and Museumsinsel cluster in the historic city centre – **Mitte**. It also encompasses the maze-like historic Jewish quarter around Hackescher Markt, which now teems with fashionable boutiques, bars and restaurants. North of here, residential **Prenzlauer Berg** has a lively cafe and restaurant scene, while to the south loom the contemporary high-rises of **Potsdamer Platz**. Further south, gritty but cool **Kreuzberg** is party central, as is student-flavoured **Friedrichshain** east across the Spree River. Western Berlin's hub is **Charlottenburg**, with great shopping and a swish royal palace.

⊙ Historic Mitte

★ Reichstag   HISTORIC BUILDING
(Map p262; www.bundestag.de; Platz der Republik 1, Service Center: Scheidemannstrasse; ⊘ lift ride 8am-midnight, last entry 11pm, Service Center 8am-8pm Apr-Oct, to 6pm Nov-Mar; 🚌 100, ⑤ Bundestag, ⑱ Hauptbahnhof, Brandenburger Tor) **FREE** One of Berlin's most iconic buildings, the 1894 Reichstag was burned, bombed, rebuilt, buttressed by the Berlin Wall, wrapped in fabric and eventually turned into the home of Germany's parliament, the Bundestag, by Lord Norman Foster. Its most distinctive feature, the glittering glass dome, is accessible by lift (reservations mandatory, see www.bundestag.de) and affords fabulous 360-degree city views. Those without a reservation can try scoring left-over tickets in the Service Center. Bring ID.

★ Brandenburger Tor & Pariser Platz
                                LANDMARK
(Map p262; Pariser Platz; ⊘ 24hr; ⑤ Brandenburger Tor, ⑱ Brandenburger Tor) **FREE** A symbol of division during the Cold War, the landmark Brandenburg Gate now epitomises German reunification. Modelled after the Acropolis in Athens, the triumphal arch was completed in 1791 as the royal city gate and is crowned by the Quadriga sculpture – a winged goddess of victory piloting a horse-drawn chariot.

Holocaust Memorial   MEMORIAL
(Memorial to the Murdered European Jews; Map p266; ☑ 030-2639 4336; www.stiftung-denkmal.de; Cora-Berliner-Strasse 1; audioguide adult/concession €4/2; ⊘ field 24hr, information centre 10am-8pm Tue-Sun Apr-Sep, to 7pm Oct-Mar, last entry 45min before closing; ⑤ Brandenburger Tor, ⑱ Brandenburger Tor) **FREE** Inaugurated in 2005, this football-field-sized memorial by American architect Peter Eisenman consists of 2711 sarcophagi-like concrete columns rising in sombre silence from undulating ground. You're free to access this maze at any point and make your individual journey through it. For context visit the subterranean **Ort der Information**; the exhibits will leave no one untouched. Audioguides are available.

Hitler's Bunker   HISTORIC SITE
(Map p266; cnr In den Ministergärten & Gertrud-Kolmar-Strasse; ⊘ 24hr; ⑤ Brandenburger Tor, ⑱ Brandenburger Tor) Berlin was burning and Soviet tanks were advancing relentlessly when Adolf Hitler committed suicide on 30 April 1945, alongside Eva Braun, his long-time female companion, hours after their marriage. Today, a parking lot covers the site, revealing its dark history only via

GERMANY BERLIN

BERLIN IN...

One Day

Book ahead for an early lift ride to the **Reichstag** dome, then snap a picture of the **Brandenburger Tor (Gate)** before stumbling around the **Holocaust Memorial** and admiring the contemporary architecture of **Potsdamer Platz**. Ponder Cold War madness at **Checkpoint Charlie**, then head to **Museumsinsel** to admire Queen Nefertiti and the Ishtar Gate. Finish up with a night of mirth and gaiety around **Hackescher Markt**.

Two Days

Kick off day two coming to grips with what life was like in divided Berlin at the **Gedenkstätte Berliner Mauer**. Intensify the experience at the **DDR Museum** or on a walk along the **East Side Gallery**. Spend the afternoon soaking up the urban spirit of **Kreuzberg** with its sassy shops and street art, grab dinner along the canal, drinks around Kottbusser Tor and finish up with a night of clubbing.

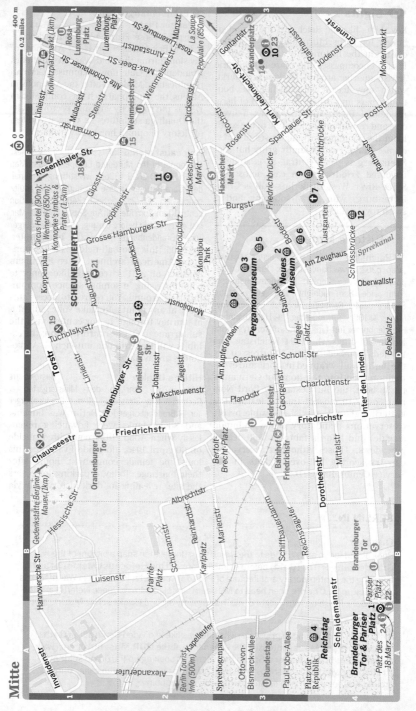

Mitte

Mitte

an information panel with a diagram of the vast bunker network, construction data and the site's post-WWII history.

Checkpoint Charlie HISTORIC SITE
(Map p266; cnr Zimmerstrasse & Friedrichstrasse; ⊙24hr; ⑤Kochstrasse, Stadtmitte) Checkpoint Charlie was the principal gateway for foreigners and diplomats between the two Berlins from 1961 to 1990. Unfortunately, this potent symbol of the Cold War has become a tacky tourist trap, although a free open-air exhibit that illustrates milestones in Cold War history is one redeeming aspect.

◉ Museumsinsel & Scheunenviertel

Museumsinsel (Museum Island) is Berlin's most important treasure trove, spanning 6000 years' worth of art, artefacts, sculp-ture and architecture from Europe and beyond. It segues into the Scheunenviertel (Barn Quarter), a compact and charismatic quarter filled with idyllic courtyards, bleeding-edge art galleries, local designer boutiques, shabby-chic bars and even a belle époque ballroom. Since reunification, the Scheunenviertel has also reprised its historic role as Berlin's main Jewish quarter.

★**Pergamonmuseum** MUSEUM
(Map p262; ☎030-266 424 242; www.smb. museum; Bodestrasse 1-3; adult/concession €12/6; ⊙10am-6pm Fri-Wed, to 8pm Thu; ☐100, ☒Hackescher Markt, Friedrichstrasse) Even while undergoing renovation, the Pergamonmuseum still opens a fascinating window onto the ancient world. The palatial three-wing complex unites a rich feast of classical sculpture and monumental architecture from Greece, Rome, Babylon and the Middle East, including such famous stunners as the radiant-blue **Ishtar Gate** from Babylon, the Roman **Market Gate of Miletus** and the **Caliph's Palace** of Mshatta. Note that the namesake Pergamon Altar will be off limits until 2019.

★**Neues Museum** MUSEUM
(New Museum; Map p262; ☎030-266 424 242; www.smb.museum; Bodestrasse 1-3; adult/concession €12/6; ⊙10am-6pm Fri-Wed, to 8pm Thu; ☐100, 200, ☒Hackescher Markt) David Chipperfield's reconstruction of the bombed-out Neues Museum is now the residence of Queen Nefertiti, the show-stopper of the Egyptian Museum that also features mummies, sculptures and sarcophagi. Pride of place of the Museum of Pre- and Early History in the same building goes to Trojan antiquities, a Neanderthal skull and a 3000-year-old gilded conical ceremonial hat. Museum tickets are only valid for admission during a designated half-hour time slot. Skip the queue by buying advance tickets online.

Berliner Dom CHURCH
(Berlin Cathedral; Map p262; ☎030-2026 9136; www.berlinerdom.de; Am Lustgarten; adult/concession/under 18yr €7/4/free; ⊙9am-8pm Sun Apr-Sep, to 7pm Oct-Mar; ☐100, 200, ☒Hackescher Markt) Pompous yet majestic, the Italian Renaissance–style former church of the royal court (1905) does triple duty as house of worship, museum and concert hall. Inside it's gilt to the hilt and outfitted with a lavish marble-and-onyx altar, a 7269-pipe Sauer organ and elaborate royal sarcophagi. Climb up the 267 steps to the gallery for glorious city views.

MORE MUSEUMSINSEL TREASURES

While the Pergamonmuseum and the Neues Museum are the highlights of Museumsinsel (Museum Island), the other three museums are no slouches in the treasure department either. Fronting the Lustgarten park the **Altes Museum** (Old Museum; Map p262; 030-266 424 242; www.smb.museum; Am Lustgarten; adult/concession €10/5; 10am-6pm Tue, Wed & Fri-Sun, to 8pm Thu; 100, 200, Friedrichstrasse, Hackescher Markt) presents Greek, Etruscan and Roman antiquities. At the northern tip of the island, the **Bodemuseum** (Map p262; 030-266 424 242; www.smb.museum; Am Kupfergraben/Monbijoubrücke; adult/concession €10/5; 10am-6pm Tue, Wed & Fri-Sun, to 8pm Thu; Hackescher Markt) has a prized collection of European sculpture from the Middle Ages to the 18th century. Finally, there's the **Alte Nationalgalerie** (Old National Gallery; Map p262; 030-266 424 242; www.smb.museum; Bodestrasse 1-3; adult/concession €10/5; 10am-6pm Tue, Wed & Fri-Sun, to 8pm Thu; 100, 200, Hackescher Markt), one thematic focus of which is on 19th-century European painting. A combined day pass for all five museums costs €18 (concession €9).

DDR Museum
MUSEUM

(GDR Museum; Map p262; 030-847 123 731; www.ddr-museum.de; Karl-Liebknecht-Strasse 1; adult/concession €6/4; 10am-8pm Sun-Fri, to 10pm Sat; ; 100, 200, Hackescher Markt) This interactive museum does a delightful job at pulling back the iron curtain on an extinct society. Find out that East German kids were put through collective potty training, engineers earned little more than farmers and everyone, it seems, went on nudist holidays. A highlight is a simulated ride in a Trabi.

Fernsehturm
LANDMARK

(TV Tower; Map p262; 030-247 575 875; www.tv-turm.de; Panoramastrasse 1a; adult/child €13/8.50, Fast View ticket €19.50/11.50; 9am-midnight Mar-Oct, 10am-midnight Nov-Feb; Alexanderplatz, Alexanderplatz) Germany's tallest structure, the 368m-high TV Tower is as iconic to Berlin as the Eiffel Tower is to Paris. On clear days, views from the panorama level at 203m are unbeatable. The upstairs Restaurant Sphere (mains €14 to €28) makes one revolution per hour. To skip the line, buy tickets online.

Hackesche Höfe
HISTORIC SITE

(Map p262; 030-2809 8010; www.hackesche-hoefe.com; Rosenthaler Strasse 40/41, Sophienstrasse 6; M1, Hackescher Markt) **FREE** Thanks to its congenial mix of cafes, galleries, boutiques and entertainment venues, this attractively restored complex of eight interlinked courtyards is hugely popular with the tourist brigade. **Court I**, festooned with patterned art nouveau tiles, is the prettiest. **Court VII** leads off to the romantic **Rosenhöfe**, a single courtyard with a sunken rose garden and tendril-like balustrades.

Neue Synagoge
SYNAGOGUE

(Map p262; 030-8802 8300; www.centrum judaicum.de; Oranienburger Strasse 28-30; adult/concession €3.50/3, dome €2/1.50; 10am-8pm Sun & Mon, to 6pm Tue-Thu, to 5pm Fri, 10am-6pm Sun & Mon Nov-Feb, 10am-2pm Fri Oct-Mar); Oranienburger Tor, Oranienburger Strasse) The original New Synagogue, finished in 1866 in what was then the predominantly Jewish part of the city, was Germany's largest synagogue at that time. It was destroyed in World War II and rebuilt after the Berlin Wall fell. Now this space doubles as a museum and cultural centre documenting local Jewish life.

Gedenkstätte Berliner Mauer
MEMORIAL

(Berlin Wall Memorial; 030-467 986 666; www.berliner-mauer-gedenkstaette.de; Bernauer Strasse btwn Schwedter Strasse & Gartenstrasse; visitor center 9.30am-7pm Apr-Oct, to 6pm Nov-Mar, open-air exhibit 8am-10pm; Nordbahnhof, Bernauer Strasse, Eberswalder Strasse) **FREE** The central memorial site of German division extends for 1.4km along Bernauer Strasse and incorporates a section of original Wall, vestiges of the border installations and escape tunnels, a chapel and a monument. It's the only place where you can see how border fortifications developed over time. Multimedia stations, 'archaeological windows' and markers provide context and details about events that took place along here. For a great overview climb up the viewing platform at the Documentation Centre near Ackerstrasse.

Potsdamer Platz & Tiergarten

Berlin newest quarter, Potsdamer Platz was forged in the 1990s from ground once bisected by the Berlin Wall and is a show-case of contemporary architecture, with Helmut Jahn's **Sony Center** being the most eye-catching structure.

The adjacent **Kulturforum** harbours art museums and the world-famous Berliner Philharmonie. With its rambling paths and hidden beer gardens, the Tiergarten, one of Europe's largest city parks, makes for a perfect sightseeing break.

★ **Gemäldegalerie** GALLERY
(Gallery of Paintings; Map p268; ☑ 030-266 424 242; www.smb.museum/gg; Matthäikirchplatz 8; adult/concession €10/5; ⏱ 10am-6pm Tue, Wed & Fri-Sun, to 8pm Thu; 🚌 M29, M41, 200, Ⓢ Potsdamer Platz, Ⓡ Potsdamer Platz) The principal Kulturforum museum boasts one of the world's finest and most comprehensive collections of European art from the 13th to the 18th centuries. Wear comfy shoes when exploring the 72 galleries: a walk past masterpieces by Rembrandt, Dürer, Hals, Vermeer, Gainsborough and many more old masters covers almost 2km.

Topographie des Terrors MUSEUM
(Topography of Terror; Map p266; ☑ 030-2548 0950; www.topographie.de; Niederkirchner Strasse 8; ⏱ 10am-8pm, grounds until dusk or 8pm latest; ♿; Ⓢ Potsdamer Platz, Ⓡ Potsdamer Platz) FREE In the same spot where the most feared institutions of Nazi Germany (including the Gestapo headquarters and the SS central command) once stood, this compelling exhibit chronicles the stages of terror and persecution, puts a face on the perpetrators and details the impact these brutal institutions had on all of Europe. A second exhibit outside zeroes in on how life changed for Berlin and its people after the Nazis made it their capital.

Kreuzberg & Friedrichshain

Kreuzberg has a split personality: while its western section (around Bergmannstrasse) has an upmarket, genteel air, eastern Kreuzberg (around Kottbusser Tor) is a multicultural mosaic and raucous nightlife hub. You'll find more after-dark action along with some Cold War relics (including Karl-Marx-Allee, East Berlin's showcase socialist boulevard) in student-flavoured Friedrichshain across the Spree.

East Side Gallery HISTORIC SITE
(Map p266; www.eastsidegallery-berlin.de; Mühlenstrasse btwn Oberbaumbrücke & Ostbahnhof; ⏱ 24hr; Ⓢ Warschauer Strasse, Ⓡ Ostbahnhof, Warschauer Strasse) FREE The year was 1989. After 28 years, the Berlin Wall, that grim and grey divider of humanity, finally met its maker. Most of it was quickly dismantled along the Spree, but a 1.3km stretch became the East Side Gallery, the world's largest open-air mural collection. In more than 100 paintings, dozens of international artists translated the era's global euphoria and optimism into a mix of political statements, drug-induced musings and truly artistic visions.

Jüdisches Museum MUSEUM
(Jewish Museum; Map p266; ☑ 030-2599 3300; www.jmberlin.de; Lindenstrasse 9-14; adult/concession €8/3; ⏱ 10am-10pm Mon, to 8pm Tue-Sun, last admission 1hr before closing; Ⓢ Hallesches Tor, Kochstrasse) In a landmark building by American-Polish architect Daniel Libeskind, Berlin's Jewish Museum offers a chronicle of the trials and triumphs in 2000 years of Jewish history in Germany. The exhibit smoothly navigates through all major periods, from the Middle Ages via the Enlightenment to the community's current renaissance. Find

GERMANY BERLIN

RECONSTRUCTION OF THE BERLIN CITY PALACE

In July 2013 construction of the Humboldt-Forum finally got underway on Schlossplatz. The facade of the humungous project will replicate the baroque Berliner Stadtschloss (Berlin City Palace), which was blown up by the East German government in 1950 and replaced 26 years later with an asbestos-riddled multipurpose hall called Palace of the Republic, which itself met the wrecking ball in 2006. The modern interior will be a forum for science, education and intercultural dialogue, and will shelter the Museum of Ethnology and the Museum of Asian Art – both currently in the outer suburb of Dahlem – as well as the Central State Library and university collections. Projected completion date is 2019. Get a sneak preview at the **Humboldt-Box** (Map p262; ☑ 0180-503 0707; www.humboldt-box.com; Schlossplatz; admission €2; ⏱ 10am-7pm; 🚌 100, 200, Ⓢ Hausvogteiplatz), the oddly shaped structure next to the construction site, which also offers great views from the rooftop cafe terrace.

Kreuzberg & Friedrichshain

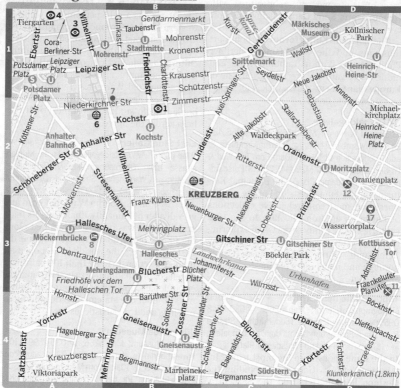

out about Jewish cultural contributions, holiday traditions, the difficult road to emancipation, and outstanding individuals such as the philosopher Moses Mendelssohn, jeans inventor Levi Strauss and the painter Felix Nussbaum.

Stasimuseum Berlin
MUSEUM

(☎030-553 6854; www.stasimuseum.de; Haus 1, Ruschestrasse 103; adult/concession €5/4; ⊙10am-6pm Mon-Fri, noon-6pm Sat & Sun; ⑤Magdalenenstrasse) The former head office of the Ministry of State Security is now a museum, where you can marvel at cunningly low-tech surveillance devices (hidden in watering cans, rocks, even neckties), a prisoner transport van with teensy, lightless cells and the obsessively neat offices of Stasi chief Erich Mielke.

Stasi Prison
MEMORIAL

(Gedenkstätte Hohenschönhausen; ☎030-9860 8230; http://en.stiftung-hsh.de; Genslerstrasse 66; adult/concession €5/2.50; ⊙German tours hourly 11am-3pm Mon-Fri Mar-Oct, 11am, 1pm & 3pm Mon-Fri Nov-Feb, hourly 10am-4pm Sat & Sun year-round, English tours 2.30pm Wed, Sat & Sun; ⊠M5 to Freienwalder Strasse) Victims of Stasi persecution often ended up in this grim remand prison, now a memorial site officially called Gedenkstätte Hohenschönhausen. Tours reveal the full extent of the terror and cruelty perpetrated upon thousands of suspected regime opponents, many utterly innocent. A new exhibit documents the history of the prison. To get here, take tram M5 from Alexanderplatz to Freienwalder Strasse, then walk 10 minutes along Freienwalder Strasse.

City West & Charlottenburg

The glittering heart of West Berlin during the Cold War, Charlottenburg has been eclipsed by historic Mitte and other eastern districts since reunification, but is now trying hard to stage a comeback with major

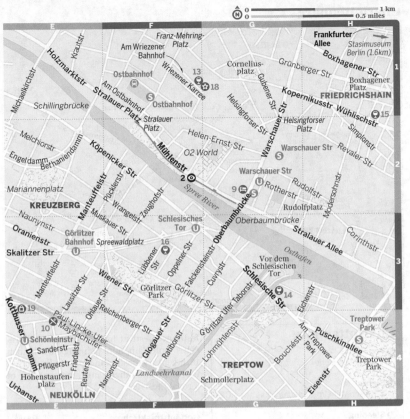

Kreuzberg & Friedrichshain

redevelopment around Zoologischer Garten (Zoo station). Its main artery is the 3.5km-long Kurfürstendamm (Ku'damm for short), Berlin's busiest shopping strip. The main tourist attraction is the nicely restored Schloss Charlottenburg.

Charlottenburg

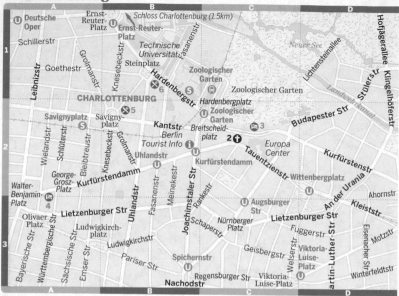

Charlottenburg

⭐**Schloss Charlottenburg** PALACE
(📞030-320 910; www.spsg.de; Spandauer Damm 10-22; day pass adult/concession €15/11; ⊙ hours vary by bldg; 🚌M45, 109, 309, Ⓢ Richard-Wagner-Platz, Sophie-Charlotte-Platz) The grandest of Berlin's surviving royal pads consists of the main palace and three smaller buildings dotted around the lovely palace park. The Schloss palace has origins as the summer residence of Sophie Charlotte, wife of King Friedrich I, and was later enlarged by Frederick the Great. Highlights include opulently furnished private royal apartments, richly

festooned festival halls, collections of precious porcelain and paintings by French 18th-century masters and lots of silver, vases, tapestries and other items representative of a royal lifestyle.

Kaiser-Wilhelm-Gedächtniskirche CHURCH
(Kaiser Wilhelm Memorial Church; Map p268; 📞030-218 5023; www.gedaechtniskirche.com; Breitscheidplatz; ⊙ church 9am-7pm, memorial hall 10am-6pm Mon-Fri, 10am-5.30pm Sat, noon-5.30pm Sun; 🚌100, Ⓢ Zoologischer Garten, Kurfürstendamm, 🚆Zoologischer Garten) 🆓 The bombed-out tower of this landmark church, consecrated in 1895, serves as an antiwar memorial, standing quiet and dignified amid the roaring traffic. The adjacent octagonal hall of worship, added in 1961, has amazing midnight-blue glass walls and a giant 'floating' Jesus.

🚶 Tours

Most of the following English-language walking tours don't require reservations; just check the website for the current meeting points.

Alternative Berlin Tours WALKING
(📞0162 819 8264; www.alternativeberlin.com) Pay-what-you-want twice-daily subculture tours that get beneath the skin of the city,

plus a street-art workshop, an alternative pub crawl and the hardcore 'Twilight Tour'.

Berlin Walks
WALKING
(📞030-301 9194; www.berlinwalks.de; adult €12-15, concession €10-12) Berlin's longest-running English-language walking tour company also does tours of Sachsenhausen Concentration Camp and Potsdam.

Fat Tire Bike Tours
BICYCLE
(Map p262; 📞030-2404 7991; www.fattirebike tours.com/berlin; Panoramastrasse 1a; adult/concession €24/22; Ⓢ Alexanderplatz, Ⓡ Alexanderplatz) Has classic city, Nazi and Berlin Wall tours as well as a fascinating 'Raw: Berlin Exposed' tour that gets under the city's urban, subcultural skin. Tours leave from the TV Tower main entrance. E-bike tours available. Reservations recommended (and for some tours required).

Trabi Safari
CAR
(Map p266; 📞030-2759 2273; www.trabi-safari.de; Zimmerstrasse 97; per person €34-60, Wall Ride €79-89; Ⓢ Kochstrasse) Catch the *Good Bye, Lenin!* vibe on tours of Berlin's classic sights or the 'Wild East' with you driving or riding as a passenger in a convoy of GDR-made Trabant cars (Trabi) with live commentary (in English by prior arrangement) piped into your vehicle.

🛏 Sleeping

While hotels in Charlottenburg often have special deals, remember that staying here puts you a U-Bahn ride away from most major sights (which are in Mitte) and happening nightlife in Friedrichshain or Kreuzberg.

Historic Mitte & Scheunenviertel

Wombats City Hostel Berlin
HOSTEL €
(Map p262; 📞030-8471 0820; www.wombats-hostels.com; Alte Schönhauser Strasse 2; dm/d €26/78; @🛜; Ⓢ Rosa-Luxemburg-Platz) Sociable and central, Wombats gets hostelling right. From backpack-sized in-room lockers to individual reading lamps and a guest kitchen with dishwasher, the attention to detail here is impressive. Spacious ensuite rooms are as much part of the deal as freebie linen and a welcome drink, best enjoyed with fellow party pilgrims at the 7th-floor Wombar.

★Circus Hotel
HOTEL €€
(📞030-2000 3939; www.circus-berlin.de; Rosenthaler Strasse 1; d €85-120; @🛜; Ⓢ Rosenthaler Platz) At our favourite budget boutique hotel, none of the mod rooms are alike, but all feature upbeat colours, thoughtful design details, sleek oak floors and quality beds. Baths have walk-in rain showers. Unexpected perks include a roof terrace with summertime yoga, bike rentals and a fabulous breakfast buffet (€9) served until 1pm. Simply good value all around.

Hotel Amano
HOTEL €€
(Map p262; 📞030-809 4150; www.amanogroup. de; Auguststrasse 43; d €90-190; ⓅⓍ@🛜; Ⓢ Rosenthaler Platz) This budget designer hotel has inviting public areas, dressed in brushed-copper walls and cocoa-hued banquettes, and efficiently styled rooms, where white furniture teams up with oak floors and natural-toned fabrics to create crisp cosiness. Space-cravers should book an apartment with kitchenette. Breakfast is €15.

Casa Camper
HOTEL €€€
(Map p262; 📞030-2000 3410; www.casacamper. com; Weinmeisterstrasse 1; r/ste from €194/338; Ⓟ🛜; Ⓢ Weinmeisterstrasse) Catalan shoemaker Camper has translated its concept of chic yet sensible footwear into this style-pit of trend-conscious travellers. Rooms are mod if minimalist and come with day-lit bathrooms and beds that invite hitting the snooze

ⓘ DISCOUNT CARDS

If you're on a budget, various ticket deals and passes can help you stretch your euros further.

The **Museumspass Berlin** (www. visitberlin.de; adult/concession €24/12) buys admission to the permanent exhibits of about 50 museums for three consecutive days, including big draws like the Pergamonmuseum. Sold at tourist offices and participating museums.

The **Berlin Welcome Card** (www. berlin-welcomecard.de; travel in AB zones 48/72hr €18.50/25.50, 48hr incl Potsdam & up to 3 children under 15yr €20.50, 72hr incl Museumsinsel €40.50) entitles you to unlimited public transport and up to 50% discount to 200 sights, attractions and tours for periods of two, three or five days. Sold online, at tourist offices, at U-Bahn and S-Bahn vending machines and on buses.

button. Minibars are eschewed for a top-floor lounge with stellar views, free breakfast and 24/7 snacks and drinks.

🛏 Kreuzberg & Friedrichshain

★ **Grand Hostel Berlin**   HOSTEL €
(Map p266; ☑030-2009 5450; www.grand hostel-berlin.de; Tempelhofer Ufer 14; dm from €14, d €58; @🖘; ⑤Möckernbrücke) Afternoon tea in the library bar? Check. Rooms with stucco-ornamented ceilings? Got 'em. Canal views? Yup. OK, the Grand Hostel may be no five-star hotel, but it is one of Berlin's most supremely comfortable and atmospheric hostels. Ensconced in a fully renovated 1870s building are private rooms and dorms with quality single beds (linen costs €3.60) and large lockers.

★ **Michelberger Hotel**   HOTEL €€
(Map p266; ☑030-2977 8590; www.michelberger hotel.com; Warschauer Strasse 39; d €105-196; 🖘; ⑤Warschauer Strasse, ⓡWarschauer Strasse) The ultimate in creative crash pads, Michelsberger perfectly encapsulates Berlin's offbeat DIY spirit without being self-consciously cool. Rooms don't hide their factory pedigree, but are comfortable and come in sizes suitable for lovebirds, families or rock bands. Staff are friendly and clued-up, and there's a popular

restaurant and live music in the lobby on some nights. Optional breakfast is €16.

🛏 City West & Charlottenburg

25hours Hotel Bikini Berlin   HOTEL €€
(Map p268; ☑030-120 2210; www.25hours-hotels. com; Budapester Strasse 40; r from €80; ❄@🖘; ⑤Zoologischer Garten, ⓡZoologischer Garten) The 'urban jungle' theme of this hip lifestyle outpost is a reflection of its location between the city's zoo and main shopping district. Rooms are stylish, if a tad compact, with the nicer ones facing the animal park.

Hotel Askanischer Hof   HOTEL €€
(Map p268; ☑030-881 8033; www.askanischer-hof. de; Kurfürstendamm 53; d incl breakfast €80-160; 🖘; ⑤Adenauerplatz) If you're after character and vintage flair, you'll find heaps of both at this 17-room jewel with a Roaring Twenties pedigree. An ornate oak door leads to a quiet oasis where no two rooms are alike, but all are filled with antiques, lace curtains, frilly chandeliers and time-worn oriental rugs. The quaint Old Berlin charms make a popular setting for fashion shoots.

🍴 Eating

Berlin is a snacker's paradise, with Turkish (your best bet), wurst (sausage), Greek, Italian and Chinese *Imbiss* (snack) stalls throughout the city. For a local snack, try a ubiquitous *Currywurst* (slivered sausage drizzled with ketchup and curry powder). Excellent farmers markets include those at **Kollwitzplatzmarkt** (Kollwitzstrasse; ◷noon-7pm Thu, 9am-4pm Sat; ⑤Senefelderplatz) in Prenzlauer Berg and the **Türkenmarkt** (Turkish Market; Map p266; www.tuerkenmarkt.de; Maybachufer; ◷11am-6.30pm Tue & Fri; ⑤Schön-leinstrasse, Kottbusser Tor) in Kreuzberg.

🍴 Historic Mitte & Scheunenviertel

Chèn Chè   VIETNAMESE €€
(Map p262; www.chenche-berlin.de; Rosenthaler Strasse 13; dishes €7-11; ◷noon-midnight; ☑; ⑤Rosenthaler Platz, ⓡM1) Settle down in the charming Zen garden or beneath the hexagonal chandelier of this exotic Vietnamese teahouse and pick from the small menu of steaming *pho* (soups), curries and noodle dishes served in traditional clay pots. Exquisite tea selection and small store.

Schwarzwaldstuben GERMAN €€
(Map p262; 030-2809 8084; Tucholskystrasse
48; mains €7-14; 9am-midnight; M1, Oranienburger Strasse) In the mood for a Hansel
and Gretel moment? Then join the other
'lost kids' for satisfying southern German
food amid tongue-in-cheek forest decor.
Thumbs up for the *Spätzle* (mac 'n' cheese),
Maultaschen (ravioli-like pasta) and giant
schnitzel, all best washed down with a crisp
Rothaus Tannenzäpfle beer, straight from
the Black Forest.

Weinbar Rutz GERMAN €€€
(Map p262; 030-2462 8760; www.rutz-
weinbar.de; Chausseestrasse 8; bar mains €16-25,
3-/4-course menu €44/54; 4-11pm Tue-Sat;
Oranienburger Tor) Below his high-concept
gourmet temple, Michelin-starred Marco
Müller operates a more down-to-earth wine
bar where the menu has a distinct earthy
and carnivorous bent. Many of the meats
and sausages are sourced from Berlin and
surrounds. Finish up with a Berlin cheesecake with walnuts and elderberry ice cream.

✕ Prenzlauer Berg

Konnopke's Imbiss GERMAN €
(030-442 7765; www.konnopke-imbiss.de; Schönhauser Allee 44a; sausages €1.40-1.90; 9am-8pm
Mon-Fri, 11.30am-8pm Sat; Eberswalder Strasse,
M1, M10) Brave the inevitable queue at this
famous sausage kitchen, ensconced in the
same spot below the elevated U-Bahn track
since 1930, but now equipped with a heated
pavilion and an English menu. The 'secret'
sauce topping its classic *Currywurst* comes
in a four-part heat scale from mild to wild.

La Soupe Populaire GERMAN €€
(030-4431 9680; www.lasoupepopulaire.de;
Prenzlauer Allee 242; mains €14-21; noon-midnight Thu-Sat; Rosa-Luxemburg-Strasse, M2)
Local top toque Tim Raue's newest gastro
destination embraces the soulful goodness
of German home cooking, with a best seller
being his riff on *Königsberger Klopse* (veal
meatballs in caper sauce). It's all served in
an industrial-chic space within a defunct
19th-century brewery where patrons sit at
vintage tables overlooking a gallery space
showcasing changing contemporary art.

✕ Kreuzberg

Cafe Jacques INTERNATIONAL €€
(Map p266; 030-694 1048; Maybachufer 14;
mains €12-20; 6pm-late; Schönleinstrasse) A

favourite with off-duty chefs and local foodies, Jacques infallibly charms with flatter-
ing candlelight, arty-elegant decor, fantastic
wine and uberfriendly staff. It's the perfect
date spot but, quite frankly, you only have
to be in love with good food to appreciate
the French- and North African–inspired
blackboard menu. The cold appetiser platter is big enough for sharing, fish and meat
are always tops and the pasta is homemade.
Reservations essential.

Max und Moritz GERMAN €€
(Map p266; 030-6951 5911; www.maxundmoritz
berlin.de; Oranienstrasse 162; mains €9.50-17;
5pm-midnight; Moritzplatz) The patina of
yesteryear hangs over this ode-to-old-school
brewpub named for the cheeky Wilhelm
Busch cartoon characters. Since 1902 it has
packed hungry diners and drinkers into its
rustic tile-and-stucco ornamented rooms for
sudsy home brews and granny-style Berlin
fare. A menu favourite is the *Kutschergu-
lasch* (goulash cooked with beer).

Defne TURKISH €€
(Map p266; 030-8179 7111; www.defne-restaurant.
de; Planufer 92c; mains €8-20; 4pm-1am
Apr-Sep, 5pm-1am Oct-Mar; Kottbusser Tor,
Schönleinstrasse) If you thought Turkish cuisine stopped at the doner kebab, canal-side
Defne will teach you otherwise. The appetiser platter alone elicits intense cravings
(fabulous walnut-chilli paste!), but inventive
mains such as *ali nacik* (sliced lamb with
puréed eggplant and yoghurt) also warrant
repeat visits. Lovely summer terrace.

✕ City West & Charlottenburg

Dicke Wirtin GERMAN €€
(Map p268; 030-312 4952; www.dicke-wirtin.de;
Carmerstrasse 9; mains €6-16; from 11am-late;
Savignyplatz) Old Berlin charm oozes from
every nook and cranny of this been-here-
forever pub which pours eight draught beers
(including the superb Kloster Andechs) and
nearly three dozen homemade schnapps
varieties. Hearty local fare like roast pork,
fried liver or breaded schnitzel keeps brains
balanced. Bargain lunches.

Restaurant am Steinplatz GERMAN €€€
(Map p268; 030-312 6589; www.marriott.de;
Hardenbergstrasse 12; mains €16-26; breakfast,
lunch & dinner; M45, Ernst-Reuter-Platz, Bahnhof Zoologischer Garten, Bahnhof Zoologischer
Garten) The 1920s gets a 21st-century makeover both in the kitchen and the decor at

WORTH A TRIP

SCHLOSS & PARK SANSSOUCI

Easily reached in half an hour from central Berlin, the former royal Prussian seat of **Potsdam** lures visitors to its splendid Unesco-recognised palaces and parks dreamed up by 18th-century King Friedrich II (Frederick the Great).

Headlining the roll call of royal pads is **Schloss Sanssouci** (☑0331-969 4200; www.spsg.de; Maulbeerallee; adult/concession incl audioguide €12/8; ☺10am-6pm Tue-Sun Apr-Oct, to 5pm Nov-Mar; ☒650, 695), a celebrated rococo palace and the king's favourite summer retreat. Standouts on the audioguided tour include the whimsically decorated concert hall, the intimate library and the domed Marble Hall. Admission is limited and by timed ticket only; book online (http://tickets.spsg.de) to avoid wait times and/or disappointment. Tours run by the Potsdam **tourist office** (☑0331-2755 8899; www.potsdam-tourism.com; ☺9.30am-8pm Mon-Sat, 10am-4pm Sun) guarantee entry.

Schloss Sanssouci is surrounded by a sprawling park dotted with numerous other palaces, buildings, fountains, statues and romantic corners. The one building not to be missed is the **Chinesisches Haus** (Chinese House; ☑0331-969 4200; www.spsg.de; Am Grünen Gitter; admission €2; ☺10am-6pm Tue-Sun May-Oct; ☒605, 606 to Schloss Charlottenhof, ☒91 to Schloss Charlottenhof), an adorable clover-leaf-shaped pavilion decorated with exotically dressed gilded figures shown sipping tea, dancing and playing musical instruments.

Another park highlight is the **Neues Palais** (New Palace; ☑0331-969 4200; www.spsg.de; Am Neuen Palais; adult/concession incl audioguide €8/6; ☺10am-6pm Wed-Mon Apr-Oct, to 5pm Nov-Mar; ☒605 or 606 to Neues Palais, ☒Potsdam Charlottenhof) at the far western end. It has built-to-impress dimensions and is filled with opulent private and representative rooms, some of which are closed for restoration.

Each building charges separate admission; a day pass to all costs €19 (concession €14).

On a nice day, it's worth exploring Potsdam's watery landscape and numerous other palaces on a **boat cruise** (☑0331-275 9210; www.schiffahrt-in-potsdam.de; Lange Brücke 6; ☺10am-7pm Apr-Oct). The most popular one is the 90-minute *Schlösserundfahrt* (palace cruise; €13). Boats leave from docks near the Hauptbahnhof.

Regional trains leaving from Berlin-Hauptbahnhof and Zoologischer Garten need only 30 minutes to reach Potsdam Hauptbahnhof. The S-Bahn S7 from central Berlin makes the trip in about 40 minutes. You'll need an ABC ticket (€3.20) for either service.

this stylish outpost. The dining room is anchored by an open kitchen where veteran chef Marcus Zimmer uses mostly regional products to execute classic Berlin recipes. Even rustic beer-hall dishes such as *Eisbein* (boiled pork knuckle) are imaginatively reinterpreted and beautifully plated.

 Drinking & Nightlife

With no curfew, Berlin is a notoriously late city, where bars stay packed from dusk to dawn and beyond and some clubs don't hit their stride until 6am. Kreuzberg and Friedrichshain are currently the edgiest bar-hopping grounds, with swanky Mitte and Charlottenburg being more suited for date nights than late nights. For listings consult the biweekly city magazines *Zitty* (www.zitty.de) or *Tip* (www.tip.de), or check internet platforms such as www.residentadvisor.net.

Prater　　　　BEER GARDEN
(☑030-448 5688; www.pratergarten.de; Kastanienallee 7-9; ☺noon-late Apr-Sep, weather permitting; ☒Eberswalder Strasse) This place has seen beer-soaked nights since 1837, making it Berlin's oldest beer garden. It's kept much of its traditional charm and is still perfect for guzzling a custom-brewed Prater pilsner beneath the ancient chestnut trees (self-service). Kids can romp around the small play area. In foul weather or winter, the adjacent beer hall is a fine place to sample classic Berlin dishes (mains €8 to €19).

Weinerei　　　　WINE BAR
(☑030-440 6983; www.weinerei.com; Veteranenstrasse 14; ☺8pm-late; ☎; ☒Rosenthaler Platz, ☒M1) This living-room-style wine bar works on the honour principle: you 'rent' a wine glass for €2, then help yourself to as much vino as you like and in the end decide what

you want to pay. Please be fair and do not take advantage of this fantastic concept.

Madame Claude
PUB

(Map p266; ☑ 030-8411 0859; www.madameclaude. de; Lübbener Strasse 19; ☺ from 7pm; Ⓢ Schlesisches Tor, Görlitzer Bahnhof) Gravity is literally upended at this David Lynchian booze burrow where the furniture dangles from the ceiling and the moulding is on the floor. There are concerts, DJs and events every night, including eXperimondays, Wednesday's music quiz night and open-mike Sundays. The name honours a famous French prostitute – *très* apropos given the place's bordello pedigree.

Hops & Barley
PUB

(Map p266; ☑ 030-2936 7534; Wühlischstrasse 40; ☺ from 5pm Mon-Fri, from 3pm Sat & Sun; Ⓢ Warschauer Strasse, Ⓡ Warschauer Strasse) Conversation flows as freely as the unfiltered pilsner, malty *Dunkel* (dark), fruity *Weizen* (wheat) and potent cider produced right at this congenial microbrewery inside a former butcher's shop. For variety, the brewmeisters produce seasonal blackboard specials such as a malty Bernstein or a robust Indian Pale Ale.

Würgeengel
BAR

(Map p266; www.wuergeengel.de; Dresdener Strasse 122; ☺ from 7pm; Ⓢ Kottbusser Tor) For a swish night out, point the compass to Würgeengel, a stylish art deco–style bar with lots of chandeliers and shiny black surfaces. It's always busy but especially so after the final credits roll at the adjacent Babylon cinema.

Klunkerkranich
BAR

(www.klunkerkranich.de; Karl-Marx-Strasse 66; ☺ 10am-midnight Mon-Sat, noon-midnight Sun, weather permitting; Ⓢ Rathaus Neukölln) Open only in the warmer months, Klunkerkranich (German for 'wattled crane') is a club-garden-beach-bar combo that 'roosts' amid potted plants on the rooftop parking deck of the Neukölln Arcaden shopping mall. It's a great place for sundowners while chilling to local DJs or bands.

Berghain/Panorama Bar
CLUB

(Map p266; www.berghain.de; Wriezener Bahnhof; ☺ midnight Fri-Mon morning; Ⓡ Ostbahnhof) Only world-class spin masters heat up this hedonistic bass-junkie hellhole inside a labyrinthine ex-power plant. Hard-edged minimal techno dominates the ex-turbine hall (Berghain) while house dominates at Panorama Bar one floor up. Strict door, no cameras. Check the web-site for midweek concerts and record-release parties at the main venue and the adjacent **Kantine am Berghain** (Map p266; ☑ 030-2936 0210; www.berghain.de; Am Wriezener Bahnhof; ☺ hours vary; Ⓡ Ostbahnhof).

Clärchens Ballhaus
CLUB

(Map p262; ☑ 030-282 9295; www.ballhaus. de; Augustrasse 24; ☺ 11am-late, dancing from 9pm or 9.30pm; Ⓜ M1, Ⓡ Oranienburger Strasse) Yesteryear is right now at this late, great 19th-century dance hall where groovers and grannies hoof it across the parquet without even a touch of irony. There are different sounds nightly – salsa to swing, tango to disco – and a live band on Saturday.

Club der Visionäre
CLUB

(Map p266; ☑ 030-6951 8942; www.clubder visionaere.com; Am Flutgraben 1; ☺ from 2pm Mon-Fri, from noon Sat & Sun; Ⓢ Schlesisches Tor, Ⓡ Treptower Park) It's cold beer, crispy pizza and fine electro at this summertime chill and party playground in an old canal-side boatshed. Park yourself beneath the weeping willows, stake out some turf on the upstairs deck or hit the teensy dance floor. At weekends party people invade. The toilets suck.

☆ Entertainment

Berliner Philharmonie
CLASSICAL MUSIC

(Map p268; ☑ tickets 030-2548 8301; www.berliner-philharmoniker.de; Herbert-von-Karajan-Strasse 1; ☑ 200, Ⓢ Potsdamer Platz, Ⓡ Potsdamer Platz) This world-famous concert hall has supreme acoustics and, thanks to Hans Scharoun's clever terraced vineyard design,

---

GAY & LESBIAN BERLIN

Berlin's legendary liberalism has spawned one of the world's biggest and most diverse GLBT playgrounds. The historic 'gay village' is near Nollendorfplatz in Schöneberg (Motzstrasse and Fuggerstrasse especially, get off U-Bahn station Nollendorfplatz), where the rainbow flag has proudly flown since the 1920s. The crowds skews older and leather. Current hipster central is Kreuzberg, where freewheeling party pens cluster around Mehringdamm and Oranienstrasse. Check *Siegessäule* (www.siegesaeule.de), the weekly freebie 'bible' to all things gay and lesbian in town, for the latest happenings.

SACHSENHAUSEN CONCENTRATION CAMP

A mere 35km north of Berlin, Sachsenhausen was built by prisoners and opened in 1936 as a prototype for other concentration camps. By 1945 some 200,000 people had passed through its sinister gates, initially mostly political opponents but later also Roma and Sinti, Jews and prisoners of war (POWs). Tens of thousands died from hunger, exhaustion, illness, exposure, medical experiments and executions. The camp became a **memorial site** (☑ 03301-200 200; www.stiftung-bg.de; Strasse der Nationen 22; ☺ 8.30am–6pm mid-Mar–mid-Oct, to 4.30pm mid-Oct–mid-Mar, most exhibits closed Mon) FREE in 1961. A tour of the grounds, remaining buildings and exhibits will leave no one untouched.

Unless you're on a guided tour, pick up a leaflet (€0.50) or, better yet, an audioguide (€3, including leaflet) at the visitor centre to get a better grasp of this huge site. Note that although the grounds are open daily, indoor exhibits are closed on Mondays.

The S-Bahn S1 makes the trip to Oranienburg thrice hourly (€3.20, 45 minutes), from where it's a 2km signposted walk or a ride on hourly bus 804 to the camp.

not a bad seat in the house. It's the home turf of the Berliner Philharmoniker, which will be led by Sir Simon Rattle until 2018. Chamber-music concerts take place at the adjacent Kammermusiksaal.

ℹ Information

Visit Berlin (Map p262; www.visitberlin.de; Brandenburger Tor, Pariser Platz), the Berlin tourist board, operates four walk-in offices, info desks at the airports, and a **call centre** (☑ 030-2500 2333; ☺ 9am-7pm Mon-Fri, 10am-6pm Sat, 10am-2pm Sun) with multilingual staff who field general questions and make hotel and ticket bookings. You'll find the walk-in offices at the following locations:

Brandenburger Tor (Map p262; Pariser Platz, Brandenburger Tor; ☺ 9.30am-7pm Apr-Oct, to 6pm Nov-Mar; ⓢ Brandenburger Tor, ⓡ Brandenburger Tor)

Hauptbahnhof (Hauptbahnhof, Europaplatz entrance, ground fl; ☺ 8am-10pm; ⓢ Hauptbahnhof, ⓡ Hauptbahnhof)

Neues Kranzler Eck (Map p268; Kurfürstendamm 22, Neues Kranzler Eck; ☺ 9.30am-8pm Mon-Sat; ⓢ Kurfürstendamm)

TV Tower (Map p262; TV Tower, ground fl; ☺ 10am-6pm Apr-Oct, to 4pm Nov-Mar; 🚌 100, 200, ⓢ Alexanderplatz, ⓡ Alexanderplatz)

ℹ Getting There & Away

AIR

Most visitors arrive in Berlin by air. Since the opening of the new Berlin Brandenburg Airport has been delayed indefinitely, flights continue to land at the city's **Tegel** (TXL; ☑ 030-6091 1150; www.berlin-airport.de) and **Schönefeld** (SXF; ☑ 030-6091 1150; www.berlin-airport.de) airports.

BUS

Most long-haul buses arrive at the **Zentraler Omnibusbahnhof** (ZOB; ☑ 030-302 5361; www.iob-berlin.de; Masurenallee 4-6; ⓢ Kaiserdamm, ⓡ Messe/ICC Nord) near the trade fair grounds in far western Berlin. The U2 U-Bahn line links to the city centre. Some bus operators also stop at Alexanderplatz and other points around town.

TRAIN

Berlin has several train stations but most trains converge at the Hauptbahnhof (main train station) in the heart of the city.

ℹ Getting Around

TO/FROM THE AIRPORT
Tegel

Bus TXL bus to Alexanderplatz (€2.60, 40 minutes) via Haupbahnhof every 10 minutes. Bus X9 for Kurfürstendamm and Zoologischer Garten (Zoo station; €2.60, 20 minutes).

U-Bahn Closest U-station is Jakob-Kaiser-Platz, served by bus 109 and X9. From here, the U7 goes straight to Schöneberg and Kreuzberg (€2.60).

Schönefeld

The airport train station is about 400m from the terminals. Free shuttle buses run every 10 minutes; walking takes five to 10 minutes.

ℹ BUS TOUR ON THE CHEAP

Get a crash course in 'Berlinology' by hopping on bus 100 or 200 at Zoologischer Garten or Alexanderplatz and letting the landmarks whoosh by for the price of a standard bus ticket (€2.60, day pass €6.80). Bus 100 goes via the Tiergarten, 200 via Potsdamer Platz. Without traffic and getting off, trips take about 30 minutes.

Airport-Express Regular Deutsche Bahn regional trains, identified as RE7 and RB14 in timetables, go to central Berlin twice hourly (€3.20, 30 minutes).

S-Bahn S9 runs every 20 minutes and is handy for Friedrichshain or Prenzlauer Berg. For the Messe (trade-fair grounds), take the S45 to Südkreuz and change to the S41. Tickets cost €3.20.

PUBLIC TRANSPORT

One ticket is valid on all forms of public transport, including the U-Bahn, buses, trams and ferries. Most trips within Berlin require an AB ticket (€2.60), which is valid for two hours (interruptions and transfers allowed, but not round trips).

Tickets are available from bus drivers, vending machines at U- and S-Bahn stations (English instructions available), vending machines aboard trams and from station offices. Expect to pay cash (change given) and be sure to validate (stamp) your ticket or risk a €40 fine.

Services operate from 4am until just after midnight on weekdays, with half-hourly *Nachtbuses* (night buses) in between. At weekends the U-Bahn and S-Bahn run all night long (except the U4 and U55).

For trip planning, check the website or call the 24-hour **hotline** (☑ 030-194 49; www.bvg.de).

TAXI

You can order a **taxi** (☑ 030-20 20 20, 030-44 33 11) by phone, flag one down or pick one up at a rank. Flag fall is €3.40, then it's €1.79 per kilometre up to 7km and €1.28 for each kilometre after that. Tip about 10%. Short trips of 2km cost €4 provided you flag down a cab and request a *Kurzstrecke* before the driver has activated the meter.

CENTRAL GERMANY

Central Germany straddles the states of Thuringia and Saxony, both in the former East Germany. It takes in towns like Weimar, Eisenach and Erfurt that have been shaped by some of the biggest names in Germany history, including Goethe and Martin Luther. Further east, Dresden is a town that defines survival while Leipzig can be justifiably proud of doing its part in bringing about the downfall of East Germany. Expect this region to enlighten, inspire and, above all, surprise you.

Dresden

☑ 0351 / POP 512,000

Proof that there is life after death, Dresden has become one of Germany's most visited cities, and for good reason. Restorations have returned its historic core to its 18th-century heyday when it was famous throughout Europe as 'Florence on the Elbe'. Scores of Italian artists, musicians, actors and master craftsmen flocked to the court of Augustus the Strong, bestowing countless masterpieces upon the city.

The devastating bombing raids in 1945 levelled most of these treasures. But Dresden is a survivor and many of the most important landmarks have since been rebuilt, including the elegant Frauenkirche. Today there's a constantly evolving arts and cultural scene and zinging pub and nightlife quarters, especially in the Outer Neustadt.

⊙ Sights

Dresden straddles the Elbe River, with the attraction-studded Altstadt (old town) in the south and the Neustadt (new town) pub and student quarter to the north.

Frauenkirche CHURCH
(www.frauenkirche-dresden.de; Neumarkt; audioguide €2.50; ⊙ usually 10am-noon & 1-6pm) FREE
The domed Frauenkirche – Dresden's most beloved symbol – has literally risen from the city's ashes. The original graced its skyline for two centuries before collapsing after the February 1945 bombing. After reunification a grassroots movement helped raise funds to rebuild the landmark. A spitting image of the original, it may not bear the gravitas of age but that only slightly detracts from its festive beauty inside and out. The altar, reassembled from nearly 2000 fragments, is especially striking.

Zwinger MUSEUM
(☑ 0351-4914 2000; www.skd.museum; Theaterplatz 1; adult/under 17yr €14/free; ⊙ 10am-6pm Tue-Sun) The sprawling Zwinger, one of the most ravishing baroque buildings in Germany, today houses several important museums. The most important collection, the **Gemäldegalerie Alte Meister** (Old Masters Gallery), displays a roll call of such art-world darlings as Botticelli, Titian, Rubens, Vermeer and Dürer. A key work is the 500-year-old *Sistine Madonna* by Raphael. Fans of precious porcelain from Meissen and East Asia gravitate to the **Porzellansammlung**, while techno types will like the historic scientific instruments (globes, clocks, telescopes, etc) at the **Mathematisch-Physikalischer Salon**.

GRÜNES GEWÖLBE

Dresden's fortress-like Renaissance city palace was home to Saxon rulers from 1485 to 1918 and now shelters Augustus the Strong's dazzling collection of precious objects, a real-life 'Aladdin's Cave' spilling over with trinkets wrought from gold, ivory, silver, diamonds and jewels. There's so much of it that displays are spread over two separate museums: the **Historisches Grünes Gewölbe** (Historic Green Vault; ☑0351-4914 2000; www.skd.museum; Residenzschloss; adult/under 17yr incl audioguide €14/free; ☺10am-6pm Wed-Mon) and the modern **Neues Grünes Gewölbe** (New Green Vault; ☑0351-4914 2000; www.skd.museum; Residenzschloss; adult/under 17yr incl audioguide €14/free; ☺10am-6pm Wed-Mon).

If you only have time for one, make it the former, largely because objects are displayed in a series of lavishly decorated baroque-style rooms just as they were during Augustus' time. Admission is by timed ticket only and visitor numbers are limited. It's best to get advance tickets online or show up before the ticket office opens.

Don't be too disappointed, though, if you can't get into the historic chambers, for trinkets displayed in the modern New Green Vault are just as stunning.

Combination tickets to both Green Vaults cost €23 (free under age 17) and are also good for the other palace collections (coins, armour, prints and drawings) as well as the Hausmannturm (tower).

Semperoper HISTORIC BUILDING
(☑0351-320 7360; www.semperoper-erleben. de; Theaterplatz 2; tour adult/concession €10/6; ☺varies) One of Germany's most famous opera houses, the Semperoper opened in 1841 and has hosted premieres of famous works by Richard Strauss, Carl Maria von Weber and Richard Wagner. Guided 45-minute tours operate almost daily (the 3pm tour is in English); exact times depend on the rehearsal and performance schedule. Buy advance tickets online to skip the queue.

Albertinum MUSEUM
(☑0351-4914 2000; www.skd.museum; enter from Brühlsche Terrasse or Georg-Treu-Platz 2; adult/concession/under 17yr €10/7.50/free; ☺10am-6pm Tue-Sun; P) After massive renovations following severe 2002 flood damage, the Renaissance-era former arsenal is now the stunning home of the **Galerie Neue Meister** (New Masters Gallery), which displays an arc of paintings by prime practitioners from the 18th to the 20th centuries – Caspar David Friedrich to Claude Monet and Gerhard Richter – in gorgeous rooms orbiting a light-filled courtyard.

⌂ Tours

NightWalk Dresden WALKING
(☑0172 781 5007; www.nightwalk-dresden.de; Albertplatz; tours €13; ☺tour 9pm) Dresden is not all about baroque beauties, as you will discover on this intriguing 'behind the scenes' walking tour of its most interesting quarter, the Outer Neustadt. See fabulous street art, learn about what life was like in the former East Germany and visit fun pubs and bars. The meeting point is normally at Albertplatz but call ahead and confirm.

Grosse Stadtrundfahrt BUS
(☑0351-899 5650; www.stadtrundfahrt.com; Theaterplatz; day pass adult/concession €20/18; ☺9.30am-10pm Apr-Oct, to 8pm Nov-Mar) Narrated hop-on, hop-off tour with 22 stops, every 15 to 20 minutes, and optional short guided tours tick off all major sights.

⌂ Sleeping

Hostel Mondpalast HOSTEL €
(☑0351-563 4050; www.mondpalast.de; Louisenstrasse 77; dm €13-19.50, d €56, linen €2; @) Check in at the out-of-this-world bar-cafe (with cheap drinks) before being 'beamed up' to your room in the Moon Palace – each one designed to reflect a sign of the zodiac. Bonus points for the bike rentals and the well-equipped kitchen. Breakfast is €6.50.

★ Aparthotel am Zwinger APARTMENT €€
(☑0351-8990 0100; www.pension-zwinger.de; Maxstrasse 3; apt €60-112; ☺reception 7am-10pm Mon-Fri, 9.30am-6pm Sat & Sun or by arrangement; P@☂) Self-caterers, families and space-cravers will appreciate these bright, functional and stylish rooms and apartments with basic kitchens. Units are spread over several buildings, but all are super central and fairly quiet. Breakfast costs €9.50.

Hotel Martha Dresden HOTEL €€
(☑ 0351-817 60; www.hotel-martha-dresden.de; Nieritzstrasse 11; d €113-121; 🛜) Fifty rooms with big windows, wooden floors and Biedermeier-inspired furnishings combine with an attractive winter garden and a smiley welcome to make this a pleasant place to hang your hat. Breakfast costs €10. The entire hotel is wheelchair accessible. Bike rentals are available.

🍴 Eating & Drinking

The Neustadt has oodles of cafes and restaurants, especially along Königsstrasse and the streets north of Albertplatz. The latter is also the centre of Dresden's nightlife. Altstadt restaurants are more tourist-geared and pricier.

Villandry MEDITERRANEAN €€
(☑ 0351-899 6724; www.villandry.de; Jordanstrasse 8; mains €9-22; ⊙ 6.30-11.30pm Mon-Sat) The folks in the kitchen here sure know how to coax maximum flavour out of even the simplest ingredients, and to turn them into super tasty Mediterranean treats for your eyes and palate. Meals are best enjoyed in the lovely courtyard.

Cafe Alte Meister INTERNATIONAL €€
(☑ 0351-481 0426; www.altemeister.net; Theaterplatz 1a; mains €9-20; ⊙ 10am-1am) If you've worked up an appetite from museum-hopping or need a break from culture overload, retreat to this elegant filling station between the Zwinger and the Semperoper for creative and seasonal bistro fare in its artsy interior or on the terrace. At night, the ambience is a bit more formal.

Raskolnikoff INTERNATIONAL €€
(☑ 0351-804 5706; www.raskolnikoff.de; Böhmische Strasse 34; mains €7-24; ⊙ 10am-2am Mon-Fri, 9am-2am Sat & Sun) An artist squat before the Wall came down, Raskolnikoff now brims with grown-up artsy-bohemian flair, especially in the sweet little garden at the back. The seasonally calibrated menu showcases the fruits of regional terroir in globally inspired dishes, and the beer is brewed locally. Upstairs are seven handsomely done-up rooms (single/double €45/62) and one studio with kitchenette (€55/72).

Twist BAR
(☑ 0351-795 150; Salzgasse 4; ⊙ from 6pm Mon-Sat) 'Twist' is indeed the name of the game at this sky bar where classic cocktails are given – often radical – new interpretations. On the 6th floor of the Innside Hotel you'll be at eye level with the Frauenkirche dome.

ℹ️ Information

Tourist Office (☑ 0351-501 501; www.dresden. de) There are branches inside the Hauptbahnhof (Wiener Platz; ⊙ 8am-8pm) and Frauenkirche (Neumarkt 2; ⊙ 10am-7pm Mon-Fri, to 6pm Sat, to 3pm Sun). Both book rooms and tours, rent out audioguides and sell the Dresden Cards.

ℹ️ Getting There & Away

Dresden Airport (DRS; www.dresden-airport.de) is about 9km north of the city centre and linked by the S2 train several times hourly (€2.20, 20 minutes).

Direct train destinations include Leipzig (from €23.80, 70 to 100 minutes) and Berlin (€40, 2¼ hours). The S1 train runs to Meissen (€5.90, 35 minutes). Most trains stop at Dresden-Hauptbahnhof and at Dresden-Neustadt across the Elbe River.

ℹ️ Getting Around

For public transport info in Dresden, check www. dvb.de/en or call the hotline at ☑ 0351-8657 1011.

Leipzig

☑ 0341 / POP 530,500

Bustling Leipzig is an important business and transport centre, a trade-fair mecca, and – aside from Berlin – the most dynamic city in eastern Germany. Relatively low rent and throbbing nightlife are making it an attractive place to live for students and young professionals. Leipzig played a leading role in the 1989 democratic revolution and has plenty in store for history buffs keen on learning about life behind the Wall. The one-time home of Bach, Wagner and Mendelssohn, the city also looks back on a long and illustrious music tradition that continues to flourish today, as do its art and literary scenes. Another famous figure to pass through was Goethe, who set a key scene of *Faust* in the cellar of his favourite local watering hole.

⦿ Sights

Don't rush from sight to sight – wandering around Leipzig is a pleasure in itself, with many of the blocks around the central Markt criss-crossed by historic shopping arcades, including the classic **Mädlerpassage**.

MEISSEN

Straddling the Elbe around 25km upstream from Dresden, Meissen is the hub of European porcelain, which was first cooked up in 1710 in its imposing castle, the **Albrechtsburg** (☑ 03521-470 70; www.albrechtsburg-meissen.de; Domplatz 1; adult/concession incl audioguide €8/4; ☺ 10am-6pm Mar-Oct, to 5pm Nov-Feb). An exhibit on the 2nd floor chronicles how it all began. Highlights of the adjacent **cathedral** (☑ 03521-452 490; www.dom-zu-meissen.de; Domplatz 7; adult/concession €4/2.50; ☺ 9am-6pm Apr-Oct, 10am-4pm Nov-Mar) include medieval stained-glass windows and an altarpiece by Lucas Cranach the Elder. Both squat atop a ridge overlooking Meissen's cute Altstadt (old town).

Since 1863, porcelain production has taken place in a custom-built factory, about 1km south of the Altstadt. Next to it is the **Erlebniswelt Haus Meissen** (☑ 03521-468 208; www.meissen.com/de/meissen-besuchen/erlebniswelt-haus-meissen; Talstrasse 9; adult/concession €9/5; ☺ 9am-6pm May-Oct, to 5pm Nov-Apr), a vastly popular porcelain museum where you can witness the astonishing artistry and craftsmanship that makes Meissen porcelain unique.

For details and further information about the town, stop by the **tourist office** (☑ 03521-419 40; www.touristinfo-meissen.de; Markt 3; ☺ 10am-6pm Mon-Fri, 10am-4pm Sat & Sun Apr-Oct, 10am-5pm Mon-Fri, 10am-3pm Sat Nov, Dec, Feb & Mar).

Half-hourly S1 trains run to Meissen from Dresden's Hauptbahnhof and Neustadt train stations (€5.90, 35 minutes). For the Erlebniswelt, get off at Meissen-Triebischtal. Boats operated by **Sächsische Dampfschiffahrt** (☑ 03521-866 090; www.saechsische-dampfschiffahrt.de; one way/return €13.50/17.50; ☺ May-Sep) make the trip to Meissen from the Terrassenufer in Dresden in two hours. Consider going one way by boat and the other by train.

★ **Nikolaikirche** CHURCH
(Church of St Nicholas; www.nikolaikirche-leipzig.de; Nikolaikirchhof 3; ☺ 10am-6pm Mon-Sat & during services 9.30am, 11.15am & 5pm Sun) The Church of St Nicholas has Romanesque and Gothic roots but since 1797 has sported a striking neoclassical interior with palm-like pillars and cream-coloured pews. The church played a key role in the nonviolent movement that led to the downfall of the East German government. As early as 1982 it hosted 'peace prayers' every Monday at 5pm (still held today), which over time inspired and empowered local citizens to confront the injustices plaguing their country.

Zeitgeschichtliches Forum MUSEUM
(Forum of Contemporary History; ☑ 0341-222 00; www.hdg.de/leipzig; Grimmaische Strasse 6; ☺ 9am-6pm Tue-Fri, 10am-6pm Sat & Sun) FREE This fascinating exhibit tells the political history of the German Democratic Republic (GDR) from division and dictatorship to fall-of-the-Wall ecstasy and post-Wende blues. It's essential viewing for anyone seeking to understand the late country's political power apparatus, the systematic oppression of regime critics, milestones in inter-German and international relations, and the opposition movement that led to its downfall.

Bach-Museum Leipzig MUSEUM
(☑ 0341-913 70; www.bachmuseumleipzig.de; Thomaskirchhof 16; adult/concession/under 16yr €8/6/free; ☺ 10am-6pm Tue-Sun) This interactive museum does more than tell you about the life and accomplishments of heavy-weight musician Johann Sebastian Bach. Learn how to date a Bach manuscript, listen to baroque instruments or treat your ears to any composition he ever wrote. The 'treasure room' downstairs displays rare original manuscripts.

Thomaskirche CHURCH
(☑ 0341-222 240; www.thomaskirche.org; Thomaskirchhof 18; tower €2; ☺ church 9am-6pm, tower 1pm, 2pm & 4.30pm Sat, 2pm & 3pm Sun Apr-Nov) The composer Johann Sebastian Bach worked in the Thomaskirche as a cantor from 1723 until his death in 1750, and his remains lie buried beneath a bronze plate in front of the altar. The Thomanerchor, once led by Bach, has been going strong since 1212 and now includes 100 boys aged eight to 18. The church tower can be climbed.

Stasi Museum MUSEUM
(☑ 0341-961 2443; www.runde-ecke-leipzig.de; Dittrichring 24; ☺ 10am-6pm) FREE In the GDR the walls had ears, as is chillingly documented in this exhibit in the former Leipzig headquarters of the East German secret police (the

Stasi), a building known as the Runde Ecke (Round Corner). English-language audioguides aid in understanding the all-German displays on propaganda, preposterous disguises, cunning surveillance devices, recruitment (even among children), scent storage and other chilling machinations that reveal the GDR's all-out zeal when it came to controlling, manipulating and repressing its own people.

🛏 Sleeping

Motel One
HOTEL €

(☑0341-337 4370; www.motel-one.de; Nikolaistrasse 23; d from €69; P❄🛜) The older of two Motel One outposts in Leipzig has a five-star location opposite the Nikolaikirche and also gets most other things right, from the Zeitgeist-capturing lobby-lounge to the snug but smartly designed rooms. No surprise it's often booked out. Breakfast costs €7.50.

arcona Living Bach14
HOTEL, STUDIOS €€

(☑0341-496 140; www.bach14.arcona.de; Thomaskirchhof 13/14; d from €110; 🛜) In this musically themed marvel, you'll sleep sweetly in sleek rooms decorated with sound-sculpture lamps, Bach manuscript wallpaper and colours ranging from subdued olive to perky raspberry. The quietest ones are in the garden wing, while those in the historic front section have views of the famous Thomaner church.

★Steigenberger Grandhotel Handelshof
HOTEL €€€

(☑0341-350 5810; www.steigenberger.com/Leipzig; Salzgässchen 6; r from €160; ❄@🛜) Behind the imposing historic facade of a 1909 municipal trading hall, this luxe lodge outclasses most of Leipzig's hotels with its super central location, charmingly efficient team and modern rooms dressed in crisp white-silver-purple colours. The stylish bi-level spa is the perfect bliss-out station.

🍴 Eating

Aside from locations listed here, another good place to head to is restaurant row on popular Muenzgasse, just south of the city centre. Take tram 10 or 11 to 'Hohe Strasse'.

Sol y Mar
MEDITERRANEAN, ASIAN €€

(☑0341-961 5721; www.solymar-leipzig.de; Gottschedstrasse 4; mains €5-14; ⊙9am-late; 🛜) The soft lighting, ambient sounds and sensuous interior (including padded pods for noshing in a reclining position) make this a popular place to chill and dine on feel-good food from around the Med and Asia. Weekday lunch

specials from €4.90, Sunday brunch and expansive summer terrace.

★Auerbachs Keller
GERMAN €€€

(☑0341-216 100; www.auerbachs-keller-leipzig.de; Mädlerpassage, Grimmaische Strasse 2-4; mains Keller €10-27, Weinstuben €33-35; ⊙Keller noon-11pm daily, Weinstuben 6-11pm Mon-Sat) Founded in 1525, Auerbachs Keller is one of Germany's best-known restaurants. It's cosy and touristy but the food's actually quite good and the setting memorable. There are two sections: the vaulted Grosser Keller for hearty Saxonian dishes and the four historic rooms of the Historische Weinstuben for upscale German fare. Reservations highly advised.

Max Enk
MODERN GERMAN €€€

(☑0341-9999 7638; www.max-enk.de; Neumarkt 9-19; mains €20-26, 1-/2-/3-course lunch €10/12/15; ⊙noon-2pm & 6pm-1am Mon-Fri, noon-1am Sat, 11.30am-4pm Sun) People share laughs over hand-picked wines and plates of elegant comfort food kicked into high gear at this sleek outpost. The Wiener schnitzel is a reliable standby, the quality meats are grilled to perfection and the weekday multicourse lunches are a steal.

🍷 Drinking & Entertainment

Party activity centres on three main areas: the boisterous Drallewatsch pub strip, the more upmarket theatre district around Gottschedstrasse, and the mix of trendy and alt-vibe joints along Karl-Liebknecht-Strasse (aka 'Südmeile').

Moritzbastei
CAFE, BAR

(☑0341-702 590; www.moritzbastei.de; Universitätsstrasse 9; ⊙10am-late Mon-Fri, from 9am Sun, parties almost nightly; 🛜) This legendary (sub)cultural centre in a warren of cellars of the old city fortifications keeps an all-ages crowd happy with parties, concerts, art and readings. It harbours stylish cocktail and wine bars as well as a daytime cafe (dishes €2 to €5) that serves delicious coffee along with healthy and wallet-friendly fare. Summer terrace, too.

Flowerpower
PUB

(☑0341-961 3441; www.flower-power.de; Riemannstrasse 42; ⊙7pm-5am; 🛜) It's party time any time at this long-running psychedelic flashback to the '60s (cool pinball machines). Admission is always free and the music tends to be older than the crowd. If you've overdone it, you can even crash upstairs for the night for €15.

Cafe Waldi
CAFE, BAR

(📞0341-462 5667; www.cafewaldi.de; Petersstein-weg 10; ⏰11.30am-late Mon-Fri, 9am-late Sat & Sun) Despite its great-grandma's living room look – complete with big sofas, cuckoo clocks and mounted antlers – Waldi is an up-to-the-minute hang-out where you can eat breakfast until 4pm, fuel up on coffee and a light meal, or nurse cocktails and pints until the wee hours. On weekends, DJs rock the upstairs area with house, indie and hip hop.

ℹ Information

Tourist Office (📞0341-710 4260, room referral 0341-710 4255; www.leipzig.travel; Katharinenstrasse 8; ⏰9.30am-6pm Mon-Fri, to 3pm Sat, to 3pm Sun) Room referral, ticket sales, maps and general information. Also sells the Leipzig Card (1/3 days €9.90/19.90).

ℹ Getting There & Away

Leipzig-Halle Airport (LEJ; www.leipzig-halle-airport.de) is about 21km west of Leipzig and linked to town by half-hourly S-Bahn train (€4.30, 35 minutes).

High-speed trains frequently serve Frankfurt (€80, 3½ hours), Dresden (€28, 1¼ hours) and Berlin (€47,1¼ hours), among others.

Weimar

📞03643 / POP 65,500

Wandering around Weimar's enchanting old streets, you can sense the presence of such notables as Goethe, Schiller, Bach, Liszt and Nietzsche, who once made their home here. There are plenty of statues, plaques and museums to remind you of their legacy, along with parks and gardens to take a break from the intellectual onslaught.

◉ Sights

★**Goethe-Nationalmuseum**
MUSEUM

(📞03643-545 400; www.klassik-stiftung.de; Frauenplan 1; adult/concession/under 16yr €12/8.50/free; ⏰9am-6pm Tue-Sun Apr-Oct, to 4pm Nov-Mar) This museum has the most comprehensive and insightful exhibit about Johann Wolfgang von Goethe, who is to the Germans what Shakespeare is to the British. It incorporates his home of 50 years, left pretty much as it was upon his death in 1832. This is where Goethe worked, studied, researched and penned *Faust* and other immortal works. In a modern annex, documents and objects shed light on the man

and his achievements, not only in literature but also in art, science and politics.

If you're a Goethe fan, you'll get the chills when seeing his study and the bedroom where he died, both preserved in their original state. To get the most from your visit, use the audioguide (free).

Schiller-Museum
MUSEUM

(📞03643-545 400; www.klassik-stiftung.de; Schillerstrasse 12; adult/concession/under 16yr €7.50/6/free; ⏰9.30am-6pm Tue-Sun Apr-Oct, to 4pm Nov-Mar) The dramatist Friedrich von Schiller (and close friend of Goethe's) lived in Weimar from 1799 until his early death in 1805. Study up on the man, his family and life in Thuringia in a recently revamped exhibit before plunging on to the private quarters, including the study with his deathbed and the desk where he wrote *Wilhelm Tell* and other famous works.

Bauhaus Museum
MUSEUM

(📞03643-545 400; www.klassik-stiftung.de; Theaterplatz 1; adult/concession/under 16yr €4.50/3/free; ⏰10am-6pm Apr-Oct, to 4pm Nov-Mar) Considering that Weimar is the 1919 birthplace of the influential Bauhaus school of art, design and architecture, this museum is a rather modest affair. A new, representative museum is expected to open in 2018.

Park an der Ilm
PARK

The sprawling Park an der Ilm provides a bucolic backdrop to the town and is also home to a trio of historic houses, most notably the **Goethe Gartenhaus** (where Goethe lived from 1776 to 1782), the **Römisches Haus** (the local duke's summer retreat, with period rooms and an exhibit on the park) and the **Liszt-Haus** (where the composer resided in 1848 and again from 1869 to 1886, and wrote the *Faust Symphony*).

⌷ Sleeping

★**Casa dei Colori**
B&B €€

(📞03643-489 640; www.casa-colori.de; Eisfeld 1a; d incl breakfast €95-125; 🅿🛜) Possibly Weimar's most charming boutique *Pension* (B&B or small hotel), the Casa convincingly imports cheerfully exuberant Mediterranean flair to central Europe. The mostly good-sized rooms are dressed in bold colours and come with a small desk, a couple of comfy armchairs and a stylish bathroom.

Amalienhof
HOTEL €€

(📞03643-5490; www.amalienhof-weimar.de; Amalienstrasse 2; d incl parking €97-125; 🅿🛜) The

EISENACH

On the edge of the Thuringian forest, Eisenach is the birthplace of Johann Sebastian Bach, but even the town's **museum** (☑03691-793 40; www.bachhaus.de; Frauenplan 21; adult/concession €8.50/4.50; ☺10am-6pm) dedicated to the great composer plays second fiddle to its main attraction: the awe-inspiring 11th-century **Wartburg** (☑03691-2500; www.wartburg-eisenach.de; Auf der Wartburg 1; tour adult/concession €9/5, museum & Luther study only €5/3; ☺tours 8.30am-5pm Apr-Oct, 9am-3.30pm Nov-Mar, English tour 1.30pm) castle.

Perched high above the town (views!), the humungous pile hosted medieval minstrel song contests and was the home of Elisabeth, a Hungarian princess later canonised for her charitable deeds. Its most famous resident, however, was **Martin Luther**, who went into hiding here in 1521 after being excommunicated and placed under papal ban. During this 10-month stay, he translated the New Testament from Greek into German, contributing enormously to the development of the written German language. His modest study is part of the guided tour. Back in town, there's an exhibit about the man and his historical impact in the **Lutherhaus** (☑03691-298 30; www.lutherhaus-eisenach.de; Lutherplatz 8; adult/concession €6/4; ☺10am-5pm, closed Mon Nov-Mar), where he lived as a schoolboy.

Arrive before 11am to avoid the worst of the crowds. From April to October, bus 10 runs hourly from 9am to 5pm from the Hauptbahnhof (central train station) to the Eselstation stop, from where it's a steep 10-minute walk up to the castle.

Regional trains run frequently to Erfurt (€11.10, 45 minutes) and Weimar (€14.40, one hour). The **tourist office** (☑03691-792 30; www.eisenach.de; Markt 24; ☺10am-6pm Mon-Fri, to 5pm Sat & Sun) can help with finding accommodation.

charms of this hotel are manifold: classy antique furnishings, richly styled rooms that point to history without burying you in it, and a late breakfast buffet for those who take their holidays seriously. It's a splendid choice.

✖ Eating & Drinking

JoHanns Hof　　　　　　　GERMAN €€
(☑03643-493 617; www.restaurant-weimar.com; Scherfgasse 1; mains €12-25, lunch special €6.50; ☺11.30am-2.30pm & 5-11pm Mon-Sat) JoHanns is a breezy and elegant port of call for in-spired modern German cuisine and perfectly prepared choice cuts of steak, paired with a carefully curated selection of wines from the nearby Saale-Unstrut region. For a break from sightseeing, tuck into the value-priced weekday lunch specials in the cosy courtyard.

Residenz-Café　　　　INTERNATIONAL €€
(☑03643-594 08; www.residenz-cafe.de; Grüner Markt 4; breakfast €2.90-6.40, mains €5-12; ☺8am-1am; ☑) Locally adored 'Resi' is a Viennese-style coffeehouse and a jack of all trades – everyone should find something to their taste here no matter where the hands on the clock. The 'Lovers' Breakfast' comes with sparkling wine, the cakes are delicious and the salads crisp, but perhaps the most creativity goes into the weekly specials.

ℹ Information

Tourist Office (☑03643-7450; www.weimar.de; Markt 10; ☺9.30am-7pm Mon-Sat, to 3pm Sun Apr-Oct, 9.30am-6pm Mon-Fri, to 2.30pm Sat & Sun Nov-Mar) Sells the WeimarCard (per day €14.50) for free or discounted museum admissions and travel on city buses and other benefits.

ℹ Getting There & Away

Frequent direct train connections include Erfurt (€5.30, 15 minutes), Eisenach (€15.30, one hour), Leipzig (€19.20, 1¾ hours), Dresden (€47, 2½ hours) and Berlin-Hauptbahnhof (€58, 2¼ hours). The town centre is a 20-minute walk or ride on bus 1 away.

Erfurt

☑0361 / POP 205,000

A little river courses through this pretty medieval pastiche of sweeping squares, time-worn alleyways, a house-lined bridge and lofty church spires. Erfurt also boasts one of Germany's oldest universities, founded by rich merchants in 1392, where Martin Luther studied philosophy before becoming a monk at the local monastery. It's a refreshingly untouristed spot and well worth exploring.

◉ Sights

All of Erfurt's main sights cluster in the old town, about a 10-minute walk from the train station (or quick ride on tram 3, 4 or 6). The most striking panorama unfolds on the vast Domplatz where two churches – the Marien-dom and the Severikirche – form a photo-genic ensemble lorded over by the vast and well-preserved Petersberg citadel.

Mariendom
CHURCH

(St Mary's Cathedral; ☑0361-646 1265; www.dom-erfurt.de; Domplatz; ☺9.30am-6pm Mon-Sat, 1-6pm Sun May-Oct, to 5pm Nov-Apr) The cathe-dral where Martin Luther was ordained a priest has origins as a simple 8th-century chapel that grew into the stately Gothic pile you see today. Standouts in its treasure-filled interior include the stained-glass windows; the Wolfram, an 850-year-old bronze cande-labrum in the shape of a man; the Gloriosa bell (1497); a Romanesque stucco Madonna; and the intricately carved choir stalls.

The steps buttressing the cathedral make for a dramatic backdrop for the popular **Domstufen-Festspiele**, a classical music festival held in July or August.

Krämerbrücke
BRIDGE

(Merchants' Bridge) Flanked by cute half-timbered houses on both sides, this charm-ing 1325 stone bridge is the only one north of the Alps that's still inhabited. To this day people live above little shops with attractive displays of chocolate and pottery, jewellery and basic souvenirs. See the bridge from above by climbing the tower of the **Ägidien-kirche** (usually open 11am to 5pm) punctu-ating its eastern end.

Augustinerkloster
CHURCH

(Augustinian Monastery; ☑0361-576 600; www.augustinerkloster.de; Augustinerstrasse 10; tour adult/concession €6/4; ☺tours 9.30am-5pm Mon-Sat, 11am & noon Sun Apr-Oct, 9.30am-3.30pm Mon-Fri, to 2pm Sat, 11am Sun Nov-Mar) It's Luther lore galore at the very monastery where the reformer lived from 1505 to 1511, and where he was ordained as a monk and read his first Mass. You're free to roam the grounds, visit the church with its ethereal Gothic stained-glass windows and attend the prayer servic-es. Guided tours of the monastery itself take in the cloister, a re-created Luther cell and an exhibit on Luther's life in Erfurt. You can sleep here, too. Enter on Comthurgasse.

⌷ Sleeping

Opera Hostel
HOSTEL €

(☑0361-6013 1360; www.opera-hostel.de; Walk-mühlstrasse 13; dm €13-20, s/d/tr €49/60/81, linen €2.50; @ 🛜) Run with smiles and aplomb, this upmarket hostel in a historic building above a steakhouse scores big with wal-let-watching global nomads. Rooms are bright and spacious, many with an extra sofa for chilling, and you can make friends in the communal kitchen and on-site lounge-bar. From the train station, take bus 51 (direction: Hochheim) to 'Alte Oper'.

Pension Rad-Hof
PENSION €

(☑0361-602 7761; www.rad-hof.de; Kirchgasse 1b; d €66; @ 🛜) The owners of this cyclist-friendly guesthouse, next to the Augustinian monas-tery and near the pub quarter, have gone the extra mile in renovating the building with natural materials, such as wood and mud. No two rooms are alike.

Hotel Brühlerhöhe
HOTEL €€

(☑0361-241 4990; www.hotel-bruehlerhoehe-erfurt.de; Rudolfstrasse 48; d from €85; P 🛜) This Prussian officers' casino turned chic city hotel gets high marks for its opulent breakfast spread (€12.50) and smiley, quick-on-their-feet staff. Room are modern but cosy with chocolate brown furniture, thick carpets and sparkling baths. It's a 10-minute walk or short tram ride into the town centre.

✕ Eating & Drinking

Pub and cafes abound in the narrow lanes of the Andreasviertel north of the Dom.

Zwiesel
GERMAN €

(Michaelisstrasse 31; mains €6-9; ☺6pm-late Mon-Thu, 3pm-late Fri-Sun) A combination of home-style food, cold beer, an epic cocktail list and an easy-going vibe has been the winning formula at Lars Schirmer's popular locals' hang-out. On colder days the art-decorated vaulted cellar beckons while in summer the action moves into the beer garden.

Henner
SANDWICHES €

(☑0361-654 6691; www.henner-sandwiches.de; Weitergasse 8; dishes €3.50-8; ☺8am-5pm Mon-Fri; ☑) This upbeat bistro makes a great daytime pit stop for freshly made sand-wiches, homemade soups and crisp salads.

Zum Wenigemarkt 13
GERMAN €€

(☑0361-642 2379; www.wenigemarkt-13.de; Weni-gemarkt 13; mains €9-17; ☺11.30am-11pm) Run by a dynamic family, this upbeat restaurant serves traditional and updated takes on Thuringian cuisine starring regionally hunted and gathered ingredients when possible. Tender salt-encrusted pork roast and trout drizzled with tangy caper white-wine sauce are both menu stars.

❶ Information

Tourist Office (☑ 0361-664 00; www.erfurt-tourismus.de; Benediktsplatz 1; ⊘ 10am-6pm Mon-Sat, to 2pm Sun Apr-Dec, 10am-6pm Mon-Fri, to 4pm Sat, to 2pm Sun Jan-Mar) Sells the ErfurtCard (€12.90 per 48 hours), which includes a city tour, public transport and free or discounted admissions.

❶ Getting There & Around

Fast trains leave frequently for Berlin (€61, 2¾ hours; some with change in Leipzig), Dresden (€51, 2¾ hours) and Frankfurt-am-Main (€55, 2¼ hours). Regional trains to Weimar (€5.30, 15 minutes) and Eisenach (€11.80, 45 minutes) depart at least once hourly. From Erfurt's central station, trams 3, 4 and 6 run via Anger and Fischmarkt to Domplatz.

BAVARIA

From the cloud-shredding Alps to the fertile Danube plain, Bavaria (Bayern) is a place that keeps its clichéd promises. Story-book castles bequeathed by an oddball king poke through dark forest, cowbells tinkle in flower-filled meadows, the thwack of palm on Lederhosen accompanies the clump of frothy stein on timber, and medieval walled towns go about their time-warped business.

But there's so much more than the chocolate-box idyll. Learn about Bavaria's state-of-the-art motor industry in Munich, discover its Nazi past in Nuremberg and Berchtesgaden, sip world-class wines in Würzburg or take a mind-boggling train ride up Germany's highest mountains. Destinations are often described as possessing 'something for everyone'. In Bavaria, this is no exaggeration.

Munich

☑ 089 / POP 1.38 MILLION

If you're looking for Alpine clichés, they're all here, but Munich also has plenty of unexpected cards down its dirndl. Folklore and age-old traditions exist side by side with sleek BMWs, designer boutiques

and high-powered industry. Its museums include world-class collections of artistic masterpieces, and its music and cultural scenes are second only to Berlin's.

◉ Sights

◉ Altstadt

★**Marienplatz** SQUARE
(Ⓢ Marienplatz) The heart and soul of the Altstadt, Marienplatz, is a popular gathering spot and packs a lot of personality into a compact frame. It's anchored by the Mariensäule (Mary's Column), built in 1638 to celebrate the victory over Swedish forces during the Thirty Years' War. At 11am and noon (also 5pm March to October), the square jams up with tourists craning their necks to take in the cute carillon in the Neues Rathaus (New Town Hall).

St Peterskirche CHURCH
(Church of St Peter; Rindermarkt 1; admission church free, tower adult/child €2/1; ⊘ tower 9am-7pm Mon-Fri, from 10am Sat & Sun May-Oct, closes 1hr earlier Nov-Apr; Ⓢ Marienplatz, 🚊 Marienplatz) Some 306 steps divide you from the best view of central Munich from the 92m tower of St Peterskirche, Munich's oldest church (1150). Inside awaits a virtual textbook of art through the centuries. Worth taking a closer peek at are the Gothic St-Martin-Altar, the baroque ceiling fresco by Johann Baptist Zimmermann and rococo sculptures by Ignaz Günther.

Central Munich

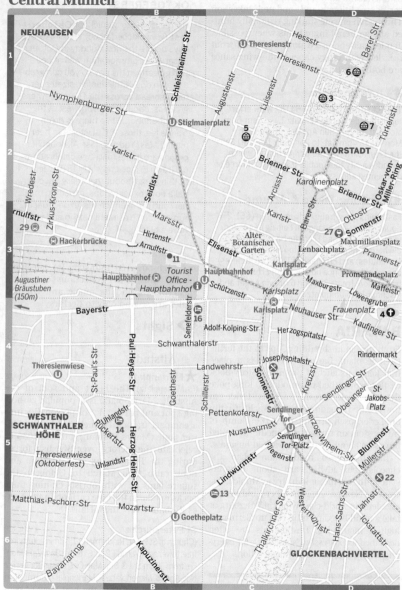

Viktualienmarkt MARKET
(🕓Mon-Fri&Satmorning; Ⓢ Marienplatz, Ⓡ Marienplatz) Fresh fruits and vegetables, piles of artisan cheeses, tubs of exotic olives, hams and jams, chanterelles and truffles – Viktualienmarkt is a feast of flavours and one of central Europe's finest gourmet markets.

Frauenkirche CHURCH
(Church of Our Lady; ☑089-290 0820; www.muenchner-dom.de; Frauenplatz 1; 🕓7am-7pm

500 m
0.25 miles

Geschwister-Scholl-Platz
Chinesischer Turm (150m)
Universität
Eisbach Creek
Schellingstr
Kaulbachstr
Amalienstr
Ludwigstr
Schönfeldstr
Englischer Garten
Hofgartensemped
Von-der-Tann-Str
Jägerstr
Ludwigstr
Galeriestr
Prinzregentenstr
Hofgarten
Karl-Scharnagl-Ring
Odeonsplatz
Hofgartenstr
Theatinerstr
Residenzmuseum
2 🏛🏛 8
Max-Joseph-Platz
Marstallplatz
Maximilianstr
19
Train Station
ALTSTADT
Tourist Office
Marienplatz
Neuturmstr
Thomas-Wimmer-Ring
24
Marienplatz
1 25
Marienplatz
Petersplatz
15 9
Tal
Dreifaltigkeits Platz
Isartor 21
Mariannen Platz
20 10
Frauenstr
Reichenbachplatz
18
Klenzestr
Baaderstr
26
Buttermelcherstr
Cornelliusstr
Kohlstr
Gärtnerplatzviertel
Klenzestr
Erhardtstr
Fraunhoferstr
28
Zeppelinstr
23
12
Fraunhoferstr
Isar
Gebsat
Lilienstr

taller than its onion-domed twin towers, which reach a skyscraping 99m.

◎ Maxvorstadt, Schwabing & Englischer Garten

North of the Altstadt, Maxvorstadt is home to Munich's main university and top-drawer art museums. It segues into equally cafe-filled Schwabing, which rubs up against the vast **Englischer Garten**, one of Europe's biggest city parks and a favourite playground for locals and visitors alike.

Alte Pinakothek   MUSEUM
(☎089-238 0526; www.pinakothek.de; Barer Strasse 27; adult/child €4/2, Sun €1, audioguide €4.50;

Sat-Wed, to 8.30pm Thu, to 6pm Fri; Ⓢ Marienplatz) The landmark Frauenkirche, built between 1468 and 1488, is Munich's spiritual heart and the Mt Everest among its churches. No other building in the central city may stand

⊙10am-8pm Tue, to 6pm Wed-Sun; 🖥Pinakotheken, 🏛Pinakotheken) Munich's main repository of old European masters is crammed with all the major players that decorated canvases between the 14th and 18th centuries. This neoclassical temple was masterminded by Leo von Klenze and is a delicacy even if you can't tell your Rembrandt from your Rubens. The collection is world famous for its exceptional quality and depth, especially when it comes to German masters. Note that some sections are closed for renovation.

Neue Pinakothek   MUSEUM
(☑089-2380 5195; www.pinakothek.de; Barer Strasse 29; adult/child €7/5, Sun €1; ⊙10am-6pm Thu-Mon, to 8pm Wed; 🖥Pinakotheken, 🏛Pinakotheken) The Neue Pinakothek harbours a well-respected collection of 19th- and early 20th-century paintings and sculpture, from rococo to *Jugendstil* (art nouveau). All the world-famous household names get wall space here, including crowd-pleasing French Impressionists such as Monet, Cézanne and Degas as well as Van Gogh, whose bold pigmented *Sunflowers* (1888) radiates cheer.

Pinakothek der Moderne   MUSEUM
(☑089-2380 5360; www.pinakothek.de; Barer Strasse 40; adult/child €10/7, Sun €1; ⊙10am-6pm Tue, Wed & Fri-Sun, to 8pm Thu; 🖥Pinakotheken, 🏛Pinakotheken) Germany's largest modern art museum unites four significant collections under a single roof: 20th-century art, applied design from the 19th century to today, a graphics collection and an architecture museum. It's housed in a spectacular building by Stephan Braunfels, whose four-storey interior centres on a vast eye-like dome from where soft natural light filters throughout blanched white galleries.

Lenbachhaus   MUSEUM
(Municipal Gallery; ☑089-2333 2000; www.lenbachhaus.de; Luisenstrasse 33; adult/concession incl

---

NO WAVE GOODBYE

Munich is famous for beer, sausages and surfing. Yep, you read that right. Just go to the southern tip of the Englischer Garten at Prinzregentenstrasse and you'll see scores of people leaning over a bridge to cheer on wetsuit-clad daredevils as they 'hang 10' on an artificially created wave in the Eisbach creek. It's only a single wave, but it's a darn fine one.

---

audioguide €10/5; ⊙10am-9pm Tue, to 6pm Wed-Sun; 🖥Königsplatz, 🚇Königsplatz) Reopened to rave reviews after a four-year renovation that saw the addition of a new wing by Lord Norman Foster, this glorious gallery is once again the go-to place to admire the vibrant expressionist canvases of Kandinsky, Franz Marc, Paul Klee and other members of the groundbreaking modernist artist group called Blue Rider, founded in Munich in 1911.

◉ Further Afield

Schloss Nymphenburg   PALACE
(www.schloss-nymphenburg.de; adult/concession/under 18yr €6/5/free; ⊙9am-6pm Apr-mid-Oct, 10am-4pm mid-Oct-Mar; 🏛Schloss Nymphenburg) The Bavarian royal family's summer residence and its lavish gardens sprawl around 5km northwest of the city centre. A self-guided tour kicks off in the Gallery of Beauties, where 38 portraits of attractive females chosen by an admiring King Ludwig I peer prettily from the walls. Other highlights include the Queen's Bedroom with the sleigh bed on which Ludwig II was born, and the King's Chamber resplendent with trompe l'œil ceiling frescoes.

BMW Museum   MUSEUM
(☑089-125 016 001; www.bmw-welt.de; Am Olympiapark 2; adult/concession €8/6; ⊙museum 10am-6pm Tue-Sun, BMW Welt 9am-6pm Tue-Sun; 🚇Petuelring) The silver-bowl-shaped museum comprises seven themed 'houses' that examine the development of BMW's product line and include sections on motorcycles and motor racing. Even if you're not a petrol head, the interior design – with its curvy retro feel, futuristic bridges, squares and huge backlit wall screens – is reason enough to visit.

The museum is linked to two more architecturally stunning buildings: the BMW Headquarters (closed to the public) and the BMW-Welt showroom (admission free). Plant tours are available from 9am to 4.30pm on weekdays.

⊊ Tours

Radius Tours & Bike Rental   GUIDED
(☑089-5502 9374; www.radiustours.com; Arnulfstrasse 3; ⊙office 8.30am-6pm Apr-Oct, to 2pm Nov-Mar) Entertaining and informative English-language tours include the donation-based city tour, a Third Reich tour and a beer-themed tour. Also does day trips to Neuschwanstein, Nuremberg and Salzburg. Rents bikes for €17 for 24 hours.

MUNICH RESIDENZ

Generations of Bavarian rulers expanded a medieval fortress into this vast and palatial compound that served as their primary residence and seat of government from 1508 to 1918. Today it's an Aladdin's cave of fanciful rooms and collections through the ages that can be seen on an audioguided tour of what is called the **Residenzmuseum** (☑ 089-290 671; www.residenz-muenchen.de; adult/concession/under 18yr €7/6/free; ⊙ 9am-6pm Apr–mid-Oct, 10am-5pm mid-Oct–Mar, last entry 1hr before closing; Ⓢ Odeonsplatz). Allow at least two hours to see everything at a gallop.

Highlights include the fresco-smothered **Antiquarium** banqueting hall and the exuberantly rococo **Reiche Zimmer** (Ornate Rooms). The **Schatzkammer** (Residence Treasury; adult/concession/under 18yr with parents €7/6/free; ⊙ 9am-6pm Apr–mid-Oct, 10am-5pm mid-Oct–Mar, last entry 1hr before closing; Ⓢ Odeonsplatz) displays a veritable banker's bonus worth of jewel-encrusted bling of yesteryear, from golden toothpicks to finely crafted swords, miniatures in ivory to gold entombed cosmetics trunks. A combined ticket for the Residenzmuseum and Schatzkammer is adult/concession €11/9.

City Bus 100   BUS

Ordinary city bus that runs from the Hauptbahnhof to the Ostbahnhof via 21 sights, including the Residenz and the Pinakothek museums.

🛏 Sleeping

Book way ahead during Oktoberfest and the busy summer. Many budget places cluster in the cheerless streets around the train station.

Wombats City Hostel Munich   HOSTEL €

(☑ 089-5998 9180; www.wombats-hostels.com; Senefelderstrasse 1; dm €19-29, d €76; P @ 🛜; Ⓢ Hauptbahnhof, 🚇 Hauptbahnhof) Munich's top hostel is a professionally run affair with a whopping 300 dorm beds plus private rooms. Dorms are painted in cheerful pastels and outfitted with wooden floors, ensuite facilities, sturdy lockers and comfy pine bunks, all in a central location near the train station. A free welcome drink awaits in the bar. Breakfast costs €3.90.

★ Hotel Laimer Hof   HOTEL €€

(☑ 089-178 0380; www.laimerhof.de; Laimer Strasse 40; s/d from €65/85; P @ 🛜; 🚇 Romanplatz) Just a five-minute amble from Schloss Nymphenburg, this tranquil refuge is run by a friendly team who take time to get to know their guests. No two of the 23 rooms are alike, but all boast antique touches, oriental carpets and golden beds. Free bike rentals and coffee and tea in the lobby. Breakfast costs €10.

Hotel Uhland   HOTEL €€

(☑ 089-543 350; www.hotel-uhland.de; Uhlandstrasse 1; s/d from €75/95; P 🛜; Ⓢ Theresienwiese) The Uhland is an enduring favourite with regulars who like their hotel to feel like a home away from home. Free wi-fi and parking, a breakfast buffet with organic products, and minibar drinks that won't dent your budget are just some of the thoughtful features. Rooms have extra large waterbeds.

Flushing Meadows   DESIGN HOTEL €€

(☑ 089-5527 9170; www.flushingmeadowshotel. com; Fraunhoferstrasse 32; studios €115-165; ⊙ reception 6am-11pm; P ❄ 🛜; Ⓢ Fraunhoferstrasse) Urban explorers keen on up-to-the-minute design cherish this new contender on the top two floors of a former postal office in the hip Glockenbachviertel. Each of the 11 concrete-ceilinged lofts reflects the vision of a locally known creative type, while three of the five penthouse studios have a private terrace. Breakfast costs €11.

Hotel Cocoon   DESIGN HOTEL €€

(☑ 089-5999 3907; www.hotel-cocoon.de; Lindwurmstrasse 35; s/d from €69/89; Ⓢ Sendlinger Tor, 🚇 Sendlinger Tor) Fans of retro design will strike gold in this central lifestyle hotel. Things kick off in the reception with its faux '70s veneer and dangling '60s ball chairs, and continue in the rooms. All are identical, decorated in retro oranges and greens and equipped with LCD TV, iPod dock and a 'laptop cabin'. The glass showers actually stand in the sleeping area, with only a kitschy Alpine meadow scene veiling life's vitals. Breakfast costs €9.

Louis Hotel   HOTEL €€€

(☑ 089-411 9080; www.louis-hotel.com; Viktualienmarkt 6/Rindermarkt 2; r €159-289; Ⓢ Marienplatz) An air of relaxed sophistication pervades the scene-savvy Louis, where good-sized rooms are furnished in nut and oak,

BEER HALLS & BEER GARDENS

Beer drinking is not just an integral part of Munich's entertainment scene, it's a reason to visit. Following are a few options:

Augustiner Bräustuben (☑089-507 047; www.braeustuben.de; Landsberger Strasse 19; ⊘10am-midnight; ⊠Holzapfelstrasse) Depending on the wind, an aroma of hops envelops you as you approach this traditional beer hall inside the actual Augustiner brewery. The Bavarian grub (mains €7.50 to €14) here is superb, especially the *Schweinshaxe* (pork knuckle). Different specials daily to boot.

Hofbräuhaus (☑089-290 136 100; www.hofbraeuhaus.de; Am Platzl 9; ⊘9am-11.30pm; ⑤Marienplatz, ⊠Kammerspiele, ⊠Marienplatz) The mothership of all beer halls is a warren of woodsy, vaulted rooms filled with beer-swilling revelers swaying to the inevitable oompah band and tucking into gut-busting Bavarian fare (mains €7.50 to €18). It's just as crazy fun as you imagined it to be. For more quiet, head to the big, flag-festooned hall upstairs.

Chinesischer Turm (☑089-383 8730; www.chinaturm.de; Englischer Garten 3; ⊘10am-11pm; ⊠Chinesischer Turm, ⊠Tivolistrasse) This one's hard to ignore because of its Englischer Garten (English Garden) location and pedigree as Munich's oldest beer garden (since 1791). Camera-toting tourists and laid-back locals, picnicking families and suits sneaking a brew clomp around the wooden pagoda, serenaded by an oompah band.

natural stone and elegant tiles and equipped with the gamut of 'electronica', including iPod docks and flatscreens with Sky TV. All have small balconies facing either the courtyard or the Viktualienmarkt. Views are also terrific from the rooftop bar and restaurant. Breakfast costs €24.50.

✗ Eating

Schmalznudel
CAFE €

(Cafe Frischhut; ☑089-2602 3156; Prälat-Zistl-Strasse 8; pastries €1.70; ⊘7am-6pm Mon-Fri, 5am-5pm Sat; ⑤Marienplatz, ⊠Marienplatz) Officially called Cafe Frischhut, this little cult joint is mostly known by its nickname, *Schmalznudel*, an oily type of doughnut which is the only thing served here. Best enjoyed with a pot of steaming coffee.

Wirtshaus in der Au
BAVARIAN €€

(☑089-448 1400; Lilienstrasse 51; mains €9-20; ⊘5pm-midnight Mon-Fri, from 10am Sat & Sun; ⊠Deutsches Museum) This traditional Bavarian restaurant has a solid 21st-century vibe but it's the time-honoured dumpling that's the top speciality here, although carnivores might prefer the roast duck or another hearty menu item. Once a brewery, the space-rich dining room has chunky tiled floors, a lofty ceiling and a crackling fireplace in winter. When spring springs, the beer garden fills.

Wirtshaus Fraunhofer
BAVARIAN €€

(☑089-266 460; www.fraunhofertheater.de; Fraunhoferstrasse 9; mains €7.50-19; ⊘4pm-1am; ☑; ⊠Müllerstrasse) With its screechy parquet floors, stuccoed ceilings, wood panelling and virtually no trace that the last century even happened, this wonderfully characterful inn is perfect for exploring the region with a fork. The menu is a seasonally adapted checklist of southern German favourites, but also features at least a dozen vegetarian dishes.

Vegelangelo
VEGETARIAN €€

(☑089-2880 6836; www.vegelangelo.de; Thomas-Wimmer-Ring 16; mains €10-19; ⊘noon-2pm Tue-Thu, 6pm-late Mon-Sat; ☑; ⊠Isartor, ⊠Isartor) Reservations are recommended at this petite vegie spot where Indian odds and ends, a piano and a small Victorian fireplace distract little from the superb meat-free cooking, all of which can be adapted to suit vegans. There's a menu-only (3/4 courses €24/30) policy Fridays and Saturdays. Cash only.

Café Cord
INTERNATIONAL €€

(☑089-5454 0780; www.cafe-cord.tv; Sonnenstrasse 19; mains €10-20; ⊘11am-1am Mon-Sat; ⑤Karlsplatz, ⊠Karlsplatz, ⊠Karlsplatz) Clean-cut Cord is a good stop for a light lunch or coffee, or an ideal first stop on the club circuit. In summer the super delicious global fare (mains €10 to €20) tastes best in the romantic, twinkling courtyard.

Kochspielhaus INTERNATIONAL €€
(☑ 089-5480 2738; www.kochspielhaus.de; Rumfordstrasse 5; breakfast €10-16, mains €13-26; ☺ 7am-8pm Sun & Mon, 6.30am-midnight Tue-Sat; ⓢ Fraunhoferstrasse) Attached to a gourmet bakery called Backspielhaus, this modern-country-style lair accented with massive candles packages only super fresh, top-quality ingredients into clever pasta, meat and fish dishes. Also a great spot for breakfast, especially in summer when the white outdoor tables and benches beckon.

Les Deux Brasserie INTERNATIONAL €€
(☑ 089-710 407 373; www.lesdeux-muc.de; Maffaistrasse 3a; mains €6.50-17; ☺ noon-10pm; ⓢ Marienplatz) Below the eponymous fine-dining restaurant, Les Deux' ground-floor brasserie is perfect for taking a tasty break without breaking the budget. Choose from such classics as mini burgers, club sandwich or Icelandic cod and chips or go for one of the more elaborate weekly specials. If the weather permits, tables spill into the courtyard.

 Drinking & Nightlife

Apart from the beer halls and gardens, Munich has no shortage of lively pubs. The Glockenbachviertel, the Gärtnerplatzviertel, Maxvorstadt and Schwabing are good places to follow your ears.

Zephyr Bar COCKTAIL BAR
(www.zephyr-bar.de; Baaderstrasse 68; ☺ 8pm-1am Mon-Thu, to 3am Fri & Sat; ⓢ Fraunhoferstrasse) At one of Munich's best bars, Alex Schmaltz whips up courageous potions with unusual ingredients such as homemade cucumber-dill juice, sesame oil or banana-parsley purée. Cocktail alchemy at its finest, and a top gin selection to boot. No reservations.

Niederlassung BAR
(☑ 089-3260 0307; www.niederlassung.org; Buttermelcherstrasse 6; ☺ 7pm-1am Tue-Thu, to 3am Fri & Sat, to midnight Sun; ⓢ Fraunhoferstrasse, ⓡ Isartor) From Adler Dry to Zephyr, this gin joint stocks an impressive 80 varieties of juniper juice in an unpretentious setting filled with books and sofas and humming with indie sounds. There's even a selection of different tonic waters to choose from. Happy hour from 7pm to 9pm and after midnight.

Rote Sonne CLUB
(☑ 089-5526 3330; www.rote-sonne.com; Maximiliansplatz 5; ☺ from 11pm Thu-Sun; ⓡ Lenbachplatz) Named for a 1969 Munich cult movie starring It-Girl Uschi Obermaier, the Red Sun is a

fiery nirvana for fans of electronic sounds. A global roster of DJs keeps the wooden dance floor packed and sweaty until the sun rises.

Atomic Café CLUB
(www.atomic.de; Neuturmstrasse 5; ☺ from 10pm Wed-Sat; ⓡ Kammerspiele) This bastion of indie sounds with funky '60s decor is known for bookers with a knack for catching upwardly hopeful bands before their big break. Otherwise, it's party time; long-running Britwoch is the hottest Wednesday club night in town.

❶ Information

Tourist Office (☑ 089-2339 6500; www.muenchen.de) Branches include Hauptbahnhof (Bahnhofplatz 2; ☺ 9am-8pm Mon-Sat, 10am-6pm Sun) and Marienplatz (Marienplatz 2; ☺ 10am-7pm Mon-Fri, to 5pm Sat, to 2pm Sun).

❶ Getting There & Away

AIR

Munich Airport (MUC; www.munich-airport.de) is about 30km northeast of town and linked to the Hauptbahnhof every 10 minutes by S-Bahn (S1 and S8; €10.40, 40 minutes) and every 20 minutes by the Lufthansa Airport Bus (€10.50, 45 minutes, between 5am and 8pm).

Ryanair flies into Memmingen's **Allgäu Airport** (FMM; www.allgaeu-airport.de), 125km to the west. The Allgäu-Airport-Express travels up to seven times daily between here and Munich Hauptbahnhof (€17, €12 if bought online, 1½ hours).

BUS

Buses, including the Romantic Road Coach, depart from **Zentraler Omnibusbahnhof** (Central Bus Station, ZOB; Arnulfstrasse 21) at S-Bahn station Hackerbrücke near the main train station.

TRAIN

All services leave from the Hauptbahnhof, where **Euraide** (www.euraide.de; Desk 1, Reisezentrum, Hauptbahnhof; ☺ 10am-7pm Mon-Fri Aug-Apr)

GERMANY MUNICH

GAY & LESBIAN MUNICH

In Munich, the rainbow flag flies especially proudly along Müllerstrasse and the adjoining Glockenbachviertel. Keep an eye out for the freebie mags *Our Munich* and *Sergej*, which contain up-to-date listings and news about the community and gay-friendly establishments around town. The website **Gay Tourist Office** (www.gaytouristoffice.de) also has handy information and can book gay-friendly lodging.

DACHAU CONCENTRATION CAMP

About 16km northwest of central Munich, **Dachau** (Dachau Concentration Camp Memorial Site; ☑ 08131-669 970; www.kz-gedenkstaette-dachau.de; Peter-Roth-Strasse 2a, Dachau; museum admission free; ⊙ 9am-5pm Tue-Sun) opened in 1933 as the first Nazi concentration camp. All in all, it 'processed' more than 200,000 inmates, killing between 30,000 and 40,000. It is now a haunting memorial that will stay long in your memory. Expect to spend two to three hours exploring the grounds and exhibits. For deeper understanding, pick up an audioguide (€3.50), join a 2½-hour tour and watch the 22-minute English-language documentary at the main museum.

From the Hauptbahnhof take the S2 to Dachau station (two-zone ticket; €5.20, 25 minutes), then catch bus 726 (direction: Saubachsiedlung) to the KZ-Gedenkstätte stop.

is a friendly English-speaking travel agency. Frequent fast and direct service include trains to Nuremberg (€55, 1¼ hours), Frankfurt (€101, 3¼ hours), Berlin (€130, six hours) and Vienna (€91.20, four hours), as well as twice-daily trains to Prague (€69.10 six hours).

❶ Getting Around

For public transport information, consult www.mvv-muenchen.de.

Garmisch-Partenkirchen

☑ 08821 / POP 26,700

An outdoor paradise for skiers and hikers, Garmisch-Partenkirchen is blessed with a fabled setting a snowball's throw from Germany's highest peak, the 2962m-high Zugspitze. Garmisch has a more cosmopolitan feel, while Partenkirchen retains an old-world Alpine village vibe. The towns were merged for the 1936 Winter Olympics.

◉ Sights

Zugspitze   MOUNTAIN

(www.zugspitze.de; return adult/child May-Sep €51/29.50, Oct-Apr €42.50/23; ⊙ train 8.15am-2.15pm) On good days, views from Germany's rooftop extend into four countries. The round trip starts in Garmisch aboard a cogwheel train (Zahnradbahn) that chugs along the mountain base to the Eibsee, an idyllic forest lake. From here, the Eibsee-Seilbahn, a super steep cable car, swings to the top at 2962m. When you're done admiring the views, the Gletscherbahn cable car brings you to the Zugspitz glacier at 2600m, from where the cogwheel train heads back to Garmisch.

The trip to the Zugspitze summit is as memorable as it is popular; beat the crowds by starting early in the day and, if possible, skip weekends altogether.

🛏 Sleeping & Eating

Reindl's Partenkirchner Hof   HOTEL €€€

(☑ 08821-943 870; www.reindls.de; Bahnhofstrasse 15; d €130-230; ⊙ restaurant noon-2.30pm & 6.30-11pm; ℗ 🐾 @ 🛜) Though Reindl's doesn't look worthy of its five stars from the outside, this elegant, tri-winged luxury hotel is stacked with perks, a wine bar and a top-notch gourmet restaurant. Rooms are studies in folk-themed elegance and some enjoy gobsmacking mountain views.

Bräustüberl   GERMAN €€

(☑ 08821-2312; www.braeustueberl-garmisch.de; Fürstenstrasse 23; mains €8.50-19) This quintessentially Bavarian tavern is the place to cosy up with some local nosh, served by dirndl-trussed waitresses, while the enormous enamel coal-burning stove revives chilled extremities. Live music on Saturdays.

❶ Information

Tourist Office (☑ 08821-180 700; www.gapa.de; Richard-Strauss-Platz 2; ⊙ 9am-6pm Mon-Sat, 10am-noon Sun) Friendly staff hand out maps, brochures and advice.

❶ Getting There & Away

Numerous tour operators run day trips to Garmisch-Partenkirchen from Munich but there's also at least hourly direct train service (€20.10, 1¼ hour).

Berchtesgaden

☑ 08652 / POP 7600

Steeped in myth and legend, Berchtesgaden and the surrounding countryside (the Berchtesgadener Land) is almost preternaturally beautiful. Framed by six formidable mountain ranges and home to Germany's second-highest mountain, the Watzmann

(2713m), its dreamy, fir-lined valleys are filled with gurgling streams and peaceful Alpine villages. Alas, Berchtesgaden's history is also indelibly tainted by the Nazi period. The area is easily visited on a day trip from Salzburg.

◉ Sights

Eagle's Nest   HISTORIC SITE
(Kehlsteinhaus; ☑ 08652-2929; www.kehlsteinhaus. de; Obersalzberg; adult/child €16.10/9.30; ⊗ buses 7.40am-4pm mid-May–Oct) The Eagle's Nest is a mountaintop retreat built as a 50th-birthday gift for Hitler. It took some 3000 workers only two years to carve the precipitous 6km-long mountain road, cut a 124m-long tunnel and a brass-panelled lift through the rock, and build the lodge itself (now a restaurant). It can only be reached by special shuttle bus from the Kehlsteinhaus bus station. Avoid peak hours (10am to 1pm).

On clear days, views from the top are breathtaking. If you're not driving, bus 838 makes the trip to the shuttle bus stop from the Berchtesgaden Hauptbahnhof every half hour.

At the mountain station, you'll be asked to book a spot on a return bus. Allow at least two hours to get through lines, explore the lodge and the mountaintop, and perhaps have a bite to eat. Don't panic if you miss your bus – just go back to the mountain station kiosk and rebook.

Dokumentation Obersalzberg   MUSEUM
(☑ 08652-947 960; www.obersalzberg.de; Salzbergstrasse 41, Obersalzberg; adult/child €3/ free, audioguide €2; ⊗ 9am-5pm daily Apr-Oct, 10am-3pm Tue-Sun Nov-Mar, last entry 1hr before closing) In 1933 the quiet mountain village of Obersalzberg (3km from Berchtesgaden) became the second seat of Nazi power after Berlin, a dark period that's given the full historical treatment at this excellent exhibit. It documents the forced takeover of the area, the construction of the compound and the daily life of the Nazi elite. All facets of Nazi terror are dealt with, including Hitler's near-mythical appeal, his racial politics, the resistance movement, foreign policy and the death camps. A section of the underground bunker network is open for perusal. Half-hourly bus 838 from Berchtesgaden Hauptbahnhof will get you there.

Königssee   LAKE
(☑ 08652-963 696; www.seenschifffahrt.de; Schönau; return boat adult/child €13.90/7; ⊗ boats 8am-5.15pm mid-Apr–mid-Oct) Cross-ing the serenely picturesque, emerald green Königssee makes for some unforgettable memories and once-in-a-lifetime photo opportunities. Cradled by steep mountain walls some 5km south of Berchtesgaden, the Königssee is Germany's highest lake (603m), with drinkably pure waters shimmering into fjordlike depths. Bus 841 makes the trip out here from the Berchtesgaden Hauptbahnhof roughly every hour.

☞ Tours

Eagle's Nest Tours   TOUR
(☑ 08652-649 71; www.eagles-nest-tours.com; Königsseer Strasse 2; adult/child €53/35; ⊗ 1.15pm mid-May–Oct) This highly reputable outfit offers a fascinating overview of Berchtesgaden's Nazi legacy.

🛏 Sleeping & Eating

Hotel Edelweiss   HOTEL €€€
(☑ 08652-979 90; www.edelweiss-berchtesgaden. com; Maximilianstrasse 2; d €200-236) Smack dab in the town centre, the Edelweiss is Berchtesgaden's sleek new contender. The style is modern Bavarian, meaning a combination of traditional woodsy flair and such hip factors as a luxe spa, a rooftop terrace restaurant-bar with wonderful mountain views and an outdoor infinity pool. Rooms are XL-sized and most have a balcony.

HITLER'S MOUNTAIN RETREAT

Of all the German towns tainted by the Third Reich, the Berchtesgaden area carries a burden heavier than most. Hitler fell in love with the secluded Alpine village of Obersalzberg while vacationing here in the 1920s and later bought a small country home that was enlarged into an imposing residence – the Berghof.

After seizing power in 1933, the Führer established a second seat of power here and brought much of the party brass with him. They drove out the locals and turned the compound into a *Führersperrgebiet* (an off-limits area). Many important decisions, about war and peace and the Holocaust, were made here.

In the final days of WWII, British and American bombers levelled much of Obersalzberg, although the Eagle's Nest, Hitler's mountaintop eyrie, was left strangely unscathed.

SCHLOSS NEUSCHWANSTEIN

Appearing through the mountaintops like a misty mirage, **Schloss Neuschwanstein** (🎫 tickets 08362-930 830; www.neuschwanstein.de; Neuschwansteinstrasse 20; adult/concession/under 18yr €12/11/free, incl Hohenschwangau €23/21/free; ⊘ 9am-6pm Apr–mid-Oct, 10am-4pm mid-Oct–Mar) was the model for Disney's *Sleeping Beauty* castle. Ludwig II planned this sugary fairy-tale pile himself, with the help of a stage designer rather than an architect. He envisioned it as a giant set on which to re-create the world of Germanic mythology, inspired by the operatic works of his friend Richard Wagner. The most impressive room is the **Sängersaal** (Minstrels' Hall), the wall frescoes depict scenes from the opera *Tannhäuser*.

Other completed sections include Ludwig's Tristan and Isolde–themed **bedroom**, dominated by a huge Gothic-style bed crowned with intricately carved cathedral-like spires; a gaudy **artificial grotto** (another allusion to *Tannhäuser*); and the Byzantine-style **Thronsaal** (Throne Room) with an incredible mosaic floor containing over two million stones. The tour ends with a 20-minute film on the castle and its creator.

For the postcard view of Neuschwanstein, walk 10 minutes up to **Marienbrücke** (Mary's Bridge).

Bräustübl　　　　　　　BAVARIAN **€€**
(🎫 08652-976 724; www.braeustueberl-berchtesgaden.de; Bräuhausstrasse 13; mains €6.50-15; ⊘ 10am-1am) Past the vaulted entrance painted in Bavaria's white and blue diamonds, this cosy beer hall–beer garden is run by the local brewery. Expect a carnivorous feast with such favourite rib-stickers as pork roast and the house speciality: baked veal head (tastes better than it sounds). On Friday and Saturday, a traditional band kicks into knee-slapping action.

ℹ Information

Regional Tourist Office (🎫 08652-896 70; www.berchtesgaden.com; Königsseer Strasse 2; ⊘ 8.30am-6pm Mon-Fri, 9am-5pm Sat, 9am-3pm Sun Apr–mid-Oct, reduced hours mid-Oct–Mar) Near the train station, this office has information about the entire Berchtegaden region.

ℹ Getting There & Away

Bus 840 connects the train stations in Berchtesgaden and Salzburg twice hourly (50 minutes). Travelling from Munich by train involves a change to a bus at Freilassing (€32.80, 2½ hours).

Romantic Road

Stretching 400km from the vineyards of Würzburg to the foot of the Alps, the Romantic Road (Romantische Strasse) is by far the most popular of Germany's themed holiday routes. It passes through more than two-dozen cities and towns, most famously Rothenburg ob der Tauber.

ℹ Getting There & Around

Frankfurt and Munich are the most popular gateways for exploring the Romantic Road, especially if you decide to take the **Romantic Road Coach** (🎫 0719-126 268, 0171-653 234; www.touring-travel.eu). From April to October this special service runs one coach daily in each direction between Frankfurt and Füssen (for Neuschwanstein) via Munich; the entire trip takes around 12 hours. There's no charge for breaking the journey and continuing the next day. Note that buses get incredibly crowded in summer.

Tickets are available for the entire route or for short segments. Buy them online or from travel agents, EurAide (p289) in Munich or *Reisezentrum* offices in larger train stations.

Füssen

🎫 08362 / POP 14,900

In the foothills of the Alps, Füssen itself is a charming town, although most visitors skip it and head straight to Schloss Neuschwanstein and Hohenschwangau, the two most famous castles associated with King Ludwig II. You can see both on a long day trip from Munich, although only when spending the night, after all the day trippers have gone, will you sense a certain Alpine serenity.

◎ Sights

The castles are about 4km outside of Füssen.

Schloss Hohenschwangau　　　　CASTLE
(🎫 08362-930 830; www.hohenschwangau.de; adult/concession/under 18yr €12/11/free, incl Neuschwanstein €23/21/free; ⊘ 8am-5.30pm Apr–mid-Oct, 9am-3.30pm mid-Oct–Mar) King Ludwig II grew up at the lovely sun-yellow Schloss

Hohenschwangau and later enjoyed spending summers here until his death in 1886. His father, Maximilian II, built this palace in a neo-Gothic style atop 12th-century ruins left by Schwangau knights. Far less showy than Neuschwanstein, Hohenschwangau has a distinctly lived-in feel where every piece of furniture is a used original. After his father died, Ludwig's main alteration was having stars, illuminated with hidden oil lamps, painted on the ceiling of his bedroom.

🛏 Sleeping & Eating

Altstadthotel Zum Hechten HOTEL €€
(✆08362-916 00; www.hotel-hechten.com; Ritterstrasse 6; d €94-100; P🐾) This is one of Füssen's oldest hotels and a barrel of fun. Public areas are traditional in style while the bedrooms have a contemporary feel with beautifully patterned parquet floors, a large bed and sunny colours. The small but classy spa is great for relaxing after a day on the trail.

Restaurant Ritterstub'n GERMAN €€
(✆08362-7759; www.restaurant-ritterstuben.de; Ritterstrasse 4; mains €5.50-16; ⏱11.30am-11pm Tue-Sun) This convivial pit stop has value-priced salads, snacks, lunch specials, fish, schnitzel and gluten-free dishes, and even a cute kids menu. The medieval-knight theme can be a bit grating but kids often love eating their fish sticks with their fingers or seeing mum and dad draped in a big bib.

ⓘ Information

Tourist Office (✆08362-938 50; www.fuessen. de; Kaiser-Maximilian-Platz; ⏱9am-6pm Mon-Fri, 10am-2pm Sat, 10am-noon Sun May-Oct,

---

ⓘ CASTLE TICKETS & TOURS

Both Hohenschwanstein and Neuschwanstein must be seen on guided 35-minute tours (in German or English). Timed tickets are only available from the **Ticket-Center** (✆08362-930 830; www. hohenschwangau.de; Alpenseestrasse 12; ⏱8am-5.30pm Apr–mid-Oct, 9am-3.30pm mid-Oct–Mar) at the foot of the castles and may be reserved online until two days prior to your visit (recommended).

If visiting both castles on the same day, the Hohenschwangau tour is scheduled first with enough time for the steep 30- to 40-minute walk between the castles. The footsore can travel by bus or by horse drawn carriage.

9am-5pm Mon-Fri, 10am-2pm Sat Nov-Apr) Can help find lodging.

ⓘ Getting There & Away

Füssen is the southern terminus of the Romantic Road Coach.

Regional trains run from Munich to Füssen every two hours with onward service to the castles on bus 78 or 73 (€27.90, 2½ hours). It's possible to do this as a day trip if leaving Munich around 8am.

Rothenburg ob der Tauber

✆09861 / POP 11,000

With its jumble of half-timbered houses enclosed by Germany's best-preserved ramparts, Rothenburg ob der Tauber lays on the medieval cuteness with a trowel. It's an essential stop on the Romantic Road but, alas, overcrowding can detract from its charm. Visit early or late in the day (or, ideally, stay overnight) to experience this historic wonderland sans crowds.

⊙ Sights

★ **Jakobskirche** CHURCH
(Church of St Jacob; Klingengasse 1; adult/child €2/0.50; ⏱9am-5.30pm Mon-Sat, 10.45am-5.30pm Sun) Rothenburg's majestic 500-year-old Lutheran parish church shelters the **Heilig Blut Altar** (Sacred Blood Altar), a supremely intricate altarpiece by medieval master carver Tilman Riemenschneider (it's up the stairs behind the organ).

Rathausturm HISTORIC BUILDING
(Town Hall Tower; Marktplatz; adult/concession €2/0.50; ⏱9.30am-12.30pm & 1-5pm daily Apr-Oct, noon-3pm Sat & Sun Jan-Mar & Nov, 10.30-2pm & 2.30-6pm daily Dec) Climb the 220 steps of the medieval town hall to the viewing platform of the Rathausturm to be rewarded with widescreen views of the Tauber.

Stadtmauer HISTORIC SITE
(Town Wall) Follow in the footsteps of sentries on a walk along Rothenburg's original 15th-century town fortifications. A 2.5km stretch of it is accessible, but even a short walk 5m to 7m above the ground delivers tremendous views over the town's red roofs.

Mittelalterliches Kriminalmuseum MUSEUM
(Medieval Crime & Punishment Museum; ✆09681-5359; www.kriminalmuseum.rothenburg.de; Burggasse 3-5; adult/child €5/3; ⏱10am-6pm May-Oct, shorter hours Nov-Apr) Medieval implements of

torture and punishment are on show at this gruesomely fascinating museum. Exhibits include chastity belts, masks of disgrace for gossips, a cage for cheating bakers, a neck brace for quarrelsome women and a beer-barrel pen for drunks. You can even snap a selfie of yourself in the stocks!

🛏 Sleeping & Eating

Altfränkische Weinstube   HOTEL €€
(📞 09861-6404; www.altfraenkische.de; Klosterhof 7; d €82-118; 🗟) This characterful inn has six romantic country-style rooms with exposed half-timber, bathtubs and most with four-poster or canopied beds. From 6pm onwards, the tavern serves up sound regional fare (mains €7 to €16) with a dollop of medieval cheer.

Mittermeier
Restaurant & Hotel   DESIGN HOTEL €€€
(📞 09861-945 430; www.blauesau.eu; Vorm Würzburger Tor 7; d €80-200; ⊘ restaurant 6-10.30pm Mon-Sat; 🅿 🗟) You'll sleep well in this smartly designed hotel just outside the town wall. The kitchen ninjas in the vaulted cellar restaurant pair punctilious craftsmanship with top-notch ingredients, sourced regionally whenever possibly (dinner mains €22 to €38). The focus is on grills paired with creative sides and superb wines from Franconia and beyond. Breakfast costs €10.

Gasthof Butz   GERMAN €
(📞 09861-2201; Kapellenplatz 4; mains €7-15; ⊘ 11.30am-2pm & 6-9pm; 🗟) For a quick goulash, schnitzel or roast pork, lug your weary legs to this locally adored, family-run inn in a former brewery. In summer two flowery beer gardens beckon. It also rents a dozen simply furnished rooms (double €36 to €75).

ℹ Information

Tourist Office (📞 09861-404 800; www.tourismus.rothenburg.de; Marktplatz 2; ⊘ 9am-6pm Mon-Fri, 10am-5pm Sat & Sun May-Oct, 9am-5pm Mon-Fri, 10am-1pm Sat Nov-Mar) Offers free internet access.

ℹ Getting There & Away

The Romantic Road Coach pauses in town for 45 minutes.

There are hourly trains to/from Steinach, a transfer point for service to Würzburg (€12.90, 1¼ hours).

Würzburg

📞 0931 / POP 127,000

Tucked in among river valleys lined with vineyards, Würzburg beguiles long before you reach the city centre and is renowned for its art, architecture and delicate wines. Its crowning architectural glory is the Residenz, one of the finest baroque structures in Germany and a Unesco World Heritage Site.

⊙ Sights

Festung Marienberg   FORTRESS
(📞 0931-355 170; tour adult/concession €3.50/2.50; ⊘ tours 11am, 2pm, 3pm & 4pm Tue-Sun, also 10am & 1pm Sat & Sun mid-Mar–Oct, 11am, 2pm & 3pm Sat & Sun Nov-mid-Mar) Enjoy panoramic city and vineyard views from this hulking fortress, the construction of which was initiated around 1200 by the local prince-bishops who governed here until 1719. Dramatically illuminated at night, the structure was only penetrated once, by Swedish troops during the Thirty Years' War, in 1631. Inside, the **Fürstenbaumuseum** (closed November to mid-March) sheds light on its former residents' pompous lifestyle, while the **Mainfränkisches Museum** presents city history and works by local late-Gothic master carver Tilmann Riemenschneider and other famous artists. The fortress is a 30-minute walk up the hill through the vineyards from the Alte Mainbrücke via the Tellsteige trail.

Dom St Kilian   CHURCH
(📞 0931-3866 2900; www.dom-wuerzburg.de; Domstrasse 40; ⊘ 10am-7pm Mon-Sat, 1-6pm Sun) Würzburg's freshly renovated Romanesque cathedral has impressive dimensions, an airy feel, and precious sculpture and tombstones affixed to slender pillars. A highlight is the **Schönbornkapelle** by Balthasar Neumann.

🛏 Sleeping & Eating

Würzburg's many *Weinstuben* (wine taverns) are great for sampling the local vintages.

Hotel Zum Winzermännle   HOTEL €€
(📞 0931-541 56; www.winzermaennle.de; Domstrasse 32; s €60-80, d €90-110; 🅿 @) This family-run converted winery is a feel-good retreat in the city's pedestrianised heart. Rooms are well furnished if a little on the old-fashioned side; some among those facing the quiet courtyard have balconies. Communal areas are bright and often seasonally decorated. Breakfast costs €5.

RESIDENZ

The vast Unesco-listed **Würzburg Residenz** (www.residenz-wuerzburg.de; Balthasar-Neumann-Promenade; adult/concession/under 18yr €7.50/6.50/free; ☺9am-6pm Apr-Oct, 10am-4.30pm Nov-Mar, 45-minute English tours 11am & 3pm, also 4.30pm Apr-Oct), built by 18th-century starchitect Balthasar Neumann as the home of the local prince-bishops, is one of Germany's most important and beautiful baroque palaces. Top billing goes to the brilliant zigzagging **staircase** lidded by what still is the world's largest fresco, a masterpiece by Giovanni Battista Tiepolo.

Most of the palace can be explored on your own. Besides the staircase, feast your eyes on the ice white stucco-adorned **Weisser Saal** (White Hall) before entering the **Kaisersaal** (Imperial Hall), canopied by yet another impressive Tiepolo fresco. Other stunners include the gilded stucco **Spiegelkabinett** (Mirror Hall), covered with a unique mirrorlike glass painted with figural, floral and animal motifs (accessible by tour only). The **Hofkirche** (Court Church) is another Neumann and Tiepolo coproduction. Its marble columns, gold leaf and profusion of angels match the Residenz in splendour and proportions.

Alte Mainmühle
GERMAN €€

(☎0931-167 77; www.alte-mainmuehle.de; Mainkai 1; mains €8-23; ☺9.30am-midnight) Tourists and locals alike cram into this old mill, accessed straight from the old bridge, to savour modern twists on Franconian classics (including delicious grilled sausages). In summer the double terrace beckons – the upper one delivers pretty views of the bridge and Marienberg Fortress. In winter retreat to the snug timber dining room.

Backöfele
GERMAN €€

(☎0931-590 59; www.backoefele.de; Ursulinergasse 2; mains €7-19.50; ☺noon-midnight Mon-Thu, to 1am Fri & Sat, to 11pm Sun) This old-timey warren has been spreading hearty Franconian food love for nearly 40 years. Find your favorite table in the cobbled courtyard or one of four historic rooms, each candlelit and uniquely furnished with local flair.

ℹ Information

Tourist Office (☎0931-372 398; www.wuerzburg.de; Marktplatz 9; ☺10am-6pm Mon-Fri, 10am-2pm Sat Apr-Dec, 10am-2pm Sun May-Oct, 10am-5pm Mon-Fri, 10am-2pm Sat Jan-Mar) Trip planning and room reservations.

ℹ Getting There & Away

The Romantic Road Coach stops next to the Hauptbahnhof.

Frequent trains run to Bamberg (€20.10, one hour), Frankfurt (€35, 1¼ hour), Nuremberg (from €20.30, one hour) and Rothenburg ob der Tauber (via Steinach; €12.90, 1¼ hour).

Nuremberg

☎0911 / POP 510,000

Nuremberg (Nürnberg) woos visitors with its wonderfully restored medieval Altstadt, its grand castle and, in December, its magical *Christkindlmarkt* (Christmas market).

The town played a key role during the Nazi years. It was here that the fanatical party rallies were held, the boycott of Jewish businesses began and the anti-Semitic Nuremberg Laws were enacted. After WWII the city was chosen as the site of the Nuremberg Trials of Nazi war criminals.

◉ Sights

The city centre is best explored on foot but the Nazi-related sights are a tram ride away.

Hauptmarkt
SQUARE

This bustling square in the heart of the Altstadt is the site of daily markets as well as the famous *Christkindlmarkt*. At the eastern end is the ornate Gothic **Frauenkirche** (church). Daily at noon crowds crane their necks to witness the clock's figures enact a spectacle called the *Männleinlaufen*. Rising from the square like a Gothic spire is the sculpture-festooned **Schöner Brunnen** (Beautiful Fountain). Touch the golden ring in the ornate wrought-iron gate for good luck.

Kaiserburg
CASTLE

(Imperial Castle; ☎0911-244 6590; www.kaiserburg-nuernberg.de; Auf der Burg; adult/concession/under 18yr incl museum €5.50/4.50/free, tower & well €3.50/2.50/free; ☺9am-6pm Apr-Sep, 10am-4pm

CHRISTMAS MARKETS

Beginning in late November every year, central squares across Germany are transformed into Christmas markets (*Christkindlmarkt*; also known as *Weihnachtsmärkte*). Folks stamp about between the wooden stalls, perusing seasonal trinkets (from hand-carved ornaments to plastic angels) while warming themselves with *Glühwein* (mulled, spiced red wine) and grilled sausages. Locals love 'em and, not surprisingly, the markets are popular with tourists, so bundle up and carouse for hours. Markets in Nuremberg, Dresden, Cologne and Munich are especially famous.

Oct-Mar) This enormous castle complex above the Altstadt poignantly reflects Nuremberg's medieval might. Don't miss a tour of the residential wing to see the lavish Knights' and Imperial Hall, a Romanesque double chapel and an exhibit on the inner workings of the Holy Roman Empire. This segues to the **Kaiserburg Museum**, which focuses on the castle's military and building history. Elsewhere, enjoy panoramic views from the **Sinwell Tower** or peer 48m down into the **Deep Well**.

Germanisches Nationalmuseum   MUSEUM
(German National Museum; ☎0911-133 10; www.gnm.de; Kartäusergasse 1; adult/concession €8/5; ⊙10am-6pm Tue & Thu-Sun, to 9pm Wed) Spanning prehistory to the early 20th century, the Germanisches Nationalmuseum is the country's most important museum of German culture. It features works by German painters and sculptors, an archaeological collection, arms and armour, musical and scientific instruments, and toys.

Memorium Nuremberg Trials   MEMORIAL
(☎0911-3217 9372; www.memorium-nuremberg.de; Bärenschanzstrasse 72; adult/concession incl audioguide €5/3; ⊙10am-6pm Wed-Mon) Göring, Hess, Speer and 21 other Nazi leaders were tried for crimes against peace and humanity by the Allies in Schwurgerichtssaal 600 (Court Room 600) of this still-working courthouse. Today the room forms part of an engaging exhibit detailing the background, progression and impact of the trials using film, photographs, audiotape and even the original defendants' dock. To get here, take the U1 towards Bärenschanze and get off at Sielstrasse.

Reichsparteitagsgelände   HISTORIC SITE
(Luitpoldhain; ☎0911-231 5666; www.museen-nuernberg.de; Bayernstrasse 110; grounds free, documentation centre adult/concession incl audioguide €5/3; ⊙grounds 24hr, documentation centre 9am-6pm Mon-Fri, 10am-6pm Sat & Sun) If you've ever wondered where the infamous black-and-white images of ecstatic Nazi supporters hailing their Führer were taken, it was here in Nuremberg. Much of the grounds were destroyed during Allied bombing raids, but enough remain to get a sense of the megalomania behind it, especially after visiting the excellent **Dokumentationszentrum** (Documentation Centre) served by tram 9 from the Hauptbahnhof.

🛏 Sleeping

★**Hotel Drei Raben**   BOUTIQUE HOTEL €€
(☎0911-274 380; www.hoteldreiraben.de; Königstrasse 63; d from €135; [P 🌐 🛜]) The design of this classy charmer builds upon the legend of the three ravens perched on the building's chimney stack, who tell stories from Nuremberg lore. Art and decor in the 'mythical theme' rooms reflect a particular tale, from the life of Albrecht Dürer to the first railway.

Hotel Elch   HOTEL €€
(☎0911-249 2980; www.hotel-elch.com; Irrerstrasse 9; d from €89; 🛜) This snug, romantic 12-room gem of a hotel occupies a 14th-century, half-timbered house near the Kaiserburg. The antique flair is offset by contemporary art, glazed terracotta bathrooms and multihued chandeliers. The downstairs restaurant specialises in schnitzel.

🍴 Eating

Don't leave Nuremberg without trying its famous finger-sized *Nürnberger Bratwürste*.

Goldenes Posthorn   GERMAN €€
(☎0911-225 153; www.die-nuernberger-bratwurst.de; Glöckleinsgasse 2, cnr Sebalder Platz; mains €7-20; ⊙11am-11pm; 🍴) Push open the heavy copper door to find a real culinary treat that has hosted royals, artists and professors (including Albrecht Dürer) since 1498. You can't go wrong sticking with the miniature local sausages, but the pork shoulder and also the house speciality – vinegar-marinated ox cheeks – are highly recommended as well.

Hexenhäusle   GERMAN €€
(☎0911-4902 9095; www.hexenhaeusle-nuernberg.com; Vestnertorgraben 4; mains €7-11; ⊙11am-11pm) The half-timbered 'Witches

Hut' ranks among Nuremberg's most enchanting inns and beer gardens. Tucked next to a sturdy town gate at the foot of the castle, it serves the gamut of grilled fare and other Franconian rib-stickers with big mugs of local Zirndorfer and Tucher beer.

ⓘ Information

Tourist Office (☑ 0911-233 60; www.tourismus. nuernberg.de) Both branches, at Hauptmarkt (Hauptmarkt 18; ⊘ 9am-6pm Mon-Sat year-round, 10am-4pm Sun May-Oct) and in the Künstlerhaus (Königstrasse 93; ⊘ 9am-7pm Mon-Sat, 10am-4pm Sun), sell the Nuremberg Card (€23) with two days of free museum entry and public transport. Staff also offer maps, info and advice.

ⓘ Getting There & Away

Nuremberg **airport** (NUE; www.airport-nuernberg.de), 5km north of the city centre, is served by the U2 from Hauptbahnhof (€2.50, 12 minutes).

Rail connections from Nuremberg include Frankfurt (€55, two hours) and Munich (€55, 1½ hours).

ⓘ Getting Around

For public transport information, see www.vgn.de.

Bamberg

☑ 0951 / POP 70,000

Off the major tourist routes, Bamberg is one of Germany's most delightful and authentic towns. It has a bevy of beautifully preserved historic buildings, palaces and churches in its Unesco-recognised Altstadt, a lively student population and its own style of beer.

⊙ Sights

Bamberger Dom CATHEDRAL
(www.erzbistum-bamberg.de; Domplatz; ⊘ 8am-6pm Apr-Oct, to 5pm Nov-Mar) Beneath the quartet of spires, Bamberg's cathedral is packed with artistic treasures, most famously the lifesize equestrian statue of the **Bamberger Reiter** (Bamberg Horseman), whose true identity remains a mystery. It overlooks the **tomb of cathedral founders**, Emperor Heinrich II and his wife Kunigunde, splendidly carved by Tilmann Riemenschneider. The **marble tomb of Clemens II** in the west choir is the only papal burial site north of the Alps. Nearby, the **Virgin Mary altar** by Veit Stoss also warrants closer inspection.

Altes Rathaus HISTORIC BUILDING
(Old Town Hall; Obere Brücke) Like a ship in dry dock, Bamberg's 1462 Old Town Hall was built on an artifical island in the Regnitz River, allegedly because the local bishop had refused to give the town's citizens any land for its construction. Inside is a collection of precious porcelain but even more enchanting are the richly detailed frescoes adorning its facades – note the cherub's leg cheekily sticking out from its east facade.

Neue Residenz PALACE
(New Residence; ☑ 0951-519 390; www.schloesser.bayern.de; Domplatz 8; adult/child €4.50/3.50; ⊘ 9am-6pm Apr-Sep, 10am-4pm Oct-Mar) This splendid episcopal palace gives you an eyeful of the lavish lifestyle of Bamberg's prince-bishops who, between 1703 and 1802, occupied its 40-odd rooms that can only be seen on guided 45-minute tours (in German). Tickets are also good for the Bavarian State Gallery, with works by Lucas Cranach the Elder and other old masters. The baroque **Rose Garden** delivers fabulous views over Bamberg's sea of red-tiled roofs.

🛏 Sleeping

Hotel Wohnbar BOUTIQUE HOTEL €
(☑ 0951-5099 8844; www.wohnbar-bamberg.de; Stangsstrasse 3; d from €59; 🛜) 'Carpe Noctem' (Seize the Night) is the motto of this charming 10-room retreat with boldly coloured, contemporary rooms near the university quarter. Those in the 'economy' category are a very tight squeeze – avoid.

Hotel Europa HOTEL €€
(☑ 0951-309 3020; www.hotel-europa-bamberg.de; Untere Königstrasse 6-8; d from €119; 🛜) This spick-and-span but unfussy affair just outside the Altstadt gets kudos for its friendliness, comfy beds and opulent breakfast, served in the winter garden or sunny courtyard. Rooms at the front are noisier but may overlook the cathedral and the red-tiled roofs of the Altstadt. Some are a bit small.

🍴 Eating & Drinking

Obere Sandstrasse near the cathedral and Austrasse near the university are both good eat and drink streets. Bamberg's unique style of beer is called *Rauchbier* (smoked beer), the distinctive flavour of which is created by drying malted barley over smouldering beechwood.

★ **Schlenkerla** GERMAN €€
(✆ 0951-560 60; www.schlenkerla.de; Dominikanerstrasse 6; mains €8-15; ⏱ 9.30am-11.30pm)
Beneath wooden beams as dark as the superb *Rauchbier* poured straight from oak barrels, locals and visitors dig into scrumptious Franconian fare at this legendary flower-festooned tavern near the cathedral.

Spezial-Keller GERMAN €€
(✆ 0951-548 87; www.spezial-keller.de; Sternwartstrasse 8; dishes €6-13; ⏱ 3pm-late Tue-Fri, from noon Sat, from 10am Sun) The walk into the hills past the cathedral to this delightful beer garden is well worth it, both for the malty *Rauchbier* and the sweeping views of the Altstadt. In winter the action moves into the cosy tavern warmed by a traditional wood-burning tiled stove.

ⓘ Information

Tourist Office (✆ 0951-297 6200; www.bamberg.info; Geyerswörthstrasse 5; ⏱ 9.30am-6pm Mon-Fri, to 4pm Sat, to 2.30pm Sun) Staff rent the multimedia iTour Guide (four/eight hours €8.50/12) for self-guided city tours.

ⓘ Getting There & Away

Getting to and from Bamberg by train usually involves a change in Würzburg.

Regensburg

✆ 0941 / POP 138,000

In a scene-stealing locale on the wide Danube River, Regensburg has relics of historic periods reaching back to the Romans, yet doesn't get the tourist mobs you'll find in other equally attractive German cities. Though big on the historical wow factor, today's Regensburg is a laid-back and unpretentious student town with a distinct Italianate flair.

◉ Sights

Steinerne Brücke BRIDGE
(Stone Bridge) An incredible feat of engineering for its day, Regensburg's 900-year-old Stone Bridge was at one time the only fortified crossing of the Danube. A small historical exhibit in the southern tower traces the bridge's milestones.

Dom St Peter CHURCH
(www.bistum-regensburg.de; Domplatz; ⏱ 6.30am-7pm Jun-Sep, to 6pm Apr, May & Oct, to 5pm Nov-Mar) It takes a few seconds for your eyes to adjust to the dim interior of Regens-

burg's soaring landmark, the Dom St Peter, one of Bavaria's grandest Gothic cathedrals, with stunning kaleidoscopic stained-glass windows and an opulent, silver-sheathed main altar.

The cathedral is the home of the Domspatzen, a 1000-year-old boys choir that accompanies the 10am Sunday service (only during the school year). The Domschatzmuseum (Cathedral Treasury) brims with monstrances, tapestries and other church treasures.

Altes Rathaus HISTORIC BUILDING
(Old Town Hall; ✆ 0941-507 3440; Rathausplatz; adult/concession €7.50/4; ⏱ English tours 3pm Apr-Oct, 2pm Nov-Mar, German tours every half hour) From 1663 to 1806, the Reichstag (imperial assembly) held its gatherings at Regensburg's old town hall, an important role commemorated by an exhibit in today's **Reichstagsmuseum**. Tours take in the lavish assembly hall and the original **torture chambers** in the cellar.

⌖ Sleeping

Elements Hotel HOTEL €€
(✆ 0941-3819 8600; www.hotel-elements.de; Alter Kornmarkt 3; d from €105; ⊛ ⓢ) Four elements, four rooms, and what rooms they are! 'Fire' blazes in plush crimson, while 'Water' is splashed with portholes and a Jacuzzi, 'Air' is playful and light and natural wood, and stone and leather reign in colonial-inspired 'Earth'. Breakfast costs €15.

Petit Hotel Orphée HOTEL €€
(✆ 0941-596 020; www.hotel-orphee.de; Wahlenstrasse 1; d €75-175; ⓢ) Behind a humble door lies a world of genuine charm, unexpected extras and ample attention to detail. The striped floors, wrought-iron beds, original sinks and common rooms with soft cushions and well-read books give the feel of a lovingly attended home. Check-in and breakfast is nearby in the Cafe Orphée at Untere Bachgasse 8. Additional rooms are above the cafe.

✗ Eating & Drinking

Historische Wurstkuchl GERMAN €
(✆ 0941-466 210; www.wurstkuchl.de; Thundorferstrasse 3; 6 sausages €8.40; ⏱ 8am-7pm) This titchy eatery has been serving the city's traditional finger-size sausages, grilled over beech wood and dished up with sauerkraut and sweet grainy mustard, since 1135 and lays claim to being the world's oldest sausage kitchen.

Leerer Beutel EUROPEAN €€
(☑0941-589 97; www.leerer-beutel.de; Bertold-strasse 9; mains €12-18; ⊙6pm-1am Mon, 11am-1am Tue-Sat, 11am-3pm Sun) Subscriber to the slow-food ethos, the cavernous restaurant at the eponymous cultural centre offers an imaginatively mixed menu of Bavarian, Tyrolean and Italian dishes, served indoors or out on the car-free cobbles. From Tuesday to Friday, clued-up locals invade for the two-course lunches for €6.50.

Spitalgarten BEER GARDEN
(☑0941-847 74; www.spitalgarten.de; St Katharinenplatz 1; ⊙9am-midnight) A veritable thicket of folding chairs and slatted tables by the Danube, this is one of the best places in town for some alfresco quaffing. It claims to have brewed beer (today's Spital) here since 1350, so it probably knows what it's doing by now.

ℹ Information

Tourist Office (☑0941-507 4410; www.regensburg.de; Rathausplatz 4; ⊙9am-6pm Mon-Fri, to 4pm Sat year-round, 9.30am-4pm Sun Apr-Oct, 9.30am-2.30pm Sun Nov-Mar; ☎) In the historic Altes Rathaus. Sells tickets, tours, rooms and an audioguide for self-guided tours.

ℹ Getting There & Away

Frequent trains leave for Munich (€26.70, 1½ hours) and Nuremberg (€20.10, one hour), among others.

STUTTGART & THE BLACK FOREST

The high-tech urbanite pleasures of Stuttgart, one of the engines of the German economy, form an appealing contrast to the historic charms of Heidelberg, home to the country's oldest university and a romantic ruined castle. Beyond lies the myth-shrouded Black Forest (*Schwarzwald* in German), a pretty land of misty hills, thick forest and cute villages, with youthful and vibrant Freiburg as its only major town.

Stuttgart

☑ 0711 / POP 591,000

Stuttgart residents enjoy an enviable quality of life that's to no small degree rooted in its fabled car companies – Porsche and Mercedes – which show off their pedigree in two excellent museums. Hemmed in by

BOHEMIAN BEANS

Stuttgart's most interesting neighbourhood is a short stroll from the city centre. The **Bohnenviertel** (Bean District) takes its name from the diet of the poor tanners, dyers and craftsmen who lived here. Today the district's cobbled lanes and gabled houses harbour idiosyncratic galleries, workshops, bookstores, wine taverns, cafes and a red-light district.

vine-covered hills, the city has also plenty in store for fans of European art.

◉ Sights

Königsstrasse, a long, pedestrianised shopping strip, links the Hauptbahnhof to the city centre. In the city centre are the Schloss and the art museums. The Mercedes-Benz Museum is about 5km northeast and the Porsche Museum 7km north of here.

Staatsgalerie Stuttgart GALLERY
(☑0711-470 400; www.staatsgalerie-stuttgart.de; Konrad-Adenauer-Strasse 30-32; permanent collection adult/concession/under 20yr €5/3/free; ⊙10am-6pm Tue, Wed & Fri-Sun, to 8pm Thu) The neoclassical-meets-contemporary Staatsgalerie bears British architect James Stirling's curvy, colourful imprint. Alongside big-name exhibitions, the gallery harbours a representative collection of European art from the 14th to the 21st centuries as well as American post-WWII avant-gardists.

Neues Schloss PALACE
(☑in Ludwigsburg 07141-182 004; www.neues-schloss-stuttgart.de; Schlossplatz; tour adult/concession €8/4) Duke Karl Eugen von Württemberg's answer to Versailles was the exuberant three-winged Neues Schloss, a baroque-neoclassical royal residence that now houses state-government ministries. A bronze statue of Emperor Wilhelm I looking dashing on his steed graces nearby **Karlsplatz**. Check the website for the tour schedule.

Mercedes-Benz Museum MUSEUM
(☑0711-1730 000; www.mercedes-benz-classic.com; Mercedesstrasse 100; adult/concession €8/4; ⊙9am-6pm Tue-Sun, last admission 5pm; ☒S1 to Neckarpark) A futuristic swirl on the cityscape, the Mercedes-Benz Museum takes a chronological spin through the Mercedes empire. Look out for legends like the 1885 Daimler Riding Car, the world's first gasoline-powered

vehicle and the record-breaking Lightning Benz that hit 228km/h at Daytona Beach in 1909.

Porsche Museum MUSEUM

(www.porsche.com/museum; Porscheplatz 1; adult/concession €8/4; ⊘9am-6pm Tue-Sun; ⓡNeuwirtshaus) Like a pearly white spaceship preparing for lift-off, the barrier-free Porsche Museum is every little boy's dream. Groovy audioguides race you through the history of Porsche from its 1948 beginnings. Break to glimpse the 911 GT1 that won Le Mans in 1998.

🛏 Sleeping

Hostel Alex 30 HOSTEL €

(☑0711-838 8950; www.alex30-hostel.de; Alexanderstrasse 30; dm €25-29, d €74; ⓟⓦ) Fun-seekers on a budget should thrive at this popular hostel within walking distance of the city centre. Rooms are spotless, citrus-bright and contemporary, and the bar, sun deck and communal kitchen ideal for swapping stories with fellow travellers. Breakfast costs €8.

Der Zauberlehrling BOUTIQUE HOTEL €€€

(☑0711-237 7770; www.zauberlehrling.de; Rosenstrasse 38; s/d from €135/180; ⓟⓦ) The dreamily styled rooms at the 'Sorcerer's Apprentice' offer soothing quarters after a day on the road. Each one interprets a different theme (Mediterranean siesta, sunrise, One Thousand and One Nights) through colour, furniture and features such as canopy beds, clawfoot tubs, tatami mats or fireplaces. Breakfast costs €19.

🍴 Eating & Drinking

Stuttgart is a great place to sample Swabian specialities such as *Spätzle* (homemade noodles) and *Maultaschen* (a hearty ravioli in broth). Local wines edge out beer in popularity.

Hans-im-Glück-Platz is a hub of bars, while clubs line Theodor-Heuss-Strasse and wine taverns abound in the Bohnenviertel.

Stuttgarter Markthalle MARKET €

(Market Hall; www.markthalle-stuttgart.de; Dorotheenstrasse 4; ⊘7am-6.30pm Mon-Fri, to 5pm Sat) Self-caterers can try the Markthalle, which sells picnic fixings, and has Italian and Swabian restaurants.

Weinhaus Stetter GERMAN €€

(☑0711-240 163; www.weinhaus-stetter.de; Rosenstrasse 32; mains €4-14.50; ⊘3-11pm Mon-Fri, noon-3pm & 5.30-11pm Sat) This traditional wine tavern in the Bohnenviertel quarter serves up no-nonsense Swabian cooking, such as flavoursome *Linsen und Saiten* (lentils with sausage) and beef roast with onion, in a convivial ambience. The attached wine shop sells 650 different vintages.

Academie der Schönen Künste FRENCH €€

(☑0711-242 436; www.academie-der-schoensten-kuenste.de; Charlottenstrasse 5; mains €11-20; ⊘8am-midnight Mon-Sat, to 8pm Sun) A breakfast institution since the 1970s, the Academy has evolved into a darling French-style bistro where dishes revolve around market-fresh fare but also include such tried-and-true classics as coq au vin and *Flammekuche* (Alsatian pizza). Sit inside among bright canvases or in the charismatic couryard.

Cube INTERNATIONAL €€€

(☑0711-280 4441; www.cube-restaurant.de; Kleiner Schlossplatz 1; mains lunch €9-20, dinner €27-35; ⊘11.30am-midnight) The food is stellar but it actually plays second fiddle to the dazzling decor, refined ambience and stunning views at this glass-fronted cube atop the Kunstmuseum. Lunches are perky, fresh and international, while dinners feature more complex Pacific Rim–inspired cuisine. The lunch special for €9 is a steal.

★ Palast der Republik BEER GARDEN

(☑0711-226 4887; www.facebook.com/Palast Stuttgart; Friedrichstrasse 27; ⊘11am-3am; ⓢFriedrichsbau) The palace in question is more like a little kiosk but that's not stopping everyone from students to bankers from making this place *the* local hot spot for chilling under the trees, cold beer in hand.

ℹ Information

Tourist Office (☑0711-222 8253; www.stuttgart-tourist.de; Königstrasse 1a; ⊘9am-8pm Mon-Fri, to 6pm Sat, 11am-6pm Sun)

ℹ Getting There & Away

Stuttgart Airport (SGT; www.stuttgart-airport.com), a major hub for Germanwings, is 13km south of the city and linked to the Hauptbahnhof by S2 and S3 trains (€3.70, 30 minutes).

Trains head to all major German cities, including Frankfurt (€63, 1¼ hours) and Munich (€57, 2¼ hours).

ℹ Getting Around

For public transport information, check www.vvs.de.

Heidelberg

☑ 06221 / POP 149,000

Germany's oldest and most famous university town is renowned for its lovely Altstadt, its plethora of pubs and its evocative half-ruined castle. Millions of visitors are drawn each year to this photogenic assemblage, thereby following in the footsteps of Mark Twain, who kicked off his European travels in 1878 in Heidelberg, later recounting his bemused observations in *A Tramp Abroad.*

◉ Sights

Heidelberg's sites cluster in the Altstadt, which starts to reveal itself only after a charm-free 15-minute walk east from the main train station or a short ride on bus 32 or 38.

★ Schloss Heidelberg   CASTLE

(☑ 06221-658 880; www.schloss-heidelberg.de; adult/child incl Bergbahn €6/4, audioguide €4; ⊙ grounds 24hr, castle 8am-6pm, English tours hourly 11.15am-4.15pm Mon-Fri, 10.15am-4.15pm Sat & Sun Apr-Oct, fewer tours Nov-Mar) Towering over the Altstadt, Heidelberg's ruined Renaissance castle cuts a romantic figure, especially when illuminated at night and seen across the Neckar River. Attractions include the world's largest wine cask and fabulous views. Get there either via a steep, cobbled trail in about 10 minutes or by taking the cogwheel train from Kornmarkt station (tickets include Schloss entry). After 6pm you can stroll the grounds for free.

Alte Brücke   BRIDGE

(Karl-Theodor-Brücke) The 200m-long 'Old Bridge', built in 1786, connects the Altstadt with the river's right bank and the **Schlangenweg** (Snake Path), the switchbacks of which lead to the **Philosophenweg** (Philosophers' Walk). A stroll along here delivers romantic views of the town and Heidelberg Castle.

Heiliggeistkirche   CHURCH

(☑ 06221-980 30; www.ekihd.de; Marktplatz; tower adult/concesssion €2/1; ⊙ 11am-5pm Mon-Sat, 12.30-5pm Sun) For bird's-eye views, climb 208 stairs to the top of the tower of Heidelberg's famous 15th-century church, which was shared by Catholics and Protestants from 1706 until 1936 (it's now Protestant).

Studentenkarzer   HISTORIC SITE

(Student Jail; ☑ 06221-543 554; www.uni-heidelberg.de/fakultaeten/philosophie/zegk/fpi/karzerhd.html; Augustinergasse 2; adult/concession €3/2.50; ⊙ 10am-6pm daily Apr-Oct, 10am-4pm Mon-Sat Nov-Mar) From 1823 to 1914, students convicted of misdeeds such as public inebriation, loud nocturnal singing, freeing the local pigs or duelling were sent to this student jail for at least 24 hours. Judging by the inventive wall graffiti, some found their stay highly amusing.

☞ Tours

The tourist office runs English-language **walking tours** (adult/concession €7/5; ⊙ English tours 10.30am Thu-Sat Apr-Oct) of the Altstadt.

🛏 Sleeping & Eating

Steffis Hostel   HOSTEL €

(☑ 06221-778 2772; www.hostelheidelberg.de; Alte Eppelheimer Strasse 50; dm €18-24, s/d without bathroom €45/56; ⊙ reception 8am-10pm; ℗@⊚) In a 19th-century tobacco factory near the main train station, Steffis offers bright, well-lit dorms and rooms (all with shared bathrooms), a colourful lounge that's ideal for meeting fellow travellers, a spacious kitchen and an ineffable old-school hostel vibe. Breakfast costs €3.

Perks include free wi-fi, tea, coffee and bicycles. It's situated a block north of the Hauptbahn-hof, three floors above a Lidl supermarket; access is via an industrial-size lift.

★ Arthotel Heidelberg   BOUTIQUE HOTEL €€

(☑ 06221-650 060; www.arthotel.de; Grabengasse 7; d €125-200; ℗✳⊚) This charmer is a winning blend of historic setting and sleek contemporary design. The light-flooded red and black lobby is mere overture to the symphony of the 24 rooms. Equipped with huge bathrooms (tubs!), they're spacious and purist – except for three that sport painted ceilings from 1790. Breakfast costs €12.90.

KulturBrauerei   GERMAN €€

(☑ 06221-502 980; www.heidelberger-kulturbrauerei.de; Leyergasse 6; mains €11-26.50; ⊙ 7am-11pm or later) With its wood-plank floor, chairs from a Spanish monastery and black iron chandeliers, this brewpub is an atmospheric spot to tuck into regional specialities such as *Schäufele* (pork shoulder) or to quaff the house brew in the enchanting beer garden.

★ Herrenmühle Heidelberg   GERMAN €€€

(☑ 06221-602 909; www.herrenmuehle-heidelberg.de; Hauptstrasse 239; mains €22-29, 3-/5-course dinner €48/69; ⊙ 6-10pm Mon-Sat) A flour mill from 1690 has been turned into an elegant and highly cultured place to enjoy upscale 'country-style' cuisine, including fish, under thick wooden beams, a candle flickering romantically at each table. Book ahead.

ℹ Information

Tourist Office (www.heidelberg-marketing.de) There are branches at Hauptbahnhof (☎ 06221-584 4444; ⊙ 9am-7pm Mon-Sat, 10am-6pm Sun Apr-Oct, 9am-6pm Mon-Sat Nov-Mar), right outside the main train station, and on Marktplatz (Marktplatz 10; ⊙ 8am-5pm Mon-Fri, 10am-5pm Sat), in the old town. Aside from loads of helpful information both also stock a useful walking-tour map (€1.50).

ℹ Getting There & Away

There are at least hourly InterCity (IC) trains to/from Frankfurt (€22, 55 minutes) and Stuttgart (€27, 40 minutes).

Black Forest

The Black Forest (Schwarzwald) gets its name from its dark canopy of evergreens. Let winding backroads take you through misty vales, fairy-tale woodlands and villages that radiate earthy authenticity. It's not nature wild and remote, but bucolic and picturesque. And, yes, there are many, many places to buy cuckoo clocks.

ℹ Getting Around

One of Germany's most scenic roads is the Schwarzwald-Hochstrasse (B500), which meanders for 60km between Baden-Baden and Freudenstadt.

Regional trains link Alpirsbach, Schiltach, Hausach and other Black Forest villages. In Hausach, there's a connection with the Schwarzwaldbahn line which takes in Baden-Baden and Triberg.

Baden-Baden

☎ 07221 / POP 53,600

The northern gateway to the Black Forest, Baden-Baden is one of Europe's most famous spa towns whose mineral-rich waters have cured the ills of celebs from Queen Victoria to Victoria Beckham. An air of old-world luxury hangs over this beautiful town that's also home to a palatial casino.

🏃 Activities

★ Friedrichsbad   SPA

(☎ 07221-275 920; www.carasana.de; Römerplatz 1; 3hr ticket €25, incl soap-&-brush massage €37; ⊙ 9am-10pm, last admission 7pm) If it's the body of Venus and the complexion of Cleopatra you desire, abandon modesty (and clothing) to wallow in thermal waters at this palatial 19th-century marble-and-mosaic-festooned spa. As Mark Twain put it, 'after 10 minutes you forget time; after 20 minutes, the world', as you slip into the regime of steaming, scrubbing, hot-cold bathing and dunking in the Roman-Irish bath.

Caracalla Spa   SPA

(☎ 07221-275 940; www.carasana.de; Römerplatz 11; 2/3/4hr €15/18/21; ⊙ 8am-10pm, last admission 8pm) This modern glass-fronted spa has a cluster of indoor and outdoor pools, grottoes and surge channels, making the most of the mineral-rich spring water. For those who dare to bare, saunas range from the rustic 'forest' to the roasting 95°C 'fire' variety.

🛏 Sleeping & Eating

Schweizer Hof   HOTEL €€

(☎ 07221-304 60; www.schweizerhof.de; Lange Strasse 73; d €99-119) Sitting on one of Baden-Baden's smartest streets, this above-par hotel is a real find, with dapper rooms,

---

THE BATTLE OF THE BIRDS

Triberg being Germany's undisputed cuckoo-clock capital, it's not surprising that two giant timepieces battle for title of world's largest cuckoo clock.

The older and more charming contender calls itself the **1. Weltgrösste Kuckucksuhr** (First World's Largest Cuckoo Clock; ☎ 07722-4689; www.1weltgroesstekuckucksuhr.de; Untertalstrasse 28, Schonach; adult/concession €1.20/0.60; ⊙ 9am-noon & 1-6pm) and can be found in Schonach. It kicked into gear in 1980 and took a local clockmaker three years to build by hand.

It has since been eclipsed in size by its cousin at the **Eble Uhren-Park** (☎ 07722-962 20; www.uhren-park.de; Schonachbach 27; admission €2; ⊙ 9am-6pm Mon-Sat, 10am-6pm Sun), which occupies an entire house on the B33 between Triberg and Hornberg. Although undeniably bigger (and listed in the *Guinness Book of World Records*), it's more of a gimmick to lure shoppers inside a large clock shop.

chandelier-lit spaces, and a garden with sun lounges for chilling.

Rizzi INTERNATIONAL €€€
(☑ 07221-258 38; www.rizzi-baden-baden.de; Augustaplatz 1; mains lunch €9-24, dinner €14-52; ☺ noon-1am) A summertime favourite, this pink villa's tree-shaded patio is the place to sip excellent wines while tucking into choice steaks. Other menu faves include delicious burgers, homemade pastas and 'Rizzi-style sushi'.

ℹ Information

Branch Tourist Office (Kaiserallee 3; ☺ 10am-5pm Mon-Sat, 2-5pm Sun) In the Trinkhalle. Sells events tickets.

Triberg

☑ 07722 / POP 4800
Cuckoo-clock capital, black forest–cake pilgrimage site and Germany's highest waterfall – Triberg is a torrent of Schwarzwald superlatives and attracts a ton of guests.

◉ Sights

★ **Triberger Wasserfälle** WATERFALL
(adult/concession/family €4/3/9.50; ☺ Mar-early Nov, 25-30 Dec) Niagara they ain't but Germany's highest waterfalls do exude their own wild romanticism. The Gutach River feeds the seven-tiered falls, which drop a total of 163m and are illuminated until 10pm.

🛏 Sleeping & Eating

Parkhotel Wehrle HISTORIC HOTEL €€€
(☑ 07722-860 20; www.parkhotel-wehrle.de; Gartenstrasse 24; d €155-179; 🅿 🛜 🐾) Hemingway once waxed lyrical about the trout he ordered at the venerable restaurant (mains €13 to €32, open 6pm to 9pm daily, noon to 2pm Sunday) that's attached to this 400-year-old hotel with integrated spa. Often with a baroque or Biedermeier touch, quarters are roomy and beautifully furnished with antiques; the best have Duravit whirlpool tubs.

Café Schäfer CAFE €
(☑ 07722-4465; www.cafe-schaefer-triberg.de; Hauptstrasse 33; cakes €3-4; ☺ 9am-6pm Mon, Tue, Thu & Fri, 8am-6pm Sat, 11am-6pm Sun) Confectioner Claus Schäfer uses the original 1915 recipe for black forest gateau to prepare this sinful treat that layers chocolate cake (perfumed with cherry brandy), whipped cream and sour cherries and wraps it all in more cream and shaved chocolate. Trust us, it's worth the calories.

SOARING ABOVE THE FOREST

Freiburg seems tiny as you drift up above the city and a tapestry of meadows and forest on the **Schauinslandbahn** (return adult/concession €12/11, one way €8.50/8; ☺ 9am-5pm Oct-Jun, to 6pm Jul-Sep) to the 1284m **Schauinsland peak** (www.bergwelt-schauinsland.de). The lift provides a speedy link between Freiburg and the Black Forest highlands.

ℹ Information

Tourist Office (☑ 07722-866 490; www.triberg.de; Wallfahrtstrasse 4; ☺ 9am-5pm Mon-Fri) Inside the Schwarzwald-Museum.

Freiburg im Breisgau

☑ 0761 / POP 220.300
Sitting plump at the foot of the Black Forest's wooded slopes and vineyards, Freiburg is a sunny, cheerful university town whose Altstadt is a story-book tableau of gabled town houses, cobblestone lanes and cafe-rimmed plazas. Party-loving students spice up the local nightlife and give Freiburg its relaxed air.

◉ Sights

★ **Freiburger Münster** CATHEDRAL
(Freiburg Minster; ☑ 0761-202 790; www.freiburger muenster.info; Münsterplatz; tower adult/concession €2/1.50; ☺ 10am-5pm Mon-Sat, 1-7.30pm Sun, tower 10am-4.45pm Mon-Sat, 1-5pm Sun) With its lacy spires, cheeky gargoyles and dizzying entrance portal, Freiburg's 11th-century minster cuts an impressive figure above the central market square. It has dazzling kaleidoscopic stained-glass windows that were mostly financed by medieval guilds, and a high altar with a masterful triptych by Dürer protege Hans Baldung Grien. The tower can be climbed.

Rathausplatz SQUARE
(Town Hall Square) Join locals relaxing in a cafe by the fountain in chestnut-shaded Rathausplatz, Freiburg's prettiest square, then pull out that camera to snap pictures of the ox-blood-red 16th-century **Altes Rathaus** (Old Town Hall) with the tourist office, the step-gabled 19th-century **Neues Rathaus** (New Town Hall) and the medieval **Martinskirche** with a modern interior.

Augustinermuseum
MUSEUM

(☑0761-201 2531; Augustinerplatz 1; adult/concession/under 18yr €7/5/free; ⊙10am-5pm Tue-Sun) Dip into the past as represented by artists working from the Middle Ages to the 19th century at this superb museum in a sensitively modernised monastery. The Sculpture Hall on the ground floor is especially impressive for its fine medieval sculpture and masterpieces by Renaissance artists Hans Baldung Grien and Lucas Cranach the Elder. Head upstairs for eye-level views of mounted gargoyles.

🛏 Sleeping

Black Forest Hostel
HOSTEL €

(☑0761-881 7870; www.blackforest-hostel.de; Kartäuserstrasse 33; dm €17-27, s/d €35/58, linen €4; ⊙reception 7am-1am; @) Funky budget digs with chilled common areas, a shared kitchen, bike rental and spacey stainless-steel showers. It's a five-minute walk from the town centre.

Hotel Minerva
HOTEL €€

(☑0761-386 490; www.minerva-freiburg.de; Poststrasse 8; d €130-165; P ☎) All curvaceous windows and polished wood, this art nouveau charmer is five minutes' trudge from the Altstadt. The convivial rooms are painted in sunny shades and feature free wi-fi. The sauna is another plus.

🍴 Eating & Drinking

Stalls spilling over with fresh produce and flowers set up around the Freiburg Minster from Monday to Saturday between 7.30am and 1.30pm.

Markthalle
FOOD HALL €

(www.markthalle-freiburg.de; Martinsgasse 235; light meals €4-8; ⊙8am-8pm Mon-Thu, to midnight Fri & Sat) Eat your way around the world – curry to sushi, oysters to antipasti – at the food counters in this historic market hall nicknamed 'Fressgässle'.

Hausbrauerei Feierling
BREWPUB €€

(☑0761-243 480; www.feierling.de; Gerberau 46; mains €6-12; ⊙11am-midnight Mon-Thu, to 1am Fri & Sun; ☑) Thumbs up for the Feierling house brew which has kept beer lovers lubricated for over a quarter century. In summer grab a table in the lovely beer garden and stave off a hangover with honest-to-goodness German classics or try one of the flavour-packed vegetarian alternatives.

MEAL WITH A VIEW

Enjoy views of the city from the rooftop terrace of the self-service bistro atop the Karstadt department store at Kaiser-Joseph-Strasse 165. Bonus: free wi-fi.

Kreuzblume
FRENCH, GERMAN €€€

(☑0761-311 94; www.hotel-kreuzblume.de; Konviktstrasse 31; 2-/3-/4-course dinner €32.50/39/47; ⊙noon-2pm Fri-Sun, 6-10pm Wed-Sun) On a flower-festooned lane, this pocket-sized restaurant with clever backlighting and a menu fizzing with bright, sunny flavours attracts a rather food-literate clientele. Each dish combines just a few hand-picked ingredients in bold and tasty ways. Service is tops.

Schlappen
CAFE, PUB

(Löwenstrasse 2; ⊙11am-1am Mon-Wed, to 2am Thu, to 3am Fri & Sat, 3pm-1am Sun) In historic digs and crammed with antiques and vintage theatre posters, this evergreen pub has made the magic happen for generations of students. Check out the skeleton in the men's toilet. Summer terrace.

ℹ Information

Tourist Office (☑0761-388 1880; www.freiburg.de; Rathausplatz 2-4; ⊙8am-8pm Mon-Fri, 9.30am-5pm Sat, 10.30am-3.30pm Sun Jun-Sep, 8am-6pm Mon-Fri, 9.30am-2.30pm Sat, 10am-noon Sun Oct-May) Well stocked with 1:50,000-scale cycling maps, city maps (€1) and the useful booklet Freiburg – Official Guide (€4.90). Can make room bookings (€3).

ℹ Getting There & Away

Freiburg shares **EuroAirport** (BSL; www.euroairport.com) with Basel, Switzerland, and Mulhouse, France, and is served hourly by the Airport Bus (one way/return €26/42, 55 minutes).

Train connections include InterCity Express (ICE) trains to Basel (€25.20, 45 minutes) and Baden-Baden (€30, 45 minutes).

FRANKFURT & THE RHINELAND

Defined by the mighty Rhine, fine wines, medieval castles and romantic villages, Germany's heartland speaks to the imagination. Even Frankfurt, which may seem all buttoned-up business, reveals itself as a laid-back metropolis with fabulous museums and pulsating nightlife.

Frankfurt-am-Main

☑ 069 / POP 700,800

Unashamedly high-rise, Frankfurt-on-the-Main (pronounced 'mine') is a true capital of finance and business and hosts some of Europe's key trade fairs. But despite its business demeanour, Frankfurt consistently ranks high among Germany's most liveable cities thanks to its rich collection of museums, expansive parks and greenery, a lively student scene and excellent public transport.

◉ Sights

★ Römerberg   SQUARE
(Kaisersaal adult/concession €2/0.50; ⊙ Kaisersaal 10am-1pm & 2-5pm; ℝ Dom/Römer) The Römerberg is Frankfurt's old central square. Ornately gabled half-timbered buildings, reconstructed after WWII, give an idea of how beautiful the city's medieval core once was. Looming above it all is grand old **old town hall** (*Römer*) where scores of Holy Roman Emperors celebrated their coronations. For a who's who, visit the imposing **Kaisersaal** (Imperial Hall; enter from Limpurgerstrasse).

Kaiserdom   CATHEDRAL
(Imperial/Frankfurt Cathedral; www.dom-frankfurt.de; Domplatz 14; tower adult/concession €3.50/1.50; tower 9am-8pm Sat-Thu, 1-8pm Fri, tower 9am-6pm Apr-Oct, 11am-5pm Thu-Mon Nov-Mar; ℝ Dom/Römer) Dominated by an elegant Gothic **tower** (95m; can be climbed), begun in the 1400s and completed in the 1860s, Frankfurt's red sandstone cathedral is an island of calm amid the bustle of the city centre. From 1356 to 1792, the Holy Roman Emperors were elected (and, after 1562, consecrated and crowned) in the **Wahlkapelle** at the end of the right aisle (look for the modern 'skull' altar).

Museumsufer Frankfurt   MUSEUM
(www.museumsufer-frankfurt.de; btwn Eiserner Steg & Friedensbrücke; ⑤ Schweizer Platz) Collectively known as the Museumsufer, more than a dozen museums line up along the south bank of the Main River. The most famous is the Städel Museum, a renowned art gallery, but fans of architecture, archaeology, applied arts, film and ethnology will also get their fill. Bus 46, which leaves from the Hauptbahnhof several times hourly, links most museums.

★ Städel Museum   MUSEUM
(☑ 069-605 098 117; www.staedelmuseum.de; Schaumainkai 63; adult/concession/under 12yr/ family €14/12/free/24; ⊙ 10am-6pm Tue, Wed, Sat & Sun, to 9pm Thur & Fri; ⑤ Schweizer Platz) Founded in 1815, this world-renowned art gallery has a truly outstanding collection of European art from the Middle Ages to today. Feast your eyes on stunning works by some of the biggest names, including Dürer, Rembrandt, Rubens, Renoir, Picasso and Cézanne. Contemporary art by such hotshots as Gerhard Richter and Francis Bacon is shown in a recently added subterranean extension lit by circular skylights.

Main Tower   VIEWPOINT
(☑ 069-3650 4878; www.maintower.de; Neue Mainzer Strasse 52-58; elevator adult/child/family €6.50/4.50/17.50; ⊙ 10am-9pm Sun-Thu, to 11pm Fri & Sat Apr-Oct, 10am-7pm Sun-Thu, to 9pm Fri & Sat Nov-Mar, cocktail lounge 9pm-midnight Tue-Thu, to 1am Fri & Sat; ℝ Alte Oper) Frankfurt's skyline wouldn't be the same without the Main Tower, at 200m one of the tallest and most distinctive high-rises in town. A good place to get a feel for 'Mainhattan' is 200m above street level, on the **observation platform** reached by lift in a mere 45 seconds. Be prepared for airport-type security. Closes during thunderstorms.

🛏 Sleeping

As at the stock exchange, supply and demand regulate room rates in Frankfurt. In other words, if a big trade show is in town (and it often is) prices can triple. In general, rates drop on weekends.

Frankfurt Hostel   HOSTEL €
(☑ 069-247 5130; www.frankfurt-hostel.com; Kaiserstrasse 74, 3rd fl; dm €18-22, s/d from €39/49; @ 🤶; ℝ Frankfurt Hauptbahnhof) Reached via a prewar marble-and-tile lobby and a mirrored lift, this lively, 200-bed hostel has a chill-out area for socialising, a small shared kitchen, wooden floors and a free breakfast buffet.

25hours Hotel by Levi's   HOTEL €€
(☑ 069-256 6770; www.25hours-hotels.com; Niddastrasse 58; d weekday/weekend from €99/70, during fairs up to €390; ✳@🤶; ℝ Hauptbahnhof) A hit with creative types for its playful design inspired by Levi's (yes, the jeans brand) and such hip factors as a rooftop terrace, free bike and Mini rentals, and a Gibson Music Room where anyone can jam on drums and guitars. Rooms are themed by decade, from the 1930s (calm colours) to the 1980s (tiger-print walls, optical-illusion carpets). Breakfast costs €16.

Frankfurt-am-Main

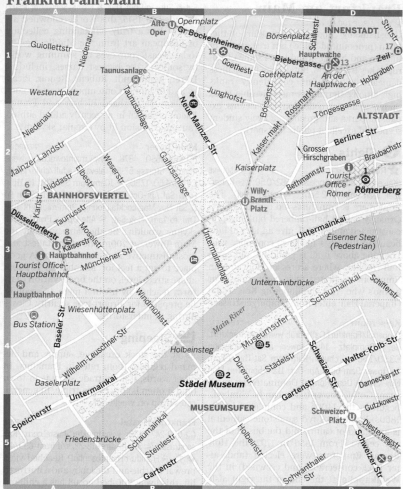

GERMANY FRANKFURT-AM-MAIN

Adina Apartment Hotel   HOTEL €€€
(☎069-247 4740; www.adina.eu/adina-apart-
ment-hotel-frankfurt; Wilhelm-Leuschner-Strasse
6; studio/apt from €199/245; P❋🛜🏊; ⑤Wil-
ly-Brandt-Platz) Those in need of plenty of
elbow room love the spacious and warmly
furnished studios and apartments in this
high-rise overlooking the Main River. The
one- and two-bedroom units come with full
kitchens, handy for self-caterers and families. Wi-fi is charged at €14.50 per 24 hours.
Breakfast costs €21.

🍴 Eating & Drinking

The pedestrian strip west of Hauptwache
square is nicknamed Fressgass thanks to its
many (average) eateries. Cosy apple-wine
taverns cluster in Alt-Sachsenhausen.

Kleinmarkthalle   MARKET €
(www.kleinmarkthalle.de; Hasengasse 5; ⏰8am-
6pm Mon-Fri, to 4pm Sat; ⑤Dom/Römer) This
traditional market hall is a bustling beehive of artfully arranged stalls selling quality fruit, veg, meat, spices and delectable
cheese. Feed acute tummy rumbles with

delectable baked goods, wurst (sausage) in a bun, and even sushi and tapas.

Almas TURKISH €€

(☎069-6642 6666; www.almas-restaurants.de; Wallstrasse 22; mains €11-18; ☺5pm-midnight Tue-Thu, to 2am Fri & Sat, 10am-3pm Sun; ⑤Südbahnhof) With its elegantly exotic decor, Almas wouldn't look out of place in Istanbul and has a wide menu of Turkish specialities beyond the doner kebab to go with its candle-lit, linen-draped tables. Everything tastes genuine, fresh and inflected with an authentic medley of spices.

Metropol Cafe am Dom INTERNATIONAL €€

(☎069-288 287; www.metropolcafe.de; Weckmarkt 13-15; mains €6-15.80; ☺9am-1am Tue-Sun; ⑤Dom/Römer) Homemade food inspired by the cuisines of the world is the name of the game at this bistro in a quiet spot next to the cathedral. It's popular with locals for its two-course lunches (€8.90), preferably enjoyed on the flowery terrace. In the evening a hipsterish crowd invades.

Leonhard's FAST FOOD €€

(☎069-219 1579; www.leonhards-restaurant.de; Zeil 116-26, 7th fl, Galeria Kaufhof; meals from €5; ☺9.30am-9pm Mon-Sat; ☑; ⑤Hauptwache) High atop the Galeria Kaufhof department store, this upscale food court with outdoor terrace serves up everything from coffee and baked goods to freshly prepared fish and meat dishes.

☆ Entertainment

Jazzkeller JAZZ

(www.jazzkeller.com; Kleine Bockenheimer Strasse 18a; admission €5-25; ☺8pm-2am Tue-Thu, 10pm-3am Fri, 9pm-2am Sat, 8pm-1am Sun; ⑤Alte Oper) A great jazz venue with mood, since 1952. Check out the walls for photos of jazz greats

GERMANY FRANKFURT-AM-MAIN

LOCAL KNOWLEDGE

APPLE-WINE TAVERNS

Apple-wine taverns are Frankfurt's great local tradition. They serve *Ebbelwei* (Frankfurt dialect for *Apfelwein*), an alcoholic apple cider, along with local specialities like *Handkäse mit Musik* (literally, 'hand-cheese with music'). This is a round cheese soaked in oil and vinegar and topped with onions; your bowel supplies the music. Anything with *Grüne Sosse*, a sensational local herb sauce, is also a winner. **Fichtekränzi** (☑ 069-612 778; www.fichtekraenzi. de; Wallstrasse 5; dishes €2.80-14.50; ☺ 5pm-midnight; ☒; ☒ Lokalbahnhof) and **Adolf Wagner** (☑ 069-612 565; www. apfelwein-wagner.com; Schweizer Strasse 71; mains €8.50-13.90; ☺ 11am-midnight; ☒; ☒ Südbahnhof) in Alt-Sachsenhausen are recommended.

who've played here over the years. Concerts begin at 9pm (8pm Sunday), except on DJ night (Friday) when there's dancing to Latin and funk. Hidden away in a cellar across from Goethestrasse 27.

Nachtleben CLUB
(☑ 069-206 50; www.nachtleben.net; Kurt-Schumacher-Strasse 45; ☺ 10.30am-2am Mon-Wed, to 4am Thu-Sat; ☒ Konstablerwache) Tucked away in the southeastern corner of Konstablerwache, Nachtleben has a sedate cafe (open 7am to 2am Sunday) with a terrace on the ground floor and a basement club without 'show-me' attitude that gets bustling about 1am. Concerts showcase alt and indie bands, parties range from Britpop to techno to hip hop, depending on the night.

🛍 Shopping

Zeil MALL
(☒ Hauptwache) For some epic shopping, stroll along the pedestrianised Zeil, which is lined by department stores, high-street chains and malls, including the architecturally striking MyZeil. The strip is bookended by two squares called Konstablerwache and Hauptwache, both named after guardhouses of which only the one on Hauptwache survives.

ℹ Information

Tourist Office (☑ 069-2123 8800; www. frankfurt-tourismus.de) Two branches: Hauptbahnhof (Main Hall, main train station; ☺ 8am-

9pm Mon-Fri, 9am-6pm Sat & Sun) and Römer (Römerberg 27; ☺ 9.30am-5.30pm Mon-Fri, to 4pm Sat & Sun; ☒ Frankfurt Hauptbahnhof), a smallish office in the central square.

ℹ Getting There & Away

AIR

Frankfurt Airport (FRA; www.frankfurt-airport. com), 12km southwest of the city centre, is Germany's busiest. S-Bahn lines S8 and S9 shuttle between the airport's regional train station (Regionalbahnhof) and the city centre (€4.35, 11 minutes) several times hourly.

Note that **Frankfurt-Hahn Airport** (HHN; www. hahn-airport.de), served by Ryanair, is actually 125km west of Frankfurt, near the Mosel Valley.

BUS

The Romantic Road Coach and long-distance buses leave from the south side of the Hauptbahnhof.

TRAIN

There are direct trains to pretty much everywhere, including Berlin (€123, four hours) and Munich (€101, 3½ hours).

ℹ Getting Around

For public transport information, go to www.rmv. de/en.

The Romantic Rhine Valley

Between Koblenz and Bingen, the Rhine cuts deeply through the Rhenish slate mountains. Nicknamed the 'Romantic Rhine', the stretch is justifiably a highlight for many Germany explorers. This is where hillsides cradle craggy cliffs and nearly vertical terraced vineyards. Idyllic villages appear around each bend, their neat half-timbered houses and church steeples seemingly plucked from the world of fairy tales. High above the river, busy with barge traffic, are the famous medieval castles, some ruined, some restored, all vestiges from a mysterious past.

Although Koblenz and Mainz are logical starting points, the area can also be explored on a long day trip from Frankfurt.

ℹ Getting There & Around

Each mode of transport on the Rhine has its own advantages and all are equally enjoyable. Try combining several.

BOAT

From about Easter to October (winter services are very limited), passenger ships run by

Köln-Düsseldorfer (KD; ✆ 0221-2088 318; www.k-d.com) link villages on a set timetable. You're free to get on and off as you like.

CAR

There are no bridges between Koblenz and Bingen but you can easily change banks by using a car ferry. There are five routes: Bingen–Rüdesheim, Niederheimbach–Lorch, Boppard–Filsen, Oberwesel–Kaub and St Goar–Goarshausen.

TRAIN

Villages on the Rhine's left bank (eg Bacharach and Boppard) are served hourly by local trains on the Koblenz–Mainz run. Right-bank villages such as Rüdesheim, St Goarshausen and Braubach are linked hourly to Koblenz' Hauptbahnhof and Frankfurt by the RheingauLinie train.

Bacharach

One of the prettiest of the Rhine villages, Bacharach conceals its considerable charms behind a 14th-century town wall. Beyond the thick arched gateways awaits a beautiful medieval old town graced with half-timbered town houses lining Oberstrasse, the main thoroughfare. There's no shortage of atmospheric places to eat and sample the local vintages.

For gorgeous views of village, vineyards and river, take a stroll atop the **medieval ramparts**, which are punctuated by guard towers. An especially scenic panorama unfolds from the **Postenturm** at the north end of town, from where you can also espy the filigreed ruins of the **Wernerkapelle**, a medieval chapel, and the turrets of the 12th-century hilltop **Burg Stahleck**, a castle turned **youth hostel** (✆ 06743-1266; www.jugendherberge.de; Burg Stahleck; s/d €27/43). Another good place to stay is the **Rhein Hotel** (✆ 06743-1243; www.rhein-hotel-bacharach.de;

Langstrasse 50; d €78-136; P ❄ 🛜), which has 14 well-lit, soundproofed rooms with original artwork and a respected restaurant.

St Goar & St Goarshausen

These twin towns face each other across the Rhine. On the left bank, St Goar is lorded over by **Burg Rheinfels** (www.st-goar.de; adult/child €4/2; ⌚ 9am-6pm mid-Mar–late Oct, to 5pm until 9 Nov), one of the largest and most impressive river castles. Its labyrinthine ruins reflect the greed and ambition of the local count who built the behemoth in 1245 to levy tolls on passing ships.

Today an inexpensive ferry links St Goar with St Goarshausen and the most fabled spot along the Romantic Rhine, the **Loreley Rock**. This vertical slab of slate owes its fame to a mythical maiden whose siren songs are said to have lured sailors to their death in the river's treacherous currents.

A classy spot to spend the night is **Romantik Hotel Schloss Rheinfels** (✆ 06741-8020; www.schloss-rheinfels.de; d incl breakfast €130-245; P @ 🛜 🍽), right by the castle. Its three restaurants enjoy a fine reputation but there are plenty more down in the village.

Braubach

Framed by forested hillsides, vineyards and Rhine-side rose gardens, the 1300-year-old town of Braubach, on the right bank, is centred on the small, half-timbered market square. High above are the dramatic towers, turrets and crenellations of the 700-year-old **Marksburg** (✆ 0049-2627-536; www.marksburg.de; adult/student/6-18yr €6/5/4; ⌚ 10am-5pm late Mar-Oct, 11am-4pm Nov-late Mar) which – unique among the Rhine fortresses – was never destroyed. Tours (in English at 1pm and 4pm

---

ROMANCING THE RHINE

The Romantic Rhine Valley villages have plenty more charmers that deserve at least a quick spin. Just pick one at random and make your own discoveries. The following are some teasers:

Boppard Roman ruins and a cable car to the stunning Vierseenblick viewpoint (left bank).

Oberwesel Famous for its 3km-long medieval town wall punctuated by 16 guard towers (left bank).

Assmannshausen Relatively untouristed village known for its red wines, sweeping views and good hikes (right bank).

Rüdesheim Day-tripper-deluged but handy launch pad for the mighty Niederwalddenkmal monument and Eberbach Monastery (right bank).

from late March through early November)
take in the citadel, the Gothic hall and the
large kitchen, plus a grisly torture chamber.

Koblenz

Founded by the Romans, Koblenz sits at
the confluence of the Rhine and Moselle
Rivers, a point known as **Deutsches Eck**
(German Corner) and dominated by a bombastic 19th-century statue of Kaiser Wilhelm I on horseback. On the right Rhine
bank high above the Deutsches Eck – and
reached by an 850m-long **Seilbahn** (Cable
car; www.seilbahn-koblenz.de; return adult/child
€9/4, incl fortress €11.80/5.60; ⊘10am-6pm or
7pm Apr-Oct, to 5pm Nov-Mar) – is the venerable
fortress of **Festung Ehrenbreitstein** (www.
diefestungehrenbreitstein.de; adult/child €6/3, incl
cable car €11.80/5.60, audioguide €2; ⊘10am-
6pm Apr-Oct, to 5pm Nov-Mar), one of Europe's
mightiest citadels. Views are great and
there's a restaurant and a regional museum
inside.

Moselle Valley

Like a vine right before harvest, the Moselle hangs heavy with visitor fruit. Castles
and towns with half-timbered buildings are
built along the sinuous river below steep,
rocky cliffs planted with vineyards. It's one
of Germany's most evocative regions, with
stunning views revealed at every river bend.
Unlike the Romantic Rhine, it's spanned
by plenty of bridges. The most scenic section unravels between Bernkastel-Kues and
Cochem, 50km apart and linked by the B421.

Cochem

Easily reached by train or boat from Koblenz, Cochem is one of the most popular
destinations on the Moselle thanks to its
fairy-tale-like **Reichsburg** (☑02671-255;
www.burg-cochem.de; Schlossstrasse 36; tours
adult/concession/child €5/4.50/3; ⊘9am-5pm
mid-Mar–Oct, 10am-3pm Nov & Dec, 11am, noon
& 1pm Wed, Sat & Sun Jan–mid-Mar). Like many
others, the 11th-century original fell victim
to frenzied Frenchmen in 1689, then stood
ruined for centuries until a wealthy Berliner
snapped it up for a pittance in 1868 and had
it restored to its current – if not always architecturally faithful – glory. The 40-minute
tours (in German but English leaflet available) take in decorative rooms reflecting 1000
years' worth of tastes and styles.

The **tourist office** (☑02671-600 40; www.
ferienland-cochem.de; Endertplatz 1; ⊘9am-5pm
Mon-Fri Apr-Oct, 9am-1pm & 2-5pm Mon-Fri Nov-Mar,
9am-3pm Sat May–mid-Jul, 9am-5pm mid-Jul–Oct,
10am-3pm Sun Jul-Oct) has information about
the entire region.

Cochem is 55km from Koblenz via the scenic B327 and B49. Regional trains shuttling
between Trier (€12.90, 45 minutes) and Koblenz (€11.30, 50 minutes) stop here as well.

Beilstein

Picture-perfect Beilstein is little more than
a cluster of higgledy-piggledy houses surrounded by steep vineyards. Its historic
highlights include the **Marktplatz** and
the ruined hilltop castle **Burg Metternich**
(views!). The **Zehnthauskeller** (☑02673-900
907; www.zehnthauskeller.de; Marktplatz; ⊘11am-
evening Tue-Sun) **FREE** houses a romantically
dark, vaulted wine tavern owned by the
same family that also runs two local hotels.
Meals are available for €2.20 to €9. There is
no tourist office.

Bus 716 goes from Cochem to Beilstein
(€3.65, 20 minutes) almost hourly in season,
although the approach by boat is more scenic (€12, one hour).

Bernkastel-Kues

This charming twin town straddles the Moselle about 50km downriver from Trier and
is close to some of the river's most famous
vineyards. Bernkastel, on the right bank, is
a symphony in half-timber, stone and slate
and teems with wine taverns.

Get your heart pumping by hoofing
it up to **Burg Landshut**, a ruined 13th-
century castle on a bluff above town. Allow 30
minutes to be rewarded with glorious valley
views and a cold drink at the beer garden.

The **tourist office** (☑06531-500 190; www.
bernkastel.de; Gestade 6, Bernkastel; ⊘9am-5pm
Mon-Fri, 10am-5pm Sat, 10am-1pm Sun May-Oct,
9.30am-4pm Mon-Fri Nov-Apr) is in Bernkastel.

Coming from Trier, drivers should follow
the B53. Using public transport involves
catching the regional train to Wittlich and
switching to bus 300.

Trier

☑0651 / POP 106,700

This handsome, leafy Moselle town is home
to Germany's finest ensemble of Roman
monuments – including thermal baths and

BURG ELTZ

At the head of the beautiful Eltz Valley, **Burg Eltz** (02672-950 500; www.burg-eltz.de; Wierschem; tour adult/student/family €9/6.50/26; 9.30am-5.30pm Apr-Oct) is one of Germany's most romantic medieval castles. Never destroyed, this vision of turrets, towers, oriels, gables and half-timber has squatted atop a rock framed by thick forest for nearly 900 years and is still owned by the original family. The decorations, furnishings, tapestries, fireplaces, paintings and armour you see during the 45-minute tour are also many hundreds of years old.

By car, you can reach Burg Eltz via Munstermaifeld. Alternatively, take a boat or train to Moselkern village and approach the castle via a lovely 5km walk (or €24 taxi ride).

an amphitheatre – as well as architectural gems from later ages.

⊙ Sights

Porta Nigra   GATE
(adult/student/child €3/2.10/1.50; 9am-6pm Apr-Sep, to 5pm Mar & Oct, to 4pm Nov-Feb) This brooding 2nd-century city gate – blackened by time (hence the name, Latin for 'black gate') – is a marvel of engineering since it's held together by nothing but gravity and iron clamps.

Amphitheatre   HISTORIC SITE
(Olewiger Strasse; adult/concession/child €3/2.10/1.50; 9am-6pm Apr-Sep, to 5pm Mar & Oct, to 4pm Nov-Feb) Trier's Roman amphitheatre could accommodate 20,000 spectators for gladiator tournaments and animal fights. Beneath the arena are dungeons where prisoners sentenced to death waited next to starving beasts for the final showdown.

Kaiserthermen   HISTORIC SITE
(Imperial Baths; Weberbachstrasse 41; adult/student/child €3/2.10/1.50; 9am-6pm Apr-Sep, to 5pm Mar & Oct, to 4pm Nov-Feb) Get a sense of the layout of this vast Roman thermal bathing complex with its striped brick-and-stone arches from the corner lookout tower, then descend into an underground labyrinth consisting of hot- and cold-water baths, boiler rooms and heating channels.

Trierer Dom   CATHEDRAL
(0651-979 0790; www.dominformation.de; Liebfrauenstrasse 12, cnr of Domfreihof; 6.30am-6pm Apr-Oct, to 5.30pm Nov-Mar) Trier's cathedral is considered the oldest bishop's church in Germany and looms above a palace built during Roman times. Today's edifice is a study in nearly 1700 years of church architecture, with Romanesque, Gothic and baroque elements. Intriguingly, its floorplan is that of a 12-petalled flower, a symbol of the Virgin Mary.

Konstantin Basilika   CHURCH
(0651-425 70; www.konstantin-basilika.de; Konstantinplatz 10; 10am-6pm Apr-Oct, 11am-noon & 3-4pm Tue-Sat, noon-1pm Sun Jan-Mar) Constructed around AD 310 as Constantine's throne room, the brick-built basilica is now a typically austere Protestant church. With built-to-impress dimensions (67m long and 36m high), it's the largest single-room Roman structure still in existence.

🛏 Sleeping

Hotel Deutscher Hof   HOTEL €€
(0651-977 80; www.hotel-deutscher-hof.de; Südallee 25; s/d from €60/75; P @ 🛜) This comfortable value-priced pad a short walk south of the city centre oozes warmth and comfort in its softly lit and warmly decorated rooms. In summer there's a nice terrace for enjoying breakfast, while on colder days the sauna and steam baths beckon. Breakfast costs €8.

Hotel Villa Hügel   BOUTIQUE HOTEL €€€
(0651-937 100; www.hotel-villa-huegel.de; Bernhardstrasse 14; d including breakfast €146-194; P @ 🛜 🏊) A stylish, 33-room hillside villa where you can begin the day with sparkling wine at a lavish breakfast buffet and end it luxuriating in the 12m indoor pool and Finnish sauna. Rooms, decorated with honey-toned woods, are calming and create a sense of wellbeing. Served by buses 2 and 82.

✕ Eating & Drinking

In the warm months cafes fill the old city's public squares, including the Kornmarkt. The Olewig wine district, 3km southeast of the city centre, is reached by buses 6, 16 and 81.

de Winkel   PUB €
(0651-436 1878; www.de-winkel.de; Johannisstrasse 25; mains €6-9.50; 6pm-1am Tue-Thu, to 2am Fri & Sat) Winny and Morris have presided over this locally adored watering hole for over

15 years. Join the locals for Pils and a bite, for instance the crispy chicken wings called 'Flieten' in Trier dialect.

Weinstube Kesselstadt   GERMAN €€
(📞 0651-411 78; www.weinstube-kesselstatt.de; Liebfrauenstrasse 10; dishes €4.50-12; ⏰ 10am-midnight) Sampling the local wines is a great pleasure in this charming setting, in summer on the cathedral-facing terrace. The standard menu showcases quality products from the region and is augmented by specials starring seasonal bounty like mushrooms, game or asparagus. Order at the bar.

Zum Domstein   ROMAN €€
(📞 0651-744 90; www.domstein.de; Hauptmarkt 5; mains €9-19, Roman dinner €17-36; ⏰ 8.30am-midnight) At this old-timey restaurant you can either dine like an ancient Roman or feast on more conventional German and international fare. Roman dishes are based on the recipes of a 1st-century local chef named Marcus Gavius Apicius.

ℹ️ Information

Tourist Office (📞 0651-978 080; www. trier-info.de; ⏰ 9am-6pm Mon-Sat Mar-Dec, 10am-5pm Sun May-Oct, to 3pm Sun Mar, Apr, Nov & Dec, shorter hours Jan & Feb) Next to the Porta Nigra. Has excellent brochures in English and sells Moselle-area walking and cycling maps, concert tickets and boat excursions.

ℹ️ Getting There & Away

Frequent direct train connections include Koblenz (€22.10, 1½ to two hours), Cologne (€33, three hours) and Luxembourg (€17.30, 50 minutes).

Cologne

📞 0221 / POP 1 MILLION

Cologne (Köln) offers lots of attractions, led by its famous cathedral, the filigree twin spires of which dominate the skyline. The city's museum landscape is especially strong when it comes to art but also has something in store for fans of chocolate, sports and Roman history. Its people are well known for their joie de vivre and it's easy to have a good time right along with them year-round in the beer halls of the Altstadt.

👁 Sights

⭐ **Kölner Dom**   CHURCH
(Cologne Cathedral; 📞 0211-1794 0200; www. koelner-dom.de; tower adult/concession/family

€3/1.50/6; ⏰ 6am-9pm Mon-Sat May-Oct, to 7.30pm Nov-Apr, 1-3.30pm Sun year-round, tower 9am-6pm May-Sep, to 5pm Mar-Apr & Oct, to 4pm Nov-Feb) Cologne's geographical and spiritual heart – and its single-biggest tourist draw – is the magnificent Kölner Dom. With its soaring twin spires, this is the Mt Everest of cathedrals, jam-packed with art and treasures.

For an exercise fix, climb the 509 steps up the Dom's south tower to the base of the steeple that dwarfed all buildings in Europe until Gustave Eiffel built a certain tower in Paris. A good excuse to take a breather on your way up is the 24-tonne **Peter Bell** (1923), the largest free-swinging working bell in the world.

The Dom is Germany's largest cathedral and must be circled to truly appreciate its dimensions. Note how its lacy spires and flying buttresses create a sensation of lightness and fragility despite its mass and height. Soft light filters through the medieval stained-glass windows as well a much-lauded new one by contemporary artist Gerhard Richter in the transept.

The pièce de résistance among the cathedral's bevy of treasures is the **Shrine of the Three Kings** behind the main altar, a richly bejewelled and gilded sarcophagus said to hold the remains of the kings who followed the star to the stable in Bethlehem where Jesus was born. The bones were spirited out of Milan in 1164 as spoils of war by Emperor Barbarossa's chancellor and instantly turned Cologne into a major pilgrimage site.

Other highlights include the **Gero Crucifix** (970), notable for its monumental size and an emotional intensity rarely achieved in those early medieval days; the **choir stalls** from 1310, richly carved from oak; and the **altar painting** (c 1450) by Cologne artist Stephan Lochner.

⭐ **Römisch-Germanisches Museum**   MUSEUM
(Roman Germanic Museum; 📞 0221-2212 4438; www.museenkoeln.de; Roncalliplatz 4; adult/concession €9/5; ⏰ 10am-5pm Tue-Sun) Sculptures and ruins displayed outside the entrance are merely the overture to a full symphony of Roman artefacts found along the Rhine. Highlights include the giant **Poblicius tomb** (AD 30–40), magnificent 3rd-century **Dionysus mosaic**, and astonishingly well-preserved glass items. Insight into daily Roman life is gained from toys, tweezers, lamps and jewellery, the designs of which have changed surprisingly little since.

COLOGNE CARNIVAL

Ushering in Lent in late February or early March, Cologne's Carnival (Karneval) rivals Munich's Oktoberfest for exuberance, as people dress in creative costumes and party in the streets. Things kick off the Thursday before the seventh Sunday before Easter, culminate on Monday *(Rosenmontag)*, when there are televised street parades, and end on Ash Wednesday.

★Museum Ludwig MUSEUM
(☎0221-2212 6165; www.museum-ludwig.de; Heinrich-Böll-Platz; adult/child €11/7.50, more during special exhibits; ⏲10am-6pm Tue-Sun) A mecca of 20th-century art, Museum Ludwig presents a tantalising mix of works from all major phases. Fans of German expressionism (Beckmann, Dix, Kirchner) will get their fill here as much as those with a penchant for Picasso, American pop art (Warhol, Lichtenstein) and Russian avant-garde painter Alexander Rodchenko. Rothko and Pollock are highlights of the abstract collection, while Gursky and Tillmanns are among the reasons the photography section is a must-see.

Wallraf-Richartz-Museum & Fondation Corboud MUSEUM
(☎0221-2212 1119; www.wallraf.museum; Obenmarspforten; adult/concession €13/8; ⏲10am-6pm Tue-Sun, to 9pm Thu) A famous collection of European paintings from the 13th to the 19th centuries, the Wallraf-Richartz-Museum occupies a postmodern cube designed by the late OM Ungers. Works are presented chronologically, with the oldest on the 1st floor where standouts include brilliant examples from the Cologne School, known for its distinctive use of colour. The most famous painting is Stefan Lochner's *Madonna of the Rose Bower*.

Schokoladenmuseum MUSEUM
(Chocolate Museum; ☎0221-931 8880; www.schokoladenmuseum.de; Am Schokoladenmuseum 1a; adult/concession/family €9/6.50/25; ⏲10am-6pm Tue-Fri, 11am-7pm Sat & Sun, last entry 1hr before closing) At this high-tech temple to the art of chocolate-making, exhibits on the origin of the 'elixir of the gods', as the Aztecs called it, and the cocoa-growing process are followed by a live-production factory tour and a stop at a chocolate fountain for a sample.

Tours

KD River Cruises BOAT
(☎0221-258 3011; www.k-d.com; Frankenwerft 35; adult/child €9.50/6; ⏲10.30am-5pm Apr-Oct) One of several companies offering one-hour spins taking in the splendid Altstadt panorama; other options include brunch and sunset cruises.

Sleeping

Station Hostel for Backpackers HOSTEL €
(☎0221-912 5301; www.hostel-cologne.de; Marzellenstrasse 44-56; dm €17-20, s/d from €39/55; @📶) Near the Hauptbahnhof, this is a hostel as hostels should be: central, convivial and economical. A lounge gives way to clean, colourful rooms sleeping one to six people. There's lots of free stuff, including linen, internet access, lockers, city maps and guest kitchen.

Stern am Rathaus HOTEL €€
(☎0221-2225 1750; www.stern-am-rathaus.de; Bürgerstrasse 6; d €105-135; 📶) This small, contemporary hotel has eight nicely spruced-up, luxuriously panelled rooms spread over three floors. It's in a quiet side street smack-dab in the Altstadt yet close to sights and plenty of restaurants. Kudos for the extra comfortable beds, the personalised service and the high-quality breakfast buffet.

Excelsior Hotel Ernst HOTEL €€€
(☎0221-2701; www.excelsiorhotelernst.com; Trankgasse 1-5; d from €230; ❄@📶) Luxury is taken very seriously at this traditional hotel with a pedigree going back to 1863. Some of the plushly furnished rooms overlook the majestic Cologne cathedral. If that doesn't wow enough, perhaps a meal at the Michelin-starred restaurant will. Breakfast costs €32.

Eating & Drinking

There are plenty of beer halls and restaurants in the tourist-adored Altstadt, but for a more local vibe head to student-flavoured Zülpicher Viertel or the Belgisches Viertel, both in the city centre. Local breweries turn out a variety called *Kölsch*, which is relatively light and served in skinny 200mL glasses.

Freddy Schilling BURGERS €
(☎0221-1695 5515; www.freddyschilling.de; Kyffhäuserstrasse 34; burgers €5.50-10; ⏲noon-11pm Sun-Tue, to 11pm Fri & Sat) A wholewheat bun

Cologne

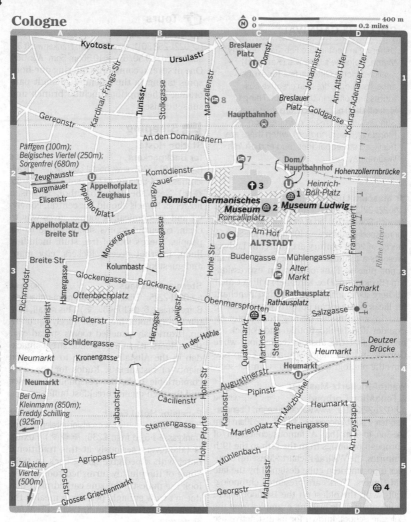

provides a solid framework for the moist patties made with beef from happy cows and drizzled with Freddy's homemade 'special' sauce. Pair it with a side of Rosi's: small butter-and-rosemary-tossed potatoes.

Bei Oma Kleinmann
GERMAN €€

(☎0221-232 346; www.beiomakleinmann.de; Zülpicher Strasse 9; mains €13-21; ⊗5pm-1am Tue-Sat, to midnight Sun) Named for its long-time owner, who was still cooking almost to her last day at age 95 in 2009, this perennially booked restaurant serves a mind-boggling variety of schnitzel, made either with pork or veal and paired with homemade sauces and sides. Pull up a seat at the small wooden tables for a classic Cologne night out.

Sorgenfrei
MODERN EUROPEAN €€€

(☎0221-355 7327; www.sorgenfrei-koeln.com; Antwerpener Strasse 15; mains €17-35, 2-course lunch €17, 3-/4-course dinner €35/43; ⊗noon-3pm Mon-Fri, 6pm-midnight Mon-Sat) A huge wine-by-the-glass menu is but one draw of this Belgische Viertel fine-dining treasure. Dishes are prepared with the same attention to detail yet lack of pretension found throughout this small restaurant. Hardwood floors

Cologne

encourage a casual vibe that goes well with salads and simple mains at lunch and more complex creations for dinner.

★ **Päffgen** BEER HALL
(☑ 0221-135 461; www.paeffgen-koelsch.de; Friesenstrasse 64-66; ⊙10am-midnight Sun-Thu, to 12.30am Fri & Sat) Busy, loud and boisterous, Päffgen has been pouring Kölsch since 1883 and hasn't lost a step since. In summer you can enjoy the refreshing brew and local specialities (€1.10 to €10.70) beneath starry skies in the beer garden.

Früh am Dom BEER HALL
(☑ 0221-261 3215; www.frueh-am-dom.de; Am Hof 12-14; ⊙8am-midnight) This warren of a beer hall near the Dom epitomises Cologne earthiness. Tuck into hearty meals (€2.50 to €20) sitting inside amid loads of knick-knacks or on the flower-filled terrace next to a fountain. It's also known for gut-filling breakfasts (€4.30 to €9.50).

ⓘ **Information**

Tourist Office (☑ 0221-346 430; www.cologne-tourism.com; Kardinal-Höffner-Platz 1; ⊙9am-8pm Mon-Sat, 10am-5pm Sun) Near the cathedral.

ⓘ **Getting There & Away**

AIR
Köln Bonn Airport (CGN; Cologne-Bonn Airport; ☑ 02203-404 001; www.koeln-bonn-airport.de; Kennedystrasse) is about 18km southeast of the

city centre and connected to the Hauptbahnhof by the S-Bahn S13 train every 20 minutes (€2.80, 15 minutes).

TRAIN
Services to and from Cologne are fast and frequent in all directions. A sampling: Berlin (€117, 4¼ hours), Frankfurt (€71, 1¼ hours), Düsseldorf (€11.30, 30 minutes), Bonn (€7.70, 30 minutes) and Aachen (€16.80, one hour). ICE trains leave for Brussels to connect with the Eurostar for London or Paris.

ⓘ **Getting Around**

For public transport information, see www.vrs.de.

Düsseldorf

☑ 0211 / POP 596,000
Düsseldorf dazzles with boundary-pushing architecture, zinging nightlife and an art scene to rival many a metropolis. It's a posh and modern city whose economy is dominated by banking, advertising, fashion and telecommunications. However, a couple of hours of partying in the boisterous pubs of the Altstadt, the historical quarter along the Rhine, is all you need to realise that locals have no problem letting their hair down once they slip out of those Boss jackets.

⊙ **Sights**

K20 Grabbeplatz MUSEUM
(☑ 0211-838 1130; www.kunstsammlung.de; Grabbeplatz 5; adult/child €12/9.50; ⊙10am-6pm Tue-Fri, 11am-6pm Sat & Sun) A collection that spans the arc of 20th-century artistic vision gives the K20 an enviable edge in the art world. It encompasses major works by Picasso, Matisse and Mondrian and more than 100 paintings and drawings by Paul Klee. Americans represented include Jackson Pollock, Andy Warhol and Jasper John. Düsseldorf's own Joseph Beuys has a major presence as well.

K21 Ständehaus MUSEUM
(☑ 0211-838 1630; www.kunstsammlung.de; Ständehausstrasse 1; adult/child €12/9.50; ⊙10am-6pm Tue-Fri, 11am-6pm Sat & Sun) A stately 19th-century parliament building forms a fabulous dichotomy to the cutting-edge art of the K21, a collection showcasing only works created after the 1980s. Large-scale film and video installations and groups of works share space with site-specific rooms by an international cast of artists including Andreas Gursky, Candida Höfer, Bill Viola and Nam June Paik.

GERMANY DÜSSELDORF

BONN

South of Cologne on the Rhine River, Bonn served as West Germany's capital from 1949 until 1990. For visitors, the birthplace of Ludwig van Beethoven has plenty in store, not least the great composer's birth house, a string of top-rated museums and the lovely riverside setting.

The **Beethoven-Haus** (⌨0228-981 7525; www.beethoven-haus-bonn.de; Bonngasse 24-26; adult/concession €6/4.50; ☉10am-6pm Apr-Oct, 10am-5pm Mon-Sat, 11am-5pm Sun Nov-Mar), where the composer was born in 1770, is big on memorabilia concerning his life and music. A highlight is his last piano, which was outfitted with an amplified sounding board to accommodate his deafness. Tickets are also good for an adjacent interactive Beethoven-themed 3D multimedia show.

Bonn's most stellar museums line up neatly on Museumsmeile (Museum Mile) in the heart of the former government quarter along Willy-Brandt-Allee just south of the city centre (take U-Bahn lines 16, 63 and 66). A top contender is the **Kunstmuseum Bonn** (Bonn Art Museum; ⌨0228-776 260; www.kunstmuseum-bonn.de; Friedrich-Ebert-Allee 2; adult/concession €7/3.50; ☉11am-6pm Tue & Thu-Sun, to 9pm Wed), which presents 20th-century art, including a standout collection of works by August Macke and other Rhenish expressionists. History buffs gravitate to the **Haus der Geschichte** (Museum of History; ⌨0228-916 50; www.hdg.de; Willy-Brandt-Allee 14; ☉9am-7pm Tue-Fri, 10am-6pm Sat & Sun) [FREE] for an engaging romp through Germany's post-WWII history.

The **tourist office** (⌨0228-775 000; www.bonn.de; Windeckstrasse 1; ☉10am-6pm Mon-Fri, to 4pm Sat, to 2pm Sun) is just off Münsterplatz and a three-minute walk, along Poststrasse, from the Hauptbahnhof (central train station).

The U-Bahn lines 16 and 18 (€7.70, one hour) and regional trains (€7.70, 30 minutes) link Cologne and Bonn several times hourly.

Medienhafen ARCHITECTURE

(Am Handelshafen) This once-dead old harbour area has been reborn as the Medienhafen, an increasingly hip quarter filled with architecture, restaurants, bars, hotels and clubs. Once-crumbling warehouses have turned into high-tech office buildings and now rub shoulders with bold new structures designed by celebrated international architects, including Frank Gehry.

🛏 Sleeping

Backpackers-Düsseldorf HOSTEL €

(⌨0211-302 0848; www.backpackers-duesseldorf. de; Fürstenwall 180; dm incl small breakfast €18-24, linen €2; [P]@🛜) Düsseldorf's cute indie hostel sleeps 60 in clean four- to 10-bed dorms outfitted with individual backpack-sized lockers.

Max Hotel Garni HOTEL €€

(⌨0211-386 800; www.max-hotelgarni.de; Adersstrasse 65; s/d/tr €75/90/110; @🛜) Upbeat, contemporary and run with personal flair, this charmer is a favourite Düsseldorf bargain. The 11 rooms are good sized and decked out in bright hues and warm woods. Rates include coffee, tea, soft drinks and a regional public transport pass, but breakfast costs €7.50. The reception isn't always staffed, so call ahead to arrange an arrival time.

Sir & Lady Astor HOTEL €€

(⌨0211-173 370; www.sir-astor.de; Kurfürstenstrasse 18 & 23; s/d from €75/80; ✳@🛜) Never mind the ho-hum setting on a residential street near the Hauptbahnhof: this unique twin boutique hotel brims with class, originality and charm. Check-in is at Sir Astor, furnished in 'Scotland-meets-Africa' style, while Lady Astor across the street goes more for French floral sumptuousness. With a huge fan base and only 21 rooms in total, book early.

🍴 Eating & Drinking

The local beverage of choice is *Altbier*, a dark and semisweet beer typical of Düsseldorf.

⭐ Brauerei im Füchschen GERMAN €€

(⌨0211-137 470; www.fuechschen.de; Ratinger Strasse 28; snacks €1.80-6.90, mains €8.50-15.30; ☉9am-1am Mon-Thu, to 2am Fri & Sat, to midnight Sun) Boisterous, packed and drenched with local colour – the 'Little Fox' in the Altstadt is all you expect a Rhenish beer hall to be. The kitchen makes a mean *Schweinshaxe* (roast pork leg). The high-ceilinged interior echoes with the mirthful roar of people enjoying their meals. This is one of the best *Altbier* breweries in town.

Sila Thai
THAI €€€

(☑ 0211-860 4427; www.sila-thai.com; Bahnstrasse 76; mains €17-25; ⊘ noon-3pm & 6pm-1am) Even simple curries become culinary poetry at this Thai gourmet temple with its fairy-tale setting of carved wood, rich fabrics and imported sculpture. Like a trip to Thailand without the passport. Reservations advised.

★ Zum Uerige
BEER HALL

(☑ 0211-866 990; www.uerige.de; Berger Strasse 1; ⊘ 10am-midnight) This cavernous brewpub is the quintessential Düsseldorf haunt to try the city's typical *Altbier*. The suds flow so quickly from giant copper vats that the waitstaff – called *Köbes* – simply carry huge trays of brew and plonk down a glass whenever they spy an empty. Even on a cold day, there are groups all over the street outside.

ⓘ Information

Tourist Office (☑ 0211-1720 2844; www.duesseldorf-tourismus.de) There are two tourist offices, the main one at the Hauptbahnhof (Immermannstrasse 65b; ⊘ 9.30am-7pm Mon-Fri, to 5pm Sat) and another in the Altstadt (cnr Marktstrasse & Rheinstrasse; ⊘ 10am-6pm), the historic centre.

ⓘ Getting There & Away

Düsseldorf International Airport (DUS; www.dus-int.de) is linked to the city centre by the S-Bahn line 1 (€2.50, 10 minutes).

Regional trains travel to Cologne (€11.30, 30 minutes), Bonn (€16.80, one hour) and Aachen (€20.70, 1½ hours). Fast ICE train links include Berlin (€111, 4¼ hours), Hamburg (€82, 3½ hours) and Frankfurt (€82, 1½ hours).

ⓘ Getting Around

For public transport information, go to www.vrr.de.

Aachen

☑ 0241 / POP 236,000

A spa town with a hopping student population and tremendous amounts of character, Aachen is most famous for its ancient cathedral. It makes for an excellent day trip from Cologne or Düsseldorf or a worthy overnight stop.

◉ Sights

★ Aachener Dom
CHURCH

(☑ 0241-447 090; www.aachendom.de; Münsterplatz; tours adult/concession €4/3; ⊘ 7am-7pm Apr-Dec, to 6pm Jan-Mar, tours 11am-5.30pm Mon-Fri, 1-5pm Sat & Sun, 2pm tour in English) It's impossible to overestimate the significance of Aachen's magnificent cathedral. The burial place of Charlemagne, it's where more than 30 German kings were crowned and where pilgrims have flocked since the 12th century. Before entering the church, stop by the new **Dom Visitors Centre** (☑ 0241-4770 9127; Klosterplatz 2; ⊘ 10am-1pm Mon, to 5pm Tue-Sun Jan-Mar, 10am-1pm Mon, to 6pm Tue-Sun Apr-Dec) for info and tickets for tours and the cathedral treasury.

The oldest and most impressive section is Charlemagne's palace chapel, the **Pfalzkapelle**. Completed in 800 (the year of the emperor's coronation), it's an octagonal dome encircled by a 16-sided ambulatory supported by antique Italian pillars. The colossal brass chandelier was a gift from Emperor Friedrich Barbarossa during whose reign Charlemagne was canonised in 1165.

Pilgrims have poured into Aachen ever since, drawn as much by the cult surrounding Charlemagne as by four prized relics, including the loincloth purportedly worn by Jesus at his crucifixion. To accommodate these floods of the faithful, a Gothic **choir** was docked to the chapel in 1414 and filled with such priceless 11th-century treasures as the **pala d'oro** (a gold-plated altar-front) and the jewel-encrusted gilded copper **pulpit**. At the far end is the gilded **shrine of Charlemagne** that has held the emperor's remains since 1215. In front, the equally fanciful **shrine of St Mary** shelters the four relics.

Unless you join a guided tour, you'll barely catch a glimpse of Charlemagne's white marble **throne** in the upstairs gallery. It served as the coronation throne of those 30 German kings between 936 and 1531. The tours themselves are fascinating for the level of detail they reveal about the church.

Rathaus
HISTORIC BUILDING

(Town Hall; ☑ 0241-432 7310; Markt; adult/concession incl audioguide €5/3; ⊘ 10am-6pm) Fifty life-size statues of German rulers, including 30 kings crowned in town between 936 and 1531 AD, adorn the facade of Aachen's splendid Gothic town hall. It was built in the 14th century atop the foundations of Charlemagne's palace, of which only the eastern tower, the **Granusturm**, survives. Inside, the undisputed highlight is the **Krönungssaal** (coronation hall) with its epic 19th-century **frescoes** and replicas of the **imperial insignia**: a crown, orb and sword (the originals are in Vienna).

Domschatzkammer MUSEUM
(Cathedral Treasury; ☎0241-4770 9127; adult/
child €5/4; ⊙10am-1pm Mon, to 5pm Tue-Sun
Jan-Mar, 10am-1pm Mon, to 6pm Tue-Sun Apr-Dec)
The cathedral treasury is a veritable mother lode of gold, silver and jewels. Items of
particular importance include a silver and
golden bust of Charlemagne, a 10th-century
bejewelled processional cross known as the
Lotharkreuz and a 1000-year-old relief-
decorated **ivory situla** (a pail for holy water).

Tours

Old Town Guided Tour WALKING TOUR
(adult/child €8/4; ⊙11am Sat Apr-Dec) The tourist office runs 90-minute English-language
walking tours.

Sleeping & Eating

Aachen's students have their own 'Latin
Quarter' along Pontstrasse northeast of the
Markt.

Hotel Drei Könige HOTEL €€
(☎0241-483 93; www.h3k-aachen.de; Büchel 5; s
€90-130, d €120-160, apt €130-240; ⊙reception
staffed 7am-11pm; 🛜) The radiant Mediterranean decor is an instant mood enhancer
at this family-run favourite with its doesn't-
get-more-central location. Some rooms are a
tad twee but the two-room apartment sleeps
up to four. Breakfast, on the 4th floor, comes
with dreamy views over the rooftops and the
cathedral.

Aquis Grana City Hotel HOTEL €€
(☎0241-4430; www.hotel-aquis-grana.de; Büchel
32; d €85-165; 🅿🛜) The best quarters at this
gracious hotel have terrace and balcony
views of the town hall. But even in the most
modest of the 98 rooms, you couldn't be any
closer to the heart of town. The hotel offers
a full range of services, including a bar and
a restaurant.

Cafe Van den Daele CAFE €
(☎0241-357 24; www.van-den-daele.de; Büchel 18;
treats from €3) Leather-covered walls, tiled
stoves and antiques forge the yesteryear flair
of this rambling cafe institution. Come for all-
day breakfast, a light lunch, divine cakes or
just to pick up a bag of homemade *Printen,*
Aachen's riff on traditional *Lebkuchen.*

Am Knipp GERMAN €€
(☎0241-331 68; www.amknipp.de; Bergdriesch 3;
mains €9-20; ⊙5-11pm Wed-Mon) Hungry graz-
ers have stopped by this traditional inn since
1698, and you too will have a fine time en-

joying hearty German cuisine served amid
a flea market's worth of knick-knacks or, if
weather permits, in the big beer garden.

ℹ Information

Tourist Office (☎0241-180 2960; www.
aachen-tourist.de; Friedrich-Wilhelm-Platz;
⊙9am-6pm Mon-Fri, to 4pm Sat & Sun
Apr-Dec, 9am-6pm Mon-Fri, to 2pm Sat Jan-
Mar, 10am-2pm Sun Easter-Dec) Maps, general
information, rooms, tours, tickets and more.

ℹ Getting There & Away

Regional trains frequently head to Cologne
(€16.80, 55 minutes), Düsseldorf (€20.70, 1½
hours) and beyond.

HAMBURG & THE NORTH

Germany's windswept, maritime-flavoured
north is dominated by Hamburg, a metropolis shaped by water and commerce since the
Middle Ages. Bremen is a fabulous stop with
fairy-tale character, and not only because of
the famous Brothers' Grimm fairy tale starring a certain donkey, dog, cat and rooster.
Those with a sweet tooth should not miss a
side trip to Lübeck, renowned for its superb
marzipan.

Hamburg

☎040 / POP 1.75 MILLION
'The gateway to the world' might be a bold
claim, but Germany's second-largest city and
biggest port has never been shy. Hamburg has
engaged in business with the world ever since
it joined the Hanseatic League trading bloc
back in the Middle Ages. Today this 'harbour-
polis' is the nation's premier media hub and
among its wealthiest cities. It's also the site
of Europe's largest urban-renewal project, the
HafenCity, which is efficiently transforming
the old docklands into a bold new city quarter. Hamburg's maritime spirit infuses the
entire city: from architecture to menus to
the cry of gulls, you always know you're near
the water. The city has given rise to vibrant
neighbourhoods awash with multicultural
eateries, as well as the gloriously seedy Reeperbahn party and red-light district.

◉ Sights

Rathaus HISTORIC BUILDING
(☎040-428 312 064; Rathausmarkt 1; tours adult/
under 14yr €4/free; ⊙tours half-hourly 10am-3pm

Mon-Fri, to 5pm Sat, to 4pm Sun, English tours depend on demand; §Rathausmarkt, Jungfernstieg) Hamburg's baroque Rathaus is one of Europe's most opulent, renowned for the Emperor's Hall and the Great Hall, with its spectacular coffered ceiling. The 40-minute tours take in only a fraction of this beehive of 647 rooms.

North of here, you can wander through the Alsterarkaden, the Renaissance-style arcades sheltering shops and cafes alongside a canal.

★Hamburger Kunsthalle MUSEUM

(☑040-428 131 200; www.hamburger-kunsthalle. de; Glockengiesserwall; adult/concession €12/6; ⊙10am-6pm Tue, Wed & Fri-Sun, to 9pm Thu; §Hauptbahnhof) One of Germany's most prestigious art collections, the Kunsthalle displays works from the Middle Ages to today in two buildings. In the original brick one from 1869 you can admire old masters (Rembrandt, Ruisdael), 19th-century Romantics (Friedrich, Runge) and classical modernist works (Beckmann, Munch). A stark white concrete cube – the Galerie der Gegenwart – showcases mostly German artists working since the 1960s, including Neo Rauch, Jenny Holzer, Candida Höfer and Reinhard Mucha.

Chilehaus HISTORIC BUILDING

(☑040-349 194 247; www.chilehaus.de; Fischertwiete 2; §Messberg) Looking like a giant ocean liner in dry dock, the brown-brick Chilehaus is a leading example of German expressionist architecture. It was designed by Fritz Höger in 1924 for a merchant who derived his wealth from trading with Chile.

St Michaelis CHURCH

(Church of St Michael; ☑040-376 780; www. st-michaelis.de; tower adult/6-15yr €5/3.50, crypt €4/2.50, combo ticket €7/4; ⊙10am-8pm May-Oct, to 6pm Nov-Apr, last admission 30min before closing; ⊠Stadthausbrücke) 'Der Michel', as it is affectionately called, is one of Hamburg's most recognisable landmarks and northern Germany's largest Protestant baroque church. Ascending the **tower** (by steps or lift) rewards visitors with great panoramas across the city and canals. The **crypt** has an engaging multimedia exhibit on the city's history.

★Speicherstadt NEIGHBOURHOOD

(Am Sandtorkai; ⊙24hr; §Rödingsmarkt, Messberg) The seven-storey red-brick warehouses lining the Speicherstadt archipelago are a famous Hamburg symbol and the largest continuous warehouse complex in the world,

CRUISING ON THE CHEAP

This maritime city offers a bewildering array of boat trips, but there's no need to fork over €18 for a cruise to see the port. Instead, hop on one of the public ferries for the price of a standard public transport ticket (€3). The handiest line is ferry 62, which leaves from Landungsbrücken (pier 3) and travels west to Finkenwerder. Get off at the **Dockland** station to climb to the roof of this stunning office building shaped like a parallelogram for views of the container terminal, then continue to Neumühlen/Oevelgönne to look at old ships in the **museum harbour** and relax on the sandy Elbe beach with a beer from Strandperle (p323).

recognised by Unesco as a World Heritage Site. Its distinctive architecture is best appreciated on a leisurely wander or a ride on a flat tour boat (called *Barkasse*). Many buildings contain shops, cafes and small museums.

Miniatur Wunderland MUSEUM

(☑040-300 6800; www.miniatur-wunderland.de; Kehrwieder 2; adult/under 16yr €12/6; ⊙9.30am-6pm Mon, Wed, Thu, to 7pm Fri, to 9pm Tue, 8am-9pm Sat, 8.30am-8pm Sun; §Messberg) Even the worst cynics are quickly transformed into fans of this vast miniature world. When you see an A380 plane swoop out of the sky and land at the fully functional model of Hamburg's airport you can't help but gasp and say some variation of OMG! In busy times prepurchase your ticket online to skip the queues.

HafenCity NEIGHBOURHOOD

(☑040-3690 1799; www.hafencity.com; InfoCenter, Am Sandtorkai 30; ⊙InfoCenter 10am-6pm Tue-Sun; §Baumwall, Überseequartier) HafenCity is a vast new city quarter taking shape east of the harbour. When fully completed, it's expected to be home to 12,000 people and offer work space for 40,000. It's a showcase of modern architecture with the biggest eye-catcher being the Elbphilharmonie, a vast concert hall jutting into the harbour atop a protected tea-and-cocoa warehouse. After many delays, it's expected to open in 2017. For the low-down, visit the HafenCity InfoCenter, which also runs free guided tours.

GERMANY HAMBURG

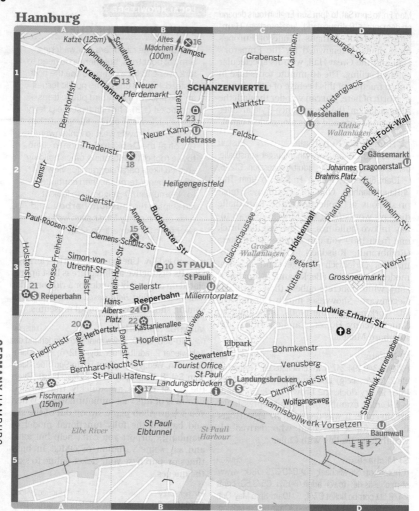

Fischmarkt

MARKET

(Grosse Elbstrasse 9; ⊙5-9.30am Sun Apr-Oct, 7-9.30am Sun Nov-Mar; ☐112 to Fischmarkt, ☐Reeperbahn) Here's the perfect excuse to stay up all Saturday night. Every Sunday in the wee hours, some 70,000 locals and visitors descend upon the famous Fischmarkt in St Pauli. The market has been running since 1703, and its undisputed stars are the boisterous *Marktschreier* (market criers) who hawk their wares at full volume. Live bands also entertainingly crank out cover versions of ancient German pop songs in the adjoining Fischauktionshalle (Fish Auction Hall).

Auswanderermuseum BallinStadt

MUSEUM

(Emigration Museum; ☑040-3197 9160; www. ballinstadt.de; Veddeler Bogen 2; adult/concession/5-12yr €12.50/10/7; ⊙10am-6pm Apr-Oct, 10am-4.30pm Nov-Mar; ☐Veddel) Sort of a bookend for New York's Ellis Island, Hamburg's excellent emigration museum in the original halls looks at the conditions that drove about 5 million people to leave Germany for the US and South America in search of better lives from 1850 until the 1930s. Multilingual displays address the hardships endured before and during the voyage and

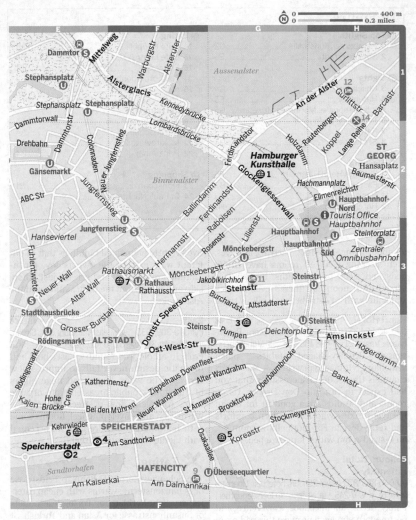

upon arrival in the New World. Although about 4km east of the city centre, Ballinstadt is easily reached by S-Bahn line S3.

Internationales Maritimes Museum

MUSEUM

(☑ 040-3009 3300; www.internationales-maritimes-museum.de; Koreastrasse 1; adult/concession €12/8.50; ⊙ 10am-6pm Tue, Wed & Fri-Sun, to 8pm Thu; ⑤ Messberg) Hamburg's maritime past – and future – is fully explored in this excellent private museum that sprawls over 10 floors of a revamped brick shipping warehouse. Considered the world's largest private collection of maritime treasures, it includes a mind-numbing 26,000 model ships, 50,000 construction plans, 5000 illustrations, 2000 films, 1.5 million photographs and much more.

🛏 Sleeping

Superbude St Pauli

HOTEL, HOSTEL €

(☑ 040-807 915 820; www.superbude.de; Juliusstrasse 1-7; dm/d from €16/60; @ 🐱; ⑤ Sternschanze, 🔁 Sternschanze, Holstenstrasse) The young and forever-young mix and mingle without a shred of prejudice at this rocking design hotel–hostel combo that's

Hamburg

all about living, laughing, partying and, yes, even sleeping well. All rooms have comfy beds and sleek private baths, breakfast is served until noon and there's even a 'rock star suite' with an Astra beer as a pillow treat.

Henri Hotel HOTEL €€
(☑ 040-554 357 557; www.henri-hotel.com; Bugenhagenstrasse 21; r €98-138; ☎; ⑤ Mönckebergstrasse) Kidney-shaped tables, plush armchairs, vintage typewriters – the Henri channels the 1950s so successfully that you half expect to run into Don Draper. Its 65 rooms and studios are a good fit for urban lifestyle junkies who like modern comforts and retro design. For more elbow room get an L-sized room with a king-size bed.

25hours Hotel HafenCity HOTEL €€
(☑ 040-855 870; www.25hours-hotel.de; Überseeallee 5; r €97-245; ℗☺☎; ⑤ Überseequartier) Funky decor, an infectious irreverence and postmodern vintage flair make this pad a top choice among global nomads. Sporting maritime flourishes, the decor channels an old-timey seaman's club in the lobby, the excellent restaurant and the 170 cabin-style rooms. Enjoy views of the emerging HafenCity neighbourhood from the rooftop sauna. Breakfast costs €14.

★ **Hotel Wedina** HOTEL €€
(☑ 040-280 8900; www.hotelwedina.de; Gurlittstrasse 23; d €125-245; ℗@☎; ⑤ Hauptbahnhof) Margaret Atwood, Jonathan Franzen and Martin Walser are among the literary greats who've stayed at this loveable lair and left behind signed books. Rooms spread over

five brightly pigmented buildings that in different ways express the owners' love for literature, architecture and art. It's just a hop, skip and jump from the train station and the Alster lakes.

East HOTEL €€
(☑ 040-309 933; www.east-hamburg.de; Simon-von-Utrecht-Strasse 31; d €113-209; ✱☎; ⑤ St Pauli) In an old iron foundry, East's bold and dramatic design never fails to impress new arrivals. The walls, lamps and huge pillars of this hotel's public areas emulate organic forms (droplets, flowers, trees), giving it a warm, rich and enveloping feel. Rooms come with handmade furniture and are accented with tactile fabrics and leather.

✕ Eating

The Schanzenviertel (U-Bahn to Feldstrasse or Schanzenstern) swarms with cheap eateries; try Schulterblatt for Portuguese outlets or Susannenstrasse for Asian and Turkish. St Georg's Lange Reihe (U-Bahn to Hauptbahnhof) offers many characterful eating spots to suit every budget. Fish restaurants around the Landungsbrücken tend to be overrated and touristy.

★ **Fischbrötchenbude Brücke 10** FISH €
(☑ 040-6504 6899; www.bruecke-10.de; Landungsbrücken, Pier 10; sandwiches €2.50-7.50; ☺10am-10pm Mon-Sat, 9am-10pm Sat; ⑤ Landungsbrücken, ℝ Landungsbrücken) There are a gazillion fish-sandwich vendors in Hamburg, but we're going to stick our neck out and say that this vibrant, clean and contemporary out-

TOP THREE HAMBURG MARKETS

St Pauli Nachtmarkt (Spielbudenplatz; ⊘ 4-10pm Wed; ⑤ St Pauli) This after-dark farmers and gourmet market with colourful bounty and fun snack stands lures locals and visitors to the heart of St Pauli.

Flohschanze (Neuer Kamp 30; ⊘ 8am-4pm Sat; ⑤ Feldstrasse) Hamburg's best flea market is nirvana for thrifty trinket hunters and vintage junkies, with hundreds of vendors holding forth outdoors in the hip Karolinenviertel.

Isemarkt (www.isemarkt.com; btwn U-Bahn stations Hoheluft & Eppendorfer Baum; ⊘ 8.30am-2pm Tue & Fri; ⑤ Eppendorfer Baum, Hoheluft) Winding for over 1km beneath the elevated U-Bahn tracks, the twice-weekly Isemarkt in Eppendorf is literally the longest farmers market in Germany with some 200 vendors offering quality anything.

post makes the best. Try a classic *Bismarck* (pickled herring) or *Matjes* (brined) or treat yourself to a bulging shrimp sandwich.

Café Mimosa CAFE €
(☑ 040-3202 7989; www.cafemimosa.de; Clemens-Schultz-Strasse 87; mains €3.50-12; ⊘ 10am-7pm Tue-Sun; ⑤ St Pauli) This gem of a neighbourhood cafe is the go-to place for warm brioches, some of the yummiest cakes in town plus daily changing lunch specials. Sit inside among theatrical flourishes or grab a sidewalk table.

Café Koppel VEGETARIAN €
(www.cafe-koppel.de; Lange Reihe 66; mains €5-10; ☑; ⑤ Hauptbahnhof) Set back from busy Lange Reihe, with a garden in summer, this vegie cafe is a refined oasis, where you can hear the tinkling of spoons in coffee cups midmorning on the mezzanine floor. The menu could be an ad for the fertile fields of northern Germany as there are baked goods, salads, soups and much more made with fresh seasonal ingredients.

Altes Mädchen MODERN GERMAN €€
(☑ 040-800 077 750; www.altes-maedchen.com; Lagerstrasse 28b; mains €9-22; ⊘ from noon Mon-Sat, from 10am Sun; ⑤ Sternschanze) The lofty red-brick halls of a 19th-century animal market have been upcycled into a hip culinary destination that includes a coffee roastery, a celebrity-chef restaurant, and this tarted-up brewpub with a central bar, in-house bakery and beer garden.

Erikas Eck GERMAN €€
(☑ 040-433 545; www.erikas-eck.de; Sternstrasse 98; mains €6-18; ⊘ 5pm-2pm; ⑧ Sternschanze) This pit-stop institution originally fed hungry workers from the nearby abattoir (today the central meat market) and now serves wallet-friendly but waist-expanding

portions of schnitzel and other trad German fare to a motley crowd of clubbers, cabbies and cops 21 hours a day.

Nil INTERNATIONAL €€€
(☑ 040-439 7823; www.restaurant-nil.de; Neuer Pferdemarkt 5; mains €15.50-24; ⊘ 6-10.30pm Wed-Mon; ⑤ Feldstrasse) Despite the name, this contempo tri-level restaurant doesn't do Egyptian fare but proffers a varied and inspired slow-food menu steered by the seasons and whatever regional suppliers have in store. Flavour pairings can be adventurous (scallops with kohlrabi) but usually produce tantalising results.

🍸 Drinking & Entertainment

Partying in Hamburg concentrates on the Schanzenviertel and St Pauli, a few streets further south. Most people start the night in the former, then move on to the clubs and bars of the latter around midnight. Online sources: www.szene-hamburg.de and www.neu.clubkombinat.de.

Katze BAR
(☑ 040-5577 5910; Schulterblatt 88; ⊘ 3pm-midnight Mon-Thu, 6pm-3am Fri, 1pm-3am Sat, 3pm-midnight Sun; ⑤ Sternschanze) Small and sleek, this 'kitty' (Katze means 'cat') gets the crowd purring for well-priced cocktails (best caipirinhas in town) and great music (there's dancing on weekends). It's one of the most popular among the watering holes on this main Schanzenviertel booze strip.

Strandperle BAR
(☑ 040-880 1112; www.strandperle-hamburg.de; Oevelgönne 60; ⊘ 10am-11pm Mon-Fri, 9am-11pm Sat & Sun May-Sep, weather permitting, shorter hours otherwise; ⬜ 112) The mother of Hamburg's beach bars is a must for primo beer, burgers and people-watching. All ages and

ST PAULI & THE REEPERBAHN

No discussion of Hamburg is complete without mentioning St Pauli, home to one of Europe's most (in)famous red-light districts. Sex shops, table-dance bars and strip clubs still line its main drag, the Reeperbahn, and side streets, but the popularity of prostitution has declined dramatically in the internet age. Today St Pauli is Hamburg's main nightlife district, drawing people of all ages and walks of life to live-music and dance clubs, chic bars and theatres.

In fact, street walkers are not even allowed to hit the pavement before 8pm and then are confined to certain areas, the most notorious being the gated Herbertstrasse (no women, and no men under 18 years allowed). Nearby, the cops of the Davidwache police station keep an eye on the lurid surrounds. A short walk west is the side street called Grosse Freiheit, where the Beatles cut their teeth at the Indra Club (No 64) and the Kaiserkeller (No 36). Both are vastly different venues today, but there's a small monument to the Fab Four in a courtyard behind No 35.

classes gather and mingle, especially at sunset, right on the Elbe as huge freighters glide past and you wiggle your toes in the sand. Get there by taking ferry 62 from Landungsbrücken or bus 112 from Altona station to Neumühlen/Oevelgönne.

★ **Golden Pudel Club**   LIVE MUSIC
(☎040-3197 9930; www.pudel.com; St-Pauli-Fischmarkt 27; ☉nightly; ⏭Reeperbahn) In a 19th-century bootleggers' jail, this tiny bar-club is run by members of the legendary ex-punk band Die Goldenen Zitronen and is an essential stop on the St Pauli party circuit. Night after night it gets packed to the rafters for its countercultural vibe, quality bands and DJs, and relaxed crowd.

Molotow   LIVE MUSIC
(☎040-430 1110; www.molotowclub.com; Holstenstrasse 5; ⏭Reeperbahn) The legendary indie club still rocks on as hot 'n heavy as ever after moving to new digs after its Reeperbahn location was torn down in 2013.

Prinzenbar   CONCERT VENUE
(Kastanienallee 20; ⑤St Pauli, ⏭Reeperbahn) With its cheeky cherubs, stucco flourishes and wrought-iron galleries, this intimate club has chapel looks but is in fact a former cinema that now hosts stylish electro parties, concerts, queer parties and indie nights in the heart of St Pauli.

Hasenschaukel   LIVE MUSIC
(☎040-1801 2721; www.hasenschaukel.de; Silbersackstrasse 17; ☉from 9pm Tue-Sun; ⏭Reeperbahn) The booking policy at this unhurried pocket-size club with plush decor skews

towards lo-fi indie-folk-rock and usually features pre-stardom international artists along with DJ sets. Grab a vegan midnight snack if the vintage doll lamps get too trippy after a few beers.

ℹ Information

Tourist Office (www.hamburg-tourism.de) Branches include Hauptbahnhof (Kirchenallee exit; ☉9am-7pm Mon-Sat, 10am-6pm Sun; ⑤Hauptbahnhof, ⏭Hauptbahnhof) and St Pauli Landungsbrücken (btwn piers 4 & 5; ☉9am-6pm Sun-Wed, to 7pm Thu-Sat; ⑤Landungsbrücken); note this latter branch doesn't make hotel bookings.

ℹ Getting There & Away

AIR

Hamburg Airport (HAM; www.airport.de) is linked to the city centre every 10 minutes by the S-Bahn line S1 (€3, 25 minutes). A taxi takes about a half hour and cost around €25.

BUS

The **Zentraler Omnibusbahnhof** (ZOB, Central Bus Station; ☎040-247 576; www.zob-hamburg.de; Adenauerallee 78), southeast of the Hauptbahnhof, has many domestic and international departures by Euroline, Flixbus and many other operators.

TRAIN

Hamburg is a major train hub with four mainline train stations: the Hauptbahnhof, Dammtor, Altona and Harburg. Frequent trains serve Lübeck (€13.70, 45 minutes), Bremen (from €28, 55 minutes), Berlin-Hauptbahnhof (€78, 1¾ hours), Copenhagen (€85.40, 4¾ hours) and many other cities.

ⓘ Getting Around

For public transport information, go to www.hvv. de. The city is divided into zones. Fare zone A covers the city centre, inner suburbs and airport.

Lübeck

🕿 0451 / POP 214,000

Compact and charming Lübeck makes for a great day trip from Hamburg. Looking like a pair of witches' hats, the pointed towers of its landmark Holstentor (Holsten Gate) form the gateway to its historic centre that sits on an island embraced by the arms of the Trave River. The Unesco-recognised web of cobbled lanes flanked by gabled merchants' homes and spired churches is an enduring reminder of Lübeck's role as the one-time capital of the medieval Hanseatic League trading power. Today it enjoys fame as Germany's marzipan capital.

◉ Sights

A good place to start a wander around Lübeck's old town is from the Holsten Gate. Hüxstrasse is lined by pleasant boutiques and cafes. For a breath of seaside air, take a short train ride to the Baltic port and resort of Travemünde.

★ Holstentor   LANDMARK
(Holsten Gate) Built in 1464 Lübeck's charming red-brick city gate is a national icon. Its pointed slate-covered towers, linked by a stepped gable, have graced postcards, paintings and posters, and the old 50 Deutschmark note. Its crooked appearance is the result of an insufficient foundation that caused the south tower to sag until the movement could be halted in the 1930s. The museum inside sheds light on the history of the gate and on Lübeck's medieval mercantile glory days.

Marienkirche   CHURCH
(St Mary's Church; 🕿 0451-397 700; Marienkirchhof; adult/concession €2/1.50; ⊙10am-6pm Apr-Sep, to 5pm Oct, to 4pm Tue-Sun Nov-Mar) This fine Gothic church boasts the world's highest brick-vaulted roof and was the model for dozens of churches in northern Germany. Crane your neck to take in the painted cross-vaulted ceilings supported by slender, ribbed pillars. Also note the astronomical clock in the north aisle next to modern glass windows inspired by a medieval Dance of Death mural destroyed in WWII. Another bombing raid

brought down the church's bells, which have been left where they fell in 1942.

Petrikirche   CHURCH
(Church of St Peter; 🕿 0451-397 730; www.st-petri-luebeck.de; Petrikirchhof 1; tower adult/child €3/2; ⊙9am-9pm Apr-Sep, 10am-7pm Oct-Mar) Thanks to a lift, even the fitness-phobic get to enjoy panoramic views from the 50m-high platform in the tower of the 13th-century Petrikirche. No longer an active parish, the starkly whitewashed interior hosts exhibits and events.

🛏 Sleeping

Hotel an der Marienkirche   HOTEL €
(🕿 0451-799 410; www.hotel-an-der-marienkirche. de; Schüsselbuden 4; d from €89; 🕿) After a recent renovation, this small, good-value hotel exudes cheery, contemporary Scandinavian flair and is equipped with top-quality latex mattresses and crispy linen. One of the 18 rooms even has a view of the namesake church.

Hotel Lindenhof   HOTEL €€
(🕿 0451-872 100; www.lindenhof-luebeck.de; Lindenstrasse 1a; d from €94; 🅿@🕿) Most of the 66 rooms at this family-run hotel in a quiet side street won't hold a ton of luggage, but the opulent breakfast buffet, friendly service and little extras (such as free biscuits and newspapers) propel the Lindenhof into a superior league.

🍴 Eating

Schiffergesellschaft   GERMAN €€
(🕿 0451-767 76; www.schiffergesellschaft.com; Breite Strasse 2; mains €10-25) In the historic seafarer's guild hall, Lübeck's cutest – if not

> **DON'T MISS**
>
> ## SWEET TEMPTATIONS
>
> **Niederegger** (🕿 0451-530 1126; www.niederegger.de; Breite Strasse 89; ⊙9am-7pm Mon-Fri, 9am-6pm Sat, 10am-6pm Sun) is Lübeck's mecca for marzipan, which has been made locally for centuries. The shop's elaborate displays are a feast for the eyes, and there's even a museum where you'll learn that marzipan was considered medicine in the Middle Ages. The on-site cafe serves sandwiches and salads alongside sweet treats.

ANNE FRANK & BERGEN-BELSEN

The Nazi-built camp at **Bergen-Belsen** (Bergen-Belsen Memorial Site; ☑ 05051-475 90; www.bergen-belsen.de; Anne-Frank-Platz, Lohheide; ☉ documentation centre 10am-6pm Apr-Sep, 10am-5pm Oct-Mar, grounds until dusk) **FREE** began its existence in 1940 as a prisoner of war (POW) camp, but became a concentration camp after being taken over by the *Schutzstaffel* (SS) in 1943, initially to imprison Jews as hostages in exchange for German POWs held abroad. In all, 70,000 prisoners perished here, most famously Anne Frank. Victims were buried in mass graves scattered across the parklike cemetery grounds. The modern **Documentation Centre** poignantly chronicles the fates of the people who passed through here – before, during and after incarceration. A small section deals with Anne Frank, and there's also a **memorial grave stone** for her and her sister, Margot, near the cemetery's Jewish Monument.

The memorial site is in the countryside about 60km northeast of Hanover and a bit complicated to reach if you don't have your own wheels. See the website for detailed driving and public transport directions.

its best – restaurant is a veritable museum. Ships' lanterns, old model ships and revolving Chinese-style silhouette lamps dangle from the beamed ceiling of this wood-lined dining room. White-aproned waitstaff deliver regional specialities to tables here or in the hidden garden out the back. Book ahead at dinnertime.

Remise　　　　　　　　　　CAFE **€€**
(☑ 0451-777 73; www.remise-luebeck.de; Wahmstrasse 43-45; mains €12-20; ☉ noon-late Mon-Fri, 9am-late Sat & Sun) This charming owner-run restaurant in a former roastery specialises in grass-fed beef but also does creative pastas, regional fare and salads. In fine weather, snag a table in the vine-draped courtyard. Locals invade on 2-4-1 Monday evenings.

Brauberger　　　　　　　GERMAN **€€**
(☑ 0451-702 0606; Alfstrasse 36; snacks €1.50-5, mains €11-18; ☉ 5pm-midnight Mon-Thu, to late Fri & Sat) The air is redolent of hops at this traditional German brewery. Get a stein of the sweet, cloudy house brew *(Zwickelbier)* and tuck into a sizeable schnitzel or other traditional fare.

❶ Information

Tourist Office (☑ 0451-889 9700; www.luebeck-tourismus.de; Holstentorplatz 1; ☉ 9am-7pm Mon-Fri, 10am-4pm Sat, 10am-3pm Sun May-Aug, slightly reduced hours otherwise) Sells the HappyDay Card (per 24/48/72 hours €11/13/16) with discounts and free public transport. Also has a cafe and internet terminals.

❶ Getting There & Away

Ryanair and Wizzair serve **Lübeck Airport** (LBC; www.flughafen-luebeck.de).

Regional trains connect to Hamburg twice hourly (€13.50, 45 minutes).

Bremen

☑ 0421 / POP 548,000

It's a shame the donkey, dog, cat and rooster in Grimm's *Town Musicians of Bremen* never actually made it here – they would have fallen in love with the place. This little city is big on charm, from the fairy-tale character statue to a jaw-dropping expressionist laneway and impressive town hall. On top of that, the Weser riverside promenade is a relaxing, bistro-and-beer-garden–lined refuge and the lively student district ('Das Viertel') along Ostertorsteinweg is filled with indie boutiques, cafes, art-house cinemas and alt-flavoured cultural venues.

◉ Sights

Bremen's key historic sights cluster around Markt and can easily be explored on foot.

★ **Markt**　　　　　　　　　　SQUARE
Bremen's Unesco-recognised Markt is striking, especially because of its ornate, gabled and sculpture-festooned Rathaus (town hall; 1410). In front stands a 5.5m-high medieval statue of the knight **Roland** (1404), the symbolic protector of Bremen's civic rights and freedoms. On the town hall's western side, you'll find a sculpture of the Town Musicians of Bremen (1951).

Dom St Petri
CHURCH

(St Petri Cathedral; www.stpetridom.de; Markt; tower €1, Lead Cellar adult/concession €1.40/1; ⊙10am-6pm Mon-Fri & Sun, to 2pm Sat Jun-Sep, 10am-5pm Mon-Fri, to 2pm Sat, 2-5pm Sun Oct-Mar, tower closed Nov-Easter) Bremen's protestant main church has origins in the 8th century and got its ribbed vaulting, chapels and two high towers in the 13th century. Aside from the imposing architecture, the intricately carved pulpit and the baptismal font in the western crypt deserve a closer look. For panoramic views, climb the 265 steps to the top of the south tower. A separate entrance leads to the church's **Bleikeller**, a cellar where open coffins reveal eight bodies mummified in the incredibly dry air.

Böttcherstrasse
STREET

(www.boettcherstrasse.de) The charming medieval coopers' lane was transformed into a prime example of mostly expressionist architecture in the 1920s at the instigation of coffee merchant Ludwig Roselius. Its redbrick houses sport unique facades, whimsical fountains, statues and a carillon; many house artesanal shops and art museums. Its most striking feature is Bernhard Hoetger's golden **Lichtbringer** (Bringer of Light) relief that keeps an eye on the north entrance.

Schnoor
NEIGHBOURHOOD

This maze of narrow, winding alleys was once the fishermen's quarter and later a red-light district. Now its doll's-house-sized cottages contain boutiques, restaurants, cafes and galleries. Though tourist-geared, there are some lovely corners to explore around here on a leisurely amble.

🛏 Sleeping

Townside Hostel Bremen
HOSTEL €

(☑ 0421-780 15; www.townside.de; Am Dobben 62; dm €15-25, s/d €54/76; 🛜) This bright, professionally run hostel is right in the middle of Bremen's nightlife quarter and handy to Werder Bremen's stadium. Breakfast costs €5.50. Take tram 10 from Hauptbahnhof to Humboldtstrasse or tram 2 or 3 to Sielwall.

Hotel Überfluss
DESIGN HOTEL €€€

(☑ 0421-322 860; www.hotel-ueberfluss.com; Langenstrasse 72; d €139-169, ste €345; ✳🛜✳) Just metres above river level, this cutting-edge cool hotel is a good choice for design-minded urban nomads. Black, white and chrome create a sleek, postmodern vibe that extends to the rooms that feature open bathrooms and Yves Rocher products. Suites have river views and a private sauna and whirlpool – perfect for a honeymoon. Breakfast costs €12.50.

🍴 Eating & Drinking

Tourist-oriented places cluster around Markt, which is pretty dead after dark. Das Viertel has an alternative, student-flavoured feel, while the waterfront promenade, Schlachte, is pricier and more mainstream.

Engel Weincafe
CAFE €

(☑ 0421-6964 2390; www.engelweincafe-bremen.de; Ostertorsteinweg 31; dishes €4-11; ⊙8am-1am

---

WORTH A TRIP

BACK TO THE ROOTS IN BREMERHAVEN

'Give me your tired, your poor, your huddled masses', invites the *State of Liberty* in New York harbour. Well, Bremerhaven is one place that most certainly did just that. More than seven million of those landing at Ellis Island departed from here between 1830 and 1974, and the **Deutsches Auswandererhaus** (German Emigration Centre; ☑ 0471-902 200; www.dah-bremerhaven.de; Columbusstrasse 65; adult/child 4-16yr €12.60/6.90; ⊙10am-6pm Mar-Oct, to 5pm Nov-Feb) does a superb job of chronicling and commemorating some of their stories. You relive the stages of the journey and the emigrants' travelling conditions aboard a movie-set-like steamer, clutching the biographical details of one particular traveller. Once you've 'landed', you have to go through immigration at Ellis Island and travel on to a miniature replica of New York's Grand Central Station to start your new life.

A somewhat less engaging new exhibit reverses the theme and tells the story of immigration *to* Germany since the 17th century.

Bremerhaven is some 70km north of Bremen and is served by regional train (€12, 35 minutes). From the station, take bus 502, 505, 506, 508 or 509 to 'Havenwelten' to get to the museum and the harbour with its many old vessels (including a WWII sub) and striking contemporary architecture.

HANOVER'S HERRENHÄUSER GÄRTEN

Proof that Hanover is not all buttoned-down business are the grandiose baroque **Royal Gardens of Herrenhausen** (☑0511-1683 4000; www.herrenhaeuser-gaerten.de; Herrenhäuser Strasse; gardens adult/concession/under 12yr €8/4/free; ⊗9am-6pm Apr-Oct, to 4.30pm Nov-Mar, grotto 9am-5.30pm Apr-Oct, to 4pm Nov-Mar), which rank among the most important historic garden landscapes in Europe. Inspired by the park at Versailles, the sprawling grounds are perfect for slowing down and smelling the roses for a couple of hours, especially on a blue-sky day.

With its fountains, neat flowerbeds, trimmed hedges and shaped lawns, the 300-year-old **Grosser Garten** (Great Garden) is the centrepiece of the experience. Don't miss the **Niki de Saint Phalle Grotto** near the northern end, which provides a magical backdrop for the whimsical statues, fountains and coloured tile by this late French artist (1930–2002). South of here, the **Grosse Fontäne** (Big Fountain; the tallest in Europe) jets water up to 80m high. In summer fountains are synchronised during the **Wasserspiele** (water games). During the **Illuminations** the gardens and fountains are atmospherically lit at night.

Across Herrenhäuser Strasse, the **Berggarten** is redolent with a mind-boggling assortment of global flora, while east of the Grosser Garten, beyond a small canal, the lake-dotted **Georgengarten** counts the **Wilhelm-Busch-Museum** (☑0511-1699 9911; www.wilhelm-busch-museum.de; Georgengarten; adult/concession €4.50/2.50; ⊗11am-6pm Tue-Sun), with its wealth of caricature by Busch, Honoré Daumier, William Hogarth and many others, among its treasures.

If you're curious about Hanover's other sights, stop by the **tourist office** (☑information 0511-1234 5111, room reservations 0511-1234 5555; www.hannover.de; Ernst-August-Platz 8; ⊗9am-6pm Mon-Fri, 10am-3pm Sat & Sun).

Mon-Fri, 10am-1am Sat & Sun; 🛜🎢) Exuding the nostalgic vibe of a former pharmacy, this popular hang-out gets a good crowd no matter where the hands on the clock. Come for breakfast, a hot lunch special, crispy *Flammekuche* (French pizza), carpaccio or pasta, or just some cheese and a glass of wine.

Casa
MEDITERRANEAN €€

(☑0421-326 430; www.casa-bremen.com; Ostertorsteinweg 59; mains €10-27; ⊗11.30am-midnight Mon-Fri, 10am-midnight Sat & Sun; 🎢) This long-standing local favourite evokes a slight Mediterranean vibe, both in its looks and through its menu, which includes salads, pastas and an inspired selection of tapas. Top marks, though, go to the lava-grill fish and meat dishes (including a signature burger), made with quality organic meats.

Luv
INTERNATIONAL €€

(☑0421-165 5599; www.restaurant-luv.de; Schlachte 15-18; mains €9-37; ⊗11am-late Mon-Fri, 10am-late Sun) This upbeat bistro has a lounge-bar feel and a menu strong on salads and pasta complemented by mostly meaty mains, including a respectable lava-grill burger, a giant Wiener Schnitzel and locally caught fish. In good weather sit beneath the twinkling lights at the outdoor tables overlooking the Weser River.

Café Sand
CAFE

(☑0421-556 011; www.cafe-sand.de; Strandweg 106; ⊗from noon Mon-Sat, from 10am Sun, closing hours vary) On an island in the Weser River, this beach cafe makes you feel light years away from the city. It's favoured by everyone from swimmers and tanners to families and fans of Werder Bremen football club. Get here on foot via the Wilhelm-Kaisen-Brücke (bridge) or by ferry from the Osterdeich (return €2.20, from 3pm Friday, noon Saturday, 10am Sunday until at least 6pm).

ℹ Information

Tourist Office (☑0421-308 0010; www.bremen-tourism.de) Branches include Hauptbahnhof (⊗9am-7pm Mon-Fri, 9.30am-5pm Sat & Sun), handily located at the main train station and Markt (Langenstrasse 2-4; ⊗10am-6.30pm Mon-Sat, to 4pm Sun Apr-Oct, closes at 4pm Sat Nov-Mar), a full-service tourist office with friendly staff, near Markt.

ℹ Getting There & Around

Bremen Airport (BRE; www.airport-bremen.de) is about 3.5km south of the city and served by tram 6 (€2.50, 15 minutes).

Train connections include regional trains to Bremerhaven (€12, 35 minutes), InterCity (IC) trains to Hamburg (€28, one hour) and Cologne (€67, three hours).

SURVIVAL GUIDE

ℹ Directory A–Z

ACCOMMODATION

Reservations are a good idea, especially between June and September, around major holidays, festivals, cultural events and trade shows. Local tourist offices will often go out of their way to find something in your price range.

BUSINESS HOURS

Banks 9am to 4pm Monday to Friday, often extended hours Tuesday or Thursday
Bars 6pm to 1am
Cafes 8am to 8pm
Clubs 10pm to 4am
Post offices 9am to 6pm Monday to Friday, some Saturday mornings
Restaurants 11am to 9pm or 10pm (varies widely, 3pm to 6pm break common in rural areas)
Shops 9.30am to 8pm Monday to Saturday (shorter hours in suburbs and rural areas, possible lunchtime break)

DISCOUNT CARDS

Tourist offices in many cities sell Welcome Cards entitling visitors to free or reduced admission on museums, sights and tours, plus unlimited local public transport for the period of their validity (usually 24 or 48 hours). They can be good value if you want to fit a lot in.

GAY & LESBIAN TRAVELLERS

➡ Germany is a magnet for *schwule* (gay) and *lesbische* (lesbian) travellers, with the rainbow flag flying especially proudly in Berlin and Cologne, and with sizeable communities in Hamburg, Frankfurt and Munich.
➡ Generally speaking, attitudes towards homosexuality tend to be more conservative in rural areas, among older people and in the eastern states.

INTERNET RESOURCES

Deutschland Online (www.magazine-deutschland.de)

COUNTRY FACTS

Area 356,866 sq km
Capital Berlin
Country Code ☎ 49
Currency Euro (€)
Emergency ☎ 112
Language German
Money ATMs common, cash preferred for most purchases
Population 81.1 million
Visas Schengen rules apply

Facts About Germany (www.tatsachen-ueber-deutschland.de)
German National Tourist Office (www.germany.travel)
Online German Course (www.deutsch-lernen.com)

LEGAL MATTERS

➡ Drivers need to carry their driving licence at all times. The permissible blood-alcohol limit is 0.05%; stiff fines and a confiscated licence and even jail time are possible if caught driving over the limit.
➡ Drinking in public is not illegal, but please be discreet about it.
➡ Cannabis possession is a criminal offence and punishment may range from a warning to a court appearance.

MONEY

➡ Cash is king in Germany, so always carry some with you and plan to pay in cash almost everywhere.
➡ ATMs (*Geldautomat*) linked to international networks such as Cirrus, Plus, Star and Maestro are widely available. Check with the issuer about fees.
➡ Credit cards are becoming more widely accepted, but it's best not to assume that you'll be able to use one – enquire first.

PUBLIC HOLIDAYS

In addition to the following nationwide holidays, individual states observe additional (usually religious) holidays.
Neujahrstag (New Year's Day) 1 January
Ostern (Easter) Good Friday, Easter Sunday and Easter Monday
Christi Himmelfahrt (Ascension Day) Forty days after Easter
Maifeiertag/Tag der Arbeit (Labour Day) 1 May

Pfingsten (Whit/Pentecost Sunday & Monday) Fifty days after Easter

Tag der Deutschen Einheit (Day of German Unity) 3 October

Weihnachtstag (Christmas Day) 25 December

Zweiter Weihnachtstag (Boxing Day) 26 December

TELEPHONE

German phone numbers consist of an area code (three to six digits) followed by the local number (three to nine digits). Mobile phones work on GSM900/1800.

Country code ⬦49

International access code ⬦00

Directory inquiries ⬦11837 for an English-speaking operator (charged at €1.99 per minute)

Getting There & Away

AIR

Huge Frankfurt Airport (p308) is Germany's busiest, with Munich (p289) a close second and Düsseldorf (p315) getting a good share of departures as well. Airports in Berlin, Hamburg and Cologne are comparatively small.

LAND

Bus

Bus travel is becoming increasingly popular in Germany thanks to a new crop of companies offering good-value connections within Germany and beyond aboard comfortable buses with snack bars and free wi-fi. For routes, times and prices, check www.buslinien-suche.de (also in English).

The largest Europewide bus network is maintained by **Eurolines** (www.eurolines.com), a consortium of national bus companies.

Car & Motorcycle

➡ When bringing your own vehicle to Germany, you need a valid driving licence, car registration and proof of third-party insurance. Foreign cars must display a nationality sticker unless they have official European plates. You also need to carry a warning (hazard) triangle and a first-aid kit.

➡ Most German cities now have environmental zones that may only be entered by vehicles (including foreign ones) displaying an *Umweltplakette* (emissions sticker). Check with your motoring association or buy one at www.umwelt-plakette.de.

Train

➡ Germany has an efficient railway network with excellent links to other European destinations. Ticketing is handled by **Deutsche Bahn** (⬦01806 99 66 33; www.bahn.de).

➡ Seat reservations are a good idea for Friday and Sunday travel on long-distance trains and highly recommended during the peak summer season and around major holidays.

➡ Eurail and Interrail passes are valid on all German national trains.

SEA

➡ Germany's main ferry ports are Kiel, Lübeck and Travemünde in Schleswig-Holstein, and Rostock and Sassnitz (on Rügen Island) in Mecklenburg–Western Pomerania. All have services to Scandinavia and the Baltic states. There are no direct ferries between Germany and the UK.

➡ For details and tickets, go to www.ferry-booker.com or www.ferrysavers.com.

Getting Around

Germany has an excellent and comprehensive public transport system. Regional bus services fill the gaps in areas not well served by the rail network.

AIR

Unless you're flying from one end of the country to the other, say from Berlin or Hamburg to Munich, planes are only marginally quicker than trains once you factor in the check-in and transit times.

BICYCLE

➡ Cycling is allowed on all roads except autobahns (motorways). Helmets are not compulsory (not even for children).

➡ Bicycles may be taken on most trains but require a *Fahrradkarte* (separate ticket) and a reservation if travelling on an InterCity (IC)/EuroCity (EC) train. They are not allowed on InterCity Express (ICE) trains.

➡ Most towns and cities have a private bicycle-hire station, often at or near the train station. A growing number have automated bike-rental systems.

BOAT

From April to October, boats operate on set timetables along sections of the Rhine, the Elbe and the Danube.

BUS

➡ Domestic buses cover an extensive nation-wide network.

➡ In some rural areas buses may be your only option for getting around without your own vehicle. The frequency of services varies from 'rarely' to 'constantly'. Commuter-geared routes offer limited or no service in the evenings and on weekends.

➡ In cities, buses generally converge at the *Busbahnhof* or *Zentraler Omnibus Bahnhof* (ZOB; central bus station), which is often near the Hauptbahnhof (central train station).

CAR & MOTORCYCLE

➡ Driving is on the right side of the road.

➡ With few exceptions, no tolls are charged on public roads.

➡ Unless posted otherwise, speed limits are 50km/h in cities, 100km/h on country roads and no limit on the autobahn.

➡ Cars are impractical in urban areas. Leaving your car in a central *Parkhaus* (car park) can cost €20 per day or more.

➡ Visitors from most countries do not need an International Driving Permit to drive in Germany; bring your licence from home.

➡ To hire a car, you'll usually need to be over 25 years old and in possession of a valid driving license and a major credit card. Automatic transmissions are rare and must be booked well in advance.

LOCAL TRANSPORT

➡ Public transport is excellent within big cities and small towns and may include buses, *Strassenbahn* (trams), S-Bahn (light rail) and U-Bahn (underground/subway trains).

➡ Tickets cover all forms of transit, and fares are determined by zones or time travelled, sometimes both. *Streifenkarte* (multiticket trips) and *Tageskarte* (day passes) offer better value than single-ride tickets.

➡ Most tickets must be validated (stamped) upon boarding.

TRAIN

➡ Germany's train network is almost entirely run by **Deutsche Bahn** (www.bahn.com), although there is a growing number of routes operated by private companies.

➡ Of the several train types, ICE trains are the fastest and most comfortable. IC trains (EC if they cross borders) are almost as fast but older and less snazzy. Regional Express (RE) and Regionalbahn (RB) trains are regional. S-Bahn are suburban trains operating in large cities and conurbations.

MILESTONES IN GERMAN HISTORY

800 Charlemagne is crowned emperor by the pope, laying the foundation for the Holy Roman Empire, which will last until 1806.

1241 Hamburg and Lübeck sign a trading agreement, creating the base for the powerful Hanseatic League that dominates politics and trade across much of Europe throughout the Middle Ages.

1455 Johannes Gutenberg invents moveable type, which for the first time allows books to be published in larger quantities.

1517 Martin Luther challenges Catholic-church practices by posting his Ninety-Five Theses and ushering in the Reformation.

1618–48 The Thirty Years' War pits Protestants against Catholics in a far-reaching, bloody war that leaves Europe's population depleted and vast regions reduced to wasteland.

1871 A united Germany is created with Prussia at its helm, Berlin as its capital and Wilhelm I as its emperor.

1914–18 WWI: Germany, Austria-Hungary and Turkey go to war against Britain, France, Italy and Russia. Germany is defeated.

1933 Hitler comes to power, ushering in 12 years of Nazi terror that culminates in WWII and the systematic annihiliation of Jews, Roma, Sinti and other people deemed 'undesirable'.

1949 Germany is divided into a democratic West Germany under the western Allies (the US, UK and France) and a socialist East Germany under the Soviet Union.

1961 The East German government erects the Berlin Wall, dividing the country into two for the next 28 years.

1989 The Berlin Wall collapses; Germany is reunited the following year.

ESSENTIAL FOOD & DRINK

As in Britain, Germany has redeemed itself gastronomically over the past decade. These days culinary offerings are often slimmed down and healthier as many chefs let the trifecta of seasonal-regional-organic ingredients steer their menus. International flavours and cooking techniques further add pizazz to tried-and-trusted specialities, while vegan and vegetarian selections are becoming commonplace. Of course, if you crave traditional comfort food, you'll still find plenty of pork, potatoes and cabbage on the menus, especially in the countryside. Here are our top-five classic German culinary treats:

➡ **Sausage** (wurst) Favourite snack food, links come in 1500 varieties, including finger-sized *Nürnbergers*, crunchy *Thüringers* and tomato-sauce-drowned *Currywurst*.

➡ **Schweinshaxe** The mother of all pork dishes, this one presents itself as entire knuckle roasted to crispy perfection.

➡ **Königsberger Klopse** A simple but elegant plate of golf-ball-sized veal meatballs in a caper-laced white sauce and served with a side of boiled potatoes and beetroot.

➡ **Bread** Get Germans talking about bread and often their eyes will water as they describe their favourite type – usually hearty and wholegrained in infinite variations.

➡ **Black forest cake** (Schwarzwälder Kirschtorte) Multilayered chocolate sponge cake, whipped cream and kirsch confection, topped with cherries and chocolate shavings.

➡ At larger stations, you can store your luggage in a *Schliessfach* (locker) or a *Gepäckaufbewahrung* (left-luggage office).

➡ Seat reservations for long-distance travel are highly recommended, especially if you're travelling on a Friday or Sunday afternoon, during holiday periods or in summer. Reservations can be made online and at ticket counters as late as 10 minutes before departure.

➡ Buy tickets online (www.bahn.de) or at stations from vending machines or *Reisezentrum* (ticket offices). Only conductors on ICE and IC/EC trains sell tickets on board at a surcharge.

Greece

Best Places to Eat

➡ To Maridaki (p363)

➡ To Steki tou Yianni (p371)

➡ Paparouna (p349)

➡ Funky Gourmet (p341)

➡ M-Eating (p353)

Best Places to Stay

➡ Aroma Suites (p358)

➡ Casa Leone (p363)

➡ Marco Polo Mansion (p366)

➡ Amfitriti Pension (p344)

➡ Siorra Vittoria (p374)

Why Go?

The alluring combination of history and ravishing beauty that has made Greece (Ελλάδα) one of the most popular destinations on the planet always seems to beckon. Within easy reach of magnificent archaeological sites such as the Acropolis, Delphi, Delos and Knossos are breathtaking beaches and relaxed tavernas serving everything from ouzo to octopus. Hiking trails criss-cross Mt Olympus, the Zagorohoria and islands like Crete and Corfu.

Wanderers can island-hop to their heart's content (each island has its own character), while party types can enjoy pulsating nightlife in Greece's vibrant modern cities and on islands such as Mykonos and Santorini. Add welcoming locals with an enticing culture to the mix and it's easy to see why most visitors head home vowing to come back. Travellers to Greece inevitably end up with a favourite site they long to return to – get out there and find yours.

When to Go
Athens

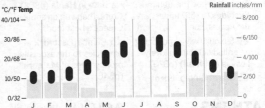

May & Jun Greece opens the shutters in time for Orthodox Easter; the best months to visit.

Jul & Aug Be prepared to battle summer crowds, high prices and soaring temperatures.

Sep & Oct The tourist season winds down; an excellent, relaxing time to head to Greece.

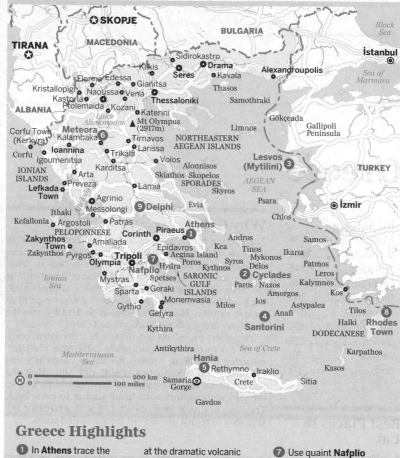

Greece Highlights

1 In **Athens** trace the ancient to the modern from the Acropolis to booming nightclubs.

2 Island-hop through the **Cyclades** (p350) under the Aegean sun.

3 Sip ouzo while munching on grilled octopus in lovely **Lesvos (Mytilini)** (p370).

4 Stare dumbfounded at the dramatic volcanic caldera of incomparable **Santorini** (p356).

5 Stroll the lovely Venetian Harbour in **Hania** (p362), Crete, then sup on some of Greece's best food.

6 Climb russet rock pinnacles to the exquisite monasteries of **Meteora** (p346).

7 Use quaint **Nafplio** (p344) as a base for exploring the back roads and ruins of the Peloponnese.

8 Lose yourself within the medieval walls of the Old Town in **Rhodes Town** (p365).

9 Search for the oracle amid the dazzling ruins of **Delphi** (p346).

ATHENS   AΘHNA

POP 3.8 MILLION

Ancient and modern, with equal measures of grunge and grace, bustling Athens is a heady mix of history and edginess. Iconic monuments mingle with first-rate muse- ums, lively cafes and alfresco dining, and it's downright fun. With Greece's financial diffi- culties Athens has revealed its more restive aspect, but take the time to look beneath the surface and you'll discover a complex metropolis full of vibrant subcultures.

One Week

Explore **Athens'** museums and ancient sites on day one before spending a couple of days in the **Peloponnese** visiting Nafplio, Mycenae and Olympia; ferry to the **Cyclades** and enjoy Mykonos and spectacular Santorini.

One Month

Give yourself some more time in Athens and the Peloponnese, then visit the **Ionian Islands** for a few days. Explore the villages of Zagorohoria before travelling back to Athens via **Meteora** and **Delphi**. Take a ferry from Piraeus south to **Mykonos**, then island-hop via Santorini to **Crete**. After exploring Crete, take the ferry east to **Rhodes**, then north to **Kos**, **Samos** and **Lesvos**. Wrap up in relaxed, cosmopolitan **Thessaloniki**.

◉ Sights

★ Acropolis
HISTORIC SITE

(☑ 210 321 0219; http://odysseus.culture.gr; adult/child/concession €12/free/6; ⊙ 8am-8pm Apr-Oct, to 5pm Nov-Mar; Ⓜ Akropoli) The Acropolis is the most important ancient site in the Western world. Crowned by the **Parthenon**, it stands sentinel over Athens, visible from almost everywhere within the city. Its monuments of Pentelic marble gleam white in the midday sun and gradually take on a honey hue as the sun sinks, while at night they stand brilliantly illuminated above the city. A glimpse of this magnificent sight cannot fail to exalt your spirit.

★ Acropolis Museum
MUSEUM

(☑ 210 900 0901; www.theacropolismuseum.gr; Dionysiou Areopagitou 15, Makrygianni; adult/child free; ⊙ 8am-4pm Mon, to 8pm Tue-Sun, to 10pm Fri Apr-Oct, 9am-5pm Mon-Thu, to 10pm Fri, 9am-8pm Sat & Sun Nov-Mar; Ⓜ Akropoli) The long-awaited Acropolis Museum opened with much fanfare in 2009 in the southern foothills of the Acropolis. Ten times larger than the former on-site museum, the imposing modernist building brings together the surviving treasures of the Acropolis, including items formerly held in other museums or storage, as well as pieces returned from foreign museums. The **restaurant** has superb views (and is surprisingly good value) and there's a fine museum **shop**.

★ Ancient Agora
HISTORIC SITE

(☑ 210 321 0185; http://odysseus.culture.gr; Adrianou; adult/child €4/free, free with Acropolis pass; ⊙ 11am-3pm Mon, from 8am Tue-Sun; Ⓜ Monastiraki) The heart of ancient Athens was the Agora, the lively, crowded focal point of administrative, commercial, political and social activity. Socrates expounded his philosophy here, and in AD 49 St Paul came here to win converts to Christianity. The site today is a lush, refreshing respite with beautiful monuments and temples, and a fascinating **museum**.

★ Roman Agora & Tower of the Winds
RUIN

(☑ 210 324 5220; cnr Pelopida & Eolou, Monastiraki; adult/child €2/1, free with Acropolis pass; ⊙ 8am-3pm; Ⓜ Monastiraki) The entrance to the Roman Agora is through the well-preserved **Gate of Athena Archegetis**, which is flanked by four Doric columns. It was erected sometime during the 1st century AD and financed by Julius Caesar. The well-preserved, extraordinary **Tower of the Winds** was built in the 1st century BC by a Syrian astronomer named Andronicus.

★ Temple of Olympian Zeus
RUIN

(☑ 210 922 6330; adult/child €2/free, free with Acropolis pass; ⊙ 8am-8pm Apr-Oct, 8.30am-3pm Nov-Mar; Ⓜ Syntagma, Akropoli) You can't miss this striking marvel, smack in the centre of Athens. It is the largest temple in Greece and was begun in the 6th century BC by Peisistratos, but was abandoned for lack of funds. Various other leaders had stabs at completing it, but it was left to Hadrian to complete the work in AD 131. In total, it took more than 700 years to build.

★ Panathenaic Stadium
HISTORIC SITE

(☑ 210 752 2984; www.panathenaicstadium.gr; Leoforos Vasileos Konstantinou, Pangrati; adult/child €3/1.50; ⊙ 8am-7pm Mar-Oct, to 5pm Nov-Feb; Ⓜ Akropoli) The grand Panathenaic Stadium lies between two pine-covered hills between the neighbourhoods of Mets and Pangrati. It was originally built in the 4th century BC as a venue for the Panathenaic athletic contests. It's said that at Hadrian's inauguration in AD 120, 1000 wild animals were sacrificed in the arena. Later, the seats

Central Athens

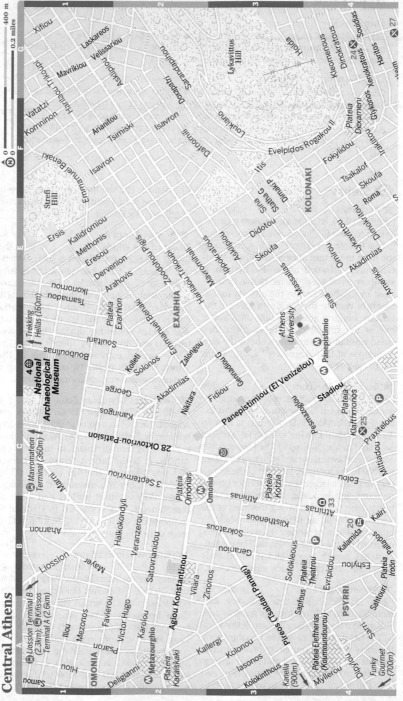

400 m
0.2 miles

Liossion Terminal B (2.3km); Kifissos Terminal A (2.6km)

Mavromateon Terminal (360m)

Trekking Hellas (160m)

4 National Archaeological Museum

OMONIA

EXARHIA

KOLONAKI

PSYRRI

Lykavittos Hill

Loukiano

Strefi Hill

Athens University

Panepistimio

Plateia Omonias

Omonia

Plateia Kotzia

Plateia Exarhion

Plateia Karaïskaki

Metaxourghio

Agiou Konstantinou

Pireos (Tsaldari Panagi)

Plateia Theatrou

Plateia Eleftherias (Koumoundourou)

Funky Gourmet (700m)

Kanella (900m)

Panepistimiou (El Venizelou)

Stadiou

Plateia Klafthmonos

Plateia Dexameni

28 Oktovriou-Patision

3 Septemvriou

Xifiou

Laskareos

Velissariou

Mavrikiou

Hatziioannou Tirkoki

Vatatzi

Komninon

Emmanuel Benaki

Arianitou

Tsimiski

Isavron

Isavron

Doxapatri

Sarandapihou

Asklipiou

Dafnomili

Itis

Dimaki P

Sina

Statha G

Didotou

Skoufa

Ippokratous

Asklipiou

Mavromihali

Harilaou Trikoupi

Zodohou Pigis

Ersis

Kalidromiou

Methonis

Eresou

Dervenion

Arahovis

Ikonomou

Tsamadou

Soultani

Kolleti

Solonos

Akadimias

Nikitara

Fidiou

Gennadiou G

Zalongou

George

Kaningos

Akadimias

Marni

Aharnon

Halkokondyli

Veranzerou

Satovrianidou

Vilara

Zinonos

Geraniou

Sofokleous

Sokratous

Klisthenous

Athinas

Athinas

Sapfous

Evripidou

Eshylou

Kalamida

Kairi

Eolou

Miltiadou

Praxitelous

Pesmazoglou

Sina

Amerikis

Lykavittou

Akadimias

Omirou

Plateia Iroön

Sahtouri

Sarri

Diplou

Myllerou

Kolokinthous

Iasonos

Kolonou

Kallergi

Zinonos

Deligianni

Karolou

Victor Hugo

Favierou

Mezonos

Iliou

Psaron

Hilou

Samou

Mayer

Liossion

Aharnon

Evelpidos Rogakou II

Fokylidou

Tsakalof

Skoufa

Roma

Dinokratou

Kleomenous

Dinokratous

Souidias

Haritos

Iraklitou

Glykonos Xenokratous

Ippiou

Eratosthenous

27

24

25

33

20

Satovrianidou

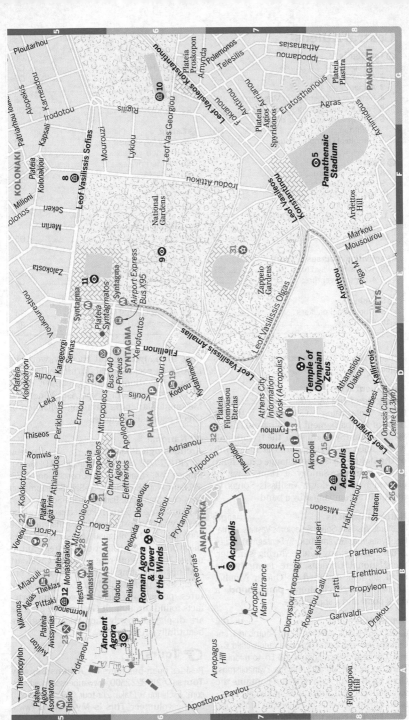

Central Athens

were rebuilt in Pentelic marble by Herodes Atticus.

Parliament & Changing of the Guard
BUILDING
(Plateia Syntagmatos; Ⓜ Syntagma) **FREE** In front of the parliament building on Plateia Syntagmatos (Syntagma Sq), the traditionally costumed *evzones* (guards) of the **Tomb of the Unknown Soldier** change every hour on the hour. On Sunday at 11am, a whole platoon marches down Vasilissis Sofias to the tomb, accompanied by a band.

National Gardens
GARDENS
(Leoforos Vasilissis Sofias & Leoforos Vasilissis Amalias, Syntagma; ⊙7am-dusk; Ⓜ Syntagma) **FREE** A delightful, shady refuge during summer, the National Gardens were formerly the royal gardens designed by Queen Amalia. There's a large children's **playground**, a duck pond and a shady **cafe**.

Benaki Museum
MUSEUM
(☑210 367 1000; www.benaki.gr; Koumbari 1, cnr Leoforos Vasilissis Sofias, Kolonaki; adult/child €7/free, Thu free; ⊙9am-5pm Wed & Fri, to midnight Thu & Sat, to 3pm Sun; Ⓜ Syntagma, Evangelismos) Greece's finest private museum contains the vast collection of Antonis Benakis, accumulated during 35 years of collecting in Europe and Asia. The collection includes Bronze Age

finds from Mycenae and Thessaly; works by El Greco; ecclesiastical furniture brought from Asia Minor; pottery, copper, silver and woodwork from Egypt, Asia Minor and Mesopotamia; and a stunning collection of Greek regional costumes.

★ National Archaeological Museum
MUSEUM
(☑210 821 7717; www.namuseum.gr; 28 Oktovriou-Patision 44, Exarhia; adult/concession €7/3; ⊙1-8pm Mon, 8am-8pm Tue-Sat, 8am-3pm Sun Apr-Oct, 1-8pm Mon, 9am-4pm Tue-Sun Nov-Mar; Ⓜ Viktoria, 🚌2, 4, 5, 9 or 11 Polytechnio stop) One of the world's most important museums, the National Archaeological Museum houses the world's finest collection of Greek antiquities. Treasures offering a view of Greek art and history, dating from the Neolithic era to classical periods, include exquisite sculptures, pottery, jewellery, frescoes and artefacts found throughout Greece. The exhibits are displayed largely thematically and are beautifully presented.

☞ Tours
Besides open-bus tours try **Athens Segway Tours** (☑210 322 2500; www.athenssegwaytours.com; Eschinou 9, Plaka; 2hr tour €59; Ⓜ Akropoli) or the volunteer **This is My Athens** (www.

thisisathens.org). Get out of town on the cheap with **Athens: Adventures** ([📞] 210 922 4044; www.athensadventures.gr). Hike or kayak with **Trekking Hellas** ([📞] 210 331 0323; www.trek king.gr; Saripolou 10, Exarhia; [Ⓜ] Viktoria).

✵ Festivals

Hellenic Festival — PERFORMING ARTS
(www.greekfestival.gr; ⊙ Jun-Sep) The ancient theatre at Epidavros and Athens' Theatre of Herodes Atticus are the headline venues of Greece's annual cultural festival featuring a top line-up of local and international music, dance and theatre.

🛏 Sleeping

Book well ahead for July and August.

★ Athens Backpackers — HOSTEL €
([📞] 210 922 4044; www.backpackers.gr; Makri 12, Makrygianni; dm incl breakfast €24-29, 2-/4-/6-person apt €95/125/155; [❄][@][🛜]; [Ⓜ] Akropoli) The popular rooftop bar with cheap drinks and Acropolis views is a major drawcard of this modern and friendly Australian-run backpacker favourite, right near the Acropolis metro. There's a BBQ in the courtyard, a well-stocked kitchen and a busy social scene. Spotless dorms with private bathrooms and lockers have bedding, but use of towels costs €2. The same management runs well-priced modern apartments nearby.

Tempi Hotel — HOTEL €
([📞] 210 321 3175; www.tempihotel.gr; Eolou 29, Monastiraki; d/tr €55/65, s/d without bathroom €37/47; [❄][🛜]; [Ⓜ] Monastiraki) Location and affordability are the strengths of this older, family-run place on pedestrian Eolou. Front balconies overlook Plateia Agia Irini, the scene of some of Athens' best nightlife, and side views get the Acropolis. Basic rooms have satellite TV, but bathrooms are primitive. Top-floor rooms are small and quite a hike. There is a communal kitchen.

AthenStyle — HOSTEL €
([📞] 210 322 5010; www.athenstyle.com; Agias Theklas 10, Psyrri; dm €18-26, s/d €51/76, apt from €86; [❄][@]; [Ⓜ] Monastiraki) This bright and arty place has friendly staff, well-equipped studio apartments and hostel beds within walking distance of the Monastiraki metro, major sights and nightlife. Each dorm has lockers; some balconies have Acropolis views. Murals bedeck reception, and the cool basement lounge, with its pool table, home cinema and internet corner, holds art exhi-

ⓘ CHEAPER BY THE HALF-DOZEN

The €12 ticket at the Acropolis (valid for four days) includes entry to the other significant ancient sites: Ancient Agora, Roman Agora, Keramikos, Temple of Olympian Zeus and the Theatre of Dionysos.

Enter the sites free on the first Sunday of the month from November to March, and on certain holidays. Anyone aged under 18 years or with an EU student card gets in free.

bitions. The small Acropolis-view rooftop bar hosts evening happy hours.

Hera Hotel — BOUTIQUE HOTEL €€
([📞] 210 923 6682; www.herahotel.gr; Falirou 9, Makrygianni; d incl breakfast €120-165, ste €225; [❄][@][🛜]; [Ⓜ] Akropoli) This elegant boutique hotel, a short walk from the Acropolis and Plaka, was totally rebuilt but the formal interior design is in keeping with the lovely neoclassical facade. There's lots of brass and timber, and stylish classic furnishings. The rooftop garden, restaurant and bar have spectacular views.

Plaka Hotel — HOTEL €€
([📞] 210 322 2096; www.plakahotel.gr; Kapnikareas 7, cnr Mitropoleos, Monastiraki; d incl breakfast €125-200; [❄][🛜]; [Ⓜ] Monastiraki) It's hard to beat the Acropolis views from the rooftop garden, as well as those from top-floor rooms. Tidy rooms have light timber floors and furniture, and satellite TV, though bathrooms are on the small side. Though called the Plaka Hotel, it's actually closer to Monastiraki.

Central Hotel — BUSINESS HOTEL €€
([📞] 210 323 4357; www.centralhotel.gr; Apollonos 21, Plaka; d/tr incl breakfast from €105/150; [❄][@][🛜]; [Ⓜ] Syntagma) This stylish hotel has been tastefully decorated in light, contemporary tones. It has comfortable rooms with all the mod cons and good bathrooms. There is a lovely roof terrace with Acropolis views, a small spa and sun lounges. As its name suggests, Central Hotel is in a great location between Syntagma and Plaka.

Hotel Adonis — HOTEL €€
([📞] 210 324 9737; www.hotel-adonis.gr; 3 Kodrou St, Plaka; s/d/tr incl breakfast €70/88/105; [❄][@][🛜]; [Ⓜ] Syntagma) This comfortable pension on a quiet pedestrian street in Plaka has basic,

CONTEMPORARY ART

Athens is not all about ancient art. For a taste of the contemporary, visit:

Taf (The Art Foundation; ☑ 210 323 8757; www.theartfoundation.gr; Normanou 5, Monastiraki; ☺ 1pm-midnight; Ⓜ Monastiraki) Eclectic art and music gallery.

Six DOGS (☑ 210 321 0510; www.sixdogs.gr; Avramiotou 6, Monastiraki; Ⓜ Monastiraki) Theatre meets gallery meets live music venue.

Onassis Cultural Centre (☑ 213 017 8000, box office 210 900 5800; www.sgt.gr; Leoforos Syngrou 107-109, Neos Kosmos; Ⓜ Syngrou-Fix) Multimillion-euro visual and performing-arts centre.

National Museum of Contemporary Art (☑ 210 924 2111; www.emst.gr; Athens Conservatory, cnr Vassileos Georgiou B 17-19 & Rigillis, Kolonaki; adult/child €3/free; ☺ 11am-7pm Tue, Wed & Fri-Sun, to 10pm Thu; Ⓜ Syntagma) Soon to move to its new location on Syngrou.

clean rooms with TVs. Bathrooms are small but have been excellently renovated. Take in great Acropolis views from 4th-floor rooms and the rooftop terrace where breakfast is served. No credit cards.

Hotel Cecil
HOTEL €€

(☑ 210 321 7079; www.cecilhotel.gr; Athinas 39, Monastiraki; s/d/tr/q incl breakfast from €60/65/95/120; ❄@☎; Ⓜ Monastiraki) This charming old hotel on busy Athinas has beautiful high, moulded ceilings, polished timber floors and an original cage-style lift. The simple rooms are tastefully furnished, but don't have fridges. Two connecting rooms with a shared bathroom are ideal for families.

✗ Eating

Eat streets include Mitropoleos, Adrianou and Navarchou Apostoli in Monastiraki, the area around Plateia Psyrri, and Gazi, near Keramikos metro.

The fruit and vegetable **market** (Varvakios Agora; Athinas, btwn Sofokleous & Evripidou; ☺ 7am-3pm Mon-Sat; Ⓜ Monastiraki, Panepistimio, Omonia) is opposite the meat market.

★ Mani Mani
GREEK €

(☑ 210 921 8180; www.manimani.com.gr; Falirou 10, Makrygianni; mains €9-15; ☺ 2.30-11.30pm Mon-Fri, from 1pm Sat, 1-5.30pm Sun, closed Jul & Aug; Ⓜ Akropoli) Head upstairs to the relaxing, cheerful dining rooms of this delightful modern restaurant, which specialises in regional cuisine from Mani in the Peloponnese. The ravioli with Swiss chard, chervil and cheese, and the tangy Mani sausage with orange are standouts. Almost all dishes can be ordered as half portions (at half-price), allowing you to sample widely.

Oikeio
MEDITERRANEAN €

(☑ 210 725 9216; Ploutarhou 15, Kolonaki; mains €7-13; ☺ 1pm-2.30am Mon-Sat; Ⓜ Evangelismos) With excellent home-style cooking, this modern taverna lives up to its name (meaning 'homey'). It's decorated like a cosy bistro on the inside, and tables on the footpath allow people-watching without the normal Kolonaki bill. Pastas, salads and international fare are tasty, but try the *mayirefta* (ready-cooked meals) specials such as the excellent stuffed zucchini. Book ahead.

Tzitzikas & Mermingas
MEZEDHES €

(☑ 210 324 7607; Mitropoleos 12-14, Syntagma; mezedhes €6-11; ☺ noon-11pm; Ⓜ Syntagma) Greek merchandise lines the walls of this cheery, modern *mezedhopoleio* that sits smack in the middle of central Athens. It serves a tasty range of delicious and creative mezedhes (like the honey-drizzled, bacon-wrapped cheese one) to a bustling crowd of locals.

Kalnterimi
TAVERNA €

(☑ 210 331 0049; www.kalnterimi.gr; Plateia Agion Theodoron, cnr Skouleniou, Monastiraki; mains €6-9; ☺ noon-midnight; Ⓜ Panepistimio) Find your way behind the Church of Agii Theodori to this hidden open-air taverna offering Greek food at its most authentic. Everything is fresh cooked and delicious: you can't go wrong. Hand-painted tables spill onto the footpath along a pedestrian street and give a feeling of peace in one of the busiest parts of the city.

Filippou
TAVERNA €

(☑ 210 721 6390; Xenokratous 19, Kolonaki; mains €8-12; ☺ noon-11pm, closed Sat night & Sun; Ⓜ Evangelismos) Why mess with what works? Filippou has been dishing out yummy Greek dishes since 1923. A chance for a little soul cooking, with white linen, in the heart of Kolonaki.

Kanella TAVERNA €
(☑210 347 6320; Leoforos Konstantinoupoleos 70, Gazi; dishes €7-10; ⊗1.30pm-late; Ⓜ Keramikos) Homemade village-style bread, mismatched retro crockery and brown-paper tablecloths set the tone for this trendy, modern taverna serving regional Greek cuisine. Friendly staff serve daily specials such as lemon lamb with potatoes, and an excellent zucchini and avocado salad.

Thanasis SOUVLAKI €
(☑210 324 4705; Mitropoleos 69, Monastiraki; gyros €2.50; ⊗8.30am-2.30am; Ⓜ Monastiraki) In the heart of Athens' souvlaki hub, at the end of Mitropoleos, Thanasis is known for its kebabs on pitta with grilled tomato and onions.

★ Café Avyssinia MEZEDHES €€
(☑210 321 7047; www.avissinia.gr; Kynetou 7, Monastiraki; mains €10-16; ⊗11am-1am Tue-Sat, to 7pm Sun; Ⓜ Monastiraki) Hidden away on colourful Plateia Avyssinias, in the middle of the flea market, this bohemian *mezedhopoleio* gets top marks for atmosphere, food and friendly service. It specialises in regional Greek cuisine, from warm fava to eggplants baked with tomato and cheese, and has a great selection of ouzo, *raki* (Cretan fire water) and *tsipouro* (a distilled spirit similar to ouzo but usually stronger).

★ Funky Gourmet MEDITERRANEAN €€€
(☑210 524 2727; www.funkygourmet.com; Paramithias 3, cnr Salaminas, Keramikos; set menu from €70; ⊗7.30-11.30pm Tue-Sat; Ⓜ Metaxourgio) Noveau gastronomy meets fresh Mediterranean ingredients at this Michelin-starred restaurant. Elegant lighting, refinement and sheer joy in food make this a worthwhile stop for any foodie. The degustation menus can be paired with wines. Book ahead.

🍷 Drinking & Entertainment

Kolonaki has a mind-boggling array of cafes off Plateia Kolonakiou on Skoufa and Tsakalof. Another cafe-thick area is Adrianou, along the Ancient Agora.

Athenians know how to party. Expect people to show up after midnight. Head to Monastiraki (around Plateia Agia Irini, Plateia Karytsi or Kolokotroni), Gazi (around Voutadon and the Keramikos metro station) or Kolonaki (around Ploutarhou and Haritos or Skoufa and Omirou) and explore!

Gay bars cluster in Gazi near the railway line on Leoforos Konstantinoupoleos and Megalou Alexandrou, as well as Makrygianni, Psyrri, Metaxourghio and Exarhia. Check out www.athensinfoguide.com or www.gayguide.gr.

Although Exarhia has a bohemian bar scene, the neighbourhood has been affected recently by street demonstrations.

For events listings try: www.breathtakingathens.gr, www.elculture.gr, www.tickethour.com, www.tickethouse.gr and www.ticketservices.gr. The Kathimerini supplement inside the *International Herald Tribune* contains event listings and a cinema guide. In summer, dance clubs move to the beachfront near Glyfada.

🛍 Shopping

Find boutiques around Syntagma, from the Attica department store past Voukourestiou and on Ermou; designer brands and cool shops in Kolonaki; and souvenirs, folk art and leather in Plaka and Monastiraki with its fun **Monastiraki Flea Market** (Adrianou, Monastiraki; ⊗daily; Ⓜ Monastiraki).

GREECE ATHENS

ℹ UNCERTAIN TIMES

➡ Due to the financial difficulties in Greece, opening hours, prices and even the existence of some establishments have fluctuated much more than usual.

➡ The government was running many archaeological sites on their shorter winter hours (closing around 3pm).

➡ With businesses associated with tourism, opening hours can always be haphazard; if trade is good, they're open, if not, they shut.

➡ 'High season' is usually July and August. If you turn up in 'shoulder seasons' (May and June; September and October) expect to pay significantly less. Things may be dirt cheap or closed in winter.

➡ If in doubt, call ahead.

ISLAND IN A DAY: AEGINA & HYDRA   ΑΙΓΙΝΑ & ΥΔΡΑ

For islands within easy reach of Athens, head to the Saronic Gulf. **Aegina** (eh-yee-nah; www.aeginagreece.com), just a half hour from Piraeus is home to the impressive **Temple of Aphaia**, said to have served as a model for the construction of the Parthenon. The catwalk queen of the Saronics, **Hydra** (ee-drah; www.hydra.gr, www.hydraislandgreece.com) is a delight, an hour and a half from Piraeus. Its picturesque horseshoe-shaped harbour town with gracious stone mansions stacked up the rocky hillsides is known as a retreat for artists, writers and celebrities. There are no motorised vehicles – apart from sanitation trucks – leading to unspoilt trails along the coast and into the mountains.

From Hydra, you can return to Piraeus, or carry on to Spetses and the Peloponnese (Metohi, Ermione and Porto Heli). Check **Hellenic Seaways** (www.hsw.gr) and **Aegina Flying Dolphins** (www.aegeanflyingdolphins.gr).

ℹ Information

DANGERS & ANNOYANCES

Crime has risen in Athens with the onset of the financial crisis. Though violent crime remains relatively rare, travellers should stay alert on the streets, especially at night.

➜ Streets surrounding Omonia have become markedly seedier, with an increase in prostitutes and junkies; avoid the area, especially at night.

➜ Watch for pickpockets on the metro and at the markets.

➜ When taking taxis, ask the driver to use the meter or negotiate a price in advance. Ignore stories that the hotel you've chosen is closed or full: they're angling for a commission from another hotel.

➜ Bar scams are commonplace, particularly in Plaka and Syntagma. Beware the over-friendly!

➜ With the recent financial reforms in Greece have come strikes in Athens (check http://livingingreece.gr/strikes). Picketers tend to march in Plateia Syntagmatos.

EMERGENCY

SOS Doctors (☑1016, 210 821 1888; ⊙24hr) Pay service with English-speaking doctors.
Visitor Emergency Assistance (☑112) Toll-free 24-hour service in English.

INTERNET RESOURCES

Official visitor site (www.breathtakingathens.gr)

TOURIST INFORMATION

Athens City Information Kiosk (Acropolis) (☑210 321 7116; Acropolis; ⊙9am-9pm May-Sep; Ⓜ Akropoli)
Athens City Information Kiosk (Airport) (☑210 353 0390; ⊙8am-8pm; Ⓜ Airport) Maps, transport information and all Athens info.

EOT (Greek National Tourist Organisation; ☑210 331 0347, 210 331 0716; www.visitgreece.gr; Dionysiou Areopagitou 18-20, Makrygianni; ⊙8am-8pm Mon-Fri, 10am-4pm Sat & Sun May-Sep, 9am-7pm Mon-Fri Oct-Apr; Ⓜ Akropoli) Free Athens map, transport information and *Athens & Attica* booklet.

ℹ Getting There & Away

AIR

Modern **Eleftherios Venizelos International Airport** (ATH; ☑210 353 0000; www.aia.gr) is 27km east of Athens.

BOAT

Most ferries, hydrofoils and high-speed catamarans leave from the massive port at Piraeus. Some depart from smaller ports at Rafina/Lavrio.

BUS

Athens has two main intercity **KTEL** (☑14505; www.ktel.org) bus stations: **Liossion Terminal B** (☑210 831 7153; Liossion 260, Thymarakia; Ⓜ Agios Nikolaos), 5km north of Omonia with buses to central and northern Greece (Delphi, Meteora) and **Kifissos Terminal A** (☑210 512 4910; Kifisou 100, Peristeri; Ⓜ Agios Antonios), 7km north of Omonia, with buses to Thessaloniki, the Peloponnese, Ionian Islands and western Greece. The KTEL website and tourist offices have timetables.

Buses for southern Attica (Rafina, Lavrio, Sounio) leave from the **Mavromateon Terminal** (☑210 880 8000, 210 822 5148; cnr Leoforos Alexandras & 28 Oktovriou-Patision, Pedion Areos; Ⓜ Viktoria), about 250m north of the National Archaeological Museum.

CAR & MOTORCYCLE

The airport has car rental, and Syngrou, just south of the Temple of Olympian Zeus, is dotted with car-hire firms, though driving in Athens is treacherous.

TRAIN

Intercity trains to central and northern Greece depart from the central **Larisis train station** (Stathmos Larisis; ☑ 14511; www.trainose. gr), about 1km northwest of Plateia Omonias (Omonia Sq), and served by the metro. For the Peloponnese, take the suburban rail to Kiato and change for other OSE services, or check for available lines at the Larisis station.

ⓘ Getting Around

TO/FROM THE AIRPORT
Bus

Tickets cost €5. Twenty-four-hour services:
Piraeus Port Bus X96, 1½ hours, every 20 minutes
Plateia Syntagmatos Bus X95, 60 to 90 minutes, every 15 minutes (the Syntagma stop is on Othonos)
Terminal A (Kifissos) Bus Station Bus X93, 35 minutes, every 30 minutes

Metro

Blue line 3 links the airport to the city centre in around 40 minutes; it operates from Monastiraki from 5.50am to midnight, and from the airport from 5.30am to 11.30pm. Tickets (€8) are valid for all public transport for 70 minutes. Fare for two passengers is €14 total.

Taxi

Fixed fares are posted. Expect day/night €35/50 to the city centre, and €47/65 to Piraeus. Both trips often take at least an hour, longer with heavy traffic. Check www.athensairport taxi.com for more info.

PUBLIC TRANSPORT

The metro, tram and bus system makes getting around central Athens and to Piraeus easy. Athens' road traffic can be horrendous. Get maps and timetables at the tourist offices or **Athens Urban Transport Organisation** (OASA; ☑ 185; www.oasa.gr).

Tickets good for 70 minutes (€1.20), or a 24-hour/five-day travel pass (€4/10) are valid for all forms of public transport except for airport services; the three-day tourist ticket (€20) includes airport transport. Bus/trolleybus-only tickets cannot be used on the metro.

Children under six travel free; people under 18 or over 65 pay half-fare. Buy tickets in metro stations, transport kiosks, or most *periptera* (kiosks). Validate the ticket in the machine as you board.

Bus & Trolleybus

Buses and electric trolleybuses operate every 15 minutes from 5am to midnight.

To get to Piraeus: from Syntagma and Filellinon to Akti Xaveriou catch bus 040; from the Omonia end of Athinas to Plateia Themistokleous, catch bus 049.

Metro

Trains operate from 5am to midnight (Friday and Saturday to around 2am), every three to 10 minutes. Get timetables at www.stasy.gr.

TAXI

Taxis are generally reasonable, with small surcharges for port, train and bus station pick-ups, baggage over 10kg or radio taxi. Insist on a metered rate (except for posted flat rates at the airport).
Athina 1 (☑ 210 921 2800)

PIRAEUS PORT   ΠΕΙΡΑΙΆΣ

Greece's main port and ferry hub fills seemingly endless quays with ships, hydrofoils and catamarans heading all over the country. All ferry companies have online timetables and booths on the quays. EOT (Greek National Tourist Organisation) in Athens has a weekly schedule, or check www.openseas.gr. Schedules are reduced in April, May and October, and are radically cut in winter, especially to smaller islands. When buying tickets, confirm the departure point – some Cyclades boats leave from Rafina or Lavrio, and Patras port serves Italy and the Ionian Islands. Igoumenitsa also serves Corfu.

The fastest and most convenient link to Athens is the metro (€1.20, 40 minutes, every 10 minutes, 5am to midnight), near the ferries. Piraeus has a station for Athens' suburban rail.

Left luggage at the metro station costs €3 per 24 hours.

The **X96 (Plateia Karaïskak; tickets €5)** Piraeus–Athens Airport Express leaves from the southwestern corner of Plateia Karaïskaki. **Bus 040** goes to Syntagma in downtown Athens.

TRAIN

Suburban Rail (☑1110; www.trainose.gr) A fast suburban rail links Athens with the airport, Piraeus, the outer regions and the northern Peloponnese. It connects to the metro at Larisis, Doukissis Plakentias and Nerantziotissa stations, and goes from the airport to Kiato.

THE PELOPONNESE
ΠΕΛΟΠΟΝΝΗΣΟΣ

The Peloponnese encompasses a breathtaking array of landscapes, villages and ruins, where much of Greek history has played out.

Nafplio   Ναυπλιο

POP 14,200

Elegant Venetian houses and neoclassical mansions dripping with crimson bougainvillea cascade down Nafplio's hillside to the azure sea. Vibrant cafes, shops and restaurants fill winding pedestrian streets. Crenulated Palamidi Fortress perches above it all. What's not to love?

⊙ Sights

Palamidi Fortress   FORT
(☑27520 28036; adult/child €4/free; ⊙8am-7.30pm May–mid-Oct, to 3pm mid-Oct–Apr) This vast and spectacular citadel stands on a 216m-high outcrop of rock with excellent views down onto the sea and surrounding land. It was built by the Venetians between 1711 and 1714, and is regarded as a masterpiece of military architecture.

**Peloponnese Folklore
Foundation Museum**   MUSEUM
(☑27520 28379; www.pli.gr; Vasileos Alexandrou 1; admission €2; ⊙9.30am-2.30pm Wed-Mon) Nafplio's award-winning museum is a beautifully arranged collection of folk costumes and household items from Nafplio's history. Established by the philanthropic owner, it's not to be missed. A lovely gift shop is on the ground floor.

⌸ Sleeping

The Old Town is *the* place to stay, but it has few budget options. Cheaper spots dot the road to Argos and Tolo.

Hotel Byron   PENSION €
(☑27520 22351; www.byronhotel.gr; Platonos 2; d incl breakfast €50-70; ⊛) Occupying a fine Venetian building, the Byron is a reliable

favourite, with friendly management, neat rooms, iron bedsteads and period furniture.

★**Amfitriti Pension**   PENSION €€
(☑27520 96250; www.amfitriti-pension.gr; Kapodistriou 24; d incl breakfast from €60; ⊛❀☎) Quaint antiques fill these intimate rooms in a house in the Old Town. You can also enjoy stellar views at its nearby sister hotel, **Amfitriti Belvedere**, which is chock full of brightly coloured tapestries and emits a feeling of cheery serenity.

Pension Marianna   HOTEL €€
(☑27520 24256; www.pensionmarianna.gr; Potamianou 9; s incl breakfast €50, d €65-75, tr €85, q €100; ℗❀☎) For value and hospitality, it doesn't get better than this. The welcoming owner-hosts, the warm Zotos brothers, epitomise Greek *filoxenia* (hospitality) and serve up conviviality, travel advice and delicious breakfasts (comprising homemade produce where possible). The comfortable, squeaky-clean rooms open onto terraces where you can feast on the killer view from your hilltop position.

✗ Eating

Nafplio's Old Town streets are loaded with standard tavernas, with best eats around Vasilissis Olgas.

Antica Gelateria di Roma   GELATERIA €
(☑27520 23520; www.anticagelateria.gr; cnr Farmakopoulou & Komninou; snacks from €2; ⊙10am-11pm) The only 'true' gelato shop in Nafplio, where Italian gelati maestros Marcello, Claudia or Monica Raffo greet you with: '*Bongiorno* – this is an *Italian* gelati shop!' Only natural and local products are used and it's all made on the premises.

To Kentrikon   CAFE €
(☑27520 29933; Plateia Syntagmatos; mains €4-10; ⊙8am-midnight) Relax under the shady trees on this pretty square during extensive breakfasts.

Alaloum   GREEK €€
(☑27520 29883; Papanikolaou 10; mains €10-18; ⊙noon-3pm & 7pm-1am) Situated in a lovely spot overlooking a leafy square, Alaloum serves up excellent (and very generous portions of) Greek Mediterranean fare.

ⓘ Information

Staikos Tours (☑27520 27950; Bouboulinas 50; ⊙9am-1pm & 3-7pm) A helpful outfit offering Avis rental cars and full travel services

> **DON'T MISS**
>
> ### ART & CULTURAL CENTRE
>
> Nafplio's marquee arts and cultural centre, **Fougaro** (☑ 27520 96005; www.fougaro.gr; Asklipiou 98), opened with fanfare in 2012 in an impeccably renovated factory, which now houses an art shop, library, cafe and exhibition spaces, and holds performing-arts programs.

like occasional day-long **boat trips** (www.pegasus-cruises.gr) to Spetses, Hydra and Monemvasia.

❶ Getting There & Away

KTEL Argolis Bus Station (☑ 27520 27323; www.ktel-argolidas.gr; Syngrou) has the following services:

Argos (for Peloponnese connections) €1.60, 30 minutes, half-hourly

Athens €13.10, 2½ hours, hourly (via Corinth)

Epidavros €2.90, 45 minutes, two Monday to Saturday

Mycenae €2.90, one hour, three daily

Epidavros Επίδαυρος

Spectacular World Heritage–listed **Epidavros** (☑ 27530 22009; admission €6; ⊗ 8am-8pm Apr-Oct, to 5pm Nov-Mar) was the sanctuary of Asclepius, god of medicine. Amid pine-covered hills, the magnificent **theatre** is still a venue during the Hellenic Festival, but don't miss the peaceful **Sanctuary of Asclepius**, an ancient spa and healing centre.

Go as a day trip from Nafplio (€2.90, 45 minutes, two buses Monday to Saturday).

Mycenae Μυκήνες

Although settled as early as the 6th millennium BC, **Ancient Mycenae** (☑ 27510 76585; adult/child €8/free; ⊗ 8am-6pm Apr-Oct, to 3pm Nov-Mar), pronounced mih-*kee*-nes, was at its most powerful from 1600 to 1200 BC. Mycenae's grand entrance, the **Lion Gate**, is Europe's oldest monumental sculpture.

Three buses go daily to Mycenae from Argos (€1.60, 30 minutes) and Nafplio (€2.90, one hour).

Mystras Μυστρας

Magical **Mystras** (☑ 23315 25363; adult/child €5/free; ⊗ 8.30am-7pm or 8pm Mon-Sat, to 5.30pm Sun Apr-Oct, to 3pm Nov-Mar) was once the effective capital of the Byzantine Empire. Ruins of palaces, monasteries and churches, most of them dating from between 1271 and 1460, nestle at the base of the Taÿgetos Mountains, and are surrounded by verdant olive and orange groves. Allow half a day to explore.

While only 7km from Sparta, staying in the village nearby allows you to get there early before it heats up. Enjoy exquisite views and a beautiful swimming pool at **Hotel Byzantion** (☑ 27310 83309; www.byzantionhotel.gr; s/d/tr €40/50/65; 🅿❋@☀).

Camp at **Castle View** (☑ 27310 83303; www.castleview.gr; camp sites per adult/tent/car €6/4/4, 2-person bungalow €25; ⊗ Apr-Oct; 🛜☀), about 1km before Mystras village and set in olive trees. Buses will stop outside if you ask.

Olympia Ολυμπία
POP 1000

Tucked alongside the Kladeos River, in fertile delta country, the modern town of Olympia supports the extensive ruins of the same name. The first Olympics were staged here in 776 BC, and every four years thereafter until AD 393, when Emperor Theodosius I banned them.

Ancient Olympia (☑ 26240 22517; adult/child €6/free, site & museum €9/free; ⊗ 8am-8pm Mon-Fri, to 3pm Sat & Sun, reduced hours winter) is dominated by the immense ruined **Temple of Zeus**, to whom the games were dedicated. Don't miss the statue of **Hermes of Praxiteles**, a classical-sculpture masterpiece, at the exceptional **Archaeological Museum** (adult/child €6/free; ⊗ 10am-5pm Mon, 8am-8pm Tue-Sun Apr-Oct, to 3pm Nov-Mar).

Sparkling-clean **Pension Posidon** (☑ 26240 22567; www.pensionposidon.gr; Stefanopoulou 9; s/d/tr incl breakfast €35/45/55; ❋) and quiet, spacious **Hotel Pelops** (☑ 26240 22543; www.hotelpelops.gr; Varela 2; s/d/tr incl breakfast €40/50/70; ⊜❋@☀) offer the best value in the centre. Family-run **Best Western Europa** (☑ 26240 22650; www.hoteleuropa.gr; Drouva 1; s/d/tr incl breakfast €85/110/120; 🅿❋@🛜☀) above town has sweeping vistas from room balconies and the wonderful swimming pool.

Pitch your tent in the leafy grove at **Camping Diana** (☑ 26240 22314; www.campingdiana.gr; camp sites per adult/car/tent €8/5/6; ⊗ year-round; ☀), 250m west of town.

Catch buses at the stop on the north end of town. Northbound buses go via Pyrgos (€2.30, 30 minutes), where you connect to buses for Athens, Corinth and Patra. Two buses go east from Olympia to Tripoli (€14.30, three hours) – you must reserve ahead at **KTEL Pyrgos** (☑ 26210 20600; www. ktelileias.gr). Local trains run daily to Pyrgos (€1, 30 minutes).

CENTRAL GREECE
ΚΕΝΤΡΙΚΗ ΕΛΛΑΔΑ

Central Greece's dramatic landscape of deep gorges, rugged mountains and fertile valleys is home to the magical stone pinnacle-topping monasteries of Meteora and the iconic ruins of ancient Delphi, where Alexander the Great sought advice from the Delphic oracle. Established in 1938, **Parnassos National Park** (www.en.parnassosnp.gr), to the north of Delphi, attracts naturalists, hikers (it's part of the E4 European long-distance path) and skiers.

Delphi   Δελφοί
POP 2800

Modern Delphi and its adjoining ruins hang stunningly on the slopes of Mt Parnassos overlooking the shimmering Gulf of Corinth.

According to mythology, Zeus released two eagles at opposite ends of the world and they met here, thus making Delphi the centre of the world. By the 6th century BC, **Ancient Delphi** (☑ 22650 82312; www.culture. gr; site or museum adult/child €6/free, combined €9; ☺ 8am-3pm, longer hours summer) had become the Sanctuary of Apollo. Thousands of pilgrims flocked here to consult the female oracle who sat at the mouth of a fume-emitting chasm. After sacrificing a sheep or goat, pilgrims would ask a question, and a priest would translate the oracle's response into verse. Wars, voyages and business transactions were undertaken on the strength of these prophecies.

From the entrance, take the Sacred Way up to the **Temple of Apollo**, where the oracle sat. From here the path continues to the well-preserved theatre and stadium.

Opposite the main site and down the hill some 100m, don't miss the **Sanctuary of Athena** and the much-photographed **Tholos**, a 4th-century-BC columned rotunda of Pentelic marble.

In the town centre, **Rooms Pitho** (☑ 22650 82850; www.pithohotel.gr; Vasileon Pavlou & Friderikis 40a; s/d/tr incl breakfast from €40/55/65; ❈ ☢) is friendly and quiet and **Hotel Hermes** (☑ 22650 82318; www.hermeshotel.com.gr; Vasileon Pavlou & Friderikis 27; s/d incl breakfast €45/55; ❈) has spacious rooms sporting balconies with excellent valley views. **Hotel Apollonia** (☑ 22650 82919; www. hotelapollonia.gr; Syngrou 37-39; s/d incl breakfast €75/90; ❈ @ ☢) is a bit more upmarket.

Apollon Camping (☑ 22650 82762; www. apolloncamping.gr; camp sites per person/tent €8.50/4; ℗ @ ☢ ❈) is just 2km west of town, with a restaurant, pool and minimarket.

Specialities at **Taverna Vakhos** (☑ 22650 83186; www.vakhos.com; Apollonos 31; mains €6-11; ☺ noon-midnight; ☢) include stuffed zucchini flowers and rabbit stew. Locals pack **Taverna Gargadouas** (☑ 22650 82488; Vasileon Pavlou & Friderikis; mains €7-10; ☺ noon-midnight) for grilled meats and slow-roasted lamb.

The KTEL **bus stop** (☑ 22650 82317; www. ktel-fokidas.gr; Vasileon Pavlou & Friderikis), post office and banks are all on modern Delphi's main street, Vasileon Pavlou & Friderikis. Six buses a day go to Athens Liossion Terminal B (€15.10, three hours). For Meteora/Kalambaka, take a bus to Lamia (€9.10, two hours, one daily) or Trikala (€14, 4½ hours, one daily) to transfer.

Meteora   Μετεωρα

Meteora (meh-*teh*-o-rah) should be a certified Wonder of the World with its magnificent late-14th-century monasteries perched dramatically atop enormous rocky pinnacles. Try not to miss it.

⊙ Sights

While there were once monasteries on all 24 pinnacles, only six are still occupied: **Megalou Meteoron** (Grand Meteoron; ☑ 24320 22278; admission €3; ☺ 9am-5pm Wed-Mon Apr-Oct, to 4pm Thu-Mon Nov-Mar), **Varlaam** (☑ 24320 22277; admission €3; ☺ 9am-4pm Sat-Thu Apr-Oct, closed Thu Nov-Mar), **Agiou Stefanou** (☑ 24320 22279; admission €3; ☺ 9am-1.30pm & 3.30-5.30pm Tue-Sun Apr-Oct, 9.30am-1pm & 3-5pm Nov-Mar), **Agias Triados** (Holy Trinity; ☑ 24320 22220; admission €3; ☺ 9am-5pm Fri-Wed Apr-Oct, 10am-3pm Fri-Tue Nov-Mar), **Agiou Nikolaou** (Monastery of St Nikolaou Anapafsa; ☑ 24320 22375; admission €3; ☺ 9am-3.30pm Sat-Thu Apr-Oct, to 2pm Nov-Mar) and **Agias Varvaras Rousanou** (admission

€3; ⊘9am-6pm Thu-Tue Apr-Oct, to 2pm Nov-Mar). Strict dress codes apply (no bare shoulders or knees and women must wear skirts; you can borrow a long skirt at the door). Walk the footpaths between monasteries, drive the back asphalt road, or take the bus (€1.20, 20 minutes) that departs from Kalambaka and Kastraki at 9am, and returns at 1pm (12.40pm on weekends).

Meteora's stunning rocks are also a climbing paradise. Licensed mountain guide **Lazaros Botelis** (☑69480 43655, 24320 79165; meteora.guide@gmail.gr; Kastraki) shows the way.

🛏 Sleeping & Eating

The tranquil village of Kastraki, 2km from Kalambaka, is the best base for visiting.

Doupiani House PENSION €
(☑24320 75326; www.doupianihouse.com; s/d/tr incl breakfast from €45/55/65; P✳@🛜) The delightful Doupiani House has the lot: spotless, tastefully decorated rooms, with balconies or garden access. Its location – just outside the village – provides a window to Meteora; it boasts one of the region's best panoramic views. There's breakfast on the terrace, birdsong and attentive hosts, Toula and Thanasis.

Vrachos Camping CAMPGROUND €
(☑24320 22293; www.campingmeteora.gr; camp sites per tent €7.50; ✳) A well-shaded campground on the Kalambaka–Kastraki road with excellent facilities.

Taverna Paradisos TAVERNA €
(☑24320 22723; mains €6.50-9; ⊘noon-3pm & 7-11pm) The traditional meals at roomy Paradisos will have you exclaiming *nostimo!* (delicious!) all the way through your dishes, thanks to local and high-quality ingredients and owner-chef Koula's magic touch. Excellent fried zucchini.

ℹ Getting There & Around

Local buses shuttle between Kalambaka and Kastraki (€1.20). Hourly buses go from Kalambaka's **KTEL bus station** (☑24320 22432; www.ktel-trikala.gr; Ikonomou) to the transport hub of Trikala (€2.30, 30 minutes), from where buses go to Ioannina (€12.50, three hours, two daily) and Athens (€29, five hours, six daily).

From Kalambaka **train station** (☑24320 22451; www.trainose.gr), trains run to Athens (regular/IC €18/29, 5½/4½ hours, both twice daily) and Thessaloniki (€15.20, four hours, one daily). You may need to change in Paleofarsalos.

MT OLYMPUS ΟΛΥΜΠΟΣ ΟΡΟΣ

Just as it did for the ancients, Greece's highest mountain, **Olympus** (www.olympusfd.gr), the cloud-covered lair of the Greek pantheon, fires the visitor's imagination today. The highest of Olympus' eight peaks is **Mytikas** (2917m), popular with trekkers, who use **Litohoro** (305m), 5km inland from the Athens–Thessaloniki highway, as their base. The main route up takes two days, with a stay overnight at one of the **refuges** (⊘May-Oct). Good protective clothing is essential, even in summer. **EOS Litohoro** (Greek Alpine Club; ☑23520 82444, 23520 84544; http://eoslitohorou.blogspot.com; ⊘9.30am-12.30pm & 6-8pm Mon-Sat Jun-Sep) has information.

NORTHERN GREECE
ΒΟΡΕΙΑ ΕΛΛΑΔΑ

Northern Greece is graced with magnificent mountains, thick forests, tranquil lakes and archaeological sites. It's easy to get off the beaten track and experience aspects of Greece noticeably different to other mainland areas and the islands.

Thessaloniki Θεσσαλονικη
POP 325,182
Dodge cherry sellers in the street, smell spices in the air and enjoy waterfront breezes in Thessaloniki (thess-ah-lo-*nee*-kih), also known as Salonica. The second city of Byzantium and of modern Greece boasts countless Byzantine churches, a smattering of Roman ruins, engaging museums, shopping to rival Athens, fine restaurants and a lively cafe scene and nightlife.

◉ Sights

Check out the seafront **White Tower** (Lefkos Pyrgos; ☑2310 267 832; www.lpth.gr; ⊘8.30am-3pm Tue-Sun) and wander *hammams* (Turkish baths), Ottoman and Roman sites including Galerius' **Rotunda** (☑2310 218 720; Plateia Agiou Georgiou; ⊘9am-5pm Tue-Sun) **FREE**, and churches such as the enormous, revered 5th-century **Church of Agios Dimitrios** (☑2310 270 008; Agiou Dimitriou 97; ⊘8am-10pm) with its crypt containing the relics of the city's patron saint.

Thessaloniki

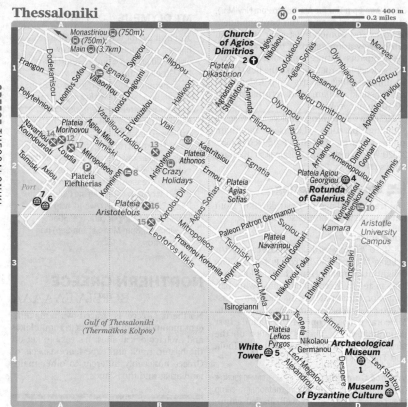

Thessaloniki

◎ Top Sights
1 Archaeological Museum D4
2 Church of Agios Dimitrios C1
3 Museum of Byzantine Culture D4
4 Rotunda of Galerius D2
5 White Tower C4

◎ Sights
6 Thessaloniki Centre of
    Contemporary Art A2
7 Thessaloniki Museum of
    Photography A2

⊨ Sleeping
8 City Hotel B2
9 Colors Rooms & Apartments A1
10 Rent Rooms Thessaloniki D2

⊗ Eating
11 Dore Zythos C4
12 Kouzina Kioupia A2
13 Modiano Market B2
14 Paparouna A2
15 To Mikraki B3
16 Turkenlis B2
17 Zythos A2

The award-winning **Museum of Byzantine Culture** (☏ 2313 306 400; www.mbp.gr; Leof Stratou 2; adult/child €4/free, with Archaeological Museum €8; ◷ 8am-8pm Apr-Oct, 9am-4pm Nov-Mar) beautifully displays splendid sculptures, mosaics, icons and other intriguing artefacts. The **Archaeological Museum** (☏ 2310 830 538; www.amth.gr; Manoli Andronikou 6; adult/child €6/free, with Museum of Byzantine Culture €8; ◷ 8am-5pm Apr-Oct, 9am-4pm Nov-Mar) showcases prehistoric, ancient Macedonian and Hellenistic finds.

The compelling **Thessaloniki Centre of Contemporary Art** (☏ 2310 593 270; www.cact.

gr; Warehouse B1; adult/child €3/1.50; ⊙10am-4pm Tue-Sun, hours vary) and hip **Thessaloniki Museum of Photography** (☑2310 566 716; www.thmphoto.gr; Warehouse A, Port; adult/child €2/1; ⊙11am-7pm Tue-Sun), beside the port, are worth a look.

🛏 Sleeping

Colors Rooms & Apartments APARTMENT €
(☑2310 502 280; www.colors.com.gr; Valaoritou 21; s/d/ste €45/55/65; ❄️🛜) Valaoritou party people, you finally have somewhere nice to crash. These 15 sparkling-new apartments rival more expensive hotel rooms, with cool lighting, minimalist decor and mod cons including iPhone docks with radio. Four of the apartments are self-catering. A pastry breakfast (€5 extra) is brought to your room, or you can eat in the 1st-floor reception/coffee area.

Rent Rooms Thessaloniki HOSTEL €
(☑2310 204 080; www.rentrooms-thessaloniki. com; Konstantinou Melenikou 9, near Kamara; dm/s/d/tr/q incl breakfast €19/38/49/67/82; ❄️🛜) This well-kept Kamara-area hostel has a relaxing back-garden cafe with Rotunda views, where breakfast and drinks are served. Some dorms and rooms have mini kitchens; all have bathrooms. The friendly staff provides local info and can assist with bike rental.

City Hotel BUSINESS HOTEL €€
(☑2310 269 421; www.cityhotel.gr; Komninon 11; d/tr/ste incl breakfast from €70/90/110; ❄️@🛜) This sleek four-star place near Plateia Eleftherias, east of Ladadika, has handsome rooms (some wheelchair-friendly) with subdued elegance. There's a big American-style breakfast and spa centre.

✗ Eating & Drinking

Thessaloniki is a great food town. Tavernas dot Plateia Athonos and cafes pack Leoforos Nikis, and the Ladadika quarter is tops for restaurants and bars. Head to **Modiano Market** (Vassiliou Irakliou or Ermo; ⊙7am-6pm) for fresh produce. Thessaloniki is known for its sweets: shop around!

★**Paparouna** MODERN GREEK €
(☑2310 510 852; www.paparouna.com; cnr Pangaiou 4 & Doxis; mains €5-11; ⊙10am-2am) The ever-popular Paparouna spills onto the pavement in Ladadika, sporting vibrant colours, checkerboard floor, cheerful staff and an intriguing menu that changes seasonally. Charismatic chef and owner Antonis Ladas occasionally plays Latin, soul and jazz inside.

★**Kouzina Kioupia** TAVERNA €
(☑2310 553 239; www.kouzina-kioupia.gr; Plateia Morihovou 3-5; mains €4-7; ⊙1pm-1am Mon-Sat, to 6pm Sun) Bright, friendly and spilling onto the plaza, this welcoming taverna fills with happy local families and tables full of friends. Straightforward taverna dishes are served with flare, and a good time is had by all. Occasional live music.

★**To Mikraki** TAVERNA €
(☑2310 270 517; Proxenou Koromila 2; mains €4-7.50; ⊙12.30-6pm Mon-Sat) This friendly storefront in a bastion of chic cafes offers top home-cooked Greek fare with smiling familiarity. A true neighbourhood hang-out. Look behind the counter to see the day's specials.

Zythos TAVERNA €
(Katouni 5; mains €8-12; ⊙noon-3pm & 7pm-midnight) Popular with locals, this excellent taverna with friendly staff serves up delicious standards, interesting regional specialities, good wines by the glass and beers on tap. Its second outlet is **Dore Zythos** (☑2310 279 010; Tsirogianni 7; mains €10-18; ⊙lunch & dinner), near the White Tower.

Turkenlis BAKERY €
(Aristotelous 4; sweets €1-3; ⊙8am-8pm) Renowned for *tzoureki* (sweet bread) and a mind-boggling array of sweet-scented confections.

ℹ Information

Check www.enjoythessaloniki.com for current events.
Tourist Police (☑2310 554 871; 5th fl, Dodekanisou 4; ⊙7.30am-11pm)

ℹ Getting There & Away

AIR
Makedonia International Airport (SKG; ☑2310 473 212; www.thessalonikiairport.com) is 16km southeast of the centre and served by local bus 78 (€2, one hour, from 5am to 10pm with a few night buses; www.oasth.gr). Taxis cost €25 or more (20 minutes). Olympic Air, Aegean Airlines and Astra Airlines (p378) fly throughout Greece; many airlines fly internationally.

BOAT
Weekly ferries go to, among others, Limnos (€20, eight hours), Lesvos (€30, 14 hours), Chios (€32, 19 hours) and Samos (€40, 20 hours). Check port area travel agencies such as **Karacharisis Travel & Shipping Agency** (☑2310 513 005; b_karachari@tincewind_techpath.gr; Navarhou

WORTH A TRIP

ZAGOROHORIA & VIKOS GORGE ΤΑ ΖΑΓΟΡΟΧΩΡΙΑ & ΧΑΡΑΔΡΑ ΤΟΥ ΒΙΚΟΥ

Try not to miss the spectacular **Zagori region**, with its deep gorges, abundant wildlife, dense forests and snow-capped mountains. Some 46 charming villages, famous for their grey-slate architecture, and known collectively as the Zagorohoria, are sprinkled across a large expanse of the Pindos Mountains north of Ioannina. These beautifully restored gems were once only connected by stone paths and arching footbridges, but paved roads now wind between them. Get information on walks from Ioannina's **EOS** (Greek Alpine Club; ☑ 26510 22138; www.orivatikos.gr; Smyrnis 15; ☺ hours vary) office.

Monodendri is a popular departure point for treks through dramatic 12km-long, 900m-deep Vikos Gorge, with its sheer limestone walls. Exquisite inns with attached tavernas abound in remote (but popular) twin villages **Megalo Papingo** and **Mikro Papingo**. It's best to explore by rental car from Ioannina.

Koundourioti 8; ☺ 8am-8.30pm) and www.openseas.gr.

BUS

The **main KTEL bus station** (☑ 2310 595 408; www.ktelmacedonia.gr; Giannitson 244), 3.7km west of the centre, services Athens (€42, 6¼ hours, 11 daily), Ioannina (€32, 4¾ hours, six daily) and other destinations. For Athens *only* you can also get on buses near the train station at **Monastiriou Bus Station** (☑ 2310 500 111; Monastiriou 69). Buses to the Halkidiki Peninsula leave from the **Halkidiki bus terminal** (☑ 2310 316 555; www.ktel-chalkidikis.gr; Karakasi 68).

KTEL serves Sofia, and small bus companies, across from the courthouse (Dikastirion), serve international destinations including Skopje, Sofia and Bucharest. Try **Simeonidis Tours** (☑ 2310 540 970; www.simeonidistours.gr; 26 Oktovriou 14; ☺ 9am-9pm Mon-Fri, to 2pm Sat). **Crazy Holidays** (☑ 2310 241 545; www.crazy-holidays.gr; Aristotelous 10) also serves İstanbul.

TRAIN

The **train station** (☑ 2310 599 421; www.trainose.gr; Monastiriou) serves Athens (regular/IC €36/48, 6¾/5½ hours, seven/10 daily) and other domestic destinations. International trains go to Skopje and Sofia, and beyond.

CYCLADES   ΚΥΚΛΑΔΕΣ

The Cyclades (kih-*klah*-dez) are Greek islands to dream about. Named after the rough *kyklos* (circle) they form around the island of Delos, they are rugged outcrops of rock in the azure Aegean, speckled with white cubist buildings and blue-domed Byzantine churches. Throw in sun-blasted golden beaches, more than a dash of hedonism and a fascinating culture, and it's easy to see why many find the Cyclades irresistible.

Mykonos   Μύκονος

POP 10,190

Mykonos is the great glamour island of the Cyclades and happily flaunts its sizzling style and reputation. The high-season mix of good-time holidaymakers, cruise-ship crowds (which can reach 15,000 a day) and posturing fashionistas throngs through Mykonos Town, a traditional Cycladic maze, delighting in its authentic cubist charms and its pricey cafe-bar-shopping scene. It remains a mecca for gay travellers and the well bankrolled, but can get super-packed in high season.

☉ Sights

The island's most popular beaches, thronged in summer, are on the southern coast. **Platys Gialos** has wall-to-wall sun lounges, while nudity is not uncommon at **Paradise Beach**, **Super Paradise**, **Elia** and more secluded **Agrari**.

Hora   TOWN

(Mykonos Town) Mykonos Town is a captivating labyrinth that's home to chic boutiques and whiter-than-white houses decked with bougainvillea and geraniums, plus a handful of small museums and photogenic churches. **Little Venice**, where the sea laps up to the edge of the restaurants and bars, and Mykonos' famous hilltop **windmills** should be high on the must-see list.

🛏 Sleeping

Book well ahead in high season. Prices plummet outside of July and August, and most hotels close in winter.

Mykonos has two camping areas, both on the south coast – Paradise Beach and **Mykonos Camping** (☑ 22890 25915; www.mycamp.gr; Paraga Beach; camp sites per adult/child/tent €10/5/10, dm €20, bungalow per person €15-30; P🗑🛜🏊). Minibuses from both meet the ferries and buses go regularly into town.

Paradise Beach Camping   CAMPGROUND, APARTMENT €
(☑ 22890 22852; www.paradisemykonos.com; camp sites per person/tent €10/5; @🛜🏊) There are lots of options here, including camping, beach cabins and apartments, as well as bars, a swimming pool, games etc. It is skin-to-skin mayhem in summer with a real party atmosphere.

★ Carbonaki Hotel   BOUTIQUE HOTEL €€
(☑ 22890 24124; www.carbonaki.gr; 23 Panahrantou, Hora; s/d/tr/q from €120/142/180/206; 🗑🛜) This family-run boutique hotel in central Mykonos is a delightful oasis with bright, comfortable rooms, relaxing public balconies and sunny central courtyards. Chill out in the jacuzzi and small sauna. Some wheelchair access and great low-season discounts.

Manto Hotel   HOTEL €€
(☑ 22890 22330; www.manto-mykonos.gr; Evagelistrias 1, Hora; s/d incl breakfast from €60/85; ☺year-round; 🗑🛜) Buried in the heart of Hora, cheerful Manto is an excellent affordable option (for Mykonos), with well-kept colourful rooms, some with balconies, an inviting breakfast room and friendly owners.

Hotel Philippi   PENSION €€
(☑ 22890 22294; www.philippihotel.com; Kalogera 25, Hora; s/d from €80/100; ☺Apr-Oct; 🗑🛜) A verdant courtyard-garden makes this a welcome choice in the heart of Hora. Bright, clean rooms open onto a railed verandah overlooking the garden.

Fresh Hotel   BOUTIQUE HOTEL €€€
(☑ 22890 24670; www.hotelfreshmykonos.com; Kalogera 31, Hora; d incl breakfast from €160; ☺mid-May–Oct; 🗑@🛜) In the heart of town with a leafy central garden, stylish breakfast room, bar and jacuzzi, rooms have wood floors and minimalist slate-and-white decor.

🍴 Eating

High prices don't necessarily reflect high quality in Mykonos Town. Cafes line the waterfront; you'll find good food and coffee drinks at **Kadena** (☑ 22890 29290; Hora; mains €10-20; ☺8am-late; 🛜). Souvlaki shops dot Enoplon Dynameon and Fabrika Sq (Plateia Yialos). Most places stay open late during high season.

Suisse Cafe   CAFE €
(☑ 22890 27462; Matoyani, Hora; snacks €4-6; ☺9am-late; 🛜) Top-notch breakfasts, crêpes and people-watching.

Nautilus   GREEK €€
(☑ 22890 27100; www.nautilus-mykonos.gr; Kalogera 6, Hora; mains €11-16; ☺7pm-1am Mar-Nov) The whitewashed terrace spills out onto the street and Greek fusion dishes incorporate top ingredients.

To Maereio   GREEK $$
(☑ 22890 28825; Kalogera 16, Hora; dishes €14-21; ☺noon-3pm & 7pm-midnight) A small but

---

ℹ CYCLADIC CONNECTIONS

Once high season kicks in, a batch of companies run daily catamarans and ferries up and down the Cyclades. You can start from Piraeus (for Athens), Iraklio in Crete, or just about anywhere in-between.

For example, one boat heads south daily from Piraeus to Paros, Naxos, Ios and Santorini, returning along the same route. There's also a daily run from Piraeus to Syros, Tinos and Mykonos. Occasional ferries also move east–west, connecting islands laterally.

Heading north from Iraklio, another catamaran runs to Santorini, Ios, Paros, Mykonos and return.

It can all get a bit much to comprehend (the schedules are constantly changing!), so check www.openseas.gr or www.gtp.gr. Out of season, boats stop running, or go on very reduced schedules. Sometimes flying ends up being easier.

Mykonos

Tinos; Syros;
Rafina; Piraeus;
Thessaloniki

Ikaria; Samos;
Patmos

5 km
2.5 miles

AEGEAN
SEA

Dragonisi

Cape
Evros

Cape
Goni

Cape
Kalafatis

Lia Beach
Kalafatis Beach

Merchias
Bay

Profitis Ilias
Anomeritis
(351m)

Fokos
Beach

Cape
Mavros

Mersini
Bay

Mersini
Beach

Kalo
Livadi
Beach

Cape
Mavrokefalas

Ano Mera

Elia
Elia
Beach

Moni Panagias
Tourlianis

Agrari
Beach

Panormos
Bay

Agios Sostis
Beach

Panormos
Beach

Ftelia
Beach

Lake
Marathi

275m

Super
Paradise
Beach

Paradise
Beach

Marathi

Paraga
Beach

372m

Tourlos

Vothonas

Platys
Gialos

Psarou

Platys
Gialos Beach

New Port

Tourlos
Beach

Old Port

Hora
(Mykonos Town)

Vrissi

Psarou
Beach

Cape
Armenistis

Houlakia
Beach

Agios
Stefanos

Malaliamos
Beach

Agios Stefanos
Beach

Ornos

Nea
Mykonos

Cape
Alogomandra

Korfos

Kapari

Agios
Ioannis
Beach

Kapari
Beach

Naxos; Paros; Iraklio;
Ios; Santorini

Excursion Boat

Delos

DELOS   ΔΗΛΟΣ

Southwest of Mykonos, the island of **Delos** (22890 22259; museum & sites adult/child €5/free; ⊙8am-8pm Apr-Oct, to 3pm Nov-Mar), a Unesco World Heritage Site, is the Cyclades' archaeological jewel. Go! The mythical birthplace of twins Apollo and Artemis, splendid Ancient Delos was a shrine-turned-sacred-treasury and commercial centre. It was inhabited from the 3rd millennium BC and reached its apex of power around the 5th century BC.

Ruins include the **Sanctuary of Apollo**, containing temples dedicated to him, and the famous **Terrace of the Lions**, guarding the sacred area (the originals are in the island's museum). The **Sacred Lake** (dry since 1925) is where Leto gave birth to Apollo and Artemis, while the **Theatre Quarter** is where private houses with magnificent mosaics were built around the Theatre of Delos. The climb up Mt Kynthos (113m) is a highlight.

Take a sunhat, sunscreen and sturdy footwear. The island's cafeteria sells food and drinks. Staying overnight is forbidden.

Boats from Mykonos to Delos (€18 return, 30 minutes) go between 9am and 5pm in summer, and return between noon and 8pm. In Hora (Mykonos Town) buy tickets at the old wharf kiosk or at **Delia Travel** (22890 22322; www.mykonos-delia.com; Akti Kambani), **Sea & Sky** (22890 22853; sea-sky@otenet.gr; Akti Kambani) or Mykonos Accommodation Centre. Sometimes in summer boats go from Tinos and Naxos.

GREECE MYKONOS

selective menu of Mykonian favourites keeps this cosy place popular.

M-Eating   MEDITERRANEAN €€€
(22890 78550; www.m-eating.gr; Kalogera 10, Hora; mains €15-26; ⊙7pm-midnight) Attentive service and relaxed luxury are the hallmarks of this creative restaurant specialising in fresh Greek products prepared with flair. Sample anything from tenderloin stuffed with Metsovo cheese to shrimp ravioli with crayfish sauce. Don't miss the Mykonian honey pie, or for beer lovers the Volcano microbrew from Santorini.

Drinking & Entertainment

Folks come to Mykonos to party. Each major beach has at least one beach bar that gets going during the day. Night action in town starts around 11pm and warms up by 1am, and revellers often relocate from Mykonos Town to **Cavo Paradiso** (22890 27205; www.cavoparadiso.gr; Paradise Beach) in the wee hours. Hora offers an action-packed bar hop: from cool sunset cocktails in Little Venice to sweaty trance dancing. Wherever you go, bring a bankroll (cover alone runs around €20) – the high life doesn't come cheap. Long feted as a gay travel destination, there are many gay-centric clubs and hang outs.

ℹ Information

Mykonos Accommodation Centre (22890 23408; www.mykonos-accommodation.com;

1st fl, Enoplon Dynameon 10, Hora) Very helpful for all things Mykonos (accommodation, guided tours, island info), including gay-related aspects. The website is loaded.

ℹ Getting There & Around

AIR

Mykonos Airport (JMK; 22890 22490) Daily flights connect Mykonos Airport to Athens, plus a growing number of international flights wing directly in from May to September. The airport is 3km southeast of the town centre; €1.60 by bus from the southern bus station, €9 by taxi.

BOAT

Year-round ferries serve mainland ports Piraeus (€35, 4¾ hours, one or two daily) and Rafina (sometimes quicker if you are coming directly from Athens airport), and nearby islands, Tinos and Andros. In the high season, Mykonos is well connected with all neighbouring islands, including Paros and Santorini. Hora is loaded with ticket agents.

Mykonos has two ferry quays: the Old Port, 400m north of town, where some conventional ferries and smaller fast ferries dock, and the New Port, 2km north of town, where the bigger fast ferries and some conventional ferries dock. When buying outgoing tickets, double-check which quay your ferry leaves from.

Local Boats

In summer, *caiques* (small fishing boats) from Mykonos Town and Platys Gialos putter to Paradise, Super Paradise, Agrari and Elia Beaches.

BUS

The northern bus station is near the Old Port. It serves Agios Stefanos, Elia, Kalafatis and Ano Mera. The southern bus station, on Fabrika Sq a 300m walk up from the windmills, serves the airport, Agios Ioannis, Psarou, Platys Gialos and Paradise Beach. There's also a pick-up point near the New Port.

CAR & TAXI

Car hire starts at €45 per day in high season. Scooters/quads are €20/40. Avis and Sixt are among agencies at the airport.

Taxi (☑ 22400 23700, airport 22400 22400)

Naxos   Ναξος

POP 12,089

The largest of the Cyclades islands, beautiful, raw Naxos could probably survive without tourism. Green and fertile, with vast central mountains, Naxos produces olives, grapes, figs, citrus, corn and potatoes. Explore its fascinating main town, excellent beaches, remote villages and striking interior.

Naxos Town (Hora), on the west coast, is the island's capital and port.

◉ Sights

★ **Kastro**   NEIGHBOURHOOD

(Naxos Town) Behind the waterfront, get lost in the narrow alleyways scrambling up to the spectacular hilltop 13th-century *kastro*, where the Venetian Catholics lived. You'll get super views, and there's a well-stocked **archaeological museum** (☑ 22850 22725; adult/child €3/free; ⊗ 8am-3pm Tue-Sun).

★ **Temple of Apollo**   ARCHAEOLOGICAL SITE

(The Potara) **FREE** From Naxos Town harbour, a causeway leads to Palatia Islet and the striking, unfinished Temple of Apollo, Naxos' most famous landmark. Simply two marble columns with a crowning lintel, it makes an arresting sight, and people gather at sunset for views back to Naxos' whitewashed houses and 13th-century *kastro* on the hilltop.

GREEK HISTORY IN A NUTSHELL

With its strategic position at the crossroads of Europe and Asia, Greece has endured a vibrant and turbulent history. During the Bronze Age (3000–1200 BC in Greece), the advanced Cycladic, Minoan and Mycenaean civilisations flourished. The Mycenaeans were swept aside in the 12th century BC by the warrior-like Dorians, who introduced Greece to the Iron Age.

By 800 BC, when Homer's *Odyssey* and *Iliad* were first written down, Greece was undergoing a cultural and military revival with the evolution of the city states, the most powerful of which were Athens and Sparta, and the development of democracy. The unified Greeks repelled the Persians twice, which was followed by an era of unparalleled growth and prosperity known as the Classical (or Golden) Age.

The Golden Age

During this period, Pericles commissioned the Parthenon, Sophocles wrote *Oedipus the King* and Socrates taught young Athenians to think. The era ended with the Peloponnesian War (431–404 BC), when the militaristic Spartans defeated the Athenians. They failed to notice the expansion of Macedonia under King Philip II, who conquered the war-weary city states.

Philip's son, Alexander the Great, marched triumphantly into Asia Minor, Egypt, Persia and parts of what are now Afghanistan and India. In 323 BC he met an untimely death at the age of 33, and his generals divided his empire between themselves.

Roman Rule & the Byzantine Empire

Roman incursions into Greece began in 205 BC. By 146 BC Greece and Macedonia had become Roman provinces. In the centuries that followed, Venetians, Franks, Normans, Slavs, Persians, Arabs and, finally, Turks, took turns chipping away at the Byzantine Empire.

The Ottoman Empire & Independence

After the end of the Byzantine Empire in 1453, when Constantinople fell to the Turks, most of Greece became part of the Ottoman Empire. The Greeks fought the War of Independence from 1821 to 1832, and in 1827 Ioannis Kapodistrias was elected the first Greek president.

DON'T MISS

KITRON-TASTING IN HALKI

The historic village of **Halki** is a top spot to try *kitron*, a liqueur unique to Naxos. While the exact recipe is top secret, visitors can taste it and stock up on supplies at **Vallindras Distillery** (☑22850 31220; ⊙10am-10pm Jul & Aug, to 6pm May, Jun, Sep & Oct) in Halki's main square. There are free tours of the old distillery's atmospheric rooms, which contain ancient jars and copper stills. *Kitron* tastings round off the trip.

★ **Temple of Demeter**   TEMPLE
(Dimitra's Temple; ☑22850 22725; ⊙8.30am-3pm Tue-Sun) FREE Surrounded by mountains, and gleaming in a gorgeous verdant valley sweeping to the sea, the impressive Temple of Demeter remains remarkably powerful. The ruins and reconstructions are not large, but they are historically fascinating, and the location is unparalleled – it's clear that this is a place for the worship of the goddess of the harvest. The site museum holds additional reconstructions of temple features. Signs point the way from the village of **Sangri** about 1.5km south to the site.

◉ Beaches

The popular beach of **Agios Georgios** is just a 10-minute walk south from the main waterfront. **Agia Anna Beach**, 6km from town, and **Plaka Beach** are lined with accommodation and packed in summer. Beyond, wonderful sandy beaches continue as far south as **Pyrgaki Beach**.

◉ Villages

A hire car or scooter will help reveal Naxos' dramatic and rugged landscape. The **Tragaea** region has tranquil villages, churches atop rocky crags and huge olive groves. Between Melanes and Kinidaros are the island's famous **marble quarries**. You'll find two ancient abandoned **kouros** (youth) statues, signposted a short walk from the road. Little **Apiranthos** settlement, perches on the slopes of **Mt Zeus** (1004m), the highest peak in the Cyclades, and has a few intermittently open **museums**. The historic village of **Halki**, one-time centre of Naxian commerce, is well worth a visit.

Lovely waterside **Apollonas** near Naxos' northern tip has a **beach**, taverna and another mysterious 10.5m **kouros** from the 7th century BC, abandoned and unfinished in an ancient marble quarry.

🛏 Sleeping

Nikos Verikokos Studios   HOTEL €
(☑22850 22025; www.nikos-verikokos.com; Naxos Town; s/d/tr €40/50/60; ⊙year-round; ❊☎) Friendly Nikos maintains immaculate rooms in the heart of the old town. Some have balconies and sea views, most have little kitchenettes. Offers port pick-up with pre-arrangement.

Camping Maragas   CAMPGROUND €
(☑22850 42552; www.maragascamping.gr; Agia Anna Beach; camp sites €9, d/studio from €40/60) South of Naxos Town.

Hotel Glaros   BOUTIQUE HOTEL €€
(☑22850 23101; www.hotelglaros.com; Agios Georgios Beach; d €115-125, ste from €150; ⊙Apr-Oct; ❊@☎) Edgy yet homey, simple yet plush, this well-run and immaculate hotel has a seaside feel with light blues and whites and handpainted wooden furnishings. Service is efficient and thoughtful and the beach is only a few steps away. Breakfast is €7.

🍴 Eating & Drinking

Hora's waterfront is lined with eating and drinking establishments. Head into Market St in the Old Town, just down from the ferry quay, to find quality tavernas. South, only a few minutes' walk away, Main Sq is home to other excellent eateries, some of which stay open year-round.

Meze 2   SEAFOOD €
(☑22850 26401; Harbour, Naxos Town; mains €6-13; ⊙noon-midnight Apr-Oct) It would be easy to dismiss this waterfront restaurant as a tourist trap, but don't. Its Cretan and Naxian menu and fantastic service make it stand out from the bunch. The seafood is superb; try stuffed squid, grilled sardines, fisherman's *saganaki* (seafood baked with tomato sauce and feta) or mussels in ouzo and garlic. The salads are creative and filling, particularly the Naxian potato salad. Yum!

L'Osteria   ITALIAN €€
(☑22850 24080; Naxos Town; mains €10-15; ⊙7pm-midnight) This authentic Italian

eatery is tucked in a small alley uphill from the harbour and beneath the *kastro* walls. Plunk yourself down in the relaxed courtyard and prepare to be gastronomically wowed. The menu changes daily with dishes like salmon lasagne and the ravioli is homemade. Need we say more?

ℹ Information

There's no official tourist information office. Try the website www.naxos-greece.net for more information.

Zas Travel (☑ 22850 23330; www.zastravel.com; Harbour, Naxos Town; ☺9am-9pm) Sells ferry tickets and organises accommodation, tours and car hire. Reduced hours in winter.

ℹ Getting There & Around

AIR

Naxos Airport (JNX) serves Athens daily. The airport is 3km south of town; there are no buses – a taxi costs €15, or arrange hotel pick-up.

BOAT

There are myriad high-season daily ferry and hydrofoil connections to most Cycladic islands and Crete, plus Piraeus ferries (€31, five hours) and catamarans (€48, 3¾ hours). Reduced services in winter.

BUS

Buses travel to most villages regularly in high season from in front of the **bus information office** (☑ 22850 22291; www.naxosdestinations.com; Harbour) on the port. Buy tickets at the office or its ticket machine.

CAR & MOTORCYCLE

Having your own wheels is a good idea for exploring Naxos. Car (€4 to€65) and motorcycle (€25 to €30) rentals line Hora's port and main streets.

Santorini (Thira)
Σαντορινη (Θηρα)

POP 13,500

Stunning Santorini may well have conquered a corner of your imagination before you've even set eyes on it. The startling sight of the submerged caldera almost encircled by sheer lava-layered cliffs – topped off by clifftop towns that look like a dusting of icing sugar – will grab your attention and not let it go. If you turn up in high season, though, be prepared for relentless crowds and commercialism – Santorini survives on tourism.

◉ Sights & Activities

★ Fira
VILLAGE

Santorini's vibrant main town with its snaking narrow streets full of shops and restaurants perches on top of the caldera. The stunning caldera views from Fira and its neighbouring hamlet Firostefani are matched only by tiny Oia.

Museum of Prehistoric Thira MUSEUM
(☑ 22860 23217; Mitropoleos, Fira; admission €3; ☺8.30am-3pm Tue-Sun) On the southern edge of Fira, this museum houses extraordinary finds excavated from Akrotiri and is all the more impressive when you realise just how old they are. Most impressive is the glowing gold ibex figurine, dating from the 17th century BC and in amazingly mint condition. Also look for fossilised olive tree leaves from within the caldera from 60,000 BC.

★ Oia
VILLAGE

At the north of the island, the postcard-perfect village of Oia (ee-ah), famed for its sunsets, is less hectic than Fira and a must-visit. Its caldera-facing tavernas are superb spots for a meal. A path from Fira to Oia along the top of the caldera takes three to four hours to walk; otherwise take a taxi or bus. Beat the crowds in the early morning or late evening.

★ Ancient Akrotiri
ARCHAEOLOGICAL SITE
(☑ 22860 81366; adult/child €5/free; ☺8am-3pm Tue-Sun) In 1967, excavations began at the site of Akrotiri. What they uncovered was phenomenal: an ancient Minoan city buried deep beneath volcanic ash from the catastrophic eruption of 1613 BC. Today, the site retains a strong sense of place and reverent awe. Housed within a cool, protective structure, wooden walkways allow you to pass through various parts of the city.

★ Santo Wines
WINERY
(☑ 22860 22596; www.santowines.gr; Pyrgos; ☺10am-7pm) Santorini's lauded wines are its crisp, clear dry whites, such as the delectable *asyrtiko*, and the amber-coloured, unfortified dessert wine Vinsanto. At Santo Wines you can sample a range of wines and browse local products including fava beans, tomatoes, capers and preserves.

◔ Around the Island

Santorini's known for its multihued beaches. The black-sand beaches of Perissa,

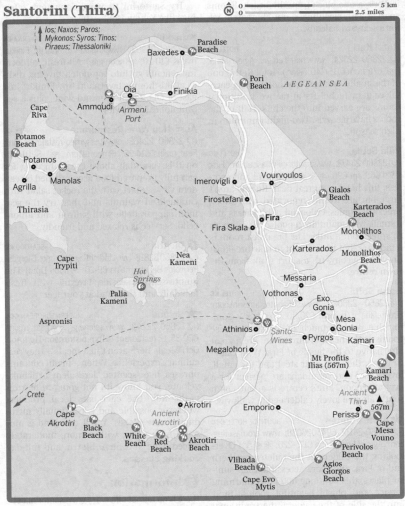

Map label: Santorini (Thira)

Scale: 0 — 5 km / 0 — 2.5 miles

Ios; Naxos; Paros; Mykonos; Syros; Tinos; Piraeus; Thessaloniki

AEGEAN SEA

Paradise Beach · Baxedes · Pori Beach · Oia · Finikia · Ammoudi · Armeni Port · Cape Riva · Potamos Beach · Potamos · Manolas · Agrilla · Thirasia · Imerovigli · Vourvoulos · Firostefani · Gialos Beach · Karterados Beach · Fira · Monolithos · Fira Skala · Karterados · Monolithos Beach · Cape Trypiti · Nea Kameni · Hot Springs · Messaria · Palia Kameni · Vothonas · Exo Gonia · Aspronisi · Mesa Gonia · Athinios · Santo Wines · Pyrgos · Kamari · Megalohori · Mt Profitis Ilias (567m) · Kamari Beach · Crete · Ancient Thira 567m · Cape Akrotiri · Akrotiri · Ancient Akrotiri · Emporio · Perissa · Cape Mesa Vouno · Black Beach · White Beach · Red Beach · Akrotiri Beach · Perivolos Beach · Vlihada Beach · Agios Giorgos Beach · Cape Evo Mytis

Perivolos, **Agios Giorgos** and **Kamari** sizzle – beach mats are essential. **Red Beach**, near Ancient Akrotiri, has impressive red cliffs and smooth, hand-sized pebbles submerged under clear water.

On a mountain between Perissa and Kamari are the atmospheric ruins of **Ancient Thira** (admission €4; ⏱8am-2.30pm Tue-Sun), first settled in the 9th century BC.

Of the volcanic islets, only **Thirasia** is inhabited. Visitors can clamber over lava on **Nea Kameni** then swim in warm springs in the sea at **Palia Kameni**. Many excursions get you there; small boats are at Fira Skala port.

🛏 Sleeping

Santorini's sleeping options are exorbitant in high season, especially anywhere with a caldera view. Many hotels offer free port and airport transfers. Check www.airbnb.com for deals.

Stelios Place   HOTEL €
(☏22860 81860; www.steliosplace.com; Perissa; d/tr/q €55/70/90; 🅿❄🛜🏊) This hotel has a great position set back from the main drag

in Perissa one block from the beach. Rooms sparkle with cleanliness, not character. Ask for a seaward balcony.

Hotel Keti
HOTEL €€

(☑ 22860 22324; www.hotelketi.gr; Agiou Mina, Fira; d/tr from €115/140; ❄️ 🛜) Hotel Keti is one of the smaller 'sunset view' hotels in a peaceful caldera niche. Its attractive traditional rooms are carved into the cliffs. Half of the rooms have jacuzzis. Two-night minimum in high season.

Villa Soula
HOTEL €€

(☑ 22860 23473; www.santorini-villasoula.gr; Fira; s & d €68, apt €95; ❄️ 🛜 🏊) Cheerful and spotless, this hotel is a great deal. Rooms aren't large but are freshly renovated with small, breezy balconies. Colourful public areas and a small, well-maintained pool give you room to spread out a little. The breakfast room is a tad dark, but you can opt to take breakfast on your balcony. It's a short walk from the town centre.

Hotel Sofia
HOTEL €€

(☑ 22860 22802; www.sofiahotelsantorini.com; Firostefani; d/tr from €70/105; ❄️ 🛜 🏊) Comfortable, with a touch of character, these rooms at the heart of Firostefani are a great alternative to the bustle of Fira. With caldera views, they're a near steal and the small, lovely pool and verandahs are perfect for a lazy afternoon. Fira's centre is about 1.5km south, along a lovely caldera-edge walkway.

★ Aroma Suites
BOUTIQUE HOTEL €€€

(☑ 22860 24112, 6945026038; www.aromasuites. com; Agiou Mina, Fira; d €175-220; ❄️ @ 🛜) Overlooking the caldera at the quieter southern end of Fira, and more accessible than similar places, this boutique hotel has charming service and plush, beautiful rooms. Built into the side of the caldera, the traditional interiors are made all the more lovely with strong colour touches, canopied beds, local art, books and stereos. Balconies offer a feeling of complete seclusion.

✗ Eating & Drinking

Overpriced, indifferent food geared towards tourists is still an unfortunate feature of summertime Fira. Prices tend to double at spots with caldera views. Cheaper eateries cluster around Fira's square. Popular bars and clubs line Erythrou Stavrou in Fira. Many diners head to Oia, legendary for its superb sunsets. Good-value tavernas line the waterfronts at Kamari and Perissa.

Try Santorini Brewing Company's offerings like Yellow Donkey beer.

Krinaki
TAVERNA €€

(☑ 22860 71993; www.krinaki-santorini.gr; Finikia; mains €10-20; ⊙ noon-late) All-fresh, all-local ingredients go into top-notch taverna dishes at this homey taverna in tiny Finikia, just east of Oia. Local beer and wine, plus a sea (but not caldera) view.

Assyrtico Wine Restaurant
GREEK €€

(☑ 22860 22463; www.assyrtico-restaurant.com; Fira; mains €14-25; ⊙ noon-11pm; 🛜) Settle in on this verandah above the main drag for carefully prepared food accompanied by caldera views. Start with the rocket salad with caramelised walnuts and then try the seafood pappardelle with saffron and limoncello. Service is relaxed and friendly.

Ta Dichtia
SEAFOOD €€

(☑ 22860 82818; www.tadichtia.com; Agios Giorgos-Perivolos Beach; mains €9-20; ⊙ noon-11pm) The quintessential seaside taverna with fresh fish daily and soft sand at your feet.

★ Selene
MODERN EUROPEAN €€€

(☑ 22860 22249; www.selene.gr; Pyrgos; mains €20-35; ⊙ restaurant 7-11pm, bistro noon-11pm Apr-Oct) Meals here aren't just meals – they're a culinary experience. When a menu contains phrases like 'scented Jerusalem artichoke velouté', you know it's not going to be run-of-the-mill. The chef uses local products wherever possible and is continually introducing new dishes. You'll now find a museum here along with a more moderately priced wine and meze **bistro**, and full-day **cooking classes**.

🛈 Information

There is no tourist office. Try www.santorini.net for more information.

Dakoutros Travel (☑ 22860 22958; www. dakoutrostravel.gr; Fira; ⊙ 8.30am-10pm) On the main street, just before Plateia Theotokopoulou.

🛈 Getting There & Around

AIR
Santorini Airport (JTR; ☑ 22860 28405; www. santoriniairport.com) Santorini Airport has daily flights to Athens, a growing number of other domestic destinations and direct international flights from throughout Europe. The airport is 5km southeast of Fira; frequent buses (€1.50) and taxis (€15) will get you there.

BOAT

The new Port of Athinios, where most ferries dock, is 10km south of Fira by road. Ferries are met by buses and taxis. The old port of Fira Skala, used by cruise ships and excursion boats, is directly below Fira and accessed by cable car (adult/child €4/2 one way), donkey (€5, up only) or by foot (588 steps).

There are daily ferries (€33.50, nine hours) and fast boats (€60, 5¼ hours) to Piraeus; daily connections in summer to Mykonos, Ios, Naxos, Paros and Iraklio; and ferries to the smaller islands in the Cyclades as well as Iraklio (Crete).

BUS

The bus station and **taxi stand** (☑22860 22555, 22860 23951) are just south of Fira's main square, Plateia Theotokopoulou. Buses go frequently to Oia, Kamari, Perissa and Akrotiri. Athinios Port buses (€2.20, 30 minutes) usually leave Fira, Kamari and Perissa one to 1½ hours before ferry departures.

CAR & MOTORCYCLE

A car (from €40 per day) or scooter is good for getting out of town. Outlets abound.

CRETE   KPHTH

POP 550,000

Crete is Greece's largest, most southerly island and its size, distance and independent history give it the feel of a different country. With its dramatic landscape, myriad mountain villages, unique cultural identity and some of the best food in Greece, Crete is a delight to explore.

The island is split by a dramatic chain of mountains running east to west. Major towns are on the more hospitable northern coast, while most of the southern coast is too precipitous to support large settlements. The rugged mountainous interior, dotted with caves and sliced by dramatic gorges, offers rigorous hiking and climbing. Small villages like Magarites, a potters' village near Mt Idi, offer a glimpse into traditional life.

Iraklio   Ηρακλειο

POP 174,000

Iraklio (ee-*rah*-klee-oh; often spelt Heraklion), Crete's capital and economic hub, is a bustling modern city and the fifth-largest in Greece. It has a lively city centre, an excellent archaeological museum and is close to Knossos, Crete's major visitor attraction.

IRAKLIO MARKET

An Iraklio institution, just south of the Lion Fountain, narrow **Odos 1866** (1866 St) is part market, part bazaar and, despite being increasingly tourist-oriented, it's a fun place to browse and stock up on picnic supplies from fruit and vegetables, creamy cheeses and honey to succulent olives and fresh breads. Other stalls sell pungent herbs, leather goods, hats, jewellery and some souvenirs. Cap off a spree with lunch at **Giakoumis** (Theodosaki 5-8; mains €6-13; ⊙noon-11pm) or another nearby taverna (avoid those in the market itself).

Other towns are more picturesque, but in a pinch, you can stay over in Iraklio.

Iraklio's harbours face north with the landmark **Koules Venetian Fortress**. Plateia Venizelou, known for its **Lion (Morosini) Fountain**, is the heart of the city, 400m south of the old harbour up 25 Avgoustou.

⊙ Sights & Activities

★Heraklion

Archaeological Museum   MUSEUM
(☑2810 279000; http://odysseus.culture.gr; Xanthoudidou 2; adult/child €6/free, incl Knossos €10; ⊙8am-8pm Apr-Oct, 11am-5pm Mon, 8am-3pm Tue-Sun Nov-Mar) This outstanding museum is one of the largest and most important in Greece. There are artefacts spanning 5500 years from neolithic to Roman times, but it's rightly most famous for its extensive Minoan collection. The beautifully restored museum makes a gleaming showcase for the artefacts, and greatly enhances any understanding of Crete's rich history. Don't skip it.

The treasure trove includes pottery, jewellery, sarcophagi, plus several famous frescoes from the sites of Knossos, Phaestos, Zakros, Malia and Agia Triada.

Cretan Adventures   OUTDOORS
(☑2810 332772; www.cretanadventures.gr; 3rd fl, Evans 10) This well-regarded local company organises hiking tours, mountain biking and extreme outdoor excursions.

🛏 Sleeping

Staying in nearby Arhanes offers a chance to see Cretan wine country. Try **Arhontiko** (☑2810 881550; www.arhontikoarhanes.gr; apt

Crete

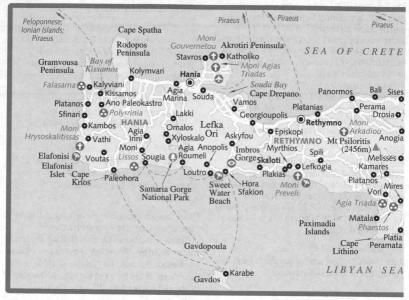

€75-95; ✶ 🤖) with its beautifully kitted-out apartments.

Kronos Hotel
HOTEL €

(☏ 2810 282240; www.kronoshotel.gr; Sofokli Venizelou 2; s/d €49/60; ✶ @ 🤖) After a thorough makeover this waterfront hotel pole-vaulted to the top of the budget hotel category. Rooms have double-glazed windows to block out noise, as well as balconies, phone, a tiny TV and a fridge. Some doubles have sea views (€66).

Rea Hotel
HOTEL €

(☏ 2810 223638; www.hotelrea.gr; Kalimeraki 1, cnr Hortatson; d with/without bathroom €45/35, tr €54; ✶ 🤖) Popular with backpackers, the family-run Rea has an easy, friendly atmosphere. Rooms all have small TVs and balconies, but some bathrooms are shared. Family rooms are available. There's a book exchange and a communal fridge.

Lato Boutique Hotel
BOUTIQUE HOTEL €€

(☏ 2810 228103; www.lato.gr; Epimenidou 15; d incl breakfast €89-136, q from €124; P ✶ @ 🤖) Iraklio goes Hollywood – with all the sass but sans attitude – at this mod boutique hotel overlooking the old harbour, easily recognised by its jazzy facade. Rooms here sport rich woods, warm reds and vinyl floors, plus custom furniture, pillow-top mattresses, a playful lighting scheme and a kettle for making coffee or tea. Back rooms overlook a modernist metal sculpture.

✖ Eating & Drinking

Eateries, bars and cafes surround Plateia Venizelou (Lion Fountain) and the El Greco Park area. The old harbour offers seafood options.

Fyllo...Sofies
CAFE €

(☏ 2810 284774; www.fillosofies.gr; Plateia Venizelou 33; snacks €3-7; ☉ 5am-late; 🤖) With a terrace spilling towards the Morosini Fountain, this been-here-forever cafe is *the* go-to place for *bougatsa*: a traditional pastry filled with cream or *myzithra* (sheep's milk cheese) and sometimes served with ice cream or sprinkled with honey and nuts.

Ippokambos
SEAFOOD €

(☏ 2810 280240; Sofokli Venizelou 3; mains €6-13; ☉ noon-midnight Mon-Sat; 🤖) Locals give this unpretentious *ouzerie* an enthusiastic thumbs up and we are only too happy to follow suit. Fish is the thing here, freshly caught, simply but expertly prepared and sold at fair prices. In summer, park yourself on the covered waterfront terrace.

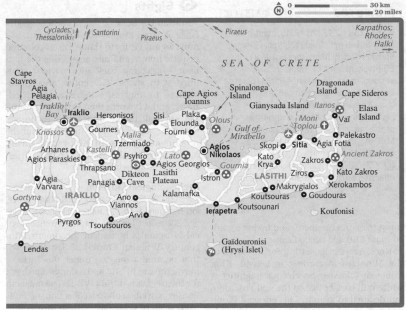

ℹ Information

Visit www.heraklion.gr for city information.
Skoutelis Travel (☎ 2810 280808; www.
skoutelisrentacar.gr; 25 Avgoustou 24) Airline
and ferry bookings, excursions around Crete
and to Santorini, accommodation help and
car hire.
Tourist Office (☎ 2810 228225; Xanthoulidou
1; ⊗ 9am-3pm Mon-Fri) Meagre selection of
brochures and maps.

ℹ Getting There & Around

AIR

Flights from Iraklio's **Nikos Kazantzakis International Airport** (HER; ☎ 2810 397800; www.
heraklion-airport.info) serve Athens, Thessaloniki and Rhodes plus destinations all over Europe.
The airport is 5km east of town. Bus 1 travels
between the airport and city centre (€1.20)
every 15 minutes from 6.15am to 10.45pm.

BOAT

Daily ferries from Iraklio's **ferry port** (☎ 2810
244956) service Piraeus (€39, eight hours), and
catamarans head to Santorini and other Cycladic islands. Ferries sail east to Rhodes (€28, 14
hours) via Agios Nikolaos, Sitia, Kasos, Karpathos and Halki. Services are reduced in winter.
See www.openseas.gr.

BUS

KTEL (www.bus-service-crete-ktel.com) runs
the buses on Crete. Main Bus Station A, just
inland from the new harbour, serves eastern
and western Crete (Agios Nikolaos, Ierapetra,
Sitia, Malia, Lasithi Plateau, Hania, Rethymno
and Knossos). It has useful tourist information
and a left-luggage service. Bus Station B, 50m
beyond the Hania Gate, serves the southern
route (Phaestos, Matala and Anogia).

Knossos   Κνωσσος

Crete's most famous historical attraction is
the **Palace of Knossos** (☎ 2810 231940; adult/
child €6/free, incl Heraklion Archaeological Museum
€10; ⊗ 8am-8pm Jun-Oct, to 5pm Nov-May), 5km
south of Iraklio, and the grand capital of Minoan Crete. Excavation on Knossos (k-nos-
os) started in 1878 with Cretan archaeologist
Minos Kalokerinos, and continued from
1900 to 1930 with British archaeologist
Sir Arthur Evans. Today, it's hard to make
sense, in the extensive restorations, of what
is Evans' interpretation and what actually
existed in Minoan times. But the setting is
gorgeous and the ruins and re-creations impressive, incorporating an immense palace,
courtyards, private apartments, baths, lively
frescoes and more. Going to the Heraklion
Archaeological Museum (p359) in Iraklio

PHAESTOS ΦΑΙΣΤΟΣ

Phaestos (☑ 28920 42315; adult/child €4/free, incl Agia Triada €6/free; ⊙ 8am-8pm Apr-Oct, 8.30am-3pm Nov-Mar), 63km southwest of Iraklio, is Crete's second-most important Minoan palatial site. More unreconstructed and moody than Knossos, Phaestos (fes-*tos*) is also worth a visit for its stunning views of the surrounding Mesara plain and Mt Psiloritis (2456m; also known as Mt Ida). The smaller site of **Agia Triada** (☑ 27230 22448; adult/child €3/free, incl Phaestos €6/free; ⊙ 10am-3pm) is 3km west.

(most treasures are there) and taking a guided tour (€10) add needed context.

Knossos was the setting for the myth of the Minotaur. According to legend, King Minos of Knossos was given a magnificent white bull to sacrifice to the god Poseidon, but decided to keep it. This enraged Poseidon, who punished the king by causing his wife Pasiphae to fall in love with the animal. The result of this odd union was the Minotaur – half-man and half-bull – who was imprisoned in a labyrinth beneath the king's palace at Knossos, munching on youths and maidens, before being killed by Theseus.

Buses to Knossos (€1.50, 20 minutes, three per hour) leave from Bus Station A in Iraklio.

Hania Χανιά

POP 54,000

Crete's most romantic, evocative and alluring town, Hania (hahn-*yah*; often spelt Chania) is the former capital and the island's second-largest city. There is a rich mosaic of Venetian and Ottoman architecture, particularly in the area of the old harbour, which lures tourists in droves.

Modern Hania with its university retains the exoticism of a city playing with East and West and has some of the best hotels and restaurants on the island. It's an excellent base for exploring nearby idyllic beaches and a spectacular mountainous interior.

◉ Sights

Venetian Harbour HISTORIC QUARTER

FREE A stroll around the old harbour is a must for any visitor to Hania. Pastel-coloured historic homes and businesses line the harbour, zigzagging back into narrow lanes lined with shops. The entire area is ensconced in impressive **Venetian fortifications**, and it is worth the 1.5km walk around the sea wall to the **Venetian lighthouse**. On the eastern side of the inner harbour the prominent **Mosque of Kioutsouk Hasan** (also known as the Mosque of Janissaries) houses regular exhibitions.

Archaeological Museum MUSEUM

(☑ 28210 90334; Halidon 30; adult/child €2/free, incl Byzantine & Postbyzantine Collection €3/free; ⊙ 8.30am-3pm Tue-Sun) Hania's Archaeological Museum is housed in the superb 16th-century Venetian Church of San Francisco that became a mosque under the Turks, a movie theatre in 1913 and a munitions depot for the Germans during WWII. The museum houses a well-displayed collection of finds from western Crete dating from the neolithic to the Roman eras. Artefacts from 3400 to 1200 BC include tablets with Linear A script. There is also exquisite pottery from the Geometric Age (1200–800 BC) and a case of bull figurines.

◉ Sleeping

Hania's old harbour is loaded with great hotels that can book up, even on winter weekends; reserve ahead.

Ionas Hotel BOUTIQUE HOTEL €€

(☑ 28210 55090; www.ionashotel.com; cnr Sarpaki & Sorvolou; d incl breakfast €60-90; ❇ ❐) One of the new breed of boutique hotels in the quieter Splantzia quarter, Ionas is housed in a historic building with contemporary interior design and friendly owners. The nine rooms are kitted out with all mod cons (including a smallish jacuzzi in one), and share a terrace. Original touches include a Venetian archway in the entrance, and walls from the mid-16th century.

Palazzo Duca APARTMENT €€

(☑ 28210 70460; www.palazzoduca.gr; Douka 27-29; d/ste from €80/110) This reader favourite small hotel is tucked back into the streets of Hania's old harbour and has super-comfy studies and apartments with kitchenettes. Some offer port views or small balconies.

Pension Lena
PENSION €€

(☑28210 86860; www.lenachania.gr; Ritsou 5; d €65; ✳🛜) Run by the friendly Lena, this pension near Nea Hora beach has tastefully done rooms with an old-world feel and a scattering of antiques, though the front rooms are the most appealing. Lena also offers three independent houses.

★ Casa Leone
BOUTIQUE HOTEL €€€

(☑28210 76762; www.casa-leone.com; Parodos Theotokopoulou 18; d/ste incl breakfast from €125/160; ✳🛜) This Venetian residence has been converted into a classy and romantic family-run boutique hotel. The rooms are spacious and well appointed, with balconies overlooking the harbour. There are honeymoon suites, with classic drape-canopy beds and sumptuous curtains.

✕ Eating & Drinking

Look beyond the waterfront tourist-traps for some of the best eats on the island. The Splantzia neighbourhood is popular with discerning locals. Nightclubs dot the port, and atmospheric Fagotto Jazz Bar (☑28210 71877; Angelou 16; ⊙7pm-2am) has occasional live music.

★ Taverna Tamam
TAVERNA €

(☑28210 96080; Zambeliou 49; mains €7-12; ⊙noon-midnight; ☑) This excellent, convivial taverna in a converted Turkish bathhouse fills with chatting locals at tables spilling out onto the street. Meals incorporate mid-Eastern spices, and include tasty soups and a superb selection of vegetarian specialities.

★ Bougatsa tou Iordanis
CRETAN €

(☑28210 88855; Apokoronou 24; bougatsa €3) You haven't lived til you've eaten the *bougatsa* at this little storefront dedicated to the flaky, sweet-cheesy treat. It's cooked fresh in enormous slabs and carved up in front of your eyes. Pair it with a coffee and you're set for the morning.

Pallas
CAFE €

(Akti Tombazi 15-17; mains €8-16; ⊙8am-midnight; 🛜) For coffee and breakfast at Hania's old harbour, head to local favourite Pallas, with a 2nd-floor dining room, superb views and a brunch menu to match.

★ To Maridaki
CRETAN €€

(☑28210 08880; Daskalogianni 33; dishes €7-12; ⊙noon-midnight Mon-Sat) This modern seafood *mezedhopoleio* (mezedhes restaurant) is not to be missed. In a cheerful, bright dining room, happy visitors and locals alike tuck into impeccable, local seafood and Cretan specialities. Ingredients are fresh, the fried calamari is to die for, the house white wine is crisp and delicious, and the complimentary panna cotta to finish the meal is transcendent. What's not to love?

ℹ Information

For more information visit www.chania.gr.
Local Tourist Office (☑28210 41665; tourism@chania.gr; Milonogianni 53; ⊙9am-2pm) Modest selection at the town hall.
Tellus Travel (☑28210 91500; www.tellustravel.gr; Halidon 108; ⊙8am-11pm) Major agency hires cars, changes money, arranges air and boat tickets, accommodation and excursions.

WORTH A TRIP

RETHYMNO & MONI ARKADIOU

Rethymno (*reth*-im-no), on the coast between Iraklio and Hania, is one of the island's architectural treasures, due to its stunning **fortress** and mix of Venetian and Turkish houses in the **old quarter**. It's worth a stop to explore the area around the old Venetian harbour, and shop in its interesting arts and crafts boutiques.

Moni Arkadiou (Arkadi Monastery; ☑28310 83136; www.arkadimonastery.gr; admission €2.50; ⊙9am-8pm Jun-Aug, shorter hour Sep-May), in the hills some 23km southeast of Rethymno, has deep significance for Cretans. A potent symbol of human resistance, it was the site of a tragic and momentous stand-off between the Turks and the Cretans in 1866, and considered a spark plug in the struggle towards freedom from Turkish occupation. Arkadiou's most impressive structure, its **Venetian church** (1587), has a striking Renaissance facade marked by eight slender Corinthian columns and topped by an ornate triple-belled tower. Its high mountain valley is beautiful, especially around sunset.

WORTH A TRIP

SOUTHWEST COAST VILLAGES

Crete's southern coastline at its western end is dotted with remote, attractive little villages that are brilliant spots to take it easy for a few days.

From Paleohora heading east are Sougia, Agia Roumeli, Loutro and Hora Sfakion. No road links the coastal resorts, but a once-daily boat from Paleohora to Sougia (€8, one hour), Agia Roumeli (€14, 1½ hours), Loutro (€15, 2½ hours) and Hora Sfakion (€16, three hours) connects the villages in summer. See www.sfakia-crete.com/sfakia-crete/ferries.html. In summer three buses daily connect Hania and Hora Sfakion (€7.60, two hours), two daily to Sougia (€7.10, 1¾ hours). If you're a keen hiker, it's also possible to walk right along this southern coast.

Paleohora This village is isolated on a peninsula with a sandy beach to the west and a pebbly beach to the east. On summer evenings the main street is closed to traffic and the tavernas move onto the road. If you're after a relaxing few days, Paleohora is a great spot to chill out. Stay at **Joanna's** (☑ 69785 83503, 28230 41801; www.joannas-palaiochora.com; studio €40-55; ☺ Apr-Nov; P ✿ 🛜) spacious, spotless studios.

Sougia At the mouth of the **Agia Irini gorge**, Sougia (soo-yah) is a laid-back and refreshingly undeveloped spot with a wide curve of sand-and-pebble beach. The 14.5km (six hour) walk from Paleohora is popular, as is the Agia Irini gorge walk, which ends (or starts!) in Sougia. It's possible to get here by ferry, by car or on foot. Stay at **Santa Irene Apartments** (☑ 28230 51342; www.santa-irene.gr; apt €60-80; ☺ late Mar-early Nov; P ✿ 🛜), a smart beachside complex with its own cafe.

Agia Roumeli At the mouth of the Samaria Gorge, Agia Roumeli bristles with gorge-walkers from mid-afternoon until the ferry comes to take them away. Once they are gone, this pleasant little town goes into quiet mode until the first walkers turn up in the early afternoon the following day. Right on the waterfront, **Paralia Taverna & Rooms** (☑ 28250 91408; www.taverna-paralia.com; Agia Roumeli; d from €30; ✿ 🛜) offers excellent views, tasty Cretan cuisine, cold beer and simple, clean rooms.

Loutro This tiny village is a particularly picturesque spot, curled around the only natural harbour on the southern coast of Crete. With no vehicle access, the only way in is by boat or on foot. **Hotel Porto Loutro** (☑ 28250 91433; www.hotelportoloutro.com; s/d incl breakfast €50/60; ☺ mid-Mar–Oct; ✿ @) has tasteful rooms with balconies overlooking the harbour. The village beach, excellent walks, rental kayaks and boat transfers to excellent Sweetwater Beach fill peaceful days.

Hora Sfakion Renowned in Cretan history for its rebellious streak, Hora Sfakion is an amiable town. WWII history buffs know this as the place where thousands of Allied troops were evacuated by sea after the Battle of Crete. Hora Sfakion's seafront tavernas serve fresh seafood and unique *Sfakianes pites*, which look like crêpes filled with sweet or savoury local cheese. **Hotel Stavris** (☑ 28250 91220; www.hotel-stavris-sfakia-crete.com; s/d/tr from €28/33/38; ✿ 🛜) has simple rooms and breakfast outside in its courtyard.

❶ Getting There & Away

AIR

Hania Airport (CHQ; www.chaniaairport.com) serves Athens, Thessaloniki and seasonally cities around Europe. The airport is 14km east of town on the Akrotiri Peninsula. Taxis cost €20; buses cost €2.30.

BOAT

The port is at Souda, 9km southeast of Hania. Once-nightly **Anek** (www.anek.gr) ferries serve Piraeus (€35, nine hours). Frequent buses

(€1.65) and taxis (€10) connect the town and Souda.

BUS

Frequent buses from the **main bus station** (www.bus-service-crete-ktel.com; Kydonias 73-77; left luggage per bag per day €2) run along Crete's northern coast to Iraklio (€13.80, 2¾ hours, half-hourly) and Rethymno (€6.20, one hour, half-hourly); buses run less frequently to Paleohora, Omalos and Hora Sfakion. Buses for beaches west of Hania leave from the eastern side of Plateia 1866.

Samaria Gorge
Φαραγγι Της Σαμαριας

Samaria Gorge (☑ 28210 45570; www.samaria gorge.eu; adult/child €5/2.50; ⊙ 7am-sunset May-late Oct) is one of Europe's most spectacular gorges and a superb (very popular) hike. Walkers should take rugged footwear, food, drinks and sun protection for this strenuous five- to six-hour trek. You can do the walk as part of an excursion tour, or independently by taking the Omalos bus from the main bus station in Hania (€6.90, one hour) to the head of the gorge at Xyloskalo (1230m). It's a 16.7km walk (all downhill) to Agia Roumeli on the coast, from where you take a boat to Hora Sfakion (€10, 1¼ hours) and then a bus back to Hania (€7.60, 1½ hours).

You are not allowed to spend the night in the gorge, so you need to complete the walk in a day, or beat the crowds and stay over in one of the nearby villages. Other gorges, such as **Imbros** (admission €2; ⊙ year-round), also make for fine walking, and are less crowded.

DODECANESE
ΔΩΔΕΚΑΝΗΣΑ

Strung out along the coast of western Turkey, the 12 main islands of the Dodecanese (*dodeca* means 12) have suffered a turbulent past of invasions and occupations that have endowed them with a fascinating diversity. Conquered successively by the Romans, the Arabs, the Knights of St John, the Turks, the Italians, then liberated from the Germans by British and Greek commandos in 1944, the Dodecanese became part of Greece in 1947. These days, tourists rule.

Rhodes
Ροδος
POP 98,000

Rhodes (Rodos in Greek) is the largest island in the Dodecanese. According to mythology, the sun god Helios chose Rhodes as his bride and bestowed light, warmth and vegetation upon her. The blessing seems to have paid off, for Rhodes produces more flowers and sunny days than most Greek islands. Throw in an east coast of virtually uninterrupted sandy beaches and it's easy to understand why sun-starved northern Europeans flock here in droves. The old town is magnificent.

Rhodes Town
POP 56,000

Rhodes' capital is Rhodes Town, on the northern tip of the island. Its magnificent **Old Town**, the largest inhabited medieval town in Europe, is enclosed within massive walls and is a delight to explore. To the north is **New Town**, the commercial centre. The **town beach**, which looks out at Turkey runs around the peninsula at the northern end of New Town.

The main port, **Commercial Harbour**, is east of the Old Town, and is where the big interisland ferries dock. Northwest of here is **Mandraki Harbour**, lined with excursion boats and smaller ferries, hydrofoils and catamarans. It was the supposed site of the **Colossus of Rhodes**, a 32m-high bronze statue of Apollo built over 12 years (294–282 BC). The statue stood for a mere 65 years before being toppled by an earthquake.

◎ Sights

A wander around Rhodes' Unesco World Heritage–listed Old Town is a must. It is reputedly the world's finest surviving example of medieval fortification, with 12m-thick

GREECE SAMARIA GORGE

THE KNIGHTS OF ST JOHN

Island-hopping in the Dodecanese you'll quickly realise that the Knights of St John left behind a passel of castles. Originally formed as the Knights Hospitaller in Jerusalem in 1080 to provide care for poor and sick pilgrims, the knights relocated to Rhodes (via Cyprus) after the loss of Jerusalem in the First Crusade. They ousted the ruling Genoese in 1309, built a stack of castles in the Dodecanese to protect their new home, then set about irking the neighbours by committing acts of piracy against Ottoman shipping. Sultan Süleyman the Magnificent, not a man you'd want to irk, took offence and set about dislodging the knights from their strongholds. Rhodes finally capitulated in 1523 and the remaining knights relocated to Malta. They set up there as the Sovereign Military Hospitaller of Jerusalem, of Rhodes, and of Malta.

walls. A mesh of Byzantine, Turkish and Latin architecture, the Old Town is divided into the Kollakio (the Knights' Quarter, where the Knights of St John lived during medieval times), the Hora and the Jewish Quarter. The Knights' Quarter contains most of the medieval historical sights while the Hora, often referred to as the Turkish Quarter, is primarily Rhodes Town's commercial sector with shops and restaurants, thronged by tourists.

The **Knights' Quarter** is in the northern end of the Old Town. The cobbled **Avenue of the Knights** (Ippoton) is lined with magnificent medieval buildings, the most imposing of which is the **Palace of the Grand Masters** (22410 23359; admission €6; 8.30am-3pm Tue-Sun), which was restored, but never used, as a holiday home for Mussolini. From the palace, explore the **D'Amboise Gate**, the most atmospheric of the fortification gates, which takes you across the moat.

The beautiful 15th-century Knight's Hospital, closer to the seafront, now houses the excellent **Archaeological Museum** (22410 65256; Plateia Mousiou; admission €6; 8am-3pm Tue-Sun). The splendid building was restored by the Italians and has an impressive collection that includes the ethereal marble statue *Aphrodite of Rhodes*.

The pink-domed **Mosque of Süleyman**, at the top of Sokratous, was built in 1522 to commemorate the Ottoman victory against the knights, then rebuilt in 1808.

🛏 Sleeping

Mango Rooms PENSION €
(22410 24877; www.mango.gr; Plateia Dorieos 3, Old Town; d/tr €60/72; ✻@🖧) Set in a square in Old Town, these are spotless, simple rooms with safety deposit box, fridge and bathroom. Downstairs is a restaurant and internet cafe.

LINDOS
••••••••••••••••••••••••••••••••••
The **Acropolis of Lindos** (22440 31258; admission €6; 8am-6pm Tue-Sun Jun-Aug, to 2.40pm Sep-May), 47km south from Rhodes Town, is an ancient city spectacularly perched atop a 116m-high rocky outcrop. Below is the town of Lindos, a tangle of streets with elaborately decorated 17th-century houses.

★**Marco Polo Mansion** BOUTIQUE HOTEL €€
(22410 25562; www.marcopolomansion.gr; Agiou Fanouriou 40, Old Town; d incl breakfast €80-180; Apr-Oct; ✻🖧) We love the vivid style in this 15th-century former Ottoman official's house, with its heavy antique furniture and eastern rugs, and stained-glass windows washing the ox-blood walls in blue light. The rooms are spectacularly romantic with huge beds and tasteful furnishings. Try the split-level ex-harem bedroom. There's a top restaurant, too!

Hotel International HOTEL €€
(22410 24595; www.international-hotel.gr; 12 Kazouli St, New Town; s/d incl breakfast €50/70; ✻🖧) In New Town, the International is a friendly family-run operation with immaculately clean and good-value rooms only a few minutes from Rhodes' main town beach. It's a 10-minute stroll to Old Town, and prices drop by a third out of high season.

Nikos & Takis Hotel BOUTIQUE HOTEL €€€
(22410 70773; www.nikostakishotel.com; Panetiou 29; d/ste incl breakfast from €170/180; year-round; P✻@🖧) Soaked in shades of ochre, this hilltop eyrie in the heart of the Knights' Quarter abounds in eclectic style: a melange of Moorish and high-fashion influences with frescoed arched doors, a gorgeous pebble mosaic courtyard and palace or sea views. Its eight individually designed suites are fit for royalty with four-poster beds, silk drapes, traditional wooden ceilings and tangerine-hued walls.

Service is sensational and breakfast is lavishly made to order.

🍴 Eating & Drinking

Old Rhodes is rife with tourist traps; look in the backstreets. Head further north into New Town for better value restaurants and bars.

To Meltemi TAVERNA €
(Kountourioti 8; mains €10-15; noon-6pm; P✻🚶) With wide sea views and just yards from the beach, this breezy taverna has a cosy, nautically themed interior, or you can dine on the semi-alfresco terrace. Staff are charming and the menu swimming in feisty salads, salted mackerel, calamari and octopus.

Pizanias TAVERNA €€
(22410 22117; Sofokleous 24; mains €8-18; noon-midnight Feb-Oct) This atmospheric little taverna tucked back into the heart of

Old Town is known for its fresh seafood and delicious fava. Dine under the trees and the night sky.

ⓘ Information

For information, visit www.rodos.gr.

Tourist Information Office (EOT; ☑ 22410 44335; www.ando.gr/eot; cnr Makariou & Papagou; ⊙8am-2.45pm Mon-Fri) Brochures, maps, transport information and *Rodos News*, a free English-language newspaper.

Triton Holidays (☑ 22410 21690; www.tritondmc.gr; Plastira 9, Mandraki; ⊙9am-8pm) Air and sea travel, hire cars, accommodation and tours throughout the Dodecanese. It also sells tickets to Turkey.

ⓘ Getting There & Around

AIR

Many flights daily connect Rhodes' **Diagoras Airport** (RHO; ☑ 22410 88700; www.rhodes-airport.org) and Athens, plus less-regular flights to Karpathos, Kastellorizo, Thessaloniki, Iraklio and Samos. International flights, budget airlines and charter flights swarm in summer. The airport is on the west coast, 16km southwest of Rhodes Town; 25 minutes and €2.20 by bus, €22 by taxi.

BOAT

Rhodes is the main port of the Dodecanese and there is a complex array of departures. Most of the daily boats to Piraeus (€59, 13 hours) sail via the Dodecanese, but some go via Karpathos, Crete and the Cyclades. In summer, catamaran services run up and down the Dodecanese daily from Rhodes to Symi or Halki, Kos, Kalymnos, Nisyros, Tilos, Patmos and Leros. Check www.openseas.gr, **Dodekanisos Seaways** (☑ 22410 70590; Afstralias 3) and **Blue Star Ferries** (☑ 21089 19800; www.bluestarferries.com). Excursion boats at the harbour also go to Symi.

To Turkey

Ferries connect Rhodes and Marmaris in Turkey (one way/return including port taxes €50/75, 50 minutes). Check www.marmarisinfo.com. For Fethiye, Turkey (one way/return including port taxes €50/75, 90 minutes) see www.alaturkaturkey.com.

BUS

Rhodes Town has two bus stations a block apart next to the New Market. The **west-side bus station** (☑ 22410 26300) serves the airport, Kamiros (€5, 55 minutes) and the west coast. The **east-side bus station** (☑ 22410 27706; www.ktelrodou.gr) serves the east coast, Lindos (€5, 1½ hours) and the inland southern villages.

ⓘ BOATS TO TURKEY

Turkey is so close that it looks like you could swim there from many of the Dodecanese and Northeastern Aegean islands. Here are the boat options:

Marmaris or Fethiye from Rhodes

Bodrum from Kos

Kuşadasi (near Ephesus) from Samos

Çeşme (near İzmir) from Chios

Dikili (near Ayvalık) from Lesvos

Kos   Κως

POP 19,872

Bustling Kos, only 5km from the Turkish peninsula of Bodrum, is popular with history buffs as the birthplace of Hippocrates (460–377 BC), the father of medicine. The island also attracts an entirely different crowd – hordes of sun-worshipping beach lovers from northern Europe who pack the place in summer.

⊙ Sights & Activities

Busy Kos Town has lots of **bicycle paths** and renting a bike along the pretty waterfront is great for seeing the sights. Near the Castle of the Knights is **Hippocrates Plane Tree** (Plateia Platanou, Kos Town) FREE, under which the man himself is said to have taught his pupils. The modern town is built on the vast remains of the ancient Greek one – explore the ruins!

★ **Asklepeion**   ARCHAEOLOGICAL SITE
(☑ 22420 28763; adult/child €4/free; ⊙8am-7.30pm Tue-Sun) On a pretty pine and olivegrove-clad hill 4km southwest of Kos Town stand the extensive ruins of the renowned healing centre that taught the principles of Hippocrates' way. Doctors and healers come from all over the world to visit.

Castle of the Knights   FORTRESS
(☑ 22420 27927; Kos Town; admission €4; ⊙8am-2.30pm Tue-Sun) Reach the once impregnable Castle of the Knights by crossing a bridge over Finikon from **Plateia Platanou**. The castle, which had massive outer walls and an inner keep, was built in the 14th century and separated from the town by a moat (now Finikon). Damaged by an earthquake in 1495 and restored in the 16th century,

it was the knights' most stalwart defence against the encroaching Ottomans.

Ancient Agora
RUIN

(Kos Town) FREE The ancient agora, with the ruins of the **Shrine of Aphrodite** and **Temple of Hercules**, is an open site south of the Castle of the Knights. A massive 3rd-century-BC stoa, with some reconstructed columns, stands on its western side.

🛏 Sleeping

Hotel Afendoulis
HOTEL €

(☑ 22420 25321; www.afendoulishotel.com; Evripilou 1, Kos Town; s/d €30/50; ☉ Mar-Nov; ✱ @ 🛜) Peaceful Afendoulis has unfailingly friendly staff and sparkling rooms with white walls, small balconies, flat-screen TVs, hairdryers and spotless bathrooms. Downstairs there's an open breakfast room and flowery terrace with wrought-iron tables and chairs for enjoying the feast of homemade jams and marmalades.

★Hotel Sonia
HOTEL €€

(☑ 22420 28798; www.hotelsonia.gr; Irodotou 9, Kos Town; s/d/tr €45/60/75; ☉ year-round; ✱ 🛜) On a peaceful street, this pension has sparkling rooms with parquet floors, flat-screen TVs, fridges, chic bathrooms and an extra bed if you need it. There's a relaxing communal verandah with wrought-iron chairs, spacious private balconies and a decent library. Room 4 has the best sea view.

✗ Eating & Drinking

Restaurants line the central waterfront of the old harbour in Kos Town, but back-streets harbour better value. Nightclubs dot Diakon and Nafklirou, just north of the *agora*.

H2O
INTERNATIONAL €

(☑ 22420 47200; www.kosaktis.gr; Vasileos Georgiou 7, Kos Town; mains €10-20; ☉ 11am-midnight; ✱ 🛜 ✎) The city's glitziest waterfront eatery at Kos Aktis Art Hotel is patronised by fashionistas and makes for a great stop for a healthy lunch or dinner, out on the decked terrace facing Bodrum. Choose from bruschetta, grilled veg, battered shrimp and chicken risotto, or simply plump for a sundowner mojito.

ℹ ISLAND SHORTCUTS

If long ferry rides eat into your holiday too much, check Aegean Airlines, Olympic Air, Astra Airlines and Sky Express (see p378) for flights. But beware baggage limits: Sky Express in particular only allows teeny bags.

Arap
TURKISH €

(☑ 22420 28442; Platani Sq, Kos Town; mains €7-15; ☉ noon-midnight) Located in the Turkish quarter, called Platani, on the way towards the Asklepeion, this casual grill-house is tops for heaping portions of tender kebabs and delicious dips with fresh pitta. It's a bit of a dreary 2.5km walk from the centre; bike it or catch a cab.

ℹ Information

Visit www.kos.gr, www.kosinfo.gr or www.travel-to-kos.com for information.

ℹ Getting There & Around

AIR

Daily flights to Athens serve **Ippokratis Airport** (KGS; ☑ 22420 51229), as do flights to Rhodes and Kalymnos, and international flights and charters in summer. The airport is 28km southwest of Kos Town; buses cost €4, taxis €30.

BICYCLE

Hire bikes at the harbour to get around town.

BOAT

Kos has services to Piraeus and all islands in the Dodecanese, the Cyclades, Samos and Thessaloniki run by: **Blue Star Ferries** (☑ 22420 28914; Kos Town), **Anek Lines** (☑ 22420 28545) and **ANE Kalymnou** (☑ 22420 29900). Catamarans are run by Dodekanisos Seaways at the interisland ferry quay. Local passenger and car ferries run to Pothia on Kalymnos from Mastihari. For tickets, visit **Fanos Travel & Shipping** (☑ 22420 20035; www.kostravel.gr; 11 Akti Kountourioti, Kos Town) on the harbour.

To Turkey

In summer excursion boats depart daily for Bodrum in Turkey (€20 return, one hour).

BUS

There is a good public bus system on Kos, with the bus station on Kleopatras, near the ruins at the back of town.

NORTHEASTERN AEGEAN ISLANDS

ΤΑ ΝΗΣΙΑ ΤΟΥ ΒΟΡΕΙΟ ΑΝΑΤΟΛΙΚΟ ΑΙΓΑΙΟΥ

One of Greece's best-kept secrets, these far-flung islands are strewn across the northeastern corner of the Aegean, closer to Turkey than mainland Greece. They harbour unspoilt scenery, welcoming locals, fascinating independent cultures, and remain relatively calm even when other Greek islands are sagging with tourists at the height of summer.

Samos   Σάμος

POP 32,820

A lush mountainous island only 3km from Turkey, Samos has a glorious history as the legendary birthplace of Hera, wife and sister of god-of-all-gods Zeus. Samos was an important centre of Hellenic culture, and the mathematician Pythagoras and story-teller Aesop are among its sons. The island has beaches that bake in summer, and a hinterland that is superb for hiking. Spring brings with it pink flamingos, wildflowers, and orchids that the island grows for export, while summer brings throngs of package tourists.

Vathy (Samos Town)   Βαθύ Σάμος

POP 2030

Busy Vathy is an attractive working port town. Most of the action is along Themistokleous Sofouli, the main street that runs along the waterfront. The main square, Plateia Pythagorou, in the middle of the waterfront, is recognisable by its four palm trees and statue of a lion.

The first-rate **Archaeological Museum** (✆22730 27469; adult/child €3/free, Sun Nov-Mar free; ☉8.30am-3.30pm Tue-Sun) is one of the best in the islands. **Cleomenis Hotel** (✆22730 23232; Kallistratous 33; d incl breakfast from €35) offers great, simple rooms close to the beach northeast of town. Elegant **Ino Village Hotel** (✆22730 23241; www.ino villagehotel.com; Kalami; d incl breakfast €70-145; P❀⏀✲) in the hills north of the ferry quay has **Elea Restaurant** with terrace views over town and the harbour.

ITSA Travel (✆22730 23605; www.itsatravel samos.gr; Themistokleous Sofouli; ☉8am-8pm), opposite the quay, is helpful with travel inquiries, excursions, accommodation and luggage storage.

Pythagorio   Πυθαγόρειο

POP 1300

Little Pythagorio, 11km south of Vathy, is where you'll disembark if you've come by boat from Patmos. It is a small, enticing town with a yacht-lined harbour and a busy, holiday atmosphere, overwhelming to some.

The 1034m-long **Evpalinos Tunnel** (✆22730 61400; Pythagorio; adult/child €4/free; ☉8am-2pm Tue-Sun), built in the 6th century BC, was dug by political prisoners and used as an aqueduct to bring water from Mt Ampelos (1140m).

Ireon (adult/child €4/free; ☉8.30am-3pm Tue-Sun), the legendary birthplace of the goddess Hera, is 8km west of Pythagorio. The temple at this Unesco World Heritage Site was enormous – four times the size of the Parthenon – though only one column remains.

Polyxeni Hotel (✆22730 61590; www. polyxenihotel.com; d €45-70; ❀⏀) is a fun place to stay in the heart of the waterfront action. Tavernas and bars line the waterfront.

The cordial **municipal tourist office** (✆22730 61389; deap5@otenet.gr; Lykourgou Logotheti; ☉8am-9.30pm) is two blocks from the waterfront on the main street. The **bus stop** is two blocks further inland on the same street.

Around Samos

Samos is an island of forests, mountains, wildlife and over 30 villages, harboring excellent, cheap tavernas. The captivating villages of **Vourliotes** and **Manolates**, on the slopes of imposing **Mt Ampelos**, northwest of Vathy, are excellent walking territory and have many marked pathways.

Karlovasi, on the northwest coast, is another ferry port and interesting in its own right. Spend the night near the beach at immaculate, friendly **Hesperia Hotel Apartments** (✆22730 30706; www.hesperiahotel.gr; Karlovasi; studio/apt €50/65). The beaches south of Karlovasi, like **Potami Beach** are tops. Other choice beaches include **Tsamadou** on the north coast, **Votsalakia** in the southwest and **Psili Ammos** to the east of Pythagorio. The latter is sandy and stares straight out at Turkey, barely a couple of kilometres away. Beautiful **Bollos Beach** near Skoureika village is even more off the beaten path.

ℹ Getting There & Around

AIR

Daily flights connect Athens with Samos Airport (SMI), 4km west of Pythagorio. Several-weekly flights serve Iraklio, Rhodes, Chios and Thessaloniki. Charter flights wing in from Europe in summer.

Buses (€2) run nine times daily and taxis to Vathy/Pythagorio cost €25/6.

BOAT

Samos has two main ports: Vathy in the northeast (bigger ferries) and Pythagorio on the southeast coast (boats arriving from the south). Buses between the two take 25 minutes. Boats to Limnos, Chios and Lesvos also leave from Karlovasi. Double-check where your boat is leaving from.

A maritime hub, Samos offers daily ferries to Piraeus (€40, 12 hours), plus ferries heading north to Chios and west to the Cyclades. In summer high-speed services head south to Patmos and Kos.

To Turkey

There are daily ferries to Kuşadası (for Ephesus) in Turkey (€35/45 one way/return, plus €10 port taxes). Day excursions are also available from April to October. Check with ITSA Travel (p369) for up-to-date details.

BUS

You can get to most of the island's villages and beaches by bus.

CAR & MOTORCYCLE

Rental cars and scooters are available all over (cars/scooters from €60/30 per day), and give you more freedom.

Lesvos (Mytilini)
Λεσβος (Μυτιληνη)

POP 93,500

Lesvos, or Mytilini as it is often called, tends to do things in a big way. The third-largest of the Greek Islands after Crete and Evia, Lesvos produces half the world's ouzo and is home to over 11 million olive trees. Mountainous yet fertile, the island has world-class local cuisine, and presents excellent hiking and birdwatching opportunities, but remains refreshingly untouched in terms of tourism.

Mytilini   Μυτιλήνη

POP 29,650

The capital and main port, Mytilini, is a lively student town with great eating and drinking options, plus eclectic churches and grand 19th-century mansions and museums. It is built between two harbours (north and south) with an imposing fortress on the promontory to the east. All ferries dock at the southern harbour, and most of the town's action is around this waterfront.

◉ Sights

Check with the tourist office to see if Teriade Museum (☑ 22510 23372; www.museum teriade.gr; Varia), with its fine art collection has completed its renovations, which were ongoing at the time of research. Also ask for a complete list of the numerous local museums, including some dedicated to olive oil and ouzo.

Archaeological Museum   MUSEUM

(Old Archaeological Museum; adult/child incl New Archaeological Museum €3/2; ⏰ 8.30am-3pm Tue-Sun) One block north of the quay, this museum has impressive finds from neolithic to Roman times, including ceramic somersaulting female figurines and gold jewellery.

Fortress   FORTRESS

(adult/child €2/free; ⏰ 8.30am-2.30pm Tue-Sun) Mytilini's imposing early Byzantine fortress

---

SAPPHO, LESBIANS & LESVOS

Sappho, one of Greece's great ancient poets, was born on Lesvos during the 7th century BC. Most of her work was devoted to love and desire, and the objects of her affection were often female. Because of this, Sappho's name and birthplace have come to be associated with female homosexuality.

These days, Lesvos is visited by many lesbians paying homage to Sappho. The whole island is very gay-friendly, in particular the southwestern beach resort of Skala Eresou, which is built over ancient Eresos, where Sappho was born. The village is well set up to cater to lesbian needs and has a 'Women Together' festival held annually in September. See www.womensfestival.eu and www.sapphotravel.com for details.

was renovated in the 14th century by Genoese overlord Francisco Gatelouzo, and then the Turks enlarged it again. It's popular for a stroll and is flanked by pine forests.

🛏 Sleeping

★Alkaios Rooms
PENSION €

(☑ 22510 47737, 69455 07089; www.alkaios rooms.gr; Alkaiou 16 & 30; s/d/tr incl breakfast €35/45/55; ❄ 🛜) This collection of 30 clean, well-kept rooms nestled discreetly in several renovated traditional buildings is Mytilini's most attractive budget option. It's a two-minute walk up from Paradosiaka Bougatsa Mytilinis on the waterfront.

Hotel Lesvion
HOTEL €€

(☑ 22510 28177; www.lesvion.gr; Harbour; s/d/tr from €45/60/70; ❄ 🛜) The well-positioned Lesvion, smack on the harbour, has friendly service and attractive modern rooms, some with excellent port-view balconies.

Theofilos Paradise Boutique Hotel
BOUTIQUE HOTEL €€

(☑ 22510 43300; www.theofilosparadise.gr; Skra 7; s/d/q/ste incl breakfast from €70/95/135/120; P ❄ @ 🛜 🌊) This smartly restored 100-year-old mansion is elegant, cheerful and good value, with modern amenities, along with a traditional *hammam* (Turkish bath). The 22 rooms are spread among three adjacent buildings surrounding a courtyard.

🍴 Eating & Drinking

Hit the streets in the bend in the harbour (Plateia Sapphou), around Ladadika, for zippy bars, cafes and creative eats.

★To Steki tou Yianni
TAVERNA €

(☑ 22510 28244; Agiou Therapodos; mains €6-14; ⊘noon-3pm & 8pm-late) Head up behind the giant Agios Therapon church to this wonderful, welcoming taverna where Yianni dishes out whatever's freshest. All the produce is local, the cheeses delectable, and the fish or meat top quality. Go with the flow... this is a local hang-out, with folks arriving after 9pm. Sip a local ouzo and see what Yianni brings you.

Averoff Restaurant
GREEK €

(☑ 22510 22180; Kountourioti, Harbour; mains €6-10; ⊘10am-10pm) No-frills eatery in the middle of the waterfront, specialising in generous *may-irefta* (ready-cooked) plates, such as chicken and potatoes, stuffed tomatoes and *briam* (oven-baked vegetable casserole).

❶ Information

See www.lesvos.net and www.greeknet.com for information.

Tourist Office (EOT; ☑ 22510 42512; Aristar-hou 6; ⊘9am-1pm Mon-Fri) Near the quay; offers brochures and maps.

Zoumboulis Tours (☑ 22510 37755; Koun-touriotou 69; ⊘8am-8pm) Sells ferry and plane tickets, runs boat trips to Turkey and rents rooms.

Molyvos (Mithymna)
Μόλυβος (Μήθυμνα)

POP 1500

The gracious, historic town of Mithymna (known by locals as Molyvos), 62km north of Mytilini Town, winds beautifully from the picturesque **old harbour**, up through cobbled streets canopied by flowering vines to the impressive **Byzantine-Genoese Castle** (admission €2; ⊘8am-3pm Tue-Sun) on the hilltop, from which you get tremendous views out to Turkey and around the lush valleys. Ravishing to the eye, Molyvos is well worth a wander, or is a peaceful place to stay.

Eftalou hot springs (☑ 22530 72200; Ef-talou; old common/new private bathhouse €4/5; ⊘old bathhouse 6am-9pm), 4km from town on the beach, is a superb bathhouse complex with steaming, pebbled pools. The scenery on the northern coast is extraordinary, as are its tiny villages.

Airy, friendly **Nassos Guest House** (☑ 22530 71432; www.nassosguesthouse.com; Ar-ionis; d/tr without bathroom €20/35; 🛜) offers shared facilities and a communal kitchen in an old Turkish house with rapturous views. **Molyvos Queen** (☑ 22530 71452; www.molyvos-queen.gr; apt from €60; ❄ 🛜) has full apartments with sea or castle views.

From the bus stop, walk towards town 100m to the helpful **municipal tourist office** (☑ 22530 71347; www.visitmolivos.com; ⊘hours vary).

Buses to Mithymna (€6.90) take 1¾ hours from Mytilini; a rental car is a better option with so much to explore.

Around the Island

Hire a car and tour the incredible countryside. Southern Lesvos is dominated by **Mt Olympus** (968m), and grove-covered valleys. Visit wonderful mountain village **Agiasos**, with its artisan workshops making everything from handcrafted furniture to pottery. **Plomari** in the far south is the land of ouzo distilleries; tour fascinating **Varvagianni Ouzo** (☎ 22520 32741; ☺ 9am-4pm Mon-Fri, by appointment Sat & Sun) **FREE**.

Western Lesvos is known for its **petrified forest** (www.petrifiedforest.gr; admission €2; ☺ 9am-5pm Jul-Sep, Fri-Sun Oct-Jun), with petrified wood at least 500,000 years old, and for the gay-friendly town of **Skala Eresou**, the birthplace of Sappho (see p370). You can stay over in peaceful **Sigri**, with its broad beaches to the southwest.

ⓘ Getting There & Around

AIR

Written up on flight schedules as Mytilene, Lesvos' Odysseas Airport (MJT) has daily connections with Athens and Thessaloniki. **Sky Express** (☎ 28102 23500; www.skyexpress.gr) flies to Iraklio, Limnos, Chios, Samos, Rhodes and Ikaria (but beware its strict baggage policy). The airport is 8km south of Mytilini town; taxis cost €10, bus €1.60.

BOAT

In summer daily fast boats leave Mytilini Town for Piraeus (€41, 11 to 13 hours) via Chios. Other ferries serve Chios, Ikaria Limnos, Thessaloniki and Samos. Check www.openseas.gr.

To Turkey

There are regular ferries each week to Dikili port (which serves Ayvalık) and to Fokias (which serves İzmir). Stop by Zoumboulis Tours (p371) for ticketing and schedules.

BUS

The long-distance bus station in Mytilini Town is beside Agia Irinis Park, near the domed church. The local bus station is opposite Plateia Sapphou, the main square.

CAR

It's worth renting a car in Lesvos to explore the vast island. There are several outlets at the airport and many in town.

SPORADES ΣΠΟΡΑΔΕΣ

Scattered to the southeast of the Pelion Peninsula, to which they were joined in prehistoric times, the 11 islands that make up the Sporades group have similarly mountainous terrain and dense vegetation, and are surrounded by scintillatingly clear seas.

The main ports for the Sporades are Volos and Agios Konstantinos on the mainland.

Skiathos Σκιαθος

POP 6150

Lush and green, Skiathos has a beach resort feel about it. Charter flights bring loads of package tourists, but the island still oozes enjoyment and is downright mellow in winter. Skiathos Town, with its quaint **old harbour**, and some excellent beaches are on the hospitable south coast.

◉ Sights & Activities

Moni Evangelistrias (Monastery of the Annunciation; museum admission €2; ☺ 10am-dusk), the most famous of the island's monasteries was a hilltop refuge for freedom fighters during the War of Independence, and the Greek flag was first raised here, in 1807.

Skiathos has superb beaches, particularly on the south coast. **Koukounaries** is popular with families, and has a wonderful protected **marshland** for water fowl. A stroll over the headland, **Big Banana Beach** is stunning, but if you want an all-over tan, head a tad further to **Little Banana Beach**, where bathing suits are a rarity. Beautiful **Lalaria** on the north coast is accessible only by boat.

At the Old Port in Skiathos Town, **boat excursions** go to nearby beaches (€10), around Skiathos Island (€25) and on full-day trips to Skopelos, Alonnisos and the Alonissos Marine Park (€35).

🛌 Sleeping

Hotel Mato HOTEL €
(☎ 24270 22186; www.matoskiathos.gr; 25th Martiou 30; d incl breakfast €60; ✴ ⓢ) Cosy Hotel Mato is in the centre of the picturesque pedestrianised old town, and remains open all year. Friendly proprietor Popi keeps the place spick and span and cooks fab breakfasts with farm-fresh eggs.

Hotel Bourtzi BOUTIQUE HOTEL €€€
(☎ 24270 21304; www.hotelbourtzi.gr; Moraitou 8; d incl breakfast from €174; Ⓟ ✴ ⓢ ⌷) On upper Papadiamanti, the swank Bourtzi escapes much of the town noise and features high-design rooms and an inviting garden and pool. Minimum seven-night stay in summer.

🍴 Eating & Drinking

Seafood joints line Skiathos' Old Harbour, cafes and bars wrap around the whole waterfront.

MOVIES UNDER THE STARS

Summertime in Greece means open-air cinema. Athens has **Aigli Cinema** (☑210 336 9369; www.aeglizappiou.gr; Zappeio Gardens, Syntagma; Ⓜ Syntagma) and **Cine Paris** (☑210 322 0721; www.cineparis.gr; Kydathineon 22, Plaka; Ⓜ Syntagma), among others, and Skiathos boasts **Cinema Attikon** (☑69727 06305, 24720 22352; tickets €7). Catch current English-language movies under the stars, sip a beer and practise speed-reading Greek subtitles. Many other islands have similar cinemas – ask around.

**Taverna-Ouzerie
Kabourelia** TAVERNA €
(Old Harbour; mains €4-9; ⊙noon-midnight; 🗑) Poke your nose into the open kitchen to glimpse the day's catch at this popular year-round eatery at the old port, with perfect fish grills at moderate prices. Grilled octopus and *taramasalata* are just two of several standout mezedhes.

O Batis TAVERNA €
(☑24270 22288; Old Harbour; mains €4-9; ⊙noon-midnight) This popular fish taverna on the path above the old port is a local standby for reliable and well-priced fresh fish, *gavros* (marinated small fish), and fine mezedhes. Cosy atmosphere and a good selection of island wines, year-round.

ⓘ Information

See www.skiathosinfo.com for information.

ⓘ Getting There & Around

AIR
Skiathos Airport (JSI) is 2km northeast of Skiathos Town, and has summertime daily flights to Athens and charter flights from northern Europe. Taxis cost €6 to €15 depending on where you're headed.

BOAT
Frequent daily hydrofoils serve mainland ports Volos (€38, 1¼ hours) and Agios Konstantinos (€37, two hours), as do cheaper ferries. Hydrofoils/ferries serve Skopelos (€10/6, 20/40 minutes) and Alonnisos (€17/11, 1½/2½ hours). See **Hellenic Seaways** (☑24270 22209; www.hsw.gr) or **NEL Lines** (☑24270 22018; www.nel.gr).

Water taxis around Skiathos depart from the Old Harbour.

BUS
Crowded buses ply the south-coast road between Skiathos Town and Koukounaries (€2) every 30 minutes between 7.30am and 11pm year-round, stopping at all the beaches along the way. The bus stop is at the eastern end of the harbour.

IONIAN ISLANDS
ΤΑ ΕΠΤΑΝΗΣΑ

The idyllic cypress- and fir-covered Ionian Islands stretch down the western coast of Greece from Corfu in the north to Kythira, off the southern tip of the Peloponnese. Mountainous, with dramatic cliff-backed beaches, soft light and turquoise water, they're more Italian in feel, offering a contrasting experience to other Greek islands.

Corfu Κέρκυρα
POP 101,080

Many consider Corfu, or Kerkyra (*ker-kih-rah*) in Greek, to be Greece's most beautiful island – the unfortunate consequence of which is that it's overbuilt and often overrun with crowds. Look beyond them to find its core splendour.

Corfu Town Κέρκυρα
POP 31,359

Built on a promontory and wedged between two fortresses, Corfu's **Old Town** is a tangle of narrow walking streets through gorgeous Venetian buildings. Explore the winding alleys and surprising plazas in the early morning or late afternoon to avoid the hordes of day trippers seeking souvenirs.

⊙ Sights

★**Palaio Frourio** FORTRESS
(Old Fortress; ☑26610 48310; adult/concession €4/2; ⊙8am-8pm Apr-Oct, 8.30am-3pm Nov-Mar) Constructed by the Venetians in the 15th century on the remains of a Byzantine castle and further altered by the British, this spectacular landmark offers respite from the crowds and superb views of the region. Climb to the summit of the inner outcrop, which is crowned by a lighthouse for a 360-degree panorama. The gatehouse contains a Byzantine **museum**.

IONIAN PLEASURES

Paxi (Παξοί) Paxi lives up to its reputation as one of the Ionians' most idyllic and picturesque islands. At only 10km by 4km it's the smallest of the main holiday islands and makes a fine escape from Corfu's quicker-paced pleasures.

Kefallonia (Κεφαλλονιά) Tranquil cypress- and fir-covered Kefallonia, the largest Ionian island, is breathtakingly beautiful with rugged mountain ranges, rich vineyards, soaring coastal cliffs and golden beaches. It has not succumbed to package tourism to the extent that some of the other Ionian Islands have and remains low-key outside resort areas.

Ithaki (Ιθάκη) Odysseus' long-lost home in Homer's *Odyssey*, Ithaki (ancient Ithaca) remains a verdant, pristine island blessed with cypress-covered hills and beautiful turquoise coves. It's best reached from Kefallonia.

Lefkada (Λευκάδα) Lefkada has some of the best beaches in Greece, if not the world, and an easygoing way of life.

★ **Palace of St Michael & St George**   PALACE
Originally the residence of a succession of British high commissioners, this palace now houses the world-class **Museum of Asian Art** (☑ 2661030443; www.matk.gr; adult/child incl audioguide €3/free, with Antivouniotissa Museum & Old Fortress €8; ⊙ 8.30am-3.30pm Tue-Sun), founded in 1929. Expertly curated with extensive, informative English-language placards, the collection's approximately 10,000 artefacts collected from all over Asia include priceless prehistoric bronzes, ceramics, jade figurines, coins and works of art in onyx, ivory and enamel. Additionally, the palace's **throne room** and **rotunda** are impressively adorned in period furnishings and art.

★ **Church of Agios Spyridon**   CHURCH
(Agios Spyridonos; ⊙ 7am-8pm) FREE The sacred relic of Corfu's beloved patron saint, St Spyridon, lies in an elaborate silver casket in the 16th-century basilica.

Antivouniotissa Museum   MUSEUM
(☑ 26610 38313; www.antivouniotissamuseum.gr; off Arseniou; adult/child €2/1; ⊙ 9am-3.30pm Tue-Sun) The exquisite timber-roofed 15th-century **Church of Our Lady of Antivouniotissa** holds an outstanding collection of Byzantine and post-Byzantine icons and artefacts dating from the 13th to the 17th centuries.

Mon Repos Estate   PARK
(Kanoni Peninsula; ⊙ 8am-7pm May-Oct, to 5pm Nov-Apr) FREE On the southern outskirts of town on the Kanoni Peninsula, an extensive wooded parkland estate surrounds an elegant neoclassical villa housing the **Museum of Palaeopolis** (☑ 26610 41369; www.corfu.

gr; adult/concession €3/2; ⊙ 8am-7pm Tue-Sun May-Oct), with entertaining archaeological displays and exhibits on the history of Corfu Town. Paths lead through lush grounds to the ruins of two Doric temples; the first is truly a ruin, but the southerly **Temple of Artemis** is serenely impressive.

🛏 Sleeping

Accommodation prices fluctuate wildly depending on season; book ahead.

★ **Siorra Vittoria**   BOUTIQUE HOTEL €€
(☑ 26610 36300; www.siorravittoria.com; Stefanou Padova 36; s/d incl breakfast from €95/135, ste €165-190; P ※ 🛜) Expect luxury and style at this quiet, 19th-century mansion where painstakingly restored traditional architecture and modern amenities meet. Marble bathrooms, crisp linens and genteel service make for a relaxed stay. Breakfast in the peaceful garden beneath an ancient magnolia tree. The Vittoria suite encompasses the atelier and has views of the sea.

★ **Bella Venezia**   BOUTIQUE HOTEL €€
(☑ 26610 46500; www.bellaveneziahotel.com; N Zambeli 4; s/d incl breakfast from €100/120; ☻ ※ 🛜) In a neoclassical former girls' school, the Venezia has comfy rooms and an elegant ambience. Conscientious staff welcome you, and the gazebo breakfast room in the garden is delightful.

Hermes Hotel   HOTEL €€
(☑ 26610 39268; www.hermes-hotel.gr; Markora 12; s/d/tr from €50/70/90; ※ 🛜) In a busy part of the new town, overlooking the market, Hermes offers simple, tidy rooms with double glazing, which are especially atmospheric in the old wing.

✕ Eating & Drinking

Corfu has excellent restaurants. Cafes and bars line the arcaded Liston. Try Corfu Beer.

★ To Tavernaki tis Marinas
TAVERNA €

(☑69816 56001; 4th Parados, Agias Sofias 1; mains €6-16; ☺noon-midnight) Restored stone walls, smooth hardwood floors and cheerful staff lift the ambience of this taverna a cut above the rest. Check daily specials or choose anything from *mousakas* (baked layers of eggplant or zucchini, minced meat and potatoes topped with cheese sauce) or grilled sardines to steak. Accompany it all with a dram of ouzo or *tsipouro* (a spirit similar to ouzo).

Chrisomalis
TAVERNA €

(☑26610 30342; N Theotoki 6; mains €8-13; ☺noon-midnight) Smack in the heart of the old town, this ma-and-pa operation dishes out the classics. Cruise inside to choose from what's fresh.

★ La Cucina
ITALIAN €€

(☑26610 45029; Guilford 17; mains €13-25; ☺7-11pm) A long-established favourite, well-run La Cucina shines for its creative cuisine, with hand-rolled pasta dishes at the fore.

The original Guilford location is cosy warm tones and murals, while the **Moustoxidou** (☑26610 45799; cnr Guilford & Moustoxidou; ☺7-11pm) annexe (with identical menu) is chic in glass and grey.

To Dimarchio
ITALIAN, GREEK €€

(☑26610 39031; Plateia Dimarchio; mains €9-25; ☺noon-midnight) Relax in a luxuriant rose garden on a charming square. Attentive staff serve elegant, inventive dishes, both Italian and Greek, prepared with the freshest ingredients.

ⓘ Information

Tourist Police (☑26610 30265; 3rd fl, Samartzi 4) Off Plateia San Rocco.

Around the Island

To explore the island fully your own transport is best. Much of the coast just north of Corfu Town is overwhelmed with beach resorts, the south is quieter, and the west has a beautiful, if popular, coastline. The **Corfu Trail** (www.thecorfutrail.com) traverses the island north to south.

North of Corfu Town, in **Kassiopi**, **Manessis Apartments** (☑26610 34990; www.manessiskassiopi.com; Kassiopi; 4-person apt €70-100; ☀⟨) offers water-view apartments.

South of Corfu Town, **Achillion Palace** (☑26610 56210; www.achillion-corfu.gr; Gastouri; adult/child €7/2, audio guide €3; ☺8am-8pm Apr-Oct, 8.45am-4pm Nov-Mar) pulls 'em in for over-the-top royal bling. Don't miss a dinner at one of the island's best tavernas, **Klimataria** (Bellos; ☑26610 71201; mains €8-14; ☺7pm-midnight) in nearby **Benitses**.

To gain an aerial view of the gorgeous cypress-backed bays around **Paleokastritsa**, the west coast's main resort, go to the quiet village of **Lakones**. Backpackers head to **Pelekas Beach** for low-key **Sunrock** (☑26610 94637; www.sunrockhostel.com; Pelekas Beach; dm/r per person incl breakfast & dinner €18/25; @⟨), a full-board hostel. Further south, good beaches surround tiny **Agios Gordios**, which has the famous **Pink Palace** (☑26610 53103; www.thepinkpalace.com; Agios Gordios Beach; dm & r per person incl breakfast & dinner €21-50; ☀@) backpackers and is party central.

ⓘ Getting There & Around

AIR

Ioannis Kapodistrias Airport (CFU; ☑26610 89600; www.corfu-airport.com) is 2km southwest of Corfu Town. **Olympic Air** (☑801 801 0101; www.olympicair.com), **Aegean Airlines** (☑26610 27100; www.aegeanair.com) and Astra Airlines (p378) fly daily to Athens and a few times weekly to Thessaloniki. **Sky Express** (☑2810 223500; www.skyexpress.gr) operates seasonal routes to other Ionian Islands and Crete (but beware its strict baggage policy). Charter planes and budget airlines fly internationally in summer. Bus 19 serves the airport (€1.50); taxis cost €7 to €10.

BOAT

Neo Limani port lies west of the Neo Frourio (New Fortress). Ferries go to Igoumenitsa (€10, 1½ hours, hourly). In summer daily ferries and hydrofoils go to Paxi, and ferries to Italy (Bari, Brindisi and Venice) also stop in Patra (€35, six hours); some stop in Kefallonia and Zakynthos. **Petrakis Lines** (Ionian Cruises; ☑26610 31649; Ethnikis Antistaseos 4, Corfu Town) goes to Saranda, Albania. Check www.openseas.gr.

BUS

Blue buses (€1.10 to €1.50) for villages near Corfu Town leave from Plateia San Rocco. Services to other destinations (around Corfu

€1.60 to €4.40) and daily buses to Athens (€45, 8½ hours) and Thessaloniki (€35, eight hours) leave from Corfu's **long-distance bus station** (☑ 26610 28927; www.ktelkerkyras.gr; Ioannou Theotoki, Corfu Town).

SURVIVAL GUIDE

ℹ Directory A–Z

ACCOMMODATION
Accommodation Types

Hotels Range from basic business lodging to high-end boutique extravaganzas.

Pensions and guesthouses Often include breakfast and are usually owner-operated.

Domatia Rooms for rent; owners greet ferries and buses shouting 'room!'.

Youth hostels In most major towns and on some islands.

Campgrounds Generally open April to October; standard facilities include hot showers, kitchens, restaurants and minimarkets, and often a swimming pool. Check out **Panhellenic Camping Association** (☑ 21036 21560; www. greececamping.gr). Wild camping is forbidden.

Mountain refuges Listed in *Greece Mountain Refuges & Ski Centres*, available free from EOT and EOS (Ellinikos Orivatikos Syndesmos, Greek Alpine Club) offices.

BUSINESS HOURS

Banks 8am to 2.30pm Monday to Thursday, 8am to 2pm Friday

Bars 8pm to late

Cafes 10am to midnight

Clubs 10pm to 4am

Post offices Rural areas 7.30am to 2pm Monday to Friday; urban offices 7.30am to 8pm Monday to Friday, 7.30am to 2pm Saturday

Restaurants 11am to 3pm and 7pm to 1am

Shops 8am to 3pm Monday, Wednesday and Saturday; 8am to 2.30pm and 5pm to 8.30pm Tuesday, Thursday and Friday (all day in summer in resorts). Sunday permitted in major tourist areas and central Athens.

CUSTOMS REGULATIONS

It is strictly forbidden to export antiquities (anything over 100 years old) without an export permit.

INTERNET ACCESS

Wi-fi is common at most sleeping and eating venues, ports, airports and some city squares.

ESSENTIAL FOOD & DRINK

Nutritious and flavourful, the food is one of the great pleasures of travelling in Greece. The country's rich culinary heritage draws from a fusion of mountain village food, island cuisine, flavours introduced by Greeks from Asia Minor, and influences from various invaders and historical trading partners. The essence of classic Greek cuisine lies in fresh, seasonal home-grown produce and generally simple, unfussy cooking that brings out the rich flavours of the Mediterranean.

➡ **Savoury appetisers** Known as mezedhes (literally, 'tastes'; meze for short), standards include tzatziki (yoghurt, cucumber and garlic), *melitzanosalata* (aubergine dip), *taramasalata* (fish-roe dip), dolmadhes (stuffed vine leaves; dolmas for short), *fasolia* (beans) and *oktapodi* (octopus).

➡ **Cheap eats** Gyros is pork or chicken shaved from a revolving stack of sizzling meat and wrapped in pitta bread with tomato, onion, fried potatoes and lashings of tzatziki. Souvlaki is skewered meat, usually pork.

➡ **Taverna staples** You'll find *mousaka* (layers of aubergine and mince, topped with béchamel sauce and baked) on every menu, alongside *moschari* (oven-baked veal and potatoes), *keftedhes* (meatballs), *stifado* (meat stew), *pastitsio* (baked dish of macaroni with minced meat and béchamel sauce) and *yemista* (either tomatoes or green peppers stuffed with minced meat and rice).

➡ **Sweets** Greeks are serious about their sweets, with *zaharoplasteia* (sweet shops) in even the smallest villages. Try variations on baklava (thin layers of pastry filled with honey and nuts). Or go simple: delicious Greek yogurt drizzled with honey.

➡ **Top tipples** Legendary aniseed-flavoured ouzo sipped slowly, turns a cloudy white when ice or water is added. *Raki*, the Cretan fire water, is produced from grape skins. Greek coffee, a legacy of Ottoman rule, is a favourite pastime.

COUNTRY FACTS

Area 131,944 sq km

Capital Athens

Country Code ☑ 30

Currency Euro (€)

Emergency ☑ 112

Language Greek

Money Cash is king, ATMs are common except in small villages, and credit cards only sporadically accepted.

Population 10.7 million

Visas Generally not required for stays up to 90 days. Member of Schengen Convention.

INTERNET RESOURCES

Ancient Greece (www.ancientgreece.com)
Greek Ferries (www.openseas.gr, www.greek ferries.gr)
Greek National Tourist Organisation (www. gnto.gr, visitgreece.gr, www.discovergreece. com)
Greek Travel Pages (www.gtp.gr)
Virtual Greece (www.greecevirtual.gr)

MONEY

➡ ATMs are everywhere except small villages.
➡ Cash is widely used and your best bet, especially in the countryside; credit cards are not always accepted in small villages.
➡ Service charge is included on the bill in restaurants, but it is the custom to 'round up the bill'; same for taxis.

POST

➡ Tahydromia (post offices; www.elta.gr) are easily identified by their yellow sign.
➡ Postcards and airmail letters within the EU cost €0.60, to other destinations €0.80.

PUBLIC HOLIDAYS

New Year's Day 1 January
Epiphany 6 January
First Sunday in Lent February
Greek Independence Day 25 March
Orthodox Good Friday March/April (varies)
Orthodox Easter Sunday 12 April 2015, 1 May 2016, 16 April 2017, 8 April 2018, 28 April 2019
May Day (Protomagia) 1 May
Whit Monday (Agiou Pnevmatos) 50 days after Easter Sunday
Feast of the Assumption 15 August
Ohi Day 28 October
Christmas Day 25 December
St Stephen's Day 26 December

TELEPHONE

➡ Organismos Tilepikoinonion Ellados, known as OTE (o-teh), public phones abound. Phonecards are sold at OTE shops and newspaper kiosks; pressing the 'i' button brings up instructions in English.

➡ Mobile coverage is widespread. Visitors with GSM 900/1800 phones can make roaming calls; purchase a local SIM card, which requires a passport to register, if you're staying awhile and have an unlocked mobile.

➡ For directory inquiries within Greece, call ☑ 131; for international inquiries ☑ 161. Area codes are part of the 10-digit number within Greece.

TIME

Greece is in the Eastern European time zone: two hours ahead of GMT/UTC and three hours ahead on daylight-saving time (last Sunday in March through to last Sunday in October).

ⓘ Getting There & Away

Regular ferry connections shuttle between Greece and the Italian ports of Ancona, Bari, Brindisi and Venice. Similarly, ferries operate between the Greek islands of Rhodes, Kos, Samos, Chios and Lesvos and the Aegean coast of Turkey.

Overland, it's possible to reach Albania, Bulgaria, the Former Yugoslav Republic of Macedonia (FYROM), Romania and Turkey from Greece. If you've got your own wheels, you can drive through border crossings with these four countries. There are train and bus connections with Greece's neighbours, but check ahead, as these have been affected by the financial crisis.

See www.seat61.com for more information on ferry travel.

SLEEPING PRICE RANGES

Accommodation is nearly always negotiable (and deeply reduced) outside peak season, especially for longer stays. Prices quoted in listings are for high season (July and August) with a private bathroom.

€ less than €60 (€80 in Athens)

€€ €60 to €150 (€80 to €150 in Athens)

€€€ more than €150

EATING PRICE RANGES

Price ranges are based on the average cost of a main dish:

€ less than €10

€€ €10 to €20

€€€ more than €20

AIR

Most visitors arrive by air, mostly into Athens. There are 17 international airports in Greece; most handle only summer charter flights to the islands.

There's a growing number of direct scheduled services into Greece by European budget airlines – **Olympic Air** (www. olympicair.com) and **Aegean Airlines** (www.aegeanair.com) also fly internationally.

LAND
Border Crossings

You can drive or ride through the following border crossings.

Albania Kakavia (60km northwest of Ioannina); Sagiada (28km north of Igoumenitsa); Mertziani (17km west of Konitsa); Krystallopigi (14km west of Kotas)

Bulgaria Promahonas (109km northeast of Thessaloniki); Ormenio (41km from Serres); Exohi (50km north of Drama)

Former Yugoslav Republic of Macedonia (FYROM) Evzoni (68km north of Thessaloniki); Niki (16km north of Florina); Doïrani (31km north of Kilkis)

Turkey Kipi (43km east of Alexandroupolis); Kastanies (139km northeast of Alexandroupolis)

Bus

Private companies and KTEL Macedonia run buses from Thessaloniki to İstanbul, Skopje and Sofia; see p350.

Albania is served by **Albatrans** (☑+355 42 259 204; www.albatrans.com.al) and **Euro Interlines** (☑+355 42251866, 210 523 4594; www.eurointerlines.com).

Bus and tour companies run buses between Greece and Sofia, Bulgaria; Budapest, Hungary; Prague, Czech Republic; and Turkey. See Simeonidis Tours (p350), **Dimidis Tours** (www.dimidistours.gr) and **Tourist Service** (www.tourist-service.com).

Train

Both international and domestic **train routes** (www.trainose.gr) have been severely curtailed due to financial problems. Check the current

situation well in advance. Trains go from Thessaloniki to Bulgaria (Sofia) and FYROM (Skopje).

SEA

Check ferry routes and schedules at www.greekferries.gr and www.openseas.gr.

If you are travelling on a rail pass, check to see if ferry travel between Italy and Greece is included. Some ferries are free, others give a discount. On some routes you will need to make reservations.

Albania

For Saranda, **Petrakis Lines** (☑26610 38690; www.ionian-cruises.com) has daily hydrofoils to Corfu (25 minutes).

Italy

Routes vary, check online.

Ancona Patra (20 hours, three daily, summer)

Bari Patra (14½ hours, daily) via Corfu (eight hours) and Kefallonia (14 hours); also to Igoumenitsa (11½ hours, daily). Some go via Zakynthos.

Brindisi Patra (15 hours, April to early October) via Igoumenitsa

Venice Patra (30 hours, up to 12 weekly, summer) via Corfu (25 hours)

Turkey

Boat services operate between Turkey's Aegean coast and the Greek Islands; see p367.

🛈 Getting Around

Greece has a comprehensive transport system and is easy to get around.

AIR

It's sometimes cheaper to fly than take the ferry, especially if you book ahead online. Domestic airlines include the following.

Aegean Airlines (☑801 112 0000; www.aegeanair.com)

Astra Airlines (☑2310 489 392; www.astra-airlines.gr) Airline based in Thessaloniki.

Hellenic Seaplanes (☑210 647 0180; www.hellenic-seaplanes.com) Charters with planned routes to the islands.

Olympic Air (☑801 801 0101; www.olympicair.com) Partly merged with Aegean.

Sky Express (☑2810 223500; www.skyexpress.gr) Cretan airline with flights around Greece. Beware harsh baggage restrictions.

BICYCLE

➡ Greece has very hilly terrain and the summer heat can be stifling. In addition, most drivers totally disregard road rules. Bicycles are carried for free on ferries.

➡ See www.cyclegreece.gr for bicycle tour ideas.

➜ Rental bicycles are available at most tourist centres, but are generally for pedalling around town rather than for serious riding. Prices range from €10 to €20 per day.

BOAT

For many, the idea of meandering from island to island by boat is the ultimate Greek Island dream. Beware that in high season you might find it just as stressful as rush hour back home.

Ferries come in all shapes and sizes, from state-of-the-art 'superferries' that run on the major routes, to ageing open ferries that operate local services to outlying islands. Newer high-speed ferries slash travel times, but cost more; they are often catamarans or hydrofoils.

You may have the option of 'deck class', which is the cheapest ticket, or 'cabin class' with air-con assigned seats. On larger ferries there are lounges and restaurants for everyone serving fast food or snacks.

Boat operations are highly seasonal and based on the tourist trade. Services pick up from April, and slow down by November. In winter they are reduced or cut entirely. Weather (especially wind) can result in last-minute cancellations, even in summer. If you are prone to seasickness, book seats in the centre rear of the boat, or with a window.

Be flexible. Boats seldom arrive early, but often arrive late! And some don't come at all.

Tickets can be bought at the dock, but in high season, boats are often full – plan ahead. Check www.openseas.gr or www.gtp.gr for schedules, costs and links to individual boat company websites.

The Greek Ships app for smartphones tracks ferries in real time.

BUS

Long-distance buses are operated by **KTEL** (www.ktel.org). Fares are fixed by the government and service routes can be found on the company's website or regional websites (listed in our coverage). Buses are comfortable, generally run on time, are reasonably priced and offer frequent services on major routes. Buy tickets at least an hour in advance. Buses don't have toilets

Main Ferry Routes

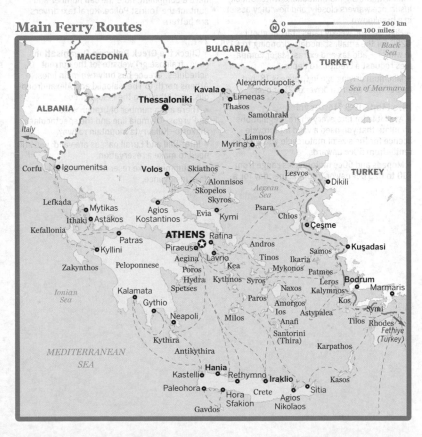

or refreshments, but stop for a break every couple of hours.

CAR & MOTORCYCLE
➡ A great way to explore areas in Greece that are off the beaten track, but be careful on highways – Greece has the highest road-fatality rate in Europe. The road network is decent, but freeway tolls are fairly hefty.

➡ Almost all islands are served by car ferries, but they are expensive; costs vary by the size of the vehicle.

➡ The Greek automobile club, **ELPA** (www.elpa.gr), generally offers reciprocal services to members of other national motoring associations. If your vehicle breaks down, dial 🗷104.

➡ EU-registered vehicles are allowed free entry into Greece for six months without road taxes being due; a green card (international third-party insurance) is all that's required.

Hire Cars
➡ Available throughout Greece, you'll get better rates with local rental-car companies than with the big multinational outfits. Check insurance waivers closely, and how they assist in a breakdown.

➡ High-season weekly rates start at about €280 for the smallest models, dropping to €175 in winter – add tax and extras. Major companies request a credit-card deposit.

➡ Minimum driving age in Greece is 18, but most firms require a driver of 21 or over.

Hire Mopeds & Motorcycles
➡ Available for hire everywhere. Regulations stipulate that you need a valid motorcycle licence for the size of motorcycle you wish to rent – from 50cc upwards.

➡ Mopeds and 50cc motorcycles range from €10 to €25 per day or from €25 per day for a 250cc motorcycle. Outside high season, rates drop considerably.

Road Rules
➡ Drive on the right.

➡ Overtake on the left (not all Greeks do this!).

➡ Compulsory to wear seatbelts in the front seats, and in the back if they are fitted.

➡ Drink-driving laws are strict; a blood alcohol content of 0.05% incurs a fine of around €150 and over 0.08% is a criminal offence.

PUBLIC TRANSPORT
All major towns have a local bus system. Athens is the only city with a metro system.

TAXI
➡ Taxis are widely available and reasonably priced. Yellow city cabs are metered; rates double between midnight and 5am. Grey rural taxis do not have meters; settle on a price before you get in.

➡ Athens taxi drivers are gifted in their ability to make a little bit extra with every fare. If you have a complaint, note the cab number and contact the Tourist Police. Rural taxi drivers are better.

TRAIN
➡ Check the **Greek Railways Organisation** (www.trainose.gr) website for the current schedules. Greece has only two main lines: Athens north to Thessaloniki and Alexandroupolis, and Athens to the Peloponnese.

➡ There are a number of branch lines, eg Pyrgos–Olympia line and the spectacular Diakofto–Kalavryta mountain railway.

➡ Inter-Rail and Eurail passes are valid; you still need to make a reservation.

➡ In summer make reservations at least two days in advance.

Ireland

Includes ➡

Best Traditional Pubs

➡ Stag's Head (p390)

➡ Kyteler's Inn (p394)

➡ O'Connor's (p399)

➡ Crown Liquor Saloon (p408)

➡ Peadar O'Donnell's (p412)

➡ Crane Bar (p403)

Best Places to Eat

➡ Fade Street Social (p389)

➡ Market Lane (p396)

➡ Quay Street Kitchen (p403)

➡ Barking Dog (p408)

Why Go?

Few countries have an image so plagued by cliché. From shamrocks and *shillelaghs* (Irish fighting sticks) to leprechauns and loveable rogues, there's a plethora of platitudes to wade through before you reach the real Ireland.

But it's well worth looking beyond the tourist tat, for the Emerald Isle is one of Europe's gems, a scenic extravaganza of lakes, mountains, sea and sky. From picture-postcard County Kerry to the rugged coastline of Northern Ireland (part of the UK, distinct from the Republic of Ireland), there are countless opportunities to get outdoors and explore, whether cycling the Causeway Coast or hiking the hills of Killarney and Connemara.

There are cultural pleasures too in the land of Joyce and Yeats, U2 and the Undertones. Dublin, Cork and Belfast all have world-class art galleries and museums, while you can enjoy foot-stomping traditional music in the bars of Galway and Killarney. So push aside the shamrocks and experience the real Ireland.

When to Go

Dublin

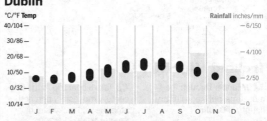

Late Mar Spring flowers everywhere, landscape is greening, St Patrick's Day festivities beckon.

Jun Best chance of dry weather, long summer evenings, Bloomsday in Dublin.

Sep & Oct Summer crowds thin, autumn colours reign, surf's up on the west coast.

ATLANTIC OCEAN

Troon

Cairnryan

Giant's Causeway **3**

Carrick-a-Rede Island

Bushmills

Ballycastle

Lough Foyle

Coleraine

Derry/Londonderry

Letterkenny

Glens of Antrim

A26

A6

Larne

North Channel

Glencolumbcille

Slieve League ▲

Donegal

NORTHERN IRELAND

Newtownabbey

Lough Neagh

Belfast **7**

Douglas; Liverpool

Omagh

N15

Bundoran

Lower Lough Erne

Sligo

Enniskillen

Newry

Mourne Mountains

Irish Sea

Ballycastle

N59

N26

Lough Feeagh

Dundalk

Liverpool; Douglas

Westport

N17

Longford

M1

Drogheda

Connemara

Lough Corrib

Mullingar

Clifden

Athlone

Dublin **1**

Holyhead

Galway **2**

Burren Village

M6

The Curragh

M4

N7

Dun Laoghaire **5**

Aran Islands **8**

The Burren

N18

Doolin

Cliffs of Moher

Donegal Point

Ennis

Portlaoise

Glendalough

Naas

Gleanealy

Lugnaquilla Mountain

M11

Wicklow Head

M7

Carlow

Limerick

M8

Kilkenny

N9

St George's Channel

Mouth of the Shannon

Rock of Cashel

Dingle Peninsula

N69

Tralee

Gap of Dunloe **6**

N20

Clonmel

IRELAND

Wexford

Fishguard (Wales)

Dingle

Carrantuohil ▲

Killarney

Blarney

Waterford

Rosslare

Caherciveen

N71

Skellig Michael **4**

N22

Cork

Ballinskelligs

Beara Peninsula

Cobh

ATLANTIC OCEAN

Mizen Head Peninsula

Kinsale

Clear Island

Baltimore

Roscoff (France)

Cherbourg & Roscoff (France)

0 ——— 100 km
0 ——— 50 miles

N

Ireland Highlights

1 Meander through the museums, pubs and literary haunts of **Dublin**.

2 Hang out in bohemian **Galway** (p401), with its hip cafes and live-music venues.

3 Hike the Causeway Coast and clamber across the **Giant's Causeway** (p410).

4 Take a boat trip to the 6th-century monastery perched atop the wild rocky islet of **Skellig Michael** (p399).

5 Sip a pint of Guinness while listening to live music in one of Dublin's **traditional pubs** (p390).

6 Cycle through the spectacular lake and mountain

scenery of the **Gap of Dunloe** (p398).

7 Discover the industrial history of the city that built the world's most famous ocean liner at **Titanic Belfast** (p405).

8 Wander the wild, limestone shores of the remote and craggy **Aran Islands** (p403).

ITINERARIES

One Week

Spend a couple of days in **Dublin** ambling through the excellent national museums, and gorging yourself on Guinness and good company in Temple Bar. Get medieval in **Kilkenny** before heading on to **Cork** and discovering why they call it 'The Real Capital'. Head west for a day or two exploring the scenic **Ring of Kerry** and enchanting **Killarney**.

Two Weeks

Follow the one-week itinerary, then make your way north from Killarney to bohemian **Galway**. Using Galway as your base, explore the alluring **Aran Islands** and the hills of **Connemara**. Finally, head north to see the **Giant's Causeway** and experience the optimistic vibe in fast-changing **Belfast**.

DUBLIN

POP 1.27 MILLION

Sultry rather than sexy, Dublin exudes personality as only those who've managed to turn careworn into carefree can. The halcyon days of the Celtic Tiger (the Irish economic boom of the late 1990s), when cash cascaded like a free-flowing waterfall, have long since disappeared, and the city has once again been forced to grind out a living. But Dubliners still know how to enjoy life. They do so through their music, art and literature – things that Dubs often take for granted but, once reminded, generate immense pride.

There are world-class museums, superb restaurants and the best range of entertainment available anywhere in Ireland – and that's not including the pub, the ubiquitous centre of the city's social life and an absolute must for any visitor. And should you wish to get away from it all, the city has a handful of seaside towns at its edges that make for wonderful day trips.

◉ Sights

Dublin's finest Georgian architecture, including its famed doorways, is found around **St Stephen's Green** (⊙dawn-dusk; ▣all city centre; ▣St Stephen's Green) **FREE** and **Merrion Square** (⊙dawn-dusk; ▣7 & 44 from city centre) **FREE** just south of Trinity College; both are prime picnic spots when the sun shines.

★**Trinity College**　　　　HISTORIC BUILDING
(☑01-896 1000; www.tcd.ie; College Green; ⊙8am-10pm; ▣all city centre) **FREE** This calm retreat from the bustle of contemporary Dublin is Ireland's most prestigious university, founded by Elizabeth I in 1592. Not only is it the city's most attractive historic real estate, but it's also home to one of the world's most famous – and most beautiful – books, the gloriously illuminated **Book of Kells**. There's no charge to wander around the grounds on your own, but the student-led **walking tours** (trinitytours@csc.tcd.ie; per person €5, incl Book of Kells €10; ⊙10.15am-3.40pm Mon-Sat, to 3pm Sun mid-May–Sep, fewer midweek tours Oct-Apr), departing from the College Green entrance, are recommended.

The college was established on land confiscated from an Augustinian priory in an effort to stop the brain drain of young Protestant Dubliners, who were skipping across to Continental Europe for an education and were becoming 'infected with popery'. Trinity went on to become one of Europe's most outstanding universities, producing a host of notable graduates – how about Jonathan Swift, Oscar Wilde and Samuel Beckett at the same alumni dinner?

It remained completely Protestant until 1793, but even when the university relented and began to admit Catholics, the Church forbade it; until 1970, any Catholic who enrolled here could consider themselves excommunicated.

The campus is a masterpiece of architecture and landscaping beautifully preserved in Georgian style; the elegant Regent House entrance on College Green is guarded by statues of the writer Oliver Goldsmith (1730–74) and the orator Edmund Burke (1729–97). Through the gate, most of the buildings date from the 18th and 19th centuries, elegantly laid out around a series of interlinked squares.

The newer parts include the brutalist **Berkeley Library**, a masterpiece of modern architecture, and the 1978 **Arts & Social Science Building**, which backs onto Nassau St and provides an alternative entrance to the college. Like the Berkeley Library, it was designed by Paul Koralek; it also houses the **Douglas Hyde Gallery of Modern**

Dublin

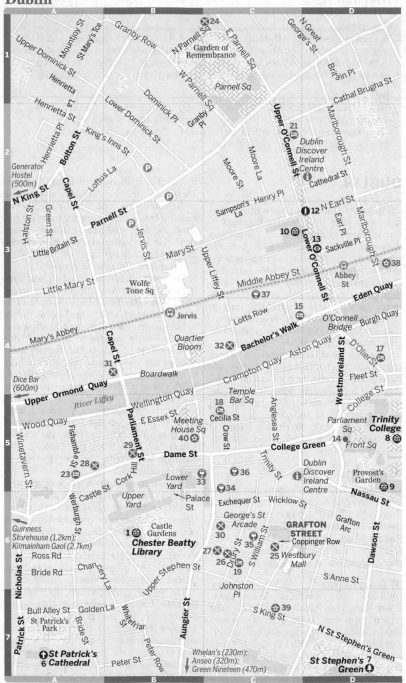

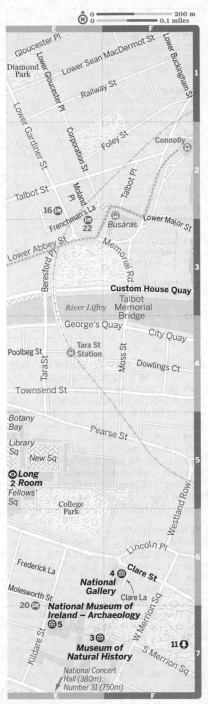

Art (www.douglashydegallery.com; Trinity College; 11am-6pm Mon-Wed & Fri, to 7pm Thu, to 4.45pm Sat) FREE.

★**Long Room**　　　　NOTABLE BUILDING
(East Pavilion, Library Colonnades; adult/student/child €10/8/free; 9.30am-5pm Mon-Sat year-round, noon-4.30pm Sun Oct-Apr, 9.30am-4.30pm Sun May-Sep; all city centre) The Old Library – built in a rather severe style by Thomas Burgh between 1712–32 – contains Trinity College's greatest treasures in its stunning, barrel-vaulted Long Room, a 65m-long temple of learning lined with gleaming bookshelves and marble busts. It houses about 250,000 of the library's oldest volumes, including the breathtaking *Book of Kells*. Other displays include a rare copy of the Proclamation of the Irish Republic, which was read by Pádraig Pearse at the beginning of the Easter Rising in 1916.

Admission includes temporary exhibitions on display in the East Pavilion.

Also here is the so-called **harp of Brian Ború**, which was definitely not in use when the army of this early Irish hero defeated the Danes at the Battle of Clontarf in 1014. It does, however, date from around 1400, making it one of the oldest harps in Ireland.

★**National Museum of Ireland – Archaeology**　　　　MUSEUM
(www.museum.ie; Kildare St; 10am-5pm Tue-Sat, 2-5pm Sun; all city centre) FREE Among the highlights of the National Museum's archaeology branch are its superb collection of **prehistoric gold objects**; the exquisite 8th-century **Ardagh Chalice** and **Tara Brooch**, the world's finest examples of Celtic art; and ancient objects recovered from Ireland's bogs, including remarkably well-preserved human bodies. Other exhibits focus on early Christian art, the Viking period and medieval Ireland. There's a lot to see, so ask if there's a guided tour available, or buy a guidebook to help you navigate the exhibits.

★**Guinness Storehouse**　　　　BREWERY, MUSEUM
(www.guinness-storehouse.com; St James's Gate, South Market St; adult/student/child €18/14.50/6.50, connoisseur experience €30, discounts for online booking; 9.30am-5pm Sep-Jun, to 7pm Jul & Aug; ; 21A, 51B, 78, 78A or 123 from Fleet St, St James's) The most popular visit in town is the beer-lover's Disneyland, a multimedia bells-and-whistles homage to the country's most famous export and the city's most enduring symbol. The old grain storehouse, the only part of the

Dublin

massive, 26-hectare St James's Gate Brewery open to the public, is a suitable cathedral in which to worship the black gold; it rises seven impressive storeys high around a stunning central atrium. At the top is the **Gravity Bar**, with panoramic views of Dublin.

★ **Chester Beatty Library**   MUSEUM
(☏01-407 0750; www.cbl.ie; Dublin Castle; ◷10am-5pm Tue-Fri, 11am-5pm Sat, 1-5pm Sun year-round, 10am-5pm Mon May-Sep, free tours 1pm Wed, 3pm & 4pm Sun; ▣50, 51B, 77, 78A or 123) FREE This world-famous library, in the grounds of Dublin Castle, houses the collection of mining engineer Sir Alfred Chester Beatty (1875–1968), bequeathed to the Irish State on his death. Spread over two floors, the breathtaking collection includes more than 20,000 manuscripts, rare books, miniature paintings, clay tablets, costumes and other objects of artistic, historical and aesthetic importance, including fragments of early Christian gospels dating from AD 150–200.

★ **Kilmainham Gaol**   MUSEUM
(www.heritageireland.com; Inchicore Rd; adult/child €6/2; ◷9.30am-6pm Apr-Sep, 9.30am-5.30pm Mon-Sat, 10am-6pm Sun Oct-Mar; ▣23, 25, 25A, 26, 68 or 69 from city centre) If you have *any* desire to understand Irish history – especially the juicy bits about resistance to English rule – then a visit to this former prison is a must. This threatening grey building, built between 1792 and 1795, has played a role in virtually every act of Ireland's painful path to independence. An excellent audiovisual introduction to the building is followed by a thought-provoking guided tour of the eerie prison, the largest unoccupied building of its kind in Europe.

★ **National Gallery**   MUSEUM
(www.nationalgallery.ie; West Merrion Sq; ◷9.30am-5.30pm Mon-Wed, Fri & Sat, 9.30am-8.30pm Thu, noon-5.30pm Sun; ▣7 & 44 from city centre) FREE A magnificent Caravaggio and a breathtaking collection of works by Jack B Yeats – William Butler's younger brother – are the main reasons to visit the National Gallery, but not the only ones. Its excellent collection is strong in Irish art, but there are also high-quality collections of every major European school of painting. There are free guided tours at 12.30pm and 1.30pm on Sundays.

★ St Patrick's Cathedral
CHURCH

(www.stpatrickscathedral.ie; St Patrick's Close; adult/child €5.50/free; ⏰9am-5pm Mon-Sat, 9-10.30am & 12.30-2.30pm Sun year-round, longer hours Mar-Oct; 🚌50, 50A or 56A from Aston Quay, 54 or 54A from Burgh Quay) It was at this cathedral, reputedly, that St Paddy himself dunked the Irish heathens into the waters of a well, so the church that bears his name stands on one of the earliest Christian sites in the city. Although there's been a church here since the 5th century, the present building dates from 1190 or 1225 (opinions differ) and it has been altered several times, most notably in 1864 when the flying buttresses were added.

★ Museum of Natural History
MUSEUM

(National Museum of Ireland – Natural History; www.museum.ie; Merrion St; ⏰10am-5pm Tue-Sat, 2-5pm Sun; 🚌7 & 44 from city centre) **FREE** Dusty, weird and utterly compelling, this window into Victorian times has barely changed since Scottish explorer Dr David Livingstone opened it in 1857 (before disappearing into the African jungle). The creaky-floored interior is crammed with some two million stuffed animals, skeletons, fossils and other specimens from around the world, ranging from West African apes to pickled insects in jars. Some are free-standing, others behind glass, but everywhere you turn the animals of the 'dead zoo' are still and staring.

O'Connell St
HISTORIC SITE

(⏰24hr; 🚌all city centre) Dublin's grandest avenue is dominated by the needle-like, 120m-tall **Monument of Light**, better known as 'The Spire'. It rises from the spot once occupied by a statue of Admiral Nelson, which was blown up by the Irish Republican Army (IRA) in 1966. Nearby is the 1815 **General Post Office** (www.anpost.ie; ⏰8am-8pm Mon-Sat; 🚌all city centre, 🚆Abbey), an important landmark of the 1916 Easter Rising, when the Irish Volunteers used it as a base for attacks against the British army.

🛏 Sleeping

Hotel rooms in Dublin aren't as expensive as they were during the Celtic Tiger years, but demand is still high and booking is highly recommended, especially if you want to stay in the city centre or within walking distance of it.

🏛 North of the Liffey

★ Isaacs Hostel
HOSTEL €

(☎01-855 6215; www.isaacs.ie; 2-5 Frenchman's Lane; dm/tw from €14/58; @🛜; 🚌all city centre, 🚆Connolly) The north side's best hostel – hell, for atmosphere alone it's the best in town – is in a 200-year-old wine vault just around the corner from the main bus station. With summer barbecues, live music in the lounge, internet access and colourful dorms, this terrific place generates consistently good feedback from backpackers and other travellers.

★ Generator Hostel
HOSTEL €

(☎01-901 0222; www.generatorhostels.com; Smithfield Sq; dm/tw from €16/70; @🛜) This European chain brings its own brand of funky, fun design to Dublin's hostel scene, with bright colours, comfortable dorms (including women-only) and a lively social scene. Good location on a pedestrian mall next to Old Jameson Distillery.

Abbey Court Hostel
HOSTEL €

(☎01-878 0700; www.abbey-court.com; 29 Bachelor's Walk; dm/d from €16/78; 🛜; 🚌all cross-city) Spread over two buildings, this large, well-run hostel has 33 clean beds with good storage. Its excellent facilities include a dining hall, conservatory and barbecue area. Doubles with bathroom are in the newer building where a light breakfast is provided in the adjacent cafe. Not surprisingly, this is a popular spot; reservations are advised.

Anchor House
B&B €€

(☎01-878 6913; www.anchorhousedublin.com; 49 Lower Gardiner St; s/d €95/105; 🅿🛜; 🚌all city centre, 🚆Connolly) Most B&Bs in these parts offer pretty much the same stuff: TV, half-decent shower, clean linen and tea- and coffee-making facilities. The Anchor does all that, but it also has an elegance you won't find in many other B&Bs along this stretch. This lovely Georgian guesthouse, with its delicious wholesome breakfasts, comes highly recommended by readers. They're dead right.

Gresham Hotel
HOTEL €€€

(☎01-874 6881; www.gresham-hotels.com; Upper O'Connell St; r from €145; 🅿✳@🛜; 🚌all cross-city) This landmark hotel shed its traditional granny's parlour look with a major overhaul some years ago. Despite its brighter, smarter, modern appearance and a fabulous open-plan foyer, its loyal clientele – elderly groups on shopping breaks and well-heeled

Americans – continues to find it charming. Rooms are spacious and well serviced, and the location is unbeatable.

South of the Liffey

Barnacles
HOSTEL €

(☑01-671 6277; www.barnacles.ie; 19 Lower Temple Lane; dm/tw from €17/64; P🤝; 🖵all city centre) If you're here for a good time and not a long time, then this Temple Bar hostel is the ideal spot to meet fellow revellers; tap up the helpful and knowledgeable staff for the best places to cause mischief; and sleep off the effects of said mischief whilst being totally oblivious to the noise outside, which is constant.

Rooms are quieter at the back. Top facilities include a comfy lounge with an open fire. Linen and towels are provided. A contender for the south side's best hostel, it also has a discount deal with a nearby covered car park.

Ashfield House
HOSTEL €

(☑01-679 7734; www.ashfieldhouse.ie; 19-20 D'Olier St; dm/tw from €14/70; @🤝; 🖵all city centre) A stone's throw from Temple Bar and O'Connell Bridge, this modern hostel in a converted church has a selection of tidy four- and six-bed rooms, one large dorm and 25 rooms with private bathroom. It's more like a small hotel, but without the price tag. A continental-style breakfast is included – a rare beast indeed for hostels. Maximum stay is six nights.

Kinlay House
HOSTEL €

(☑01-679 6644; www.kinlaydublin.ie; 2-12 Lord Edward St; dm/s/q from €16/26/68; 🤝; 🖵all city centre) An institution among the city's hostels, this former boarding house for boys has massive, mixed 24-bed dorms, as well as smaller rooms. Its bustling location next to Christ Church Cathedral and Dublin Castle is a bonus, but some rooms suffer from noise. There are cooking facilities and a cafe, and breakfast is included. Not for the faint-hearted.

★ Brooks Hotel
HOTEL €€

(☑01-670 4000; www.sinnotthotels.com; 59-62 Drury St; r from €140; P❄; 🖵all cross-city, 🚌St Stephen's Green) About 120m west of Grafton St, this small, plush place has an emphasis on familial, friendly service. The decor is nouveau classic with high-veneer-panelled walls, decorative bookcases and old-fashioned sofas, while bedrooms are extremely comfortable and come fitted out in subtly coloured furnishings. The clincher though, is the king- and superking-size beds in all rooms, complete with…a pillow menu.

Buswell's Hotel
HOTEL €€

(☑01-614 6500; www.buswells.ie; 23-27 Molesworth St; r from €141; P❄@; 🖵all cross-city, 🚌St Stephen's Green) This Dublin institution, open since 1882, has a long association with politicians, who wander across the road from Dáil Éireann to wet their beaks at the hotel bar. The 69 bedrooms have all been given the once-over, but have kept their Georgian charm intact.

★ Number 31
GUESTHOUSE €€€

(☑01-676 5011; www.number31.ie; 31 Leeson Close; s/d/tr incl breakfast €240/280/320; P🤝; 🖵all city centre) The city's most distinctive property is the former home of modernist architect Sam Stephenson, who successfully fused '60s style with 18th-century grace. Its 21 bedrooms are split between the retro coach house, with its fancy rooms, and the more elegant Georgian house, where rooms are individually furnished with tasteful French antiques and big comfortable beds.

Eating

The most concentrated restaurant area is Temple Bar but, apart from a handful of good places, the bulk of eateries offer bland, unimaginative fodder and cheap set menus for tourists. Better food and service can usually be found on either side of Grafton St, while the top-end restaurants are clustered around Merrion Sq and Fitzwilliam Sq. Fast-food chains dominate the north side, though some fine cafes and eateries are finally appearing there, too.

North of the Liffey

Soup Dragon
FAST FOOD €

(www.soupdragon.com; 168 Capel St; mains €5-8; ⊙8am-5pm Mon-Fri; 🖵all city centre, 🚌Jervis) Queues are a regular feature outside this fabulous spot that specialises in soups-on-the-go, but it also does excellent curries, stews, pies and salads. The all-day breakfast options are excellent – we especially like the mini-breakfast quiche of sausage, egg and bacon. Bowls come in three different sizes and prices include fresh bread and a piece of fruit.

★ Chapter One
MODERN IRISH €€€

(☑01-873 2266; www.chapteronerestaurant.com; 18 North Parnell Sq; 2-course lunch €29, 4-course dinner €70; ⊙12.30-2pm Tue-Fri, 7.30-10.30pm Tue-Sat; 🖵3, 10, 11, 13, 16, 19 or 22 from city centre) Michelin-starred Chapter One is our choice for the city's best eatery. It successfully combines flawless haute cuisine with a relaxed, welcoming atmosphere that is at the heart of Irish hospitality. The food is French-inspired contemporary Irish, the menus change regularly and the service is top-notch. The three-course pre-theatre menu (€36.50) is a favourite with those heading to the Gate around the corner.

Winding Stair
MODERN IRISH €€€

(📞01-873 7320; www.winding-stair.com; 40 Lower Ormond Quay; 2-course lunch €19, mains €23-27; ⊙noon-5pm & 5.30-10.30pm; 🚇all city centre) Housed within a beautiful Georgian building that was once home to the city's most beloved bookshop (the ground floor still is one), the Winding Stair's conversion to elegant restaurant has been faultless. The wonderful Irish menu – creamy fish pie, bacon and organic cabbage, steamed mussels, and Irish farmyard cheeses – coupled with an excellent wine list make for a memorable meal.

🍴 South of the Liffey

Green Nineteen
IRISH €

(📞01-478 9626; www.green19.ie; 19 Lower Camden St; mains €9-14; ⊙8.30am-11pm; 📶; 🚇all city centre) 🌿 A firm favourite on Camden St's corridor of cool is this sleek hipster canteen that specialises in locally sourced, organic grub – without the fancy price tag. Braised lamb chump, corned beef, pot roast chicken and the ubiquitous burger are the meaty part of the menu, which also includes salads and vegie options. We love it.

Queen of Tarts
CAFE €

(www.queenoftarts.ie; 4 Cork Hill; mains €5-10; ⊙8am-7pm Mon-Fri, 9am-7pm Sat & Sun; 🚇all city centre) Pocket-sized Queen of Tarts offers a mouth-watering array of savoury tarts, filled focaccias, fruit crumbles and brownies. There

are also great healthy breakfasts and weekend brunch specials such as potato-and-chive cake with mushroom and egg, plus the coffee is splendid and the service sweet. There's a bigger version around the corner on **Cow's Lane** (www.queenoftarts.ie; 3-4 Cow's Lane; mains €5-10; ⊙8am-7pm Mon-Fri, 9am-7pm Sat & Sun; 🚇all cross-city).

Simon's Place
CAFE €

(George's St Arcade, S Great George's St; sandwiches €5; ⊙8.30am-5pm Mon-Sat; 🖊; 🚇all city centre) Simon hasn't had to change the menu of doorstep sandwiches and wholesome vegetarian soups since he first opened shop more than two decades ago – and why should he? His grub is as heartening and legendary as he is. It's a great place to sip a coffee and watch life go by in the old-fashioned arcade.

★ Fade Street Social
MODERN IRISH €€

(📞01-604 0066; www.fadestreetsocial.com; Fade St; mains €19-32, tapas €5-12; ⊙12.30-2.30pm Mon-Fri, 5-10.30pm daily; 📶; 🚇all city centre) 🌿 Two eateries in one, courtesy of renowned chef Dylan McGrath: at the front, the buzzy Gastro Bar, which serves up gourmet tapas from a beautiful open kitchen. At the back, the more muted Restaurant does Irish cuts of meat – from veal to rabbit – served with homegrown, organic vegetables. Three-course lunch and early evening menu €25. Reservations suggested.

Coppinger Row
MEDITERRANEAN €€

(www.coppingerrow.com; Coppinger Row; mains €17-26; ⊙noon-5.30pm & 6-11pm Mon-Sat, 12.30-4pm & 6-9pm Sun; 🚇all city centre) Virtually all of the Mediterranean basin is represented on this restaurant's ever-changing, imaginative menu. Choices include the likes of pan-fried sea bass with roast baby fennel,

---

FREE THRILLS

Dublin is not a cheap city, but there are plenty of attractions that won't bust your budget.

➡ Wander the grounds at **Trinity College** (College Green; college grounds free, Old Library adult/child €9/free, walking tours per person €10; ⊙ 9.30am-5pm Mon-Sat year-round, 9.30am-4.30pm Sun May-Sep, noon-4.30pm Sun Oct-Apr, walking tours twice per hour 10.15am-3.40pm Mon-Sat, to 3pm Sun mid-May–Sep), Dublin's oldest and most beautiful university.

➡ Discover the world's finest collection of prehistoric gold artefacts at the **National Museum of Archaeology** (p385).

➡ Explore the **Chester Beatty Library** (p386), with its collection of oriental and religious art.

➡ Gaze at Irish and European paintings at the **National Gallery** (p386).

➡ Laze at **St Stephen's Green** (p383), the city's most picturesque public park.

tomato and olives; or rump of lamb with spiced aubergine and dried apricots. A nice touch are the filtered still and sparkling waters (€1), where 50% of the cost goes to cancer research.

L'Gueuleton   FRENCH €€
(www.lgueuleton.com; 1 Fade St; mains €16-27; ⊘12.30-3.30pm & 5.30-10pm Mon-Sat, noon-3.30pm & 5.30-9pm Sun; 🚇all city centre) Dubliners have a devil of a time pronouncing the name (which means 'a gluttonous feast' in French) and have had their patience tested with the no-reservations-get-in-line-and-wait policy, but they just can't get enough of this restaurant's robust (read: meaty and filling) take on French rustic cuisine that makes twisted tongues and sore feet a small price to pay.

🍸 Drinking & Nightlife

Temple Bar, Dublin's 'party district', is almost always packed with raucous stag (bachelor) and hen (bachelorette) parties, scantily clad girls and loud guys from Ohio wearing Guinness T-shirts. If you're just looking to get smashed and hook up with someone from another country, there's no better place in Ireland. If that's not your style, there's plenty to enjoy beyond Temple Bar. In fact, most of the best old-fashioned pubs are outside the district.

★Stag's Head   PUB
(www.louisfitzgerald.com/stagshead; 1 Dame Ct; ⊘10.30am-1am Mon-Sat, to midnight Sun; 🚇all city centre) The Stag's Head was built in 1770, remodelled in 1895 and thankfully not changed a bit since then. It's a superb pub, so picturesque that it often appears in films and also featured in a postage-stamp series on Irish bars. A bloody great pub, no doubt.

Grogan's Castle Lounge   PUB
(www.groganspub.ie; 15 South William St; ⊘10.30am-11.30pm Mon-Thu, 10.30am-12.30am Fri & Sat, 12.30-11pm Sun) This place is known simply as Grogan's (after the original owner), and it is a city-centre institution. It has long been a favourite haunt of Dublin's writers and painters, as well as others from the alternative bohemian set, most of whom seem to be waiting for the 'inevitable' moment when they are finally recognised as geniuses.

George   GAY
(www.thegeorge.ie; 89 S Great George's St; ⊘2-11.30pm Mon, 2pm-2.30am Tue-Fri, 12.30pm-2.30am Sat, 12.30pm-1.30am Sun) The purple mother of Dublin's gay bars is a long-standing institution, having lived through the years when it was the only place in town where the gay crowd could, well, be gay. There are other places to go, but the George remains the best, if only for tradition's sake. Shirley's legendary Sunday night bingo is as popular as ever.

Dice Bar   BAR
(☑01-674 6710; www.thatsitdublin.com; 79 Queen St; ⊘3pm-midnight Mon-Thu, to 1am Fri & Sat, to 11.30pm Sun; 🚌25, 25A, 66, 67 from city centre, 🚊Museum) Co-owned by Huey from the Fun Lovin' Criminals, the Dice Bar looks like something you might find on New York's Lower East Side. Its dodgy locale, black-and-red painted interior, dripping candles and distressed seating, combined with rocking DJs most nights, make it a magnet for Dublin hipsters. It has Guinness and local craft beers.

Anseo   BAR
(28 Lower Camden St; ⊘10.30am-11.30pm Mon-Thu, 10.30am-12.30am Fri & Sat, 11am-11pm Sun; 🚇all city centre) Unpretentious, unaffected and incredibly popular, this cosy alternative bar – which is pronounced 'an-shuh', the Irish for 'here' – is a favourite with those who live by the credo that to try too hard is far worse than not trying at all. Wearing cool like a loose garment, the punters thrive on the mix of chat and terrific DJs.

Globe   BAR
(☑01-671 1220; www.theglobe.ie; 11 S Great George's St; ⊘5pm-2.30am Mon-Fri, 4pm-2.30am Sat, 4pm-1am Sun; 🛜; 🚇all city centre) The granddaddy of the city's hipster bars, the Globe has held on to its groover status by virtue of tradition and the fact that the formula is brilliantly simple: wooden floors, plain brick walls and a no-attitude atmosphere that you just can't fake.

Twisted Pepper CLUB
(📋01-873 4800; www.bodytonicmusic.com/
thetwistedpepper; 54 Middle Abbey St; ⊙bar 4pm-
late, cafe 8.30am-6pm; 🚇all city centre, 🚉Abbey)
Dublin's hippest venue comes in four parts:
DJs spin great tunes in the basement; the
stage is for live acts; the mezzanine is a secluded bar area above the stage; and the cafe
is where you can get an Irish breakfast all
day. All run by the Bodytonic crew, one of the
most exciting music and production crowds
in town.

☆ Entertainment

For events, reviews and club listings, pick
up a copy of the fortnightly music review
Hot Press (www.hotpress.com), or for free
cultural events, check out the weekly e-zine
Dublin Event Guide (www.dublinevent
guide.com). Friday's *Irish Times* has a pull-
out section called 'The Ticket' that has
reviews and listings of all things arty.

Whelan's LIVE MUSIC
(📋01-478 0766; www.whelanslive.com; 25 Wexford St; 🚌bus 16, 122 from city centre) A Dublin
institution, providing a showcase for Irish
singer-songwriters and other lo-fi performers since the 1990s, Whelan's combines a
traditional pub upstairs and a popular live-
music venue on the ground floor. The old-
fashioned ambience belies a progressive
music booking policy, with a program that
features many breaking new acts from rock
and indie to folk and trad.

Abbey Theatre THEATRE
(📋01-878 7222; www.abbeytheatre.ie; Lower Abbey
St; 🚇all city centre, 🚉Abbey) Ireland's renowned
national theatre, founded by WB Yeats in
1904, has been reinvigorated in recent years
by director Fiach MacConghaill, who has introduced lots of new blood to what was in
danger of becoming a moribund corpse. The
current program has a mix of Irish classics
(Synge, O'Casey etc), established international names (Shepard, Mamet) and new talent
(O'Rowe, Carr et al).

National Concert Hall LIVE MUSIC
(📋01-417 0000; www.nch.ie; Earlsfort Tce; 🚇all
city centre) Ireland's premier orchestral hall
hosts a variety of concerts year-round, including a series of lunchtime concerts from
1.05pm to 2pm on Tuesdays, June to August.

Gaiety Theatre THEATRE
(📋01-677 1717; www.gaietytheatre.com; South King
St; 🚇all city centre) The Gaiety's program of
plays is strictly of the fun-for-all-the-family
type: West End hits, musicals, Christmas
pantomimes and classic Irish plays for those
simply looking to be entertained.

Irish Film Institute CINEMA
(📋01-679 5744; www.ifi.ie; 6 Eustace St; 🚇all city
centre) The Irish Film Institute (IFI) has a
couple of screens and shows classics and
new art-house films, although we question
some of its selections: weird and controversial can be a little tedious. The complex also
has a bar, a cafe and a bookshop.

ℹ Information

All Dublin tourist offices provide walk-in services
only – no phone enquiries. For tourist information
by phone call 📋1850 230 330 from within the
Republic.

Dublin Discover Ireland Centre (www.visit
dublin.com; St Andrew's Church, 2 Suffolk St;
⊙9am-5.30pm Mon-Sat, 10.30am-3pm Sun)
The main tourist information centre; there's a
second branch on O'Connell St (14 O'Connell
St; ⊙9am-5pm Mon-Sat).

Grafton Medical Centre (📋01-671 2122; www.
graftonmedical.ie; 34 Grafton St; ⊙8.30am-
6pm Mon-Fri, 11am-2pm Sat) One-stop shop with
male and female doctors and physiotherapists.

Hickey's Pharmacy (📋01-873 0427; 55 Lower
O'Connell St; ⊙8am-10pm Mon-Fri, 8.30am-
10pm Sat, 10am-10pm Sun) Open till 10pm
every night.

St James's Hospital (📋01-410 3000; www.
stjames.ie; James's St) Dublin's main 24-hour
accident and emergency department.

ℹ Getting There & Away

AIR

Dublin Airport (p415), about 13km north of
the city centre, is Ireland's major international
gateway, with direct flights from Europe, North
America and Asia. Budget airlines such as Ryanair and Flybe land here.

BOAT

There are direct ferries from Holyhead in Wales
to Dublin Port, 3km northeast of the city centre,
and to Dun Laoghaire, 13km southeast. Boats
also sail direct to Dublin Port from Liverpool and
from Douglas, on the Isle of Man.

BUS

The private company **Citylink** (www.citylink.ie)
has nonstop services from Dublin Airport (picking up in the city centre at Bachelor's Walk, near
O'Connell Bridge) to Galway (€13, 2½ hours,
hourly).

BOOK OF KELLS

The world-famous *Book of Kells*, dating from around AD 800 and thus one of the oldest books in the world, was probably produced by monks at St Colmcille's Monastery on the remote island of Iona. It contains the four gospels of the New Testament, written in Latin, as well as prefaces, summaries and other text. If it were merely words, the Book of Kells would simply be a very old book – it's the extensive and amazingly complex illustrations (the illuminations) that make it so wonderful. The superbly decorated opening initials are only part of the story, for the book has smaller illustrations between the lines.

Aircoach (www.aircoach.ie) operates a service from O'Connell St in the Dublin city centre, via Dublin Airport to Belfast.

Busáras (☑ 01-836 6111; www.buseireann.ie; Store St) pronounced buh-*saw*-ras, is Dublin's main bus station; it's just north of the Liffey.

Belfast €17, 2½ hours, hourly
Cork €15, 3¾ hours, six daily
Galway €14.50, 3¾ hours, hourly
Kilkenny €13.50, 2¼ hours, six daily
Rosslare Europoort €23, four hours, five daily

TRAIN

Connolly station is north of the Liffey, with trains to Belfast, Sligo and Rosslare. Heuston station is south of the Liffey and west of the city centre, with trains for Cork, Galway, Killarney, Limerick, and most other points to the south and west. Visit www.irishrail.ie for timetables and fares.

Belfast €38, 2¼ hours, eight daily
Cork €64, 2¾ hours, hourly
Galway €36, 2¾ hours, nine daily
Killarney €67, 3¼ hours, seven daily

ⓘ Getting Around

TO/FROM THE AIRPORT

Aircoach (www.aircoach.ie; one way/return €7/12) Buses every 10 to 15 minutes between 6am and midnight, hourly from midnight until 6am.

Airlink Express (☑ 01-873 4222; www.dublin bus.ie; one way/return €6/3) Bus 747 runs every 10 to 20 minutes from 5.45am to 11.30pm between the airport, central bus station (Busáras) and the Dublin Bus office on Upper O'Connell St.

Taxi There is a taxi rank directly outside the arrivals concourse. It should take about 45 minutes to get into the city centre by taxi and cost about €25, including a supplementary charge of €3 (not applied when going to the airport).

BICYCLE

Rental rates begin at around €13/70 per day/week; you'll need a €50 to €200 cash deposit and photo ID.

Dublinbikes (www.dublinbikes.ie) A pay-as-you-go service similar to London's: cyclists purchase a Smart Card (€5 for three days, €20 for one year, plus a €150 credit-card deposit) either online or at any of more than 40 stations throughout the city centre, and bike use is then free for the first 30 minutes, increasing gradually thereafter (eg €3.50 for up to three hours).

Neill's Wheels (www.rentabikedublin.com; per day/week €12.50/70) Various outlets, including Kinlay House and Isaacs Hostel.

PUBLIC TRANSPORT
Bus

Dublin Bus (www.dublinbus.ie) Local buses cost from €0.70 to €3.05 for a single journey. You must pay the exact fare when boarding; drivers don't give change. The Freedom Pass (€30) allows three days' unlimited travel on all Dublin buses including Airlink and Dublin Bus hop-on/hop-off tour buses.

Train

Dublin Area Rapid Transport (DART; ☑ 01-836 6222; www.irishrail.ie) Provides quick rail access as far north as Howth and south to Bray; Pearse and Tara St stations are handy for central Dublin. Single fares cost €2.15 to €3.05; a one-day pass costs €11.10.

Tram

Luas (www.luas.ie) Runs on two (unconnected) lines; the green line runs from the eastern side of St Stephen's Green southeast to Sandyford, and the red line runs from Tallaght to Connolly station, with stops at Heuston station, the National Museum and Busáras. Single fares range from €1.70 to €3 depending on how many zones you travel through; a one-day pass is €6.40.

TAXI

Taxis in Dublin are expensive; flag fall costs €4.10, plus €1.03 per kilometre. For taxi service, call **National Radio Cabs** (☑ 01-677 2222; www.radiocabs.ie).

THE SOUTHEAST

Kilkenny

POP 24,400

Kilkenny (Cill Chainnigh) is the Ireland of many visitors' imaginations. Its majestic riverside castle, tangle of 17th-century passageways, rows of colourful, old-fashioned shopfronts and centuries-old pubs with traditional live music all have a timeless appeal, as does its splendid medieval cathedral. But Kilkenny is also famed for its contemporary restaurants and rich cultural life.

◉ Sights

★ **Kilkenny Castle**   CASTLE
(www.kilkennycastle.ie; adult/child €6/2.50, audio guides €5, parkland admission free; ⊙9.30am-5pm Mar-Sep, to 4.30pm Oct-Feb, parkland daylight hours) Rising above the River Nore, Kilkenny Castle is one of Ireland's most visited heritage sites. Stronghold of the powerful Butler family, it has a history dating back to the 12th century, though much of its present look dates from the 19th century. Highlights of the guided tour include the painted roof beams of the Long Gallery and the collection of Victorian antiques. There's an excellent tearoom in the former castle kitchens, all white marble and gleaming copper.

★ **St Canice's Cathedral**   CATHEDRAL
(www.stcanicescathedral.ie; St Canice's Pl; cathedral €4, round tower €3, combined €6; ⊙9am-6pm Mon-Sat, 1-6pm Sun, shorter hours Sep-May) Ireland's second-largest medieval cathedral (after St Patrick's in Dublin), with its iconic round tower, has a long and fascinating history. Legend has it that the first monastery was built here in the 6th century by St Canice, Kilkenny's patron saint. Outside the cathedral, a 30m-high round tower rises amid ancient tombstones. It was built sometime between AD 700 and 1000 on the site of an earlier Christian cemetery; those aged over 12 can admire the view from the top.

National Craft Gallery &
Kilkenny Design Centre   GALLERY
(www.nationalcraftgallery.ie; Castle Yard; ⊙10am-5.30pm Tue-Sat, 11am-5.30pm Sun; ⓐ) Contemporary Irish crafts are showcased at these imaginative galleries, set in the former Kilkenny Castle stables that also house the shops of the Kilkenny Design Centre. Ceramics dominate, but exhibits often feature furniture, jewellery and weaving from the members of the Crafts Council of Ireland. Family days are held the second Saturday of every month with free hands-on workshops for children at 10am and 12.30pm. For additional workshops and events, check the website.

✦ Festivals & Events

Kilkenny is rightly known as the festival capital of Ireland, with several world-class events throughout the year.

Kilkenny Arts Festival   ART
(www.kilkennyarts.ie; ⓐ) In August the city comes alive with theatre, cinema, music, literature, visual arts, children's events and street spectacles for 10 action-packed days.

Kilkenny Rhythm & Roots   MUSIC
(www.kilkennyroots.com) More than 30 pubs and other venues participate in hosting this major music festival in May, with an emphasis on country and 'old-time' American roots music.

⬛ Sleeping

Kilkenny Tourist Hostel   HOSTEL €
(☎056-776 3541; www.kilkennyhostel.ie; 35 Parliament St; dm/tw from €17/42; @ ⓐ) Inside an ivy-covered 1770s Georgian town house, this cosy, 60-bed IHH hostel has a sitting room warmed by an open fireplace, and a timber-and leadlight-panelled dining room adjoining the self-catering kitchen.

Butler House   BOUTIQUE HOTEL €€
(☎056-772 2828; www.butler.ie; 16 Patrick St; s/d from €90/145; P @ ⓐ) You can't stay in Kilkenny Castle, but this historic mansion is the next best thing. Once the home of the earls of Ormonde, who built the castle, today it houses a boutique hotel with aristocratic trappings including sweeping staircases, marble fireplaces, an art collection and impeccably trimmed gardens.

Celtic House   B&B €€
(☎056-776 2249; www.celtic-house-bandb.com; 18 Michael St; r €70; P @ ⓐ) Artist and author Angela Byrne extends one of Ireland's warmest welcomes at her spick-and-span B&B. Some of the bright rooms have sky-lit bathrooms, others have views of the castle, and Angela's landscapes adorn many of the walls. Book ahead.

✗ Eating

Gourmet Store SANDWICHES €
(56 High St; sandwich & coffee €5; ⏱ 9am-6pm Mon-Sat) In this crowded little deli, take-away sandwiches are assembled from choice imported meats and cheeses (plus a few top-notch locals).

★ Foodworks BISTRO, CAFE €€
(☎ 056-777 7696; www.foodworks.ie; 7 Parliament St; mains €8-21; ⏱ noon-9.30pm Wed-Fri, noon-10pm Sat, 12.30-4.30pm Sun; ☎) ⏷ The owners of this cool and casual bistro keep their own pigs and grow their own salad leaves, so it would be churlish not to try their pulled pork brioche with beetroot slaw – and you'll be glad you did. Delicious food, excellent coffee and friendly service make this a justifiably popular venue; best to book a table.

Cafe Sol MODERN IRISH €€
(☎ 056-776 4987; www.restaurantskilkenny.com; William St; mains lunch €10-14, 2-/3-course dinner €23/27; ⏱ 11am-9.30pm Mon-Thu, 11am-10pm Fri & Sat, noon-9pm Sun; ☎) ⏷ Leisurely lunches stretch until 5pm at this much-loved restaurant. Local organic produce is featured in dishes that emphasise what's fresh each season. The flavours are frequently bold and have global influences. Service, albeit casual, is excellent and the whole place exudes a modern Med-bistro look.

☕ Drinking & Nightlife

★ Kyteler's Inn PUB
(www.kytelersinn.com; 27 St Kieran's St; ⏱ 11am-midnight Sun-Thu, to 2am Fri & Sat, live music 6.30pm Mar-Oct) Dame Alice Kyteler's old house was built back in 1224 and has seen its share of history: she was charged with witchcraft in 1323. Today the rambling bar includes the orignal building, complete with vaulted ceiling and arches. There is a beer garden, courtyard and a large upstairs room for the live bands, ranging from trad to blues.

Tynan's Bridge House PUB
(St John's Bridge; ⏱ 10.30am-11.30pm Mon-Thu, 10.30am-12.30am Fri & Sat, 11.30am-11pm Sun) This historic 1703 Georgian pub flaunting a brilliant blue facade is the best traditional pub in town with its horseshoe bar, original tilework, regular clientele of crusty locals – and no TV! There is trad music on Wednesdays and Sundays at 9pm.

☆ Entertainment

Watergate Theatre THEATRE
(www.watergatetheatre.com; Parliament St) The top theatre venue hosts drama, comedy and musical performances. If you're wondering why intermission lasts 18 minutes, it's so patrons can nip into **John Cleere's pub** (www.cleeres.com; 22 Parliament St; ⏱ 11.30am-11.30pm Mon-Thu, to 12.30am Fri & Sat, 1-11pm Sun) for a pint.

ⓘ Information

Tourist Office (www.kilkennytourism.ie; Rose Inn St; ⏱ 9.15am-5pm Mon-Sat) Stocks excellent guides and walking maps. Located in Shee Alms House, dating from 1582 and built in local stone by benefactor Sir Richard Shee to help the poor.

ⓘ Getting There & Away

BUS
Buses depart from the train station. Services include Cork (€19, three hours, two daily) and Dublin (€13.50, 2¼ hours, six daily).

TRAIN
Kilkenny train station (Dublin Rd) is east of the town centre along John St, next to the MacDonagh Junction shopping mall. Services include Dublin Heuston (€25, 1¾ hours, eight daily) and Galway (€47, 3½ hours, one daily, change at Kildare).

THE SOUTHWEST

Cork
POP 119,230

Ireland's second city is first in every important respect, at least according to the locals, who cheerfully refer to it as the 'real capital of Ireland'. The compact city centre is surrounded by interesting waterways and is chock full of great restaurants fed by arguably the best foodie scene in the country.

⊙ Sights

★ English Market MARKET
(www.englishmarket.ie; Princes St; ⏱ 9am-5.30pm Mon-Sat) It could just as easily be called the Victorian Market for its ornate vaulted ceilings and columns, but the English Market is a true gem, no matter what you name it. Scores of vendors sell some of the very best local produce, meats, cheeses and takeaway food in the region. On decent days, take your lunch to nearby **Bishop Lucey Park**, a popular alfresco eating spot.

WORTH A TRIP

ROCK OF CASHEL

The **Rock of Cashel** (www.heritage ire land.com; adult/child €6/2; ☉9am-5.30pm mid-Mar–mid-Oct, to 7pm mid-Jun–Aug, to 4.30pm mid-Oct–mid-Mar) is one of Ireland's most spectacular archaeological sites. A prominent green hill, banded with limestone outcrops, it rises from a grassy plain on the outskirts of Cashel town and bristles with ancient fortifications. For more than 1000 years it was a symbol of power, and the seat of kings and churchmen who ruled over the region. Sturdy walls circle an enclosure that contains a complete round tower, a roofless abbey and the finest 12th-century Romanesque chapel in Ireland.

Cashel Lodge & Camping Park (☎062-61003; www.cashel-lodge.com; Dundrum Rd; campsite per person €10, dm/s/d €20/40/65; P ☎) is a good place to stay, with terrific views of the Rock. Bus Éireann runs six buses daily between Cashel and Cork (€15, 1¾ hours).

Crawford Municipal Art Gallery

GALLERY

(☎021-480 5042; www.crawfordartgallery.ie; Emmet Pl; ☉10am-5pm Mon-Wed, Fri & Sat, to 8pm Thu) **FREE** Cork's public gallery houses a small but excellent permanent collection covering the 17th century to the modern day. Highlights include works by Sir John Lavery, Jack B Yeats and Nathaniel Hone, and a room devoted to Irish women artists from 1886 to 1978 – don't miss the works by Mainie Jellet and Evie Hone.

Cork City Gaol

MUSEUM

(☎021-430 5022; www.corkcitygaol.com; Convent Ave, Sun's Well; adult/child €8/4.50; ☉9.30am-5pm Apr-Oct, 10am-4pm Nov-Mar) This imposing former prison is well worth a visit, if only to get a sense of how crap life was for prisoners a century ago. An audio tour guides you around the restored cells, which feature models of suffering prisoners and sadistic-looking guards. It's very moving, bringing home the harshness of the 19th-century penal system. The most common crime was that of poverty; many of the inmates were sentenced to hard labour for stealing loaves of bread.

🛏 Sleeping

Oscar's Hostel

HOSTEL €

(☎085 175 3458; www.oscarshostel.com; 111 Lower Glanmire Rd; dm/tw €20/44; ☎) Pretty much brand new at the time of research, this small (32-bed) hostel is set on a busy street just 200m east of the train station and 15 minutes' walk from the city centre. Facilities are good, with a well-equipped modern kitchen, comfy common rooms and bike storage, though the bedrooms are basic.

Brú Bar & Hostel

HOSTEL €

(☎021-455 9667; www.bruhostel.com; 57 MacCurtain St; dm/tw from €17/40; @☎) This buzzing hostel has its own internet cafe, with free access for guests, and a fantastic bar, popular with backpackers and locals alike. The dorms (each with a bathroom) have four to six beds and are both clean and stylish – ask for one on the upper floors to avoid bar noise. Breakfast is free.

★ Garnish House

B&B €€

(☎021-427 5111; www.garnish.ie; Western Rd; s/d from €89/98; P☎) Attention is lavished upon guests at this award-winning B&B. The legendary breakfast menu (30 choices) includes fresh fish and French toast. Typical of the touches here is the delicious porridge, which comes with creamed honey and your choice of whiskey or Baileys. Enjoy it out on the garden terrace. The 14 rooms are very comfortable; reception is open 24 hours.

★ River Lee Hotel

HOTEL €€€

(☎021-425 2700; www.doylecollection.com; Western Rd; r from €155; P☎☎) This modern riverside hotel brings a touch of luxury to the city centre. It has gorgeous public areas with huge sofas, a designer fireplace and a stunning five-storey glass-walled atrium, and superb service. There are well-equipped bedrooms (nice and quiet at the back, but request a corner room for extra space) and possibly the best breakfast buffet in Ireland.

🍴 Eating

Quay Co-op

VEGETARIAN €

(☎021-431 7026; www.quaycoop.com; 24 Sullivan's Quay; mains €5-11; ☉8am-9pm Mon-Sat, noon-9pm Sun; 🖘) 🌿 Flying the flag for alternative Cork, this place offers a range of self-service vegetarian dishes, all organic, including big breakfasts and rib-sticking soups and casseroles. It also caters for

Cork

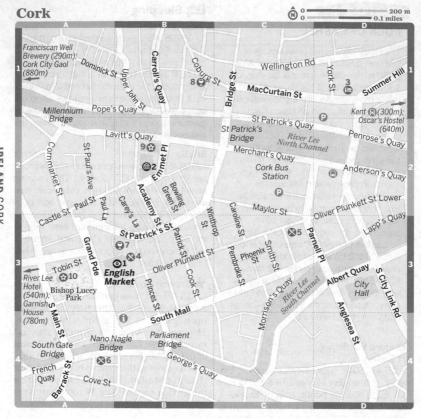

gluten-, dairy- and wheat-free needs, and is amazingly child-friendly.

★ Market Lane
IRISH, INTERNATIONAL €€

(☑ 021-427 4710; www.marketlane.ie; 5 Oliver Plunkett St; mains €12-26; ☉ noon-10.30pm Mon-Sat, 1-9pm Sun; 🛜 🖶) 🖉 It's always hopping at this bright corner bistro with an open kitchen and long wooden bar. The broad menu changes often to reflect what's fresh – look out for braised pork marinated in Cork dry gin, and steaks with awesome aioli. The €10 lunch menu is a steal. No reservations; sip a drink at the bar while you wait for a table.

Farmgate Cafe
CAFE, BISTRO €€

(www.farmgate.ie; English Market, Princes St, mains €6-15; ☉ 8.30am-4.30pm Mon-Fri, to 5pm Sat) 🖉 An unmissable experience at the heart of the English Market, the Farmgate is perched on a balcony overlooking the market below, the source of all that fresh local produce on your plate, everything from rock oysters to the

lamb for an Irish stew. Up the stairs and turn left for table service, right for counter service.

🍷 Drinking & Nightlife

In Cork pubs, drink Guinness at your peril, even though Heineken now owns both of the local stout legends, Murphy's and Beamish (and closed down the latter's brewery). Cork's microbrewery, the Franciscan Well Brewery, makes quality beers, including Friar Weisse, popular in summer.

Franciscan Well Brewery
PUB

(www.franciscanwellbrewery.com; 14 North Mall; ☉ 3-11.30pm Mon-Thu, to 12.30am Fri & Sat, to 11pm Sun; 🛜) The copper vats gleaming behind the bar give the game away: the Franciscan Well brews its own beer. The best place to enjoy it is in the enormous beer garden at the back. The pub holds regular beer festivals with other small (and often underappreciated) Irish breweries.

Sin É   PUB
(www.corkheritagepubs.com; 8 Coburg St; ⊙ 12.30-
11.30pm Sun-Thu, to 12.30am Fri & Sat) You could
easily while away an entire day at this great
old place, which is everything a craic-filled
pub should be – long on atmosphere and
short on pretension. There's music most
nights (regular sessions Tuesday at 9.30pm,
Friday and Sunday at 6.30pm), much of it
traditional, but with the odd surprise.

Mutton Lane Inn   PUB
(www.corkheritagepubs.com; Mutton Lane;
⊙ 10.30am-11.30pm Mon-Thu, 10.30am-12.30am
Fri & Sat, 2-11pm Sun) Tucked down the tiniest
of laneways off St Patrick's St, this inviting
pub, lit by candles and fairy lights, is one of
Cork's most intimate drinking holes. It's minuscule so try to get in early to bag the snug,
or perch on beer kegs outside.

☆ Entertainment

Cork's cultural life is generally of a high cali-
bre. To see what's happening grab *WhazOn?*
(www.whazon.com), a free monthly booklet
available from the tourist office, newsagen-
cies, shops, hostels and B&Bs.

Cork Opera House   OPERA
(☑ 021-427 0022; www.corkoperahouse.ie; Emmet
Pl; ⊙ box office 10am-7pm Mon-Sat, from 6pm Sun
performance nights, 10am-5.30pm Mon-Sat non-
performance nights) This leading venue has
been entertaining the city for more than 150

years with everything from opera and ballet
to stand-up and puppet shows. Around the
back, the **Half Moon Theatre** (☑ 021-427 0022;
www.corkoperahouse.ie/category/genre/half-moon-
theatre; Emmet Pl) presents contemporary
theatre, dance, art and occasional club nights.

Triskel Arts Centre   ARTS CENTRE
(☑ 021-472 2022; www.triskelart.com; Tobin St; tickets €15-20; ⊙ cafe 10am-5pm Mon-Sat) Expect a
varied program of live music, installation art,
photography and theatre at this intimate venue. There's also a **cinema** (from 6.30pm) and
a great **cafe**.

ⓘ Information

Cork City Tourist Office (☑ 021-425 5100;
www.corkcity.ie; Grand Pde; ⊙ 9am-6pm
Mon-Sat year-round, plus 10am-5pm Sun Jul &
Aug) Souvenir shop and information desk. Sells
Ordnance Survey maps. Stena Line ferries has
a desk here.

ⓘ Getting There & Around

BICYCLE
Cycle Scene (☑ 021-430 1183; www.cycle
scene.ie; 396 Blarney St) has bikes for hire from
€15/80 per day/week.

BOAT
Brittany Ferries (☑ 021-427 7801; www.brittany
ferries.ie; 42 Grand Pde) has regular sailings from
Cork to Roscoff (France). The ferry terminal is at
Ringaskiddy, about 15 minutes by car southeast
of the city centre along the N28.

BUS
Aircoach (☑ 01-844 7118; www.aircoach.ie)
provides a direct service to Dublin city (€16)
and Dublin Airport (€20) from St Patrick's Quay
(three hours, hourly). **Cork bus station** (cnr
Merchants Quay & Parnell Pl) is east of the city
centre. Services include Dublin (€15, 3¾ hours,
six daily), Kilkenny (€21, three hours, two daily)
and Killarney (€27, two hours, hourly).

TRAIN
Cork's **Kent train station** (☑ 021-450 4777)
is across the river. Destinations include Dublin
(€64, 2¼ hours, eight daily), Galway (€57, four
to six hours, seven daily, two or three changes
needed) and Killarney (€28, 1½ to two hours,
nine daily).

Around Cork

If you need proof of the power of a good
yarn, then join the queue to get into the 15th-
century **Blarney Castle** (☑ 021-438 5252;

www.blarneycastle.ie; adult/child €12/5; ⊙9am-5.30pm daily year-round, to 6pm Mon-Sat May & Sep, to 7pm Mon-Sat Jun-Aug; P), one of Ireland's most inexplicably popular tourist attractions. Tourists are here, of course, to plant their lips on the **Blarney Stone**, which supposedly gives one the gift of gab – a cliché that has entered every lexicon and tour route. Blarney is 8km northwest of Cork and buses run every half hour from Cork bus station (€7.30 return, 30 minutes).

Killarney

POP 14,200

Killarney is a well-oiled tourism machine set in a sublime landscape of lakes, forests and 1000m peaks. Its manufactured tweeness is renowned, the streets filled with tour-bus visitors shopping for soft-toy shamrocks and countless placards pointing to trad-music sessions. However, it has many charms beyond its proximity to waterfalls, woodlands, mountains and moors. In a town that's been practising the tourism game for more than 250 years, competition keeps standards high, and visitors on all budgets can expect to find superb restaurants, great pubs and good accommodation.

◎ Sights & Activities

Most of Killarney's attractions are just outside the town. The mountain backdrop is part of **Killarney National Park** (www.killarneynationalpark.ie), which takes in beautiful Lough Leane, Muckross Lake and Upper Lake. Besides **Ross Castle** and **Muckross House**, the park also has much to explore by foot, bike or boat.

In summer the **Gap of Dunloe**, a gloriously scenic mountain pass squeezed between Purple Mountain and Carrauntuohill (at 1040m, Ireland's highest peak), is a tourist bottleneck. Rather than join the crowds taking pony-and-trap rides, **O'Connors Tours** (☑064-663 0200; www.gapofdunloetours.com; 7 High St, Killarney; ⊙Mar-Oct) can arrange a bike and boat circuit (€15; highly recommended) or bus and boat tour (€30) taking in the Gap.

🛏 Sleeping

Súgán Hostel   HOSTEL €
(☑064-663 3104; www.killarneysuganhostel.com; Lewis Rd; dm €12-15, tw €38; 🛜) Behind its pub-like front, 250-year-old Súgán is an amiably eccentric hostel with an open fire in the cosy common room, low, crazy-cornered ceilings and hardwood floors. Note that it's an alcohol-free zone, which is either a good thing or a bad thing, depending on your point of view.

Fleming's White Bridge
Caravan & Camping Park   CAMPGROUND €
(☑086 363 0266; www.killarneycamping.com; White Bridge, Ballycasheen Rd; campsites €10-25; ⊙mid-Mar–Oct; 🛜) A lovely, sheltered, family-run campsite about 2km southeast of the town centre off the N22, Fleming's has a games room, bike hire, campers' kitchen, laundry and free trout fishing on the river that runs alongside. Your man Hillary at reception can arrange bus, bike and boat tours, if he doesn't talk the legs off you first!

★**Crystal Springs**   B&B €€
(☑064-663 3272; www.crystalspringsbb.com; Ballycasheen Cross; s/d from €45/70; P🛜) The timber deck of this wonderfully relaxing B&B overhangs the River Flesk, where trout anglers can fish for free. Rooms are richly furnished with patterned wallpapers and walnut timber; private bathrooms (most with spa baths) are huge. The glass-enclosed breakfast room also overlooks the rushing river. It's about a 15-minute stroll into town.

Kingfisher Lodge   B&B €€
(☑064-663 7131; www.kingfisherlodgekillarney.com; Lewis Rd; s/d/f €70/90/120; ⊙mid-Feb–Nov; P@🛜) Lovely back gardens are a highlight at this immaculate B&B, whose 11 rooms are done up in vivid yellows, reds and pinks. Owner Donal Carroll is a certified walking guide with a wealth of knowledge on hiking in the area.

🍴 Eating

Jam   CAFE €
(☑064-663 7716; www.jam.ie; 77 Old Market Lane; mains €4-11; ⊙8am-5.30pm Mon-Sat, 10am-5.30pm Sun; 🍴) 🌿 Duck down the alley to this local hideout for a changing menu of hot meals like Kerry shepherd's pie, deli items, and coffee and cake. It's all made with locally sourced produce and there are a few tables under an awning out front. There are branches in Kenmare and Cork.

Smoke House   STEAK, SEAFOOD €€
(☑087 233 9611; High St; lunch mains €11-16, dinner mains €15-29; ⊙noon-10pm Mon-Fri, 9am-10pm Sat & Sun) One of Killarney's busiest restaurants, this tiled bistro was the first

establishment in Ireland to cook with a Josper (Spanish charcoal oven). Stylish salads include Norwegian king crab, and its Kerry surf 'n' turf burger – with prawns and house-made barbecue sauce – has a local following. Early bird three-course dinner is €25.

Brícín IRISH €€
(www.bricin.com; 26 High St; mains €19-26; ⊗6-9.30pm Tue-Sat) Decorated with fittings from a convent, an orphanage and a school, this Celtic deco restaurant doubles as the town museum, with Jonathan Fisher's 18th-century views of the national park taking pride of place. Try the house speciality, boxty (traditional potato pancake). Two-course dinner for €19 before 6.45pm.

🍷 Drinking & Nightlife

★O'Connor's PUB
(High St; ⊗10.30am-11pm Mon-Thu, 10.30am-12.30am Fri & Sat, 12.30-11pm Sun) This tiny traditional pub with leaded-glass doors is one of Killarney's most popular haunts. Live music plays every night; good bar food is served daily in summer. In warmer weather, the crowds spill out to the adjacent lane.

Courtney's PUB
(www.courtneysbar.com; Plunkett St; ⊗5-11.30pm Sun-Thu, 5pm-12.30am Fri, 2pm-12.30am Sat) Inconspicuous on the outside, inside this timeless pub bursts at the seams with traditional music sessions many nights year-round. This is where locals come to see their old mates perform and to kick off a night on the town.

Killarney Grand BAR, CLUB
(www.killarneygrand.com; Main St; ⊗7.30pm-2.30am Mon-Sat, to 1.30am Sun) There's traditional live music from 9pm to 11pm, bands from 11.30pm to 1.30am and a disco from 11pm at this Killarney institution. Entry is free before 11pm.

ℹ️ Information

Tourist Office (☑064-663 1633; www.killarney. ie; Beech Rd; ⊗9am-5pm Mon-Sat; 🖥️) Can handle almost any query, especially dealing with transport intricacies.

ℹ️ Getting There & Around

BIKE
O'Sullivan's (www.killarneyrentabike.com; Beech Rd; per day/week €15/80) offers bike rental; opposite the tourist office.

WORTH A TRIP

SKELLIG MICHAEL
Portmagee (an 80km drive west of Killarney) is the jumping-off point for an unforgettable experience: the Skellig Islands, two tiny rocks 12km off the coast. The vertiginous climb up uninhabited Skellig Michael inspires an awe that monks could have clung to life in the meagre beehive-shaped stone huts that cluster on the tiny patch of level land on top. From spring to late summer, weather permitting, boat trips run from Portmagee to Skellig Michael; the standard rate is around €50 per person, departing 10am and returning 3pm. Advance booking is essential; there are a dozen boat operators, including **Casey's** (☑066-947 2437; www.skelligislands.com; Portmagee) and **Sea Quest** (☑066-947 6214; www.skelligsrock.com).

BUS
Operating from the train station, Bus Éireann has regular services to Cork (€27, two hours, hourly), Galway via Limerick (€26, 3¾ hours, four daily) and Rosslare Harbour (€29, seven hours, three daily).

TAXI
Taxis can be found at the taxi rank on College St. A cab from the edge of town (eg Flesk campsite) into the town centre costs around €9.

TRAIN
Travelling by train to Cork (€28, 1½ to two hours, nine daily) or Dublin (€67, 3¼ hours, seven daily) sometimes involves changing at Mallow.

Ring of Kerry
The Ring of Kerry, a 179km circuit around the dramatic coastal scenery of the Iveragh Peninsula, is one of Ireland's premier tourist attractions. Most travellers tackle the ring by bus on guided day trips from Killarney, but you could spend days wandering here.

The Ring is dotted with picturesque villages (**Sneem** and **Portmagee** are worth a stop), **prehistoric sites** (ask for a guide at Killarney tourist office) and spectacular **viewpoints**, notably at Beenarourke just west of Caherdaniel, and Ladies' View (between Kenmare and Killarney). The **Ring of Skellig**, at the end of the peninsula, has

WORTH A TRIP

CLIFFS OF MOHER

Star of a million tourist brochures, the Cliffs of Moher in County Clare are one of the most popular sights in Ireland. But like many an ageing star, you have to look beyond the famous facade to appreciate its inherent attributes. In summer the site is overrun with day trippers, but there are good rewards if you're willing to walk along the clifftops for 10 minutes to escape the crowds.

The landscaped **Cliffs of Moher Visitor Centre** (www.cliffsofmoher.ie; adult/child €6/free; ☉9am-9pm Jul-Aug, to 7pm May-Jun & Sep & Oct, (to 6pm Mar-Apr & Oct, to 5pm Nov-Feb) has exhibitions about the cliffs and their natural history. A number of bus tours leave Galway every morning for the Cliffs of Moher, including **Burren Wild Tours** (☑087 877 9565; www.burren walks.com; departs Galway Coach Station; adult/student €25/20; ☉10am-5pm).

fine views of the Skellig Islands and is not as busy as the main route. You can forgo driving completely by walking part of the 200km **Kerry Way** (www.kerryway.com), which winds through the Macgillycuddy's Reeks mountains past Carrauntuohill (1040m), Ireland's highest mountain.

◉ Sights

Kerry Bog Village Museum MUSEUM
(www.kerrybogvillage.ie; adult/child €6.50/4.50; ☉9am-6pm) On the N70 between Killorglin and Glenbeigh, this museum recreates a 19th-century bog village, typical of the small communities that carved out a precarious living in the harsh environment of Ireland's ubiquitous peat bogs. You'll see the thatched homes of the turfcutter, blacksmith, thatcher and labourer, as well as a dairy. You can meet rare Kerry Bog ponies.

Derrynane National Historic Park HISTORIC SITE
(☑066-947 5113; www.heritageireland.ie; Derry-nane; adult/child €3/1; ☉10.30am-6pm May-Sep, 10am-5pm Wed-Sun Oct-late Nov) Derrynane House was the family home of Daniel O'Connell, the early-19th-century campaigner for Catholic emancipation. His ancestors

bought the house and surrounding parkland, having grown rich on smuggling with France and Spain. It's largely furnished with O'Connell memorabilia, including the restored triumphal chariot in which he lapped Dublin after his release from prison in 1844.

🛏 Sleeping & Eating

There are plenty of hostels and B&Bs along the Ring. It's wise to book ahead, though, as some places are closed out of season and others fill up quickly.

Mannix Point Camping & Caravan Park CAMPGROUND €
(☑066-947 2806; www.campinginkerry.com; Mannix Point; backpackers per person €8.50, campervan €23; ☉Mar-Oct; 🖅) Mortimer Moriarty's award-winning coastal site has an inviting kitchen, campers' sitting room with a peat fire (no TV but regular music sessions), a barbecue area and even a birdwatching platform. And the sunsets are stunning.

★**Smuggler's Inn** INN €€
(☑066-947 4330; www.the-smugglers-inn.com; Cliff Rd; d €80-130; ☉Apr-Oct; 🅿🖅) Across from the Waterville Golf Links at the water's edge, Smuggler's Inn is a diamond find (once you do find it: it's hard to spot if you're coming from the north). Rooms are freshly renovated – try for room 15, with a glassed-in balcony overlooking Ballinskelligs Bay.

Moorings INN €€
(☑066-947 7108; www.moorings.ie; s/d from €60/80; 🅿🖅) The Moorings is a friendly local hotel, bar and restaurant, with 16 rooms split between modern sea-view choices and simpler options, most refreshingly white. The nautical-themed **restaurant** (mains €20-25; ☉6-10pm Tue-Sun Apr-Oct) specialises in excellent seafood, while the **Bridge Bar** (mains €10-25; ☉food served noon-9pm) serves superb fish and chips.

❶ Getting Around

Bus Éireann runs a once-daily Ring of Kerry bus service (No 280) from late June to late August. Buses leave Killarney at 11.30am and stop at Killorglin, Glenbeigh, Caherciveen (€16.40, 1¾ hours), Waterville, Caherdaniel and Molls Gap (€21.50), arriving back at Killarney at 4.45pm.

Travel agencies and hostels in Killarney offer daily coach tours of the Ring for about €20 to €25 year-round, lasting from 10.30am to 5pm.

THE WEST COAST

Galway

POP 75,500

Arty and bohemian, Galway (Gaillimh) is legendary around the world for its entertainment scene. Students make up a quarter of the city's population and brightly painted pubs heave with live music on any given night. Here, street life is more important than sightseeing – cafes spill out onto cobblestone streets filled with a frenzy of fiddles, banjos, guitars and Bodhráns (handheld goatskin drums), while jugglers, painters, puppeteers and magicians in outlandish masks enchant passers-by.

⊙ Sights

★**Galway City Museum**   MUSEUM
(www.galwaycitymuseum.ie; Spanish Pde; ⊙ 10am-5pm Tue-Sat year-round, noon-5pm Sun Easter-Sep) FREE This modern museum has exhibits on the city's history from 1800 to 1950, including an iconic Galway Hooker fishing boat, a collection of *currachs* (boats made from animal hides) and a controversial statue of Galway-born writer and hellraiser Pádraic Ó Conaire (1883–1928), which was previously in Eyre Sq.

★**Spanish Arch**   HISTORIC SITE
The Spanish Arch is thought to be an extension of Galway's medieval city walls, designed to protect ships moored at the nearby quay while they unloaded goods such as wine and brandy from Spain. Today it reverberates to the beat of bongo drums, and the lawns and riverside form a gathering place for locals and visitors on a sunny day. Many watch kayakers manoeuvre over the tidal rapids of the River Corrib.

Lynch's Castle   HISTORIC BUILDING
(cnr Shop & Upper Abbeygate Sts) Considered the finest town castle in Ireland, this old stone town house was built in the 14th century, though much of what you see today dates from around 1600. Stonework on the facade (the real attraction here) includes ghoulish

gargoyles and the coats of arms of Henry VII, the Lynches (the most powerful of the 14 ruling Galway 'tribes') and the Fitzgeralds of Kildare.

★☆ Festivals

Galway International Arts Festival   ART
(www.giaf.ie) A two-week extravaganza of art, music, theatre and comedy in mid-July.

Galway Oyster Festival   FOOD, DRINK
(www.galwayoysterfest.com) Going strong for more than 50 years now, this festival draws thousands of visitors in late September.

🛏 Sleeping

★**Kinlay Hostel**   HOSTEL €
(☑ 091-565 244; www.kinlayhouse.ie; Merchants Rd; dm/d €29/70; @ 🛜) Easygoing staff, a full range of facilities and a cream-in-the-doughnut location just off Eyre Sq make this a top choice. Spanning two huge, brightly lit floors, amenities include two self-catering kitchens and two cosy TV lounges. Some rooms have bay views.

Snoozles Tourist Hostel   HOSTEL €
(☑ 091-530 064; www.snoozleshostelgalway.ie; Forster St; dm/d €18/50; @ 🛜) Dorms and private rooms all have bathrooms at this new hostel. It's ideal for the over-burdened as it sits near the train and bus stations. Extras include a barbecue terrace, pool table and more.

★**Heron's Rest**   B&B €€
(☑ 091-539 574; www.theheronsrest.com; 16a Longwalk; s/d from €70/140; 🛜) Ideally located on the banks of the Corrib, the endlessly thoughtful hosts here will give you deck chairs so you can sit outside and enjoy the scene. Other touches include holiday-friendly breakfast times (8am to 11am), decanters of port and more. Rooms, all with water views, are small and cute.

St Martins B&B   B&B €€
(☑ 091-568 286; www.stmartins.ie; 2 Nun's Island Rd; s/d from €50/80; @ 🛜) This beautifully kept, renovated older house right on the canal has a flower-filled garden overlooking the William O'Brien Bridge and the River Corrib. The four rooms have all the comforts and the breakfast is a few cuts above the norm (fresh-squeezed OJ). Owner Mary Sexton wins rave reviews.

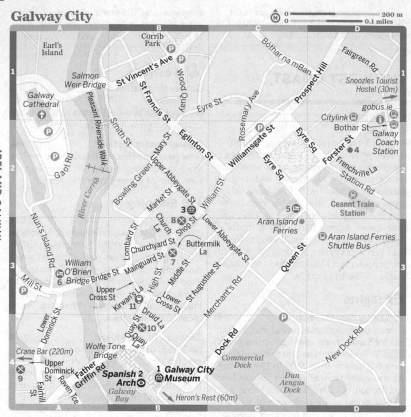

Galway City

IRELAND GALWAY

Galway City

✕ Eating & Drinking

★ McCambridge's
CAFE, GROCER €

(www.mccambridges.com; 38/39 Shop St; snacks from €3, mains €7-13; ☺ cafe 9am-5.30pm Mon-Wed, 9am-10pm Thu-Sat, 10.30am-6pm Sun, grocery 9am-6pm Mon-Sat) The long-running food hall here has a superb selection of prepared salads, hot foods and other more exotic treats. Create the perfect picnic or enjoy your selections at the tables out front. The upstairs cafe is simply fabulous – modern Irish fare flavours the ever-changing menu. Creative sandwiches, salads, silky soups and savoury meals are featured.

Griffin's
CAFE, BAKERY €

(www.griffinsbakery.com; Shop St; mains €4-8; ☺ 8am-6pm Mon-Sat) A local institution, which, although it's been run by the Griffin family since 1876, remains as fresh as a bun hot out of the oven. The small bakery counter is laden with treats, including great scones. But the real pleasure lies upstairs in the cafe where you can choose from sandwiches, hot specials, luscious desserts and more.

★**Quay Street Kitchen**   IRISH €€
(☑091-865 680; The Halls, Quay St; mains €8-18; ⊙11.45am-10.30pm; ☎☑) Fast and friendly service makes a great first impression at this always-busy bistro. The menu doesn't disappoint either, with a selection of steak, lamb and seafood, good vegetarian and vegan dishes, and hearty daily specials such as pork, leek and stout sausages with mashed potato and onion gravy.

★**Oscar's**   SEAFOOD €€
(☑091-582 180; www.oscarsbistro.ie; Upper Dominick St; mains €15-25; ⊙6.30-9.30pm Mon-Sat, 6-9pm Sun) Galway's best seafood restaurant is just west of the tourist bustle. The long and ever-changing menu has a huge range of local specialities, from shellfish to white fish (which make some superb fish and chips). The flavours are bold, not unlike the bright red accents inside and out.

★**Séhán Ua Neáchtain**   PUB
(www.tighneachtain.com; 17 Upper Cross St; ⊙noon-11.30pm Mon-Thu, noon-midnight Fri & Sat, noon-11pm Sun) Painted a bright cornflower blue, this 19th-century pub, known simply as Neáchtain's (*nock*-tans) or Naughtons, has a wraparound string of tables outside, many shaded by a large tree. It's a place where a polyglot mix of locals plop down and let the world pass them by – or stop and join them for a pint. Good lunches.

★**Crane Bar**   PUB
(www.thecranebar.com; 2 Sea Rd; ⊙10.30am-11.30pm Mon-Thu, 10.30am-12.30am Fri & Sat, noon-11pm Sun) An atmospheric old pub west of the Corrib, the Crane is the best spot in Galway to catch an informal *céilidh* (session of traditional music and dancing) most nights. Talented bands play its rowdy, good-natured upstairs bar; downstairs at times it seems right out of *The Far Side*.

ℹ **Information**

Tourist Office (www.discoverireland.ie; Forster St; ⊙9am-5.45pm daily Easter-Sep, closed Sun Oct-Easter) Large, efficient regional information centre that can help arrange local accommodation and tours.

ℹ **Getting There & Around**

BICYCLE
On Yer Bike (www.onyourbikecycles.com; 40 Prospect Hill; ⊙9am-5.30pm Mon-Sat) Bike hire from €10 per day.

BUS
Bus Éireann buses depart from outside the train station. **Citylink** (www.citylink.ie; ticket office Forster St; ⊙office 9am-6pm; ☎) and **GoBus** (www.gobus.ie; Galway Coach Station; ☎) use the **coach station** (New Coach Station; Bothar St) a block northeast. Citylink has buses to Clifden (€14, 1½ hours, five daily) and Dublin (€13, 2½ hours, hourly). Bus Éireann runs buses to Killarney via Limerick (€26, 3¾ hours, four daily).

TRAIN
Trains run to and from Dublin (€36, 2¾ hours, nine daily). You can connect with other trains at Athlone.

Aran Islands

The windswept Aran Islands are one of western Ireland's major attractions. As well as their rugged beauty – they are an extension of The Burren's limestone plateau – the Irish-speaking islands have some of the country's oldest Christian and pre-Christian ruins.

There are three main islands in the group, all inhabited year-round. Most visitors head for the long and narrow (14.5km by a maximum 4km) **Inishmór** (or Inishmore). The land slopes up from the relatively sheltered northern shores of the island and plummets on the southern side into the raging Atlantic. **Inishmaan** and **Inisheer** are much smaller and receive far fewer visitors.

The **tourist office** (☑099-61263; Kilronan; ⊙10am-5pm May & Jun, 10am-5.45pm Jul & Aug, 11am-5pm Sep-Apr) operates year-round at Kilronan, the arrival point and major village of Inishmór. You can leave your luggage here and change money. Around the corner is a Spar supermarket with an ATM (many places do not accept credit cards).

Inishmór

Three spectacular forts stand guard over Inishmór, each believed to be around 2000 years old. Chief among them is **Dún Aengus** (Dún Aonghasa; www.heritageireland.ie; adult/child €3/1; ⊙9.45am-6pm Apr-Oct, 9.30am-4pm Nov-Mar, closed Mon & Tue Jan & Feb), which has three massive drystone walls that run right up to sheer drops to the ocean below.

It is protected by remarkable *chevaux de frise*, fearsome and densely packed defensive stone spikes. A small visitor centre has displays that put everything in context. A slightly strenuous 900m walkway wanders uphill to the fort itself.

Kilronan Hostel (☑ 099-61255; www.kilronan hostel.com; Kilronan; dm €15-30, tw €42; @ 🛜), perched above Tí Joe Mac's pub, is a friendly hostel just a two-minute walk from the ferry. **Kilmurvey House** (☑ 099-61218; www.kilmurvey house.com; Kilmurvey; s/d from €55/90; ⊙ Apr-Sep) offers B&B in a grand 18th-century stone mansion on the path leading to Dún Aengus.

❶ Getting There & Away

AIR

Aer Arann Islands (☑ 091-593 034; www.aer arannislands.ie) Offers return flights to each of the islands several times daily (hourly in summer) for adult/child €49/27; the flights take about 10 minutes, and groups of four or more can get group rates. A connecting minibus from the Victoria Hotel in Galway costs €3 one way.

BOAT

Aran Island Ferries (www.aranislandferries. com; Galway Ticket Office, Merchant's Rd; adult/child return from €25/13; ⊙ 8am-5pm) The crossing can take up to one hour and is subject to cancellation in high seas. Boats leave from Rossaveal, 40km west of Galway City on the R336. Buses from Galway (adult/child €7/4) connect with the sailings; ask when you book.

Ferries to the Arans (primarily Inisheer) also operate from Doolin.

Connemara

With its shimmering black lakes, pale mountains, lonely valleys and more than the occasional rainbow, Connemara in the northwestern corner of County Galway is one of the most gorgeous corners of Ireland. It's prime hillwalking country with plenty of wild terrain, none more so than the Twelve Bens, a ridge of rugged mountains that form part of **Connemara National Park** (www. connemaranationalpark.ie; off N59; ⊙ visitor centre 9am-5.30pm Mar-Oct, park 24hr) **FREE**.

Connemara's 'capital', **Clifden** (An Clochán), is an appealing Victorian-era country town with an oval of streets offering evocative strolls. Right in the centre of town is cheery **Clifden Town Hostel** (☑ 095-21076; www.clifdentownhostel.com; Market St; dm €17-22, d from €40), while the gorgeous **Dolphin Beach B&B** (☑ 095-21204; www.dolphinbeach

house.com; Lower Sky Rd; s/d from €90/130, dinner €40; P 🛜) is 5km west of town.

From Galway, **Lally Tours** (☑ 091-562 905; www.lallytours.com; 4 Forster St; tours from adult/child €20/12) runs day-long coach tours of Connemara.

NORTHERN IRELAND

☑ 028 / POP 1.8 MILLION

When you cross from the Republic into Northern Ireland you notice a couple of changes: the accent is different, the road signs are in miles, and the prices are in pounds sterling. But there's no border checkpoint, no guards, not even a sign to mark the crossing point – the two countries are in a customs union, so there's no passport control and no customs declarations. All of a sudden, you're in the UK.

Dragged down for decades by the violence and uncertainty of the Troubles, Northern Ireland today is a nation rejuvenated. The 1998 Good Friday Agreement laid the groundwork for peace and raised hopes for the future, and since then this UK province has seen a huge influx of investment and redevelopment. Belfast has become a happening place with a famously wild nightlife; Derry has come into its own as a cool, artistic city; and the stunning Causeway Coast gets more and more visitors each year.

There are plenty of reminders of the Troubles – notably the 'peace lines' that divide Belfast – and the passions that have torn Northern Ireland apart over the decades still run deep. But despite occasional setbacks there is an atmosphere of determined optimism.

Belfast

POP 280,900

Once lumped with Beirut, Baghdad and Bosnia as one of the four Bs for travellers to avoid, Belfast has pulled off a remarkable transformation from bombs-and-bullets pariah to hip-hotels-and-hedonism party town. Despite the economic downturn, the city's skyline is in a constant state of flux as redevelopment continues. The old shipyards are giving way to luxury waterfront apartments in the Titanic Quarter; and Victoria Sq, Europe's biggest urban regeneration project, has added a massive city-centre shopping mall to the city's list of tourist attractions: Victorian architecture, a glittering waterfront lined with modern art, foot-stomping music in packed-out pubs and the UK's second-biggest arts festival.

The city centre is compact, and the imposing City Hall in Donegall Sq is the central landmark. The principal shopping district is north of the square. North again, around Donegall St and St Anne's Cathedral, is the bohemian Cathedral Quarter.

South of the square, the so-called Golden Mile stretches for 1km along Great Victoria St, Shaftesbury Sq and Botanic Ave to Queen's University and the leafy suburbs of South Belfast; this area has dozens of restaurants and bars and most of the city's budget and midrange accommodation.

⊙ Sights

★ Titanic Belfast   EXHIBITION

(www.titanicbelfast.com; Queen's Rd; adult/child £15.50/7.25; ⊙9am-7pm Apr & Jun-Aug, 9am-6pm May & Sep, 10am-5pm Oct-Mar) The head of the slipway where the *Titanic* was built is now occupied by the gleaming, angular edifice of Titanic Belfast, an all-singing all-dancing multimedia extravaganza that charts the history of Belfast and the creation of the world's most famous ocean liner. Cleverly designed exhibits enlivened by historic images, animated projections and soundtracks chart Belfast's rise to turn-of-the-20th-century industrial superpower, followed by a high-tech ride through a noisy, smells-and-all re-creation of the city's shipyards.

You can then explore every detail of the *Titanic's* construction, from a computer 'fly-through' from keel to bridge, to replicas of the passenger accommodation. Perhaps most poignant are the few flickering images that constitute the only film footage of the ship in existence.

★ SS Nomadic   HISTORIC SITE

(www.nomadicbelfast.com; Queen's Rd; adult/child £8.50/5; ⊙10am-6pm daily Apr-Sep, to 5pm Tue-Sun Oct-Mar) The SS *Nomadic* is the only surviving vessel of the White Star Line (the shipping company that owned the *Titanic*). The little steamship once served as a tender to the giant Olympic Class ocean liners; now beautifully restored, it is home to an exhibition on the ship's history and its part in the *Titanic* story. After the one-hour guided tour that points out the original fittings, you are free to roam at will – don't miss the 1st-class toilets!

Built in Belfast in 1911, the *Nomadic* ferried 1st- and 2nd-class passengers between Cherbourg Harbour and the ocean liners that were too big to dock at the French port. On 10 April 1912 it delivered 142 1st-class passengers to the ill-fated *Titanic*. Having been requisitioned in both world wars, the ship ended up as a floating restaurant in Paris in the 1980s and '90s. In 2006 it was rescued from the breaker's yard and brought to Belfast, where it has a berth in the Hamilton Graving Dock, just northeast of the Odyssey Complex.

★ Ulster Museum   MUSEUM

(www.nmni.com/um; Stranmillis Rd; ⊙10am-5pm Tue-Sun; ♿) **FREE** Following a major revamp, the Ulster Museum is now one of Northern Ireland's don't-miss attractions. You could spend several hours browsing the beautifully designed displays, but if you're pressed for time don't miss the Armada Room, with artefacts retrieved from the wreck of the Spanish galleon *Girona*; Takabuti, a 2500-year-old Egyptian mummy; and the Bann Disc, a superb example of Celtic design dating from the Iron Age.

★ Crown Liquor Saloon   HISTORIC BUILDING

(www.nationaltrust.org.uk; 46 Great Victoria St; ⊙11.30am-11pm Mon-Wed, 11.30am-midnight Thu-Sat, 12.30-10pm Sun) **FREE** There are not too many historical monuments that you can enjoy while savouring a pint of beer, but the National Trust's Crown Liquor Saloon is one of them. Belfast's most famous bar was refurbished by Patrick Flanagan in the late 19th century and displays Victorian decorative flamboyance at its best (he was looking to pull in a posh clientele from the newfangled train station and Grand Opera House across the street).

West Belfast   HISTORIC SITE

Though scarred by three decades of civil unrest, the former battleground of West Belfast is one of the most compelling places to visit

Belfast

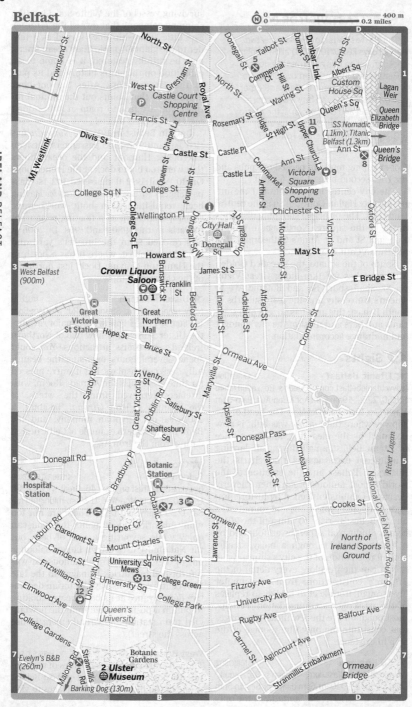

Belfast

in Northern Ireland. Falls Rd and Shankill Rd are adorned with famous **murals** expressing local political and religious passions, and divided by the infamous **Peace Line** – a 4km-long barrier that divides Catholic and Protestant districts. Take a taxi tour of the district, or pick up a map from the tourist office and explore on foot.

🎊 Festivals & Events

Féile An Phobail CULTURAL
(www.feilebelfast.com; ⊘ early Aug) Said to be the largest community festival in Ireland, the Féile takes place in West Belfast over 10 days. Events include an opening carnival parade, street parties, theatre performances, concerts and historical tours of the City and Milltown cemeteries.

Festival at Queen's ART
(www.belfastfestival.com) For three weeks in late October/early November, Belfast hosts the second-largest arts festival in the UK, in and around Queen's University.

🛏 Sleeping

Many B&Bs are concentrated in the pleasant university district of South Belfast, which is well stocked with restaurants and pubs.

★ **Vagabonds** HOSTEL €
(☑ 028-9023 3017; www.vagabondsbelfast.com; 9 University Rd; dm £13-16, tw & d £40; @ 🛜) Comfy bunks, lockable luggage baskets, private shower cubicles and a relaxed atmosphere are what you get at one of Belfast's best hostels, run by a couple of experienced travellers. Conveniently located close to both Queen's and the city centre.

★ **Tara Lodge** B&B €€
(☑ 028-9059 0900; www.taralodge.com; 36 Cromwell Rd; s/d from £79/89; P @ 🛜) This B&B is a cut above the average, feeling more like a boutique hotel with its clean-cut, minimalist decor, friendly and efficient staff, delicious breakfasts (including porridge with Bushmills whiskey) and 24 bright and cheerful rooms. It's in a great location too, on a quiet side street just a few paces from the buzz of Botanic Ave.

★ **Old Rectory** B&B €€
(☑ 028-9066 7882; www.anoldrectory.co.uk; 148 Malone Rd; s/d £55/86; P @ 🛜) A lovely Victorian villa with lots of original stained glass, this former rectory has five spacious bedrooms, a comfortable drawing room with leather sofa, and fancy breakfasts (wild-boar sausages, scrambled eggs with smoked salmon, vegie fry-ups, freshly squeezed OJ).

Evelyn's B&B B&B €€
(☑ 028-9066 5209; www.evelynsbandb.co.uk; 17 Wellington Park Tce; d from £50; 🛜) A friendly host and her even friendlier dog are the custodians of this delightful B&B, with period features including cast-iron bedsteads, a Victorian roll-top bath (the two doubles share the bathroom) and an Aga in the kitchen. Hard to find, but worth seeking out – it's on narrow Wellington Lane, leading off Wellington Park Tce (look for the purple door).

🍴 Eating

There are lots of inexpensive eating places along Botanic Ave in South Belfast, and many pubs offer good-value meals.

Maggie May's CAFE €
(www.maggiemaysbelfastcafe.co.uk; 50 Botanic Ave; mains £3-8; ⊘ 8am-11pm Mon-Sat, 9am-11pm Sun; 🖉 🖶) This is a classic little cafe with cosy wooden booths, murals of old Belfast and a host of hungover students wolfing down huge Ulster fries at lunchtime. The breakfast menu runs from a vegie fry-up to French toast and maple syrup, while lunch

BELFAST CITY TOURS

Many operators, including **Harpers** (☑07711 757178; www.harperstaxitours.co.nr; from £30) and **Paddy Campbell's** (☑07990 955227; www.belfastblackcabtours.co.uk; from £30), offer guided taxi tours of West Belfast, with an even-handed account of the Troubles. They run daily for around £10 per person based on a group of three to six, or £30 total for one or two, and pick-up can be arranged.

There are a number of walking tours available, including the three-hour **Belfast Pub Crawl** (☑07712 603764; www.belfastcrawl.com; per person £8; ☉7.30pm Fri & Sat), taking in four of the city's historic pubs, and the three-hour **Titanic Tour** (☑07852 716655; www. titanictours-belfast.co.uk; adult/child £30/15; ☉on demand), visiting various *Titanic* sites.

can be soup and a sandwich or beef lasagne; there's a good range of vegetarian dishes, too. BYOB.

There's a newer branch in Stranmillis (☑028-9066 8515; www.maggiemaysbelfastcafe. co.uk; 2 Malone Rd; mains £3-8; ☉8am-11pm Mon-Sat, 9am-11pm Sun).

John Hewitt Bar & Restaurant
PUB FOOD €

(www.thejohnhewitt.com; 51 Donegall St; mains £7-9; ☉food served noon-3pm Mon-Thu, to 5.30pm Fri & Sat;) Named for the Belfast poet and socialist, this is a modern pub with a traditional atmosphere and a well-earned reputation for excellent food. The menu changes weekly, but includes a soup of the day, inventive beef and chicken dishes, and a couple of vegetarian options. It's also a great place for a drink.

★Barking Dog
BISTRO €€

(☑028-9066 1885; www.barkingdogbelfast.com; 33-35 Malone Rd; mains £11-16; ☉noon-3pm & 5.30-10pm Mon-Sat, noon-9pm Sun) Chunky hardwood, bare brick, candlelight and quirky design create the atmosphere of a stylishly restored farmhouse. The menu completes the feeling of cosiness and comfort with simple but sensational dishes such as the bistro's signature burger of meltingly tender beef shin wrapped in caramelised onion and horseradish cream. Superb service, too.

★OX
IRISH €€

(☑028-9031 4121; www.oxbelfast.com; 1 Oxford St; mains £16-22; ☉noon-2.45pm & 5.45-10pm Tue-Fri, 1-2.45pm & 5.45-10pm Sat) A high-ceilinged space walled with cream-painted brick and furnished with warm golden wood creates a theatre-like ambience for the open kitchen at the back, where Michelin-trained chefs turn out some of Belfast's finest and best-value cuisine. The restaurant works with local suppliers and focuses on fine Irish beef, sustainable seafood, and seasonal vegetables and fruit. Three-course lunch/pretheatre costs £18/20.

🍷 Drinking & Nightlife

Belfast's pub scene is lively and friendly, with the older traditional pubs complemented by a rising tide of stylish designer bars.

★Crown Liquor Saloon
PUB

(www.nicholsonspubs.co.uk; 46 Great Victoria St; ☉11.30am-11pm Mon-Wed, 11.30am-midnight Thu-Sat, 12.30-10pm Sun) Belfast's most famous bar has a wonderfully ornate Victorian interior. Despite being a tourist attraction (p405), it still fills up with crowds of locals at lunchtime and in the early evening.

★Muriel's Cafe-Bar
BAR

(☑028-9033 2445; 12-14 Church Lane; ☉11am-1am Mon-Fri, 10am-1am Sat, 10am-midnight Sun) Hats meet harlotry (ask who Muriel was) in this delightfully snug and welcoming wee bar with retro-chic decor, old sofas and armchairs, heavy fabrics in shades of olive and dark red, gilt-framed mirrors and a cast-iron fireplace. Gin is Muriel's favourite tipple and there's a range of exotic brands to mix with your tonic. The food menu is pretty good, too.

Bittle's Bar
PUB

(103 Victoria St; ☉11.30am-11pm Mon-Thu, 11.30am-midnight Fri & Sat, 12.30-11pm Sun) A cramped and staunchly traditional bar, Bittle's is a 19th-century triangular red-brick building decorated with gilded shamrocks. The wedge-shaped interior is covered in paintings of Ireland's literary heroes by local artist Joe O'Kane. Pride of place on the back wall is a large canvas depicting Yeats, Joyce, Behan, Beckett and Wilde. It has an excellent range of craft beers.

QUB Student Union
CLUB

(www.mandelahall.com; Queen's Students Union, University Rd;) The student union has various bars and music venues hosting club nights, live bands and stand-up comedy. The monthly **Shine** (www.shine.net; admission £20; ☺ 1st Sat of month) is one of the city's best club nights with resident and guest DJs pumping out harder and heavier dance music than most of Belfast's other clubs.

☆ Entertainment

The Visit Belfast Welcome Centre issues *Whatabout?*, a free monthly guide to Belfast events. Another useful guide is *The Big List* (www.thebiglist.co.uk).

Queen's Film Theatre CINEMA
(www.queensfilmtheatre.com; 20 University Sq) A two-screen art-house cinema close to the university and a major venue for the Belfast Film Festival.

Lyric Theatre THEATRE
(www.lyrictheatre.co.uk; 55 Ridgeway St) This stunning modern theatre opened to great dramatic and architectural acclaim in 2011; it is built on the site of the old Lyric Theatre, where Hollywood star Liam Neeson first trod the boards (he is now a patron).

ℹ Information

Visit Belfast Welcome Centre (☎ 028-9024 6609; www.visit-belfast.com; 9 Donegall Sq N; ☺ 9am-5.30pm Mon-Sat, 11am-4pm Sun year-round, 9am-7pm Mon-Sat Jun-Sep; ☏) Provides information about the whole of Northern Ireland, and books accommodation anywhere in Ireland and Britain. Services include left luggage (not overnight), currency exchange and free wi-fi.

ℹ Getting There & Away

AIR
Belfast International Airport (p415) is 30km northwest of the city, and has flights from the UK, Europe and New York. George Best Belfast City Airport (p415) is 6km northeast of the city centre, with flights from the UK only.

BOAT
Stena Line ferries to Belfast from Cairnryan and Liverpool dock at **Victoria Terminal** (West Bank Rd), 5km north of the city centre; exit the M2 motorway at junction 1. Ferries from the Isle of Man arrive at **Albert Quay** (Corry Rd), 2km north of the centre.

Other car ferries to and from Scotland dock at Larne, 30km north of Belfast.

BUS
Europa Bus Centre, Belfast's main bus station, is behind the Europa Hotel and next door to Great Victoria St train station; it's reached via the Great Northern Mall beside the hotel. It's the main terminus for buses to Derry, Dublin and destinations in the west and south of Northern Ireland.

Ballycastle £12, two hours, three daily on weekdays, two on Saturday

Derry £12, 1¾ hours, half-hourly

Dublin £15, three hours, hourly

Aircoach (www.aircoach.ie) operates a service from Glengall St, near Europa Bus Centre, to Dublin city centre and Dublin Airport.

TRAIN
Belfast has two main train stations: Great Victoria St, next to the Europa Bus Centre, and Belfast Central, east of the city centre. If you arrive by train at Central Station, your rail ticket entitles you to a free bus ride into the city centre. A local train also connects with Great Victoria St.

Derry £11.50, 2¼ hours, seven or eight daily

Dublin £30, two hours, eight daily Monday to Saturday, five on Sunday

Larne Harbour £6.90, one hour, hourly

ℹ Getting Around

BICYCLE
Belfast Bike Tours (☎ 07812 114235; www.belfastbiketours.com; per person £15; ☺ 10.30am & 2pm Mon, Wed, Fri & Sat Apr-Sep, Sat only Oct-Mar) hires out bikes for £15 per day. Credit-card deposit and photo ID are required.

BUS
A short trip on a city bus costs £1.40 to £2.20; a one-day ticket costs £3.70. Most local bus services depart from Donegall Sq, near the City Hall, where there's a ticket kiosk; otherwise, buy a ticket from the driver.

The Causeway Coast

Ireland isn't short of scenic coastlines, but the **Causeway Coast** between Portstewart and Ballycastle – climaxing in the spectacular rock formations of the Giant's Causeway – and the **Antrim Coast** between Ballycastle and Belfast, are as magnificent as they come.

From April to September the **Ulsterbus** (☎ 028-9066 6630; www.translink.co.uk) Antrim Coaster (bus 252) links Larne with Coleraine (£12, four hours, two daily) via the Glens of Antrim, Ballycastle, the Giant's Causeway, Bushmills, Portrush and Portstewart.

From Easter to September the Causeway Rambler (bus 402) links Coleraine and Carrick-a-Rede (£6, 40 minutes, seven daily) via Bushmills, the Giant's Causeway, White Park Bay and Ballintoy. The ticket allows unlimited travel in both directions for one day.

There are several hostels along the coast, including **Sheep Island View Hostel** (☑028-2076 9391; www.sheepislandview.com; 42a Main St; campsites/dm/d £6/15/40; P@🛜), **Ballycastle Backpackers** (☑028-2076 3612; www.ballycastlebackpackers.net; 4 North St; dm/tw from £15/40; P@🛜) and **Bushmills Youth Hostel** (☑028-2073 1222; www.hini.org.uk; 49 Main St; dm/tw from £18.50/41; ⊗closed 11am-2pm Jul & Aug, 11am-5pm Mar-Jun, Sep & Oct; @).

◉ Sights

★ Giant's Causeway   LANDMARK
(www.nationaltrust.org.uk; ⊗dawn-dusk) `FREE`
This spectacular rock formation – Northern Ireland's only Unesco World Heritage Site – is one of Ireland's most impressive and atmospheric landscape features, a vast expanse of regular, closely packed, hexagonal stone columns looking for all the world like the handiwork of giants. The phenomenon is explained in the **Giant's Causeway Visitor Experience** (☑028-2073 1855; www.giantscausewaycentre.com; adult/child £8.50/4.25; ⊗9am-9pm Jul & Aug, to 7pm Apr-Jun & Sep, to 6pm Feb-Mar & Oct, to 5pm Nov-Jan; 🛜), a spectacular new ecofriendly building half-hidden in a hillside above the sea.

Visiting the Giant's Causeway itself is free of charge but you pay to use the car park and the visitor centre. (The admission fee is reduced by £1.50 if you arrive by bus, bike or on foot.)

From the centre it's an easy 10- to 15-minute walk downhill to the Causeway itself, but a more interesting approach is to follow the clifftop path northeast for 2km to the Chimney Tops headland, then descend the Shepherd's Steps to the Causeway. For the less mobile, a minibus shuttles from the visitors centre to the Causeway (£2 return).

★ Carrick-a-Rede
Rope Bridge   BRIDGE
(www.nationaltrust.org.uk; Ballintoy; adult/child £5.60/2.90; ⊗10am-7pm Jun-Aug, to 6pm Mar-May, Sep & Oct) The main attraction on the stretch of coast between Ballycastle and the Giant's Causeway is the famous (or notorious) Carrick-a-Rede Rope Bridge. The 20m-long, 1m-wide bridge of wire rope spans the chasm between the sea cliffs and the little island of Carrick-a-Rede, swaying gently 30m above the rock-strewn water. Crossing the bridge is perfectly safe, but it can be frightening if you don't have a head for heights, especially if it's breezy (in high winds the bridge is closed).

Once on the island there are good views of Rathlin Island and Fair Head to the east. The island has sustained a salmon fishery for centuries; fishermen stretch their nets out from the tip of the island to intercept the passage of salmon migrating along the coast to their home rivers. The fishermen put the bridge up every spring as they have done for the last 200 years – though it's not, of course, the original bridge.

There's a small National Trust information centre and cafe at the car park.

Derry/Londonderry

POP 107,900

Northern Ireland's second city comes as a pleasant surprise to many visitors. Derry was never the prettiest of places, and it certainly lagged behind Belfast in terms of investment and redevelopment, but in preparation for its year in the limelight as UK City of Culture 2013, the city centre was given a handsome makeover. The new **Peace Bridge**, Ebrington Sq, and the redevelopment of the waterfront and Guildhall area make the most of the city's riverside setting. And Derry's determined air of can-do optimism has made it the powerhouse of the North's cultural revival.

There's a lot of history to absorb here, from the Siege of Derry to the Battle of the Bogside – a stroll around the 17th-century city walls is a must, as is a tour of the Bogside murals. The city's lively pubs are home to a burgeoning live-music scene. But perhaps the biggest attraction is the people themselves: warm, witty and welcoming.

Derry or Londonderry? The name you use for Northern Ireland's second-largest city can be a political statement, but today most people just call it Derry, whatever their politics. The 'London' prefix was added in 1613 in recognition of the Corporation of London's role in the 'plantation' of Ulster with Protestant settlers.

In 1968 resentment at the long-running Protestant domination of the city council boiled over into a series of (Catholic-dominated) civil-rights marches. In August 1969 fighting between police and local youths in the poor Catholic Bogside district prompted the UK government to send British troops into Derry. In January 1972 'Bloody Sunday' resulted in the deaths of 13 unarmed Catholic civil-rights marchers in

Derry at the hands of the British army, an event that marked the beginning of the Troubles in earnest.

◉ Sights

★ Derry's City Walls LANDMARK

(www.derryswalls.com) Completed in 1619, Derry's city walls are 8m high and 9m thick, with a circumference of about 1.5km, and are the only city walls in Ireland to survive almost intact – you can walk the parapet all the way round. Derry's nickname, the Maiden City, derives from the fact that the walls have never been breached by an invader.

★ Tower Museum MUSEUM

(☑ 028-7137 2411; www.derrycity.gov.uk/museums; Union Hall Pl; adult/child £4/2; ⊙ 10am-6pm) This award-winning museum is housed in a replica 16th-century tower house. Head straight to the 5th floor for a view from the top of the tower, then work your way down through the excellent **Armada Shipwreck** exhibition, and the **Story of Derry**, where well-thought-out exhibits and audiovisuals lead you through the city's history from the founding of the monastery of St Colmcille (Columba) in the 6th century to the Battle of the Bogside in the late 1960s.

The Armada Shipwreck exhibition tells the story of *La Trinidad Valenciera* – a ship of the Spanish Armada that was wrecked at Kinnagoe Bay in Donegal in 1588. It was dis-covered by the City of Derry Sub-Aqua Club in 1971 and excavated by marine archaeologists. On display are bronze guns, pewter tableware and personal items – a wooden comb, an olive jar, a shoe sole – recovered from the site, along with a 2.5-tonne siege gun bearing the arms of Phillip II of Spain showing him as king of England. Allow at least two hours to do the museum justice.

★ People's Gallery Murals MURALS

(Rossville St) The 12 murals that decorate the gable ends of houses along Rossville St, near Free Derry Corner, are popularly referred to as the People's Gallery. They are the work of Tom Kelly, Will Kelly and Kevin Hasson, known as 'the Bogside Artists'. The three men have spent most of their lives in the Bogside, and lived through the worst of the Troubles. They can be clearly seen from the northern part of the City Walls.

🛏 Sleeping

Derry City
Independent Hostel HOSTEL €
(☑ 028-7128 0542; www.derry-hostel.co.uk; 12 Princes St; dm/d £16/42; @ 🐾) Run by experienced backpackers and decorated with souvenirs from their travels around the world, this small, friendly hostel is set in a Georgian town house, just a short walk northwest of the bus station. If you've been

---

OTHER IRISH PLACES WORTH A VISIT

Some other places in Ireland you might like to consider for day trips or longer visits:

Dingle (65km west of Killarney) The charms of this special spot have long drawn runaways from across the world, making this port town a surprisingly cosmopolitan and creative place. There are loads of cafes, bookshops and art and craft galleries, and a friendly dolphin called Fungie who has lived in the bay for 25 years.

Glendalough (50km south of Dublin) Nestled between two lakes, haunting Glendalough (Gleann dá Loch, meaning 'Valley of the Two Lakes') is one of the most significant monastic sites in Ireland and one of the loveliest spots in the country.

Kinsale (28km south of Cork) This picturesque yachting harbour is one of the many gems that dot the coastline of County Cork, and has been labelled the gourmet capital of Ireland; it certainly contains more than its fair share of international-standard restaurants.

Slieve League (120km southwest of Derry/Londonderry) The awe-inspiring cliffs at Slieve League, rising 300m above the Atlantic Ocean, are one of Ireland's top sights. Experienced hikers can spend a day walking along the top of the cliffs via the slightly terrifying One Man's Path to Malinbeg, near Glencolumbcille.

Sligo (140km north of Galway) William Butler Yeats (1865–1939) was born in Dublin and educated in London, but his poetry is infused with the landscapes, history and folklore of his mother's native Sligo (Sligeach). He returned many times and there are plentiful reminders of his presence in this sweet, sleepy town.

here before, note that it has moved to a new location around the corner.

★ **Merchant's House** B&B €€
(☑ 028-7126 9691; www.thesaddlershouse.com; 16 Queen St; s/d £70/75; @ 🕏) This historic, Georgian-style town house is a gem of a B&B. It has an elegant lounge and dining room with marble fireplaces and antique furniture, TV, coffee-making facilities, homemade marmalade at breakfast and even bathrobes in the bedrooms (only one has a private bathroom). Call at **Saddler's House** (☑ 028-7126 9691; www.thesaddlershouse.com; 36 Great James St; s/d £75/80; @🕏) first to pick up a key.

Abbey B&B B&B €€
(☑ 028-7127 9000; www.abbeyaccommodation.com; 4 Abbey St; s/d/f from £54/64/79; @ 🕏) There's a warm welcome waiting at this family-run B&B just a short walk from the walled city, on the edge of the Bogside. The six rooms are stylishly decorated and include family rooms able to sleep four.

✕ Eating

★ **Primrose Cafe** CAFE €
(15 Carlisle Rd; mains £7-8; ⊙ 8am-5pm Mon-Sat, 11am-3pm Sun; 🖐) The latest addition to Derry's cafe culture, the Primrose has prospered by sticking to the classics and doing them really well – from pancakes with maple syrup to Irish stew, and a Sunday brunch that ranges from eggs Benedict to the full Ulster fry. Even with the outdoor terrace at the back, it can be hard to find a seat.

Café del Mondo CAFE, IRISH €€
(☑ 028-7136 6877; www.cafedelmondo.org; Craft Village, Shipquay St; mains lunch £6-7, dinner £13-22; ⊙ 8.30am-6pm Mon, 8.30am-1am Tue-Sat, noon-5pm Sun, closed Sun & Mon Nov-Mar; 🕏 🖐) 🖐 A bohemian cafe that serves excellent fairtrade coffee as well as hearty homemade soups, artisan breads and hot lunch specials that use organic, locally sourced produce. A restaurant menu is served in the evening (best to book), offering steak, venison, seafood and a couple of vegetarian dishes.

Brown's in Town IRISH €€
(☑ 028-7136 2889; www.brownsrestaurant.com; 21-23 Strand Rd; mains £16-22; ⊙ noon-3pm Mon-Sat, 5.30-10.30pm Tue-Sat, 5-8.30pm Sun) There's a definite art-deco feel to the decor in Brown's city centre restaurant, bringing a much-needed touch of glamour and sophistication to Derry's downtown restaurant scene. The early bird three-course

dinner menu (£20, till 7.30pm Tuesday to Thursday, till 7pm Friday and Saturday) is terrific value.

🍷 Drinking & Entertainment

★ **Peadar O'Donnell's** PUB
(www.peadars.com; 63 Waterloo St; ⊙ 11.30am-1.30am Mon-Sat, 12.30pm-12.30am Sun) A backpackers' favourite, Peadar's has traditional music sessions every night and often on weekend afternoons as well. It's done up as a typical Irish pub-cum-grocer, down to the shelves of household items, shopkeepers, scales on the counter and a museum's-worth of old bric-a-brac.

Sandino's Cafe-Bar LIVE MUSIC
(www.sandinos.com; 1 Water St; admission £3-6; ⊙ 11.30am-1am Mon-Sat, 1pm-midnight Sun) From the posters of Che to the Free Palestine flag to the fairtrade coffee, this relaxed cafe-bar exudes a liberal, left-wing vibe. There are live bands on Friday nights and occasionally midweek, and DJ sessions on Saturdays, plus regular theme nights and events.

Playhouse THEATRE
(www.derryplayhouse.co.uk; 5-7 Artillery St; ⊙ box office 10am-5pm Mon-Fri, to 4pm Sat, plus 45min before show) Housed in beautifully restored former school buildings with an award-winning modern extension at the rear, this community arts centre stages music, dance and theatre by local and international performers.

ℹ️ Information

Derry Tourist Information Centre (☑ 028-7126 7284; www.visitderry.com; 44 Foyle St; ⊙ 9.30am-5pm Mon-Fri, 10am-4pm Sat & Sun year-round, longer hours Apr-Oct; 🕏) Covers all of Northern Ireland and the Republic as well as Derry. It sells books and maps, and can book accommodation throughout Ireland. It has a bureau de change, bike hire and free wi-fi.

ℹ️ Getting There & Away

BUS

The **bus station** (☑ 028-7126 2261; Foyle St) is just northeast of the walled city.

Belfast £12, 1¾ hours, every 30 minutes Monday to Saturday, 11 services on Sunday

Dublin £20, four hours, every two hours daily

Airporter (☑ 028-7126 9996; www.airporter. co.uk; 1 Bay Rd, Culmore Rd) Runs direct from Derry to Belfast International Airport (£20, 1½ hours) and George Best Belfast City Airport (£20, two hours) hourly Monday to Friday (six or seven daily Saturday and Sunday). Buses depart from Airporter office, 1.5km north of the city centre, next to Da Vinci's Hotel.

TRAIN
Derry's train station (always referred to as Londonderry in Northern Ireland timetables) is on the eastern side of the River Foyle; a free Rail Link bus connects with the bus station.

Belfast £11.50, 2¼ hours, seven or eight daily Monday to Saturday, four on Sunday

SURVIVAL GUIDE

 Directory A–Z

ACCOMMODATION
Hostels in Ireland can be booked solid in summer. An Óige (meaning 'youth') and Hostelling International Northern Ireland (HINI) are branches of Hostelling International (HI); An Óige has 26 hostels in the Republic, while HINI has six in the North. Other hostel associations include Independent Holiday Hostels (IHH), a cooperative group with about 120 hostels throughout the island, and the Independent Hostel Owners (IHO) association, which has more than 100 members around Ireland.

From June to September a dorm bed at most hostels costs €15 to €25 (£13 to £20), except for the more expensive hostels in Dublin, Belfast and a few other places.

Typical B&Bs cost around €35 to €45 (£25 to £40) per person a night (sharing a double room), though more luxurious B&Bs can cost upwards

of €55 (£45) per person. Most B&Bs are small, so in summer they quickly fill up.

Commercial camping grounds typically charge €12 to €25 (£10 to £20) for a tent or campervan and two people. Unless otherwise indicated, prices quoted for 'campsites' are for a tent, car and two people.

The following are useful resources:

An Óige (www.anoige.ie) Hostelling International (HI)–associated national organisation with 26 hostels scattered around the Republic.

Family Homes of Ireland (www.familyhomes.ie) Lists family-run guesthouses and self-catering properties.

HINI (www.hini.org.uk) HI-associated organisation with six hostels in Northern Ireland.

Independent Holiday Hostels of Ireland (IHH; www.hostels-ireland.com) Over 100 tourist-board approved hostels throughout Ireland.

Independent Hostel Owners of Ireland (IHO; www.independenthostelsireland.com) Independent hostelling association.

ACTIVITIES
Ireland is great for outdoor activities, and tourist offices have a wide selection of information covering birdwatching, surfing (great along the west coast), scuba diving, cycling, fishing, horse riding, sailing, canoeing and many other activities.

Walking is particularly popular, although you must come prepared for wet weather. There are now well over 20 waymarked trails throughout Ireland, one of the more popular being the 200km **Kerry Way** (www.kerryway.com).

ESSENTIAL FOOD & DRINK

Ireland's recently acquired reputation as a gourmet destination is thoroughly deserved, with a host of chefs and producers leading a foodie revolution that has made it easy to eat well on all budgets.

➡ **Champ** Northern Irish dish of mashed potatoes with spring onions (scallions).

➡ **Colcannon** Potatoes mashed with milk, cabbage and fried onion.

➡ **Farl** Triangular flatbread in Northern Ireland and Donegal.

➡ **Irish stew** Lamb stew with potatoes, onions and thyme.

➡ **Soda bread** Wonderful bread – white or brown, sweet or savoury – made from very soft Irish flour and buttermilk.

➡ **Stout** Dark, almost black beer made with roasted barley; famous brands are Guinness in Dublin, and Murphy's and Beamish & Crawford in Cork.

➡ **Irish whiskey** Around 100 different types are produced by only four distilleries: Jameson, Bushmills, Cooley and recently reopened Kilbeggan.

BUSINESS HOURS

Hours in both the Republic and Northern Ireland are roughly the same.

Banks 10am to 4pm Monday to Friday (to 5pm Thursday)

Offices 9am to 5pm Monday to Friday

Post offices Northern Ireland 9am to 5.30pm Monday to Friday, 9am to 12.30pm Saturday; Republic 9am to 6pm Monday to Friday, 9am to 1pm Saturday. Smaller post offices may close at lunch and one day per week.

Pubs Northern Ireland 11.30am to 11pm Monday to Saturday, 12.30pm to 10pm Sunday. Pubs with late licences open until 1am Monday to Saturday and midnight Sunday; Republic 10.30am to 11.30pm Monday to Thursday, 10.30am to 12.30am Friday and Saturday, noon to 11pm Sunday. Pubs with bar extensions open to 2.30am Thursday to Saturday. All pubs close Christmas Day and Good Friday.

Restaurants Noon to 10.30pm; many close one day of the week.

Shops 9am to 5.30pm or 6pm Monday to Saturday (to 8pm on Thursday and sometimes Friday), noon to 6pm Sunday (in bigger towns only). Shops in rural towns may close at lunch and one day per week.

INTERNET RESOURCES

Failte Ireland (www.discoverireland.ie) Official tourism site

Northern Ireland Tourist Board (www.discover northernireland.com) Official tourism site

Entertainment Ireland (www.entertainment.ie) Countrywide entertainment listings

MONEY

The Irish Republic uses the euro (€), while Northern Ireland uses the British pound sterling (£).

Banks offer the best exchange rates; exchange bureaux, open longer, have worse rates and higher commissions. Post offices generally have exchange facilities and are open on Saturday morning.

In Northern Ireland several banks issue their own Northern Irish pound notes, which are equivalent to sterling but not readily accepted in mainland Britain. Many hotels, restaurants and shops in Northern Ireland accept euros.

Tipping

Fancy hotels and restaurants usually add a 10% or 15% service charge onto bills. Simpler places usually don't add a service charge; if you decide to tip, just round up the bill (or add 10% at most). Taxi drivers do not have to be tipped, but if you do, 10% is more than generous.

PUBLIC HOLIDAYS

The main public holidays in the Republic, Northern Ireland and both:

New Year's Day 1 January

St Patrick's Day 17 March

Easter (Good Friday to Easter Monday inclusive) March/April

May Holiday First Monday in May

Christmas Day 25 December

St Stephen's Day (Boxing Day) 26 December

Northern Ireland

Spring Bank Holiday Last Monday in May

Orangemen's Day 12 July (following Monday if 12th is on the weekend)

August Bank Holiday Last Monday in August

Republic of Ireland

June Holiday First Monday in June

August Holiday First Monday in August

October Holiday Last Monday in October

TELEPHONE

The mobile- (cell-) phone network in Ireland runs on the GSM 900/1800 system compatible with the rest of Europe and Australia, but not the USA. Mobile numbers in the Republic begin with ☑ 085, ☑ 086 or ☑ 087 (☑ 07 in Northern Ireland). A local pay-as-you-go SIM for your mobile will cost from around €10, but may work out free after the standard phone-credit refund (make sure your phone is compatible with the local provider).

To call Northern Ireland from the Republic, do not use ☑ 0044 as for the rest of the UK. Instead, dial ☑ 048 and then the local number. To dial the Republic from Northern Ireland, however, use the full international code ☑ 00 353, then the local number.

VISAS

If you're a European Economic Area (EEA) national, you don't need a visa to visit (or work in) either the Republic or Northern Ireland. Citizens of Australia, Canada, New Zealand, South Africa and the US can visit the Republic for up to three months, and Northern Ireland for up to six months.

There are no border controls or passport checks between the Republic of Ireland and Northern Ireland.

ⓘ Getting There & Away

AIR

There are nonstop flights from Britain, Continental Europe and North America to Dublin, Shannon and Belfast International, and nonstop connections from Britain and Europe to Cork. International departure tax is normally included in the price of your ticket.

International airports in Ireland:

Belfast International Airport (BFS; ☑ 028-9448 4848; www.belfastairport.com) Located 30km northwest of the city; flights within/and from the UK, Europe and New York.

Dublin Airport (☑ 01-814 1111; www.dublin airport.com) Dublin Airport, 13km north of the centre, is Ireland's major international gateway airport, with direct flights from Europe, North America and Asia.

George Best Belfast City Airport (BHD; ☑ 028-9093 9093; www.belfastcityairport.com; Airport Rd) Located 6km northeast of the city centre; flights within/and from the UK.

Shannon Airport (SNN; ☑ 061-712 000; www.shannonairport.com; ⊛) Has many facilities, including a free observation area for those stuck waiting. Almost everything, including ATMs and currency exchange, is on one level.

SEA

The main ferry routes between Ireland and the UK and mainland Europe:

➡ Belfast to Liverpool (England; 8½ hours)

➡ Belfast to Cairnryan (Scotland; 1¾ hours)

➡ Cork to Roscoff (France; 14 hours)

➡ Dublin to Liverpool (England; fast/slow four/8½ hours)

➡ Dublin and Dun Laoghaire to Holyhead (Wales; fast/slow 1½/three hours)

➡ Larne to Cairnryan (Scotland; 1½ hours)

➡ Larne to Troon (Scotland; 1½ hours; March to October only)

➡ Larne to Fleetwood (England; six hours)

➡ Rosslare to Cherbourg and Roscoff (France; 20½ hours)

➡ Rosslare to Fishguard and Pembroke (Wales; 3½ hours)

Competition from budget airlines has forced ferry operators to discount heavily and offer flexible fares, meaning great bargains at quiet times of the day or year. For example, the popular route across the Irish Sea between Dublin and Holyhead can cost as little as €15 (£12) for a foot passenger and €90 (£75) for a car plus up to four passengers.

A very useful online tool is www.ferrybooker.com, a single site covering all sea-ferry routes and operators out of the UK (the mainstay of sea travel to Ireland).

Main operators include the following:

Brittany Ferries (www.brittanyferries.com) Cork to Roscoff; every Saturday April to October.

Irish Ferries (www.irishferries.com) It has Dublin to Holyhead ferries (up to four per day year-round); and France to Rosslare (three times per week, mid-February to December).

Isle of Man Steam Packet Company (www.steam-packet.com) Isle of Man to Dublin and Belfast, twice weekly in summer.

P&O Irish Sea (www.poirishsea.com) Daily sailings year-round from Dublin to Liverpool, and Larne to Cairnryan. Larne to Troon runs from March to October only.

EATING PRICE RANGES

The following price indicators are used to indicate the cost of a main course at dinner:

Republic of Ireland

€ less than €12

€€ €12 to €25

€€€ more than €25

Northern Ireland

£ less than £12

££ £12 to £20

£££ more than £20

BUS & RAIL PASSES

There are a number of bus- or train-only and bus-and-rail passes worth considering if you plan on doing a lot of travel using public transport.

Open Road Pass (Bus) Three days' travel out of six consecutive days (€57) to 15 days out of 30 (€249) on all Bus Éireann services.

Irish Explorer (Bus & Rail) Eight days' travel out of 15 consecutive days (€245) on trains and buses within the Republic.

Irish Explorer (Rail) Five days' travel out of 15 consecutive days (€160) on trains in the Republic.

Trekker Four consecutive days' travel (€110) on all trains in the Republic.

Bus Rambler (Bus) One day's unlimited travel (£9) on Northern Ireland buses, after 9.15am, July and August only.

Sunday Day Tracker One day's unlimited travel (£7) on Northern Ireland trains, on Sundays only.

Children aged under 16 pay half-price for all these passes and for all normal tickets. Children aged under three travel for free on public transport. You can buy the above passes at most major train and bus stations in Ireland.

Stena Line (www.stenaline.com) Daily sailings from Holyhead to Dublin Port and Dun Laoghaire, and from Belfast to Liverpool and Cairnryan.

Discounts & Passes

Britrail Pass Has an option to add on Ireland for an extra fee, including ferry transit.

Eurail Pass Holders get a 50% discount on Irish Ferries crossings to France.

InterRail Pass Holders get a 50% discount on Irish Ferries and Stena Line services.

❶ Getting Around

Travelling around Ireland looks simple, as the distances are short and there's a dense network of roads and railways. But in Ireland, getting from A to B seldom uses a straight line, and public transport can be expensive (particularly trains), infrequent or both. For these reasons having your own transport – either car or bicycle – can be a major advantage.

BICYCLE

Ireland's compact size, relative flatness and scenic landscapes make it an ideal cycling destination. Dodgy weather and the occasional uneven road surface are the only concerns. A good tip for cyclists in the west is that the prevailing winds make it easier to cycle from south to north.

Buses will carry bikes, but only if there's room. For trains, bear in mind:

➡ Intercity trains charge up to €10 per bike.

➡ Bikes are transported in the passenger compartment.

➡ Book in advance (www.irishrail.ie), as there's only room for three bikes per service.

BUS

The Republic of Ireland's national bus line, **Bus Éireann** (☑ 01-836 6111; www.buseireann.ie), operates services all over the Republic and into Northern Ireland. Fares are much cheaper than train fares. Return trips are usually only slightly more expensive than one-way fares, and special deals (eg same-day returns) are often available. Most intercity buses in Northern Ireland are operated by **Ulsterbus** (☑ 028-9066 6600; www.ulsterbus.co.uk).

CAR & MOTORCYCLE

The majority of hire companies won't rent you a car if you're under 23 and haven't had a valid driving licence for at least a year. Some companies will not hire to those aged 74 or over. Your own local licence is usually sufficient to hire a car for up to three months.

TRAIN

The Republic of Ireland's railway system, **Irish Rail** (Iarnród Éireann; ☑ 1850 366 222; www.irishrail.ie), has routes radiating out from Dublin, but there is no direct north–south route along the west coast. Tickets can be twice as expensive as the bus, but travel times may be dramatically reduced. Special fares are often available, and a midweek return ticket sometimes costs just a bit more than the single fare; the flip side is that fares may be significantly higher on Friday and Sunday. **Rail Users Ireland** (www.railusers.ie) can be more informative than the official website.

Northern Ireland Railways (NIR; ☑ 028-9089 9411; www.nirailways.co.uk; Belfast Central Station) has four lines from Belfast, one of which links up with the Republic's rail system.

Italy

Best Places to Eat

➡ Pizzeria Gino Sorbillo (p480)

➡ Casa Coppelle (p433)

➡ Osteria Ballarò (p489)

➡ L'Osteria di Giovanni (p468)

➡ Osteria de' Poeti (p460)

Best Museums & Galleries

➡ Vatican Museums (p423)

➡ Galleria degli Uffizi (p463)

➡ Museo Archeologico Nazionale (p476)

➡ Museo e Galleria Borghese (p425)

➡ Gallerie dell'Accademia (p451)

Why Go?

A favourite destination since the days of the 18th-century Grand Tour, Italy may appear to hold few surprises. Its iconic monuments and masterpieces are known the world over, while cities such as Rome, Florence and Venice need no introduction.

Yet Italy is far more than the sum of its sights. Its fiercely proud regions maintain customs and culinary traditions dating back centuries, resulting in passionate festivals and delectable food at every turn. And then there are those timeless landscapes, from Tuscany's gentle hillsides to icy Alpine peaks, vertiginous coastlines and spitting southern volcanoes.

Drama is never far away in Italy and its theatrical streets and piazzas provide endless people-watching, ideally over a leisurely lunch or cool evening drink. This is, after all, the land of *dolce far niente* (sweet idleness) where simply hanging out is a pleasure and time seems to matter just that little bit less.

When to Go

Rome

Apr & May Perfect spring weather; ideal for exploring vibrant cities and blooming countryside.

Jun & Jul Summer means beach weather and a packed festival calendar.

Oct Enjoy mild temperatures, autumn cuisine and the *vendemia* (grape harvest).

Italy Highlights

1 See awe-inspiring art and iconic monuments in **Rome**.

2 Take to the water past Gothic palaces, domed churches and crumbling piazzas in **Venice** (p450).

3 Explore the exquisite Renaissance time capsule that is **Florence** (p462).

4 Work up an appetite for the world's best pizza in the backstreets of **Naples** (p476).

5 Visit regal palaces and museums in **Turin** (p442).

6 Admire glorious Gothic architecture and renaissance art in **Siena** (p472).

7 Bask in inspiring sea views on the **Amalfi Coast** (p485).

8 Enjoy an open-air opera in one of Italy's most romantic cities, **Verona** (p448).

9 Feast on foodie delights and medieval architecture in hedonistic **Bologna** (p460).

10 Revel in drama at an ancient Greek theatre in **Syracuse** (p491).

ITINERARIES

One Week

A one-week whistle-stop tour of Italy is enough to take in the country's three most famous cities. After a couple of days exploring the unique canalscape of **Venice**, head south to **Florence**, Italy's great Renaissance city. Two days will whet your appetite for the artistic and architectural treasures that await in **Rome**.

Two Weeks

After the first week, continue south for some sea and southern passion. Spend a day dodging traffic in **Naples**, a day investigating the ruins at **Pompeii**, and a day or two admiring the **Amalfi Coast**. Then backtrack to Naples for a ferry to **Palermo** and the gastronomic delights of Sicily.

ROME

POP 2.86 MILLION

Even in this country of exquisite cities, Rome is special. Pulsating, seductive and utterly disarming, the Italian capital is an epic, monumental metropolis that will steal your heart and haunt your soul. They say a lifetime's not enough (*Roma, non basta una vita*), but even on a short visit you'll be swept off your feet by its artistic and architectural masterpieces, its operatic piazzas, romantic corners and cobbled lanes. Yet while history reverberates all around, modern life is lived to the full – and it's this intoxicating mix of past and present, of style and urban grit that makes Rome such a compelling place.

⊙ Sights

◉ Ancient Rome

⭐**Colosseum**   RUIN

(Colosseo; Map p426; ☑06 3996 7700; www.coopculture.it; Piazza del Colosseo; adult/reduced incl Roman Forum & Palatino €12/7.50; ⊗8.30am-1hr before sunset; Ⓜ Colosseo) Rome's great gladiatorial arena is the most thrilling of the city's ancient sights. Inaugurated in AD 80, the 50,000-seat Colosseum, originally known as the Flavian Amphitheatre, was clad in travertine and covered by a huge canvas awning held aloft by 240 masts. Inside, tiered seating encircled the arena, itself built over an underground complex (the hypogeum) where animals were caged and stage sets prepared. Games involved gladiators fighting wild animals or each other.

⭐**Palatino**   ARCHAEOLOGICAL SITE

(Palatine Hill; Map p426; ☑06 3996 7700; www.coopculture.it; Via di San Gregorio 30 & Via Sacra; adult/reduced incl Colosseum & Roman Forum €12/7.50; ⊗8.30am-1hr before sunset; Ⓜ Colosseo) Sandwiched between the Roman Forum and the Circo Massimo, the Palatino is an atmospheric area of towering pine trees, majestic ruins and memorable views. It was here that Romulus supposedly founded the city in 753 BC, and Rome's emperors lived in unabashed luxury. Look out for the **stadio** (stadium; Map p426), the ruins of the **Domus Flavia** (Map p426), the imperial palace, and the grandstand views over the Roman Forum from the **Orti Farnesiani** (Map p426).

⭐**Roman Forum**   ARCHAEOLOGICAL SITE

(Foro Romano; Map p426; ☑06 3996 7700; www.coopculture.it; Largo della Salara Vecchia & Via Sacra; adult/reduced incl Colosseum & Palatino €12/7.50; ⊗8.30am-1hr before sunset; Ⓠ Via dei Fori Imperiali) Nowadays an impressive – if rather confusing – sprawl of ruins, the Roman Forum was ancient Rome's showpiece centre, a grandiose district of temples, basilicas and vibrant public spaces. The site, which was originally an Etruscan burial ground, was first developed in the 7th century BC, growing over time to become the social, political and commercial hub of the Roman Empire. Landmark sights include the **Arco di Settimio Severo** (Arch of Septimius Severus; Map p426), the **Curia** (Map p426),

ⓘ COLOSSEUM TICKETS

To avoid queues at the Colosseum, buy your ticket from the Palatino entrance (about 250m away at Via di San Gregorio 30) or at the Roman Forum (Largo della Salara Vecchia). You can also book online at www.coopculture.it (€2 booking fee).

Greater Rome

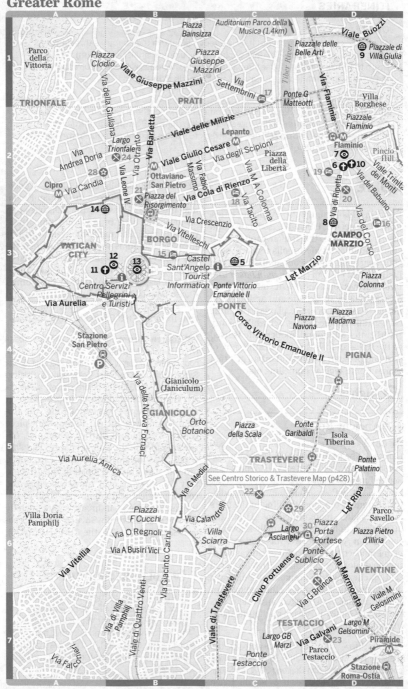

Parco della Vittoria

TRIONFALE

Piazza Clodio

Viale Giuseppe Mazzini

Piazza Bainsizza

Auditorium Parco della Musica (1.4km)

Piazzale delle Belle Arti

Viale Buozzi

Piazzale di Villa Giulia **9**

Piazza Giuseppe Mazzini

Via Settembrini **17**

Ponte G Matteotti

Via Flaminia

Villa Borghese

Via della Giuliana

PRATI

Viale delle Milizie

Piazzale Flaminio

Via Andrea Doria

Largo Trionfale **24**

Via Barletta

Lepanto

Viale Giulio Cesare

Via degli Scipioni

Piazza della Libertà

Flaminio **7**

6 **10**

Pincio Hill

Via Otranto

Via Leone IV

Ottaviano-San Pietro

Via Fabio Massimo

Via M A Colonna

19

Via di Ripetta

Viale Trinità dei Monti

Cipro

Via Candia

28

21

Piazza del Risorgimento

Via Cola di Rienzo

Via Tacito

18

8

CAMPO MARZIO

Via del Babuino

20

Via del Corso

14

Via Crescenzio

BORGO

Via Vitelleschi

15

Castel Sant'Angelo Tourist Information

5

16

VATICAN CITY

12

13

11

Centro Servizi Pellegrini e Turisti

Ponte Vittorio Emanuele II

Lgt Marzio

Piazza Colonna

Via Aurelia

Stazione San Pietro

PONTE

Piazza Navona

Piazza Madama

Corso Vittorio Emanuele II

PIGNA

Via delle Nuova Fornaci

Gianicolo (Janiculum)

GIANICOLO

Orto Botanico

Piazza della Scala

Ponte Garibaldi

Isola Tiberina

Ponte Palatino

Via Aurelia Antica

Via G Medici

TRASTEVERE

See Centro Storico & Trastevere Map (p428)

22

Lgt Ripa

Parco Savello

Villa Doria Pamphilj

Piazza F Cucchi

Via Calandrelli

29

30

Piazza Porta Portese

Piazza Pietro d'Illiria

Via O Regnoli

Villa Sciarra

Largo Ascianghi

Via O Busiri Vici

Via Giacinto Carini

Ponte Sublicio

Lgt Marmorata

AVENTINE

Via Vitelia

Clivo Portuense

27

Viale M Gelosimini

Via di Villa Pamphilj

Via di Quattro Venti

Viale di Trastevere

Via G Branca

TESTACCIO

Largo M Gelsomini

Via Fal...

Largo GB Marzi

Via Galvani

23

Pirámide

Ponte Testaccio

Parco Testaccio

Stazione Roma-Ostia

Tiber River

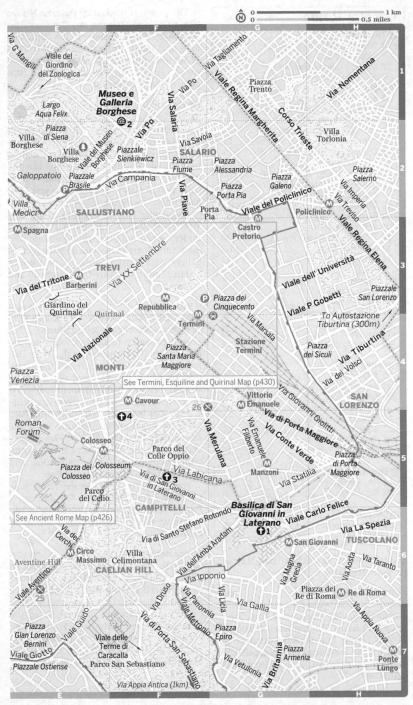

N 0 ——— 1 km
0 ——— 0.5 miles

Viale G Mangili

Viale del
Giardino
del Zoologica

Largo
Aqua Felix

**Museo e
Galleria
Borghese** 2

Via Po

Via Salaria

Via Tagliamento

Viale Regina Margherita

Piazza
Trento

Via Nomentana

Corso Trieste

Villa
Torlonia

Piazza
Salerno

Piazza
di Siena

Via Savoia

SALARIO

Piazza
Sienkiewicz

Villa
Borghese

Viale del Museo Borghese

Piazzale

Galoppatoio

Piazzale
Brasile

Via Campania

Piazza
Fiume

Piazza
Alessandria

Piazza
Galeno

Via Imperia

Via Treviso

Villa
Medici

SALLUSTIANO

Via Piave

Piazza
Porta Pia

Porta
Pia

Viale del Policlinico

Policlinico

Viale Regina Elena

M Spagna

Castro
Pretorio

Via del Tritone

Barberini

TREVI

Via XX Settembre

Viale dell' Università

Viale P Gobetti

Piazzale
San Lorenzo

Giardino del
Quirinale

Quirinal

M
Repubblica

P Piazza dei
Cinquecento

Via Marsala

To Autostazione
Tiburtina (300m)

Via Nazionale

Termini

Piazza
Venezia

Piazza
Santa Maria
Maggiore

MONTI

Stazione
Termini

Piazza
dei Siculi

Via Tiburtina

Via dei Volsci

See Termini, Esquiline and Quirinal Map (p430)

M Cavour

26

Vittorio
Emanuele

Via Giovanni Giolitti

SAN
LORENZO

Roman
Forum

4

Via Merulana

Via di Porta Maggiore

Via Emanuele
Filiberto

Via Conte Verde

Piazza
di Porta
Maggiore

Colosseo

Parco del
Colle Oppio

Piazza del
Colosseo

Colosseum

Via di San Giovanni
in Laterano

3

Via Labicana

Manzoni

Via Statilia

Parco
del Celio

CAMPITELLI

See Ancient Rome Map (p426)

**Basilica di San
Giovanni in
Laterano** 1

Viale Carlo Felice

Via La Spezia

Via del
Cerchi

Circo
Massimo

Villa
Celimontana

CAELIAN HILL

Via di Santo Stefano Rotondo

Via dell'Amba Aradam

M San Giovanni

TUSCOLANO

Via Magna
Grecia

Via Aosta

Via Taranto

Aventine Hill

Via Ipponio

Via Licia

Via Gallia

Piazza dei
Re di Roma

M Re di Roma

Viale Aventino

25

Via Druso

Via Panonnia

Viale Metronio

Piazza
Epiro

Via Appia Nuova

M

Piazza
Gian Lorenzo
Bernini

Viale Guido

Viale delle
Terme di
Caracalla

Via di Porta San Sebastiano

Piazza
Armenia

Via Britannia

Via Vetulonia

Ponte
Lungo

Viale Giotto

Piazzale Ostiense

Parco San Sebastiano

Via Appia Antica (1km)

Greater Rome

and the **Casa delle Vestali** (House of the Vestal Virgins; Map p426).

Piazza del Campidoglio   PIAZZA
(Map p426; ⊡ Piazza Venezia) Designed by Michelangelo in 1538, this is one of Rome's most beautiful piazzas. You can reach it from the Roman Forum, but the most dramatic approach is via the **Cordonata** (Map p426), the graceful staircase that leads up from Piazza d'Ara Coeli.

The piazza is flanked by **Palazzo Nuovo** (Map p426) and **Palazzo dei Conservatori** (Map p426), together home to the Capitoline Museums, and **Palazzo Senatorio** (Map p426), seat of Rome's city council. In the centre is a copy of an equestrian **statue** (Map p426) of Marcus Aurelius.

★ **Capitoline Museums**   MUSEUM
(Musei Capitolini; Map p426; ☑ 06 06 08; www.museicapitolini.org; Piazza del Campidoglio 1; adult/reduced €11.50/9.50; ☉ 9am-8pm Tue-Sun, last admission 7pm; ⊡ Piazza Venezia) Dating to 1471, the Capitoline Museums are the world's oldest national museums. Their collection of classical sculpture is one of Italy's finest, including crowd-pleasers such as the iconic *Lupa capitolina* (Capitoline Wolf), a sculpture of Romulus and Remus under a wolf, and the *Galata morente* (Dying Gaul). There's also a formidable picture gallery with masterpieces by the likes of Titian, Tintoretto, Van Dyck, Rubens and Caravaggio.

Il Vittoriano   MONUMENT
(Map p426; Piazza Venezia; ☉ 9.30am-5.30pm summer, to 4.30pm winter; ⊡ Piazza Venezia) **FREE**
Love it or loathe it, as most locals do, you can't ignore Il Vittoriano (aka the Altare della Patria; Altar of the Fatherland), the mountain of white marble overlooking Piazza Venezia. Begun in 1885 to honour Italy's first king, Victor Emmanuel II, it incorporates the **Museo Centrale del Risorgimento** (Map p426; www.risorgimento.it; Il Vittoriano, Piazza Venezia; adult/reduced €5/2.50; ☉ 9.30am-6.30pm, closed 1st Mon of month; ⊡ Piazza Venezia), a museum documenting Italian unification, and the **Tomb of the Unknown Soldier**.

For Rome's best 360-degree views, take the **Roma dal Cielo** (Map p426; Il Vittoriano, Piazza Venezia; adult/reduced €7/3.50; ☉ 9.30am-6.30pm Mon-Thu, to 7.30pm Fri-Sun; ⊡ Piazza Venezia) lift to the top.

Bocca della Verità   MONUMENT
(Map p428; Piazza Bocca della Verità 18; donation €0.50; ☉ 9.30am-5.50pm summer, to 4.50pm winter; ⊡ Piazza Bocca della Verità) A round piece of marble that was once part of a fountain, or possibly an ancient manhole cover, the *Bocca della Verità* (Mouth of Truth) is one of Rome's most popular curiosities. Legend has it that if you put your hand in the carved mouth and tell a lie, it will bite your hand off.

The mouth lives in the portico of the **Chiesa di Santa Maria in Cosmedin**, a beautiful medieval church.

◉ The Vatican

The world's smallest sovereign state, the Vatican is the modern vestige of the Papal States, the papal empire that encompassed Rome and much of central Italy until Italian unification in 1861. It was formally established under the terms of the 1929 Lateran Treaty, signed by Mussolini and Pope Pius XI.

★ St Peter's Basilica BASILICA
(Basilica di San Pietro; Map p420; www.vatican. va; St Peter's Sq; ⊘7am-7pm summer, to 6.30pm winter; Ⓜ Ottaviano-San Pietro) FREE In this city of outstanding churches, none can hold a candle to the Basilica di San Pietro, Italy's most spectacular cathedral. Built atop an earlier 4th-century church, it was completed in 1626 after 150 years of construction. It contains many spectacular works of art, including three of Italy's most celebrated masterpieces: Michelangelo's *Pietà*, his soaring dome, and Bernini's 29m-high baldachin over the papal altar.

Note that the basilica attracts up to 20,000 people on a busy day, so expect queues in peak periods.

St Peter's Square PIAZZA
(Piazza San Pietro; Map p420; Ⓜ Ottaviano-San Pietro) Overlooked by St Peter's Basilica, the Vatican's central square was laid out be-

> ⓘ **QUEUE-JUMPING AT THE VATICAN MUSEUMS**
>
> ➡ Book tickets online at http:// mv.vatican.va (€4 booking fee).
>
> ➡ Time your visit: Wednesday mornings are good as everyone is at the Pope's weekly audience at St Peter's; afternoon is better than the morning; avoid Mondays, when many other museums are shut.

tween 1656 and 1667 to a design by baroque artist Gian Lorenzo Bernini. Seen from above, it resembles a giant keyhole with two semicircular colonnades, each consisting of four rows of Doric columns, encircling a giant ellipse that straightens out to funnel believers into the basilica. The effect was deliberate – Bernini described the colonnades as representing 'the motherly arms of the church'.

★ Vatican Museums MUSEUM
(Musei Vaticani; Map p420; ☑06 6988 4676; http://mv.vatican.va; Viale Vaticano; adult/reduced €16/8, free last Sun of month; ⊘9am-4pm Mon-Sat, to 12.30pm last Sun of month; Ⓜ Ottaviano-San Pietro) Founded by Pope Julius II in the early 16th century and enlarged by successive pontiffs, the Vatican Museums boast one of the world's greatest art collections. Exhibits, which are displayed along about 7km of halls and corridors, range from Egyptian mummies and Etruscan bronzes to ancient

ITALY ROME

VATICAN MUSEUMS ITINERARY

Follow this three-hour itinerary for the museums' greatest hits:

At the top of the escalator after the entrance, head out to the **Cortile della Pigna**, a courtyard named after the Augustan-era bronze pine cone in the monumental niche. Cross the courtyard into the long corridor that is the **Museo Chiaramonti** and head left up to the **Museo Pio Clementino**, home of the Vatican's finest classical statuary. Follow through the **Cortile Ottagono** (Octagonal Courtyard) onto the **Sala Croce Greca** (Greek Cross Room) from where stairs lead up to the 1st floor.

Continue through the **Galleria dei Candelabri** (Gallery of the Candelabra), **Galleria degli Arazzi** (Tapestry Gallery) and **Galleria delle Carte Geografiche** (Map Gallery) to the **Sala di Costantino**, the first of the four **Stanze di Raffaello** (Raphael Rooms) – the others are the **Stanza d' Eliodoro**, the **Stanza della Segnatura**, home to Raphael's superlative *La Scuola di Atene* (The School of Athens), and the **Stanza dell'Incendio di Borgo**. Anywhere else these frescoed chambers would be the star attraction, but here they're the warm-up act for the museums' grand finale, the **Sistine Chapel**.

Originally built in 1484 for Pope Sixtus IV, this towering chapel boasts two of the world's most famous works of art: Michelangelo's ceiling frescoes (1508–1512) and his *Giudizio Universale* (Last Judgment; 1535–1541).

ST PETER'S BASILICA DOME

Rising imperiously over Rome's skyline, **St Peter's Basilica Dome** (Map p420; with/without lift €7/5; ☉ 8am-5.45pm summer, to 4.45pm winter; M Ottaviano-San Pietro) was Michelangelo's greatest architectural achievement. To climb it, the entrance is to the right of the basilica. You can walk the 551 steps to the top, or take a small lift halfway up and then tramp the last 320 steps. Either way, it's a steep, narrow climb that's not recommended for those who suffer from claustrophobia or vertigo. Make it to the top, though, and you're rewarded with stunning views from a lofty perch 120m above St Peter's Sq.

busts, old masters and modern paintings. Highlights include the spectacular collection of classical statuary in the Museo Pio-Clementino, a suite of frescoed rooms by Raphael, and the Michelangelo-painted Sistine Chapel.

◉ Historic Centre

★ Pantheon   CHURCH
(Map p428; Piazza della Rotonda; ☉ 8.30am-7.30pm Mon-Sat, 9am-6pm Sun; ☐ Largo di Torre Argentina) FREE A striking 2000-year-old temple, now church, the Pantheon is the best preserved of Rome's ancient monuments, and one of the most influential buildings in the Western world. Built by Hadrian over Marcus Agrippa's earlier 27 BC temple, it has stood since AD 120, and although its greying, pockmarked exterior is looking its age, it's still an exhilarating experience to pass through its vast bronze doors and gaze up at the largest unreinforced concrete dome ever built.

★ Piazza Navona   PIAZZA
(Map p428; ☐ Corso del Rinascimento) With its ornate fountains, baroque *palazzi* (mansions) and colourful cast of street artists, hawkers and tourists, Piazza Navona is central Rome's showcase square. Built over the 1st-century Stadio di Domiziano (Domitian's Stadium), it was paved over in the 15th century and for almost 300 years hosted the city's main market. Its grand centrepiece, Bernini's **Fontana dei Quattro Fiumi** (Fountain of the Four Rivers; Map p428), is an ornate, showy work depict-

ing personifications of the rivers Nile, Ganges, Danube and Plate.

Campo de' Fiori   PIAZZA
(Map p428; ☐ Corso Vittorio Emanuele II) Noisy, colourful 'Il Campo' is a major focus of Roman life: by day it hosts a much-loved market, while at night it morphs into a raucous open-air pub. For centuries it was the site of public executions, and it was here that philosopher monk Giordano Bruno was burned at the stake for heresy in 1600. The spot is today marked by a sinister statue of the hooded monk, created by Ettore Ferrari and unveiled in 1889.

Galleria Doria Pamphilj   MUSEUM
(Map p428; ☑ 06 679 73 23; www.dopart.it; Via del Corso 305; adult/reduced €11/7.50; ☉ 9am-7pm, last admission 6pm; ☐ Via del Corso) Hidden behind the grimy grey exterior of Palazzo Doria Pamphilj, this wonderful gallery boasts one of Rome's richest private art collections, with works by Raphael, Tintoretto, Brueghel, Titian, Caravaggio, Bernini and Velázquez. Masterpieces abound, but the undisputed star is Velázquez' portrait of an implacable Pope Innocent X, who grumbled that the depiction was 'too real'. Compare it with Gian Lorenzo Bernini's sculptural interpretation of the same subject.

★ Trevi Fountain   FOUNTAIN
(Fontana di Trevi; Map p430; Piazza di Trevi; M Barberini) The Fontana di Trevi, scene of Anita Ekberg's dip in *La Dolce Vita*, is Rome's largest and most famous fountain. A flamboyant baroque ensemble of mythical figures, wild horses and cascading rock falls, it takes up the entire side of the 17th-century Palazzo Poli.

The famous tradition is to toss a coin into the water, thus ensuring that one day you'll return to the Eternal City. On average about €3000 is thrown in every day.

Spanish Steps   STAIRCASE
(Scalinata della Trinità dei Monti; Map p430; Piazza di Spagna; M Spagna) Rising from Piazza di Spagna, the Spanish Steps have been attracting visitors since the 18th century. The piazza was named after the nearby Spanish Embassy, but the staircase, designed by Italian Francesco De Sanctis and built in 1725 with French money, leads to the French **Chiesa della Trinità dei Monti** (Map p430; visite.guidate.tdm@gmail.com; Piazza Trinità dei Monti; ☉ 6.30am-8pm Tue-Sun, tours Italian Sat 11am, French Sun/Tue 9.15/11am; M Spagna). At

the the foot of the stairs, the boat-shaped **Barcaccia** (1627) (Map p430) fountain is believed to be by Pietro Bernini (father of Gian Lorenzo Bernini).

Piazza del Popolo
PIAZZA

(Map p420; M Flaminio) This dazzling piazza was laid out in 1538 to provide a grandiose entrance to what was then Rome's main northern gateway. It has since been remodelled several times, most recently by Giuseppe Valadier in 1823.

Guarding its southern approach are Carlo Rainaldi's twin 17th-century churches, **Chiesa di Santa Maria dei Miracoli** (Map p420; M Flaminio) and **Chiesa di Santa Maria in Montesanto** (Map p420; M Flaminio). In the centre, the 36m-high **obelisk** (Map p420; M Flaminio) was brought by Augustus from ancient Egypt and originally stood in Circo Massimo.

Museo dell'Ara Pacis
MUSEUM

(Map p420; ☑ 06 06 08; http://en.arapacis.it; Lungotevere in Augusta; adult/reduced €10.50/8.50, audioguide €4; ⊙ 9am-7pm, last admission 6pm; M Flaminio) The first modern construction in Rome's historic centre since WWII, Richard Meier's controversial and widely detested glass-and-marble pavilion houses the *Ara Pacis Augustae* (Altar of Peace), Augustus' great monument to peace. One of the most important works of ancient Roman sculpture, the vast marble altar – measuring 11.6m by 10.6m by 3.6m – was completed in 13 BC.

⊚ Trastevere

Trastevere is one of central Rome's most vivacious neighbourhoods, a tightly packed warren of ochre *palazzi,* ivy-clad facades and photogenic lanes. Originally working class, it's now a trendy hang-out full of bars and restaurants.

★ Basilica di Santa Maria in Trastevere
BASILICA

(Map p428; Piazza Santa Maria in Trastevere; ⊙ 7.30am-9pm; ⛫ Viale di Trastevere, ⛫ Viale di Trastevere) Nestled in a quiet corner of Trastevere's focal square, this is said to be the oldest church dedicated to the Virgin Mary in Rome. In its original form it dates to the early 3rd century, but a major 12th-century makeover saw the addition of a Romanesque bell tower and glittering facade. The portico came later, added by Carlo Fontana in 1702.

Inside, the 12th-century mosaics are the headline feature.

⊚ Villa Borghese

Accessible from Piazzale Flaminio, Pincio Hill and the top of Via Vittorio Veneto, Villa Borghese is Rome's best-known park.

★ Museo e Galleria Borghese
MUSEUM

(Map p420; ☑ 06 3 28 10; www.galleriaborghese. it; Piazzale del Museo Borghese 5; adult/reduced €11/6.50; ⊙ 9am-7pm Tue-Sun; ⛫ Via Pinciana) If you only have the time (or inclination) for one art gallery in Rome, make it this one. Housing what's generally considered the 'queen of all private art collections', it boasts paintings by Caravaggio, Botticelli and Raphael, as well as some spectacular sculptures by Bernini. There are highlights at every turn, but look out for Bernini's *Ratto di Proserpina* (Rape of Persephone) and Canova's *Venere vincitrice* (Conquering Venus).

To limit numbers, visitors are admitted at two-hourly intervals, so you'll need to book your ticket and get an entry time.

Museo Nazionale Etrusco di Villa Giulia
MUSEUM

(Map p420; www.villagiulia.beniculturali.it; Piazzale di Villa Giulia; adult/reduced €8/4; ⊙ 8.30am-7.30pm Tue-Sun; ⛫ Via delle Belle Arti) Italy's finest collection of Etruscan treasures is considerably displayed in Villa Giulia, Pope Julius III's 16th-century pleasure palace, and the nearby Villa Poniatowski. Exhibits, many of which came from burial tombs in the surrounding Lazio region, range from bronze

---

❶ ROMA PASS

A cumulative sightseeing and transport card, available online or from tourist information points and participating museums, the **Roma Pass** (www.roma pass.it) comes in two forms:

Classic (€36; valid for three days) Provides free admission to two museums or sites, as well as reduced entry to extra sites, unlimited city transport, and discounted entry to other exhibitions and events.

48-hour (€28; valid for 48 hours) Gives free admission to one museum or site, and then as per the classic pass.

Ancient Rome

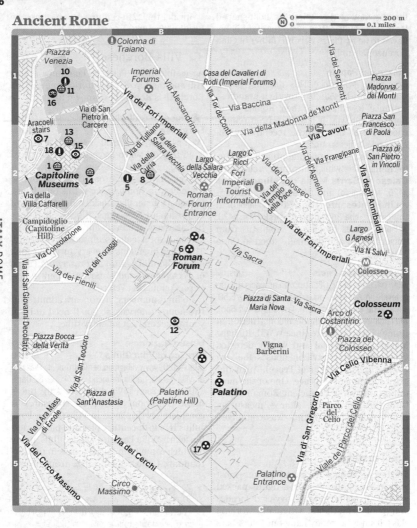

Ancient Rome

figurines and black *bucchero* tableware to temple decorations, terracotta vases and a dazzling display of sophisticated jewellery.

Must-sees include a polychrome terracotta statue of Apollo, the 6th-century BC *Sarcofago degli Sposi* (Sarcophagus of the Betrothed) and the *Euphronios Krater,* a celebrated Greek vase.

◉ Termini & Esquiline

The largest of Rome's seven hills, the Esquiline (Esquilino) extends from the Colosseum up to Stazione Termini, Rome's main transport hub.

★ Museo Nazionale Romano: Palazzo Massimo alle Terme   MUSEUM

(Map p430; ⏻ 06 3996 7700; www.coopculture. it; Largo di Villa Peretti 1; adult/reduced €7/3.50; ⊙ 9am-7.45pm Tue-Sun; Ⓜ Termini) One of Rome's great unheralded museums, this is a fabulous treasure trove of classical art. The ground and 1st floors are devoted to sculpture with some breathtaking pieces – check out the *Pugile* (Boxer), a 2nd-century BC Greek bronze; the graceful 2nd-century BC *Ermafrodite dormiente* (Sleeping Hermaphrodite); and the idealised *Il discobolo* (Discus Thrower). It's the magnificent and vibrantly coloured frescoes on the 2nd floor, however, that are the real highlight.

Basilica di Santa Maria Maggiore   BASILICA

(Map p430; Piazza Santa Maria Maggiore; basilica/museum/loggia/archaeological site free/€3/5/5; ⊙ 7am-7pm, museum & loggia 9am-5.30pm; 🚇 Piazza Santa Maria Maggiore) One of Rome's four patriarchal basilicas, this monumental 5th-century church stands on the summit of the Esquiline Hill, on the spot where snow is said to have miraculously fallen in the summer of AD 358. Much altered over the centuries, it's something of an architectural hybrid, with a 14th-century Romanesque belfry, an 18th-century baroque facade, a largely baroque interior and a series of glorious 5th-century mosaics.

Basilica di San Pietro in Vincoli   BASILICA

(Map p420; Piazza di San Pietro in Vincoli 4a; ⊙ 8am-12.20pm & 3-7pm summer, to 6pm winter; Ⓜ Cavour) Pilgrims and art lovers flock to this 5th-century basilica for two reasons: to marvel at Michelangelo's colossal *Moses* (1505) sculpture and to see the chains that supposedly bound St Peter when he was imprisoned in the Carcere Mamertino (near the Roman Forum).

Access to the church is via a flight of steps through a low arch that leads up from Via Cavour.

◉ San Giovanni & Caelian Hill

★ Basilica di San Giovanni in Laterano   BASILICA

(Map p420; Piazza di San Giovanni in Laterano 4; basilica/cloister free/€5; ⊙ 7am-6.30pm, cloister 9am-6pm; Ⓜ San Giovanni) For a thousand years this monumental cathedral was the most important church in Christendom. Commissioned by the Emperor Constantine and consecrated in AD 324, it was the first Christian basilica built in the city and, until the late 14th century, was the pope's main place of worship. It's still Rome's official cathedral and the pope's seat as the bishop of Rome.

The basilica has been revamped several times, most notably by Borromini in the 17th century, and by Alessandro Galilei, who added the vast 18th-century facade.

Basilica di San Clemente   BASILICA

(Map p420; www.basilicasanclemente.com; Via di San Giovanni in Laterano; excavations adult/reduced €10/5; ⊙ 9am-12.30pm & 3-6pm Mon-Sat, 12.15-6pm Sun; 🚇 Via Labicana) Nowhere better illustrates the various stages of Rome's turbulent past than this fascinating multilayered church. The ground-level 12th-century basilica sits atop a 4th-century church, which, in turn, stands over a 2nd-century pagan temple and 1st-century Roman house. Beneath everything are foundations dating from the Roman Republic.

🛏 Sleeping

🛏 Ancient Rome

Nicolas Inn   B&B €€

(Map p426; ⏻ 06 9761 8483; www.nicolasinn.com; 1st fl, Via Cavour 295; s €95-160, d €100-180; ❋ 🔊; Ⓜ Cavour) This sunny B&B offers a warm welcome and convenient location, a stone's throw from the Roman Forum. Run by a friendly couple, it has four big rooms, each with homely furnishings, colourful pictures and large en suite bathrooms. No children under five.

Centro Storico & Trastevere

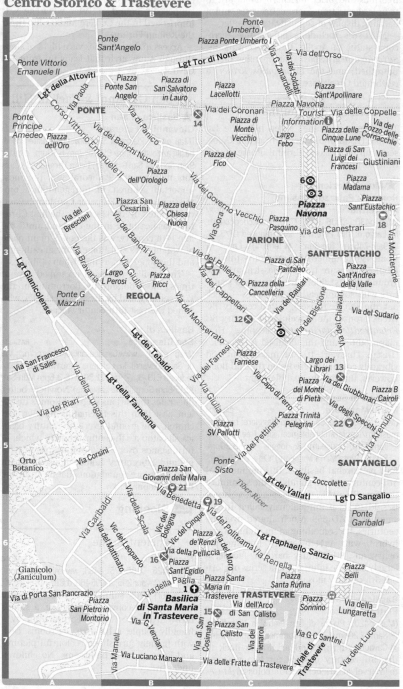

Centro Storico & Trastevere

◎ Top Sights

1 Basilica di Santa Maria in Trastevere	B6
2 Pantheon	E2
3 Piazza Navona	D2

◎ Sights

4 Bocca della Verità	F7
5 Campo de' Fiori	C4
6 Fontana dei Quattro Fiumi	D2
7 Galleria Doria Pamphilj	F3

▣ Sleeping

8 Arco del Lauro	E7
9 La Casa di Kaia	E7
Maria-Rosa Guesthouse	(see 9)

✕ Eating

10 Armando al Pantheon	E2
11 Casa Coppelle	E1
12 Forno di Campo de' Fiori	C4
13 Forno Roscioli	D4
14 Gelateria del Teatro	B2
15 Paris	C7
16 Trattoria degli Amici	B6

⦿ Drinking & Nightlife

17 Barnum Cafe	C3
18 Caffè Sant'Eustachio	D3
19 Freni e Frizioni	C6
20 La Casa del Caffè Tazza d'Oro	E2
21 Ma Che Siete Venuti a Fà	B5
22 Open Baladin	D5

⊨ The Vatican

★ Le Stanze di Orazio   B&B **€€**

(Map p420; ☑ 06 3265 2474; www.lestanzediorazio.com; Via Orazio 3; r €85-125; ❄ @ ☎; Ⓜ Lepanto) This small boutique B&B is excellent value for money. Its five bright rooms feature soothing tones and playful decor – think shimmering rainbow wallpaper, lilac accents and grey designer bathrooms. There's a small breakfast area and rooms come with kettles and tea-making kit.

Hotel Bramante   HISTORIC HOTEL **€€**

(Map p420; ☑ 06 6880 6426; www.hotelbramante.com; Vicolo delle Palline 24-25; s €100-160, d €140-240, tr €175-260, q €190-300; ❄ ☎; ☐ Borgo Sant'Angelo) Nestled under the Vatican walls, the Bramante exudes country-house charm with its cosy internal courtyard, eggshell blue walls, wood-beamed ceilings and antique furniture. It's housed in the 16th-century building where architect Domenico Fontana once lived.

Termini, Esquiline and Quirinal

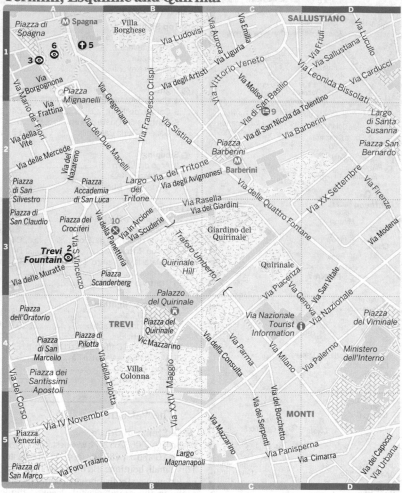

Termini, Esquiline and Quirinal

◉ Top Sights
1 Museo Nazionale Romano: Palazzo Massimo alle Terme	F3
2 Trevi Fountain	A3

◉ Sights
3 Barcaccia	A1
4 Basilica di Santa Maria Maggiore	F5
5 Chiesa della Trinità dei Monti	A1
6 Spanish Steps	A1

🛌 Sleeping
7 Beehive	H2
8 Blue Hostel	F5
9 Daphne Inn	C2

✪ Eating
10 San Crispino	B3

✪ Entertainment
11 Teatro dell'Opera di Roma	E3

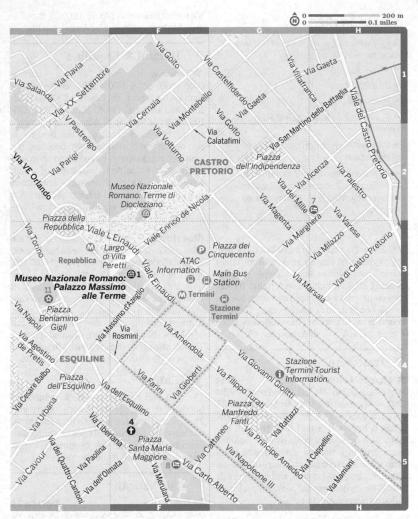

ITALY ROME

🛏 Historic Centre

Okapi Rooms
HOTEL €

(Map p420; ☎ 06 3260 9815; www.okapirooms.it; Via della Penna 57; s €65-80, d €85-120, tr €110-140, q €120-180; ❄️✳️🛜; Ⓜ Flaminio) The Okapi is a smart, value-for-money choice near Piazza del Popolo. Rooms, spread over six floors of a narrow townhouse, are simple and airy with cream walls, terracotta floors and the occasional stone frieze. Some are smaller than others and several have small terraces. No breakfast.

Hotel Panda
PENSION €

(Map p420; ☎ 06 678 01 79; www.hotelpanda.it; Via della Croce 35; s €65-80, d €85-130, tr €120-150, q €160-190; ❄️✳️🛜; Ⓜ Spagna) Near the Spanish Steps, in an area where a bargain is a Bulgari watch bought at the sales, the Panda flies the flag for budget accommodation. It's a friendly place with high-ceilinged rooms and simple, tasteful decor. Air-con is free in summer, but €6 in other periods.

Daphne Inn
BOUTIQUE HOTEL €€

(Map p430; ☎ 06 8745 0086; www.daphne-rome. com; Via di San Basilio 55; s €115-180, d €130-240, ste

ROME FOR FREE

Tuck your wallet away, some of Rome's most famous sights are free:

➜ Trevi Fountain

➜ Spanish Steps

➜ Pantheon

➜ St Peter's Basilica and all of Rome's churches

➜ Vatican Museums on the last Sunday of the month

➜ All state museums and monuments, including the Colosseum and Capitoline Museums, on the first Sunday of the month

€190-290, without bathroom s €70-130, d €90-160; ❋ ☎; Ⓜ Barberini) Run by an American-Italian couple, the Daphne has helpful English-speaking staff and chic, comfortable rooms. They come in various shapes and sizes, but the overall look is smart contemporary. There's a second branch, Daphne Trevi, offering more of the same at Via degli Avignonesi 20.

Trastevere

★ **Arco del Lauro** B&B €

(Map p428; ☎ 346 2443212, 9am-2pm 06 9784 0350; www.arcodellauro.it; Via Arco de' Tolomei 27; s €75-125, d €95-145; ❋ ☎; ☐ Viale di Trastevere, ☐ Viale di Trastevere) A real find, this fab six-room B&B occupies a centuries-old *palazzo* (mansion) on a narrow cobbled street. Its gleaming white rooms combine rustic charm with a modern low-key look and comfortable beds. The owners extend a warm welcome and are always ready to help.

Maria-Rosa Guesthouse B&B €

(Map p428; ☎ 338 7700067; www.maria-rosa.it; Via dei Vascellari 55; s €45-65, d €60-80, tr €95-120; @ ☎; ☐ Viale di Trastevere, ☐ Viale di Trastevere) This is a delightful B&B on the 3rd floor of a Trastevere townhouse. It's a simple affair with two guestrooms sharing a single bathroom and a small living room, but the homey decor, pot plants and books create a lovely, warm atmosphere. The owner, Sylvie, also has a further three rooms on the floor above at **La Casa di Kaia** (Map p428; ☎ 338 7700067; www.kaia-trastevere.it; Via dei Vascellari

55; without bathroom s €45-55, d €60-75; ☎; ☐ Viale di Trastevere, ☐ Viale di Trastevere). No lift.

Termini & Esquiline

★ **Beehive** HOSTEL €

(Map p430; ☎ 06 4470 4553; www.the-beehive.com; Via Marghera 8; dm €25-30, s €60-70, d €80-100, without bathroom s €40-50, d €60-80, tr €75-105; ❋ ☎; Ⓜ Termini) ✎ More boutique chic than backpacker crash pad, the Beehive is one of the best hostels in town. Beds are in a spotless, eight-person mixed dorm or in one of six private double rooms, some of which have air-con. Original artworks and funky modular furniture add colour, and there's a cafe where pop-up vegan dinners are occasionally organised.

Blue Hostel HOSTEL €

(Map p430; ☎ 340 9258503; www.bluehostel.it; 3rd fl, Via Carlo Alberto 13; d €60-140, apt €100-180; ❋ ☎; Ⓜ Vittorio Emanuele) A hostel in name only, this pearl offers small, hotel-standard rooms, each with its own en suite bathroom, and decorated in tasteful low-key style: beamed ceilings, wooden floors, French windows, black-and-white framed photos. There's also an apartment, with kitchen, that sleeps up to four. No lift and no breakfast.

✗ Eating

The best and most atmospheric neighbourhoods to dine in are the historic centre and Trastevere. There are also excellent choices in studenty San Lorenzo and once-working-class Testaccio. Watch out for overpriced tourist traps around Termini and the Vatican.

✗ The Vatican

Fa-Bìo SANDWICHES €

(Map p420; ☎ 06 6452 5810; www.fa-bio.com; Via Germanico 43; sandwiches €5; ⏱ 10am-5.30pm Mon-Fri, to 4pm Sat) ✎ Sandwiches, salads and smoothies are all prepared with speed, skill and organic ingredients at this tiny takeaway. Locals in the know come here to grab a quick lunchtime bite, and if you can squeeze in the door you'd do well to follow suit.

Hostaria Dino e Tony TRATTORIA €€

(Map p420; ☎ 06 3973 3284; Via Leone IV 60; meals €25-30; ⏱ 12.30-3pm & 7-11pm, closed Sun & Aug; Ⓜ Ottaviano-San Pietro) An authentic old-school trattoria, Dino e Tony offers simple, no-frills

Roman cooking. Kick off with the monumental antipasto, a minor meal in its own right, before plunging into its signature *rigatoni all'amatriciana* (pasta tubes with pancetta, chilli and tomato sauce). No credit cards.

Historic Centre

★ Forno Roscioli   PIZZA, BAKERY €
(Map p428; Via dei Chiavari 34; pizza slices from €2, snacks from €1.50; ☉7am-7.30pm Mon-Sat; 🚇Via Arenula) This is one of Rome's top bakeries, much loved by lunching locals who crowd here for luscious sliced pizza, prize pastries and hunger-sating *supplì* (fried rice balls). There's also a counter serving hot pastas and vegetable side dishes.

Forno di Campo de' Fiori   PIZZA, BAKERY €
(Map p428; Campo de' Fiori 22; pizza slices about €3; ☉7.30am-2.30pm & 4.45-8pm Mon-Sat; 🚇Corso Vittorio Emanuele II) This buzzing bakery on Campo de' Fiori does a roaring trade in *panini* and delicious fresh-from-the-oven *pizza al taglio* (by the slice). Aficionados swear by the *pizza bianca* ('white' pizza with olive oil, rosemary and salt), but the *panini* and *pizza rossa* ('red' pizza, with olive oil, tomato and oregano) taste plenty good, too.

★ Casa Coppelle   RISTORANTE €€
(Map p428; ☎06 6889 1707; www.casacoppelle. it; Piazza delle Coppelle 49; meals €35-40; ☉12-3.30pm & 6.30-11.30pm; 🚇Corso del Rinascimento) Intimate and romantic, Casa Coppelle serves modern Italian and French-inspired food on a small piazza near the Pantheon. There's a full range of starters and pastas, but the real tours de force are the deliciously tender steaks and meat dishes. Service is quick and attentive. Book ahead.

Armando al Pantheon   TRATTORIA €€
(Map p428; ☎06 6880 3034; www.armandoal pantheon.it; Salita dei Crescenzi 31; meals €40; ☉12.30-3pm & 7-11pm Mon-Fri, 12.30-3pm Sat; 🚇Largo di Torre Argentina) A Roman institution, wood-panelled Armando is a rare find – a genuine family-run trattoria in the touristy Pantheon area. It's been on the go for more than 50 years and has served its fair share of celebs, but the focus remains fixed on traditional, earthy Roman food. Reservations recommended.

Al Gran Sasso   TRATTORIA €€
(Map p420; ☎06 321 48 83; www.algransasso.com; Via di Ripetta 32; meals €35; ☉12.30-2.30pm & 7.30-11.30pm Sun-Fri; 🚇Flaminio) A top lunchtime spot, this is a classic, dyed-in-the-wool trattoria specialising in old-school country cooking. It's a relaxed place with a welcoming vibe, garish murals on the walls (strangely often a good sign) and tasty, value-for-money food. The fried dishes are excellent, or try one of the daily specials, chalked up on the board outside.

Trastevere

Trattoria degli Amici   TRATTORIA €€
(Map p428; ☎06 580 60 33; www.trattoriadegli amici.org; Piazza Sant'Egidio 6; meals €35; ☉12.30-3pm & 7.30-11.30pm; 🚇Viale di Trastevere, 🚇Viale di Trastevere) Boasting a prime location on a pretty piazza, this cheerful trattoria is staffed by volunteers and people with disabilities who welcome guests with a warmth not always apparent in this touristy neck of the woods. Grab a squareside table and dig into fried starters and fresh, well-prepared Italian classics.

ROME'S TOP GELATO

Fatamorgana (Map p420; Via Roma Libera 11, Piazza San Cosimato; cones & tubs from €2; ☉noon-midnight summer, to 10.30pm winter; 🚇Viale di Trastevere, 🚇Viale di Trastevere) Creative flavours at one of Rome's new breed of gourmet gelaterie.

Il Gelato (Map p420; Viale Aventino 59; gelati €2-4.50; ☉10am-midnight summer, 11am-9pm winter; 🚇Viale Aventino) An oupost of the gelato empire built by Rome's ice-cream king, Claudio Torcè.

Gelateria del Teatro (Map p428; Via dei Coronari 65; gelati from €2.50; ☉11.30am-midnight; 🚇Corso del Rinascimento) Seasonal fruit and spicy chocolate flavours in the heart of the *centro storico* (historic centre).

San Crispino (Map p430; ☎06 679 39 24; Via della Panetteria 42; tubs from €2.70; ☉11am-12.30am Mon-Thu & Sun, to 1.30am Fri & Sat; 🚇Barberini) Near the Trevi Fountain; specialises in natural, seasonal flavours.

WORTH A TRIP

VIA APPIA ANTICA

Completed in 190 BC, the Appian Way connected Rome with Brindisi on Italy's southern Adriatic coast. It's now a much-sought-after address but it has a dark history – Spartacus and 6000 of his slave rebels were crucified here in 71 BC, and it was here that the early Christians buried their dead in the catacombs. See where at the **Catacombe di San Sebastiano** (☎06 785 03 50; www.catacombe.org; Via Appia Antica 136; adult/reduced €8/5; ☉10am-5pm Mon-Sat, closed Dec; 🚌Via Appia Antica) or **Catacombe di San Callisto** (☎06 513 01 51; www.catacombe.roma.it; Via Appia Antica 110 & 126; adult/reduced €8/5; ☉9am-noon & 2-5pm, closed Wed & Feb; 🚌Via Appia Antica).

To get to Via Appia Antica, take bus 660 from Colli Albani metro station (line A) or bus 118 from Piramide (line B).

Paris RISTORANTE €€€
(Map p428; ☎06 581 53 78; www.ristoranteparis.it; Piazza San Calisto 7a; meals €45-55; ☉7.30-11pm Mon, 12.30-3pm & 7.30-11pm Tue-Sun; 🚌Viale di Trastevere, 🚊Viale di Trastevere) An old-school restaurant set in a 17th-century building with tables on a small piazza, Paris – named for its founder, not the French capital – is the best place outside the Ghetto to sample Roman-Jewish cuisine. Signature dishes include *gran fritto vegetale con baccalà* (deep-fried vegetables with salt cod) and *carciofi alla giudia* (fried artichoke).

Testaccio

Pizzeria Da Remo PIZZA €
(Map p420; ☎06 574 62 70; Piazza Santa Maria Liberatrice 44; pizzas from €5.50; ☉7pm-1am Mon-Sat; 🚌Via Marmorata) For an authentic Roman experience, join the noisy crowds at this popular pizzeria. It's a spartan place, but the thin-crust Roman pizzas are the business, and there's a cheerful, boisterous vibe. To order, tick your choices on the sheet of paper slapped down by an overstretched waiter. Expect to queue after 8.30pm.

Flavio al Velavevodetto TRATTORIA €€
(Map p420; ☎06 574 41 94; www.ristorante velavevodetto.it; Via di Monte Testaccio 97-99; meals €35; ☉12.30-3pm & 7.45-11pm; 🚌Via Galvani) This welcoming eatery is the sort of place that gives Roman trattorias a good name. Housed in a rustic Pompeian-red villa, complete with covered courtyard and open-air terrace, it specialises in earthy, no-nonsense Roman food. Expect antipasti of cheeses and cured meats, huge helpings of homemade pastas, and uncomplicated meat dishes.

Termini & Esquiline

★**Panella l'Arte del Pane** BAKERY, CAFE €
(Map p420; ☎06 487 24 35; Via Merulana 54; snacks about €3.50; ☉8am-11pm Mon-Thu, to midnight Fri & Sat, 8.30am-4pm Sun; Ⓜ Vittorio Emanuele) With a magnificent array of *pizza al taglio, arancini* (Sicilian rice balls), focaccia, fried croquettes and pastries, this smart bakery-cum-cafe is good any time of the day. The outside tables are ideal for a leisurely breakfast or chilled evening drink, or you can perch on a high stool and lunch on something from the sumptuous counter display.

🍷 Drinking & Nightlife

Much of the drinking action is in the *centro storico* (historic centre): Campo de' Fiori is popular with students and can get messy, while the area around Piazza Navona hosts a more upmarket scene. Over the river, Trastevere is another favored spot with dozens of bars and pubs.

Rome's clubbing scene is centred on Testaccio and the Ostiense area, although you'll also find places in Trastevere and the historic centre. Admission to clubs is often free, but drinks are expensive.

★**Circolo degli Artisti** CLUB
(☎06 7030 5684; www.circoloartisti.it; Via Casilina Vecchia 42; free-€15 depending on the event; ☉depends on event; 🚌Ponte Casilino) The Circolo offers one of Rome's best nights out. Friday means Miss Loretta's disco night with '80s anthems and dance-floor classics, while Saturday sees Screamadelica unleash rock, retro and electro beats. Regular gigs are staged and, outside, there's a cool garden bar. To get here, take bus 105 from Termini.

★**Barnum Cafe** CAFE
(Map p428; www.barnumcafe.com; Via del Pellegrino 87; ☉9am-10pm Mon, 8.30am-2am Tue-Sat; 📶; 🚌Corso Vittorio Emanuele II) A relaxed, friendly spot to check your email over a freshly

squeezed orange juice or spend a pleasant hour reading a newspaper on one of the tatty old armchairs in the white bare-brick interior. Come evenings and the scene is cocktails, smooth tunes and dressed-down locals.

Caffè Sant'Eustachio CAFE
(Map p428; www.santeustachioilcaffe.it; Piazza Sant'Eustachio 82; ⏱8.30am-1am Sun-Thu, to 1.30am Fri, to 2am Sat; 🚇Corso del Rinascimento) This small, unassuming cafe, generally three deep at the bar, is reckoned to serve the best coffee in town. Created by beating the first drops of espresso and several teaspoons of sugar into a frothy paste, then adding the rest of the coffee, it's superbly smooth and guaranteed to put some zing into your sightseeing.

Open Baladin BAR
(Map p428; www.openbaladinroma.it; Via degli Specchi 6; ⏱noon-2am; 🛜; 🚇Via Arenula) A hip, shabby-chic lounge bar near Campo de' Fiori, Open Baladin is a leading light in Rome's thriving beer scene with more than 40 beers on tap and up to 100 bottled brews, many from artisanal microbreweries. There's also a decent food menu with *panini,* burgers and daily specials.

La Casa del Caffè
Tazza d'Oro CAFE
(Map p428; www.tazzadorocoffeeshop.com; Via degli Orfani 84-86; ⏱7am-8pm Mon-Sat, 10.30am-7.30pm Sun; 🚇Via del Corso) A busy, stand-up cafe with burnished 1940s fittings, this is one of Rome's best coffee houses. Its espresso hits the mark nicely and there's a range of delicious coffee concoctions, including a cooling *granita di caffè* (a crushed-ice coffee drink served with whipped cream).

Ma Che Siete Venuti a Fà PUB
(Map p428; www.football-pub.com; Via Benedetta 25; ⏱11am-2am; 🚇Piazza Trilussa) Named after a football chant, which translates politely as 'What did you come here for?', this pint-sized Trastevere pub is a beer-buff's paradise, packing in a huge number of international craft beers, both bottled and on tap.

Freni e Frizioni BAR
(Map p428; ☎06 4549 7499; www.freniefrizioni.com; Via del Politeama 4-6; ⏱6.30pm-2am; 🚇Piazza Trilussa) This cool Trastevere bar is housed in a former mechanic's workshop – hence its name, which means 'brakes and clutches'. It draws a young *spritz*-loving crowd that

swells onto the small piazza outside to sip well-priced cocktails (from €7) and to enjoy the daily *aperitivo* (apéritif; 7pm to 10pm).

☆ Entertainment

Rome has a thriving cultural scene, with a year-round calendar of concerts, performances and festivals. A useful listings guide is *Trova Roma,* a free insert with *La Repubblica* newspaper every Thursday. Upcoming events are also listed on www.turismoroma.it and www.auditorium.com.

Auditorium Parco
della Musica CONCERT VENUE
(☎06 8024 1281; www.auditorium.com; Viale Pietro de Coubertin 30; 🚇Viale Tiziano) Rome's main concert venue, this modernist complex combines architectural innovation with perfect acoustics. Designed by Renzo Piano, its three concert halls and 3000-seat open-air arena host everything from classical-music concerts to tango exhibitions, book readings and film screenings.

To get to the auditorium, take tram 2 from Piazzale Flaminio.

Alexanderplatz JAZZ
(Map p420; ☎06 3972 1867; www.alexanderplatzjazzclub.com; Via Ostia 9; ⏱8.30pm-2am, concerts 9.45pm; Ⓜ Ottaviano-San Pietro) Small and intimate, Rome's best-known jazz joint attracts top Italian and international performers and a respectful, cosmopolitan crowd. Book a table if you want to dine to the tunes.

Teatro dell'Opera
di Roma OPERA
(Map p430; ☎06 481 70 03; www.operaroma.it; Piazza Beniamino Gigli; ballet €12-80, opera €17-160; ⏱9am-5pm Tue-Sat, to 1.30pm Sun; Ⓜ Repubblica) Rome's premier opera house boasts a plush and gilt interior, a Fascist 1920s exterior and an impressive history: it premiered Puccini's *Tosca* and Maria Callas once sang here. Opera and ballet performances are staged between September and June.

Big Mama BLUES
(Map p420; ☎06 581 25 51; www.bigmama.it; Vicolo di San Francesco a Ripa 18; ⏱9pm-1.30am, shows 10.30pm, closed Jun-Sep; 🚇Viale di Trastevere, 🚇Viale di Trastevere) Head to this cramped Trastevere basement for a mellow night of Eternal City blues. A long-standing venue, it also stages jazz, funk, soul and R&B, as well as popular Italian cover bands.

ITALY ROME

DAY TRIPS FROM ROME

Ostia Antica

An easy train ride from Rome, Ostia Antica is one of Italy's most under appreciated archaeological sites. The ruins of ancient Rome's main seaport, the **Scavi Archeologici di Ostia Antica** (☑ 06 5635 0215; www.ostiaantica.beniculturali.it; Viale dei Romagnoli 717; adult/reduced €10/6; ☺ 8.30am-6.15pm Tue-Sun summer, earlier closing winter), are spread out and you'll need a few hours to do them justice. Highlights include the **Terme di Nettuno** (Baths of Neptune) and steeply stacked **amphitheatre**.

To get to Ostia take the Ostia Lido train (25 minutes, half-hourly) from Stazione Porta San Paolo next to Piramide metro station. The journey is covered by standard public-transport tickets.

Tivoli

Tivoli, 30km east of Rome, is home to two Unesco-listed sites.

Five kilometres from Tivoli proper, **Villa Adriana** (☑ 0774 38 27 33; www.villaadriana.beniculturali.it; adult/reduced €8/4, incl temporary exhibition €11/7; ☺ 9am-1hr before sunset) was Emperor Hadrian's sprawling 1st-century summer residence. One of the largest and most sumptuous villas in the Roman Empire, it was subsequently plundered for building materials, but enough remains to convey its magnificence.

Up in Tivoli's hilltop centre, the Renaissance **Villa d'Este** (☑ 0774 31 20 70; www.villadestetivoli.info; Piazza Trento; adult/reduced €8/4; ☺ 8.30am-1hr before sunset Tue-Sun) is famous for its elaborate gardens and fountains.

Tivoli is accessible by Cotral bus (€2.30, 50 minutes, every 15 to 20 minutes) from Ponte Mammolo metro station. To get to Villa Adriana from Tivoli town centre, take CAT bus 4 or 4X (€1, 10 minutes, half-hourly) from Largo Garibaldi.

🔒 Shopping

Rome boasts the usual cast of flagship chain stores and glitzy designer outlets, but what makes shopping here fun is its legion of small, independent shops: family-run delis, small-label fashion boutiques, artisans' studios and neighbourhood markets.

Porta Portese Market　　MARKET
(Map p420; Piazza Porta Portese; ☺ 6am-2pm Sun; 🚊 Viale di Trastevere, 🚊 Viale di Trastevere) To see another side of Rome, head to this mammoth flea market. With thousands of stalls selling everything from rare books and fell-off-a-lorry bikes to Peruvian shawls and MP3 players, it's crazily busy and a lot of fun. Keep your valuables safe and wear your haggling hat.

ℹ Information

DANGERS & ANNOYANCES

Rome is not a dangerous city, but petty theft can be a problem. Watch out for pickpockets around the big tourist sites, at Stazione Termini and on crowded public transport – the 64 Vatican bus is notorious.

INTERNET ACCESS

Free wi-fi is widely available in hostels, B&Bs and hotels; some also provide laptops/computers. Many bars and cafes now also offer wi-fi.

MEDICAL SERVICES

Ospedale Santo Spirito (☑ 06 6 83 51; Lungotevere in Sassia 1) Near the Vatican.

Pharmacy (☑ 06 488 00 19; Piazza dei Cinquecento 51; ☺ 7am-11.30pm Mon-Fri, 8am-11.30pm Sat & Sun) There's also a pharmacy in Stazione Termini, next to platform 1, open 7.30am to 10pm daily.

TOURIST INFORMATION

For phone enquiries, the Comune di Roma runs a multilingual **tourist information line** (☑ 06 06 08; ☺ 9am-9pm).

For information about the Vatican, contact the **Centro Servizi Pellegrini e Turisti** (Map p420; ☑ 06 6988 1662; St Peter's Sq; ☺ 8.30am-6.15pm Mon-Sat).

There are tourist information points at **Fiumicino** (Terminal 3, International Arrivals; ☺ 8am-7.30pm) and **Ciampino** (International Arrivals, baggage claim area; ☺ 9am-6.30pm) airports, and at the following locations:

Castel Sant'Angelo Tourist Information (Map p420; Piazza Pia; ☺ 9.30am-7.15pm)

Fori Imperiali Tourist Information (Map p426; Via dei Fori Imperiali; ⊘9.30am-7.15pm)

Piazza Navona Tourist Information (Map p428; ⊘9.30am-7pm) Near Piazza delle Cinque Lune.

Stazione Termini Tourist Information (Map p430; ⊘8am-7.45pm) In the hall adjacent to platform 24.

Trevi Fountain Tourist Information (Map p428; Via Marco Minghetti; ⊘9.30am-7pm) This tourist point is closer to Via del Corso than the fountain.

Via Nazionale Tourist Information (Map p430; Via Nazionale; ⊘9.30am-7.15pm)

USEFUL WEBSITES

060608 (www.060608.it) Comprehensive information on sights, upcoming events, transport etc.

Coop Culture (www.coopculture.it) Information and ticket booking for many major sights.

Roma Turismo (www.turismoroma.it) Rome's official tourist website, with extensive listings and up-to-date information.

ⓘ Getting There & Away

AIR

Leonardo da Vinci (Fiumicino; ☑06 6 59 51; www.adr.it/fiumicino) Rome's main international airport, better known as Fiumicino, is 30km west of the city.

Ciampino (☑06 6 59 51; www.adr.it/ciampino) This smaller airport, 15km southeast of the centre, is the hub for low-cost carrier.

Ryanair (☑895 895 8989; www.ryanair.com).

BOAT

The nearest port to Rome is at Civitavecchia, about 80km to the north. Ferries sail here from Spain and Tunisia, as well as Sicily and Sardinia.

Book tickets at the Termini-based **Agenzia 365** (☑06 474 09 23; www.agenzie365.it; ⊘7am-9pm), at travel agents or online at www.traghettiweb.it. You can also buy directly at the port.

Half-hourly trains connect Civitavecchia and Roma Termini (€5 to €10, 40 minutes to 1¼ hours).

BUS

Long-distance national and international buses use the **Autostazione Tiburtina** (Piazzale Tiburtina; Ⓜ Tiburtina).

Get tickets at the Autostazione or at travel agencies.

Interbus (☑091 34 25 25; www.interbus.it) To/from Sicily.

Marozzi (☑080 579 01 11; www.marozzivt.it) To/from Sorrento, Bari and Puglia.

SENA (☑861 1991900; www.sena.it) To/from Siena, Bologna and Milan.

Sulga (☑800 099661; www.sulga.it) To/from Perugia, Assisi and Ravenna.

CAR & MOTORCYCLE

Rome is circled by the Grande Raccordo Anulare (GRA), to which all autostradas (motorways) connect, including the main A1 north–south artery, and the A12, which runs to Civitavecchia and Fiumicino airport.

Car hire is available at the airport and Stazione Termini.

TRAIN

Rome's main station is **Stazione Termini** (Piazza dei Cinquecento; Ⓜ Termini). It has regular connections to other European countries, all major Italian cities and many smaller towns.

Left luggage (Stazione Termini; 1st 5hr €6, 6-12hr per hour €0.90, 13hr & over per hour €0.40; ⊘6am-11pm) is on the lower-ground floor under platform 24.

Rome's other principal train stations are Stazione Tiburtina and Stazione Roma-Ostiense.

ⓘ Getting Around

TO/FROM THE AIRPORTS
Fiumicino

The easiest way to get to/from Fiumicino is by train, but there are also bus services. The set taxi fare to the city centre is €48 (valid for up to four people with luggage).

FL1 Train (one way €8) Connects to Trastevere, Ostiense and Tiburtina stations, but not Termini. Departures from the airport every 15 minutes (hourly on Sunday and public holidays) between 5.57am and 10.42pm; from Tiburtina every 15 minutes between 5.46am and 7.31pm, then half-hourly to 10.02pm.

Leonardo Express Train (one way €14) Runs to/from Stazione Termini. Departures from the airport every 30 minutes between 6.38am and 11.08pm; from Termini between 5.50am and 10.50pm. Journey time is 30 minutes.

Ciampino

The best option from Ciampino is to take one of the regular bus services into the city centre. The set taxi fare to the city centre is €30.

SIT Bus (☑06 591 68 26; www.sitbusshuttle.com; from/to airport €4/6) Regular departures from the airport to Via Marsala outside Stazione Termini between 7.15am and 10.30pm, and from Termini between 4.30am and 9.30pm. Get tickets on the bus. Journey time is 45 minutes.

Terravision Bus (www.terravision.eu; one way €6 or €4 online) Twice-hourly departures to/from Via Marsala outside Stazione Termini. From the airport services are between 8.15am

A BRIEF HISTORY OF ITALY

Ancient Times

The Etruscans were the first major force to emerge on the Italian peninsula. By the 7th century BC they dominated central Italy, rivalled only by the Greeks from the southern colony of Magna Graecia. Both thrived until the emerging city of Rome began to flex its muscles.

Founded in the 8th century BC (legend has it by Romulus), Rome flourished, becoming a republic in 509 BC and growing to become the dominant force in the Western world. The end came for the republic when internal rivalries led to the murder of Julius Caesar in 44 BC and his great-nephew Octavian took power as Augustus, the first Roman emperor.

The empire's golden age came in the 2nd century AD, but a century later it was in decline. Diocletian split the empire into eastern and western halves, and when his successor, Constantine (the first Christian emperor), moved his court to Constantinople, Rome's days were numbered. In 476 the western empire fell to Germanic tribes.

City States & the Renaissance

The Middle Ages was a period of almost constant warfare as powerful city-states fought across central and northern Italy. Eventually Florence, Milan and Venice emerged as regional powers. Against this fractious background, art and culture thrived, culminating in an explosion of intellectual and artistic activity in 15th-century Florence – the Renaissance.

Unification

By the end of the 16th century most of Italy was in foreign hands – the Austrian Habsburgs in the north and the Spanish Bourbons in the south. Three centuries later, Napoleon's brief Italian interlude inspired the unification movement, the Risorgimento. With Count Cavour providing the political vision and Garibaldi the military muscle, the movement brought about the 1861 unification of Italy. Ten years later Rome was wrested from the papacy to become Italy's capital.

Birth of a Republic

Italy's brief Fascist interlude was a low point. Mussolini gained power in 1925 and in 1940 entered WWII on Germany's side. Defeat ensued and Il Duce was killed by partisans in April 1945. A year later, Italians voted in a national referendum to abolish the monarchy and create a constitutional republic.

The Modern Era

Italy's postwar era has been largely successful. A founding member of the European Economic Community, it survived a period of domestic terrorism in the 1970s and enjoyed sustained economic growth in the 1980s. But the 1990s heralded a period of crisis as corruption scandals rocked the nation, paving the way for billionaire media mogul Silvio Berlusconi to enter the political arena.

Recent economic crises have hit Italy hard and since Berlusconi was forced from office in 2011, successive prime ministers have struggled to cope with the country's sluggish economy. At the time of writing, centre-left PM Matteo Renzi was in the hot seat, battling to face down the increasingly militant unions and to calm social tensions.

and 12.15am; from Via Marsala between 4.30am and 9.20pm. Buy tickets at Terracafè in front of the Via Marsala bus stop. Journey time is 40 minutes.

PUBLIC TRANSPORT

Rome's public transport system includes buses, trams, metro and a suburban train network.

Tickets are valid for all forms of public transport, except for routes to Fiumicino airport. Buy tickets at *tabaccherie* (tobacconists), news-stands or vending machines; they come in various forms:

Single (BIT; €1.50) Valid for 100 minutes, but only one metro journey.
Daily (BIG; €6)

Three-day (BTI; €16.50)
Weekly (CIS; €24)

Bus

Buses and trams are run by **ATAC** (☑ 06 5 70 03; www.atac.roma.it).

The **main bus station** (Map p430) is on Piazza dei Cinquecento, where there's an **information booth** (Map p430; ☉7.30am-8pm). Other important hubs are Largo di Torre Argentina and Piazza Venezia.

Buses generally run from about 5.30am until midnight, with limited services throughout the night.

Metro

Rome has two principal metro lines, A (orange) and B (blue), which cross at Termini.

Trains run between 5.30am and 11.30pm (1.30am on Friday and Saturday).

TAXI

Official licensed taxis are white with an ID number and *Roma capitale* on the sides.

Always go with the metered fare, never an arranged price (apart from the set fares to/from the airports). Official rates are posted in taxis.

You can hail a taxi, but it's often easier to phone for one or wait at a taxi rank. There are ranks at the airports, Stazione Termini, Largo di Torre Argentina, Piazza della Repubblica, the Colosseum, and Piazza del Risorgimento near the Vatican Museums.

La Capitale (☑ 06 49 94)
Radio Taxi (☑ 06 35 70; www.3570.it)
Samarcanda (☑ 06 55 51; www.samarcanda.it)

NORTHERN ITALY

Italy's well-heeled north is a fascinating area of historical wealth and natural diversity. Bordered by the northern Alps and boasting some of the country's most spectacular coastline, it also encompasses Italy's largest lowland area, the fertile Po Valley plain. Glacial lakes in the far north offer stunning scenery, while cities like Venice, Milan and Turin harbour artistic treasures and lively cultural scenes.

Genoa

POP 597,000

Genoa (Genova) is an absorbing city of aristocratic *palazzi,* dark, malodorous alleyways, Gothic architecture and industrial sprawl. Formerly a powerful maritime republic known as La Superba (Christopher Columbus was born here in 1451), Genoa is still an important transport hub, with ferry links to destinations across the Med and train links to the Cinque Terre.

⊙ Sights

**Musei di
Strada Nuova**   MUSEUM
(www.museidigenova.it; Via Garibaldi; combined ticket adult/reduced €9/7; ☉9am-7pm Tue-Fri, 10am-7pm Sat & Sun) Skirting the northern edge of what was once the city limits, pedestrianised Via Garibaldi (formerly called the Strada Nuova) was planned by Galeazzo Alessi in the 16th century. It quickly became the city's most sought-after quarter, lined with the palaces of Genoa's wealthiest citizens. Three of these *palazzi* – Rosso, Bianco and Doria-Tursi – today comprise the Musei di Strada Nuova. Between them, they hold the city's finest collection of old masters.

**Cattedrale di
San Lorenzo**   CATHEDRAL
(Piazza San Lorenzo; ☉8am-noon & 3-7pm) Genoa's zebra-striped Gothic-Romanesque cathedral owes its continued existence to the poor quality of a British WWII bomb that failed to ignite here in 1941; it still sits on the right side of the nave like an innocuous museum piece.

The cathedral, fronted by three arched portals, twisting columns and crouching lions, was first consecrated in 1118. The two bell towers and cupola were added later in the 16th century.

⊨ Sleeping & Eating

★**Hotel Cairoli**   HOTEL €
(☑010 246 14 54; www.hotelcairoligenova.com; Via Cairoli 14/4; d €65-120, tr €85-130, q €90-150; ✳@⊚) For five-star service at three-star prices, book at this artful hideaway. Rooms, on the 3rd floor of a towering *palazzo,* are themed on modern artists and feature works inspired by the likes of Mondrian, Dorazio and Alexander Calder. Add in a library, chill-out area, internet point, small gym and terrace, and you have the ideal bolt-hole.

B&B Palazzo Morali   B&B €
(☑010 246 70 27; www.palazzomorali.com; Piazza della Raibetta; s/d €75/85; ✳⊚) Stay in rarefied splendour at this antique-clad B&B near the Porto Antico. On the top two floors of a lofty building, its palatial rooms (some with

shared bathroom) are embellished with gold-leafed four-poster beds, gilt-framed mirrors and Genoese art.

La Cremeria delle Erbe

GELATERIA €

(Piazza delle Erbe 15-17; cones from €2; ⊗ 11am-1am Mon-Thu & Sun, to 2am Fri & Sat) A contender for the 'best ice cream in Genoa' mantle. On agreeably shabby Piazza delle Erbe, this gelateria snares late-night diners and boozers with its array of lush, creamy flavours and generous scoops.

★ Trattoria della Raibetta

TRATTORIA €€

(☑ 010 246 88 77; www.trattoriadellaraibetta.it; Vico Caprettari 10-12; meals €35; ⊗ noon-2.30pm & 7.30-11pm Tue-Sun) The most authentic Genoese food can be found in the family-run joints hidden in the warren of streets near the cathedral. This, a snug trattoria with a low brick-vaulted ceiling, serves regional classics such as *trofiette al pesto* alongside excellent fresh seafood.

❶ Information

There are several tourist offices across town, including at the **airport** (☑ 010 601 52 47; arrivals hall; ⊗ 9am-6.20pm summer, to 5.50pm winter) and **Via Garibaldi** (☑ 010 557 29 03; www.visit genoa.it; Via Garibaldi 12r; ⊗ 9am-6.20pm).

❶ Getting There & Around

AIR

Genoa's **Cristoforo Colombo Airport** (☑ 010 6 01 51; www.airport.genova.it) is 6km west of the city. To get to/from it, the **Volabus** (www.amt. genova.it; one way €6) shuttle connects with Stazione Brignole and Stazione Principe. Buy tickets on board.

BOAT

Ferries sail to/from Spain, Sicily, Sardinia, Corsica and Tunisia from the **Terminal Traghetti** (Ferry Terminal; Via Milano 51), west of the city centre.

Grandi Navi Veloci (GNV; ☑ 010 209 45 91; www.gnv.it) Ferries to Sardinia (Porto Torres, €74) and Sicily (Palermo, €90). Also to Barcelona (Spain), Tunis (Tunisia) and Tangier (Morocco).

Moby Lines (☑ 199 303040; www.mobylines. it) Ferries year-round to Corsica (Bastia, €39) and Sardinia (Olbia, €73).

Tirrenia (☑ 89 21 23; www.tirrenia.it) To/from Sardinia (Porto Torres €60; Olbia from €41; Arbatax €91).

BUS

Buses to international and regional destinations depart from Piazza della Vittoria, south of Stazione Brignole. Book tickets at **Geotravels** (Piazza della Vittoria 57; ⊗ 9am-12.30pm & 3-7pm Mon-Fri, 9am-noon Sat).

Local buses are run by **AMT** (www.amt.genova. it). Tickets, which are also valid on the metro, cost €1.50.

TRAIN

Genoa has two main stations: Stazione Brignole and Stazione Principe.

From Principe Trains run to Turin (€9 to €16, two hours, at least hourly), Milan (€10.30 to €16.50, 1¾ hours, hourly), Pisa (€9 to €11, two to 3½ hours, up to 15 daily) and Rome (€25 to €48, 4½ to five hours, nine daily).

From Brignole Trains serve Riomaggiore (€7, 1½ to two hours, 18 daily) and the other Cinque Terre villages.

Cinque Terre

Liguria's eastern Riviera boasts some of Italy's most dramatic coastline, the highlight of which is the Unesco-listed **Parco Nazionale delle Cinque Terre** (Cinque Terre National Park) just west of La Spezia. Running for 18km, this awesome stretch of plunging cliffs and vine-covered hills is named after its five tiny villages: Riomaggiore, Manarola, Corniglia, Vernazza and Monterosso.

✦ Activities

The Cinque Terre offers excellent hiking. The best known path is the 12km **Sentiero Azzurro** (Blue Trail), a one-time mule trail that links all five villages. To walk it (or any of the national park's trails) you'll need a **Cinque Terre Trekking Card** (1/2 days €7.50/14.50), or a **Cinque Terre Treno Card** (1/2 days €12/23), which also provides unlimited train travel between La Spezia and the five villages. Both cards are available at all park offices.

At the time of writing the Sentiero Azzurro was closed between Riomaggiore and Vernazza, after it sustained severe damage during heavy rainfall in 2011 and a rockfall in September 2012. Authorities hoped to have it re-opened by mid-2015, but check www.parco nazionale5terre.it for the current situation.

The Sentiero Azzurro is just one of a network of footpaths and cycle trails that crisscross the park; details are available from the park offices.

If water sports are more your thing, you can hire snorkelling gear and kayaks at the **Diving Center 5 Terre** (www.5terrediving.it; Via San Giacomo) in Riomaggiore.

ℹ Information

There are park information offices at the train stations of all five villages and also at La Spezia station. They generally open 8am to 8pm daily in summer, 9am to 5pm winter.

Online information is available at www.cinque terre.it and www.cinqueterre.com.

ℹ Getting There & Away

BOAT

Between July and September, **Golfo Paradiso** (📞 0185 77 20 91; www.golfoparadiso.it) runs boats from Genoa's Porto Antico to Vernazza and Monterosso (€18 one way, €33 return).

From late March to October, the **Consorzio Marittimo Turistico 5 Terre** (📞 0187 73 29 87; www.navigazionegolfodeipoeti.it) operates four daily services between La Spezia and Riomaggiore, Manarola, Vernazza and Monterosso. One-way tickets cost €12 to Riomaggiore or Manarola, €16 to Vernazza or Monterosso. Return trips are covered by a daily ticket (weekdays/weekends €25/27).

TRAIN

From Genoa Brignole, trains run to Riomaggiore (€6.80, 1½ to two hours, 18 daily), stopping at each of the villages.

From La Spezia, one to three trains an hour run up the coast between 4.30am and 11.46pm. If you're using this route and want to stop at all the villages, get the Cinque Terre Treno Card.

Monterosso

The largest and most developed of the villages, Monterosso boasts the coast's only sandy beach, as well as a wealth of eating and accommodation options.

🛌 Sleeping & Eating

★**Hotel Pasquale**   HOTEL €€
(📞 0187 81 74 77; www.hotelpasquale.it; Via Fegina 4; s €80-145, d €135-190, tr €180-250; ⊗ Mar–mid-Nov; ❄☎) Offering soothing views and stylish, modern guest rooms, this friendly seafront hotel is built into Monterosso's medieval sea walls. To find it, exit the train station and go left through the tunnel towards the *centro storico*.

Ristorante Belvedere   SEAFOOD €€
(📞 0187 81 70 33; www.ristorante-belvedere.it; Piazza Garibaldi 38; meals €30; ⊗ noon-3pm & 6.15-10.30pm Wed-Mon) With tables overlooking the beach, this unpretentious seafood restaurant is a good place to try the local bounty. Start with *penne con scampi* (pasta tubes with scampi) before diving into a rich *zuppa di pesce* (fish soup).

Vernazza

Perhaps the most attractive of the five villages, Vernazza overlooks a small, picturesque harbour.

From near the harbour, a steep, narrow staircase leads up to the **Castello Doria** (admission €1.50; ⊗ 10am-7pm), the oldest surviving fortification in the Cinque Terre. Dating to around 1000, it's now largely ruined except for the circular tower in the centre of the esplanade, but the castle is well worth a visit for the superb views it commands.

To spend a romantic night in Vernazza, **L'Eremo sul Mare** (📞 339 268 56 17; www.eremosulmare.com; d €70-100; ❄☎) is a charming cliffside villa with just three rooms and a lovely panoramic terrace. It's a 15-minute walk from the village; follow the Sentiero Azzurro towards Corniglia.

Corniglia

Corniglia, the only village with no direct sea access, sits atop a 1000m-high rocky promontory surrounded by vineyards. To reach it from the train station, either take on the 365-step staircase or hop on a bus (€2, or free with a Cinque Terre card).

Once up in the village, you can enjoy dazzling 180-degree sea views from the **Belvedere di Santa Maria**, a heart-stopping lookout point. To find it, follow Via Fieschi through the village until you eventually reach the clifftop balcony.

Manarola

One of the busiest of the villages, Manarola tumbles down to the sea in a helter-skelter of pastel-coloured buildings, cafes, trattorias and restaurants.

🛌 Sleeping & Eating

Ostello 5 Terre   HOSTEL €
(📞 0187 92 00 39; www.hostel5terre.com; Via Riccobaldi 21; dm €21-24, d €55-65, f €92-132; @☎)

Manarola's hostel sits at the top of the village next to the Chiesa di San Lorenzo. Open for 11 months of the year (it closes mid-January to mid-February), it has single-sex, six-bed dorms, each with their own bathroom, and several double and family rooms.

Hotel Ca' d'Andrean HOTEL €€
(☎ 0187 92 00 40; www.cadandrean.it; Via Doscovolo 101; s €80-90, d €90-150; ☉ Mar–mid-Nov; ❉ ⍟) An excellent family-run hotel in the upper part of Manarola. Rooms are big and cool, with white-grey tones and designer bathrooms, and some have private terraces. Breakfast (€7) is optional. No credit cards.

Il Porticciolo SEAFOOD €€
(☎ 0187 92 00 83; www.ilporticciolo5terre.it; Via Renato Birolli 92; meals €30; ☉ 11.30am-11pm) One of several restaurants lining the main route down to the harbour, this is a popular spot for an alfresco seafood feast. Expect seaside bustle and a fishy menu featuring classic crowd-pleasers such as spaghetti with mussels and crispy fried squid.

Riomaggiore

The Cinque Terre's largest and easternmost village, Riomaggiore acts as the unofficial HQ.

For a taste of classic seafood and local wine, search out **Dau Cila** (☎ 0187 76 00 32; www.ristorantedaucila.com; Via San Giacomo 65; meals €40; ☉ 8am-2am Mar-Oct), a smart restaurant-cum-wine bar perched within pebble-lobbing distance of Riomaggiore's twee harbour.

Turin

POP 902,200

With its regal *palazzi*, baroque piazzas, cafes and world-class museums, the dynamic, cultured city of Turin (Torino) is a far cry from the dour industrial centre it's often portrayed as. For centuries it was the seat of the royal Savoy family, and between 1861 and 1864, it was Italy's first post-unification capital. More recently, it hosted the 2006 Winter Olympics and was European Capital of Design in 2008.

◉ Sights

★ **Mole Antonelliana** LANDMARK
(Via Montebello 20; Panoramic Lift adult/reduced €7/5, incl Museo €14/11; ☉ Panoramic Lift 10am-8pm Tue-Fri & Sun, to 11pm Sat) The symbol of Turin, this 167m tower with its distinctive aluminium spire appears on the Italian two-cent coin. It was originally intended as a synagogue when construction began in 1862, but was never used as a place of worship, and nowadays houses the Museo Nazionale del Cinema.

For dazzling 360-degree views, take the **Panoramic Lift** up to the 85m-high outdoor viewing deck.

Museo Nazionale del Cinema MUSEUM
(www.museocinema.it; Via Montebello 20; adult/reduced €10/8, incl Panoramic Lift €14/11; ☉ 9am-8pm Tue-Fri & Sun, to 11pm Sat) Housed in the Mole Antonelliana, this enjoyable museum takes you on a fantastic tour through cinematic history. Memorabilia on display includes Marilyn Monroe's black lace bustier, Peter O'Toole's robe from *Lawrence of Arabia* and the coffin used by Bela Lugosi's Dracula. At the heart of the museum, the vast Temple Hall is surrounded by 10 interactive 'chapels' devoted to various film genres.

Museo Egizio MUSEUM
(Egyptian Museum; www.museoegizio.it; Via Accademia delle Scienze 6; adult/reduced €7.50/3.50; ☉ 8.30am-7.30pm Tue-Sun) Opened in 1824, this legendary museum in the Palazzo dell'Accademia delle Scienze houses the most important collection of Egyptian treasure outside Cairo. Two of its many highlights include a statue of Ramses II (one of the world's most important pieces of Egyptian art) and over 500 items found in 1906 in the tomb of royal architect Kha and his wife Merit (from 1400 BC).

The museum underwent a major overhaul and work was completed in 2015.

Piazza Castello PIAZZA
Turin's central square shelters a wealth of museums, theatres and cafes. Essentially baroque, it was laid out from the 14th century to serve as the seat of the Savoy dynasty. Dominating it is the part-medieval part-baroque **Palazzo Madama**, the original seat of the Italian parliament. To the north, statues of Castor and Pollux guard the entrance to **Palazzo Reale**, the royal palace built for Carlo Emanuele II in the mid-1600s.

Cattedrale di San Giovanni Battista CATHEDRAL
(Piazza San Giovanni; ☉ 8am-noon & 3-7pm) Turin's 15th-century cathedral houses the famous

Shroud of Turin *(Sindone),* supposedly the cloth used to wrap the crucified Christ. A copy is on permanent display in front of the altar, while the real thing is kept in a vacuum-sealed box and rarely revealed.

🛏 Sleeping

Tomato
Backpackers Hotel HOSTEL €
(📞 011 020 94 00; www.tomato.to.it; Via Pellico 11; dm/s/d/tr €25/38/56/72; 📶) 🍃 This eco-friendly hostel in the trendy San Salvario area east of the train station is one of the few central places that caters to budget travellers. And it does so with style, offering pristine dorms, smart private rooms, a kitchen and a communal lounge. There's a relaxed, inclusive vibe and a long list of extras including laundry facilities and left luggage.

★ Art Hotel Boston BOUTIQUE HOTEL €€€
(📞 011 50 03 59; www.hotelbostontorino.it; Via Massena 70; s €80-150, d €110-400; 🌐📶) The Boston's austere classical facade gives no inkling of the artistic interiors that await inside. Public areas are filled with original works by Warhol, Lichtenstein and Aldo Mondino, while individually styled guest rooms are themed on subjects as diverse as Lavazza coffee, Ayrton Senna and Pablo Picasso.

🍴 Eating

Grom GELATERIA €
(www.grom.it; Piazza Pietro Paleocapa 1/D; cones & cups from €2.50; ⏲ 11am-11pm Sun-Thu, to 1am Fri & Sat summer, to midnight Fri & Sat winter) 🍃 At the vanguard of the gourmet gelato trend that has spread across Italy in recent years, the Grom chain founded its first store here in 2003. Long queues testify to its success and the quality of the ice cream.

L'Hamburgheria
di Eataly BURGERS €
(Piazza Solferino 16a; meals €10-15; ⏲ noon-midnight) This upmarket burger bar adds a dash of style to fast-food dining with its smart brick-and-steel interior and select menu. House speciality are the gourmet burgers, all made from locally sourced Piedmontese beef, but you can also grab a hot dog or kebab, as well as an Italian craft beer to quench your thirst.

La Cantinella RISTORANTE, PIZZA €€
(📞 011 819 33 11; www.lacantinella-restaurant.com; Corso Moncalieri 3/A; meals €40; ⏲ 7.30pm-1am) In-the-know locals flock to this intimate res-

taurant over the river from Piazza Vittorio Veneto. There's a full menu of pastas and pizzas, but the star performers are the steaks and spitting-hot grilled meats. Round things off with a delectably creamy chestnut mousse.

🍷 Drinking & Nightlife

Early evening is the time to make for one of the city's cafes to enjoy an *apericena,* Turin's answer to an aperitif. Order a drink (usually €5 to €10) and tuck into the sumptuous buffet included in the price. Popular precincts include Piazza Emanuele Filiberto, Piazza Savoia and Piazza Vittorio Veneto.

ℹ Information

Piazza Carlo Felice Tourist Office (📞 011 53 51 81; Piazza Carlo Felice; ⏲ 9am-6pm) On the piazza in front of Stazione Porta Nuova.
Piazza Castello Tourist Office (📞 011 53 51 81; www.turismotorino.org; Piazza Castello; ⏲ 9am-6pm) Central and multilingual.

ℹ Getting There & Around

From Turin's **Torino Airport** (www.turin-airport.com), 16km northwest of the city centre, airlines fly to Italy's main airports and destinations across Europe.

Sadem (www.sadem.it; one way €6.50, on bus €7.50) runs an airport shuttle (40 minutes, half-hourly) to/from Porta Nuova train station.

Trains connect with Milan (€12.20 to €24, one to two hours, up to 30 daily), Florence (€52, three hours, nine daily), Genoa (€12.20 to €19, two hours, up to 15 daily) and Rome (€72, 4¼ hours, 14 daily).

Milan
POP 1.32 MILLION

Few Italian cities polarise opinion like Milan, Italy's financial and fashion capital. Some people love the cosmopolitan, can-do atmosphere, the vibrant cultural scene and sophisticated shopping; others grumble that it's dirty, ugly and expensive. Certainly, it lacks the picture-postcard beauty of many Italian towns, but in among the urban hustle are some truly great sights: Leonardo da Vinci's *Last Supper,* the immense Duomo and La Scala opera house.

👁 Sights

★ Duomo CATHEDRAL
(www.duomomilano.it; Piazza del Duomo; roof terraces adult/reduced stairs €7/3.50, lift €12/6, Battistero di San Giovanni €6/4; ⏲ Duomo

ITALY MILAN

Central Milan

◎ **Top Sights**
1 Duomo...C3
2 Teatro alla Scala C2

◎ **Sights**
3 Museo del Novecento C3
4 Museo Teatrale alla Scala C2
5 Pinacoteca di Brera C1

🛏 **Sleeping**
6 Ostello Bello A4

🍽 **Eating**
7 Luini..C3

🎭 **Entertainment**
Teatro alla Scala............................ (see 2)
8 Teatro alla Scala Box Office C3

🛍 **Shopping**
9 Cavalli e Nastri..................................C2
10 Peck...B3

7am-6.40pm, roof terraces 9am-6.30pm, Battiste-ro di San Giovanni 10am-6pm Tue-Sun; Ⓜ Duomo) A vision in pink Candoglia marble, Milan's extravagant Gothic cathedral aptly reflects the city's creativity and ambition. Commissioned in 1387 and finished nearly 600 years later, it boasts a pearly white facade adorned with 135 spires and 3200 statues,

and a vast interior punctuated by the largest stained-glass windows in Christendom. Underground, you can see the remains of the saintly Carlo Borromeo in the crypt and explore ancient ruins in the Battiste-ro di San Giovanni. Up top, the spired roof terraces command stunning views.

Museo del Novecento GALLERY
(☑02 8844 4061; www.museodelnovecento.org; Piazza del Duomo 12; adult/reduced €5/3; ⊘2.30-7.30pm Mon, 9.30am-7.30pm Tue, Wed, Fri & Sun, to 10.30pm Thu & Sat; Ⓜ Duomo) Overlooking Piazza del Duomo, with fabulous views of the cathedral, is Mussolini's **Arengario**, from where he would harangue huge crowds in his heyday. Now it houses Milan's museum of 20th-century art. Built around a futuristic spiral ramp (an ode to the Guggenheim), the lower floors are cramped, but the heady collection, which includes the likes of Umberto Boccioni, Campigli, de Chirico and Marinetti, more than distracts.

★ Teatro alla Scala THEATRE
(La Scala; www.teatroallascala.org; Via Filodrammatici 2; Ⓜ Cordusio, Duomo) Giuseppe Piermarini's grand 2800-seat theatre was inaugurated in 1778 with Antonio Salieri's *Europa Riconosciuta,* replacing the previous theatre, which burnt down in a fire after a carnival gala. Costs were covered by the sale of *palchi* (private boxes), of which there are six gilt-and-crimson tiers.

In the theatre's **museum** (La Scala Museum; ☑02 8879 7473; Largo Ghiringhelli 1; admission €6; ⊘9am-12.30pm & 1.30-5.30pm), harlequin costumes and a spinet inscribed with the command 'Inexpert hand, touch me not!' hint at centuries of Milanese musical drama.

★ The Last Supper ARTWORK
(Il Cenacolo Vinciano; ☑02 9280 0360; www.vivaticket.it; Piazza Santa Maria delle Grazie 2; adult/reduced €6.50/3.25, plus booking fee €1.50; ⊘8.15am-7pm Tue-Sun) Milan's most famous mural, Leonardo da Vinci's *The Last Supper* is hidden away on a wall of the refectory adjoining the **Basilica di Santa Maria delle Grazie.** Depicting Christ and his disciples at the dramatic moment when Christ reveals he's aware of his betrayal, it's a masterful psychological study and one of the world's most iconic images.

To see it you must book in advance or sign up for a guided city tour.

Pinacoteca di Brera GALLERY
(☑02 7226 3264; www.brera.beniculturali.it; Via Brera 28; adult/reduced €9/6; ⊘8.30am-7.15pm Tue-Thu, Sat & Sun, to 9.15pm Fri; Ⓜ Lanza) Located upstairs from the centuries-old Accademia di Belle Arti (still one of Italy's most prestigious art schools), this gallery houses Milan's most impressive collection of old masters, much of the bounty 'lifted' from Venice by Napoleon. Rembrandt, Goya and Van Dyck all have a place in the collection, but you're here to see the Italians: Titian, Tintoretto, glorious Veronese, groundbreaking Mantegna, the Bellini brothers and a Caravaggio.

🛏 Sleeping

Ostello Bello HOSTEL €
(☑02 3658 2720; www.ostellobello.com; Via Medici 4; dm €28-35, d/tr/q €98/130/160; ❋🛜; 🚇Via Torino) A breath of fresh air in Milan's stiffly suited centre, this is the best hostel in town. Entrance is through its lively bar-cafe, open to nonguests, where you're welcomed with a smile and complimentary drink. Beds are in mixed dorms or spotless private rooms, and there's a kitchen, small terrace, and basement lounge equipped with guitars, board games and table football.

Hotel Aurora HOTEL €€
(☑02 204 79 60; www.hotelauroramilano.com; Corso Buenos Aires 18; s €60-135, d €80-140; ❋🛜; Ⓜ Porta Venezia) Clean, quiet rooms in a strategic location await at this modest two-star hotel. The decor is business-like and fairly unforgettable, but the rates compare well with other places in town and rooms are comfortable enough. No breakfast.

Antica Locanda Leonardo HOTEL €€€
(☑02 4801 4197; www.anticalocandaleonardo.com; Corso Magenta 78; s €95-170, d €158-395; ❋@🛜; Ⓜ Conciliazione) A charmer hidden in a 19th-century residence near Leonardo's *Last Supper.* Rooms exude homey comfort, from the period furniture and parquet floors to the plush drapes, while breakfast is served in the small, scented garden.

🍴 Eating & Drinking

Local specialities include *risotto alla milanese* (saffron-infused risotto cooked in bone-marrow stock) and *cotoletta alla milanese* (breaded veal cutlet).

Luini FAST FOOD €
(www.luini.it; Via Santa Radegonda 16; panzerotti €2.70; ⊘10am-3pm Mon, to 8pm Tue-Sun; Ⓜ Duomo) This historic joint is the go-to place for *panzerotti*, delicious pizza-dough parcels stuffed with a combination of mozzarella, spinach, tomato, ham or spicy salami, and then fried or baked in a wood-fired oven.

Rinomata
GELATERIA €

(Ripa di Porta Ticinese; cones & tubs €2.50-4.50; ⊙noon-2am; Ⓜ Porta Genova) If dining in Navigli, skip dessert and grab an ice cream from this hole-in-the-wall gelateria. Its fabulous interior features old-fashioned fridges and glass-fronted cabinets filled with cones – and the gelato is good, too.

Al Bacco
ITALIAN €€

(☑02 5412 1637; Via Marcona 1; meals €35; ⊙12.30-2.30pm & 7.30-11pm Mon-Fri, 7pm-1am Sat; 🚊 Corso XXII Marzo) Search out this cosy, Slow Food–recommended restaurant east of the city centre – a block north of Corso XXII Marzo – for lovingly prepared Milanese classics. Try *tortino di riso giallo allo zafferano* (yellow rice tart with saffron) followed by *cotoletta alla milanese* (breaded veal cutlet).

BQ Navigli
BAR

(Birra Artigianale di Qualità; Via Alzaia Naviglio Grande 44; ⊙6pm-2am; Ⓜ Porta Genova) This Navigli canalside bar has a fine selection of craft beers, ranging from light lagers to robust hop-heavy bitters. Soak it all up with *panini* and *piadine* (stuffed pitta breads).

☆ Entertainment

Teatro alla Scala
OPERA

(☑02 8 87 91; www.teatroallascala.org; Piazza della Scala; ballet €11-127, opera €13-210; Ⓜ Duomo) La Scala's opera season runs from early December through July, but you can see theatre, ballet and concerts year-round, except for August. Tickets can be bought online or by phone up to two months before the performance, and then from the central **box office**

FOOTBALL IN MILAN

Milan is home to two of Italy's most successful *calcio* (football) teams: AC Milan and Internazionale (Inter). During the season (September to May), the two clubs play on alternate Sundays at the **Stadio Giuseppe Meazza** (Via Piccolomini 5; Ⓜ Lotto), aka the San Siro. Match tickets (from €19) are available from branches of Banca Intesa (AC Milan) and Banca Popolare di Milano (Inter).

To get to the stadium on match days, take the free shuttle bus from the Lotto (MM1) metro station.

(Galleria del Sagrato, Piazza del Duomo; ⊙noon-6pm; Ⓜ Duomo).

Blue Note
JAZZ

(☑02 6901 6888; www.bluenotemilano.com; Via Borsieri 37; tickets €22-40; ⊙concerts 9pm & 11.30pm; Ⓜ Zara, Garibaldi) Top-class jazz acts from around the world perform here; get tickets by phone, online or at the door from 7.30pm. It also does a popular easy-listening Sunday brunch (€35 per adult, or €70 for two adults and two children under 12).

🛍 Shopping

The Quadrilatero d'Oro (the area around Via della Spiga, Via Sant'Andrea, Via Monte Napoleone and Via Alessandro Manzoni) is the place to go for big-name designer brands. Hip younger labels can be found in Brera and Corso Magenta, while Corso Porta Ticinese and Navigli are home to Milan's street scene. Chain stores line Corso Vercelli and Corso Buenos Aires.

Peck
FOOD, WINE

(☑02 802 31 61; www.peck.it; Via Spadari 9; ⊙3.30-7.30pm Mon, 9.30am-7.30pm Tue-Sat; Ⓜ Duomo) Milan's historic deli is smaller than its reputation suggests, but what it lacks in space it makes up for in variety, with a mind-boggling selection of *parmigiano reggiano* (Parmesan) and myriad other treasures: chocolates, pralines, pastries, freshly made gelato, seafood, caviar, pâtés, fruit and vegetables, truffle products, olive oils and balsamic vinegars.

Cavalli e Nastri
CLOTHING

(☑02 7200 0449; www.cavallienastri.com; Via Brera 2; ⊙3.30-7.30pm Mon, 10.30am-7.30pm Tue-Sat; Ⓜ Montenapoleone) This gorgeously colourful Brera shop is known for its vintage clothes and accessories. It specialises in lovingly curated frocks, bags, jewellery and even shoes, sourced from early and mid-20th-century Italian fashion houses, and priced accordingly.

ℹ Information

Useful websites include www.turismo.milano.it and www.hellomilano.it.

24-Hour Pharmacy (☑02 669 09 35; Galleria delle Partenze, Stazione Centrale; Ⓜ Centrale FS) Located on 1st floor of the central station.

Milan Tourist Office (☑02 7740 4343; www.visitamilano.it; Piazza Castello 1; ⊙9am-6pm Mon-Fri, 9am-1.30pm & 2-6pm Sat, to 5pm Sun; Ⓜ Cairoli)

Stazione Centrale Tourist Office (☑02 7740 4318; ⊙9am-5pm Mon-Fri, to 12.30pm Sat &

Sun; Ⓜ Centrale FS) On the 2nd floor by the side of platform 21.

ⓘ Getting There & Away

AIR

Linate Airport (✆ 02 23 23 23; www.milano linate-airport.com) Located 7km east of the city centre; domestic and some European flights.

Malpensa Airport (✆ 02 23 23 23; www. milanomalpensa-airport.com) About 50km northwest of the city; northern Italy's main international airport.

Orio al Serio (✆ 035 32 63 23; www.sacbo. it) Bergamo airport receives regular European flights and has direct transport links to Milan.

TRAIN

Regular trains depart Stazione Centrale for Venice (€37.50, 2½ hours), Bologna (€40, one hour), Florence (€50, 1¾ hours), Rome (€86, three hours) and other Italian and European cities.

Most regional trains also stop at Stazione Nord in Piazzale Cadorna.

ⓘ Getting Around

TO/FROM THE AIRPORT
Malpensa

Malpensa Shuttle (✆ 02 5858 3185; www. malpensashuttle.it; one way €10) Coaches run to/from Piazza Luigi di Savoia next to Stazione Centrale. Departures run from the station every 20 minutes between 3.45am and 12.30am; from the airport 5am to 12.30am. Journey time 50 minutes.

Malpensa Express (✆ 02 7249 4949; www. malpensaexpress.it; one way €12) From 4.28am to 12.26am, trains run every 30 minutes between Terminal 1, Cadorna Stazione Nord (35 minutes) and Stazione Centrale (45 minutes). Passengers for Terminal 2 will need to take the free shuttle bus to/from Terminal 1.

Linate

Air Bus (www.atm-mi.it; one way €5) Half-hourly departures from Piazza Luigi di Savoia between 6am and 11pm; from the airport between 6.30am and 11.30pm. Journey time 25 minutes.

Orio al Serio

Orio Bus Express (✆ 02 3391 0794; www. autostradale.it; one way €5) This Autostradale service departs Piazza Luigi di Savoia approximately every half hour between 2.45am and 11.30pm; from Orio between 4.30am and 1am. The journey takes one hour.

PUBLIC TRANSPORT

Milan's metro, buses and trams are run by **ATM** (✆ 02 4860 7607; www.atm.it). Tickets (€1.50)

are valid for one underground ride or up to 90 minutes' travel on city buses and trams. A day ticket costs €4.50. Buy them at metro stations, *tabaccherie* and newsstands.

The Lakes

Ringed by snowcapped mountains, gracious towns and landscaped gardens, the Italian lake district is an enchanting corner of the country.

Lago Maggiore

Snaking across the Swiss border, Lago Maggiore, the westernmost of the three main lakes, retains the belle époque air of its 19th-century heyday when it was a popular retreat for artists and writers.

Its headline sights are the Borromean islands, accessible from **Stresa** on the lake's western bank. **Isola Bella** is dominated by the 17th-century **Palazzo Borromeo** (✆ 0323 3 05 56; www.isoleborromee.it; adult/reduced €13/6.50, incl Isola Madre €18.50/8.50, Galleria dei Quadri €3/2; ⊙ 9am-5.30pm mid-Mar–mid-Oct), a grand baroque palace with a picture gallery (Galleria dei Quadri) and beautiful tiered gardens. Over the water, **Palazzo Madre** (✆ 0323 3 12 61; www.isoleborromee.it; adult/reduced €11/6, incl Isola Bella €18.50/8.50; ⊙ 9am-6pm mid-Mar–mid-Oct) lords it over **Isola Madre**.

In Stresa's pedestrianised centre, **Nonna Italia** (✆ 0323 93 39 22; www.nonnaitalia.net; Via Garibaldi 32; pizzas €5-8, meals €25-30) is a welcoming trattoria serving creative regional cooking. Nearby, the family-run **Hotel Fiorentina** (✆ 0323 3 02 54; www.hotelfiorentino.com; Via Bolongaro 9; s €50-60, d €80-90; ❄🤶) has warm, modest rooms.

For further information, contact Stresa's **tourist office** (✆ 0323 3 13 08; www.stresa turismo.it; Piazza Marconi 16; ⊙ 10am-12.30pm & 3-6.30pm summer, reduced hours winter).

ⓘ Getting There & Around

The easiest way to get to Stresa is by train from Milan (€8.30, one hour, up to 14 daily).

Between April and September, **Saf** (✆ 0323 55 21 72; www.safduemila.com) operates an Alibus shuttle to/from Malpensa airport (€12, one hour, six daily).

Navigazione Lago Maggiore (✆ 800 551801; www.navigazionelaghi.it) operates ferries across the lake. From Stresa, a return ticket to Isola Bella costs €6.80, to Isola Madre €10.

Lago di Como

Lago di Como, overshadowed by steep wooded hills and snowcapped peaks, is the most spectacular and least visited of the lakes. At its southwestern tip, **Como** is a prosperous town with a charming medieval centre and good ferry links.

Just over a kilometre from Como's centre, the sumptuous 18th-century **Villa Olmo** (☑031 57 61 69; www.grandimostrecomo. it; Via Cantoni 1; gardens free, villa dependent upon exhibition; ☺villa during exhibitions 9am-12.30pm & 2-5pm Mon-Sat, gardens 7.30am-11pm summer, to 7pm winter) is a local landmark and one of the lake's many waterside villas.

For lunch head to the characterful **Osteria del Gallo** (☑031 27 25 91; www.osteriadel gallo-como.it; Via Vitani 16; meals €25-30; ☺12.30-3pm Mon, to 9pm Tue-Sat). Also in the medieval centre, the modish **Avenue Hotel** (☑031 27 21 86; www.avenuehotel.it; Piazzole Terragni 6; d/ste from €170/220; ✹⑤) offers slick four-star accommodation.

You can get more local information at the **infopoint** (www.comotourism.it; Como San Giovanni train station; 9am-5pm Wed-Mon summer, to 4.30pm winter).

ⓘ Getting There & Around

Regional trains run to Como San Giovanni from Milan's Stazione Centrale and Porta Garibaldi (€4.60, one hour, hourly).

Navigazione Lago di Como (☑800 551801; www.navigazionelaghi.it) operates year-round ferries from the jetty near Piazza Cavour.

Lago di Garda

The largest and most developed of the lakes, Lago di Garda straddles the border between Lombardy and the Veneto. A good base is **Sirmione**, a picturesque village on its southern shores. Here you can investigate the **Rocca Scaligera** (Castello Scaligero; adult/reduced €4/2; ☺8.30am-7pm Tue-Sat, to 1.30pm Sun), a medieval castle, and enjoy views over the lake's placid blue waters.

There are an inordinate number of eateries crammed into Sirmione's historic centre. One of the best is **La Fiasca** (☑030 990 61 11; www.trattorialafiasca.it; Via Santa Maria Maggiore; meals €30; ☺noon-2.30pm & 7-10.30pm Thu-Tue), an authentic trattoria serving flavoursome lake fish.

Sirmione can be visited on a day trip from Verona, but if you want to overnight, **Hotel Marconi** (☑030 91 60 07; www.hotelmarconi. net; Via Vittorio Emanuele II 51; s €45-75, d €80-140; ᴾ✹⑤) has stylishly understated rooms and relaxing lake views.

Get information from the **tourist office** (☑030 91 61 14; iat.sirmione@tiscali.it; Viale Marconi 8; ☺9am-12.30pm & 3-6.30pm, closed Sat afternoon & Sun winter) outside the medieval walls.

ⓘ Getting There & Around

Regular buses run to Sirmione from Verona (€3.50, one hour, hourly).

Navigazione Lago di Garda (☑800 551801; www.navigazionelaghi.it) operates the lake's fleet of ferries.

Verona

POP 260,000

Wander Verona's atmospheric streets and you'll understand why Shakespeare set *Romeo and Juliet* here – this is one of Italy's most beautiful and romantic cities. Known as *piccola Roma* (little Rome) for its importance in ancient times, its heyday came in the 13th and 14th centuries when it was ruled by the Della Scala (aka Scaligeri) family, who built *palazzi* and bridges, sponsored Giotto, Dante and Petrarch, oppressed their subjects and feuded with everyone else.

⊙ Sights

Roman Arena   RUIN

(☑045 800 32 04; www.arena.it; Piazza Brà; adult/reduced €10/7.50, incl Museo Maffeiano €11/8, or with VeronaCard €1, first Sun of month Oct-May; ☺1.30-7.30pm Mon, 8.30am-7.30pm Tue-Sun) Verona's Roman amphitheatre, built of pinktinged marble in the 1st century AD, survived a 12th-century earthquake to become the city's legendary open-air opera house, with seating for 30,000 people. You can visit the arena year-round, though it's at its best during the summer **opera festival**.

Casa di Giulietta   MUSEUM

(Juliet's House; ☑045 803 43 03; Via Cappello 23; adult/reduced €6/4.50; ☺1.30-7.30pm Mon, 8.30am-7.30pm Tue-Sun) Never mind that Romeo and Juliet were completely fictional characters, and that there's hardly room for two on the narrow stone balcony: romantics flock to this 14th-century house to add their lovelorn pleas to the graffiti on the courtyard gateway.

WORTH A TRIP

PADUA

Were it just for Padua's medieval centre and lively university atmosphere, the city would be a rewarding day trip from Venice. But what makes a visit so special is the **Cappella degli Scrovegni** (Scrovegni Chapel; ☑ 049 201 00 20; www.cappelladegliscrovegni.it; Piazza Eremitani 8; adult/reduced €13/6, night ticket €8/6, or with PadovaCard €1; ⊙ 9am-7pm, also 7-10pm various periods through year), home to a remarkable cycle of Giotto frescoes. Considered one of the defining masterpieces of early Renaissance art, this extraordinary work consists of 38 colourful panels, painted between 1303 and 1305, depicting episodes from the life of Christ and the Virgin Mary. Note that visits to the chapel must be booked in advance.

For information about the town's other sights, there are tourist offices at the **train station** (☑ 049 201 00 80; Piazza di Stazione; ⊙ 9am-7pm Mon-Sat, 10am-4pm Sun) and **Galleria Pedrocchi** (☑ 049 201 00 80; www.turismopadova.it; Vicolo Pedrocchi; ⊙ 9am-7pm Mon-Sat).

To fuel your wanderings, join the university crowd for a cheerful, no-nonsense lunch at **L'Anfora** (☑ 049 65 66 29; Via dei Soncin 13; meals €25-30; ⊙ noon-3pm & 7-11pm Mon-Sat). Trains leave for Padova from Venice (€4.05, 50 minutes) every 20 minutes or so.

Piazza delle Erbe SQUARE

Originally a Roman forum, Piazza delle Erbe is ringed with buzzing cafes and some of Verona's most sumptuous buildings, including the elegantly baroque **Palazzo Maffei**, which now houses several shops at its northern end.

Just off the piazza, the monumental arch known as the **Arco della Costa** is hung with a whale's rib. Legend holds that the rib will fall on the first just person to walk beneath it. So far, it remains intact, despite visits by popes and kings.

Piazza dei Signori SQUARE

Verona's beautiful open-air salon is ringed by a series of elegant Renaissance *palazzi*. Chief among these are the **Palazzo degli Scaligeri** (aka Palazzo Podestà), the 14th-century residence of Cangrande I Della Scala; the arched **Loggia del Consiglio**, built in the 15th century as the city council chambers; and the brick-and-tufa stone **Palazzo della Ragione**.

In the middle of the piazza is a statue of **Dante**, who was given refuge in Verona after he was exiled from Florence in 1302.

🛏 Sleeping & Eating

★ **Corte delle Pigne** B&B €€

(☑ 333 7584141; www.cortedellepigne.it; Via Pigna 6a; s €60-90, d €90-130, tr & q €110-150; P ❄ 🛜) In the heart of the historic centre, this three-room B&B is set around a quiet internal courtyard. It offers tasteful rooms and plenty of personal touches: a communal sweet

jar, luxury toiletries, and even a Jacuzzi for one lucky couple.

Hotel Aurora HOTEL €€

(☑ 045 59 47 17; www.hotelaurora.biz; Piazzetta XIV Novembre 2; d €100-250, tr €130-280; ❄ 🛜) This friendly three-star hotel is right in the thick of it, overlooking Piazza delle Erbe. Its light-filled rooms, some of which have piazza views, offer a mix of modern and classic decor. Breakfast can be enjoyed on the the sunny open-air terrace.

Hostaria La Vecchia Fontanina TRATTORIA €

(☑ 045 59 11 59; www.ristorantevecchiafontanina. com; Piazzetta Chiavica 5; meals €25; ⊙ noon-2.30pm & 7-10.30pm Mon-Sat) With tables on a pint-sized piazza, cosy indoor rooms and excellent food, this historic eatery stands out from the crowd. The menu features typical Veronese dishes alongside a number of more unusual creations, such as *bigoli con ortica e ricotta affumicata* (thick spaghetti with nettles and smoked ricotta) and several heavenly desserts.

Al Pompiere TRATTORIA €€

(☑ 045 803 05 37; www.alpompiere.com; Vicolo Regina d'Ungheria 5; meals €45; ⊙ 12.40-2pm & 7.40-10.30pm Mon-Sat) The *pompiere* (firefighter's hat) is still on the wall, but the focal point at this local hot spot is the vast cheese selection and famed house-cured *salumi* (cured meats) platter. Make a meal of the starters with wine by the glass, or graduate to plates of risotto and oven-cooked pork knuckle. Reserve ahead.

☆ Entertainment

Performances during the summer opera festival are held at the **Arena** (📞045 800 51 51; www.arena.it; box office Via Dietro Anfiteatro 6b; opera tickets €12-208; ⊘ box office 9am-noon Mon-Sat & 3.15-5.45pm Mon-Fri, longer hours during opera festival).

ℹ️ Information

Tourist Office (📞045 806 86 80; www.tourism.verona.it; Via degli Alpini 9; ⊘9am-7pm Mon-Sat, 10am-4pm Sun) Just off Piazza Brà. Knowledgeable and helpful, with an accommodation booking desk open from 10am to 6pm Monday to Saturday.

ℹ️ Getting There & Around

An Aerobus (€6, 20 minutes, every 20 minutes from 5.15am to 11.35pm) links **Verona Villafranca Airport** (📞045 809 56 66; www.aeroportoverona.it), 12km outside town, with the train station. From there, buses 11, 12, 13 and 510 (90, 92, 93, 98 evenings and Sundays) run to Piazza Brà.

Trains connect with Milan (€12 to €17, one hour 20 minutes to two hours, up to three hourly), Venice (€8.50 to €18.50, 50 minutes to 2¼ hours, twice hourly) and Bologna (€10 to €18.50, 50 minutes to 1½ hours, 20 daily).

Venice

POP 264,500

Venice (Venezia) is a hauntingly beautiful city. At every turn you're assailed by unforgettable images: tiny bridges arching over limpid canals; chintzy gondolas sliding past working barges; towers and distant domes silhouetted against the watery horizon. Its celebrated sights are legion, and its labyrinthine alleyways exude a unique, almost eerie atmosphere, redolent of cloaked passions and dark secrets. Parts of the Cannaregio, Dorsoduro and Castello *sestieri* (districts) rarely see many tourists, and you can lose yourself for hours in the lanes between the Accademia and train station.

Many of the city's treasures date to its time as a powerful medieval republic known as La Serenissima.

◉ Sights

◉ San Marco

★**Basilica di San Marco**   BASILICA
(St Mark's Basilica; Map p452; 📞041 270 83 11; www.basilicasanmarco.it; Piazza San Marco; ⊘9.45am-5pm Mon-Sat, 2-5pm Sun Apr-Oct, to 4pm Sun Nov-Mar; ⊛San Marco) **FREE** With its tapering spires, Byzantine domes, luminous mosaics and lavish marblework, Venice's signature church is an unforgettable sight. It was originally built to house St Mark's corpse, but the first chapel burnt down in 932 and a new basilica was constructed over it in 1094. For the next 500 years it was a work in progress as successive doges added mosaics and embellishments looted from the east.

Of the many jewels inside, look out for the **Pala d'Oro** (Map p452; admission €2; ⊘9.45am-5pm Mon-Sat, 2-5pm Sun Apr-Oct, to 4pm Nov-Mar; ⊛San Marco), a stunning gold altarpiece.

Piazza San Marco   PIAZZA
(Map p452; ⊛San Marco) This grand showpiece square beautifully encapsulates the splendour of Venice's past and its tourist-fuelled present. Flanked by the arcaded **Procuratie Vecchie** and **Procuratie Nuove**, it's filled for much of the day with tourists, pigeons and tour guides. To get a bird's-eye view, the Basilica di San Marco's free-standing 99m **campanile** (Bell Tower; Map p452; www.

basilicasanmarco.it; Piazza San Marco; admission €8; ⊙9am-9pm summer, to 7pm spring & autumn, 9.30am-3.45pm winter; ⚑ San Marco) commands stunning 360-degree panoramas.

★**Palazzo Ducale** MUSEUM
(Ducal Palace; Map p452; ✆041 271 59 11; www. palazzoducale.visitmuve.it; Piazzetta San Marco 52; adult/reduced €17/10; ⊙8.30am-7pm Apr-Oct, to 5.30pm Nov-Mar; ⚑ San Zaccaria) This grand Gothic palace was the Doge's official residence from the 9th century, and seat of the Venetian Republic's government (and prisons) for nearly seven centuries. The Doge's Apartments are on the 1st floor, but it's the lavishly decorated 2nd-floor chambers that are the real highlight. These culminate in the echoing **Sala del Maggior Consiglio** (Grand Council Hall), home to the Doge's throne and a 22m-by-7m *Paradise* painting by Tintoretto's son Domenico.

★**Ponte dei Sospiri** BRIDGE
(Map p452) One of Venice's most photographed sights, the Bridge of Sighs connects Palazzo Ducale to the 16th-century Priggione Nove (New Prisons). It's named after the sighs that condemned prisoners – including Giacomo Casanova – emitted as they were led down to the cells.

⊙ Dorsoduro

★**Gallerie dell'Accademia** GALLERY
(Map p452; ✆041 520 03 45; www.gallerieaccademia. org; Campo della Carità 1050; adult/reduced €11/8, first Sun of the month free; ⊙8.15am-2pm Mon, to 7.15pm Tue-Sun; ⚑ Accademia) Venice's historic gallery traces the development of Venetian art from the 14th to 18th centuries with works by Bellini, Titian, Tintoretto, Veronese and Canaletto, among others. Housing it, the former Santa Maria della Carità convent

ITALY VENICE

Greater Venice

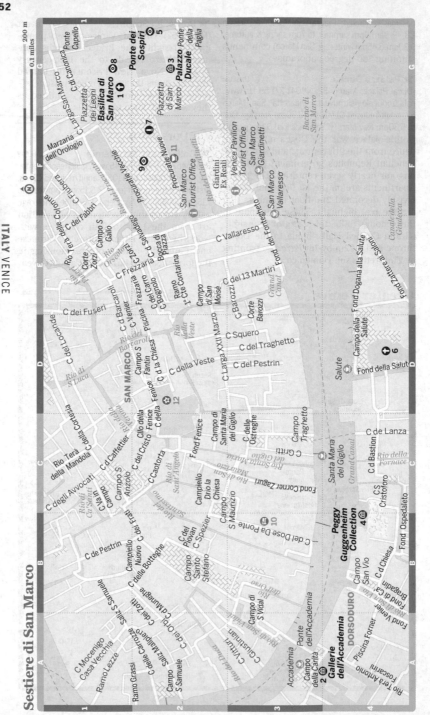

ITALY VENICE

Sestiere di San Marco

200 m
0.1 miles

Ponte dei Sospiri

Basilica di San Marco ❶✚

Palazzo Ducale ❸🏛

❽◉

❺

❷

Marzaria dell'Orologio

Piazzetta dei Leoni

C di Canonica

Larga San Marco

Ponte Capello

Piazzetta di San Marco

❼❶

❾◉ ❶❶

Procuratie Nuove

San Marco Tourist Office

Procuratie Vecchie

Bacino di San Marco

Giardini Ex Reali

Venice Pavilion Tourist Office

San Marco Giardinetti

San Marco Vallaresso

Rio dei Giardinetti

Rio del Fonteghetto

C Vallaresso

Fond del Fonteghetto

C dei 13 Martiri

Grand Canal

C del Corte Contarina

Campo di San Moisè

C Barozzi

Corte Barozzi

C Squero

C del Traghetto

C del Pestrin

C Larga XXII Marzo

Fond Zattere ai Saloni

Canale della Giudecca

Fond Dogana alla Salute

Campo della Salute

Salute

❻✚

Fond della Salute

C de Lanza

C d Bastion

Rio della Fornace

Santa Maria del Giglio

Grand Canal

Campo Traghetto

Campo di Santa Maria del Giglio

C delle Ostreghe

Fond Corner Zaguri

Fond Fenice

CS Cristoforo

Fond Ospedaleto

Peggy Guggenheim Collection

❹🏛

Campo San Vio

C d Chiesa

Fond di Ca' Bragadin

DORSODURO

Fond Venier

Rio di San Maurizio

❶❷✦

SAN MARCO

Campo S Fantin

C della Fenice

Cllo della Fenice

C del Cristo

C della Veste

C dei Fuseri

C dei Fabbri

C Frezzaria

C del Carro

C del Bognolo

Ramo 1ª Cte Contarina

Bocca di Piazza

Campo S Gallo

Rio Orseolo

Corte Zorzi

Rio Terà delle Colonne

C Tera 2 Aprile

C del Locande

Rio di S Luca

Rio Tera della Mandola

C della Cortesia

C degli Avvocati

Campo S Luca

C Caotorta

C del Cristo

C de Caffettier

C del Forno

C de la Chiesa

Rio dei Barcaroli

Rio della Verona

Campo S Angelo

Rio di Sant'Angelo

Campiello Drio la Chiesa

Campo S Maurizio

❶⓪🏠

C del Dose Da Ponte

C Barcaroli

C Vernier

C Frezzaria

Piscina Frezzaria

Rio della Veste

C d Barcaroli

C degli Avvocati

Campo S Anzolo

Rio di Ca' Garzoni

C del Spezier

Campo Santo Stefano

C dell Botteghe

Campiello Nuovo

C del Pestrin

C de Pestrin

C del Piovan

Campiello S Stefano

Rio del Orso

Campo S Samuele

C Mocenigo Casa Vecchia

Ramo Lezze

Ramo Grassi

C del Zotti

Salز S Samuele

Salz Malipiero

C delle Carozze

Salز d'Muneghe

C del Orbi

C Giustinian

C Vittori

Piscina Forner

Rio Terà Foscarini

Rio Terà A Foscarini

Accademia

Campo della Carità

Gallerie dell'Accademia

❷🏛

Ponte dell'Accademia

Campo S Vidal

Rio di San Vidal

Fond di Ca' Bragadin

Sestiere di San Marco

complex maintained its serene composure for centuries until Napoleon installed his haul of Venetian art trophies here in 1807. Since then there's been nonstop visual drama inside its walls.

★ **Peggy Guggenheim Collection**   MUSEUM
(Map p452; ☑041 240 54 11; www.guggenheim-venice.it; Palazzo Venier dei Leoni 704; adult/reduced €15/9; ⊙10am-6pm Wed-Mon; ⛴Accademia) After losing her father on the *Titanic,* heiress Peggy Guggenheim became one of the great collectors of the 20th century. Her palatial canalside home, Palazzo Venier dei Leoni, showcases her stockpile of surrealist, futurist and abstract expressionist art with works by up to 200 artists, including her ex-husband Max Ernst, Jackson Pollock (among her many rumoured lovers), Picasso and Salvador Dalí.

Basilica di Santa Maria della Salute   BASILICA
(La Salute; Map p452; ☑041 241 10 18; www.seminariovenezia.it; Campo della Salute 1b; admission free, sacristy adult/reduced €3/1.50; ⊙9am-noon & 3-5.30pm; ⛴Salute) Guarding the entrance to the Grand Canal, this 17th-century domed church was commissioned by Venice's plague survivors as thanks for salvation. Baldassare Longhena's uplifting design is an engineering feat that defies simple logic, and in fact the church is said to have mystical curative properties. Titian

eluded the plague until age 94, leaving a legacy of masterpieces in the Salute's sacristy.

◎ San Polo & Santa Croce

I Frari   CHURCH
(Basilica di Santa Maria Gloriosa dei Frari; Campo dei Frari, San Polo 3072; adult/reduced €3/1.50; ⊙9am-6pm Mon-Sat, 1-6pm Sun; ⛴San Tomà) This soaring Italian-brick Gothic church features marquetry choir stalls, Canova's pyramid mausoleum, Bellini's achingly sweet *Madonna with Child* triptych in the sacristy and Longhena's creepy Doge Pesaro funereal monument – yet visitors are inevitably drawn to the small altarpiece. This is Titian's 1518 *Assumption,* in which a radiant red-cloaked Madonna reaches heavenward, steps onto a cloud and escapes this mortal coil. Titian himself died in 1576 and is buried here near his celebrated masterpiece.

◎ Giudecca

Chiesa del Santissimo Redentore   CHURCH
(Church of the Redeemer; Campo del SS Redentore 194; adult/reduced €3/1.50, or Chorus Pass; ⊙10am-5pm Mon-Sat; ⛴Redentore) Built to celebrate the city's deliverance from the Black Death, Palladio's *Il Redentore* was completed under Antonio da Ponte (of Rialto bridge fame) in 1592. Inside there are works by Tintoretto, Veronese and Vivarini, but the most striking is Paolo Piazza's 1619 *Gratitude of Venice for Liberation from the Plague.*

◎ The Islands

Murano   ISLAND
(⛴4.1, 4.2) Murano has been the home of Venetian glass making since the 13th century. Tour a factory for a behind-the-scenes

---

ⓘ NAVIGATING VENICE

Venice is not an easy place to navigate and even with a map you're bound to get lost. The main area of interest lies between Santa Lucia train station (signposted as the *ferrovia*) and Piazza San Marco (St Mark's Sq). The path between the two – Venice's main drag – is a good 40- to 50-minute walk.

It also helps to know that the city is divided into six *sestieri* (districts): Cannaregio, Castello, San Marco, Dorsoduro, San Polo and Santa Croce.

ITALY VENICE

ITALY VENICE

Sestiere di San Polo

N

0   200 m
0   0.1 miles

CASTELLO

SAN MARCO

SANTA CROCE

SAN POLO

Strada Nuova

RIALTO

Grand Canal

Rialto-Mercato

Ponte di Rialto

Rialto

Ca' d'Oro

Ca' d'Oro

San Silvestro

San Silvestro

Riva del Carbon

Rio di San Salvador

C Bembo

C Larga Mazzini

Salizz Pio X

Campo San Bartolomeo

Corte del Tentor

Campo San Tomà

Campo della Fava

C d Fava

Saliz San Lio

C de la Bissa

C dei Stagneri

Marzaria

Via 2 Aprile

C de la Malvasia

C de Carminati

C Scaletta

C d Tasca

Campo Santa Marina

C Pindemonte

Ponte d Panada

Campo Santa Marina

C Castelli

C Widman

C dei Bondì

C d Madonna

C Bondì

C d Posta

C del Traghetto

Rio Terà di Franceschi

Campiello della Cason

Salizz del Pistor

Rio Terà Bembo

C del Verde

C dell'Oca

C del Forno

Campo Santa Sofia

Campo dei SS Apostoli

Campo dei Santi Apostoli

Rio dei Santi Apostoli

C d Maca

Zen

Corte Leon Bianco

Campiello del Remer

Salizz San Canciano

Campo San Canciano

Campo Santa Maria Nova

Campo dei Miracoli

C del Fumo

Rio di S Giovanni Crisostomo

Rio dei Santi Apostoli

C Modena

C dell'Aseo

Rio di San Domenego dei Vedbadori

Campo San Giacometto

Rialto-Mercato

Campo Cesare Battisti

Ruga dei Oresi

Campo San Giovanni

Ruga Vecchia di S Giovanni

C dei Cinque

C Sturion

C d Paradiso

Campo S Silvestro

C Dolera

D Mezzo

C dei Morti Schiria

R dei Morti Schiria

C d Botteri

Fond del Vin

Grand Canal

Fond dell'Olio

Campo delle Beccarie

C delle Beccarie

C dell'Angelo

C del Boteri

C Raspi

Campo Sansoni

Campiello Sansoni

Ponte Raspi

C dei Bottari

Ruga Ravano

Ponte delle Tette

Campo Sant'Aponal

Campo Sant'Aponal

C del Perdon

C della Madona

C del Traghetto della Madonneta

C dei SC dei Cavalli

Rio dei Meloni

Rio dei Meloni

Rio del Meloni

C dei Miani

Campo San Cassian

Rio di San Cassian

C d Regina

C d Chiesa

Campo San Cassian

C d M orti

C della Rosa

C Corner

C del Ravano

C del Tozzi

Fond Rimpetto Mocenigo

Rio delle Torri

Rio delle Torri

Ponte Storte

Campo

Campiello Albrizzi

C Albrizzi

Campo Santa Maria Mater Dòmini

C Lunga

C Filosi

C del Cristo

C d Modena

C d Chiesa

Salizz di San Stae

Fond delle Grue

Saliz Cammnati

C del Forno

Rio de Ca' Pesaro

Rio della Pescaria

Rio di San Stae

Campo

C Pezzana

C del Scaleter

C del Scaleter

Campo San Polo

Saliz S Polo

Rio di San Polo

Rio di San Polo

C Corner

C Larga

C Cornal

C d Saoneri

C Noto

C Rio Terà

Rio Terà

C d Albanesi

Campiello Sant'Agostin

Campo Sant'Agostin

C del Tentor

C Dona

C della Vida

Fond Contarini

Zen

Rio dei Frari

C del Meio

C Zambelli

C Colombo

C Larga

C del Tentor

Rio Terà dell'Isola

C dell'Isola

SANTA CROCE

8

4

5

10

11

9

6

1

7

Sestiere di San Polo

look at production or visit the **Museo del Vetro** (Glass Museum; ☎ 041 527 47 18; www. museovetro.visitmuve.it; Fondamenta Giustinian 8; adult/reduced €10/7.50; ☉10am-6pm Apr-Oct, to 5pm Nov-Mar; 🚤Museo) near the Museo *vaporetto* (water bus) stop. Note that at the time of writing the museum was undergoing a major overhaul.

Burano   ISLAND
(🚤12) Burano, with its cheery pastel-coloured houses, is renowned for its hand-made lace. These days, however, much of the lace sold in local shops is imported.

Torcello   ISLAND
(🚤Torcello) Torcello, the republic's original island settlement, was largely abandoned due to malaria and now counts no more than 80 residents. Its mosaic-clad Byzantine cathedral, the **Basilica di Santa Maria Assunta** (☎041 73 01 19; Piazza Torcello; adult/reduced €5/4, incl museum €8/6, incl campanile €9; ☉10.30am-6pm Mar-Oct, to 5pm Nov-Feb; 🚤Torcello), is Venice's oldest.

Lido di Venezia   ISLAND
(🚤1, 2, 5.1, 5.2, 6, 8, 10, 14, N) The main draw here is the beach, but the water can be polluted and the public areas are often unkempt. Some of the beaches at the southern end of the island, such as those at Alberoni, are an exception. If you want to stay closer to the *vaporetto* stops, you'll pay about €10 to hire a chair and umbrella in the more easily accessible and cleaner areas of the beach.

🏊 Activities

Official **gondola** rates start at €80 (8am to 7pm) or €100 (7pm to 8am). Prices are per gondola for 40 minutes; maximum six people. Additional time is charged in 20-minute increments (day/night €40/50).

🎭 Festivals & Events

Carnevale   CARNIVAL
(www.carnevale.venezia.it) Masquerade madness stretches over two weeks in February before Lent. Tickets to masked balls start at €140, but there's a free-flowing wine fountain to commence Carnevale, public costume parties in every *campo* (square) and a Grand Canal flotilla marking the end of festivities.

**Palio delle Quattro
Antiche Repubbliche Marinare**   CULTURAL
(Regatta of the Four Ancient Maritime Republics) The four historical maritime rivals – Pisa, Venice, Amalfi and Genoa – take turns to host this historic regatta in early June.

Venice Biennale   ART
(www.labiennale.org) This major exhibition of international visual arts is held every odd-numbered year from June to November.

Festa del Redentore   RELIGIOUS
(Feast of the Redeemer; www.turismovenezia.it) Walk on water across the Giudecca Canal to Il Redentore via a wobbly pontoon bridge on the third Saturday and Sunday in July, then watch the fireworks from the Zattere.

**Venice International
Film Festival**   FILM
(Mostra del Cinema di Venezia; www.labiennale. org/en/cinema) The only thing hotter than a Lido beach in August is the film festival's star-studded red carpet, usually rolled out from the last weekend in August through the first week of September.

Regata Storica   CULTURAL
(www.regatastoricavenezia.it) Sixteenth-century costumes, eight-oared gondolas and ceremonial barques feature in this historical procession (usually held in September), which reenacts the arrival of the Queen of Cyprus and precedes gondola races.

🛏 Sleeping

🏠 San Marco

★**Novecento**   BOUTIQUE HOTEL €€€
(Map p452; ☎041 241 37 65; www.novecento. biz; Calle del Dose 2683/84; d €160-340; ✴🕸; 🚤Santa Maria del Giglio) Sporting a boho-chic

look, the Novocento is a real charmer. Its nine individually designed rooms ooze style with Turkish kilim pillows, Fortuny draperies and 19th-century carved bedsteads. Outside, its garden is a lovely spot to linger over breakfast.

Dorsoduro

Hotel La Calcina   HOTEL €€€
(☑ 041 520 64 66; www.lacalcina.com; Fondamenta Zattere ai Gesuati 780; s €100-190, d €170-370; ❄ ⃰; ☑ Zattere) A historic waterfront landmark, this classy three-star hotel boasts a panoramic rooftop terrace, an elegant canalside restaurant, and airy, parquet-floored rooms, several facing the Giudecca Canal and Redentore church. Book ahead for rooms with views, especially No 2, where John Ruskin stayed while he wrote his classic 1876 *The Stones of Venice.*

San Polo & Santa Croce

L'Imbarcadero   HOSTEL €
(☑ 392 341 08 61; www.hostelvenice.net; cnr Imbarcadero Riva de Biasio & Calle Zen, Santa Croce; dm €18-27; ⃰; ☑ Riva de Biasio) A five-minute walk from the train station, this friendly hostel in Santa Croce offers spacious mixed and female-only dorms with single beds and the occasional Grand Canal view.

★ Ca' Angeli   BOUTIQUE HOTEL €€
(Map p454; ☑ 041 523 24 80; www.caangeli.it; Calle del Traghetto de la Madoneta 1434, San Polo; d €95-225, ste from €200; ❄ ⃰; ☑ San Silvestro) Murano-glass chandeliers, polished parquet floors and grandstand canal views await at this refined retreat. Guestrooms are a picture, with beamed ceilings, antique carpets and big bathrooms, while the dining room, where hearty organic breakfasts are served, looks out onto the Grand Canal.

Pensione Guerrato   PENSION €€
(Map p454; ☑ 041 528 59 27; www.pension eguerrato.it; Calle Drio la Scimia 240a, San Polo; d/tr/q €145/165/185; ❄ ⃰; ☑ Rialto Mercato)

> ### ⓘ TOILETS IN VENICE
> You'll find public toilets at the train station, Piazzale Roma, Accademia bridge, Campo San Bartolomeo and behind Piazza San Marco. To use them you'll need €1.50 in change (€1 at the station).

In a 1227 tower that was once a hostel for knights headed to the Third Crusade, smart guestrooms haven't lost their sense of history – some have frescoes or glimpses of the Grand Canal. A prime Rialto market location and helpful owners add to the package. Wi-fi in lobby. No lift.

★ Oltre il Giardino   BOUTIQUE HOTEL €€€
(Map p454; ☑ 041 275 00 15; www.oltreilgiardino-venezia.com; Fondamenta Contarini, San Polo 2542; d €180-250, ste €200-500; ❄ ⃰; ☑ San Tomà) Live the dream in this garden villa, the 1920s home of Alma Mahler, the composer's widow. Hidden behind a lush walled garden, its six high-ceilinged guestrooms brim with historic charm and modern comfort, marrying precious antiques with discreet mod cons and pale ivory backdrops.

Cannaregio

Hotel Bernardi   HOTEL €
(Map p454; ☑ 041 522 72 57; www.hotelbernardi.com; SS Apostoli Calle dell'Oca 4366; s €48-110, d €57-90, f €75-140, without bathroom s €25-32, d €45-62; ❄ ⃰) Hospitable owners, a convenient location just off the main thoroughfare and keen prices mean that the Bernardi is always heavily booked. Some of the best rooms – think timber-beamed ceilings, Murano chandeliers and gilt furniture – are in the annexe round the corner.

Giardino dei Melograni   GUESTHOUSE €€
(☑ 041 822 61 31; www.pardesrimonim.net; Ghetto Nuovo, Cannaregio 2873/c; s €70-100, d €80-180, tr €110-210, q €140-240; ❄ ⃰; ☑ Ferrovia Santa Lucia) Run by Venice's Jewish community, to which all proceeds go, the 'Garden of Pomegranates' is a sparkling kosher residence. It's located on the charming Campo Ghetto Nuovo just a short walk from the train station, and offers 14 bright, modern rooms.

✗ Eating

Venetian specialities include *risi e bisi* (pea soup thickened with rice) and *sarde in saor* (fried sardines marinated in vinegar and onions). Also look out for *cicheti,* traditional Venetian bar snacks.

✗ Dorsoduro

Grom   GELATERIA €
(☑ 041 099 17 51; www.grom.it; Campo San Barnaba 2461; gelati €2.50-5.50; ⊙ 10.30am-11pm Sun-

Thu, 10am-12.30am Fri & Sat, shorter hours winter; ⊠ Ca' Rezzonico) One of several Grom branches across town. The consistently good gelato, made with prime, seasonal ingredients (lemons from the Amalfi Coast, pistachios from Sicily, hazelnuts from Piedmont), makes for a perfect pick-me-up.

Ristorante La Bitta RISTORANTE €€
(⊘ 041 523 05 31; Calle Lunga San Barnaba 2753a; meals €35-40; ⊘ 6.45-10.45pm Mon-Sat; ⊠ Ca' Rezzonico) A cosy, woody restaurant near lively Campo Santa Margherita. The daily menu arrives on an artist's easel, and the hearty rustic fare looks like a still life and tastes like a carnivore's dream: steak comes snugly wrapped in bacon, veal is braised with *chiodini* mushrooms. Reservations essential. Cash only.

San Polo & Santa Croce

★**All'Arco** VENETIAN €
(Map p454; ⊘ 041 520 56 66; Calle dell'Ochialer 436, San Polo; cicheti from €1.50; ⊘ 8am-8pm Wed-Fri, to 3pm Mon, Tue & Sat; ⊠ Rialto-Mercato) Search out this authentic neighbourhood *osteria* (casual tavern or eatery presided over by a host) for some of the best *cicheti* in town. Armed with ingredients from the nearby Rialto market, father-son team Francesco and Matteo serve miniature masterpieces such as poached white asparagus with seasoned pancetta, and *otrega* (butterfish) *crudo* (raw) with mint-and-olive-oil marinade.

Osteria La Zucca MODERN ITALIAN €€
(Map p454; ⊘ 041 524 15 70; www.lazucca.it; Calle del Tentor 1762, Santa Croce; meals €35; ⊘ 12.30-2.30pm & 7-10.30pm Mon-Sat; ⊠ San Stae) With its menu of seasonal vegetarian creations and classic meat dishes, this cosy wood-panelled restaurant consistently hits the mark. Herbs and spices are used to great effect in dishes such as cinnamon-tinged pumpkin flan and lamb with dill and *pecorino* (sheep's milk cheese). The small interior can get toasty, so reserve canalside seats in summer.

Birraria La Corte RISTORANTE, PIZZA €€
(Map p454; ⊘ 041 275 05 70; Campo San Polo 2168, San Polo; pizzas €7-14, meals €35; ⊘ noon-3pm & 6-10.30pm; ☎; ⊠ San Tomà) This one-time bull stable became a brewery in the 19th century to keep Venice's Austrian occupiers occupied, and beer and beef remain reliable bets.

There's also pizza and much coveted piazza side seating.

Vecio Fritolin VENETIAN, SEAFOOD €€€
(Map p454; ⊘ 041 522 28 81; www.veciofritolin. it; Calle della Regina 2262, Santa Croce; traditional 3-course set menu €38, meals €45; ⊘ 7.30-10.30pm Tue, noon-2.30pm & 7-10.30pm Wed-Sun; ⊠ San Stae) ⊘ Traditionally, a *fritolin* was an eatery where diners sat at a communal table and tucked into fried fish. This is the modern equivalent, albeit smarter and more sophisticated. The menu includes meat and vegetable dishes, but the star act is the top-quality seafood, sourced daily from the nearby Rialto market.

Cannaregio

Dalla Marisa VENETIAN €€
(⊘ 041 72 02 11; Fondamenta di San Giobbe 652b; set menus lunch/dinner €15/35; ⊘ noon-3pm daily & 7-11pm Tue & Thu-Sat; ⊠ Crea) At this Cannaregio institution, you'll be seated where there's room and have whatever Marisa's cooking, though you will be informed whether the fixed-price menu is meat- or fish-based when you book. Venetian regulars confess Marisa's *fegato alla veneziana* (Venetian calf's liver) is better than their grandmothers'. No credit cards.

Trattoria da Bepi
Già "54" VENETIAN €€
(Map p454; ⊘ 041 528 50 31; www.dabepi.it; Campo SS. Apostoli 4550; meals €30-40; ⊘ noon-2.30pm & 7-10pm Fri-Wed; ⊠ Ca' d'Oro) One of the better eateries on the touristy main drag (actually it's just a few metres off it near Santi Apostoli), this is a classic old-school trattoria with a few outside tables and a cheerfully cluttered wood-lined interior. The food is traditional Venetian with an emphasis on seafood.

★**Anice Stellato** VENETIAN €€€
(⊘ 041 72 07 44; www.osterianicestellato.com; Fondamenta della Sensa 3272; bar snacks €13.50, meals €45-50; ⊘ 10.30am-3.30pm & 6.30pm-midnight Wed-Sun; ⊠ Madonna dell'Orto) ⊘ Tin lamps, unadorned rustic tables and a small wooden bar set the scene for quality seafood at this excellent canalside *bacaro* (traditional Venetian *osteria*). You can munch on barside *cicheti* or go for the full à la carte menu and swoon over juicy scampi in *saor* (vinegar marinade) and grilled tuna.

ITALY VENICE

⚲ Drinking & Nightlife

Cantina Do Spade
BAR

(Map p454; ☑041 521 05 83; www.cantinadospade.com; Calle delle Do Spade 860, San Polo; ⊙10am-3pm & 6-10pm; 🖘; 🚊Rialto) Since 1488 this cosy, brick-clad bar has kept Venice in good spirits, and the young, laid-back management extends a warm welcome to *spritz*-sipping Venetian regulars and visiting connoisseurs drinking double-malt beer and bargain Venetian cab franc. Come early for market-fresh *fritture* (batter-fried seafood).

Al Mercà
WINE BAR

(Map p454; Campo Cesare Battisti 213, San Polo; ⊙10am-2.30pm & 6-9pm Mon-Thu, to 9.30pm Fri & Sat; 🚊Rialto) Discerning drinkers throng to this cupboard-sized counter on a Rialto market square to sip on top-notch *prosecco* (type of sparkling wine) and Denominazione di origine controllata (DOC; a type of trademark for a product from a specific region) wines by the glass (from €2). Arrive by 6.30pm for mini-*panini* (€1 to €2.50) and easy bar access, or mingle with crowds stretching to the Grand Canal docks.

Il Caffè Rosso
CAFE

(☑041 528 79 98; Campo Santa Margherita 2963, Dorsoduro; ⊙7am-1am Mon-Sat; 🖘; 🚊Ca' Rezzonico) Affectionately known as 'il rosso', this red-fronted cafe has been at the centre of the bar scene on Campo Santa Margherita since the late 1800s. It's at its best in the early evening, when locals snap up the sunny piazza seating to sip on inexpensive *spritzes* (a type of cocktail made with *prosecco*).

★El Rèfolo
BAR

(www.elrefolo.it; Via Garibaldi, Castello 1580; ⊙11.30am-1am) A popular hangout in the Castello district. Like many Venetian bars, the action is centred on the street outside, particularly around 7pm when locals drop by to chat over a glass of *prosecco* (€2.50) and snack on cured meats and cheese.

Caffè Florian
CAFE

(Map p136; ☑041 520 56 41; www.caffeflorian.com; Piazza San Marco 56/59; drinks €10-25; ⊙9am-midnight; 🚊San Marco) One of Venice's most famous cafes, Florian maintains rituals (if not prices) established c 1720: white-jacketed waiters serve cappuccino on silver trays, lovers canoodle in plush banquettes and the orchestra strikes up a tango as the sunset illuminates San Marco's mosaics.

☆ Entertainment

Upcoming events are listed in the *Shows & Events* guide (€1), available at tourist offices, and at www.veneziadavivere.com.

★Teatro La Fenice
OPERA

(Map p452; ☑041 78 65 11, theatre tours 041 78 66 75; www.teatrolafenice.it; Campo San Fantin 1965; theatre visits adult/reduced €9/6, concert/opera tickets from €15/45; ⊙tours 9.30am-6pm; 🚊Santa Maria del Giglio) La Fenice, one of Italy's top opera houses, hosts a rich program of opera, ballet and classical music. With advance booking you can tour the theatre, but the best way to see it is with the *loggionisti* (opera buffs in the cheap top-tier seats). Get tickets at the theatre, online or through **HelloVenezia** (☑041 24 24; Piazzale Roma; ⊙7am-8pm for transport tickets, 8.30am-6.30pm for events tickets; 🚊Piazzale Roma).

ℹ Information

Airport Tourist Office (☑041 529 87 11; www.turismovenezia.it; Marco Polo Airport, arrivals hall; ⊙8.30am-7.30pm)

Ospedale Civile (☑041 529 41 11; Campo SS Giovanni e Paolo 6777; 🚊Ospedale) Venice's main hospital; for emergency care and dental treatment.

Piazzale Roma Tourist Office (☑041 529 87 11; www.turismovenezia.it; Piazzale Roma, Ground fl, multistorey car park; ⊙8.30am-2.30pm; 🚊Santa Chiara)

Police Station (Santa Croce 500; 🚊Santa Chiara)

San Marco Tourist Office (Map p452; ☑041 529 87 11; www.turismovenezia.it; Piazza San Marco 71f; ⊙8.30am-7pm; 🚊San Marco)

Station Tourist Office (☑041 529 87 11; www.turismovenezia.it; Stazione di Santa Lucia; ⊙8.30am-7pm; 🚊Ferrovia Santa Lucia)

Venice Pavilion Tourist Office (Map p452; ☑041 529 87 11; www.turismovenezia.it; Ex Giardini Reali, San Marco 30124; ⊙8.30am-7pm; 🚊San Marco)

ℹ Getting There & Away

AIR

Most flights arrive at and depart from **Marco Polo Airport** (VCE; ☑flight information 041 260 92 60; www.veniceairport.it), 12km outside Venice. Ryanair flies to/from **Treviso Airport** (TSF; ☑0422 31 51 11; www.trevisoairport.it; Via Noalese 63), about 30km away.

BOAT

Venezia Lines (☑041 882 11 01; www.venezialines.com) operates high-speed boats to/from several ports in Croatia between mid-April and early October.

BUS

ACTV (☑ 041 24 24; www.actv.it) buses service surrounding areas. Get tickets and information at the **bus station** (Piazzale Roma).

TRAIN

Trains serve Venice's Stazione di Santa Lucia from Padua (€4.05 to €13, 50 minutes, every 10 minutes) and Verona (€7.50 to €18.50, 1¼ to 2¼ hours, half-hourly) as well as Bologna, Milan, Rome and Florence.

Direct international trains run to/from points in France, Germany, Austria and Switzerland.

ⓘ Getting Around

TO/FROM THE AIRPORT
Marco Polo Airport

Alilaguna (☑ 041 240 17 01; www.alilaguna. it) operates three boat lines (approximately half-hourly) to the city centre. Tickets cost €15 to Venice, €8 to Murano.

Orange To Piazza San Marco via Rialto and the Grand Canal.

Blue Stops include Murano, the Lido, San Marco and Giudecca.

Red To Murano, the Lido and San Marco.

An **ATVO** (☑ 0421 59 46 71; www.atvo.it) shuttle bus goes to/from Piazzale Roma (one way/return €6/11, 20 minutes, half-hourly), as does ACTV bus 5 (one way/return €6/11, 25 minutes, every 15 minutes).

Treviso Airport

ATVO buses run to/from Piazzale Roma (one way/return €10/18, 70 minutes, nine daily).

BOAT

The city's main mode of public transport is the *vaporetto* (water bus). Tickets, available from ACTV booths at major *vaporetti* stops and the HelloVenezia booth on Piazzale Roma, cost €7 for a single trip, €18 for 12 hours, €20 for 24 hours, €25 for 36 hours, €30 for two days, €35 for three days and €50 for seven days. Useful routes:

1 Piazzale Roma to the train station and down the Grand Canal to San Marco and the Lido.

2 San Zaccaria (near San Marco) to the Lido via Giudecca, Piazzale Roma, the train station and Rialto.

4.1 To/from Murano via Fondamente Nove, the train station, Piazzale Roma, Redentore and San Zaccaria.

To cross the Grand Canal where there's no nearby bridge, take a *traghetto gondola* (€2 per crossing).

Trieste

POP 204,800

Italy's last city before Slovenia, Trieste merits a quick stopover. There are few must-see sights, but its imposing seafront *palazzi* lend it an impressive grandeur and the historic centre buzzes with bars and cafes. Hanging over everything is a palpable Mittel-European air, a hangover of its time an an important Austro-Hungarian port.

⊙ Sights & Activities

Piazza dell'
Unità d'Italia   PIAZZA

Italy's largest sea-facing piazza is a triumph of Austro-Hungarian town planning and contemporary civil pride. Flanked by the city's grandest *palazzi* (including Palazzo del Municipio), Trieste's 19th-century city hall, this vast public space is a good place for a drink or a chat, or simply for a quiet moment staring out at ships on the horizon.

No 2 Tram   TOUR

(www.triestetrasporti.it; Piazza Oberdan; hourly/daily ticket €1.30/€4.30; ⊙ departures every 20min 7am-8pm) For wonderful views, jump on this vintage tram to Villa Opicina. For most of the 5km journey from Piazza Oberdan it's a regular tram, but a funicular section tackles the steep gradient as it heads up into the Carso. It's a short but significant trip – Villa Opicina was once almost entirely Slovenian-speaking and today retains a decidedly un-Italian feel.

🛏 Sleeping & Eating

★**L'Albero Nascosto**   BOUTIQUE HOTEL €€

(☑ 040 30 01 88; www.alberonascosto.it; Via Felice Venezian 18; s €85, d €125-145; ❋ 🖻) A delightful little hotel in the middle of the old town, Nascosto is a model of discreet style. Rooms are spacious and tastefully decked out with parquet floors, original artworks, books and a vintage piece or two; most also have a small kitchen corner. Breakfasts are simple but thoughtful, with local cheeses, top-quality preserves and Illy coffee on tap.

Buffet da Siora Rosa   BUFFET €

(☑ 040 30 14 60; Piazza Hortis 3; meals €25; ⊙ 8am-10pm Tue-Sat) Opened before WWII, the family-run Siora Rosa is one Trieste's traditional buffets (bar-restaurants). Sit outside or in the wonderfully retro interior and tuck into boiled pork, sauerkraut and other Germanic and Hungarian offerings, or opt for something fishly like *baccalà* (salted cod) with polenta.

❶ Information

Tourist Office (📞 040 347 83 12; www.turismofvg.it; Via dell'Orologio 1; ⏰ 9am-7pm Mon-Sat, to 1pm Sun)

❶ Getting There & Around

Trains run to Trieste from Venice (€13.25 to €19, two to 3¾ hours, 25 daily). From the train station, bus 30 heads down to Piazza dell'Unità d'Italia and the seafront.

National and international buses operate from the **bus station** (📞 040 42 50 20; www.autostazionetrieste.it; Via Fabio Severo 24). These include services to Croatia (Pula, Zagreb, Dubrovnik), Slovenia (Ljubljana) and further afield.

Bologna
POP 384,200

Bologna is one of Italy's great unsung destinations. Its medieval centre is an eye-catching ensemble of red-brick *palazzi,* Renaissance towers and 40km of arcaded porticoes, and there are enough sights to excite without exhausting. A university town since 1088 (Europe's oldest), it's also a prime foodie destination, home to the eponymous bolognese sauce *(ragù)* as well as tortellini, lasagne and *mortadella* (Bologna sausage).

◉ Sights

★ Basilica di San Petronio
CHURCH

(Piazza Maggiore; ⏰ 7.45am-2pm & 3-6.30pm) Bologna's hulking Gothic basilica is the world's fifth-largest church, measuring 132m by 66m by 47m. Work began on it in 1390, but it was never finished and still today its main facade remains incomplete. Inside, look out for the huge sundial that stretches 67.7m down the eastern aisle. Designed in 1656 by Gian Cassini and Domenico Guglielmi, this was instrumental in discovering the anomalies of the Julian calendar and led to the creation of the leap year.

Torre degli Asinelli
TOWER

(Piazza di Porta Ravegnana; admission €3; ⏰ 9am-6pm, to 5pm Oct-May) Bologna's two leaning towers are the city's main symbol. The taller of the two, the 97.6m-high Torre degli Asinelli is open to the public, though it's not advisable for the weak-kneed (there are 498 steps) or for superstitious students (local lore says if you climb it you'll never graduate). Built by the Asinelli family between 1109 and 1119, it today leans 1.3m off vertical.

Its shorter twin, the 48m-high **Torre Garisenda** is sensibly out of bounds given its drunken 3.2m tilt.

Quadrilatero
AREA

To the east of Piazza Maggiore, the grid of streets around Via Clavature (Street of Locksmiths) sits on what was once Roman Bologna. Known as the Quadrilatero, this compact district is a great place for a wander with its market stalls, cafes and lavishly stocked delis.

🛏 Sleeping & Eating

Albergo delle Drapperie
HOTEL €€

(📞 051 22 39 55; www.albergodrapperie.com; Via delle Drapperie 5; s €64-115, d €102-160, ste €130-180; ❋ 🛜) In the atmospheric Quadrilatero neighbourhood, the Drapperie is snugly ensconced in the upper floors of a large building. Buzz in at ground level and climb the stairs to discover 19 attractive rooms with wood-beamed ceilings, the occasional brick arch and colourful ceiling frescoes. Breakfast is €5 extra.

Hotel University Bologna
HOTEL €€

(📞 051 22 97 13; www.hoteluniversitybologna.com; Via Mentana 7; d €70-250; ❋ 🛜) Student digs never felt so good. This low-key hotel offers a hospitable welcome and decent three-star rooms in the heart of the university district.

Trattoria del Rosso
TRATTORIA €

(📞 051 23 67 30; www.trattoriadelrosso.com; Via A Righi 30; meals €20-25; ⏰ noon-midnight) The Rosso, said to be the city's oldest trattoria, is a great example of what they do so well in Bologna. A bustling, workaday eatery, it serves healthy portions of homestyle local fare at honest prices and without a frill in sight.

★ Osteria de' Poeti
RISTORANTE €€

(📞 051 23 61 66; www.osteriadepoeti.com; Via de' Poeti 1b; meals €35-40; ⏰ 12.30-2.30pm & 7.30pm-3am Tue-Fri, 7.30pm-3am Sat, 12.30-2.30pm Sun) In the wine cellar of a 14th-century *palazzo,* this historic eatery is one place to get to grips with Bologna's much-lauded cuisine. Take a table by the stone fireplace and order from the selection of traditional staples such as *tortelloni al doppio burro e salvia* (home-made ravioli with butter and sage).

ℹ Information

Tourist Office (☑ 051 23 96 60; www.bologna turismo.info; Piazza Maggiore 1e; ⊙ 9am-7pm Mon-Sat, 10am-5pm Sun) Also has an office at the airport.

ℹ Getting There & Around

AIR
European and domestic flights serve **Guglielmo Marconi Airport** (☑ 051 647 96 15; www.bologna-airport.it), 8km northwest of the city.

From the airport, an Aerobus shuttle (€6, 30 minutes, every 15 to 30 minutes) connects with the train station; buy tickets on board.

BUS
Buses 25 and 30 are among several that connect the train station with the centre.

TRAIN
Bologna is a major rail hub. From the station on Piazza delle Medaglie d'Oro, there are regular high-speed trains to Milan (€33 to €40, one to two hours), Venice (€30, 1½ hours), Florence (€24, 40 minutes) and Rome (€56, 2½ hours).

Ravenna

POP 158,800

A rewarding and worthwhile day trip from Bologna, Ravenna is famous for its early Christian mosaics. These Unesco-listed treasures have been impressing visitors since the 13th century, when Dante described them in his *Divine Comedy* (much of which was written here).

◉ Sights

Ravenna's mosaics are spread over five sites in the centre: the Basilica di San Vitale, the Mausoleo di Galla Placida, the Basilica di Sant'Appollinare Nuovo, the Museo Arcivescovile and the Battistero Neoniano. These are covered by a single ticket (€9.50, or €11.50 between March and June), available at any of the sites. The website www.ravenna mosaici.it gives further information.

On the northern edge of the *centro storico* (historic centre), the sombre exterior of the 6th-century **Basilica di San Vitale** (Via Fiandrini; ⊙ 9am-7pm summer, 9.30am-5pm winter) hides a dazzling interior with mosaics depicting Old Testament scenes. In the same complex, the small **Mausoleo di Galla Placidia** (Via Fiandrini; ⊙ 9am-7pm summer, 9.30am-5pm winter) contains the city's oldest mosaics.

Adjoining Ravenna's unremarkable cathedral, the **Museo Arcivescovile** (Piazza Arcivescovado; ⊙ 9am-7pm summer, 10am-5pm winter) boasts an exquisite 6th-century ivory throne, while next door in the **Battistero Neoniano** (Piazza del Duomo; ⊙ 9am-7pm summer, 10am-5pm winter), the baptism of Christ is represented in the domed roof mosaic. To the east, the **Basilica di Sant'Apollinare Nuovo** (Via di Roma; ⊙ 9am-7pm summer, 10am-5pm winter) boasts, among other

---

ITALIAN ART & ARCHITECTURE

Italy is littered with architectural and artistic reminders of its convoluted history. **Etruscan** tombs and **Greek** temples tell of glories long past, **Roman** amphitheatres testify to ancient bloodlust and architectural brilliance, and **Byzantine** mosaics reveal influences sweeping in from the East.

The **Renaissance** left an indelible mark, giving rise to some of Italy's greatest masterpieces: Filippo Brunelleschi's dome atop Florence's Duomo, Botticelli's *The Birth of Venus* and Michelangelo's Sistine Chapel frescoes. Contemporaries Leonardo da Vinci and Raphael further brightened the scene.

Caravaggio revolutionised the late-16th-century art world with his controversial and highly influential painting style. He worked in Rome and the south, where **baroque** art and architecture flourished in the 17th century.

In the late 18th and early 19th centuries, **neoclassicism** saw a return to sober classical lines. Its main Italian exponent was sculptor Antonio Canova.

In sharp contrast to backward-looking neoclassicism, early-20th-century **futurism** sought new ways to express the dynamism of the machine age, while Italian **rationalism** saw the development of a linear, muscular style of architecture.

Continuing in this modernist tradition are Italy's two contemporary **starchitects**: Renzo Piano, the visionary behind Rome's Auditorium, and Rome-born Massimiliano Fuksas.

things, a superb mosaic depicting a procession of martyrs headed towards Christ and his apostles.

Five kilometres southeast of the city, the apse mosaic of **Basilica di Sant'Apollinare in Classe** (Via Romea Sud; adult/reduced €5/2.50; ⊙8.30am-7.30pm Mon-Sat, 1-7.30pm Sun) is a must-see. Take bus 4 from Piazza Caduti per la Libertà.

✕ Eating

La Gardela   TRATTORIA €
(☑0544 21 71 47; Via Ponte Marino 3; meals €25; ⊙noon-2.30pm & 7-10pm Fri-Wed) Economical prices and formidable home cooking mean this bustling trattoria can be crowded, but in a pleasant, gregarious way. Professional waiters glide by with plates of Italian classics: think thin-crust pizzas, risottos, and pasta with *ragù*.

❶ Information

Tourist Office (☑0544 3 54 04; www.turismo. ravenna.it; Via Salara 8-12; ⊙8.30am-6pm Mon-Sat, 10am-6pm Sun)

❶ Getting There & Around

Regional trains run to/from Bologna (€7.10, 1½ hours, hourly) and destinations on the east coast.

TUSCANY & UMBRIA

Tuscany and its lesser-known neighbour, Umbria, are two of Italy's most beautiful regions. Tuscany's fabled landscape of rolling vine-covered hills dotted with cypress trees and stone villas has long been considered the embodiment of rural chic, while its historic cities and hilltop towns are home to a significant portfolio of the world's medieval and Renaissance art.

To the south, the predominantly rural region of Umbria, dubbed the 'green heart of Italy', harbours some of the country's best-preserved historic *borghi* (villages) and many important artistic, religious and architectural treasures.

Florence

POP 377,200

Visitors have rhapsodised about the beauty of Florence (Firenze) for centuries, and once here you'll appreciate why. This Renaissance time capsule is busy year-round, but even the inevitable crowds of tourists fail to diminish its lustre. A list of the city's famous sons reads like a Renaissance who's who – under 'M' alone you'll find Medici, Machiavelli and Michelangelo – and its treasure trove of galleries, museums and churches showcases a magnificent array of Renaissance art.

The city's golden age came under the Medici family between the 14th and 17th centuries. Later, it served as capital of the newly unified Italy from 1865 to 1870.

◉ Sights

◎ Piazza del Duomo & Around

★ Duomo   CATHEDRAL
(Cattedrale di Santa Maria del Fiore; www.opera duomo.firenze.it; Piazza del Duomo; ⊙10am-5pm Mon-Wed & Fri, to 4.30pm Thu, to 4.45pm Sat, 1.30-4.45pm Sun) FREE Florence's Duomo is the city's most iconic landmark. Capped by Filippo Brunelleschi's red-tiled **cupola** (Dome; Piazza del Duomo; incl cupola, baptistry, campanile, crypt & museum adult/reduced €10/ free; ⊙8.30am-6.20pm Mon-Fri, to 5pm Sat), it's a staggering construction and its breathtaking pink, white and green marble facade and graceful *campanile* (bell tower) dominate the medieval cityscape. Sienese architect Arnolfo di Cambio began work on it 1296, but construction took almost 150 years and it wasn't consecrated until 1436. In the echoing interior, look out for frescoes by Vasari and Zuccari and up to 44 stained-glass windows.

Campanile   BELL TOWER
(www.operaduomo.firenze.it; Piazza del Duomo; adult/reduced inc cathedral dome & baptistry €10/ free; ⊙8.30am-7.30pm) Begun in 1334 by Giotto, the Duomo's soaring bell tower rises nearly as high as the dome. Its elaborate Gothic facade, including 16 life-size statues, was worked on by a who's who of 14th-century artists, including Giotto, Andrea Pisano, Donatello and Luca Della Robbia. Climb its 414 steps for nearly the same superb views as those from Brunelleschi's dome, but without the snaking queues.

**Battistero di
San Giovanni**   LANDMARK
(Baptistry; Piazza di San Giovanni; adult/reduced €10/free incl cupola, campanile & museum; ⊙8.15-10.15am & 11.15am-7pm Mon-Sat, 8.30am-2pm Sun &

1st Sat of month) Across from the Duomo is the 11th-century Romanesque baptistry, an octagonal striped structure of white and green marble with three sets of doors conceived as panels on which to tell the story of humanity and the Redemption. Most celebrated of all are Lorenzo Ghiberti's gilded bronze doors at the eastern entrance, known as the *Porta del Paradiso* (Gate of Paradise). What you see today, though, are copies – the originals are in the Grande Museo del Duomo.

◉ Piazza della Signoria & Around

Piazza della Signoria   PIAZZA

The hub of local life since the 13th century, this animated piazza is where Florentines flock to meet friends and chat over early-evening *aperitivi* at historic cafes. Presiding over eveything is **Palazzo Vecchio**, Florence's city hall, and the 14th-century **Loggia dei Lanzi**, an open-air gallery showcasing Renaissance sculptures, including Giambologna's *Rape of the Sabine Women* (c 1583), Benvenuto Cellini's bronze *Perseus* (1554) and Agnolo Gaddi's *Seven Virtues* (1384–89).

★**Palazzo Vecchio**   MUSEUM

(☑055 276 82 24; www.musefirenze.it; Piazza della Signoria; museum adult/reduced €10/8, tower €10/8, museum & tower €14/12, archaeology tour €2; ☺museum 9am-midnight Mon-Wed & Fri-Sun, to 2pm Thu summer, 9am-7pm Mon-Wed & Fri-Sun, to 2pm Thu winter, tower 9am-9pm Fri-Wed, to 2pm Thu summer, 10am-5pm Fri-Wed, to 2pm Thu winter) This fortress palace, with its crenellations and 94m-high tower, was designed by Arnolfo di Cambio between 1298 and 1314 for the *signoria* (city government). From the top of the **Torre d'Arnolfo** (tower), you can revel in unforgettable rooftop views, while inside, Michelangelo's *Genio della Vittoria* (Genius of Victory) sculpture graces the **Salone dei Cinquecento**, a magnificent painted hall created for the city's 15th-century ruling Consiglio dei Cinquecento (Council of 500).

★**Galleria degli Uffizi**   GALLERY

(Uffizi Gallery; www.uffizi.firenze.it; Piazzale degli Uffizi 6; adult/reduced €8/4, incl temporary exhibition €12.50/6.25; ☺8.15am-6.50pm Tue-Sun) Home to the world's greatest collection of Italian Renaissance art, Florence's premier gallery occupies Palazzo degli Uffizi,

BEST OF THE UFFIZI

Cut to the quick of the gallery's collection and start by getting to grips with pre-Renaissance Tuscan art in **Room 2**, home to several shimmering alterpieces by Giotto et al. Then work your way on to **Room 8** and Piero della Francesca's iconic profile portrait of the Duke and Duchess of Urbino.

More familiar images await in the **Sala di Botticelli**, including the master's great Renaissance masterpiece, *La nascita di Venere* (The Birth of Venus). Continue on to **Room 15** for a couple of works by Leonardo da Vinci and then on to **Room 35** for Michelangelo's *Doni Tondi*.

a handsome palace built between 1560 and 1580 to house government offices. The collection, which was bequeathed to the city by the Medici family in 1743 on condition that it never leave Florence, contains some of Italy's best-known paintings, including Piero della Francesco's profile portaits of the Duke and Duchess of Urbino and Sandro Botticelli's *La nascita di Venere* (The Birth of Venus).

Ponte Vecchio   BRIDGE

Dating to 1345, Ponte Vecchio was the only Florentine bridge to survive destruction at the hands of retreating German forces in 1944. Above the jewellers' shops on the eastern side, the **Corridoio Vasariano** is a 16th-century passageway between the Uffizi and Palazzo Pitti that runs around, rather than through, the medieval **Torre dei Mannelli** at the bridge's southern end.

★**Museo del Bargello**   MUSEUM

(www.polomuseale.firenze.it; Via del Proconsolo 4; adult/reduced €4/2; ☺8.15am-4.50pm summer, to 1.50pm winter, closed 1st, 3rd & 5th Sun & 2nd & 4th Mon of month) It was behind the stark walls of Palazzo del Bargello, Florence's earliest public building, that the *podestà* meted out justice from the late 13th century until 1502. Today the building safeguards Italy's most comprehensive collection of Tuscan Renaissance sculpture with some of Michelangelo's best early works and a hall full of Donatello's.

Florence

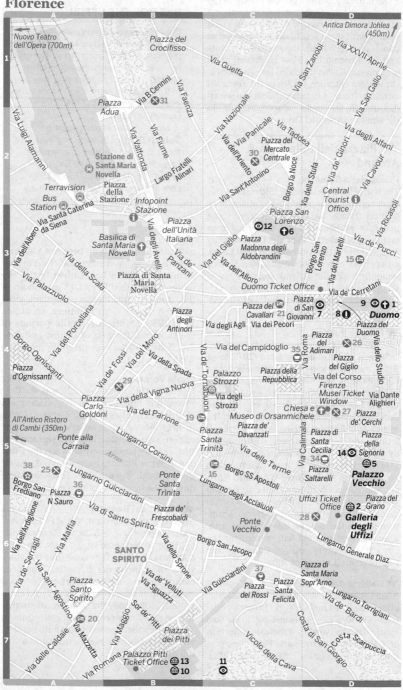

Nuovo Teatro
dell'Opera (700m)

Antica Dimora Johlea
(450m)

Piazza del
Crocifisso

Via Guelfa

Via XXVII Aprile

Via B Cennini

31

Via Faenza

Via San Zanobi

Via San Gallo

Piazza
Adua

Via Fiume

Via Valfonda

Via Nazionale

Via Panicale

Via Taddea

Via degli Alfani

Via' Ginori

Via Cavour

Via dell'Ariento

30

Piazza del
Mercato
Centrale

Borgo la Noce

Via della Stufa

Stazione di
Santa Maria
Novella

Largo Fratelli
Alinari

Via Sant'Antonino

Central
Tourist
Office

Terravision
Bus
Station

Piazza
della
Stazione

Via Santa Caterina
da Siena

Infopoint
Stazione

Piazza San
Lorenzo

12

6

Borgo San
Lorenzo

Via de' Pucci

Piazza
dell'Unità
Italiana

Piazza
Madonna degli
Aldobrandini

Via de' Martelli

15

Basilica di
Santa Maria
Novella

Via degli Aveli

Via de'
Panzani

Via del Giglio

Via dell'Alloro

Via de' Cerretani

Via della Scala

Piazza di Santa
Maria
Novella

Duomo Ticket Office

Via Palazzuolo

Piazza del
Cavallari

21

Piazza
di San
Giovanni

7

9

8

1

Duomo

Via del Porcellana

Piazza
degli
Antinori

Via degli Agli

Via dei Pecori

Piazza del
Duomo

26

Borgo Ognissanti

Via de' Fossi

Via del Moro

Via della Spada

Via del Campidoglio

35

Piazza
del
Adimari

Via Roma

Piazza
d'Ognissanti

Via della Vigna Nuova

Palazzo
Strozzi

Piazza della
Repubblica

Piazza
del Giglio

Via dello Studio

29

Via degli
Strozzi

Via del Corso
Firenze

Piazza
Carlo
Goldoni

Via del Parione

19

Musei Ticket
Window

Via Dante
Alighieri

All'Antico Ristoro
di Cambi (350m)

Lungarno Corsini

Piazza
Santa
Trinità

Museo di Orsanmichele

Chiesa e
27

Piazza
de' Cerchi

Ponte alla
Carraia

Arno

Piazza de'
Davanzati

Via Calimala

Piazza di
Santa
Cecilia

Piazza
della
Signoria

38

25

Ponte
Santa
Trinita

Via delle Terme

14

5

Borgo San
Frediano

Piazza
N Sauro

36

16

Borgo SS Apostoli

Lungarno degli Acciaiuoli

Piazza
Saltarelli

34

Palazzo
Vecchio

Via dell'Ardiglione

Via de' Serragli

Lungarno Guicciardini

Piazza de'
Frescobaldi

Uffizi Ticket
Office

2

Piazza del
Grano

Via Maffia

Via di Santo Spirito

Borgo San Jacopo

Ponte
Vecchio

28

Galleria
degli
Uffizi

Via Sant' Agostino

SANTO
SPIRITO

Via dello Sprone

Via Guicciardini

37

Piazza di
Santa Maria
Sopr'Arno

Lungarno Generale Diaz

Via de' Velluti

Piazza
dei Rossi

Piazza
Santa
Felicità

Lungarno Torrigiani

Piazza
Santo
Spirito

Via Sguazza

Via de' Bardi

Via delle Caldaie

Via Mazzetta

20

Sor de' Pitti

Via Maggio

Piazza
dei Pitti

11

Vicolo della Cava

Costa di San Giorgio

Costa Scarpuccia

Via Romana

Palazzo Pitti
Ticket Office

13

10

⬆ N
0 ——————— 200 m
0 ——————— 0.1 miles

Florence

◉ Top Sights

◉ Sights

🛏 Sleeping

⊗ Eating

◉ Drinking & Nightlife

◉ Entertainment

◉ San Lorenzo

Basilica di San Lorenzo BASILICA

(Piazza San Lorenzo; admission €4.50, incl Biblioteca Medicea Laurenziana €7; ⊙ 10am-5.30pm Mon-Sat, plus 1.30-5pm Sun winter) Considered one of the most harmonious examples of Renaissance architecture in Florence, this unfinished basilica was the Medici parish

ⓘ CUT THE QUEUES

➡ Book tickets for the Uffizi and Galleria dell'Accademia, as well as several other museums, through **Firenze Musei** (Florence Museums; 🕿 055 29 48 83; www. firenzemusei.it). Note that this entails a booking fee of €4 per museum.

➡ Alternatively, the **Firenze Card** (€72, valid for 72 hours) allows you to bypass both advance booking and queues. This can be purchased online, at the Via Cavour tourist office, at Palazzo Pitti, Palazzo Vecchio or the Uffizi. Check details at www.firenzecard.it.

church and mausoleum – many members of the family are buried here. It was designed by Brunelleschi in 1425 for Cosimo the Elder, who lived nearby, and built over an earlier 4th-century church. In the solemn interior look out for Brunelleschi's austerely beautiful **Sagrestia Vecchia** (Old Sacristy) with its sculptural decoration by Donatello.

**Museo delle
Cappelle Medicee**   CHAPEL
(Medici Chapels; 🕿 055 294 883; www.polo museale.firenze.it; Piazza Madonna degli Aldobrandini; adult/reduced €6/3; ⏰ 8.15am-1.50pm, closed 2nd & 4th Sun & 1st, 3rd & 5th Mon of month) Nowhere is Medici conceit expressed so explicitly as in their mausoleum, the Medici Chapels. Sumptuously adorned with granite, precious marble, semiprecious stones and some of Michelangelo's most beautiful sculptures, it is the burial place of 49 members of the dynasty.

◎ San Marco

★ **Galleria
dell'Accademia**   GALLERY
(www.polomuseale.firenze.it; Via Ricasoli 60; adult/reduced €8/4; ⏰ 8.15am-6.50pm Tue-Sun) A lengthy queue marks the door to this gallery, built to house one of the Renaissance's most iconic masterpieces, Michelangelo's *David*. Fortunately, the world's most famous statue is worth the wait. The subtle detail of the real thing – the veins in his sinewy arms, the leg muscles, the change in expression as you move around the statue – *is* impressive.

◎ Oltrarno

Palazzo Pitti   MUSEUM
(www.polomuseale.firenze.it; Piazza dei Pitti; ⏰ 8.15am-6.50pm Tue-Sun, reduced hours winter) Commissioned by banker Luca Pitta and designed by Brunelleschi in 1457, this vast Renaissance palace was later bought by the Medici family. Over the centuries, it served as the residence of the city's rulers until the Savoys donated it to the state in 1919. Nowadays, it houses several museums including the art-rich **Galleria Palatina** (incl Appartamenti Reali & Galleria d'Arte Moderna adult/reduced €8.50/4.25; ⏰ 8.15am-6.50pm Tue-Sun summer, reduced hours winter). Behind it, you can explore the palace's 17th-century gardens, the **Giardino di Boboli** (incl Museo degli Argenti, Museo delle Porcellane & Galleria del Costume adult/reduced €7/3.50; ⏰ 8.15am-7.30pm summer, reduced hours winter).

★✫ Festivals & Events

Scoppio del Carro   FIREWORKS
A cart of fireworks is exploded in front of the cathedral at 11am on Easter Sunday.

**Maggio Musicale
Fiorentino**   PERFORMING ARTS
(www.operadifirenze.it) Italy's oldest arts festival features world-class performances of theatre, classical music, jazz and dance; April to June.

Festa di San Giovanni   RELIGIOUS
Florence celebrates its patron saint, John, with a *calcio storico* (historic football) match on Piazza di Santa Croce and fireworks over Piazzale Michelangelo; 24 June.

⏢ Sleeping

★ **Hotel Dalí**   HOTEL €
(🕿 055 234 07 06; www.hoteldali.com; Via dell'Oriuolo 17; d €90, s/d without bathroom €40/70, apt from €95; 🅿 🛜) A warm welcome from hosts Marco and Samanta awaits at this lovely small hotel. A stone's throw from the Duomo, it has 10 sunny rooms, some overlooking a leafy inner courtyard, decorated in a low-key, modern way and equipped with kettles, coffee and tea. No breakfast, but there is free parking available.

★ **Hotel Cestelli**   HOTEL €
(🕿 055 21 42 13; www.hotelcestelli.com; Borgo SS Apostoli 25; d €70-100, f €80-115, without bathroom s €40-60, d €50-80; ⏰ closed 4 weeks Jan-Feb,

2-3 weeks Aug; 🕿) Housed in a 12th-century *palazzo* a stiletto hop from fashionable Via de' Tornabuoni, this intimate eight-room hotel is a gem. Rooms reveal an understated style, tastefully combining polished antiques with spangly chandeliers, vintage art and silk screens. Owners Alessio and Asumi are a mine of local information and are happy to share their knowledge. No breakfast.

Relais del Duomo　　　　　B&B €
(🕿055 21 01 47; www.relaisdelduomo.it; Piazza dell'Olio 2; s €40-90, d €70-130; ❋🕿) Location is the prime selling point of this B&B on a quiet, traffic-free street around the corner from the Duomo. Its four elegant, pastel-coloured rooms come with parquet floors and simple, down-to-earth decor.

Academy Hostel　　　　　HOSTEL €
(🕿055 239 86 65; www.academyhostel.eu; Via Ricasoli 9r; dm €32-36, s/d €42/100, d without bathroom €85; ❋@🕿) This classy 10-room hostel sits on the 1st floor of Baron Ricasoli's 17th-century *palazzo*. The inviting lobby area was once a theatre and 'dorms' sport maximum four or six beds, high moulded ceilings and brightly coloured lockers. No credit cards for payments under €150.

★**Palazzo**
Guadagni Hotel　　　　　HOTEL €€
(🕿055 265 83 76; www.palazzoguadagni.com; Piazza Santo Spirito 9; d €150, extra bed €45; ❋🕿) This delightful hotel overlooking Florence's liveliest summertime square is legendary – Zefferelli shot scenes from *Tea with Mussolini* here. Housed in an artfully revamped Renaissance palace, it has 15 spacious, tastefully styled rooms and an impossibly romantic loggia terrace with wicker chairs and predictably dreamy views.

Hotel Scoti　　　　　PENSION €€
(🕿055 29 21 28; www.hotelscoti.com; Via de' Tornabuoni 7; s/d/tr/q €75/130/160/185; 🕿) Wedged between the designer stores on Florence's smartest shopping strip, this hidden *pensione* (small hotel) is a splendid mix of old-fashioned charm and value for money. Its 16 traditionally styled rooms are spread across the 2nd floor of a towering 16th-century *palazzo*, with some offering lovely rooftop views. The star of the show, though, is the frescoed lounge from 1780. Breakfast costs €5.

Antica
Dimora Johlea　　　　　B&B €€
(🕿055 463 32 92; www.johanna.it; Via San Gallo 80; d €90-220; ❋@🕿) A way out from the centre, this impeccable residence is a lovely retreat. There's an air of old-world elegance about the six guest rooms with their four-poster beds, creaking parquet floors, high ceilings and period furniture. Help yourself to a drink from the honesty bar and head up to the small terrace to enjoy views over to the Duomo.

Hotel Morandi
alla Crocetta　　　　　BOUTIQUE HOTEL €€
(🕿055 234 47 47; www.hotelmorandi.it; Via Laura 50; s/d/tr/q €105/170/197/227; P❋🕿) This medieval convent-turned-hotel away from the madding crowd in San Marco is a stunner. Rooms are refined and traditional in look – think antique furnishings, wood beams and oil paintings – with a quiet, old-world ambience. Pick of the bunch is frescoed room 29, the former chapel.

✗ Eating

Classic Tuscan dishes include *ribollita*, a heavy vegetable soup, and *bistecca alla fiorentina* (Florentine steak served rare). Chianti is the local tipple.

★**Mercato Centrale**　　　MARKET, FAST FOOD €
(🕿055 239 97 98; www.mercatocentrale.it; Piazza del Mercato Centrale 4; dishes €7-15; ⊗10-1am, food stalls noon-3pm & 7pm-midnight; 🕿) The food court concept has arrived in Florence. The 1st floor of the covered Mercato Centrale has been transformed into a vibrant food fair with a dedicated bookshop, a cookery school, wine bars and stalls selling everything from steaks and grilled burgers to smoothies, pizzas, gelato, pastries and fresh pasta. Load up and sit at the nearest free table.

'Ino　　　　　SANDWICHES €
(www.inofirenze.com; Via dei Georgofili 3r-7r; panini €5-8; ⊗11.30am-4.30pm summer, noon-3.30pm Mon-Fri, 11.30am-4.30pm Sat & Sun winter) ❢ Artisanal ingredients sourced locally and mixed creatively is the secret behind this gourmet sandwich bar near the Uffizi. Create your own filling or go for a house special such as *finocchiona* (a local Tuscan salami) paired with herbed *pecorino* and pepper mustard.

TOP FIVE GELATERIE

La Carraia (Piazza Nazario Sauro 25r; cones & tubs €1.50-6; ⊗11am-11pm summer, to 10pm winter) Fantastic gelateria next to Ponte Carraia.

Gelateria dei Neri (Via de' Neri 22r; cones & tubs from €1.80; ⊗9am-midnight) An old-fashioned shop serving fresh, vibrant flavours.

Gelateria Vivoli (Via dell'Isola delle Stinche 7; tubs €2-10; ⊗7.30am-midnight Tue-Sun summer, to 9pm winter) Select from the huge choice on offer and scoff it in the pretty piazza opposite.

Grom (www.grom.it; cnr Via del Campanile & Via delle Oche; cones €2.50-4.50, tubs €2.50-5.50; ⊗10am-midnight summer, to 11pm winter) Delectable flavours and organic seasonal ingredients.

Vestri (☑055 234 03 74; www.vestri.it; Borgo degli Albizi 11r; cones & tubs from €1.80; ⊗10.40am-8pm Mon-Sat) Specialises in chocolate.

I Due Fratellini   SANDWICHES €
(www.iduefratellini.com; Via dei Cimatori 38r; panini €3; ⊗9am-8pm Mon-Sat) This hole-in-the-wall counter has been dishing out *panini* since 1875. Roll fillers range from ham and salsa to fishy combos such as anchovy with parsley sauce.

Trattoria Cibrèo   TUSCAN €€
(www.edizioniteatrodelsalecibreofirenze.it; Via dei Macci 122r; meals €30; ⊗12.50-2.30pm & 6.50-11pm Tue-Sat, closed Aug) Dine here and you'll instantly understand why a queue gathers outside before it opens. Once inside, revel in top-notch Tuscan cuisine: perhaps *pappa al pomodoro* (a thick soupy mash of tomato, bread and basil) followed by *polpettine di pollo e ricotta* (chicken and ricotta meatballs). No reservations, no credit cards, no coffee, and arrive early to snag a table.

Del Fagioli   TUSCAN €€
(☑055 24 42 85; Corso Tintori 47r; meals €25-30; ⊗12.30-2.30pm & 7.30-10.30pm Mon-Fri, closed Aug) This cosy, woody eatery near the Basilica di Santa Croce is the archetypal Tuscan trattoria. It opened in 1966 and has been serving well-priced soups and boiled meats to throngs of appreciative local workers and residents ever since. No credit cards.

**All'Antico Ristoro
di' Cambi**   TUSCAN €€
(☑055 21 71 34; www.anticoristorodicambi.it; Via Sant'Onofrio 1r; meals €35; ⊗noon-2.30pm & 6-10.30pm Mon-Sat) Founded as a wine shop in 1950, this Oltrarno institution sticks closely to the traditional, with its long list of fine

Tuscan wines, dried meats hanging from brick-vaulted ceilings and a glass case proudly displaying its highly regarded *bistecca alla fiorentina*. Meat aficionados will also enjoy the succulent *tagliata di cinta senese* (steak of Senese pork).

Accademia Ristorante   TUSCAN €€
(☑055 21 73 43; www.ristoranteaccademia.it; Piazza San Marco 7r; pizzas €7-18, meals €35-40; ⊗noon-3pm & 7-11pm) Friendly staff, cheerful decor and consistently good food mean that this family-run restaurant is perennially packed. The focus is traditional regional cuisine, so expect antipasti of crostini, cured meats and cheeses, homemade pastas, meaty mains and a good selection of wood-fired pizzas.

Trattoria I Due G   TUSCAN €€
(☑055 21 86 23; www.trattoriai2g.com; Via B Cennini 6r; meals €30; ⊗noon-2.30pm & 7.30-10pm Mon-Sat) Near the train station, this is a quintessential family-run trattoria specialising in earthy Tuscan cooking. Start off with a classic *parpadelle al cinghiale* (pasta ribbons with a boar-meat sauce) before getting your teeth into a tasty hunk of tender chargrilled steak.

★**L'Osteria di Giovanni**   TUSCAN €€€
(☑055 28 48 97; www.osteriadigiovanni.it; Via del Moro 22; meals €50; ⊗7-10pm Mon-Fri, noon-3pm & 7-10pm Sat & Sun) It's not the decor that stands out at this smart neighbourhood eatery, it's the cuisine: sumptuous Tuscan. Imagine truffles, tender steaks and pastas such as *pici al sugo di salsicccia e cavolo nero* (thick spaghetti with a sauce

of sausage and black cabbage). Throw in a complimentary glass of *prosecco* and you'll want to return time and again.

Drinking & Nightlife

★ Il Santino
WINE BAR
(Via Santo Spirito 60r; ⊙ 12.30-11pm) This pocket-sized wine bar is packed every evening. Inside, squat modern stools contrast with old brick walls, but the real action is outside, from around 9pm, when the buoyant wine-loving crowd spills onto the street.

Le Volpi e l'Uva
WINE BAR
(www.levolpieluva.com; Piazza dei Rossi 1; ⊙ 11am-9pm Mon-Sat) This intimate spot with a marble-topped bar crowning two oak wine barrels chalks up an impressive list of Italian wines, from Tuscan Chianti's to rich Piedmontese reds and chardonnays from the Valle d'Aosta. To attain true bliss, nibble on *crostini* or Tuscan cheeses as you sip.

Caffè Rivoire
CAFE
(Piazza della Signoria 4; ⊙ 7am-11pm Tue-Sun) Dating to 1872, this pricey number offers unbeatable people-watching on Piazza della Signoria – an ideal antidote to art overload brought on in the nearby Uffizi. Speciality of the house is its exquisite chocolate.

Gilli
CAFE
(www.gilli.it; Piazza della Repubblica 39r; ⊙ 7.30am-1.30am) The city's grandest cafe, Gilli has been serving excellent coffee and delicious cakes since 1733. Claiming a table on the piazza is molto expensive – we prefer standing at the spacious Liberty-style bar.

☆ Entertainment

Florence's definitive monthly listings guide, *Firenze Spettacolo* (www.firenzespettacolo.it), is sold at news-stands and has a small English-language section on the final pages.

Concerts, opera and dance are performed at the **Nuovo Teatro dell'Opera** (☑ 055 277 93 50; www.operadifirenze.it; Viale Fratelli Rosselli 15), also the venue for events during Maggio Musicale Fiorentino.

For live music in intimate surrounds, search out **La Cité** (www.lacitelibreria.info; Borgo San Frediano 20r; ⊙ 8am-2am Mon-Sat, 3pm-2am Sun; 🛜).

ℹ Information

24-Hour Pharmacy (Stazione di Santa Maria Novella)

Dr Stephen Kerr: Medical Service (☑ 055 28 80 55, 335 8361682; www.dr-kerr.com; Piazza Mercato Nuovo 1; ⊙ 3-5pm Mon-Fri, or by appointment 9am-3pm Mon-Fri) Resident British doctor.

Infopoint Stazione (☑ 055 21 22 45; www.firenzeturismo.it; Piazza della Stazione 5; ⊙ 9am-7pm Mon-Sat, to 2pm Sun)

Central Tourist Office (☑ 055 29 08 32; www.firenzeturismo.it; Via Cavour 1r; ⊙ 9am-6pm Mon-Sat)

ℹ Getting There & Away

AIR
The main airport serving Florence is **Pisa International Airport** (Galileo Galilei Airport; ☑ 050 84 93 00; www.pisa-airport.com). There's also a small city airport 5km north of town, **Florence Airport** (Aeroport Vespucci; ☑ 055 306 13 00; www.aeroporto.firenze.it; Via del Termine).

BUS
The main bus station, **Autostazione Busitalia-Sita Nord** (☑ 800 37 37 60; Via Santa Caterina da Siena 17r; ⊙ 5.40am-8.40pm Mon-Sat, 6.20am-8pm Sun), is just southwest of the train station. Buses leave for Siena (€7.80, 1¼ hours, at least hourly) and San Gimignano via Poggibonsi (€6.80, 1¼ to two hours, up to 16 daily).

TRAIN
Florence's **Stazione di Santa Maria Novella** (Piazza della Stazione) is on the main Rome–Milan line. There are regular direct services to/from Pisa (€8, 45 minutes to 1½ hours), Rome (€21 to €36, 1½ to 3½ hours), Venice (€22 to €45, two hours) and Milan (€28 to €50, 1¾ to four hours).

ℹ Getting Around

TO/FROM THE AIRPORT
Terravision (www.terravision.eu; single/return €6/10) Terravision buses run to Pisa International Airport fom the bus stop outside Stazione di Santa Maria Novella on Via Luigi Alamanni. Buy tickets online, on board, or at the Terravision desk in Deanna Cafè.

Volainbus (☑ 800 424500; www.ataf.net; one way €6) The Volainbus shuttle runs between the bus station and Florence Airport. Departures are roughly every 20 minutes between 5.30am and 12.30am. Journey time is about 25 minutes.

PUBLIC TRANSPORT

City buses are operated by ATAF. Get tickets (€1.20 or €2 if bought on board) at *tabaccherie* and news-stands. They are valid for 90 minutes on any bus.

Pisa

POP 88,600

A handsome university city, Pisa is best known as the home of an architectural project gone terribly wrong. However, the Leaning Tower is just one of a number of noteworthy sights in its compact medieval centre.

Pisa's golden age came in the 12th and 13th centuries when it was a maritime power to rival Genoa and Venice.

◉ Sights

★ Leaning Tower   TOWER

(Torre Pendente; www.opapisa.it; Piazza dei Miracoli; admission €18; ⊙ 9am-8pm summer, 10am-5pm winter) One of Italy's signature sights, the Torre Pendente truly lives up to its name, leaning a startling 3.9 degrees off the vertical. The 56m-high tower, officially the Duomo's *campanile* (bell tower), took almost 200 years to build, but was already listing when it was unveiled in 1372. Over time, the tilt, caused by a layer of weak subsoil, steadily worsened until it was finally halted by a major stabilisation project in the 1990s.

★ Duomo   CATHEDRAL

(www.opapisa.it; Piazza dei Miracoli; ⊙ 10am-8pm summer, 10am-12.45pm & 2-5pm winter) **FREE** Pisa's magnificent Romanesque Duomo was begun in 1064 and consecrated in 1118. Its striking tiered exterior, with cladding of green and cream marble bands, gives on to a vast columned interior capped by a gold wooden ceiling. The elliptical dome, the first of its kind in Europe at the time, was added in 1380.

Note that while admission is free, you'll need an entrance coupon from the ticket office or a ticket from one of the other Piazza dei Miracoli sights.

★ Battistero   RELIGIOUS SITE

(Baptistry; www.opapisa.it; Piazza dei Miracoli; adult/reduced €5/3, combination ticket with Camposanto & Museo delle Sinópie adult/reduced €7/8, 2/3 sights adult/reduced €4/5; ⊙ 8am-8pm summer, 10am-5pm Nov-Feb) Pisa's unusual round baptistry has one dome piled on top of another, each roofed half in lead, half in tiles,

ⓘ LEANING TOWER VISITS

Access to the Leaning Tower is limited to 40 people at a time. To avoid disappointment, book online, or go straight to a ticket office when you arrive in Pisa to book a slot for later in the day. Visits last 30 minutes and involve a steep climb up 300-odd occasionally slippery steps. All bags must be deposited at the free left-luggage desk next to the ticket office.

and topped by a gilt bronze John the Baptist (1395). Construction began in 1152, but it was remodelled and continued by Nicola and Giovanni Pisano more than a century later and finally completed in the 14th century. Inside, the hexagonal marble pulpit (1260) by Nicola Pisano is the highlight.

🛏 Sleeping & Eating

★ Hotel Pisa Tower   HOTEL €

(☑ 050 520 00 19; www.hotelpisatower.com; Via Pisano 23; d €75-90, tr €90-100, q €110-119; ❄ ☎) Superb value for money, a superlative location and spacious, high-ceilinged rooms – this polished newcomer is one of Pisa's best deals. Chandeliers, marble floors and old framed prints adorn the classically attired interiors, while out back, a pristine lawn adds a soothing dash of green.

Hostel Pisa Tower   HOSTEL €

(☑ 050 520 24 54; www.hostelpisatower.it; Via Piave 4; dm €20-25; @ ☎) This super friendly hostel occupies a suburban villa a couple of minutes' walk from Piazza dei Miracoli. It's a bright, cheery place with female and mixed dorms, a communal kitchen and a terrace overlooking a small back garden.

Hotel Bologna   HOTEL €€

(☑ 050 50 21 20; www.hotelbologna.pisa.it; Via Giuseppe Mazzini 57; d/tr/q €148/188/228; P ❄ ☎) Nicely placed away from the Piazza dei Miracoli mayhem, this four-star hotel is an oasis of peace and tranquillity. Its big, bright rooms have wooden floors and colour-coordinated furnishings, and some are nicely frescoed.

Osteria La Toscana   OSTERIA €€

(☑ 050 96 90 52; Via San Frediano 10; meals €25-30; ⊙ 7-11pm daily & noon-3pm Sat & Sun) This relaxed spot is one of several excellent eateries on Via San Frediano, a lively street off Piazza dei Cavalieri. Subdued lighting, bare brown walls and background jazz set the stage for ample pastas and delectable grilled meats served with a smile and quiet efficiency.

biOsteria 050
VEGETARIAN €€

(☑ 050 54 31 06; www.biosteria050.it; Via San Francesco 36; meals €25-30; ⊘ 12.30-2.30pm & 7.30-10.30pm Tue-Sat, 7.30-10.30pm Mon & Sun; ☑) ✔ Everything that Marco and Raffaele at Zero Cinquanta cook up is strictly seasonal, local and organic, with products from farms within a 50km radius of Pisa. Feast on dishes like risotto with almonds and asparagus or go for one of the excellent-value lunch specials.

ℹ Information

Check www.pisaunicaterra.it or pop into the **tourist office** (☑ 050 4 22 91; www.pisaunicaterra.it; Piazza Vittorio Emanuele II 16; ⊘10am-1pm & 2-4pm) in the city centre.

ℹ Getting There & Around

Pisa International Airport (www.pisa-airport.com) is linked to the city centre by the PisaMover bus (€1.30, eight minutes, every 10 minutes).

Terravision buses link the airport with Florence (one way/return €6/10, 70 minutes, 18 daily).

Frequent trains run to Lucca (€3.40, 30 minutes), Florence (€8, 45 minutes to 1¼ hours) and La Spezia (€7 to €12, 45 minutes to 1½ hours) for the Cinque Terre.

Lucca
POP 89,200

Lucca is a love-at-first-sight type of place. Hidden behind monumental Renaissance walls, its historic centre is chock-full of handsome churches, excellent restaurants and tempting *pasticcerie* (pastry shops). Founded by the Etruscans, it became a city-state in the 12th century and stayed that way for 600 years. Most of its streets and monuments date from this period.

◉ Sights

City Wall
WALL

Lucca's monumental *mura* (wall) was built around the old city in the 16th and 17th centuries and remains in almost perfect condition. Twelve metres high and 4km long, the ramparts are crowned with a tree-lined footpath that looks down on the *centro storico* and out towards the Apuane Alps. This path is a favourite location for the locals' daily *passeggiata* (traditional evening stroll).

Cattedrale di
San Martino
CATHEDRAL

(www.museocattedralelucca.it; Piazza San Martino; adult/reduced €3/2, with museum & Chiesa e Battistero dei SS Giovanni & Reparata €7/5; ⊘9.30am-5pm Mon-Fri, to 6pm Sat, 11.30am-5pm Sun) Lucca's predominantly Romanesque cathedral dates to the start of the 11th century. Its stunning facade was constructed in the prevailing Lucca-Pisan style and designed to accommodate the preexisting *campanile*. The reliefs over the left doorway of the portico are believed to be by Nicola Pisano, while inside, treasures include the **Volto Santo** (literally, Holy Countenance) crucifix sculpture and a wonderful 15th-century tomb in the **sacristy**.

🛏 Sleeping & Eating

★**Piccolo Hotel Puccini**
HOTEL €

(☑ 0583 5 54 21; www.hotelpuccini.com; Via di Poggio 9; s/d €75/100; ✳🐾) In an enviable central position, this welcoming three-star hotel hides behind a discreet brick exterior. Its small guestrooms reveal an attractive look with wooden floors, vintage ceiling fans and colourful, contemporary design touches.

Alla Corte
degli Angeli
BOUTIQUE HOTEL €€

(☑ 0583 46 92 04; www.allacortedegliangeli.com; Via degli Angeli 23; s/d/ste €150/250/400; ✳@🐾) This boutique hotel oozes charm. Set in a 15th-century townhouse, its lovely beamed lounge gives onto 21 sunny rooms adorned with frescoed ceilings, patches of exposed brick and landscape murals. Breakfast is €10 extra.

Da Felice
PIZZA €

(www.pizzeriadafelice.it; Via Buia 12; focaccias €1-3, pizza slices €1.30; ⊘11am-8.30pm Mon, 10am-8.30pm Tue-Sat) This buzzing spot behind Piazza San Michele is where the locals come for wood-fired pizza, *cecina* (salted chickpea pizza) and *castagnacci* (chestnut cakes).

La Pecora Nera
TRATTORIA €€

(☑ 0583 46 97 38; www.lapecoraneralucca.it; Piazza San Francesco 1; pizzas €5.50-9, meals €25-30; ⊘7-11pm Wed-Fri, 11am-3pm & 7-11pm Sat & Sun)

SAN GIMIGNANO

This tiny hilltop town deep in the Tuscan countryside is a mecca for day trippers from Florence and Siena. Its nickname is the 'Medieval Manhattan', courtesy of the 14 11th-century towers that soar above its pristine *centro storico* (historic centre).

Palazzo Comunale (☑0577 99 03 12; Piazza del Duomo 2; adult/reduced €6/5; ☺9am-6.30pm summer, 11am-5pm winter) houses San Gimignano's art gallery, the **Pinacoteca**, and tallest tower, the **Torre Grossa**.

Overlooking **Piazza del Duomo**, the **Collegiata** (Duomo, Basilica di Santa Maria Assunta; Piazza del Duomo; adult/reduced €4/2; ☺10am-7pm Mon-Fri, to 5pm Sat, 12.30-7pm Sun summer, to 4.30pm winter), San Gimignano's Romanesque cathedral, boasts a series of superb 14th-century frescoes.

For a traditional Tuscan lunch, head to **Ristorante La Mandragola** (☑0577 94 03 77; www.locandalamandragola.it; Via Diaccetto 7; set menus €14-25, meals €35; ☺noon-2.30pm & 7.30-9.30pm, closed Thu Nov-early Mar).

The **tourist office** (☑0577 94 00 08; www.sangimignano.com; Piazza del Duomo 1; ☺9am-1pm & 3-7pm summer, 9am-1pm & 2-6pm winter) is on Piazza del Duomo, up Via San Giovanni from the bus stops.

Regular buses link San Gimignano with Florence (€7, 1¼ to two hours, up to 16 daily) via Poggibonsi. There are also services to/from Siena (€6, 1¼ hours, hourly).

A pretty *centro storico* piazza sets the scene for alfresco dining at this laid-back trattoria. Staffed in part by young disabled people, it's a lovely spot for a pizza or dinner of earthy Tuscan fare.

ℹ Information

Tourist Office (☑0583 58 31 50; www.luccaitinera.it; Piazzale Verdi; ☺9am-7pm summer, to 5pm winter) Free hotel reservations, bicycle hire and a left-luggage service.

ℹ Getting There & Away

Regional trains run to/from Florence (€7, 1½ hours, every 30 to 90 minutes) and Pisa (€8, one hour, half-hourly).

Siena

POP 54,200

Siena is one of Italy's most enchanting medieval towns. Its walled centre is a beautifully preserved warren of dark lanes punctuated with Gothic *palazzi*, and at its heart is Piazza del Campo (Il Campo), the sloping square that is the venue for the city's famous annual horse race, Il Palio.

In the Middle Ages, the city was a political and artistic force to be reckoned with, a worthy rival for its larger neighbour Florence.

◉ Sights

⭐ **Piazza del Campo**   PIAZZA

This sloping piazza, popularly known as Il Campo, has been Siena's civic and social centre since being staked out by the Consiglio dei Nove (Council of Nine) in the mid-12th century. It was built on the site of a former Roman marketplace, and its pie-piece paving design is divided into nine sectors to represent the number of members of the council. At its lowest point, the graceful Gothic **Palazzo Comunale** houses the town's finest museum, the Museo Civico.

Museo Civico   MUSEUM

(Palazzo Comunale, Piazza del Campo; adult/reduced €9/8; ☺10am-7pm summer, to 6pm winter) Siena's most famous museum occupies rooms richly frescoed by artists of the Sienese school. These are unusual in that they were commissioned by the governing body of the city, rather than by the Church, and many depict secular subjects instead of the favoured religious themes of the time. The highlight is Simone Martini's celebrated *Maestà* (Virgin Mary in Majesty; 1315) in the **Sala del Mappamondo** (Hall of the World Map).

⭐ **Duomo**   CATHEDRAL

(www.operaduomo.siena.it; Piazza del Duomo; summer/winter €4/free, when floor displayed €7;

⊙10.30am-7pm Mon-Sat, 1.30-6pm Sun summer, 10.30am-5.30pm Mon-Sat, 1.30-5.30pm Sun winter) A triumph of Romanesque-Gothic architecture, Siena's cathedral is one of Italy's most awe-inspiring churches. According to tradition it was consecrated in 1179, but work continued on it for centuries and many of Italy's top artists contributed: Giovanni Pisano designed the intricate white, green and red marble facade; Nicola Pisano carved the elaborate pulpit; Pinturicchio painted frescoes; and Michelangelo, Donatello and Gian Lorenzo Bernini all produced sculptures. Also of note is the extraordinary inlaid floor.

Battistero di San Giovanni

BAPTISTRY

(Piazza San Giovanni; admission €4; ⊙10.30am-7pm summer, to 5.30pm winter) Behind the Duomo, down a steep flight of steps, is the Baptistry, richly decorated with frescoes. At its centre is a hexagonal marble font by Jacopo della Quercia, decorated with bronze panels depicting the life of St John the Baptist by artists including Lorenzo Ghiberti *(Baptism of Christ* and *St John in Prison)* and Donatello *(The Head of John the Baptist Being Presented to Herod)*.

Museo dell'Opera del Duomo

MUSEUM

(www.operaduomo.siena.it; Piazza del Duomo 8; admission €7; ⊙10.30am-7pm summer, to 5.30pm winter) The collection here showcases artworks that formerly adorned the cathedral, including 12 statues of prophets and philosophers by Giovanni Pisano that originally stood on the facade. These were designed to be viewed from ground level, which is why they look so distorted as they crane uncomfortably forward. The museum's highlight is Duccio di Buoninsegna's striking *Maestà* (1311), which was painted on both sides as a screen for the Duomo's high altar.

🎉 Festivals & Events

Il Palio

PAGEANT, HORSE RACE

Dating from the Middle Ages, this spectacular annual event (held on 2 July and 16 August) includes a series of colourful pageants and a wild horse race in Piazza del Campo. Ten of Siena's 17 *contrade* (town districts) compete for the coveted *palio* (silk banner). Each *contrada* has its own traditions, symbol and colours, plus its own church and *palio* museum.

🛏 Sleeping & Eating

★Hotel Alma Domus

HOTEL €

(☎0577 4 41 77; www.hotelalmadomus.it; Via Camporegio 37; s €40-52, d €60-€122, q €95-140; 🖳🖬) Owned by the church and still home to several Dominican nuns, this convent hotel is a lovely, peaceful oasis. Rooms, on the 3rd and 4th floors, represent excellent value for money, with a smart, modern look and pristine bathrooms. Some, for which you'll pay more, have views over to the Duomo.

Antica Residenza Cicogna

B&B €

(☎0577 28 56 13; www.anticaresidenzacicogna.it; Via delle Terme 76; s €70-95, d 95-115, ste €120-155; 🖳🖬🖬) Charming host Elisa welcomes guests to her 13th-century family *palazzo.* The seven guestrooms are clean and well maintained, with painted ceilings, brick floors and the occasional patch of original fresco. There's also a tiny lounge where you can relax over complimentary Vin Santo and *cantuccini* (hard, sweet almond biscuits).

Osteria Nonna Gina

TRATTORIA €

(☎0577 28 72 47; www.osterianonnagina.com; Pian dei Mantellini 2; meals €25; ⊙12.30-2.30pm & 7.30-10.30pm Tue-Sun) This cheery eatery is the picture of an old-school family-run trattoria. An oddment of accumulated clutter provides the decor as family members run between the kitchen and cosy dining room delivering steaming plates of pasta and Tuscan stews.

Morbidi

DELI €

(www.morbidi.com; Via Banchi di Sopra 75; lunch buffet €12; ⊙8am-8pm Mon-Thu, to 9pm Fri & Sat) Duck under the ground-floor deli for Morbidi's excellent lunch buffet. For a mere €12 you can pick and choose from antipasti, salads, risottos, pastas and a dessert of the day. Bottled water is supplied, wine and coffee cost extra.

★Enoteca I Terzi

MODERN TUSCAN €€

(☎0577 4 43 29; www.enotecaiterzi.it; Via dei Termini 7; meals €35-40; ⊙11am-1am summer, 11am-4pm & 6.30pm-midnight winter, closed Sun) Close to the Campo, this historic *enoteca* (wine bar) is a favourite with locals, who linger over working lunches, *aperitivi*, and casual dinners featuring top-notch Tuscan *salumi* (cured meats), delicate handmade pasta and wonderful wines.

ℹ️ Information

Tourist Office (📞 0577 28 05 51; www.
terresiena.it; Piazza del Duomo 1; ⏱ 9am-6pm
daily summer, 10am-5pm Mon-Sat, to 1pm Sun
winter) Opposite the Duomo. Reserves accommodation, organises car and scooter hire, and
sells train tickets (commission applies). Also
takes bookings for a range of day tours.

ℹ️ Getting There & Away

Siena Mobilità (📞 800 922984; www.siena
mobilita.it) buses run to/from Florence (€8, 1¼
hours, at least hourly), San Gimignano (€6, 1¼
hours, hourly), either direct or via Poggibonsi,
and Pisa International Airport (€14, two hours,
one daily).

Sena (www.sena.it) operates services to/from
Rome Tiburtina (€24, three hours, nine daily),
two of which continue to Fiumicino Airport; also
to Milan (€36, 4½ hours, four daily), Perugia
(€18, 1½ hours, two daily) and Venice (€32, 5½
hours, two daily).

Ticket offices are in the basement under the
bus station on Piazza Gramsci.

Perugia

POP 166,000

With its hilltop medieval centre and international student population, Perugia is
Umbria's largest and most cosmopolitan
city. In July music fans inundate the city
for the prestigious **Umbria Jazz festival**
(www.umbriajazz.com), and in the third week
of October the **Eurochocolate** (www.euro
chocolate.com) festival lures chocoholics from
across the globe.

Perugia has a dramatic and bloody past. In
the Middle Ages, art and culture thrived: both
Perugino and Raphael, his student, worked
here, as powerful local dynasties fought for
control of the city.

👁 Sights

Perugia's sights are in the hilltop historic centre, concentrated on the main strip,
Corso Vannucci, and Piazza IV Novembre, a
handsome medieval piazza.

**Cattedrale di
San Lorenzo**   CATHEDRAL
(Piazza IV Novembre; ⏱ 7.30am-noon & 3.30-
6.45pm Mon-Sat, 8am-1pm & 4-7pm Sun) Overlooking Piazza IV Novembre is Perugia's
stark medieval cathedral. A church has
stood here since the 900s, but the version
you see today was begun in 1345 from de-

signs created by Fra Bevignate. Building
continued until 1587, although the main
facade was never completed. Inside you'll
find dramatic late Gothic architecture, an
altarpiece by Signorelli and sculptures by
Duccio. The steps in front of the facade are
where seemingly all of Perugia congregates;
they overlook the piazza's centrepiece: the
delicate pink-and-white marble **Fontana
Maggiore** (Great Fountain; Piazza IV Novembre).

⭐ **Palazzo dei Priori**   PALACE
(Corso Vannucci) Flanking Corso Vannucci,
this Gothic palace, constructed between
the 13th and 14th centuries, is architecturally striking with its tripartite windows,
ornamental portal and fortress-like crenellations. It was formerly the headquarters
of the local magistracy, but now houses the
city's main art gallery, the Galleria Nazionale
dell'Umbria. Also of note is the **Nobile Collegio del Cambio** (Exchange Hall; www.perugia
cittamuseo.it; Palazzo dei Priori, Corso Vannucci 25;
admission €4.50, incl Nobile Collegio della Mercan-
zia €5.50; ⏱ 9am-12.30pm & 2.30-5.30pm Mon-
Sat, 9am-1pm Sun), Perugia's medieval money
exchange, with its Perugino frescoes.

**Galleria Nazionale
dell'Umbria**   MUSEUM
(📞 075 5866 8410; www.gallerianazionaleumbria.
it; Palazzo dei Priori, Corso Vannucci 19; adult/
reduced €6.50/3.25; ⏱ 8.30am-7.30pm Tue-Sun)
Umbria's foremost art gallery is housed in
Palazzo dei Priori on the city's main strip.
Its collection, one of central Italy's richest,
numbers almost 3000 works, ranging from
Byzantine-inspired 13th-century paintings
to Gothic works by Gentile da Fabriano and
Renaissance masterpieces by hometown
heroes Pinturicchio and Perugino.

🛏 Sleeping & Eating

Primavera Minihotel   HOTEL €
(📞 075 572 16 57; www.primaveraminihotel.it; Via
Vincioli 8; s €55-65, d €75-105, tr €95-120; 🌫 ❄ 🅿)
This welcoming hotel is tucked in a quiet
corner of the *centro storico*. Magnificent
views complement the bright rooms, decorated with period furnishings and characterful features like exposed stone, beams
and wood floors. Breakfast costs €5 to €8
extra. English, French and Italian spoken.

Hotel Morlacchi   PENSION €
(📞 075 572 03 19; www.hotelmorlacchi.it; Via Tiberi
2; s €60-66, d €80-92, tr €90-115; 🅿) A friendly,

WORTH A TRIP

ORVIETO

Strategically located on the main train line between Rome and Florence, this spectacularly sited hilltop town has one major drawcard: its extraordinary Gothic **Cattedrale di Orvieto** (☑0763 34 24 77; www.opsm.it; Piazza Duomo 26; admission €3; ⊙9.30am-6pm Mon-Sat, 1-5.30pm Sun summer, 9.30am-1pm & 2.30-5pm Mon-Sat, 2.30-4.30pm Sun winter), built over 300 years from 1290. The facade is stunning, and the ethereally beautiful interior contains Luca Signorelli's awe-inspiring *Giudizio Universale* (The Last Judgment) fresco cycle.

For a filling meal, search out the **Trattoria del Moro Aronne** (☑0763 34 27 63; www.trattoriadelmoro.info; Via San Leonardo 7; meals €25-30; ⊙noon-2.30pm & 7.30-9.30pm Wed-Mon).

For information, the **tourist office** (☑0763 34 17 72; www.orvieto.regioneumbria.eu; Piazza Duomo 24; ⊙8.15am-1.50pm & 4-7pm Mon-Fri, 10am-1pm & 3-6pm Sat & Sun) is opposite the cathedral.

Trains run to/from Florence (€15.40 to €19.50, 2¼ hours, hourly) and Rome (€7.50 to €13.50, 1¼ hours, hourly). From Perugia (€7 to €14.50, 1¾ to three hours, up to 13 daily), you'll need to change trains at Terontola-Cortona or Orte.

If you arrive by train, you'll need to take the **funicular** (€1.30; ⊙every 10min 7.15am-8.30pm Mon-Sat, every 15mins 8am-8.30pm Sun) up to the town centre.

old-school *pensione* near Piazza IV Novembre. The cosy, low-ceilinged rooms, spread over several floors of a 17th-century townhouse, are modest but comfortable with antiques and original artworks.

Pizzeria Mediterranea PIZZA €
(Piazza Piccinino 11/12; pizzas €4.50-12; ⊙12.30-2.30pm & 7.30-11pm;) A classic pizzeria with a wood-fired oven and bustling atmosphere, this popular spot does the best pizzas in town. Served bubbling hot, they come with light, Neapolitan-style bases and flavoursome toppings. Expect queues at the weekend.

Sandri CAFE, PASTICCERIA €
(Corso Vannucci 32; pastries €2.50; ⊙7.30am-11pm) This city institution has been serving coffee and cake since 1860. Its delicately frescoed, chandelier-lit interior provides the perfect backdrop for exquisite-looking pastries, chocolates and cakes, enticingly presented in wall-to-ceiling cabinets.

Osteria a Priori OSTERIA €€
(☑075 572 70 98; www.osteriaapriori.it; Via dei Priori 39; meals around €30; ⊙12.30-2.30pm & 7.30-10pm Mon-Sat) 🍴 Located above an *enoteca*, this fashionable *osteria* specialises in local wines and fresh regional cuisine prepared with seasonal ingredients. Umbrian cheeses and cured meats feature alongside truffles, roast meats and autumnal mushrooms.

Weekday lunch is a snip at €9. Reservations recommended.

❶ Information

Tourist office (☑075 573 64 58; http://turismo.comune.perugia.it; Piazza Matteotti 18; ⊙9am-7pm). City maps are available here. For information about what's on in town, buy a copy of *Viva Perugia* (€1) from a local newsstand.

❶ Getting There & Around

Perugia's bus station is on Piazza dei Partigiani, from where an elevator connects with Piazza Italia in the historic centre.

Sena (☑861 1991900; www.sena.it) Buses serve Florence (€21, two hours, two daily) and destinations in Tuscany.

Sulga (☑800 099661; www.sulga.it) Buses run to/from Rome (€17, 2½ hours, four to five daily) and Fiumicino Airport (€22, 3¾ hours, two to four daily).

Umbria Mobilità (☑075 963 76 37; www.umbriamobilita.it) Operates buses to regional destinations, including Assisi (€4.20, 45 minutes, eight daily).

Direct trains connect with Florence (€14, 1½ to 2¼ hours, eight daily). To get to the centre from the train station, take the minimetrò (€1.50) to the Pincetto stop just below Piazza Matteotti. Alternatively, jump on bus G (€1.50, €2 on bus) to Piazza Italia or bus C to behind the Cattedrale di San Lorenzo.

Assisi

POP 28,100

The birthplace of St Francis (1182–1226), the medieval town of Assisi is a major destination for millions of pilgrims. The main sight is the Basilica di San Francesco, one of Italy's most visited churches, but the hilltop historic centre is also well worth a look.

◎ Sights

★ Basilica di San Francesco
BASILICA

(www.sanfrancescoassisi.org; Piazza di San Francesco; ⊙ upper church 8.30am-6.45pm, lower church & tomb 6am-6.45pm) FREE Visible for miles around, the Basilica di San Francesco is the crowning glory of Assisi's Unesco World Heritage ensemble. It's divided into an upper church, the **Basilica Superiore**, with a celebrated cycle of Giotto frescoes, and beneath, the older **Basilica Inferiore**, where you'll find frescoes by Cimabue, Pietro Lorenzetti and Simone Martini. Also here, in the Basilica's crypt, is St Francis' tomb.

Basilica di Santa Chiara
BASILICA

(Piazza Santa Chiara; ⊙ 6.30am-noon & 2-7pm summer, to 6pm winter) Built in a 13th-century Romanesque style, with steep ramparts and a striking pink-and-white facade, this church is dedicated to St Clare, a spiritual contemporary of St Francis and founder of the Sorelle Povere di Santa Chiara (Order of the Poor Ladies), now known as the Poor Clares. She is buried in the church's crypt, alongside the Crocifisso di San Damiano, a Byzantine cross before which St Francis was praying when he heard from God in 1205.

⨳ Sleeping & Eating

Hotel Alexander
HOTEL €€

(☑ 075 81 61 90; www.hotelalexanderassisi.it; Piazza Chiesa Nuova 6; s €60-80, d €99-140; ⧉ 🛜) On a small cobbled piazza by the Chiesa Nuova, the Hotel Alexander offers eight spacious rooms and a communal terrace with wonderful rooftop views. The modern decor – pale wooden floors and earthy brown tones – contrasts well with the wood-beamed ceilings and carefully preserved antiquity all around.

Trattoria da Erminio
TRATTORIA €€

(☑ 075 81 25 06; www.trattoriadaerminio.it; Via Montecavallo 19; fixed-price menus €18, meals €25-30; ⊙ noon-2.30pm & 7-9pm Fri-Wed) This charming backstreet trattoria is known for its grilled meats, prepared on a huge fireplace in the small dining area. In summer tables on the pretty cobbled street are hot property, and no wonder – this is old-fashioned Umbrian dining at its rustic best. You'll find it in the upper town near Piazza Matteotti.

❶ Information

Tourist Office (☑ 075 813 86 80; www.assisi.regioneumbria.eu; Piazza del Comune 22; ⊙ 9.30am-7pm daily summer, 8am-2pm & 3-6pm Mon-Fri, 9am-7pm Sat, 9am-6pm Sun winter) Stop by here for maps, leaflets and info on accommodation.

❶ Getting There & Away

It is better to travel to Assisi by bus rather than train. Buses arrive at and depart from Piazza Matteotti in the centro storico.

Sulga (www.sulga.it) Buses serve Rome (€18, three hours, one daily).

Umbria Mobilità (www.umbriamobilita.it) Buses run to/from Perugia (€4, 45 minutes, eight daily).

The train station is 4km from Assisi proper in Santa Maria degli Angeli. If you arrive by train, take bus C (€1.30, €2 on board, half-hourly) to Piazza Matteotti. Regional trains run to Perugia (€2.50, 20 minutes, hourly).

SOUTHERN ITALY

A sun-bleached land of spectacular coastlines and rugged landscapes, southern Italy is a robust contrast to the more genteel north. Its stunning scenery, baroque towns and classical ruins exist alongside ugly urban sprawl and scruffy coastal development, sometimes in the space of just a few kilometres.

Yet for all its flaws, *il mezzogiorno* ('the midday sun,' as southern Italy is known) is an essential part of every Italian itinerary, offering charm, culinary good times and architectural treasures.

Naples

POP 989,100

Naples (Napoli) is dirty, noisy, dishevelled and totally exhilarating. Founded by Greek colonists, it became a thriving Roman city and was later the Bourbon capital of the Kingdom of the Two Sicilies. In the 18th century it was one of Europe's great cities, something you'll readily believe as you marvel at its profusion of baroque *palazzi*.

⊙ Sights

★ Museo Archeologico Nazionale
MUSEUM

(☑ 081442 2149; http://cir.campania.beniculturali.it/museoarcheologiconazionale; Piazza Museo Nazionale 19; adult/reduced €8/4; ⊙ 9am-7.30pm Wed-Mon; Ⓜ Museo, Piazza Cavour) Naples' premier museum showcases one of the world's finest collections of Greco-Roman artefacts. Originally a cavalry barracks and later seat of the city's university, the museum was established by the Bourbon king Charles VII in the late 18th century to house the antiquities he inherited from his mother, Elisabetta Farnese, as well as treasures looted from Pompeii and Herculaneum. Star exhibits include the celebrated *Toro Farnese* (Farnese Bull) sculpture and a series of awe-inspiring mosaics from Pompeii's Casa del Fauno.

★ Cappella Sansevero
CHAPEL

(☑ 081 551 84 70; www.museosansevero.it; Via Francesco de Sanctis 19; adult/reduced €7/5; ⊙ 9.30am-6.30pm Mon & Wed-Sat, to 2pm Sun; Ⓜ Dante) It's in this Masonic-inspired baroque chapel that you'll find Giuseppe Sanmartino's incredible sculpture, *Cristo velato* (Veiled Christ), its marble veil so realistic that it's tempting to try to lift it and view Christ underneath. It's one of several artistic wonders, which also include Francesco Queirolo's sculpture *Disinganno* (Disillusion), Antonio Corradini's *Pudicizia* (Modesty) and riotously colourful frescoes by Francesco Maria Russo, the latter untouched since their creation in 1749.

Complesso Monumentale di Santa Chiara
BASILICA, MONASTERY

(☑ 081 551 66 73; www.monasterodisantachiara.eu; Via Santa Chiara 49c; basilica free, Complesso Monumentale adult/reduced €6/4.50; ⊙ basilica 7.30am-1pm & 4.30-8pm, Complesso Monumentale 9.30am-5.30pm Mon-Sat, 10am-2.30pm Sun; Ⓜ Dante) Vast, Gothic and cleverly deceptive, the mighty **Basilica di Santa Chiara** stands at the heart of this tranquil monastery complex. The church was severely damaged in World War II and what you see today is actually a 20th-century re-creation

of Gagliardo Primario's 14th-century original. Adjoining it are the basilica's **cloisters**, lavished with wonderfully colourful 17th-century maiolica tiles and frescoes.

★ Certosa e Museo di San Martino
MONASTERY, MUSEUM

(☑ 081 229 45 10; www.polomusealenapoli.beniculturali.it; Largo San Martino 5; adult/reduced €6/3; ⊙ 8.30am-7.30pm Thu-Tue; Ⓜ Vanvitelli, funicular Montesanto Morghen) The high point (quite literally) of the Neapolitan baroque, this charterhouse-turned-museum was founded as a Carthusian monastery in the 14th century. Centred on one of Italy's finest cloisters, it has been decorated, adorned and altered over the centuries by some of Italy's finest talent, most importantly Giovanni Antonio Dosio in the 16th century and baroque master Cosimo Fanzago a century later. Nowadays, it's a superb repository of Neapolitan artistry.

Palazzo Reale di Capodimonte
GALLERY

(☑ 081 749 91 11; www.polomusealenapoli.beniculturali.it; Via Miano 2; adult/reduced €7.50/3.75; ⊙ 8.30am-7.30pm Thu-Tue; ▣ Via Capodimonte) Originally designed as a hunting lodge for Charles VII of Bourbon, this monumental palace is now home to the **Museo Nazionale di Capodimonte**, southern Italy's largest

Central Naples

N 0 — 400 m
0 — 0.2 miles

Museo Archeologico Nazionale 2

Palazzo Reale di Capodimonte (1.9km)

Via S Guiseppe dei Nudi

Via Tommasi

Via Francesco Saverio Correra

Museo

Via Foria

Via Maria Longo

Piazza Museo Nazionale

Piazza Cavour

Via Santa Maria di Costantinopoli

Largo Regina Coeli

Via Santissimi Apostoli

Via d'Anticaglia

Via Pisanelli

Vico Giganti

Duomo

Via Broggia

Via della Sapienza

Via Atri

Via San Paolo

Via Duomo

Via dei Tribunali

Via Enrico Pessina

Via Bellini

Via del Sole

Piazza San Gaetano

Vico Zuroli

Via della Zite

Via G Brombeis

Vico S Domenico Soriano

Piazza Bellini

Piazza Luigi Miraglia

Via G Maffei

Via Nilo

Via Vicaria Vecchia

Via Montesanto

Via Port'Alba

Dante

Cappella Sansevero 1

Via San Biagio dei Librai

Piazza Museo Filangieri

Via Tarsia

Piazza Dante

Palazzo dei Di Sangrio

Piazzetta del Nilo

Vico S Severino

Via d'Alagno

Via Pellegrini

Via San Sebastiano

Via Benedetto Croce

Via B Capasso

Duomo (under construction)

Piazza Nicola Amore

Via Toledo

Via D Capitelli

Piazza del Gesù Nuovo

Via Mezzocannone

Via G Paladino

Stazione Centrale (1.1km); Circumvesuviana (1.1km)

Via Pasquale Scura

Via Santa Chiara

Largo Giusso

Via Pignasecca

Via T Caravita

Piazza Monteoliveto

Largo Banchi Nuovi

Via S Liborio

Piazza Carità

Via Donnalbina

Via Sedile di Porto

Corso Umberto I

Piazzetta Orefici

Via Formale

Via Monteoliveto

Via Nuova Marina

Via G Simonelli

Via D Cerriglio

Piazza Bovio

Via G C Cortese

Vico P Galluppi

Toledo

Piazza Matteotti

Università

Via Concezione a Montecalvario

Via C Battisti

Via A Diaz

Via Alside De Gasperi

Medmar

Tirrenia

Via Montecalvario

Via Bracco

Via D Fiorentini

Via Graziella

Via A Depretis

Via S Nicola alla Dogana

Calata Porta di Massa

Toledo

Via Potracarrese a Montecalvario

Via S Tommaso d'Aquino

Via F Gioia

Via S Bartolomeo

Via Cristoforo Colombo

Varco Immacolatella

Via Speranzella

Via S Giacomo

Via Medina

Piazza Francese

Via Toledo

Piazza del Municipio

Piazza Francese

Via P E Imbriani

Chiaia (under construction)

Via Vittorio Emanuele III

Municipio (under construction)

Via Santa Brigida

Vico d'Aflitto

Funicolare Centrale

Molo Angioino

San Carlo

Castel Nuovo

SNAV

Tirrenia

Piazza Trieste e Trento

Parco Castello

Alilauro

Caremar

Molo Beverello

Piazza del Plebiscito

Via A F Acton

Central Naples

and richest art gallery. Its vast collection – much of which Charles inherited from his mother, Elisabetta Farnese, and moved here in 1759 – ranges from exquisite 12th-century altarpieces to works by Botticelli, Caravaggio, Titian and Andy Warhol.

The palace was started in 1738 and took more than a century to complete.

✵ Festivals & Events

Festa di San Gennaro   RELIGIOUS
The faithful flock to the Duomo to witness the miraculous liquefaction of San Gennaro's blood on the Saturday before the first Sunday in May. Repeat performances take place on 19 September and 16 December.

Maggio dei Monumenti   CULTURAL
A month-long cultural feast, with a bounty of concerts, performances, exhibitions, guided tours and other events across the city in May.

⎙ Sleeping

**B&B Cappella
Vecchia**   B&B €
(✆081 240 51 17; www.cappellavecchia11.it; Vico Santa Maria a Cappella Vecchia 11; s €50-70, d €75-100, tr €90-120; ❄@🕾; 🚌C24 to Piazza dei Martiri) Run by a super helpful young couple, this B&B makes a great base in the smart Chia district. It has six simple, comfy rooms with funky bathrooms, plays of colour, and Neapolitan themes, from *malocchio* (evil eye) to *spaccanapoli* (the main artery through Naples' historic centre). Breakfast is served in the spacious communal area.

Hostel of the Sun   HOSTEL €
(✆081 420 63 93; www.hostelnapoli.com; Via G Melisurgo 15; dm €16-22, d €50-70; ❄@🕾; 🚌R2 to Via Depretis) The award-wining HOTS is an ultrafriendly hostel near the port. Located on the 7th floor (have €0.05 for the lift), it's a bright, sociable place with multicoloured dorms, a cute in-house bar, and pristine private rooms, with or without ensuite bathrooms.

**★Hotel Piazza
Bellini**   BOUTIQUE HOTEL €€
(✆081 45 17 32; www.hotelpiazzabellini.com; Via Santa Maria di Costantinopoli 101; s €70-150, d €80-170; ❄@🕾; Ⓜ Dante) Only steps away from buzzing Piazza Bellini, this sharp, contemporary hotel occupies a 16th-century *palazzo*, its mint white spaces spiked with original maiolica tiles and the work of emerging artists. Rooms offer pared-back cool, with designer fittings, chic bathrooms and mirror frames drawn straight on the wall. Some also feature panoramic balconies.

Casa D'Anna   GUESTHOUSE €€
(✆081 44 66 11; www.casadanna.it; Via Cristallini 138; s €67-102, d €95-145; ❄🕾; Ⓜ Piazza Cavour, Museo) Everyone from artists to Parisian fashionistas adores this elegant guesthouse, lavished with antiques, books and original artwork. Its four guestrooms skillfully blend classic and contemporary design features of the highest quality, while the lush communal terrace is perfect for an alfresco tête-à-tête. Note, there's a two-night minimum stay.

**Art Resort
Galleria Umberto**   HOTEL €€
(✆081 497 62 81; www.artresortgalleriaumberto. it; 4th fl, Galleria Umberto I 83; r €94-193; ❄@🕾) For a taste of Neapolitan glitz, book into this lofty four-star hotel on the upper floor of the Galleria Umberto I. Rooms are quiet and lavishly attired with frescoes, marble floors and gilt-framed paintings, as are the

POMPEII & HERCULANEUM

On 24 August AD 79, Mt Vesuvius erupted, submerging the thriving port of Pompeii in lapilli (burning fragments of pumice stone) and Herculaneum in mud. Both places were quite literally buried alive, leaving thousands of people dead. The Unesco-listed ruins of both provide remarkable models of working Roman cities, complete with streets, temples, houses, baths, forums, taverns, shops and even a brothel.

Pompeii

A stark reminder of the malign forces that lie deep inside Vesuvius, the ruins of ancient **Pompeii** (☎081 857 53 47; www.pompeiisites.org; entrances at Porta Marina, Piazza Esedra & Piazza Anfiteatro; adult/reduced €11/5.50, incl Herculaneum €20/10; ⏲8.30am-7.30pm summer, to 5pm winter) make for one of Europe's most compelling archaeological sites. The remains first came to light in 1594, when the architect Domenico Fontana stumbled across them while digging a canal, but systematic exploration didn't begin until 1748. Since then 44 of Pompeii's original 66 hectares have been excavated.

There's a huge amount to see at the site. Start with the **Terme Suburbane**, a public bathhouse decorated with erotic frescoes just outside **Porta Marina**, the most impressive of the city's original seven gates. Once inside the walls, continue down **Via Marina** to the grassy **foro** (forum). This was the ancient city's main piazza and is today flanked by limestone columns and what's left of the **basilica**, the 2nd-century-BC seat of the city's law courts and exchange. Opposite the basilica, the **Tempio di Apollo** is the oldest and most important of Pompeii's religious buildings, while at the forum's northern end the **Granai del Foro** (Forum Granary) stores hundreds of amphorae and a number of body casts. These were made in the 19th century by pouring plaster into the hollows left by disintegrated bodies.

A short walk away, the **Lupanare** (Brothel) pulls in the crowds with its collection of red-light frescoes. To the south, the 2nd-century-BC **Teatro Grande** is a 5000-seat theatre carved into the lava mass on which Pompeii was originally built.

Other highlights include the **Anfiteatro**, the oldest-known Roman amphitheatre in existence; the **Casa del Fauno**, Pompeii's largest private house, where many of the mosaics

baroque-styled public spaces. Outside of office hours, you'll need €0.10 for the lift.

Romeo Hotel LUXURY HOTEL €€€
(☎081 017 50 01; www.romeohotel.it; Via Cristoforo Colombo 45; r €150-330, ste €240-650; ❄@📶) All A-list art, glass and steel, this top-end design hotel brings a touch of glamour to the scruffy port area. Rooms vary in size, but all are luxe and supremely comfortable, and the best offer memorable bay views. A Michelin-starred restaurant, sushi bar and fab spa add to the experience.

✕ Eating

Neapolitans are justifiably proud of their pizzas. There are any number of toppings but locals favour the *margherita* (tomato, basil and mozzarella) or *marinara* (tomatoes, garlic and oregano).

★Pizzeria Gino Sorbillo PIZZA €
(☎081 44 66 43; www.accademiadellapizza.it; Via dei Tribunali 32; pizzas from €4; ⏲noon-1am Mon-Sat; Ⓜ Dante) Day in, day out, this legendary pizzeria is besieged by hungry hordes. Once in, the frenetic atmosphere does nothing to diminish the taste of the pizzas, which are supremely good. If it's too crowded, try the 'quieter' Sorbillo a few doors away at Via dei Tribunali 38.

Di Matteo PIZZA €
(☎081 45 52 62; www.pizzeriadimatteo.com; Via dei Tribunali 94; snacks from €0.50, pizzas from €2.50; ⏲9am-midnight Mon-Sat; 🚌C55 to Via Duomo) One of Naples' hard-core pizzerias, Di Matteo is fronted by a popular street-front stall that sells some of the city's best fried snacks, from *pizza fritta* (Neopolitan fried pizza) to nourishing *arancini* (stuffed rice balls). Inside, expect trademark sallow

now in Naples' Museo Archeologico Nazionale originated; and the **Villa dei Misteri**, home to the Dionysiac frieze, the most important fresco still on site.

To get to Pompeii, take the Circumvesuviana train to Pompeii Scavi-Villa dei Misteri (€2.90, 35 minutes from Naples; €2.20, 30 minutes from Sorrento) near the main Porta Marina entrance.

Herculaneum

Smaller and less daunting than Pompeii, **Herculaneum** (☑ 081 732 43 27; www.pompeiisites. org; Corso Resina 187, Ercolano; adult/reduced €11/5.50, incl Pompeii €20/10; ☉ 8.30am-7.30pm summer, to 5pm winter) can reasonably be visited in a morning or afternoon.

A modest fishing port and resort for wealthy Romans, Herculaneum, like Pompeii, was destroyed by the Vesuvius eruption. But because it was much closer to the volcano, it drowned in a 16m-deep sea of mud and debris rather than in the lapilli and ash that rained down on Pompeii. This essentially fossilised the town, ensuring that even delicate items like furniture and clothing were well preserved. Excavations began after the town was rediscovered in 1709 and continue to this day.

There are a number of fascinating houses to explore. Notable among them are the **Casa d'Argo**, a noble residence centred on a porticoed, palm-treed garden; the aristocratic **Casa di Nettuno e Anfitrite**, named after the extraordinary mosaic of Neptune in the nymphaeum (fountain and bath); and the **Casa dei Cervi**, with its marble deer, murals, and beautiful still-life paintings.

Marking the sites' southernmost tip, the 1st-century-AD **Terme Suburbane** is a wonderfully preserved baths complex with deep pools, stucco friezes and bas-reliefs looking down on marble seats and floors.

To reach Herculaneum, take the Circumvesuviana train to Ercolano (€2.20, 15 minutes from Naples; €2.20, 45 minutes from Sorrento), from where it's a 500m walk from the station; follow signs downhill to the *scavi* (ruins).

lighting, surly waitstaff and lip-smacking pizzas.

Trattoria Castel dell'Ovo
SEAFOOD €€

(☑ 081 764 63 52; Via Luculliana 28; meals €25-30; ☉ 1-3pm & 7.30pm-midnight Fri-Wed) Naples isn't all about pizza. Seafood is a citywide passion and the most atmospheric place to try it is the Borgo Marinaro. Here, fronting the marina and nestled among larger, smarter restaurants, this modest family-run trattoria serves tasty, no-nonsense fish dishes to locals and visitors alike.

Da Michele
PIZZA €

(☑ 081 553 92 04; www.damichele.net; Via Cesare Sersale 1; pizzas from €4; ☉ 10.30am-midnight Mon-Sat) Veteran pizzeria Da Michele continues to keep things plain and simple: unadorned marble tabletops, brisk service and two types of pizza – *margherita* or *marinara*. Both are delicious. Just show up, take a ticket and wait (patiently) for your turn.

★ Pintauro
PASTICCERIA €

(☑ 348 778 16 45; Via Toledo 275; sfogliatelle €2; ☉ 8am-2pm & 2.30-8pm Mon-Sat, 9am-2pm Sun Sep-May) Of Neapolitan *dolci* (sweets), the cream of the crop is the *sfogliatella*, a shell of flaky pastry stuffed with creamy, scented ricotta. This local institution has been selling *sfogliatelle* since the early 1800s, when its founder supposedly brought them to Naples from their culinary birthplace on the Amalfi Coast.

La Stanza del Gusto
OSTERIA €€

(☑ 081 40 15 78; www.lastanzadelgusto.com; Via Costantinopoli 100; fixed-price menu €13, tasting menus €35-65; ☉ 5.30pm-midnight Mon, 11am-midnight Tue-Sat; Ⓜ Dante) Focused on top-quality ingredients and artisinal producers, this foodie address offers a trendy ground-floor 'cheese bar', a more-formal restaurant upstairs and a small basement deli. Frankly, the tasting menus aren't great value, but the 'cheese room' is perfect for

OTHER SOUTHERN SPOTS WORTH A VISIT

Lecce Known as the Florence of the South; a lively university town famous for its ornate baroque architecture.

Matera A prehistoric town set on two rocky ravines, studded with primitive cave dwellings, known as *sassi*.

Aeolian Islands An archipelago of seven tiny islands off Sicily's northeastern coast. Lipari is the largest and the main hub, while Stromboli is the most dramatic, with its permanently spitting volcano.

formaggi (cheese), *salumi* and wine by the glass.

Drinking & Nightlife

Caffè Mexico   CAFE
(Piazza Dante 86; ⊙5.30am-9pm Mon-Sat; Ⓜ Dante) Naples' best (and best-loved) coffee bar – even the local cops stop by for a quick pick-me-up – is a retro-tastic combo of old-school baristas, orange espresso machine and velvety, full-flavoured *caffè*. The espresso is served *zuccherato* (sweetened), so request it *amaro* if you fancy a bitter hit.

Caffè Gambrinus   CAFE
(⊘081 41 75 82; www.grancaffegambrinus.com; Via Chiaia 12; ⊙7am-1am; ⊠R2 to Via San Carlo) Grand, chandeliered Gambrinus is Naples' oldest and most venerable cafe. Oscar Wilde knocked back a few here and Mussolini had some of the rooms shut to keep out left-wing intellectuals. Sure, the prices may be steep, but the *aperitivo* nibbles are decent and sipping a *spritz* while soaking up elegant Piazza Triesto e Trento is a moment worth savouring.

Intra Moenia   CAFE
(⊘081 29 07 20; Piazza Bellini 70; ⊙10am-2am; ⎙; Ⓜ Dante) Despite the sloppy service, this ivy-clad literary cafe on Piazza Bellini is a good spot for chilling out. Browse limited-edition books on Neapolitan culture, pick up a vintage-style postcard, or simply sip a *prosecco* and people-watch on the piazza. Wine costs from €4 a glass and there's a range of bruschette, salads and snacks to tide off the munchies.

 Entertainment

Teatro San Carlo   OPERA, BALLET
(⊘081 797 23 31; www.teatrosancarlo.it; Via San Carlo 98; ⊙box office 10am-5.30pm Mon-Sat, to 2pm Sun; ⊠R2 to Via San Carlo) One of Italy's top opera houses, the San Carlo stages a year-round program of opera, ballet and concerts. Bank on anything from €30 to €400 for opera tickets, less for ballet and concerts.

Information

Travellers should be careful about walking alone late at night near Stazione Centrale and Piazza Dante. Petty theft is also widespread so watch out for pickpockets (especially on the city's public transport) and scooter thieves.

TOURIST INFORMATION

Ospedale Loreto-Mare (⊘081 254 21 11; Via Amerigo Vespucci; ⊠ Corso Garibaldi) This hospital is on the waterfront, near the train station.

Police Station (Questura; ⊘081 794 11 11; Via Medina 75) Has an office for foreigners. To report a stolen car, call ⊘113.

Piazza del Gesù Nuovo (⊘081 551 27 01; Piazza del Gesù Nuovo 7; ⊙9am-5pm Mon-Sat, to 1pm Sun; Ⓜ Dante).

Stazione Centrale (⊘081 26 87 79; Stazione Centrale; ⊙8.30am-8.30pm; ⊠ Piazza Garibaldi).

Via San Carlo (⊘081 40 23 94; Via San Carlo 9; ⊙9am-5pm Mon-Sat, to 1pm Sun; ⊠R2 to Via San Carlo).

Getting There & Away

AIR

Naples Capodichino (⊘081 789 61 11; www.gesac.it) Capodichino airport, 7km northeast of the city centre, is southern Italy's main airport. It's served by a number of major airlines and low-cost carriers, including easyJet, which operates flights to Naples from London, Paris, Berlin and several other European cities.

BOAT

Naples, the bay islands, the Amalfi Coast, Sicily and Sardinia are served by a comprehensive ferry network. Departure points:

Calata Porta di Massa Next to Molo Angioino; slow ferries to Capri, Procida and Ischia.

Molo Beverello For Sorrento, Capri, Ischia and Procida. Some services also leave from Molo Mergellina.

Molo Angioino Beside Molo Beverello; for Sicily and Sardinia.

Tickets can be bought online or at Molo Beverello. For longer journeys try **Ontano Tours** (☑ 081 551 71 64; www.ontanotour.it; Molo Angioino; ⊘ 8.30am-8pm Mon-Fri, to 1.30pm Sat). As a rough guide, bank on €19 for the 50-minute jet crossing to Capri, and €12.50 for the 35-minute sail to Sorrento. Services are pared back in winter and adverse sea conditions may affect schedules.

Alilauro (☑ 081 497 22 01; www.alilauro.it)

Caremar (☑ 081 551 38 82; www.caremar.it)

Medmar (☑ 081 333 44 11; www.medmargroup.it)

NLG (☑ 081 552 07 63; www.navlib.it)

Siremar (☑ 081 497 29 99; www.siremar.it)

SNAV (☑ 081 428 55 55; www.snav.it)

Tirrenia (☑ 892 123; www.tirrenia.it)

BUS

SITA Sud (☑ 089 40 51 45; www.sitasud trasporti.it) runs buses to/from Amalfi (€4.10, two hours, up to four daily Monday through Saturday). They arrive at and depart from Varco Immacolatella on the seafront.

From the Metropark near the train station on Corso Arnaldo Lucci, **Marino** (☑ 080 311 23 35; www.marinobus.it) runs up to four daily buses to/from Bari (from €13, three to 3¾ hours). Get tickets from Bar Ettore at Piazza Garibaldi 95.

TRAIN

Most trains arrive at or depart from Stazione Centrale (Piazza Garinaldi) or Stazione Garibaldi underneath Stazione Centrale.

There are about 40 daily trains to Rome (€11 to €34.50, 1¼ to 2½ hours), many of which continue northwards.

Circumvesuviana (☑ 800 211388; www.eavsrl. it) – follow signs from the main train station – operates half-hourly trains to Sorrento (€4.10, 65 minutes) via Ercolano (€2.20, 15 minutes) for Herculaneum, and Pompeii (€2.90, 35 minutes).

⊕ Getting Around

TO/FROM THE AIRPORT

The **Alibus** (☑ 800 639525; www.anm.it) airport shuttle (€3, 45 minutes, every 20 minutes) runs to/from Piazza Garibaldi or Molo Beverello. Buy tickets on board.

PUBLIC TRANSPORT

You can travel around Naples by bus, metro and funicular. Journeys are covered by the Unico Napoli ticket, which comes in various forms:

Standard Valid for 90 minutes, €1.30

Daily €3.70

Weekend daily €3.10

Note that these tickets are only valid for Naples city, they don't cover travel on the Circumvesuviana trains to Herculaneum, Pompeii and Sorrento.

Capri
POP 14,100

The most visited of the islands in the Bay of Naples, Capri deserves more than a quick day trip. Beyond the glamorous veneer of chichi cafes and designer boutiques is an island of rugged seascapes, desolate Roman ruins and a surprisingly unspoiled rural inland.

Ferries dock at Marina Grande, from where it's a short funicular ride up to Capri, the main town. A further bus ride takes you up to Anacapri.

⊙ Sights

Grotta Azzurra CAVE
(Blue Grotto; admission €13; ⊘ 9am-1hr before sunset) Capri's single most famous attraction is the Grotto Azzura, a stunning sea cave illuminated by an other-worldly blue light.

The easiest way to visit is to take a tour from Marina Grande. This costs €26.50, comprising the return boat trip, a rowing boat into the cave and the cave's admission fee. Allow a good hour.

Giardini di Augusto GARDENS
(Gardens of Augustus; admission €1; ⊘ 9am-1hr before sunset) Escape the crowds by seeking out these colourful gardens near the 14th-century Certosa di San Giacomo. Founded by the Emperor Augustus, they rise in a series of flowered terraces to a viewpoint offering breathtaking views over to the **Isole Faraglioni**, a group of three limestone stacks that rise vertically out of the sea.

Villa Jovis RUIN
(Jupiter's Villa; Via Amaiuri; admission €2; ⊘ 9am-1pm, closed Tue 1st-15th of month, closed Sun rest of month) Some 2km east of Capri along Via Tiberio, Villa Jovis was the largest and most sumptuous of the island's 12 Roman villas and Tiberius' main Capri residence. A vast pleasure complex, now reduced to ruins, it famously pandered to the emperor's debauched tastes, and included imperial quarters and extensive bathing areas set in dense gardens and woodland.

★ Seggiovia del Monte Solaro
CHAIRLIFT

(☎ 081 837 14 38; www.capriseggiovia.it; single/return €7.50/10; ☺ 9.30am-5pm summer, to 3.30pm winter) A fast and painless way to reach Capri's highest peak, Anacapri's Seggiovia del Monte Solaro chairlift whisks you to the top of the mountain in a tranquil, beautiful ride of just 12 minutes. The views from the top are outstanding – on a clear day, you can see the entire Bay of Naples, the Amalfi Coast and the islands of Ischia and Procida.

🛏 Sleeping & Eating

Hotel Villa Eva
HOTEL €€

(☎ 081 837 15 49; www.villaeva.com; Via La Fabbrica 8; d €100-160, tr €150-210, apt per person €55-70; ☺ Easter-Oct; 🅿🛜🏊) Nestled amid fruit and olive trees in the countryside near Anacapri, Villa Eva is an idyllic retreat, complete with swimming pool, lush gardens and sunny rooms and apartments. Stained-glass windows and vintage fireplaces add character, while the location ensures peace and quiet.

Hotel La Tosca
PENSION €€

(☎ 081 837 09 89; www.latoscahotel.com; Via Dalmazio Birago 5; s €50-100, d €75-160; ☺ Apr-Oct; 🅿🛜) Away from the glitz of Capri's town centre, this charming one-star place is hidden down a quiet back lane overlooking the Certosa di San Giacomo. The rooms are airy and comfortable, with pine furniture, light tiles, striped fabrics and large bathrooms. Several also have private terraces.

Lo Sfizio
TRATTORIA, PIZZA €€

(☎ 081 837 41 28; Via Tiberio 7; pizzas €7-11, meals €30; ☺ noon-3pm & 7pm-midnight Wed-Mon Apr-Dec) On the path up to Villa Jovis, this trattoria-cum-pizzeria is ideally placed for a post sightseeing meal. It's a relaxed, down-to-earth place with a few roadside tables and a typical island menu, ranging from pizza and handmade pasta to grilled meats and baked fish.

Pulalli
RISTORANTE €€

(☎ 081 837 41 08; Piazza Umberto 1; meals €35-40; ☺ noon-3pm & 7-11.30pm daily Aug, closed Tue Sep-Jul) Climb Capri's clock-tower steps to the right of the tourist office and your reward is this lofty local hang-out where fabulous wine meets a discerning selection of cheese, charcuterie, and more substantial fare such as *risotto al limone* (lemon risotto). Try for a seat on the terrace or, best of all, the coveted table on its own balcony.

ℹ Information

Information is available online at www.capritourism.com or from one of the three tourist offices: **Marina Grande** (☎ 081 837 06 34; www.capritourism.com; Quayside, Marina Grande; ☺ 9am-2pm & 3-6.50pm Mon-Sat, 9am-1pm & 2-7pm Sun), **Capri Town** (☎ 081 837 06 86; www.capritourism.com; Piazza Umberto I; ☺ 9am-7pm Mon-Sat, 9am-1pm & 2-7pm Sun) or **Anacapri** (☎ 081 837 15 24; www.capritourism.com; Via Giuseppe Orlandi 59, Anacapri; ☺ 9am-3pm).

ℹ Getting There & Around

There are year-round boats to Capri from Naples and Sorrento. Timetables and fare details are available online at www.capritourism.com.

From Naples Regular services depart from Molo Beverello. Tickets cost €19 (jetfoils), €12 (ferries).

From Sorrento Jetfoils cost €17 to €18.50, slower ferries €14.50.

On the island, buses run from Capri Town to/from Marina Grande, Anacapri and Marina Piccola. Single tickets cost €1.80 on all routes, including the funicular.

Sorrento
POP 16,700

Despite being a popular package-holiday destination, Sorrento manages to retain a laid-back southern Italian charm. There are very few sights to speak of, but its small *centro storico* is an atmospheric place to explore. Sorrento's relative proximity to the Amalfi Coast, Pompeii and Capri also make it a good base for exploring the area.

◉ Sights & Activities

You'll probably spend most of your time in the *centro storico*, a handsome area thick with souvenir stores, cafes, churches and restaurants.

Villa Comunale Park
PARK

(☺ 8am-midnight summer, to 10.30pm winter) This landscaped park commands stunning views across the water to Mt Vesuvius. A popular green space to while away the sunset hours, it's a lively spot, with benches, operatic buskers and a small bar.

> **❶ UNICO COSTIERA**
>
> Bus travel along the Amalfi Coast is covered by the Unico Costiera travel card, available for durations of 45 minutes (€2.50), 90 minutes (€3.80), 24 hours (€7.50) and 72 hours (€18). Buy the cards from bars, *tabaccherie* (tobacconists) and SITA or Circumvesuviana ticket offices.

Bagni Regina Giovanna
BEACH

Sorrento lacks a decent beach, so consider heading to Bagni Regina Giovanna, a rocky beach with clear, clean water about 2km west of town, set among the ruins of the Roman Villa Pollio Felix.

🛏 Sleeping & Eating

Casa Astarita
B&B €

(☑ 081 877 49 06; www.casastarita.com; Corso Italia 67; d €70-120, tr €100-150; ✳🤖🛜) Housed in a 16th-century *palazzo* on Sorrento's main strip, this charming B&B reveals a colourful, eclectic look with original vaulted ceilings, brightly painted doors and maiolica-tiled floors. Its six simple but well-equipped rooms surround a central parlour, where breakfast is served on a large rustic table.

Ulisse
HOSTEL €

(☑ 081 877 47 53; www.ulissedeluxe.com; Via del Mare 22; dm €18-28, d €50-120; ℗✳🤖🛜) Although it calls itself a hostel, the Ulisse is about as far from a backpackers pad as a hiking boot from a stiletto. True, there are two single-sex dorms, but most rooms are plush, spacious affairs with Regency-style fabrics, marble floors and large en suite bathrooms. Breakfast is included in some rates, but costs €10 with others.

Raki
GELATERIA €

(www.rakisorrento.com; Via San Cesareo 48; cones & tubs from €2; ⊙11am-late) There are numerous gelaterie in Sorrento, but this new kid on the block is making a mark with its homemade preservative-free ice cream in a number of exciting flavours. Try ricotta, walnut and honey, or vanilla and ginger, which packs a surprisingly spicy punch.

O'Puledrone
SEAFOOD €€

(☑ 081 012 41 34; Via Marina Grande 150; meals €25-30; ⊙noon-3pm & 6.30pm-late Easter-Oct) The small harbour at Marina Grande is the place for seafood. This no-frills trattoria, run by a cooperative of local fishers, is as good a spot as any for fried fish starters, pastas and a mountainous *risotto alla pescatora* (seafood risotto).

❶ Information

The main **tourist office** (☑ 081 807 40 33; www. sorrentotourism.com; Via Luigi De Maio 35; ⊙8.30am-7pm Mon-Sat summer, to 4.10pm winter) is near Piazza San Antonino, but there are also information points at the **Circumvesuviana station** (⊙10am-1pm & 3-7pm summer, to 5pm winter) and on **Piazza Tasso** (cnr Corso Italia & Via Correale; ⊙10am-1pm & 4-9pm summer, to 7pm winter).

❶ Getting There & Away

Circumvesuviana trains run half-hourly between Sorrento and Naples (€4.10, 65 minutes) via Pompeii (€2.20, 30 minutes) and Ercolano (€2.20, 45 minutes). A daily ticket covering stops at Ercolano, Pompeii and Sorrento costs €6.30 (€3.50 on weekends).

Regular SITA buses leave from the Circumvesuviana station for the Amalfi Coast, stopping at Positano (€2.50, 40 minutes) and Amalfi (€3.80, 90 minutes).

From Marina Piccola, jetfoils (€18.50) and fast ferries (€17) sail to Capri (25 minutes, up to 16 daily).There are also summer sailings to Naples (€12.50, 35 minutes), Positano (return €32) and Amalfi (return €34).

Amalfi Coast

Stretching 50km along the southern side of the Sorrentine Peninsula, the Unesco-protected Amalfi Coast (Costiera Amalfitana) is a postcard-perfect vision of shimmering blue water fringed by vertiginous cliffs, on which whitewashed villages and terraced lemon groves cling.

❶ Getting There & Away

SITA buses run from Sorrento to Positano (€2.50, 40 minutes) and Amalfi (€3.80, 90 minutes), and from Salerno to Amalfi (€3.80, 75 minutes).

Boat services generally run between April and October.

Alicost (☑ 089 87 14 83; www.alicost.it) Operates daily boats from Salerno (Molo Manfredi) to Amalfi (€8), Positano (€12) and Capri (€22).

Travelmar (☑ 089 87 29 50; www.travelmar. it) Has up to seven daily sailings from Salerno (Piazza Concordia) to Amalfi (€8) and Positano (€12).

WORTH A TRIP

RAVELLO

Elegant Ravello sits high in the clouds overlooking the coast. From Amalfi, it's a nerve-tingling half-hour bus ride (€2.50, up to three an hour), but once you've made it up, you can unwind in the ravishing gardens of **Villa Rufolo** (☑ 089 85 76 21; www.villarufolo.it; Piazza Duomo; adult/reduced €5/3; ☺ 9am-5pm) and bask in awe-inspiring views at **Villa Cimbrone** (☑ 089 85 80 72; Via Santa Chiara 26; adult/reduced €7/4; ☺ 9am-7.30pm summer, to sunset winter).

Positano

POP 3950

Approaching Positano by boat, you're greeted by an unforgettable view of colourful, steeply stacked houses clinging to near-vertical green slopes. In town, the main activities are hanging out on the small beach, drinking and dining on flower-laden terraces and browsing the expensive boutiques.

The **tourist office** (☑ 089 87 50 67; Via del Saracino 4; ☺ 9am-7pm Mon-Sat, to 2pm Sun summer, 9am-4pm Mon-Sat winter) can provide information on walking in the densely wooded Lattari Mountains.

🛏 Sleeping & Eating

Pensione Maria Luisa PENSION €
(☑ 089 87 50 23; www.pensionemarialuisa.com; Via Fornillo 42; r €70-80, with sea view €95; ☺ Mar-Oct; @ 🛜) The Maria Luisa is a friendly old-school *pensione*. Rooms feature shiny blue tiles and simple, no-frills decor; those with private balconies are well worth the extra €15 for the bay views. If you can't bag a room with a view, there's a small communal terrace offering the same sensational vistas. Breakfast is an additional €5.

Hostel Brikette HOSTEL €
(☑ 089 87 58 57; www.hostel-positano.com; Via Marconi 358; dm €24-50, d €65-145, apt €80-220; ✳ 🛜) Positano's year-round hostel is a bright, cheerful place. It has wonderful views and a range of sleeping options, from dorms to doubles and apartments. Conveniently, it also offers a daily hostelling option that allows day trippers use of the hostel's facilities, including showers, wi-fi and left luggage, for €10. Breakfast isn't included.

C'era una volta TRATTORIA, PIZZA €
(☑ 089 81 19 30; Via Marconi 127; pizzas €6, meals €25; ☺ noon-3pm & 6.30pm-late) Up in the high part of town, this authentic trattoria is a good bet for honest, down-to-earth Italian grub. Alongside regional staples, including *gnocchi alla sorrentina* (gnocchi served in a tomato and basil sauce), there's a decent selection of pizzas (to eat in or take-away) and a full menu of pastas and fail-safe mains.

Next2 RISTORANTE €€
(☑ 089 812 35 16; www.next2.it; Viale Pasitea 242; meals €45; ☺ 6.30-11.30pm) Understated elegance meets creative cuisine at this contemporary set-up. Local and organic ingredients are put to impressive use in beautifully presented dishes such as ravioli stuffed with aubergine and prawns or seabass with tomatoes and lemon-scented peas. Desserts are wickedly delicious and the alfresco sea-facing terrace is summer perfection.

Amalfi

POP 5170

Amalfi, the main hub on the coast, makes a convenient base for exploring the surrounding coastline. It's a pretty place with a tangle of narrow alleyways, stacked whitewashed houses and sun-drenched piazzas, but it can get very busy in summer as day trippers pour in to peruse its loud souvenir shops and busy eateries.

The **tourist office** (☑ 089 87 11 07; www.amalfitouristoffice.it; Corso delle Repubbliche Marinare 33; ☺ 9am-1pm & 2-6pm Mon-Sat) can provide information about sights, activities and transport.

◎ Sights

Cattedrale di Sant'Andrea CATHEDRAL
(☑ 089 87 10 59; Piazza del Duomo; ☺ cathedral 7.30am-7.45pm, cloister 9am-7.45pm) A melange of architectural styles, Amalfi's cathedral, one of the few relics of the town's past as an 11th-century maritime superpower, makes a striking impression at the top of its sweeping flight of stairs. Between 10am and 5pm entrance is through the adjacent **Chiostro del Paradiso**, a 13th-century cloister, where you have to pay an admission fee of €3.

Grotta dello Smeraldo CAVE
(admission €5; ☺ 9.30am-4pm) Four kilometres west of Amalfi, this grotto is named after the

BARI

Most travellers visit Puglia's regional capital to catch a ferry. And while there's not a lot to detain you, it's worth taking an hour or so to explore Bari Vecchia (Old Bari). Here, among the labyrinthine lanes, you'll find the **Basilica di San Nicola** (www.basilicasan nicola.it; Piazza San Nicola; ⊘ 7am-8.30pm Mon-Sat, to 10pm Sun), the impressive home to the relics of St Nicholas (aka Santa Claus).

For lunch, **Terranima** (✆ 080 521 97 25; www.terranima.com; Via Putignani 213/215; meals €30; ⊘ 11.30am-3.30pm & 6.30-10.30pm Mon-Sat, 11.30am-3.30pm Sun) serves delicious Puglian food.

Regular trains run to Bari from Rome (€39 to €43, four to six hours). Marino buses arrive from Naples (from €13, three to 3¾ hours).

Ferries sail to Greece, Croatia, Montenegro and Albania from the port, accessible by bus from the train station. Ferry companies have offices at the port, or you can get tickets at the **Morfimare** (✆ 080 578 98 15; www.morfimare.it; Corso de Tullio 36-40) travel agency.

eerie emerald colour that emanates from the water. Stalactites hang down from the 24m-high ceiling, while stalagmites grow up to 10m tall. Buses regularly pass the car park above the cave entrance (from where you take a lift or stairs down to the rowing boats). Alternatively, Coop Sant'Andrea runs boats from Amalfi (€10 return, plus cave admission). Allow 1½ hours for the return trip.

🍴 Sleeping & Eating

Hotel Lidomare   HOTEL €€
(✆ 089 87 13 32; www.lidomare.it; Largo Duchi Piccolomini 9; s/d €50/120; ❋ 🕾) Family run, this old-fashioned hotel has real character. The large, luminous rooms have an air of gentility, with their appealingly haphazard decor, vintage tiles and fine antiques. Some have Jacuzzi bathtubs, others have sea views and a balcony, some have both. Breakfast is laid out, rather unusually, on top of a grand piano.

Hotel Centrale   HOTEL €€
(✆ 089 87 26 08; www.amalfihotelcentrale.it; Largo Piccolomini 1; d €85-140; ❋ @ 🕾) For the money, this is one of the best-value hotels in Amalfi. The entrance is on a tiny little piazza in the *centro storico,* but many of the small but tastefully decorated rooms overlook Piazza del Duomo. The aquamarine ceramic tiling lends it a vibrant, fresh look and the views from the rooftop terrace are magnificent.

Trattoria Il Mulino   TRATTORIA, PIZZA €€
(Via delle Cartiere 36; pizzas €6-11, meals €30; ⊘ 11.30am-4pm & 6.30pm-midnight Tue-Sun) A TV-in-the-corner, kids-running-between-the-

tables sort of place, this is about as authentic an eatery as you'll find in Amalfi. There are few surprises on the menu, just hearty, honest pastas, grilled meats and fish. For a taste of local seafood try the *scialatielli alla pescatore* (ribbon pasta with prawns, mussels, tomato and parsley).

Marina Grande   SEAFOOD €€€
(✆ 089 87 11 29; www.ristorantemarinagrande. com; Viale Delle Regioni 4; tasting menu lunch/ dinner €25/60, meals €45; ⊘ noon-3pm & 6.30-11pm Tue-Sun Mar-Oct) 🌱 Run by the third generation of the same family, this beachfront restaurant serves fish so fresh it's almost flapping. It prides itself on its use of locally sourced organic produce which, in Amalfi, means high-quality seafood. Reservations recommended.

Sicily

Everything about the Mediterranean's largest island is extreme, from the beauty of its rugged landscape to its hybrid cuisine and flamboyant architecture. Over the centuries Sicily has seen off a catalogue of foreign invaders, from the Phoenicians and ancient Greeks to the Spanish Bourbons and WWII Allies. All have contributed to the island's complex and fascinating cultural landscape.

ℹ️ Getting There & Away

AIR

Flights from mainland Italian cities and an increasing number of European destinations serve Sicily's two main airports: Palermo's **Falcone-Borsellino**

Airport (☑ 091 702 02 73; www.gesap.it) and Catania's **Fontaross Airport** (☑ 095 723 91 11; www.aeroporto.catania.it).

BOAT

Regular car and passenger ferries cross to Sicily (Messina) from Villa San Giovanni in Calabria. Ferries also sail from Genoa, Livorno, Civitavecchia, Naples, Salerno and Cagliari, as well as Malta and Tunisia.

Following are the major routes and the companies that operate them:

TO	DEPARTURE POINT	COMPANIES
Catania	Naples	TTT Lines
Messina	Salerno	Caronte & Tourist
Palermo	Cagliari	Tirrenia
Palermo	Civitavecchia	Grandi Navi Veloci
Palermo	Genoa	Grandi Navi Veloci
Palermo	Naples	Tirrenia, Grandi Navi Veloci
Palermo	Salerno	Grimaldi Lines

BUS

Bus services between Rome and Sicily are operated by **SAIS Trasporti** (www.saistrasporti.it) and **Segesta** (☑ 091 34 25 25; www.buscenter. it), departing from Rome Tiburtina. There are daily buses to Messina, Catania, Palermo and Syracuse.

TRAIN

Direct trains run from Rome, Naples and Reggio di Calabria to Messina and on to Palermo and Catania.

Palermo

POP 678,500

Still bearing the bruises of its WWII battering, Palermo is a compelling and chaotic city. It takes a little work, but once you've acclimatised to the congested and noisy streets you'll be rewarded with some of southern Italy's most imposing architecture, impressive art galleries, vibrant street markets and an array of tempting restaurants and cafes.

◎ Sights

A good starting point is the **Quattro Canti**, a road junction where Palermo's four central districts converge. Nearby, **Piazza Pretoria** is dominated by the ostentatious **Fontana Pretoria**.

La Martorana
CHURCH
(Chiesa di Santa Maria dell'Ammiraglio; Piazza Bellini 3; admission €2; ⊙8.30am-1pm & 3.30-5.30pm Mon-Sat, 8.30-9.45am & 11.45am-1pm Sun) On the southern side of Piazza Bellini, this luminously beautiful 12th-century church was endowed by King Roger's Syrian emir, George of Antioch, and was originally planned as a mosque. Delicate Fatimid pillars support a domed cupola depicting Christ enthroned amid his archangels. The interior is best appreciated in the morning, when sunlight illuminates magnificent Byzantine mosaics.

Chiesa Capitolare di San Cataldo
CHURCH
(Piazza Bellini 3; admission €2.50; ⊙9.30am-12.30pm & 3-6pm) This 12th-century church in Arab-Norman style is one of Palermo's most striking buildings. With its dusky pink bijou domes, solid square shape, blind arcading and delicate tracery, it illustrates perfectly the synthesis of Arab and Norman architectural styles. The interior, while more austere, is still beautiful, with its inlaid floor and lovely stone-and-brickwork in the arches and domes.

Cattedrale di Palermo
CATHEDRAL
(www.cattedrale.palermo.it; Corso Vittorio Emanuele; cathedral free, monumental area €7; ⊙7am-7pm Mon-Sat, 8am-1pm & 4-7pm Sun) A feast of geometric patterns, ziggurat crenulations, maiolica cupolas and blind arches, Palermo's cathedral has suffered aesthetically from multiple reworkings over the centuries, but remains a prime example of Sicily's unique Arab-Norman architectural style. The interior, while impressive in scale, is essentially a marble shell, the most interesting features of which are the royal Norman tombs (in the **Monumental Area** to the left as you enter) and **treasury**, home to Constance of Aragon's gem-encrusted 13th-century crown.

Palazzo dei Normanni
PALACE
(Palazzo Reale; www.fondazionefedericosecondo. it; Piazza Indipendenza 1; adult/reduced Fri-Mon €8.50/6.50, Tue-Thu €7/5; ⊙8.15am-5.40pm Mon-Sat, to 1pm Sun) Home to Sicily's regional parliament, this venerable palace dates to the 9th century. However, it owes its current look (and name) to a major Norman makeover, during which spectacular mosaics were added to its royal apartments and magnificent chapel, the Cappella Palatina. Visits to the apartments, which are off limits from Tuesday to Thursday, take in the mosaic-lined

Sala dei Venti, and **Sala di Ruggero II**, King Roger's 12th-century bedroom.

★**Cappella Palatina** CHAPEL

(Palatine Chapel; www.fondazionefedericosecondo. it; adult/reduced Fri-Mon €8.50/6.50, Tue-Thu €7/5; ☉8.15am-5.40pm Mon-Sat, 8.15-9.45am & 11.15am-1pm Sun) This priceless jewel of a chapel, designed by Roger II in 1130, is Palermo's top tourist attraction. On the mid level of Palazzo dei Normanni's three-tiered loggia, it glitters with stunning gold mosaics, its aesthetic harmony further enhanced by the inlaid marble floors and wooden *muqarnas* ceiling, a masterpiece of Arabic-style honeycomb carving that reflects Norman Sicily's cultural complexity.

Note that queues are likely, and that you'll be refused entry if you're wearing shorts, a short skirt or a low-cut top.

★**Teatro Massimo** THEATRE

(☑tour reservations 091 605 35 80; www.teatro massimo.it; Piazza Giuseppe Verdi; guided tours adult/reduced €8/5; ☉9.30am-5pm Tue-Sun) Palermo's grand neoclassical opera house took over 20 years to complete and has become one of the city's iconic landmarks. The closing scene of *The Godfather: Part III*, with its visually stunning juxtaposition of high culture, crime, drama and death, was filmed here. Guided 25-minute tours are offered in English, Spanish, French and Italian daily, except Monday.

🛏 Sleeping

★**A Casa di Amici Hostel** HOSTEL €

(☑091 765 46 50; www.acasadiamici.com; Via Dante 57; dm €15-23, d €46-70; ❈☎) Vibrant, friendly and full of uplifting paintings left by former guests, this funky hostel-cum-guesthouse is a great choice. Beds are in single-sex or mixed dorms, or in several imaginatively decorated rooms, each themed on a musical instrument. There's a kitchen and a yoga room, and multilingual owner Claudia provides helpful maps and advice.

B&B Panormus B&B €

(☑091 617 58 26; www.bbpanormus.com; Via Roma 72; s €45-70, d €60-83, tr €75-120; ❈☎) Keen prices, a charming host and convenient location help make this one of the city's most popular B&Bs. Its five high-ceilinged rooms, each with its own private bathroom down the passageway, are decorated in an elegant

Liberty style and come with double-glazed windows and flat-screen TVs.

Butera 28 APARTMENT €€

(☑333 3165432; www.butera28.it; Via Butera 28; apt per day €60-180, per week €380-1150; ❈☎) Delightful multilingual owner Nicoletta rents 11 comfortable apartments in the 18th-century Palazzo Lanzi Tomasi, the last home of Giuseppe Tomasi di Lampedusa, author of *The Leopard*. Units range from 30 to 180 sq metres, most sleeping a family of four or more. Four apartments face the sea, most have laundry facilities and all have well-equipped kitchens.

🍴 Eating & Drinking

Three local specialities to try are *arancini*, *panelle* (chickpea fritters) and *cannoli* (pastry tubes filled with sweetened ricotta and candied fruit).

For an adrenalin-charged food experience, head to one of Palermo's markets: Capo on Via Sant'Agostino or Ballarò in the Albergheria quarter, off Via Maqueda.

Touring Café CAFE €

(☑091 32 27 26; Via Roma 252; arancino €1.70; ☉6.15am-11pm Mon-Fri, to midnight Sat & Sun) Don't let the gleaming Liberty-style mirrored bar and array of picture-perfect pastries distract you. You come here for the *arancini*, great fist-sized rice balls stuffed with *ragù*, spinach or butter, and fried to a perfect golden orange.

Trattoria Il Maestro del Brodo TRATTORIA €

(☑091 32 95 23; Via Pannieri 7; meals €25; ☉12.30-3.30pm Tue-Sun & 8-11pm Fri & Sat) This no-frills trattoria in the Vucciria offers delicious soups, an array of ultrafresh seafood, and a sensational antipasto buffet (€8) featuring a dozen-plus homemade delicacies: *sarde a beccafico* (stuffed sardines), eggplant *involtini* (rolls), smoked fish, artichokes with parsley, sun-dried tomatoes, olives and more.

★**Osteria Ballarò** SICILIAN €€

(☑091 791 01 84; www.osteriaballaro.it; Via Calascibetta 25; meals €35-40; ☉12.30pm-3.15pm & 7pm-midnight) A hot new foodie address, this classy restaurant-cum-wine bar marries an atmospheric setting with fantastic island cooking. Bare stone columns, exposed-brick walls and vaulted ceilings set the stage for delicious seafood *primi*, local wines and memorable Sicilian *dolci*. Reservations recommended.

For a faster meal, you can snack on street food at the bar or take away from the hole-in-the-wall counter outside.

Kursaal Kalhesa   BAR

(☑ 091 616 00 50; www.kursaalkalhesa.it; Foro Umberto I 21; ⊗ 6.30pm-1am Tue-Sun) Recently reopened after a restyling, Kursaal Kalhesa has long been a noted city nightspot. Touting itself as a restaurant, wine bar and jazz club, it draws a cool, in-the-know crowd who come to hang out over *aperitivi,* dine alfresco or catch a gig under the high vaulted ceilings – it's in a 15th-century *palazzo* on the city's massive sea walls.

ℹ Information

There are several information points across town, the most useful at the airport, **Piazza Bellini** (☑ 091 740 80 21; promozioneturismo@comune.palermo.it; ⊗ 8.30am-6.30pm Mon-Sat) and **Piazza Castelnuovo** (⊗ 8.30am-1pm Mon-Sat).

Ospedale Civico (☑ 091 666 11 11; www.ospedalecivicopa.org; Piazza Nicola Leotta) Emergency facilities.

Police Station (Questura; ☑ 091 21 01 11; Piazza della Vittoria 8).

ℹ Getting There & Away

National and international flights arrive at Falcone-Borsellino Airport (p487), 31km west of Palermo.

The ferry terminal is northeast of the historic centre, off Via Francesco Crispi.

The intercity bus terminal is in Piazza Cairoli, to the side of the train station. Following are the main bus companies:

Cuffaro (☑ 091 616 15 10; www.cuffaro.info; Via Paolo Balsamo 13) Services to Agrigento (€9, two hours, three to eight daily).

Interbus (☑ 091 616 79 19; www.interbus.it; Piazza Cairoli) To/from Syracuse (€13.50, 3¼ hours, three daily).

SAIS Autolinee (☑ 091 616 60 28; www.saisautolinee.it; Piazza Cairoli) To/from Catania (€15, 2¾ hours, 10 to 14 daily) and Messina (€26, 2¾ hours, three to six daily).

Trains serve Messina (€12 to €19.50, 2½ to 3½ hours, hourly), Agrigento (€8.50, two hours, 11 daily), Naples (€50 to €59, 9¼ hours, three daily) and Rome (€59 to €62, 11½ to 12¾ hours, four daily).

ℹ Getting Around

TO/FROM THE AIRPORT

Prestia e Comandè (☑ 091 58 63 51; www.prestiaecomande.it) operates a bus service from outside the train station to the airport. Buses run half-hourly between 5am and 10.30pm (11pm from the airport). Tickets for the 50-minute journey cost €6.30 and are available online or on the bus.

BUS

Walking is the best way to get around Palermo's centre, but if you want to take a bus, most stop outside or near the train station. Tickets cost €1.40 (€1.80 on board) and are valid for 90 minutes.

Taormina

POP 11,100

Spectacularly perched on a clifftop terrace overlooking the Ionian Sea and Mt Etna, this sophisticated town has attracted socialites, artists and writers ever since Greek times. Its pristine medieval core, proximity to beaches, grandstand coastal views and chic social scene make it a hugely popular summer holiday destination.

⊙ Sights & Activities

The principal pastime in Taormina is wandering the pretty hilltop streets, browsing the shops on **Corso Umberto**, the pedestrianised main strip, and eyeing up fellow holidaymakers.

For the beach, you'll need to take the **funivia** (cable car; Via Luigi Pirandello; one way €3; ⊗ 8.45am-1am Mon, 7.45am-1am Tue-Sun) down to Lido Mazzarò and Isola Bella.

★ Teatro Greco   RUIN

(☑ 094 22 32 20; Via Teatro Greco; adult/reduced €8/4; ⊗ 9am to 1hr before sunset) Taormina's premier sight is this perfect horseshoe-shaped theatre, suspended between sea and sky, with Mt Etna looming on the southern horizon. Built in the 3rd century BC, it's the most dramatically situated Greek theatre in the world and the second largest in Sicily (after Syracuse). In summer it's used to stage international arts and film festivals.

SAT   BUS TOUR

(☑ 0942 2 46 53; www.satexcursions.it; Corso Umberto I 73) One of a number of agencies that organises day trips to Mt Etna (from €35), Syracuse (€45), Palermo (€55) and Agrigento (€52).

🛏 Sleeping & Eating

★ Isoco Guest House   GUESTHOUSE €

(☑ 0942 2 36 79; www.isoco.it; Via Salita Branco 2; r €95-120; ⊗ Mar-Nov; ※ @ 🖱) Each of the five rooms in this welcoming, gay-friendly guesthouse is dedicated to an artist, from Botticelli to graffiti pop designer Keith Haring and photo legend Herb Ritts. Outside there's a garden where breakfast is served around a large table, and a roof terrace with a hot tub and stunning sea views.

Hostel Taormina HOSTEL€

(☑ 0942 62 55 05; www.hosteltaormina.com; Via Circonvallazione 13; dm €18-23, r €49-85; ✳ ☎) Friendly and laid-back, this year-round hostel occupies a house with a roof terrace commanding panoramic sea views. It's a snug, homey set-up with accommodation in three dorms, a private room and a couple of apartments. There's also a communal kitchen, a relaxed vibe and the owners go out of their way to help.

Tiramisù RISTORANTE, PIZZA €€

(☑ 0942 2 48 03; Via Cappuccini 1; pizzas €7-14, meals €35; ☺ 12.30pm-midnight Wed-Fri, 1-3.30pm & 7.30pm-midnight Sat & Sun) Head to this stylish place near Porta Messina for excellent seafood, tasty wood-fired pizzas and traditional island dishes such as *rigatoni alla Norma*, a classic mix of pasta, aubergines, basil, tomato and ricotta. When dessert rolls around, don't miss the trademark tiramisu.

ℹ Information

Tourist Office (☑ 094 22 32 43; Palazzo Corvaja, Piazza Santa Caterina; ☺ 8.30am-2.15pm & 3.30-6.45pm Mon-Fri, also 9am-1pm & 4-6.30pm Sat summer) Has plenty of practical information.

ℹ Getting There & Away

Taormina is best reached by bus. From the bus terminus on Via Luigi Pirandello, Interbus services leave for Messina (€4.30, 55 minutes to 1¾ hours, up to six daily), Catania (€5, 1¼ hours, six to 10 daily) and Catania's Fontanaross Airport (€8, 1½ hours, six daily).

Mt Etna

The dark silhouette of Mt Etna (3350m) broods ominously over Sicily's east coast, more or less halfway between Taormina and Catania. One of Europe's highest and most volatile volcanoes, it erupts frequently, most recently in summer 2014.

To get to Etna by public transport, take the AST bus from Catania (at 8.15am daily, also 11.20am June to September). This departs from in front of the train station (returning at 4.30pm; €6 return) and drops you at the Rifugio Sapienza (1923m), where you can pick up the **Funivia dell'Etna** (☑ 095 91 41 41; www.funiviaetna.com; return €30, incl bus & guide €60; ☺ 9am-5.45pm summer, to 3.45pm winter) to 2500m. From there buses courier you up to the crater zone (2920m). If you want to walk, allow up to four hours for the round trip.

Gruppo Guide Alpine Etna Sud (☑ 095 791 47 55; www.etnaguide.com) is one of many outfits offering guided tours. Bank on around €70 to €80 for a full-day excursion.

Further Etna information is available from Catania's **tourist office** (☑ 095 742 55 73; www.comune.catania.it; Via Vittorio Emanuele II 172; ☺ 8.15am-7.15pm Mon-Sat).

Syracuse

POP 122,300

A tumultuous past has left Syracuse (Siracusa) a beautiful baroque centre and some of Sicily's finest ancient ruins. Founded in 734 BC by Corinthian settlers, it became the dominant Greek city-state on the Mediterranean and was known as the most beautiful city in the ancient world. A devastating earthquake in 1693 destroyed most of the city's buildings, paving the way for a city-wide baroque makeover.

◉ Sights

Ortygia AREA

Connected to the modern town by bridge, Ortygia, Syracuse's historic centre, is an atmospheric warren of elaborate baroque *palazzi*, lively piazzas and busy trattorias. At its heart, the city's 7th-century **Duomo** (Piazza del Duomo; admission €2; ☺ 9am-6.30pm Mon-Sat summer, to 5.30pm winter) lords it over Piazza del Duomo, one of Sicily's loveliest public spaces. The cathedral was built over a preexisting 5th-century-BC Greek temple, incorporating most of the original columns in its three-aisled structure. The sumptuous baroque facade was added in the 18th century.

Parco Archeologico della Neapolis ARCHAEOLOGICAL SITE

(☑ 0931 6 62 06; Viale Paradiso 14; adult/reduced €10/5, incl Museo Archeologico €13.50/7; ☺ 9am-6pm) For the classicist, Syracuse's real attraction is this archaeological park, with its pearly white 5th-century-BC **Teatro Greco**. Hewn out of the rocky hillside, this

16,000-capacity amphitheatre staged the last tragedies of Aeschylus (including *The Persians*), which were first performed here in his presence. In late spring it's brought to life with an annual season of classical theatre.

★ Museo Archeologico Paolo Orsi
MUSEUM

(☑ 093 146 40 22; Viale Teocrito 66; adult/reduced €8/4, incl Parco Archeologico €13.50/7; ⊙ 9am-6pm Tue-Sat, to 1pm Sun) About 500m east of the archaeological park, this modern museum contains one of Sicily's largest and most interesting archaeological collections. Allow plenty of time to investigate the four sectors charting the area's prehistory, as well as Syracuse's development from foundation to the late Roman period.

🛏 Sleeping & Eating

★ B&B dei Viaggiatori, Viandanti e Sognatori
B&B €

(☑ 0931 2 47 81; www.bedandbreakfastsicily.it; Via Roma 156; s €35-50, d €55-70, tr €75-80, q €90-100; ❋ ☎) Decorated with verve and boasting a prime Ortygia location, this relaxed B&B exudes a homey boho feel, with books and antique furniture juxtaposed against bright walls. Rooms are colourful and imaginatively decorated, while up top, the sunny roof terrace offers sweeping sea views.

B&B L'Acanto
B&B €

(☑ 0931 44 95 55; www.bebsicily.com; Via Roma 15; s €35-50, d €55-70, tr €75-80, q €90-100; ❋ ☎) Set around an internal courtyard in the heart of Ortygia, L'Acanto is a popular, value-for-money B&B. Its five rooms are simply decorated and enlivened with patches of exposed stone, vintage furniture and the occasional mural.

Palazzo del Sale
B&B €€

(☑ 093 16 59 58; www.palazzodelsale.com; Via Santa Teresa 25; d €100-120, ste €115-135; ❋ ☎) Housed in a historic *palazzo*, the seven rooms at this designer B&B are hot property in summer, so be sure to book ahead. All are well sized, with high ceilings, original touches and good beds. Coffee and tea are always available in the comfortable communal lounge.

★ Sicily
PIZZA €

(☑ 392 9659949; www.sicilypizzeria.it; Via Cavour 67; pizzas €4.50-12; ⊙ 7.15pm-midnight Tue-Sun) Experimenting with pizzas is something you do at your peril in culinary-conservative Sicily. But that's what they do, and do well, at this funky retro-chic pizzeria. So if you're game for wood-fired pizzas topped with moreish combos like sausage, cheese, Swiss chard, pine nuts, sun-dried tomatoes and raisins, this is the place for you.

Sicilia in Tavola
SICILIAN €

(☑ 392 4610889; Via Cavour 28; meals €25; ⊙ 12.30-2.30pm & 7.30-10.30pm Tue-Sun) One of a number of popular eateries on Via Cavour, this tiny trattoria enjoys a strong local reputation on the back of its homemade pasta and fresh seafood. To taste for yourself, try the *fettuccine allo scoglio* (pasta ribbons with mixed seafood). Reservations are recommended.

❶ Information

Check out the useful website www.siracusa turismo.net.

Tourist Office (☑ 0800 055500; infoturismo@ provsr.it; Via Roma 31; ⊙ 8am-8pm Mon-Sat, 9am-7pm Sun) For on-the-ground information, drop into this office in Ortygia.

❶ Getting There & Around

Buses are a better bet than trains, serving a terminus close to the train station. Interbus runs services to/from Catania's Fontanaross Airport (€6, 1¼ hours, hourly), Catania (€6, 1½ hours, hourly) and Palermo (€13.50, 3¼ hours, three daily).

Direct trains connect with Taormina (€8.50, two hours, eight daily) and Messina (€9.50 to €15.50, 2¾ hours, seven daily).

Sd'a trasporti runs three lines of electric buses, the most useful of which is the red No 2 line, which links Ortygia with the train station and archaeological zone. Tickets, available on board, cost €0.50.

Agrigento

POP 59,000

Seen from a distance, Agrigento doesn't bode well, with rows of unsightly apartment blocks crowded onto the hillside. But behind the veneer, the city boasts a small but attractive medieval core and, down in the valley, one of Italy's greatest ancient sites, the Valley of the Temples (Valle dei Templi).

Founded around 581 BC by Greek settlers, the city was an important trading centre under the Romans and Byzantines.

For maps and information, ask at the **tourist office** (☑ 0922 59 31 11; www.provincia. agrigento.it; Piazzale Aldo Moro 1; ⊙ 9am-1pm &

2.30-7pm Mon-Fri, 9am-1pm Sat) in the Provincia building.

◎ Sights

★ Valley of the Temples
ARCHAEOLOGICAL SITE

(Valle dei Templi; ☑0922 62 16 11; www.parco valledeitempli.net; adult/reduced €10/5, incl Museo Archeologico €13.50/7; ⊙8.30am-7pm) Sicily's most enthralling archaeological site, the Parco Valle dei Templi encompasses the ruins of the ancient city of Akragas. The highlight is the stunning **Tempio della Concordia** (Temple of Concord), one of the best-preserved Greek temples in existence and one of a series built on a ridge to act as beacons for homecoming sailors.

The 13-sq-km park, 3km south of Agrigento, is split into an eastern zone, with the most spectacular temples, and, over the road, the western sector.

🛏 Sleeping & Eating

PortAtenea
B&B €

(☑349 093 74 92; www.portatenea.com; Via Atenea, cnr Via C Battisti; s €39-50, d €59-75, tr €79-95; ✳🢒) Conveniently located near the train and bus stations, this five-room B&B is an excellent choice. It wins plaudits for its panoramic roof terrace overlooking the Valley of the Temples, and spacious, well-appointed rooms.

Trattoria Concordia
TRATTORIA €€

(☑0922 2 26 68; Via Porcello 8; meals €25-30; ⊙noon-3pm & 7-10.30pm Mon-Fri, 7-11pm Sat) This cosy side-alley eatery is a quintessential family-run trattoria. The look is rustic with rough stone walls and a low wood-beamed ceiling, and the food abundant and full of flavour. Kick off with the antipasto *rustico* (a heaving plate of frittata, sweet-and-sour aubergine, ricotta, salad, olives and more) before following with a juicy grilled steak.

❶ Getting There & Around

The bus is the easiest way to get to and from Agrigento. Intercity buses arrive on Piazzale F Rosselli, from where it's a short walk downhill to the train station on Piazza Gugliemo Marconi, where you can catch local bus 1, 2 or 3 to the Valley of the Temples (€1.20).

Cuffaro runs buses to/from Palermo (€9, two hours, three to eight daily) and SAIS Trasporti services go to Catania (€13.50, three hours, hourly).

SURVIVAL GUIDE

❶ Directory A–Z

ACCOMMODATION

➡ The bulk of Italy's accommodation is made up of *alberghi* (hotels) and *pensioni*. Other options are hostels, campgrounds, B&Bs, *agriturismi* (farm stays), mountain *rifugi* (Alpine refuges), monasteries and villa/apartment rentals.

➡ Prices fluctuate enormously between seasons. High-season rates apply at Easter, in summer (mid-June to August) and over the Christmas to New Year period.

➡ Many places in coastal resorts close between November and March.

B&Bs

➡ Quality varies, but the best offer comfort greater than you'd get in a similarly priced hotel room.

➡ Prices typically range from about €70 to €180 for a double room.

Camping

➡ Most Italian campgrounds are major complexes with on-site supermarkets, restaurants and sports facilities.

➡ In summer expect to pay up to €20 per person, and a further €25 for a tent pitch.

➡ Useful resources include www.campeggi. com, www.camping.it and www.italcamping.it.

Convents & Monasteries

Basic accommodation is often available in convents and monasteries. See www.monastery stays.com, a specialist online booking service.

Farm Stays

➡ An *agriturismo* is a good option for a country stay, although you'll usually need a car to get there.

SLEEPING PRICE RANGES

In this chapter prices quoted are for rooms with a private bathroom and, unless otherwise stated, include breakfast. The following price indicators apply (for a high-season double):

€ less than €110 (under €120 in Rome and Venice)

€€ €110–€200 (€120–€250 in Rome, €120–€220 in Venice)

€€€ more than €200 (more than €250 in Rome & €220 in Venice)

ITALY DIRECTORY A-Z

ⓘ HOTEL TAX

Most Italian hotels apply a *tassa di soggiorno* (room occupancy tax) which is charged on top of your regular hotel bill. The exact amount, which varies from city to city, depends on your type of accommodation, but as a rough guide reckon on €1 to €3 per person per night in a one-star hotel, €3 to €3.50 in a B&B, €3 to €4 in a three-star hotel etc.

Prices quoted in accommodation reviews do not include the tax.

➙ Accommodation varies from spartan billets on working farms to palatial suites at luxury retreats.

➙ For listings check out www.agriturist.it or www.agriturismo.com.

Hostels

➙ Official HI-affiliated *ostelli per la gioventù* (youth hostels) are run by the **Italian Youth Hostel Association** (Associazione Italiana Alberghi per la Gioventù; Map p420; ☑ 06 487 11 52; www.aighostels.it). A valid HI card is required for these; you can get a card in your home country or directly at hostels.

➙ There are also many excellent private hostels offering dorms and private rooms.

➙ Dorm rates are typically between €15 and €30, with breakfast usually included.

Hotels & Pensioni

➙ A *pensione* is a small, often family-run, hotel. In cities, they are often in converted apartments.

➙ Hotels and *pensioni* are rated from one to five stars. As a rule, a three-star room will come with an en suite bathroom, air-con, hairdryer, minibar, safe and wi-fi.

➙ Many city-centre hotels offer discounts in August to lure clients from the crowded coast. Check websites for deals.

ACTIVITIES

Cycling Tourist offices can provide details on trails and guided rides. The best time is spring. Favourite areas include Tuscany, the flatlands of Emilia-Romagna, and the peaks around Lago Maggiore and Lago del Garda.

Hiking Thousands of kilometres of *sentieri* (marked trails) criss-cross the country. The hiking season is from June to September. The Italian Parks organisation (www.parks.it) lists walking trails in Italy's national parks.

Skiing Italy's ski season runs from December through to March. Prices are generally high, particularly in the top Alpine resorts – the Apennines are cheaper. A popular option is to buy a *settimana bianca* (literally 'white week') package deal, covering accommodation, food and ski passes.

BUSINESS HOURS

In reviews, the hours listed are the most commonly applied ones. Where necessary, summer/winter variations are noted. The following are the general hours for various business types:

Banks 8.30am to 1.30pm and 2.45pm to 4.30pm Monday to Friday.

Bars & Cafes 7.30am to 8pm, sometimes until 1am or 2am.

Clubs 10pm to 4am.

Museums & Galleries Generally operate summer and winter hours. Typically, summer hours apply from late March/April to October. At some places, closing time is set in relation to sunset.

Pharmacies Keep shop hours; outside of these, they open on a rotation basis – all are required to post a list of places open in the vicinity.

Post offices Major offices 8am to 7pm Monday to Friday, to 1.15pm Saturday; branch offices often close at 2pm Monday to Friday, 1pm Saturday.

Restaurants Noon to 3pm and 7.30pm to 11pm; most restaurants close one day a week.

Shops 9am to 1pm and 3.30pm to 7.30pm (or 4pm to 8pm) Monday to Saturday; in larger cities chain stores and supermarkets may stay open at lunchtime and on Sundays.

FOOD

➙ On the bill expect to be charged for *pane e coperto* (bread and cover charge). This is standard and is added even if you don't ask for or eat the bread.

➙ *Servizio* (service charge) of 10% to 15% might or might not be added; if it's not, tourists are expected to leave around 10%.

➙ Restaurants are nonsmoking.

GAY & LESBIAN TRAVELLERS

➙ Homosexuality is legal in Italy. It's well tolerated in major cities, but overt displays of affection could attract a negative response.

➙ Italy's main gay and lesbian organisation is **Arcigay** (☑ 051 1095 7241; www.arcigay.it; Via Don Minzoni 18, Bologna), based in Bologna.

INTERNET ACCESS

➙ Most hotels, hostels, B&Bs and *pensioni* offer free wi-fi.

➙ Public wi-fi is available in many large cities, but you'll generaly need an Italian mobile number to register for it.

➙ Internet cafes are thin on the ground. Charges are typically around €5 per hour.

→ To use internet points you must present photo ID.

INTERNET RESOURCES

The following websites will whet your appetite for a trip to Italy:

Italia (www.italia.it) Mix of practical and inspirational information.

Lonely Planet (www.lonelyplanet.com/italy) Destination information, hotel booking, traveller forum and more.

Delicious Italy (www.deliciousitaly.com) Articles on Italian food and food-related news, events etc.

MONEY

ATMs Known as *bancomat*, ATMs are widespread and will accept cards displaying the appropriate sign. Visa and MasterCard are widely recognised, as are Cirrus and Maestro; American Express is less common.

Credit cards Credit cards are widely accepted, although American Express less than Visa and MasterCard. Many trattorias, pizzerias and *pensioni* will only take cash, however. Don't assume museums, galleries and the like will accept credit cards. If your credit/debit card is lost, stolen or swallowed by an ATM, telephone toll free to block it: **Amex** (☑800 928391), **MasterCard** (☑800 870866) or **Visa** (☑800 819014).

Tipping If *servizio* is not included, leave 10% in restaurants, a euro or two in pizzerias. It's not necessary in bars or cafes, but many people leave small change if drinking at the bar.

PUBLIC HOLIDAYS

Most Italians take their annual holiday in August. This means that many businesses and shops close down for at least part of the month, usually around Ferragosto (15 August). Easter is another busy holiday. Individual towns also have holidays to celebrate their patron saints.

Countrywide public holidays:

ESSENTIAL FOOD & DRINK

Italian cuisine is highly regional in nature and wherever you go you'll find local specialities. That said, some staples are ubiquitous:

→ **Pizza** There are two varieties: Roman, with a thin crispy base; and Neapolitan, with a higher, more doughy base. The best are always prepared in a *forno a legna* (wood-fired oven).

→ **Pasta** This comes in hundreds of shapes and sizes and is served with everything from thick meat-based sauces to fresh seafood.

→ **Gelato** Classic flavours include *fragola* (strawberry), *pistacchio* (pistachio), *nocciola* (hazelnut) and *stracciatella* (milk with chocolate shavings).

→ **Wine** Ranges from big-name reds such as Piedmont's Barolo and Tuscany's Brunello di Montalcino to sweet Sicilian Malvasia and sparkling *prosecco* from the Veneto.

→ **Caffè** Italians take their coffee seriously, drinking cappuccino only in the morning, and espressos whenever, ideally standing at a bar.

Eat Like an Italian

A full Italian meal consists of an antipasto, a *primo* (first course; pasta or rice dish), *secondo* (second/main course; usually meat or fish) with an *insalata* (salad) or *contorno* (vegetable side dish), *dolce* (dessert) and coffee. Most Italians only eat a meal this large at Sunday lunch or on a special occasion, and when eating out it's fine to mix and match and order, say, a *primo* followed by an *insalata* or *contorno*.

Italians are late diners, often not eating until after 9pm.

Where to Eat & Drink

For a full meal there are several options: **trattorias** are traditional, often family-run places serving local food and wine; **ristoranti** (restaurants) are more formal, with greater choice and smarter service; **pizzerias**, which usually open evenings only, often serve a full menu alongside pizzas.

At lunchtime **bars** and **cafes** sell *panini* (bread rolls), and many serve an evening *aperitivo* (aperitif) buffet. At an **enoteca** (wine bar) you can drink wine by the glass and snack on cheese and cured meats. Some also serve hot dishes. For a slice of pizza search out a **pizza al taglio** joint.

New Year's Day (Capodanno) 1 January

Epiphany (Epifania) 6 January

Easter Monday (Pasquetta) March/April

Liberation Day (Giorno delle Liberazione) 25 April

Labour Day (Festa del Lavoro) 1 May

Republic Day (Festa della Repubblica) 2 June

Feast of the Assumption (Ferragosto) 15 August

All Saints' Day (Ognisanti) 1 November

Feast of the Immaculate Conception (Immacolata Concezione) 8 December

Christmas Day (Natale) 25 December

Boxing Day (Festa di Santo Stefano) 26 December

SAFE TRAVEL

Italy is generally a safe country, but petty theft is prevalent. Be on your guard against pickpockets in popular tourist centres such as Rome, Florence, Venice and Naples.

TELEPHONE

➡ Area codes are an integral part of all Italian phone numbers and must be dialled even when calling locally.

➡ To call Italy from abroad, dial ☑ 0039 and then the area code, including the first zero.

➡ To call abroad from Italy, dial ☑ 00, then the relevant country code followed by the telephone number.

➡ Italian mobile phone numbers are nine or 10 digits long and start with a three-digit prefix starting with a ☑ 3.

➡ Skype is available on many hostel computers.

Mobile Phones

➡ Italy uses the GSM 900/1800 network, which is compatible with European and Australian devices, but not all North American cell phones.

COUNTRY FACTS

Area 301,230 sq km

Capital Rome

Currency Euro (€)

Emergency ☑ 112

Language Italian

Money ATMs are widespread; credit cards widely accepted

Population 60.78 million

Telephone Country code ☑ 39, international access code ☑ 00

Visas Schengen rules apply

EATING PRICE RANGES

The following price ranges refer to the cost of a two-course meal, glass of house wine and *coperto* (cover charge):

€ less than €25

€€ €25–€45

€€€ more than €45

➡ If you can unlock your device (check with your service provider), the cheapest way to make calls is to buy an Italian SIM card. These are available from **TIM** (www.tim.it), **Tre** (www.tre.it), **Wind** (www.wind.it) and **Vodafone** (www.vodafone.it). You'll need ID when you buy one.

VISAS

➡ Schengen visa rules apply for entry to Italy.

➡ Unless staying in a hotel/B&B/hostel etc, all foreign visitors are supposed to register with the local police within eight days of arrival.

➡ A *permesso di soggiorno* (permit to stay) is required by all non-EU nationals who stay in Italy longer than three months. You must apply within eight days of arriving in Italy. Check documentary requirements on www.poliziadistato.it.

➡ EU citizens do not require a *permesso di soggiorno*.

❶ Getting There & Away

Getting to Italy is straightforward. It is well served by international airlines and European low-cost carriers, and there are plenty of bus, train and ferry routes into the country.

Flights, tours and rail tickets can be booked online at lonelyplanet.com/bookings.

AIR

There are direct intercontinental flights to/from Rome and Milan. European flights also serve regional airports. Italy's national carrier is **Alitalia** (www.alitalia.com).

Italy's principal airports:

Leonardo da Vinci (www.adr.it/iumicino) Italy's main airport; also known as Rome Fiumicino Airport.

Rome Ciampino (www.adr.it/ciampino) Rome's second airport.

Milan Malpensa (www.milanomalpensa-airport.com) Northern Italy's principal hub.

Venice Marco Polo (www.veniceairport.it) Venice's main airport.

Pisa International (www.pisa-airport.com) Gateway for Florence and Tuscany.

MAIN INTERNATIONAL FERRY ROUTES

FROM	TO	COMPANY	MIN-MAX FARE (€)	DURATION (HR)
Ancona	Igoumenitsa	Minoan, Superfast, Anek	69-100	16½-22
Ancona	Patra	Minoan, Superfast, Anek	69-100	22-29
Ancona	Split	Jadrolinija, SNAV	48-57.50	10¾
Bari	Bar	Montenegro	50-55	9
Bari	Corfu	Superfast	78-93	9
Bari	Dubrovnik	Jadrolinija	48-57.50	10-12
Bari	Igoumenitsa	Superfast	78-93	8-12
Bari	Patra	Superfast	78-93	16
Brindisi	Igoumenitsa	Endeavor	52-83	8
Brindisi	Patra	Endeavor	56-94	14
Brindisi	Corfu	Endeavor	52-83	6½-11½
Brindisi	Kefallonia	Endeavor	56-94	12½
Civitavecchia	Barcelona	Grimaldi	45-90	20
Genoa	Barcelona	GNV	90	19½
Genoa	Tunis	GNV	111	23½
Venice	Igoumenitsa	Superfast	66-82	15
Venice	Patras	Superfast	66-82	18-21½

Naples Capodichino (www.gesac.it) Southern Italy's main airport.

Catania Fontanarossa (www.aeroporto. catania.it) Sicily's largest airport.

LAND
Bus

Eurolines (www.eurolines.it) operates buses from European destinations to many Italian cities.

Train

Milan and Venice are Italy's main international rail hubs. International trains also run to/from Rome, Genoa, Turin, Verona, Padua, Bologna, Florence and Naples. Main routes:

Milan To/from Paris, Marseille, Geneva, Zürich and Vienna.

Rome To/from Munich and Vienna.

Venice To/from Paris, Munich, Innsbruck, Salzburg and Vienna.

Voyages-sncf (☑ 0844 848 5848; http://uk. voyages-sncf.com) can provide fare information on journeys from the UK to Italy, most of which require a change at Paris. Another excellent resource is www.seat61.com.

Eurail and Inter-Rail passes are valid in Italy.

SEA
➡ Ferries serve Italian ports from across the Mediterranean. Timetables are seasonal, so always check ahead.

➡ For routes, companies and online booking try www.traghettiweb.it.

➡ Prices quoted in this chapter are for a one-way *poltrona* (reclinable seat).

➡ Holders of Eurail and Inter-Rail passes should check with the ferry company if they are entitled to a discount or free passage.

➡ Major ferry companies include: **Anek Lines** (www.anekitalia.com), **Endeavor Lines** (www. endeavor-lines.com), **GNV** (www.gnv.it), **Jadrolinija** (www.jadrolinija.hr), **Minoan Lines** (www.minoan.it), **Montenegro Lines** (www. montenegrolines.net), **SNAV** (www.snav.it) and **Superfast** (www.superfast.com).

🅘 Getting Around

BICYCLE
➡ Bikes can be taken on regional and certain international trains carrying the bike logo, but you'll need to pay a supplement (€3.50 on regional trains, €12 on international trains). Bikes can be carried free if dismantled and stored in a bike bag.

➡ Bikes generally incur a small supplement on ferries, typically €10 to €15.

BOAT
Navi (large ferries) sail to Sicily and Sardinia; *traghetti* (smaller ferries) and *aliscafi* (hydrofoils) cover the smaller islands.

The main embarkation points for Sardinia are Genoa, Civitavecchia and Naples; for Sicily, Naples and Villa San Giovanni in Calabria.

ⓘ ADMISSION PRICES

As of July 2014, admission to state-run museums, galleries, monuments and sites is free to minors under 18. People aged between 18 and 25 are entitled to a discount. To get it, you'll need proof of your age, ideally a passport or ID card.

Admission is free to everyone on the first Sunday of each month.

Following are the major domestic ferry companies:

GNV (☏ 010 209 45 91; www.gnv.it) To/from Sardinia and Sicily.

Moby Lines (☏ 199 303040; www.moby.it) To/from Sardinia and Elba.

Sardinia Ferries (☏ 199 400500; www. corsica-ferries.it) To/from Sardinia.

SNAV (☏ 081 428 55 55; www.snav.it) To/from Aeolian Islands, Capri and Bay of Naples islands.

Tirrenia (☏ 892 123; www.tirrenia.it) To/from Sardinia and Sicily.

BUS

➡ Italy boasts an extensive and largely reliable bus network.

➡ Buses are not necessarily cheaper than trains, but in mountainous areas they are often the only choice.

➡ In larger cities, companies have ticket offices or operate through agencies, but in villages and small towns tickets are sold in bars or on the bus.

➡ Reservations are only necessary for high-season long-haul trips.

CAR & MOTORCYCLE

➡ Italy's roads are generally good, and there's an extensive network of toll autostradas (motorways).

➡ All EU driving licences are recognised in Italy. Holders of non-EU licences should get an International Driving Permit (IDP) through their national automobile association.

➡ Traffic restrictions apply in most city centres.

➡ To hire a car you'll require a driving licence (plus IDP if necessary) and credit card. Age restrictions vary, but generally you'll need to be 21 or over.

➡ If driving your own car, carry your vehicle registration certificate, driving licence and proof of third-party liability insurance cover.

➡ For further details, see the website of Italy's motoring organisation **Automobile Club d'Italia** (ACI; www.aci.it).

➡ ACI provides 24-hour roadside assistance: call ☏ 803 116 from a landline or Italian mobile, ☏ 800 116 800 from a foreign mobile.

TRAIN

Italy has an extensive rail network. Trains are relatively cheap, and many are fast and comfortable. Most services are run by **Trenitalia** (☏ 892021; www.trenitalia.com) but **Italo** (☏ 06 07 08; www.italotreno.it) also operates high-speed trains.

There are several types of train:

InterCity (IC) Trains between major cities. **Le Frecce** Fast trains: Frecciarossa, Frecciargento and Frecciabianca.

Regionale or interregionale (R) Slow local services.

Tickets

➡ InterCity and Frecce trains require a supplement, which is incorporated in the ticket price. If you have a standard ticket and board an InterCity you'll have to pay the difference on board.

➡ Frecce trains require prior reservation.

➡ Generally, it's cheaper to buy train tickets in Italy.

➡ If your ticket doesn't include a reservation with an assigned seat, you must validate it before boarding by inserting it into one of the machines dotted around stations.

➡ Some services offer 'ticketless' travel; book and pay for your seat on www.trenitalia.com and then communicate your booking code to the controller on board.

The Netherlands

Best Places to Eat

➡ Greetje (p507)
➡ De Jong (p517)
➡ Foodhallen (p506)
➡ Karaf (p520)
➡ Café Sjiek (p521)

Best Places to Stay

➡ King Kong Hostel (p517)
➡ Dylan (p506)
➡ Trash Deluxe (p521)
➡ Hotel New York (p517)
➡ Hotel de Plataan (p514)

Why Go?

Old and new intertwine in the Netherlands. The legacies of great Dutch artists Rembrandt, Vermeer and Van Gogh, beautiful 17th-century canals, windmills, tulips and quaint brown cafes lit by flickering candles coexist with ground-breaking contemporary architecture, cutting-edge fashion, homewares, design and food scenes, phenomenal nightlife and a progressive mindset.

Much of the Netherlands is famously below sea level and the pancake-flat landscape offers idyllic cycling. Locals live on bicycles and you can too. Rental outlets are ubiquitous throughout the country, which is crisscrossed with dedicated cycling paths. Allow plenty of time to revel in the magical, multifaceted capital Amsterdam, to venture further afield to charming canal-laced towns such as Leiden and Delft, and to check out Dutch cities like exquisite Maastricht, with its city walls, ancient churches and grand squares, and the pulsing port city of Rotterdam, currently undergoing an urban renaissance. It's a very big small country.

When to Go
Amsterdam

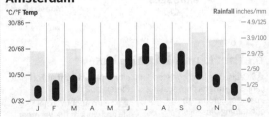

Mar–May Colour explodes as billions of bulbs bloom.

Jul Mild summer temps and long daylight hours keep you outside cycling and drinking.

Dec–Feb When the canals freeze, the Dutch passion for ice skating is on display nationwide.

Map labels

Waddeneilanden

FRISIAN ISLANDS

Schiermonnikoog

Ameland

Terschelling

Dokkumer Ee

Vlieland

Leeuwarden

Groningen

Winschoterdiep

Ems Kanaal

Texel

Waddenzee

Sneek

Assen

NORTH
SEA

Den
Helder

IJsselmeer

Dwingelderveld
National Park

Emmen

Alkmaar

Zwolle

IJssel

Bad
Bentheim

Zaanse
Schans ⑦

Edam

Deventer

Enschede

IJmuiden

Amsterdam ①

Haarlem

Keukenhof
Gardens ⑥

Schiphol

Aalsmeer

Hoge Veluwe
National Park

Twente Kanaal

Amersfoort

Leiden ⑤

⑧ **Randstad**

Veluwezoom
National Park

Utrecht

Den Haag ⑤

Hoek van
Holland

Delft ④

Gouda

Lek

Arnhem

Rotterdam
The Hague Airport

Waal

Europoort

Rotterdam ②

Kinderdijk

Nijmegen

Dordrecht

De Biesbosch
National Park

Schouwen-
Duiveland

Bergse Maas

Den Bosch

Maas

Willemstad

Breda

Domburg

Noord-
Beveland

Roosendaal

Walcheren

Zuid-Beveland

Tilburg

Eindhoven
Airport

Middelburg

Oosterschelde

Eindhoven

Venlo

Düsseldorf

Westerschelde

Perkpolder

Zeeuws-
Vlaanderen

Roermond

Julianakanaal

Antwerp

Ghent

Cologne

BRUSSELS

Maastricht ③

Aachen

Liège (8km)

N   0 ——— 50 km
     0 ——— 25 miles

Netherlands Highlights

① Cruise the Unesco-listed canals of **Amsterdam** soaking up one of Europe's most enchanting old cities.

② Marvel at the astonishing **Markthal Rotterdam** (p518), an architectural highlight of the Netherlands' hip-and-happening 'second city'.

③ Explore the centuries-old tunnels below the resplendent city of **Maastricht** at Fort Sint Pieter (p521).

④ Learn about Vermeer's life and work at the **Vermeer Centrum Delft** (p514).

⑤ Discover the tree-lined boulevards, classy museums and palatial Binnenhof buildings of **Den Haag** (p512).

⑥ Delve into the museums in picturesque **Leiden** (p511)

and dazzling tulip displays of **Keukenhof Gardens** (p512).

⑦ Watch windmills twirl and meet the millers at the delightful **Zaanse Schans** (p510).

⑧ Follow dikes along shimmering canals or tour the tulip fields of the **Randstad** on the world's best network of cycling (p513) routes.

One Week

Spend three days canal exploring, museum hopping and cafe crawling in **Amsterdam**. Work your way through the ancient towns of the **Randstad** and the contemporary vibe of **Rotterdam**, and save a day for the grandeur of **Maastricht**.

Two Weeks

Allow four days for Amsterdam's many delights, plus a day trip to the old towns of the north, and a day or two exploring some of the region's smaller towns. Then add a day each at beautiful **Delft**, regal **Den Haag** (The Hague), student-filled **Utrecht** and buzzing **Rotterdam**. Finish off with two days in historic Maastricht.

AMSTERDAM

📞 020 / POP 811,185

World Heritage–listed canals lined by gabled houses, candlelit cafes, whirring bicycles, lush parks, monumental museums, colourful markets, diverse dining, quirky shopping and legendary nightlife make the free-spirited Dutch capital one of Europe's great cities.

Amsterdam has been a liberal place since the Netherlands' Golden Age, when it was at the forefront of European art and trade. Centuries later, in the 1960s, it again led the pack – this time in the principles of tolerance, with broad-minded views on drugs and same-sex relationships taking centre stage.

Explore its many worlds-within-worlds, where nothing ever seems the same twice.

⊙ Sights

Amsterdam is compact and you can roam the city on foot, but there's also an excellent public transport network.

⊙ City Centre

Crowned by the **Royal Palace** (Koninklijk Paleis; Map p502; 📞620 40 60; www.paleis amsterdam.nl; Dam; adult/child €10/free; ⊙11am-5pm; 🚊4/9/16/24 Dam), the square that puts the 'Dam' in Amsterdam anchors the city's oldest quarter, which is also home to its infamous Red Light District.

Begijnhof   HISTORIC BUILDING
(Map p502; 📞622 19 18; www.begijnhof amsterdam.nl; off Gedempte Begijnensloot; ⊙9am-5pm; 🚊1/2/5/13/17 Spui) FREE This enclosed former convent dates from the early 14th century. It's a surreal oasis of peace, with tiny houses and postage-stamp gardens around a well-kept courtyard. The Beguines were a Catholic order of unmarried or widowed women who cared for the elderly and lived a religious life without taking monastic vows. The last true Beguine died in 1971.

⊙ Canal Ring

Amsterdam's Canal Ring was built during the 17th-century after the seafaring port grew beyond its medieval walls, and authorities devised a ground-breaking expansion plan.

Wandering here amid architectural treasures and their reflections on the narrow waters of the Prinsengracht, Keizersgracht and Herengracht can cause days to vanish.

★ Anne Frank Huis   MUSEUM
(📞556 71 00; www.annefrank.org; Prinsengracht 267; adult/child €9/4.50; ⊙9am-9pm, hours vary seasonally; 🚊13/14/17 Westermarkt) The Anne Frank Huis draws almost one million visitors annually (prepurchase tickets online to minimise the queues). With its reconstruction of Anne's melancholy bedroom and her actual diary – sitting alone in its glass case, filled with sunnily optimistic writing tempered by quiet despair – it's a powerful experience.

The focus of the museum is the *achterhuis* (rear house), also known as the **Secret Annexe**, a dark and airless space where the Franks and others observed complete silence during the daytime, outgrew their clothes, pasted photos of Hollywood stars on the walls and read Dickens, before being mysteriously betrayed and sent to their deaths. Opening hours vary according to the season.

⊙ Museumplein

Amsterdam's big three museums fan out around the grassy expanse of Museumplein, in the Old South neighbourhood.

★ Van Gogh Museum   MUSEUM
(Map p504; 📞570 52 00; www.vangoghmuseum. nl; Paulus Potterstraat 7; adult/child €15/free,

Central Amsterdam

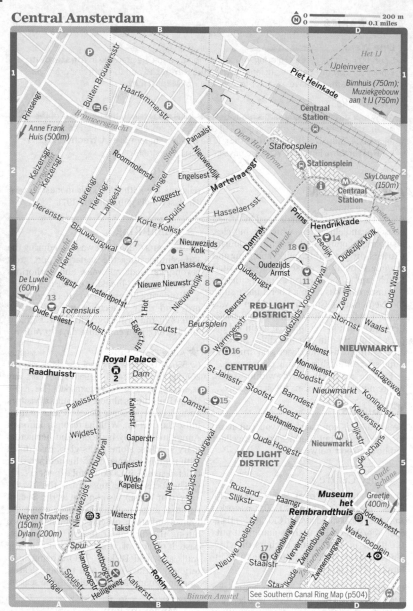

audioguide €5; ⊘9am-6pm Sat-Thu, to 10pm Fri; ☏; 🚊2/3/5/12 Van Baerlestraat) Framed by a gleaming new glass entrance hall, the world's largest Van Gogh collection offers a superb line-up of masterworks. Trace the artist's life from his tentative start through his giddy-coloured sunflower phase, and on to the black cloud that descended over him and his work. There are also paintings by contemporaries Gauguin, Toulouse-Lautrec, Monet and Bernard.

Queues can be huge; pre-booked e-tickets and discount cards expedite the process with fast-track entry. Opening hours vary seasonally.

★ **Rijksmuseum**　　　　　　　MUSEUM
(National Museum; Map p504; ☑ 900 07 45; www. rijksmuseum.nl; Museumstraat 1; adult/child €17.50/ free; ◷ 9am-5pm; ☒ 2/5 Hobbemastraat) The Rijksmuseum is the Netherlands' premier art trove, splashing Rembrandts, Vermeers and 7500 other masterpieces over 1.5km of galleries. To avoid the biggest crowds, come after 3pm. Or prebook tickets online, which provides fast-track entry.

The Golden Age works are the highlight. Feast your eyes on still lifes, gentlemen in ruffled collars and landscapes bathed in pale yellow light. Rembrandt's *The Night Watch* (1642) takes pride of place.

Initially titled *Company of Frans Banning Cocq* (the militia's leader), the name *The Night Watch* was bestowed years later due to a layer of grime that gave the impression it was evening. Other must-sees are the Delftware (blue-and-white pottery), intricately detailed dolls' houses and the brand-new Asian Pavilion. The

sculpture-studded gardens around the exterior are free to visit.

Stedelijk Museum　　　　　　　MUSEUM
(Map p504; ☑ 573 29 11; www.stedelijk.nl; Museumplein 10; adult/child €15/free, audio guide €5; ◷ 10am-6pm Fri-Wed, to 10pm Thu; ☏; ☒ 2/3/5/12 Van Baerlestraat) Built in 1895 to a neo-Renaissance design by AM Weissman, the Stedelijk Museum is the permanent home of the National Museum of Modern Art. Amassed by postwar curator Willem Sandberg, the modern classics here are among the world's most admired. The permanent collection includes all the blue chips of 19th- and 20th-century painting – Monet, Picasso and Chagall among them – as well as sculptures by Rodin, abstracts by Mondrian and Kandinsky, and much, much more.

Vondelpark　　　　　　　PARK
(Map p504; www.vondelpark.nl; ☒ 2/5 Hobbemastraat) **FREE** The lush urban idyll of the Vondelpark is one of Amsterdam's most magical places – sprawling, English-style gardens, with ponds, lawns, footbridges and winding footpaths. On a sunny day, an open-air party atmosphere ensues when tourists, lovers, cyclists, in-line skaters, pram-pushing parents, cartwheeling children, football-kicking teenagers, spliff-sharing friends and champagneswilling picnickers all come out to play.

◉ **De Pijp**

Immediately south of the Canal Ring, villagey De Pijp is dubbed Amsterdam's 'Latin Quarter'. Increasingly hip cafes, restaurants and bars spill out around its colourful street market, Albert Cuypmarkt (p508).

Heineken Experience　　　　　　　BREWERY
(Map p504; ☑ 523 94 35; www.heineken experience.com; Stadhouderskade 78; adult/ child €18/12.50; ◷ 10.30am-9pm Jul & Aug, 11am-7.30pm Mon-Thu, 10.30am-9pm Fri-Sun Sep-Jun; ☒ 16/24 Stadhouderskade) On the site of the company's old brewery, the crowning glory of this self-guided 'Experience' (samples aside) is a multimedia exhibit where you 'become' a beer by getting shaken up, sprayed with water and subjected to heat. True beer connoisseurs will shudder, but it's a lot of fun. Admission includes a 15-minute shuttle boat ride to the Heineken Brand Store near Rembrandtplein. Prebooking tickets online saves you €2 on the entry fee and allows you to skip the ticket queues.

THE NETHERLANDS AMSTERDAM

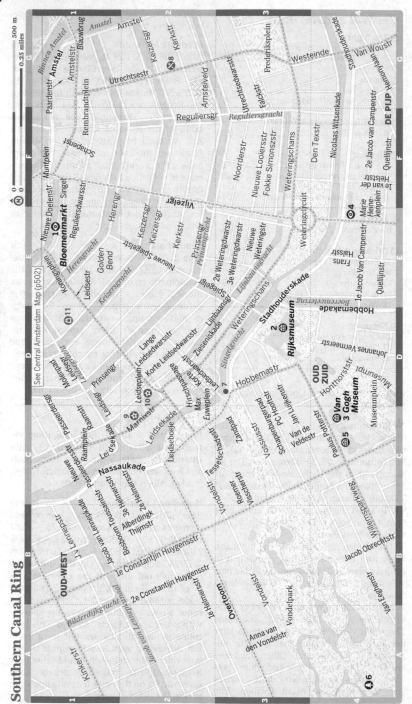

Southern Canal Ring

THE NETHERLANDS AMSTERDAM

Southern Canal Ring

◉ Nieuwmarkt & Plantage

The streets around the Rembrandt House are prime wandering territory, offering a vibrant mix of old Amsterdam, canals and quirky shops and cafes.

★ **Museum het Rembrandthuis**   MUSEUM
(Rembrandt House Museum; Map p502; ☑ 520 04 00; www.rembrandthuis.nl; Jodenbreestraat 4; adult/child €12.50/4; ◷10am-6pm; ◙9/14 Waterlooplein) You almost expect to find the master himself at the Museum het Rembrandthuis, where Rembrandt van Rijn ran the Netherlands' largest painting studio, only to lose the lot when profligacy set in, enemies swooped and bankruptcy came a-knocking. The museum has scores of etchings and sketches. Ask for the free audio guide at the entrance. You can buy advance tickets online, though it's not as vital here as at some of the other big museums. There's also a mind-boggling collection of Rembrandt's possessions: seashells, weaponry, Roman busts and military helmets.

✶ Activities

Canal Motorboats   BOAT RENTAL
(☑020 422 70 07; www.canalmotorboats.com; Zandhoek 10a; 1st hr €50; ◷9am-sunset; ◙48 Barentszplein) This operator has small, electric aluminium boats (maximum six passengers) that are easy to drive (no boat licence required). Staff give you a map and plenty of advice, and will come and rescue you if need be. Credit-card imprint or €150 cash deposit required. Reduced rates after the first hour.

☞ Tours

Amsterdam's **canal boats** (p510) are a relaxing way to tour the town. Avoid steamed-up glass windows by choosing boats with open seating areas, such as **Blue Boat Company** (Map p504; ☑679 13 70; www.blueboat.nl; Stadhouderskade 30; 75-minute tour adult/child €16/8.50; ◷half-hourly 10am-6pm Mar-Oct, hourly Nov-Feb; ◙1/2/5 Leidseplein).

Yellow Bike   CYCLING
(Map p502; ☑620 69 40; www.yellowbike.nl; Nieuwezijds Kolk 29; bike rental per day €12, city/countryside tours €25/31.50; ◷9.30am-5pm; ◙1/2/5/13/17 Nieuwezijds Kolk) The original. Choose from city tours or the longer countryside tour through the pretty Waterland district to the north.

🛏 Sleeping

Book ahead for summer and weekends year-round. Many cheaper places cater specifically to party animals with general mayhem around the clock. Others exude refined old-world charm. Wi-fi is near universal but lifts/elevators are not.

St Christopher's at the Winston   HOSTEL €€
(Map p502; ☑623 13 80; www.winston.nl; Warmoesstraat 129; dm €38-43, s €95, d €124-144; 🖳; ◙4/9/16/24/25 Dam) This place hops 24/7 with rock 'n' roll rooms and a busy club, bar, beer garden and smoking deck downstairs. En-suite dorms sleep up to eight. Most private rooms are 'art' rooms: local artists were given free rein, with super-edgy (entirely stainless steel) to questionably raunchy results. Rates include breakfast (and ear plugs!).

Hotel Brouwer   HOTEL €€
(Map p502; ☑624 63 58; www.hotelbrouwer.nl; Singel 83; s €71-79, d €115-128, tr €148-178; 🏧🖳; ◙1/2/5/13/17 Nieuwezijds Kolk) A bargain-priced (for Amsterdam) favourite, Brouwer has just eight rooms in a house dating back to 1652. Each chamber is named for a Dutch painter and furnished with simplicity, but all have canal views. There's a mix of Delft-blue tiles and early-20th-century decor, plus a tiny lift. Staff dispense friendly advice. Reserve well in advance. Cash only.

RED LIGHT DISTRICT

Just southeast of Centraal Station, on and around the parallel neon-lit canals Oudezijds Voorburgwal and Oudezijds Achterburgwal, the warren of medieval alleyways making up Amsterdam's Red Light District (locally known as De Wallen) is a carnival of vice, seething with skimpily clad prostitutes in brothel windows, raucous bars, haze-filled 'coffeeshops', strip shows, sex shows, mind-boggling museums and shops selling everything from cartoonish condoms to S&M gear and herbal highs.

The area is generally safe, but keep your wits about you and don't photograph or film prostitutes in the windows – out of respect, and to avoid having your camera flung in a canal by the women's enforcers. Seriously.

Hotel The Exchange
BOUTIQUE HOTEL €€

(Map p502; ☑ 523 00 89; www.hoteltheexchange. com; Damrak 50; d 1-/2-/3-/4-/5-star from €93/110/128/162/196; @ ☎; ☒ 1/2/5/13/17 Nieuwezijds Kolk) The Exchange's 61 rooms have been dressed 'like models' in eye-popping style by students from the Amsterdam Fashion Institute. Anything goes, from oversized button-adorned walls to a Marie Antoinette dress tented over the bed. If you like plain decor, this isn't your place. Rooms range from small and viewless to spacious sanctums, but all have en-suite bathrooms.

Frederic Rentabike
HOUSEBOAT €€

(Map p502; ☑ 624 55 09; www.frederic.nl; Brouwersgracht 78; houseboat from €145; ☎; ☒ 18/21/22 Brouwersstraat) Frederic offers nicely outfitted houseboats on the Prinsengracht, Brouwersgracht and Bloemgracht that are bona fide floating holiday homes with all mod cons. On land, the company also has various rooms and apartments in central locations. (And yes, bikes, too.)

★ Dylan
HOTEL €€€

(☑ 530 20 10; www.dylanamsterdam.com; Keizersgracht 384; d/ste from €350/500; ❋@☎; ☒ 1/2/5 Spui) Exquisite boutique hotel the Dylan occupies an 18th-century Keizersgracht canal house ensconcing a herringbone-paved, topiary-filled inner courtyard. Bespoke furniture such as silver-leaf and mother-of-pearl drinks cabinets adorn its 40 individually decorated rooms and suites (some duplex). Its Michelin-starred Restaurant Vinkeles also hosts private chef's tables aboard its boat, the *Muze*, as it cruises the canals.

✖ Eating

Amsterdam abounds with eateries. Superb streets for hunting include Utrechtsestraat, near Rembrandtplein; Amstelveenseweg, along the Vondelpark's western edge; and any of the little streets throughout the western canals.

★ Foodhallen
FOOD HALL €

(www.foodhallen.nl; Bellamyplein 51; most dishes €5-15; ☉ 11am-8pm Sun-Wed, to 9pm Thu-Sat; ☒ 17 Ten Katestraat) Inside the converted tram sheds housing the cultural and design complex De Hallen, this glorious international food hall has 20 stands surrounding an airy open-plan eating area. Some are offshoots of popular Amsterdam eateries, such as the Butcher (burgers) and Wild Moa Pies; look out for De Ballenbar (*bitterballen*). It's adjacent to the lively street market Ten Katemarkt.

Vleminckx
FAST FOOD €

(Map p502; Voetboogstraat 31; fries €2.10-4.10, sauces €0.60; ☉ noon-7pm Sun & Mon, 11am-7pm Tue, Wed, Fri & Sat, 11am-9pm Thu; ☒ 1/2/5 Koningsplein) This hole-in-the-wall takeaway has drawn the hordes for its monumental *frites* (French fries) since 1887. The standard is smothered in mayonnaise, though you can ask for ketchup, peanut sauce or a variety of spicy toppings.

De Luwte
INTERNATIONAL €€

(☑ 625 85 48; www.restaurantdeluwte.nl; Leliegracht 26; mains €19.50-28.50; ☉ 6-11pm; ☒ 13/17 Westermarkt) Fabulously designed with a vertical 'living wall' garden and recycled timbers, the star of the show here is the artfully presented, Mediterranean-inspired food: slow-cooked rack of pork with risotto croquettes; cod with creamed pumpkin and truffle polenta with mushroom foam; or the house-specialty black Angus tomahawk steak for two. Great cocktails, too.

Buffet van Odette
CAFE €€

(☑ 423 60 34; www.buffet-amsterdam.nl; Prinsengracht 598; lunch mains €7.50-15.50, dinner €14.50-20.50; ☉ kitchen 10am-10pm; ☑; ☒ 7/10 Spiegelgracht) Not a buffet but an airy, white-tiled, sit-down cafe with a beautiful canal-side terrace, where Odette and Yvette show how good simple cooking can taste when you start with great ingredients and a dash of creativity. Soups, sandwiches, pastas and quiches are mostly organic, with smart little extras like pine nuts or truffle cheese.

★ **Greetje**   CONTEMPORARY DUTCH €€€
(☑779 74 50; www.restaurantgreetje.nl; Peperstraat 23-25; mains €23-27; ☉6-10pm Sun-Fri, to 11pm Sat; ⊟22/34/35/48 Prins Hendrikkade) 🍴
Using market-fresh organic produce, Greetje resurrects and re-creates traditional Dutch recipes like beet-crusted North Sea cod, Veluwe deer stew with red cabbage and Elstar apple, or roasted Alblasserwaard pheasant with melted duck liver. A good place to start is the two-person Big Beginning, with a sampling of hot and cold starters.

Tempo Doeloe   INDONESIAN €€€
(Map p504; ☑625 67 18; www.tempodoeloe restaurant.nl; Utrechtsestraat 75; mains €23.50-38.50, rijsttafel & set menus €28.50-49; ☉6-11.30pm Mon-Sat; ☑; ⊟4 Prinsengracht) Consistently ranked among Amsterdam's finest Indonesian restaurants, Tempo Doeloe's setting and service are elegant without being overdone. The same applies to the rijsttafel: a ridiculously overblown affair at many places, here it's a fine sampling of the range of flavours found in the country. Warning: dishes marked 'very hot' are indeed like napalm. The wine list is excellent.

🍷 **Drinking & Nightlife**

In addition to the Medieval Centre and Red Light District, party hotspots include Rembrandtplein and Leidseplein, both awash with bars, clubs, coffeeshops and pubs.

To truly experience the unique Dutch quality of *gezellig* (conviviality/cosiness), head to a history-steeped *bruin café* (brown cafe, ie pub, named for the nicotine-stained walls). Many serve food.

Around town, look out for local (often very potent) organic brews by **Brouwerij 't**

DON'T MISS

JORDAAN
....
A densely populated *volksbuurt* (district for the common people) until to mid-20th century, the intimate Jordaan is now one of Amsterdam's most desirable addresses. The neighbourhood is a pastiche of modest 17th- and 18th-century merchants' houses and humble workers' homes squashed in a grid of tiny lanes peppered with bite-sized cafes and shops. There's a handful of small-scale museums (houseboat museum, tulip museum) but the real pleasure here is simply losing yourself in its charming canal-side backstreets.

IJ (www.brouwerijhetij.nl; Funenkade 7; ☉2-8pm; ⊟10 Hoogte Kadijk) 🍴 and **Brouwerij De Prael** (Map p502; ☑408 44 69; http://deprael.nl; Oudezijds Armsteeg 26; ☉noon-midnight Tue & Wed, to 1am Thu-Sat, to 11pm Sun; ⊟4/9/16/24/25 Centraal Station). Both also have atmospheric pubs.

★ **In 't Aepjen**   BROWN CAFE
(Map p502; Zeedijk 1; ☉noon-1am Mon-Thu, to 3am Fri & Sat; ⊟4/9/16/24 Centraal Station) Candles burn even during the day at this bar based in a mid-16th-century house, which is one of two remaining wooden buildings in the city. The name allegedly comes from the bar's role in the 16th and 17th centuries as a crash pad for sailors from the Far East, who often toted *aapjes* (monkeys) with them.

Wynand Fockink   TASTING HOUSE
(Map p502; www.wynand-fockink.nl; Pijlsteeg 31; ☉3-9pm; ⊟4/9/16/24 Dam) This small tasting house (dating from 1679) serves scores of jenever and liqueurs in an arcade behind Grand Hotel Krasnapolsky. Although there are no seats or stools, it's an intimate place to knock back a shot-glass or two. Guides give an English-language tour of the distillery every Saturday at 2pm (€17.50, reservations not required).

SkyLounge   COCKTAIL BAR
(http://doubletree3.hilton.com; Oosterdoksstraat 4; ☉11am-1am Sun-Thu, to 3am Fri & Sat; ⊟1/2/4/5/9/14/16/24 Centraal Station) An unrivalled 360-degree panorama of Amsterdam extends from the glass-walled SkyLounge on the 11th floor of the DoubleTree Amsterdam Centraal Station hotel – and just gets better when you head out to its vast SkyTerrace, with an outdoor bar and timber decking strewn

with sofas. Deliberate over more than 500 different cocktails; DJs regularly hit the decks.

Air
CLUB

(www.air.nl; Amstelstraat 16-24; ⊙ Thu-Sun, hours vary; 🚊 4/9/14 Rembrandtplein) One of Amsterdam's 'it' clubs, Air has an environmentally friendly design by Dutch designer Marcel Wanders including a unique tiered dance floor. Bonuses include lockers and refillable cards that preclude fussing with change at the bar. The awesome sound system attracts cutting-edge DJs spinning everything from disco to house and techno to hip hop. Dress to impress.

Coffeeshops

In the Netherlands, 'coffeeshops' are where one buys pot (marijuana).

Dampkring
COFFEESHOP

(Map p502; www.dampkring-coffeeshop-amsterdam.nl; Handboogstraat 29; ⊙ 10am-1am; 📶; 🚊 1/2/5 Koningsplein) With an interior that resembles a larger-than-life lava lamp, Dampkring is a consistent Cannabis Cup winner, and known for having the most comprehensive menu in town (including details about smell, taste and effect). Its name means the ring of the earth's atmosphere where smaller items combust.

Grey Area
COFFEESHOP

(Map p502; www.greyarea.nl; Oude Leliestraat 2; ⊙ noon-8pm; 🚊 1/2/5/13/14/17 Dam) Owned by a couple of laid-back American guys, this tiny shop introduced the extra-sticky, flavoursome 'Double Bubble Gum' weed to the city's smokers. Organic coffee includes free refills.

COFFEESHOP DOS & DON'TS

➡ Do ask at the bar for the menu of cannabis-related goods on offer, usually packaged in small bags. You can also buy ready-made joints; most shops offer rolling papers, pipes or bongs to use.

➡ Don't light up anywhere besides a coffeeshop without checking that it's OK to do so.

➡ Don't use alcohol and tobacco products – these are not permitted in coffeeshops.

➡ Don't ask for hard (illegal) drugs.

☆ Entertainment

Find out what's on at I Amsterdam (www.iamsterdam.com).

For tickets, including last-minute discounts, head to Uitburo (Map p504; ☑ 621 13 11; www.aub.nl; Leidseplein 26; ⊙ 10am-6pm Mon-Wed, Fri & Sat, to 9pm Thu, noon-6pm Sun; 🚊 1/2/5/7/10 Leidseplein).

Melkweg
LIVE MUSIC

(Map p504; www.melkweg.nl; Lijnbaansgracht 234a; ⊙ 6pm-1am; 🚊 1/2/5/7/10 Leidseplein) In a former dairy, the nonprofit 'Milky Way' is a dazzling galaxy of diverse music. One night it's electronica, the next reggae or punk, and next heavy metal. Roots, rock and mellow singer-songwriters all get stage time, too. Check out the website for cutting-edge cinema, theatre and multimedia offerings.

Muziekgebouw aan 't IJ
CONCERT VENUE

(☑ 788 20 00; www.muziekgebouw.nl; Piet Heinkade 1; tickets free-€33; ⊙ box office noon-6pm Mon-Sat & 90min before performance; 🚊 26 Muziekgebouw) Behind this multidisciplinary performing-arts venue's hi-tech exterior, the dramatically lit main hall has a flexible stage layout and great acoustics. Its jazz stage, Bimhuis (☑ 788 21 88; www.bimhuis.nl; Piet Heinkade 3; tickets free-€28; 🚊 26 Muziekgebouw), is more intimate. Under-30s can get €10 tickets at the box office 30 minutes before showtime, or online via http://earlybirds.muziekgebouw.nl. Everyone else should try the Last Minute Ticket Shop (www.lastminuteticketshop.nl) for discounts.

🔒 Shopping

The ultimate pleasure of shopping in Amsterdam is discovering some tiny shop selling something you'd find nowhere else. In the Western Canal Ring, the 'nine little streets' making up the Negen Straatjes (Nine Streets; www.de9straatjes.nl; 🚊 1/2/5 Spui) are dotted with them.

Markets of just about every description are scattered across the city, including Amsterdam's largest and busiest, De Pijp's Albert Cuypmarkt (www.albertcuypmarkt.nl; Albert Cuypstraat, btwn Ferdinand Bolstraat & Van Woustraat; ⊙ 9am-5pm Mon-Sat; 🚊 16/24 Albert Cuypstraat); the Bloemenmarkt (Flower Market; Map p504; Singel, btwn Muntplein & Koningsplein; ⊙ 9am-5.30pm Mon-Sat, 11am-5.30pm Sun; 🚊 1/2/5 Koningsplein), a 'floating' flower market (on pilings), with bulbs galore; and Waterlooplein Flea Market (Map p502; www.

waterloopleinmarkt.nl; Waterlooplein; ☺9am-6pm Mon-Sat; ⓖ9/14 Waterlooplein).

★ **Droog**   DESIGN, HOMEWARES
(Map p502; www.droog.com; Staalstraat 7; ☺11am-6pm Tue-Sun; ⓖ4/9/14/16/24 Muntplein) *Droog* means 'dry' in Dutch, and this slick local design house's products are strong on dry wit. You'll find all kinds of smart items you never knew you needed, like super-powerful suction cups. Also here is a gallery space, whimsical blue-and-white cafe, and fairy-tale-inspired courtyard garden that Alice in Wonderland would love, as well as a top-floor apartment (double €275 per night).

Young Designers United   CLOTHING
(YDU; Map p504; www.ydu.nl; Keizersgracht 447; ☺1-6pm Mon, 10am-6pm Tue, Wed, Fri & Sat, 10am-8pm Thu; ⓖ1/2/5 Keizersgracht) Racks are rotated regularly at this affordable boutique showcasing young designers working in the Netherlands. You might spot durable basics by Agna K, minimalist knits by Andy ve Eirn, geometric dresses by Fenny Faber and soft, limited-edition knits by Mimoods. Accessorise with YDU's select range of jewellery and bags.

**Condomerie Het
Gulden Vlies**   SPECIALTY SHOP
(Map p502; condomerie.com; Warmoesstraat 141; ☺11am-6pm Mon-Sat, 1-5pm Sun; ⓖ4/9/14/16/24 Dam) Perfectly positioned for the Red Light District, this boutique sells condoms in every imaginable size, colour, flavour and design (horned devils, marijuana leaves, Delftware tiles...), along with lubricants and saucy gifts.

Kokopelli   SMART SHOP
(Map p502; www.kokopelli.nl; Warmoesstraat 12; ☺11am-10pm; ⓖ4/9/16/24/25 Centraal Station) Were it not for its trade in 'magic truffles' (similar to now-outlawed psilocybin mushrooms aka magic mushrooms) you might swear this large, beautiful space was a fashionable clothing or homewares store. There's a coffee and juice bar and a chill-out lounge area overlooking Damrak.

ⓘ Information

Tourist Office (VVV; Map p502; ☏702 60 00; www.iamsterdam.nl; Stationsplein 10; ☺9am-5pm Mon-Sat, to 4pm Sun; ⓖ4/9/16/24/25 Centraal Station) Maps, guides and transit passes.

> **ⓘ I AMSTERDAM CARD**
>
> The **I Amsterdam Card** (www.iamsterdam.com; per 24/48/72hr €47/57/67) provides admission to more than 30 museums, a canal cruise, and discounts at shops, attractions and restaurants. Also includes a GVB transit pass. Available at VVV offices (tourist offices) and some hotels.

ⓘ Getting There & Away

AIR
Most major airlines serve Schiphol (p523), 18km southwest of the city centre.

BUS
Eurolines connects with all major European capitals. Buses arrive at Amsterdam Duivendrecht train station, 7.5km southeast of the centre, which has an easy metro link to Centraal Station (about a 15-minute trip).

   Eurolines' ticket office (www.eurolines.nl; Rokin 38a; ☺9am-5pm Mon-Sat; ⓖ4/9/14/16/24 Dam) is near the Dam.

TRAIN
Amsterdam's main train station is fabled **Centraal Station**, with extensive services to the rest of the country and major European cities.

   For domestic destinations, visit the Dutch national train service, **Nederlandse Spoorwegen** (NS; www.ns.nl). **NS International** (www.nsinternational.nl) operates many international services.

ⓘ Getting Around

TO/FROM THE AIRPORT
Taxi To Amsterdam from Schiphol Airport takes 25 to 45 minutes and costs about €55.

Trains To Centraal Station leave every few minutes, take 15 to 20 minutes, and cost €4/8 per single/return.

BICYCLE
Amsterdam is cycling nirvana. The city has more bicycles (881,000) than residents (811,000). About 80,000 bicycles are stolen each year, so always lock up.

Bike City (☏626 37 21; www.bikecity.nl; Bloemgracht 68-70; bike rental per day from €14; ☺9am-6pm; ⓖ13/14/17 Westermarkt) These black bikes have no advertising on them, so you can free-wheel like a local.

WORTH A TRIP

ZAANSE SCHANS

The working, inhabited village Zaanse Schans functions as an open-air **windmill gallery** (www.dezaanseschans.nl; site free, windmills adult/child €3.50/2; ⊘windmills 10am-5pm Apr-Nov, hours vary Dec-Mar) FREE on the Zaan river. Popular with tourists, its mills are completely authentic and operated with enthusiasm and love. You can explore the windmills at will, seeing the vast moving parts first-hand.

The impressive **Zaans Museum** (☑075-616 28 62; www.zaansmuseum.nl; Schansend 7; adult/child €9/5; ⊘10am-5pm; ⊛) shows how wind and water were harnessed.

Trains (€3, 17 minutes, four per hour) run from Amsterdam Centraal Station (direction Alkmaar) to Koog Zaandijk, from where it's a well-signposted 1.5km walk.

BOAT

Canal Bus (☑217 05 00; www.canal.nl; Weteringschans 26; day pass adult/child €22/11; ⊘10am-6pm; ⊛; ⓠ1/2/5 Leidseplein) Offers a unique hop-on, hop-off service, with docks around the city near big museums and attractions.

PUBLIC TRANSPORT

Public transport in Amsterdam uses the OV-chipkaart. Rides cost €2.90 when bought on board. Unlimited-ride passes are available for one to seven days (€7.50 to €32) and are valid on trams, most buses and the metro.

GVB Information Office (www.gvb.nl; Stationsplein 10; ⊘7am-9pm Mon-Fri, 8am-9pm Sat & Sun; ⓠ1/2/4/5/9/14/16/24 Centraal Station) Amsterdam's local transit authority, GVB, has an information office where you can get tickets, maps and the like. It's across the tram tracks from Centraal Station's main entrance.

TAXI

Amsterdam taxis are expensive, even over short journeys. Try **Taxicentrale Amsterdam** (TCA; ☑777 77 77; www.tcataxi.nl).

THE RANDSTAD

One of the most densely populated places on the planet, the Randstad stretches from Amsterdam to Rotterdam and is crammed with classic Dutch towns and cities such as Den Haag, Utrecht, Leiden and Delft. A cycling network links the towns amid tulip fields.

Haarlem

☑023 / POP 150,000

Just 15 minutes by train from Amsterdam, Haarlem's canals and cobblestone streets filled with gabled buildings, grand churches, museums, cosy bars, good restaurants and antique shops draw scores of day trippers.

◉ Sights

Haarlem's centre radiates out from the **Grote Markt**. The **Town Hall** (Grote Markt 2) is worth a look, as is the cathedral, **Grote Kerk van St Bavo** (www.bavo.nl; Oude Groenmarkt 22; adult/child €2.50/1.25; ⊘10am-5pm Mon-Sat).

Frans Hals Museum GALLERY
(www.franshalsmuseum.nl; Groot Heiligland 62; adult/child €15.50/free; ⊘11am-5pm Tue-Sat, from noon Sun; ⊛) A short stroll south of Grote Markt, the Frans Hals Museum is a must for anyone interested in the Dutch Masters. Kept in a poorhouse where Hals spent his final years, the collection focuses on the 17th-century Haarlem School; its pride and joy are eight group portraits of the Civic Guard that reveal Hals' exceptional attention to mood and psychological tone. Look out for works by other greats such as Pieter Brueghel the Younger and Jacob van Ruysdael.

✗ Eating & Drinking

Restaurants line Schagchelstraat, while cafes cluster along Lange Veerstraat, and around the Grote Markt. The Saturday morning market here is one of the Netherlands' best; there's a smaller market on Monday.

De Haerlemsche Vlaamse FAST FOOD €
(Spekstraat 3; frites €2-3; ⊘11am-6.30pm Mon-Wed & Fri, to 9pm Thu, to 5pm Sat, noon-5pm Sun) Practically on the doorstep of the Grote Kerk, this miniscule *frites* (French fries) joint is a local institution. Line up for its crispy, golden fries made from fresh potatoes and one of a dozen sauces including three kinds of mayonnaise.

★ Jopenkerk BREWERY
(www.jopenkerk.nl; Gedempte Voldersgracht 2; ⊘brewery & cafe 10am-1am, restaurant 5.30pm-late Tue-Sat) Haarlem's most atmospheric place to drink and/or dine is this independent

brewery inside a stained-glass-windowed, 1910-built church. Enjoy brews like citrusy Hopen, fruity Lente Bier or chocolatey Koyt and classic snacks (*bitterballen*, cheeses) beneath the gleaming vats, or head to the mezzanine for mains (€16.50 to €23.50) made from locally sourced, seasonal ingredients and Jopenkerk's beers, with pairings available.

ℹ Getting There & Away

Trains serve Haarlem's stunning art deco station, a 10-minute walk north of the centre. Destinations include:

Amsterdam (€4.10, 15 minutes, five to eight per hour)

Den Haag (€8.20, 35 to 40 minutes, four to six per hour)

Rotterdam (€11.90, 50 minutes, four to six per hour).

Leiden

📞 071 / POP 122,000

Vibrant Leiden is renowned for being Rembrandt's birthplace, the home of the Netherlands' oldest university (and 20,000 students) and the place America's pilgrims raised money to lease the leaky *Mayflower* that took them to the New World in 1620. Beautiful 17th-century buildings line its canals.

◉ Sights

The best way to experience Leiden is by strolling the historic centre, especially along the Rapenburg canal.

Pieterskerk   CHURCH
(Pieterskerkhof; admission €2; ⏱11am-6pm) Crowned by its huge steeple, Pieterskerk is often under restoration – a good thing as it has been prone to collapse since it was built in the 14th century.

The precinct here is as old Leiden as you'll get and includes the gabled old **Latin School** (Lokhorststraat 16), which – before it became a commercial building – was graced by a pupil named Rembrandt from 1616 to 1620. Across the plaza, look for the **Gravensteen** (Pieterskerkhof 6), which dates to the 13th century and was once a prison. The gallery facing the plaza was where judges watched executions.

Lakenhal   MUSEUM
(www.lakenhal.nl; Oude Singel 32; adult/child €7.50/free; ⏱10am-5pm Tue-Fri, noon-5pm Sat & Sun) Get your Rembrandt fix at the 17th-century Lakenhal, which houses the Municipal Museum, with an assortment of works by old masters, as well as period rooms and temporary exhibits. The 1st floor has been restored to the way it would have looked when Leiden was at the peak of its prosperity.

Rijksmuseum van Oudheden   MUSEUM
(National Museum of Antiquities; www.rmo.nl; Rapenburg 28; adult/child €9.50/3; ⏱10am-5pm Tue-Sun; 🅿) This museum has a world-class collection of Greek, Roman and Egyptian artefacts, the pride of which is the extraordinary **Temple of Taffeh**, a gift from former Egyptian president Anwar Sadat to the Netherlands for helping to save ancient Egyptian monuments from flood.

🛏 Sleeping & Eating

The city-centre canals and narrow old streets teem with choices. Saturday's market sprawls along Nieuwe Rijn.

Nieuw Minerva   HOTEL €€
(📞512 63 58; www.nieuwminerva.nl; Boommarkt 23; s/d from €84/88; @🅿) Located in canal-side houses dating from the 16th century, this central hotel has a mix of 40 regular (ie nothing special) and very fun themed rooms, including a room with a bed in which King Lodewijk Bonaparte (aka Louis Bonaparte) slept, the 'room of angels' – a luminous vision of white, the 'Delft blue room', and the Rembrandt room.

Oudt Leyden   PANCAKES €
(www.oudtleyden.nl; Steenstraat 49; pancakes €8-15, mains €12.50-24.50; ⏱11.30am-9.30pm; 📞🚼) Get ready to meet giant Dutch-style pancakes with creative fillings that make kids and adults alike go wide-eyed. Whether you're feeling savoury (marinated salmon, sour cream and capers), sweet (apple, raisins, almond paste, sugar and cinnamon) or simply adventurous (ginger and bacon!), this welcoming cafe hits the spot every time.

Proeverij de Dames   CAFE €€
(www.proeverijdedames.nl; Nieuwe Rijn 37; lunch mains €7-9.50, dinner €17-20.50; ⏱10am-10pm) Run by two women with excellent taste, this stylish canal-side cafe/wine bar opening out to a terrace has an excellent range of coffees and wines by the glass. There's a long list of small plates for nibbling, sharing or combining into a meal. House-made baked goods include double-chocolate cake and apple pie.

DON'T MISS

KEUKENHOF GARDENS

One of the Netherlands' top attractions is near Lisse, between Haarlem and Leiden. **Keukenhof** (www.keukenhof.nl; Lisse; adult/child €16/8, parking €6; ⊘8am-7.30pm mid-Mar–mid-May, last entry 6pm; 🐦) is the world's largest bulb-flower garden, attracting nearly 800,000 visitors during a season almost as short-lived as the blooms on the millions of multicoloured tulips, daffodils and hyacinths.

Special buses link Keukenhof with Amsterdam's Schiphol airport and Leiden's Centraal Station in season; combination tickets covering entry and transport are available (adult/child €23.50/12.50). Pre-purchase tickets online to help avoid huge queues.

ℹ Information

Tourist Office (⌨516 60 00; www.vvvleiden.nl; Stationsweg 41; ⊘7am-7pm Mon-Fri, 10am-4pm Sat, 11am-3pm Sun) Across from the train station.

ℹ Getting There & Away

Buses leave from directly in front of Centraal Station.

Train destinations include:

Amsterdam (€8.80, 34 minutes, six per hour)
Den Haag (€3.40, 10 minutes, six per hour)
Schiphol Airport (€5.70, 15 minutes, six per hour).

Den Haag

⌨070 / POP 501,000

Flanked by wide, leafy boulevards, Den Haag (The Hague), officially known as 's-Gravenhage (Count's Hedge), is the Dutch seat of government (although Amsterdam is the capital). Embassies and various international courts of justice give the city a worldly air. Around 5km northwest, the long beach at **Scheveningen**, pronounced – if possible – as s'chay-fuhninger, is horribly overdeveloped; the hype tapers off to the south past the harbour.

👁 Sights

★**Mauritshuis**　　　　MUSEUM
(www.mauritshuis.nl; Plein 29; adult/child €14/free, combined ticket with Galerij Prins Willem V €17.50;

⊘1-6pm Mon, 10am-5pm Tue, Wed & Fri-Sun, to 8pm Thu) For a comprehensive introduction to Dutch and Flemish Art, visit the Mauritshuis, a jewel-box of a museum in an old palace and brand-new wing. Almost every work is a masterpiece, among them Vermeer's *Girl with a Pearl Earring*, Rembrandts including a wistful self-portrait in the year of his death, 1669, and *The Anatomy Lesson of Dr Nicolaes Tulp*. A five-minute walk southwest, the newly restored **Galerij Prins Willem V** (www.mauritshuis.nl; Buitenhof 35; adult/child €5/2.50, combined ticket with Mauritshuis €17.50; ⊘noon-5pm Tue-Sun) contains 150 old masters (Steen, Rubens, Potter, et al).

★**Binnenhof**　　　　PALACE
The Binnenhof's central courtyard (once used for executions) is surrounded by parliamentary buildings. The splendid 17th-century North Wing is still home to the Upper Chamber of the **Dutch Parliament**. The Lower Chamber formerly met in the ballroom, in the 19th-century wing; it now meets in a modern building on the south side. A highlight of the complex is the restored 13th-century **Ridderzaal** (Knights' Hall). To see the buildings you need to join a tour through visitor organisation **ProDemos** (⌨757 02 00; www.prodemos.nl; Hofweg 1; 45-minute Ridderzaal tour €5, 90-minute government tour €10; ⊘9.30am-5pm Mon-Sat, tours by reservation).

Afterwards, stroll around the **Hofvijver**, where the reflections of the Binnenhof and the Mauritshuis have inspired countless snapshots.

Escher in Het Paleis Museum　　　　MUSEUM
(www.escherinhetpaleis.nl; Lange Voorhout 74; adult/child €9/6.50; ⊘11am-5pm Tue-Sun) The Lange Voorhout Palace was once Queen Emma's winter residence. Now it's home to the work of Dutch graphic artist MC Escher. The permanent exhibition features notes, letters, drafts, photos and fully mature works covering Escher's entire career, from his early realism to the later phantasmagoria. There are some imaginative displays, including a virtual reality reconstruction of Escher's impossible buildings.

Gemeentemuseum　　　　MUSEUM
(Municipal Museum; www.gemeentemuseum.nl; Stadhouderslaan 41; adult/child €17/free; ⊘10am-5pm Tue-Sun) Admirers of De Stijl, and in particular of Piet Mondrian, mustn't miss the Berlage-designed Gemeentemuseum. It houses a large collection of works by neoplasticist

artists and others from the late 19th century, as well as extensive exhibits of applied arts, costumes and musical instruments. Take tram 17 from CS and HS to the Statenwartier stop.

🛏 Sleeping & Eating

Expats on expense accounts support a diverse and thriving cafe culture. The cobbled streets and canals off Denneweg are an excellent place to start wandering.

Corona HOTEL €€
(☑ 363 79 30; www.corona.nl; Buitenhof 39-42; s €90-120, d €145-175; 🅿 @ 🛜) In a bullseye location by the Binnenhof, 1km southwest of Centraal Station, this well-run property occupies three 17th-century, recently renovated townhouses. The 36 rooms span a range of styles that mix classic details with modernity. On-site parking (€20) by reservation.

Zebedeüs CAFE €€
(www.zebedeus.nl; Rond de Grote Kerk 8; lunch mains €5-13.50, dinner €16.50-22.50; ⊙11am-10pm) 🍴 Built right into the walls of the Grote Kerk, this organic cafe serves huge, fresh sandwiches (smoked trout, pulled pork) all day, and creative evening dishes like catfish with pancetta, duck breast with smoked garlic and caramel jus, and mushroom and lentil burgers with celeriac and mash. In fine weather, the best seats are at the chestnut-tree-shaded tables outside.

De Basiliek FRENCH, ITALIAN €€
(☑ 360 61 44; www.debasiliek.nl; Korte Houtstraat 4a; mains €18.50-22.50, 2-/3-course market menu €27.50/30; ⊙noon-4pm & 6-10pm Mon-Fri, 6-10pm Sat) Behind a smart facade framed by black awnings, classy De Basiliek crafts intricate dishes such as roast hare with red cabbage and figs, or duck cannoli with asparagus and truffle oil. The stellar wine list has full-bottle, half-bottle and by-the-glass options.

🛍 Shopping

Grote Markstraat is fittingly the street for large stores. Enticing boutiques line Hoogstraat, Noordeinde, Heulstraat and especially Prinsestraat.

Stanley & Livingstone BOOKS
(☑ 365 73 06; www.stanley-livingstone.eu; Schoolstraat 21; ⊙hours vary) Quaint travel bookshop.

ℹ Information

Tourist Office (VVV; ☑ 361 88 60; www.denhaag.com; Spui 68; ⊙noon-8pm Mon, 10am-8pm Tue-Fri, 10am-5pm Sat, noon-5pm Sun; 🛜) On the ground floor of the public library in the landmark New Toen Hall.

ℹ Getting There & Around

A day pass for local trams costs €7.70.

Most trains use Den Haag Centraal Station (CS), but some through trains only stop at Den

---

THE NETHERLANDS BY BIKE

The Netherlands has more than 32,000km of dedicated bike paths *(fietspaden)*, which makes it the most bike-friendly place on the planet. You can crisscross the country on the motorways of cycling: the LF routes. Standing for *landelijke fietsroutes* (long-distance routes), but virtually always simply called LF, they cover approximately 4500km. All are well marked by distinctive green-and-white signs.

The best overall maps are the widely available Falk/VVV *Fietskaart met Knooppunten-netwerk* (cycling network) maps, an easy-to-use series of 20, with keys in English, that blanket the country in 1:50,000 scale, and cost €9. Every bike lane, path and other route is shown, along with distances. Comprehensive cycling website **Nederland Fietsland** (www.nederlandfietsland.nl) has route planners and downloadable GPS tracks, and lists every bike-rental outlet in the country.

Bike Rentals

Bicycle hire is available all over the Netherlands at hotels, independent rental outlets and train stations. Prices average around €15 per 24 hours. You'll need to show ID and leave a deposit (€50 to €150).

On Trains

You may bring your bicycle onto any train outside peak hours (6.30am to 9am and 4pm to 6.30pm Monday to Friday) as long as there is room. Bicycles require a day pass *(dagkaart fiets*; €6).

Haag HS (Holland Spoor) station just south of the centre.

Services include:

Amsterdam (€11.20, 50 minutes, up to six per hour)

Rotterdam (€4.70, 25 minutes, up to six per hour); also accessible by metro

Schiphol Airport (€8.20, 30 minutes, up to six per hour)

Delft

🗐 015 / POP 99,737

Compact and charming, Delft makes a perfect Dutch day trip. Founded around 1100, it maintains tangible links to its romantic past despite the pressures of modernisation and tourist hordes. Many of the canal-side vistas could be scenes from the *Girl with a Pearl Earring*, the novel about Delft-born Golden Age painter Johannes Vermeer.

◉ Sights

The **town hall** and the **Waag** on the **Grote Markt** are right out of the 17th century.

Oude Kerk   CHURCH

(Old Church; www.oudeennieuwekerkdelft.nl; Heilige Geestkerkhof 25; adult/child incl Nieuwe Kerk €6.50/ free; ⊙9am-6pm Apr-Oct, 11am-4pm Nov-Mar, closed Sun) The Gothic Oude Kerk, founded in 1246, is a surreal sight: its 75m-high tower leans nearly 2m from the vertical due to subsidence caused by its canal location, hence its nickname Scheve Jan ('Leaning Jan'). One of the tombs inside the church is Vermeer's.

Nieuwe Kerk   CHURCH

(New Church; www.oudeennieuwekerkdelft.nl; Markt; adult/child incl Oude Kerk €6.50/free, Nieuwe Kerk tower €3.75/2.25; ⊙9am-6pm Mon-Sat Apr-Oct, hours vary Nov-Mar) Construction on Delft's Nieuwe Kerk began in 1381; it was finally completed in 1655. Amazing views extend from the 108.75m-high tower: after climbing its 376 narrow, spiralling steps you can see as far as Rotterdam and Den Haag on a clear day. It's the resting place of William of Orange (William the Silent), in a mausoleum designed by Hendrick de Keyser.

Municipal Museum het Prinsenhof   MUSEUM

(http://prinsenhof-delft.nl; St Agathaplein 1; adult/ child €10/5; ⊙11am-5pm, closed Mon Nov-May) Opposite the Oude Kerk, the former convent where William of Orange (William the Silent) was assassinated in 1584 (the bullet hole in the wall is preserved) is now a museum dis-playing various objects telling the story of the Eighty Years' War with Spain, as well as 17th-century paintings. An artist-in-residence paints interpretations of Dutch masterpieces; relax in the serene gardens.

★Vermeer Centrum Delft   MUSEUM

(www.vermeerdelft.nl; Voldersgracht 21; adult/child €8/4; ⊙10am-5pm) As the place where Vermeer was born, lived, and worked, Delft is 'Vermeer Central' to many art-history and old-masters enthusiasts. Along with viewing life-sized images of Vermeer's oeuvre, you can tour a replica of Vermeer's studio, which reveals the way the artist approached the use of light and colour in his craft. A 'Vermeer's World' exhibit offers insight into his environment and upbringing, while temporary exhibits show how his work continues to inspire other artists.

De Candelaer   STUDIO

(www.candelaer.nl; Kerkstraat 13; ⊙9.30am-6pm Mon-Sat, 11am-6pm Sun) The most central and modest Delftware outfit is de Candelaer, just off the Markt. It has five artists, a few of whom work most days. When it's quiet they'll give you a detailed tour of the manu-facturing process.

🛏 Sleeping & Eating

★Hotel de Plataan   BOUTIQUE HOTEL €€

(🗐212 60 46; www.hoteldeplataan.nl; Doelenplein 9-11; s/d from €105/115; 🖥) On a pretty canal-side square in the old town, this family-run gem has small but elegant standard rooms and wonderfully opulent theme rooms, including the 'Garden of Eden'; the Eastern-style 'Amber', with a Turkish massage shower; or the desert-island 'Tamarinde'. Modesty alert: many en suites are only partially screened from the room. Rates include breakfast and secure parking.

De Visbanken   SEAFOOD €

(www.visbanken.nl; Camaretten 2; dishes €2-7; ⊙10am-6pm Mon, 9am-6pm Tue-Fri, 9am-5pm Sat, 10am-5pm Sun) Fish has been sold on this spot since 1342. Display cases in the old open-air pavilion entice with fresh and marinated, smoked and fried fishy treats.

Stads-Koffyhuis   CAFE €

(http://stads-koffyhuis.nl; Oude Delft 133; mains €6.25-12.50; ⊙9am-7pm Mon-Fri, to 6pm Sat) The most idyllic seats at this delightful cafe are on the terrace, aboard a barge moored out front. Tuck into award-winning bread rolls, with fillings such as aged artisan Gouda with apple sauce, mustard, fresh figs and walnuts, or house-specialty pancakes, while admiring possibly the best view of the Oude Kerk, just ahead at the end of the canal.

Spijshuis de Dis   CONTEMPORARY DUTCH €€
(☑213 17 82; www.spijshuisdedis.com; Beestenmarkt 36; mains €17-24.50; ☺5-10pm Tue-Sat; ☑🖰) Fresh fish and amazing soups served in bread bowls take centre stage at this romantic foodie haven, but meat eaters and vegetarians are well catered for, too. Creative starters include smoked, marinated mackerel on sliced apple with horseradish. Don't skip the Dutch pudding served in a wooden shoe.

🍷 Drinking & Nightlife

Locus Publicus   BROWN CAFE
(www.locuspublicus.nl; Brabantse Turfmarkt 67; ☺11am-1am Mon-Thu, to 2am Fri & Sat, noon-1am Sun) Cosy little Locus Publicus is filled with cheery locals quaffing their way through the 175-strong beer list. There's great people-watching from the front terrace.

ⓘ Information

Tourist Office (VVV; ☑215 40 51; www.delft. nl; Kerkstraat 3; ☺hours vary) Sells excellent walking-tour brochures.

ⓘ Getting There & Away

The area around the train station is a vast construction site while the lines are moved underground; completion is due in 2016.

Services include:

Amsterdam (€12.70, one hour, up to six per hour)
Den Haag (€2.40, 12 minutes, up to six per hour)
Rotterdam (€3.20, 12 minutes, four per hour)

Rotterdam

☑010 / POP 619,879

Bold new initiatives, myriad urban regeneration projects, and electrifying dining and nightlife all make Rotterdam one of the most happening cities in Europe right now. The Netherlands' exhilarating 'second city' has a diverse, multi-ethnic community, an absorbing maritime tradition centred on Europe's busiest port, and a wealth of top-class museums.

Central Rotterdam was largely levelled during WWII and spent the following decades rebuilding. It maintains a progressive, perpetual-motion approach to architecture, with an anything-goes philosophy.

Rotterdam is split by the vast Nieuwe Maas shipping channel, which is crossed by a series of tunnels and bridges, notably the dramatic Erasmusbrug. On the north side of the water, the city centre is easily strolled.

◉ Sights & Activities

Rotterdam is a veritable open-air gallery of modern, postmodern and contemporary architecture, with mind-bending late-20th-century icons and eye-popping new additions.

Just 3km southwest of the centre, **Delfshaven**, once the official seaport for the city of Delft, survived the war and retains its historic character. Before leaving the Netherlands for America, the Pilgrims prayed for the last time at the Oude Kerk (p514); they're honoured at local brewery **Stadsbrouwerij De Pelgrim** (www.pelgrim bier.nl; Aelbrechtskolk 12; ☺noon-midnight Wed-Sat). A reconstructed 18th-century **windmill**

MARITIME ROTTERDAM

Harbour tours, museums and exhibits bring Rotterdam's centuries-old maritime heritage to life.

Maritiem Museum Rotterdam (Maritime Museum; www.maritiemmuseum.nl; Leuvehaven 1; adult/child €8.50/4.50; ☺10am-5pm Tue-Sat, 11am-5pm Sun year-round, plus 10am-5pm Mon Jul & Aug) This comprehensive museum looks at the Netherlands' rich maritime traditions through an array of models that any youngster would love to take into the tub, plus interesting and explanatory displays.

Haven Museum (www.maritiemmuseum.nl; Leuvehaven 50; ☺10am-4pm Tue-Sat, 11am-4pm Sun) Just south of the Maritime Museum, the Haven Museum comprises all manner of old and historic ships moored in the basin. You can always wander the quays; when the visitor centre is open you can learn more about what's tied up.

Spido (www.spido.nl; Willemsplein 85; adult/child €11.25/6.90) Harbour tours lasting 75 minutes depart from the pier at Leuvehoofd near the Erasmusbrug (by Leuvehaven metro stop). There are up to 10 departures daily in July and August, fewer in the rest of the year.

Rotterdam

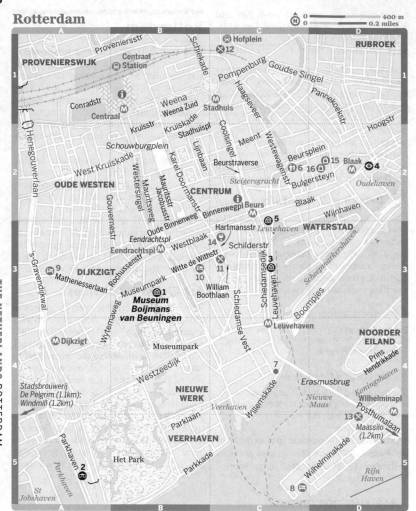

(☑010 477 9181; Voorhaven 210; ☺1-5pm Wed, 10am-4pm Sat, hours vary) **FREE** overlooks the water. Take tram 4 or 8, or the metro.

★Museum Boijmans
van Beuningen
MUSEUM

(www.boijmans.nl; Museumpark 18-20; adult/child €15/free, Wed free; ☺11am-5pm Tue-Sun) Among Europe's very finest museums, the Museum Boijmans van Beuningen has a permanent collection spanning all eras of Dutch and European art, including superb old masters. Among the highlights are *The Marriage*

Feast at Cana by Hieronymus Bosch, the *Three Maries at the Open Sepulchre* by Van Eyck, the minutely detailed *Tower of Babel* by Pieter Brueghel the Elder, and *Portrait of Titus* and *Man in a Red Cap* by Rembrandt.

Overblaak Development
NOTABLE BUILDING

Designed by Piet Blom and built from 1978 to 1984, this development near Blaak metro station is marked by its pencil-shaped tower and 'forest' of 45-degree-tilted, cube-shaped apartments on hexagonal pylons. One apartment, the **Kijk-Kubus Museum-House**

Rotterdam

(www.kubuswoning.nl; Overblaak 70; admission €3; ⊙11am-5pm), is open to the public; the **Stay-okay Rotterdam** youth hostel occupies the super-sized cube at the southern end.

Euromast VIEWPOINT
(www.euromast.nl; Parkhaven 20; adult/child from €9.25/5.90; ⊙9.30am-10pm Apr-Sep, from 10am Oct-Mar) A 1960-built landmark, the 185m Euromast offers unparalleled 360-degree views of Rotterdam from its 100m-high observation deck. Extra diversions here include a brasserie and summertime abseiling (€52.50). The tower's two suites start from €385 including breakfast.

RiFO10 SURFING
(www.rif010.nl; Steigersgracht) From early 2016, surfers, bodyboarders, stand-up paddleboarders and kayakers can take a wild 14-second ride on a naturally purified, barrelling 1.5m-high wave in an inner-city canal. Its water-level beach-house cafe provides up-close views of the action.

🛏 Sleeping

⭐**King Kong Hostel** BOUTIQUE HOSTEL €
(☑818 87 78; www.kingkonghostel.com; Witte de Withstraat 74; dm/d/q from €22.50/75/110; @🛜) Outdoor benches made from salvaged timbers and garden hoses by Sander Bokkinga sit outside King Kong, a design haven on Rotterdam's coolest street. Artist-designed rooms and dorms are filled with vintage and industrial furniture; fab features include hammocks, lockers equipped with device-charging points, a gourmet self-catering kitchen, roof garden and barbecue area, and Netflix.

Hotel Van Walsum HOTEL €€
(☑436 32 75; www.hotelvanwalsum.nl; Mathenesserlaan 199-201; s/d/tr/q from €70/85/110/125; P🛜) In a group of grand townhouses dating from 1895, but with mod-cons including a lift/elevator, this warm, welcoming family-run hotel is just 10 minutes' walk from the centre, with great public transport connections. Comfortable rooms are decorated in autumnal hues; there's a charming back garden and secure parking (per day €15). Rates include breakfast.

⭐**Hotel New York** HISTORIC HOTEL €€€
(☑439 05 00; www.hotelnewyork.nl; Koninginnenhoofd 1; d €99-270; @🛜) An art nouveau showpiece, the Holland-America passenger-ship line's former HQ has sweeping vistas, superb dining options including an oyster bar, a barber shop, and a water taxi ferrying guests across the Nieuwe Maas to the city centre. Rooms retain original, painstakingly restored fittings and decor; styles range from standard to timber-panelled suites in the old boardrooms with fireplaces.

🍴 Eating

Rotterdam's food scene is booming. The stunning new Markthal Rotterdam (p518) has sit-down and take-away eating options galore.

⭐**De Jong** CONTEMPORARY DUTCH €€
(☑465 79 55; www.restaurantdejong.nl; Rampoortstraat 38; 4-course menu €40; ⊙6-11pm Wed-Sun; 🍴) In the hip Station Hofplein complex – the former train station of the disused Hofpleinlijn railway, whose viaduct arches are being transformed into cultural and creative

THE NETHERLANDS ROTTERDAM

spaces – adventurous chef Jim De Jong wows diners with surprise four-course menus (meat/fish or vegetarian; no à la carte) made from seasonal produce including herbs and flowers from the restaurant's garden.

Ter Marsch & Co BURGERS, STEAK €€
(www.termarschco.nl; Witte de Withstraat 70; burgers €7-12.50, mains €21-40; ⊘noon-10pm) Butcher shop–turned–bar/restaurant Ter Marsch & Co sizzles up monumental burgers (such as Scottish black Angus, pancetta and truffle mayo) and succulent steaks.

HMB INTERNATIONAL €€
(⌨760 06 20; www.hmb-restaurant.nl; Holland Amerika Kade 104; mains €15-17.50, 3-course lunch menu €35, 4-/5-/6-course dinner menu €49/57/65; ⊘noon-3.30pm & 5-10pm Tue-Fri, 5-10pm Sat) On the ground floor of the glitzy 'vertical city' De Rotterdam, the Netherlands' largest building, with dazzling views of the Erasmusbrug, chic HMB serves artistically presented contemporary cuisine (veal meatballs with truffled potatoes; foie gras with eel and apple) at impressively reasonable prices. Afterwards, head to the terrace of the building's 7th-floor cocktail bar.

Bazar MIDDLE EASTERN €€
(www.bazarrotterdam.nl; Witte de Withstraat 16; mains €8.50-16; ⊘8am-11pm Mon-Thu, to midnight Fri, 9am-midnight Sat & Sun) Beneath the exotic Hotel Bazar, this lantern-lit, souq-style stalwart dishes up dolmades, couscous, hummus, felafel, kebabs, Turkish pizza, baked feta with mint and parsley, Persian lamb and more. Tables spill onto the pavement terrace.

🍷 Drinking & Nightlife

★De Witte Aap BROWN CAFE
(www.dewitteaap.nl; Witte de Withstraat 78; ⊘1pm-4am; 🕸) Anchoring this artist-filled 'hood, the fabulous 'White Monkey' has live music on Wednesdays and DJs on Saturdays and is always crowded with locals. The front opens right up and a huge awning keeps inclement weather at bay.

Café LaBru BAR
(http://cafelabru.nl; Hartmansstraat 18a; ⊘2pm-1am Sun-Thu, to 2am Fri & Sat) Hard-to-find whisky, gin, rum, tequila and craft beers are on the menu at this super-cool vintage- and retro-adorned bar.

Maassilo CLUB
(www.maassilo.com; Maashaven Zuidzijde 1-2; ⊘11pm-6am Fri & Sat, hours vary Sun-Thu) Pump-

in' club inside a century-old grain silo with a capacity of 6000. Check the agenda to see what party's on when.

Shopping

Brand-name shops and department stores line Lijnbaan, Beursplein and the semi-subterranean Beurstraverse. Alternative shops congregate along Meent and its surrounds, as well as Nieuwemarkt, Pannekoekstraat, Oude Binnenweg and Nieuwe Binnenweg.

★Markthal Rotterdam FOOD & DRINK
(http://markthalrotterdam.nl; Nieuwstraat; ⊘10am-8pm Mon-Thu & Sat, to 9pm Fri, noon-6pm Sun) The Netherlands' inaugural indoor food market hit headlines around the world when it opened in 2014 due to its extraordinary inverted-U-shaped design, with glass-walled apartments arcing over the foodhall's fantastical fruit- and vegetable-muralled ceiling. There's a tantalising array of produce, prepared food and drinks; shops continue downstairs, while the **Blaak** (⊘8am-5pm Tue & Sat) street market unfurls outside twice weekly.

ⓘ Information

Tourist Office (⌨790 01 85; www.rotterdam.info; Coolsingel 197; ⊘9.30am-6pm) Main tourist office; there's a smaller branch at the main train station (Centraal Station; ⊘9am-5.30pm).

ⓘ Getting There & Away

Completed in 2014, Rotterdam's Centraal Station is an architectural stunner. There are direct services to Brussels and Paris; from late 2016, Eurostar trains linking Amsterdam with London will stop here.

Major services:
Amsterdam via Leiden (€14.80, 65 minutes, five per hour)
Amsterdam high speed (€17.10, 42 minutes, two per hour)
Schiphol airport (€11.90–€14.20, 20 to 50 minutes, five per hour)
Utrecht (€10.10, 40 minutes, four per hour)

ⓘ Getting Around

Rotterdam's trams, buses and metro are operated by **RET** (www.ret.nl). Most converge in front of Centraal Station, where there's an **information booth** (⊘7am-10pm) that also sells tickets. Day passes are available for varying durations (one/two/three days €7.10/10.70/14.20). A single-ride ticket purchased from a bus driver or tram conductor costs €3.

Utrecht

030 / POP 330,772

One of the Netherlands' oldest cities, Utrecht retains a beautiful old-world city centre, ringed by unique 13th-century canal wharves below street level. Canal-side streets brim with shops, restaurants and cafes. Its spirited student community of 70,000 is the country's largest.

Utrecht's train station (the country's busiest) and adjoining, maze-like Hoog Catharijne shopping centre are being transformed by a vast construction project (www. nieuwhc.nl), due for completion in 2016.

◎ Sights

Focus your wanderings on the **Domplein** and south along the tree-lined **Oudegracht**. The tourist office has a useful booklet covering Utrecht's myriad small museums, which feature everything from waste water to old trains.

Domtoren   HISTORIC BUILDING
(Cathedral Tower; www.domtoren.nl; Domplein; tower tour adult/child €9/5; ⊙11am-4pm) Finished in the 14th century after almost 300 years' construction, the cathedral and its tower are Utrecht's most striking medieval landmarks. In 1674 the North Sea winds reached hurricane force and blew down the cathedral's nave, leaving the tower and transept behind.

The Domtoren is 112m high, with 50 bells. It's worth the tough haul up 465 steps to the top for unbeatable city views; on a clear day you can see Amsterdam.

Centraal Museum   MUSEUM
(www.centraalmuseum.nl; Nicolaaskerkhof 10; adult/child €9/4; ⊙11am-5pm Tue-Sun; 🛜) The Centraal Museum has a wide-ranging collection. It displays applied arts dating back to the 17th century, as well as paintings by some of the Utrecht School artists and a bit of De Stijl to boot – including the world's most extensive Gerrit Rietveld collection, a dream for all minimalists. There's even a 12th-century Viking longboat that was dug out of the local mud, plus a sumptuous 17th-century dollhouse. Admission includes entry to the **Dick Bruna House** (www.centraalmuseum.nl; Nicolaaskerkhof 10; ⊙11am-5pm Tue-Sun), the studio of author and illustrator Dick Bruna, creator of belov-

WORTH A TRIP

OTHER DUTCH DESTINATIONS WORTH A VISIT

Other Netherlands highlights worth considering for day trips or longer visits:

Alkmaar Although touristy, its cheese ceremony (Fridays from first Friday of April to the first Friday of September) dates from the 17th century.

Deventer A sleepy Hanseatic League town with over 1000 16th- and 17th-century buildings.

Kinderdijk & Dordrecht A good day trip by fast ferry from Rotterdam is to visit Kinderdijk's Unesco-listed windmills then Dordrecht's medieval canals.

Gouda The perfect little Dutch town.

Texel Largest of the Frisian Islands, with endless walks along dune-backed beaches and excellent local seafood.

ed cartoon rabbit Miffy (Nijntje in Dutch). Entry to the Unesco-recognised house by Utrecht architect Gerrit Rietveld, **Rietveld-Schröderhuis** (reservations 030 236 2310; www.centraalmuseum.nl; Prins Hendriklaan 50; ⊙11am-5pm Wed-Sun), is also included.

⛏ Sleeping

B&B Utrecht   GUESTHOUSE €
(06 5043 4884; www.hostelutrecht.nl; Lucas Bolwerk 4; dm/s/d/tr from €19.50/57.50/65/90; ⊛🛜) Straddling the border between hostel and hotel, this spotless inn in an elegant old building has a communal kitchen and free breakfast, lunch and dinner ingredients. Wifi, scanners, printers etc are also free, along with a huge range of musical instruments and DVDs.

Mary K Hotel   HOTEL €€
(230 48 88; www.marykhotel.com; Oudegracht 25; d from €120; 🛜) ⵌ A bevy of Utrecht artists decorated the rooms at this ideally situated canal house. Rooms come in three basic sizes ('cosy', medium and large) but no two are alike. All make use of the original 18th-century features and you may find a timber beam running through your bathroom or a stuffed animal snoozing in the rafters.

HOLLAND OR THE NETHERLANDS?

'Holland' is a popular synonym for the Netherlands, yet it only refers to the combined provinces of Noord (North) and Zuid (South) Holland. Amsterdam is Noord-Holland's largest city; Haarlem is the provincial capital. Rotterdam is Zuid-Holland's largest city; Den Haag is its provincial capital. The rest of the country is not Holland, even if locals themselves often make the mistake.

✖ Eating & Drinking

GYS CAFE €

(http://gysutrecht.nl; Voorstraat 77; dishes €7-10; ⊙10am-10pm Mon-Sat; 🛜) 🖉 Organic produce at this bright, airy, design-filled cafe is used in burgers (such as tofu with grilled peppers and hummus, or lamb with pumpkin and mint), sandwiches (such as tempeh with sweet potato, avocado and watercress, or smoked mackerel with beetroot mousse), soups, salads and hot dishes like eggplant schnitzel with salsa, plus tasting platters.

★ Karaf INTERNATIONAL €€

(🗹 233 11 04; www.restaurantkaraf.nl; Lange Nieuwstraat 71; mains €18-23.50; ⊙5-10pm) Exquisitely presented dishes such as seabass in smoked butter, and Scottish grouse stuffed with Merquez sausage served with mulberry jus are among the reasons Karaf became an instant hit following its recent opening – along with its cool, contemporary Dutch dining room and stunning wine list.

't Oude Pothuys BROWN CAFE

(www.pothuys.nl; Oudegracht 279; ⊙3pm-2am Mon & Tue, noon-3am Wed-Sun) In a darkened barrel-vaulted medieval cellar, this wonderfully cosy pub has nightly music, from jam sessions and emerging bands to funk and soul, jazz and blues, electro and established acts. Enjoy drinks on the canal-side pier.

ℹ Information

Tourist Office (VVV; 🗹 0900 128 87 32; www.visit-utrecht.com; Domplein 9; ⊙noon-5pm Sun & Mon, 10am-5pm Tue-Sat) Sells Domtoren tickets.

ℹ Getting There & Away

Utrecht's train station is a major connection point, including for Germany.

Key services:

Amsterdam (€7.40, 30 minutes, four per hour)
Cologne (€29-44, two hours, up to seven direct services per day)
Maastricht (€23.10, two hours, hourly)
Rotterdam (€10.10, 40 minutes, up to four per hour)

THE SOUTH

Actual hills rise on the Netherlands' southern edge, where Belgium and Germany are within range of a tossed wooden shoe. The star here is Maastricht.

Maastricht

🗹 043 / POP 121,906

In the far-flung south, the grand old city of Maastricht is well worth the journey from Amsterdam and the pearls of the Ranstad, and you can easily continue to Belgium and Germany.

Among Maastricht's 1650 listed historic buildings, look for Spanish and Roman ruins, French and Belgian architectural twists, splendid food and the cosmopolitan flair that made Maastricht the location for the signing of the namesake treaty, which created the modern EU in 1992.

It's at its most exuberant during **carnaval**, from the Friday before Shrove Tuesday until late Wednesday.

◉ Sights

Maastricht's delights are scattered along both banks of the Maas and reward walkers.

Ringed by grand cafes, museums and churches, the large **Vrijthof** square is a focal point. Intimate **Onze Lieve Vrouweplein** is a cafe-filled square named after its church, which still attracts pilgrims. The arched stone footbridge **Sint Servaasbrug** dates from the 13th-century and links Maastricht's centre with the Wyck district.

Bonnefantenmuseum MUSEUM

(www.bonnefanten.nl; Ave Cèramique 250; adult/child €9/4.50; ⊙11am-5pm Tue-Sun) The Bonnefantenmuseum features a 28m tower that's a local landmark. Designed by Aldo Rossi, the museum opened in 1995, and is well laid out with collections divided into departments, each on its own floor: Old Masters and medieval sculpture are on one floor, contemporary art by Limburg artists on the next, linked by a dramatic sweep of stairs. Make time for the world-class Neuteling collection of medieval art.

Sint Servaasbasiliek CHURCH
(www.sintservaas.nl; basilica free, treasury adult/child €4/free; ⏲10am-4.30pm) FREE Sint Servaasbasiliek, a pastiche of architecture dating from 1000, dominates the Vrijthof. The **Treasury** is filled with gold artwork from the 12th century. Don't miss the **shrine to St Servatius**, a Catholic diplomat who died here in 384, and be sure to duck around the back to the serene cloister **garden**.

★Fort Sint Pieter FORTRESS
(☎325 21 21; www.maastrichtunderground.nl; Luikerweg 80; tour adult/child €6.20/5; ⏲English tours 12.30pm) Much of Maastricht is riddled with defensive tunnels dug into the soft sandstone over the centuries. The best place to see them is Fort Sint Pieter, now restored to its 1701 appearance. This is a really beautiful area, pastoral despite the ominous walls – the fort is an arresting sight looming over the charming hillside – and it's a fine 2km walk south of town.

Sleeping

Stayokay Maastricht HOSTEL €
(☎750 17 90; www.stayokay.com/maastricht; Maasboulevard 101; dm €21.50-37, tw €59-89; @ 📶) A vast terrace right on the Maas is the highlight of this stunner of a hostel with 199 beds in dorms and private rooms. It's 1km south of the centre in a sprawling park.

★Trash Deluxe BOUTIQUE HOTEL €€
(☎852 55 00; www.trashdeluxe.nl; Boschstraat 55; d €85-115, f €200; 📶) The name says it all. Across two historic buildings in a fabulous town-centre location (light sleepers should ask for a room at the back), this artist-designed hotel utilises recycled materials (rubber conveyor belts, industrial lighting, packing crates etc) in its ultrastylish, spacious and spotless rooms such as Glass, Metal and Concrete. Service is first rate.

Eating & Drinking

Excellent restaurants are even more common than old fortifications in Maastricht.

Bisschopsmolen BAKERY, CAFE €
(www.bisschopsmolen.nl; Stenebrug 1-3; dishes €4-8.50; ⏲9.30am-5.30pm Tue-Sat, 11am-4.30pm Sun) A working 7th-century water wheel powers a vintage flour mill that supplies its adjoining bakery. Specialties including spelt loaves and *vlaai* (seasonal fruit pies) come direct from the ovens that are on view out the back. You can dine onsite at the cafe, and, if it's not busy, self-tour the mill and see how flour's been made for eons.

★Café Sjiek DUTCH €€
(www.cafesjiek.nl; St Pieterstraat 13; mains €12.50-34.50; ⏲kitchen 5pm-11pm Mon-Fri, noon-11pm Sat & Sun; 📶) Traditional local fare at this cosy spot ranges from *zoervleis* (horse meat) with apple sauce to hearty venison stew, fresh fish and Rommedoe cheese with pear

ESSENTIAL FOOD & DRINK

- **Vlaamse frites** Iconic French fries smothered in mayonnaise or myriad other sauces.
- **Cheese** The Dutch consume almost 19kg of cheese per person per year, nearly two-thirds of which is Gouda. The tastiest hard, rich *oud* (old) varieties have strong, complex flavours.
- **Seafood** Street stalls sell seafood snacks including raw, slightly salted *haring* (herring) cut into bite-sized pieces and served with onion and pickles.
- **Indonesian** The most famous meal is a rijsttafel (rice table): an array of spicy savoury dishes such as braised beef, pork satay and ribs served with rice.
- **Kroketten** Croquettes are crumbed, deep-fried dough balls with various fillings, such as meat-filled *bitterballen*.
- **Beer** Big names like Heineken are ubiquitous; small brewers like De Drie Ringen and Gulpener are the best.
- **Jenever** Dutch gin is made from juniper berries and drunk chilled from a tulip-shaped shot glass. *Jonge* (young) jenever is smooth; strongly flavoured *oude* (old) jenever can be an acquired taste.

syrup and rye bread. It doesn't take reservations and is always busy, but you can wait at the bar. In summer there's a bevy of tables in the park across the street.

Take One BROWN CAFE
(www.takeonebiercafe.nl; Rechtstraat 28; ⊙4pm-2am Thu-Mon) Cramped and narrow from the outside, this eccentric 1930s tavern has well over 100 beers from the most obscure parts of the Benelux. It's run by a husband-and-wife team who help you select the beer most appropriate to your taste. The Bink Blonde is sweet, tangy and very good.

ⓘ Information

Tourist Office (VVV; ☑ 325 21 21; www.vvv maastricht.nl; Kleine Straat 1; ⊙ hours vary) In the 15th-century Dinghuis; offers excellent walking-tour brochures.

ⓘ Getting There & Away

Trains to Brussels and Cologne require a change in Liège.
   Domestic services include:

Amsterdam (€25, 2½ hours, two per hour)
Utrecht (€23.10, two hours, two per hour)

SURVIVAL GUIDE

ⓘ Directory A–Z

ACCOMMODATION

Always book accommodation ahead, especially during high season. The tourist offices operate booking services; when booking for two, make it clear whether you want two single (twin) beds or a double bed.

   Many Dutch hotels have steep, perilous stairs but no lifts/elevators, although most top-end and some midrange hotels are exceptions.

Stayokay (www.stayokay.com) is the Dutch hostelling association. A youth-hostel card costs €17.50 at the hostels; nonmembers pay an extra €2.50 per night and after six nights you become a member. The usual HI discounts apply.

BUSINESS HOURS

Banks & government offices 9am to 5pm Monday to Friday
Bars and cafes 11am to 1am
Clubs Mostly 10pm to 4am
Museums Many closed Monday
Post offices 9am to 6pm Monday to Saturday
Restaurants 10am or 11am to 10pm, often with a break between 3pm and 6pm

---

SLEEPING PRICE RANGES

Prices quoted include private bathrooms unless otherwise stated and are high-season rates. Breakfast is not included unless specified.

€ less than €80
€€ €80 to €160
€€€ more than €160

Shops Noon to 6pm Monday, 9am to 6pm Tuesday, Wednesday, Friday and Saturday (often Sunday too in large cities), to 9pm Thursday; supermarkets to 8pm or 10pm

DISCOUNT CARDS

Museumkaart (Museum Card; www.museum kaart.nl; adult/child €55/30, plus for 1st registration €5) Free and discounted entry to some 400 museums all over the country for one year. Purchase at participating museum ticket counters or at Uitburo ticket shops.

INTERNET RESOURCES

Lonely Planet (www.lonelyplanet.com/the-netherlands)
Netherlands Board of Tourism (www.holland.com)
Windmill Database (www.molendatabase.nl)

LEGAL MATTERS

Drugs are actually illegal in the Netherlands. Possession of soft drugs up to 5g is tolerated but larger amounts can get you jailed. Hard drugs are treated as a serious crime.

   Smoking is banned in all public places. In a uniquely Dutch solution, you can still smoke tobacco-free pot in coffeeshops.

MONEY
ATMs

Automatic teller machines proliferate outside banks, inside supermarkets and at train stations.

Credit Cards

Most hotels, restaurants and large stores accept major international cards. Some establishments,

---

TIPPING

Tipping is not essential as restaurants, hotels, bars etc include a service charge on their bills. A little extra is always welcomed though – anything from rounding up to the nearest euro to adding on 10% of the bill.

COUNTRY FACTS

Area 41,526 sq km

Capital Amsterdam

Country Code 31

Currency Euro (€)

Emergency 112

Language Dutch, English widespread

Money ATMs are common; cash pre-ferred for small purchases

Visas Schengen rules apply

however, including the Dutch railway, don't ac-cept non-European credit cards – check first.

PUBLIC HOLIDAYS

Nieuwjaarsdag New Year's Day
Goede Vrijdag Good Friday
Eerste Paasdag Easter Sunday
Tweede Paasdag Easter Monday
Koningsdag (King's Day) 27 April
Bevrijdingsdag (Liberation Day) 5 May
Hemelvaartsdag Ascension Day
Eerste Pinksterdag Whit Sunday (Pentecost)
Tweede Pinksterdag Whit Monday
Eerste Kerstdag (Christmas Day) 25 December
Tweede Kerstdag (Boxing Day) 26 December

SAFE TRAVEL

The Netherlands is a safe country, but be sensi-ble all the same and *always* lock your bike. Never buy drugs on the street: it's illegal and fatalities can and do occur. And don't light up joints just anywhere – stick to coffeeshops.

TELEPHONE

Country code 31
International access code 00

ⓘ Getting There & Away

AIR

Huge **Schiphol airport** (AMS; www.schiphol.nl) is the Netherlands' main international airport. **Rotterdam The Hague Airport** (RTM; www. rotterdamthehagueairport.nl) and budget airline hub **Eindhoven Airport** (EIN; www.eindhoven airport.nl) are small.

LAND
Bus

European bus network **Eurolines** (www.eurolines. com) serves a dozen destinations across the Netherlands including the major cities.

Car & Motorcycle

You'll need the vehicle's registration papers, third-party insurance and an international driver's permit in addition to your domestic licence. The national auto club, **ANWB** (www. anwb.nl), has offices across the country and will provide info if you can show an auto-club card from your home country (eg AAA in the US or AA in the UK).

Train

International train connections are good. All Eu-rail and Inter-Rail passes are valid on the Dutch national train service, **Nederlandse Spoorwe-gen** (NS; www.ns.nl).

Many international services are operated by **NS International** (www.nsinternational.nl). In addition, **Thalys** (www.thalys.com) fast trains serve Brussels (where you can connect to the Eurostar) and Paris. From December 2016, direct Eurostar services will link Amsterdam, Schiphol airport and Rotterdam with London.

The high-speed line from Amsterdam (via Schiphol and Rotterdam) speeds travel times to Antwerp (1¼ hours), Brussels (two hours) and Paris (3¼ hours). German ICE high-speed trains run six direct services per day between Amsterdam and Cologne (2½ hours) via Utrecht. Many continue on to Frankfurt (four hours) via Frankfurt airport.

In peak periods, it's wise to reserve seats in advance. By tickets online at **SNCB Europe** (www.b-europe.com).

ⓘ TRAIN TIPS

Be aware of the following when buying train tickets:

➡ Only some ticket machines accept cash, and those are coins-only, so you need a pocketful of change.

➡ Ticket machines that accept plastic will not work with credit and ATM cards without embedded chips (even then, not all international cards will work). The exceptions are a limited number of machines at Schiphol airport and Amsterdam Centraal.

➡ Ticket windows do not accept credit or ATM cards, but do accept paper euros. Queues are often long and there is a surcharge for using a ticket window.

➡ To buy domestic and international train tickets online with an international credit card, visit **SNCB Europe** (www. b-europe.com). You may need to print a paper copy of the ticket pdf.

SEA

Several companies operate car/passenger ferries between the Netherlands and the UK:

DFDS Seaways (www.dfdsseaways.co.uk) DFDS Seaways has overnight sailings (15 hours) between Newcastle and IJmuiden, 30km northwest of Amsterdam, linked to Amsterdam by bus (one-way €6, 40 minutes).

P&O Ferries (www.poferries.com) P&O Ferries operates an overnight ferry every evening (11¾ hours) between Hull and Europoort, 39km west of central Rotterdam. Book bus tickets (€10, 40 minutes) to/from the city when you reserve your berth.

Stena Line (www.stenaline.co.uk) Stena Line has overnight crossings between Harwich and Hoek van Holland, 31km northwest of Rotterdam, linked to central Rotterdam by train (€5.50, 30 minutes).

ⓘ Getting Around

BOAT

Ferries connect the mainland with the five Frisian Islands, including Texel. Other ferries span the Westerschelde in the south of Zeeland, providing road links to the bit of the Netherlands south of here as well as to Belgium. These are popular with people using the Zeebrugge ferry terminal and run frequently year-round.

CAR & MOTORCYCLE
Hire

You must be at least 23 years of age to hire a car in the Netherlands. Outside Amsterdam, car-hire companies can be in inconvenient locations if you're arriving by train.

Road Rules

Traffic travels on the right and the minimum driving age is 18 for vehicles and 16 for motorcycles. Seat belts are required and children under 12 must ride in the back if there's room. Trams always have the right of way and, if turning right, bikes have priority.

Speed limits are generally 50km/h in built-up areas, 80km/h in the country, 100km/h on

---

CONNECTIONS

Train connections to neighbouring countries are excellent. Amsterdam is linked to Cologne, Brussels and Paris by high-speed trains. From late 2016, Amsterdam and Rotterdam will have direct Eurostar services to/from London. Maastricht is right on the Belgian and German borders, with connections to Cologne and Brussels.

EATING PRICE RANGES

The following price categories are for the cost of a main course:

€ less than €12

€€ €12 to €25

€€€ more than €25

---

major through-roads, and 130km/h on freeways (variations are clearly indicated). Hidden speeding cameras are everywhere and they will find you through your rental car company.

LOCAL TRANSPORT

National public transport info is available in English at **9292** (www.9292ov.nl), which has an excellent smartphone app.

The universal form of transport payment in the Netherlands is the **OV-chipkaart** (www.ov-chipkaart.nl). Visitors can buy a disposable card, good for one hour, from specified vending machines in stations, at ticket windows or on board where available (correct change required). You can also buy disposable OV-chipkaarts good for unlimited use for one or more days and this is often the most convenient option, and cheaper than single-use chip cards.

Fares are also lower with refillable 'anonymous' OV-chipkaarts (€7.50 plus €3 if bought at a ticket window). These store the value of your payment and deduct the cost of trips as you use them. Purchase cards and top up at machines, newsagents or ticket windows.

When you enter *and* exit a bus, tram or train, you hold the card against a reader at the doors or station gates. The system then calculates your fare and deducts it from the card.

TRAIN

The train network is run by NS. First-class sections are barely different from 2nd-class areas, but they are less crowded. Trains are fast and frequent and serve most places of interest. Distances are short. The high-speed line between Schiphol and Rotterdam Centraal requires a 1st-/2nd-class supplement of €3/2.30. Most train stations have lockers operated by credit cards (average cost €5).

Tickets

Enkele reis One way; you can break your journey along the direct route.

Dagretour Day return; costs the same as two one-way tickets.

Dagkaart Day pass (€50.80); allows unlimited train travel throughout the country. Only good value if you're planning to spend the day on the train.

Portugal

Best Places to Eat

➡ Belcanto (p534)

➡ Botequim da Mouraria (p543)

➡ DOP (p553)

➡ Fangas Mercearia Bar (p548)

➡ Restaurante O Barradas (p541)

Best Places to Stay

➡ Memmo Alfama (p533)

➡ Gallery Hostel (p552)

➡ Nice Way Sintra Palace (p538)

➡ Duas Quintas (p541)

➡ Albergaria do Calvario (p543)

Why Go?

With medieval castles, frozen-in-time villages, captivating cities and golden-sand bays, the Portuguese experience can mean many things. History, terrific food and wine, lyrical scenery and all-night partying are just the beginning.

Portugal's cinematically beautiful capital, Lisbon, and its soulful northern rival, Porto, are two of Europe's most charismatic cities. Both are a joy to stroll, with gorgeous river views, rattling trams and tangled lanes hiding boutiques and vintage shops, new-wave bars, and a seductive mix of restaurants, fado (traditional Portuguese song) clubs and open-air cafes.

Beyond the cities, Portugal's landscape unfolds in all its beauty. Here, you can stay overnight in converted hilltop fortresses fronting age-old vineyards, hike amid granite peaks or explore medieval villages in the little-visited hinterland. More than 800km of coast shelters some of Europe's best beaches. You can gaze out over dramatic end-of-the-world cliffs, surf Atlantic breaks off dune-covered beaches or laze on sandy islands fronting the ocean.

When to Go
Lisbon

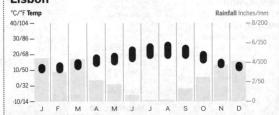

Apr & May Sunny days and wildflowers set the stage for hiking and outdoor activities.

Jun–Aug Lovely and lively, with a packed festival calendar and steamy beach days.

Late Sep & Oct Crisp mornings and sunny days; prices dip, crowds disperse.

Portugal Highlights

1 Follow the sound of fado spilling from the lamplit lanes of the **Alfama** (p535), an enchanting old-world neighbourhood in the heart of Lisbon.

2 Take in the laid-back charms of **Tavira** (p540), before hitting some of the Algarve's prettiest beaches.

3 Catch live music in a backstreet bar in **Coimbra** (p547), a festive university town with a stunning medieval centre.

4 Explore the wooded hills of **Sintra** (p537), studded with fairy-tale-like palaces, villas and gardens.

5 Conquer the trails of the ruggedly scenic **Parque Nacional da Peneda-Gerês** (p557).

6 Enjoy heady beach days in **Lagos** (p540), a surf-loving town with a vibrant drinking and dining scene.

7 Explore the Unesco World Heritage–listed centre of **Porto** (p549), sampling velvety ports at riverside wine lodges.

ITINERARIES

One Week

Devote three days to **Lisbon**, including a night of fado (traditional Portuguese song) in the Alfama, bar-hopping in Bairro Alto and Unesco-gazing and pastry-eating in Belém. Spend a day taking in the wooded wonderland of **Sintra**, before continuing to **Coimbra**, Portugal's own Cambridge. End your week in **Porto**, gateway to the magical wine-growing region of the Douro valley.

Two Weeks

On week two, stroll the historic lanes of **Évora** and visit the nearby megaliths. Take in the picturesque castle town of **Monsaraz** before hitting the beaches of the Algarve. Travel along the coast, visiting the pretty riverfront town of **Tavira** and the dramatic cliffs of **Sagres**. End the grand tour back in sunny **Lisbon**.

LISBON

POP 552,700

Spread across steep hillsides that overlook the Rio Tejo, Lisbon has captivated visitors for centuries. Windswept vistas at breathtaking heights reveal the city in all its beauty: Roman and Moorish ruins, white-domed cathedrals and grand plazas lined with sun-drenched cafes. The real delight of discovery, though, is delving into the narrow cobblestone lanes.

As bright-yellow trams clatter through curvy tree-lined streets, *lisboêtas* (residents of Lisbon) stroll through lamplit old quarters, much as they've done for centuries. Village-life gossip is exchanged over fresh bread and wine at tiny patio restaurants as fado singers perform in the background. In other parts of town, Lisbon reveals her youthful alter ego at stylish dining rooms and lounges, late-night street parties, riverside nightspots and boutiques selling all things classic and cutting-edge.

Just outside Lisbon, there's more to explore: enchanting woodlands, gorgeous beaches and seaside villages – all ripe for discovery.

◉ Sights

◉ Baixa & Alfama

Alfama is Lisbon's Moorish time capsule: a medina-like district of tangled alleys, hidden palm-shaded squares and narrow terracotta-roofed houses that tumble down to the glittering Tejo.

Castelo de São Jorge　　　CASTLE
(http://castelodesaojorge.pt; adult/child €8.50/5; ⊙9am-9pm Mar-Oct, 9am-6pm Nov-Feb) Towering dramatically above Lisbon, the hilltop fortifications of Castelo de São Jorge sneak into almost every snapshot. Roam its snaking ramparts and pine-shaded courtyards for superlative views over the city's red rooftops to the river.

Sé　　　CATHEDRAL
(⊙9am-7pm Tue-Sat, 9am-5pm Mon & Sun) **FREE** One of Lisbon's icons is the fortress-like *sé*, built in 1150 on the site of a mosque soon after Christians recaptured the city from the Moors.

FREE LISBOA

Aside from the **Castelo de São Jorge**, many sights in Lisbon have free entrance on Sundays from 10am to 2pm. For a free cultural fix on other days, make for Belém's **Museu Colecção Berardo** (p530) for outstanding contemporary art exhibits and the fortresslike **Sé** (cathedral), which was built on the site of a mosque in 1150. For Roman ruins, take a free tour of the **Núcleo Arqueológico** (Rua Augusta 96; ⊙10am-6pm Mon-Sat) **FREE**, which contains a web of tunnels hidden under the Baixa. The **Museu de Design e da Moda** (www.mude.pt; Rua Augusta 24; ⊙10am-6pm Tue-Sun) **FREE** exhibits eye-catching furniture, industrial design and couture dating to the 1930s.

Central Lisbon

200 m
0.1 miles

Miradouro da Senhora do Monte (170m)

R dos Lagares

Cç de Sto André

Santa Clara dos Cogumelos (600m)

Costa do Castelo

CASTELO

Lg das Olarias

R do Terreirinho

R dos Cavaleiros

Cç do Monte

2

1

Esplanada do Castelo

Costa do Castelo

Martim Moniz

R da Mouraria

Lg Martim Moniz

R do São Pedro Mártir

R dos Condes de Monsanto

Cç Marquês de Tancos

R de São Lázaro

R da Palma

Tram 28/Largo Martim Moniz

R da Madalena

Lg Adelino Amaro da Costa

R do Arco da Graça

R dos Fanqueiros

BAIXA

Cç de Santano

Cç do Garcia

R Barros Queiros

Dom Duarte

Rossio
Pç da Figueira

R da Betesga

R de Santa Justa

R da Assunção

10

13

Lg de São Domingos

26

Pç Dom Pedro IV (Rossio)

ROSSIO

R de Áurea

R do Carmo

R das Portas de Santo Antão

R Jardim do Regedor

Y Lisboa

15

R 1 de Dezembro

Estação do Rossio (Rossio Train Station)

R do Duque

R da Condessa

R da Oliveira

R da Trindade

Elevador da Lavra

Parque Eduardo VII

Pç dos Restauradores

Restauradores

Av da Liberdade

Ask Me Lisboa

11

R Nova da Trindade

Lg Trindade Coelho

São Jorge (300m); Cinemateca Portuguesa (650m); Lisbon Dreams (1km); Casa Amora (1.2km); Museu Calouste Gulbenkian & Centro de Arte Moderna (3km)

R da Glória

R das Talpas

R Dom Pedro V

R Luísa Todi

Tv de S Pedro

R do Teixeira

Elevador da Glória

3

Tv da Boa Hora

Tv da Água da Flor

BAIRRO ALTO

R da Rosa

R Luz Soriano

R da Misericórdia

R das Gáveas

R do Norte

R do Diário de Notícias

R da Barroca

Tv da Queimada

R da Atalaia

Tv dos Fiéis de Deus

30

27

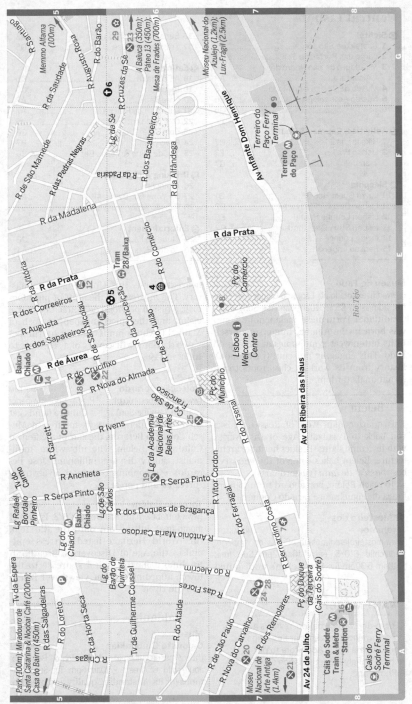

PORTUGAL LISBON

Central Lisbon

Museu do Fado   MUSEUM
(www.museudofado.pt; Largo do Chafariz de Dentro; admission €5; ◷10am-6pm Tue-Sun) Fado (traditional Portuguese melancholic song) was born in the Alfama. Immerse yourself in its bittersweet symphonies at Museu do Fado. This engaging museum traces fado's history from its working-class roots to international stardom.

◎ Belém

This quarter, 6km west of Rossio, whisks you back to Portugal's Age of Discoveries with its iconic sights. Besides heritage architecture, Belém bakes some of the country's best *pastéis de nata* (custard tarts).

To reach Belém, hop aboard tram 15 from Praça da Figueira or Praça do Comércio.

★**Mosteiro dos
Jerónimos**   MONASTERY
(www.mosteirojeronimos.pt; Praça do Império; adult/child €10/5, entry 10am-2pm Sun free; ◷10am-6.30pm Tue-Sun) Belém's undisputed heart-stealer is this Unesco-listed monastery. The *mosteiro* is the stuff of pure fantasy; a fusion of Diogo de Boitaca's creative vision and the spice and pepper dosh of Manuel I, who commissioned it to trumpet Vasco da Gama's discovery of a sea route to India in 1498.

**Museu
Colecção Berardo**   MUSEUM
(www.museuberardo.pt; Praça do Império; ◷10am-7pm Tue-Sun) FREE Culture fiends get their contemporary art fix for free at Museu Colecção Berardo, the star of the Centro Cultural de Belém. The ultrawhite, minimalist gallery displays billionaire José Berardo's eye-popping collection of abstract, surrealist and pop art.

Torre de Belém   TOWER
(www.torrebelem.pt; adult/child €6/3, 1st Sun of month free) Jutting out onto the Rio Tejo, this World Heritage–listed fortress epitomises the Age of Discoveries. Breathe in to climb a narrow spiral staircase to the tower, affording sublime views over Belém and the river.

◎ Saldanha

**Museu
Calouste Gulbenkian**   MUSEUM
(http://museu.gulbenkian.pt; Avenida de Berna 45; adult/child €5/free; ◷10am-6pm Tue-Sun) Famous for its outstanding quality and breadth,

---

WANT MORE?
....

For in-depth information, reviews and recommendations at your fingertips, head to the Apple App Store to purchase Lonely Planet's *Lisbon City Guide* iPhone app.

PORTUGAL LISBON

Museu Calouste Gulbenkian showcases an epic collection of Western and Eastern art – from Egyptian treasures to Old Master and Impressionist paintings.

Centro de
Arte Moderna
MUSEUM

(Modern Art Centre; www.cam.gulbenkian.pt; Rua Dr Nicaulau de Bettencourt; adult/chilld €5/ free; ⊙10am-6pm Tue-Sun) Situated in a sculpture-dotted garden, the Centro de Arte Moderna reveals a stellar collection of 20th-century Portuguese and international art.

◉ Santa Apolónia & Lapa

The museums listed here are west and east of the city centre, but are well worth visiting.

Museu Nacional
do Azulejo
MUSEUM

(www.museudoazulejo.pt; Rua Madre de Deus 4; adult/child €5/2.50, 1st Sun of month free; ⊙10am-6pm Tue-Sun) Housed in a sublime 16th-century convent, the museum covers the entire *azulejo* (hand-painted tile) spectrum. Star exhibits feature a 36m-long panel depicting pre-earthquake Lisbon, a Manueline cloister with weblike vaulting and exquisite blue-and-white *azulejos*, and a gold-smothered baroque chapel.

Museu Nacional
de Arte Antiga
MUSEUM

(Ancient Art Museum; www.museuarteantiga.pt; Rua das Janelas Verdes; adult/child €6/3, 1st Sun of month free; ⊙2-6pm Tue, 10am-6pm Wed-Sun) Set in a lemon-fronted, 17th-century palace, the Museu Nacional de Arte Antiga is Lapa's biggest draw. It presents a star-studded collection of European and Asian paintings and decorative arts.

◉ Parque das Nações

The former Expo '98 site, this revitalised 2km-long waterfront area in the northeast equals a family fun day out, packed with public art, gardens and kid-friendly attractions.

Take the metro to **Oriente station** – a stunner designed by star Spanish architect Santiago Calatrava.

Oceanário
AQUARIUM

(www.oceanario.pt; Doca dos Olivais; adult/child €14/9; ⊙10am-8pm) The closest you'll get to scuba-diving without a wetsuit, Lisbon's

---

Oceanário is mind-blowing. No amount of hyperbole, where 8000 species splash in 7 million litres of seawater, does it justice. Huge wraparound tanks make you feel as if you are underwater, as you eyeball zebra sharks, honeycombed rays, gliding mantas and schools of neon fish.

Pavilhão
do Conhecimento
MUSEUM

(www.pavconhecimento.pt; Living Science Centre; adult/child €8/5; ⊙10am-6pm Tue-Fri, 11am-7pm Sat & Sun) Kids won't grumble about science at the interactive Pavilhão do Conhecimento, where they can launch hydrogen rockets, lie unhurt on a bed of nails, experience the gravity on the moon and get dizzy on a high-wire bicycle.

☞ Tours

Lisbon Walker
WALKING TOUR

(☎218 861 840; www.lisbonwalker.com; Rua dos Remédios 84; 3hr walk adult/child €15/ free; ⊙10am & 2.30pm) This excellent company, with well-informed, English-speaking guides, offers themed walking tours through Lisbon, which depart from the northwest corner of Praça do Comércio.

PORTUGAL LISBON

Transtejo
CRUISE

(📞 210 422 417; www.transtejo.pt; Terreiro do Paço ferry terminal; adult/child €20/10; ⊘ Apr-Oct) These 2½-hour river cruises are a laid-back way to enjoy Lisbon's sights with multilingual commentary.

⭐ Festivals & Events

The **Festa de Santo António** (Festival of Saint Anthony), from 12 June to 13 June, culminates the three-week **Festas de Lisboa**, with processions and dozens of street parties; it's liveliest in the Alfama.

🛏 Sleeping

Boutique hotels with river views, cosy B&Bs and palatial castle hotels – it's all in the mix in Lisbon. Book well ahead in summer.

🛏 Baixa, Rossio & Cais do Sodré

Lisbon
Destination Hostel
HOSTEL €

(📞 213 466 457; http://destinationhostels.com; 2nd fl, Rossio Train Station; dm €23-34, d €40-80; @ 🛜) Housed in Lisbon's loveliest train station, the stylish Lisbon Destination Hostel features a glass ceiling that lights the spacious plant-filled common area. Rooms are crisp and well kept, and there are loads of activities (bar crawls, beach day trips etc), plus facilities including a shared kitchen, game consoles and a 24-hour self-service bar. Breakfast is top notch and includes crêpes and fresh fruit.

CYCLING THE TEJO

A **cycling/jogging path** courses along the Tejo for 7km, between Cais do Sodré and Belém. Complete with artful touches – including the poetry of Pessoa printed along parts of it – the path takes in ageing warehouses, weathered docks and open-air restaurants and nightspots.

A handy place to rent bikes is a short stroll from Cais do Sodré: **Bike Iberia** (📞 213 470 347; www.bikeiberia.com; Largo Corpo Santo 5; bike hire per 2hr/day from €7.50/14; ⊘ 9.30am-5pm).

Travellers House
HOSTEL €

(📞 210 115 922; www.travellershouse.com; Rua Augusta 89; dm €20-28, s €40, d €70-90; @ 🛜) Travellers enthuse about this super-friendly hostel set in a converted 250-year-old house on Rua Augusta. As well as cosy dorms, there's a retro lounge with beanbags, an internet corner and a communal kitchen.

Sunset
Destination Hostel
HOSTEL €

(📞 210 997 735; http://destinationhostels.com; Cais do Sodré Train Station; dm €22-28, d €32-69; @ 🛜 ✉) This beautifully designed river-facing hostel has comfy rooms, a swanky dining room, a top-notch kitchen and a roof pool terrace with impressive river views.

Lisbon
Lounge Hostel
HOSTEL €

(📞 213 462 061; www.lisbonloungehostel.com; Rua de São Nicolau 41; dm/d €25/64; @ 🛜) Lisbon Lounge Hostel has artfully designed dorms, a slick lounge complete with faux moose head and a fun team. Three-course dinners, bike hire, walking tours and DJ nights are all part and parcel of these nicely chilled Baixa digs.

Lavra Guest House
GUESTHOUSE €€

(📞 218 820 000; www.lavra.pt; Calçada de Santano 198; d not incl breakfast €59-69; 🛜) Set in a former convent that dates back two centuries, this place has stylishly set rooms with wood floors and tiny balconies. Some bathrooms are cramped. It's a short stroll from the Elevador da Lavra, or a steep climb from Largo de São Domingos.

Lisbon
Story Guesthouse
GUESTHOUSE €€

(📞 218 879 392; www.lisbonstoryguesthouse.com; Largo de São Domingos 18; d €50-80, without bathroom €60-80; @ 🛜) 🚭 Overlooking Largo de São Domingos, Lisbon Story is a small, welcoming guesthouse with nicely maintained, light-drenched rooms, some of which sport Portuguese themes (the Tejo, tram 28, fado etc). The shoe-free lounge, with throw pillows and low tables, is a great place to chill, as is the terrace.

Pensão Imperial
GUESTHOUSE €€

(📞 213 420 166; Praça dos Restauradores 78; d €50-70, tr €90-100) Cheery Imperial has a terrific location in Rossio, but you'll need to grin and lug it, as there's no lift. The rooms with high ceilings and wooden furniture are nothing flash, but some have flower-draped balconies overlooking the *praça* (town square). Bathrooms are shared, though some rooms have a shower or sink.

Alfama

Alfama Patio Hostel　　　HOSTEL €
(☑ 218 883 127; http://alfama.destinationhostels. com; Rua das Escolas Gerais 3; dm €21-25, s/d €32/64; @ 🛜) In the heart of the Alfama, this beautifully run hostel is a great place to meet other travellers, with loads of activities (from pub crawls through the Bairro Alto to day trips to the beach), plus regular barbecues on the hostel's laid-back garden-like patio. There's a stylish lounge and fantastic staff.

★Memmo Alfama　　　BOUTIQUE HOTEL €€€
(☑ 210 495 660; http://memmoalfama.com; Travessa Merceeiras 27; r €150-400; ❄ 🛜) Slip down a narrow alley to reach this gorgeous boutique newcomer to Alfama, a stunning conversion of a shoe polish factory. The rooms are an ode to whitewashed minimalism, but it's the view down to the Tejo from the roof terrace that will really blow you away.

Chiado, Bairro Alto & Príncipe Real

★Living Lounge　　　HOSTEL €
(☑ 213 461 078; www.livingloungehostel.com; 2nd fl, Rua do Crucifixo 116; dm €16-20, s €35, d €60; @ 🛜) The Living Lounge has a stylish design, attractive rooms, friendly staff and excellent amenities (full kitchen, wi-fi, bicycle hire). The nightly dinners and wide range of tours provide a fine opportunity to meet other travellers.

Casa do Bairro　　　B&B €€
(☑ 914 176 969; http://shiadu.com; Beco Caldeira 1; d/tr/f €104/114/129; ❄ 🛜) This small, welcoming guesthouse has bright rooms furnished in an attractive contemporary style, and staff have great tips on the city. Some rooms are small, and bathrooms can be rather cramped. It's hard to find (it's located on a staircase lane), so get good directions before arriving. The owners also operate four other B&Bs in Lisbon, and one in Porto.

Avenida de Liberdade, Rato & Marquês de Pombal

★Casa Amora　　　GUESTHOUSE €€
(☑ 919 300 317; http://solisbon.com; Rua João Penha 13; d €105-170; ❄ 🛜) Casa Amora has 10 beautifully designed guestrooms, with eye-catching art and iPod docks. There's a lovely garden patio where the first-rate breakfast is served. It's located in the peaceful neighbourhood of Amoreiras, a few steps from one of Lisbon's prettiest squares.

Lisbon Dreams　　　GUESTHOUSE €€
(☑ 213 872 393; www.lisbondreamsguesthouse. com; Rua Rodrigo da Fonseca 29; s/d without bathroom €55/60; @ 🛜) On a quiet street lined with jacaranda trees, Lisbon Dreams offers terrific value for its bright, modern rooms with high ceilings and excellent mattresses. The green apples are a nice touch, and there are attractive common areas to unwind in. All bathrooms are shared, but are spotlessly clean.

Eating

In addition to creative newcomers, you'll find inexpensive, traditional dining rooms home to classic Portuguese fare.

Baixa, Rossio & Cais do Sodré

A Palmeira　　　PORTUGUESE €
(Rua do Crucifixo 69; mains €7-10; ⊙ 11am-9pm Mon-Fri) Popular among Baixa's lunching locals, A Palmeira dishes up good, honest Portuguese fare, from grilled fish to beef stew, in an old-fashioned tiled interior. Look for the palm on the sign.

Povo　　　PORTUGUESE €
(Rua Nova do Carvalho 32; small plates €4-8; ⊙ noon-2am Tue-Sat, 6pm-1am Sun & Mon) On bar-lined Rua Nova do Carvalho, Povo serves up tasty Portuguese comfort food in the form of *petiscos* (small plates). There's also outdoor seating and live fado nights (Thursdays are best).

Oito Dezoito　　　PORTUGUESE €€
(☑ 961 330 226; www.oitodezoito.pt; Rua de São Nicolau 114; mains €12-20; ⊙ noon-2am Mon-Sat) It's named after the time it takes a sunray to reach the earth, and Oito Dezoito (Eight

Eighteen) shines with its Italian-inspired cuisine. Clean lines and charcoal and cream tones create a sleek backdrop for brunch, lunch or dishes like tender roast lamb with pomegranate and chestnut sauce. Wines are available by the glass.

✕ Alfama

Pois Café
CAFE €

(www.poiscafe.com; Rua de São João da Praça 93; mains €7-10; ⊙1-11pm Mon, 11am-11pm Tue-Sun; 🖘) Boasting a laid-back vibe, Pois Café has creative salads, sandwiches and fresh juices, plus a delicious daily special (soup and main for €9.50). Its sofas invite lazy afternoons spent reading novels and sipping coffee.

★Santa Clara
dos Cogumelos
INTERNATIONAL €€

(☑218 870 661; www.santaclaradoscogumelos. com; Campo de Santa Clara 7; petiscos €5-8, mains €14-18; ⊙7.30-11pm Tue-Fri, 12.30-3.30pm & 7.30-11pm Sat; ✎) If you're a mushroom fan, this novel restaurant in the old market hall on Campo de Santa Clara is simply magic. The menu is an ode to the humble *cogumelo* (mushroom). Go for *petiscos* (tapas) like organic shiitake with garlic and coriander, mains like risotto with porcini and black trumpets, and perhaps mushroom ice cream with brownies for dessert.

Páteo 13
PORTUGUESE €€

(Calçadinha de Santo Estêvão 13; mains €8-12; ⊙11am-11pm Tue-Sun) Follow the scent of chargrilled fish to this local favourite tucked away on a small, festively decorated plaza in the Alfama.

✕ Chiado, Bairro Alto & Príncipe Real

Mercado da Ribeira
MARKET €

(Avenida 24 de Julho; ⊙10am-midnight Sun-Wed, 10am-2am Thu-Sat) Doing trade in fresh fruit and veg, fish and flowers since 1892, this oriental dome-topped market hall is the word on everyone's lips since *Time Out* transformed half of it into a gourmet food court in 2014. Now it's like Lisbon in microcosm, with everything from Garrafeira Nacional wines to Conserveira de Lisboa fish, Arcádia chocolate and Santini gelato.

Cafe Tati
CAFE €

(☑213 461 279; http://cafetati.blogspot.com; Rua da Ribeira Nova 36; mains €7-8; ⊙11am-1am Tue-Sun; 🖘) Cafe Tati has undeniable charm amid its smattering of well-lit stone-arched rooms with stencilled walls. Along with inventive *tostas* (Parma ham and raclette) and salads (goat cheese and green apple), there are appetising daily specials.

Tagide Wine &
Tapas Bar
FUSION €€

(☑213 404 010; Largo da Academia Nacional de Belas Artes 20; tapas €4-9; ⊙12.30-3pm & 7pm-midnight Tue-Thu, 12.30-3pm & 7pm-1am Fri, 2pm-1am Sat) Not to be confused with the pricier Tagide next door, this casual, slickly modern tapas bar has pretty views to the river. Small sharing plates are imaginative and packed with flavour. Three-course lunch specials, which include a glass of wine and coffee, cost €12.50.

★Belcanto
PORTUGUESE €€€

(☑213 420 607; Largo de São Carlos 10; mains €42, tasting menu €90-145, 2-/3-course lunch €45/60; ⊙12.30-3pm & 7.30-11pm Tue-Sat) Shining brighter than any other Lisbon restaurant with two Michelin stars, José Avillez' Belcanto wows diners with its well-edited, creative menu, polished service and first-rate sommelier. Signatures like sea bass with seaweed and bivalves, and rosemary-smoked beef loin with bone marrow and garlic purée elevate Portuguese to a whole new level. Reservations are essential.

✕ Belém

Antiga Confeitaria
de Belém
PATISSERIE €

(Rua de Belém 86-88; pastries €1-2.50; ⊙8am-11pm) Since 1837, this patisserie has been transporting locals to sugar-coated nirvana with heavenly *pastéis de belém*. The crisp pastry nests are filled with custard cream, baked at 200°C for that perfect golden crust, then lightly dusted with cinnamon.

Enoteca
de Belém
PORTUGUESE €€

(☑213 631 511; Travessa do Marta Pinto 10; mains €12-17; ⊙1-11pm Tue-Sun) Tucked down a quiet lane just off Belém's main thoroughfare, this wine bar serves tasty Portuguese classics (try the octopus or the grilled Iberian pork), matched by an excellent selection of full-bodied Douro reds and refreshing Alentejan whites.

🍷 Drinking & Nightlife

All-night street parties in Bairro Alto, sunset drinks from high-up terraces, and sumptuous art deco cafes scattered about Chiado – Lisbon has many enticing options for imbibers.

Lisbon's small gay scene is headquartered in Príncipe Real, though you'll also find a few gay bars in Bairro Alto. Lux draws both a gay and straight crowd.

Pensão Amor   BAR
(www.pensaoamor.pt; Rua Nova do Carvalho 36; ⊘ noon-3am Mon-Wed, noon-4am Thu-Sat) Set inside a former brothel, this cheeky bar pays homage to its passion-filled past with colourful wall murals, a library of erotic-tinged works, and a small stage where you can sometimes catch burlesque shows.

BA Wine Bar
Bairro Alto   WINE BAR
(Rua da Rosa 107; ⊘ 6-11pm Tue-Sun) One of the nicest ways to kick-start an evening is over a glass of Portuguese wine (there are 150 to choose from) and tapas at this intimate, friendly wine bar in the heart of Bairro Alto.

Noobai Café   BAR
(Miradouro de Santa Catarina; ⊘ noon-midnight) Great views, winning cocktails and a festive crowd make Noobai a popular draw for a sundowner.

Park   BAR
(Calçada do Combro 58; ⊘ 1pm-2am Tue-Sat, 1-8pm Sun) If only all multi-storey car parks were like this... Climb up to the top floor, which has been transformed into one of Lisbon's hippest rooftop bars and offers sweeping views reaching right down to the Tejo.

A Ginjinha   GINJINHA BAR
(Largo de Saõ Domingos 8; ⊘ 9am-10pm) Hipsters, old men in flat caps, office workers and tourists all meet at this microscopic *ginjinha* (cherry liqueur) bar for that moment of cherry-licking, pip-spitting pleasure.

Lux-Frágil   CLUB
(www.luxfragil.com; Avenida Infante Dom Henrique, Santo Apolónia; ⊘ 11pm-6am Thu-Sat) Lisbon's ice-cool, must-see club, Lux hosts

---

PORTUGUESE SOUL

Infused by Moorish song and the ditties of homesick sailors, bluesy, bittersweet **fado** (traditional Portuguese song) encapsulates the Lisbon psyche like nothing else. The uniquely Portuguese style was born in the Alfama, still the best place in Lisbon to hear it live. Minimum consumption charges range from €15 to €25 per person.

A Baîuca (☑ 218 867 284; Rua de São Miguel 20; ⊘ 8pm-midnight Thu-Mon) On a good night, walking into A Baîuca is like gatecrashing a family party. It's a special place with *fado vadio*, where locals take a turn and spectators hiss if anyone dares to chat during the singing.

Clube de Fado (☑ 218 852 704; www.clube-de-fado.com; Rua de São João da Praça 92; ⊘ 8pm-2am) Hosts the cream of the fado crop in vaulted, dimly lit surrounds. Big-name *fadistas* perform here alongside celebrated guitarists.

Mesa de Frades (☑ 917 029 436; Rua dos Remédios 139A; ⊘ 7pm-2am Mon-Sat) A magical place to hear fado, tiny Mesa de Frades used to be a chapel. It's tiled with exquisite *azulejos* (hand-painted tiles) and has just a handful of tables. Reserve ahead.

---

big-name DJs spinning electro and house. It's run by ex-Frágil maestro Marcel Reis and part-owned by John Malkovich. Grab a spot on the terrace to see the sun rise over the Tejo.

☆ Entertainment

For the latest goings-on, pick up the weekly *Time Out Lisboa* (www.timeout.pt) from bookstores, or the free monthly *Follow Me Lisboa* from the tourist office.

Zé dos Bois   LIVE MUSIC
(www.zedosbois.org; Rua da Barroca 59; ⊘ 7pm-2am) Focusing on tomorrow's performing arts and music trends, Zé dos Bois is an experimental venue with a graffitied courtyard, and an eclectic line-up of theatre, film, visual arts and live music.

Cinemas

Lisbon's cinematic standouts are the grand **São Jorge** (Avenida da Liberdade 175) and, just around the corner, **Cinemateca Portuguesa** (www.cinemateca.pt; Rua Barata Salgueiro 39); both screen offbeat, art-house, world and old films.

Sport

Lisbon's football teams are Benfica, Belenenses and Sporting. Euro 2004 led to the upgrading of the 65,000-seat **Estádio da Luz** (☑ 217 219 555; www.slbenfica.pt) and the construction of the 54,000-seat **Estádio Nacional** (☑ 214 197 212; Cruz Quebrada). State-of-the-art stadium **Estádio José de Alvalade** (Rua Prof Fernando da Fonseca) seats 54,000 and is just north of the university. Take the metro to Campo Grande.

ℹ Information

EMERGENCY

Police Station (☑ 217 654 242; Rua Capelo 13)
Tourist Police (☑ 213 421 634; Palácio Foz, Praça dos Restauradores; ⊘ 24hr)

INTERNET ACCESS

Most hostels and midrange guesthouses offer wireless (usually free). Loads of cafes and restaurants also offer wi-fi – just ask for the *codigo* (access code).
Portugal Telecom (Avenida Fontes Pereira de Melo 40, Loja 4; ⊘ 9am-7pm) Has rows of booths.

MEDICAL SERVICES

British Hospital (☑ 217 213 410; www.british-hospital.pt; Rua Tomás da Fonseca) English-speaking staff and English-speaking doctors.

MONEY

Cota Câmbios (Praça Dom Pedro IV 41) The best bet for changing cash or travellers cheques is a private exchange bureau like this one.

POST

Main Post Office (Praça dos Restauradores 58; ⊘ 8am-10pm Mon-Fri, 9am-6pm Sat) Also has an ATM.
Post Office (Praça do Município 6) Central post office.

TOURIST INFORMATION

Ask Me Lisboa (☑ 213 463 314; www.askmelisboa.com; Palácio Foz, Praça dos Restauradores; ⊘ 9am-8pm) The largest and most helpful tourist office. Can book accommodation or reserve rental cars.

Lisboa Welcome Centre (☑ 210 312 810; www.visitlisboa.com; Praça do Comércio; ⊘ 9am-8pm) Main branch of Turismo de Lisboa, providing free city maps, brochures, and hotel and tour booking services. Buy the Lisboa Card here.
Y Lisboa (☑ 213 472 134; www.askmelisboa.com; Rua Jardim do Regedor 50; ⊘ 10am-7pm)

USEFUL WEBSITES

Go Lisbon (www.golisbon.com) Up-to-date info on sightseeing, eating, nightlife and events.
Time Out (www.timeout.pt) Details on upcoming gigs and cultural events, interesting commentary; in Portuguese.
Visit Lisboa (www.visitlisboa.com) Lisbon's comprehensive tourism website, with the lowdown on sightseeing, transport and accommodation.

ℹ Getting There & Away

AIR

Around 6km north of the centre, **Aeroporto de Lisboa** (Lisbon Airport; ☑ 218 413 500; www.ana.pt) operates direct flights to many European cities.

BUS

Lisbon's long-distance bus terminal is **Sete Rios** (Rua das Laranjeiras), conveniently linked to both Jardim Zoológico metro station and Sete Rios train station. The big carriers, **Rede Expressos** (☑ 707 223 344; www.rede-expressos.pt) and **Eva** (☑ 707 223 344; www.eva-bus.com), run frequent services to almost every major town.

The other major terminal is **Gare do Oriente** (at Oriente metro and train station), concentrating on services to the north and to Spain. The biggest companies operating from here are **Renex** (☑ 218 956 836; www.renex.pt) and the Spanish operator **Avanza** (☑ 218 940 250; www.avanzabus.com).

TRAIN

Santa Apolónia station is the terminus for northern and central Portugal. You can catch trains from Santa Apolónia to Gare do Oriente train station, which has departures to the Algarve and international destinations. Cais do Sodré station is for Belém, Cascais and Estoril. Rossio station is the terminal for trains to Sintra via Queluz.

For fares and schedules, visit www.cp.pt.

ℹ Getting Around

TO/FROM THE AIRPORT

The **AeroBus** (www.yellowbustours.com; one way €3.50) runs every 20 minutes from 7am to 11pm, taking 30 to 45 minutes between the airport and Cais do Sodré.

A metro station on the red line gives convenient access to downtown. Change at Alameda (green line) to reach Rossio and Baixa. A taxi into town is about €15.

PUBLIC TRANSPORT

A 24-hour Bilhete Carris/Metro (€6) gives unlimited travel on all buses, trams, metros and funiculars. Pick it up from Carris kiosks and metro stations.

Bus, Tram & Funicular

Buses and trams run from 6am to 1am, with a few all-night services. Pick up a transport map from tourist offices or Carris kiosks. A single ticket costs more if you buy it on board (€2.85/1.80/3.60 for tram/bus/funicular), and much less (€1.40 per ride) if you buy a refillable Viva Viagem card (€0.50), available at Carris offices and in metro stations.

There are three funiculars: Elevador da Bica; Elevador da Glória; Elevador do Lavra.

Don't leave the city without riding tram 28 from Largo Martim Moniz through the narrow streets of the Alfama; tram 12 goes from Praça da Figueira out to Belém.

Ferry

Car, bicycle and passenger ferries leave frequently from the Cais do Sodré ferry terminal to Cacilhas (€1.20, 10 minutes). From Terreiro do Paço terminal, catamarans zip across to Montijo (€2.75, every 30 minutes) and Seixal (€2.35, every 30 minutes).

Metro

The **metro** (www.metrolisboa.pt; single/day ticket €1.40/6; ☺ 6.30am-1am) is useful for hops across town and to the Parque das Nações. Buy tickets from metro ticket machines, which have English-language menus.

AROUND LISBON

Sintra

POP 26,200

Lord Byron called this hilltop town a 'glorious Eden' and, although best appreciated at dusk when the coach tours have left, it *is* a magnificent place. Less than an hour west of Lisbon, Sintra was the traditional summer retreat of Portugal's kings. Today, it's a fairy-tale setting of stunning palaces and manors surrounded by rolling green countryside.

◉ Sights & Activities

Although the whole town resembles a historical theme park, there are several compulsory eye-catching sights.

★ Quinta da Regaleira
VILLA, GARDENS

(www.regaleira.pt; Rua Barbosa du Bocage; adult/child €6/3; ☺ 10am-8pm high season, shorter hours in low season) This magical villa and gardens is a neo-Manueline extravaganza, dreamed up by Italian opera-set designer, Luigi Manini, under the orders of Brazilian coffee tycoon, António Carvalho Monteiro, aka Monteiro dos Milhões (Moneybags Monteiro). The villa is surprisingly homely inside, despite its ferociously carved fireplaces, frescoes and Venetian glass mosaics. Keep an eye out for mythological and Knights Templar symbols.

Palácio Nacional de Sintra
PALACE

(www.parquesdesintra.pt; Largo Rainha Dona Amélia; adult/child €9.50/7.50; ☺ 9.30am-7pm, shorter hours in low season) The star of Sintra-Vila is this palace, with its iconic twin conical chimneys and lavish interior. The whimsical interior is a mix of Moorish and Manueline styles, with arabesque courtyards, barley-twist columns and 15th- and 16th-century geometric *azulejos* (hand-painted tiles) that figure among Portugal's oldest.

Castelo dos Mouros
CASTLE

(www.parquesdesintra.pt; adult/child €7.50/6; ☺ 9.30am-8pm, shorter hours in low season) Soaring 412m above sea level, this mist-enshrouded ruined castle looms high above the surrounding forest. When the clouds peel away, the vistas over Sintra's palace-dotted hill and dale to the glittering Atlantic are – like the climb – breathtaking.

Palácio Nacional da Pena
PALACE

(www.parquesdesintra.pt; adult/child €14/11; ☺ 10am-7pm, shorter hours in low season) Rising up from a thickly wooded peak and often enshrouded in swirling mist, Palácio Nacional da Pena is a wacky confection of onion domes, Moorish keyhole gates, writhing stone snakes and crenellated towers in pinks and lemons.

🛏 Sleeping

★Nice Way
Sintra Palace   HOSTEL €
(☑219 249 800; www.sintrapalace.com; Rua Sotto Mayor 22; dm €18-22, d with/without bathroom €60/50; ⊚) In a rambling mansion north of the main square, you'll find stylishly outfitted rooms, great countryside views and a lovely garden. The flickering fireplace on cold nights sweetens the deal. There's also a friendly vibe, making it a good place to meet other travellers. The fully equipped two-bedroom cottage is excellent value for families at around €75 per night.

Hotel Nova Sintra   GUESTHOUSE €€
(☑219 230 220; www.novasintra.com; Largo Afonso de Albuquerque 25; s/d €75/95; ❄⊚) This renovated late-19th-century mansion is set above the main road. The big drawcard is the sunny terrace overlooking Sintra, where you can take breakfast. Front-facing doubles offer picturesque views, back rooms more peaceful slumber. Some rooms are rather small.

🍴 Eating

Saudade   CAFE €
(Avenida Dr Miguel Bombardo 8; mains €5-7; ⊙8.30am-8pm; ⊚) This former bakery, where Sintra's famous *queijadas* (mini cheesecakes in a crispy pastry shell) were made, has cherub-covered ceilings and a rambling interior, making it a fine spot for pastries or lighter fare (with a different soup, salad, fish- and meat-dish of the day). A gallery in the back features changing art exhibitions.

Dom Pipas   PORTUGUESE €€
(Rua João de Deus 62; mains €7-13; ⊙noon-3pm & 7.30-10pm Tue-Sun) A local favourite, Dom Pipas serves up excellent Portuguese dishes, amid *azulejos* and rustic country decor. It's behind the train station (left out of the station, first left, then left again to the end).

ℹ Information

Turismo (☑219 231 157; Praça da Republica; ⊙9.30am-6pm) Near the centre of Sintra-Vila, this helpful multilingual office has expert insight into Sintra and the surrounding areas. There's also a small train station (☑211 932 545; ⊙10am-12.30pm & 2.30-6pm) branch, often overrun by those arriving by rail.

ℹ Getting There & Away

The Lisbon–Sintra railway terminates in Sintra, a 1km scenic walk northeast of the town's historic centre. Sintra's bus station, and another train station, are a further 1km east in the new town Portela de Sintra. Frequent shuttle buses link the historic centre with the bus station.

Train services (€2.55, 40 minutes, every 15 minutes) run between Sintra and Lisbon's Rossio station.

ℹ Getting Around

A handy bus for accessing the castle is the hop-on, hop-off Scotturb bus 434 (€5), which runs from the train station via Sintra-Vila to Castelo dos Mouros (10 minutes), Palácio da Pena (15 minutes), and back.

A taxi to Pena or Monserrate costs around €8 one way.

Cascais
POP 34,000

Cascais is a handsome seaside resort with elegant buildings, an atmospheric Old Town and a happy abundance of restaurants and bars.

⦿ Sights & Activities

Cascais' three sandy bays – **Praia da Conceição**, **Praia da Rainha** and **Praia da Ribeira** – are great for a sunbake or a tingly Atlantic dip, but attract crowds in summer.

The sea roars into the coast at **Boca do Inferno** (Hell's Mouth), 2km west of Cascais. Spectacular **Cabo da Roca**, Europe's westernmost point, is 16km from Cascais and Sintra and is served by buses from both towns.

Casa das Histórias
Paula Rego   GALLERY
(www.casadashistoriaspaularego.com; Avenida da República 300; adult/child €3/free; ⊙10am-7pm Tue-Sun) FREE The Casa das Histórias Paula Rego showcases the disturbing, highly evocative paintings of one of Portugal's finest living artists.

Museu Condes
de Castro Guimarães   MUSEUM
(⊙10am-5pm Tue-Sun) FREE This whimsical early-19th-century mansion complete with castle turrets and Arabic cloister sits in the grounds of the Parque Marechal Carmona.

🛏 Sleeping & Eating

Agarre o Momento GUESTHOUSE €€
(📞214 064 532; www.agarreomomento.com; Rua Joaquim Ereira 458; d/tr/q €60/90/120; @🛜) This welcoming guesthouse in a peaceful residential neighbourhood has bright, airy rooms plus a garden, shared kitchen and bike rental. It's a 15-minute walk (1.5km) north of the station, or a short taxi ride.

Casa Vela GUESTHOUSE €€€
(📞214 868 972; www.casavelahotel.com; Rua dos Bem Lembrados 17; d €135-169; 🅿❄🛜🏊) The friendly Casa Vela has earned many admirers for its bright and attractive rooms set with modern furnishings. Some rooms have a balcony overlooking the lovely gardens and pool. It's in a peaceful neighbourhood about a 10-minute walk to the old town centre.

House of Wonders CAFE €
(Largo da Misericordia 53; light meals €4-8; ⊙10am-midnight, shorter hours in low season; 🛜🍴) Tucked away in the old quarter, this charming Dutch-owned cafe is a traveller's delight. Aside from a warm, welcoming ambience and an artwork-filled interior, you'll find beautifully presented salads, quiches, soups and desserts.

ℹ Information

Turismo (📞214 822 327; www.visiteestoril. com; Rua Visconde da Luz 14; ⊙9am-1pm & 2-7pm Mon-Sat) Sells a map of Cascais.

ℹ Getting There & Away

Trains run frequently to Cascais via Estoril (€2.15, 40 minutes) from Cais do Sodré station in Lisbon.

THE ALGARVE

It's easy to see the allure of the Algarve: breathtaking cliffs, golden sands, scalloped bays and long sandy islands. Although overdevelopment has blighted parts of the coast, head inland and you'll land solidly in lovely Portuguese countryside once again. Algarve highlights include the riverside town of Tavira, party-loving Lagos and windswept Sagres. Faro is the regional capital.

Faro

POP 65,0000

Faro is an attractive town with a palm-clad waterfront, well-maintained plazas and a small pedestrianised centre sprinkled with outdoor cafes. There are no beaches in Faro itself, though it's an easy jaunt by ferry to picturesque beaches nearby. A boat trip through the Parque Natural da Ria Formosa is another highlight.

⊙ Sights & Activities

Ilha Deserta ISLAND
Ferries go out to Ilha da Barreta (aka Ilha Deserta), a long narrow strip of sand just off the mainland.

Parque Natural da Ria Formosa NATURE RESERVE
For visits to the Ria Formosa Natural Park, sign up for a boating or birdwatching tour with the environmentally friendly outfits of **Ria Formosa** (📞918 720 002; www. formosamar.pt) and **Lands** (📞289 817 466; www.lands.pt), both in the Clube Naval in Faro's marina.

🛏 Sleeping & Eating

⭐**Casa d'Alagoa** HOSTEL €
(📞289 813 252; www.farohostel.com; Praça Alexandre Herculano 27; dm not incl breakfast €19-25, d €70; 🛜) Housed in a renovated mansion, this welcome addition to Faro's budget scene has all the elements of today's sophisticated hostel: it's funky, laid-back and cool.

Hotel Eva HOTEL €€€
(📞289 001 000; www.tdhotels.pt; Avenida da República 1; s/d/ste €145/175/265; 🅿❄🛜🏊) Eva has spacious, pleasant rooms. Those facing east have balconies and views. There's a rooftop swimming pool for more marina-gazing.

Gengibre e Canela VEGETARIAN €
(📞289 882 424; Travessa da Mota 10; buffet €7.50; ⊙noon-3pm Mon-Sat; 🍴) Give the taste buds a break from meat and fish dishes and veg out (literally) at this Zen-like vegetarian restaurant. The buffet changes daily; there may be vegetable lasagne, *feijoada* (bean casserole) and tofu dishes.

Adega Nova
PORTUGUESE €€

(☑ 289 813 433; www.restauranteadeganova.com; Rua Francisco Barreto 24; mains €7.50-18; ☺ 11.30am-11pm) Dishing up simply grilled fish and meat, this popular place has plenty of country charm. It has a lofty beamed ceiling, rustic cooking implements on display and long, communal tables and bench seats. Service is efficient.

ℹ Information

Turismo (www.visitalgarve.pt; Rua da Misericórdia 8) This efficient, busy place offers information on Faro.

ℹ Getting There & Away

Faro airport has both domestic and international flights.

From the bus station, just west of the centre, there are at least six daily express coaches to Lisbon (€20, four hours), plus several slower services, and frequent buses to other coastal towns. There are also international buses to Madrid (€39, eight hours).

The train station is a few minutes' walk west of the bus station. Five trains run daily to Lisbon's Sete Rios station (€23.50, 3¼ hours).

ℹ Getting Around

The airport is 6km from the centre. Buses 14 and 16 (€2.20) run into town until 9pm. A taxi from the airport to the town centre costs about €12.

Tavira
POP 26,200

Set on either side of the meandering Rio Gilão, Tavira is a charming town with a hilltop castle, an old Roman bridge and a smattering of Gothic churches. The pretty sands of Ilha da Tavira are a short boat ride away.

◉ Sights & Activities

Castelo
CASTLE

FREE Tavira's ruined castle rises high and mighty above the town. Possibly dating back to Neolithic times, rebuilt by Phoenicians and later taken over by the Moors, most of what now stands is a 17th-century reconstruction. The octagonal tower offers fine views over Tavira. Note that the ramparts and steps are without railing.

Igreja da Misericórdia
CHURCH

(Rua da Galeria; ☺ 9am-1pm & 2-6pm Mon-Sat) FREE Built in the 1540s, this church is the Algarve's most important Renaissance monument, with a magnificent carved, arched doorway topped by statues of Nossa Senhora da Misericórdia, São Pedro and São Paulo.

Ilha da Tavira
ISLAND, BEACH

An island beach connected to the mainland by a ferry at Quatro Águas. Walk the 2km or take the (summer-only) bus from the bus station.

🛏 Sleeping & Eating

Calçada Guesthouse
GUESTHOUSE €€

(☑ 926 563 713, 927 710 771; www.calcadaguesthouse.com; Calçada de Dona Ana 12; r €85-100; ✳ 🛜) Two British expats renovated and run this stylish, centrally located spot. It has bright, homely rooms and a gorgeous roof terrace for gazing out across Tavira's rooftops. Breakfast costs extra (€8.50), and children are welcome. Minimum-night stays sometimes apply.

Casa Simão
PORTUGUESE €

(João Vaz Corte Real 10; mains €6-11; ☺ noon-3pm & 7-10pm Mon-Sat) We'll be upfront: this old-style, barn-like eatery has harsh lighting and zero romance, but that's because the delightful family owners concentrate on down-to-earth fare – they whip up great-value meals such as *javali estufado* (wild boar stew) and grills. Go for the daily specials.

ℹ Information

Turismo (☑ 281 322 511; www.visitalgarve.pt; Praça da República 5; ☺ 9am-6pm Mon-Fri, 9am-1pm & 2-6pm Sat & Sun, to 7pm Jul & Aug) Provides local and some regional information and has accommodation listings. Changeable hours.

ℹ Getting There & Away

Some 15 trains run daily between Faro and Tavira (€3.15, 40 minutes).

Lagos
POP 31,100

In summer, the pretty fishing port of Lagos has a party vibe; its picturesque cobbled streets and pretty nearby beaches, including

Meia Praia to the east and **Praia da Luz** to the west, are packed with revellers and sun-seekers.

🏃 Activities

Blue Ocean DIVING
(☑964 665 667; www.blue-ocean-divers.de) For those who want to go diving or snorkelling. Offers a half-day discovery experience (€30), a full-day dive (€90) and a divemaster PADI scuba course (€590). It also offers kayak safaris (half-/full day €30/45, child under 12 years half price).

Kayak Adventures KAYAKING
(☑913 262 200; http://kayakadventureslagos.com) Has kayaking trips from Batata Beach, including snorkelling, between April and October. Trips last three hours (€25).

🛏 Sleeping

Hotel Mar Azul GUESTHOUSE €
(☑282 770 230; www.hotelmarazul.eu; Rua 25 de Abril 13; s €50-60, d €60-85; ❄@🛜) This little gem is one of Lagos' best-value spots. It's a central, well-run and delightfully welcoming place, with comfortable, neat rooms, some with sea views. A simple breakfast is an added bonus.

Albergaria Marina Rio HOTEL €€€
(☑282 780 830; www.marinario.com; Avenida dos Descobrimentos; s €105-130, d €108-133; P❄@🛜🏊) Overlooking the harbour, this hotel has comfortable rooms with contemporary decor and balconies. On the downside, it faces the road and backs onto the bus station. Most rooms are twins. There's a tiny pool and roof terrace.

🍴 Eating

★A Forja PORTUGUESE €€
(☑282 768 588; Rua dos Ferreiros 17; mains €8-15; ⊙noon-3pm & 6.30-10pm Sun-Fri) The secret is out. This buzzing place pulls in the crowds – locals, tourists and expats – for its hearty, top-quality traditional food served in a bustling environment at great prices. Plates of the day are always reliable, as are the fish dishes.

Casinha do Petisco SEAFOOD €€
(Rua da Oliveira 51; mains €7-13; ⊙6-11pm Mon-Sat) Blink – or be late – and you'll miss this tiny traditional gem. It's cosy and simply decorated and comes highly recommended

by locals for its seafood grills and shellfish dishes.

ℹ Information

Turismo (☑282 763 031; www.visitalgarve.pt; Praça Gil Eanes; ⊙9am-6pm) The very helpful staff offers excellent maps and leaflets.

ℹ Getting There & Away

Bus and train services depart frequently for other Algarve towns, and around eight times daily to Lisbon (€25.50, four hours).

ℹ Getting Around

A **bus service** (tickets €1.20-1.60; ⊙7am-8pm Mon-Sat) provides useful connections to the beaches of Meia Praia and Luz. Rent bicycles and motorbikes from **Motorent** (☑282 769 716; www.motorent.pt; Rua Victor Costa e Silva; bike/motorcycle per 3 days from €21/60).

Silves

POP 11,000
The one-time capital of Moorish Algarve, Silves is a pretty town of jumbled orange rooftops scattered above the banks of the Rio Arade. Clamber around the ramparts of its fairy-tale **castle** for superb views.

🛏 Sleeping & Eating

★Duas Quintas RURAL INN €€
(☑282 449 311; www.duasquintas.com; São Estevão; d/studio €95/120; 🛜🏊) Set among orange groves and rolling hills, this utterly charming converted farmhouse has six pleasant rooms, a living space, terraces and a pool.

**★Restaurante
O Barradas** PORTUGUESE €€€
(☑282 443 308; www.obarradas.com; Palmeirinha; mains €8.50-25; ⊙6-10pm Thu-Tue; 🅿) 🌿 The star choice for foodies is this delightful converted farmhouse run by Luís and his German wife Andrea, with a romantic candlelit garden for warm-weather dining. They take pride in careful sourcing and use organic fish, meat and fruits in season. Luís is a winemaker so you can be assured of some fine wines.

ℹ Getting There & Away

Silves train station is 2km from town; trains from Lagos (€2.90, 35 minutes) stop eight times daily (from Faro, change at Tunes), to be met by local buses. Frequent trains connect Silves and Albufeira-Ferreiras (€2.45, 30 minutes).

Sagres

POP 2100

The small, elongated village of Sagres has an end-of-the-world feel with its sea-carved cliffs and empty, wind-whipped fortress high above the ocean. This coast is ideal for surfing; hire windsurfing gear at sand-dune fringed Praia do Martinhal.

Visit Europe's southwestern-most point, the **Cabo de São Vicente** (Cape St Vincent), 6km to the west. A solitary lighthouse stands on this barren cape.

◎ Sights & Activities

Fortaleza de Sagres   FORTRESS
(adult/child €3/1.50; ⊙9.30am-8pm May-Sep, 9.30am-5.30pm Oct-Apr) Blank, hulking and forbidding, Sagres' fortress offers breathtaking views over the sheer cliffs, and all along the coast to Cabo de São Vicente. According to legend, this is where Henry the Navigator established his navigation school and primed the early Portuguese explorers.

Mar Ilimitado   BOAT TOUR
(☑916 832 625; www.marilimitado.com; Porto da Baleeira) ✔ Mar Ilimitado, a team of marine biologists, offers a variety of 'educational' boat trips from dolphin-spotting trips (€32) to excursions up to Cabo de São Vicente (€20) and seabird watching (€40).

DiversCape   DIVING
(☑965 559 073; www.diverscape.com; Porto da Baleeira) Diving centres are based at the port. Recommended is the PADI-certified DiversCape, which organises snorkelling expeditions (€25, two hours), plus dives of between 12m and 30m around shipwrecks.

Sagres Natura   SURFING
(☑282 624 072; www.sagresnatura.com; Rua São Vicente) Recommended surf school. Also rents out bodyboards (€10 per day), surfboards (€15) and wetsuits (€5). The company also offers canoeing trips (€35), and bikes can be hired (€15).

⊨ Sleeping & Eating

Casa Azul   B&B €
(☑282 624 856; www.casaazulsagres.com; Rua Dom Sebastião; d €65-125, apt €75-200; ❄ @ �)

As blue as its name suggests, Casa Azul is a popular surfer crash pad, with bright and breezy rooms decked out with splashes of bold colour. The apartments are big enough for families and come with kitchenettes and barbecue decks.

Casa do Cabo de Santa Maria   GUESTHOUSE €€
(☑282 624 722; www.casadocabodesantamaria. com; Rua Patrão António Faústino; d €50-70, apt €70-110; ℙ � ⍰) These squeaky-clean, welcoming rooms and apartments might not have sweeping views, but they are handsome and nicely furnished – excellent value (breakfast not included).

❶ Information

Turismo (☑282 624 873; www.cm-vilado-bispo.pt; Rua Comandante Matoso; ⊙9am-6pm, hours subject to change) Situated on a patch of green lawn, 100m east of Praça da República.

❶ Getting There & Away

Frequent buses run daily to Sagres from Lagos (€3.80, one hour), with fewer on Sunday. One continues to Cabo de São Vicente on weekdays.

CENTRAL PORTUGAL

The vast centre of Portugal is a rugged swathe of rolling hillsides, whitewashed villages, and olive groves and cork trees. Richly historic, it is scattered with prehistoric remains and medieval castles. It's also home to one of Portugal's most architecturally rich towns, Évora, as well as several spectacular walled villages. There are fine local wines and, for the more energetic, plenty of outdoor exploring in the dramatic Beiras region.

Évora

POP 54,300

Évora is an enchanting place to delve into the past. Inside the 14th-century walls, Évora's narrow, winding lanes lead to a striking medieval cathedral, a Roman temple and a picturesque town square. These old-fashioned good looks are the backdrop to a lively student town surrounded by wineries and dramatic countryside.

◉ Sights & Activities

Igreja de São Francisco　　　CHURCH
(Praça 1 de Maio) `FREE` Évora's best-known church is a tall and huge Manueline-Gothic structure, completed around 1510 and dedicated to St Francis. Legend has it that the Portuguese navigator Gil Vicente is buried here.

Sé　　　CATHEDRAL
(Largo do Marquês de Marialva; admission €1.50, with cloister €2.50; ⊙9am-5pm) Guarded by a pair of rose granite towers, Évora's fortresslike medieval cathedral has fabulous cloisters and a museum jam-packed with ecclesiastical treasures.

Templo Romano　　　RUIN
(Temple of Diana; Largo do Conde de Vila Flor) Once part of the Roman Forum, the remains of this temple dating from the 2nd or early 3rd century are a heady slice of drama right in town.

⌷ Sleeping

Hostel Namaste　　　HOSTEL €
(☑266 743 014; www.hostelnamasteevora.pt; Largo Doutor Manuel Alves Branco 12; dm/s/d €17/30/45; ☎) Maria and Carla Sofia are the kind souls who run these welcoming digs in the historic Arabic quarter. Rooms are bright, spotlessly clean and decorated with splashes of art and colour, and there's a lounge, library, kitchen and bike hire. Breakfast costs an extra €4.

★Albergaria do Calvario　　　BOUTIQUE HOTEL €€€
(☑266 745 930; www.albergariadocalvario.com; Travessa dos Lagares 3; s €98-110, d €108-120; ℗☎) Unpretentiously elegant, discreetly attentive and comfortable (but not can't-put-your-feet-up-uber-luxurious), this place has an ambience that travellers adore. The delightful staff leave no service stone unturned and breakfasts are among the region's best, with locally sourced organic produce, homemade cakes and egg dishes.

✕ Eating

Pastelaria Conventual Pão de Rala　　　PATISSERIE €
(Rua do Cicioso 47; pastries from €2; ⊙7.30am-7.30pm) Out of the centre but still within the walls, this delightful spot specialises in heavenly pastries and convent cakes, all made on the premises.

★Botequim da Mouraria　　　PORTUGUESE €€
(☑266 746 775; Rua da Mouraria 16A; mains €13-16.50; ⊙noon-3pm & 6-10pm Mon-Fri, noon-3pm Sat) Poke around the old Moorish quarter to find this cosy spot serving some of Évora's finest food and wine. There are no reservations, just 12 stools at a counter.

Vinho e Noz　　　PORTUGUESE €€
(Ramalho Orgião 12; mains around €12; ⊙noon-10pm Mon-Sat) A delightful family runs this unpretentious place, which has professional service, a large wine list and good-quality cuisine.

Dom Joaquim　　　PORTUGUESE €€
(☑266 731 105; Rua dos Penedos 6; mains €12-15; ⊙noon-3pm & 7-10.45pm Tue-Sat, noon-3pm Sun) Amid stone walls and modern artwork, Dom Joaquim serves excellent traditional cuisine including meats (game and succulent, fall-off-the-bone lamb) and seafood dishes, such as *caçao* (dogfish).

⌸ Drinking

Bookshelf　　　CAFE
(Rua de Machede 19; ⊙8am-8pm) A bit boho, a bit retro, this incredibly friendly cafe does a fine line in speciality teas, juices, homemade cakes and light meals.

Páteo　　　BAR
(Rua 5 de Outubro, Beco da Espinhosa; ⊙11am-2am; ☎) Right in Évora's medieval heart, this bar has a pretty tree-shaded patio for nursing a glass of Alentejo wine. The food is pretty good, too.

❶ Information

Turismo (☑266 777 071; www.cm-evora.pt; Praça do Giraldo 73; ⊙9am-7pm Apr-Oct, 9am-6pm Nov-Mar) This helpful, central tourist office dishes out a great town map.

❶ Getting There & Away

Regular trains go direct to Lisbon (€12, 80 minutes) and indirectly, via Pinhal Novo, to Faro (€26, 3¾ to 4¼ hours) and Lagos (€29, five hours). The train station is 600m south of the Jardim Público.

Monsaraz

POP 782

In a dizzy setting high above the plain, this walled village has a moody medieval feel and magnificent views. The biennial

Monsaraz Museu Aberto, held in July on even-numbered years, features exhibitions and concerts.

Housed inside a fine Gothic building beside the parish church, the **Museu de Arte Sacra** (Museum of Sacred Art; Praça Dom Nuno Álvares Pereira; adult/child €1.80/1.20; ☺10am-6pm) contains a small collection of 14th-century wooden religious figures, 18th-century vestments and silverware.

Situated 3km north of town is the granite, 5.6m-tall **Menhir do Outeiro** `FREE`, one of the tallest megalithic monuments ever discovered.

A rustic, pin-drop peaceful retreat, whitewashed **St Condestável** (✆969 713 213, 266 557 181; www.condestavel-monsaraz.com; Rua Direita 4; r €60-70, ste €85; ❋☎) dates to the 17th century and offers five cool rooms with heavy carved wooden beds. Some have fine views over the plains to the lake of Alqueva.

On its hilltop perch, **Sabores de Monsaraz** (✆969 217 800; www.saboresdemonsaraz.com; Largo de S Bartolomeu; ☺12.30-3.30pm Tue, 12.30-3.30pm & 7.30-10.30pm Wed-Sun; 🖋) is a family-friendly tavern dishing up Alentejano home-cooking – meltingly tender black pork and *migas com bacalhau e coentros* (codfish with bread and coriander) and the like.

The **tourist office** (✆927 997 316; Rua Direita; ☺10am-12.30pm & 2-5.30pm) can offer advice on accommodation.

Up to four daily buses connect Monsaraz with Reguengos de Monsaraz (€3, 35 minutes, Monday to Friday), with connections to Évora.

Peniche

POP 16,000

Popular for its nearby surfing beaches and also as a jumping-off point for Berlenga Grande, part of the beautiful Ilhas Berlengas nature reserve, the coastal city of Peniche remains a working port, giving it a slightly grittier and more 'lived-in' feel than its beach-resort neighbours. It has a walled historic centre and lovely beaches east of town.

From the bus station, it's a 10-minute walk west to the historic centre.

◉ Sights

Fortaleza FORT
(☺9am-12.30pm & 2-5.30pm Tue-Fri, from 10am Sat & Sun) `FREE` Dominating the south of the peninsula, Peniche's imposing 16th-century fortress was used in the 20th century as one of dictator Salazar's infamous jails for political prisoners.

Baleal BEACH
About 5km to the northeast of Peniche is this scenic island-village, connected to the mainland village of Casais do Baleal by a causeway. The fantastic sweep of sandy beach here offers some fine surfing. Surf schools dot the sands, as do several bar-restaurants.

Berlenga Grande ISLAND
Sitting about 10km offshore from Peniche, Berlenga Grande is a spectacular, rocky and remote island, with twisting, shocked-rock formations and gaping caverns.

OTHER PORTUGUESE TOWNS WORTH A VISIT

Time not an issue? Consider tacking on a day trip or staying overnight at these Portuguese gems.

Guimarães Birthplace of Afonso Henriques, the first independent king of Portugal, this beautiful medieval town in the south of Portugal's northern Minho region is a warren of labyrinthine lanes and plazas crowned by a 1000-year-old castle.

Elvas A Unesco heritage town in the east of the Alentejo and hugging the Spanish border, with impressive star-shaped fortifications, a lovely plaza and quaint museums.

Chaves A pretty spa town straddling the mountain-fringed banks of the Rio Tâmega in Portugal's northern Trás-os-Montes region, with a well-preserved historic centre and 16-arch Roman bridge.

Batalha & Alcobaça Situated slightly inland from the Atlantic and in the heart of the country, this Estremadura duo beckon with their charming centres and two of Portugal's most stunning monasteries.

Monsanto The crowning glory of the central Beiras region is this spectacular craggy cliff-top village, perched like an eyrie above the boulder-strewn landscape.

❖ Activities

Surfing

Surf camps offer week-long instruction as well as two-hour classes, plus board and wet-suit hire. Well-established names include **Baleal Surfcamp** (☑ 262 769 277; www.baleal surfcamp.com; Rua Amigos do Baleal 2; 1-/3-/5-day course €60/95/145) and **Peniche Surf-camp** (☑ 962 336 295; www.penichesurfcamp. com; Avenida do Mar 162, Casais do Baleal).

Diving

There are good diving opportunities around Peniche, and especially around Berlenga. Expect to pay about €65 to €75 for two dives (less around Peniche) with **Acuasuboeste** (☑ 918 393 444; Porto de Pesca; diving intro course €80, single dives €25-35) or **Haliotis** (☑ 262 781 160; www.haliotis.pt; Casal Ponte; single-/double-dive trip €35/75).

🛏 Sleeping

Peniche Hostel   HOSTEL €

(☑ 969 008 689; www.penichehostel.com; Rua Arquitecto Paulino Montês 6; dm/d €20/50; @ 🛜) This cosy little hostel, only steps from the tourist office and a five-minute walk from the bus station, has colourfully decorated and breezy rooms. Surfboards and bikes are available for hire, and there's an attached surf school.

🍴 Eating & Drinking

Restaurante
A Sardinha   SEAFOOD €

(☑ 262 781 820; Rua Vasco da Gama 81; mains €6-14; ⊘ 11.30am-4pm & 6.30-10.30pm) This no-frills place on a narrow street parallel to Largo da Ribeira does a roaring trade in mains like simply grilled fish and *caldeira-da* (fish stew) done well.

Java House   CAFE, BAR

(Largo da Ribeira 14; ⊘ 9am-3am Mon-Thu, to 4am Fri & Sat; 🛜) The most popular joint in town, this place deals in everything from early-morning coffees to sandwiches and crêpes. The lights dim later in the evening, and DJs strut their stuff.

❶ Getting There & Away

Peniche's **bus station** (☑ 968 903 861; Rua Dr Ernesto Moreira) is located 400m northeast of the tourist office (cross the Ponte Velha connecting the town to the isthmus). Destinations include Coimbra (€14, 2¾ hours, three daily), Leiria (€12.20, two hours, three daily), Lisbon (€8.60, 1½ hours, every one to two hours) and Óbidos (€3.15, 40 minutes, six to eight daily).

Óbidos

POP 3100

This exquisite walled village was a wedding gift from Dom Dinis to his wife Dona Isabel (beats a fondue set), and its historic centre is a delightful place to wander. Highlights include the **Igreja de Santa Maria** (Praça de Santa Maria; ⊘ 9.30am-12.30pm & 2.30-7pm) **FREE**, with fine 17th-century *azulejos,* and views from the town walls.

From mid-July to mid-August, Óbidos hosts the **Mercado Medieval** (www. mercadomedievalobidos.pt), featuring jousting matches, wandering minstrels and abundant medieval mayhem.

🛏 Sleeping & Eating

Hostel Argonauta   HOSTEL €

(☑ 262 958 088; www.hostelargonauta.com; Rua Adelaide Ribeirete 14; dm/d €25/50; 🛜) In a pretty spot just outside the walls, this feels more like a friend's place than a hostel. Run with good cheer, it has an arty, colourful dorm with wood-stove heating and beds as well as bunks; there's also a cute double with a great view.

Petrarum Domus   PORTUGUESE €€

(☑ 262 959 620; Rua Direita; mains €9-18; ⊘ noon-1am Mon-Thu, to 2am Fri & Sat, to midnight Sun) Amid age-old stone walls, Petrarum serves up hearty dishes like pork with mushrooms, mixed seafood sautés and several *bacalhau* (dried salt-cod) plates.

❶ Information

Turismo (☑ 262 959 231; www.obidos.pt; ⊘ 9.30am-7.30pm) Just outside Porta da Vila, near the bus stop, with helpful multilingual staff offering town brochures and maps in four languages.

❶ Getting There & Away

There are direct buses Monday to Friday from Lisbon (€8, 70 minutes).

Nazaré

POP 16,000

Nazaré has a bustling coastal setting with narrow cobbled lanes running down to a wide, cliff-backed beach. The town centre is jammed with seafood restaurants and bars; expect huge crowds in July and August.

Sights & Activities

The **beaches** here are superb, although swimmers should be aware of dangerous currents. Climb or take the funicular to the clifftop **Sítio**, with its cluster of fishermen's cottages and great view.

Sleeping & Eating

Many townspeople rent out rooms; doubles start at €35. Ask around near the seafront at Avenida da República.

Magic Art Hotel HOTEL €
(✍ 262 569 040; http://hotelmagic.pt; Rua Mouzinho de Albuquerque 58; s €70-85, d €75-90; P ❂ 🛜) Close to the action, this breezy, newish hotel has gone for the chic modern look. Clean-lined, well-equipped white rooms with artily presented photos of old-time Nazaré contrast with appealing black slate bathrooms.

Hotel Oceano GUESTHOUSE €€
(✍ 262 561 161; www.adegaoceano.com; Avenida da República 51; d €60-85; ❂🛜) This cordial little oceanfront place offers compact rooms, with flatscreen TV and excellent modern bathrooms. Those at the front have nice views across the beach to the cliffs and waterfront. As it's close to the action, street noise can be a problem.

⭐ **A Tasquinha** SEAFOOD €
(✍ 262 551 945; Rua Adrião Batalha 54; mains €6-10; ⊙ noon-3pm & 7-10.30pm Tue-Sun) This exceptionally friendly family affair serves high quality seafood in a pair of snug but pretty tiled dining rooms. Expect queues on summer nights.

Information

Turismo (✍ 262 561 194; www.cm-nazare.pt; Centro Cultural da Nazaré, Avenida Manuel Remígio; ⊙ 9.30am-12.30pm & 2.30-6.30pm, shorter hours in low season) On the beachfront strip, in the cultural centre in the old fish market.

Getting There & Away

Nazaré has numerous bus connections to Lisbon (€10.50, two hours).

Tomar

POP 16,000

A charming town straddling a river, Tomar has the notoriety of being home to the Knights Templar; check out their headquarters, the outstanding monastery **Convento de Cristo** (www.conventocristo.pt; Rua Castelo dos Templários; adult/child €6/free; ⊙ 9am-6.30pm), a steep climb above town. Other rarities include the country's best-preserved medieval **synagogue** (Rua Dr Joaquim Jacinto 73; ⊙ 10am-7pm Tue-Sun, shorter hours in low season) **FREE**. The town is backed by the dense greenery of the **Mata Nacional dos Sete Montes** (Seven Hills National Forest).

Sleeping & Eating

Residencial União GUESTHOUSE €
(✍ 249 323 161; www.residencialuniao.pt; Rua Serpa Pinto 94; s/d €30/50; 🛜) Tomar's most atmospheric budget choice, this once-grand town house on the main pedestrian drag features large and sprucely maintained rooms with antique furniture and fixtures.

Restaurante Tabuleiro PORTUGUESE €€
(✍ 249 312 771; Rua Serpa Pinto 140; mains €8-12; ⊙ noon-3pm & 7-10pm Mon-Sat; ❂) Located just off Tomar's main square, this family-friendly local hang-out features warm, attentive service, good traditional food and ample portions.

Information

Turismo (✍ 249 329 823; www.cm-tomar.pt; Rua Serpa Pinto; ⊙ 10am-1pm & 3-7pm Apr-Sep, 9.30am-1pm & 2.30-6pm Oct-Mar) Offers a good town map and an accommodation list.

Getting There & Away

Frequent trains run to Lisbon (€9.65, two hours).

Coimbra

POP 107,000

Coimbra is a dynamic, fashionable, yet comfortably lived-in city, with a student life centred on the magnificent 13th-century university. Aesthetically eclectic, there are elegant shopping streets, ancient stone walls and backstreet alleys with hidden *tascas* (taverns) and fado bars. Coimbra was the birth and burial place of Portugal's first king, and was the country's most important city when the Moors captured Lisbon.

◉ Sights & Activities

★ Sé Velha   CATHEDRAL
(Old Cathedral; ☑ 239 825 273; Largo da Sé Velha; admission €2; ⊙10am-6pm, closed Sun low season) Coimbra's stunning 12th-century cathedral is one of Portugal's finest examples of Romanesque architecture. The main portal and facade are exceptionally striking. Its crenellated exterior and narrow, slit-like lower windows serve as reminders of the nation's embattled early days, when the Moors were still a threat. These buildings were designed to be useful as fortresses in times of trouble.

Velha Universidade   UNIVERSITY
(Old University; www.uc.pt; adult/child €9/free, incl tower €12.50/free; ⊙9am-7.30pm mid-Mar-Oct, 9.30am-1pm & 2-5.30pm mid-Oct-mid-Mar) In every way the city's high point, the Old University consists of a series of remarkable 16th-to-18th-century buildings, all set around the vast **Patio des Escolas**, entered by way of the elegant 17th-century **Porta Férrea**, which occupies the same site as the main gate to Coimbra's Moorish stronghold. The highlight is the magnificent **library**.

Go Walks   WALKING TOUR
(☑ 910 163 118; www.gowalksportugal.com; Rua do Sargento Mor 4; half-/full-day tour €25/40) ⬦ Various themed walking tours – from fado to Jewish Coimbra – run by enthusiastic, knowledgeable students who speak good English (French and Spanish also bookable).

O Pioneiro
do Mondego   KAYAKING
(☑ 239 478 385; www.opioneirodomondego.com; guided tour per person €22.50) ⬦ Rents out kayaks for paddling the Mondego between Penacova and Torres de Mondego, an 18km trip.

WORTH A TRIP

ROMAN RUINS

Conimbriga, 16km south of Coimbra, is the site of the well-preserved ruins of a **Roman town** (⊙10am-7pm), including mosaic floors, elaborate baths and trickling fountains. It's a fascinating place to explore, with a **museum** (www.conimbriga.pt; adult/child incl Roman Ruins €4.50/free; ⊙10am-7pm) that describes the once-flourishing and later abandoned town. Frequent buses run to Condeixa, 2km from the site; there are also two direct buses from Coimbra.

★★ Festivals & Events

Queima das Fitas   FIESTA
(www.queimadasfitas.org) Coimbra's biggest bash is Queima das Fitas, a boozy week of fado and revelry that takes place during the first week in May when students celebrate the end of the academic year.

🛏 Sleeping

Hotel Vitória   HOTEL €
(☑ 234 824 049; www.hotelvitoria.pt; Rua da Sota 9; s/d/tr €45/59/75; ❄🛜) This friendly family-run *residencial* has had a slick makeover. The newest rooms have a clean-line Nordic feel and lots of light. Try for a 3rd floor room for the best views of the old town or river. There's a great family room available too, and a downstairs restaurant.

Casa Pombal   GUESTHOUSE €
(☑ 239 835 175; www.casapombal.com; Rua das Flores 18; d with/without bathroom €68/54; @🛜) In a lovely old-town location, this winning, Dutch-run guesthouse squeezes tons of charm into a small space. A delicious breakfast is served in the gorgeous blue-tiled breakfast room.

Riversuites   HOTEL €
(☑ 239 440 582; www.riversuiteshotel.com; Avenida João das Regras 82; d €40-52, tr €65, q €75; ❄🛜) Just across the bridge from the centre, this excellent hotel has slick, modern rooms (not suites) and comforts. A decent breakfast is included, and the showers are just great.

✗ Eating & Drinking

A colourful stop for self-caterers, the **Mercado Municipal Dom Pedro V** (Rua Olímpio Nicolau Rui Fernandes; ⏱7am-7pm Mon-Sat) 🥕 is full of lively fruit and vegetable stalls and butcher shops displaying Portuguese cuts of meat (hooves, claws and all).

Adega Paço
dos Condes   PORTUGUESE €
(☑239 825 605; Rua do Paço do Conde 1; mains €5-10; ⏱11.30am-3pm & 6.30-11pm Mon-Sat) Usually crowded with students and Coimbra locals, this straightforward family-run grill is one of the city's best budget eateries.

★Fangas
Mercearia Bar   TAPAS €€
(☑934 093 636; http://fangas.pt; Rua Fernandes Tomás 45; petiscos €4-7; ⏱noon-4pm & 7pm-1am Tue-Sun; 🍴) Top-quality deli produce is used to produce delightful *petiscos* (tapas) in this bright, cheery dining room, the best place to eat in the old town. Service is slow but friendly and staff will help you choose from a delicious array of tasty platters – sausages, stuffed vegetables, conserves – and interesting wines. Book ahead as this small space always fills quickly.

Zé Manel dos Ossos   TASCA €€
(Beco do Forno 12; mains €7-15; ⏱noon-3pm & 7.30-10pm Mon-Fri, noon-3pm Sat) Tucked down a nondescript alleyway, this little gem, papered with scholarly doodles and scribbled poems, serves a terrific *feijoada à leitão* (a stew of beans and suckling pig).

Restaurante Zé Neto   PORTUGUESE €€
(Rua das Azeiteiras 8; mains €9-11; ⏱9am-3pm & 7pm-midnight Mon-Sat) This marvellous family-run place specialises in homemade Portuguese standards, including *cabrito* (kid).

★Café Santa Cruz   CAFE
(www.cafesantacruz.com; Praça 8 de Maio; ⏱7.30am-midnight Mon-Sat) One of Portugal's most atmospheric cafes, Santa Cruz is set in a dramatically beautiful high-vaulted former chapel, with stained-glass windows, graceful stone arches, and a Ché mosaic where the altar would have been, while the terrace grants lovely views of Praça 8 de Maio.

Bar Quebra Costas   BAR
(Rua Quebra Costas 45; ⏱noon-4am Mon-Fri, 2pm-4am Sat) This Coimbra classic has a sunny cobblestoned terrace, an artsy interior, friendly service, chilled-out tunes and the occasional jazz session.

☆ Entertainment

Coimbra-style fado is more cerebral than the Lisbon variety, and its adherents are staunchly protective.

Á Capella   FADO
(☑239 833 985; www.acapella.com.pt; Rua Corpo de Deus; admission incl one drink €10; ⏱9pm-2am) A 14th-century chapel turned candlelit cocktail lounge, this place regularly hosts the city's most renowned fado musicians. There's a show every night at 10pm.

ℹ Information

Turismo Praça República (www.turismodecoimbra.pt; Praça da República; ⏱9am-12.30pm & 2-6pm Mon-Fri) On the eastern side of town.
Turismo Universidade (☑239 834 158; www.turismodecoimbra.pt; Praça da Porta Férrea; ⏱10am-1pm & 2-6pm Apr-Oct, shorter hours in low season) Adjacent to the Velha Universidade ticket desk, just outside the Porta Férrea.

ℹ Getting There & Away

There are frequent trains to Lisbon (€24, two to 2½ hours) and Porto (€9.50 to €17, one hour to 1¾ hours). There are also regular services to Faro and Évora via Lisbon. The main train stations are Coimbra B, 2km northwest of the centre, and central Coimbra A. Most long-distance trains call at Coimbra B. The bus station (Avenida Fernão Magalhães) is about 400m northeast of the centre.

Luso & the Buçaco Forest

POP 2000

This sylvan region harbours a lush forest of century-old trees surrounded by countryside that's dappled with heather, wildflowers and leafy ferns. There's even a fairy-tale **palace** (☑231 937 970; www.almeidahotels.com; Mata Nacional do Buçaco; 7-/8-course meal €35/40; ⏱lunch & dinner; 🛎) here, a 1907 neo-Manueline extravagance, where deep-pocketed visitors can dine or stay overnight. The palace lies amid the Mata Nacional do Buçaco, a forest criss-crossed with trails, dotted with crumbling chapels and graced with ponds, fountains and exotic trees. Buçaco was chosen as a retreat by 16th-century monks, and it surrounds the lovely spa town of Luso. From the centre, it's a 2km walk through forest up to the palace.

The **Maloclinic Spa** (www.maloclinicterm asluso.com; Rua Álvaro Castelões; ⊘8am-1pm & 2-7pm daily high season, 9am-1pm & 2-6pm Mon-Sat low season) offers a range of soothing treatments.

🛏 Sleeping & Eating

Alegre Hotel   BOUTIQUE HOTEL **€€**
(✆231 930 256; www.alegrehotels.com; Rua Emídio Navarro 2; s/d €45/55; ᴘ🕈🌊) This grand, atmospheric, pinkish-coloured 19th-century town house has large doubles with plush drapes, decorative plaster ceilings and polished period furniture. Its appeal is enhanced by an elegant entryway, formal parlour and pretty vine-draped garden with pool.

ℹ Information

Turismo (✆231 939 133; Rua Emídio Navarro 136; ⊘9.30am-1pm & 2.30-6pm) Has accommodation information, town and forest maps, internet access, and is helpful.

ℹ Getting There & Away

Buses to/from Coimbra (€3.50, 45 minutes) run four times daily each weekday and twice daily on Saturdays. Trains to/from Coimbra B station (€2.50, 25 minutes) run several times daily; it's a 15-minute walk to town from the station.

Serra da Estrela

The forested Serra da Estrela has a raw natural beauty and offers some of the country's best hiking. This is Portugal's highest mainland mountain range (1993m), and the source of its two great rivers: Rio Mondego and Rio Zêzere. The town of Manteigas makes a great base for hiking and exploring the area (plus skiing in winter). The **main park office** (✆275 980 060; pnse@icnf.pt; Rua 1 de Maio 2, Manteigas; ⊘9am-12.30pm & 2-5.30pm Mon-Fri) provides details of popular walks in the Parque Natural da Serra da Estrela – some of which leave from town or just outside it; additional offices are at Seia, Gouveia and Guarda.

🛏 Sleeping

Hotel Berne   HOTEL **€**
(✆275 981 351; www.hotelberne.com; Quinta de Santo António, Manteigas; d/tr/q €65/80/105; ᴘ🕈🌊) Going for a Swiss feel, this lovely hotel at the bottom of town has cheerful, spotless, wood-accented rooms, many with views of Manteigas and the mountains above. There is a great restaurant and a spacious lounge.

★**Casa das Penhas Douradas**   HOTEL **€€€**
(✆275 981 045; www.casadaspenhasdouradas. pt; Penhas Douradas; s €120-140, d €135-160; ᴘ🕈@🕈🌊) On its mountaintop perch between Manteigas and Seia, this hotel gets everything right. The rooms all have great natural light, views, and some come with sloping ceilings or appealing terraces. An enlightened attitude to guest comfort means all sorts of welcome details, such as a heated pool, bikes and kayaks, books and DVDs, and spa and massage treatments are available.

ℹ Getting There & Around

Two regular weekday buses connect Manteigas with Guarda, from where there are onward services to Coimbra and Lisbon.

THE NORTH

Beneath the edge of Spanish Galicia, northern Portugal is a land of lush river valleys, sparkling coastline, granite peaks and virgin forests. This region is also gluttony for wine lovers: it's the home of the sprightly *vinho verde* wine (a young, slightly sparkling white or red wine) and ancient vineyards along the dramatic Rio Douro. Gateway to the north is Porto, a beguiling riverside city blending both medieval and modern attractions. Smaller towns and villages also offer cultural allure, from majestic Braga, the country's religious heart, to the seaside beauty Viana do Castelo.

Porto
POP 238,000

From across the Rio Douro at sunset, romantic Porto looks like a pop-up town, acolourful tumbledown dream with medieval relics, soaring bell towers, extravagant baroque churches and stately beaux-arts buildings piled on top of one another, illuminated by streaming shafts of sun. If you squint you might be able to make out the open windows, the narrow lanes and the staircases zigzagging to nowhere.

Porto

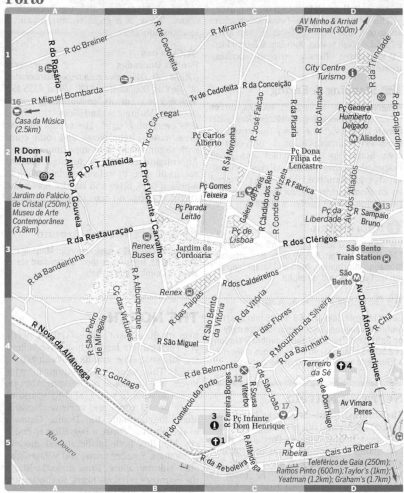

A lively walkable city with chatter in the air and a tangible sense of history, Porto's old-world riverfront district is a Unesco World Heritage Site. Across the water twinkle the neon signs of Vila Nova de Gaia, the headquarters of the major port manufacturers.

◎ Sights & Activities

Perfect for a languid stroll, the **Ribeira** district – Porto's riverfront nucleus – is a remarkable window into the city's history. Along the riverside promenade, *barcos rabelos* (the traditional boats used to ferry port wine down the Douro) bob beneath the shadow of the photogenic Ponte de Dom Luís I.

A few kilometres west of the city centre, the seaside suburb of **Foz do Douro** is a prime destination on hot summer weekends. It has a long beach promenade and a smattering of oceanfront bars and restaurants.

★ **Palácio da Bolsa**   MONUMENT
(Stock Exchange; Rua Ferreira Borges; tours adult/child €7/4; ⊙ 9am-6.30pm Apr-Oct, 9am-12.30pm & 2-5.30pm Nov-Mar) This splendid neoclassical monument (built from 1842

PORTUGAL PORTO

eventually reach the hulking, hilltop fortress of the cathedral. Founded in the 12th century, it was largely rebuilt a century later and then extensively altered during the 18th century. However, you can still make out the church's Romanesque contours. Inside, a rose window and a 14th-century Gothic cloister remain from its early days.

Igreja de São Francisco
CHURCH

(Praça Infante Dom Henrique; adult/child €3.50/1.75; ⊙9am-8pm Jul-Sep, to 7pm Mar-Jun & Oct, to 6pm Nov-Feb) Sitting on Praça Infante Dom Henrique, Igreja de São Francisco looks from the outside to be an austerely Gothic church, but inside it hides one of Portugal's most dazzling displays of baroque finery. Hardly an inch escapes unsmothered, as otherworldly cherubs and sober monks are drowned by nearly 100kg of gold leaf.

Jardim do Palácio de Cristal
PARK

(Rua Dom Manuel II; ⊙8am-9pm Apr-Sep, 8am-7pm Oct-Mar) FREE Sitting atop a bluff, this gorgeous botanical garden is one of Porto's best-loved escapes, with lawns interwoven

to 1910) honours Porto's past and present money merchants. Just past the entrance is the glass-domed **Pátio das Nações** (Hall of Nations), where the exchange once operated. But this pales in comparison with rooms deeper inside; to visit these, join one of the half-hour guided tours, which set off every 30 minutes.

Sé
CATHEDRAL

(Terreiro da Sé; cloisters adult/student €3/2; ⊙9am-12.30pm & 2.30-7pm Apr-Oct, to 6pm Nov-Mar) FREE From Praça da Ribeira rises a tangle of medieval alleys and stairways that

with sun-dappled paths and dotted with fountains, sculptures, giant magnolias, camellias, cypress and olive trees. It's actually a mosaic of small gardens that open up little by little as you wander – as do the stunning views of the city and Douro River.

Museu de Arte Contemporânea
MUSEUM

(www.serralves.pt; Rua Dom João de Castro 210; adult/child museums & park €8.50/free, park €4/free; ⊙10am-7pm Tue-Fri, 10am-8pm Sat & Sun, shorter hours in winter) This arrestingly minimalist, whitewashed space was designed by the eminent Porto-based architect Álvaro Siza Vieira. Cutting-edge exhibitions are showcased in the **Casa de Serralves**, a delightful pink art deco mansion, and there's a fine permanent collection featuring works from the late 1960s to the present. Both museums are accessible on a single ticket and sit within the marvellous 18-hectare **Parque de Serralves**.

Museu Nacional Soares dos Reis
MUSEUM

(www.museusoaresdosreis.pt; Rua Dom Manuel II 44; adult/child €5/free, 10am-2pm Sun free; ⊙10am-6pm Wed-Sun, 2-6pm Tue) Porto's best art museum presents a stellar collection ranging from Neolithic carvings to Portugal's take on modernism, all housed in the formidable Palácio das Carrancas.

Teleférico de Gaia
CABLE CAR

(www.gaiacablecar.com; one way/return €5/8; ⊙10am-8pm high season, 10am-6pm low season) Don't miss a ride on the Teleférico de Gaia, an aerial gondola that provides fine views over the Douro and Porto on its short, five-minute jaunt. It runs between the southern end of the Ponte Dom Luís I and the riverside.

Taste Porto Food Tours
GUIDED TOUR

(⊙967 258 750; www.tasteportofoodtours.com; adult/child €55/40; ⊙tours 10.30am Tue-Sat, 4pm Tue-Fri) Hungry? Good. Loosen a belt notch for these superb half-day food tours, where you'll sample everything from Porto's best slow-roast pork sandwich to éclairs, fine wines, cheese and coffee.

We Hate Tourism Tours
GUIDED TOUR

(⊙913 776 598; http://wehatetourismtours.com/oporto; full-day tours around €40) If you want to sidestep tourist traps and beeline to

the city's soul, WHTT is the real deal, with guides such as André buzzing with passion for Porto.

✹ Festivals & Events

Serralves Em Festa
CULTURAL

(www.serralvesemfesta.com) This huge event runs for 40 hours nonstop over one weekend in early June. Parque de Serralves hosts the main events, with concerts, avant-garde theatre and kiddie activities. Other open-air events happen all over town.

Festa de São João
RELIGIOUS

(St John's Festival) Porto's biggest party. For one night in June the city erupts into music, competitions and riotous parties; this is also when merrymakers pound each other on the head with squeaky plastic mallets (you've been warned).

Noites Ritual Rock
MUSIC

A weekend-long rock extravaganza in late August.

🛏 Sleeping

★ Gallery Hostel
HOSTEL €

(⊙224 964 313; www.gallery-hostel.com; Rua Miguel Bombarda 222; dm €22-24, d €64, tr €80; ❄⃝🕾) A true travellers' hub, this hostel-gallery has clean and cosy dorms and doubles; a sunny, glass-enclosed back patio; a grassy terrace; a cinema room; a shared kitchen and a bar-music room. Throw in its free walking tours, homemade dinners on request, port wine tastings and concerts, and you'll see why it's booked up so often – reserve ahead.

Tattva Design Hostel
HOSTEL €

(⊙220 944 622; www.tattvadesignhostel.com; Rua do Cativo 26-28; dm €10-20, d €47-60, q €75-100; ◉🕾) Tattva knows precisely what makes backpackers tick. The facilities are superb and the attractive rooms have thoughtful touches – big lockers, good lighting, privacy curtains, and a bathroom and balcony in every room. The open-air rooftop lounge is a great place for a sundowner. Plus it offers free walking tours.

6 Only
GUESTHOUSE €€

(⊙222 013 971; www.6only.pt; Rua Duque de Loulé 97; r €70-80; ◉🕾) This beautifully restored guesthouse has just six rooms, all with simple but stylish details that effortlessly blend old (such as wrought-iron decorative balconies)

THROUGH THE GRAPEVINES OF THE DOURO

Portugal's best-known river flows through the country's rural heartland. In the upper reaches, port-wine grapes are grown on steep terraced hills, punctuated by remote stone villages and, in spring, splashes of dazzling white almond blossom.

The Rio Douro is navigable right across Portugal. Highly recommended is the train journey from Porto to Pinhão (€11, 2½ hours, five daily), the last 70km clinging to the river's edge; trains continue to Pocinho (from Porto €13.50, 3¼ hours). **Porto Tours** (☑ 222 000 045; www.portotours.com; Calçada Pedro Pitões 15, Torre Medieval; ⊙ 10am-7pm), situated next to Porto's cathedral, can arrange tours, including idyllic Douro cruises.

Cyclists and drivers can choose river-hugging roads along either bank, and can visit wineries along the way (check out www.dourovalley.eu for an extensive list of wineries open to visitors). You can also stay overnight in scenic wine lodges among the vineyards.

with contemporary. There's a lounge, a Zen-like courtyard and friendly staff.

ROSA ET
AL Townhouse
GUESTHOUSE **€€**

(☑ 916 000 081; www.rosaetal.pt; Rua do Rosário 233; r €98-228; ☏) This gorgeously done up townhouse in the thick of Porto's art district has six suites with hardwood floors and free-standing claw-foot tubs, and a lovely garden out back. The restaurant serves delicious brunch and afternoon tea at weekends There are rotating exhibits, cooking workshops and other fun events. Breakfast costs an extra €30 per room.

Yeatman
RESORT **€€€**

(☑ 220 134 200; www.the-yeatman-hotel.com; Rua do Choupelo 88; s €270-320, d €285-335, ste €615-1100; ✽☏☲) Named for one of Taylor's original founders, the Yeatman is Porto's only true five-star resort, terraced and tucked into the Gaia hillside with massive Douro and Porto views. There's a Michelin-starred chef, huge guest rooms and suites with private terrace, a decanter-shaped pool, sunken Roman baths in the fantastic Caudalie spa, and all the amenities you could desire.

✗ Eating

★ Mercado do Bolhão
MARKET **€**

(Rua Formosa; ⊙ 7am-5pm Mon-Fri, to 1pm Sat) The 19th-century, wrought-iron Mercado do Bolhão does a brisk trade in fresh produce, including cheeses, olives, smoked meats, sausages, breads and more. At its lively best on Friday and Saturday mornings, the market is also sprinkled with inexpensive stalls where you can eat fish so fresh it was probably swimming in the Atlantic that morning, or sample local wines and cheeses.

Casa Guedes
TASCA **€**

(Praça dos Poveiros 130; mains €4-9; ⊙ 8am-midnight Mon-Sat) Come for tasty, filling and cheap meals, or for the famous pork sandwiches, served all day.

Flor dos
Congregados
PORTUGUESE **€€**

(Travessa dos Congregados 11; mains €8-16; ⊙ 6.30-11pm Mon-Wed, noon-3pm & 6.30-11pm Thu-Sat) Tucked away down a narrow alley, this softly lit, family-run restaurant brims with stone-walled, wood-beamed, art-slung nooks. The frequently changing blackboard menu goes with the seasons.

Café Majestic
CAFE **€€**

(Rua Santa Catarina 112; mains €10-18; ⊙ 9am-midnight) Porto's best-known tea shop is packed with prancing cherubs, opulently gilded woodwork and leather seats. The gold-braided waiters will serve you an elegant breakfast, afternoon tea or light meals – from a classic *francesinha* sandwich to salads at the healthier end of the spectrum. There's a pavement terrace.

★ DOP
PORTUGUESE **€€€**

(☑ 222 014 313; www.ruipaula.com; Largo de S Domingos 18; tasting menu €65; ⊙ 7-11pm Mon, 12.30-3pm & 7-11pm Tue-Sat) Housed in the Palácio das Artes, DOP is one of Porto's most stylish addresses, with its high ceilings and slick, monochrome interior. Much-feted chef Rui Paula puts a creative, seasonal twist on outstanding ingredients.

▼ Drinking & Nightlife

The bar-lined Rua Galeira de Paris and nearby streets are packed with revellers most nights. Down by the water, the open-air bar scene on Praça da Ribeira is great for drinks with a view.

Rota do Chá   TEAHOUSE
(www.rotadocha.pt; Rua Miguel Bombarda 457; tea €2.50; ⊗11am-8pm Mon-Thu, noon-midnight Fri & Sat, 1-8pm Sun) This proudly bohemian cafe has a verdant but rustic back garden where students and the gallery crowd sit around low tables sampling from an enormous 300+ tea menu divided by region.

Casa do Livro   LOUNGE
(Rua Galeria de Paris 85; ⊗9.30pm-4am) Vintage wallpaper, gilded mirrors and walls of books give a discreet charm to this nicely lit beer and wine bar. On weekends, DJs spin funk, soul, jazz and retro sounds in the back room.

Vinologia   WINE BAR
(Rua de São João 46; ⊗4pm-midnight) This cosy wine bar is an excellent place to sample the fine quaffs of Porto, with over 200 different ports on offer. If you fall in love with a certain wine, you can usually buy a whole bottle (or even send a case home).

☆ Entertainment

★Casa da Música   LIVE MUSIC
(House of Music; ☑220 120 220; www.casadamusica.com; Avenida da Boavista 604) Grand and minimalist, sophisticated yet populist, Porto's music mecca is the Casa da Música, with a shoebox-style concert hall at its heart, meticulously engineered to accommodate everything from jazz duets to Beethoven's Ninth.

Maus Hábitos   PERFORMING ARTS
(www.maushabitos.com; 4th fl, Rua Passos Manuel 178; ⊗noon-2am Wed & Thu, noon-4am Fri & Sat) Maus Hábitos or 'Bad Habits' is an arty, nicely chilled haunt hosting a culturally ambitious agenda. Changing exhibitions and imaginative installations adorn the walls, while live bands and DJs work the small stage.

❶ Information

City Centre Turismo (☑223 393 472; www.visitporto.travel; Rua Clube dos Fenianos 25; ⊗9am-8pm high season, 9am-7pm low season) The main city *turismo* has a detailed city map, a transport map and the *Agenda do Porto* cultural calendar, among other printed materials.

Post Office (Praça General Humberto Delgado) Across from the main tourist office.

Santo António Hospital (☑222 077 500; www.chporto.pt; Largo Prof Abel Salazar) Has English-speaking staff.

Tourist Police (☑222 081 833; Rua Clube dos Fenianos 11; ⊗8am-2am) Multilingual station beside the main city *turismo*.

❶ Getting There & Away

AIR

Porto's airport (p559) is connected by daily flights from Lisbon and London, and has direct links from other European cities, particularly with EasyJet and Ryanair.

BUS

Porto has many private bus companies leaving from different terminals; the main tourist office can help. In general, for Lisbon and the Algarve, the choice is **Renex** (www.renex.pt; Campo Mártires de Pátria 37) or **Rede Expressos** (☑222 006 954; www.rede-expressos.pt; Rua Alexandre Herculano 366). **Eurolines** (www.eurolines.com) runs buses to Madrid (via Guarda; €50, 10 hours) and Santiago de Compostela (via Braga; €33, five hours) in Spain.

Bus companies operate from or near Praceto Régulo Magauanha, off Rua Dr Alfredo Magalhães: **Transdev-Norte** (www.transdev.pt) goes to Braga (€6); **AV Minho** (www.avminho.pt) to Viana do Castelo (€8).

TRAIN

Porto is a northern Portugal rail hub. Most international trains, and all intercity links, start at Campanhã, 2km east of the centre.

At São Bento, you can book tickets to any other destination.

❶ Getting Around

TO/FROM THE AIRPORT

The metro's 'violet' E line provides handy service to the airport. A one-way ride to the centre costs €1.85 and takes about 45 minutes. A daytime taxi costs €20 to €25 to/from the centre.

PUBLIC TRANSPORT

Save money on transport by purchasing a refillable **Andante Card** (€0.60), valid for transport on buses, metro, funicular and tram. You can buy them from STCP kiosks or newsagents. A

TASTING PORT WINE

Sitting just across the Rio Douro from Porto, **Vila Nova de Gaia** is woven into the city's fabric by stunning bridges and a shared history of port-wine making. Since the mid-18th century, port-wine bottlers and exporters have maintained their lodges here.

Today, some 30 of these lodges clamber up the river bank and most open their doors to the public for cellar tours and tastings. Among the best are **Taylor's** (📞223 742 800; www.taylor.pt; Rua do Choupelo 250; tour €5; ☺10am-6pm Mon-Fri, to 5pm Sat & Sun), **Graham's** (📞223 776 484; www.grahams-port.com; Rua do Agro 141; tour €5-20; ☺9.30am-6pm Apr-Oct, 9.30am-5.30pm Nov-Mar) and **Ramos Pinto** (📞223 707 000; www.ramospinto.pt; Av Ramos Pinto 400; tour & tasting €5; ☺10am-6pm daily May-Oct, 10am-6pm Mon-Fri Apr, 9am-5pm Mon-Fri Nov-Mar).

24-hour ticket for the entire public transport network, excluding trams, costs €7.

Bus

Central hubs of Porto's extensive bus system include Jardim da Cordoaria, Praça da Liberdade and São Bento station. Tickets purchased on the bus are one way €1.20/€1.85 with/without the Andante Card.

Funicular

The panoramic **Funicular dos Guindais** (one way €2; ☺8am-10pm, shorter hours in winter) shuttles up and down a steep incline from Avenida Gustavo Eiffel to Rua Augusto Rosa.

Metro

Porto's **metro** (www.metrodoporto.pt) currently comprises six metropolitan lines that all converge at the Trinidade stop. Tickets cost €1.20 with an Andante Card. There are also various 24-hour passes (from €4.15) available.

Tram

Porto has three antique trams that trundle around town. The most useful line, 1E, travels along the Douro towards the Foz district. A single tram ticket costs €2.50.

TAXI

To cross town, expect to pay between €5 and €8. There's a 20% surcharge at night, and an additional charge to leave city limits, which includes Vila Nova de Gaia. There are taxi ranks throughout the centre or you can call a **taxi** (📞225 076 400).

Viana do Castelo

POP 38,000

The jewel of the Costa Verde (Green Coast), Viana do Castelo has both an appealing medieval centre and lovely beaches just outside the city. In addition to its natural beauty, Viana do Castelo whips up some excellent seafood and hosts some magnificent traditional festivals, including the spectacular **Festa de Nossa Senhora da Agonia** in August.

◉ Sights

The stately heart of town is **Praça da República**, with its delicate fountain and grandiose buildings, including the 16th-century **Misericórdia**, a former almshouse.

Monte de Santa Luzia　　　　　　　　HILL

There are two good reasons to visit Viana's 228m, eucalyptus-clad hill. One is the wondrous view down the coast and up the Lima valley. The other is the fabulously over-the-top, 20th-century, neo-Byzantine **Templo do Sagrado Coração de Jesus** (Temple of the Sacred Heart of Jesus; ☺11am-1pm & 3-8pm) FREE. You can get a little closer to heaven on its graffiti-covered roof, via a lift, followed by an elbow-scraping stairway – take the museum entrance on the ground floor.

Praia do Cabedelo　　　　　　　　　BEACH

(☺ferry 9am-6pm) This is one of the Minho's best beaches: a 1km-long arch of blonde, powdery sand, which folds into grassy dunes backed by a grove of wind-blown pines. It's across the river from town, best reached on a five-minute ferry trip (one way/return €1.40/2.80; half-price for under-12s, free for children under six) from the pier south of Largo 5 de Outubro.

🛌 Sleeping & Eating

Ó Meu Amor　　　　　　　　GUESTHOUSE €

(📞258 406 513; www.omeuamor.com; Rua do Poço 19; s/d without bathroom €25/45; @🖀) Top choice in town right in the historic centre, this hideaway in a rambling town house full of nooks and crannies has nine adorable rooms with shared bathrooms. Guests can use the kitchen and cosy living room.

Margarida da Praça
GUESTHOUSE €€

(☎258 809 630; www.margaridadapraca.com; Largo 5 de Outubro 58; s €60-75, d €78-88; @ 🛜) Fantastically whimsical, this boutique inn offers thematic rooms in striking pinks, sea greens and whites, accented by stylish floral wallpaper, candelabra lanterns and lush duvets. The equally stylish lobby glows with candlelight in the evening.

Taberna do Valentim
SEAFOOD €€

(Campo do Castelo; mains €9.75-12.50; ⊗12.30-3pm & 7.30-10pm Mon-Sat) This bright and buzzing seafood restaurant serves fresh grilled fish by the kilo and rich seafood stews – *arroz de tamboril* (monkfish rice) and *caldeirada* (fish stew).

O Pescador
SEAFOOD €€

(☎258 826 039; Largo de São Domingos 35; mains €9.50-15.50; ⊗noon-3pm & 7-10pm Mon-Sat, noon-3pm Sun) A simple, friendly, family-run restaurant admired by locals for its good seafood and tasty lunch specials (from €6.50).

🛈 Getting There & Away

Five to 10 trains go daily to Porto (€7 to €8, 1½ hours), as well as express buses (€8, one to 1½ hours).

Braga

POP 143,000

Portugal's third-largest city boasts a fine array of churches, their splendid baroque facades looming above the old plazas and narrow lanes of the historic centre. Lively cafes, trim little boutiques and some good restaurants add to the appeal.

🛈 Sights

Sé
CATHEDRAL

(www.se-braga.pt; Rua Dom Paio Mendes; ⊗8am-7pm high season, 9am-6pm low season) FREE Braga's extraordinary cathedral, the oldest in Portugal, was begun when the archdiocese was restored in 1070 and completed in the following century. It's a rambling complex made up of differing styles, and architecture buffs could spend half a day happily distinguishing the Romanesque bones from Manueline musculature and baroque frippery.

Escadaria do Bom Jesus
RELIGIOUS SITE

At Bom Jesus do Monte, a hilltop pilgrimage site 5km from Braga, is an extraordinary stairway, with allegorical fountains, chapels and a superb view. City bus 2 runs frequently from Braga to the site, where you can climb the steps (pilgrims sometimes do this on their knees) or ascend by funicular railway (one way/return €1.20/2).

🛏 Sleeping

Pop Hostel
HOSTEL €

(☎253 058 806; http://bragapophostel.blogspot.co.uk; Rua do Carmo 61; dm/d from €17/40; @ 🛜) This small cosy hostel in a top-floor apartment is a great recent addition to Braga, with a colourfully decked lounge, a hammock on the balcony and a friendly owner who knows all the great eating and drinking spots in town. Bike hire and tours available.

★Portuguez Inn
GUESTHOUSE €€

(☎962 130 549; www.portuguezinn.pt; Rua Dom Frei Caetano Brandão 154; per 2/4 people €96/156; 🅿 ❄ 🛜) This hideaway in the historic centre bills itself as 'the world's smallest guesthouse'. Small it is, but its six levels offer a stylish micro-world that features a 1st-century Roman sewer in the basement, a cosy top-floor living room and Portuguese touches such as woollen blankets, ceramic swallows, handmade soaps and cotton dolls.

Hotel Bracara Augusta
BOUTIQUE HOTEL €€

(☎253 206 260; www.bracaraaugusta.com; Avenida Central 134; s/d €79/99; 🅿 ❄ @ 🛜) This stylish, grand town house offers bright, modern rooms with parquet floors, classic decor and marble bathrooms.

🍴 Eating

Anjo Verde
VEGETARIAN €

(Largo da Praça Velha 21; mains €7.50-8.60; ⊗noon-3pm & 7.30-10.30pm Mon-Sat) Braga's vegetarian offering serves generous, elegantly presented plates in a lovely, airy dining room. Vegetarian lasagne, risotto and vegetable tarts are among the choices. Mains can be bland, but the spiced chocolate tart is a superstar.

Cozinha da Sé
PORTUGUESE €€

(Rua Dom Frei Caetano Brandão 95; mains €10-14; ⊗lunch & dinner Wed-Sun, dinner Tue) Contemporary artwork hangs from the exposed stone walls at this intimate cheery Braga pick. Traditional standouts include baked *bacalhau* (dried salt-cod) and *açorda de marisco* (seafood stew in a bread bowl).

ℹ Information

Turismo (☎ 253 262 550; www.cm-braga.pt; Avenida da Liberdade 1; ◎ 9am-7pm Mon-Fri, 9am-12.30pm & 2-5.30pm Sat & Sun Jun-Sep, shorter hours in low season) Braga's helpful tourist office is in an art-deco-style building facing the fountain.

ℹ Getting There & Away

Trains arrive regularly from Lisbon (€33, 3½ to 4½ hours), Coimbra (€16 to €20, 1¾ to 2½ hours) and Porto (€3.10, 50 minutes), and there are daily connections north to Viana do Castelo. Car hire is available at **AVIC** (☎ 253 203 910; Rua Gabriel Pereira de Castro 28; ◎ 9am-7pm Mon-Fri, 9am-12.30pm Sat), with prices starting at €35 per day.

Parque Nacional da Peneda-Gerês

Spread across four impressive granite massifs, this vast park encompasses boulder-strewn peaks, precipitous valleys, gorse-clad moorlands and forests of oak and pine. It also shelters more than 100 granite villages that, in many ways, have changed little since Portugal's founding in the 12th century. For nature lovers, the stunning scenery here is unmatched in Portugal for camping, hiking and other outdoor adventures. The park's main centre is at **Vila do Gerês**, a sleepy, hot-springs village.

☆ Activities

Hiking

There are trails and footpaths through the park, some between villages with accommodation. Leaflets detailing these are available from the park offices.

Day hikes around Vila do Gerês are popular. An adventurous option is the **old Roman road** from Mata do Albergaria (10km up-valley from Vila do Gerês), past the **Vilarinho das Furnas** reservoir to Campo do Gerês. More distant destinations include **Ermida** and **Cabril**, both with simple accommodation.

Cycling & Horse Riding

Mountain bikes can be hired in Campo do Gerês (15km northeast of Vila do Gerês) from **Equi Campo** (☎ 253 161 405; www.equicampo.com; ◎ 9am-7pm daily Jun-Aug, 9am-7pm Sat & Sun Sep-May). Guides here also lead horse-riding trips, hikes and combination hiking/climbing/abseiling excursions.

Water Sports

Rio Caldo, 8km south of Vila do Gerês, is the base for water sports on the Caniçada Reservoir. English-run **AML** (☎ 253 391 779; www.aguamontanha.com; Lugar de Paredes) rents kayaks, pedal boats, rowing boats and small motorboats. It also organises kayaking trips along the Albufeira de Salamonde.

🛏 Sleeping & Eating

Vila do Gerês has plenty of *pensões* (guesthouses), but you may find vacancies are limited; many are block-booked by spa patients in summer.

Parque Campismo de Cerdeira   CAMPGROUND €
(☎ 253 351 005; www.parquecerdeira.com; per person/tent/car €5.90/5/5, bungalow €70; ◎ year-round; ▣🐾🏊) In Campo de Gêres, this place has oak-shaded sites, a laundry, a pool, a minimarket and a particularly good restaurant. The ecofriendly bungalows open onto unrivalled mountain views.

★ **Peneda Hotel**   HOTEL €€
(☎ 251 460 040; www.penedahotel.pt; Lugar da Peneda, Arcos de Valdevez; s/d €70/75; ▣🐾) Once a nest for Igreja Senhora de Peneda's pilgrims, this mountain lodge features a waterfall backdrop, a gushing creek beneath and ultra-cosy rooms with blonde-wood floors, French windows and views of quaint Peneda village across the ravine. There's also a decent restaurant.

Beleza da Serra   GUESTHOUSE €€
(☎ 253 391 457; www.bserra.com; Lugar do Bairro 25, Vilar da Veiga; d/tr €62.50/78.50; ▣❄🐾) A great base for hiking and kayaking, this friendly waterfront guesthouse overlooks the Caniçada Reservoir, 4.5km south of Vila do Gerês. It has simple, clean, comfortable rooms and a restaurant dishing up regional food.

ⓘ Information

The head park office is **Adere-PG** (☑ 258 452 250; www.adere-pg.pt; Largo da Misericórdia 10; ⓧ 9am-12.30pm & 2.30-6pm Mon-Fri) in Ponte de Barca. Obtain park information and reserve cottages and other park accommodation here.

ⓘ Getting There & Away

Because of the lack of transport within the park, it's good to have your own wheels. You can rent cars in Braga (p557).

SURVIVAL GUIDE

ⓘ Directory A–Z

ACCOMMODATION

Portugal offers outstanding value by and large. Budget places provide some of Western Europe's cheapest digs, while you'll find atmospheric accommodation in converted castles, mansions and farmhouses.

Seasons

High season Mid-June to mid-September
Mid-season May to mid-June and mid-September to October
Low season November to April

Ecotourism & Farmstays

Turismo de Habitação (www.turihab.pt) is a private network of historic, heritage or rustic properties, ranging from 17th-century manors to quaint farmhouses or self-catering cottages. Doubles run from €60 to €120.

Pousadas

These are government-run former castles, monasteries or palaces, often in spectacular locations. For details, contact tourist offices or **Pousadas de Portugal** (www.pousadas.pt).

Guesthouses

The most common types are the *residencial* and the *pensão*, usually simple, family-owned

---

COUNTRY FACTS

Area 91,470 sq km

Capital Lisbon

Country Code ☑ 351

Currency Euro (€)

Emergency ☑ 112

Language Portuguese

Money ATMs are widespread; banks open Monday to Friday

Visas Schengen rules apply

---

operations. Some have cheaper rooms with shared bathrooms. Double rooms with private bathroom typically run €40 to €60.

Hostels

Portugal has a growing number of cool backpacker digs, particularly in Lisbon. Nationwide, Portugal has over 30 **pousadas da juventude** (www.pousadasjuventude.pt) within the Hostelling International (HI) system. The average price for a dorm room is about €20.

Camping

For detailed listings of camp sites nationwide, pick up the **Roteiro Campista** (www.roteiro-campista.pt), updated annually and sold at bookshops. Some of the swishest places are run by **Orbitur** (www.orbitur.pt).

BUSINESS HOURS

Opening hours vary throughout the year. We provide high-season opening hours; these hours will generally decrease in the shoulder and low seasons.

Banks 8.30am to 3pm Monday to Friday
Bars 7pm to 2am
Cafes 9am to 7pm
Malls 10am to 10pm
Nightclubs 11pm to 4am Thursday to Saturday
Post offices 8.30am to 4pm Monday to Friday
Restaurants noon to 3pm and 7pm to 10pm
Shops 9.30am to noon and 2pm to 7pm Monday to Friday, 10am to 1pm Saturday

INTERNET RESOURCES

Lonely Planet (www.lonelyplanet.com/portugal)
Portugal Tourism (www.visitportugal.com)

MONEY

There are numerous banks with ATMs located throughout Portugal. Credit cards are accepted

---

SLEEPING PRICE RANGES

The following price ranges refer to a double room with private bathroom in high season. Unless otherwise stated breakfast is included in the price.

€ less than €60

€€ €60 to €120

€€€ more than €120

in midrange and top-end hotels, restaurants and shops.

PUBLIC HOLIDAYS

New Year's Day 1 January

Carnaval Tuesday February/March – the day before Ash Wednesday

Good Friday March/April

Liberty Day 25 April – celebrating the 1974 revolution

Labour Day 1 May

Corpus Christi May/June – 9th Thursday after Easter

Portugal Day 10 June – also known as Camões and Communities Day

Feast of the Assumption 15 August

Republic Day 5 October – commemorating the 1910 declaration of the Portuguese Republic

All Saints' Day 1 November

Independence Day 1 December – commemorating the 1640 restoration of independence from Spain

Feast of the Immaculate Conception 8 December

Christmas Day 25 December

TELEPHONE

Portugal's country code is ☎351. There are no regional area codes. Mobile phone numbers within Portugal have nine digits and begin with ☎9.

For general information, dial ☎118, and for reverse-charge (collect) calls dial ☎120.

Phonecards are sold at post offices, newsagents and tobacconists in denominations of €5 and €10.

ⓘ Getting There & Away

AIR

TAP (www.flytap.com) is Portugal's international flag carrier as well as its main domestic airline. Portugal's main airports:

Faro Airport (FAO; ☎289 800 800; www.ana.pt)

Lisbon Airport (LIS; ☎218 413 500; www.ana.pt)

Porto Airport (OPO; ☎229 432 400; www.ana.pt)

ESSENTIAL FOOD & DRINK

➜ **Seafood** Char-grilled *lulas* (squid), *polvo* (octopus) or *sardinhas* (sardines). Other treats: *cataplana* (seafood and sausage cooked in a copper pot), *caldeirada* (hearty fish stew) and *açorda de mariscos* (bread stew with shrimp).

➜ **Cod for all seasons** The Portuguese have dozens of ways to prepare *bacalhau* (salted cod). Try *bacalhau a brás* (grated cod fried with potatoes and eggs), *bacalhau espiritual* (cod soufflé) or *bacalhau com natas* (baked cod with cream and grated cheese).

➜ **Field & fowl** *Porco preto* (sweet 'black' pork), *leitão* (roast suckling pig), *alheira* (bread and meat sausage – formerly Kosher), *cabrito assado* (roast kid) and *arroz de pato* (duck risotto).

➜ **Drink** Port and red wines from the Douro valley, *alvarinho* and *vinho verde* (crisp, semi-sparkling wine) from the Minho and great, little-known reds from the Alentejo and the Beiras (particularly the Dão region).

➜ **Pastries** The *pastel de nata* (custard tart) is legendary, especially in Belém. Other delicacies: *travesseiros* (almond and egg pastries) and *queijadas* (mini-cheese pastries).

LAND

Bus

UK–Portugal and France–Portugal Eurolines services cross to Portugal via northwest Spain. Some operators:

Alsa (www.alsa.es)

Avanza (www.avanzabus.com)

Damas (www.damas-sa.es)

Eurolines (www.eurolines.com)

Eva (☎289 899 760; www.eva-bus.com)

Train

The most popular train link from Spain is on the Sud Express, operated by **Renfe** (www.renfe.com), which has a nightly sleeper service between Madrid and Lisbon.

Two other Spain–Portugal crossings are at Valença do Minho and at Caia (Caya in Spain), near Elvas.

CONNECTIONS

Travelling overland from Portugal entails a trip through Spain. Good places to cross the (invisible) border include the ferry crossing from Vila Real de Santo António in the Algarve, with onward connections to Seville. There are also links from Elvas (going across to Badajoz) and rail links from Valença do Minho in the north (heading up to Santiago de Compostela in Galicia).

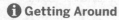 Getting Around

AIR

TAP Portugal (p559) has daily Lisbon–Porto and Lisbon–Faro flights (taking less than one hour) year-round.

BICYCLE

Bicycles can be taken free on all regional and inter-regional trains as accompanied baggage. They can also go on a few suburban services on weekends. Most domestic bus lines won't accept bikes.

BUS

A host of small bus operators, most amalgamated into regional companies, run a dense network of services across the country. Among the largest companies are **Rede Expressos** (☑ 707 223 344; www.rede-expressos.pt), **Rodonorte** (☑ 259 340 710; www.rodonorte.pt) and the Algarve line Eva (p559).

Most bus-station ticket desks will give you a computer printout of fares, and services and schedules are usually posted at major stations.

Classes

Expressos Comfortable, fast buses between major cities

Rápidas Quick regional buses

Carreiras Marked CR, slow, stopping at every crossroad

CAR & MOTORCYCLE
Automobile Associations

Automóvel Clube de Portugal (ACP; ☑ 213 180 100; www.acp.pt) has a reciprocal arrangement with better-known foreign automobile clubs, including AA and RAC. It provides medical, legal and breakdown assistance. The 24-hour emergency help number is ☑ 707 509 510.

Hire

To hire a car in Portugal you must be at least 25 years old and have held your home licence for more than one year. To hire a scooter of up to 50cc you must be over 18 years old and have a valid driving licence.

Road Rules

The various speed limits for cars and motorcycles are 50km/h within cities and public centres, 90km/h on normal roads and 120km/h on motorways.

Drink-driving laws are strict in Portugal, with a maximum legal blood-alcohol level of 0.05%.

TRAIN

Caminhos de Ferro Portugueses (CP; www.cp.pt) is the statewide train network and is generally efficient.

There are four main types of long-distance service. Note that international services are marked 'IN' on timetables.

Regional (marked R on timetables) Slow trains that stop everywhere.

Interregional (IR) Reasonably fast trains.

Intercidade (IC)/**Rápido** Express trains.

Alfa Pendular Deluxe, fastest and most expensive service.

Spain

Best Places to Eat

➡ El Celler de Can Roca (p598)

➡ Simply Fosh (p613)

➡ Tickets (p594)

➡ Arzak (p603)

➡ Mercado de San Miguel (p572)

Best Places to Stay

➡ Hotel Meninas (p568)

➡ Don Gregorio (p580)

➡ Can Cera (p613)

➡ Barceló Raval (p592)

➡ Hospedería La Gran Casa Mudéjar (p581)

Why Go?

Passionate, sophisticated and devoted to living the good life, Spain is at once a stereotype come to life and a country more diverse than you ever imagined.

Spanish landscapes stir the soul, from the jagged Pyrenees and wildly beautiful cliffs of the Atlantic northwest to charming Mediterranean coves, while astonishing architecture spans the ages at seemingly every turn. Spain's cities march to a beguiling beat, rushing headlong into the 21st century even as timeless villages serve as beautiful signposts to Old Spain. And then there's one of Europe's most celebrated (and varied) gastronomic scenes.

But, above all, Spain lives very much in the present. Perhaps you'll sense it along a crowded after-midnight street when all the world has come out to play. Or maybe that moment will come when a flamenco performer touches something deep in your soul. Whenever it happens, you'll find yourself nodding in recognition: *this* is Spain.

When to Go
Madrid

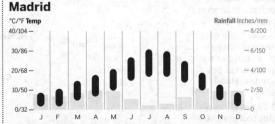

Mar & Apr Spring wildflowers, Semana Santa processions and mild southern temps.

May & Sep Mild and often balmy weather but without the crowds of high summer.

Jun–Aug Spaniards hit the coast in warm weather, but quiet corners still abound.

Spain Highlights

① Explore the **Alhambra** (p624), an exquisite Islamic palace complex in Granada.

② Visit Gaudí's singular work in progress, Barcelona's **La Sagrada Família** (p588), a cathedral that truly defies imagination.

③ Wander amid the horseshoe arches of Córdoba's **Mezquita** (p621), close to perfection wrought in stone.

④ Eat your way through **San Sebastián** (p603), a gourmand's paradise with an idyllic setting.

⑤ Join the pilgrims making their way to magnificent **Santiago de Compostela** (p606).

⑥ Soak up the scent of orange blossom, admire the architecture and surrender to the party atmosphere in sunny **Seville** (p616).

⑦ Discover the impossibly beautiful Mediterranean beaches and coves of **Menorca** (p612).

⑧ Spend your days in some of Europe's best art galleries and nights amid its best nightlife in **Madrid** (p564).

⑨ Be carried away by the soulful strains of live **flamenco** (p575).

ITINERARIES

One Week

Marvel at **Barcelona's** art nouveau–influenced modernista architecture and seaside style before taking the train to **San Sebastián**, with a stop in **Zaragoza** on the way. Head on to **Bilbao** for the Guggenheim Museum and end the trip living it up in **Madrid's** legendary night scene.

One Month

Fly into **Seville** and embark on a route exploring the town and picture-perfect **Ronda**, **Granada** and **Córdoba**. Take the train to **Madrid**, from where you can check out **Toledo**, **Salamanca** and **Segovia**. Make east for the coast and **Valencia**, detour northwest into the postcard-perfect villages of **Aragón** and the **Pyrenees**, then travel east into Catalonia, spending time in **Tarragona** before reaching **Barcelona**. Take a plane or boat for the **Balearic Islands**, from where you can get a flight home.

MADRID

POP 3.26 MILLION

No city on earth is more alive than Madrid, a beguiling place whose sheer energy carries a simple message: *madrileños* (people from Madrid) know how to live. Explore the old streets of the centre, relax in the plazas, soak up the culture in Madrid's excellent art museums, and spend at least one night in the city's legendary nightlife scene.

◉ Sights & Activities

Museo del Prado   MUSEUM
(Map p566; www.museodelprado.es; Paseo del Prado; adult/child €14/free, free 6-8pm Mon-Sat & 5-7pm Sun, audioguides €3.50, admission plus official guidebook €23; ⊙10am-8pm Mon-Sat, 10am-7pm Sun; 🛈; ⓜBanco de España) Welcome to one of the world's premier art galleries. The more than 7000 paintings held in the Museo del Prado's collection (although only around 1500 are currently on display) are like a window onto the historical vagaries of the Spanish soul, at once grand and imperious in the royal paintings of Velázquez, darkly tumultuous in *Las pinturas negras* (The Black Paintings) of Goya, yet also outward-looking with sophisticated works of art from all across Europe.

Museo Thyssen-Bornemisza   MUSEUM
(Map p570; ☑902 760511; www.museothyssen. org; Paseo del Prado 8; adult/concession/child €10/7/free, Mon free; ⊙10am-7pm Tue-Sun, noon-4pm Mon; ⓜBanco de España) The Thyssen is one of the most extraordinary private collections of predominantly European art in the world. Where the Prado or Reina Sofía enable you to study the body of work of a particular artist in depth, the Thyssen is the place to immerse yourself in a breathtaking breadth of artistic styles. Most of the big names are here, sometimes with just a single painting, but the Thyssen's gift to Madrid and the art-loving public is to have them all under one roof.

Centro de Arte
Reina Sofía   MUSEUM
(Map p570; ☑91 774 10 00; www.museoreina sofia.es; Calle de Santa Isabel 52; adult/concession €8/free, free Sun, 7-9pm Mon & Wed-Sat; ⊙10am-9pm Mon, Wed, Thu & Sat, 10am-7pm Sun, closed Tue; ⓜAtocha) Home to Picasso's *Guernica*, arguably Spain's single most famous artwork, the Centro de Arte Reina Sofía is Madrid's premier collection of contemporary art. In addition to plenty of paintings by Picasso, other major drawcards are works by Salvador Dalí (1904–89) and Joan Miró (1893–1983). The collection principally spans the 20th century up to the 1980s. The occasional non-Spaniard artist makes an appearance (including Francis Bacon's *Lying Figure;* 1966), but most of the collection is strictly peninsular.

Caixa Forum   MUSEUM, ARCHITECTURE
(Map p570; www.fundacio.lacaixa.es; Paseo del Prado 36; ⊙10am-8pm; ⓜAtocha) **FREE** This extraordinary structure is one of Madrid's most eye-catching landmarks. Seeming to hover above the ground, this brick edifice is topped by an intriguing summit of rusted iron. On an adjacent wall is the *jardín colgante* (hanging garden), a lush vertical wall of greenery almost four storeys high. Inside there are four floors of exhibition and performance space awash in stainless steel and with soaring ceilings. The exhibitions here are always worth checking out and include

photography, contemporary painting and multimedia shows.

Palacio Real PALACE

(Map p566; ☎91 454 88 00; www.patrimonio nacional.es; Calle de Bailén; adult/concession €10/5, guide/audioguide/pamphlet €7/4/1, EU citizens free last 3 hours Mon-Thu; ⊙10am-8pm Apr-Sep, to 6pm Oct-Mar; ⓂÓpera) Spain's lavish Palacio Real is a jewel box of a palace, although it's used only occasionally for royal ceremonies; the royal family moved to the modest Palacio de la Zarzuela years ago.

When the Alcázar burned down on Christmas Day 1734, Felipe V, the first of the Bourbon kings, decided to build a palace that would dwarf all of its European counterparts. Felipe died before the palace was finished, which is perhaps why the Italianate baroque colossus has a mere 2800 rooms, just one-quarter of the original plan.

Plaza Mayor SQUARE

(Map p570; Plaza Mayor; ⓂSol) Madrid's grand central square, a rare but expansive opening in the tightly packed streets of central Madrid, is one of the prettiest open spaces in Spain, a winning combination of imposing architecture, picaresque historical tales and vibrant street life coursing across its cobblestones. At once beautiful in its own right and a reference point for so many Madrid days, it also hosts the city's main tourist office (p577), a Christmas market in December and arches leading to many laneways that lead out into the labyrinth.

★Parque del Buen Retiro GARDENS

(Map p566; ⊙6am-midnight May-Sep, to 11pm Oct-Apr; ⓂRetiro, Príncipe de Vergara, Ibiza, Atocha) The glorious gardens of El Retiro are as beautiful as any you'll find in a European city. Littered with marble monuments, landscaped lawns, the occasional elegant building (the Palacio de Cristal is especially worth seeking out) and abundant greenery, it's quiet and contemplative during the week but comes to life on weekends. Put simply, this is one of our favourite places in Madrid.

Ermita de San Antonio de la Florida GALLERY

(Map p566; Glorieta de San Antonio de la Florida 5; ⊙9.30am-8pm Tue-Sun, hours vary Jul & Aug; ⓂPríncipe Pío) `FREE` The frescoed ceilings of the Ermita de San Antonio de la Florida

---

MUSEO DEL PRADO ITINERARY: ICONS OF SPANISH ART

The Museo del Prado collection can be overwhelming in scope, but if your time is limited, zero in on the museum's peerless collection of Spanish art.

Francisco José de Goya y Lucientes (Goya) is found on all three floors of the Prado, but we recommend starting at the southern end of the ground or lower level. In room 65, Goya's *El dos de mayo* and *El tres de mayo* rank among Madrid's most emblematic paintings; they bring to life the 1808 anti-French revolt and subsequent execution of insurgents in Madrid. Alongside, in rooms 67 and 68, are some of his darkest and most disturbing works, *Las pinturas negras;* they are so called in part because of the dark browns and black that dominate, but more for the distorted animalesque appearance of their characters.

There are more Goyas on the 1st floor in rooms 34 to 37. Among them are two more of Goya's best-known and most intriguing oils: *La maja vestida* and *La maja desnuda*. These portraits, in room 36, of an unknown woman, commonly believed to be the Duquesa de Alba (who may have been Goya's lover), are identical save for the lack of clothing in the latter. There are further Goyas on the top floor.

Having studied the works of Goya, turn your attention to Velázquez. Of all his works, *Las meninas* (room 12) is what most people come to see. Completed in 1656, it is more properly known as *La fam/lia de Felipe IV* (The Family of Felipe IV). The rooms surrounding *Las meninas* contain more fine works by Velázquez: watch in particular for his paintings of various members of royalty who seem to spring off the canvas – Felipe II, Felipe IV, Margarita de Austria (a younger version of whom features in *Las meninas*), El Príncipe Baltasar Carlos and Isabel de Francia – on horseback. In room 9a, seek out his masterful *La Rendición de Breda*.

Further, Bartolomé Esteban Murillo (room 17), José de Ribera (room 9), the stark figures of Francisco de Zurbarán (room 10a) and the vivid, almost surreal works of El Greco (room 8b) should all be on your itinerary.

Madrid

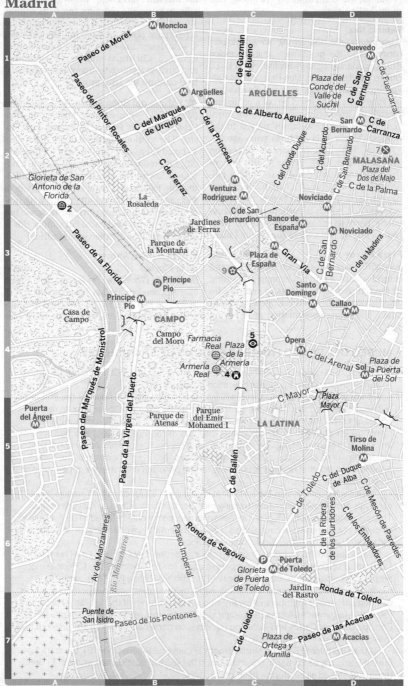

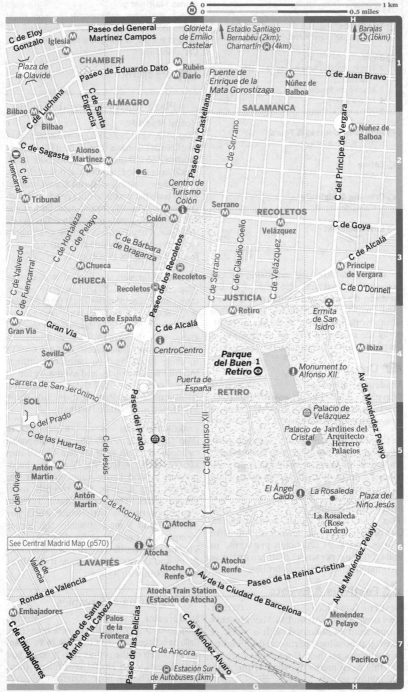

Madrid

are one of Madrid's most surprising secrets. Recently restored and also known as the **Panteón de Goya**, the southern of the two small chapels is one of the few places to see Goya's work in its original setting, as painted by the master in 1798 on the request of Carlos IV. Simply breathtaking.

📖 Courses

Academia Inhispania   LANGUAGE COURSE
(Map p570; ☎91 521 22 31; www.inhispania.com; Calle Marqués de Valdeiglesias 3; Ⓜ Sol) Intensive four-week courses start at €525.

Academia Madrid Plus   LANGUAGE COURSE
(Map p570; ☎91 548 11 16; www.madridplus.es; 6th fl, Calle del Arenal 21; Ⓜ Ópera) Four-week courses start from €340, and go up to €800 for intensive courses.

International House   LANGUAGE COURSE
(Map p566; ☎902 141517; www.ihmadrid.es; Calle de Zurbano 8; Ⓜ Alonso Martínez) Intensive courses cost €594 (20 hours per week) to €804 (30 hours per week). Staff can organise accommodation with local families.

🎊 Festivals & Events

Fiesta de San Isidro   CULTURAL
(www.esmadrid.com) Around 15 May Madrid's patron saint is honoured with a week of nonstop processions, parties and bullfights. Free concerts are held throughout the city, and this week marks the start of the city's bullfighting season.

Suma Flamenca   FLAMENCO
(www.madrid.org/sumaflamenca) A soul-filled flamenco festival that draws some of the biggest names in the genre to the Teatros del Canal in June.

🛏️ Sleeping

🛏️ Plaza Mayor & Royal Madrid

Hostal Madrid   HOSTAL, APARTMENT €
(Map p570; ☎91 522 00 60; www.hostal-madrid. info; Calle de Esparteros 6; s €35-62, d €45-78, d apt per night €55-150, per month €1200-2500; ✳️🖂; Ⓜ Sol) Economic crisis or no economic crisis, the 24 rooms at this well-run *hostal* (budget hotel) have been wonderfully renovated with exposed brickwork, brand-new bathrooms and a look that puts many three-star hotels to shame. They also have terrific apartments (some recently renovated and ranging in size from 33 sq metres to 200 sq metres).

★**Hotel Meninas**   BOUTIQUE HOTEL €€
(Map p570; ☎91 541 28 05; www.hotelmeninas. com; Calle de Campomanes 7; s/d from €89/109; ✳️🖂; Ⓜ Ópera) This is a classy, cool choice. The colour scheme is blacks, whites and greys, with dark-wood floors and splashes of fuchsia and lime green. Flat-screen TVs in every room, modern bathroom fittings, internet access points, and even a laptop in some rooms, round out the clean lines and latest innovations. Past guests include Viggo Mortensen and Natalie Portman.

Praktik Metropol   BOUTIQUE HOTEL €€
(Map p570; ☎91 521 29 35; www.hotelpraktik metropol.com; Calle de la Montera 47; s/d from €65/79; ✳️🖂; Ⓜ Gran Vía) You'd be hard-pressed to find better value anywhere in Europe than here in this recently over-hauled hotel. The rooms have a fresh, contemporary look with white wood furnishings, and some (especially the corner rooms) have brilliant views down to Gran Vía and out over the city. It's spread over six floors and there's a roof terrace if you don't have a room with a view.

🛏️ La Latina & Lavapiés

Mad Hostel   HOSTEL €
(Map p570; ☎91 506 48 40; www.madhostel.com; Calle de la Cabeza 24; dm €16-23; ✳️@🖂; Ⓜ Antón Martín) From the people who brought you Cat's Hostel, Mad Hostel is similarly filled with life. The 1st-floor courtyard – with

retractable roof – recreates an old Madrid *corrala* (traditional internal or communal patio) and is a wonderful place to chill, while the four- to eight-bed rooms are smallish but clean. There's a small, rooftop gym.

★ Posada del León de Oro
BOUTIQUE HOTEL €€

(Map p570; ☑ 91 119 14 94; www.posadadelleon deoro.com; Calle de la Cava Baja 12; r from €121; ✲ 🛜; Ⓜ La Latina) This rehabilitated inn has muted colour schemes and generally large rooms. There's a *corrala* in its core, and thoroughly modern rooms along one of Madrid's best-loved streets. The downstairs bar is terrific.

🛏 Sol, Santa Ana & Huertas

★ Hotel Alicia
BOUTIQUE HOTEL €€

(Map p570; ☑ 91 389 60 95; www.room-mate hoteles.com; Calle del Prado 2; d €100-175, ste from €200; ✲ 🛜; Ⓜ Sol, Sevilla, Antón Martín) One of the landmark properties of the designer Room Mate chain of hotels, Hotel Alicia overlooks Plaza de Santa Ana with beautiful, spacious rooms. The style (the work of designer Pascua Ortega) is a touch more muted than in other Room Mate hotels, but the supermodern look remains intact, the

downstairs bar is oh-so-cool, and the service is young and switched on.

🛏 Malasaña & Chueca

Life Hotel
HOTEL €

(Map p570; ☑ 91 531 42 96; www.antiguaposada delpez.com; Calle de Pizarro 16; s/d from €39/55; ✲ 🛜; Ⓜ Noviciado) If only all places to stay were this good. This place inhabits the shell of an historic Malasaña building, but the rooms are slick and contemporary with designer bathrooms. You're also just a few steps up the hill from Calle del Pez, one of Malasaña's most happening streets. It's an exceptionally good deal, even when prices head upwards.

★ Only You Hotel
BOUTIQUE HOTEL €€

(Map p570; ☑ 91 005 22 22; www.onlyyouhotels. com; Calle de Barquillo 21; d from €157; ✲ @ 🛜; Ⓜ Chueca) This stunning new boutique hotel makes perfect use of a 19th-century Chueca mansion. The look is classy and contemporary and is the latest project by respected interior designer Lázaro Rosa Violán. Nice touches include all-day à la carte breakfasts and a portable router that you can carry with you out into the city to stay connected.

MADRID'S BEST PLAZAS

A royal palace that once had aspirations to be the Spanish Versailles. Sophisticated cafes watched over by apartments that cost the equivalent of a royal salary. The **Teatro Real** (Map p570; ☑ 902 24 48 48; www.teatro-real.com; Plaza de Oriente; Ⓜ Ópera), Madrid's opera house and one of Spain's temples to high culture. Some of the finest sunset views in Madrid... Welcome to **Plaza de Oriente** (Map p566; Ⓜ Ópera), a living, breathing monument to imperial Madrid.

On the other hand, the intimate **Plaza de la Villa** (Map p570; Ⓜ Ópera) is one of Madrid's prettiest. Enclosed on three sides by wonderfully preserved examples of 17th-century barroco *madrileño* (Madrid-style baroque architecture – a pleasing amalgam of brick, exposed stone and wrought iron), it was the permanent seat of Madrid's city government from the Middle Ages until recent years, when Madrid's city council relocated to the grand Palacio de Cibeles on **Plaza de la Cibeles** (Map p570; Ⓜ Banco de España).

Plaza de Santa Ana (Map p570; Ⓜ Sevilla, Sol, Antón Martín) is a delightful confluence of elegant architecture and irresistible energy. It presides over the upper reaches of the Barrio de las Letras and this literary personality makes its presence felt with the statues of the 17th-century writers Calderón de la Barca and Federico García Lorca, and in the **Teatro Español** (Map p570; ☑ 91 360 14 84; www.teatroespanol.es; Calle del Príncipe 25; Ⓜ Sevilla, Sol, Antón Martín), formerly the Teatro del Príncipe, at the plaza's eastern end. Apart from anything else, the plaza is the starting point for many a long Huertas night.

Central Madrid

400 m
0.2 miles

G
Plaza de la Villa de Paris
C de Bárbara de Braganza
C de Piamonte
C del Almirante
C de Prim
Paseo de los Recoletos
Paseo del Prado
Paseo del Prado
⊙5
C de Alcalá
Banco de España
C de Marqués de Cubas
C de Zorrilla

F
Plaza de las Salesas
C de Fernando VI
C de Santo Tomé
C de Bárbara de Braganza
⊙31
C de Belén
C de San Gregorio
C de San Lucas
C de Gravina
CHUECA
⊟15
C de Augusto Figueroa
C de Barquillo
Plaza del Rey
C del Marqués del Valdeiglesias
C de los Madrazo
C de Marqués de Cubas
C de Zorrilla

E
C de la Santa Brígida
C de la Farmacia
C de Hortaleza
C de Pelayo
Chueca Ⓜ
C de Chueca
Plaza de Chueca
⊗19
C de San Marcos
C de San Bartolomé
C de la Libertad
Plaza de Vásquez de Mella
C de las Infantas
8
C del Marqués del Valdeiglesias
C de la Reina
Gran Vía
36
C del Clavel
C del Caballero de Gracia
C de la Virgen de los Peligros
Sevilla Ⓜ
C de los Cedaceros
C de Alcalá
Sevilla Ⓜ
C de Arlabán

D
C Santa Bárbara
C de Colón
C de Valverde
C de Fuencarral
C de Hortaleza
C de Hernán Cortés
Gran Vía
C del Valverde
Ⓜ17
Plaza de la Red de San Luis
⊗42
C de los Jardines
CENTRO
C de la Aduana
C de la Montera
C de Alcalá
Carrera de San Jerónimo

C
C de Andrés Borrego
C de la Madera
C del Pez
C de Pizarro
⊗13
C del Barco
C de la Puebla
C de la Corredera Baja de San Pablo
C del Molino de Viento
C de San Roque
Plaza de Santa María Soledad
C del Barco
C de la Salud
C de Tudescos
Gran Vía
C de la Abada
C de Chinchilla
Plaza del Carmen
C del Carmen
C de Preciados
⊗21
Sol Ⓜ
C del Maestro Victoria
Travesía del Arenal
⊗39

B
MALASAÑA
C de Manzana
C de Antonio Grilo
C García Molinos
C de San Bernardo
Noviciado Ⓜ
C Poza
C de las Mi
C Jesús del Valle
C del Marqués de Leganés
C de la Flor Alta
Plaza de Santo Domingo
C de Santo Domingo
C de la Luna
C de Silva
Callao Ⓜ
Plaza del Callao
C del Callao
C de Preciados
C Conchas
Plaza de San Martín
Plaza de las Descalzas
32
C del Arenal
C de los Coloreros

A
España Ⓜ
C de los Reyes
Banco de España
Cuesta de San Vicente
C de la Princesa
Gran Vía
C de Isabel la Católica
⊟46
C de Leganitos
C del Fomento
C de Torija
C de la Bola
⊗29
C del Reloj
C de Campomanes
12
Cuesta de Santo Domingo
C de Arrieta
⊗44
Ópera Ⓜ
9
48
C de Vergara
C de San Nicolás

1 2 3 4

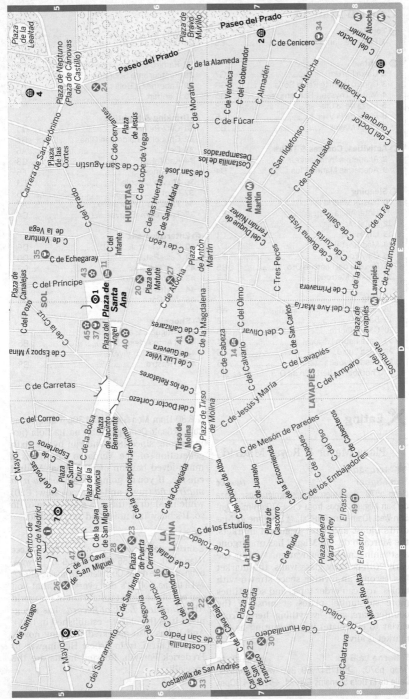

Eating

Plaza Mayor & Royal Madrid

★ Mercado de San Miguel
TAPAS €€

(Map p570; www.mercadodesanmiguel.es; Plaza de San Miguel; tapas from €1; ◷10am-midnight Sun-Wed, 10am-2am Thu-Sat; Ⓜ Sol) One of Madrid's oldest and most beautiful markets, the Mercado de San Miguel has undergone a stunning major renovation. Within the early-20th-century glass walls, the market has become an inviting space strewn with tables. You can order tapas and sometimes more substantial plates at most of the counter-bars, and everything here (from caviar to chocolate) is as tempting as the market is alive.

Taberna La Bola
MADRILEÑO €€

(Map p570; ☎91 547 69 30; www.labola.es; Calle de la Bola 5; mains €16-24; ◷1.30-4.30pm & 8.30-11pm Mon-Sat, 1.30-4.30pm Sun, closed Aug; Ⓜ Santo Domingo) Taberna La Bola (going strong since 1870 and run by the sixth generation of the Verdasco family) is a much-loved bastion of traditional Madrid cuisine. If you're going to try *cocido a la madrileña* (meat-and-chickpea stew; €20) while in Madrid, this is a good place to do so. It's busy and noisy and very Madrid.

★ Restaurante Sobrino de Botín
CASTILIAN €€€

(Map p570; ☎91 366 42 17, 91 366 42 17; www.botin.es; Calle de los Cuchilleros 17; mains €19-27; Ⓜ La Latina, Sol) It's not every day that you can eat in the oldest restaurant in the world (the *Guinness Book of Records* has recognised it as the oldest – established in 1725). And it has also appeared in many novels about Madrid, from Ernest Hemingway to Frederick Forsyth. Roasted meats are the speciality.

La Latina & Lavapiés

**Enotaberna del
León de Oro** SPANISH €€
(Map p570; ☎91 119 14 94; www.posadadel
leondeoro.com; Calle de la Cava Baja 12; mains

€13-18; ⊙1-4pm & 8pm-midnight daily; Ⓜ La
Latina) The stunning restoration work that
brought to life the Posada del León de Oro
(p569) also bequeathed to La Latina a
fine new bar-restaurant. The emphasis is
on matching carefully chosen wines with

A TAPAS TOUR OF MADRID

Madrid's home of tapas is La Latina, especially along Calle de la Cava Baja and the surrounding streets.

Almendro 13 (Map p570; ☎91 365 42 52; Calle del Almendro 13; mains €7-15; ⊙12.30-4pm & 7.30pm-midnight Sun-Thu, 12.30-5pm & 8pm-1am Fri & Sat; Ⓜ La Latina) Almendro 13 is a charming, wildly popular *taberna* (tavern) where you come for traditional Spanish tapas with an emphasis on quality rather than frilly elaborations. Cured meats, cheeses, omelettes and many variations on these themes dominate the menu – a full *racion* of the famously good *huevos rotos* (literally, 'broken eggs') served with *jamón* (ham) and thin potato slices is a meal in itself.

Juana La Loca (Map p570; ☎91 364 05 25; Plaza de la Puerta de Moros 4; tapas from €4.50, mains €8-19; ⊙noon-1am Tue-Sun, 8pm-1am Mon; Ⓜ La Latina) Juana La Loca does a range of creative tapas with tempting options lined up along the bar, and more on the menu that they prepare to order. But we love it above all for its *tortilla de patatas* (potato and onion omelette), which is distinguished from others of its kind by the caramelised onions – simply wonderful.

Txirimiri (Map p570; ☎91 364 11 96; www.txirimiri.es; Calle del Humilladero 6; tapas from €4; ⊙noon-4.30pm & 8.30pm-midnight, closed Aug; Ⓜ La Latina) This *pintxo* (Basque tapas) bar is a great little discovery just down from the main La Latina tapas circuit. Wonderful wines, gorgeous *pinchos* (tapas; the *tortilla de patatas* is superb) and fine risottos add up to a pretty special combination.

Casa Revuelta (Map p570; ☎91 366 33 32; Calle de Latoneros 3; tapas from €2.60; ⊙10.30am-4pm & 7-11pm Tue-Sat, 10.30am-4pm Sun, closed Aug; Ⓜ Sol, La Latina) Casa Revuelta puts out some of Madrid's finest tapas of *bacalao* (cod) bar none – the fact that the octogenarian owner, Señor Revuelta, painstakingly extracts every fish bone in the morning and serves as a waiter in the afternoon wins the argument for us. Early on a Sunday afternoon, as the Rastro crowd gathers here, it's filled to the rafters.

Casa Labra (Map p570; ☎91 532 14 05; www.casalabra.es; Calle de Tetuán 11; tapas from €0.90; ⊙9.30am-3.30pm & 5.30-11pm; Ⓜ Sol) Casa Labra has been going strong since 1860, an era that the decor strongly evokes. Locals love their *bacalao* and ordering it here – either as deep-fried tapas (*una tajada de bacalao* goes for €1.30) or as *una croqueta de bacalao* (€0.90 per croquette) – is a Madrid rite of initiation. As the lunchtime queues attest, they go through more than 700kg of cod every week.

Ramiro's Tapas Wine Bar (Map p570; ☎91 843 73 47; Calle de Atocha 51; tapas from €4.50, raciones from €10; ⊙1-4.30pm & 8-11.30pm Mon-Sat, 1-4.30pm Sun; Ⓜ Antón Martín) One of the best tapas bars to open in Madrid in recent years, this fine gastrobar offers up traditional tapas with subtle but original touches. Most of the cooking comes from Castilla y León but they do exceptional things with cured meats, foie gras and prawns.

Estado Puro (Map p570; ☎91 330 24 00; www.tapasenestadopuro.com; Plaza Neptuno (Plaza de Cánovas del Castillo) 4; tapas €2-12.50; ⊙noon-midnight Mon-Sat, to 4pm Sun; Ⓜ Banco de España, Atocha) Most places to eat along or around the Paseo del Prado are either tourist traps or upmarket temples to fine dining, but this place bucks the trend. A slick but casual tapas bar attached to the NH Paseo del Prado hotel, Estado Puro serves up fantastic tapas, many of which have their origins in Catalonia's world-famous El Bulli restaurant, such as the *tortilla española siglo XXI* (21st-century Spanish omelette, served in a glass).

creative dishes (such as baby squid with potato emulsion and rucula pesto) in a casual atmosphere. It's a winning combination.

Casa Lucio SPANISH €€
(Map p570; ☑91 365 32 52; www.casalucio.es; Calle de la Cava Baja 35; mains €10-30; ☉1-4pm & 8.30pm-midnight Sun-Fri, 8.30pm-midnight Sat, closed Aug; ⓂLa Latina) Lucio has been wowing *madrileños* with his light touch, quality ingredients and home-style local cooking for ages – think roasted meats and, a Lucio speciality, eggs in abundance. There's also *rabo de toro* (bull's tail) during the Fiestas de San Isidro Labrador and plenty of *rioja* (red wine) to wash away the mere thought of it. The lunchtime *guisos del día* (stews of the day), including *cocido* on Wednesdays, are also popular.

Sol, Santa Ana & Huertas

★Casa Alberto SPANISH, TAPAS €€
(Map p570; ☑91 429 93 56; www.casaalberto.es; Calle de las Huertas 18; tapas from €3.25, raciones €8.50-16, mains €14-21; ☉1.30-4pm & 8pm-midnight Tue-Sat, 1.30-4pm Sun; ⓂAntón Martín) One of the most atmospheric old *tabernas* of Madrid, Casa Alberto has been around since 1827. The secret to its staying power is vermouth on tap, excellent tapas at the bar and fine sit-down meals; Casa Alberto's *rabo de toro* is famous among aficionados.

Malasaña & Chueca

Bazaar CONTEMPORARY SPANISH €
(Map p570; www.restaurantbazaar.com; Calle de la Libertad 21; mains €6.50-10; ☉1.15-4pm & 8.30-11.30pm Sun-Wed, 1.15-4pm & 8.15pm-midnight Thu-Sat; ⓂChueca) Bazaar's popularity among the well heeled and famous shows no sign of abating. Its pristine white interior design, with theatre-style lighting and wall-length windows, may draw a crowd that looks like it stepped out of the pages of *Hola!* magazine, but the food is extremely well priced and innovative and the atmosphere is casual.

Albur TAPAS, SPANISH €€
(Map p566; ☑91 594 27 33; www.restaurantealbur.com; Calle de Manuela Malasaña 15; mains €13-18; ☉12.30-5pm & 7.30pm-1am Mon-Thu, 12.30-5pm & 7.30pm-2am Fri, 12.30pm-2am Sat, 12.30pm-1am Sun; ⓂBilbao) One of Malasaña's best deals, this place has a wildly popular tapas bar and a classy but casual restaurant out the back. Albur is known for terrific rice dishes and tapas, and has a well-chosen wine list. The restaurant waiters never seem to lose their cool, and their extremely well-priced rice dishes are the stars of the show, although in truth you could order anything here and leave well satisfied.

🍷 Drinking & Nightlife

The essence of Madrid lives in its streets and plazas, and bar-hopping is a pastime enjoyed by young and old alike. If you're after the more traditional, with tiled walls and flamenco tunes, head to Huertas. For gay-friendly drinking holes, Chueca is the place. Malasaña caters to a grungy, funky crowd, while La Latina has friendly bars that guarantee atmosphere most nights of the week. In summer, the terrace bars that pop up all over the city are unbeatable.

The bulk of Madrid bars open until 2am Sundays to Thursdays, and till 3am or 3.30am Fridays and Saturdays. Don't expect dance clubs or *discotecas* (nightclubs) to get going until after 1am at the earliest. Standard entry fee is €12, which usually includes the first drink, although megaclubs and swankier places charge a few euros more.

★La Venencia BAR
(Map p570; ☑91 429 73 13; Calle de Echegaray 7; ☉1-3.30pm & 7.30pm-1.30am; ⓂSol, Sevilla) La Venencia is a *barrio* (district) classic, with fine sherry from Sanlúcar and manzanilla from Jeréz poured straight from the dusty wooden barrels, accompanied by a small selection of tapas with an Andalucian bent. Otherwise, there's no music, no flashy decorations; it's all about you, your *fino* (sherry) and your friends. As one reviewer put it, it's 'a classic among classics'.

Museo Chicote COCKTAIL BAR
(Map p570; www.museo-chicote.com; Gran Vía 12; ☉5pm-3am Mon-Thu, to 3.30am Fri & Sat; ⓂGran Vía) The founder of this Madrid landmark (complete with 1930s-era interior) is said to have invented more than 100 cocktails, which the likes of Hemingway, Ava Gardner, Grace Kelly, Sophia Loren and Frank Sinatra have all enjoyed at one time or another. It's at its best after midnight, when a lounge atmosphere takes over, couples cuddle on the curved benches and some of the city's best DJs do their thing.

Café Comercial　　　　CAFE
(Map p566; Glorieta de Bilbao 7; ⊘7.30am-midnight Mon-Thu, 7.30am-2am Fri, 8.30am-2am Sat, 9am-midnight Sun; ☎; Ⓜ Bilbao) This glorious old Madrid cafe proudly fights a rearguard action against progress with heavy leather seats, abundant marble and old-style waiters. It dates back to 1887 and has changed little since those days, although the clientele has broadened to include just about anyone, from writers and their laptops to old men playing chess.

Teatro Joy Eslava　　　　CLUB
(Joy Madrid; Map p570; ☎91 366 37 33; www.joy-eslava.com; Calle del Arenal 11; admission €12-15; ⊘11.30pm-6am; Ⓜ Sol) The only things guaranteed at this grand old Madrid dance club (housed in a 19th-century theatre) are a crowd and the fact that it'll be open (it claims to have operated every single day for the past 29 years). The music and the crowd are a mixed bag, but queues are long and invariably include locals and tourists, and even the occasional *famoso* (celebrity). Every night's a little different.

Delic　　　　BAR
(Map p570; www.delic.es; Costanilla de San Andrés 14; ⊘11.30am-midnight Mon-Fri, 1.30pm-midnight Sat; Ⓜ La Latina) We could go on for hours about this long-standing cafe-bar, but we'll reduce it to its most basic elements: nursing an exceptionally good mojito (€8) or three on a warm summer's evening at Delic's outdoor tables on one of Madrid's prettiest plazas is one of life's great pleasures. Bliss.

Taberna Tempranillo　　　　WINE BAR
(Map p570; Calle de la Cava Baja 38; ⊘1-3.30pm & 8pm-midnight Tue-Sun, 8pm-midnight Mon; Ⓜ La Latina) You could come here for the tapas, but we recommend Taberna Tempranillo primarily for its wines, of which it has a selection that puts many Spanish bars to shame, and many are sold by the glass. It's not a late-night place, but it's always packed in the early evening and on Sundays after El Rastro.

Roof　　　　COCKTAIL BAR
(Map p570; ☎91 701 60 20; www.memadrid.com; Plaza de Santa Ana 14; admission €25; ⊘9pm-1.30am Mon-Thu, 8pm-3am Fri & Sat; Ⓜ Antón Martín, Sol) High above the Plaza de Santa Ana, this sybaritic open-air (7th-floor) cocktail bar has terrific views over Madrid's rooftops. The high admission price announces straight away that riff-raff are not welcome and it's

a place for sophisticates, with chill-out areas strewn with cushions, funky DJs and a dress policy designed to sort out the classy from the wannabes. If you suffer from vertigo, consider the equally classy **Midnight Rose** on the ground floor.

Café Belén　　　　BAR
(Map p570; Calle de Belén 5; ⊘3.30pm-2am Sun-Thu, 3.30pm-3.30am Fri & Sat; Ⓜ Chueca) Café Belén is cool in all the right places – lounge and chill-out music, dim lighting, a great range of drinks (the mojitos are especially good) and a low-key crowd that's the height of casual sophistication. In short, it's one of our favourite Chueca watering holes.

Kapital　　　　CLUB
(Map p570; ☎91 420 29 06; www.grupo-kapital.com; Calle de Atocha 125; admission from €18; ⊘5.30-10.30pm & midnight-6am Fri & Sat, midnight-6am Thu & Sun; Ⓜ Atocha) One of the most famous megaclubs in Madrid, this seven-storey club has something for everyone: from cocktail bars and dance music to karaoke, salsa, hip hop and more chilled spaces for R&B and soul, as well as an area devoted to 'Made in Spain' music. It's such a big place that a cross-section of Madrid society (VIPs and the Real Madrid set love this place) hangs out here without ever getting in each other's way.

☆ Entertainment
Flamenco
Las Tablas　　　　FLAMENCO
(Map p566; ☎91 542 05 20; www.lastablasmadrid.com; Plaza de España 9; admission incl drink €27; ⊘8pm & 10pm; Ⓜ Plaza de España) Las Tablas has a reputation for quality flamenco and reasonable prices; it could just be the best choice in town. Most nights you'll see a classic flamenco show, with

plenty of throaty singing and soul-baring dancing. Antonia Moya and Marisol Navarro, leading lights in the flamenco world, are regular performers here.

Casa Patas   FLAMENCO

(Map p570; ☑ 91 369 04 96; www.casapatas.com; Calle de Cañizares 10; admission incl drink €34; ◉ shows 10.30pm Mon-Thu, 9pm & midnight Fri & Sat; Ⓜ Antón Martín, Tirso de Molina) One of the top flamenco stages in Madrid, this *tablao* (flamenco venue) always offers flawless quality that serves as a good introduction to the art. It's not the friendliest place in town, especially if you're only here for the show, and you're likely to be crammed in a little, but no one complains about the standard of the performances.

Villa Rosa   FLAMENCO

(Map p570; ☑ 91 521 36 89; www.tablaoflamenco villarosa.com; Plaza de Santa Ana 15; admission €32; ◉ 11pm-6am Mon-Sat, shows 8.30pm & 10.45pm Sun-Thu, 8.30pm, 10.45pm & 12.15am Fri & Sat; Ⓜ Sol) The extraordinary tiled facade (the 1928 work of Alfonso Romero, who was responsible for the tile work in Madrid's Plaza de Toros) of this long-standing nightclub is a tourist attraction in itself; the club even appeared in the Pedro Almodóvar film *Tacones Lejanos* (High Heels; 1991). It's been going strong since 1914 and has seen many manifestations – it made its name as a flamenco venue and has recently returned to its roots with well-priced shows and meals that won't break the bank.

Jazz & Other Live Music

★ Café Central   JAZZ

(Map p570; ☑ 91 369 41 43; www.cafecentral madrid.com; Plaza del Ángel 10; admission €12-18; ◉ 12.30pm-2.30am Sun-Thu, 12.30pm-3.30am Fri & Sat; Ⓜ Antón Martín, Sol) In 2011, the respected jazz magazine *Down Beat* included this art-deco bar on the list of the world's best jazz clubs, the only place in Spain to earn the prestigious accolade (said by some to be the jazz equivalent of earning a Michelin star) and with well over 9000 gigs under its belt, it rarely misses a beat.

★ Sala El Sol   LIVE MUSIC

(Map p570; ☑ 91 532 64 90; www.elsolmad.com; Calle de los Jardines 3; admission incl drink €10, concert tickets €8-25; ◉ midnight-5.30am Tue-Sat Jul-Sep; Ⓜ Gran Vía) Madrid institutions don't come any more beloved than Sala El Sol. It opened in 1979, just in time for *la movida madrileña,* and quickly established itself as a leading stage for all the icons of the era, such as Nacha Pop and Alaska y los Pegamoides. *La movida* may have faded into history, but it lives on at El Sol, where the music rocks and rolls and usually resurrects the '70s and '80s, while soul and funk also get a run.

Sport

Estadio Santiago Bernabéu   FOOTBALL

(☑ 91 398 43 00, 902 291709; www.realmadrid. com; Avenida de Concha Espina 1; tour adult/child €19/13; ◉ 10am-7pm Mon-Sat, 10.30am-6.30pm Sun, except match days; Ⓜ Santiago Bernabéu) The home of **Real Madrid**, Estadio Santiago Bernabéu is a temple to football and is one of the world's great sporting arenas. For a self-guided **tour** of the stadium, buy your ticket at ticket window 10 (next to gate 7). Tickets for matches start at around €40 and can be bought online at www.real madrid.com, while the all-important telephone number for booking tickets (which you later pick up at gate 42) is ☑ 902 324 324, which only works if you're calling from within Spain.

🛍 Shopping

El Rastro   MARKET

(Map p570; Calle de la Ribera de Curtidores; ◉ 8am-3pm Sun; Ⓜ La Latina, Puerta de Toledo, Tirso de Molina) A Sunday morning at El Rastro is a Madrid institution. You could easily spend an entire morning inching your way down the Calle de la Ribera de Curtidores and through the maze of streets that hosts El Rastro flea market every Sunday morning. Cheap clothes, luggage, old flamenco records, even older photos of Madrid, faux designer purses, grungy T-shirts, household goods and electronics are the main fare. For every 10 pieces of junk, there's a real gem (a lost masterpiece, an Underwood typewriter) waiting to be found.

A word of warning: pickpockets love El Rastro as much as everyone else, so keep a tight hold on your belongings and don't keep valuables in easy-to-reach pockets.

Antigua Casa Talavera   CERAMICS

(Map p570; Calle de Isabel la Católica 2; ◉ 10am-1.30pm & 5-8pm Mon-Fri, 10am-1.30pm Sat; Ⓜ Santo Domingo) The extraordinary tiled facade of this wonderful old shop conceals an Aladdin's cave of ceramics from all over Spain. This is not the mass-produced stuff aimed at a tourist market, but comes from the small family potters of Andalucía and

Toledo, ranging from the decorative (tiles) to the useful (plates, jugs and other kitchen items). The old couple who run the place are delightful.

El Arco Artesanía   HANDICRAFTS

(Map p570; www.artesaniaelarco.com; Plaza Mayor 9; ⊙11am-9pm; M Sol, La Latina) This original shop in the southwestern corner of Plaza Mayor sells an outstanding array of home-made designer souvenirs, from stone and glass work to jewellery and home fittings. The papier mâché figures are gorgeous, but there's so much else here to turn your head.

El Flamenco Vive   FLAMENCO

(Map p570; www.elflamencovive.es; Calle Conde de Lemos 7; ⊙10.30am-2pm & 5-9pm Mon-Sat; M Ópera) This temple to flamenco has it all, from guitars and songbooks to well-priced CDs, polka-dotted dancing costumes, shoes, colourful plastic jewellery and literature about flamenco. It's the sort of place that will appeal as much to curious first-timers as to serious students of the art. It also organises classes in flamenco guitar.

❶ Information

DISCOUNT CARDS

Madrid Card (☑91 360 47 72; www.madrid card.com; 1/2/3 days adult €45/55/65, child age 6-12yr €32/38/42) If you intend to do some intensive sightseeing and travelling on public transport, the Madrid Card includes free entry to more than 50 museums in and around Madrid, free walking tours and discounts in a number of restaurants, shops, bars and car rental. The Madrid Card can be bought online (slightly cheaper), or from a list of sales outlets on the website.

EMERGENCY

Emergency (☑112)

Policía Nacional (☑091)

Servicio de Atención al Turista Extranjero (Foreign Tourist Assistance Service; ☑91 548 80 08, 91 548 85 37, 902 102112; www.es madrid.com/satemadrid; Calle de Leganitos 19; ⊙9am-midnight; M Plaza de España, Santo Domingo) To report thefts or other crime-related matters, your best bet is the Servicio de Atención al Turista Extranjero, which is housed in the central police station or *comisaría* (commissioner's office) of the National Police. Here you'll find specially trained officers working alongside representatives from the tourism ministry. They can also assist in cancelling credit cards, as well as contacting your embassy or your family.

MEDICAL SERVICES

Farmacia Mayor (☑91 366 46 16; Calle Mayor 13; ⊙24hr; M Sol) Open around the clock.

Unidad Medica (Anglo American; ☑91 435 18 23; www.unidadmedica.com; Calle del Conde de Aranda 1; ⊙9am-8pm Mon-Fri, 10am-1pm Sat; M Retiro) A private clinic with a wide range of specialisations and where all doctors speak Spanish and English, with some also speaking French and German. Each consultation costs around €125.

SAFE TRAVEL

Madrid is a generally safe city, although you should, as in most European cities, be wary of pickpockets on transport and around major tourist sights. You're most likely to fall foul of pickpockets in the most heavily touristed parts of town, notably the Plaza Mayor and surrounding streets, the Puerta del Sol, El Rastro and around the Museo del Prado. Be wary of jostling on crowded buses and the metro and, as a general rule, dark, empty streets are to be avoided; luckily, Madrid's most lively nocturnal areas are generally busy with crowds having a good time.

TOURIST INFORMATION

Centro de Turismo de Madrid (Map p570; ☑91 588 16 36; www.esmadrid.com; Plaza Mayor 27; ⊙9.30am-8.30pm; M Sol) Excellent city tourist office with a smaller office underneath Plaza de Colón (Map p566; www. esmadrid.com; ⊙9.30am-8.30pm; M Colón) and the Palacio de Cibeles (Map p566; ⊙10am-8pm Tue-Sun; M Plaza de España), as well as information points at Plaza de la Cibeles (Map p570; ⊙9.30am-8.30pm; M Banco de España), Plaza del Callao (Map p570; M Callao), closed for renovations at the time of writing, outside the Centro de Arte Reina Sofía (Map p566; cnr Calle de Santa Isabel & Plaza del Emperador Carlos V; ⊙9.30am-8.30pm; M Atocha) and at the T2 and T4 terminals at Barajas airport.

Comunidad de Madrid (www.turismomadrid. es) The regional Madrid government maintains this useful site for the entire Madrid region.

❶ Getting There & Away

AIR

Barajas Airport (☑902 404704; www.aena. es; M Aeropuerto T1, T2 & T3; Aeropuerto T4) Madrid's Adolfo Suarez Barajas Airport lies 15km northeast of the city and has four terminals. Terminal 4 (T4) deals mainly with flights of Iberia and its partners (eg British Airways, American Airlines and Vueling), while the remainder leave from the conjoined T1, T2 and (rarely) T3.

ÁVILA

Ávila's old city, just over an hour from Madrid, is surrounded by imposing city walls comprising eight monumental gates, 88 watchtowers and more than 2500 turrets. It's one of the best-preserved medieval bastions in Spain.

Murallas (adult/child under 12yr €5/free; ⊙10am-8pm Tue-Sun; 🖼) Ávila's splendid 12th-century walls stretch for 2.5km atop the remains of earlier Roman and Muslim battlements and rank among the world's best-preserved medieval defensive perimeters. Two sections of the walls can be climbed – a 300m stretch that can be accessed from just inside the **Puerta del Alcázar**, and a longer 1300m stretch that runs the length of the old city's northern perimeter. The admission price includes a multilingual audioguide.

Catedral del Salvador (Plaza de la Catedral; admission €4; ⊙10am-7.30pm Mon-Fri, 10am-8pm Sat, noon-6.30pm Sun) Ávila's 12th-century cathedral is both a house of worship and an ingenious fortress: its stout granite apse forms the central bulwark in the historic city walls. The sombre Gothic-style facade conceals a magnificent interior with an exquisite early-16th-century altar frieze showing the life of Jesus, plus Renaissance-era carved choir stalls and a museum with an El Greco painting and a splendid silver monstrance by Juan de Arfe. Push the buttons to illuminate the altar and the choir stalls.

Hotel El Rastro (☑920 35 22 25; www.elrastroavila.com; Calle Cepedas; s/d €35/55; ❄🐾) This atmospheric hotel occupies a former 16th-century palace with original stone, exposed brickwork and a natural earth-toned colour scheme exuding a calm understated elegance. Each room has a different form, but most have high ceilings and plenty of space. Note that the owners also run a marginally cheaper, same-name *hostal* around the corner.

Centro de Recepción de Visitantes (☑920 35 40 00, ext 790; www.avilaturismo.com; Avenida de Madrid 39; ⊙9am-8pm) Municipal tourist office.

BUS

ALSA (☑902 422242; www.alsa.es) One of the largest Spanish companies with many services throughout Spain. Most depart from Estación Sur but some buses headed north (including to Bilbao and Zaragoza, and some services to Barcelona) leave from the Intercambiador de Avenida de América with occasional services from T4 of Madrid's Barajas Airport.

Avanzabus (☑902 020052; www.avanzabus. com) Services to Extremadura (eg Cáceres), Castilla y León (eg Salamanca and Zamora) and Valencia via Cuenca, as well as Lisbon, Portugal. All leave from the Estación Sur.

Estación Sur de Autobuses (☑91 468 42 00; www.estaciondeautobuses.com; Calle de Méndez Álvaro 83; Ⓜ Méndez Álvaro) Estación Sur de Autobuses, just south of the M30 ring road, is the city's principal bus station. It serves most destinations to the south and many in other parts of the country. Most bus companies have a ticket office here, even if their buses depart from elsewhere.

TRAIN

High-speed Tren de Alta Velocidad Española (AVE) services connect Madrid with Seville (via Córdoba), Valladolid (via Segovia), Toledo, Valencia (via Cuenca), Málaga and Barcelona (via Zaragoza and Tarragona).

Estación de Chamartín (Ⓜ Chamartín) North of the city centre, Estación de Chamartín has numerous long-distance rail services, especially those to/from northern Spain. This is also where long-haul international trains arrive from Paris and Lisbon.

Puerta de Atocha (Ⓜ Atocha Renfe) The largest of Madrid's train stations is at the southern end of the city centre. The bulk of trains for Spanish destinations depart from Atocha, especially those going south.

Renfe (☑902 240202; www.renfe.es) For all train bookings.

ℹ Getting Around

TO/FROM THE AIRPORT
Bus

AeroCITY (☑91 747 75 70; www.aerocity.com; per person from €20, express service from €35 per minibus) This excellent, private minibus service takes you door-to-door between central Madrid and the airport (T1 in front of Arrivals Gate 2, T2 between gates 5 and 6, and T4 arrivals hall). It operates 24 hours and you can book by phone or online. You can reserve a seat or the entire minibus; the latter operates like a taxi.

Exprés Aeropuerto (Airport Express; www.emtmadrid.es; per person €5; ⊘24hr; 🚇) The Exprés Aeropuerto runs between Puerta de Atocha train station and the airport. Buses run every 13 to 23 minutes from 6am to 11.30pm, and every 35 minutes throughout the rest of the night. The trip takes 40 minutes. From 11.55pm until 5.35am, departures are from the Plaza de la Cibeles, not the train station.

Metro

Line 8 of the metro (entrances in T2 and T4) runs to the Nuevos Ministerios transport interchange, which connects with lines 10 and 6. It operates from 6.05am to 2am. A one-way ticket to/from the airport costs €4.50. The journey from the airport to Nuevos Ministerios takes around 15 minutes, around 25 minutes from T4.

Taxi

There is now a fixed rate for taxis from the airport to the city centre (€30). If you're going to an airport hotel, you'll pay €20.

PUBLIC TRANSPORT

Metro (www.metromadrid.es) Madrid's modern metro is a fast, efficient and safe way to navigate Madrid, and generally easier than getting to grips with bus routes. There are numerous colour-coded lines in central Madrid and colour maps showing the metro system are available from any metro station or online.

TAXI

You can pick up a taxi at ranks throughout town or simply flag one down. Flag fall is €2.40 from 6am to 9pm Monday to Friday, €2.90 the rest of the time. Several supplementary charges, usually posted inside the taxi, apply; these include €3 from taxi ranks at train and bus stations.

CASTILLA Y LEÓN

Salamanca

POP 155,619

Whether floodlit by night or bathed in midday sun, Salamanca is a dream destination. This is a city of rare architectural splendour, awash with golden sandstone overlaid with Latin inscriptions in ochre, and with an extraordinary virtuosity of plateresque and Renaissance styles. The monumental highlights are many, with the exceptional Plaza Mayor (illuminated to stunning effect at night) an unforgettable highlight. But this is also Castilla's liveliest city, home to a massive Spanish and international student population who throng the streets at night and provide the city with youth and vitality.

◉ Sights & Activities

★ Plaza Mayor   SQUARE

Built between 1729 and 1755, Salamanca's exceptional grand square is widely considered to be Spain's most beautiful central plaza. The square is particularly memorable at night when illuminated (until midnight) to magical effect. Designed by Alberto Churriguera, it's a remarkably harmonious and controlled baroque display. The medallions placed around the square bear the busts of famous figures.

Catedral Nueva & Catedral Vieja   CHURCH

(www.catedralsalamanca.org) Curiously, Salamanca is home to two cathedrals: the newer and larger cathedral was built beside the old Romanesque one instead of on top of it, as was the norm. The **Catedral Nueva** (Plaza de Anaya; ⊘9am-8pm) ᖴᖇᗴᗴ, completed in 1733, is a late-Gothic masterpiece that took 220 years to build. Its magnificent Renaissance doorways stand out.

The largely Romanesque **Catedral Vieja** (Plaza de Anaya; admission €4.75; ⊘10am-7.30pm) is a 12th-century temple with a stunning 15th-century altarpiece whose 53 panels depict scenes from the life of Christ and Mary, topped by a representation of the *Final Judgement*.

★ Universidad Civil   HISTORIC BUILDING

(Calle de los Libreros; adult/concession €4/2, Mon morning free; ⊘9.30am-1.30pm & 4-6.30pm Mon-Sat, 10am-1.30pm Sun) The visual feast of the entrance facade is a tapestry in sandstone, bursting with images of mythical heroes, religious scenes and coats of arms.

FIND THE FROG

The facade of the Universidad Civil is an ornate mass of sculptures and carvings, and hidden among this 16th-century plateresque creation is a tiny stone frog. Legend says that those who find the frog will have good luck in studies, life and love. If you don't want any help, look away now... It's sitting on a skull on the pillar that runs up the right-hand side of the facade.

It's dominated by busts of Fernando and Isabel. Founded initially as the Estudio General in 1218, the university reached the peak of its renown in the 15th and 16th centuries. Behind the facade, the highlight of an otherwise modest collection of rooms lies upstairs: the extraordinary **university library**, the oldest university library in Europe.

🛏 Sleeping

⭐Hostal Concejo   HOSTAL €
(☑ 923 21 47 37; www.hconcejo.com; Plaza de la Libertad 1; s/d €45/60; P ✳ 🛜) A cut above the average *hostal,* the stylish Concejo has polished-wood floors, tasteful furnishings, light-filled rooms and a superb central location. Try and snag one of the corner rooms (like number 104) with its traditional glassed-in balcony, complete with a table, chairs and people-watching views.

Microtel Placentinos   BOUTIQUE HOTEL €€
(☑ 923 28 15 31; www.microtelplacentinos.com; Calle de Placentinos 9; s/d incl breakfast Sun-Thu €57/73, Fri & Sat €88/100; ✳ 🛜) One of Salamanca's most charming boutique hotels, Microtel Placentinos is tucked away on a quiet street and has rooms with exposed stone walls and wooden beams. The service is faultless, and the overall atmosphere is one of intimacy and discretion. All rooms have a hydromassage shower or tub and there's a summer-only outside whirlpool spa.

⭐Don Gregorio   BOUTIQUE HOTEL €€€
(☑ 923 21 70 15; www.hoteldongregorio.com; Calle de San Pablo 80; r/ste incl breakfast from €180/300; P ✳ 🛜) A palatial hotel with part of the city's Roman Wall flanking the garden. Rooms are decorated in soothing shades of cappuccino with crisp white linens and extravagant extras, including private saunas, espresso machines and two TVs (in the suites), complimentary mini-bar, king-size beds and vast hydromassage tubs (in the standard rooms). Sumptuous antiques and medieval tapestries adorn the public areas.

🍴 Eating & Drinking

La Cocina de Toño   TAPAS €€
(www.lacocinadetoño.es; Calle Gran Via 20; tapas €1.30-3.80, mains €7-20; ⊗ 2-4pm & 8-10pm Tue-

Sat, 2-5pm Sun) This place owes its loyal following to its creative *pinchos* (snacks) and half-servings of dishes such as escalope of foie gras with roast apple and passionfruit gelatin. The restaurant serves more traditional fare as befits the decor, but the bar is one of Salamanca's gastronomic stars. Slightly removed from the old city, it draws a predominantly Spanish crowd.

Mesón Las Conchas   CASTILIAN €€
(Rúa Mayor 16; mains €10-21; ⊗ bar 8am-midnight, restaurant 1-4pm & 8pm-midnight; 🖶) Enjoy a choice of outdoor tables, an atmospheric bar or the upstairs, wood-beamed dining area. The bar caters mainly to locals who know their *embutidos* (cured meats). For sit-down meals, there's a good mix of roasts, *platos combinados* and *raciones* (full-plate-size tapas). It serves a couple of cured meat platters (€35 for two people), and a highly rated oven-baked turbot.

⭐Tío Vivo   MUSIC BAR
(www.tiovivosalamanca.com; Calle del Clavel 3-5; ⊗ 3.30pm-late) Sip drinks by flickering candlelight to a background of '80s music, enjoying the whimsical decor of carousel horses and oddball antiquities. There is live music Tuesday to Thursday from midnight, sometimes with a €5 admission.

ℹ Information

Municipal & Regional Tourist Office (☑ 923 21 83 42; www.turismodesalamanca.com; Plaza Mayor 14; ⊗ 9am-2pm & 4.30-8pm Mon-Fri, 10am-8pm Sat, 10am-2pm Sun) The Regional Tourist Office shares an office with the municipal office on Plaza Mayor. An audio city barcode guide (www.audioguiasalamanca.es) is available with the appropriate app.

ℹ Getting There & Away

The bus and train stations are a 10- and 15-minute walk, respectively, from Plaza Mayor.

BUS

Buses include the following destinations: Madrid (regular/express €16.45/24.05, 2½ to three hours, hourly), Ávila (€7.60, 1½ hours, five daily) and Segovia (€14, 2½ hours, four daily).

TRAIN

There are regular departures to Madrid's Chamartín station (€23.20, 2½ hours) via Ávila (€11.75, 1¼ hours).

Segovia

POP 56,660

Unesco World Heritage–listed Segovia has a stunning monument to Roman grandeur and a castle said to have inspired Walt Disney, and is otherwise a city of warm terracotta and sandstone hues set amid the rolling hills of Castilla.

◉ Sights

★ Acueducto
ROMAN AQUEDUCT

Segovia's most recognisable symbol is El Acueducto (Roman Aqueduct), an 894m-long engineering wonder that looks like an enormous comb plunged into Segovia. First raised here by the Romans in the 1st century AD, the aqueduct was built with not a drop of mortar to hold the more than 20,000 uneven granite blocks together. It's made up of 163 arches and, at its highest point in Plaza del Azoguejo, rises 28m high.

★ Alcázar
CASTLE

(www.alcazardesegovia.com; Plaza de la Reina Victoria Eugenia; adult/concession/child under 6yr €5/3/free, tower €2, EU citizens free 3rd Tue of month; ⊙10am-7pm; ⚑) Rapunzel towers, turrets topped with slate witches' hats and a *deep* moat at its base make the Alcázar a prototype fairy-tale castle, so much so that its design inspired Walt Disney's vision of Sleeping Beauty's castle. Fortified since Roman days, the site takes its name from the Arabic *al-qasr* (fortress). It was rebuilt in the 13th and 14th centuries, but the whole lot burned down in 1862. What you see today is an evocative, over-the-top reconstruction of the original.

Catedral
CHURCH

(Plaza Mayor; adult/child €3/2, free 9.30am-1.15pm Sun; ⊙9.30am-6.30pm) In the heart of town, the resplendent late-Gothic cathedral was started in 1525 and completed a mere 200 years later. The Cristo del Consuelo **chapel** houses a magnificent Romanesque doorway preserved from the original church that burned down.

Iglesia de Vera Cruz
CHURCH

(Carretera de Zamarramala; admission €1.75; ⊙10.30am-1.30pm & 4-7pm Tue-Sun Dec-Oct) This 12-sided church is one of the best preserved of its kind in Europe. Built in the early 13th century by the Knights Templar and based on Jerusalem's Church of the Holy Sepulchre, it once housed a piece of the *Vera Cruz* (True Cross), now in the nearby village church of Zamarramala (on view only at Easter).

🛏 Sleeping

Hostal Fornos
HOSTAL €

(☑921 46 01 98; www.hostalfornos.com; Calle de la Infanta Isabel 13; s/d €41/55; ❄) This tidy little *hostal* is a cut above most other places in this price category. It has a bright cheerful atmosphere and rooms with a fresh white-linen-and-wicker look. Some rooms are larger than others, but the value is excellent. On the downside, some readers have complained of street noise.

★ Hospedería La Gran Casa Mudéjar
HISTORIC HOTEL €€

(☑921 46 62 50; www.lacasamudejar.com; Calle de Isabel la Católica 8; r €80; ❄@🖥) Spread over two buildings, this place has been magnificently renovated, blending genuine, 15th-century Mudéjar carved wooden ceilings in some rooms with modern amenities. In the newer wing, the rooms on the top floors have fine mountain views out over the rooftops of Segovia's old Jewish quarter. Adding to the appeal, there's a small spa and the **restaurant** comes highly recommended.

✖ Eating

★ Restaurante El Fogón Sefardí
SEPHARDIC €€

(☑921 46 62 50; www.lacasamudejar.com; Calle de Isabel la Católica 8; mains €20-25, tapas from €2.50; ⊙1.30-4.30pm & 5.30-11.30pm) Located within the Hospedería La Gran Casa Mudéjar, this is one of the most original places in town. Sephardic and Jewish cuisine is served either on the intimate patio or in the splendid dining hall with its original, 15th-century Mudéjar flourishes. The theme in the bar is equally diverse. Stop here for a taste of the award-winning tapas. Reservations recommended.

Casa Duque
GRILL €€

(☑921 46 24 87; www.restauranteduque.es; Calle de Cervantes 12; mains €9-20; ⊙12.30-4.30pm & 8.30-11.30pm) *Cochinillo asado* (roast pig) has been served at this atmospheric *mesón*

SPAIN

BURGOS & LEÓN – A TALE OF TWO CATHEDRALS

Burgos and León are cathedral towns par excellence, and both are well connected by train and bus to Madrid.

Burgos

Catedral (Plaza del Rey Fernando; adult/child under 14yr incl multilingual audioguide €6/1.50; ☺10am-6pm) This Unesco World Heritage–listed cathedral is a masterpiece. A former modest Romanesque church, work began on a grander scale in 1221. Remarkably, within 40 years most of the French Gothic structure had been completed. You can enter the cathedral from Plaza de Santa María for free, and have access to the **Capilla del Santísimo Cristo**, with its much-revered 13th-century crucifix, and the **Capilla de Santa Tecla**, with its extraordinary ceiling. However, we recommend that you visit the cathedral in its entirety.

Hotel Norte y Londres (☑947 26 41 25; www.hotelnorteylondres.com; Plaza de Alonso Martínez 10; s/d €66/100; ℗@🛜) Set in a former 16th-century palace and with under-stated period charm, this fine hotel promises spacious rooms with antique furnishings, polished wooden floors and pretty balconies; those on the 4th floor are more modern. The bathrooms are exceptionally large, the service exceptionally efficient.

Cervecería Morito (Calle Sombrerería 27; tapas €3, raciones €5-7; ☺12.30-3.30pm & 7-11.30pm) Cervecería Morito is the undisputed king of Burgos tapas bars and it's always crowded, deservedly so. A typical order is *alpargata* (lashings of cured ham with bread, tomato and olive oil) or the *pincho de morcilla* (small tapa of local blood sausage). The presentation is surprisingly nouvelle, especially the visual feast of salads.

Municipal Tourist office (☑947 28 88 74; www.aytoburgos.es; Plaza de Santa María; ☺10am-8pm) Pick up its 24-hour, 48-hour and 72-hour guides to Burgos; they can also be downloaded as PDFs online.

León

Catedral (www.catedraldeleon.org; adult/concession/child under 12yr €5/4/free; ☺8.30am-1.30pm & 4-8pm Mon-Sat, 8.30am-2.30pm & 5-8pm Sun) León's 13th-century cathedral, with its soaring towers, flying buttresses and breathtaking interior, is the city's spiritual heart. Whether spotlit by night or bathed in glorious sunshine, the cathedral, arguably Spain's premier Gothic masterpiece, exudes a glorious, almost luminous quality. The show-stopping facade has a radiant rose window, three richly sculpted doorways and two muscular towers. After going through the main entrance, lorded over by the scene of the Last Supper, an extraordinary gallery of *vidrieras* (stained-glass windows) awaits.

Panteón Real (admission €5; ☺10am-1.30pm & 4-6.30pm Mon-Sat, 10am-1.30pm Sun) Attached to the Real Basílica de San Isidoro, Panteón Real houses the remaining sarcophagi, which rest with quiet dignity beneath a canopy of some of the finest Romanesque frescoes in Spain. Motif after colourful motif of biblical scenes drench the vaults and arches of this extraordinary hall, held aloft by marble columns with intricately carved capitals.

The pantheon also houses a small **museum** where you can admire the shrine of San Isidoro, a mummified finger of the saint (!) and other treasures.

La Posada Regia (☑987 21 31 73; www.regialeon.com; Calle de Regidores 9-11; s/d incl breakfast €55/90; ▦🛜) This place has the feel of a *casa rural* despite being in the city centre. The secret is a 14th-century building, magnificently restored (wooden beams, exposed brick and understated antique furniture), with individually styled rooms and supremely comfortable beds and bathrooms. As with anywhere in the Barri Gòtic, weekend nights can be noisy.

Municipal Tourist Office (☑987 87 83 27; Plaza de San Marcelo; ☺9.30am-2pm & 5-7.30pm)

(tavern) since the 1890s. For the uninitiated, try the *menú segoviano* (€32), which includes *cochinillo*, or the *menú gastronómico* (€39). Downstairs is the informal *cueva* (cave), where you can get tapas and full-bodied *cazuelas* (stews). Reservations recommended.

ℹ Information

Centro de Recepción de Visitantes (Tourist Office; ✆ 921 46 67 20; www.turismodesegovia.com; Plaza del Azoguejo 1; ◷ 10am-7pm Sun-Fri, 10am-8pm Sat) Segovia's main tourist office runs two-hour guided tours, departing daily at 11.15am for a minimum of four people (€13.50 per person). Reserve ahead.

Regional Tourist Office (www.segoviaturismo.es; Plaza Mayor 10; ◷ 9am-8pm Sun-Thu, 9am-9pm Fri & Sat)

ℹ Getting There & Away

BUS

The bus station is just off Paseo de Ezequiel González. Buses run half-hourly to Segovia from Madrid's Paseo de la Florida bus stop (€8, 1½ hours). Buses depart to Ávila (€6, one hour, eight daily) and Salamanca (€14, 2½ hours, four daily), among other destinations.

TRAIN

There are a couple of options by train: just two normal trains run daily from Madrid to Segovia (€8, two hours), leaving you at the main train station 2.5km from the aqueduct. The faster option is the high-speed Avant (€12.50, 28 minutes), which deposits you at the new Segovia-Guiomar station, 5km from the aqueduct.

CASTILLA-LA MANCHA

Toledo

POP 85,593

Though one of the smaller of Spain's provincial capitals, Toledo looms large in the nation's history and consciousness as a religious centre, bulwark of the Spanish church, and once-flourishing symbol of a multicultural medieval society. The old town today is a treasure chest of churches, museums, synagogues and mosques set in a labyrinth of narrow streets, plazas and inner patios in a lofty setting high above the Río Tajo. Crowded by day, Toledo changes dramatically after dark when the streets take on a moody, other-worldly air.

◉ Sights

★ **Catedral** CATHEDRAL
(Plaza del Ayuntamiento; adult/child €8/free; ◷ 10.30am-6.30pm Mon-Sat, 2-6.30pm Sun) Toledo's cathedral reflects the city's historical significance as the heart of Catholic Spain and it's one of the most extravagant cathedrals in the country. The heavy interior, with sturdy columns dividing the space into five naves, is on a monumental scale. Every one of the numerous side chapels has artistic treasures, and other highlights include the *coro* (choir), Capilla Mayor, Transparente, *sacristía* and bell tower (for €3 extra).

Alcázar FORTRESS, MUSEUM
(Museo del Ejército; Calle Alféreces Provisionales; adult/child €5/free; ◷ 11am-5pm) At the highest point in the city looms the foreboding Alcázar. Rebuilt under Franco, it has been reopened as a vast military museum. The usual displays of uniforms and medals are here, but the best part is the exhaustive historical section, with an in-depth overview of the nation's history in Spanish and English.

★ **Sinagoga del Tránsito** SYNAGOGUE
(museosefardi.mcu.es; Calle Samuel Leví; adult/child €3/1.50, free Sat after 2pm & all day Sun, combined ticket with Museo del Greco €5; ◷ 9.30am-8pm Tue-Sat Apr-Sep, to 6.30pm Tue-Sat Oct-Mar, 10am-3pm Sun) This magnificent synagogue was built in 1355 by special permission of Pedro I. The synagogue now houses the **Museo Sefardí**. The vast main prayer hall has been expertly restored and the Mudéjar decoration and intricately carved pine ceiling are striking. Exhibits provide an insight into the history of Jewish culture in Spain, and include archaeological finds, a memorial garden, costumes and ceremonial artefacts.

★ **Monasterio San Juan de los Reyes** MONASTERY
(Calle San Juan de los Reyes 2; admission €2.50; ◷ 10am-6.30pm Jun-Sep, to 5.30pm Oct-May) This imposing 15th-century Franciscan monastery and church was provocatively founded in the heart of the Jewish quarter by the Catholic monarchs Isabel and Fernando to demonstrate the supremacy of their faith. The rulers had planned to be buried here but eventually ended up in their prize conquest, Granada.

The highlight is the amazing two-level cloister, a harmonious fusion of late ('flamboyant') Gothic downstairs and Mudéjar architecture upstairs, with superb statuary, arches, vaulting, elaborate pinnacles and gargoyles surrounding a lush garden with orange trees and roses.

🛏 Sleeping & Eating

Hostal Alfonso XII   HOSTAL €
(☑925 25 25 09; www.hostal-alfonso12.com; Calle de Alfonso XII; s €27-40, d €35-50; ❋ 🛜) In a great location in the *Judería* this quality *hostal* occupies an 18th-century Toledo house, meaning twisty passages and stairs, and compact rooms in curious places. It's got plenty of charm.

Casa de Cisneros   BOUTIQUE HOTEL €€
(☑925 22 88 28, 925 22 88 28; www.hostal-casa-de-cisneros.com; Calle del Cardenal Cisneros; s/d €40/66; ❋ 🛜) Right by the cathedral, this lovely 16th-century house was once the home of the cardinal and Grand Inquisitor Cisneros (often known as Ximénes). It's a top choice, with cosy, seductive rooms with original wooden beams and walls and voguish bathrooms. Archaeological works have revealed the remains of Roman baths and part of an 11th-century Moorish palace in the basement.

⭐Kumera   MODERN SPANISH €
(☑925 25 75 53; www.restaurantekumera.com; Calle Alfonso X El Sabio 2; meals €9-10, set menus €20-35; ⊙8am-2.30am Mon-Fri, 11am-2.30am Sat & Sun) With arguably the best price-quality ratio in town, this place serves up innovative takes on local traditional dishes such as *cochinito* (suckling pig), *rabo de toro* or *croquetas* (croquettes, filled with *jamón* (cured ham), squid, cod or wild mushrooms), alongside gigantic toasts and other creatively conceived dishes. The dishes with foie gras as the centrepiece are especially memorable.

La Abadía   CASTILIAN, TAPAS €€
(www.abadiatoledo.com; Plaza de San Nicolás 3; raciones €4-15) In a former 16th-century palace, this atmospheric bar and restaurant has arches, niches and subtle lighting and is spread over a warren of brick-and-stone-clad rooms. The menu includes lightweight dishes and tapas, but the 'Menú de Montes de Toledo' (€19) is a fabulous collection of tastes from the nearby mountains.

ℹ Information

Main Tourist Office (☑925 25 40 30; www.toledo-turismo.com; Plaza del Ayuntamiento; ⊙10am-6pm) Within sight of the cathedral. There's another branch (Estación de Renfe; ⊙10am-3pm) at the train station.

Provincial Tourist Office (www.diputoledo.es; Subida de la Granja; ⊙8am-6pm Mon-Fri, 10am-5pm Sat, 10am-3pm Sun) At the top of the escalator.

ℹ Getting There & Away

For most major destinations, you'll need to backtrack to Madrid.

BUS

From Toledo's **bus station** (Avenida de Castilla La Mancha), buses depart for Madrid's Plaza Elíptica roughly every half hour (from €5.35, one hour to 1¾ hours), some direct, some villages. There are also services to Cuenca (€14.20, 2¼ hours).

TRAIN

From the pretty **train station** (☑902 240202; Paseo de la Rosa) high-speed AVE (Alta Velocidad Española; high-speed services) trains run every hour or so to Madrid (one way/return €12.70/20.30, 30 minutes).

CATALONIA

Barcelona

POP 1.62 MILLION

Barcelona is one of Europe's coolest cities. Despite two millennia of history, it's a forward-thinking place, always on the cutting edge of art, design and cuisine. Whether you explore its medieval palaces and plazas, admire the Modernista masterpieces, shop for designer fashions along its bustling boulevards, sample its exciting nightlife or soak up the sun on the beaches, you'll find it hard not to fall in love with this vibrant city.

As much as Barcelona is a visual feast, it will also lead you into culinary temptation. Anything from traditional Catalan cooking to the latest in avant-garde new Spanish cuisine will have your appetite in overdrive.

◎ Sights & Activities

◉ La Rambla

Spain's most famous boulevard, the part-pedestrianised La Rambla, explodes with life. Stretching from Plaça de Catalunya to the waterfront, it's lined with street artists, newsstands and vendors selling everything from mice to magnolias.

★**Mercat de la Boqueria** MARKET
(Map p590; ☑93 318 25 84; www.boqueria.info; La
Rambla 91; ⊙8am-8.30pm Mon-Sat, closed Sun;
Ⓜ Liceu) Mercat de la Boqueria is possibly La
Rambla's most interesting building, not so
much for its Modernista-influenced design
(it was actually built over a long period,
from 1840 to 1914, on the site of the former
St Joseph monastery), but for the action of
the food market within.

Gran Teatre del Liceu ARCHITECTURE
(Map p590; ☑93 485 99 14; www.liceubarcelo-
na.com; La Rambla dels Caputxins 51-59; tour
20/80min €5.50/11.50; ⊙guided tour 10am, short
tour 11.30am, noon, 12.30pm & 1pm; Ⓜ Liceu) If you
can't catch a night at the opera, you can still
have a look around one of Europe's greatest
opera houses, known to locals as the Liceu.
Smaller than Milan's La Scala but bigger than
Venice's La Fenice, it can seat up to 2300 people in its grand horseshoe auditorium.

◉ **Barri Gòtic**

You could easily spend several days or even
a week exploring the Barri Gòtic, Barcelona's
oldest quarter, without leaving the medieval
streets. In addition to major sights, its tangle
of narrow lanes and tranquil plazas conceal
some of the city's most atmospheric shops,
restaurants, cafes and bars.

★**La Catedral** CHURCH
(Map p590; ☑93 342 82 62; www.catedralbcn.
org; Plaça de la Seu; admission free, special visit
€6, choir admission €2.80; ⊙8am-12.45pm &
5.15-7.30pm Mon-Sat, special visit 1-5pm Mon-Sat,
2-5pm Sun & holidays; Ⓜ Jaume I) Barcelona's
central place of worship presents a magnificent image. The richly decorated main
facade, laced with gargoyles and the stone
intricacies you would expect of northern European Gothic, sets it quite apart from other
churches in Barcelona. The facade was actually added in 1870, although the rest of the
building was built between 1298 and 1460.
The other facades are sparse in decoration,
and the octagonal, flat-roofed towers are
a clear reminder that, even here, Catalan
Gothic architectural principles prevailed.

★**Museu d'Història
de Barcelona** MUSEUM
(Map p590; ☑93 256 21 00; www.museuhistoria.
bcn.cat; Plaça del Rei; adult/child €7/free, free 1st
Sun of month & 3-8pm Sun; ⊙10am-7pm Tue-Sat,
10am-8pm Sun; Ⓜ Jaume I) One of Barcelona's

most fascinating museums takes you back
through the centuries to the very foundations of Roman Barcino. You'll stroll over
ruins of the old streets, sewers, laundries
and wine- and fish-making factories that
flourished here following the town's founding by Emperor Augustus around 10 BC.
Equally impressive is the building itself,
which was once part of the Palau Reial Major (Grand Royal Palace) on Plaça del Rei,
among the key locations of medieval prince-
ly power in Barcelona.

Plaça Reial SQUARE
(Map p590; Ⓜ Liceu) One of the most photogenic squares in Barcelona, the Plaça Reial
is a delightful retreat from the traffic and
pedestrian mobs on the nearby Rambla.
Numerous eateries, bars and nightspots lie
beneath the arcades of 19th-century neoclassical buildings, with a buzz of activity at
all hours.

◉ **La Ribera**

In medieval days, La Ribera was a stone's
throw from the Mediterranean and the heart
of Barcelona's foreign trade, with homes be-
longing to numerous wealthy merchants.
Now it's a trendy district full of boutiques,
restaurants and bars.

★**Museu Picasso** MUSEUM
(Map p590; ☑93 256 30 00; www.museupicasso.
bcn.cat; Carrer de Montcada 15-23; adult/child
€14/free, temporary exhibitions adult/child €6.50/
free, 3-8pm Sun & 1st Sun of month free; ⊙9am-
7pm daily, until 9.30pm Thu; ☎; Ⓜ Jaume I) The
setting alone, in five contiguous medieval
stone mansions, makes the Museu Picasso
unique (and worth the probable queues).
The pretty courtyards, galleries and staircases preserved in the first three of these
buildings are as delightful as the collection
inside.

★**Basílica de
Santa Maria del Mar** CHURCH
(Map p590; ☑93 310 23 90; Plaça de Santa Maria
del Mar; ⊙9am-1.30pm & 4.30-8.30pm, opens at
10.30am Sun; Ⓜ Jaume I) FREE At the southwest end of Passeig del Born stands the apse
of Barcelona's finest Catalan Gothic church,
Santa Maria del Mar (Our Lady of the
Sea). Built in the 14th century with record-
breaking alacrity for the time (it took just 54
years), the church is remarkable for its architectural harmony and simplicity.

Barcelona

N

0
0.5 miles
1 km

Map labels:

SANT MARTÍ

EL CLOT
CAMP DE L'ARPA

LA DRETA DE L'EIXAMPLE

EL GUINARDÓ

SAGRADA FAMÍLIA

L'EIXAMPLE

EL FORT PIENC

GRÀCIA

EL CARMEL

SANT GERVASI DE CASSOLES

Numbered points of interest:
1, 3, 4, 8, 10, 11, 13, 16, 18, 19, 21, 22, 23

La Sagrada Família
La Pedrera
Casa Batlló

Hospital de Sant Pau
Park Güell (200m)
Camp Nou (2km)
Hospital Clínic
Parc de la Ciutadella
Estació del Nord
Arc de Triomf
Monumental

Streets and avenues:
Av Diagonal
Av Meridiana
Pg de Sant Joan
Passeig de Gràcia
Via Augusta
Gran de Gràcia
Ronda del General Mitre
Travessera de Gràcia
Travessera de Dalt
C de Mallorca
C de València
C del Consell de Cent
C de la Diputació
C del Rosselló
C de Provença
C d'Aragó
C de Balmes
C de Muntaner
C d'Aribau
C d'Enric Granados
C de Casanova
C de Viladomat
C de Londres
C de París
C de Corsega
C de Sardenya
C de Nàpols
C de Girona
C del Bruc
C de Roger de Llúria
C de Pau Claris
C de Bailèn
C de Roger de Flor
C de la Marina
C de Lepant
C de Cartagena
C de Sicília
C de Padilla
C de Pamplona
C de Zamora
C de Joan Miró
C de la Marina
Pg de Pujades
Pg de Sant Joan
Plaça de les Glòries Catalanes
Plaça de Joan Carles I
Plaça de Tetuan
Plaça de Mossèn Jacint Verdaguer
Plaça de Raspall
Plaça de Lesseps

Palau Robert Regional Tourist Office

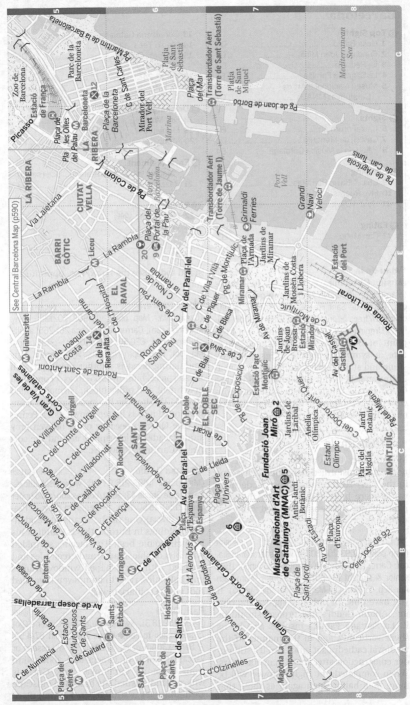

Mediterranean Sea

Zoo de Barcelona

Estació de França

Picasso

Plaça de les Olles

La Barceloneta

Parc de la Barceloneta

Pg Marítim de la Barceloneta

Platja de Sant Sebastià

Plaça del Mar

Transbordador Aeri (Torre de Sant Sebastià)

Platja de Sant Miquel

Pg de Joan de Borbó

LA RIBERA

Plaça de la Barceloneta

C de Sant Carles

Mirador del Port Vell

Marina

LA RIBERA

Pla del Palau

CIUTAT VELLA

Pg de Colom

Port de Barcelona

Via Laietana

See Central Barcelona Map (p590)

BARRI GÒTIC

Liceu

La Rambla

Plaça del Portal de la Pau

Transbordador Aeri (Torre de Jaume I)

Grimaldi Ferries

Grandi Navi Veloci

Port Vell

Pg de l'Agricola de Can Tunis

EL RAVAL

C Nou de la Rambla

Av del Paral·lel

Plaça de Montjuïc

Plaça de l'Armada

Jardins de Miramar

Estació del Port

Universitat

C de Sant Pau

C de Vila i Vila

Pg de Montjuïc

Miramar

Av de Miramar

Jardins de Mossèn Costa i Llobera

Estació del Litoral

Ronda del Litoral

C de Joaquín Costa

C de la Riera Alta

C del Carme

C de l'Hospital

Ronda de Sant Pau

C de Piquer

C de Blesa

Jardins de Joan Brossa

Estació Miramar

C de Montjuïc

Ronda de Sant Antoni

Gran Via de les Corts Catalanes

C de Villarroel

Urgell

C del Comte d'Urgell

C del Comte Borrell

C de Tamarit

C de Manso

Poble Sec

EL POBLE SEC

C de Blai

C de Salvà

Pg de l'Exposició

Estació Parc Montjuïc

Av del Castell

Castell

SANT ANTONI

Rocafort

C de Viladomat

C de Calàbria

C de Rocafort

C de Sepúlveda

Av del Paral·lel

C de Lleida

C de Ricart

Poble Sec

Jardins de Laribal

Anella Olímpica

Av del Doctor Font i Quer

Jardí Botànic

MONTJUÏC

C de Mallorca

Av de Roma

C de València

C d'Entença

Plaça de l'Univers

Fundació Joan Miró

Museu Nacional d'Art de Catalunya (MNAC)

Antic Jardí Botànic

Estadi Olímpic

Parc del Migdia

Pg del Migdia

C de Provença

C de Còrsega

Entença

Tarragona

Plaça d'Espanya

Espanya

C de Tarragona

Al Aerobús

Gran Via de les Corts Catalanes

Plaça de Sant Jordi

Plaça d'Europa

C dels Jocs de 92

Av de l'Estadi

SANTS

Plaça del Centre

Estació d'Autobusos

C de Numància

C de Bellín

Av de Josep Tarradellas

Estació

Sants

C de Guitard

C de Sants

Hostafrancs

Plaça de Sants

C de la Bordeta

C de Gavà

Magòria La Campana

C d'Olzinelles

C de Sants

Barcelona

Palau de la Música Catalana ARCHITECTURE
(Map p586; ☎93 295 72 00; www.palaumusica.org; Carrer de Sant Francesc de Paula 2; adult/child €17/free; ☺guided tours 10am-3.30pm daily; Ⓜ Urquinaona) This concert hall is a high point of Barcelona's Modernista architecture, a symphony in tile, brick, sculpted stone and stained glass. Built by Domènech i Montaner between 1905 and 1908 for the Orfeó Català musical society, it was conceived as a temple for the Catalan Renaixença (Renaissance).

◉ L'Eixample

Modernisme, the Catalan version of art nouveau, transformed Barcelona's cityscape in the early 20th century. Most Modernista works were built in L'Eixample, the grid-plan district that was developed from the 1870s on.

★ La Sagrada Família CHURCH
(Map p586; ☎93 207 30 31; www.sagradafamilia.cat; Carrer de Mallorca 401; adult/child under 11yr/senior & student €14.80/free/12.80; ☺9am-8pm Apr-Sep, to 6pm Oct-Mar; Ⓜ Sagrada Família) If you have time for only one sightseeing outing, Antoni Gaudí's masterpiece should be it. La Sagrada Família inspires awe by its sheer verticality, and in the manner of the medieval cathedrals it emulates, it's still under construction after more than 100 years. When completed, the highest tower will be more than half as high again as those that

stand today. See the boxed text, opposite, for more.

★ La Pedrera ARCHITECTURE
(Casa Milà; Map p586; ☎902 202138; www.lapedrera.com; Carrer de Provença 261-265; adult/student/child €20.50/16.50/10.25; ☺9am-8pm Mar-Oct, to 6.30pm Nov-Feb; Ⓜ Diagonal) This undulating beast is another madcap Gaudí masterpiece, built in 1905–10 as a combined apartment and office block. Formally called Casa Milà, after the businessman who commissioned it, it is better known as La Pedrera (the Quarry) because of its uneven grey stone facade, which ripples around the corner of Carrer de Provença.

★ Casa Batlló ARCHITECTURE
(Map p586; ☎93 216 03 06; www.casabatllo.es; Passeig de Gràcia 43; adult/concession/child under 7yr €21.50/18.50/free; ☺9am-9pm daily; Ⓜ Passeig de Gràcia) One of the strangest residential buildings in Europe, this is Gaudí at his hallucinogenic best. The facade, sprinkled with bits of blue, mauve and green tiles and studded with wave-shaped window frames and balconies, rises to an uneven blue-tiled roof with a solitary tower.

Park Güell PARK
(☎93 409 18 31; www.parkguell.cat; Carrer d'Olot 7; admission to central area adult/child €7/4.50; ☺8am-9.30pm daily; ☒24 or 32, Ⓜ Lesseps or Vallcarca) North of Gràcia and about 4km from Plaça de Catalunya, Park Güell is where Gaudí turned his hand to landscape gardening. It's a strange, enchanting place

LA SAGRADA FAMÍLIA HIGHLIGHTS

Roof The roof of La Sagrada Família is held up by a forest of extraordinary angled pillars. As the pillars soar towards the ceiling, they sprout a web of supporting branches, creating the effect of a forest canopy.

Nativity Facade The artistic pinnacle of the building. You can climb high up inside some of the four towers by a combination of lifts and narrow spiral staircases – a vertiginous experience.

Passion Facade The southwest Passion Facade, on the theme of Christ's last days and death, was built between 1954 and 1978 based on surviving drawings by Gaudí, with four towers and a large, sculpture-bedecked portal.

Glory Facade The Glory Facade is under construction and will, like the others, be crowned by four towers – the total of 12 representing the Twelve Apostles.

Museu Gaudí The Museu Gaudí, below ground level, includes interesting material on Gaudí's life and other works, as well as models and photos of La Sagrada Família.

Exploring La Sagrada Although essentially a building site, the completed sections and museum may be explored at leisure. Fifty-minute guided tours (€4) are offered. Alternatively, pick up an audio tour (€4), for which you need ID. Enter from Carrer de Sardenya and Carrer de la Marina. Once inside, €2.50 will get you into lifts that rise up inside towers in the Nativity and Passion Facades.

where his passion for natural forms really took flight – to the point where the artificial almost seems more natural than the natural.

◉ Montjuïc

Southwest of the city centre and with views out to sea and over the city, Montjuïc serves as a Central Park of sorts and is a great place for a jog or stroll. Buses 50, 55 and 61 all head up here. A local bus, the PM (Parc de Montjuïc) line, does a circle trip from Plaça d'Espanya to the *castell* (castle or fort). Cable cars and a funicular line also access the area.

★ Museu Nacional d'Art de Catalunya (MNAC)   MUSEUM
(Map p586; ☑ 93 622 03 76; www.museunacional.cat; Mirador del Palau Nacional; adult/senior & child under 16yr/student €12/free/8.40, 1st Sun of month free; ☉ 10am-8pm Tue-Sat, to 3pm Sun, library 10am-6pm Mon-Fri; Ⓜ Espanya) From across the city, the bombastic neobaroque silhouette of the **Palau Nacional** can be seen on the slopes of Montjuïc. Built for the 1929 World Exhibition and restored in 2005, it houses a vast collection of mostly Catalan art spanning the early Middle Ages to the early 20th century. The high point is the collection of extraordinary Romanesque frescoes.

★ Fundació Joan Miró   MUSEUM
(Map p586; ☑ 93 443 94 70; www.fundaciomiro-bcn.org; Parc de Montjuïc; adult/child €11/free; ☉ 10am-8pm Tue-Sat, to 9.30pm Thu, to 2.30pm Sun & holidays; ☐ 55, 150, funicular Paral·lel) Joan Miró, the city's best-known 20th-century artistic progeny, bequeathed this art foundation to his hometown in 1971. Its light-filled buildings, designed by close friend and architect Josep Lluís Sert (who also built Miró's Mallorca studios), are crammed with seminal works, from Miró's earliest timid sketches to paintings from his last years.

Castell de Montjuïc   FORTRESS, GARDENS
(Map p586; ☑ 93 256 44 45; www.bcn.cat/castelldemontjuic; Carretera de Montjuïc 66; adult/concession/child €5/3/free, Sun afternoons & 1st Sun of month free; ☉ 10am-8pm; ☐ 150, Telefèric de Montjuïc, Castell de Montjuïc) This forbidding *castell* dominates the southeastern heights of Montjuïc and enjoys commanding views over the Mediterranean. It dates, in its present form, from the late 17th and 18th centuries. For most of its dark history, it has been used to watch over the city and as a political prison and killing ground.

CaixaForum   GALLERY
(Map p586; ☑ 93 476 86 00; www.fundacio.lacaixa.es; Avinguda de Francesc Ferrer i Guàrdia 6-8; adult/student & child €4/free, 1st Sun of month free; ☉ 10am-8pm Mon-Fri, to 9pm Sat & Sun;

Central Barcelona

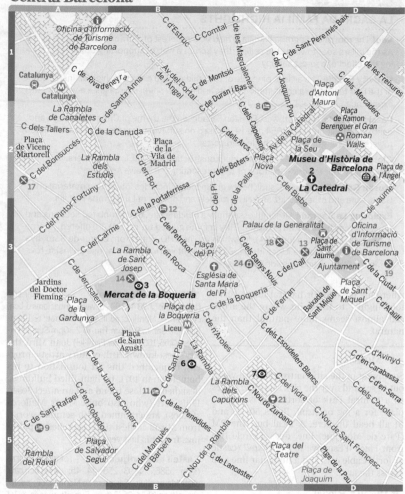

M Espanya) The Caixa building society prides itself on its involvement in (and ownership of) art, in particular all that is contemporary. Its premier art expo space in Barcelona hosts part of the bank's extensive collection from around the globe. The setting is a completely renovated former factory, the Fàbrica Casaramona, an outstanding Modernista brick structure designed by Puig i Cadafalch. From 1940 to 1993 it housed the First Squadron of the police cavalry unit – 120 horses in all.

🎉 Festivals & Events

Festes de la Mercè   CITY FESTIVAL
(www.bcn.cat/merce) The city's biggest party involves four days of concerts, dancing, *castellers* (human-castle builders), a fireworks display synchronised with the Montjuïc fountains, dances of giants on the Saturday, and *correfocs* – a parade of fireworks-spitting monsters and demons who run with the crowd – from all over Catalonia, on the Sunday. Held around 24 September.

now makes it easier to stay in La Ribera and near the beaches at La Barceloneta.

La Rambla & Barri Gòtic

Alberg Hostel Itaca   HOSTEL €
(Map p590; ☎93 301 97 51; www.itacahostel. com; Carrer de Ripoll 21; dm €21-24, tw/d €60/70, apt €90-150; @⊛; Ⓜ Jaume I) A bright, quiet hostel near the cathedral, Itaca has spacious dorms (sleeping six to 10 people) with parquet floors and spring colours, and two doubles. There's a lively vibe, and the hostel organises activities (pub crawls, flamenco concerts, free daily walking tour), making it a good option for solo travellers.

Vrabac   GUESTHOUSE €€
(Map p590; ☎663 494029; vrabacguesthouse. wordpress.com; Carrer de Portaferrissa 14; d €95-145, s/d without bathroom from €55/65; ❋⊛; Ⓜ Liceu or Catalunya) In a central location just off La Rambla, Vrabac is set in

---

Día de Sant Joan   MIDSUMMER
This is a colourful midsummer celebration on 24 June with bonfires, even in the squares of L'Eixample, and fireworks marking the evening that precedes this holiday.

⌂ Sleeping

Those looking for cheaper accommodation close to the action should check out the Barri Gòtic and El Raval. Some good lower-end *pensiones* are scattered about L'Eixample, as are a broad range of midrange and top-end places, most in easy striking distance of the Old Town. A growing range of options

a beautifully restored heritage building complete with original decorative ceilings, exposed sandstone walls and large oil paintings. Rooms vary in size and equipment – the best have elegant ceramic tile floors and sizeable balconies with private bathrooms. The cheapest are small and basic and lack a bathroom, and aren't recommended. Cash only.

El Raval

Hotel Peninsular HOTEL €
(Map p590; ☑ 93 302 31 38; www.hotelpeninsular. net; Carrer de Sant Pau 34; s/d €57/80; ❄ @ ⟨; ⓜ Liceu) An oasis on the edge of the slightly dicey Barri Xinès, this former convent (which was connected by tunnel to the Església de Sant Agustí) has a plant-draped atrium extending its height and most of its length. The 60 rooms are simple, with tiled floors and whitewash, but mostly spacious and well kept. There are some great bargains to be had on quiet dates.

★ Barceló Raval DESIGN HOTEL €€
(Map p590; ☑ 93 320 14 90; www.barceloraval.com; Rambla del Raval 17-21; r from €128; ❄ @; ⓜ Liceu) Part of the city's plans to pull the El Raval district up by the bootstraps, this oval-shaped designer hotel tower makes a 21st-century splash. The rooftop terrace offers fabulous views and the B-Lounge bar-restaurant is the toast of the town for meals and cocktails. Rooms have slick aesthetics (white with lime green or ruby-red splashes of colour), Nespresso machines and iPod docks.

Chic & Basic Ramblas DESIGN HOTEL €€
(Map p586; ☑ 93 302 71 11; www.chicandbasic ramblashotel.com; Passatge Gutenberg 7; s & d €106-116; ❄ ⟨; ⓜ Drassanes) The latest in the Chic & Basic chain is the most riotous to date, with quirky and colourful interiors that hit you from the second you walk in and see a vintage Seat 600 in the foyer. The rooms themselves are solid blocks of colour, and each loosely pays homage to an aspect of Barcelona life in the 1960s. All have balconies and small kitchens. Note that the name is misleading – the hotel is a couple of blocks into the Raval.

La Ribera & La Barceloneta

Hotel Banys Orientals BOUTIQUE HOTEL €€
(Map p590; ☑ 93 268 84 60; www.hotelbanys orientals.com; Carrer de l'Argenteria 37; s €96,

d €115.50-143; ❄ ⟨; ⓜ Jaume I) Book well ahead to get into this magnetically popular designer haunt. Cool blues and aquamarines combine with dark-hued floors to lend this clean-lined, boutique hotel a quiet charm. All rooms, on the small side, look onto the street or back lanes. There are more spacious suites in two other nearby buildings.

L'Eixample

Hostal Oliva HOSTAL €
(Map p586; ☑ 93 488 01 62; www.hostaloliva.com; Passeig de Gràcia 32; d €51-91, r without bathroom €41-71; ❄ ⟨; ⓜ Passeig de Gràcia) A picturesque antique lift wheezes its way up to this 4th-floor *hostal,* a terrific, reliable cheapie in one of the city's most expensive neighbourhoods. Some of the single rooms can barely fit a bed but the doubles are big enough, light and airy (some with tiled floors, others with parquet and dark old wardrobes).

★ Five Rooms BOUTIQUE HOTEL €€
(Map p586; ☑ 93 342 78 80; www.thefiverooms. com; Carrer de Pau Claris 72; s/d from €155/165; ❄ @ ⟨; ⓜ Urquinaona) Like they say, there are five rooms (standard rooms and suites) in this 1st-floor flat virtually on the border between L'Eixample and the old centre of town. Each is different and features include broad, firm beds, stretches of exposed brick wall, restored mosaic tiles and minimalist decor. There are also two apartments.

✖ Eating

Barcelona is foodie heaven. Although the city has a reputation as a hot spot of 'new Spanish cuisine', you'll still find local eateries serving up time-honoured local grub, from squid-ink *fideuà* (a satisfying paella-like noodle dish) through pigs' trotters, rabbit with snails, and *butifarra* (a tasty local sausage).

✖ La Rambla & Barri Gòtic

Allium CATALAN, FUSION €€
(Map p590; ☑ 93 302 30 03; Carrer del Call 17; mains €8-16; ⊙ noon-4pm Mon-Tue, to 10.30pm Wed-Sat; ⓜ Liceu) This inviting newcomer to Barri Gòtic serves beautifully prepared tapas dishes and changing specials (including seafood paella for one). The menu, which changes every two or threee weeks, focuses on seasonal, organic cuisine. Its bright, modern interior sets it apart from other neighbour-

hood options; it's also open continuously, making it a good bet for those who don't want to wait until 9pm for a meal.

La Vinateria del Call
SPANISH €€

(Map p590; ☎93 302 60 92; www.lavinateria-delcall.com; Carrer de Sant Domènec del Call 9; small plates €7-12; ⊙7.30pm-1am; Ⓜ Jaume I) In a magical setting in the former Jewish quarter, this tiny jewelbox of a restaurant serves up tasty Iberian dishes including Galician octopus, cider-cooked chorizo and the Catalan *escalivada* (roasted peppers, aubergine and onions) with anchovies. Portions are small and made for sharing, and there's a good and affordable selection of wines.

Pla
FUSION €€€

(Map p590; ☎93 412 65 52; www.elpla.cat; Carrer de la Bellafila 5; mains €18-25; ⊙7.30pm-midnight; ⓘ; Ⓜ Jaume I) One of Gòtic's long-standing favourites, Pla is a stylish, romantically lit medieval dining room where the cooks churn out such temptations as oxtail braised in red wine, seared tuna with oven-roasted peppers, and polenta with seasonal mushrooms. It has a tasting menu for €38 Sunday to Thursday.

✕ El Raval

Elisabets
CATALAN €

(Map p590; ☎93 317 58 26; Carrer d'Elisabets 2-4; mains €8-10; ⊙7.30am-11pm Mon-Thu & Sat, until 2am Fri, closed Aug; Ⓜ Catalunya) This unassuming restaurant is popular for no-nonsense local fare. The walls are dotted with old radio sets and the *menú del día* (set menu; €10.85) varies daily. If you prefer *a la carta*, try the *ragú de jabalí* (wild boar stew) and finish with *mel i mató* (a Catalan dessert made from cheese and honey). Those with a post-midnight hunger on Friday nights can probably get a meal here as late as 1am.

★ Mam i Teca
CATALAN €€

(Map p586; ☎93 441 33 35; Carrer de la Lluna 4; mains €9-12; ⊙1-4pm & 8pm-midnight Mon, Wed-Fri & Sun, closed Sat lunch; Ⓜ Sant Antoni) A tiny place with half a dozen tables, Mam i Teca is as much a lifestyle choice as a restaurant. Locals drop in and hang about at the bar, and diners are treated to Catalan dishes made with locally sourced products and adhering to Slow Food principles. Try, for example, cod fried in olive oil with garlic and red pepper, or pork ribs with chickpeas.

Bar Pinotxo
TAPAS €€

(Map p590; www.pinotxobar.com; Mercat de la Boqueria; mains €8-15; ⊙6am-4pm Mon-Sat; Ⓜ Liceu) Bar Pinotxo is arguably La Boqueria's, and even Barcelona's, best tapas bar. It sits among the half-dozen or so informal eateries within the market, and the popular owner, Juanito, might serve up chickpeas with a sweet sauce of pine nuts and raisins, a fantastically soft mix of potato and spinach sprinkled with coarse salt, soft baby squid with cannellini beans, or a quivering cube of caramel-sweet pork belly.

✕ La Ribera & Waterfront

Bormuth
TAPAS €

(Map p590; ☎93 310 21 86; Carrer del Rec 31; tapas from €3.50; ⊙5pm-midnight Mon & Tue, noon-1am Wed, Thu & Sun, noon-2.30am Fri & Sat; Ⓜ Jaume I) Opened on the pedestrian Carrer del Rec in 2013, Bormuth has tapped into the vogue for old-school tapas with modern-times service and decor, and serves all the old favourites – *patatas bravas, ensaladilla* (Russian salad), tortilla – along with some less predictable and superbly prepared numbers (try the chargrilled red pepper with black pudding). The split-level dining room is never less than animated, but there's a more peaceful space with a single long table if you can assemble a group.

Can Maño
SPANISH €

(Map p586; Carrer del Baluard 12; mains €7-12; ⊙9am-4pm Tue-Sat & 8-11pm Mon-Fri; Ⓜ Barceloneta) It may look like a dive, but you'll need to be prepared to wait before being squeezed in at a packed table for a raucous night of *raciones* (posted on a board at the back) over a bottle of *turbio* – a cloudy white plonk. The seafood is abundant with first-rate squid, shrimp and fish served at rock-bottom prices.

Cal Pep
TAPAS €€

(Map p590; ☎93 310 79 61; www.calpep.com; Plaça de les Olles 8; mains €12-20; ⊙7.30-11.30pm Mon, 1-3.45pm & 7.30-11.30pm Tue-Fri, 1-3.45pm Sat, closed last 3 weeks Aug; Ⓜ Barceloneta) It's getting a foot in the door here that's the problem – there can be queues out into the square with people trying to get in. And if you want one of the five tables out the back, you'll need to call ahead. Most people are happy elbowing their way to the bar for some of the tastiest gourmet seafood tapas in town.

DON'T MISS

SEEING AN FC BARCELONA MATCH

Football in Barcelona has the aura of religion and for much of the city's population, support of FC Barcelona is an article of faith. FC Barcelona is traditionally associated with the Catalans and even Catalan nationalism.

Tickets to FC Barcelona matches are available at **Camp Nou** (☎902 189900; www.fcbarcelona.com; Carrer d'Aristides Maillol; adult/child €23/17; ◷10am-7.30pm Mon-Sat, to 2.30pm Sun; ⓜPalau Reial), online (through FC Barcelona's official website), as well as through various city locations. Tourist offices sell them (the branch at Plaça de Catalunya is a centrally located option) as do FC Botiga stores. Tickets can cost anything from €35 to upwards of €250, depending on the seat and match. On match day the ticket windows open weekdays from 9am until half time, on Saturdays from 10am until half time; on Sundays they open two hours before kick off through half time.

✗ L'Eixample & Gràcia

★**Cerveseria Catalana**   TAPAS €

(Map p586; ☑93 216 03 68; Carrer de Mallorca 236; tapas €4-11; ◷9.30am-1.30am; ⓜPasseig de Gràcia) The 'Catalan Brewery' is good for breakfast, lunch and dinner. Come for your morning coffee and croissant, or wait until lunch to enjoy choosing from the abundance of tapas and *montaditos* (tapas on a slice of bread). You can sit at the bar, on the pavement terrace or in the restaurant at the back. The variety of hot tapas, salads and other snacks draws a well-dressed crowd of locals and outsiders.

★**Tapas 24**   TAPAS €€

(Map p586; ☑93 488 09 77; www.carlesabellan. com; Carrer de la Diputació 269; tapas €4-9; ◷9am-midnight Mon-Sat; ⓜPasseig de Gràcia) Carles Abellan, master of Comerç 24 in La Ribera, runs this basement tapas haven known for its gourmet versions of old faves. Specials include the *bikini* (toasted ham and cheese sandwich – here the ham is cured and the truffle makes all the difference) and a thick

black *arròs negre de sípia* (squid-ink black rice).

✗ Montjuïc, Sants & Poble Sec

★**Quimet i Quimet**   TAPAS €€

(Map p586; ☑93 442 31 42; Carrer del Poeta Cabanyes 25; tapas €4-11; ◷noon-4pm & 7-10.30pm Mon-Fri, noon-4pm Sat & Sun; ⓜParal·lel) Quimet i Quimet is a family-run business that has been passed down from generation to generation. There's barely space to swing a *calamar* in this bottle-lined, standing-room-only place, but it's a treat for the palate, with *montaditos* made to order. Let the folk behind the bar advise you, and order a drop of fine wine to accompany the food.

★**Tickets**   MODERN SPANISH €€€

(Map p586; www.ticketsbar.es; Avinguda del Paral·lel 164; tapas €6-15; ◷7-11.30pm Tue-Fri, 1.30-3.30pm & 7-11.30pm Sat, closed Aug; ⓜParal·lel) This is, literally, one of the sizzling tickets in the restaurant world, a tapas bar opened by Ferran Adrià, of the legendary El Bulli, and his brother Albert. And unlike El Bulli, it's an affordable venture – if you can book a table, that is (you can only book online, and two months in advance).

🍷 Drinking & Nightlife

Barcelona clubs are spread a little more thinly than bars across the city. They tend to open from around midnight until 6am. Entry can cost from nothing to €20 (one drink usually included).

Barcelona's gay and lesbian scene is concentrated in the blocks around Carrers de Muntaner and Consell de Cent (dubbed Gayxample). Here you'll find ambience every night of the week in the bars, discos and drag clubs.

🍷 Barri Gòtic

Ocaña   BAR

(Map p590; ☑93 676 48 14; www.ocana.cat; Plaça Reial 13; ◷5pm-2.30am Mon-Fri, from 11am Sat & Sun; ⓜLiceu) Named after a flamboyant artist who once lived on Plaça Reial, Ocaña is a beautifully designed space with fluted columns, stone walls, candlelit chandeliers and plush furnishings. Have a seat on the terrace and watch the passing people parade, or head downstairs to the Moorish-inspired Apotheke bar or the chic lounge a few steps away, where DJs spin for a mix of beauties and bohemians on weekend nights.

Sor Rita   BAR
(Map p590; Carrer de la Mercè 27; ⊙7pm-2.30am; Ⓜ Jaume I) A lover of all things kitsch, Sor Rita is pure eye candy, from its leopard print wallpaper to its high-heel festooned ceiling, and deliciously irreverent decorations inspired by the films of Almodóvar. It's a fun and festive scene, with special-event nights throughout the week, including tarot readings on Mondays, €5 all-you-can-eat snack buffets on Tuesdays, karaoke Wednesdays and gin specials on Thursdays.

Moog   CLUB
(Map p586; www.masimas.com/moog; Carrer de l'Arc del Teatre 3; admission €10; ⊙midnight-5am Mon-Thu & Sun, midnight-6am Fri & Sat; Ⓜ Drassanes) This fun and minuscule club is a standing favourite with the downtown crowd. In the main dance area, DJs dish out house, techno and electro, while upstairs you can groove to a nice blend of indie and occasional classic-pop throwbacks.

🍷 La Ribera

La Vinya del Senyor   WINE BAR
(Map p590; ☑93 310 33 79; www.lavinyadelsenyor. com; Plaça de Santa Maria del Mar 5; ⊙noon-1am Mon-Thu, noon-2am Fri & Sat, noon-midnight Sun; Ⓜ Jaume I) Relax on the *terrassa,* which lies in the shadow of Basílica de Santa Maria del Mar, or crowd inside at the tiny bar. The wine list is as long as *War and Peace* and there's a table upstairs for those who opt to sample by the bottle rather than the glass.

🍷 L'Eixample & Gràcia

★ Dry Martini   BAR
(Map p586; ☑93 217 50 72; www.javierdelas muelas.com; Carrer d'Aribau 162-166; ⊙1pm-2.30am Mon-Thu, 6pm-3am Fri & Sat; Ⓜ Diagonal) Waiters with a discreetly knowing smile will attend to your cocktail needs here. The house drink, taken at the bar or in one of the plush green leather lounges, is a safe bet. The gin and tonic comes in an enormous mug-sized glass – a couple of these and you're well on the way. Out the back is a restaurant, **Speakeasy** (Map p586; ☑93 217 50 80; www.javierdelas muelas.com; Carrer d'Aribau 162-166; mains €19-28; ⊙1-4pm & 8pm-midnight Mon-Fri, 8pm-midnight Sat, closed Aug; Ⓜ Diagonal).

Monvínic   WINE BAR
(Map p586; ☑932 72 61 87; www.monvinic.com; Carrer de la Diputació 249; ⊙wine bar 1.30-11pm Mon-Sat; Ⓜ Passeig de Gràcia) Proclaimed as 'possibly the best wine bar in the world' by the *Wall Street Journal,* and apparently considered unmissable by El Bulli's sommelier, Monvínic is an ode, a rhapsody even, to wine loving. The interactive wine list sits on the bar for you to browse on a digital tablet similar to an iPad and boasts more than 3000 varieties.

☆ Entertainment

Razzmatazz   LIVE MUSIC
(Map p586; ☑93 320 82 00; www.salarazzmatazz. com; Carrer de Pamplona 88; admission €12-32; ⊙midnight-3.30am Thu, to 5.30am Fri & Sat; Ⓜ Marina, Bogatell) Bands from far and wide occasionally create scenes of near hysteria in this, one of the city's classic live-music and clubbing venues. Bands can appear throughout the week (check the website), with different start times. On weekends the live music then gives way to club sounds.

★ Palau de la Música Catalana   CLASSICAL MUSIC
(Map p586; ☑93 295 72 00; www.palaumusica. org; Carrer de Sant Francesc de Paula 2; ⊙box office 9.30am-9pm Mon-Sat; Ⓜ Urquinaona) A feast for the eyes, this Modernista confection is also the city's most traditional venue for classical and choral music, although it has a wide-ranging program, including flamenco, pop and – particularly – jazz. Just being here for a performance is an experience. Sip a preconcert tipple in the foyer, its tiled pillars all a-glitter. Head up the grand stairway to the main auditorium, a whirlpool of Modernista whimsy.

🛍 Shopping

Most mainstream fashion stores are along a shopping 'axis' that runs from Plaça de Catalunya along Passeig de Gràcia, then left (west) along Avinguda Diagonal.

The El Born area in La Ribera is awash with tiny boutiques, especially those purveying young, fun fashion. There are plenty of shops scattered throughout the Barri Gòtic (stroll Carrer d'Avinyò and Carrer de Portaferrissa). For secondhand stuff, head for El Raval, especially Carrer de la Riera Baixa.

Empremtes de Catalunya   HANDICRAFTS
(Map p590; ☑93 467 46 60; Carrer dels Banys Nous 11; ⊙10am-8pm Mon-Sat, to 2pm Sun; Ⓜ Liceu) A celebration of Catalan products, this nicely designed store is a great place to browse for unique gifts. You'll find jewellery with designs inspired by Roman iconography

WORTH A TRIP

ANDORRA

This mini-country wedged between France and Spain offers by far the best ski slopes and resort facilities in all the Pyrenees. Once the snows melt, there's an abundance of great walking, ranging from easy strolls to demanding day hikes in the principality's higher, more remote reaches. Strike out above the tight valleys and you can walk for hours, almost alone.

The only way to reach Andorra is by road from Spain or France. If driving, fill up in Andorra; fuel is substantially cheaper there. There are bus services to/from Barcelona's Estació del Nord, Barcelona's airport El Prat de Llobregat, Lleida and Toulouse (France). All bus services arrive at and leave from Andorra la Vella.

(as well as works that reference Gaudí and Barcelona's Gothic era), plus pottery, wooden toys, silk scarves, notebooks, housewares and more.

Els Encants Vells MARKET
(Fira de Bellcaire; Map p586; ☑93 246 30 30; www.encantsbcn.com; Plaça de les Glòries Catalanes; ⊙8am-8pm Mon, Wed, Fri & Sat; MGlòries) In a gleaming open-sided complex near Plaça de les Glòries Catalanes, the 'Old Charms' flea market is the biggest of its kind in Barcelona. Over 500 vendors ply their wares beneath massive mirror-like panels. It's all here, from antique furniture through to secondhand clothes. A lot of it is junk, but occasionally you'll stumble across a *ganga* (bargain).

Vinçon HOMEWARES
(Map p586; ☑93 215 60 50; www.vincon.com; Passeig de Gràcia 96; ⊙10am-8.30pm Mon-Fri, 10.30am-9pm Sat; MDiagonal) An icon of the Barcelona design scene, Vinçon has the slickest furniture and household goods (particularly lighting), both local and imported. Not surprising, really, since the building, raised in 1899, belonged to the Modernista artist Ramon Casas. Head upstairs to the furniture area – from the windows and terrace you get close side views of La Pedrera.

Custo Barcelona FASHION
(Map p590; ☑93 268 78 93; www.custo-barcelona.com; Plaça de les Olles 7; ⊙10am-9pm Mon-Sat, noon-8pm Sun; MJaume I) The psychedelic decor and casual atmosphere lend this avant-garde Barcelona fashion store a youthful edge. Custo presents daring new women's and men's collections each year on the New York catwalks. The dazzling colours and cut of anything from dinner jackets to hot pants are for the uninhibited. It has five other stores around town.

ℹ Information

Purse snatching and pickpocketing are major problems, especially around Plaça de Catalunya, La Rambla and Plaça Reial.

Guàrdia Urbana (Local Police; ☑092; La Rambla 43; MLiceu)

Mossos d'Esquadra (☑088; Carrer Nou de la Rambla 80; MParal.lel) Tourists who want to report thefts need to go to the Catalan police, known as the Mossos d'Esquadra.

Oficina d'Informació de Turisme de Barcelona (Map p590; ☑93 285 38 34; www.barcelonaturisme.com; underground at Plaça de Catalunya 17-S; ⊙9.30am-9.30pm; MCatalunya) The main Barcelona tourist information office sells walking tours, bus tours, discount cards, transport passes, tickets to shows, and can help book accommodation.There's also a branch in the ajuntament (Map p590; ☑93 285 38 32; Carrer de la Ciutat 2; ⊙8.30am-8.30pm Mon-Fri, 9am-7pm Sat, 9am-2pm Sun & holidays; MJaume I), as well as in the train station and airport.

Palau Robert Regional Tourist Office (Map p586; ☑93 238 80 91, from outside Catalonia 902 400012; www.gencat.net/probert; Passeig de Gràcia 107; ⊙10am-8pm Mon-Sat, to 2.30pm Sun; MDiagonal) A host of material on Catalonia, audiovisual resources, a bookshop and a branch of Turisme Juvenil de Catalunya (for youth travel).

ℹ Getting There & Away

AIR

El Prat Airport (☑902 404704; www.aena.es) Barcelona's airport, El Prat de Llobregat, is 12km southwest of the city centre. Barcelona is a big international and domestic destination, with direct flights from North America as well as many European cities.

BOAT

Acciona Trasmediterránea (☑902 454645; www.trasmediterranea.es; MDrassanes) Regular passenger and vehicular ferries to/from the Balearic Islands, operated by Acciona

Trasmediterránea, dock along both sides of the Moll de Barcelona wharf in Port Vell.

BUS

Estació del Nord (Map p586; ☑ 902 260606; www.barcelonanord.cat; Carrer d'Ali Bei 80; Ⓜ Arc de Triomf) The main terminal for most domestic and international buses is the Estació del Nord. ALSA goes to Madrid (€32, eight hours, up to 16 daily), Valencia (€29, four to 4½ hours, nine to 14 daily) and many other destinations.

Estació d'Autobusos de Sants (Map p586; Carrer de Viriat; Ⓜ Estació Sants) Eurolines (www.eurolines.es) also offers international services from Estació del Nord and Estació d'Autobusos de Sants, which is next to Estació Sants Barcelona.

TRAIN

Estació Sants (Plaça dels Països Catalans; Ⓜ Estació Sants) Virtually all trains travelling to and from destinations within Spain stop at Estació Sants. High-speed trains to Madrid via Lleida and Zaragoza take as little as two hours and 40 minutes; prices vary wildly. Other trains run to Valencia (€35 to €45, three to 4½ hours, up to 15 daily) and Burgos (from €62 to €86, 5½ to 6½ hours, four daily).

There are also international connections with French cities from the same station.

❶ Getting Around

TO/FROM THE AIRPORT

Renfe's R2 Nord train line runs between the airport and Passeig de Gràcia (via Estació Sants) in central Barcelona (about 35 minutes). Tickets cost €4.10, unless you have a T-10 multitrip public-transport ticket.

A taxi to/from the centre, about a half-hour ride depending on traffic, costs around €30 to €35.

A1 Aerobús (Map p586; ☑ 902 100104; www.aerobusbcn.com; one way/return €5.90/10.20) The A1 Aerobús runs from Terminal 1 to Plaça de Catalunya from 6.05am to 1.05am, taking 30 to 40 minutes. A2 Aerobús does the same run from Terminal 2, from 6am to 12.30am. Buy tickets on the bus.

PUBLIC TRANSPORT

Barcelona's metro system spreads its tentacles around the city in such a way that most places of interest are within a 10-minute walk of a station. Buses and suburban trains are needed only for a few destinations. A single metro, bus or suburban train ride costs €2, but a T-10 ticket, valid for 10 rides, costs €10.30.

TAXI

Taxi (☑ Fonotaxi 93 300 11 00, Radiotaxi 93 303 30 33, Radiotaxi BCN 93 225 00 00) Barcelona's black-and-yellow taxis are plentiful and reasonably priced. The flag fall is €2.10.

Tarragona

POP 133,550

The eternally sunny port city of Tarragona is a fascinating mix of Mediterranean beach life, Roman history and medieval alleyways. Tarragona has a wealth of ruins, including a seaside amphitheatre and the town's medieval heart is one of the most beautifully designed in Spain, its maze of narrow cobbled streets encircled by steep walls and crowned with a splendid cathedral. A lively eating and drinking scene makes for an enticing stop.

◉ Sights & Activities

Museu d'Història de Tarragona RUIN
(MHT; www.museutgn.com; adult/child per site €3.30/free, all sites €11.05/free; ⊙ sites 9am-9pm Tue-Sat, 10am-3pm Sun Easter-Sep, 10am-7pm Tue-Sat, 10am-3pm Sun Oct-Easter) The Museu d'Història de Tarragona consists of various separate Unesco World Heritage Roman sites, as well as some other historic buildings around town. Buy a combined ticket and get exploring!

**★ Fòrum Provincial
Pretori i Circ Romans** RUIN
(Plaça del Rei) This sizeable complex with two separate entrances includes part of the vaults of the **Roman circus**, where chariot races were once held, as well as the **Pretori tower** on Plaça de Rei and part of the **provincial forum**, the political heart of Tarraconensis province. The circus, 300m long, stretched from here to beyond Plaça de la Font to the west.

Passeig Arqueològic Muralles WALLS
A peaceful walk takes you around part of the perimeter of the old town between two lines of city walls; the inner ones are mainly Roman and date back to the 3rd century BC, while the outer ones were put up by the British in 1709 during the War of the Spanish Succession. Prepare to be awed by the vast gateways built by the Iberians and clamber up onto the battlements from the doorway to the right of the entrance for all-encompassing views of the city. The walk starts from the **Portal del Roser** on Avenida Catalunya.

WORTH A TRIP

GIRONA

A tight huddle of ancient arcaded houses, grand churches, climbing cobbled streets and medieval baths, all enclosed by defensive walls and a lazy river, constitute a powerful reason for visiting north Catalonia's largest city, Girona (Castilian: Gerona).

Girona-Costa Brava airport, 11km south of the centre, is Ryanair's Spanish hub. There are more than 20 trains per day to Figueres (€4.10 to €5.45, 30 minutes) and Barcelona (from €8.40, 40 minutes to 1½ hours).

Catedral (www.catedraldegirona.org; Plaça de la Catedral; adult/student incl Basílica de Sant Feliu €7/5, Sun free; ⊙10am-7.30pm Apr-Oct, 10am-6.30pm Nov-Mar) The billowing baroque facade of the cathedral towers over a flight of 86 steps rising from Plaça de la Catedral. Though the beautiful double-columned Romanesque **cloister** dates to the 12th century, most of the building is Gothic, with the second-widest nave (23m) in Christendom. The 14th-century gilt-and-silver altarpiece and canopy are memorable, as are the bishop's throne and the museum, which holds the masterly Romanesque *Tapís de la creació* (Tapestry of the Creation) and a Mozarabic illuminated *Beatus* manuscript, dating from 975.

The Call Until 1492 Girona was home to Catalonia's second-most important medieval Jewish community (after Barcelona), and its Jewish quarter, the Call, was centred on Carrer de la Força. For an idea of medieval Jewish life and culture, visit the **Museu d'Història dels Jueus de Girona**. Also known as the Centre Bonastruc Ça Porta, named after Jewish Girona's most illustrious figure, a 13th-century cabbalist philosopher and mystic, the centre – a warren of rooms and stairways around a courtyard – hosts temporary exhibitions and is a focal point for studies of Jewish Spain.

Casa Cúndaro (✆972 22 35 83; www.casacundaro.com; Pujada de la Catedral 9; s/d €88/110; ✳🛜) The understated exterior of this medieval Jewish house hides five sumptuous rooms and four self-catering apartments – all combining original exposed stone walls and antique doors with modern luxuries. You couldn't wish for a more characterful base; the location right next to the cathedral is either a boon or a bane, depending on whether you enjoy the sound of church bells. Reception is at the Hotel Historic a short stroll up the hill.

El Celler de Can Roca (✆972 22 21 57; www.cellercanroca.com; Carrer Can Sunyer 48; degustation menus €150-180; ⊙1-4pm & 8.30-11pm Tue-Sat Sep-Jul) Named best restaurant in the world in 2013 by The World's 50 Best Restaurants, this place, 2km west of central Girona in a refurbished country house, is run by three brothers. The focus is 'emotional cuisine' through ever-changing takes on Catalan dishes. The style is playful and a full range of molecular gastronomy techniques is employed. The voluminous wine list arrives on a trolley. Book online 11 months in advance; if you haven't, you can join a standby list.

Tourist Office (✆972 22 65 75; www.girona.cat/turisme; Rambla de la Llibertat 1; ⊙9am-8pm Mon-Fri, 9am-2pm & 4-8pm Sat, 9am-2pm Sun) Multilingual and helpful.

★**Fòrum de la Colònia**　　　RUIN
(Carrer de Lleida) The main provincial forum occupied most of what is now the old town. Further down the hill, this local plaza was occupied by a judicial basilica (where legal disputes were settled) among other buildings. Linked to the site by a footbridge is another excavated area, which includes a stretch of Roman street. The discovery of foundations of a temple to Jupiter, Juno and Minerva suggests the forum was bigger and more important than had previously been assumed.

★**Museu Nacional Arqueològic de Tarragona**　　　MUSEUM
(www.mnat.cat; Plaça del Rei 5; adult/child €2.40/ free; ⊙9.30am-6pm Tue-Sat, 10am-2pm Sun) This excellent museum does justice to the cultural and material wealth of Roman Tarraco. Well-laid-out exhibits include part of the Roman city walls, frescoes, sculpture and pottery. The mosaic collection traces the changing trends – from simple black-and-white designs to complex full-colour creations. A highlight is the large, almost complete *Mosaic de Peixos de la Pineda*,

showing fish and sea creatures. It's open extended hours in high season.

★ **Catedral**   CATHEDRAL
(www.catedraldetarragona.com; Plaça de la Seu; adult/child €5/3; ⊙10am-7pm Mon-Sat mid-Mar–Oct, 10am-5pm Mon-Fri, 10am-7pm Sat Nov–mid-Mar) Sitting grandly atop town, Tarragona's cathedral has both Romanesque and Gothic features, as typified by the main facade. The cloister has Gothic vaulting and Romanesque carved capitals, one of which shows rats conducting a cat's funeral...until the cat comes back to life! It's a lesson about passions seemingly lying dormant until they reveal themselves. Chambers off the cloister house the **Museu Diocesà**, with an extensive collection extending from Roman hairpins to some lovely 12th- to 14th-century polychrome woodcarvings of a breastfeeding Virgin.

🍽 Sleeping & Eating

Look for tapas bars and inexpensive cafes on the Plaça de la Font. The Moll de Pescadors (Fishermen's Wharf) is the place to go for seafood restaurants.

Hotel Plaça de la Font   HOTEL €€
(☑977 24 61 34; www.hotelpdelafont.com; Plaça de la Font 26; s/d €55/75; ✳🛜) Comfortable modern rooms, with photos of Tarragona monuments above the bed, overlook a bustling terrace in a you-can't-get-more-central-than-this location, right on the popular Plaça de la Font. The ones at the front

are pretty well soundproofed and have tiny balconies for people-watching.

Hotel Lauria   HOTEL €€
(☑977 23 67 12; www.hotel-lauria.com; Rambla Nova 20; s/d incl breakfast €65/77; 🅿✳🛜🏊) Right on the Rambla Nova near where it ends at a balcony overlooking the sea, this smart hotel offers great-value modern rooms with welcome splashes of colour, large bathrooms and a small swimming pool. The rooms at the back are less exposed to the noise from the Rambla.

AQ   CATALAN €€
(☑977 21 59 54; www.aq-restaurant.com; Carrer de les Coques 7; degustation €40-50; ⊙1.30-3.30pm & 8.30-11pm Tue-Sat) This is a bubbly designer haunt alongside the cathedral with stark colour contrasts (black, lemon and cream linen), slick lines and intriguing plays on traditional cooking. One of the two degustation menus is the way to go here, or try the weekday lunch *menú* for €18.

Ares   CATALAN, SPANISH €€
(www.aresrestaurant.es; Plaça del Forum; mains €11-19; ⊙1-4pm & 8.30-11.30pm Wed-Sun) Amid a riot of colourful, exuberant Modernista decor, the cordial welcome from this husband-and-wife team guarantees good eating. Some classic Catalan dishes take their place alongside quality ingredients from across Spain: Asturian cheeses, Galician seafood, Burgos black pudding. They are complemented by some recreated Roman dishes. Quality and quantity are both praiseworthy.

SPAIN TARRAGONA

DALÍ'S CATALONIA

The first name that comes into your head when you lay your eyes on this red castle-like building, topped with giant eggs and stylised Oscar-like statues and studded with plaster-covered croissants, is Dalí. An entirely appropriate final resting place for the master of surrealism, the entrance to the **Teatre-Museu Dalí** (www.salvador-dali.org; Plaça de Gala i Salvador Dalí 5; admission incl Dalí Joies & Museu de l'Empordà adult/child under 9yr €12/free; ⊙9am-8pm Jul-Sep, 9.30am-6pm Tue-Sun Mar-Jun & Oct, 10.30am-6pm Tue-Sun Nov-Feb) is watched over by medieval suits of armour balancing baguettes on their heads; it has assured his immortality. 'Theatre-museum' is an apt label for this trip through the incredibly fertile imagination of one of the great showmen of the 20th century.

Port Lligat, a 1.25km walk from Cadaqués, is a tiny settlement around another lovely cove, with fishing boats pulled up on its beach. The **Casa Museu Dalí** started life as a mere fisherman's hut, was steadily altered and enlarged by Dalí, who lived here from 1930 to 1982 (apart from a dozen or so years abroad during and around the Spanish Civil War), and is now a fascinating insight into the lives of the (excuse the pun) surreal couple. We probably don't need to tell you that it's the house with a lot of little white chimneypots and two egg-shaped towers, overlooking the western end of the beach. You must book ahead.

ℹ Information

Tourist Office (✆ 977 25 07 95; www.tarra gonaturisme.es; Carrer Major 39; ⊙10am-2pm & 3-5pm Mon-Fri, to 7pm Sat, 10am-2pm Sun) Good place for booking guided tours of the city. Opens extended hours in high season.

ℹ Getting There & Away

BUS

The **bus station** (Plaça Imperial Tarraco) is 1.5km northwest of the old town along Rambla Nova. Destinations include Barcelona (€8.70, 1½ hours, 16 daily), Lleida (€10.70, 1¾ hours, five daily) and Valencia (€21.73, three to 4½ hours, seven daily).

TRAIN

The local train station is a 10-minute walk from the old town while fast AVE trains arrive at Camp de Tarragona station, a 15-minute taxi ride from the centre. Departures include Barcelona (both normal trains and rodalies on the R14, R15 and R16 lines, €7 to €38.20, 35 minutes to 1½ hours, every 30 minutes) and Valencia (€21.70 to €38, two to 3½ hours, 19 daily).

ARAGÓN, BASQUE COUNTRY & NAVARRA

Zaragoza

POP 679,624

Zaragoza (Saragossa) is a vibrant, elegant and fascinating city. Located on the banks of the mighty Río Ebro, the residents comprise over half of Aragón's population and enjoy a lifestyle that revolves around some of the best tapas bars in the province, as well as superb shopping and a vigorous nightlife. But Zaragoza is so much more than just a good-time city: it also has a host of historical sights spanning all the great civilisations that have left their indelible mark on the Spanish soul.

◎ Sights

★ Basílica de Nuestra Señora del Pilar   CHURCH

(Plaza del Pilar; lift admission €3; ⊙7am-9.30pm, lift 10am-1.30pm & 4-6.30pm Tue-Sun) **FREE** Brace yourself for this great baroque cavern of Catholicism. The faithful believe that it was here on 2 January AD 40 that Santiago saw the Virgin Mary descend atop a marble

pilar (pillar). A chapel was built around the remaining pillar, followed by a series of ever-more-grandiose churches, culminating in the enormous basilica. A **lift** whisks you most of the way up the north tower from where you climb to a superb viewpoint over the domes and city.

★ La Seo   CATHEDRAL

(Catedral de San Salvador; Plaza de la Seo; adult/ concession €4/3; ⊙10am-6pm Tue-Fri, 10am-noon & 3-6pm Sat, 10-11.30am & 2.30-6pm Sun Jun-Sep, shorter hours Oct-May) Dominating the eastern end of Plaza del Pilar, the La Seo was built between the 12th and 17th centuries and displays a fabulous spread of architectural styles from Romanesque to baroque. The cathedral stands on the site of Islamic Zaragoza's main mosque (which in turn stood upon the temple of the Roman forum). The admission price includes entry to La Seo's **Museo de Tapices** (Plaza de la Seo; ⊙10am-8.30pm Tue-Sun Jun-Sep, shorter hours Oct-May), an impressive collection of 14th- to 17th-century Flemish and French tapestries.

★ Aljafería   PALACE

(Calle de los Diputados; admission €3, Sun free; ⊙10am-2pm Sat-Wed, plus 4.30-8pm Mon-Wed, Fri & Sat Jul & Aug) The Aljafería is Spain's finest Islamic-era edifice outside Andalucía. Built as a pleasure palace for Zaragoza's Islamic rulers in the 11th century, it underwent its first alterations in 1118 when the city passed into Christian hands. In the 1490s the Catholic Monarchs, Fernando and Isabel, tacked on their own palace, whereafter the Aljafería fell into decay. Twentieth-century restorations brought the building back to life, and in 1987 Aragón's regional parliament was established here. Tours take place throughout the day (multilingual in July and August).

Museo Ibercaja Camón Aznar   MUSEUM

(MICAZ; www.ibercaja.es; Calle de Espoz y Mina 23; ⊙10am-2.30pm & 5-9pm Tue-Sat, 10am-2.30pm Sun) **FREE** This collection of Spanish art through the ages is dominated by an enthralling series of etchings by Goya (on the 2nd floor), one of the premier such collections in existence. You'll also find paintings by other luminaries (including Ribera and Zurbarán), which are spread over the three storeys of this Renaissance-era mansion. There are regular temporary exhibitions.

★**Museo del Foro de**
Caesaraugusta MUSEUM
(Plaza de la Seo 2; adult/concession/child under 8yr
€3/2/free; ⊙9am-8.30pm Tue-Sat, 10am-2pm Sun
Jun-Sep, shorter hours Oct-May; 🔊) The trap-
ezoidal building on Plaza de la Seo is the
entrance to an excellent reconstruction of
part of Roman Caesaraugusta's forum, now
well below ground level. The remains of porticoes, shops, a great *cloaca* (sewer) system,
and a limited collection of artefacts from the
1st century AD are on display. An interesting
multilingual 15-minute audiovisual show
breathes life into it all and culminates with
a clever 'talking head' of a statue which children, in particular, will enjoy.

★**Museo del Teatro de**
Caesaraugusta RUIN, MUSEUM
(Calle de San Jorge 12; adult/concession/child
under 8yr €4/3/free; ⊙9am-8.30pm Tue-Sat, to
1.30pm Sun; 🔊) Discovered during the excavation of a building site in 1972, the ruins of
Zaragoza's Teatro Romano (Roman theatre)
are the focus of this compelling museum.
The theatre once seated 6000 spectators,
and great efforts have been made to help
visitors reconstruct the edifice's former
splendour, including evening projections of
a **virtual performance** (May to October)
and an entertaining audiovisual production.
The theatre is visible from the surrounding
streets and the on-site (and excellent) cafe
which may be entered separately.

🛏 **Sleeping**

Hotel Río Arga HOTEL €
(☎976 39 90 65; www.hotelrioarga.es; Calle Con-
tamina 20; s/d €40/45; P🕸📶) Río Arga offers comfortable spacious rooms with easy-
on-the-eye decor and large bathrooms with
tubs. The private parking is a real boon
given this central city location. Breakfast
costs €3.75.

★**Hotel Sauce** BOUTIQUE HOTEL €€
(☎976 20 50 50; www.hotelsauce.com; Calle de Espoz y Mina 33; s €48, d €55-66; 🕸📶) This chic,
small hotel has a great central location and
overall light and airy look with white wicker,
painted furniture, stripy fabrics and tasteful watercolours on the walls. The superior
rooms are well worth the few euros extra.
Breakfast (€8) includes homemade cakes
and a much-lauded *tortilla de patatas* (potato omelette).

Sabinas APARTMENT €€
(☎976 20 47 10; www.sabinas.es; Calle de Alfonso I
43; d/apt €50/75; 🕸📶) These apartments include a contemporary-style kitchen and sitting room. The star performer is the Bayeu
Attic (€120), a two-bedroom apartment with
fabulous basilica views. It also has standard
doubles with microwave and there's a second location at Calle Francisco Bayeu 4. Reception is at nearby Hotel Sauce.

✗ **Eating & Drinking**

Zaragoza has some terrific tapas bars, with
dozens of places on or close to Plaza de Santa Marta. Otherwise the narrow streets of El
Tubo, north of Plaza de España, are tapas
central.

Calle del Temple, southwest of Plaza del
Pilar, is the spiritual home of Zaragoza's
roaring nightlife. This is where the city's students head out to drink. There are more bars
lined up along this street than anywhere
else in Aragón.

Casa Pascualillo CONTEMPORARY TAPAS €
(Calle de la Libertad 5; tapas from €1.60, mains €5-
14; ⊙noon-4pm & 7-11pm Tue-Sat, noon-4.30pm
Sun) When *Metropoli,* the weekend magazine of *El Mundo* newspaper, sought out
the best 50 tapas bars in Spain a few years
back, it's no surprise that Casa Pascualillo
made the final cut. The bar groans under the
weight of enticing tapas like El Pascualillo, a
'small' *bocadillo* (filled roll) of *jamón,* oyster
mushrooms and onion. There's a more formal restaurant attached.

★**El Ciclón** CONTEMPORARY SPANISH €€
(Plaza del Pilar 10; raciones €7-8.50, set menus
€15-20; ⊙11am-11.30pm) Opened in November 2013 by three acclaimed Spanish chefs
(all with Michelin-star restaurant experience), the dishes here are superbly prepared. Choose between set menus and tapas
and *raciones* such as the Canary Island
favourite, *papas arrugadas* (new potatoes
with a spicy coriander sauce), noodles with
mussels, and artichokes with *migas* (bread-
crumbs with garlic and olive oil) and cauli-
flower cream.

🛈 **Information**

Municipal Tourist Office (☎976 20 12 00;
www.zaragozaturismo.es; Plaza del Pilar;
⊙9am-9pm mid-Jun–mid-Oct, 10am-8pm
mid-Oct–mid-Jun; 📶) Has branch offices
around town, including the train station.

Oficina de Turismo de Aragón (www.turismo dearagon.com; Plaza de España; ⊙ 9am-2pm & 5-8pm Mon-Fri, from 10am Sat & Sun; 🐾) Has plenty of brochures on the province.

ⓘ Getting There & Away

AIR

Zaragoza-Sanjurjo Airport (☑ 976 71 23 00; www.zaragoza-airport.com) The Zaragoza-Sanjurjo airport, 8.5km west of the city, has direct Ryanair flights to/from London (Stansted), Brussels (Charleroi), Paris (Beauvais), Milan (Bergamo), Lanzarote and Seville. Iberia (www.iberia.es) and Air Europa (www.aireuropa.com) also operate a small number of domestic and international routes.

BUS

Dozens of bus lines fan out across Spain from the bus station attached to the Estación Intermodal Delicias train station.

TRAIN

Estación Intermodal Delicias (www.renfe.com; Calle Rioja 33) Zaragoza's futuristic, if rather impersonal, Estación Intermodal Delicias is connected by almost hourly high-speed AVE services to Madrid (1¼ hours) and Barcelona (from 1½ hours). There are also services to Valencia (4½ hours, three daily), Huesca (one hour), Jaca (3½ hours) and Teruel (2¼ hours).

Around Aragón

In Aragón's south, little visited **Teruel** is home to some stunning Mudéjar architecture. Nearby, **Albarracín** is one of Spain's most beautiful villages.

In the north, the Pyrenees dominate and the **Parque Nacional de Ordesa y Monte Perdido** is excellent for hiking; the pretty village of **Torla** is the gateway. South of the hamlet of **La Besurta** is the great Maladeta massif, a superb challenge for experienced climbers. This forbidding line of icy peaks, with glaciers suspended from the higher crests, culminates in **Aneto** (3404m), the highest peak in the Pyrenees. There are plenty of hiking and climbing options for all levels in these mountain parks bordering France. Another enchanting base for exploration in the region is **Aínsa**, a hilltop village of stone houses.

In Aragón's northwest, **Sos del Rey Católico** is another gorgeous stone village draped along a ridge.

San Sebastián

POP 183,300

Stylish San Sebastián (Donostia in Basque) has the air of an upscale resort, complete with an idyllic location on the shell-shaped Bahía de la Concha. The natural setting – crystalline waters, a flawless beach, green hills on all sides – is captivating. But this is one of Spain's true culinary capitals, with more Michelin stars (16) per capita than anywhere else on earth.

◉ Sights & Activities

★Playa de la Concha   BEACH
Fulfilling almost every idea of how a perfect city beach should be formed, Playa de la Concha and its westerly extension, **Playa de Ondarreta**, are easily among the best city beaches in Europe. Throughout the long summer months a fiesta atmosphere prevails, with thousands of tanned and toned bodies spread across the sands. The swimming is almost always safe.

Monte Igueldo   VIEWPOINT
The views from the summit of Monte Igueldo, just west of town, will make you feel like a circling hawk staring over the vast panorama of the Bahía de la Concha and the surrounding coastline and mountains. The best way to get there is via the old-world **funicular railway** (www.monteigueldo.es; return adult/child €3.10/2.30; ⊙ 10am-9pm Jul, 10am-10pm Aug shorter hours rest of year) to the **Parque de Atracciones** (www.monteigueldo.es; admission €2.20; ⊙ 11.15am-2pm & 4-8pm Mon-Fri, until 8.30pm Sat & Sun Jul-Sep, shorter hours rest of year), a slightly tacky mini theme park at the top of the hill. Individual rides (which include roller coasters, boat rides, carousels and pony rides) cost between €1 and €2.50 extra. Trains on the funicular railway depart every 15 minutes.

San Telmo Museoa   MUSEUM
(www.santelmomuseoa.com; Plaza Zuloaga 1; adult/student/child €5/3/free, Tue free; ⊙ 10am-8pm Tue-Sun) Both the oldest and one of the newest museums in the Basque Country, the San Telmo museum has existed since 1902 – sort of. It was actually closed for many years but after major renovation work it reopened in 2011 and is now a museum of Basque culture and society. The displays range from historical artefacts to the squiggly lines of modern art, and all the pieces reflect Basque culture and society.

🛏 Sleeping

Pensión Régil   PENSION €
(☑943 42 71 43; www.pensionregil.com; Calle de Easo 9; s/d €53/59; 🛜) The furnishings might be cheap and the decor a bit pink and floral for our liking, but just look at that price! You really won't get a much better deal in San Sebasián in high season. Add in that all rooms have private bathrooms, it's very close to Playa de la Concha and the young owner, Inaki, is a bit of a charmer and you can't go wrong.

★ Pensión Aida   BOUTIQUE HOTEL €€
(☑943 32 78 00; www.pensionesconencanto.com; Calle de Iztueta 9; s €62, d €84-90, studios €132-152; ❄@🛜) The owners of this excellent *pensión* read the rule book on what makes a good hotel and have complied exactly. The rooms are bright and bold, full of exposed stone and everything smells fresh and clean. The communal area, stuffed with soft sofas and mountains of information, is a big plus.

Pensión Amaiur   BOUTIQUE HOTEL €€
(☑943 42 96 54; www.pensionamaiur.com; Calle de 31 de Agosto 44; s €45, d €90-100; @🛜) The young and friendly owners of this top-notch guesthouse, which has a prime old-town location, have really created something different here. The look of the place is 'old-granny cottage' with bright floral wallpapers and bathrooms tiled in Andalucian blue and white.

🍴 Eating & Drinking

With 16 Michelin stars (including three restaurants with the coveted three stars) and a population of 183,000, San Sebastián stands atop a pedestal as one of the culinary capitals of the planet. As if that alone weren't enough, the city is overflowing with bars – almost all of which have bar tops weighed down under a mountain of *pintxos* (Basque tapas) that almost every Spaniard will (sometimes grudgingly) tell you are the best in country.

Do what the locals do – crawls of the city centre's bars. *Pintxos* etiquette is simple. Ask for a plate and point out what *pintxos* (more like tasty mounds of food on little slices of baguette) you want. Keep the toothpicks and go back for as many as you'd like. Accompany with *txakoli,* a cloudy white wine poured like cider to create a little fizz. When you're ready to pay, hand over the plate with all the toothpicks and tell bar staff how many drinks you've had. It's an honour system

that has stood the test of time. Expect to pay €2.50 to €3.50 for a *pintxo* and *txakoli.*

Restaurante Alberto   SEAFOOD €
(☑943 42 88 84; Calle de 31 de Agosto 19; mains €12-15, menus €15; ⊙noon-4pm & 7pm-midnight Thu-Tue) A charming old seafood restaurant with a fishmonger-style window display of the day's catch. It's small and friendly and the pocket-sized dining room feels like it was once someone's living room. The food is earthy (well, OK, salty) and good, and the service swift.

★ La Fábrica   MODERN BASQUE €€
(☑943 98 05 81; Calle del Puerto 17; mains €15-20, menus from €24; ⊙1-3.30pm & 8.30-11pm Mon-Sat, 1-3.30pm Sun) The red brick interior walls and white tablecloths lend an air of class to a resturant whose modern takes on Basque classics have been making waves with San Sebastián locals over the last couple of years. At just €24, the multidish tasting menu is about the best value deal in the city.

La Cuchara de San Telmo   CONTEMPORARY BASQUE €€
(www.lacucharadesantelmo.com; Calle de 31 de Agosto 28; pintxos from €2.50; ⊙7.30-11pm Tue, noon-3.30pm & 7.30-11pm Wed-Sun) This unfussy, hidden-away (and hard to find) bar offers miniature *nueva cocina vasca* (Basque nouvelle cuisine) from a supremely creative kitchen. Unlike many San Sebastián bars this one doesn't have any *pintxos* laid out on the bar top; instead you must order from the blackboard menu behind the counter.

Astelena   BASQUE €€
(Calle de Iñigo 1; pintxos from €2.50; ⊙1-4.30pm & 8-11pm Tue & Thu-Sat, 1-4.30pm Wed) The *pintxos* draped across the counter in this bar, tucked

into the corner of Plaza de la Constitución, stand out. Many of them are a fusion of Basque and Asian inspirations, but the best of all are perhaps the foie-gras-based treats. The great positioning means that prices are slightly elevated.

ℹ Information

Oficina de Turismo (☑ 943 48 11 66; www. sansebastianturismo.com; Alameda del Boulevard 8; ⊙ 9am-8pm Mon-Sat, 10am-7pm Sun) This friendly office offers comprehensive information on the city and the Basque Country in general.

ℹ Getting There & Away

BUS

Daily bus services leave for Bilbao (from €6.74, one hour), Bilbao Airport (€16.50, 1¼ hours), Biarritz (France; €6.75, 1¼ hours), Madrid (from €36, five hours) and Pamplona (€7.68, one hour).

TRAIN

For France you must first go to the Spanish/French border town of Irún (or sometimes trains go as far as Hendaye; Renfe from €2.65, 25 minutes), which is also served by Eusko Tren/Ferrocarril Vasco (www.euskotren.es), and change there.

Renfe Train Station (Paseo de Francia) The main Renfe train station is just across Río Urumea, on a line linking Paris to Madrid. There are several services daily to Madrid (from €47, five hours) and two to Barcelona (from €64, six hours).

Bilbao

POP 354,200

The commercial hub of the Basque Country, Bilbao (Bilbo in Basque) is best known for the magnificent Guggenheim Museum. An architectural masterpiece by Frank Gehry, the museum was the catalyst of a turnaround that saw Bilbao transformed from an industrial port city into a vibrant cultural centre. After visiting this must-see temple to modern art, spend time exploring Bilbao's Casco Viejo (Old Quarter), a grid of elegant streets dotted with shops, cafes, *pintxos* bars and several small but worthy museums.

◉ Sights

★ Museo Guggenheim   GALLERY

(www.guggenheim-bilbao.es; Avenida Abandoibarra 2; adult/student/child €13/7.50/free; ⊙ 10am-8pm, closed Mon Sep-Jun) Opened in September 1997,

Bilbao's shimmering titanium Museo Guggenheim is one of the iconic buildings of modern architecture and it almost single-handedly lifted Bilbao out of its postindustrial depression and into the 21st century – with sensation. It boosted the city's already inspired regeneration, stimulated further development and placed Bilbao firmly in the world art and tourism spotlight.

★ Museo de Bellas Artes   GALLERY

(www.museobilbao.com; Plaza del Museo 2; adult/student/child €7/5/free, free Wed; ⊙ 10am-8pm Wed-Mon) The Museo de Bellas Artes houses a compelling collection that includes everything from Gothic sculptures to 20th-century pop art. There are three main subcollections: classical art, with works by Murillo, Zurbarán, El Greco, Goya and van Dyck; contemporary art, featuring works by Gauguin, Francis Bacon and Anthony Caro; and Basque art, with works of the great sculptors Jorge de Oteiza and Eduardo Chillida, and strong paintings by the likes of Ignacio Zuloaga and Juan de Echevarria.

Casco Viejo   OLD TOWN

The compact Casco Viejo, Bilbao's atmospheric old quarter, is full of charming streets, boisterous bars and plenty of quirky and independent shops. At the heart of the Casco are Bilbao's original seven streets, **Las Siete Calles**, which date from the 1400s.

Euskal Museoa   MUSEUM

(Museo Vasco; www.euskal-museoa.org/es/hasiera; Plaza Miguel Unamuno 4; adult/child €3/free, free Thu; ⊙ 10am-7pm Mon & Wed-Fri, 10am-1.30pm & 4-7pm Sat, 10am-2pm Sun) This museum is probably the most complete museum of Basque culture and history in all of Spain. The story kicks off back in the days of prehistory and from this murky period the displays bound rapidly through to the modern age.

🛏 Sleeping & Eating

The Bilbao tourism authority has a useful **reservations department** (☑ 902 877298; www.bilbaoreservas.com) for accommodation.

★ Pensión

Iturrienea Ostatua   BOUTIQUE HOTEL €€

(☑ 944 16 15 00; www.iturrieneaostatua.com; Calle de Santa María 14; r €50-70; 🕾) Easily the most eccentric hotel in Bilbao, it's part farmyard, part old-fashioned toyshop, and a work of art in its own right. The nine rooms here

PAMPLONA & SAN FERMINES

Immortalised by Ernest Hemingway in *The Sun Also Rises,* the pre-Pyrenean city of Pamplona (Iruña in Basque) is home of the wild Sanfermines (aka Encierro or the Running of the Bulls) festival, but is also an extremely walkable city that's managed to mix the charm of old plazas and buildings with modern shops and a lively nightlife.

The Sanfermines festival is held from 6 to 14 July, when Pamplona is overrun with thrill-seekers, curious onlookers and, yes, bulls. The Encierro (Running of the Bulls) begins at 8am daily, when bulls are let loose from the Corallillos Santo Domingo. The 825m race lasts just three minutes.

Since records began in 1924, 16 people have died during Pamplona's bullrun. Many of those who run are full of bravado (and/or drink) and have little idea of what they're doing. For dedicated *encierro* news, check out www.sanfermin.com.

Animal rights groups oppose bullrunning as a cruel tradition, and the participating bulls will almost certainly all be killed in the afternoon bullfight. The PETA-organised anti-bullfighting demonstration, the Running of the Nudes, takes place two days before the first bullrun.

Tourist Office (☑ 848 42 04 20; www.turismo.navarra.es; Avenida da Roncesvalles 4; ☉ 9am-7pm Mon-Fri, 10am-2pm & 4-7pm Sat, 10am-2pm Sun) This extremely well-organised office, just opposite the statue of the bulls in the new town, has plenty of information about the city and Navarra. There are a couple of summer-only tourist info booths scattered throughout the city.

---

are so full of character that there'll be barely enough room for your own!

Hostal Begoña　　　　　BOUTIQUE HOTEL €€
(☑ 944 23 01 34; www.hostalbegona.com; Calle de la Amistad 2; s/d from €57/66; [P] [@] [☎]) The owners of this outstanding place don't need voguish labels for their very stylish and individual creation. Begoña speaks for itself with colourful rooms decorated with modern artworks, all with funky tiled bathrooms and wrought-iron beds. The common areas have mountains of books, traveller information and a rack of computers for internet usage.

★ **La Viña del Ensanche**　　　PINTXOS €
(☑ 944 15 56 15; www.lavinadelensanche.com; Calle de la Diputación 10; pintxos from €2.50, menu €30; ☉ 8.30am-11pm Mon-Fri, noon-1am Sat) Hundreds of bottles of wine line the walls of this outstanding *pintxos* bar. And when we say outstanding we mean that it could well be the best place to eat *pintxos* in all of the city.

★ **Casa Rufo**　　　　　　　BASQUE €€
(☑ 944 43 21 72; www.casarufo.com; Hurtado de Amézaga 5; mains €10-15; ☉ 1.30-4pm & 8.30-11pm Mon-Sat) Despite the emergence of numerous glitzy restaurants that are temples to haute cuisine this resolutely old-fashioned place, with its shelves full of dusty bottles of top-quality olive oil and wine, still

stands out as one of the best places to eat traditional Basque food in Bilbao.

ℹ Information

Tourist Office (www.bilbaoturismo.net) Main tourist office (☑ 944 79 57 60; Plaza Circular 1; ☉ 9am-9pm; [☎]); airport (☑ 944 71 03 01; ☉ 9am-9pm Mon-Sat, 9am-3pm Sun); Guggenheim (Alameda Mazarredo 66; ☉ 10am-7pm daily, till 3pm Sun Sep-Jun) Bilbao's friendly tourist-office staffers are extremely helpful, well informed and, above all, enthusiastic about their city. At all offices ask for the free bimonthly *Bilbao Guía*, with its entertainment listings plus tips on restaurants, bars and nightlife. At the newly opened, state-of-the-art main tourist office there's free wi-fi access, a bank of touch-screen information computers and, best of all, some humans to help answer questions.

ℹ Getting There & Away

BUS
Regular bus services operate to/from Madrid (from €31, 4¾ hours), Barcelona (€48, seven hours), Pamplona (€15, two hours) and Santander (€6.60, 1¼ hours).

TRAIN
Two Renfe trains runs daily to Madrid (€64, six hours) and Barcelona (€65, six hours) from the Abando train station. Slow **FEVE** (www.feve.es) trains run from Concordia station next door, heading west into Cantabria and Asturias.

CANTABRIA, ASTURIAS & GALICIA

With a landscape reminiscent of parts of the British Isles, 'Green Spain' offers great walks in national parks, seafood feasts in sophisticated towns and oodles of opportunities to plunge into the ice-cold waters of the Bay of Biscay.

Santillana del Mar

Some 34km west of the regional capital, Santander, Santillana del Mar (www.santillanadelmar.com) is a bijou medieval village and the obvious overnight base for visiting the nearby Cueva de Altamira. Buses run three to four times a day from Santander to Santillana del Mar.

Spain's finest prehistoric art, in the Cueva de Altamira, 2km southwest of Santillana, was discovered in 1879. It took more than 20 years, after further discoveries of cave art in France, before scientists accepted that these wonderful paintings of bison, horses and other animals really were the handiwork of primitive people many thousands of years ago. A replica cave in the museum here now enables everyone to appreciate the inspired, 14,500-year-old paintings.

Santiago de Compostela

POP 80,000

The supposed burial place of St James (Santiago), Santiago de Compostela is a bewitching city. Christian pilgrims journeying along the Camino de Santiago often end up mute with wonder on entering its medieval centre. Fortunately, they usually regain their verbal capacities over a celebratory late-night foray into the city's lively bar scene.

◎ Sights & Activities

★Catedral de
Santiago de Compostela   CATHEDRAL
(www.catedraldesantiago.es; Praza do Obradoiro; ⊙7am-8.30pm) The grand heart of Santiago, the cathedral soars above the city centre in a splendid jumble of moss-covered spires and statues. Built piecemeal over several centuries, its beauty is a mix of the original Romanesque structure (built between 1075 and 1211) and later Gothic and baroque flourishes. The tomb of Santiago beneath the main altar is a magnet for all who come to the cathedral. The artistic high point is the Pórtico de la Gloria inside the west entrance, featuring 200 masterly Romanesque sculptures.

★Museo da Catedral   MUSEUM
(Colección Permanente; www.catedralde santiago.es; Praza do Obradoiro; adult/senior, pilgrim, unemployed & student/child €6/4/free; ⊙9am-8pm Apr-Oct, 10am-8pm Nov-Mar) The Cathedral Museum spreads over four floors and includes the cathedral's large, 16th-century, Gothic/plateresque cloister. You'll see a sizeable section of Maestro Mateo's original carved stone choir (destroyed in 1604 but recently pieced back together), an impressive collection of religious art (including the *botafumeiros* – incense burners – in the 2nd-floor library), the lavishly decorated 18th-century *sala capitular* (chapter house) and, off the cloister, the Panteón de Reyes, with tombs of kings of medieval León.

Praza do Obradoiro   SQUARE
Grand Praza do Obradoiro, in front of the cathedral's west facade, earned its name from the workshops set up there while the cathedral was being built. It's free of both traffic and cafes and has a unique atmosphere.

At its northern end, the Renaissance Hostal dos Reis Católicos (admission €3; ⊙noon-2pm & 4-6pm Sun-Fri) was built in the early 16th century by order of the Catholic Monarchs, Isabel and Fernando, as a refuge for pilgrims and a symbol of the crown's power in this ecclesiastical city. Today it shelters well-off travellers instead, as a *parador* (luxurious state-owned hotel), but its four courtyards and some other areas are open to visitors.

Colexio de Fonseca   UNIVERSITY
(⊙9am-9pm Mon-Fri, 10am-8.30pm Sat) FREE Located south of Catedral de Santiago de Compostela, and in the cafe-lined Praza de Fonseca, the Colexio de Fonseca with a beautiful Renaissance courtyard and exhibition gallery was the original seat of Santiago's university (founded in 1495).

Museo das Peregrinacións
e de Santiago   MUSEUM
(www.mdperegrinacions.com; Praza das Praterías; adult/senior, pilgrim & student/child €2.50/1.50/free; ⊙10am-2pm & 5-8pm Tue-Sat, 11am-2pm Sun) The recently converted building on Praza das Praterías stages changing exhibitions on the themes of pilgrimage and Santiago (man and city), and affords close-up views of some of the cathedral's towers from its 3rd-floor windows. The museum's permanent collection – an

extensive and interesting assemblage of art, artefacts, models and memorabilia – resides in its **original building** (www.mdperegrinacions. com; Rúa de San Miguel 4; ⊙10am-8pm Tue-Fri, 10.30am-1.30pm & 5-8pm Sat, 10.30am-1.30pm Sun) **FREE** 300m away, though there are plans eventually to move it to the new site.

Cathedral Rooftop Tour   TOUR
(☑902 557812; www.catedraldesantiago.es; adult/ senior, pilgrim, unemployed & student/child €12/10/ free, combined ticket with Museo da Catedral €15/12/free; ⊙tours hourly 10am-1pm & 4-7pm, to 6pm Nov-Mar) For unforgettable bird's-eye views of the cathedral interior from its upper storeys, and of the city from the cathedral roof, take the rooftop tour, which starts in the visitor reception centre beneath the Obradoiro facade. The tours are popular, so go beforehand to book a time, or book online. One afternoon tour is usually given in English; the rest are in Spanish. Guides provide good insight into Santiago's history.

Sleeping

Meiga Backpackers   HOSTEL €
(☑981 57 08 46; www.meiga-backpackers.es; Rúa dos Basquiños 67; dm incl breakfast €15; ⊙Mar-Nov; @🕭) Clean, colourful, sociable and handily placed between the bus station and city centre, Meiga has spacious bunk dorms, a good big kitchen and lounge, and a long garden. A great choice if you're on the budget backpacking trail.

⭐**Hotel Costa Vella**   BOUTIQUE HOTEL €€
(☑981 56 95 30; www.costavella.com; Rúa da Porta da Pena 17; s €59, d €81-97; ❄🕭) Tranquil, thoughtfully designed rooms – some with typically Galician *galerías* (glassed-in balconies) – a friendly welcome and a lovely garden cafe make this old stone house a wonderful option, and the €6 breakfast is substantial. Even if you don't stay, it's an ideal spot for breakfast or coffee. Book ahead from May to September.

Parador Hostal dos Reis Católicos   HISTORIC HOTEL €€€
(☑981 58 22 00; www.parador.es; Praza do Obradoiro 1; s/d incl breakfast from €175/190; 🅿❄@🕭) Opened in 1509 as a pilgrims' hostel, and with a claim to be the world's oldest hotel, this palatial *parador*, steps from the cathedral, is Santiago's top hotel, with regal (if rather staid) rooms. If you're not staying, stop in for a look round and coffee and cakes at the elegant cafe.

WORTH A TRIP

PICOS DE EUROPA

These jagged mountains straddling Asturias, Cantabria and northeast Castilla y León amount to some of the finest walking country in Spain. They comprise three limestone massifs (the highest peak rises 2648m). The 647-sq-km **Parque Nacional de los Picos de Europa** (www.picosdeeuropa.com) covers all three massifs and is Spain's second-biggest national park.

There are numerous places to stay and eat all over the mountains. Getting here and around by bus can be slow going but the Picos are accessible from Santander and Oviedo (the latter is easier) by bus.

Eating

O Beiro   TAPAS, RACIONES €
(Rúa da Raíña 3; raciones €5-10; ⊙10am-1am Tue-Sun Mar-Dec) The house speciality is *tablas* (trays) of delectable cheeses and sausages, but there are plenty of other tapas and *raciones* at this friendly two-level wine bar. It has a terrific range of Galician wines and the fiery local grape-based liquors *orujo* and *aguardiente*.

⭐**O Curro da Parra**   CONTEMPORARY GALICIAN €€
(www.ocurrodaparra.com; Rúa do Curro da Parra 7; mains €17-23, tapas €4-8; ⊙1.30-3.30pm & 8.30-11.30pm Tue-Sat, 1.30-3.30pm Sun) With a neat little stone-walled dining room upstairs and a narrow tapas and wine bar below, O Curro da Parra serves up a broad range of thoughtfully created, market-fresh fare. You might go for pork cheeks with apple purée and spinach – or just ask what the fish and seafood of the day are. On weekday lunchtimes there's a good-value €12 *menú mercado* (market menu).

Abastos 2.0   CONTEMPORARY GALICIAN €€
(☑981 57 61 45; www.abastosdouspuntocero. es; Rúa das Ameas 3; dishes €1-10, menú €21; ⊙noon-3pm & 8-11pm Tue-Sat) This highly original and incredibly popular marketside eatery offers new dishes concocted daily from the market's offerings. You can go for small individual items, or plates to share, or a six-item *menú* that adds up to a meal for €21. The seafood is generally fantastic, but whatever you order you're likely to love

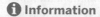

the great tastes and delicate presentation – if you can get a seat!

ℹ️ Information

Oficina de Turismo de Galicia (www.turgalicia. es; Rúa do Vilar 30-32; ⊙10am-8pm Mon-Fri, 11am-2pm & 5-7pm Sat, 11am-2pm Sun) The scoop on all things Galicia.

Oficina del Peregrino (Pilgrims' Office; ✆981 56 88 46; peregrinossantiago.es; Rúa do Vilar 3; ⊙9am-9pm May-Oct, 10am-7pm Nov-Apr) People who have covered at least the last 100km of the Camino de Santiago on foot or horseback, or the last 200km by bicycle, can obtain their 'Compostela' certificate to prove it here. The website has a good deal of useful Camino info.

Turismo de Santiago (✆981 55 51 29; www. santiagoturismo.com; Rúa do Vilar 63; ⊙9am-9pm, to 7pm approximately Nov-Mar) The efficient main municipal tourist office.

ℹ️ Getting There & Around

BUS

ALSA (✆902 422242; www.alsa.es) ALSA has services to Oviedo (from €30, five to seven hours), León (€30, six hours) and Madrid (€47 to €68, eight to 10 hours). ALSA also has direct daily services to Porto (€31, four hours).

Bus Station (✆981 54 24 16; Praza de Camilo Díaz Baliño; 🛜) The bus station is about a 20-minute walk northeast of the centre.

Castromil-Monbus (✆902 292900; www. monbus.es) Destinations throughout Galicia.

TRAIN

From the **train station** (✆981 59 18 59; Rúa do Hórreo), regional trains run up and down the coast, while a daytime Talgo and an overnight Trenhotel head to Madrid (from €50.75, 6¼ to 9½ hours).

Around Galicia

Galicia's dramatic Atlantic coastline is one of Spain's best-kept secrets, with wild and precipitous cliffs and isolated fishing villages. The lively port city of **A Coruña** has a lovely city beach and fabulous seafood (a recurring Galician theme). It's also the gateway to the stirring landscapes of the **Costa da Morte** and **Rías Altas**; the latter's highlight among many is probably **Cabo Ortegal**. Inland Galicia is also worth exploring, especially the old town of **Lugo**, surrounded by what many consider to be the world's best preserved Roman walls.

VALENCIA

POP 792.300

Spain's third-largest city is a magnificent place, content for Madrid and Barcelona to grab the headlines while it gets on with being a wonderfully liveable city with thriving cultural, eating and nightlife scenes. The star attraction is the strikingly futuristic buildings of the Ciudad de las Artes y las Ciencias, designed by local-boy-made-good Santiago Calatrava. The Barrio del Carmen also has a fistful of fabulous Modernista architecture, great museums and a large, characterful old quarter. Valencia, surrounded by the fertile fruit-and-veg farmland La Huerta, is famous as the home of rice dishes like paella, but its buzzy dining scene offers plenty more besides.

⊙ Sights & Activities

★**Ciudad de las Artes y las Ciencias** NOTABLE BUILDINGS (City of Arts & Sciences; www.cac.es; combined ticket for Oceanogràfic, Hemisfèric & Museo de las Ciencias Príncipe Felipe adult/child €36.25/27.55) The aesthetically stunning City of Arts & Sciences occupies a massive 350,000-sq-metre swath of the old Turia riverbed. It's mostly the work of world-famous, locally born architect Santiago Calatrava. He's a controversial figure for many Valencians, who complain about the expense, and various design flaws that have necessitated major repairs. Nevertheless, if your taxes weren't involved, it's awe-inspiring stuff, and pleasingly family-oriented.

★**Oceanogràfic** AQUARIUM (www.cac.es/oceanografic; adult/child €27.90/21; ⊙10am-6pm Oct-Jun, 10am-8pm Jul & Sep, 10am-midnight Aug; 🚼) For most families with children this indoor-outdoor aquarium is the highlight of a visit to Valencia's City of Arts & Sciences. There are polar zones, a dolphinarium, a Red Sea aquarium, a Mediterranean seascape – and a couple of underwater tunnels, one 70m long, where the fish have the chance to gawp back at visitors. Opening hours here are approximate; check the website by date. It opens later on Saturday.

★**Catedral** CATHEDRAL (Plaza de la Virgen; adult/child incl audioguide €5/3.50; ⊙10am-5.30pm or 6.30pm Mon-Sat, 2-5.30pm Sun, closed Sun Nov-Feb) Valencia's cathedral was built over the mosque after the 1238 reconquest. Its low, wide, brick-vaulted triple nave is mostly Gothic, with neoclassical side chapels. Highlights are rich Italianate frescoes above the altarpiece, a pair of Goyas in the **Chapel of San Francisco de Borja**, and...da-dah...in the flamboyant Gothic **Capilla del Santo Cáliz**, what's claimed to be the **Holy Grail**, the chalice from which Christ sipped during the Last Supper. It's a Roman-era agate cup, later modified, so at least the date is right.

Miguelete Bell Tower　　　　　TOWER
(adult/child €2/1; ⊘10am-7pm or 7.30pm) Left of the main portal of the Cathedral is the entrance to the Miguelete bell tower. Clamber up the 207 steps of its spiral staircase for great 360-degree city-and-skyline views.

★**La Lonja**　　　　　HISTORIC BUILDING
(Calle de la Lonja; adult/child €2/1; ⊘10am-6pm or 7pm Tue-Sat, to 3pm Sun) This splendid late-15th-century building, a Unesco World Heritage Site, was originally Valencia's silk and commodity exchange. Highlights are the colonnaded hall with its twisted Gothic pillars and the 1st-floor **Consulado del Mar** with its stunning coffered ceiling.

★**Museo de Bellas Artes**　　　　　GALLERY
(San Pío V; www.museobellasartesvalencia.gva.es; Calle de San Pío V 9; ⊘10am-7pm Tue-Sun, 11am-5pm Mon) FREE Bright and spacious, the Museo de Bellas Artes ranks among Spain's best. Highlights include the grandiose Roman *Mosaic of the Nine Muses,* a collection of magnificent late-medieval altarpieces, and works by El Greco, Goya, Velázquez, Murillo and Ribalta, plus artists such as Sorolla and Pinazo of the Valencian Impressionist school.

◉ Beaches

At the coastal end of the tram line, 3km from the centre, **Playa de las Arenas** runs north into **Playa de la Malvarrosa** and **Playa de la Patacona**, forming a wide strip of sand some 4km long. It's bordered by the **Paseo Marítimo** promenade and a string of restaurants and cafes. One block back, lively bars and discos thump out the beat in summer.

🛏 Sleeping

Pensión París　　　　　HOTEL €
(☑963 52 67 66; www.pensionparis.com; Calle de Salvà 12; s €24, d €32-44; 🖳) Welcoming, with spotless rooms – most with shared bathrooms, some with private facilities – this family-run option on a quiet street is the

antithesis of the crowded, pack-'em-in hostel. The best of the rooms have balconies and original features from this stately old building.

Ad Hoc Monumental　　　　　HOTEL €€
(☑963 91 91 40; www.adhochoteles.com; Calle Boix 4; s/d €72/84; 🖳🖳) Friendly Ad Hoc offers comfort and charm deep within the old quarter and also runs a splendid small restaurant (open for dinner Monday to Saturday). The late-19th-century building has been restored to its former splendour with great sensitivity, revealing original ceilings, mellow brickwork and solid wooden beams.

★**Caro Hotel**　　　　　HOTEL €€€
(☑963 05 90 00; www.carohotel.com; Calle Almirante 14; r €143-214; 🅿🖳🖳) Housed in a sumptuous 19th-century mansion, this sits atop some 2000 years of Valencian history, with restoration revealing a hefty hunk of the Arab wall, Roman column bases and Gothic arches. Each room is furnished in soothing dark shades, has a great king-sized bed, and varnished cement floors. Bathrooms are tops. For that very special occasion, reserve the 1st-floor grand suite, once the ballroom. Savour, too, its excellent restaurant Alma del Temple.

🍴 Eating

At weekends, locals in their hundreds head for Las Arenas, just north of the port, where a long line of restaurants overlooking the beach all serve up authentic paella in a three-course meal costing around €15.

★**Carosel** VALENCIAN €
(961 13 28 73; www.carosel.es; Calle Taula de Canvis 6; mains €7-16, menu €15; ⊙1-4pm & 9-11pm Tue-Sat, 1-4pm Sun) Jordi and his partner, Carol, run this delightful small restaurant with outdoor seating on a square. The freshest of produce from the nearby market is blended with Alicante and Valencia traditions to create salads, cocas, rices and other delicious titbits. Top value and warmly recommended.

★**Delicat** TAPAS, FUSION €€
(963 92 33 57; Calle Conde de Almodóvar 4; mains €9-14; ⊙1-4pm & 8.30-11.30pm Tue-Sat, 1-4pm Sun) At this particularly friendly, intimate option (there are only nine tables, plus the terrace in summer), Catina, up front, and her partner, Paco, on full view in the kitchen, offer an unbeatable-value, five-course menu of samplers for lunch and a range of truly innovative tapas anytime.

Lonja del Pescado FISH €€
(www.restaurantelalonjapescadovalencia.com; Calle de Eugenia Viñes 243; dishes €8-15; ⊙1-3.30pm Sat & Sun, 8-11.30pm Tue-Sun Mar-Oct, 1-3.30pm Fri-Sun, 8-11.30pm Fri & Sat Nov-Feb) One block back from the beach at Malvarrosa, this busy, informal place has plenty of atmosphere and offers unbeatable value for fresh fish. Grab an order form as you enter and fill it in at your table. The tram stops outside.

Drinking & Nightlife

The Barrio del Carmen, the university area (around Avenidas de Aragón and Blasco Ibáñez), the area around the Mercado de Abastos and, in summer, the new port area and Malvarrosa are all jumping with bars and clubs.

Café de las Horas CAFE, BAR
(www.cafedelashoras.com; Calle Conde de Almodóvar 1; ⊙10am-2am; 🐟) Offers high baroque, tapestries, music of all genres, candelabras, bouquets of fresh flowers and a long list of exotic cocktails. It does themed Sunday brunches (11am to 4pm).

Jimmy Glass MUSIC BAR
(www.jimmyglassjazz.net; Calle Baja 28; ⊙8pm-2.30am Mon-Thu, 8pm-3.30am Fri & Sat) Playing jazz from the owner's vast CD collection, Jimmy Glass also sometimes has live performances. It's just what a jazz bar should be – dim and serving jumbo measures of high-octane cocktails.

Café Museu CAFE
(Calle Museo 7; ⊙9am-11pm Mon-Thu, 9am-1.30am Fri, 11am-1.30am Sat, 11am-11pm Sun; 🐟) A real forum for bohemian souls in the Carmen district, this grungy, edgy spot has an impressive cultural program including English/Spanish conversation sessions, regular live music, theatre and more. The terrace is a popular place to knock back a few beers.

Radio City CLUB
(www.radiocityvalencia.es; Calle de Santa Teresa 19; ⊙10.30pm-3.30am Tue-Sun) Almost as much mini-cultural centre as club, Radio City, always seething, pulls in the punters with activities including cinema, flamenco and dancing to an eclectic mix. Pick up a flyer here for its younger sister, **Music Box** (Calle del Pintor Zariñena 16; ⊙midnight-7am Tue-Sat), also in the Centro Histórico, which stays open until dawn.

Information

Regional Tourist Office (963 98 64 22; www.comunitatvalenciana.com; Calle de la Paz 48; ⊙10am-6pm Mon-Fri, to 2pm Sat) A fount of information about the Valencia region.

Turismo Valencia Tourist Office (VLC; 963 15 39 31; www.turisvalencia.es; Plaza de la Reina 19; ⊙9am-7pm Mon-Sat, 10am-2pm Sun) Has several other branches around town, including Plaza del Ayuntamiento (⊙9am-7pm Mon-Sat, 10am-2pm Sun), the AVE station and airport arrivals area.

Getting There & Away

AIR

Aeropuerto de Manises (VLC; 902 40 47 04) Valencia's airport is 10km west of the city centre along the A3, towards Madrid.

BOAT

Acciona Trasmediterránea (902 45 46 45; www.trasmediterranea.es) operates car and passenger ferries to Ibiza, Mallorca and Menorca.

BUS

ALSA (www.alsa.es) Numerous buses to/from Barcelona (€29 to €35, four to five hours) and Alicante (from €20.60, 2½ hours), most passing by Benidorm.

Avanza (www.avanzabus.com) Hourly bus services to/from Madrid (€29.40, four hours).

Bus Station (96 346 62 66) Valencia's bus station is beside the riverbed on Avenida Menéndez Pidal. Bus 8 connects it to Plaza del Ayuntamiento.

TRAIN

From Valencia's Estación del Norte, major destinations include Alicante (€17 to €30, 1¾ hours, 11 to 13 daily) and Barcelona (€40 to €44, three to 4¼ hours, at least 14 daily). The AVE, the high-speed train, now links Madrid and Valencia, with up to 15 high-speed services daily and a journey time of around 1¾ hours.

Getting Around

Metro line 5 connects the airport, city centre and port. The high-speed tram leaves from the FGV tram station, 500m north of the cathedral, at the Pont de Fusta. This is a pleasant way to get to the beach, the paella restaurants of Las Arenas and the port.

BALEARIC ISLANDS

The Balearic Islands (Illes Balears in Catalan) adorn the glittering Mediterranean waters off Spain's eastern coastline. Beach tourism destinations *par excellence,* each of the islands has a quite distinct identity and they have managed to retain much of their individual character and beauty. All boast beaches second to none in the Med, but each offers reasons for exploring inland, too.

Check out websites like www.illesbalears.es and www.platgesdebalears.com.

Getting There & Away

AIR

In summer, charter and regular flights converge on Palma de Mallorca and Ibiza from all over Europe.

Air Berlin (www.airberlin.com)
Air Europa (www.aireuropa.com)
Iberia (www.iberia.es)
Vueling (www.vueling.com)

BOAT

Acciona Trasmediterránea (☑902 454645; www.trasmediterranea.es)
Baleària (☑902 160180; www.balearia.com)
Iscomar (☑902 119128; www.iscomar.com)

Compare prices and look for deals at **Direct Ferries** (www.directferries.com).

The main ferry routes to the mainland:
Ibiza (Ibiza City) To/from Barcelona (Acciona Trasmediterránea, Baleària) and Valencia (Acciona Trasmediterránea)
Ibiza (Sant Antoni) To/from Denia, Barcelona and Valencia (Baleària)

Mallorca (Palma de Mallorca) To/from Barcelona and Valencia (Acciona Trasmediterránea, Baleària) and Denia (Baleària)
Menorca (Maó) To/from Barcelona and Valencia (Acciona Trasmediterránea, Baleària)

The main interisland ferry routes:
Ibiza (Ibiza City) To/from Palma de Mallorca (Acciona Trasmediterránea and Baleària)
Mallorca (Palma de Mallorca) To/from Ibiza City (Acciona Trasmediterránea and Baleària) and Maó (Acciona Trasmediterránea and Baleària)
Mallorca (Port d'Alcúdia) To/from Ciutadella (Iscomar and Baleària)
Menorca (Ciutadella) To/from Port d'Alcúdia (Iscomar and Baleària)
Menorca (Maó) To/from Palma de Mallorca (Acciona Trasmediterránea and Baleària)

Mallorca

The sunny, warm hues of the medieval heart of Palma de Mallorca, the archipelago's capital, make a great introduction to the islands. The northwest coast, dominated by the Serra de Tramuntana mountain range, is a beautiful region of olive groves, pine forests and ochre villages, with a spectacularly rugged coastline. Most of Mallorca's best beaches are on the north and east coasts, and although many have been swallowed up by tourist developments, you can still find the occasional exception.

Palma de Mallorca

Palma de Mallorca is a graceful Mediterranean city with some world-class attractions and equally impressive culinary and nightlife scenes.

Sights & Activities

★**Catedral** CATHEDRAL
(La Seu; www.catedraldemallorca.org; Carrer del Palau Reial 9; adult/child €6/free; ⊙10am-6.15pm Mon-Fri, to 2.15pm Sat) Palma's vast cathedral is the city's major architectural landmark. Aside from its sheer scale and undoubted beauty, its stunning interior features, designed by Antoni Gaudí and renowned contemporary artist Miquel Barceló, make this unlike any cathedral elsewhere in the world. The awesome structure is predominantly Gothic, apart from the main facade, which is startling, quite beautiful and completely mongrel.

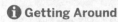

WORTH A TRIP

MENORCA

Renowned for its pristine beaches and archaeological sites, tranquil Menorca was declared a Biosphere Reserve by Unesco in 1993. **Maó** absorbs most of the tourist traffic. North of Maó, a drive across a lunar landscape leads to the lighthouse at **Cap de Favàritx**. South of the cape stretch some fine sandy bays and beaches, including **Cala Presili** and **Platja d'en Tortuga**, reachable on foot.

Ciutadella, with its smaller harbour and historic buildings, has a more distinctly Spanish feel to it and is the more attractive of the island's two main towns. A narrow country road leads south of Ciutadella (follow the 'Platges' sign from the *ronda*, or ring road) and then forks twice to reach some of the island's loveliest beaches: (from west to east) **Arenal de Son Saura**, **Cala en Turqueta**, **Es Talaier**, **Cala Macarelleta** and **Cala Macarella**. As with most beaches, you'll need your own transport.

In the centre of the island, the 357m-high **Monte Toro** has great views; on a clear day you can see Mallorca. On the northern coast, the picturesque town of **Fornells** is on a large bay popular with windsurfers.

The ports in both Maó and Ciutadella are lined with bars and restaurants.

Hostal-Residencia Oasis (☑ 630 018008; www.hostaloasismenorca.es; Carrer de Sant Isidre 33; d €40-66, tr €56-87, q €82-103; 🖥) Run by delightful friendly owners, this quiet place is close to the heart of the old quarter. Rooms, mostly with bathroom, are set beside a spacious garden courtyard. Their furnishings, though still trim, are from deep into the last century.

Tres Sants (☑ 971 48 22 08; www.grupelcarme.com; Carrer Sant Cristòfol 2; s €140-175, d €180-210; 🅿🖥🏊) Buried deep in Ciutadella's medina-like heart, Tres Sants is a slice of breezy, boho cool. The owners' attentive eye for detail shines in this beautifully converted 18th-century manor house, with frescoed walls, candlelit passageways and whitewashed rooms with nice touches like four-poster beds, sunken bathtubs and iPod docks. The subterranean pool and steam bath evokes the hotel's Roman origins.

★ **Palau de l'Almudaina**   PALACE
(Carrer del Palau Reial; adult/child €9/4, audioguide €4, guided tour €6; ⊙10am-8pm Apr-Sep, to 6pm Oct-Mar) Originally an Islamic fort, this mighty construction opposite the Catedral was converted into a residence for the Mallorcan monarchs at the end of the 13th century. The King of Spain resides here still, at least symbolically. The royal family are rarely in residence, except for the occasional ceremony, as they prefer to spend summer in the Palau Marivent (in Cala Major). At other times you can wander through a series of cavernous stone-walled rooms that have been lavishly decorated.

★ **Palau March**   MUSEUM
(Carrer del Palau Reial 18; adult/child €4.50/free; ⊙10am-6.30pm Mon-Fri, to 2pm Sat) This house, palatial by any definition, was one of several residences of the phenomenally wealthy March family. Sculptures by 20th-century greats, such as Henry Moore, Auguste Rodin, Barbara Hepworth and Eduardo Chillida, grace the outdoor terrace. Within lie many more artistic treasures from some of Spain's big names in art, such as Salvador Dalí, and Barcelona's Josep Maria Sert and Xavier Corberó, as well as an extraordinary 18th-century Neapolitan baroque *belén* (nativity scene).

★ **Es Baluard**   GALLERY
(Museu d'Art Modern i Contemporani; www.esbaluard.org; Plaça de Porta de Santa Catalina 10; adult/child €6/free, temporary exhibitions €4; ⊙10am-8pm Tue-Sat, to 3pm Sun) Built with flair and innovation into the shell of the Renaissance-era seaward walls, this contemporary art gallery is one of the finest on the island. Its temporary exhibitions are worth viewing, but the permanent collection – works by Miró, Barceló and Picasso – give the gallery its cachet.

The 21st-century concrete complex is cleverly built among the fortifications, including the partly restored remains of an 11th-century Muslim-era tower (on your right as you arrive from Carrer de Sant Pere).

★ Museu Fundación
Juan March GALLERY
(www.march.es/arte/palma; Carrer de Sant Miquel 11; ⊘10am-6.30pm Mon-Fri, 10.30am-2pm Sat) **FREE** This 17th-century mansion gives an insightful overview of Spanish contemporary art. On permanent display are some 70 pieces held by the Fundación Juan March. Together they constitute a veritable who's who of mostly 20th-century artists, including Miró, Juan Gris (of cubism fame), Dalí and the sculptors Eduardo Chillida and Julio González.

🛏 Sleeping

Hostal Pons GUESTHOUSE €
(☑971 72 26 58; www.hostalpons.com; Carrer del Vi 8, Palma de Mallorca; s €30, d €60-70, tr €85; ☎) Bang in the heart of old Palma, this is a sweet, simple family-run guesthouse. Downstairs a cat slumbers in a plant-filled patio, upstairs you'll find a book-lined lounge and rooms with rickety bedsteads and tiled floors. Cheaper rooms share communal bathrooms. The roof terrace offers peaceful respite.

Misión de San Miguel BOUTIQUE HOTEL €€
(☑971 21 48 48; www.urhotels.com; Carrer de Can Maçanet 1, Palma de Mallorca; r €75-163, ste €115-203; P ✷@☎) This 32-room boutique hotel is an astounding deal with stylish designer rooms; it does the little things well with firm mattresses and rain showers, although some rooms open onto public areas and can be a tad noisy. Its restaurant, Misa Braseria, is part of the Fosh group. Service is friendly and professional.

★ Can Cera BOUTIQUE HOTEL €€€
(☑971 71 50 12; http://cancerahotel.com; Carrer del Convent de Sant Francesc 8, Palma de Mallorca; r €165-495; ✷☎) Welcome to one of Palma's most romantic boutique bolt-holes, entered via an inner courtyard, where cobbles have been worn smooth over 700 years and a wrought-iron staircase sweeps up to guest rooms that manage the delicate act of combining history with modern design flourishes. The decor is stylish but never overblown, with high ceilings, period furnishings and richly detailed throws.

✗ Eating

Restaurant Celler
Sa Premsa SPANISH €
(☑971 72 35 29; www.cellersapremsa.com; Plaça del Bisbe Berenguer de Palou 8; mains €9-14; ⊘12.30-4pm & 7.30-11.30pm Mon-Sat) A visit to this local institution is almost obligatory. It's a cavernous tavern filled with huge old wine barrels and has walls plastered with faded bullfighting posters – you find plenty such places in the Mallorcan interior but they're a dying breed here in Palma. Mallorcan specialities dominate the menu.

Can Cera Gastro Bar MEDITERRANEAN €€
(☑971 71 50 12; www.cancerahotel.com; Carrer del Convent de Sant Francesc 8; mains €14-22, menus €18-31; ⊘1-3.30pm & 7.30-10.30pm) How enchanting: this restaurant spills out into one of Palma's loveliest inner patios at the hotel of the same name, housed in a 13th-century *palacio*. Dine by lantern light on tapas or season-focused dishes such as watermelon and tomato gazpacho and creamy rice with aioli, saffron and calamari. Note the vertical garden that attracts plenty of attention from passers-by.

★ Simply Fosh MODERN EUROPEAN €€€
(☑971 72 01 14; www.simplyfosh.com; Carrer de la Missió 7A; mains €23-29, menus €21.50-76; ⊘1-3.30pm & 7-10.30pm Mon-Sat) Lovingly prepared Mediterranean cooking with a novel flourish is the order of the day at this 17th-century convent refectory, one of the home kitchens of chef Marc Fosh, whose CV twinkles with Michelin stars. A slick, monochrome interior and courtyard provide the backdrop for high-quality, reasonably priced menus. The three-course lunch menu for €21.50 is a terrific deal.

ⓘ Information

Consell de Mallorca Tourist Office (☑971 17 39 90; www.infomallorca.net; Plaça de la Reina 2; ⊘8am-6pm Mon-Fri, 8.30am-3pm Sat; ☎) Covers the whole island.

Main Municipal Tourist Office (☑971 72 96 34; www.imtur.es; Casal Solleric, Passeig d'es Born 27; ⊘9am-8pm) Tourist office.

Around Palma de Mallorca

Mallorca's northwestern coast is a world away from the high-rise tourism on the other side of the island. Dominated by the Serra de Tramuntana, it's a beautiful region of olive groves, pine forests and small villages with shuttered stone buildings. There are a couple of highlights for drivers: the hair-raising road down to the small port of **Sa Calobra**, and the amazing trip along the peninsula leading to the island's northern tip, **Cap Formentor**.

Sóller is a good place to base yourself for hiking and the nearby village of **Fornalutx** is one of the prettiest on Mallorca.

From Sóller, it's a 10km walk to the beautiful hilltop village of **Deià**, where Robert Graves, poet and author of *I Claudius*, lived for most of his life. From the village, you can scramble down to the small shingle beach of **Cala de Deià**. Boasting a fine monastery and pretty streets, **Valldemossa** is further southwest down the coast.

Further east, **Pollença** and **Artà** are attractive inland towns. Nice beaches include those at **Cala Sant Vicenç**, **Cala Mondragó** and around **Cala Llombards**.

Ibiza

Ibiza (Eivissa in Catalan) is an island of extremes. Its formidable party reputation is completely justified, with some of the world's greatest clubs attracting hedonists from the world over. The interior and northeast of the island, however, are another world. Peaceful country drives, hilly green territory, a sprinkling of mostly laid-back beaches and coves, and some wonderful inland accommodation and eateries are light years from the ecstasy-fuelled madness of the clubs that dominate the west.

Ibiza City

Sights & Activities

Ibiza City's port area of **Sa Penya** is crammed with funky and trashy clothing boutiques and arty-crafty market stalls. From here, you can wander up into **D'Alt Vila**, the atmospheric old walled town.

★ Ramparts   HISTORIC SITE
A ramp leads from Plaça de Sa Font in Sa Penya up to the **Portal de ses Taules**, the main entrance. Above it hangs a commemorative plaque bearing Felipe II's coat of arms and an inscription recording the 1585 completion date of the fortification – seven artillery bastions joined by thick protective walls up to 22m in height.

Catedral   CATHEDRAL
(Plaça de la Catedral; ⊘ 9.30am-1.30pm & 3-8pm) Ibiza's cathedral elegantly combines several styles: the original 14th-century structure is Catalan Gothic, but the sacristy was added in 1592 and a major baroque renovation took place in the 18th century. Inside, the

Museu Diocesà (admission €1.50; ⊘ 9.30am-1.30pm Tue-Sun, closed Dec-Feb) contains centuries of religious art.

Sleeping

Many of Ibiza City's hotels and *hostales* are closed in the low season and heavily booked between April and October. Make sure you book ahead.

Vara de Rey   GUESTHOUSE €€
(✆ 971 30 13 76; www.hibiza.com; Passeig de Vara de Rey 7; s €50-65, d €65-115, ste €115-170; ※) Housed in a restored town mansion, this boho-flavoured guesthouse sits on the tree-lined Passeig de Vara de Rey boulevard. The look is shabby-chic in rooms with touches like chandeliers, wrought-iron bedsteads and diffused light. Suites notch up the romance with four-poster beds and D'Alt Vila views.

Hostal Parque   HOTEL €€
(✆ 971 30 13 58; www.hostalparque.com; Plaça des Parc 4; s €60-90, d €110-190, tr €150-190, q €180-240; ※⊗) Overlooking palm-dotted Plaça des Parc, this *hostal*'s rooms have recently been spruced up with boutique touches like wood floors, contemporary art and ultra-modern bathrooms. There's a price hike for Ático (penthouse) rooms, but their roof terraces with D'Alt Vila views are something else. Street-facing rooms might be a tad noisy for light sleepers.

★ Urban Spaces   DESIGN HOTEL €€€
(✆ 871 51 71 74; http://urbanspacesibiza.com; Carrer de la Via Púnica 32; ste €200-270; ※⊗) Ira Francis-Smith is the brains behind this design newcomer with an alternative edge. Some of the world's most prolific street artists (N4T4, INKIE, JEROM, et al) have pooled their creativity in the roomy, mural-splashed suites, with clever backlighting, proper workstations and balconies with terrific views. Extras like yoga on the roof terrace and clubber-friendly breakfasts until 1pm are surefire people-pleasers.

Eating

★ Comidas Bar San Juan   MEDITERRANEAN €
(Carrer de Guillem de Montgrí 8; mains €4-12; ⊘ 1-3.30pm & 8.30-11pm Mon-Sat) More traditional than trendy, this family-run operation, with two small dining rooms, harks back to the days before Ibiza became a byword for glam. It offers outstanding value, with fish dishes and steaks for around €10. It doesn't take

reservations, so arrive early and expect to have other people at the same table as you.

S'Ametller
IBIZAN €€

(☑971 31 17 80; www.restaurantsametller.com; Carrer de Pere Francès 12; menus €22-35; ⊘1-4pm & 8pm-1am Mon-Sat, 8pm-1am Sun) The 'Almond Tree' specialises in local, market-fresh cooking. The daily menu (for dessert, choose the house *flaó*, a mint-flavoured variant on cheesecake and a Balearic Islands speciality) is inventive and superb value. S'Ametller also offers cookery courses – including one that imparts the secrets of that *flaó*.

El Olivo
MEDITERRANEAN €€

(☑971 30 06 80; www.elolivoibiza.org; Plaça de Vila 7; mains €19-24, tapas menu €28; ⊘7pm-1am Tue-Sun) Standing head and shoulders above most places in D'Alt Vila, this slick little bistro has plenty of pavement seating. The menu goes with the seasons in clean, bright flavours as simple as rack of lamb in a fennel-mustard crust and octopus carpaccio drizzled in Ibizan olive oil – all delivered with finesse.

 ## Drinking & Nightlife

Sa Penya is the nightlife centre. Dozens of bars keep the port area jumping. Alternatively, various bars at Platja d'en Bossa combine sounds, sand, sea and sangria.

Much cheaper than a taxi, the **Discobus** (www.discobus.es; per person €3; ⊘midnight-6am Jun-Sep) does an all-night whirl of the major clubs, bars and hotels in Ibiza City, Platja d'en Bossa, Sant Rafel, Es Canar, Santa Eulària and Sant Antoni.

Teatro Pereira
LIVE MUSIC

(www.teatropereyra.com; Carrer del Comte de Rosselló 3; ⊘8am-4am) Away from the waterfront hubbub, this time warp is all stained wood and iron girders. It was once the foyer of the long-abandoned 1893 theatre at its rear. It's often packed and offers nightly live music.

CLUBBING IN IBIZA

From late May to the end of September, the west of the island is one big, nonstop dance party from sunset to sunrise and back again. Space, Pacha and Amnesia were all in *DJ Mag*'s top 10 in 2013.

The major clubs operate nightly from around midnight to 6am from mid-May or June to early October. Theme nights, fancy-dress parties and foam parties are regular features.

Entertainment Ibiza-style doesn't come cheaply. Admission can cost anything from €20 to €65 (mixed drinks and cocktails then go for around €10 to €15).

Space (www.space-ibiza.es; Platja d'en Bossa; admission €20-75; ⊘11pm-6am) In Platja d'en Bossa, aptly named Space can pack in as many as 40 DJs and up to 8000 clubbers and is considered one of the world's best clubs. Come for the terrace, electro and parties like We Love (Sundays) and Carl Cox (Tuesdays).

Pacha (www.pacha.com; Avinguda 8 d'Agost, Ibiza City; admission €20-70; ⊘11pm-6am) Going strong since 1973, Pacha is Ibiza's original glamourpuss – a cavernous club that can hold 3000 people. The main dance floor, a sea of mirror balls, heaves to deep techno. On the terrace, tunes are more relaxing. Cherry-pick your night: David Guetta works the decks at Thursday's F*** Me I'm Famous, while hippies groove at Tuesday's Flower Power.

Amnesia (www.amnesia.es; Carretera Ibiza a San Antonio Km 5, San Rafael; admission €35-75; ⊘midnight-6am) Amnesia's sound system gives your body a massage. Beats skip from techno to trance, while the decks welcome DJ royalty like Paul Van Dyk and Sven Väth. A huge glasshouse-like terrace surrounds the central dance area. Big nights include Cocoon (Mondays), Cream (Thursdays) and foam-filled Espuma (Wednesdays and Sundays).

Privilege (www.privilegeibiza.com; San Rafael; admission €20-50; ⊘11pm-6am) Welcome to the world's biggest club. Five kilometres along the road to San Rafael, Privilege is a mind-blowing space with 20 bars, an interior pool and capacity for 10,000 clubbers. The main domed dance temple is an enormous, pulsating area, where the DJ's cabin is suspended above the pool.

Bora Bora Beach Club BAR

(www.boraboraibiza.net; ⊘ noon-6am May-Sep) At Platja d'en Bossa, 4km from the old town, this is *the* place – a long beachside bar where sun and fun worshippers work off hangovers and prepare new ones. Entry's free and the ambience is chilled, with low-key club sounds wafting over the sand.

ℹ Information

Tourist Office (☑ 971 39 92 32; www.eivissa. es; Plaça de la Catedral; ⊘ 10am-2pm & 6-9pm Mon-Sat, 10am-2pm Sun) Can provide audioguides to the city; bring your passport or identity document.

Around Ibiza City

Ibiza has numerous unspoiled and relatively undeveloped beaches. **Cala de Boix**, on the northeastern coast, is the only black-sand beach on the island, while further north are the lovely beaches of **S'Aigua Blanca**.

On the north coast near Portinatx, **Cala Xarraca** is in a picturesque, secluded bay, and near Port de Sant Miquel is the attractive **Cala Benirrás**.

In the southwest, **Cala d'Hort** has a spectacular setting overlooking two rugged rock islets, Es Verda and Es Verdranell.

The best thing about rowdy **Sant Antoni**, the island's second-biggest town and north of Ibiza City, is heading to the small rock-and-sand strip on the north shore to join hundreds of others for sunset drinks at a string of chilled bars. The best known remains **Café del Mar** (www.cafedelmarmusic. com; ⊘ 4pm-1am), our favourite, but it's further north along the pedestrian walkway.

Check out rural accommodation at www. ibizaruralvillas.com and www.casasrurales ibiza.com (in Spanish). For more standard accommodation, start at www.ibizahotels guide.com.

Local buses (www.ibizabus.com) run to most destinations between May and October.

ANDALUCÍA

Images of Andalucía are so potent, so quintessentially Spanish that it's sometimes difficult not to feel a sense of déjà vu. It's almost as if you've already been there in your dreams: a solemn Easter parade, an ebullient spring festival, exotic nights in the Alhambra. In the stark light of day, the picture is no less compelling.

Seville

POP 703,000

A sexy, gutsy and gorgeous city, Seville is home to two of Spain's most colourful festivals, fascinating and distinctive *barrios* (the Barrio de Santa Cruz is particularly memorable), and a local population that lives life to the fullest. A fiery place (as you'll soon see in its packed and noisy tapas bars), it's also hot climate-wise – avoid July and August!

⊙ Sights

Catedral & Giralda CHURCH

(www.catedraldesevilla.es; adult/child €9/free; ⊘ 11am-3.30pm Mon, 11am-5pm Tue-Sat, 2.30-6pm Sun) Seville's immense cathedral, officially the biggest in the world (by volume), is awe-inspiring in its scale and sheer majesty. It stands on the site of the great 12th-century Almohad mosque, with the mosque's minaret (the Giralda) still towering beside it.

★ **Alcázar** CASTLE

(www.alcazarsevilla.org; adult/child €9.50/free; ⊘ 9.30am-7pm Apr-Sep, 9.30am-5pm Oct-Mar) If heaven really *does* exist, then let's hope it looks a little bit like the inside of Seville's Alcázar. Built primarily in the 1300s during the so-called 'dark ages' in Europe, the architecture is anything but dark. Indeed, compared to our modern-day shopping malls and throw-away apartment blocks, it could be argued that the Alcázar marked one of history's architectural high points. Unesco agreed, making it a World Heritage Site in 1987.

Archivo de Indias MUSEUM

(Calle Santo Tomás; ⊘ 9.30am-4.45pm Mon-Sat, 10am-2pm Sun) FREE On the western side of Plaza del Triunfo, the Archivo de Indias is the main archive on Spain's American empire, with 80 million pages of documents dating from 1492 through to the end of the empire in the 19th century – a most effective statement of Spain's power and influence during its Golden Age. A short film inside tells the full story of the building along with some fascinating original colonial maps and documents. The building was refurbished between 2003 and 2005.

★ **Hospital de los Venerables Sacerdotes** GALLERY

(☑ 954 56 26 96; www.focus.abengoa.es; Plaza de los Venerables 8; adult/child €5.50/2.75, Sun afternoon free; ⊘ 10am-2pm & 4-8pm) Once

ALCÁZAR HIGHLIGHTS

Patio del León (Lion Patio) The garrison yard of the original Alcázar (p616). Just off here is the Sala de la Justicia (Hall of Justice), with beautiful Mudéjar plasterwork and an *artesonado* (ceiling of interlaced beams with decorative insertions). It leads on to the pretty Patio del Yeso, which is part of the 12th-century Almohad palace reconstructed in the 19th century.

Patio de la Montería The rooms surrounding this patio are filled with interesting artefacts from Seville's history.

Cuarto Real Alto The Cuarto Real Alto (Upper Royal Quarters) are open for (heavily subscribed) tours several times a day. Highlights include the 14th-century Salón de Audiencias, still the monarch's reception room, and Pedro I's bedroom, with marvellous Mudéjar tiles and plasterwork.

Palacio de Don Pedro Also called the Palacio Mudéjar, it's the single most stunning architectural feature in Seville. At the heart of the palace is the wonderful Patio de las Doncellas (Patio of the Maidens), surrounded by beautiful arches, plasterwork and tiling. The Cámara Regia (King's Quarters), on the northern side of the patio, has stunningly beautiful ceilings and wonderful plaster- and tile work. From here you can move west into the little Patio de las Muñecas (Patio of the Dolls), the heart of the palace's private quarters, featuring delicate Granada-style decoration. The Cuarto del Príncipe (Prince's Room), to its north, has a superb wooden cupola ceiling trying to re-create a starlit night sky. The spectacular Salón de Embajadores (Hall of Ambassadors), at the western end of the Patio de las Doncellas, was the throne room. On the western side of the Salón de Embajadores is the beautiful Arco de Pavones.

Salones de Carlos V Reached via a staircase at the southeastern corner of the Patio de las Doncellas, these are the much-remodelled rooms of Alfonso X's 13th-century Gothic palace.

Patio del Crucero This patio outside the Salones de Carlos V was originally the upper storey of the patio of the 12th-century Almohad palace.

Gardens From the Salones de Carlos V you can go out into the Alcázar's large and sleepy gardens, some with pools and fountains.

a residence for aged priests, this 17th-century baroque mansion guards what is perhaps Seville's most typical *sevillano* patio – it's intimate, plant embellished and spirit-reviving. The building's other highlights are its 17th-century church, with rich religious murals, and the celebrated painting *Santa Rufina* by Diego Velázquez, which was procured for a hefty €12.5 million by the on-site Centro Velázquez foundation in 2007. Other roving art exhibitions provide an excellent support act.

Museo del Baile Flamenco MUSEUM
(www.museoflamenco.com; Calle Manuel Rojas Marcos 3; adult/senior & student €10/8; ⊙10am-7pm) The brainchild of *sevillana* flamenco dancer Cristina Hoyos, this museum spread over three floors of an 18th-century palace makes a noble effort to showcase the mysterious art, although at €10 a pop it is more than a little overpriced. Exhibits include

sketches, paintings, photos of erstwhile (and contemporary) flamenco greats, plus a collection of dresses and shawls.

Centro de Interpretación Judería de Sevilla MUSEUM
(✆954 04 70 89; www.juderiadesevilla.es; Calle Ximenez de Enciso; admission €6.50; ⊙10.30am-3.30pm 5-8pm Mon-Sat, 10.30am-7pm Sun) A reinterpretation of Seville's weighty Jewish history has been long overdue and what better place to start than in the city's former Jewish quarter. This new museum is encased in an old Sephardic Jewish house in the higgledy-piggledy Santa Cruz quarter, the one-time Jewish neighbourhood that never recovered from a brutal pogrom and massacre carried out in 1391. The events of the pogrom and other historical happenings are catalogued inside along with a few surviving mementos including documents, costumes and books. It's small but poignant.

Seville

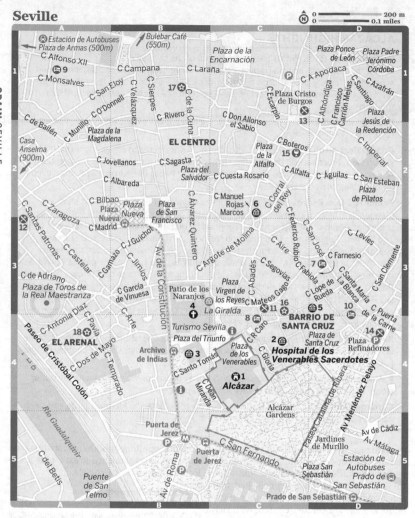

0   200 m
0   0.1 miles

✦✦ Festivals & Events

Semana Santa
HOLY WEEK

(www.semana-santa.org) Every day from Palm Sunday to Easter Sunday, large, life-sized *pasos* (sculptural representations of events from Christ's Passion) are carried from Seville's churches through the streets to the cathedral, accompanied by processions that may take more than an hour to pass. The processions are organised by more than 50 different *hermandades* or *cofradías* (brotherhoods, some of which include women).

Feria de Abril
SPRING FAIR

The April fair, held in the second half of the month (sometimes edging into May), is the jolly counterpart to the sombre Semana Santa. The biggest and most colourful of all Andalucía's ferias is less invasive (and also less inclusive) than the Easter celebration. It takes place on El Real de la Feria, in the Los Remedios area west of the Río Guadalquivir.

Bienal de Flamenco
FLAMENCO

(www.labienal.com; ☺ Sep) Most of the big names of the flamenco world participate in this major flamenco festival. Held in September in even-numbered years.

Seville

SPAIN SEVILLE

🛏 Sleeping

★ Oasis Backpackers' Hostel
HOSTEL €

(📞955 26 26 96; www.oasissevilla.com; Calle Almirante Ulloa 1; dm/d incl breakfast €15/50; ✸@🛜🏊) It's not often you get to backpack in a palace. Seville's Oasis Backpackers', a veritable oasis in the busy city centre district, is a friendly welcoming hostel with some private room options, a cafe/bar, and a rooftop deck with a small pool.

★ Hotel Amadeus
HOTEL €€

(📞954 50 14 43; www.hotelamadeussevilla.com; Calle Farnesio 6; s/d €100/114; 🅿✸🛜) Just when you thought you could never find hotels with pianos in the rooms anymore, along came Hotel Amadeus. It's run by an engaging musical family in the old *judería* (Jewish quarter) where several of the astutely decorated rooms come complete with soundproofed walls and upright pianos, ensuring you don't miss out on your daily practice.

Un Patio en Santa Cruz
HOTEL €€

(📞954 53 94 13; www.patiosantacruz.com; Calle Doncellas 15; s €65-85, d €65-120; ✸🛜) Feeling more like an art gallery than a hotel, this place has starched white walls coated in loud works of art, and strange sculptures and preserved plants. The rooms are immensely comfortable, staff are friendly, and there's a cool rooftop terrace with mosaic Moroccan tables. It's easily one of the hippest, pest and best-value hotels in town.

★ Hotel Casa 1800
LUXURY HOTEL €€€

(📞954 56 18 00; www.hotelcasa1800sevilla.com; Calle Rodrigo Caro 6; r from €195; ✸@🛜)

Straight in at number one as Seville's favourite hotel is this newly revived Santa Cruz jewel where the word *casa* (house) is taken seriously. This really is your home away from home (albeit a posh one!), with charming staff catering for your every need. Highlights include a sweet afternoon tea buffet, plus a quartet of penthouse garden suites with Giralda views.

✘ Eating

Bodega Santa Cruz
TAPAS €

(Calle Mateos Gago; tapas €2; ⊙11.30am-midnight) Forever crowded and with a mountain of paper on the floor, this place is usually standing room only, with tapas and drinks enjoyed alfresco as you dodge the marching army of tourists squeezing through Santa Cruz's narrow streets.

Vinería San Telmo
TAPAS, FUSION €€

(📞954 41 06 00; www.vineriasantelmo.com; Paseo Catalina de Ribera 4; tapas €3.50, media raciones €10; ⊙1-4.30pm & 8pm-midnight) San Telmo invented the *rascocielo* (skyscraper) tapa, an 'Empire State' of tomatoes, aubergine, goat's cheese and smoked salmon. If this and other creative nuggets such as foie gras with quail eggs and lychees, or exquisitely cooked bricks of tuna don't make you drool with expectation then you're probably dead.

★ La Brunilda
TAPAS, FUSION €€

(📞954 22 04 81; Calle Galera 5; tapas €3.50-6.50; ⊙1-4pm & 8.30-11.30pm Tue-Sat, 1-4pm Sun) Seville's crown as Andalucía's tapas capital is regularly attacked by well-armed rivals from the provinces, meaning it constantly has to reinvent itself and offer up fresh competition. Enter Brunilda, a new font of fusion tapas sandwiched into an inconspic-uous backstreet in the Arenal quarter where everything – including the food, staff and clientele – is pretty.

If you have unlimited appetite, try the whole menu. For those with smaller bellies, the creamy risotto is unmissable.

★ **Los Coloniales** CONTEMPORARY ANDALUCIAN €€
(www.tabernacoloniales.es; cnr Calle Dormitorio & Plaza Cristo de Burgos; mains €10-12; ⊘12.30pm-12.15am) The quiet ones are always the best. It might not look like much from the outside, but take it on trust that Los Coloniales is something very special. The quality plates line up like models on a catwalk: *chorizo a la Asturiana,* a divine spicy sausage in an onion sauce served on a bed of lightly fried potato; eggplants in honey; and pork tenderloin *al whiskey* (a whisky-flavoured sauce).

 Drinking & Nightlife

Bars usually open 6pm to 2am weekdays, 8pm till 3am at the weekend. Drinking and partying really get going around midnight on Friday and Saturday (daily when it's hot). In summer, dozens of open-air late-night

bars *(terrazas de verano)* spring up along both banks of the river.

Plaza del Salvador is brimful of drinkers from mid-evening to 1am.

El Garlochi BAR
(Calle Boteros 4; ⊘10pm-6am) Dedicated entirely to the iconography, smells and sounds of Semana Santa, the ubercamp El Garlochi is a true marvel. A cloud of church incense hits you as you go up the stairs, and the faces of baby Jesus and the Virgin welcome you into the velvet-walled bar, decked out with more Virgins and Jesuses.

Bulebar Café BAR
(☑954 90 19 54; Alameda de Hércules 83; ⊘4pm-late) This place gets pretty *caliente* (hot) at night but is pleasantly chilled in the early evening, with friendly staff. Don't write off its spirit-reviving alfresco breakfasts that pitch earlybirds with up-all-nighters.

☆ **Entertainment**

Seville is arguably Spain's flamenco capital and you're most likely to catch a spontaneous atmosphere (of unpredictable quality) in one of the bars staging regular nights of flamenco with no admission fee. *Soleares,* flamenco's truest *cante jondo* (deep song), was first concocted in Triana; head here to find some of the more authentic clubs.

Tablao El Arenal FLAMENCO
(www.tablaoelarenal.com; Calle Rodo 7; admission with 1 drink €38, with dinner €72; ⊘restaurant from 7pm, shows 8pm & 10pm) Of the three places in Seville that offer flamenco dinner shows this – ask any local – is the best. A smaller seating capacity (100 compared to 600 at the Palacio Andaluz) offers greater intimacy, although, as a big venue, it still lacks the grit and – invariably – *duende* (flamenco spirit) of the *peñas* (small flamenco clubs).

Casa de la Memoria FLAMENCO
(☑954 56 06 70; www.casadelamemoria.es; Calle Cuna 6; €18; ⊘shows 7.30pm & 9pm) Neither a *tablao* nor a private *peña,* this cultural centre, recently relocated from Santa Cruz to El Centro where it is accommodated in the old stables of the Palacio de la Lebrija, offers what are, without doubt, the most intimate and authentic nightly flamenco shows in Seville.

It's perennially popular and space is limited to 100, so reserve tickets a day or so in advance by calling or visiting the venue.

JAMÓN – A PRIMER

Unlike Italian prosciutto, Spanish *jamón* is a bold, deep red and well marbled with buttery fat. Like wines and olive oil, Spanish *jamón* is subject to a strict series of classifications. *Jamón serrano* refers to *jamón* made from white-coated pigs introduced to Spain in the 1950s. Once salted and semidried by the cold, dry winds of the Spanish sierra, most now go through a similar process of curing and drying in a climate-controlled shed for around a year. *Jamón serrano* accounts for approximately 90% of cured ham in Spain.

Jamón ibérico – more expensive and generally regarded as the elite of Spanish hams – comes from a black-coated pig indigenous to the Iberian Peninsula and a descendant of the wild boar. If the pig gains at least 50% of its body weight during the acorn-eating season, it can be classified as *jamón ibérico de bellota,* the most sought-after designation for *jamón.*

Casa de la Guitarra FLAMENCO
(954 22 40 93; Calle Mesón del Moro 12; tickets adult/child €17/10; shows 7.30pm & 9pm) Tiny new flamenco-only venue in Santa Cruz (no food or drinks served) where a miscued step from the performing dancers would land them in the front row of the audience. Glass display cases filled with guitars of erstwhile flamenco greats adorn the walls.

Casa Anselma FLAMENCO
(Calle Pagés del Corro 49; midnight-late Mon-Sat) If you can squeeze in past the foreboding form of Anselma (a celebrated Triana flamenco dancer) at the door, you'll quickly realise that anything can happen in here. Casa Anselma is the antithesis of a tourist flamenco *tablao*, with cheek-to-jowl crowds, thick cigarette smoke, zero amplification and spontaneous outbreaks of dexterous dancing. Pure magic. (Beware: there's no sign, just a doorway embellished with *azulejos* tiles.)

ℹ Information

Tourist Office (Avenida de la Constitución 21B; 9am-8pm Mon-Fri, 10am-2pm Sat & Sun, closed holidays) The staff at the Constitución office are well informed but often very busy.

Turismo Sevilla (www.turismosevilla.org; Plaza del Triunfo 1; 10.30am-7pm Mon-Fri) Information on all Sevilla province.

ℹ Getting There & Away

AIR

Aeropuerto San Pablo (SVQ; www.sevilla-airport.com; 24hr) Seville's airport, 7km east of the city, is Andalucía's second-busiest airport after Málaga's. Non-Spanish destinations include London, Paris, Amsterdam, Warsaw and Geneva. It is served by various budget airlines.

BUS

ALSA (www.alsa.es) Runs buses to Córdoba (€12, two hours), Granada (€23, three hours) amd Málaga (€18, 2¾ hours).

Estación de Autobuses Plaza de Armas (www.autobusesplazadearmas.es; Avenida del Cristo de la Expiración) Buses to/from the north of Sevilla province, Huelva province, Portugal and most other parts of Spain, including Madrid, leave from the main station, Estación de Autobuses Plaza de Armas. This is also the main station for Eurolines and international services to Germany, Belgium, France and beyond.

Estación de Autobuses Prado de San Sebastián (Plaza San Sebastián) Buses that do not leave from the main station, Estación de Autobuses Plaza de Armas – primarily those running inside Andalucía (except Huelva) – use the Estación de Autobuses Prado de San Sebastián. Buses from here run roughly hourly to Cádiz, Córdoba, Granada, Jerez de la Frontera, Málaga and Madrid.

TRAIN

Twenty or more superfast AVE trains, reaching speeds of 280km/h, whiz daily to/from Madrid (€76, 2½ hours). Other services include Cádiz (€16, 1¾ hours, 15 daily), Córdoba (€30, 42 minutes, more than 30 daily), Granada (€30, three hours, four daily) and Málaga (€43, two hours, 11 daily).

Estación Santa Justa (902 43 23 43; Avenida Kansas City) Seville's Estación Santa Justa is 1.5km northeast of the centre.

Córdoba

POP 328,000

Córdoba was once one of the most enlightened Islamic cities on earth, and enough remains to place it in the contemporary top three Andalucían draws. The centrepiece is the gigantic and exquisitely rendered Mezquita. Surrounding it is an intricate web of winding streets, geranium-sprouting flower boxes and cool intimate patios that are at their most beguiling in late spring.

◎ Sights & Activities

★ Mezquita MOSQUE
(957 47 05 12; www.mezquitadecordoba.org; Calle Cardenal Herrero; adult/child €8/4, 8.30-9.20am Mon-Sat free; 8.30am-7pm Mon-Sat, 8.30-10am & 2-7pm Sun Mar-Oct, 8.30am-6pm Mon-Sat, 8.30-11.30am & 3-6pm Sun Nov-Feb) It's impossible to overemphasise the beauty of Córdoba's great mosque, with its remarkably peaceful and spacious interior. The Mezquita hints, with all its lustrous decoration, at a lavish and refined age when Muslims, Jews and Christians lived side by side and enriched their city and surroundings with a heady interaction of diverse and vibrant cultures.

Alcázar de los Reyes Cristianos CASTLE
(Castle of the Christian Monarchs; Campo Santo de Los Mártires; admission €4.50, Fri free; 8.30am-8.45pm Tue-Fri, 8.30am-4.30pm Sat, 8.30am-2.30pm Sun;) Built by Alfonso XI in the 14th century on the remains of Roman and Arab predecessors, the castle began life as a palace. It hosted both Fernando and Isabel,

MEZQUITA HIGHLIGHTS

Puerta del Perdón Main entrance to the Mezquita (p621), a 14th-century Mudéjar gateway on Calle Cardenal Herrero.

Prayer Hall Divided into 11 'naves' by lines of two-tier arches striped in red brick and white stone. Their simplicity and number give a sense of endlessness to the Mezquita.

Mihrab & Maksura The arches within and around the *maksura* (the area where the caliphs and their retinues would have prayed) are the mosque's most intricate and sophisticated, forming a forest of interwoven horseshoe shapes. The portal of the mihrab itself is a sublime crescent arch.

Patio de los Naranjos & Minaret Outside the mosque, the leafy, walled courtyard and its fountain were the site of ritual ablutions before prayer. The crowning glory of the whole complex was the minaret, which at its peak towered 48m (only 22m of the minaret still survives).

The Cathedral A 16th-century construction in the Mezquita's heart.

who made their first acquaintance with Columbus here in 1486. Its terraced gardens – full of fish ponds, fountains, orange trees, flowers and topiary – are a pleasure to stroll and a joy to behold from the tower.

Centro Flamenco Fosforito   MUSEUM

(☎957 48 50 39; www.centroflamencofosforito. cordoba.es; Plaza del Potro; admission €2; ⊗8.30am-7.30pm Tue-Fri, 8.30am-2.30pm Sat, 9.30am-2.30pm Sun) Possibly the best flamenco museum in Andalucía – which is saying something – this new place benefits from a fantastic location inside the ancient Posada del Potro, an inn named-checked by Cervantes in the novel, *Don Quijote de la Mancha*. Touch-screens, fantastic archive footage and arty displays meticulously explain the building blocks of flamenco and its history, along with the singers, guitarisits and dancers who defined it. You'll walk out both enthused *and* wiser.

Medina Azahara   RUIN

(Madinat al-Zahra; admission €1.50, EU citizens free; ⊗10am-6.30pm Tue-Sat, to 8.30pm May–mid-Sep, to 2pm Sun) Even in the cicada-shrill heat and stillness of a summer afternoon, the Medina Azahara whispers of the power and vision of its founder, Abd ar-Rahman III. The self-proclaimed caliph began the construction of a magnificent new capital 8km west of Córdoba around 936, and took up full residence around 945. Medina Azahara was a resounding declaration of his status, a magnificent trapping of power. It was destroyed in the 11th century and just 10% of the site has been excavated.

A taxi costs €37 for the return trip, with one hour to view the site, or you can book a three-hour coach tour for €6.50 to €10 through many Córdoba hotels.

Hammam Baños Árabes   BATHHOUSE

(☎957 48 47 46; cordoba.hammamalandalus.com; Calle del Corregidor Luis de la Cerda 51; bath/bath & massage €24/36; ⊗2hr sessions 10am, noon, 2pm, 4pm, 6pm, 8pm & 10pm) Follow the lead of the medieval Cordobans and dip your toe in these beautifully renovated Arab baths, where you can enjoy an aromatherapy massage, with tea, hookah and Arabic sweets in the cafe afterwards.

🛏 Sleeping

⭐ Bed and Be   HOSTEL €

(☎661 420733; www.bedandbe.com; Calle Cruz Conde 22; dm/d with shared bathroom €19/60; ❇️🅿️) ✅ Hugely engaging new accommodation thanks in part to the foresight of owner, José, who also runs free evening bike tours around the city. There's an assortment of double and dorm rooms, all superclean and as gleaming white as a *pueblo blanco*. Extra value is added with a kitchen, lounge area, roof terrace and various special events regularly organised by José.

Hotel Mezquita   HOTEL €€

(☎957 47 55 85; www.hotelmezquita.com; Plaza Santa Catalina 1; s/d €42/74; ❇️🅿️) One of the best deals in town, Hotel Mezquita stands right opposite its namesake monument, amid the bric-a-brac of the tourism zone. The 16th-century mansion has large, elegant rooms with marble floors, tall doors and balconies, some affording views of the great mosque.

Hotel Hacienda
Posada de Vallina
HOTEL €€

(☑957 49 87 50; www.hhposadadevallinacordoba. com; Calle del Corregidor Luís de la Cerda 83; r from €99; P ✳ @ ⊛) In an enviable nook on the quiet side of the Mezquita (the building actually pre-dates it), this cleverly renovated hotel uses portraits and period furniture to enhance a plush and modern interior. There are two levels overlooking a salubrious patio and the rooms make you feel comfortable but in-period (ie medieval Córdoba). Columbus allegedly once stayed here.

Casa de los Azulejos
HOTEL €€

(☑957 47 00 00; www.casadelosazulejos.com; Calle Fernando Colón 5; s/d incl breakfast from €85/107; ✳ @ ⊛) Mexican and Andalucian styles converge in this stylish hotel, where the patio is all banana trees, ferns and potted palms bathed in sunlight. Colonial-style rooms feature tall antique doors, massive beds, walls in lilac and sky blue, and floors adorned with the beautiful old *azulejos* tiles that give the place its name.

 Eating

Bar Santos
TAPAS €

(Calle Magistral González Francés 3; tortilla €2.50; ⊘2pm-1.30am) The legendary Santos serves the best *tortilla de patatas* in town – and don't the *cordobeses* know it. Thick wedges are deftly cut from giant wheels of the stuff and customarily served with plastic forks on paper plates to take outside and gaze at the Mezquita. Don't miss it.

★Salmorejería
Umami
ANDALUCIAN, MODERN €€

(☑957 48 23 47; www.grupoumami.com; Calle Blanco Belmonte 6; mains €14-22; ⊘1-4pm & 8-11.30pm Mon-Sat, 1-4pm Sun) It's new, it's good and its celebrating what is probably Córdoba's most favourite dish, the locally concocted *salmorejo,* a tomato-y version of gazpacho soup that's too thick to drink. The trick (cos there's always a trick) is that Umami does a good dozen versions of the recipe including avocado, Thai and green tea flavours. The main dishes are equally creative.

Casa Mazal
JEWISH €€

(☑957 94 18 88; www.casamazal.com; Calle Tomás Conde 3; mains €12-15; ⊘12.30-4pm & 7.30-11pm) A meal here makes a fine complement to the nearby Casa de Sefarad museum, as it brings the Sephardic (Judeo-Spanish) tradition to the table. A sort of culinary diaspora, Sephardic dishes contain elements of Andalucian, Turkish, Italian and North African cuisine, with such varied items as Syrian lentil salad, honeyed eggplant fritters and *minas* (a matzo-based vegetarian lasagne) on the menu.

JEWISH CÓRDOBA

Jews were among the most dynamic and prominent citizens of Islamic Córdoba. The medieval *judería* (Jewish quarter), extending northwest from the Mezquita almost to Avenida del Gran Capitán, is today a maze of narrow streets and whitewashed buildings with flowery window boxes. Highlights include the following:

Sinagoga (Calle de los Judíos 20; ⊘9.30am-2pm & 3.30-5.30pm Tue-Sat, 9.30am-1.30pm Sun) Built in 1315, this is one of the few testaments to the Jewish presence in Andalucía, though it hasn't actually been used as a place of worship since the expulsion of Jews from Spain in 1492. It is decorated with some extravagant stuccowork that includes Hebrew inscriptions and intricate Mudéjar star and plant patterns.

Casa Andalusí (Calle de los Judíos 12; admission €2.50; ⊘10.30am-8.30pm, to 6.30pm Nov-Mar) The Casa Andalusí is a 12th-century house with a bit of an exaggerated, slightly tacky idea of Al-Andalus. It has a tinkling fountain in the patio and a variety of exhibits, mainly relating to Córdoba's medieval Muslim culture, as well as a Roman mosaic in the cellar, and a shop selling North African items.

Casa de Sefarad (www.casadesefarad.es; cnr Calle de los Judíos & Averroes; adult/reduced €4/3; ⊘11am-6pm Mon-Sat, 11am-2pm Sun) In the heart of the Judería, and once connected by underground tunnel to the Sinagoga, this small museum is devoted to the Sephardic-Judaic tradition in Spain. There is a refreshing focus on music, domestic traditions and the women intellectuals (poets, singers and thinkers) of Al-Andalus. A program of live music recitals and storytelling events runs most of the year.

ⓘ Information

Municipal Tourist Office (Plaza de Judá Levi; ⊙8.30am-2.30pm Mon-Fri)

Regional Tourist Office (Calle de Torrijos 10; ⊙9am-7.30pm Mon-Fri, 9.30am-3pm Sat, Sun & holidays) A good source of information about Córdoba province; located inside the Palacio de Congresos y Exposiciones.

ⓘ Getting There & Away

BUS

The **bus station** (☑957 40 40 40; www.estacionautobusescordoba.es; Glorieta de las Tres Culturas) is 1km northwest of Plaza de las Tendillas, behind the train station. Destinations include Seville (€10.36, 1¾ hours, six daily), Granada (€12.52, 2½ hours, seven daily) and Málaga (€12.75, 2¾ hours, five daily).

TRAIN

Córdoba's **train station** (☑957 40 02 02; Glorieta de las Tres Culturas) is on the high-speed AVE line between Madrid and Seville. Rail destinations include Seville (€10.60 to €32.10, 40 to 90 minutes, 23 or more daily), Madrid (€52 to €66.30, 1¾ to 6¼ hours, 23 or more daily), Málaga (€21 to €39.60, one to 2½ hours, nine daily) and Barcelona (€59.40 to €133, 10½ hours, four daily). For Granada (€34.30, four hours), change at Bobadilla.

Granada

ELEV 685M / POP 258,000

Granada's eight centuries as a Muslim capital are symbolised in its keynote emblem, the remarkable Alhambra, one of the most graceful architectural achievements in the Muslim world. Islam was never completely expunged here, and today it seems more present than ever in the shops, restaurants, tearooms and mosque of a growing North African community in and around the maze of the Albayzín. The tapas bars fill to bursting, while flamenco dives resound to the heart-wrenching tones of the south.

◉ Sights & Activities

★Alhambra   PALACE

(☑902 44 12 21; www.alhambra-tickets.es; adult/under 12yr €14/free, Generalife only €7; ⊙8.30am-8pm 15 Mar-14 Oct, to 6pm 15 Oct-14 Mar, night visits 10-11.30pm Tue-Sat Mar-Oct, 8-9.30pm Fri & Sat Oct-Mar) The sheer red walls of the Alhambra rise from woods of cypress and elm. Inside is one of the more splendid sights of Europe, a network of lavishly decorated palaces and irrigated gardens, a World Heritage Site and the subject of scores of legends and fantasies.

★Capilla Real   HISTORIC BUILDING

(www.capillarealgranada.com; Calle Oficios; admission €4; ⊙10.15am-1.30pm & 3.30-6.30pm Mon-Sat, 11am-1.30pm & 2.30-5.30pm Sun) The Royal Chapel adjoins Granada's cathedral and is an outstanding Christian building. Catholic Monarchs Isabel and Fernando commissioned this elaborate Isabelline Gothic–style mausoleum. It was not completed until 1521; they were temporarily interred in the Convento de San Francisco.

Museo Sefardi   MUSEUM

(☑958 22 05 78; www.museosefardidegranada.es; Placeta Berrocal 5; admission €5; ⊙10am-2pm & 5-9pm) Expelled en masse in 1492, there are very few Sephardic Jews left living in Granada today. But this didn't stop one enterprising couple from opening up a museum to their memory in 2013, the year that the Spanish government began offering Spanish citizenship to any Sephardic Jew who could prove their Iberian ancestry. The mu-

DON'T MISS

ALHAMBRA HIGHLIGHTS

Palacios Nazaríes The central palace complex is the pinnacle of the Alhambra's design, a harmonious synthesis of space, light, shade, water and greenery that sought to conjure the gardens of paradise for the rulers who dwelt here.

Patio de los Leones (Courtyard of the Lions) Glorious, recently restored patio with exceptional rooms around the perimeter.

Palacio de Carlos V Renaissance-era circle-in-a-square ground plan. Inside, the Museo de la Alhambra has a collection of Alhambra artefacts.

Generalife From the Arabic *jinan al-'arif* (the overseer's gardens), the Generalife is a soothing arrangement of pathways, patios, pools, fountains, tall trees and, in season, flowers of every imaginable hue.

ⓘ ALHAMBRA TICKETS

Up to 6600 tickets to the Alhambra are available for each day. About one-third of these are sold at the ticket office on the day, but they sell out early and you need to start queuing by 7am to be reasonably sure of getting one. It's highly advisable to book in advance (€1.40 extra per ticket).

For internet or phone bookings you need a Visa card, MasterCard or Eurocard. You receive a reference number, which you must show, along with your passport, national identity card or credit card, at the Alhambra ticket office when you pick up the ticket on the day of your visit.

The Palacios Nazaríes are open for night visits, good for atmosphere rather than detail.

Buses 30, 32 and (less directly) 34 run from near Plaza Nueva from 7am to 11pm, stopping at the ticket office and in front of the Alhambra Palace. By car, follow 'Alhambra' signs from the highway to the car park, just uphill from the ticket office.

Alhambra Advance Booking (☑902 888001, for international calls +34 958 92 60 31; www.alhambra-tickets.es) Book online or by phone.

Servicaixa (www.servicaixa.com) Buy tickets in advance from Servicaixa cash machines.

seum is tiny, but the artefacts are interesting and they're given extra resonance spike by the vivid historical portrayal related by the owners.

⊙ Albayzín

On the hill facing the Alhambra across the Darro valley, Granada's old Muslim quarter, the Albayzín, is an open-air museum in which you can lose yourself for a whole morning. The cobblestone streets are lined with gorgeous *cármenes* (large mansions with walled gardens, from the Arabic karm for garden). It survived as the Muslim quarter for several decades after the Christian conquest in 1492.

Palacio de Dar-al-Horra   PALACE
(Callejón de las Monjas) Close to the Placeta de San Miguel Bajo, off Callejón del Gallo and down a short lane, is the 15th-century Palacio de Dar-al-Horra, a romantically dishevelled mini-Alhambra that was home to the mother of Boabdil, Granada's last Muslim ruler.

Calle Calderería Nueva   STREET
Linking the upper and lower parts of the Albayzín, Calle Calderería Nueva is a narrow street famous for its *teterías* (tearooms), but also a good place to shop for slippers, hookahs, jewellery and North African pottery from an eclectic cache of shops redolent of a Moroccan souk.

Colegiata del Salvador   CHURCH
(Plaza del Salvador; admission €0.75; ⊙10am-1pm & 4.30-6.30pm) Plaza del Salvador, near the top of the Albayzín, is dominated by the Colegiata del Salvador, a 16th-century church on the site of the Albayzín's former main mosque, the patio of which still survives at the church's western end.

Mirador San Nicolás   LOOKOUT
(Callejón de San Cecilio) Callejón de San Cecilio leads to the Mirador San Nicolás, a lookout with unbeatable views of the Alhambra and Sierra Nevada. Come back here later for sunset (you can't miss the trail then!). At any time of day take care: skilful, well-organised wallet-lifters and bag-snatchers operate here. Don't be put off; there is still a terrific atmosphere with buskers and local students intermingling with camera-touting travellers.

🛏 Sleeping

Hotel Posada del Toro   BOUTIQUE HOTEL €
(☑958 22 73 33; www.posadadeltoro.com; Calle de Elvira 25; r from €54; ✳🖥) A lovely small hotel with rooms set around a tranquil central patio. Walls are washed in a delectable combination of pale pistachio, peach and cream, and the rooms are similarly enticing with parquet floors, stucco detailing Alhambra-style, rustic-style furniture and small but perfectly equipped bathrooms with double sinks and hydromassage showers. The

Granada

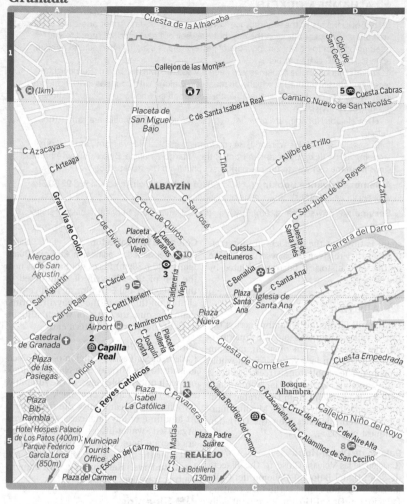

restaurant serves up Spanish dishes like Galician octopus, as well as pastas and pizza.

★ Carmen de la
Alcubilla del Caracol   HISTORIC HOTEL €€

(☑958 21 55 51; www.alcubilladelcaracol.com; Calle del Aire Alta 12; s/d €100/120; ✳@🛜) This exquisitely decorated place is located on the slopes of the Alhambra. Rooms are washed in pale pastel colours contrasting with cool cream and antiques. There are fabulous views and a pretty terraced garden. Ask for the room in the tower for a truly heady experience.

★ Hotel Hospes
Palacio de Los Patos   LUXURY HOTEL €€€

(☑958 53 57 90; www.hospes.com; Solarillo de Gracia 1; r/ste €200/400; Ⓟ✳@🛜≋) Put simply, the best hotel in Granada – if you can afford it – offering lucky guests sharp modernity and exemplary service in a palatial Unesco-protected building. You could write a novella about the many memorable features: the grand staircase, the postmodern chandeliers, the Arabian garden, the Roman emperor spa, the roses they leave on your bed in the afternoon.

11.30pm Sun-Fri, 1.30-4.30pm Sat; ✈) The best Moroccan food in a city that is well known for its Moorish throwbacks? Recline on lavish patterned seating, try the rich, fruity tagine casseroles and make your decision. Note that Arrayanes does not serve alcohol.

★ La Botillería TAPAS, FUSION €€
(✆958 22 49 28; Calle Varela 10; mains €13-20; ◷1pm-1am Wed-Sun, 1-8pm Mon) Establishing a good reputation for nouveau tapas, La Botillería is just around the corner from the legendary La Tana bar, to which it has family connections. It's a more streamlined modern place than its cousin, where you can *tapear* (eat tapas) at the bar or sit down for the full monty Andalucian style. The *solomillo* (pork tenderloin) comes in a rich, wine-laden sauce.

Carmela Restaurante TAPAS, ANDALUCIAN €€
(✆958 22 57 94; www.restaurantecarmela.com; Calle Colcha 13; tapas €5-10; ◷12.30pm-midnight) Long a bastion of traditional tapas, Granada has taken a leaf out of Seville's book in this new streamlined restaurant guarded by the statue of Jewish philosopher, Yehuba ibn Tibon, at the jaws of the Realejo quarter. Best of the new breed is the made-to-order tortilla and cured ham croquettes the size of tennis balls.

✗ Eating

Granada is one of the last bastions of that fantastic practice of free tapas with every drink, and some have an international flavour. The labyrinthine Albayzín holds a wealth of eateries tucked away in the narrow streets. Calle Calderería Nueva is a fascinating muddle of *teterías* and Arabic-influenced takeaways.

★ Arrayanes MOROCCAN €€
(✆958 22 84 01; www.rest-arrayanes.com; Cuesta Marañas 4; mains €15; ◷1.30-4.30pm & 7.30-

ANDALUCÍA'S QUIETEST BEACHES

The coast east of Almería in eastern Andalucía is perhaps the last section of Spain's Mediterranean coast where you can have a beach to yourself. This is Spain's sunniest region – even in late March it can be warm enough to strip off and take in the rays. The best thing about the region is the wonderful coastline and semidesert scenery of the **Cabo de Gata** promontory. All along the 50km coast from El Cabo de Gata village to Agua Amarga, some of the most beautiful and empty beaches on the Mediterranean alternate with precipitous cliffs and scattered villages. The main village is laid-back **San José**, with excellent beaches nearby, such as Playa de los Genoveses and Playa de Mónsul.

☆ Entertainment

Peña La Platería   FLAMENCO
(www.laplateria.org.es; Placeta de Toqueros 7) Buried in the Albayzín warren, Peña La Platería claims to be the oldest flamenco aficionados' club in Spain. It's a private affair, though, and not always open to nonmembers. Performances are usually Thursday and Saturday at 10.30pm – look presentable, and speak a little Spanish at the door, if you can.

Casa del Arte Flamenco   FLAMENCO
(☑958 56 57 67; www.casadelarteflamenco.com; Cuesta de Gomérez 11; tickets €18; ☉ shows 7.30pm & 9pm) Just what Granada needed. A new small flamenco venue that is neither *tablao* nor *peña,* but something in between. The peformers are invariably top-notch; the atmosphere depends on the tourist-aficonado ration in the audience.

Le Chien Andalou   FLAMENCO
(www.lechienandalou.com; Carrera del Darro 7; admission €6; ☉ shows 9.30pm & 11.30pm) This is one of Granada's most atmospheric venues to enjoy some vigorous castanet-clicking flamenco with a varied and professional line-up of musicians and dancers throughout the week. The cave-like surroundings of a renovated *aljibe* (well) create a fittingly moody setting and the whole place has a more genuine feel to it than the Sacromonte coach-tour traps. Book through the website.

❶ Information

Municipal Tourist Office (www.granadatur. com; Plaza del Carmen; ☉10am-7pm Mon-Sat, 10am-2pm Sun) Sleek, efficient centre opposite the city's Parque Federico García Lorca.
Regional Tourist Office (Pabellón de Acceso, Avenida del Generalife, Plaza Nueva, Alhambra; ☉8am-7.30pm Mon-Fri, 8am-2.30pm & 4-7.30pm Sat & Sun)

❶ Getting There & Away

BUS

Granada's **bus station** (Carretera de Jaén) is 3km northwest of the city centre. Destinations include Córdoba (€15, 2¾ hours direct, nine daily), Seville (€23, three hours, 10 daily), Málaga (€14, 1¾ hours, hourly) and an overnight service to Madrid's Barajas Airport (€33, five hours).

TRAIN

The **train station** (☑958 24 02 02; Avenida de Andaluces) is 1.5km west of the centre. Trains run to/from Seville (€30, three hours), Almería (€20, 2¼ hours), Ronda (€20, three hours), Algeciras (€30, 4½ hours), Madrid (€68, four to five hours), Valencia (€32, 7½ to eight hours) and Barcelona (€70, 12 hours).

Málaga

POP 558,000

The exuberant port city of Málaga may be uncomfortably close to the overdeveloped Costa del Sol, but it's a wonderful amalgam of old Andalucian town and modern metropolis. The centre presents the visitor with narrow, old streets and wide, leafy boulevards, beautiful gardens and impressive monuments, fashionable shops and a burgeoning cultural life. The city's terrific bars and nightlife, the last word in Málaga *joie de vivre,* stay open very late.

◉ Sights & Activities

★**Museo Picasso Málaga**   MUSEUM
(☑902 44 33 77; www.museopicassomalaga.org; Calle San Agustín 8; adult/child €7/3.50; ☉10am-8pm Tue-Thu & Sun, to 9pm Fri & Sat) The Museo Picasso has an enviable collection of 204 works, 155 donated and 49 loaned to the museum by Christine Ruiz-Picasso (wife of Paul, Picasso's eldest son) and Bernard Ruiz-Picasso (his grandson), and includes some wonderful paintings of the family, including the heartfelt *Paulo con gorro blanco*

(Paulo with a white cap), a portrait of Picasso's eldest son painted in the 1920s.

Don't miss the Phoenician, Roman, Islamic and Renaissance archaeological remains in the museum's basement, discovered during construction works.

★**Catedral de Málaga**   CATHEDRAL
(☑952 21 59 17; Calle Molina Lario; cathedral & museum €3.50; ⊙10am-6pm Mon-Sat, closed holidays) Málaga's cathedral was started in the 16th century when several architects set about transforming the original mosque. Of this, only the **Patio de los Naranjos** survives, a small courtyard of fragrant orange trees where the ablutions fountain used to be. The fabulous domed ceiling soars 40m into the air, while the vast colonnaded nave houses an enormous cedar-wood choir. Aisles give access to 15 chapels with gorgeous retables and a stash of 18th-century religious art.

★**Alcazaba**   CASTLE
(Calle Alcazabilla; admission €2.10, incl Castillo de Gibralfaro €3.40; ⊙9.30am-8pm Tue-Sun Apr-Oct) No time to visit Granada's Alhambra? Then Málaga's Alcazaba can provide a taster. The entrance is next to the **Roman amphitheatre**, from where a meandering path climbs amid lush greenery: crimson bougainvillea, lofty palms, fragrant jasmine bushes and rows of orange trees. Extensively restored, this palace-fortress dates from the 11th-century Moorish period and the caliphal horseshoe arches, courtyards and bubbling fountains are evocative of this influential period in Málaga's history.

Museo de Arte Flamenco   MUSEUM
(☑952 22 13 80; www.museoflamencojuanbreva. com; Calle Juan Franquelo 4; suggested donation €1; ⊙10am-2pm Tue-Sun) Fabulously laid-out over two floors in the HQ of Málaga's oldest and most prestigious *peña*, this collection of fans, costumes, posters and other flamenco paraphernalia is testimony to the city's illustrious flamenco scene.

Casa Natal de Picasso   MUSEUM
(www.fundacionpicasso.malaga.eu; Plaza de la Merced 15; admission €3; ⊙9.30am-8pm) For a more intimate insight into the painter's childhood, head to the Casa Natal de Picasso, the house where Picasso was born in 1881, which now acts as a study foundation. The house has a replica 19th-century artist's studio and small quarterly exhibitions of Picasso's work.

Personal memorabilia of Picasso and his family make up part of the display.

Castillo de Gibralfaro   CASTLE
(admission €2.10; ⊙9am-9pm Apr-Sep, to 6pm Oct-Mar) One remnant of Málaga's Islamic past is the craggy ramparts of the Castillo de Gibralfaro, spectacularly located high on the hill overlooking the city. Built by Abd ar-Rahman I, the 8th-century Cordoban emir, and later rebuilt in the 14th century when Málaga was the main port for the emirate of Granada, the castle originally acted as a lighthouse and military barracks. Nothing much is original in the castle's interior, but the airy walkway around the ramparts affords the best views over Málaga.

★**Museo Carmen Thyssen**   MUSEUM
(www.carmenthyssenmalaga.org; Calle Compañia 10; adult/child €6/free; ⊙10am-7.30pm Tue-Sun) One of the city's latest museums opened in 2011 in an aesthetically renovated 16th-century palace in the heart of the city's historic centre, the former old Moorish quarter of Málaga. The extensive collection concentrates on 19th-century Spanish and Andalucian art and includes paintings by some of the country's most exceptional painters, including Joaquín Sorolla y Bastida, Ignacio Zuloaga and Francisco de Zurbarán. Temporary exhibitions similarly focus on 19th-century art.

Beaches   BEACHES
Sandy city beaches stretch several kilometres in each direction from the port. **Playa de la Malagueta**, handy to the city centre, has some excellent bars and restaurants close by. **Playa de Pedregalejo** and **Playa del Palo**, about 4km east of the centre, are popular and reachable by bus 11 from Paseo del Parque.

🛏 Sleeping

Hotel Carlos V   HOTEL €
(☑952 21 51 20; www.hotel-carlosvmalaga.com; Calle Císter 10; s/d €36/59; ⓟ❄@) Close to the cathedral and Picasso museum, the Carlos V is enduringly popular. Renovated in 2008, bathrooms sparkle in their uniform of cream-and-white tiles. Excellent standard for the price plus helpful staff make this hotel a winner.

El Hotel del Pintor   BOUTIQUE HOTEL €€
(☑952 06 09 81; www.hoteldelpintor.com; Calle Álamos 27; s/d €54/69; ❄@📶) The red, black and white colour scheme of this friendly,

SPAIN MÁLAGA

RONDA

Perched on an inland plateau riven by the 100m fissure of El Tajo gorge and surrounded by the beautiful Serranía de Ronda, Ronda, a two-hour drive west of Málaga, is the most dramatically sited of Andalucía's *pueblos blancos* (white villages). The **Plaza de Toros** (built 1785), considered the national home of bullfighting, is a mecca for aficionados; inside is the small but fascinating Museo Taurino. The amazing 18th-century **Puente Nuevo** (New Bridge) is an incredible engineering feat crossing the gorge to the originally Muslim Old Town (La Ciudad).

Casa del Rey Moro (House of the Moorish King; Calle Santo Domingo 17; admission €4; ⊙10am-7pm) The terraces give access to La Mina, an Islamic stairway of over 300 steps that are cut into the rock all the way down to the river at the bottom of the gorge. These steps enabled Ronda to maintain water supplies when it was under attack. It was also the point where Christian troops forced entry in 1485. The steps are not well lit and are steep and wet in places. Take care.

Enfrente Arte (☑952 87 90 88; www.enfrentearte.com; Calle Real 40, Ronda; r incl breakfast €80-90; ❋@❋) On an old cobblestoned street, Belgian-owned Enfrente offers a huge range of facilities and funky modern/oriental decor. It has a bar, pool, sauna, recreation room, flowery patio with black bamboo, film room and fantastic views out to the Sierra de las Nieves. What's more, the room price includes all drinks, to which you help yourself, and a sumptuous buffet breakfast.

Parador de Ronda (☑952 87 75 00; www.parador.es; Plaza de España; r €160-171; 🅿❋@ 🛜❋) Acres of shining marble and deep-cushioned furniture give this modern *parador* a certain appeal. The terrace is a wonderful place to drink in views of the gorge with your coffee or wine, especially at night.

Bodega San Francisco (www.bodegasanfrancisco.com; Calle Ruedo Alameda; raciones €6-10; ⊙1.30-5pm & 8pm-1am Wed-Mon) With three dining rooms and tables spilling out onto the narrow pedestrian street, this may well be Ronda's top tapas bar. The menu is vast and should suit the fussiest of families, even vegetarians with nine-plus salad choices. Try the *revuelto de patatas* (scrambled eggs with potatoes and peppers). House wine is good.

Municipal Tourist Office (www.turismoderonda.es; Paseo de Blas Infante; ⊙10am-7.30pm Mon-Fri, 10.15am-2pm & 3.30-6.30pm Sat, Sun & holidays) Helpful and friendly staff with a wealth of information on the town and region.

---

small hotel echoes the abstract artwork of *malagueño* (person from Málaga) artist Pepe Bornov, whose paintings are on permanent display throughout the public areas and rooms. Although convenient for most of the city's main sights, the rooms in the front can be noisy, especially on a Saturday night.

✖ Eating

Most of the best eating places are sandwiched in the narrow streets between Calle Marqués de Larios and the cathedral.

El Piyayo　　　　　　　TAPAS €
(☑952 22 90 57; www.entreplatos.es; Calle Granada 36; raciones €6-10; ⊙12.30pm-midnight) A popular traditionally tiled bar and restaurant, famed for its *pescaitos fritos* (fried fish)

and typical local tapas, including wedges of crumbly Manchego cheese, the ideal accompaniment to a glass of hearty Rioja wine. The *berenjenas con miel de caña* (aubergine with molasses) are also good.

★ El Mesón de Cervantes　　TAPAS, ARGENTINIAN €€
(☑952 21 62 74; www.elmesondecervantes.com; Calle Álamos 11; mains €13-16; ⊙7pm-midnight Wed-Mon) Once a secret, then a whisper, now loud shout, Cervantes has catapulted itself into Málaga's *numero uno* restaurant among a growing number of impressed bloggers, tweeters and anyone else with taste buds and an internet connection.

It started as a humble tapas bar run by expat Argentinian, Gabriel Spatz (the original bar is still operating around the corner), but has now expanded into plush new digs with an open kitchen, fantastic family-style service and – no surprises – incredible meat dishes.

☆ Entertainment

Peña Juan Breva FLAMENCO
(Calle Juan Franquelo 4) You'll feel like a gate-crasher at someone else's party at this private *peña*, but persevere; the flamenco is *muy puro*. Watch guitarists who play like they've got 12 fingers and listen to singers who bellow forth as if their heart has been broken the previous night. There's no set schedule. Ask about dates when/if you visit the on-site Museo Arte de Flamenco.

Kelipe FLAMENCO
(🗹 692 829885; www.kelipe.net; Calle Pena 11; admission €20-35; ⊙shows 9pm Thu-Sat) Málaga's substantial flamenco heritage has its nexus to the northwest of Plaza de la Merced. Kelipe is a flamenco centre which puts on *muy puro* performances Thursday to Saturday; entry of €15 includes one drink and tapa – reserve ahead. Kelipe also runs intensive weekend courses in guitar and dance.

ℹ Information

Municipal Tourist Office (www.malaga turismo.com) main branch (Plaza de la Marina); Casita del Jardinero (Avenida de Cervantes 1; ⊙9am-8pm Mar-Sep, to 6pm Oct-Feb)

ℹ Getting There & Away

AIR
Málaga–Costa del Sol Airport (www.aena.es) Málaga's busy airport, the main international gateway to Andalucía, receives flights by dozens of airlines from around Europe.

BUS
Málaga's **bus station** (🗹 952 35 00 61; www.estabus.emtsam.es; Paseo de los Tilos) is 1km southwest of the city centre. Frequent buses go to Seville (€18, 2½ hours), Granada (€11, 1½ to two hours), Córdoba (€15, three hours) and Ronda (€9.50, 2½ hours).

TRAIN
The main station, **Málaga María Zambrano Train Station** (www.renfe.es; Explanada de la Estación), is around the corner from the bus station. The superfast AVE service runs to Madrid (€80, 2½ hours, 10 daily). Trains also go to Córdoba (€41, one hour, 18 daily) and Seville (€43, two hours, 11 daily).

EXTREMADURA

Cáceres
POP 95,925

The Ciudad Monumental (Old Town) of Cáceres is truly extraordinary. Narrow cobbled streets twist and climb among ancient stone walls lined with palaces and mansions, while the skyline is decorated with turrets, spires, gargoyles and enormous storks' nests. Protected by defensive walls, it has survived almost intact from its 16th-century heyday. At dusk or after dark, when the crowds have gone, you'll feel like you've stepped back into the Middle Ages.

◉ Sights

Concatedral de Santa María CATHEDRAL
(Plaza de Santa María; admission €1; ⊙10am-2pm & 5.30-9pm Mon-Sat, 9.30-11.50am & 5.30-7.15pm Sun) The Concatedral de Santa María, a 15th-century Gothic cathedral, creates an impressive opening scene on the Plaza de Santa María. At its southwestern corner is a modern **statue of San Pedro de Alcántara**, a 16th-century *extremeño* ascetic (his toes worn shiny by the hands and lips of the faithful). Inside, there's a magnificent carved 16th-century cedar **altarpiece**, several fine noble tombs and chapels, and a small ecclesiastical **museum**. Climb the **bell tower** for views over the old town.

★Torre de Bujaco TOWER
(Plaza Mayor; adult/child €2/free; ⊙10am-2pm & 5.30-8.30pm Mon-Sat, 10am-2pm Sun) As you climb up the steps to the Ciudad Monumental from the **Plaza Mayor**, turn left to climb the 12th-century Torre de Bujaco, home to an interpretative display. From the top there's a fine stork's-eye view of the Plaza Mayor.

🛏 Sleeping & Eating

★Hotel Casa Don Fernando BOUTIQUE HOTEL €€
(🗹 927 21 42 79; www.casadonfernando.com; Plaza Mayor 30; d €50-150; P ❄ 🛜) The classiest midrange choice in Cáceres, this boutique hotel sits on Plaza Mayor directly opposite the Arco de la Estrella. Spread over four floors, the designer rooms and bathrooms are tastefully chic; superior rooms (€30 more than the standards) have the best plaza views (although nights can be noisy

MOROCCO

At once African and Arab, visible from numerous points along Spain's Andalucian coast, Morocco is an exciting detour from your Western European journey. The country's attractions are endless, from the fascinating souqs and medieval architecture of Marrakesh and Fès to the Atlantic charms of Asilah and Essaouira, from the High Atlas and Rif Mountains to the soulful sand dunes of the Sahara. For further information, head to shop.lonelyplanet.com to purchase Lonely Planet's *Morocco* guide.

Casablanca and Marrakesh in particular are well-connected by air to numerous European cities, while car-and-passenger ferry services connect Tangier with Algeciras, Barcelona, Gibraltar and Tarifa, with an additional service between Nador and Almería.

especially on weekends). Attic-style top-floor rooms are good for families.

★ Restaurante
Torre de Sande FUSION €€
(☑ 927 21 11 47; www.torredesande.com; Calle Condes 3; set menus €25-35; ⊙ 1-4pm & 7pm-midnight Tue-Sat, 1-4pm Sun) Dine in the pretty courtyard on dishes like *salmorejo de cerezas del Jerte con queso de cabra* (cherry-based cold soup with goat's cheese) at this elegant gourmet restaurant in the heart of the Ciudad Monumental. More modestly, stop for a drink and a tapa at the interconnecting *tapería* (tapas bar).

❶ Information

Main Tourist Office (☑ 927 01 08 34; www.turismoextremadura.com; Plaza Mayor 3; ⊙ 8.30am-2.30pm & 4-6pm Mon-Fri, 10am-2pm Sat & Sun) Opens later in the afternoon in summer.

Regional Tourist Office (☑ 927 25 55 97; www.turismocaceres.org; Palacio Carvajal, Calle Amargura 1; ⊙ 8am-8.45pm Mon-Fri, 10am-1.45pm & 5-7.45pm Sat, 10am-1.45pm Sun) Covers Cáceres province and city.

❶ Getting There & Away

BUS

The **bus station** (Carretera de Sevilla; ⊙ 927 23 25 50) has services to Trujillo (€4.63, 40 minutes) and Mérida (€5.63, one hour).

TRAIN

Up to five trains per day run to/from Madrid (€27 to €32, four hours) and Mérida (€6, one hour).

SURVIVAL GUIDE

❶ Directory A–Z

ACCOMMODATION

Budget options include everything from dorm-style youth hostels to family-style *pensiones* and slightly better-heeled *hostales*. At the upper end of this category you'll find rooms with air-conditioning and private bathrooms. Mid-range *hostales* and hotels are more comfortable and most offer standard hotel services. Business hotels, trendy boutique hotels and luxury hotels are usually in the top-end category.

Camping

Spain has around 1000 officially graded *campings* (camping grounds) and they vary greatly in service, cleanliness and style. They're officially rated as 1st class (1ªC), 2nd class (2ªC) or 3rd class (3ªC). Camping grounds usually charge per person, per tent and per vehicle – typically €5 to €10 for each. Many camping grounds close from around October to Easter.

Campings Online (www.campingsonline.com/espana) Booking service.

Campingguía (www.campinguia.com) Comments (mostly in Spanish) and links.

Guía Camping (www.guiacampingfecc.com) Online version of the annual *Guía Camping* (€13.60), which is available in bookshops around the country.

Hotels, Hostales & Pensiones

Most options fall into the categories of hotels (one to five stars, full amenities), *hostales* (high-end guesthouses with private bathroom; one to

---

COUNTRY FACTS

Area 505,370 sq km

Capital Madrid

Country Code ☑ 34

Currency Euro (€)

Emergency ☑ 112

Languages Spanish (Castilian), Catalan, Basque, Galician (Gallego)

Money ATMs everywhere

Population 47 million

Visas Schengen rules apply

three stars) or *pensiones* (guesthouses, usually with shared bathroom; one to three stars).

Paradores (in Spain 902 54 79 79; www. parador.es) Among the more tempting hotels for those with a little fiscal room to manoeuvre are the 90 or so *paradores,* a state-funded chain of hotels in often stunning locations, among them towering castles and former medieval convents.

Youth Hostels

Albergues juveniles (youth hostels) are cheap places to stay, especially for lone travellers. Expect to pay from €15 to €28 per night, depending on location, age and season.

Red Española de Albergues Juveniles (REAJ, Spanish Youth Hostel Network; www.reaj.com) Spain's Hostelling International (HI) organisation, Red Española de Albergues Juveniles, has around 250 youth hostels throughout Spain. Official hostels require HI membership (you can buy a membership card at virtually all hostels) and some have curfews.

ACTIVITIES

Hiking

➡ Pick up Lonely Planet's *Walking in Spain* and read about some of the best treks in the country.

➡ Maps by Editorial Alpina are useful for hiking, especially in the Pyrenees. Buy at bookshops, sports shops and sometimes at petrol stations near hiking areas.

➡ GR (*Grandes Recorridos,* or long-distance) trails are indicated with red-and-white markers.

Skiing

Skiing is cheaper but less varied than in much of the rest of Europe. The season runs from December to mid-April. The best resorts are in the Pyrenees, especially in northwest Catalonia and in Aragón. The Sierra Nevada in Andalucía offers the most southerly skiing in Western Europe.

Surfing, Windsurfing & Kitesurfing

The Basque Country has good surf spots, including San Sebastián, Zarautz and the legendary left at Mundaka. Tarifa, with its long beaches and ceaseless wind, is generally considered to be the windsurfing capital of Europe. It's also a top spot for kitesurfing.

BUSINESS HOURS

Banks 8.30am to 2pm Monday to Friday; some also open 4pm to 7pm Thursday and 9am to 1pm Saturday

Central post offices 8.30am to 9.30pm Monday to Friday, 8.30am to 2pm Saturday

Nightclubs midnight or 1am to 5am or 6am

Restaurants lunch 1pm to 4pm, dinner 8.30pm to midnight or later

---

SLEEPING PRICE RANGES

Our reviews refer to double rooms with a private bathroom, except in hostels or where otherwise specified. Quoted rates are for high season, which is generally May to September (though this varies greatly from region to region).

€ less than €65 (€75 in Madrid & Barcelona)

€€ €65 to €140 (€75 to €200 in Madrid/Barcelona)

€€€ more than €140 (€200 in Madrid & Barcelona)

Shops 10am to 2pm and 4.30pm to 7.30pm or 5pm to 8pm Monday to Saturday; big supermarkets and department stores generally open from 10am to 10pm Monday to Saturday

GAY & LESBIAN TRAVELLERS

Homosexuality is legal in Spain. In 2005 the Socialists gave the country's conservative Catholic foundations a shake with the legalisation of same-sex marriages in Spain. Lesbians and gay men generally keep a fairly low profile, but are quite open in the cities. Madrid, Barcelona, Sitges, Torremolinos and Ibiza have particularly lively scenes.

INTERNET ACCESS

➡ Wi-fi is increasingly available at most hotels and in some cafes, restaurants and airports; generally (but not always) free.

➡ Good cybercafes are increasingly hard to find; ask at the local tourist office. Prices per hour range from €1.50 to €3.

INTERNET RESOURCES

Fiestas.net (www.fiestas.net) Festivals around the country.

Lonely Planet (www.lonelyplanet.com/spain) Destination information, hotel bookings, traveller forums and more.

Renfe (Red Nacional de los Ferrocarriles Españoles; www.renfe.com) Spain's rail network.

Tour Spain (www.tourspain.org) Culture, food and links to hotels and transport.

Turespaña (www.spain.info) Spanish tourist office's site.

LANGUAGE COURSES

Popular places to learn Spanish: Barcelona, Granada, Madrid, Salamanca and Seville.

Escuela Oficial de Idiomas (EOI; www.eeooi inet.com) The Escuela Oficial de Idiomas is a nationwide institution teaching Spanish and other local languages. On the website's opening

ESSENTIAL FOOD & DRINK

➡ **Paella** This signature rice dish comes in infinite varieties, although Valencia is its true home.

➡ **Cured meats** Wafer-thin slices of *chorizo, lomo, salchichón* and *jamón serrano* appear on most Spanish tables.

➡ **Tapas** These bite-sized morsels range from uncomplicated Spanish staples to pure gastronomic innovation.

➡ **Olive oil** Spain is the world's largest producer of olive oil.

➡ **Wine** Spain has the largest area of wine cultivation in the world. La Rioja and Ribera del Duero are the best-known wine-growing regions.

page, hit 'Centros' under 'Comunidad' and then 'Centros en la Red' to get to a list of schools.

MONEY

➡ Many credit and debit cards can be used for withdrawing money from *cajeros automáticos* (automatic teller machines) that display the relevant symbols such as Visa, MasterCard, Cirrus etc.

➡ Most banks will exchange major foreign currencies and offer the best rates. Ask about commissions and take your passport.

➡ Credit and debit cards can be used to pay for most purchases. You'll often be asked to show your passport or some other form of identification, or to type in your pin. The most widely accepted cards are Visa and MasterCard.

➡ Exchange offices, indicated by the word *cambio* (exchange), offer longer opening hours than banks, but worse exchange rates and higher commissions.

➡ In Spain, value-added tax (VAT) is known as IVA (ee-ba; *impuesto sobre el valor añadido*). Visitors are entitled to a refund of the 21% IVA on purchases costing more than €90.16 from any shop if they are taking them out of the EU within three months.

➡ Menu prices include a service charge. Most people leave some small change. Taxi drivers don't have to be tipped but a little rounding up won't go amiss.

➡ Travellers cheques can be changed (for a commission) at most banks and exchange offices.

PUBLIC HOLIDAYS

The two main periods when Spaniards go on holiday are Semana Santa (the week leading up to Easter Sunday) and July or August. At these times accommodation can be scarce and transport heavily booked.

There are at least 14 official holidays a year – some observed nationwide, some locally. The following are national holidays:

Año Nuevo (New Year's Day) 1 January

Viernes Santo (Good Friday) March/April

Fiesta del Trabajo (Labour Day) 1 May

La Asunción (Feast of the Assumption) 15 August

Fiesta Nacional de España (National Day) 12 October

La Inmaculada Concepción (Feast of the Immaculate Conception) 8 December

Navidad (Christmas) 25 December

Regional governments set five holidays and local councils two more. The following are common dates:

Epifanía (Epiphany) or **Día de los Reyes Magos** (Three Kings' Day) 6 January

Día de San José (St Joseph's Day) 19 March

Jueves Santo (Good Thursday) March/April. Not observed in Catalonia and Valencia.

Corpus Christi June. The Thursday after the eighth Sunday after Easter Sunday.

Día de San Juan Bautista (Feast of St John the Baptist) 24 June

Día de Santiago Apóstol (Feast of St James the Apostle) 25 July

Día de Todos los Santos (All Saints Day) 1 November

Día de la Constitución (Constitution Day) 6 December

SAFE TRAVEL

Most visitors to Spain never feel remotely threatened, but a sufficient number have unpleasant experiences to warrant an alert. The main thing to be wary of is petty theft (which may of course not seem so petty if your passport, cash, travellers cheques, credit card and camera go missing). Stay alert and you can avoid most thievery techniques. Barcelona, Madrid and Seville are the worst offenders, as are popular beaches in summer (never leave belongings unattended).

TELEPHONE

Blue public payphones are common and fairly easy to use. They accept coins, phonecards and, in some cases, credit cards. Phonecards come in €6 and €12 denominations and, like postage stamps, are sold at post offices and tobacconists.

International reverse-charge (collect) calls are simple to make: dial ☎900 99, followed by the appropriate code. For example: ☎900 99 00 61 for Australia, ☎900 99 00 44 for the UK, ☎900 99 00 11 (AT&T) for the USA etc.

To speak to an English-speaking Spanish international operator, dial ☎1008 (for calls within Europe) or ☎1005 (rest of the world).

Mobile Phones

All Spanish mobile phone companies (Telefónica's MoviStar, Orange and Vodafone) offer *prepagado* (prepaid) accounts for mobiles. The SIM card costs from €10, which includes some prepaid phone time.

Mobile phone numbers in Spain start with the number ☎6.

Phone Codes

Telephone codes in Spain are an integral part of the phone number. All numbers are nine digits and you just dial that nine-digit number.

Numbers starting with ☎900 are national toll-free numbers, while those starting ☎901 to ☎905 come with varying costs; most can only be dialled from within Spain. In a similar category are numbers starting with ☎800, ☎803, ☎806 and ☎807.

TOURIST INFORMATION

Most towns and large villages of any interest have a helpful *oficina de turismo* (tourist office) where you can get maps and brochures.

Turespaña (www.spain.info) Turespaña is the country's national tourism body.

VISAS

Spain is one of 26 member countries of the Schengen Convention and Schengen visa rules apply.

Citizens or residents of EU & Schengen countries No visa required.

Citizens or residents of Australia, Canada, Israel, Japan, New Zealand and the USA No visa required for tourist visits of up to 90 days.

Other countries Check with a Spanish embassy or consulate.

To work or study in Spain A special visa may be required – contact a Spanish embassy or consulate before travel.

ℹ️ Getting There & Away

Flights, cars and tours can be booked online at lonelyplanet.com.

ENTERING THE COUNTRY

Immigration and customs checks usually involve a minimum of fuss, although there are exceptions. Your vehicle could be searched on arrival from Morocco; they're looking for controlled substances. Expect long delays at these borders, especially in summer.

The tiny principality of Andorra is not in the EU, so border controls (and rigorous customs checks for contraband) remain in place.

AIR

Flights from all over Europe, including numerous budget airlines, serve main Spanish airports. All of Spain's airports share the user-friendly website and flight information telephone number of **Aena** (☎902 404704; www.aena. es), the national airports authority. For more information on each airport on Aena's website, choose English and click on the drop-down menu of airports. Each airport's page has details on practical information (such as parking and public transport) and a full list of (and links to) airlines using that airport.

Madrid's Aeropuerto de Barajas is Spain's busiest (and Europe's fifth-busiest) airport. Other major airports include Barcelona's Aeroport del Prat and the airports of Palma de Mallorca, Málaga, Alicante, Girona, Valencia, Ibiza, Seville, Bilbao and Zaragoza.

LAND

Spain shares land borders with France, Portugal and Andorra.

Bus

Aside from the main cross-border routes, numerous smaller services criss-cross Spain's borders with France and Portugal. Regular buses connect Andorra with Barcelona (including winter ski buses and direct services to the airport) and other destinations in Spain (including Madrid) and France.

Avanza (☎902 020999; www.avanzabus. com) Avanza runs a Lisbon to Madrid service (€42.10, 7½ hours, two daily).

Eurolines (www.eurolines.com) Eurolines is the main operator of international bus services to Spain from most of Western Europe and Morocco. Services from France include Nice to Madrid, and Paris to Barcelona.

Train

In addition to the options listed below, two or three TGV (high-speed) trains leave from

Paris-Montparnasse for Irún, where you change to a normal train for the Basque Country and on towards Madrid.

There are plans for a high-speed rail link between Madrid and Paris. In the meantime, high-speed services travel via Barcelona.

Paris to Madrid (€198 to €228, 9¾ to 17½ hours, five daily) The slow route runs via Les Aubrais, Blois, Poitiers, Irún, Vitoria, Burgos and Valladolid. It may be quicker to take the high-speed AVE train to Barcelona and change from there.

Paris to Barcelona (from €59, 6½ hours, two daily) A recently inaugurated high-speed service runs via Valence, Nimes, Montpellier, Beziers, Narbonne, Perpignan, Figueres and Girona. High-speed services also run from Lyon (from €49, five hours) and Toulouse (from €39, three hours).

Montpellier to Lorca (€79.55, 12 to 13 hours, daily) Talgo service along the Mediterranean coast via Girona, Barcelona, Tarragona and Valencia.

Lisbon to Madrid (chair/sleeper class from €36/50, nine to 10¾ hours, daily)

Lisbon to Irún (chair/sleeper class €41/56, 14 hours, daily)

Oporto to Vigo (from €14.75, 2¼ hours, two daily)

SEA

Acciona Trasmediterránea (☑ 902 454645; www.trasmediterranea.es) Most Mediterranean ferry services are run by the Spanish national ferry company, Acciona Trasmediterránea.

Brittany Ferries (☑ 0871 244 0744; www. brittany-ferries.co.uk) Services between Spain and the UK.

Grandi Navi Veloci (Map p586; ☑ in Italy 010 209 4591; www1.gnv.it; M Drassanes) High-speed luxury ferries between Barcelona and Genoa.

Grimaldi Ferries (Map p586; ☑ 902 53 13 33, in Italy 081 496 444; www.grimaldi-lines.com; M Drassanes) Barcelona to Civitavecchia (near Rome), Livorno (Tuscany) and Porto Torres (northwest Sardinia).

LD Lines (www.ldlines.co.uk) Gijón-Saint-Nazaire (France) and Gijón-Poole (UK).

❶ Getting Around

Students and seniors are eligible for discounts of 30% to 50% on most types of transport within Spain.

AIR

Air Europa (www.aireuropa.com) Madrid to Ibiza, Palma de Mallorca, Vigo, Bilbao and Barcelona as well as other routes between Spanish cities.

Iberia (www.iberia.com) Spain's national airline and its subsidiary, Iberia Regional-Air Nostrum, have an extensive domestic network.

Ryanair (www.ryanair.com) Some domestic Spanish routes include Madrid to Palma de Mallorca.

Volotea (www.volotea.com) Budget airline that flies domestically and internationally. Domestic routes take in Ibiza, Palma de Mallorca, Málaga, Valencia, Vigo, Bilbao, Zaragoza and Oviedo (but not Madrid or Barcelona).

Vueling (www.vueling.com) Spanish low-cost company with loads of domestic flights within Spain, especially from Barcelona.

BOAT

Regular ferries connect the Spanish mainland with the Balearic Islands.

BUS

Spain's bus network is operated by countless independent companies and reaches into the most remote towns and villages. Many towns and cities have one main bus station where most buses arrive and depart.

It is not necessary, and often not possible, to make advance reservations for local bus journeys. It is, however, a good idea to turn up at least 30 minutes before the bus leaves to guarantee a seat. For longer trips, you can and should buy your ticket in advance.

ALSA (☑ 902 422242; www.alsa.es) The biggest player, this company has routes all over the country in association with various other companies.

Avanza (☑ 902 020999; www.avanzabus.com) Operates buses from Madrid to Extremadura, western Castilla y León and Valencia via eastern Castilla-La Mancha (eg Cuenca), often in association with other companies.

Socibus & Secorbus (☑ 902 229292; www. socibus.es) These two companies jointly operate services between Madrid and western Andalucía, including Cádiz, Córdoba, Huelva and Seville.

CAR & MOTORCYCLE

Spain's roads vary enormously but are generally good. Fastest are the *autopistas;* on some, you have to pay hefty tolls.

Every vehicle should display a nationality plate of its country of registration and you must always carry proof of ownership of a private vehicle.

Third-party motor insurance is required throughout Europe.

A warning triangle and a reflective jacket (to be used in case of breakdown) are compulsory.

Automobile Associations

Real Automóvil Club de España (RACE; ☑ 902 404545; www.race.es) The Real Automóvil Club de España is the national automobile club. They may well come to assist you in case of a breakdown, but in any event you should obtain an emergency telephone number for Spain from your own insurer.

Driving Licences

All EU member states' driving licences are recognised. Other foreign licences should be accompanied by an International Driving Permit (although in practice local licences are usually accepted). These are available from automobile clubs in your country and valid for 12 months.

Hire

To rent a car in Spain you have to have a licence, be aged 21 or over and have a credit or debit card. Rates vary widely: the best deals tend to be in major tourist areas, including airports. Prices are especially competitive in the Balearic Islands.

FERRIES TO SPAIN

A useful website for comparing routes and finding links to the relevant ferry companies is www.ferrylines.com.

From Algeria

ROUTE	DURATION	FREQUENCY
Ghazaouet to Almería	8 hr	four weekly

From France

ROUTE	DURATION	FREQUENCY
Saint-Nazaire to Gijón	15-16 hr	three weekly

From Italy

ROUTE	DURATION	FREQUENCY
Genoa to Barcelona	18 hr	three weekly
Civitavecchia (near Rome) to Barcelona	20½ hr	six to seven weekly
Livorno (Tuscany) to Barcelona	19½ hr	three weekly
Porto Torres (Sardinia) to Barcelona	12 hr	daily

From Morocco

ROUTE	DURATION	FREQUENCY
Tangier to Algeciras	90 min	up to eight daily
Tangier to Barcelona	24-35 hr	weekly
Tangier to Tarifa	35 min	up to eight daily
Nador to Almería	6 hr	up to three daily

From the UK

ROUTE	DURATION	FREQUENCY
Plymouth to Santander	20 hr	weekly
Portsmouth to Santander	24 hr	weekly
Portsmouth to Bilbao	24 hr	twice weekly
Poole to Gijón	25 hr	weekly

CONNECTIONS

Spanish airports are among Europe's best connected, while the typical overland route leads many travellers from France over the Pyrenees into Spain. Rather than taking the main road/rail route along the Mediterranean coast (or between Biarritz and San Sebastián), you could follow lesser known, pretty routes over the mountains. There's nothing to stop you carrying on to Portugal: numerous roads and the Madrid–Lisbon rail line connect the two countries.

The most obvious sea journeys lead across the Strait of Gibraltar to Morocco (p632). The most common routes connect Algeciras or Tarifa with Tangier, from where there's plenty of transport deeper into Morocco. Car ferries also connect Barcelona with Italian ports.

There are two main rail lines to Spain from Paris, one to Madrid via the Basque Country, and another to Barcelona; both are to be upgraded to a high-speed service. The latter connects with services to the French Riviera and Switzerland.

Road Rules

➝ The blood-alcohol limit is 0.05%.

➝ The legal driving age for cars is 18. The legal driving age for motorcycles and scooters is 16 (80cc and over) or 14 (50cc and under). A licence is required.

➝ Motorcyclists must use headlights at all times and wear a helmet if riding a bike of 125cc or more.

➝ Drive on the right.

➝ In built-up areas, the speed limit is 50km/h (and in some cases, such as inner-city Barcelona, 30km/h), which increases to 100km/h on major roads and up to 120km/h on *autovías* and *autopistas* (toll-free and tolled dual-lane highways, respectively). Cars towing caravans are restricted to a maximum speed of 80km/h.

TRAIN

The national railway company is **Renfe** (☎ 902 243402; www.renfe.com). Trains are mostly modern and comfortable, and late arrivals are the exception rather than the rule. The high-speed network is in constant expansion.

Passes are valid for all long-distance Renfe trains; Inter-Rail users pay supplements on Talgo, InterCity and AVE trains. All pass-holders making reservations pay a small fee.

Among Spain's numerous types of trains:

Alaris, Altaria, Alvia, Arco and Avant Long-distance intermediate-speed services.

Cercanías For short hops and services to outlying suburbs and satellite towns in Madrid, Barcelona and 11 other cities.

Euromed Similar to the AVE trains, they connect Barcelona with Valencia and Alicante.

Regionales Trains operating within one region, usually stopping at all stations.

Talgo and Intercity Slower long-distance trains.

Tren de Alta Velocidad Española (AVE) High-speed trains that link Madrid with Barcelona, Burgos, Córdoba, Cuenca, Huesca, Lerida, Málaga, Seville, Valencia, Valladolid and Zaragoza. There are also Barcelona–Seville and Barcelona–Málaga services. In coming years Madrid–Cádiz and Madrid–Bilbao should come on line.

Trenhotel Overnight trains with sleeper berths.

Classes & Costs

➝ All long-distance trains have 2nd and 1st classes, known as *turista* and *preferente*, respectively. The latter is 20% to 40% more expensive.

➝ Fares vary enormously depending on the service (faster trains cost considerably more) and, in the case of some high-speed services such as the AVE, on the time and day of travel.

➝ Children aged between four and 12 years are entitled to a 40% discount; those aged under four travel for free (except on high-speed trains, for which they pay the same as those aged four to 12). Buying a return ticket often gives you a 10% to 20% discount on the return trip. Students and people up to 25 years of age with a Euro<26 Card (Carnet Joven in Spain) are entitled to 20% to 25% off most ticket prices.

Switzerland

Best Places to Eat

➡ Chez Vrony (p648)

➡ Alpenrose (p658)

➡ Grottino 1313 (p651)

➡ Volkshaus Basel (p660)

Best Places to Stay

➡ SYHA Basel St Alban Youth Hostel (p659)

➡ Hotel Schweizerhof (p649)

➡ Hotel Bahnhof (p648)

➡ The Hotel (p651)

Why Go?

What giddy romance Zermatt, St Moritz and other glitterati-encrusted names evoke. This is *Sonderfall Schweiz* ('special-case Switzerland'), a privileged neutral country set apart from others, proudly idiosyncratic, insular and unique. It's blessed with gargantuan cultural diversity: its four official languages alone speak volumes.

The Swiss don't do half measures: Zürich, their most gregarious urban centre, has cutting-edge art, legendary nightlife and one of the world's highest living standards. The national passion for sharing the great outdoors provides access (by public transport, no less!) to some of the world's most inspiring panoramic experiences.

So don't depend just on your postcard images of Bern's and Lucerne's chocolate-box architecture, the majestic Matterhorn or those pristine lakes – Switzerland is a place so outrageously beautiful it simply must be seen to be believed.

When to Go
Bern

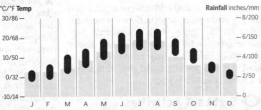

Dec–early Apr Carve through powder and eat fondue at an alpine resort.

May–Sep Hike in the shadow of the mesmerising Matterhorn and be wowed by its perfection.

Aug Celebrate Swiss National Day on 1 August and witness Swiss national pride in full force.

Switzerland Highlights

❶ Discover zesty **Zürich** (p655) via a daytime stroll along the city's sublime lake followed by a rollicking night out.

❷ Marvel at the iconic Matterhorn and wander around the car-free alpine village of **Zermatt** (p647).

❸ Enjoy the charm of famous beauties **Bern**

(p648) and **Lucerne** (p650): think medieval Old Town appeal, folkloric fountains and art.

❹ Be wowed by the Eiger's monstrous north face on a ride to the 'top of Europe', 3471m **Jungfraujoch** (p654).

❺ Board a boat in **Geneva** for a serene Lake Geneva

cruise to medieval **Lausanne** (p644).

❻ Ride one of Switzerland's iconic scenic trains, such as the **Bernina Express** (p661).

❼ Go Italian at **Lugano** (p661), with its lovely, temperate lake setting.

GENEVA

POP 189,000

The whole world seems to be in Geneva, Switzerland's second city. The UN, the International Red Cross, the World Health Organization – 200-odd governmental and nongovernmental international organisations fill the city's plush hotels with big-name guests, who feast on an extraordinary choice of cuisine and help prop up the overload of banks, jewellers and chocolate shops for which Geneva is known.

◎ Sights & Activities

The city centre is so compact it's easy to see many of the main sights on foot. Begin your explorations on the southern side of Lake Geneva and visit the **Jardin Anglais** (Quai du Général-Guisan) to see the **Horloge Fleurie** (Flower Clock). Crafted from 6500 flowers, the clock has ticked since 1955 and sports the world's longest second hand (2.5m).

★ Jet d'Eau   FOUNTAIN

(Quai Gustave-Ador) When landing by plane, this lakeside fountain is the first dramatic glimpse you get of Geneva. The 140m-tall structure shoots up water with incredible force – 200km/h, 1360 horsepower – to create the sky-high plume, kissed by a rainbow on sunny days. At any one time, 7 tonnes of water is in the air, much of which sprays spectators on the pier beneath. Two or three times a year it is illuminated pink, blue or another colour to mark a humanitarian occasion.

ITINERARIES

One Week

Starting in vibrant **Zürich**, shop famous Bahnhofstrasse, then eat, drink and be merry. Next, head to the **Jungfrau region** to explore some kick-ass alpine scenery, whether it be by hiking or skiing. Take a pit stop in beautiful **Lucerne** before finishing up in Switzerland's delightful capital, **Bern**.

Two Weeks

As above, then head west for a French flavour in **Geneva** or lakeside **Lausanne**. Stop in **Gruyères** to dip into a cheesy fondue and overdose on meringues drowned in thick double cream. Zip to **Zermatt** or across to **St Moritz** to frolic in snow or green meadows, then loop east to taste the Italian side of Switzerland at lakeside **Lugano**.

★ **Cathédrale St-Pierre** CATHEDRAL
(www.espace-saint-pierre.ch; Cour St-Pierre; admission free, towers adult/child Sfr5/2; ⊙ 9.30am-6.30pm Mon-Sat, noon-6.30pm Sun Jun-Sep, 10am-5.30pm Oct-May) FREE Begun in the 11th century, Geneva's cathedral is predominantly Gothic with an 18th-century neoclassical facade. Between 1536 and 1564 Protestant John Calvin preached here; see his seat in the north aisle. Inside the cathedral 77 steps spiral up to the attic – a fascinating glimpse at its architectural construction – from where another 40 lead to the top of the panoramic **northern** and **southern towers**.

In summer, free carillon (5pm) and organ (6pm) concerts fill the cathedral and its surrounding square with soul.

Musée International de la Croix-Rouge et du Croissant-Rouge MUSEUM
(www.micr.org; Av de la Paix 17; adult/child Sfr15/7; ⊙10am-6pm Wed-Mon Apr-Oct, 10am-5pm Nov-Mar) Compelling multimedia exhibits at Geneva's fascinating International Red Cross and Red Crescent Museum trawl through atrocities perpetuated by humanity. The litany of war and nastiness, documented in films, photos, sculptures and soundtracks, is set against the noble aims of the organisation created by Geneva businessmen and philanthropists Henri Dunant and Henri Dufour in 1864. Excellent temporary exhibitions command an additional entrance fee. Take bus 8 from Gare de Cornavin to the Appia stop.

Patek Philippe Museum WATCH MUSEUM
(☑ 022 807 09 10; www.patekmuseum.com; Rue des Vieux-Grenadiers 7; adult/child Sfr10/free; ⊙2-6pm Tue-Fri, 10am-6pm Sat) This elegant museum by one of Switzerland's leading luxury watchmakers displays exquisite timepieces and enamels from the 16th century to the present.

🛏 Sleeping

When checking in, ask for your free Public Transport Card, covering unlimited bus travel for the duration of your hotel stay.

Hôtel Bel' Esperance HOTEL €
(☑ 022 818 37 37; www.hotel-bel-esperance.ch; Rue de la Vallée 1; s/d/tr/q from Sfr110/170/210/250; ⊙reception 7am-10pm; @ 🛜) This two-star hotel is extraordinary value. Rooms are quiet and cared for, those on the 1st floor share a kitchen, and there are fridges for guests to store picnic supplies – or sausages – in! Ride the lift to the 5th floor to flop on its wonderful flower-filled rooftop terrace, complete with barbecue that can be rented (Sfr8).

Hotel Edelweiss HOTEL €€
(☑ 022 544 51 51; www.hoteledelweissgeneva.com; Place de la Navigation 2; d Sfr160-400; ✳ @ 🛜) Plunge yourself into the heart of the Swiss Alps with this Heidi-style hideout, very much the Swiss Alps *en ville* with its fireplace, wildflower-painted pine bedheads and big, cuddly St Bernard lolling over the banister. Its chalet-styled restaurant is a key address among Genevans for traditional cheese fondue.

Geneva

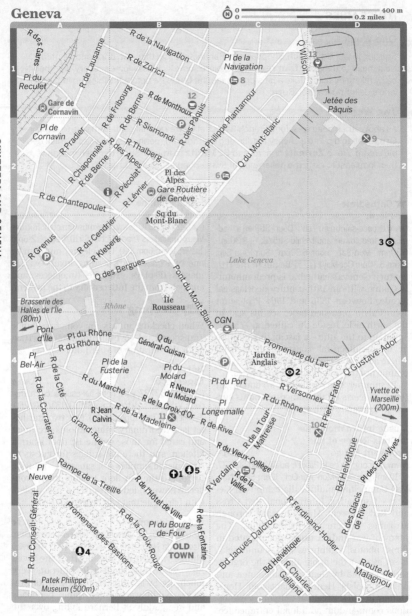

Ⓝ 0 _____ 400 m
0 _____ 0.2 miles

Hôtel Beau-Rivage   HISTORIC HOTEL €€€
(☏ 022 716 66 66; www.beau-rivage.ch; Quai du
Mont-Blanc 13; d from Sfr515; P ✳ @ ☎) Run
by the Mayer family for five generations, the
Beau-Rivage is a 19th-century jewel dripping in opulence.

✕ Eating

Eateries crowd Place du Bourg-de-Four, Geneva's oldest square, in the lovely Old Town. Otherwise, head down the hill towards the river and Place du Molard, packed with tables and chairs for much of the year. In Pâquis, there's a tasty line-up of more affordable restaurants on Place de la Navigation.

★ Buvette
des Bains   CAFETERIA €
(☑ 022 738 16 16; www.bains-des-paquis.ch; Quai du Mont-Blanc 30, Bains des Pâquis; mains Sfr14-16; ⊘ 7am-10.30pm) Meet Genevans at this earthy beach bar – rough and hip around the edges – at lakeside pool, Bains des Pâquis. Grab breakfast, a salad or the *plat du jour* (dish of the day), or dip into a *fondue au crémant* (Champagne fondue). Dining is self-service on trays and alfresco in summer. In summer pay Sfr2/1 per adult/child to access the canteen, inside the pub.

★ Le Relais
d'Entrecôte   STEAKHOUSE €€
(☑ 022 310 60 04; www.relaisentrecote.fr; Rue Pierre Fatio 6; steak & chips Sfr42; ⊘ noon-2.30pm & 7-11pm) Key vocabulary at this timeless classic where everyone eats the same dish is *à point* (medium), *bien cuit* (well done) and *saignant* (rare). It doesn't even bother with menus, just sit down, say how you like your steak cooked and wait

for it to arrive – two handsome servings (!) pre-empted by a green salad and accompanied by perfectly crisp, skinny fries.

Should you have room at the end of it all, the desserts are justly raved about. No advance reservations so arrive sharp.

★ Brasserie des
Halles de l'Île   EUROPEAN €€
(☑ 022 311 08 88; www.brasseriedeshalles delile.ch; Place de l'Île 1; mains Sfr20-50; ⊘ 10.30am-midnight Sun & Mon, to 1am Tue-Thu, to 2am Fri & Sat) At home in Geneva's old market hall on an island, this industrial-style venue cooks up a buzzing cocktail of after-work aperitifs with music, after-dark DJs and seasonal fare of fresh vegies and regional products (look for the Appellation d'Origine Contrôllée products flagged on the menu). Arrive early to snag the best seat in the house – a superb terrace hanging over the water.

♟ Drinking & Entertainment

Pâquis, the district in between the train station and lake, is particularly well endowed with bars. In summer the **paillote** (www.laterrasse.ch; Quai du Mont-Blanc 31; ⊘ 8am-midnight Apr-Sep), with wooden tables inches from the water, gets crammed.

For a dose of bohemia, head to Carouge on tram 12. This shady quarter of 17th-century houses and narrow streets has galleries, hip bars and funky shops.

Café des Arts   CAFE, BAR
(Rue des Pâquis 15; ⊘ 11am-2am Mon-Fri, 8am-2am Sat & Sun) As much a place to drink as a daytime cafe, this Pâquis hang-out lures a local crowd with its Parisian-style terrace and artsy interior. Food-wise, think meal-size salads, designer sandwiches and a great-value lunchtime *plat du jour*.

★ Yvette
de Marseille   BAR
(Rue Henri Blanvalet 13; ⊘ 5.30pm-midnight Mon & Tue, 5.30pm-1am Wed & Thu, 5.30pm-2am Fri, 6.30pm-2am Sat) No bar begs the question 'what's in the name?' more than this buzzy drinking hole. Urban and edgy, it occupies a mechanic's workshop once owned by Yvette. Note the garage door, the trap door in the floor where cars were repaired and the street number 13 (aka the departmental number of the Bouches-du-Rhône *département*, home to Marseille).

LOCAL KNOWLEDGE

PICNIC SPOTS

With mountains of fine views to pick from, Geneva is prime picnicking terrain for those reluctant to pay too much to eat. Grab a salt-studded pretzel filled with whatever you fancy (Sfr4 to Sfr6.50) from takeaway kiosk **Maison du Bretzel** (Rue de la Croix d'Or 4; pretzel Sfr4-6.50; ⊘8am-7.30pm Mon-Wed & Fri, to 9pm Thu) and head for a local picnic spot:

➜ In the contemplative shade of Henry Moore's voluptuous sculpture *Reclining Figure: Arch Leg* (1973) in the park opposite the Musée d'Art et d'Histoire.

➜ Behind the cathedral on **Terrasse Agrippa d'Abigné**, a tree-shaded park with benches, sand pit and see-saw for kids, and a fine rooftop and cathedral view.

➜ On a bench on Quai du Mont-Blanc with Mont Blanc view (sunny days only).

➜ On the world's longest bench (126m long) on chestnut tree–lined Promenade de la Treille, **Parc des Bastions**.

Chat Noir 　　　　　　　CLUB, BAR
(☑022 307 10 40; www.chatnoir.ch; Rue Vauthier 13; ⊘6pm-4am Tue-Thu, to 5am Fri & Sat) One of the busiest night spots in Carouge, the Black Cat is packed most nights thanks to its all-rounder vibe: arrive after work for an aperitif with selection of tapas to nibble on, and stay until dawn for dancing, live music and DJ sets.

 ## Shopping

Designer shopping is wedged between Rue du Rhône and Rue de Rive; the latter has lots of chain stores. Grand-Rue in the Old Town and Carouge boast artsy boutiques.

ⓘ Information

Tourist Office (☑022 909 70 00; www.geneve-tourisme.ch; Rue du Mont-Blanc 18; ⊘9am-6pm Mon-Sat, 10am-4pm Sun)

ⓘ Getting There & Away

AIR
Aéroport International de Genève (p664), 4km from town, has connections to major European cities and many others worldwide.

BOAT
CGN (Compagnie Générale de Navigation; ☑0848 811 848; www.cgn.ch) operates a web of scenic steamer services from its Jardin Anglais jetty to other villages on Lake Geneva. Many only sail May to September, including those to/from Lausanne (Sfr64, 3½ hours). Eurail and Swiss passes are valid on CGN boats or there is a one-day CGN boat pass (Sfr60).

BUS
International buses depart from the **bus station** (☑0900 320 230, 022 732 02 30; www.coach-station.com; Place Dorcière).

TRAIN
Trains run to major Swiss towns including at least every 30 minutes to/from Lausanne (Sfr21.80, 33 to 48 minutes), Bern (Sfr49, 1¾ hours) and Zürich (Sfr84, 2¾ hours).

International daily rail connections from Geneva include Paris by TGV (3¼ hours) and Milan (four hours).

ⓘ Getting Around

TO/FROM THE AIRPORT
Getting from the airport is easy with regular trains into Gare de Cornavin (Sfr2.50, eight minutes). Slower bus 10 (Sfr3.50) does the same 4km trip. A metered taxi costs Sfr35 to Sfr50.

BICYCLE
Pick up a bike at Genèveroule (www.geneveroule.ch) on Place du Rhône: the first four hours are free, then it's Sfr2 per hour. Bring ID and a Sfr20 cash deposit. Find other Genèveroule stands at Bains des Pâquis, Place de l'Octroi in Carouge, and Place de Montbrillant.

PUBLIC TRANSPORT
Buses, trams, trains and boats service the city, and ticket dispensers are found at all stops. Most services are operated by **TPG** (www.tpg.ch; Rue de Montbrillant; ⊘7am-7pm Mon-Fri, 9am-6pm Sat). Typical tickets cost Sfr3.50 (one hour); a day pass is Sfr8 when purchased after 9am.

LAKE GENEVA REGION

Lausanne

POP 130,400

In a fabulous location overlooking Lake Geneva, Lausanne is an enchanting beauty with several distinct personalities: the former fishing village of Ouchy, with its lakeside bustle; the Vieille Ville (Old Town), with charming cobblestone streets and covered staircases; and Flon, a warehouse district of bars and boutiques.

◎ Sights & Activities

★ Cathédrale de Notre Dame
CHURCH

(Place de la Cathédrale; ⊘9am-7pm Apr-Sep, to 5.30pm Oct-Mar) Lausanne's Gothic cathedral, Switzerland's finest, stands proudly at the heart of the Old Town. Raised in the 12th and 13th centuries on the site of earlier, humbler churches, it lacks the lightness of French Gothic buildings but is remarkable nonetheless. Pope Gregory X, in the presence of Rudolph of Habsburg (the Holy Roman Emperor) and an impressive following of European cardinals and bishops, consecrated the church in 1275.

Place de la Palud
SQUARE

In the heart of the Vieille Ville, this 9th-century medieval market square – pretty as a picture – was originally bogland. For five centuries it has been home to the city government, now housed in the 17th-century **Hôtel de Ville** (town hall). A fountain pierces one end of the square, presided over by a brightly painted column topped by the allegorical figure of Justice, clutching scales and dressed in blue.

Musée Olympique
MUSEUM

(☑021 621 65 11; www.olympic.org/museum; Quai d'Ouchy 1; adult/child Sfr18/10; ⊘9am-6pm May–mid-Oct daily, 10am-6pm mid-Oct–Apr Tue-Sun) Lausanne's Musée Olympique is easily the city's most lavish museum and an essential stop for sports buffs (and kids). Following a thorough revamp of its facilities, the museum reopened in 2014, with its tiered landscaped gardens and site-specific scuptural works as inviting as ever. Inside, there is a fabulous cafe with a champion lake view from its terrace, and a state-of-the-art museum recounting the Olympic story from its inception to the present day through video, interactive displays, memorabilia and temporary themed exhibitions.

⌷ Sleeping

Hotel guests get a Lausanne Transport Card providing unlimited use of public transport for the duration of their stay.

Lausanne Guest House
HOSTEL €

(☑021 601 80 00; www.lausanne-guesthouse.ch; Chemin des Épinettes 4; dm from Sfr37, s/d from Sfr90/107, with shared bathroom from Sfr80/96; ⊘reception 7.30am-noon & 3-10pm; P@⑨) ✦ An attractive mansion converted into quality backpacking accommodation near the train station. Many rooms have lake views and you can hang out in the garden or terrace. Parking is Sfr11 per day, there's a 24-hour laundry and room to leave your bike. Some of the building's energy is solar.

Lhotel
BOUTIQUE HOTEL €

(☑021 331 39 39; www.lhotel.ch; Place de l'Europe 6; r from Sfr130; ❄⑨) This smart small hotel is ideally placed for the city's lively Flon district nightlife. Rooms are simple and startlingly white, and come with iPads; breakfast costs Sfr14. There's a fab rooftop terrace and your stay gives you access to the spa at five-star Lausanne Palace & Spa nearby for Sfr55.

✕ Eating & Drinking

★ Holy Cow
BURGERS €

(www.holycow.ch; Rue Cheneau-de-Bourg 17; burger with chips & drink Sfr20; ⊘11am-10pm Mon & Tue, to 11pm Wed-Sat; ☷) A Lausanne success story, with branches in Geneva, Zürich and France, burgers (beef, chicken or vegie) feature local ingredients, creative toppings and witty names. Grab an artisanal beer, sit at a shared wooden table, and wait for your burger and fab fries to arrive in a straw basket. A second outlet can be found at **Rue des Terreaux** (Rue des Terreaux 10; burger with chips & drink Sfr20; ⊘11am-11pm Mon-Sat).

Café Romand
SWISS €

(☑021 312 63 75; www.cafe-romand.ch; Place St François 2; mains Sfr16-41.50; ⊘8am-midnight

> **DON'T MISS**
>
> ## MONTREUX
>
> This tidy lakeside town boasts Switzerland's most extraordinary castle.
>
> Originally constructed on the shores of Lake Geneva in the 11th century, **Château de Chillon** (☑ 021 966 89 10; www.chillon.ch; Av de Chillon 21; adult/child Sfr12.50/6; ⊘ 9am-7pm Apr-Sep, 9.30am-6pm Mar & Oct, 10am-5pm Nov-Feb, last entry 1hr before close) was brought to the world's attention by Lord Byron and the world has been filing past ever since. Spend at least a couple of hours exploring its numerous courtyards, towers, dungeons and halls filled with arms, period furniture and artwork.
>
> The castle is a lovely 45-minute lakefront walk from Montreux. Otherwise, trolley bus 1 passes every 10 minutes; better still, come on a CGN steamer from Montreux (Sfr17, 15 minutes).
>
> Crowds throng to the legendary (and not all-jazz) **Montreux Jazz Festival** (www.montreuxjazz.com) for a fortnight in early July. Free concerts take place every day, but big-name gigs cost Sfr75 to Sfr240. Lovers of Freddie Mercury should hightail it to the **Queen Studio Experience** (www.mercuryphoenixtrust.com; Rue du Théâtre 9, Casino Barrière de Montreux; ⊘ 10.30am-10pm) **FREE** and also to the **Freddie Mercury statue** on Place du Marché.
>
> There are frequent trains to Lausanne (Sfr12.40, 19 minutes) and other lakeside points. Make the scenic journey to Interlaken via the **GoldenPass Line** (www.goldenpass.ch; 2nd class one way Sfr57, three hours, daily; rail passes valid).

Mon-Sat) Tucked away in an unpromising looking arcade, this Lausanne legend dating to 1951 is a welcome blast from the past. Locals pour into the broad, somewhat sombre dining area filled with timber tables to revel in fondue, raclette (Sfr8.50 per serve), *cervelle au beurre noir* (brains in black butter), tripe, *pied de porc* (pork trotters) and other feisty traditional dishes.

Great Escape PUB
(☑ 021 312 31 94; www.the-great.ch; Rue Madeleine 18; ⊘ 11am-late) Everyone knows the Great Escape, a busy student pub with pub grub (great burgers) and an enviable terrace with a view over Place de la Riponne. From the aforementioned square, walk up staircase Escaliers de l'Université and turn right.

ⓘ Information

The **tourist office** (☑ 021 613 73 21; www.lausanne-tourisme.ch; Place de la Navigation 6; ⊘ 9am-7pm Apr-Sep, to 6pm Oct-Mar) neighbours Ouchy metro station; there is also a **branch** (☑ 021 613 73 73; www.lausanne-tourisme.ch; Place de la Gare 9; ⊘ 9am-7pm) at the train station.

ⓘ Getting There & Away

BOAT

The **CGN** (Compagnie Générale de Navigation; www.cgn.ch) steamer service runs from early April to mid-September to/from Geneva (Sfr43, 3½ hours) via Nyon. Other services lace the lake, including to Montreux (Sfr26, 1½ hours, up to six daily).

TRAIN

There are frequent trains to/from Geneva (Sfr21.80, 33 to 48 minutes) and Bern (Sfr32, 70 minutes).

ⓘ Getting Around

Lausanne spans several steep hillsides, so prepare for some good walks.

Buses and trolley buses service most destinations; the vital m2 Métro line (single trip/day pass Sfr2.20/8.80) connects the lake (Ouchy) with the train station (Gare), cathedral area and Flon.

Gruyères

POP 1800

Cheese and featherweight meringues drowned in thick cream are what this dreamy village is all about. Named after the emblematic gru (crane) brandished by the medieval Counts of Gruyères, it is a riot of 15th- to 17th-century houses tumbling down a hillock. Its heart is cobbled, a castle is its crowning glory and hard AOC Gruyère (the village is Gruyères, but the 's' is dropped for the cheese) has been made for centuries in its surrounding alpine pastures.

Fondue-serving cafes line the main square.

◉ Sights

A combined ticket covering the chateau and La Maison du Gruyère cheese dairy costs Sfr14.50 (no child combo ticket).

Château de Gruyères CASTLE
(☑ 026 921 21 02; www.chateau-gruyeres.ch; Rue du Château 8; adult/child Sfr10/3; ☉ 9am-6pm Apr-Oct, 10am-4.30pm Nov-Mar) This bewitching turreted castle, home to 19 different Counts of Gruyères who controlled the Sarine Valley from the 11th to 16th centuries, was rebuilt after a fire in 1493. Inside, view period furniture, tapestries and modern 'fantasy art' and watch a 20-minute multimedia film.

Don't miss the short footpath that weaves its way around the castle.

La Maison du Gruyère CHEESE DAIRY
(☑ 026 921 84 00; www.lamaisondugruyere.ch; Place de la Gare 3; adult/child Sfr7/3; ☉ 9am-7pm Jun-Sep, to 6pm Oct-May) The secret behind Gruyère cheese is revealed in Pringy, 1.5km from Gruyères. Cheesemaking takes place three to four times daily between 9am and 11am and 12.30pm to 2.30pm.

ⓘ Getting There & Away

Gruyères can be reached by train, although the village is a 10-minute walk uphill from the train station (or you can take a free bus that meets trains).

VALAIS

This is Matterhorn country, an intoxicating land that seduces the toughest of critics with its endless panoramic vistas and breathtaking views. Switzerland's 10 highest mountains rise to the sky here, while snow fiends ski and board in one of Europe's top resorts, Zermatt.

Zermatt

POP 6000

Since the mid-19th century, Zermatt has starred among Switzerland's glitziest resorts. Today it attracts intrepid mountaineers and hikers, skiers who cruise at a snail's pace, spellbound by the scenery, and style-conscious darlings flashing designer togs in the lounge bars. But all are smitten with the **Matterhorn** (4478m), the Alps' most famous peak and an unfathomable monolith synonymous with Switzerland that you simply can't quite stop looking at.

◉ Sights & Activities

Zermatt is **skiing** heaven, with mostly long, scenic red runs, plus a smattering of blues for ski virgins and knuckle-whitening blacks for experts. The main skiing areas in winter are **Rothorn, Stockhorn** and **Klein Matterhorn** – 350km of ski runs in all, with a link from Klein Matterhorn to the Italian resort of Cervinia and a **freestyle park** with half-pipe for snowboarders. **Summer skiing** (20km of runs) and **boarding** (gravity park at Plateau Rosa on the Theodul glacier) is Europe's most extensive. One-/two-day summer ski passes are Sfr82/122.

Zermatt is also excellent for **hiking**, with 400km of summer trails through some of the most incredible scenery in the Alps – the tourist office has trail maps. For Matterhorn closeups, nothing beats the highly dramatic **Matterhorn Glacier Trail** (two hours, 6.49km) from Trockener Steg to Schwarzsee; 23 information panels en route tell you everything you could possibly need to know about glaciers and glacial life.

Matterhorn Glacier Paradise CABLE CAR
(www.matterhornparadise.ch; adult/child Sfr99/49.50; ☉ 8.30am-4.20pm) Views from Zermatt's cable cars are all remarkable, but the Matterhorn Glacier Paradise is the icing on the cake. Ride Europe's highest-altitude cable car to 3883m and gawp at 14 glaciers and 38 mountain peaks over 4000m from the **Panoramic Platform** (only open in good weather). Don't miss the **Glacier Palace**, an ice palace complete with glittering ice sculptures and an ice slide to swoosh down bum first. End with some

exhilarating **snow tubing** outside in the snowy surrounds.

★**Gornergratbahn** RAILWAY
(www.gornergrat.ch; Bahnhofplatz 7; one-way adult/child Sfr42/21; ⊙7am-9.50pm) Europe's highest cogwheel railway has climbed through picture-postcard scenery to **Gornergrat** (3089m) – a 30-minute journey – since 1898. Sit on the right-hand side of the little red train to gawp at the Matterhorn. Tickets allow you to get on and off en route; there are restaurants at Riffelalp (2211m) and Riffelberg (2582m). In summer an extra train runs once a week at sunrise and sunset – the most spectacular trips of all.

🛏 Sleeping & Eating

Most places close from May to mid- (or late) June and then again from October to mid-November.

★**Hotel Bahnhof** HOTEL €
(☑027 967 24 06; www.hotelbahnhof.com; Bahnhofstrasse; dm Sfr40-45; s/d/q from Sfr80/110/235; ⊙reception 8-11.30am & 4-7pm, closed May & Oct; 🛜) Opposite the train station, these five-star budget digs have comfy beds, spotless bathrooms and family-perfect rooms for four. Dorms (Sfr5 liner obligatory) are cosy and there's a stylish lounge with armchairs to flop in and books to read. No breakfast, but feel free to prepare your own in the snazzy, open-plan kitchen.

★**Snowboat** INTERNATIONAL €
(☑027 967 43 33; www.snowboat.ch; Vispastrasse 20; mains Sfr19-26; ⊙noon-midnight) This hybrid eating-drinking, riverside address, with marigold-yellow deckchairs sprawled across its rooftop sun terrace, is a blessing. When fondue tires, head here for barbecue-sizzled burgers (forget beef, try a lamb and goat's cheese or Indonesian chicken satay burger), super-power creative salads (the Omega 3 buster is a favourite) and great cocktails. The vibe? It's 100% fun and funky.

★**Chez Vrony** SWISS €€
(☑027 967 25 52; www.chezvrony.ch; Findeln; breakfast Sfr28, mains Sfr23-45; ⊙9.15am-5pm Dec-Apr & mid-Jun–mid-Oct) Ride the *Sunnegga Express* to 2288m then ski down blue piste 6 or summer-hike 15 minutes

WORTH A TRIP

GLACIER EXPRESS

You'll have a hard time avoiding the hype for the **Glacier Express** (www.glacierexpress.ch; one-way adult/child Sfr145/73), the train that links Zermatt with the eastern towns and resorts of Graubünden, including St Moritz.

Although there is some stunning scenery of glacier-cleaved valleys and soaring peaks along the route, much of the run is down in valleys, so don't expect nonstop scenic thrills. You can shorten the eight-hour duration by starting at the rail hub of Brig instead of Zermatt or by just doing the leg between St Moritz and Chur (another rail hub).

Swiss Cards cover the entire route, while Eurail and InterRail are good for about 50% of the fare.

to Zermatt's tastiest slope-side address in the hamlet of Findeln. Keep snug in a cream blanket or lounge on a sheepskin-cushioned chaise longue and revel in the effortless romance of this century-old farmhouse with potted Edelweiss on the tables, first-class Matterhorn views and exceptional organic cuisine.

❶ Getting There & Around

CAR
Zermatt is car-free. Motorists have to park in Täsch (www.matterhornterminal.ch; first/subsequent day Sfr14.40/13.50) and ride the Zermatt Shuttle train (adult/child Sfr8/4, 12 minutes, every 20 minutes from 6am to 9.40pm) the last 5km to Zermatt.

TRAIN
Trains depart regularly from Brig – a major rail hub (Sfr32, 1½ hours), stopping at Visp en route. Zermatt is also the starting point of the popular *Glacier Express* to Graubünden.

BERN

POP 127,515

One of the planet's most underrated capitals, Bern is a fabulous find. With the genteel old soul of a Renaissance man and the heart of a high-flying 21st-century gal, the riverside city is both medieval and modern. The 15th-century Old Town is gorgeous enough to sweep you off your feet and make you forget the century (it's definitely worthy of its 1983 Unesco World Heritage Site status).

◎ Sights

Bern's flag-bedecked **medieval centre** is an attraction in its own right, with 6km of covered arcades and cellar shops and bars descending from the streets. After a devastating fire in 1405, the wooden city was rebuilt in today's sandstone. The city's 11 **decorative fountains** (1545) depict historical and folkloric characters. Most are along Marktgasse as it becomes Kramgasse and Gerechtigkeitsgasse, but the most famous lies in Kornhausplatz: the **Kindlifresserbrunnen** (Ogre Fountain) of a giant snacking...on children.

★ Zytglogge   CLOCK TOWER
(Marktgasse) Bern's most famous Old Town sight, this ornate clock tower once formed part of the city's western gate (1191–1256). Crowds congregate to watch its revolving figures twirl at four minutes before the hour, after which the chimes begin. Tours enter the tower to see the clock mechanism from May to October; contact the tourist office for details. The clock tower supposedly helped Albert Einstein hone his special theory of relativity, developed while working as a patent clerk in Bern.

Münster   CATHEDRAL
(www.bernermuenster.ch; Münsterplatz 1; tower adult/child Sfr5/2; ⊙10am-5pm Mon-Sat, 11.30am-5pm Sun May–mid-Oct, noon-4pm Mon-Fri, 10am-5pm Sat, 11.30am-4pm Sun rest of year) Bern's 15th-century Gothic cathedral boasts Switzerland's loftiest spire (100m); climb the dizzying 344-step spiral staircase for vertiginous views. Coming down, stop by the **Upper Bells** (1356), rung at 11am, noon and 3pm daily, and the three 10-tonne **Lower Bells** (Switzerland's largest). Don't miss the main portal's **Last Judgement**, which portrays Bern's mayor going to heaven, while his Zürich counterpart is shown into hell. Afterwards, wander through the adjacent **Münsterplattform**, a bijou clifftop park with a sunny pavilion cafe.

Zentrum
Paul Klee   MUSEUM
(☑031 359 01 01; www.zpk.org; Monument im Fruchtland 3; adult/child Sfr20/7, audioguide Sfr6; ⊙10am-5pm Tue-Sun) Bern's answer to the Guggenheim, Renzo Piano's architecturally bold 150m-long wave-like edifice houses an exhibition space that showcases rotating works from Paul Klee's prodigious and often-playful career. Interactive computer displays and audioguides help interpret the Swiss-born artist's work. Next door, the fun-packed **Kindermuseum Creaviva** (☑031 359 01 61; www.creaviva-zpk.org; Monument im Fruchtland 3; ⊙10am-5pm Tue-Sun) **FREE** lets kids experiment with hands-on art exhibits or create original artwork with the atelier's materials during the weekend **Five Franc Studio** (www.creaviva-zpk.org/en/art-education/5-franc-studio; admission Sfr5; ⊙10am-4.30pm Sat & Sun). Bus 12 runs from Bubenbergplatz direct to the museum.

⊨ Sleeping

Hotel Landhaus   HOTEL €
(☑031 348 03 05; www.landhausbern.ch; Altenbergstrasse 4; dm Sfr38, s Sfr80-130, d Sfr120-180, q Sfr200-220; P@ 🛜) Fronted by the river and Old Town spires, this well-run boho hotel offers a mix of stylish six-bed dorms, family rooms and doubles. Its buzzing ground-floor cafe and terrace attracts a cheery crowd. Breakfast (included with private rooms) costs Sfr8 extra for dorm-dwellers.

★ Hotel Schweizerhof   LUXURY HOTEL €€€
(☑031 326 80 80; www.schweizerhof-bern.ch; Bahnhofplatz 11; s Sfr284-640, d Sfr364-790; P ✳ @ 🛜) This classy five-star offers lavish accommodation with excellent amenities and service. A hop, skip and a jump from the train station, it's geared for both business and pleasure.

✖ Eating & Drinking

Look for interesting cafes and bistros scattered amid the arcades on Old Town streets including Zeughausgasse, Rathausgasse, Marktgasse and Kramgasse.

Altes Tramdepot   SWISS €€
(☑031 368 14 15; www.altestramdepot.ch; Am Bärengraben; mains Sfr18-37; ⊙11am-12.30am) At this cavernous microbrewery, Swiss specialities compete against wok-cooked

stir-fries for your affection, and the microbrews go down a treat: sample three different varieties for Sfr10.80, or four for Sfr14.50.

★ **Café des Pyrénées** BAR
(☑ 031 311 30 63; www.pyri.ch; Kornhausplatz 17; ⊙ 9am-11.30pm Mon-Wed, to 12.30am Thu & Fri, 8am-5pm Sat) This bohemian corner joint feels like a Parisian cafe-bar. Its central location near the tram tracks makes for good people-watching.

ⓘ Information

Tourist Office (☑ 031 328 12 12; www.bern. com; Bahnhoftplatz 10a; ⊙ 9am-7pm Mon-Sat, to 6pm Sun) Street-level floor of the train station. City tours, free hotel bookings, internet access. There's also a branch near the **Bear Park** (☑ 031 328 12 12; www.bern.com; Bärengraben; ⊙ 9am-6pm Jun-Sep, 10am-4pm Mar-May & Oct, 11am-4pm Nov-Feb).

ⓘ Getting There & Around

Frequent trains connect to most Swiss towns, including Geneva (Sfr49, 1¾ hours), Basel (Sfr39, one hour) and Zürich (Sfr49, one hour).

Buses and trams are operated by **BernMobil** (www.bernmobil.ch); many depart from the western side of Bahnhoftplatz.

CENTRAL SWITZERLAND & BERNESE OBERLAND

These two regions should come with a health warning – caution: may cause breathlessness as the sun rises and sets over Lake Lucerne, trembling in the north face of Eiger and uncontrollable bouts of euphoria at the foot of Jungfrau.

Lucerne

POP 79,500

Recipe for a gorgeous Swiss city: take a cobalt lake ringed by mountains of myth, add a medieval Old Town and sprinkle with covered bridges, sunny plazas, candy-coloured houses and waterfront promenades. Bright, beautiful Lucerne has been Little Miss Popular since the likes of Goethe, Queen Victoria and Wagner savoured her views in the 19th century.

◉ Sights

Your first port of call should be the medieval **Old Town**, with its ancient rampart walls and towers. Wander the cobblestone lanes and squares, pondering 15th-century buildings with painted facades and the two much-photographed covered bridges over the Reuss.

★ **Kapellbrücke** BRIDGE
(Chapel Bridge) You haven't really been to Lucerne until you have strolled the creaky 14th-century Kapellbrücke, spanning the Reuss River in the Old Town. The octagonal water tower is original, but its gabled roof is a modern reconstruction, rebuilt after a disastrous fire in 1993. As you cross the bridge, note Heinrich Wägmann's 17th-century triangular roof panels, showing important events from Swiss history and mythology. The icon is at its most photogenic when bathed in soft golden light at dusk.

Spreuerbrücke BRIDGE
(Spreuer Bridge; btwn Kasernenplatz & Mühlenplatz) Downriver from Kapellbrücke, this 1408 structure is darker and smaller but entirely original. Lore has it that this was the only bridge where Lucerne's medieval villagers were allowed to throw *Spreu* (chaff) into the river. Here, the roof panels consist of artist Caspar Meglinger's movie-storyboard-style sequence of paintings, *The Dance of Death*, showing how the plague affected all levels of society.

★ **Lion Monument** MONUMENT
(Löwendenkmal; Denkmalstrasse) By far the most touching of the 19th-century sights that lured so many British to Lucerne is the Lion Monument. Lukas Ahorn carved this 10m-long sculpture of a dying lion into the rock face in 1820 to commemorate Swiss soldiers who died defending King Louis XVI during the French Revolution. Mark Twain once called it the 'saddest and most moving piece of rock in the world'. For Narnia fans, it often evokes Aslan at the stone table.

Museum
Sammlung Rosengart MUSEUM
(☑ 041 220 16 60; www.rosengart.ch; Pilatusstrasse 10; adult/student Sfr18/16; ⊙ 10am-6pm Apr-Oct,

---

WORTH A TRIP

MOUNTAIN DAY TRIPS FROM LUCERNE

Among the several (heavily marketed) day trips from Lucerne, consider the one to 2132m-high **Mt Pilatus** (www.pilatus.com). From May to October, you can reach the peak on a classic 'golden round-trip'. Board the lake steamer from Lucerne to Alpnachstad, then rise with the world's steepest cog railway to Mt Pilatus. From the summit, cable cars bring you down to Kriens via Fräkmüntegg and Krienseregg, where bus 1 takes you back to Lucerne. The return trip costs Sfr97 (less with valid Swiss, Eurail or InterRail passes).

11am-5pm Nov-Mar) Lucerne's blockbuster cultural attraction is the Sammlung Rosengart, occupying a graceful neoclassical pile. It showcases the outstanding stash of Angela Rosengart, a Swiss art dealer and close friend of Picasso. Alongside works by the great Spanish master are paintings and sketches by Cézanne, Klee, Kandinsky, Miró, Matisse and Monet. Standouts include Joan Miró's electric-blue *Dancer II* (1925) and Paul Klee's childlike *X-chen* (1938).

Verkehrshaus   MUSEUM
(Swiss Museum of Transport; ☑041 370 44 44; www.verkehrshaus.ch; Lidostrasse 5; adult/ child Sfr30/15; ☉10am-6pm Apr-Oct, to 5pm Nov-Mar; ⊞) A great kid-pleaser, the fascinating interactive Verkehrshaus is deservedly Switzerland's most popular museum. Alongside space rockets, steam locomotives, bicycles and dugout canoes are hands-on activities such as flight simulators and broadcasting studios.

The museum also shelters a **planetarium** (adult/child Sfr15/9), Switzerland's largest **3D cinema** (www.filmtheater.ch; adult/ child daytime Sfr18/14, evening Sfr22/19), and its newest attraction, the **Swiss Chocolate Experience** (adult/child Sfr15/9), a 20-minute ride that whirls visitors through multimedia exhibits on the origins, history, production and distribution of chocolate, from Ghana to Switzerland and beyond.

🛏 Sleeping

Backpackers Lucerne   HOSTEL €
(☑041 360 04 20; www.backpackerslucerne.ch; Alpenquai 42; dm/d from Sfr33/78; ☉reception 7-10am & 4-11pm; @🛜) Could this be backpacker heaven? Just opposite the lake, this is a soulful place to crash with art-slung walls, bubbly staff, a well-equipped kitchen and immaculate dorms with balconies. It's a 15-minute walk southeast of the station.

There's no breakfast, but guests have kitchen access.

Hotel Waldstätterhof   HOTEL €€
(☑041 227 12 71; www.hotel-waldstaetterhof.ch; Zentralstrasse 4; s Sfr190, d Sfr290-315; 🅿🛜) Opposite the train station, this hotel with faux-Gothic exterior offers smart, modern rooms with hardwood-style floors and high ceilings, plus excellent service.

★The Hotel   HOTEL €€€
(☑041 226 86 86; www.the-hotel.ch; Sempacherstrasse 14; s/d ste from Sfr425/455; ✳@🛜) This shamelessly hip hotel, bearing the imprint of architect Jean Nouvel, is all streamlined chic, with refined suites featuring stills from movie classics on the ceilings. Downstairs, Bam Bou is one of Lucerne's hippest restaurants, and the gorgeous green park across the street is a cool place to idle.

🍴 Eating & Drinking

★Grottino 1313   ITALIAN €€
(☑041 610 13 13; www.grottino1313.ch; Industriestrasse 7; 2-course lunch menu Sfr20, 4-course dinner menu Sfr64; ☉11am-2pm & 6-11.30pm Mon-Fri, 6-11.30pm Sat, 9am-2pm Sun) Offering a welcome escape from Lucerne's tourist throngs, this relaxed yet stylish eatery serves ever-changing 'surprise' menus featuring starters like chestnut soup with figs, creative pasta dishes, meats cooked over an open fire and scrumptious desserts. The gravel-strewn, herb-fringed front patio is lovely on a summer afternoon, while the candlelit interior exudes sheer cosiness on a winter's evening.

Wirtshaus Galliker   SWISS €€
(☑041 240 10 01; Schützenstrasse 1; mains Sfr21-51; ☉11.30am-2pm & 5-10pm Tue-Sat, closed Jul–mid-Aug) Passionately run by the

Galliker family for over four generations, this old-style, wood-panelled tavern attracts a lively bunch of regulars. Motherly waitresses dish up Lucerne soul food (rösti, *chögalipaschtetli* and the like) that is batten-the-hatches filling.

Rathaus Bräuerei BREWERY
(☑ 041 410 52 57; www.braui-luzern.ch; Unter den Egg 2; ☺ 11.30am-midnight Mon-Sat, to 11pm Sun) Sip home-brewed beer under the vaulted arches of this buzzy tavern near Kapellbrücke, or nab a pavement table and watch the river flow.

❶ Information

Lake Lucerne Region Visitors Card (Vierwaldstättersee Gästekarte; www.luzern.com/visitors-card) Stamped by your hotel, this free card entitles visitors to discounts on various museums, sporting facilities, cable cars and lake cruises in Lucerne and the surrounding area.

Tourist Office (☑ 041 227 17 17; www.luzern.com; Zentralstrasse 5; ☺ 9am-7pm Mon-Sat, 9am-5pm Sun May-Oct, 8.30am-5.30pm Mon-Fri, 9am-5pm Sat, 9am-1pm Sun Nov-Apr) Reached from Zentralstrasse or platform 3 of the Hauptbahnhof. Offers city walking tours. Call for hotel reservations.

❶ Getting There & Around

Frequent trains serve Interlaken Ost (Sfr31, 1¾ hours), Bern (Sfr37, one hour), Lugano (Sfr58, 2½ hours) and Zürich (Sfr24, 50 minutes).

Trains also connect Lucerne and Interlaken Ost on the stunning GoldenPass Line via Meiringen (Sfr31, two hours).

SGV (www.lakelucerne.ch) operates boats (sometimes paddle steamers) on Lake Lucerne daily. Services are extensive. Rail passes are good for free or discounted travel.

Interlaken

POP 5660

Once Interlaken made the Victorians swoon with its dreamy mountain vistas, viewed from the chandelier-lit confines of its grand hotels. Today it makes daredevils scream with its adrenalin-loaded adventures. Straddling the glittering Lakes Thun and Brienz (thus the name), and dazzled by the pearly whites of Eiger, Mönch and Jungfrau, Interlaken boasts exceptional scenery.

◉ Sights & Activities

Switzerland is the world's second-biggest adventure-sports centre and Interlaken is its busiest hub. Sample prices are Sfr120 for rafting or canyoning, Sfr140 for hydrospeeding, Sfr130 to Sfr180 for bungee or canyon jumping, Sfr170 for tandem paragliding, Sfr180 for ice climbing, Sfr220 for hang-gliding and Sfr430 for skydiving. A half-day mountain-bike tour will set you back around Sfr25.

Harder Kulm MOUNTAIN
(www.harderkulm.ch) For far-reaching views to the 4000m giants, ride the **funicular** (adult/child return Sfr28/14; ☺ every 30min 8.10am-6.25pm late Apr-Oct, plus 7-8.30pm Jul & Aug) to 1322m Harder Kulm. Many hiking paths begin here, and the vertigo-free can enjoy the panorama from the **Zweiseensteg** (Two Lake Bridge) jutting out above the valley. The wildlife park near the valley station is home to Alpine critters, including marmots and ibex.

🛏 Sleeping

Backpackers Villa Sonnenhof HOSTEL €
(☑ 033 826 71 71; www.villa.ch; Alpenstrasse 16; dm Sfr39.50-47, s Sfr69-79, d Sfr110-148; ⓟ @ � 📶) Sonnenhof is a slick combination of ultramodern chalet and elegant art nouveau villa. Dorms are immaculate, and some have balconies with Jungfrau views. There's also a relaxed lounge, a well-equipped kitchen, a kids' playroom and a leafy garden for mountain gazing. Special family rates are available.

★ **Victoria-Jungfrau Grand Hotel & Spa** LUXURY HOTEL €€€
(☑ 033 828 26 10; www.victoria-jungfrau.ch; Höheweg 41; d Sfr400-800, ste Sfr600-1000; ⓟ @ 📶 ⚎) The reverent hush and impeccable service here (as well as the prices) evoke an era when only royalty and the seriously wealthy travelled. A perfect melding of well-preserved art nouveau features and modern luxury make this Interlaken's answer to Raffles – with plum views of Jungfrau, three first-class restaurants and a gorgeous spa to boot.

🍴 Eating & Drinking

Höheweg, east of Interlaken Ost train station, is lined with ethnic eateries with reasonable prices.

Sandwich Bar
SANDWICHES €

(Rosenstrasse 5; snacks Sfr4-9; ⊙7.30am-7pm Mon-Fri, 8am-5pm Sat) Choose your bread and get creative with fillings like air-dried ham with sun-dried tomatoes and brie with walnuts. Or try the soups, salads, toasties and locally made ice cream.

★ WineArt
MEDITERRANEAN €€

(📋033 823 73 74; www.wineart.ch; Jungfraustrasse 46; mains Sfr24-59, 5-course menu Sfr59; ⊙4pm-12.30am Mon-Sat) This is a delightful wine bar, lounge, restaurant and deli rolled into one. High ceilings, chandeliers and wood floors create a slick, elegant backdrop for season-driven Mediterranean food. Pair one of 600 wines with dishes as simple as buffalo mozzarella and rocket salad and corn-fed chicken with honey-glazed vegetables – quality and flavour are second to none.

❶ Information

Tourist Office (📋033 826 53 00; www. interlakentourism.ch; Höheweg 37; ⊙8am-7pm Mon-Fri, to 5pm Sat, 10am-4pm Sun Jul & Aug, 8am-noon & 1.30-6pm Mon-Fri, 9am-noon Sat rest of year) Halfway between the stations. There's a hotel booking board outside.

❶ Getting There & Away

There are two train stations. Interlaken West is slightly closer to the centre and is a stop for trains to Bern (Sfr27, one hour). Interlaken Ost (East) is the rail hub for all lines, including the scenic ones up into the Jungfrau region and the lovely GoldenPass Line to Lucerne (Sfr31, two hours).

Jungfrau Region

If the Bernese Oberland is Switzerland's alpine heart, the Jungfrau region is where yours will skip a beat. Presided over by glacier-encrusted monoliths Eiger, Mönch and Jungfrau (Ogre, Monk and Virgin), the scenery stirs the soul and strains the neck muscles. It's a magnet for skiers and snowboarders with its 214km of pistes, 44 lifts and much more; a one-day ski pass for either Grindelwald-Wengen or Mürren-Schilthorn costs adult/child Sfr62/31.

Come summer, hundreds of kilometres of walking trails allow you to capture the landscape from many angles, but it never looks less than astonishing.

❶ Getting There & Around

Hourly trains (www.jungfrau.ch) depart for the Jungfrau region from Interlaken Ost station. Sit in the front half of the train for Lauterbrunnen (Sfr7.40) or the back half for Grindelwald (Sfr10.80).

From Grindelwald, trains ascend to Kleine Scheidegg (Sfr31), where you can transfer for Jungfraujoch. From Lauterbrunnen, trains ascend to Wengen (Sfr6.60) and continue to Kleine Scheidegg (Sfr23) for Jungfraujoch.

You can reach Mürren two ways from Lauterbrunnen: with a bus and cable car via Stechelberg (Sfr15) or with a cable car and train via Grütschalp (Sfr11). Do a circle trip for the full experience. Gimmelwald is reached by cable car from Stechelberg and Mürren.

Many cable cars close for servicing in April and November.

Grindelwald

POP 3760

Grindelwald's charms were discovered by skiers and hikers in the late 19th century, making it one of Switzerland's oldest resorts and the Jungfrau's largest. It has lost none of its appeal over the decades, with archetypal alpine chalets and verdant pastures set against the chiselled features of the Eiger north face.

JUNGFRAU REGION HIKING 101

There are hundreds of hikes along the hundreds of kilometres of trails in the Jungfrau region; all include some of the world's most stunning scenery. Every skill and fortitude level is accommodated and options abound. Here are two to get you started.

Grütschalp to Mürren Ride the cable car up from Lauterbrunnen and follow the trail along the railway tracks. The walk to Mürren takes about an hour and is mostly level. There are unbeatable views, alpine woods and babbling glacier-fed streams.

Männlichen to Kleine Scheidegg Reach the Männlichen lift station by cable cars from Wengen and Grindelwald. Now follow the well-marked, spectacular path down to Kleine Scheidegg. It takes about 90 minutes and you have nothing but Alps in front of you.

⛷ Activities

The **Grindelwald-First** skiing area has a mix of cruisy red and challenging black runs stretching from Oberjoch at 2486m to the village at 1050m, plus 15.5km of well-groomed cross-country ski trails. In the summer it caters to hikers with 90km of trails at about 1200m, 48km of which are open year-round.

★ Kleine
Scheidegg Walk   HIKING

One of the region's most stunning day hikes is this 15km trek from Grindelwald Grund to Wengen via Kleine Scheidegg, which heads up through wildflower-freckled meadows to skirt below the Eiger's north face and reach Kleine Scheidegg, granting arresting views of the 'Big Three'. Allow around 5½ to six hours. The best map is the SAW 1:50,000 Interlaken (Sfr22.50).

Grindelwald
Sports   ADVENTURE SPORTS

(☑033 854 12 80; www.grindelwaldsports.ch; Dorfstrasse 103; ☺8.30am-6.30pm, closed Sat & Sun in low season) Opposite the tourist office, this outfit arranges mountain climbing, ski and snowboard instruction, canyon jumping and glacier bungee jumping at the Gletscherschlucht. It also houses a cosy cafe and sells walking guides.

🛏 Sleeping

Mountain Hostel   HOSTEL €

(☑033 854 38 38; www.mountainhostel.ch; Grundstrasse 58; dm Sfr37-51, d Sfr94-122; P🔊) Near Männlichen cable-car station, this is an ideal base for sports junkies, with well-kept dorms and a helpful crew. There's a beer garden, ski storage, TV lounge and mountain and e-bike rental.

★ Gletschergarten   HISTORIC HOTEL €€

(☑033 853 17 21; www.hotel-gletschergarten.ch; Obere Gletscherstrasse 1; s Sfr130-170, d Sfr230-300; P🔊) The sweet Breitenstein family make you feel at home in their rustic timber chalet, brimming with heirlooms from landscape paintings to snapshots of Elsbeth's grandfather who had 12 children (those were the days...). Decked out in pine and flowery fabrics, the rooms have balconies facing Unterer Gletscher at the front and Wetterhorn (best for sunset) at the back.

Wengen

POP 1300

Photogenically poised on a mountain ledge, Wengen has celestial views of the glacier-capped giant peaks' silent majesty as well as the shimmering waterfalls spilling into the Lauterbrunnen Valley below.

The village is car-free and can only be reached by train. It's a fabulous hub for **hiking** for much of the year as well as **skiing** in winter.

Hotel Bären (☑033 855 14 19; www.baeren-wengen.ch; s Sfr120-150, d Sfr160-290, tr Sfr280-380; 🔊) is close to the station. Loop back under the tracks and head down the hill to this snug log chalet with bright, if compact, rooms. The affable Brunner family serves a hearty breakfast.

Jungfraujoch

Jungfraujoch (3471m) is a once-in-a-life-time trip and there's good reason why two million people a year visit Europe's highest train station. Clear good weather is essential; check www.jungfrau.ch or call ☑033 828 79 31, and don't forget warm clothing, sunglasses and sunscreen.

From Interlaken Ost, the journey time is 2½ hours each way (Sfr197.60 return, discounts with rail passes). The last train back sets off at 5.45pm in summer and 4.45pm in winter. However, from May to October there's a cheaper Good Morning Ticket costing Sfr145 if you take the first train (which departs at 6.35am from Interlaken Ost) and leave the summit by 1pm.

Gimmelwald

POP 110

Decades ago some anonymous backpacker scribbled these words in the guestbook at the Mountain Hostel: 'If heaven isn't what it's cracked up to be, send me back to Gimmelwald'. Enough said. When the sun is out in Gimmelwald, this pipsqueak of a village will simply take your breath away. Sit outside and listen to the distant roar of avalanches on the sheer mountain faces arrayed before you.

The charming, spotless **Esther's Guest House** (☑033 855 54 88; www.esthersguest-house.ch; Kirchstatt; s/d Sfr60/140, apt Sfr170-250; 🔊) is run with love and care. For an extra

SWISS NATIONAL PARK

The Engadine's pride and joy is the Swiss National Park, easily accessed from Scuol, Zernez and S-chanf. Spanning 172 sq km, Switzerland's only national park is a nature-gone-wild swath of dolomitic peaks, shimmering glaciers, larch woodlands, pastures, waterfalls and high moors strung with topaz-blue lakes. This was the first national park to be established in the Alps, on 1 August 1914, and over 100 years later it remains true to its original conservation ethos, with the aims to protect, research and inform.

Given that nature has been left to its own devices for a century, the park is a glimpse of the Alps before the dawn of tourism. There are some 80km of well-marked hiking trails, where, with a little luck and a decent pair of binoculars, ibex, chamois, marmots and golden eagles can be sighted. The **Swiss National Park Centre** (☑ 081 851 41 41; www.nationalpark.ch; Zernez; exhibition adult/child Sfr7/3; ⊙ 8.30am-6pm Jun-Oct, 9am-noon & 2-5pm Nov-May) should be your first port of call for information on activities and accommodation. It sells an excellent 1:50,000 park map (Sfr20), which covers 21 walks through the park.

You can easily head off on your own, but you might get more out of one of the informative guided hikes run by the centre from late June to mid-October. These include wildlife-spotting treks to the Val Trupchun and high-alpine hikes to the Offenpass and Lakes of Macun. Most are in German, but many guides speak a little English. Expect to pay Sfr25 to Sfr35 per person. You should book ahead by phone.

Entry to the park and its car parks is free. Conservation is paramount here, so stick to footpaths and respect regulations prohibiting camping, littering, lighting fires, cycling, picking flowers and disturbing the animals.

Sfr15, you'll be served a delicious breakfast of homemade bread, cheese and yoghurt.

Mürren

POP 430

Arrive on a clear evening when the sun hangs low on the horizon, and you'll think you've died and gone to heaven. Car-free Mürren *is* storybook Switzerland.

Sleeping options include **Eiger Guesthouse** (☑ 033 856 54 60; www.eigerguesthouse. com; r Sfr110-220; �☑), by the train station, with the downstairs pub serving tasty food; and **Hotel Jungfrau** (☑ 033 856 64 64; www.hoteljungfrau.ch; d Sfr180-280, q apt Sfr550; ☑), overlooking the nursery slopes from its perch above Mürren. It dates to 1894 and has a beamed lounge with an open fire.

Schilthorn

There's a tremendous 360-degree panorama available from the 2970m **Schilthorn** (www.schilthorn.ch). On a clear day, you can see over 200 peaks, from Titlis to Mont Blanc and across to the German Black Forest. Note that this was the site of Blofeld's HQ in the underappreciated 1969 James

Bond film *On Her Majesty's Secret Service* (as the hype endlessly reminds you).

The new **Bond World 007** (http://schilt horn.ch; admission free with cable car ticket; ⊙ 8am-6pm) interactive exhibition gives you the chance to pose for photos secret-agent style and relive movie moments in a helicopter and bobsled.

From Interlaken Ost, take a Sfr121.80 excursion to Lauterbrunnen, Grütschalp, Mürren and Schilthorn and return through Stechelberg to Interlaken. A return from Lauterbrunnen (via Grütschalp) and Mürren costs Sfr107, as does the return journey via the Stechelberg cable car. A return from Mürren is Sfr77.

Ask about discounts for early morning trips. There are discounts with rail passes.

ZÜRICH

POP 380,780

Zürich, Switzerland's largest city, is an enigma. A savvy financial centre with the densest public transport system in the world, it also has a gritty, postindustrial edge that always surprises and an evocative Old Town, not to mention a lovely lakeside location.

Zürich

Zürich

◎ Sights
1 Fraumünster C3
2 Kunsthaus D3
3 Schweizerisches Landesmuseum C1

🛏 Sleeping
4 Townhouse... C2

✕ Eating
5 Café Sprüngli C3
6 Haus Hiltl B2

🍷 Drinking & Nightlife
7 Longstreet Bar................................... A1

◉ Sights

The cobbled streets of the pedestrian Old
Town line both sides of the river, while the
bank vaults beneath Bahnhofstrasse, the
city's most elegant shopping street, are said
to be crammed with gold. On Sunday all of
Zürich strolls around the lake – on a clear
day you'll glimpse the Alps in the distance.

Fraumünster   CHURCH
(www.fraumuenster.ch; Münsterhof; ◷9am-6pm
Apr-Oct, 10am-4pm Nov-Mar) The 13th-century
cathedral is renowned for its stunning, distinctive stained-glass windows, designed
by the Russian-Jewish master Marc Chagall
(1887–1985). He did a series of five windows
in the choir stalls in 1971 and the rose window in the southern transept in 1978. The
rose window in the northern transept was
created by Augusto Giacometti in 1945.

Kunsthaus   MUSEUM
(☎044 253 84 84; www.kunsthaus.ch; Heimplatz
1; adult/child Sfr15/free, Wed free; ◷10am-8pm
Wed-Fri, 10am-6pm Tue, Sat & Sun) Zürich's

impressive fine arts gallery boasts a rich collection of largely European art that stretches from the Middle Ages through a mix of Old Masters to Alberto Giacometti stick figures, Monet and Van Gogh masterpieces, Rodin sculptures and other 19th- and 20th-century art. Swiss Rail and Museum Passes don't provide free admission but the ZürichCard does.

Schweizerisches Landesmuseum
MUSEUM

(Swiss National Museum; www.musee-suisse. ch; Museumstrasse 2; adult/child Sfr10/free; ⊙10am-5pm Tue, Wed & Fri-Sun, 10am-7pm Thu) Inside a purpose-built cross between a mansion and a castle sprawls this eclectic and imaginatively presented museum. The permanent collection offers an extensive tour through Swiss history, with exhibits ranging from elaborately carved and painted sleds to household and religious artefacts to a series of reconstructed historical rooms spanning six centuries. The museum remains open while undergoing a major expansion; the new archaeology section and brand-new wing are slated to open in 2016.

🛏 Sleeping

Zürich accommodation prices are fittingly high for the main city of expensive Switzerland.

★ SYHA Hostel
HOSTEL €

(☑043 399 78 00; www.youthhostel.ch/zuerich; Mutschellenstrasse 114, Wollishofen; dm Sfr43-46, s/d Sfr119/140; @ 🛜) A bulbous, Band-Aid-pink 1960s landmark houses this busy hostel with 24-hour reception, dining hall, sparkling modern bathrooms and dependable wi-fi in the downstairs lounge. The included breakfast features miso soup and rice alongside all the Swiss standards. It's about 20 minutes south of the Hauptbahnhof. Take tram 7 to Morgental, or the S-Bahn to Wollishofen, then walk five minutes.

Townhouse
BOUTIQUE HOTEL €€

(☑044 200 95 95; www.townhouse.ch; Schützengasse 7; s Sfr195-395, d Sfr225-425; 🛜) With luxurious wallpapers, wallhangings, parquet floors and retro furniture, the 21 rooms in these stylish digs come in an assortment of sizes from 15 sq metres to 35 sq metres. Located close to the main train station, the hotel offers friendly service and welcoming touches including a DVD selection and iPod docking stations.

B2 Boutique Hotel & Spa
BOUTIQUE HOTEL €€€

(☑044 567 67 67; www.b2boutiquehotels.com; Brandschenkestrasse 152; s/d from Sfr330/380; @ 🛜) A stone's throw from Google's European headquarters, this quirky newcomer in a renovated brewery is filled with seductive features. Topping the list are the stupendous rooftop Jacuzzi pool, the spa and the fanciful library-lounge, filled floor to ceiling with an astounding 30,000 books (bought from a local antiquarian) on 13m-high shelves. Spacious rooms sport modern decor (including the odd bean-bag chair).

From the Hauptbahnhof, take tram 13 to Enge and walk five minutes west.

✗ Eating

Zürich has a thriving cafe culture and 2000-plus places to eat. Traditional local cuisine is very rich, as epitomised by the city's signature dish, Zürcher Geschnetzeltes (sliced veal in a creamy mushroom and white wine sauce).

★ Haus Hiltl
VEGETARIAN €

(☑044 227 70 00; hiltl.ch; Sihlstrasse 28; per 100g take-away/cafe/restaurant Sfr3.50/4.50/5.50; ⊙6am-midnight Mon-Sat, 8am-midnight Sun; 🥄) Guinness-certified as the world's oldest vegetarian restaurant (established 1898), Hiltl proffers an astounding smorgasbord of meatless delights, from Indian and Thai curries to Mediterranean grilled vegies to salads and desserts. Browse to your heart's content, fill your plate and weigh it, then choose a seat in the informal cafe or the spiffier adjoining restaurant (economical take-away service is also available).

Café Sprüngli
SWEETS €

(☑044 224 46 46; www.spruengli.ch; Bahnhofstrasse 21; sweets Sfr7.50-16; ⊙7am-6.30pm Mon-Fri, 8am-6pm Sat, 9.30am-5.30pm Sun) Sit down for cakes, chocolate, coffee or ice cream at this epicentre of sweet Switzerland, in business since 1836. You can have a light lunch too, but whatever you do, don't fail to check out the heavenly chocolate shop around the corner on Paradeplatz.

WORTH A TRIP

LIECHTENSTEIN

If Liechtenstein (population 37,132) didn't exist, someone would have invented it. A tiny German-speaking mountain principality (160 sq km) governed by an iron-willed monarch in the heart of 21st-century Europe, it certainly has novelty value. Only 25km long by 12km wide (at its broadest point) – just larger than Manhattan – Liechtenstein is mostly visited by people who want a glimpse of the castle and a spurious passport stamp. Stay a little longer and you can escape into its pint-sized alpine wilderness.

Vaduz

Vaduz is a postage stamp–size city with a postcard-perfect backdrop. Crouching at the foot of forested mountains, hugging the banks of the Rhine and crowned by a turreted castle, the city has a visually stunning location.

The centre itself is curiously modern and sterile, yet just a few minutes' walk brings you to traces of the quaint village that existed just 50 years ago and quiet vineyards where the Alps seem that bit closer.

Vaduz Castle is closed to the public but is worth the climb for the vistas.

Information

Liechtenstein's international phone prefix is 423.

The **Liechtenstein Center** (www.tourismus.li) offers brochures, souvenir passport stamps (Sfr3) and the **Philatelie Liechtenstein**, which will interest stamp collectors.

Getting There & Around

The nearest train stations are in the Swiss border towns of Buchs and Sargans. From each of these towns there are frequent buses to Vaduz (Sfr7.20/9.40 from Buchs/Sargans). Buses traverse the country. Single fares (buy tickets on the bus) are Sfr2.80/3.50/4.80 for one/two/three zones. Swiss Passes are valid on all main routes.

★**Alpenrose**   SWISS €€
(☑ 044 271 39 19; alpenrose.me; Fabrikstrasse 12; mains Sfr26-42; ⊙11am-midnight Wed-Fri, 6.15-11pm Sat & Sun) With its timber-clad walls, 'No Polka Dancing' warning and multi-regional Swiss cuisine, the Alpenrose exudes cosy charm. Specialities include Ticinese risotto and *Pizokel*, a savoury kind of *Spätzli* from Graubünden – as proudly noted on the menu, they've served over 20,000kg of the stuff over the past 20 years! Save room for creamy cognac parfait and other scrumptious desserts.

🍷 Drinking & Entertainment

Options abound across town, but the bulk of the more animated drinking dens are in Züri-West, especially along Langstrasse in Kreis 4 and Hardstrasse in Kreis 5.

★**Frau**
Gerolds Garten   BAR
(www.fraugerold.ch; Geroldstrasse 23/23a; ⊙11am-midnight Mon-Sat, noon-10pm Sun Apr-Oct, closed in bad weather; 🚇) Hmm, where to start? The wine bar? The margarita bar? The gin bar? Whichever poison you

choose, this wildly popular recent addition to Zürich's summertime drinking scene is pure unadulterated fun. Overhung with multicoloured streamers and sandwiched between cheery flower beds and a screeching railyard, its outdoor seating options range from picnic tables to pillow-strewn terraces to a 2nd-floor sundeck.

Longstreet Bar   BAR
(☑ 044 241 21 72; www.longstreetbar.ch; Langstrasse 92; ⊙6pm-late Wed-Fri, 8pm-4am Sat) In the heart of the Langstrasse action, the Longstreet is a music bar with a varied roll call of DJs. Try to count the thousands of light bulbs in this purple-felt-lined one-time cabaret.

Supermarket   CLUB
(☑ 044 440 20 05; www.supermarket.li; Geroldstrasse 17; ⊙11pm-late Thu-Sat) Looking like an innocent little house, Supermarket boasts three cosy lounge bars around the dance floor, a covered back courtyard and an interesting roster of DJs playing house and techno. Take a train from Hauptbahnhof to Hardbrücke.

ℹ Information

Zürich Tourism (☏ 044 215 40 00, hotel reservations 044 215 40 40; www.zuerich.com; ⊙ 8am-8.30pm Mon-Sat, 8.30am-6.30pm Sun)

ℹ Getting There & Away

AIR

Zürich Airport (p664), 9km north of the centre, is Switzerland's main airport.

TRAIN

Direct trains run to Stuttgart (Sfr64, three hours), Munich (Sfr97, 4¼ hours), Innsbruck (Sfr77, 3½ hours) and other international destinations.

There are regular direct departures to most major Swiss towns, such as Lucerne (Sfr24, 45 to 50 minutes), Bern (Sfr49, one to 1¼ hours) and Basel (Sfr32, 55 minutes to 1¼ hours).

ℹ Getting Around

TO/FROM THE AIRPORT

Up to nine trains an hour run in each direction between the airport and the main train station (Sfr6.60, nine to 14 minutes).

BICYCLE

Züri Rollt (www.schweizrollt.ch) allows visitors to borrow or rent bikes from a handful of locations, including Velostation Nord across the road from the north side of the Hauptbahnhof. Bring ID and leave Sfr20 as a deposit. Rental is free if you bring the bike back on the same day and Sfr10 a day if you keep it overnight.

PUBLIC TRANSPORT

The comprehensive, unified bus, tram and S-Bahn public transit system **ZVV** (www.zvv.ch) includes boats plying the Limmat River. Short trips under five stops are Sfr2.60, typical trips are Sfr4.20. A 24-hour pass for the city centre is Sfr8.40.

NORTHERN SWITZERLAND

With business-like Basel at its heart, this region also prides itself on having the country's finest Roman ruins (at Augusta Raurica) and a gaggle of proud castles and pretty medieval villages scattered across the rolling countryside of Aargau canton.

Basel

POP 165,570

Tucked up against the French and German borders in Switzerland's northwest corner, Basel straddles the majestic Rhine. The town is home to art galleries, 30-odd museums and avant-garde architecture, and it boasts an enchanting old town centre.

◎ Sights & Activities

Altstadt NEIGHBOURHOOD
Begin exploring Basel's delightful medieval Old Town in **Marktplatz**, dominated by the astonishingly vivid red facade of the 16th century **Rathaus**. From here, climb 400m west along Spalenberg through the former artisans' district to the 600-year-old **Spalentor** city gate, one of only three to survive the walls' demolition in 1866. Along the way, linger in captivating lanes such as Spalenberg, Heuberg and Leonhardsberg, lined by impeccably maintained, centuries-old houses.

★**Fondation Beyeler** MUSEUM
(☏ 061 645 97 00; www.fondationbeyeler.ch; Baselstrasse 101, Riehen; adult/child Sfr25/6; ⊙ 10am-6pm, to 8pm Wed) This astounding private-turned-public collection, assembled by former art dealers Hildy and Ernst Beyeler, is housed in a long, low, light-filled, open-plan building, designed by Italian architect Renzo Piano. The varied exhibits juxtapose 19th- and 20th-century works by Picasso and Rothko against sculptures by Miró and Max Ernst and tribal figures from Oceania. Take tram 6 to Riehen from Barfüsserplatz or Marktplatz.

⊨ Sleeping

Hotels are often full during Basel's trade fairs and conventions; book ahead. Guests receive a pass for free travel on public transport.

★**SYHA Basel St Alban Youth Hostel** HOSTEL €
(☏ 061 272 05 72; www.youthhostel.ch/basel; St Alban Kirchrain 10; dm/s/d Sfr44/122/136; ☏) Designed by Basel-based architects Buchner & Bründler, this swank modern hostel in a very pleasant neighbourhood is flanked by tree-shaded squares and a rushing creek. It's only a stone's throw from the Rhine, and 15 minutes on foot from the SBB Bahnhof

(or take tram 2 to Kunstmuseum and walk five minutes downhill).

★**Hotel Krafft** HOTEL **€€**
(☑ 061 690 91 30; krafftbasel.ch; Rheingasse 12; s Sfr110-150, d Sfr175-265; ☜) Design-savvy urbanites will love this renovated historic hotel. Sculptural modern chandeliers dangle in the creaky-floored dining room overlooking the Rhine, and minimalist Japanese-style tea bars adorn each landing of the spiral stairs.

✗ Eating & Drinking

Head to the **Marktplatz** for a daily market and several stands selling excellent quick bites, such as local sausages and sandwiches.

★**Volkshaus Basel** BRASSERIE, BAR **€€**
(☑ 061 690 93 11; volkshaus-basel.ch; Rebgasse 12-14; mains Sfr28-56; ⊙ 11.30am-2pm & 6-10.30pm Mon-Fri, 11.30am-10.30pm Sat) This stylish new Herzog & de Meuron–designed venue is part resto-bar, part gallery and part performance space. For relaxed dining, head for the atmospheric beer garden, in a cobblestoned courtyard decorated with columns, vine-clad walls and light-draped rows of trees. The menu ranges from brasserie classics (*steak-frites*) to more innovative offerings (shrimp and cucumber salad with sour cream–lavender dressing). The bar is open 10am to 1am Monday to Saturday.

❶ Information

Basel Tourismus (☑ 061 268 68 68; www.basel.com) SBB Bahnhof (⊙ 8.30am-6pm Mon-Fri, 9am-5pm Sat, to 3pm Sun & holidays); Stadtcasino (Steinenberg 14; ⊙ 9am-6.30pm Mon-Fri, to 5pm Sat, 10am-3pm Sun & holidays) The Stadtcasino branch organises two-hour city walking tours (adult/child Sfr18/9, in English or French upon request) starting at 2.30pm Monday to Saturday May through October, and on Saturdays the rest of the year.

❶ Getting There & Away

AIR

The **EuroAirport** (MLH or BSL; ☑ +33 3 89 90 31 11; www.euroairport.com), 5km northwest of town in France, is the main airport for Basel. It is a hub for easyJet and there are flights to major European cities.

TRAIN

Basel is a major European rail hub. The main station has TGVs to Paris (three hours) and fast ICEs to major cities in Germany.

Services within Switzerland include frequent trains to Bern (Sfr39, one hour) and Zürich (Sfr32, one hour).

❶ Getting Around

Bus 50 links the airport and Basel's main train station (Sfr4.20, 20 minutes). Trams 8 and 11 link the station to Marktplatz (Sfr3.40, day pass Sfr9).

TICINO

Switzerland meets Italy: in Ticino the summer air is rich and hot, and peacock-proud posers propel their scooters in and out of traffic. Italian weather, Italian style. Not to mention the Italian ice cream, Italian pizza, Italian architecture and Italian language.

Locarno

POP 15,480

Italianate architecture and the northern end of Lago Maggiore, plus more hours of sunshine than anywhere else in Switzerland (2300 hours, to be precise), give this laid-back town a summer resort atmosphere.

Locarno is on the northeastern corner of Lago Maggiore, which mostly lies in Italy's Lombardy region. **Navigazione Lago Maggiore** (www.navigazionelaghi.it) operates boats across the entire lake.

◉ Sights & Activities

Città Vecchia NEIGHBOURHOOD
Locarno's Italianate Old Town fans out from **Piazza Grande**, a photogenic ensemble of arcades and Lombard-style houses. A craft and fresh produce market takes over the square every Thursday.

★**Santuario della Madonna del Sasso** CHURCH
(⊙ 6.30am-6.30pm) FREE Overlooking the town, this sanctuary was built after the Virgin Mary supposedly appeared in a vision to a monk, Bartolomeo d'Ivrea, in 1480. There's a highly adorned church and several rather rough, near-life-size statue groups (including one of the Last Supper)

WORTH A TRIP

BERNINA EXPRESS

The famous **Bernina Express** (www.berninaexpress.ch; one-way Sfr84; seat reservation summer/winter Sfr14/10; ☉ mid-May–early Dec) route (6½ hours) runs from Lugano to St Moritz, Davos and the rail hub of Chur. The four-hour route from Chur to Lugano (55 tunnels, 196 bridges) climbs high into the glaciated realms of the Alps and skirts Ticino's palm-fringed lakes. From Lugano to Tirano (in Italy), a bus is used for the scenic run along Italy's Lake Como.

The train route over the Bernina Pass between Tirano and St Moritz is one of Switzerland's most spectacular and is Unesco recognised. Some trains feature open-top cars.

in niches on the stairway. The best-known painting in the church is *La Fuga in Egitto* (Flight to Egypt), painted in 1522 by Bramantino.

A **funicular** (adult one way/return Sfr4.80/7.20, child Sfr2.20/3.60; ☉ 8am-10pm) runs every 15 minutes from the town centre past the sanctuary to Orselina, but a more scenic, pilgrim-style approach is the 20-minute walk up the chapel-lined Via Crucis (take Via al Sasso off Via Cappuccini).

❶ Getting There & Away

Locarno is well linked to Ticino and the rest of Switzerland via Bellinzona, or take the scenic **Centovalli Express** (www.centovalli.ch) to Brig via Domodossola in Italy.

Lugano

POP 61,840

Ticino's lush, mountain-rimmed lake isn't its only liquid asset. Lugano is also the country's third-most-important banking centre. Suits aside, it's a vivacious city, with bars and pavement cafes huddling in the spaghetti maze of steep cobblestone streets that untangle at the edge of the lake and along the flowery promenade.

◉ Sights & Activities

The **Centro Storico** (Old Town) is a 10-minute walk downhill from the train station; take the stairs or the funicular (Sfr1.10).

Wander through the mostly porticoed lanes woven around the busy main square, **Piazza della Riforma** (which is even more lively when the Tuesday- and Friday-morning markets are held).

★ Cattedrale di San Lorenzo
CATHEDRAL

(St Lawrence Cathedral; Via San Lorenzo; ☉ 6.30am-6pm) Lugano's early-16th-century cathedral conceals some fine frescoes and ornate baroque statues behind its Renaissance facade. Out front are far-reaching views over the Old Town's jumble of terracotta rooftops to the lake and mountains.

Società Navigazione del Lago di Lugano
BOAT TOUR

(www.lakelugano.ch; Riva Vela 12; ☉ Apr-late Oct) A relaxed way to see the lake's highlights is on one of these cruises, including one-hour bay tours (Sfr27.40) and three-hour morning cruises. Visit the website for timetables.

🛏 Sleeping

Many hotels close for part of the winter.

Hotel & Hostel Montarina
HOTEL, HOSTEL €

(☎ 091 966 72 72; www.montarina.ch; Via Montarina 1; dm Sfr29, s Sfr82-92, d Sfr112-132; 🅿 🛜 🏊) Occupying a pastel-pink villa dating to 1860, this hotel/hostel duo extends a heartfelt welcome. Mosaic floors, high ceilings and wrought-iron balustrades are lingering traces of old-world grandeur. There's a shared kitchen-lounge, toys to amuse the kids, a swimming pool set in palm-dotted gardens and even a tiny vineyard. Breakfast costs an extra Sfr15.

★ Guesthouse Castagnola
GUESTHOUSE €€

(☎ 078 632 67 47; www.gh-castagnola.com; Salita degli Olivi 2; apt Sfr120-180; 🅿 🛜) Kristina and Mauro bend over backwards to please at their B&B, lodged in a beautifully restored 16th-century town house. Exposed stone, natural fabrics and earthy colours dominate in apartments kitted out with Nespreso coffee machines and flat-screen TVs. A generous breakfast (Sfr10 extra) is served in the courtyard. Take bus 2 to Castagnola, 2km east of the centre.

✗ Eating

For pizza or pasta, try any of the places around Piazza della Riforma.

Bottega
dei Sapori   CAFE €
(Via Cattedrale 6; snacks & light meals Sfr9-14; ☺ 7.30am-7.30pm Mon-Wed, to 9pm Thu-Fri, 9am-7.30pm Sat) This high-ceilinged cafe-bar does great salads, panini (for instance with air-dried beef, goat's cheese and rocket) and coffee. The tiny terrace is always packed.

★ Bottegone
del Vino   ITALIAN €€
(☑ 091 922 76 89; Via Magatti 3; mains Sfr28-42; ☺ 11am-11pm Mon-Sat) Favoured by the lunchtime banking brigade, this place has a season-driven menu that might include specialities such as ravioli stuffed with fine Tuscan Chianina beef. Knowledgeable waiters fuss around the tables and are only too happy to suggest the perfect Ticino tipple.

❶ Getting There & Away

Lugano is on the main line connecting Milan to Zürich and Lucerne. Services from Lugano include Milan (Sfr17, 75 minutes), Zürich (Sfr64, 2¾ hours) and Lucerne (Sfr60, 2½ hours).

GRAUBÜNDEN

St Moritz

POP 5150

Switzerland's original winter wonderland and the cradle of alpine tourism, St Moritz (San Murezzan in Romansch) has been luring royals, celebrities and moneyed wannabes since 1864. With its shimmering aquamarine lake, emerald forests and aloof mountains, the town looks a million dollars.

✦ Activities

With 350km of slopes, ultramodern lifts and spirit-soaring views, skiing in St Moritz is second to none, especially for confident

intermediates. The general ski pass covers all the slopes.

If cross-country skiing is more your scene, you can glide across sunny plains and through snowy woods on 220km of groomed trails.

In summer the region has excellent hiking trails.

Schweizer Skischule   SKIING
(☑ 081 830 01 01; www.skischool.ch; Via Stredas 14; ☺ 8am-noon & 2-6pm Mon-Sat, 8-9am & 4-6pm Sun) The first Swiss ski school was founded in St Moritz in 1929. Today you can arrange skiing or snowboarding tuition for Sfr120/85 per day for adults/children here.

⬛ Sleeping & Eating

Jugendherberge
St Moritz   HOSTEL €
(☑ 081 836 61 11; www.youthhostel.ch/st.moritz; Via Surpunt 60; dm/s/d/q Sfr42.50/138/164/222; ☎) On the edge of the forest, this hostel has clean, quiet four-bed dorms and doubles. There's a kiosk, children's toy room, bike hire and laundrette. Bus 9 stops in front of the hostel in high season.

Chesa Spuondas   HOTEL €€
(☑ 081 833 65 88; www.chesaspuondas.ch; Via Somplaz 47; s/d/f incl half board Sfr155/282/318; P ☎) This family hotel nestles amid meadows at the foot of forest and mountains. Rooms are in keeping with the Jugendstil villa, with high ceilings, parquet floors and the odd antique. Kids are the centre of attention here, with dedicated meal times, activities, play areas and the children's ski school a 10-minute walk away. Bus 1 from St Moritz stops nearby.

Chesa Veglia   ITALIAN €€
(☑ 081 837 28 00; www.badruttspalace.com; Via Veglia 2; mains Sfr42-60, pizza Sfr23-36, menus Sfr45-70; ☺ noon-11.30pm) This slate-roofed, chalk-white chalet restaurant dates from 1658. The softly lit interior is all warm pine and creaking wood floors, while the terrace affords lake and mountain views. Go for pizza or regional specialities such as *Bündner Gerstensuppe* (creamy barley soup) and venison medallions with *Spätzli* (egg noodles).

❶ Getting There & Away

Regular hourly trains make the scenic run to/from the rail hub of Chur (Sfr40, two hours).

St Moritz is also an end point on the much-hyped Glacier Express (p648).

The Bernina Express (p661) provides seasonal links to Lugano from St Moritz, which include the stunning Unesco-recognised train line over the Bernina Pass to Tirano in Italy.

SURVIVAL GUIDE

ⓘ Directory A–Z

ACCOMMODATION

Switzerland sports traditional and creative accommodation in every price range. Many budget hotels have cheaper rooms with shared toilet and shower facilities. From there, truly, the sky is the limit. Breakfast buffets can be extensive and tasty but are not always included in room rates. Rates in cities and towns stay constant most of the year. In mountain resorts prices are seasonal (and can fall by 50% or more outside high season).

Low season Mid-September to mid-December, mid-April to mid-June

Mid-season January to mid-February, mid-June to early July, September

High season July to August, Christmas, mid-February to Easter

BUSINESS HOURS

The reviews in this guidebook won't list hours unless they differ from the hours listed here. Hours are given for the high season (April to October) and tend to decrease in the low season.

Banks 8.30am to 4.30pm Monday to Friday

Offices 8am to noon and 2pm to 5pm Monday to Friday

Restaurants noon to 2pm and 6pm to 10pm

COUNTRY FACTS

Area 41,285 sq km

Capital Bern

Country Code ☑ 41

Currency Swiss franc (Sfr)

Emergency ambulance ☑ 144, fire ☑ 118, police ☑ 117

Languages French, German, Italian, Romansch

Money ATMs readily available

Population 8.14 million

Visas Schengen rules apply

SLEEPING PRICE RANGES

The following price ranges refer to a double room with a private bathroom, except in hostels or where otherwise specified. Quoted rates are for the high season and include breakfast, unless otherwise noted:

€ less than Sfr170

€€ Sfr170 to Sfr350

€€€ more than Sfr350

Shops 9am to 7pm Monday to Friday (sometimes with a one- to two-hour break for lunch at noon in small towns), 9am to 6pm Saturday. In cities, there's often shopping until 9pm on Thursday or Friday. Sunday sees some souvenir shops and supermarkets at some train stations open.

DISCOUNT CARDS

Swiss Museum Pass (www.museumspass.ch; adult/family Sfr155/277) Regular or long-term visitors to Switzerland may want to buy this pass, which covers entry to 480 museums countrywide.

Visitors' Cards Many resorts and cities have a visitors' card *(Gästekarte)*, which provides benefits such as reduced prices for museums, pools, public transit or cable cars, plus free local public transport. Cards are issued by your accommodation.

ELECTRICITY

The electricity current is 220V, 50Hz. Swiss sockets are recessed, three holed, hexagonally shaped and incompatible with many plugs from abroad. However, they usually take the standard European two-pronged plug.

INTERNET ACCESS

Free wi-fi hot spots can be found at airports, dozens of Swiss train stations and in many hotels and cafes. Public wi-fi (provided by Swisscom) can cost Sfr5 for 30 minutes.

INTERNET RESOURCES

MySwitzerland (www.myswitzerland.com)
Swiss Info (www.swissinfo.ch)

MONEY

➜ Swiss francs are divided into 100 centimes *(Rappen* in German-speaking Switzerland). There are notes for 10, 20, 50, 100, 200 and 1000 francs, and coins for five, 10, 20 and 50 centimes, as well as for one, two and five francs. Euros are accepted by many tourism businesses.

ESSENTIAL FOOD & DRINK

⇒ **Fondue** Switzerland's best-known dish, in which melted Emmental and Gruyère cheese are combined with white wine in a large pot and eaten with small bread chunks.

⇒ **Raclette** Another popular artery-hardener of melted cheese served with potatoes.

⇒ **Rösti** German Switzerland's national dish of fried shredded potatoes is served with everything.

⇒ **Veal** Highly rated throughout the country; in Zürich, veal is thinly sliced and served in a cream sauce (*Gschnetzeltes Kalbsfleisch*).

⇒ **Bündnerfleisch** Dried beef, smoked and thinly sliced.

⇒ **Chocolate** Good at any time of day and available seemingly everywhere.

⇒ Exchange money at large train stations.

⇒ Tipping is not necessary, given that hotels, restaurants, bars and even some taxis are legally required to include a 15% service charge in bills. You can round up the bill after a meal for good service, as locals do.

PUBLIC HOLIDAYS

New Year's Day 1 January

Easter March/April (Good Friday, Easter Sunday and Monday)

Ascension Day 40th day after Easter

Whit Sunday & Monday Seventh week after Easter

National Day 1 August

Christmas Day 25 December

St Stephen's Day 26 December

TELEPHONE

⇒ The country code for Switzerland is ☏ 41. When calling Switzerland from abroad, drop the initial zero from the number; hence to call Bern, dial ☏ 41 31 (preceded by the overseas access code of the country you're dialling from).

⇒ The international access code from Switzerland is ☏ 00. To call Britain (country code 44), start by dialling ☏ 00 44.

⇒ Save money on the normal international tariff by buying a prepaid Swisscom card worth Sfr10, Sfr20, Sfr50 or Sfr100.

EATING PRICE RANGES

The following price ranges refer to the average cost of a main meal:

€ less than Sfr25

€€ Sfr25 to Sfr50

€€€ more than Sfr50

VISAS

For up-to-date details on visa requirements, go to www.eda.admin.ch.

Visas are not required for passport holders from the UK, the EU, Ireland, the USA, Canada, Australia, New Zealand, Norway and Iceland.

ⓘ Getting There & Away

AIR

The main international airports:

Aéroport International de Genève (GVA; www.gva.ch) Geneva airport is 4km from the town centre.

Zürich Airport (ZRH; ☏ 043 816 22 11; www.zurich-airport.com) The airport is 9km north of the centre, with flights to most European capitals as well as some in Africa, Asia and North America.

LAND

Bus

Eurolines (www.eurolines.com) has buses with connections across Western Europe.

Train

Switzerland is a hub of train connections to the rest of the Continent. Zürich is the busiest international terminus, with service to all neighbouring countries. Destinations include Münich (four hours), and Vienna (eight hours), from where there are extensive onward connections to cities in Eastern Europe.

⇒ Numerous TGV trains daily connect Paris to Geneva (three hours), Lausanne (3¾ hours), Basel (three hours) and Zürich (four hours).

⇒ Nearly all connections from Italy pass through Milan before branching off to Zürich, Lucerne, Bern or Lausanne.

⇒ Most connections from Germany pass through Zürich or Basel.

➜ Swiss Federal Railways accepts internet bookings but does not post tickets outside of Switzerland.

ⓘ Getting Around

Swiss public transport is an efficient, fully integrated and comprehensive system, which incorporates trains, buses, boats and funiculars.

Marketed as the Swiss Travel System, the network has a useful website, and excellent free maps covering the country are available at train stations and tourist offices.

PASSES & DISCOUNTS

Convenient discount passes make the Swiss transport system even more appealing. For extensive travel within Switzerland, the following national travel passes generally offer better savings than Eurail or InterRail passes.

Swiss Pass This entitles the holder to unlimited travel on almost every train, boat and bus service in the country, and on trams and buses in 41 towns, plus free entry to 400-odd museums. Reductions of 50% apply on funiculars, cable cars and private railways. Different passes are available, valid between four days (Sfr272) and one month (Sfr607).

Swiss Flexi Pass This pass allows you to nominate a certain number of days – from three (Sfr260) to six (Sfr414) – during one month when you can enjoy unlimited travel.

Half-Fare Card As the name suggests, you pay only half the fare on trains with this card (Sfr120 for one month), plus you get some discounts on local-network buses, trams and cable cars.

BICYCLE

➜ **Rent-a-Bike** (www.rentabike.ch) allows you to rent bikes at 80 train stations in Switzerland. For an Sfr8 surcharge you can collect from one station and return to another.

➜ **Suisseroule** (Schweizrollt; www.schweizrollt. ch) lets you borrow a bike for free or cheaply in places like Geneva, Bern and Zürich. Bike stations are usually next to the train station or central square.

➜ Local tourist offices often have good cycling information.

BOAT

Ferries and steamers link towns and cities on many lakes, including Geneva, Lucerne, Lugano and Zürich.

BUS

➜ Yellow **post buses** (www.postbus.ch) supplement the rail network, linking towns to difficult-to-access mountain regions.

➜ Services are regular, and departures (usually next to train stations) are linked to train schedules.

➜ Swiss national travel passes are valid.

➜ Purchase tickets on board; some scenic routes over the Alps (eg the Lugano–St Moritz run) require reservations.

CAR

➜ Headlights must be on at all times, and dipped in tunnels.

➜ The speed limit is 50km/h in towns, 80km/h on main roads outside towns, 100km/h on single-lane freeways and 120km/h on dual-lane freeways.

➜ Some minor alpine passes are closed from November to May – check with the local tourist offices before setting off.

TRAIN

The Swiss rail network combines state-run and private operations. The **Swiss Federal Railway** (www.sbb.ch) is abbreviated to SBB in German, CFF in French and FFS in Italian.

➜ All major train stations are connected to each other by hourly departures, at least between 6am and midnight.

➜ Second-class seats are perfectly acceptable, but cars are often close to full. First-class carriages are more comfortable and spacious and have fewer passengers.

➜ Ticket vending machines accept most major credit cards from around the world.

➜ The SBB smartphone app is an excellent resource and can be used to store your tickets electronically.

> ## CONNECTIONS
>
> Landlocked between France, Germany, Austria, Liechtenstein and Italy, Switzerland is well linked, especially by train. Formalities are minimal when entering Switzerland by air, rail or road thanks to the Schengen Agreement. Fast, well-maintained roads run from Switzerland through to all bordering countries; the Alps present a natural barrier, meaning main roads generally head through tunnels to enter Switzerland. Switzerland can be reached by steamer from several lakes: from Germany, arrive via Lake Constance and from France via Lake Geneva. You can also cruise down the Rhine to Basel.

SWITZERLAND'S SCENIC TRAINS

Swiss trains, buses and boats are more than a means of getting from A to B. Stunning views invariably make the journey itself the destination. Switzerland boasts the following routes among its classic sightseeing journeys.

You're able to choose just one leg of the trip. Also, scheduled services often ply the same routes for standard fares; these are cheaper than the named trains, which often have cars with extra-large windows and require reservations.

Bernina Express (www.rhb.ch) Cuts 145km through Engadine from Chur to Tirano in 2¼ hours. May and October, continue onwards from Tirano to Lugano by bus.

Glacier Express (www.glacierexpress.ch) Famous train journey between Zermatt and St Moritz. The Brig–Zermatt alpine leg makes for pretty powerful viewing, as does the area between Disentis/Mustér and Brig.

Jungfrau region You can spend days ogling stunning alpine scenery from the trains, cable cars and more here.

GoldenPass Line (www.goldenpass.ch) Travels between Lucerne and Montreux. The journey is in three legs, and you must change trains twice. Regular trains, without panoramic windows, work the whole route hourly.

Centovalli Express (www.centovalli.ch) An underappreciated gem of a line (two hours) that snakes along fantastic river gorges in Switzerland and Italy, from Locarno to Domodossola. Trains run through the day and it is easy to connect to Brig and beyond from Domodossola in Italy.

→ Check the SBB website for cheap Supersaver tickets on major routes.

→ Most stations have 24-hour lockers, usually accessible from 6am to midnight.

→ Seat reservations (Sfr5) are advisable for longer journeys, particularly in the high season.

Survival Guide

Directory A–Z

Accommodation

Where you stay in Western Europe may be one of the highlights of your trip. Quirky family-run inns, manic city hostels and low-key beach resorts are just some of the places where you'll make both new memories and, more than likely, new friends.

During peak holiday periods, accommodation can be hard to find, and it's advisable to book ahead.

B&Bs & Guesthouses

In Britain and Ireland, B&Bs – where you get bed and breakfast in a private home – can be real bargains.

Elsewhere, similar private accommodation – though often without breakfast – may go under the name of pension, guesthouse, *Gasthaus*, *Zimmerfrei*, *chambre d'hôte* and so on. Although the majority of guesthouses are simple affairs, there are more luxurious ones around.

Check that the place is centrally located and not in some dull and distant suburb.

Camping

Camping is immensely popular in Western Europe and provides the cheapest form of accommodation.

➡ There's usually a charge per tent or site, per person and per vehicle.

➡ National tourist offices often provide booklets or brochures listing camping grounds throughout their countries.

➡ In large cities, most camping grounds will be some distance from the centre of town. For this reason camping is most popular with people who have their own transport. If you're on foot, the money you save by camping can quickly be eaten up by the cost of commuting to and from a town centre.

➡ Many camping grounds rent bungalows or cottages accommodating two to eight people.

➡ Camping other than at designated camping grounds is difficult; you usually need permission from the local authorities (the police or local council office) or from the owner of the land.

➡ In some countries, such as Austria, France and Germany, free camping (aka wild camping) is illegal on all but private land; in Greece it's illegal altogether. Free camping is permissible anywhere in Scotland but not the rest of Britain.

Hostels

Hostels offer the cheapest (secure) roof over your head in Western Europe, and you generally don't have to be a youngster to use them.

HOSTELLING INTERNATIONAL

Most hostels are part of the national Youth Hostel Association (YHA), which is affiliated with **Hostelling International** (HI; www.hi hostels.com).

➡ The HI website has links to all the national organisations and you can use it to book beds or rooms in advance.

➡ You can join YHA or HI in advance or at the hostels. Members usually pay about 10% less on rates.

➡ At a hostel, you get a bed in a dorm or a private room plus the use of communal facilities, which often include a kitchen where you can prepare your own meals.

➡ Hostels vary widely in character, but increased competition from other

---

BOOK YOUR STAY ONLINE

For more accommodation reviews by Lonely Planet authors, check out http://lonelyplanet.com/hotels/. You'll find independent reviews, as well as recommendations on the best places to stay. Best of all, you can book online.

forms of accommodation – particularly the emergence of privately owned hostels – has prompted many places to improve their facilities and cut back on rules and regulations.

➡ The trend is moving toward smaller dormitories with just four to six beds. Single and double rooms with private bathrooms are common and it's not unusual to find entire families at hostels.

PRIVATE HOSTELS

There are many private hostelling organisations in Western Europe and hundreds of unaffiliated backpacker hostels. Private hostels have fewer rules (eg no curfew, no daytime lockout), more self-catering facilities and a much lower number of large, noisy school groups. They often also have a much more party-friendly vibe.

However, whereas HI hostels must meet minimum safety and cleanliness standards, private hostels do not, which means that facilities vary greatly. Dorms in some private hostels can be mixed gender. Most private hostels now have small dorm rooms of three to eight beds, and private singles and doubles.

Useful resources with booking engines:

Europe's Famous Hostels (www.famoushostels.com)

Hostel World (www.hostelworld.com)

Hostels.com (www.hostels.com)

Hostelz (www.hostelz.com)

Hotels

From fabulous five-star icons to workaday cheapies, the range of hotels in Western Europe is immense. You'll often find inexpensive hotels clustered around bus and train station areas, which are always good places to start hunting; but these can be charmless and scruffy. Look for moderately priced places

closer to the interesting parts of town.

Check whether breakfast is included (often it's not). Wi-fi is increasingly free.

In southern Europe in particular, hotel owners may be open to a little bargaining if times are slack.

Booking websites:

Booking.com (www.booking.com)

Direct Rooms (www.directrooms.com)

Hotel Club (www.hotelclub.com)

Hotel Info (www.hotel.info)

Hotels.com (www.hotels.com)

HRS (www.hrs.com)

LateRooms (www.laterooms.com)

Trivago (www.trivago.com)

Rental Accommodation

Rentals can be both advantageous and fun for families travelling together or for those staying in one place for a few nights. You can have your own chic Left Bank apartment in Paris or a villa in Tuscany with a pool – and often at cheaper rates than hotels.

All rentals should be equipped with kitchens (or at least a kitchenette), which can save on the food bill and allow you to browse the neighbourhood markets and shops, eating like the locals do. Some are a little more upmarket with laundry facilities and parking.

Beware direct-rental scams: unless you book through a reputable agency, your property might not actually exist. Scammers often compile fake apartment advertisements at too-good-to-be-true prices. Never send payment to an untraceable account via a money transfer.

Try **AirBnB** (www.airbnb.com) for thousands of locations in all price ranges across Western Europe. Rentals may be an entire

apartment, a room in someone else's apartment or just a sofa. They may be offered for one night, one week or even longer.

For other leads, try the following:

Holiday Havens (www.holidayhavens.co.uk)

Homelidays (www.homelidays.com)

Vacations-Abroad (www.vacations-abroad.com)

Vacation Rentals By Owner (www.vrbo.com)

Resorts

From foreboding Irish mansions to grand Swiss hotels, Western Europe has many fabled resorts, where travellers try to avoid ever checking out. Ask about deals and packages.

Activities

Europe offers countless opportunities to indulge in active pursuits. The varied geography and climate supports the full range of outdoor activities: boating, surfing and windsurfing, skiing and snowboarding, fishing, hiking, cycling and mountaineering.

Boating

Europe's many lakes, rivers and diverse coastlines offer a variety of boating options unmatched anywhere in the world. You can houseboat in France, kayak in Switzerland, charter a yacht in Greece, row on a peaceful Alpine lake, join a cruise along the Rhine, Main and Danube rivers from Amsterdam to Vienna (and beyond), rent a sailing boat on the French Riviera or dream away on a canal boat along the extraordinary canal network of Britain (or Ireland, or France) – the possibilities are endless.

Cycling

Along with hiking, cycling is ideal for getting up close to the scenery. It's also an ideal way to get around many cities and towns.

Popular cycling areas include the Belgian Ardennes, the west of Ireland, much of the Netherlands (the world's most bike-friendly nation), the coasts of Sardinia and Puglia in Italy, anywhere in the Alps (for those fit enough), and the south of France.

Check with your airline about taking bikes in the cargo hold. Alternatively, places to hire a bicycle are myriad.

Hiking

Keen hikers can spend a lifetime exploring Western Europe's trails. Popular routes feature places to stay, often far up on some breathtakingly gorgeous peak.

Highlights include:

The Alps Spanning Switzerland, Austria, Germany and Italy, with echoes of Heidi, bell-ringing dairy cows and trails organised with Swiss precision.

Pyrenees Follow trails through hills with Gallic-Iberian flavours.

Corsica and Sardinia Sun-drenched rugged beauty, with a Mediterranean view around every corner.

Northern Portugal A glass of port awaits after a day on the trail.

Connemara Prime hillwalking on the west coast of Ireland.

In the UK, **Ramblers** (www.ramblers.org.uk) is a nonprofit organisation that promotes long-distance walking and can help you with maps and information. The British-based **Ramblers Holidays** (www.ramblersholidays.co.uk) offers hiking-oriented trips in Europe and elsewhere.

For shorter day hikes, local tourist offices are usually excellent resources. Just ask.

Every country in Western Europe has national parks and other interesting areas or attractions that may qualify as a hiker's paradise, depending on your preferences. Guided hikes are often available.

Skiing & Snowboarding

In winter Europeans take to the pistes, flocking to hundreds of resorts in the Alps and Pyrenees for downhill skiing and snowboarding. Cross-country skiing is also very popular in some areas, such as around Switzerland's St Moritz.

Equipment hire (or even purchase) can be relatively cheap, and the hassle of bringing your own skis may not be worth it.

The ski season generally lasts from early December to late March, though at higher altitudes it may extend an extra month either side. Snow conditions can vary greatly from one year to the next and from region to region, but January and February tend to be the best (and busiest) months.

For comprehensive reports on ski conditions, try **OnTheSnow** (www.onthesnow.com).

Surfing & Windsurfing

Surfing hot spots include Ireland's west coast, France (especially around Biarritz), Spain (especially around San Sebastián) and Portugal. Gear rental and lessons are readily available.

Windsurfing is a European passion, practised most places there's water and sand (which is also a commentary on the breezy nature of Western European beaches). It's easy to rent sailboards in many tourist centres, and courses are usually available for beginners.

Children

Europe is the home of Little Red Riding Hood, Cinderella, King Arthur, Tintin et al, and is a great place to travel with kids. Successful travel with young children requires some careful planning and effort. Don't try to overdo things; even for adults, packing too much sightseeing into your schedule can be counterproductive.

Most car-hire firms in Western Europe have children's safety seats for hire at a nominal cost, but it's essential that you book them in advance. High chairs and cots (cribs) are available in many restaurants and hotels but numbers are often limited.

Customs Regulations

➡ Duty-free goods are not sold to those travelling from one EU country to another.

➡ For goods purchased at airports or on ferries *outside* the EU, the usual allowances apply for tobacco (200 cigarettes, 50 cigars or 250g of loose tobacco) – although some countries have reduced this to curb smoking – and alcohol (1L of spirits or 2L of liquor with less than 22% alcohol by volume; 4L of wine).

➡ The total value of other duty-free goods (perfume, electronic devices etc) cannot exceed €430 for air and sea travellers or €300 for other travellers.

Discount Cards

Camping Card International

The **Camping Card International** (CCI; www.campingcardinternational.com) is a camping-ground ID that can be used instead of a passport when checking into a camping ground and includes third-party insurance. Many camping grounds offer a small discount (usually 5% to 10%) if you sign in with one.

Senior Cards

Museums and various other sights and attractions (including public swimming pools and spas), as well as transport companies, frequently offer discounts to retired people, old-age pensioners and/or those aged over 60. Make sure you bring proof of age.

Student, Teacher & Youth Cards

The **International Student Travel Confederation** (ISTC; https://istc.wordpress.com) issues three cards for students, teachers and under-30s, offering thousands of worldwide |discounts on transport, museum entry, youth hostels and even some restaurants:

ISIC (International Student Identity Card)

ITIC (International Teacher Identity Card)

IYTC (International Youth Travel Card).

Issuing offices include **STA Travel** (www.statravel.com). Most places, however, will also accept regular student identity cards.

The **European Youth Card** (www.euro26.org) has scores of discounts for under 30s. You don't need to be an EU citizen.

Electricity

CONTINENTAL EUROPE

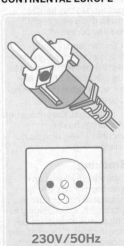

230V/50Hz

Most of Europe runs on 230V/50Hz AC (as opposed to, say, North America, where the electricity is 120V/60Hz AC). Chargers for phones, iPods and laptops *usually* can handle any type of electricity. If in doubt, read the tiny print.

BRITAIN & IRELAND

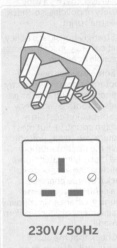

230V/50Hz

Embassies & Consulates

As a tourist, it is vitally important that you understand what your own embassy (the embassy of the country of which you are a citizen) can and cannot do. Generally speaking, embassies won't be much help in emergencies if the trouble you're in is even remotely your fault.

Remember that you are bound by the laws of the country that you are in. Your embassy will show little sympathy if you end up in jail after committing a crime locally, even if such actions are legal in your own country.

In genuine emergencies you might get some assistance, but only if other channels have been exhausted. For example, if you need to get home urgently, the embassy would expect you to

have insurance. If you have all your money and documents stolen, the embassy might assist with getting a new passport, but a loan for onward travel is almost always out of the question.

Locations

Embassies and consulates are located in Western European capitals and major cities.

You can find locations online at the following websites:

Australia (www.dfat.gov.au)

Canada (www.international.gc.ca)

New Zealand (www.mfat.govt.nz)

United Kingdom (www.gov.uk/fco)

United States (www.travel.state.gov)

Gay & Lesbian Travellers

In cosmopolitan centres in Western Europe you'll find very liberal attitudes toward homosexuality. Belgium, France, Luxembourg, the Netherlands, Spain and the UK (except Northern Ireland) have legalised same-sex marriages. Many other countries allow civil partnerships that grant all or most of the rights of marriage.

London, Paris, Berlin, Madrid, Lisbon and Amsterdam have thriving gay communities and pride events. The Greek islands of Mykonos and Lesvos are popular gay beach destinations.

Useful organisations:

Damron (http://damron.com) The USA's leading gay publisher offers guides to world cities.

International Lesbian and Gay Association (http://ilga.org) Campaigning group with some country-specific information on homosexual issues (not always up to date) and a conference calendar.

Spartacus International Gay Guide (www.spartacusworld.com) A male-only directory of gay entertainment venues and hotels in Europe and the rest of the world.

Health

It is unlikely that you will encounter unusual health problems in Western Europe, and if you do, standards of care are world-class. It's also vital to have health insurance for your trip.

Travelling tips:

➡ Bring medications in their original, clearly labelled containers.

➡ Keep a list of your prescriptions (photocopies/scans/photos of the containers are good) including generic names, so you can get replacements if your bags go on holiday – carry this info separately.

➡ If you have health problems that may need treatment, bring a signed and dated letter from your physician describing your medical conditions and medications.

➡ If carrying syringes or needles, have a physician's letter documenting their medical necessity.

➡ Carry a spare pair of contact lenses or glasses, and/or take your optical prescription with you.

Recommended Vaccinations

No jabs are necessary for Western Europe. However, the World Health Organization (WHO) recommends that all travellers should be covered for diphtheria, tetanus, measles, mumps, rubella and polio, regardless of their destination.

Insurance

It's foolhardy to travel without insurance to cover theft, loss and medical problems.

➡ Before you buy insurance, see what your existing

insurance covers, be it medical, home owner's or renter's. You may find that some aspects of travel in Western Europe are covered.

➡ If you're an EU citizen, the European Health Insurance Card (EHIC) covers you for most medical care.

➡ If you need to purchase coverage, there's a wide variety of policies, so check the small print.

➡ Strongly consider a policy that covers you for the worst possible scenario.

➡ Some policies pay doctors or hospitals directly (generally preferable, as it doesn't require you to pay out-of-pocket costs in a foreign country) but most require you to pay upfront, save the documentation and then claim later. Some policies also ask you to call back (reverse charges) to a centre in your home country, where an immediate assessment of your problem is made.

➡ Check that the policy covers ambulances or an emergency flight home.

Worldwide travel insurance is available at lonelyplanet.com/bookings. You can buy, extend and claim online any time – even if you're already on the road.

Internet Access

The number of internet cafes is plummeting. You'll still find them in tourist areas and around big train stations. Otherwise, you may end up at online gaming parlours. Libraries are another option. When in doubt, ask at a tourist office.

➡ Wi-fi (called WLAN in Germany) access is better the further north in Western Europe you go.

➡ Wi-fi is often free in hostels and midrange accommodation, while costing €20 or more at top-end hotels (though this is

finally improving, with more offering it for free).

➡ Internet access places may add a surcharge of €1 to €5 per hour for using Skype.

➡ Many destinations have free hot spots (sometimes time-limited); check with local tourist offices.

Legal Matters

Most Western European police are friendly and helpful, especially if you have been a victim of a crime. You are required by law to prove your identity if asked by police, so always carry your passport, or an identity card if you're an EU citizen.

Illegal Drugs

Narcotics are sometimes openly available in Europe, but that doesn't mean they're legal.

➡ The Netherlands is famed for its liberal attitudes, with 'coffeeshops' openly selling cannabis. However, even there it's a case of the police turning a blind eye. Possession of cannabis is decriminalised but not legalised (except for medicinal use). Don't take this relaxed attitude as an invitation to buy harder drugs; if you get caught, you'll be punished.

➡ Switzerland recently decriminalised marijuana use: the possession of up to 10g will incur a Sfr100 fine but won't result in a criminal record.

➡ In Portugal, the possession of all drugs has been decriminalised; however, selling is illegal.

Smoking

Cigarette-smoking bans have been progressively introduced across Europe. Although outdoor seating has long been a tradition at European cafes, it's gained new popularity given that most Western European countries have banned smoking in public places, including restaurants and bars. Occasionally in a few countries hotels still allow smoking in rooms so it's worth asking if you can get a nonsmoking room when reserving.

Money

For security and flexibility, diversify your source of funds. Carry an ATM card, credit card and cash.

ATMs

➜ Most countries in Western Europe have international ATMs allowing you to withdraw cash directly from your home account. This is the most common way European travellers access their money.

➜ Always have a backup option, however, as some travellers have reported glitches with ATMs in various countries, even when their card worked elsewhere across Western Europe. In some remote villages, ATMs might be scarce too.

➜ When you withdraw money from an ATM the amounts are converted and dispensed in local currency but there will be fees. Ask your bank for details.

➜ Don't forget your normal security procedures: cover the keypad when entering your PIN and make sure there are no unusual devices (which might copy your card's information) attached to the machine.

➜ If your card disappears and the screen goes blank before you've even entered your PIN, don't enter it – especially if a 'helpful' bystander tells you to do so. If you can't retrieve your card, call your bank's emergency number as soon as possible.

Cash

Nothing beats cash for convenience...or risk. If you lose it, it's gone forever and very few travel insurers will

---

EURO

The euro is the official currency used in 19 of the 28 EU states: Austria, Belgium, Cyprus, Estonia, Finland, France, Germany, Greece, the Republic of Ireland, Italy, Latvia, Lithuania, Luxembourg, Malta, the Netherlands, Portugal, Slovakia, Slovenia and Spain. Denmark, the UK, Switzerland and Sweden have held out against adopting the euro for political reasons.

The euro is divided into 100 cents and has the same value in all EU member countries. There are seven euro notes (€5, €10, €20, €50, €100, €200 and €500) and eight euro coins (€1 and €2, then €0.01, €0.02, €0.05, €0.10, €0.20 and €0.50). One side is standard for all euro coins and the other side bears a national emblem of participating countries.

---

come to your rescue. Those that do will limit the amount to somewhere around €300 or £200.

If flying into Western Europe from elsewhere, you'll find ATMs and currency exchanges in the arrivals area of the airport. There is no reason to get local currency before arriving in Western Europe, especially as exchange rates in your home country are likely to be abysmal.

Credit Cards

➜ Credit cards are often necessary for major purchases such as air or rail tickets, and offer a lifeline in certain emergencies.

➜ Visa and MasterCard are much more widely accepted in Europe than Amex and Diners Club.

➜ There are regional differences in the general acceptability of credit cards. In the UK, for example, you can usually flash your plastic in the most humble of budget restaurants; in Germany some restaurants don't take credit cards. Cards are not widely accepted off the beaten track.

➜ As with ATM cards, banks have loaded up credit cards with hidden charges for foreign purchases. Cash withdrawals on a credit card are almost always a much worse idea than using an

---

ATM card due to the fees and high interest rates. Plus, purchases in different currencies are likely to draw various conversion surcharges that are simply there to add to the bank's profit. These can run up to 5% or more. Check before leaving home.

International Transfers

In an emergency, it's quicker and easier to have money wired via **Western Union** (www.westernunion.com) or **MoneyGram** (www.money gram.com) but it can be quite costly.

Money Exchange

➜ In general, US dollars and UK pounds are the easiest currencies to exchange in Western Europe.

➜ Get rid of Scottish and Northern Ireland banknotes before leaving the UK; nobody outside it will touch them.

➜ Most airports, central train stations, big hotels and many border posts have banking facilities outside regular business hours, at times on a 24-hour basis.

➜ Post offices in Western Europe often perform banking tasks, tend to be open longer hours and

MINIMISING ATM CHARGES

When you withdraw cash from an ATM overseas there are several ways you can get hit. Firstly, most banks add a hidden 2.75% loading to what's called the 'Visa/MasterCard wholesale' or 'interbank' exchange rate. In short, they're giving you a worse exchange rate than strictly necessary. Additionally, some banks charge their customers a cash-withdrawal fee (usually 2% with a minimum €2 or more). If you're really unlucky, the bank at the foreign end might charge you as well. Triple whammy. If you use a credit card in ATMs you'll also pay interest – usually quite high – on the cash withdrawn.

If your bank levies fees, then making larger, less frequent withdrawals is better. It's also worth seeing if your bank has reciprocal agreements with banks where you are going that minimise ATM fees.

outnumber banks in remote places.

➜ The best exchange rates are usually at banks. *Bureaux de change* usually – but not always – offer worse rates or charge higher commissions. Hotels are almost always the worst places to change money.

Taxes & Refunds

Sales tax applies to many goods and services in Western Europe (although the amount – 10% to 25% – is already built into the price of the item). When non-EU residents spend more than a certain amount (about €75) they can usually reclaim that tax when leaving the country.

Making a tax-back claim is straightforward:

➜ Make sure the shop offers duty-free sales (often a sign will be displayed reading 'Tax-Free Shopping').

➜ When making your purchase ask the shop attendant for a tax-refund voucher, filled in with the correct amount and the date.

➜ The voucher can be used to claim a refund directly at international airports (beware, however, of very long lines), or be stamped at ferry ports or border crossings and mailed back for a refund.

EU residents aren't eligible for this scheme. Even an American citizen living in London is not entitled to a rebate on items bought in Paris. Conversely, an EU-passport holder living in New York is.

Tipping

Adding another 5% to 10% to a bill at a restaurant or cafe for good service is common across Western Europe, although tipping is never expected.

Travellers Cheques

Travellers cheques are rarely used.

Travel Money Cards

In recent years prepaid cards – also called travel money cards, prepaid currency cards or cash passport cards – have become a popular way of carrying money.

These enable you to load a card with as much foreign currency as you want to spend. You then use it to withdraw cash at ATMs – the money comes off the card and not out of your account – or to make direct purchases in the same way you would with a Visa or MasterCard. You can reload it via telephone or online.

One source of travel money cards is **Travelex** (www.travelex.com).

Advantages of a prepaid card:

➜ You avoid foreign-exchange fees as the money you put on the card is converted into foreign currency at the moment you load it.

➜ You can control your outlay by only loading as much as you want to spend.

➜ Security: if it's stolen your losses are limited to the balance on the card as it's not directly linked to your bank account.

➜ Lower ATM-withdrawal fees.

➜ Americans and others who carry credit cards without embedded chips (or whose chip-and-PIN cards don't work in Europe) can use these cards (which have chips and PINs) for the many European purchases that require such cards. Train-ticket-vending machines in the Netherlands are an example.

Against these you'll need to weigh the costs:

➜ Fees are charged for buying the card and then every time you load it. ATM withdrawal fees also apply.

➜ You might also be charged a fee if you don't use the card for a certain period of time or to redeem any unused currency.

➜ If the card has an expiry date, you'll forfeit any money loaded onto the card after that date.

Safe Travel

On the whole, you should experience few problems travelling in Western Europe – even alone – as the region is well developed and relatively safe. But do exercise common sense. Work out how friends and relatives at home can contact you in case of an emergency and keep in touch.

Leave a record (ie a photocopy) of your passport, credit and ATM cards and other important documents in a safe place. You can scan your documents and credit cards and post the file somewhere safe online, perhaps by emailing it to yourself. This gives you access from anywhere and saves you from having both the originals and copies lost. If things are stolen or lost, replacement is much easier when you have the vital details available.

Scams
Be aware of shopkeepers in touristy places who may short-change you. The same applies to taxi drivers. Never buy tickets other than from official vendors – they may turn out to be counterfeit.

Theft
Watch out for theft in Western Europe, including theft by other travellers. The most important things to secure are your passport, documents (such as a driving licence), tickets and money, in that order.

➡ Protect yourself from 'snatch thieves' who go for cameras and shoulder bags. They sometimes operate from motorcycles or scooters and expertly slash the strap before you have a chance to react. A small day pack is better, but watch your rear.

➡ At cafes and bars, loop the strap of your bag around your leg while seated. A jacket or bag left on the back of a chair is an invitation for theft.

➡ Pickpockets come up with endlessly creative diversions to distract you: tying friendship bracelets on your wrist, peddling trinkets,

pretending to 'find' a gold ring on the ground that they've conveniently placed there, posing as beggars or charity workers, or as tourists wanting you to take their photograph...ignore them.

➡ Beware of gangs of kids – whether dishevelled or well dressed – demanding attention, who may be trying to pickpocket you or overtly rob you.

➡ Pickpockets are most active in dense crowds, especially in busy train stations and on public transport during peak hours.

Telephone
Hotel phones notoriously have outrageous rates and hidden charges.

Mobile Phones
Travellers can easily purchase prepaid mobile phones (from £20/€30) or SIM cards (from £5/€10). GSM phones can be used throughout all countries in Western Europe. Mobile shops are everywhere.

You can bring your mobile phone from home and buy a local SIM card to enjoy cheap local calling rates if it is both unlocked and compatible with European GSM networks. Check first.

A great option is a **Toggle** (www.togglemobile.co.uk) multicountry SIM card. It allows you to have up to nine numbers in countries across much of Europe, allowing calls, text and data at local rates, plus you receive free incoming calls in some 20 countries. Purchase SIMs online or at certain phone

shops; topping up online is easy.

If you plan to use your mobile phone from home:

➡ Check international roaming rates in advance; often they are very expensive.

➡ Check roaming fees for data/internet usage; smartphone users can get socked with huge fees. You may be able to buy a data package to limit your costs.

Time
Greenwich Mean Time (UTC) Britain, Ireland, Portugal, Canary Islands (Spain).

Central European Time (GMT/ UTC + one hour) Austria, Belgium, France, Germany, Italy, Luxembourg, the Netherlands, Spain (except Canary Islands), Switzerland.

Eastern European Time (GMT/ UTC + two hours) Greece.

Daylight Saving Time/Summer Time Last Sunday in March to the last Sunday in October.

Tourist Information
Tourist offices in Western Europe are common and almost universally helpful. They can find accommodation, issue maps, advise on sights, activities, nightlife and entertainment while you're visiting, and help with more obscure queries such as where to find laundry facilities.

Visas
Most travellers will have very little to do with visas. While border procedures between EU and non-EU countries can still be thorough, citizens of Australia, Canada, Japan, New Zealand and the USA don't need visas for tourist visits to the UK, Ireland or any Schengen country. With a valid passport you should be able to visit Western

European countries for up to 90 days in a six-month period, provided you have some sort of onward or return ticket and/or 'sufficient means of support' (ie money).

For those who do require visas, it's important to remember that these will have a 'use-by' date, and you'll be refused entry after that period has elapsed. It may not be checked when entering these countries overland, but major problems can arise if it is requested during your stay or on departure and you can't produce it.

Schengen Visa Rules

As per the Schengen Agreement, there are no passport controls at borders between the following countries:

→ Austria

→ Belgium

→ Czech Republic

→ Denmark

→ Estonia

→ Finland

→ France

→ Germany

→ Greece

→ Hungary

→ Iceland

→ Italy

→ Latvia

→ Liechtenstein

→ Lithuania

→ Luxembourg

→ Malta

→ The Netherlands

→ Norway

→ Poland

→ Portugal

→ Slovakia

→ Slovenia

→ Spain

→ Sweden

→ Switzerland

New EU members Bulgaria, Croatia, Cyprus and Romania are required to join the Schengen zone (expected by 2016).

Note that Ireland and the UK are outside the Schengen zone; they are part of the separate Common Travel Area border controls (along with the Bailiwick of Guernsey, Bailiwick of Jersey and Isle of Man).

Weights & Measures

The metric system is used throughout Western Europe. In the UK, however, non-metric equivalents are common (distances continue to be given in miles and beer is sold in pints, not litres).

Transport

GETTING THERE & AWAY

The beginning of the adventure is deciding how to get to Western Europe, and in these days of cut-throat competition among airlines there are plenty of opportunities to find cheap tickets to a variety of gateway cities.

Flights, cars and tours can be booked online at lonelyplanet.com.

Air

Western Europe is well served by just about every major airline in the world.

Land

You can easily get to Western Europe from the rest of Europe by road, bus or train. The further away you're coming from, however, the more complicated it can be.

Train

It's possible to get to Western Europe by train from central and eastern Asia, but count on spending at least eight days doing it.

Four different train lines wind their way to Moscow: the Trans-Siberian (9259km from Vladivostok), the Trans-Mongolian (7621km from Beijing) and the Trans-Manchurian (8986km from Beijing) all use the same tracks across Siberia but have different routes east of Lake Baikal, while the Trans-Kazakhstan (another Trans-Siberian line) runs between Moscow and Ürümqi in northwestern China. Prices vary enormously depending on where you buy the ticket and what's included – advertised 2nd-class fares cost about €720/£555 from Beijing to Moscow.

There are many travel options between Western Europe and Moscow as well as other Eastern European countries. Poland, the Czech Republic and Hungary all have myriad rail links.

There are also rail links between Germany and Denmark with connections to other Scandinavian countries.

Sea

Ferries

Numerous ferries cross the Mediterranean between Western Europe and Africa. Options include Spain–Morocco, France–Morocco, France–Tunisia and Italy–Tunisia. There are also ferries between Greece and Israel via Cyprus. Ferries also serve Germany from all the Scandinavian countries.

The website www.ferrylines.com is a useful resource for researching ferry routes and operators.

Passenger Ships

Cruise ships have occasional transatlantic crossings. Cunard's **Queen Mary 2** (www.cunard.com) sails between

---

CLIMATE CHANGE & TRAVEL

Every form of transport that relies on carbon-based fuel generates CO_2, the main cause of human-induced climate change. Modern travel is dependent on aeroplanes, which might use less fuel per kilometre per person than most cars but travel much greater distances. The altitude at which aircraft emit gases (including CO_2) and particles also contributes to their climate change impact. Many websites offer 'carbon calculators' that allow people to estimate the carbon emissions generated by their journey and, for those who wish to do so, to offset the impact of the greenhouse gases emitted with contributions to portfolios of climate-friendly initiatives throughout the world. Lonely Planet offsets the carbon footprint of all staff and author travel.

New York, USA and South-ampton, England several times a year; the trip takes eight nights from New York to Southampton (US$3598) and seven nights from Southampton to New York (US$3098) for two people in a standard double cabin. Deals abound.

GETTING AROUND

Discount airlines are revo-lutionising the way people cover long distances within Europe. However, hopping on a plane deprives you of the fun of travelling by train and the cultural experiences of navigating train stations. Trains can sometimes work out to be quicker, taking you directly between city centres rather than further-flung airports, and are better for the environment.

Air

Dozens of tiny airports across Europe now have airline services. For instance, a trip to Italy doesn't mean choosing between Milan and Rome, but rather scores of airports up and down the 'boot'.

It's possible to put togeth-er a practical itinerary that might bounce from London to the south of Spain to Italy to Amsterdam in a two-week period, all at an affordable price and avoiding long train rides.

Airlines in Western Europe

Although many people first think of budget airlines when they consider a cheap ticket in Western Europe, you should compare all car-riers, including established ones like British Airways and Lufthansa, which serve major airports close to main destinations. Deals crop up frequently.

DISCOUNT AIRLINES

With cheap fares come many caveats.

➡ Some of the bare-bones airlines are just that – expect nonreclining seats, nonexistent legroom and nonexistent window shades.

➡ Baggage allowances are often minimal and extra baggage charges can be costly.

➡ At some small airports, customer service may be nonexistent.

➡ Convenience can be deceptive. If you really want to go to Carcassonne in the south of France, then getting a bargain-priced ticket from London will be a dream come true. But if you want to go to Frankfurt in Germany and buy a ticket to 'Frankfurt-Hahn', you will find yourself at a tiny airport 120km west of Frankfurt and almost two hours away by bus.

➡ Beware of discount airline websites showing nonstop flights that are actually connections.

Many airlines only sell their cheapest tickets online. Various websites compare fares across a range of air-lines within Europe, including the following:

CheapOair (www.cheapoair.com)

Kayak (www.kayak.com)

Skyscanner (www.skyscanner.net)

Scores of smaller low-cost airlines serve Western Europe along with major budget airlines including the following:

Air Berlin (www.airberlin.com) Hubs in Germany; service across Europe.

easyJet (www.easyjet.com) Flies to major airports across Europe.

Germanwings (www.german wings.com) Hubs in Germany; service across Europe.

Ryanair (www.ryanair.com) Flies to scores of destina-tions across Europe, but con-firm your destination airport is not a deserted airfield out in the sticks.

Vueling (www.vueling.com) Serves a broad swath of Eu-rope from its Spanish hubs.

Bicycle

A tour of Western Europe by bike may seem like a daunt-ing prospect but it can be a fantastic way to travel. The UK-based **Cyclists' Touring Club** (www.ctc.org.uk) offers members an information service on all matters asso-ciated with cycling, including cycling conditions, detailed routes, itineraries and maps.

Wearing a helmet is not always compulsory but is advised. A seasoned cyclist can average about 80km a day, but this depends on the terrain and how much you are carrying.

The key to a successful cycling trip is to travel light. What you carry should be de-termined by your destination and the type of trip you're taking. Even for the most basic trip, it's worth carrying the tools necessary for re-pairing a puncture. Bicycle shops are found everywhere, but you still might want to pack the following if you don't want to rely on others:

➡ Allen keys
➡ spanners

➡ spare brake and gear cables

➡ spare spokes

➡ strong adhesive tape

Hire

It's easy to hire bicycles in Western Europe and you can often negotiate good deals. Rental periods vary. Local tourist offices, hostels and hotels will have information on rental outlets. Occasionally you can drop off the bicycle at a different location so you don't have to double back on your route.

Urban bike-share schemes, where you check out a bike from one stand and return it to another after brief use, have taken off in cities as huge as London and Paris.

Purchase

For major cycling tours it's best to have a bike you're familiar with, so consider bringing your own rather than buying one on arrival. If you can't be bothered with the hassle of transporting it, there are plenty of places to buy bikes in Western Europe (shops sell them new and secondhand).

Transporting a Bicycle

When flying with your own bicycle, check with the airline before you buy your ticket as each one has a different policy.

Within Western Europe, bikes can often be taken onto a train with you, subject to a small supplementary fee.

Boat

The main areas of ferry service for Western Europe travellers are between Ireland and the UK; Ireland and France; the UK and the Continent (especially France, but also Belgium, the Netherlands and Spain); and Italy and Greece.

Multiple ferry companies compete on the main ferry routes, and the resulting service is comprehensive but complicated.

➡ A ferry company can have a host of different prices for the same route, depending on the time of day or year, the validity of the ticket or the length of your vehicle.

➡ It's worth planning (and booking) ahead where possible as there may be special reductions on off-peak crossings and advance-purchase tickets.

➡ Most ferry companies adjust prices according to the level of demand (so-called 'fluid' or 'dynamic' pricing), so it may pay to offer alternative travel dates.

➡ Vehicle tickets generally include the driver and a full complement of passengers.

➡ You're usually denied access to your vehicle during the voyage.

➡ Rail-pass holders are entitled to discounts or free travel on some lines.

➡ Compare fares and routes using www.ferrysavers.com.

Bus

Buses are invariably cheaper but slower and much less comfortable than trains, and not as quick or sometimes as cheap as airlines.

Europe's largest network of international buses is provided by a consortium of bus companies that operates under the name **Eurolines** (www.eurolines.com). There are many services and it's possible to travel extensive distances for less than €100. Eurolines' various affiliates offer many national and regional bus passes.

Campervan

A popular way to tour Europe is to buy or rent a campervan.

Campervans usually feature a fixed high-top or elevating roof and two to five bunk beds. Apart from the essential gas cooker, professional conversions may include a sink, a fridge and built-in cupboards. Prices and facilities vary considerably and it's certainly worth getting advice from a mechanic to see if you are being offered a fair price. Getting a mechanical check (costing from £40) is also a good idea.

London is the usual embarkation point. Good British websites to check for campervan purchases and rentals include the following:

Auto Trader (www.autotrader.co.uk)

Loot (www.loot.com)

Worldwide Motorhome Hire (www.worldwide-motorhome-hire.com)

Car

Travelling with your own vehicle allows increased flexibility and the option to get off the beaten track. Unfortunately, cars can be problematic in city centres when you have to negotiate one-way streets or find somewhere to park amid a confusing concrete jungle and a welter of expensive parking options.

Remember to never leave valuables in the vehicle.

Automobile Associations

In the event of a breakdown, you can contact the local automobile association for emergency assistance if it has an agreement with the auto club in your home country (and if you're a member!). These associations can provide a variety of roadside services such as petrol refills, flat-tyre repair and towing, plus predeparture information such as maps and itineraries and even an accommodation reservation service. Check with the main automobile association in your home country for coverage options.

Driving Licences

Proof of ownership of a private vehicle should always be carried (a Vehicle Registration Document for British-registered cars). An EU driving licence is acceptable for driving throughout Europe.

Many non-European driving licences are valid in Europe.

An International Driving Permit (IDP) is technically required in addition to a current driving licence for foreign drivers in some Western European countries (in practice, it's rare you'll be asked for it). Your national auto club can advise if you'll need one for the itinerary you plan to take and can sell you this multilingual document.

Fuel

Fuel prices can vary enormously from country to country (though it's always more expensive than in North America or Australia) and may bear little relation to the general cost of living. For fuel prices across the EU, visit the **AA Ireland** (www.theaa.ie/AA/Motoring-advice/Petrol-Prices.aspx).

Unleaded petrol and diesel are available across Western Europe. To reduce pollution, Paris and London are planning to ban diesel vehicles from 2020.

Hire

It is straightforward to rent a vehicle:

➡ All major international rental companies operate in Western Europe and will give you reliable service and a good standard of vehicle.

➡ Usually you will have the option of returning the car to a different outlet at the end of the rental period.

➡ Rates vary widely, but expect to pay somewhere between €25 and €70 per day. Prebook for the lowest rates – if you walk into an office and ask for a car on the spot, you will pay much more.

➡ For really good deals, prepay for your rental. Fly/drive combinations and other programs are worth looking into.

➡ It's imperative to understand exactly what is included in your rental agreement (collision waiver, unlimited mileage etc). Make sure you are covered with an adequate insurance policy.

➡ Check whether mileage is unlimited or whether you'll be charged for additional kilometres beyond a particular threshold – extra mileage can quickly add up.

➡ Less than 4% of European cars have automatic transmissions. If you don't want to drive a manual (stick shift), you'll need to book much further ahead, and expect to pay more than double for the car.

➡ The minimum age to rent a vehicle is usually 21 or even 23, and you'll need a credit card.

➡ If you get a ticket from one of Europe's thousands of hidden speeding cameras, they will track you down through your rental company.

RENTAL BROKERS

Rental brokers (clearing houses) can be a lot cheaper than the major car-rental firms. Good companies to try include the following:

Auto Europe (www.autoeurope.com)

AutosAbroad (www.autosabroad.com)

Carrentals.co.uk (www.carrentals.co.uk)

Holiday Autos Car Hire (www.holidayautos.com)

Kemwel (www.kemwel.com)

Insurance

Third-party motor insurance is compulsory in Europe if you are driving your own car (rental cars usually come with insurance). Most UK motor-insurance policies automatically provide this for EU countries. Get your insurer to issue a Green Card (which may cost extra), which is an internationally recognised proof of insurance, and check that it lists all the countries you intend to visit.

It's a good investment to take out a European motoring-assistance policy, such as the **AA** (www.theaa.com) Five Star Service or the **RAC** (www.rac.co.uk) European Motoring Assistance. Expect to pay about £50 for 14 days' cover, with a 10% discount for association members.

Non-Europeans might find it cheaper to arrange international coverage with their national motoring organisation before leaving home. Ask your motoring organisation for details about free services offered by affiliated organisations around Western Europe.

Every vehicle travelling across an international border should display a sticker (or number/licence plate) showing its country of registration. Car-rental/hire agencies usually ensure cars are properly equipped; if in doubt, ask.

Purchase

Britain is probably the best place to buy a vehicle as secondhand prices are good. Also, whether buying privately or from a dealer, if you're an English-speaker, the absence of language difficulties will help you establish what you are getting and what guarantees you can expect in the event of a breakdown.

Bear in mind that you will be getting a car with the steering wheel on the right-hand side in Britain, whereas in continental Europe the steering wheel is on the left.

If you're driving a right-hand-drive car, by law you'll need adjust your headlamps to avoid blinding oncoming traffic.

Leasing

Leasing a vehicle involves fewer hassles and can work out much cheaper than hiring for longer than 17 days. This program is limited to certain new cars, including **Renault** (www.renault-euro drive.com) and **Peugeot** (www.peugeot-openeurope. com), but you save money because short-term leasing is exempt from VAT, and inclusive insurance plans are cheaper than daily insurance rates.

Leasing is also open to people as young as 18 years old. To lease a vehicle your permanent address must be outside the EU. The maximum lease is five-and-a-half months; it's possible to pick up the vehicle in one country and return it in another. Leases include all on-road taxes as well as theft and collision insurance.

Road Conditions

Conditions and types of roads vary across Western Europe, but it is possible to make some generalisations.

➡ The fastest routes are four- or six-lane dual carriageways/highways, ie two or three lanes either side (motorway, autobahn, autoroute, autostrada etc).

➡ Motorways and other primary routes are great for speed and comfort but driving can be dull, with little or no interesting scenery.

➡ Some fast routes incur expensive tolls (eg in Italy, France and Spain) or have a general tax for usage (Switzerland and Austria), but there will usually be an alternative route you can take.

➡ Motorways and other primary routes are almost always in good condition.

➡ Road surfaces on minor routes are not perfect in some countries (eg Greece), although normally they will be more than adequate.

➡ Minor roads are narrower and progress is generally much slower. To compensate, you can expect much better scenery and plenty of interesting villages along the way.

Road Rules

Automobile associations can supply members with country-by-country information about motoring regulations.

➡ With the exception of Britain and Ireland, driving is on the right-hand side of the road.

➡ Take care with speed limits, as they vary from country to country.

➡ You may be surprised at the apparent disregard of traffic regulations in some places (particularly in Italy and Greece), but as a visitor it is always best to be cautious.

➡ In many countries, driving infringements are subject to an on-the-spot fine; always ask for a receipt.

➡ European drink-driving laws are particularly strict. The blood-alcohol concentration (BAC) limit when driving is generally 0.05% but in certain cases it can be as low as 0%.

➡ Some countries require compulsory in-car equipment, such as a portable breathalyser, warning triangle and fluorescent vest. These are supplied by rental companies, but you'll need to have them if you're driving your own vehicle.

Hitching

Hitching is never entirely safe in any country and we don't recommend it. Travellers who decide to hitch should understand they are taking a small but potentially serious risk. If you want to try it, it's important to remember the following:

➡ Hitch in pairs; it will be safer.

➡ Solo women should never hitch.

➡ Don't hitch from city centres; take public transport to suburban exit routes.

➡ Hitching is usually illegal on motorways – stand on the slip roads or approach drivers at petrol stations and truck stops.

➡ Look presentable and cheerful, and make a cardboard sign indicating your intended destination in the local language.

➡ Never hitch where drivers can't stop in good time or without causing an obstruction.

➡ At dusk, give up and think about finding somewhere to stay.

➡ It is sometimes possible to arrange a lift in advance: scan student noticeboards in colleges or contact car-sharing agencies. Such agencies are particularly popular in Germany where they're called *Mitfahrzentrale*. Visit www. mitfahrzentrale.de.

Motorcycle

With its good-quality winding roads, stunning scenery and an active motorcycling scene, Western Europe is ideal for motorcycle touring.

➡ The weather is not always reliable, so make sure your wet-weather gear is up to scratch.

➡ Helmets are compulsory for riders and passengers everywhere in Western Europe.

➡ On ferries, motorcyclists can sometimes be squeezed on board without a reservation, although booking ahead is advisable during peak travelling periods.

➡ Take note of local customs about parking motorcycles

on footpaths. Although this is illegal in some countries, the police often turn a blind eye as long as the vehicle doesn't obstruct pedestrians. Don't try this in Britain – excuses to traffic wardens will fall on deaf ears.

➡ If you're thinking of touring Europe on a motorcycle, contact the **British Motorcyclists Federation** (www.bmf.co.uk) for help and advice.

➡ Motorcycle and moped rental is easy in countries such as Italy, Spain and Greece and in the south of France. In tourist areas just ask around for nearby rental agencies.

Local Transport

Most Western European cities have excellent public-transport systems, which comprise some combination of metros (subways), trains, trams and buses. Service is usually comprehensive. Major airports generally have fast-train or metro links to the city centre.

Taxi

Taxis in Western Europe are metered and rates are generally high. There might also be supplements (depending on the country) for things such as luggage, the time of day, the location at which you boarded and for extra passengers.

Good public transport networks make the use of taxis almost unnecessary, but if you need one in a hurry they can usually be found idling near train stations or outside big hotels. Spain, Greece and Portugal have lower fares, which makes taking a taxi more viable.

Don't underestimate the local knowledge that can be gleaned from taxi drivers. They can often tell you about the liveliest places in town

and know all about events happening during your stay.

Tours

Package tours – whether standard or tailor-made – cater for all tastes, interests and ages. Try searching online for your own interest (eg walking) with 'Europe tour' and see what you get.

Many people have had memorable trips on tours organised by cultural institutions like the USA's **Smithsonian Institution** (www.smithsonianjourneys. org), which run tours lead by experts in fields such as art.

Train

Trains are an ideal way of getting around: they are comfortable, frequent and generally on time. The Channel Tunnel makes it possible to get from Britain to continental Europe using **Eurostar** (www.eurostar.com).

These days, Western Europe's fast, modern trains are like much-more-comfortable versions of planes. Dining cars have mostly been replaced by snack bars or trolleys, although most people buy food before boarding.

Information

Every national railway has a website with a vast amount of schedule and fare information.

➡ Major national railway companies' smartphone apps are excellent for checking schedules. Many can be used to store tickets bought online. Instead of having to print electronic tickets, the conductor can scan your phone's screen.

➡ **DB Bahn** (www.bahn.de) provides excellent schedule and fare information in English for trains across Europe.

➡ **Man In Seat Sixty-One** (www.seat61.com) has invaluable train descriptions and comprehensive practical details of journeys to the far reaches of the continent.

➡ If you plan to travel extensively by train, the **European Rail Timetable** (www.europeantimetable. eu), issued by Thomas Cook for 140 years and now produced independently, gives a condensed listing of train schedules that indicate where extra fees apply or where reservations are necessary. The timetable is updated monthly and is available online and

EURAIL & HIGH-SPEED TRAINS

Eurail likes to promote the 'hop on/hop off any train' aspect of their passes. But when it comes to the most desirable high-speed trains this is not always the case. Many require a seat reservation and the catch is that these are not always available to pass holders on all trains.

In addition, some of the high-speed services require a fairly hefty surcharge from pass users. For example, Thalys trains from Brussels to Amsterdam levy a 1st/2nd-class surcharge of €62/39; German InterCity Express (ICE) trains from Paris to Munich levy a surcharge of €30/13; Spanish Alta Velocidad Española (AVE) trains from Madrid to Seville levy a surcharge of €23.50/10.

On some high-speed routes it may work out cheaper to buy a separate ticket rather than use your pass, especially if you can find a discount fare.

DISCOUNT TRAIN TICKETS ONLINE

Many railways offer cheap ticket deals through their websites. It's always worth checking online for sales including advance-purchase reductions, one-off promotions and special circular-route tickets.

How you actually receive the discount train tickets you've purchased online varies. Common methods include the following:

➡ The ticket is sent to the passenger either as an email or as a stored graphic on an app from the train company (increasingly widespread).

➡ A reservation number is issued with the reservation which you use at a station ticket-vending machine (some UK lines).

➡ The credit card you used to purchase the tickets can be used to retrieve them at a station ticket-vending machine (in some cases, nonlocal credit-card holders must retrieve their tickets at a ticket window).

➡ If nonlocal credit cards aren't accepted online and you can't buy the discounted fares at the station (the Netherlands), purchase them online from **SNCB Europe** (www.b-europe.com) instead.

---

at selected European bookshops.

Tickets

Normal international tickets are valid for two months and you can make as many stops as you like en route. Used this way, a ticket from Paris to Vienna, for example, can serve as a mini–rail pass, as long as you stay on the route shown on the ticket.

High-Speed Trains

High-speed networks (300km/h or more) continue to expand and have given the airlines major competition on many routes.

Sample travel times:

ROUTE	DURATION
Amsterdam–Paris	3hr
Barcelona–Madrid	2¾hr
Brussels–Cologne	1¾hr
London–Paris	2¼hr
Milan–Rome	3hr
Nuremberg–Munich	1hr
Paris–Frankfurt	4hr
Paris–Marseille	3hr
Zürich–Milan	4hr

Major high-speed trains that cross borders include the following:

Eurostar (www.eurostar.com) Links beautiful St Pancras station in London to Brussels and Paris in about two hours; direct services also include London to Marseille via Lyon and Avignon. From December 2016, direct Eurostar services will link London with Amsterdam via Brussels, Antwerp, Rotterdam and Schiphol airport.

InterCity Express (ICE; www.bahn.de) The fast trains of the German railways span the country and extend to Paris, Brussels, Amsterdam, Vienna and Switzerland.

TGV (www.sncf.com) The legendary fast trains of France reach Belgium, Luxembourg, Germany, Switzerland and Italy.

Thalys (www.thalys.com) Links Paris with Brussels, Amsterdam and Cologne.

Other Trains

It does bear reiterating: you'll have a splendid holiday in Western Europe if you rely entirely on the convenient, comfortable trains.

NIGHT TRAINS

The romantic image of the European night train is becoming a lot less common with the popularity of budget airlines; however, you can still find a good network of routes from the north to Italy.

Types of accommodation:

Couchette Bunks that are comfortable enough, if lacking a bit in privacy. There are four per compartment in 1st class or six in 2nd class. A 1st-/2nd-class bunk costs about €31/21 for most international trains, in addition to the ticket, irrespective of the length of the journey.

Sleepers The most comfortable option, offering beds for one or two passengers in 1st class, and two or three passengers in 2nd class. Charges vary depending on the journey, but they are significantly more expensive than couchettes. Expect to pay at least €110 per person in addition to the fare.

Besides the national railways, you can try the following:

Caledonian Sleeper (www.scotrail.co.uk) Links London overnight with Scotland (as far north as Inverness and Aberdeen).

City Night Line (www.citynightline.de) Operates night trains from Germany and the Netherlands south through Switzerland and Austria into Italy as well as France. Trains also travel north to Scandinavia.

Thello (www.thello.com) Runs services between Paris and Italy, including Rome.

EXPRESS TRAINS

Slower but still reasonably fast express trains that cross borders are often called EuroCity (EC) or InterCity (IC). Reaching speeds of up to 200km/h or more, they are comfortable and frequent. A good example is Austria's RailJet service, which reaches Munich and Zurich.

Reservations

At weekends and during holidays and summer, it's a good idea to reserve seats on trains (which costs about €3 to €5). Standing at the end of the car for five hours is not what holiday dreams are made of, especially if you're travelling with kids or have reduced mobility. Some discounted tickets bought online may include an assigned seat on a train, but most regular tickets are good for any train on the route.

You can usually reserve ahead of time using a ticket machine at stations or at a ticket window. On many high-speed trains – such as France's TGVs – reservations are mandatory.

Pass-holders should note that reservations are a good idea for the same reasons. Just because your pricey pass lets you hop on/hop off at will, there's no guarantee that you'll have a seat.

Train Passes

Think carefully about purchasing a rail pass. Check the national railways' websites and determine what it would cost to do your trip by buying the tickets separately. More often than not, you'll find that you'll spend less than if you buy a Eurail pass.

Shop around as pass prices can vary between different outlets. Once purchased, take care of your pass as it cannot be replaced or refunded if lost or stolen. Passes get reductions on the Eurostar through the Channel Tunnel and on certain ferry

routes (eg between France and Ireland). In the USA, **Rail Europe** (www.raileurope.com) sells a variety of rail passes, as does its UK equivalent **Voyages-sncf.com** (www. uk.voyages-sncf.com); note that individual train tickets tend to be more expensive than what you'll pay buying from railways online or in stations.

EURAIL

There are so many different **Eurail** (www.eurail.com) passes to choose from and such a wide variety of areas and time periods covered that you need to have a good idea of your itinerary before purchasing one. These passes can only be bought by residents of non-European countries and are supposed to be purchased before arriving in Europe. There are two options: one for adults and one for people aged under 26. The Adult Pass is valid in both 1st- and 2nd-class coaches; a 1st-class Youth Pass is valid in both 1st- and 2nd-class coaches but the

RAIL PASS RATES

Eurail Passes

AGE	CLASS	DURATION	PRICE (€)
12-25	2nd	1 month	598
12-25	2nd	15 days	379
over 26	1st/2nd	1 month	917
over 26	1st/2nd	15 days	580
12-25	2nd	10 days in 2 months	446
12-25	2nd	15 days in 2 months	583
over 26	1st/2nd	10 days in 2 months	682
over 26	1st/2nd	15 days in 2 months	894

InterRail Passes

AGE	CLASS	DURATION	PRICE (€)
12-25	2nd	5 days in 10 days	163
12-25	2nd	10 days in 22 days	239
12-25	2nd	1 month	392
over 26	1st	5 days in 10 days	351
over 26	1st	10 days in 22 days	500
over 26	1st	1 month	836

2nd-class Youth Pass is only for 2nd-class coaches.

Eurail passes are valid for unlimited travel on national railways and some private lines in the Western European countries of Austria, Belgium, France, Germany, Greece, Ireland, Italy, Luxembourg, the Netherlands, Portugal, Spain and Switzerland (including Liechtenstein), plus several more neighbouring ones. They are also valid on some ferries between Italy and Greece. Reductions are given on some other ferry routes and on river/lake steamer services in various countries and on the Eurostar to/from the UK.

The UK is *not* covered by Eurail – it has its own Britrail pass.

Pass types include the following:

Eurail Global All the European countries (despite the much grander-sounding name) for a set number of consecutive days.

Eurail Saver Two to five people travelling together as a group for the entire trip can save about 15% on various pass types.

Eurail Selectpass Buyers choose which neighbouring countries it covers and for how long. Options are myriad and can offer significant savings over the other passes if, for example, you are only going to three or four countries. Use the Eurail website to calculate these.

INTERRAIL

The **InterRail** (www.interrail. eu) pass is available to European residents of more than six months' standing (passport identification is required), as well as citizens of Russia and Turkey. Terms and conditions vary slightly from country to country, but in the country of origin there is a discount of around 30% to 50% on the normal fares. The pass covers 30 countries.

InterRail passes are generally cheaper than Eurail, but most high-speed trains require that you also buy a seat reservation and pay a supplement of €3 to €40 depending on the route.

InterRail passes are also available for individual countries. Compare these to passes offered by the national railways.

NATIONAL RAIL PASSES

If you're intending to travel extensively within one country, check what national rail passes are available as these can sometimes save you a lot of money. In a large country such as Germany where you might be covering long distances, a pass can make sense, whereas in a small country such as the Netherlands it won't.

Language

This chapter offers basic vocabulary to help you get around Western Europe. If you read our coloured pronunciation guides as if they were English, you'll be understood.

Note that, in our pronunciation guides, the stressed syllables are indicated with italics. The abbreviations 'm' and 'f' indicate masculine and feminine gender respectively.

DUTCH

Dutch is spoken in The Netherlands and the northern part of Belgium (Flanders).

Vowels in Dutch can be long or short. Note that ew is pronounced as 'ee' with rounded lips, oh as the 'o' in 'note', uh as the 'a' in 'ago', and kh as the 'ch' in the Scottish *loch* (harsh and throaty).

Hello.	*Dag.*	dakh
Goodbye.	*Dag.*	dakh
Please.	*Alstublieft.*	al·stew·*bleeft*
Thank you.	*Dank u.*	dangk ew
Excuse me.	*Pardon.*	par·*don*
Sorry.	*Sorry.*	so·ree
Yes./No.	*Ja./Nee.*	yaa/ney
Help!	*Help!*	help
Cheers!	*Proost!*	prohst

Do you speak English?
Spreekt u Engels? spreykt ew *eng*·uhls

I don't understand.
Ik begrijp het niet. ik buh·*khreyp* huht neet

WANT MORE?

For in-depth language information and handy phrases, check out Lonely Planet's *Western Europe Phrasebook*. You'll find it at shop.lonelyplanet.com, or you can buy Lonely Planet's iPhone phrasebooks at the Apple App Store.

How much is it?
Hoeveel kost het? hoo·*veyl* kost huht

Where's ...?
Waar is ...? waar is ...

Can you show me (on the map)?
Kunt u het kunt ew huht
aanwijzen *aan*·wey·zuhn
(op de kaart)? (op duh kaart)

I'm lost.
Ik ben de weg kwijt. ik ben duh wekh kweyt

I'm ill.
Ik ben ziek. ik ben zeek

Where are the toilets?
Waar zijn de toiletten? waar zeyn duh twa·*le*·tuhn

FRENCH

French is spoken in France, Switzerland, Luxembourg and the southern part of Belgium (Wallonia).

French has nasal vowels (pronounced as if you're trying to force the sound through your nose), which are indicated in our guides with o or u followed by an almost inaudible nasal consonant sound m, n or ng. Note also that air is pronounced as in 'fair', ew as ee with rounded lips, r is a throaty sound, and zh is pronounced as the 's' in 'pleasure'. Syllables in French words are, for the most part, equally stressed.

Hello.	*Bonjour.*	bon·zhoor
Goodbye.	*Au revoir.*	o·rer·vwa
Please.	*S'il vous plaît.*	seel voo play
Thank you.	*Merci.*	mair·see
Excuse me.	*Excusez-moi.*	ek·skew·zay·mwa
Sorry.	*Pardon.*	par·don
Yes./No.	*Oui./Non.*	wee/non
Help!	*Au secours!*	o skoor
Cheers!	*Santé!*	son·tay

Do you speak English?
Parlez-vous anglais? par·lay·voo ong·glay

I don't understand.
Je ne comprends pas. zher ner kom·pron pa

How much is it?
C'est combien? say kom·byun

Where's ...?
Où est ...? oo ay ...

Can you show me (on the map)?
Pouvez-vous m'indiquer poo·vay·voo mun·dee·kay
(sur la carte)? (sewr la kart)

I'm lost.
Je suis perdu/ zher swee
perdue. (m/f) pair·dew

I'm ill.
Je suis malade. zher swee ma·lad

Where are the toilets?
Où sont les toilettes? oo son ley twa·let

GERMAN

The language of Germany, Austria and Liechtenstein also has official status, and is spoken in Switzerland, Luxembourg and Belgium.

Vowels in German can be short or long. Note that air is pronounced as in 'fair', aw as in 'saw', eu as the 'u' in 'nurse', ew as ee with rounded lips, ow as in 'now', kh as the 'ch' in the Scottish *loch* (pronounced at the back of the throat), and r is also a throaty sound.

Hello.

(in general)	*Guten Tag.*	goo·ten taak
(Austria)	*Servus.*	zer·vus
(Switzerland)	*Grüezi.*	grew·e·tsi

Goodbye. *Auf* owf
Wiedersehen. vee·der·zey·en

Please. *Bitte.* bi·te

Thank you. *Danke.* dang·ke

Excuse me. *Entschuldigung.* ent·shul·di·gung

Sorry. *Entschuldigung.* ent·shul·di·gung

Yes./No. *Ja./Nein.* yaa/nain

Help! *Hilfe!* hil·fe

Cheers! *Prost!* prawst

Do you speak English?
Sprechen Sie Englisch? shpre·khen zee eng·lish

I don't understand.
Ich verstehe nicht. ikh fer·shtey·e nikht

How much is it?
Wie viel kostet das? vee feel kos·tet das

Where's ...?
Wo ist ...? vaw ist ...

Can you show me (on the map)?
Können Sie es mir keu·nen zee es meer
(auf der Karte) (owf dair kar·te)

zeigen? tsai·gen

I'm lost.
Ich habe mich verirrt. ikh haa·be mikh fer·irt

I'm ill.
Ich bin krank. ikh bin krangk

Where are the toilets?
Wo ist die Toilette? vo ist dee to·a·le·te

GREEK

Greek is the language of mainland Greece and its islands (as well as a co-official language of Cyprus).

Note that dh is pronounced as the 'th' in 'that', and that gh and kh are both throaty sounds, similar to the 'ch' in the Scottish *loch*.

Hello.	Γεια σου.	yia su
Goodbye.	Αντίο.	a·di·o
Please.	Παρακαλώ.	pa·ra·ka·lo
Thank you.	Ευχαριστώ.	ef·kha·ri·sto
Excuse me.	Με συγχωρείτε.	me sing·kho·ri·te
Sorry.	Συγνώμη.	si·ghno·mi
Yes./No.	Ναι./Οχι.	ne/o·hi
Help!	Βοήθεια!	vo·i·thia
Cheers!	Στην υγειά μας!	stin i·yia mas

Do you speak English?
Μιλάς Αγγλικά; mi·las ang·gli·ka

I don't understand.
Δεν καταλαβαίνω. dhen ka·ta·la·ve·no

How much is it?
Πόσο κάνει; po·so ka·ni

Where's ...?
Που είναι ...; pu i·ne ...

Can you show me (on the map)?
Μπορείς να μου δείξεις bo·ris na mu dhik·sis
(στο χάρτη); (sto khar·ti)

I'm lost.
Εχω χαθεί. e·kho kha·thi

I'm ill.
Είμαι άρρωστος/ i·me a·ro·stos/
άρρωστη. (m/f) a·ro·sti

Where are the toilets?
Που είναι η τουαλέτα; pu i·ne i tu·a·le·ta

ITALIAN

The language of Italy also has official status – and is spoken – in Switzerland.

Italian vowel are generally shorter than those in English. The consonants sometimes have a stronger, more emphatic pronunciation – if the word is written with a double consonant, pronounce them stronger. Note that r is rolled and stronger than in English.

Hello.	Buongiorno.	bwon·jor·no
Goodbye.	Arrivederci.	a·ree·ve·der·chee
Please.	Per favore.	per fa·vo·re
Thank you.	Grazie.	gra·tsye
Excuse me.	Mi scusi.	mee skoo·zee
Sorry.	Mi dispiace.	mee dees·pya·che
Yes./No.	Sì./No.	see/no
Help!	Aiuto!	ai·yoo·to
Cheers!	Salute!	sa·loo·te

Do you speak English?
Parla inglese? — par·la een·gle·ze

I don't understand.
Non capisco. — non ka·pee·sko

How much is it?
Quant'è? — kwan·te

Where's ... ?
Dov'è ... ? — do·ve ...

Can you show me (on the map)?
Può mostrarmi — pwo mos·trar·mee
(sulla pianta)? — (soo·la pyan·ta)

I'm lost.
Mi sono perso/a. (m/f) — mee so·no per·so/a

I'm ill.
Mi sento male. — mee sen·to ma·le

Where are the toilets?
Dove sono i — do·ve so·no ee
gabinetti? — ga·bee·ne·tee

PORTUGUESE

Most vowel sounds in Portugal's language have a nasal version (ie pronounced as if you're trying to force the sound through your nose), which is indicated in our pronunciation guides with ng after the vowel. Note also that oh is pronounced as the 'o' in 'note', ow as in 'how', and rr is a throaty sound.

Hello.	Olá.	o·laa
Goodbye.	Adeus.	a·de·oosh
Please.	Por favor.	poor fa·vor
Thank you.	Obrigado. (m)	o·bree·gaa·doo
	Obrigada. (f)	o·bree·gaa·da
Excuse me.	Faz favor.	faash fa·vor
Sorry.	Desculpe.	desh·kool·pe
Yes./No.	Sim./Não.	seeng/nowng
Help!	Socorro!	soo·ko·rroo
Cheers!	Saúde!	sa·oo·de

Do you speak English?
Fala inglês? — faa·la eeng·glesh

I don't understand.
Não entendo. — nowng eng·teng·doo

How much is it?
Quanto custa? — kwang·too koosh·ta

Where's ...?
Onde é ...? — ong·de e ...

Can you show me (on the map)?
Pode-me mostrar — po·de·me moosh·traar
(no mapa)? — (noo maa·pa)

I'm lost.
Estou perdido/ — shtoh per·dee·doo/
perdida. (m/f) — per·dee·da

I'm ill.
Estou doente. — shtoh doo·eng·te

Where are the toilets?
Onde é a casa de — ong·de e a kaa·za de
banho? — ba·nyoo

SPANISH

Spanish is the main language of Spain. Spanish vowels are generally pronounced short. Note that r is rolled and stronger than in English, and v is pronounced as a soft 'b'.

Hello.	Hola.	o·la
Goodbye.	Adiós.	a·dyos
Please.	Por favor.	por fa·vor
Thank you.	Gracias.	gra·thyas
Excuse me.	Perdón.	per·don
Sorry.	Lo siento.	lo syen·to
Yes./No.	Sí./No.	see/no
Cheers!	¡Salud!	sa·loo
Help!	¡Socorro!	so·ko·ro

Do you speak English?
¿Habla/Hablas — a·bla/a·blas
inglés? (pol/inf) — een·gles

I don't understand.
Yo no entiendo. — yo no en·tyen·do

How much is it?
¿Cuánto cuesta? — kwan·to kwes·ta

Where's ...?
¿Dónde está ...? — don·de es·ta ...

Can you show me (on the map)?
¿Me lo puede indicar — me lo pwe·de een·dee·kar
(en el mapa)? — (en el ma·pa)

I'm lost.
Estoy perdido/a. (m/f) — es·toy per·dee·do/a

I'm ill.
Estoy enfermo/a. (m/f) — es·toy en·fer·mo/a

Where are the toilets?
¿Dónde están los — don·de es·tan los
servicios? — ser·vee·thyos

Behind the Scenes

SEND US YOUR FEEDBACK

We love to hear from travellers – your comments keep us on our toes and help make our books better. Our well-travelled team reads every word on what you loved or loathed about this book. Although we cannot reply individually to your submissions, we always guarantee that your feedback goes straight to the appropriate authors, in time for the next edition. Each person who sends us information is thanked in the next edition – the most useful submissions are rewarded with a selection of digital PDF chapters.

Visit **lonelyplanet.com/contact** to submit your updates and suggestions or to ask for help. Our award-winning website also features inspirational travel stories, news and discussions.

Note: We may edit, reproduce and incorporate your comments in Lonely Planet products such as guidebooks, websites and digital products, so let us know if you don't want your comments reproduced or your name acknowledged. For a copy of our privacy policy visit lonelyplanet.com/privacy.

OUR READERS

Many thanks to the travellers who used the last edition and wrote to us with helpful hints, useful advice and interesting anecdotes:
Amanda Pilato, Esme Sienicki, Geoff Mackay, Karyne Framand, Letitia Farrell, Melanie Basta, Shirley Farmer

AUTHOR THANKS

Alexis Averbuck

For my work on Greece, honour to Alexandra Stamopoulou for always-insightful tips and overall INSPIRATION. Margarita, Kostas and Zisis, and Anthy and Costas made Athens feel like home. Cindy Camatsos generously shared Mytilini (Lesvos) secrets and John Diakostamatis the sights and adoration of Samos. My work on Iceland was a labour of love supported by many helping hands. Big thanks to Carolyn Bain, an unstintingly generous collaborator. Yva and John became inspiring family. Ryan was, as always, a peachy partner in crime.

Kerry Christiani

A heartfelt *obrigada* to the warm, generous, kind-natured people of Portugal, who made the road to research delightfully smooth. Big thanks in particular to designer and all-round Lisbon connoisseur Jorge Moita and SIC TV journalist Rui Pedro Reis in Lisbon. Special thanks, too, to the Porto pros, especially Cristina Azevedo and Alexandra Santos. André at We Hate Tourism Tours and André at Taste Porto Food Tours were also stars, giving me the inside scoop on their beautiful city. A big *dankeschön* to all of the locals and super-efficient tourism professionals who made the road to research a breeze, especially the teams in Vienna, Innsbruck, Graz and Salzburg. I'd also like to thank my Vienna friends Chiara and Karin for good times and invaluable tips. Finally, thanks go to Christoph Unterkofler at Villa Trapp for taking time out to tell me the truth about one of Austria's most fascinating families.

Emilie Filou

Thanks to friends and family who chipped in with recommendations and joined in the research fun. Thanks also to my husband, Adolfo, for everything.

Duncan Garwood

Thanks to everyone who helped with tips and recommendations, and to the staff of Italy's tourist offices, in particular Cristina Bernasconi in Como, Manuel Testi in Ravenna, Francesca Piseddu in Milan and Michela Dibiasi in Genoa. *Grazie* also to the EDT crew in Turin; Antonello and Dora in Genoa; and Viviana in Bologna. As always, a big, heartfelt thank you to Lidia and the boys, Ben and Nick.

Anthony Ham

Special thanks to Gemma Graham, Jo Cooke, Stuart Butler, Donna Wheeler, Miles Roddis, Itziar Herrán, Francisco Palomares, Miguel Ángel Simón, Astrid Vargas and to so many Spaniards and Norwegians who were unfailingly helpful ambassadors for their country – I am deeply grateful to all of them. And it gets harder with each journey to be away from my family – to Marina, Carlota and Valentina, heartfelt thanks for enduring my absences. *Os quiero*.

Catherine Le Nevez

Hartelijk bedankt first and foremost to Julian, and to everyone throughout the Netherlands who provided insights, information and good times. *Dank u wel* in particular to Joris Rotsaert and Pamela Sturhoofd. Huge thanks too to Destination Editor Kate Morgan and all at LP. As ever, *merci encore* to my parents, brother, *belle-sœur* and *neveu*.

Sally O'Brien

Thanks to Kate Morgan for the assignment, and LP authors Nicola Williams, Kerry Christiani and Gregor Clark (for fab footprints to follow), plus all the in-house staff that made this guidebook a reality,

Andrea Schulte-Peevers

Big heartfelt thanks to all these wonderful people who've plied me with tips, insights, lodging and encouragement (in no particular order): Anke Gerber and Guido, Holm Friedrich, Guido Neumann, Tomas Kaiser, Andreas Gerber and Heinz, Walter Schulte, Kirsten Schmidt, Henrik Tidefjärd, Susan Paterson, Miriam Bers, Claudia Scheffler, Regine Schneider, Frank Engster, Heiner and Claudia Schuster, Renate Freiling, Silke Neumann.

Helena Smith

Thanks to Anne and friends for all their help in Brussels first time around, and to the friendly Use-It crew.

Neil Wilson

Many thanks to all the helpful and enthusiastic staff at tourist information centres throughout Britain and Ireland, and to the many travellers I met on the road who chipped in with advice and recommendations. Thanks also to Carol Downie, and to Steven Fallon and Keith Jeffrey, Steve Hall, Russell Leaper, Brendan Bolland, Jenny Neil and Tom and Christine Duffin. Finally, many thanks to all my co-authors and to the ever-helpful and patient editors and cartographers at Lonely Planet.

ACKNOWLEDGMENTS

Climate map data adapted from Peel MC, Finlayson BL & McMahon TA (2007) 'Updated World Map of the Köppen-Geiger Climate Classification', *Hydrology and Earth System Sciences*, 11, 1633–44.

Cover photograph: Piazza San Marco, Venice, Italy. Alan Copson/AWL ©

THIS BOOK

This 12th edition of Lonely Planet's *Western Europe* guidebook was researched and written by Alexis Averbuck, Emilie Filou, Duncan Garwood, Anthony Ham, Catherine Le Nevez, Sally O'Brien, Andrea Schulte-Peevers, Helena Smith and Neil Wilson.

This guidebook was produced by the following:

Destination Editor Kate Morgan

Book Designer Mazzy Prinsep

Product Editors Elin Berglund, Jenna Myers, Amanda Williamson

Senior Cartographer Valentina Kremenchutskaya

Assisting Book Designer Jessica Rose

Assisting Cartographer Alison Lyall

Assisting Editors Sarah Bailey, Michelle Bennett, Andrea Dobbin, Carly Hall, Kellie Langdon, Jodie Martire, Anne Mulvaney, Rosie Nicholson, Kristin Odijk, Charlotte Orr, Susan Paterson, Monique Perrin, Erin Richards, Kathryn Rowan, Kirsten Rawlings, Saralinda Turner, Jeanette Wall

Cover Researcher Campbell McKenzie

Thanks to Jo Cooke, Brendan Dempsey, Gemma Graham, Kate James, Elizabeth Jones, Claire Naylor, Karyn Noble, Martine Power, James Smart, Anna Tyler, Brana Vladisavljevic, Lauren Wellicome, Tony Wheeler

Index

Map Pages **000**
Photo Pages **000**

Map Legend

Sights

- Beach
- Bird Sanctuary
- Buddhist
- Castle/Palace
- Christian
- Confucian
- Hindu
- Islamic
- Jain
- Jewish
- Monument
- Museum/Gallery/Historic Building
- Ruin
- Shinto
- Sikh
- Taoist
- Winery/Vineyard
- Zoo/Wildlife Sanctuary
- Other Sight

Activities, Courses & Tours

- Bodysurfing
- Diving
- Canoeing/Kayaking
- Course/Tour
- Sento Hot Baths/Onsen
- Skiing
- Snorkelling
- Surfing
- Swimming/Pool
- Walking
- Windsurfing
- Other Activity

Sleeping

- Sleeping
- Camping

Eating

- Eating

Drinking & Nightlife

- Drinking & Nightlife
- Cafe

Entertainment

- Entertainment

Shopping

- Shopping

Information

- Bank
- Embassy/Consulate
- Hospital/Medical
- Internet
- Police
- Post Office
- Telephone
- Toilet
- Tourist Information
- Other Information

Geographic

- Beach
- Gate
- Hut/Shelter
- Lighthouse
- Lookout
- Mountain/Volcano
- Oasis
- Park
- Pass
- Picnic Area
- Waterfall

Population

- Capital (National)
- Capital (State/Province)
- City/Large Town
- Town/Village

Transport

- Airport
- Border crossing
- Bus
- Cable car/Funicular
- Cycling
- Ferry
- Metro station
- Monorail
- Parking
- Petrol station
- S-Bahn/S-train/Subway station
- Taxi
- T-bane/Tunnelbana station
- Train station/Railway
- Tram
- Tube station
- U-Bahn/Underground station
- Other Transport

Note: Not all symbols displayed above appear on the maps in this book

Routes

- Tollway
- Freeway
- Primary
- Secondary
- Tertiary
- Lane
- Unsealed road
- Road under construction
- Plaza/Mall
- Steps
- Tunnel
- Pedestrian overpass
- Walking Tour
- Walking Tour detour
- Path/Walking Trail

Boundaries

- International
- State/Province
- Disputed
- Regional/Suburb
- Marine Park
- Cliff
- Wall

Hydrography

- River, Creek
- Intermittent River
- Canal
- Water
- Dry/Salt/Intermittent Lake
- Reef

Areas

- Airport/Runway
- Beach/Desert
- Cemetery (Christian)
- Cemetery (Other)
- Glacier
- Mudflat
- Park/Forest
- Sight (Building)
- Sportsground
- Swamp/Mangrove

Anthony Ham

Spain Spain is one of Anthony's great loves. In 2001, Anthony (www.anthonyham. com) fell in love with Madrid on his first visit to the city. Less than a year later, he arrived on a one-way ticket, with not a word of Spanish and not knowing a single person. After 10 years living in the city, he recently returned to Australia with his Spanish-born family, but he still adores his adopted country as much as the first day he arrived.

Catherine Le Nevez

The Netherlands Catherine's wanderlust kicked in when she first roadtripped across Europe, including the Netherlands, aged four, and she's been returning to this spirited, *gezellig* country ever since, completing her Doctorate of Creative Arts in Writing, Masters in Professional Writing, and post-grad qualifications in editing and publishing along the way. Catherine has worked as a freelance writer for many years and during the past decade or so she's written scores of Lonely Planet guidebooks and articles covering destinations all over Europe and beyond. Catherine also wrote the Plan Your Trip and Survival chapters.

Sally O'Brien

Liechtenstein, Switzerland Since moving to Switzerland in 2007, Sally has revelled in swimming the country's lakes and rivers, snowboarding down its astounding mountains, scoffing its cheese and chocolate, and quaffing local-secret wines. Writing about this dreamy country for Lonely Planet and heading out on the road with her family to explore every last corner of her adopted home only adds to the fun.

Andrea Schulte-Peevers

Germany Born and raised in Germany, and educated in London and at UCLA, Andrea has travelled the distance to the moon and back in her visits to some 75 countries and now makes her home in Berlin. She's written about her native country for two decades and authored or contributed to some 80 Lonely Planet titles, including all editions of the *Germany* country guide and the *Berlin* city guide.

Helena Smith

Belgium, Luxembourg Helena Smith is the author of Lonely Planet's *Pocket Brussels & Bruges*, and was very glad to return to Europe's most eccentric country to work on this guide, as well as adding Luxembourg to her list of countries visited. When not travel writing, Helena writes about food and community at www. eathackney.com.

Neil Wilson

Britain, Ireland Neil was born in Scotland and, save for a few years spent abroad, has lived there most of his life; he is based near Dunkeld in Perthshire. An enduring passion for the great outdoors has inspired hillwalking, mountain-biking and sailing expeditions to every corner of Britain and Ireland. Neil has been a full-time author since 1988 and has written more than 70 guidebooks for various publishers, including Lonely Planet guides to Scotland, England and Ireland.

OUR STORY

A beat-up old car, a few dollars in the pocket and a sense of adventure. In 1972 that's all Tony and Maureen Wheeler needed for the trip of a lifetime – across Europe and Asia overland to Australia. It took several months, and at the end – broke but inspired – they sat at their kitchen table writing and stapling together their first travel guide, *Across Asia on the Cheap*. Within a week they'd sold 1500 copies. Lonely Planet was born.

Today, Lonely Planet has offices in Franklin, London, Melbourne, Oakland, Beijing and Delhi, with more than 600 staff and writers. We share Tony's belief that 'a great guidebook should do three things: inform, educate and amuse'.

OUR WRITERS

Alexis Averbuck

Greece Alexis lives in Hydra, Greece, takes regular reverse R&R in Athens, and makes any excuse she can to travel the isolated back roads of her adopted land. A travel writer for two decades, Alexis has lived in Antarctica for a year, crossed the Pacific by sailboat and written books on her journeys through Asia and the Americas. She's also a painter. Visit www.alexisaverbuck.com.

Kerry Christiani

Austria, Portugal Ever since her first post-grad trip to Austria, Kerry has seized every available chance to travel back to the country of Mozart, Maria and co. Hanging out in the cream of Vienna's coffee houses, road-testing Christmas markets and glimpsing the first snow of the season in the Alps were highlights this edition. Her love affair with Portugal began as a child hiking the cliffs of the Algarve. She's returned countless times since, and remains captivated by this country's creative spirit and beautifully melancholic soul. Kerry has authored/co-authored around two dozen travel guides, including Lonely Planet *Austria*, *Pocket Lisbon* and *Pocket Porto*. She tweets @kerrychristiani and lists her latest work at www.kerrychristiani.com.

Emilie Filou

France Emilie was born in Paris and spent most of her childhood holidays roaming the south of France. She now lives in London, where she works as a freelance journalist specialising in development issues in Africa. She still goes to France every year for holidays and loves feasting on local market products, especially cheese and wine. See more of Emilie's work on www.emiliefilou.com; she tweets at @emiliefilou.

Duncan Garwood

Italy Duncan is a British travel writer based near Rome. Since he moved to Italy in 1997, he has travelled extensively in his adopted homeland and worked on about 30 Lonely Planet guides, including *Rome*, *Sardinia*, *Sicily* and *Italy's Best Trips*. Memories from his most recent trip include a barbecue in a Palermo street market and catching an open-air concert in Trieste's vast central piazza.

OVER PAGE MORE WRITERS

Published by Lonely Planet Publications Pty Ltd
ABN 36 005 607 983
12th edition – October 2015
ISBN 978 1 74321 581 4
© Lonely Planet 2015   Photographs © as indicated 2015
10 9 8 7 6 5 4 3 2 1
Printed in China

Although the authors and Lonely Planet have taken all reasonable care in preparing this book, we make no warranty about the accuracy or completeness of its content and, to the maximum extent permitted, disclaim all liability arising from its use.